THE ENCYCLOPEDIA
OF MILITARY
HISTORY

from 3500 B.C. to the present

Books by T. N. Dupuy

THE BATTLE OF AUSTERLITZ

REVOLUTIONARY WAR LAND BATTLES
(with Gay M. Hammerman)

REVOLUTIONARY WAR NAVAL BATTLES
(with Grace P. Hayes)

MODERN LIBRARIES FOR MODERN COLLEGES

COLLEGE LIBRARIES IN FERMENT

MILITARY HISTORY OF THE CHINESE CIVIL WAR

MILITARY HISTORY OF WORLD WAR I

MILITARY HISTORY OF WORLD WAR II

HOLIDAYS

CIVIL WAR NAVAL ACTIONS

CIVIL WAR LAND BATTLES

CAMPAIGNS OF THE FRENCH REVOLUTION AND OF NAPOLEON

FAITHFUL AND TRUE

MILITARY LIVES—ALEXANDER THE GREAT TO WINSTON CHURCHILL

ALMANAC OF WORLD MILITARY POWER
(ed., with John A. C. Andrews and Grace P. Hayes)

A DOCUMENTARY HISTORY OF ARMS CONTROL AND DISARMAMENT
(ed., with Gay M. Hammerman)

PEOPLE AND EVENTS OF THE AMERICAN REVOLUTION
(with Gay M. Hammerman)

CONSULTANTS

D. G. E. HALL, Professor Emeritus of History, London University

JOHN D. HAYES, Rear Admiral, United States Navy, Rtd.

HAROLD C. HINTON, Professor of Political Science, George Washington University

JAMES D. HITTLE, Brigadier General, United States Marine Corps, Rtd.

W. BARTON LEACH, Brigadier General, United States Air Force Reserve, Rtd., Story Professor of Law, Harvard University

LOUIS MORTON, Professor of History, Dartmouth College

CHESTER G. STARR, Professor of History, University of Illinois

THOMAS D. STAMPS, Brigadier General, United States Army, Rtd., Professor Emeritus of Military Art and Engineering, United States Military Academy

CHARLES H. TAYLOR, H. C. Lea Professor of Medieval History, Harvard University

FREDERICK TODD, Curator Emeritus, United States Military Academy Museum

THE
ENCYCLOPEDIA
OF MILITARY
HISTORY

from 3500 B.C. to the present

R. ERNEST DUPUY and TREVOR N. DUPUY

Second Revised Edition

1817

HARPER & ROW, PUBLISHERS: New York
Cambridge, Philadelphia, San Francisco, London
Mexico City, São Paulo, Singapore, Sydney

To the memory of

THEODORE AYRAULT DODGE *and* JOHN FREDERICK CHARLES FULLER,

who pointed the way

THE ENCYCLOPEDIA OF MILITARY HISTORY FROM 3500 B.C. TO THE PRESENT (*Second Revised Edition*). Copyright © 1986 by HERO Books Partnership. All rights reserved. Printed in the United States of America. No part of this book may be used or reproduced in any manner whatsoever without written permission except in the case of brief quotations embodied in critical articles and reviews. For information address Harper & Row, Publishers, Inc., 10 East 53rd Street, New York, N.Y. 10022. Published simultaneously in Canada by Fitzhenry & Whiteside Limited, Toronto.

Library of Congress Cataloging in Publication Data

Dupuy, R. Ernest (Richard Ernest), 1887–1975.
 The encyclopedia of military history from 3500 B.C.
to the present.

 Includes indexes.
  1. Military history—Dictionaries. 2. Military art
and science—History—Dictionaries. I. Dupuy,
Trevor Nevitt, 1916–   . II. Title.
D25.A2D8 1985   355′.009   84-48158
ISBN 0-06-181235-8

86 87 88 89 90 MPC 10 9 8 7 6 5 4 3 2 1

CONTENTS

MAPS

PREFACE TO THE SECOND
REVISED EDITION

It is hard for me to realize that it has been fourteen years since the publication of the first edition of this book. Those years—including the eight since the publication of the revised edition—have gone by more quickly than a mortal likes to contemplate. Passage of time has another effect upon the author of an encyclopedia, and unfortunately it seems particularly to affect a work devoted to the recording of wars and military affairs: the work is once more outdated.

This edition, therefore, attempts to catch up with time and to make this *Encyclopedia of Military History* current as of the end of 1983 and even early 1984. It also seeks to correct those inaccuracies or omissions in the earlier editions that my colleagues at the Historical Evaluation and Research Organization and I have discovered, or have had brought to our attention. In this process of updating I have been assisted particularly by my colleague, Dr. Charles R. Smith, and also by the publisher of HERO Books, Guy P. Clifton.

Fairfax, VA   TREVOR N. DUPUY

September, 1985

PREFACE TO THE REVISED EDITION

The six years since the original Preface was written have seen the conclusion of the War in Vietnam, the beginning and end of a short but important war in the Middle East, and a series of brief revolutions, coups d'état, and politico-military developments that warrant the publication of a new edition.

Another reason for revision was the confirmation of our comment in the original Preface that such a work cannot be completely accurate. Accordingly, we have made minor corrections, and a few substantial revisions, throughout the book where inaccuracies or omissions have been brought to our attention. We welcome comments from our readers, and always seek to improve the book.

The revision was begun jointly by both of the authors, but time claimed one of us during the course of this work. I know, however, that my father would have wanted to join me in expressing our thanks for assistance not only to those who have been kind enough to send us their comments, but also to our colleagues of the Historical Evaluation and Research Organization who have given so much help in this revision, and particularly to Mrs. Grace P. Hayes.

TREVOR N. DUPUY

Dunn Loring, Va.

June, 1976

PREFACE TO THE FIRST EDITION

In writing this book, the authors have had two general purposes in mind: to present to both scholar and general reader a comprehensive survey of the history of war and of military affairs in the world throughout recorded human experience; and to provide a reliable, relatively complete, and authoritative reference work covering the entire sweep of world military history. As military historians, we were acutely aware of the lack of any work or works which even attempted to accomplish either of these purposes.

War has been a concomitant of man's existence ever since the first rival cavemen started trying to beat one another to death with club and stone. Through the ages the means and techniques of conflict have become increasingly sophisticated and complex, but there has been no change in the fundamental human objectives of war. Not even the recent advent of weapons possessing the potentiality of utter extermination has yet substantially modified man's willingness to resort to war to force his will upon others.

It is partly because this present situation demands the most thorough possible understanding of war, and partly because of the historian's belief that knowledge of the past is worthwhile in itself, that we have been impelled to accomplish our first purpose. Much has been written about war, and about the broader implications of military affairs within societies, but we know of no previous attempt to present the entire cause of the world's military history in orderly, readable form. As professional soldiers, as well as military historians, we have attempted not only to present the major facts of the world's military history, but also to interpret them—although with no intent that this should require the thoughtful reader to accept our interpretation.

As to our second purpose, our own research has made us acutely aware of the lack of any over-all reference work on military history to which other historians and other researchers could refer with reasonable confidence. We also recognize the danger of attempting to fill this void. No work which deals with the activities of men of all nations and all parts of the world since the dawn of history can hope to be either completely accurate or totally comprehensive. In part this is unavoidable; even if the authors were not subject to human error and human bias, they would be forced to rely upon sources which have all too many human shortcomings; the absolute truth can never be known about any past event. In many instances, we have been forced to choose among amazingly diverse and conflicting accounts of a single event, guided by common sense and the most objective possible evaluation of the sources. Furthermore, in such a vast undertaking, we have undoubtedly missed sources which, had we been aware of them, might have modified our presentation of some of the facts. Finally, no historical work can include everything about anything.

This question of what to include and what to exclude is a particularly difficult matter in a single-volume reference work, even a very large one. With a subject as vast as ours, we had to be arbitrary. We have tried to include everything of significance in world military history. Unfortunately, significance is not only subjective; it can change from time to time and from circumstance to circumstance. So some readers may wonder why we have included some material which they consider insignificant, and omitted other facts which they believe essential. This, however, is their opinion; what is included herein reflects the authors' joint opinion.

We recognize the fallibility of all authors, even within the parameters that they have set for themselves. To reduce such fallibility in this book to limits acceptable to other scholars—and to ourselves—we have had the good fortune to obtain advice and commentary from the distinguished consultants listed elsewhere in these pages. We are vastly indebted to them for their interest and for their assistance.

To two of our professional colleagues of the Historical Evaluation and Research Organization—Mrs. Gay M. Hammerman and Mrs. Grace P. Hayes—we owe a particular debt of gratitude. While indexing the book—in itself a stupendous task, as can be readily seen—they also read it thoroughly and gave us the benefit of their historical knowledge and experience by drawing our attention to discrepancies, errors, and questionable interpretations. They added substantially to such scholarly merit as this work may possess. Their work was greatly facilitated by research assistance from Mrs. Edith Kilroy, Mrs. Bonnie Marsh, Miss Karen Rice, and Mrs. Jonna Dupuy.

Messrs. Cass Canfield and M. S. Wyeth, Jr., of Harper & Row, have been most patient and solicitous in their editorial support and guidance, while the expert copyediting of Mr. James Fergus McRee has gone far to improve the text and to preserve the authors from being unduly influenced by their personal biases.

However, the authors alone stand responsible for the final determination of what is to be included in this book, of how it is to be presented, and for the military assessments made and opinions expressed.

We must also express our gratitude to the ladies who have spent so much time and effort, over so many years, in typing the drafts and redrafts of thousands upon thousands of manuscript pages. In particular, we are indebted to Mrs. Jean D. Brennan, Mrs. Judith B. Mitchell, and Mrs. Billie P. Davis, who have never lost either interest or good humor under the pressure of this trying task. Finally, we want to acknowledge the inspirational encouragement which we received during the ten years this book was in preparation from Laura N. Dupuy, wife of one of the authors and mother of the other.

R. ERNEST DUPUY

McLean, Va.

TREVOR N. DUPUY

January, 1970

ORGANIZATION OF THIS BOOK AND ITS USE

The schema of this encyclopedia consists of a series of chronologically and geographically organized narratives of wars, warfare, and military affairs. The course of recorded history is arbitrarily divided into twenty-one specific time periods, and one chapter is devoted to each period. Each chapter is prefaced by an introductory essay presenting a professional assessment of the principal military trends of the period, including its outstanding leaders, and the general progression of the military art in tactics, strategy, weaponry, organization, and the like. The chronological surveys of the principal wars of the period which follow are treated separately from the regional or national presentations because they possess a significance or geographical scope that extends beyond the confines of a single region. The remainder of each chapter is divided into the major geographical regions known during the era. Within these regional sections brief subsections present chronologically the principal military events affecting the affairs of each state, or nation, or people within the region.

An exhaustive General Index includes all names and events mentioned in the text, thoroughly cross-referenced. There are separate index sections for Battles and Sieges and for Wars. The indexes include the major abstract, conceptual, and topical terms associated with military affairs where it is believed that they would facilitate index search. Thus a reader in search of some specific incident, or battle, or war, or person, or type of military activity should be able, once he has located it, to relate it immediately to the local and world situation at the time, as well as to the current practice of warfare.

It is also possible to pursue the general course of the military history of a region, or nation, by following the appropriate sections from one chapter to another.

In addition to the essays on military trends at the beginning of each chapter, essays on the principal military systems of ancient and medieval history are included where appropriate. Such descriptions of national military systems are omitted in the chapters on modern military history, because these chapters cover much briefer periods, and the various military systems (such as Napoleonic, Prussian, etc.) are believed to be covered adequately in the introductory essays and in the sectional narratives.

In a work of this sort it is neither practical nor particularly useful to try to document any of the individual facts by reference citations. At the end of the book, however, there is an extensive bibliography, which includes general references as well as those of specific importance for each individual chapter.

THE ENCYCLOPEDIA OF MILITARY HISTORY

from 3500 B.C. to the present

I

THE DAWN
OF MILITARY HISTORY:
TO 600 B.C.

MILITARY TRENDS

WARFARE BEGINS

Primitive clashes of force first occurred when groups of Paleolithic men, armed with crude stone implements, fought with other groups for food, women, or land. Somewhere along the prehistoric road other drives—such as sport, the urge for dominance, or the desire for independence—became further causes for armed conflicts.

The dawn of history and the beginning of organized warfare went hand in hand. Most primitive societies learned the use of metals at the same time that they developed a system of writing. This phenomenon appeared almost simultaneously, and apparently quite independently, in Mesopotamia and Egypt sometime between 3500 and 3000 B.C., when the use of copper for weapons, household implements, and decorations began. Several hundred more years elapsed before men mastered the secret of hardening copper into bronze by mixing tin with it. Comparable development of Bronze Age culture occurred in the Indus Valley sometime before 2500 B.C., and in the Yellow River Valley of China probably several centuries later. Iron metallurgy began to replace bronze in the Middle East shortly before 1000 B.C., and in Europe soon thereafter. It was a few centuries later when the Iron Age appeared in India and China.

The ancient history which began with Bronze Age cultures is known to us largely in the terms of military history. The record is almost entirely devoted to migrations, wars, and conquests. Not until about 1500 B.C., however, are we able to visualize the actual course of any of the constant wars of the Middle East, or dimly to perceive primitive military organization and methods of combat. By the 6th century B.C. relatively comprehensive and more or less continuous records of wars become available. These records reveal that three of the five great military societies of antiquity were flourishing prior to 600 B.C., and the origins of the other two were evident.

GENERAL DEVELOPMENTS

Despite the embellishments of myth and legend, we can discern four broad general trends in warfare: (1) the introduction of military transport—on land and on water; (2) the introduction and then the relatively early decline of the chariot; (3) increasing ascendancy of the horseman—the elite in society—on the battlefield over the inchoate masses of plebeian foot soldiers; and (4) the all-important introduction of iron and steel, replacing bronze in the manufacture of weapons.

By the year 600 B.C. our knowledge is sufficient to reveal that the art of war had become highly developed in the major centers of civilization. Unquestionably there were gifted military leaders in these early centuries, but with the possible exception of **Thutmosis III** of Egypt, we can hardly more than surmise the reasons for military success.

WEAPONS

Primitive Weapons

Weapons fall into two major categories: shock and missile. The original shock weapon was the prehistoric man's club; the first missile weapon was the rock that he hurled at hunted prey or human enemy. The next important development was the leather sling for hurling small, smooth rocks with greater force for longer distances than was possible by arm power alone. In some regions the rock gradually was displaced by a light club, or throwing stick, which in turn evolved into darts, javelins, and the boomerang. The club was modified in a number of other ways. The shock-action counterpart of the javelin was the heavy pike, or thrusting spear. The basic club itself took on a variety of forms, of which the American Indian tomahawk is an axlike example, while clubs with sharpened edges became Stone Age prototypes of the sword. The bow, developed late in the Stone Age, was also invaluable to the early fighting man and to his successors over many centuries.

The most important form of protective armor devised by primitive man was the shield, held almost invariably in the left hand, or on the left arm, leaving the right arm free to wield a weapon. Shields most often were simple wooden frameworks, covered with leather hide, though some were made entirely of wood, and in Asia wicker shields were common.

Other types of protective covering for head, torso, and legs appeared before the Bronze Age. These were of leather, wicker, padded or quilted cloth, or wood.

Historic Weapons

The most important weapons improvement during the early historic period was the adoption of metal for the points, edges, or smashing surfaces in the Bronze and Iron Ages.

The first new weapons of the metallic era were the dagger, then the sword. The long thin blade which characterizes the sword could not have been created until metallurgy had sufficiently developed to permit the working of hard malleable metal. This occurred in the Bronze Age sometime before 2000 B.C., and the sword was probably introduced into warfare by the Assyrians.

Protective armor was also greatly improved during the Bronze Age. Although leather remained the basic and most common material, this was often reinforced with metal; some helmets, breastplates, and greaves were made entirely in metal—at first bronze, later iron.

TACTICS

Sometime before 1500 B.C., weapons, missions, and relative mobility began to dictate the composition of armies. Their bulk consisted of large, tight masses of infantry, wearing little or no armor, probably carrying pikes and shields. This infantry component was made up of men from the poorer classes of society, and its purpose was almost solely to provide a solid and stable base around which the more important and better-armed groups could operate. There were additional foot troops with missile weapons, either slingers or archers.

Until about 700 B.C. the elite striking force of this army of antiquity was usually a contingent of chariots. These were small armored carts, often with sharp blades projecting from the whirling spokes of the wheels, and drawn by armored horses. Great nobles and members of the royal family rode to battle in chariots and at times fought from them, though as often as not they dismounted for the actual hand-to-hand fighting.

Chariot

Cavalry, when it appeared soon after 1000 B.C., was composed of the lesser nobles, who possessed enough wealth to own horses, and to supply themselves with good weapons and armor. In some regions the principal weapon of the horseman was the bow; in others it was the javelin or spear.

There was little organization when such an army went to war. The sole objective was to reach a suitable place of battle in order to overwhelm the enemy before he was able to prevail. As time went on and the results of a number of such conflicts brought several towns, or entire regions, under the dominance of one ruler, geographical horizons widened and wars became series of battles, or even campaigns, rather than a single encounter between the forces of two small towns.

A campaign was a huge raid, in which large regions were overrun, defeated armies slaughtered, cities destroyed, and entire peoples enslaved. Men were impelled to fight through both fear and the prospect of loot and booty. There was perhaps some effort to weld units with discipline, and to prepare them for battle by training. When armies met, the infantry spearmen stayed together in large groups. The nobles in their chariots or on their horses took position in the front and on the flanks, and the swarms of lightly armed archers and slingers were out in front.

Maneuver in battle was generally accidental. As one or both armies advanced, the archers and slingers maintained harassing fire until the chariots or horsemen started to charge; the light troops then drifted to flank and rear through intervals in the heavy infantry masses. Sometimes the initial charge of chariots and horsemen would strike terror into the opposite side, in which case the battle quickly became a chase, with only the fleetest men of the pursued army escaping the slaughter. More often, the two masses simply converged to carry on the butchery in earnest. This horrible process could last for an hour or more, with the lines swaying back and forth over the growing numbers of dead and wounded, until one side suddenly sensed defeat. This quickly communicated itself through mass hysteria to all the soldiers of that side, and again only a small proportion of the defeated army would escape.

MEDITERRANEAN–MIDDLE EAST*

EGYPT, 3100–600 B.C.

c. 3100†–c. 1800. **Early Egypt.** The first identifiable figure in history was **Menes,** the warrior ruler who established a unified kingdom of Egypt. For the next 1300 years Egyptian civilization flourished along the banks of the Nile River, relatively isolated from the rest of the world. There were many military expeditions to the neighboring regions of Palestine and Nubia, with Egyptian influence reaching far up the Nile into what is now the Sudan. Internal disorders were frequent, with kings (pharaohs) often embroiled in civil wars against unruly provincial nobles. Consequently there were wide fluctuations in

---

* "Middle East" is a modern, and rather imprecise, term. In this text it is used to designate that region of southwestern Asia and eastern North Africa lying roughly between 24° and 60° east longitude, i.e., the area covered by modern Persia, Asiatic Turkey, Iraq, Arabia, the Levantine States, and Egypt.

† There are substantial differences in the dates shown by different respected authorities for the period up to 600 B.C. (and to some extent later). In the case of Menes, for instance, dates ascribed vary from about 3400 to 2900 B.C. In this and all other instances, dates shown in this text will be those which we believe are most reliable. In general we shall avoid indicating either a possible range of dates or the questionable nature of any particular date. The use of the identifying abbreviations B.C. and A.D. will not be used further in the text (as opposed to the headings) save in some instances in the latter part of the 1st century B.C. or in the early part of the 1st century A.D.

the power exercised by central authority, the rhythm of change being occasionally punctuated by the violent collapse of dynasties. Standing armies were unknown, contingents of provincial militia being assembled into active armies only temporarily when the pharaohs embarked on foreign adventures, or needed forces for internal security or to protect the frontiers.

c. 1800–c. 1600. **Hyksos Invasion.** Historic Egypt suffered its first foreign invasion during a period of internal weakness. Semitic **Hyksos** (usually translated as "shepherd kings") introduced the horse and the horse-drawn chariot in Egypt. Gradually the invaders expanded southward until (c. 1700) they completely overran Egypt. For another hundred years they maintained their sway, ruthlessly repressing frequent Egyptian uprisings.

1600. **Revolt of Thebes.** The native nobles drove the Hyksos from Upper Egypt.

1580–1557. **Reign of Amosis.** He drove the Hyksos into Palestine, again uniting Egypt under native rule. He established a strong central government, greatly reducing the former autonomy of the provincial nobles. He then reconquered Nubia, which had fallen away from Egyptian control during the Hyksos occupation. He created the first permanent army of Egyptian history and placed his main reliance upon comparatively well-drilled, disciplined archers; he adopted the dreaded Hyksos war chariot.

1546–1507. **Reigns of Amenophis I and Thutmosis I.** They extended Egyptian rule westward into Libya, further south into Nubia, and northeastward into Palestine and Syria, Egyptian armies actually reaching the banks of the Euphrates. Un-

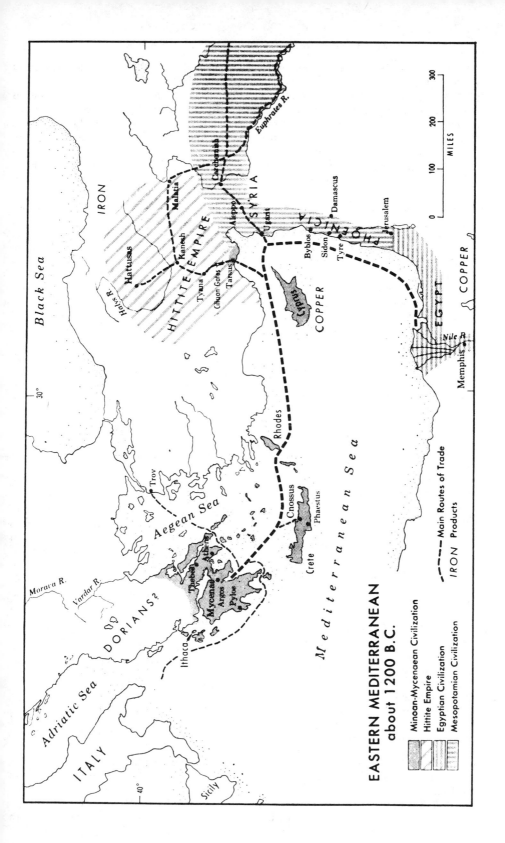

EASTERN MEDITERRANEAN
about 1200 B.C.

Minoan-Mycenaean Civilization
Hittite Empire
Egyptian Civilization
Mesopotamian Civilization

──── Main Routes of Trade
─ ─ ─ IRON Products

MILES
0   100   200   300

Black Sea

IRON

Hattusas

Halys R.

HITTITE EMPIRE

Kanesh
Malatia
Tyana
Cilician Gates
Tarsus
Aleppo

Carchemish

Euphrates R.

SYRIA

Ugarit

Damascus
Jerusalem

PHOENICIA

Byblos
Sidon
Tyre

COPPER

Cyprus

EGYPT

COPPER

Nile R.

Memphis

Rhodes

Troy

Aegean Sea

Crete

Cnossus
Phaestus

Mediterranean Sea

DORIANS?

Morava R.
Vardar R.

Thebes
Athens
Mycenae
Argos
Pylos
Ithaca

ITALY

Adriatic Sea

Sicily

30°

40°

der more peaceful successors, Egyptian control of outlying regions was relaxed.

1491–1449. Reign of Thutmosis III. For the first 20 years of his reign he was merely nominal coruler with his aunt, **Hatshepsut.** Upon her death (1472) the Hyksos King of Kadesh, in northern Palestine, led a highly organized revolt of the tribes of Palestine and Syria against the supposedly weak young Pharaoh.

1469. Battle of Megiddo. (First recorded battle of history.) Thutmosis led an Egyptian army (possibly 10,000 men) on a rapid and unexpected march into central Palestine. The rebellious chieftains assembled an army at Megiddo, southeast of Mount Carmel, sending outposts to hold the three passes leading from the south. But Thutmosis pushed through the Musmus Pass, scattering the defenders in a bold attack he himself led. In the valley beyond, the rebel army, under the King of Kadesh, was drawn up on high ground near the fortress of Megiddo. Thutmosis' army was aligned in a concave formation. While the southern wing engaged the rebels in a holding attack, Thutmosis personally led the north "horn" in an attack that seems to have driven between the rebel flank and the fortress. The result was envelopment of the rebel flank, and overwhelming victory for the Egyptians.

1470–1450. Height of Egyptian Power. After some 17 campaigns, Thutmosis had not only subdued the rebellious rulers of Palestine and Syria; he had pushed Egyptian rule to the edge of the Hittite Empire in Asia Minor, and had expanded into northwestern Mesopotamia. His fleet controlled the eastern Mediterranean.

1380–1365. Reign of Ikhnaton. Serious internal religious disputes weakened Egyptian hold over outlying regions. The warlike Hittites seized Syria, and with local allies overran much of Palestine.

1352–1319. Reign of Haremhad. Just as the Egyptian Empire seemed on the verge of dissolution, **Haremhad,** a general, seized the throne. He restored internal order and halted the erosion of the frontiers by firm defense and by sending offensive expeditions beyond the borders.

1317–1299. Reign of Seti I. A reorganized Egyptian army reconquered Palestine, but was unable to shake Hittite control of Syria.

1299–1232. Reign of Ramses II (son of Seti). He was partly successful in efforts to restore the empire to its old boundaries.

1294. Battle of Kadesh. Ramses led an army composed largely of Numidian mercenaries against the Hittite stronghold, Kadesh, on the Orontes River. In his haste to capture Kadesh before the main Hittite army could arrive, he and his advance guard were for a while cut off and surrounded by a surprise Hittite attack. Holding out until reinforcements arrived, Ramses repulsed the Hittites. He was unable to capture Kadesh, however, and eventually made peace. Ramses' superior leadership was offset by the fact that many of his enemies were evidently armed with new iron weapons, while his mercenaries were still using bronze weapons.

c. 1200. Invasions by the "Peoples of the Sea." These were seaborne raiders from Mediterranean islands and southern Europe. Most of these raids were repulsed, but some of the invaders, like the Philistines in Palestine, succeeded in establishing themselves along the coast.

1198–1167. Reign of Ramses III. When he ascended the throne, the Philistines were advancing from Palestine toward Egypt, the Libyans were approaching from the west, and the Peoples of the Sea were again harassing the Delta coast. Ramses decisively defeated all these threats, and re-established Egyptian control over Palestine. He was the last great pharaoh; in following centuries the power and influence of Egypt declined steadily; the country was frequently overrun by foreign conquerors.

c. 730. Ethiopian Conquest of Egypt. The invaders were led by King **Piankhi,** whose capital was at Napata near the Fourth Cataract of the Nile.

671–661. Assyrian Conquest. Assyrians drove out the Ethiopians (see p. 10).

661–626. Period of Turmoil. Constant Egyptian revolts finally culminated in ejection of the Assyrians (see p. 10).

609–593. Brief Egyptian Resurgence. This was under Pharaoh **Necho,** who led an Egyptian invasion of Palestine and Syria.

609. Second Battle of Megiddo (or Armageddon). Necho easily defeated a Jewish army under **Josiah,** and pushed northward to the Euphrates.

605. Battle of Carchemish. Necho was disastrously defeated by **Nebuchadnezzar** of Babylonia; the Egyptians were driven completely from Syria and Palestine.

SUMER, AKKAD AND BABYLONIA, 4000–1200 B.C.

c. 4000. Emergence of Sumer. A people of undetermined racial origin migrated southward through Asia Minor, or through the Caucasus Mountains, and settled in southern Mesopotamia. Although these Sumerians developed a civilization contemporaneously with the Egyptians, they never created a stable, unified kingdom. Sumer was divided among a number of independent, constantly warring city-states.

2350–2325. Reign of Lugalzaggisi of Erech. He created a temporary Sumerian Empire, and may have controlled all of Mesopotamia and part of Syria and Asia Minor, his realm reaching from the Persian Gulf to the Mediterranean.

c. 2325. Reign of Sargon of Akkad. He led a Semitic people to conquer Sumer. Sargon extended his empire northwestward into Asia Minor. This empire lasted nearly 300 years.

c. 2100. Turmoil in Mesopotamia. During the confusion of a new wave of migration, the Sumerians reasserted their supremacy in southern Mesopotamia for approximately two centuries.

c. 2000. Establishment of the First (Old) Babylonian Empire. A new Semitic people, probably from Syria, became dominant in Mesopotamia, with Babylon their capital.

1728–1686. Reign of Hammurabi. This able warrior and enlightened king of Babylonia, ancient history's first famous lawgiver, extended his rule over all Mesopotamia.

c. 1600–c. 1200. Hittite Destruction of the Old Babylonian Empire. In the confusion of the Hittite raids, the Kassites, an obscure barbarian mountain people from east of Babylonia, overran southern Mesopotamia, adopted the civil justice of the conquered area, and established a kingdom that lasted over 4 centuries.

HITTITE KINGDOM, 2000–1200 B.C.

c. 2000. Rise of the Hittites. An Indo-European people who apparently originated northeast of the Caucasus, the Hittites became dominant in northern and central Asia Minor. They maintained steady pressure against neighbors to the east and south. Hittite pressure probably pushed the Hyksos into Egypt (see p. 4).

c. 1590. Reign of Murshilish I. He raided extensively in Mesopotamia, overrunning the Old Babylonian Empire, bringing it to the verge of collapse. He also captured Aleppo, expanding his kingdom's southern boundaries into Syria. For the next two centuries the Hittites were occupied with internal disorders, as well as almost constant warfare with the Mitanni of northwestern Mesopotamia.

c. 1460. Defeat by Thutmosis III of Egypt. (See p. 6.) The weakened, tottering kingdom paid tribute to Egypt.

1375–1335. Reign of Shubbiluliu. The Hittites revived to re-establish control over most of Anatolia, and to conquer the Mitanni. For the next century the Hittites and Egyptians struggled for control of Syria and Palestine (see p. 6).

1281–1260. Reign of Hattushilish III. He made a treaty of peace and alliance with Ramses II (1271), accepting Egyptian sovereignty over Palestine in return for recognition of Hittite control of Syria. In his era the Hittites introduced weapons made of iron. In subsequent years the Hittite kingdom, shaken by internal disorders, declined rapidly. The great Aegean migrations of the "Peoples of the Sea" (see pp. 6 and 11) also began to threaten Hittite control of western Anatolia, while a powerful new Mesopotamian kingdom was pushing from the east.

c. 1200. Disintegration of the Hittite Kingdom.

ASSYRIA, 3000–612 B.C.

Early Assyria, 3000–727 B.C.

c. 3000. Emergence of Assyria. The Assyrian people appeared in the upland plains of northeastern Mesopotamia, along the upper reaches of the Tigris River. Flat Assyria, with no natural frontiers, was constantly threatened by neighbors on all sides, particularly the Hittites to the northwest and the Sumerian-Babylonians to the southeast.

c. 2000 – c. 1200. Military Development. The Assyrians, engaged in a never-ending struggle to maintain freedom, became the most warlike people of the Middle East (c. 1400). Initially they relied upon an informal militia system, though constant campaigning gave exceptional military proficiency to these part-time soldiers. But the Assyrian economy was severely strained by the long absence of militiamen from fields and workshops. After growing in size, wealth, and power, Assyria temporarily declined (1230–1116).

1116–1093. Reign of Tiglath-pileser I. Assyria became the leading power of the Middle East, a position she was to maintain almost continuously for five centuries. He expanded Assyrian power into the heart of Anatolia and across northern Syria to the Mediterranean.

c. 1050. Period of Retrenchment. Another wave of migrations—this time Aramean nomads—swept across Mesopotamia. The hard-pressed Assyrians finally repelled, or absorbed, the migrating tribes, and re-established control over all the main routes of the Middle East.

883–824. Reigns of Ashurnasirpal II and Shalmaneser III. They carried fire and sword across Mesopotamia, into the Kurdish mountains, and deep into Syria. Then came a brief lull in Assyrian expansion, as weak successors were unable to retain the northern conquests against vengeful foes. The Aramean tribes in Mesopotamia also became restive and unruly.

745–727. Reign of Tiglath-pileser III. He firmly re-established internal order throughout Mesopotamia, then undertook a systematic series of military expeditions around the periphery of Assyria's borders, re-establishing Assyria's frontiers on the Armenian highlands north of Lake Van and Mount Ararat, then conquering Syria, Palestine, and the lands east of the Jordan. In later years he campaigned repeatedly along the new borders he had established, maintaining order by inspiring fear. His last important operation was to invade Babylonia, reasserting vigorously the hitherto nominal Assyrian sovereignty.

ASSYRIAN MILITARY ORGANIZATION, *c.* 700 B.C.

Tiglath-pileser III established the most efficient military, financial, and administrative system the world had yet seen. The army was its heart. He abolished the militia organization and built the state around a standing regular army. The principal business of the nation became war; its wealth and prosperity were sustained by booty and by supervision of trade and finance. A semimilitary bureaucracy carried out the functions of government at home and in the conquered regions, setting the first pattern of centralized imperial control over far-flung provincial territories.

This was the first truly military society of history. No effort was spared which would contribute to the efficiency of the army, or which would assure continued Assyrian supremacy over all possible foes. The Assyrians were the first to recognize fully the advantage of iron over bronze. As early as 1000 B.C. their militia armies had been completely equipped with weapons, chariots, and armor made of iron. Tiglath-pileser saw to it that this technical superiority was maintained by constant and systematic improvement of weapons, and by the careful training of the soldiers in the use of their arms.

The bulk of the army was comprised of large masses of spearmen, slow-moving and cumbersome, but relatively more maneuverable than similar infantry formations of other peoples of the time. Their irresistible advance was the culminating phase of a typical Assyrian battle plan.

In the Assyrian Army the archers were more highly organized than their counterparts elsewhere and evidently had stronger bows, from which they fired iron-tipped arrows with deadly accuracy. They created confusion in the enemy ranks in preparation for a closely coordinated chariot and cavalry charge.

The main striking force of the Assyrian Army was the corps of horse-drawn, two-wheeled chariots. Their mission was to smash their way through the ranks of enemy infantry. Like their contemporaries, the Assyrians used chariots in simple, brute force, but employed them in larger numbers, with more determination, and in closer coordination with archers, spearmen, and cavalry.

The cavalry was the smallest element of the army, but probably the best trained and equipped. The noble horsemen fought with a combination of discipline, skill, and ingenuity not possible in the other elements of the army. Only the cavalry could be employed in the occasional maneuvers attempted in battle.

Assyrian mounted archer

The art of fortification had been well developed in the Middle East before 1000 B.C. The great walls of the large cities were almost invulnerable to the means of attack available within the limited technology of the times. The Assyrians greatly improved the techniques of siegecraft and attack of fortifications. Accompanying their armies were siege trains and various forms of specialized equipment, including materials for building large movable wooden towers (protected from the flaming arrows of defenders by dampened leather hides) and heavy battering rams. From the tops of the wooden towers, skilled archers would sweep the walls of the defenders, to prevent interference with the work of demolition, while nearby other archers, sheltered by the shields of spearmen, would fire arrows—some of them flaming—in a high trajectory over the walls, to harass the defenders and to terrify the population. The methods used by the Assyrians did not originate with them, but were apparently borrowed from the Sumerians. But it was the skill and organization of employment which brought success to Assyrian siegecraft.

The high degree of organization of the Assyrian Army is clearly evidenced by its ability to fight successfully over all kinds of terrain. The organizational details have not been preserved in the fragmentary records available to us, but their field armies may occasionally have approached a strength of 50,000 men. Forces of such size would have required large supply trains for desert or mountain operations, and could have functioned only with smoothly operating staff and logistical systems.

Terror was another factor contributing greatly to Assyrian success. Their exceptional cruelty and ferocity were possibly reflections of callousness developed over centuries of defense of their homeland against savage enemies. But theirs was also a calculated policy of terror—possibly the earliest example of organized psychological warfare. It was not unusual for them to kill every man, woman, and child in captured cities. Sometimes they would carry away entire populations into captivity.

The policies and procedures of Tiglath-pileser III were employed with vigor and ferocity by his successors and proved invaluable in maintaining security.

Assyria, 722–612 B.C.

722–705. Reign of Sargon II. He was faced by a powerful alliance of the northern provinces, combined with the neighboring tribes and nations of Armenia, the Caucasus, and Media. In a series of campaigns he reconquered the rebellious provinces, and extended his rule further north, as well as into central and southern Anatolia. He then returned to Mesopotamia to suppress brutally another Babylonian uprising.

705–681. Reign of Sennacherib. He was faced with comparable insurrections in Palestine, Syria, and Babylonia; among these major setbacks was his repulse at Jerusalem (701, or possibly in a later campaign, 684; see 2 Kings xviii and xix). This repulse was probably the result of a pestilence which ravaged his army. However, he regained the lost provinces, his successes culminating in the capture and destruction of Babylon (689).

681–668. Reign of Essarhaddon. He was able to maintain better internal order than his immediate predecessors. After repelling incursions of the Cimmerians, an Indo-European people inhabiting south Russia and the Caucasus, Essarhaddon conquered Egypt (671). Three years later he died while suppressing a revolt in that country.

668–625. Reign of Ashurbanipal (Essarhaddon's son). He put down Egyptian revolts (668 and 661) as well as undertaking a number of successful campaigns along the northern frontier. Babylonia rebelled once more under the leadership of his half-brother, **Shamash-Shu-mukin** (652). In a bitter, four-year struggle Ashurbanipal put down the revolt with typical Assyrian barbarity. Meanwhile Egypt had risen again and driven out the Assyrian garrisons, while Arabs and Elamites took advantage of Assyria's troubles to attack from the south and north. Ashurbanipal subdued the Arabs, then turned to crush and practically exterminate the Elamites. Despite his successes, the desperate struggles had exhausted the country, almost wiping out the sturdy Assyrian peasantry, the backbone of the army. Assyria, having reached the zenith of her power and magnificence, was forced now to rely largely on mercenaries, mostly

from the wild Scythian tribes who had replaced the Cimmerians along the northern frontier. Upon the death of Ashurbanipal their hordes poured across the northern frontiers, roaming almost at will across the disintegrating empire.

626. Babylonian Revolt. The rebel leader, the satrap, **Nabopolassar,** formed an alliance with **Cyaxares** of Media, also rebelling against Assyria (see p. 11).

616–612. Fall of Assyria. The Median and Babylonian allies invaded Assyria. Nineveh was captured and destroyed; the fall of the capital was the end of Assyria (612), although some resistance persisted in the northwest (612–610).

PALESTINE AND SYRIA, 1200–700 B.C.

c. 1200–c. 800. Warring States. Between the decline of the Egyptian and Hittite empires, and before the height of Assyrian power, the various tribes of Palestine and Syria coalesced into a number of petty, independent, constantly warring states. Outstanding among these were the Jewish nation, the Philistines of southwestern Palestine, the Phoenician cities of northern and western Syria, and the Aramean kingdoms of eastern Syria, of which Damascus was the most important.

c. 1100. Gideon. This most famous of the early Jewish warriors temporarily united most of the independent Israelite tribes in repelling the incursions of the Midianites, an Arabic people living east of the Jordan.

1080–1025. Rise of the Philistines. Israel was invaded and dominated by the Philistines (see p. 6).

1028–1013. Reign of Saul. The Jews rose against their oppressors. Despite many successes, internal squabbles prevented Saul from driving the Philistines completely out of Israel. He was killed by them in the **Battle of Mount Gilboa** (1013).

1010–973. Reign of David. He checked, then destroyed resurgent Philistine power. He reunited the Jews, conquered all Palestine, and apparently dominated most of Syria. He defeated all the external enemies of the Jews, but the later years of his reign were marred by several bloody internal insurrections, one led by his son **Absalom.**

973–933. Reign of Solomon. A period of peace and prosperity. After his death, the Jewish kingdom split into two parts, the kingdoms of Israel and of Judah. For two centuries Jewish history was a succession of wars in which these two rival kingdoms were either pitted against each other or against their many small neighbors.

854. Battle of Qarqar. The temporary alliance of **Ahab** of Israel and **Ben Hadad II** of Damascus postponed Assyrian conquest by a victory over Shalmaneser III.

c. 750. Assyrian Conquest. Palestine and Syria remained under foreign control for the next 27 centuries.

724–722. Revolt in Israel. Assyrian King **Shalmaneser V** heavily besieged **Samaria.** Upon his death **Sargon II** stormed the city and suppressed the revolt.

CHALDEA, 1500–600 B.C.

c. 1500–c. 700. Appearance of the Chaldeans. During the time of Assyrian supremacy, the Chaldeans, a Semitic desert people, infiltrated into southern Mesopotamia. They provided much of the vitality evidenced by Babylonia's frequent efforts to throw off the Assyrian yoke.

612. The New Babylonian, or Chaldean, Empire. Following the conquest of Assyria the Chaldeans took all of Assyria west of the Tigris, while the Medes' share was the former Assyrian provinces east of the river.

612–605. Reign of Nabopolassar. He had no difficulty in establishing his authority in Mesopotamia, but the Egyptian pharaoh, Necho, challenged his assertion of dominion over Syria and Palestine. Nabopolassar sent an army into Syria under his son **Nebuchadnezzar,** who defeated Necho at Carchemish (see p. 7).

605–561. Reign of Nebuchadnezzar. He campaigned in Syria, Palestine, and Phoenicia on several occasions, to subdue sporadic uprisings. He failed to take **Tyre,** which resisted a 13-year siege (585–573). Otherwise his long reign was relatively peaceful, and saw Babylonia reach the pinnacle of ancient Oriental culture.

MEDIA, 800–600 B.C.

c. 800–c. 625. Appearance of the Medes. These semibarbaric descendants of the Asiatic Scythians and Indo-European Iranians occupied what is now northwestern Iran, Kurdistan, and Azerbaijan. They were more or less under Assyrian control (700–625).

625–585. Reign of Cyaxares. He joined Nabopolassar of Babylonia to throw off Assyrian rule (see p. 10). His southwestern frontier secure as a result of a cordial alliance with Chaldea, Cyaxares expanded his empire rapidly to the west as far as Lydia and to the east almost as far as the Indus. This was the largest empire the world had yet seen, but it lacked the administrative machinery of Assyria, Egypt, and Chaldea.

GREECE, 1600–600 B.C.

The Early Greeks

c. 1600. The Minoans of Crete. Their highly developed and artistic civilization had spread to southern Greece and to most of the Aegean Islands.

c. 1400. The Fall of Crete. The island was overrun by invaders from the mainland, probably part of the Achaean (Indo-European) migrations from central Europe.

c. 1400–c. 1200. The Achaeans Take to the Sea. Under pressure from succeeding migration waves, the Achaeans, in company with other Mediterranean peoples, stimulated and took part in the "Peoples of the Sea" movement which so seriously affected the Mediterranean coast of the Middle East (see pp. 6 and 7).

c. 1184. The Siege of Troy. The half-legendary story of this war, as passed on to posterity by **Homer,** can be considered as the beginning of Greek history.

1100–600. Coalescence of Greece. The different peoples who had migrated into Greece, the Aegean Islands, and the west coast of Asia Minor gradually became the relatively homogeneous Greek people known to history. But for all of their cultural homogeneity, the mountainous, insular, and peninsular geography of Greece divided them politically into many tiny, independent, energetic states. Much Greek energy was consumed in a great colonization effort, in a sense merely a continuation of the migratory urge which had brought them originally into Greece. To this basic wanderlust were added the impulses of trade and the pressures of population. This colonization had important military consequences: (1) The Greeks became a seafaring people. (2) The adventurous found ample opportunity for maintaining a high standard of combat proficiency beyond the seas. (3) From combat and observation, the Greeks learned much about the strengths and weaknesses of the barbarian and civilized nations of the Mediterranean and Middle East.

Sparta, 1000–600 B.C.

c. 1000. The Founding of Sparta. The early military development of this small town in the middle of the Peloponnesian Peninsula was indistinguishable from that of other inland Greek towns.

c. 700. The Legacy of Lycurgus. Under this semilegendary leader, Sparta became, and remained, a completely military society, always maintained on a war footing. From his earliest years the Spartan citizen had only one mission in life: military service. The state was the army, and the army was the state. The result was the development of the best individual soldiers in Greece and the creation of what was, for its size and time, probably the best small army in the history of the world. The Spartan army was not significantly different from those of other Greek city-states in composition, armament, or tactics; essentially an infantry force of armored spearmen, it was composed primarily of the free-born citizens of the upper and middle classes. The principal distinguishing characteristics were the more thoroughly developed individual military skills, greatly superior organization, higher order of unit maneuverability, and the iron discipline for which the Spartans became renowned throughout Greece.

c. 700–c. 680. The First Messenian War. Sparta conquered the rich Messenian Plain to become the dominant state in southern Peloponnesus.

c. 640–620. The Second Messenian War. After a prolonged struggle Sparta again subdued Messenia and enslaved the conquered survivors.

ITALY AND ROME, 2000–600 B.C.

c. 2000. Arrival of the Ancestors of the Latins. An Indo-European people, closely related to the Greeks, migrated across the Alps from central Europe, bringing the Bronze Age to Italy.

c. 1000. Introduction of Iron. The development came with another migration.

c. 900. Arrival of the Etruscans. These were people of different racial stock who arrived in northwestern Italy by sea from the east. At the same time Greek traders and colonizers were gaining considerable influence in Sicily and southern Italy.

c. 700.* Founding of Rome. From its beginning Rome was important militarily; archaeology confirms legend. This was inevitable from its location on the border between the Indo-European settlements of Latium and the Etruscan city-states farther north. Possibly the town was established as a Latin outpost to hold off the expanding Etruscans.

c. 700–c. 500. Continuous Wars with the Etruscans. Rome in its early history may have fallen to the status of an Etruscan colony; it was for a time ruled by kings of Etruscan ancestry. A distinctive military system began to evolve during this formative period of constant combat.

SOUTH ASIA

INDIA, 2000–600 B.C.

c. 2000. The Aryan Invasions. The history of South Asia is generally considered to begin with the arrival of the Aryan invaders in the Indus Valley. They were an Indo-European people, closely related by language, religion, and customs to the Persians or Iranians. We know nothing of the details of the early conflicts between the barbaric invaders and the cultured, dark-skinned early inhabitants—Dravidians—but the Aryans slowly expanded across northern India, driving the

* It is generally agreed that Rome was founded later than the traditional date of 750 B.C.

Dravidians south. There was some amalgamation of peoples and cultures to form a new **Hindu** culture. At least one hardy band of Aryan invaders reached the very tip of India, and crossed over to Ceylon, which they conquered. They were, however, soon absorbed.

c. 1000–600. Hindu Consolidation. The predominantly Aryan Hindus firmly established themselves as masters of the Indus and upper Ganges valleys, most of their energy being absorbed by incessant warfare among their numerous tribal kingdoms or republics.

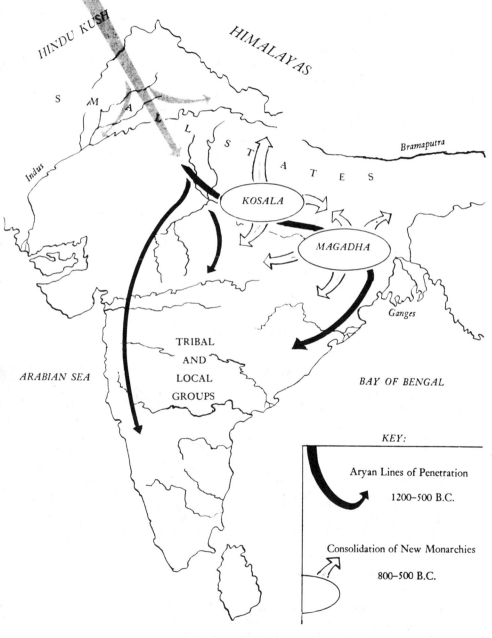

Ancient India

c. 900. Mongoloid Invaders. These brief raids presaged the future. The north Indian plain was vulnerable to invasion from the northwest. Though the fertile Ganges and Brahmaputra valleys must have been at least equally attractive to northeastern neighbors, it is of some significance that there is no record of great invasion from that direction. Formidable though they were, the Hindu Kush and Iranian highlands were fairly easily traversable by substantial military forces; the Himalayan-Tibetan complex of mountains and desolate plateaux were not.

EARLY HINDU MILITARY ORGANIZATION

Our knowledge of warfare and military practices during the period prior to 600 B.C. has been gleaned from the earliest classical literature of India—particularly the **Rigveda** and the **Mahabharata.**

The armies were made up almost entirely of footmen. The bow was their principal weapon. There was apparently no cavalry; horses were scarce and therefore were reserved for pulling the two-man war chariots of the kings and nobles. The warriors were the most honored and leading class of society. Iron weapons did not appear in India until about the 5th century B.C., which would indicate that military techniques were probably less advanced than in the Middle East.

EAST ASIA

CHINA, 1600–600 B.C.

c. 1600. Emergence of Historical China. This was in the Yellow River Valley. It is difficult to distinguish between legend and history until sometime after 900 B.C. Archaeology, however, has supported most traditional legend.

c. 1523–1027. The Shang Dynasty. The first clearly identifiable ancestors of the modern Chinese were a highly civilized people known to history by the name of

Ancient China

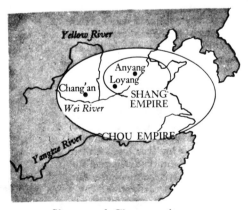

Shang and Chou empires

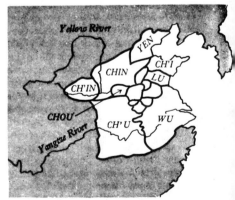

The warring states

their ruling dynasty. The Shang ruled over a relatively limited inland area around their capital, Anyang, in what is now the northern tip of Honan province. Their history is a record of wars, expansion, and internal troubles not unlike that of Egypt at about the same time. During the 12th century B.C. a semibarbaric people called **Chou** began to press eastward from the region near the junction of the Wei and Yellow rivers.

c. 1027. Establishment of the Chou Dynasty. Under **Wu Wang**, the "Martial King," the Chou defeated the Shang and absorbed their domains. Wu Wang died soon after, and his younger brother, Duke **Chou Kung,** became the regent for 7 years, during the minority of the Martial King's son. Chou Kung firmly repressed a Shang uprising and seems to have established a ruling organization comparable to that of Thutmosis III. It was largely due to this organization that the Chou Dynasty lasted for almost 900 years, despite the weakness and impotence of the kings during the latter two-thirds of that period.

c. 1000–c. 900. Chou Expansion. They drove eastward, to the sea, and pressed north to the vicinity of the present Manchurian border. Later they moved south into the lower Yangtze Valley and the coastal regions in between.

c. 800–600. Decline of Chou Power. As royal control became nominal, power gravitated to the provincial nobles, and for several centuries China's history became one of constant fighting among autonomous war lords.

EARLY CHINESE MILITARY ORGANIZATION

The art of warfare in China by about 600 B.C. was apparently as well advanced as that of the Middle East. Chinese weapons, however, were not as good as those of the Assyrians; both their bronze and iron metallurgy lagged several centuries behind the Middle East. The bronze workmanship of that period, however, was perhaps superior to that which could be found further west.

From earliest times the Chinese appear to have relied upon the bow as their principal hand weapon. Apparently the bow was always of the reflex variety, constructed of wood, horn, and sinew, and considerably longer and more powerful than those normally found in the West. Arrows were probably always made of bamboo, with metal heads appearing in historical times.

Bronze helmets appeared in China during the time of the Shang, and armor development, despite a slower start than in the Middle East, had probably caught up by about 600 B.C.

Cavalry apparently was not used by the Shang or early Chou. Chariots, however, were in use as early as 1400 B.C., and became increasingly important. Initially only the principal leaders rode and fought in chariots, which seem to have been used primarily as mobile command posts by the king or general, who was accompanied by a drummer-signaler, and also by a driver and one or more archers. But as time went on, greater advantage was taken of the shock-action capabilities of the chariot, and it became the primary instrument of war. The very strength of a state was estimated in terms of the number of war chariots it could assemble.

II

WAR BECOMES AN ART:
600—400 B.C.

MILITARY TRENDS

Significant, in this era of change and progress in all human activity, is the transition from semilegendary chronicles to serious, reliable histories. The principal military trends are thus more clear-cut. Two were of significance: (1) Within the limits of technology sound concepts evolved for the employment of weapons; and (2) as a consequence, theories of tactics and military doctrine emerged. By 400 B.C. war had assumed the major characteristics which it retained at least into the dawn of the nuclear age.

WEAPONS

Weapons themselves were essentially unchanged. There would, in fact, be relatively little modification in weapons and related implements of warfare for nearly 2,000 more years. Fundamental changes would have to await the appearance of sources of power transcending brute strength and mechanical attempts to harness the forces of gravity and of the wind.

TACTICS AND DOCTRINE ON LAND

Substantial advances were made, however, in the use of existing weapons. During the middle of the 6th century, **Cyrus the Great** made conscious effort to instill concepts of discipline and training into his army. Though these concepts had been recognized from early Mesopotamian times, they were gradually assuming greater importance among all peoples geared to military action. The principal result was to increase the value and importance of the infantry, whose unwieldy masses in earlier centuries had precluded all possibility of maneuver.

Battle formations, prebattle rituals, and religious rites, however, were stereotyped, and had their origins in the unrecorded past. Astrologers and soothsayers were consulted; offerings were made to the gods; and omens foretelling victory were anxiously sought. After haranguing the troops drawn up for battle, the general would order the advance to combat. This was usually done to the accompaniment of rousing military bands.

16

The armies approached each other in parallel lines, with the infantry in the center, chariots and cavalry generally on the flanks (sometimes in front), and with swarms of irregular slingers and bowmen usually screening the advance until the main bodies were within a hundred yards of one another. Variations in battle orders were rare, save for relative locations of cavalry and chariots, either in front or on the flanks. Just before the clash of the main lines of the opposing armies, the light troops would slip away around the flanks, or back through intervals left in the lines for this purpose. Sometimes one side would stand fast on the defensive, but more often both sides would stride purposefully toward each other, their shouts and clash of arms creating a terrible noise.

Experience had shown that last-minute maneuvers were likely to create dangerous gaps in the lines, or to expose a marching flank to missile and shock attack. Therefore tactical ingenuity was not often attempted beyond the point where an enemy would be forced to enter battle on unfavorable ground, or with only a portion of his available forces. The usual objective in battle was to outflank the enemy, since only the flanks and rear of well-armed infantry—10 to 30 ranks deep—were sensitive and vulnerable. Though we shall note a few examples of successful deviation from the parallel order of battle, such deviations more often led to failure.

Cavalry still played a great role, particularly on the wide plains of Central and Southwest Asia. Except in India and Persia, the chariot had lost much of its terror for disciplined, maneuverable footmen, and was no longer the main weapon of battle.

Cyrus of Persia won his earliest successes with foot troops—particularly expert archers—much more alert and resourceful than those in other Asiatic countries. But he discovered that he needed cavalry of his own to neutralize the effectiveness of the horsemen on whom his foes still mainly depended. The Persians quickly adapted themselves to the horse, and soon the Persian heavy cavalry and mounted archers were by far the best in the world.

As the mountains of Greece were unfavorable to cavalry movements, the Greeks in general neglected that arm, except in the northern, flatter regions of Thessaly and Macedonia. Elsewhere in the Greek peninsula, the Aegean Islands, and along the Ionian coast, the steadily improving infantry **phalanx** was relied on chiefly. This disciplined body of heavy infantry formed itself for battle in long lines which varied in depth from 8 to 16 men. The individual soldier of the phalanx was called a **hoplite**—a well-trained, disciplined soldier, kept in excellent physical condition by sport or combat. His major weapon was a pike, 8 to 10 feet long. His short sword was usually sheathed while he was in the phalanx formation. He also wore a helmet, breastplate, and greaves, and carried a round shield. In battle the hoplites in the front ranks pointed their spears toward the foe; those in the rear rested theirs on the shoulders of the men in front, forming a sort of hedge to break up flights of enemy arrows.

The phalanx and its individual units were capable of limited maneuvers in combat formation. In battle the invariable formation was a long, solid line—with narrow intervals through which light troops could pass. Battle was waged on the flattest ground available, since movement over rough ground created gaps which could be fatal.

The hoplites came from the upper and middle classes of the free citizens of the Greek states. The **psiloi,** or light troops, generally poorly armed, were neither so well trained nor disciplined. For the most part these came from the lower classes of society, but many of them were mercenaries. Along with the generally inferior cavalry, they protected the flanks of the phalanx on the march and in battle. Some of the archers and slingers, such as those from Crete and Rhodes, were quite effective. In addition to rigorous training and excellent physical condition, the Greek hoplite possessed the military advantages and disadvantages of alert, intelligent, literate free citizens of proud and independent countries. These qualities made the Greeks suspicious of regimentation, even though intellect clearly accepted the need for tactical discipline.

One aspect of the military art in which this period failed to approach the limits imposed by existing technology was in the area of engineering. Neither Persians, Greeks, nor Chinese achieved any marked improvement over the engineering techniques which had been developed by the Assyrians. Fortification had, in fact, progressed about as far as available means would permit; the art of siegecraft had failed to keep pace. Save for a few exceptional instances of surprise, ruse, or betrayal, walled cities or fortresses were impervious to everything but starvation.

Greek hoplites

NAVAL TACTICS AND DOCTRINE

The use of ships for warlike purposes had long been a common practice of seafaring peoples living along the shores of the Mediterranean and Aegean seas. Prior to the 7th century B.C., however, this had been largely limited to employing merchant ships as troop and supply transports. These short, broad-beamed craft, combining sails and oars, were essentially adjuncts of land power.

About 700 B.C. the Phoenicians introduced the first vessels designed essentially for fighting. These were speedy, oar-propelled galleys, longer and narrower than the typical merchant ship.

The Greeks, particularly the Athenians, improved the Phoenician galleys, and brought to naval warfare a skill and perfection in technique hitherto unknown in fighting on land ór sea. The Athenian **trireme** was long, low, and narrow, deriving its name from the fact that its oars were ranged in groups of three along one bank of oars, with oarsmen on each side of the vessel. Seaworthiness, comfort, cargo capacity, and range were deliberately sacrificed to achieve speed, power, and maneuverability. In addition to its oars, the trireme carried sails on its two masts as a means of auxiliary power; in battle, however, it was propelled exclusively by its 150 oarsmen.

A war fleet could not carry food and water for a long voyage; it had to be accompanied by a flotilla of supply vessels and transports. Vulnerable to storms, trireme fleets endeavored to keep near to sheltering coasts; long voyages far from land were avoided if possible.

The principal weapon of the trireme was a metal beak projecting some 10 feet in front of the prow at the water line. When this beak was rammed into the side of another vessel, the results were deadly. The difficulties of accomplishing this, however, were such that most of the Greeks usually preferred to rely upon the older tactics of pulling up alongside a foe and boarding.

Athenian sailors, however, relied upon superior seamanship, speed, and maneuverability to bring victory. When there was not an immediate opportunity to smash directly into the side of an opponent, Athenian vessels would swerve unexpectedly beside their foes, shipping their oars at the last moment, and breaking those of the surprised enemy. The disabled foe was then literally a sitting duck, to be rammed at leisure by one of the Athenian vessels. Athens' foes were never able to match this superiority in seamanship.

THEORY OF WARFARE

Economic and logistical considerations played a particularly important part in the major wars of the 5th century B.C. For Persia, the great land power, the problem was lines of communications thousands of miles long, vulnerable to harassment and interruption by sea and by land. For the smaller Greek states, particularly in their wars against Persia and among themselves, there were two main problems: (1) Their relatively complex societies were not self-sufficient, and in many instances were dependent upon distant, overwater sources of supply to maintain both peacetime and wartime economies. (2) The military security of several Greek states was based upon an extremely expensive and relatively sophisticated weapon system (the trireme fleet), which could be maintained and operated only at great cost in treasure, and in highly trained, skilled manpower.

Not the least remarkable development of this age was the serious study of wars and warfare which is suddenly discernible in the 5th century B.C. The first known histories—those of **Herodotus** and **Thucydides**—were not conscious military histories, but inevitably they dealt mainly with military events. And about the same time, in China, **Sun Tzu** was composing his treatise on *The Art of War*, revealing an understanding of the practical and philosophical fundamentals of war and of military leadership so sound and enlightened as to warrant serious study by scholars and soldiers today.

MEDITERRANEAN–
MIDDLE EAST

EGYPT, 600–525 B.C.

c. 590. **Operations in Lower Nubia.** The campaigns of **Psammetichus II** were inconclusive.

c. 586–568. **Reign of Apries.** His vain efforts to prevent the Chaldean conquest of Syria and Palestine culminated in his defeat at Jerusalem by Nebuchadnezzar (c.

580), who then consolidated control over Palestine (see p. 11). Turning west, Apries was repulsed in efforts to conquer the Greek colony of Cyrene (c. 570). He was overthrown by the revolt of **Ahmose II.**

567. **Invasion of Palestine.** Ahmose was repulsed by the aged Chaldean emperor, Nebuchadnezzar.

547–546. **Alliance with Croesus of Lydia.** Ahmose sent a large contingent of Egyptian heavy infantry to join Croesus against Cyrus of Persia. At the **Battle of Thymbra** the Egyptians stood firm in the rout of the Lydians (see below). Cyrus made separate terms with the Egyptians, who returned home with honor.

525. Persian Conquest. (See p. 21). Egypt was to remain under foreign rule for more than 24 centuries.

PERSIA, 600–400 B.C.

The Decline of Media, 600–559 B.C.

600–585. War with Lydia. A long, inconclusive war in Asia Minor ended with the Halys River accepted as the boundary.
585–559. Uneasy Balance of Power in the Middle East. This was shared between Media, Chaldean Babylonia, Egypt, and Lydia.

The Early Persian Empire, 559–400 B.C.

559. Independence of Persia. Led by their prince, **Cyrus,** the Persians, an Aryan people closely related to the Medes, revolted against **Astyages** of Media, who was deposed by Cyrus.
559–530. Reign of Cyrus the Great. His first task was the consolidation of his conquest of Media (559–550).
547. Lydian Invasion. Under their king, Croesus, they crossed the Halys into Cappadocia, a province of Persia-Media, either for the purpose of restoring Croesus' brother-in-law Astyages to the throne of Media or to try to forestall a Persian invasion of Lydia. Croesus had organized an alliance against Persia with Chaldea, Egypt, and tiny, but militarily potent, Sparta.
547 (546?). Battle of Pteria. Cyrus marched to meet Croesus, fighting a savage but indecisive winter battle. Croesus withdrew across the Halys and prepared for a new campaign. From Sardis, his capital, he sent messages to his allies, suggesting an advance into Persia when the weather improved. Cyrus invaded Lydia and (early 546) approached Sardis with a large army (but certainly no more than one-quarter of the 200,000 men reported in Xenophon's *Cyropaedia*).
546. Battle of Thymbra. Croesus hastily reassembled an even larger allied army

and marched to meet Cyrus on the nearby Plain of Thymbra. Badly outnumbered, Cyrus deployed his troops with flanks refused in a great square formation, the first recorded deviation from the normal parallel order of combat. He organized most of his army in depth, in 5 relatively short lines. The flanks were covered by chariots, cavalry, his best infantry, and a newly improvised camel corps, facing outward, perpendicular to the front. As Cyrus expected, the wings of the Lydian army wheeled inward to envelop this novel formation. As the Lydian flanks swung in, gaps appeared at the hinges of the wheeling wings. Disorder was increased by effective overhead fire of Persian archers and dart throwers, stationed within the square. Cyrus then gave the order to attack. His flank units smashed Croesus' disorganized wings; shortly afterward the Persian cavalry slashed through the gaps at the hinges. In a short time the Lydian army was routed. Cyrus pursued and captured Sardis by storm. He treated the captured with magnanimity rare for the age.
545–539. Eastward Expansion. Cyrus now turned his attention to the arid plateaux to the east, which had owed nominal allegiance to Media, but which now were attempting to re-establish independence. In a few years he reconquered most of Parthia, Sogdiana, Bactria, and Arachosia.
539–538. Conquest of Chaldea. Cyrus next invaded Babylonia, which had joined Croesus' anti-Persian alliance, defeating King **Nabonidus** and investing Babylon. For nearly 2 years the tremendous walls of the city defied Cyrus. He finally diverted the waters of the Euphrates, and his troops dashed in through the lowered stream bed, catching the defenders by surprise. The Chaldean Empire was quickly annexed to Persia.
537–530. Expedition in the East. Cyrus decided to round out his eastern dominions before dealing with Egypt and Sparta. He conquered much of the region west of the Indus River, and campaigned north as far as the Jaxartes. Here he was killed in battle against the Massagetae.

COMMENT. **Cyrus** *was the first great captain of recorded history. His conquests* *were more extensive than those of any earlier conqueror, and proved to be more permanent. This was largely due to his administrative genius and his ability to win the confidence of the conquered peoples.*

530–521. Reign of Cambyses (Son of Cyrus). An able warrior, he was an inadequate ruler. He carried out his father's ambition to conquer Egypt, defeating **Psammetichus III** at **Pelusium** (525), and also seized the Greek colony of Cyrene. He was unsuccessful, however, in an expedition up the Nile against Nubia and Ethiopia. He died while marching back to Persia to deal with an imposter who had seized the throne.

522–521. Civil War. Cambyses' cousin, **Darius,** led a successful revolt against the imposter who had usurped the throne.

521–486. Reign of Darius the Great. The wise and brilliant rule of this organizational genius assured the stability of the Persian Empire. Many subject peoples had taken advantage of Persia's internal turmoil to try to regain independence. Darius promptly and efficiently put down the revolts (521–519), then spent the remainder of his reign in consolidation. He

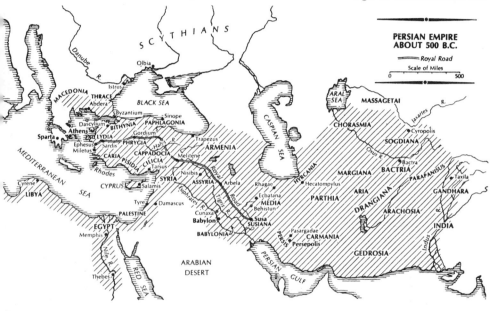

PERSIAN EMPIRE
ABOUT 500 B.C.
══ Royal Road
Scale of Miles
0   500

did not personally participate in many campaigns after his authority had been firmly established. He did, however, supervise some operations along the Indus River, north into the Pamirs of Central Asia, and against the Scythians in the steppes east of the Caspian Sea. His generals subjugated eastern Asia Minor and Armenia, and established the northern frontier of the empire along the crest of the Caucasus Mountains.

511. Invasion of Southeastern Europe. Darius personally led this expedition, which had three objectives: (1) to establish a base in Thrace for subsequent absorption of the Greek states; (2) to protect the long lines of communications leading to and from Thrace; and (3) to strike the rear of the Scythian tribes of the steppes region. (He did not realize that the Scythians of the Danube area were some 2,000 miles west of their brethren south of the Aral Sea.) The expedition, carefully prepared, utilized both land and sea forces drawn from all parts of the empire and included some Greek mercenaries. (The total strength was probably one-tenth the 700,000 attributed by Herodotus.) The navy, after building and maintaining a floating bridge over the Bosporus, patrolled the western shores of the Black Sea. Darius marched north to the Danube, where the navy constructed another floating bridge. Leaving a strong force to protect the bridge, Darius continued northward for several hundred miles, living off the country. The

Scythian horsemen refused to stand and fight, but continuously harassed the Persian Army. After two or more months of frustrating and costly marches, Darius returned to the Danube with the bulk of his army intact. The Scythians, however, had been sufficiently awed by Darius' armed might so that they made no move south of the Danube during subsequent Persian wars with Greece; Thrace and Macedonia were firmly annexed to the Persian Empire.

499–448. Graeco-Persian Wars. (See pp. 23–29.)

486–465. Reign of Xerxes. This was the beginning of a slow decline of Persia.

401–400. Revolt of Cyrus the Younger. This revolt against his brother, **Artaxerxes II,** led to the **Battle of Cunaxa** and the *Anabasis* of Xenophon (see p. 33).

PERSIAN MILITARY SYSTEM, C. 500 B.C.

How much of the military and political organization of the Persian Empire was due to the genius of Cyrus and how much to the innovations of Darius is unclear. Cyrus, the more imaginative, probably established the system which Darius then perfected.

The basis of the system was the spirit, skill, and resourcefulness of the Persians. An important weapon was the bow, used effectively by both cavalry and infantry. Insofar as possible the Persians avoided close-quarters infantry combat until their foes had been thoroughly disorganized by swarms of foot archers from the front, and the daring onrushes of horse archers against flanks and rear. The Persians were versatile in adapting their methods of warfare to all conditions of terrain. They respected the shock action of the Lydian cavalry lancers, and incorporated this concept into their mounted tactics.

Subject peoples were required to render military service. The garrisons scattered throughout the empire were principally composed of units from other regions (including many Greek mercenaries) but always included a Persian contingent. Imperial expeditionary forces were also multinational. The Persians received a surprisingly high standard of loyalty from these diverse groups, due largely to their policies of leniency toward the conquered, and of carefully supervised but decentralized administration.

The empire was divided into about 20 provinces, or satrapies, each governed by a trusted and able official. The principal military garrison in each satrapy was under the command of a general directly responsible to the emperor, which prevented dangerous accumulation of power in any region. In the emperor's court an inspector general (the "eye of the king") was responsible for the supervision of all provincial activities. This complex, but not cumbersome, system of control and of checks and balances was facilitated by a mounted-messenger system covering an excellent network of roads.

GREECE, 600–494 B.C.

Peninsular and Aegean Greece

c. 600. Ascendancy of Sparta. Her military prowess particularly dominated the Peloponnesus. This was the so-called "Age of Tyrants," and many of the Greek states were torn by civil wars between the forces of democracy and oligarchy. The tyrants were as frequently leaders of the democratic elements as they were of the oligarchy, and the word "tyrant" in those days simply meant authoritative rule by a single individual. Sparta, though far from a democratic state herself, was consistently antityrant, and sometimes intervened in the internal struggles of the other states. Though none of the other Greek states felt strong enough to challenge Sparta's ascendancy by itself, four of these (Argos, Athens, Corinth, and possibly Thebes), in shifting alliances among themselves and with smaller states, were able to preserve a balance of power.

c. 560–c. 520. Rise of Athens. Her growing

commerce, population, and wealth might have put Athens in a position to challenge Sparta, had it not been for recurrent civil strife between the forces of oligarchy and democracy.

519–507. War of Athens and Thebes. This desultory conflict resulted from Theban efforts to take advantage of Athens' difficulties and to force little Plataea, an ally of Athens, into a Boeotian League.

510–507. Spartan Intervention in Athens. The oligarchs overthrew the popular Athenian tyrant **Hippias,** with the help of **Cleomenes,** King of Sparta. Hippias fled to Persia, where he soon found favor with Darius. When the internal struggle in Athens continued, Cleomenes again intervened and captured Athens (507). The Athenians, rallying under the democratic leader **Cleisthenes,** expelled the Spartans. Cleomenes could not obtain support in Sparta for another invasion of Attica, to avenge this repulse.

494. Battle of Sepeia. Cleomenes overwhelmed Argos, then established himself as virtual tyrant in Sparta. However, in an ensuing civil war he was captured and deposed.

Ionian Greece

c. 550. Lydian Control. Some of the Greek cities on the coast of Asia Minor, with the principal exception of Miletus, were annexed to Lydia by Croesus.

546. Persian Conquest. The general **Harpagus** subdued the Ionian cities, which had tried to reassert their independence after the fall of Croesus (see p. 20).

c. 512. Unrest in Ionia. This was largely inspired by the free Greek states farther west. As a result Darius decided to conquer European Greece.

510. Ionian Revolt. Misled by false reports that Darius had been defeated by the Scythians, some of the northern Ionian cities revolted, but were quickly and firmly brought back under Persian rule. Unrest seethed in Ionia.

THE GRAECO-PERSIAN WARS, 499–448 B.C.

Ionian Revolt, 499–493 B.C.

499. Outbreak of the Revolt. This was led by the city of Miletus, which requested assistance from Greece. Sparta refused, but Athens and Eretria (on Euboea) sent small land and naval contingents.

498. Rebel Setbacks. The rebels captured Sardis, capital of the satrapy of Lydia, but **Artaphernes,** the satrap, quickly recaptured his capital and drove the Greeks back to the sea, defeating them in the **Battle of Ephesus.** The rebellious cities were unable to maintain a united front against the Persians and most were recaptured.

494. Siege of Miletus; Battle of Lade. To cut the city off from its contact with European Greece, Darius assembled a large fleet, which defeated the Ionians in a great battle off the tiny island of Lade, near Miletus. The city soon surrendered and the revolt collapsed.

493. Darius Determines to Conquer Greece. In particular he wanted to punish Athens for having supported the Ionian revolt.

492. Preparations for a Land-Sea Expedition. The Persian general **Mardonius** consolidated control over restive Thrace and Macedonia, in preparation for an invasion of Greece. His fleet, however, was wrecked during a storm off the rocky promontory of Mount Athos, so he withdrew to Asia Minor.

491. Amphibious Preparations. Darius now decided to send an amphibious force directly across the Aegean to attack Athens and Eretria. In command were Artaphernes and the Median general **Datis.** The expedition contained the cream of the Persian Army and Navy, and probably numbered nearly 50,000 men (not the 100,000 averred by Herodotus). The former Athenian tyrant Hippias was with the expedition.

CAMPAIGN AND BATTLE OF MARATHON, 490 B.C.

The Athenians first learned of the expedition when Eretria was attacked. A message asking Sparta for help was immediately sent, carried by the famed runner **Pheidippedes,** and the Athenians prepared themselves for battle. Sparta sent word that it would help, but would be delayed for nearly two weeks by a religious festival. About the same time word reached Athens that the Persians were landing near Marathon, some 26 miles away. The Athenians, about 9,000 hoplites and a smaller number of light troops, immediately marched to high ground overlooking the Persian debarkation. Here they could block the route leading from the narrow coastal plain toward Athens. They were soon joined by a small force from Plataea. **Callimachus** commanded the Athenians, and under him were 10 other generals, of whom the most respected and most experienced was **Miltiades.**

The Persians apparently knew that many Athenians, fearing defeat and the destruction of their city, were ready to surrender. They had landed at Marathon for the express purpose of drawing the Athenian troops away from the city. Having accomplished this, Artaphernes embarked with half the Persian Army, to sail around Attica for Athens, while Datis and the remainder (possibly 20,000 men) stayed ashore to hold the Athenian Army immobilized at Marathon.

Miltiades guessed the Persian plan and urged an immediate attack. After a heated council of war, Callimachus voted in support of Miltiades' bold plan and entrusted him with command of the battle.

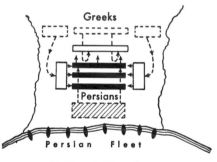

Battle of Marathon

Immediately the Athenians and Plataeans marched down the slopes to form up facing the Persian outposts, the Plataeans on the left. Miltiades had lengthened the Greek line so that the flanks rested on two small streams flowing to the sea. This thinned the center of the line substantially below the 12-man depth then favored for the phalanx, making it vulnerable to penetration by Persian cavalry charges. But Miltiades kept his wings at full phalanx depth. The result was a formation providing a powerful striking force on each flank, connected by a very thin line in the center.

The Greeks advanced across the narrow plain toward the Persian camp and beach, until within bowshot range (less than 200 yards) of the Persian archers, and then charged; the opposing archers could do no more than fire a few hastily aimed arrows before seeking safety behind the main Persian formation.

It is probable that the Greek center advanced somewhat less rapidly than the flanks, either by design or because they were exposed to the heaviest fire from the Persian archers. As the two lines met in the shock of combat, the Persians were able to throw back the thin center with relative ease. The Greek line almost immediately became concave, as the two heavy phalangial wings rapidly drove back the flanks of the lightly armored Persians. The Greek wings now began to wheel inward, compressing the Persians in a perfectly executed double envelopment. (Authorities differ as to whether this had been planned or was accidental. In any event, Miltiades had displayed his understanding of the capabilities and limitation of both armies, and of the fundamental military principles of concentration and of economy of force.)

The Persian flanks, followed by the center, took flight back to the shore, and to the transports drawn up along the beach. Datis seems to have organized some sort of a rear guard to cover the panicky embarkation of his defeated troops. This is the only explanation of his ability to get away with most of his fleet and with relatively little loss of men and transports. It was in the final confused and desperate fighting at the shore line that the Greeks lost most of their 192 killed, among these Callimachus. The Persians are reputed to have lost 6,400 killed.

Miltiades now promptly set his tired but jubilant men marching back toward Athens. In advance, in hopes that tidings of the victory would strengthen the wavering citizens sufficiently for them to hold out until the army arrived, he sent word back by a runner, reputedly Pheidippedes, on the first Marathon run. As the Athenian army arrived, the Persian fleet was only beginning to approach the shore for a landing. Realizing he was too late, Artaphernes withdrew.

That evening the Spartans arrived, to learn to their chagrin that they had missed the fight.

Persian Preparations for Invasion, 490–480 B.C.

490. Darius' Plans for Revenge. Infuriated, Darius began elaborate preparations for the complete subjugation of Greece, this time by a combined land-sea expedition.

486–484. Revolt in Egypt. This forced a temporary diversion of Persian military strength. The revolt was subdued, but meanwhile Darius had died (486).

484–481. Xerxes Resumes Preparations. Within three years Xerxes had gathered at Sardis a force of about 200,000 men— probably the largest army ever assembled up to that time. Two long floating bridges were built across the Hellespont, over which the army could march in two parallel columns. To prevent the Greek states from receiving any assistance from the powerful Greek colonies in Sicily, Xerxes made a treaty with Carthage, which agreed to attack Sicily when he began his invasion of Greece. These preparations reveal a remarkable Persian capacity for diplomacy and for strategic and administrative planning. Despite Marathon, the Greeks still feared and respected the military might of Persia, and were alarmed by reports of Xerxes' preparations. Most Athenians and most of the Peloponnesian states, led by Sparta, manfully determined to resist. Most of the remaining Greek states, convinced that Persian power was overwhelming, either endeavored to stay neutral or supported Persia.

484–483. Military Policy Debate in Athens. A lingering naval war with rival Aegina caused many citizens, led by **Themistocles,** to urge an increasing emphasis on sea power—particularly since they saw no possibility of matching Persian land power. The other party, under **Aristides,** pointed to the vulnerability of Athens to overland invasion, insisting that the largest navy in the world could not protect the city from the Persian Army. The issue was resolved by a popular vote; Aristides was defeated, and Themistocles immediately began a tremendous trireme-building program (483).

481–480. Strategic Debate between Sparta and Athens. The patriotic states now disagreed on the strategy to meet the expected invasion. The Peloponnesians urged the abandonment of all of Greece north of the Isthmus of Corinth; they felt this 4½-mile corridor could easily be defended. The Athenians, however, refused to abandon their city. Themistocles pointed out the vulnerability of the Peloponnesus to Persian sea power, and insisted that the Persian advance could be successfully disputed on land and on sea much farther north. The Spartans, recognizing the value of the Athenian navy, reluctantly agreed to Themistocles' strategy.

The Campaigns of Thermopylae and Salamis, 480 B.C.

480, Spring. The Persian Advance. The Persian host crossed the Hellespont and marched westward along the Thracian and Macedonian coasts, then south into Thessaly. In direct command, under Xerxes, was **Mardonius.** Just offshore the great Persian fleet kept pace. According to Herodotus, the fleet consisted of approximately 1,500 warships and 3,000 transports.

Greek Defensive Measures. Northern Greece was abandoned without a blow because holding the passes south of Mount Olympus required too many men. The next suitable defensive position was the defile of Thermopylae. At the West and Middle Gates of the defile, the Ledge, probably not more than 14 feet wide, provided perfect defensive positions where a few determined hoplites could indefinitely hold off any number of the more lightly armed Persians. To Thermopylae went Spartan King **Leonidas,** with about 7,000 hoplites and some archers. Save for Leonidas' bodyguard of 300 men, few of these were Spartans. The failure of the Peloponnesian states to send more troops to hold Thermopylae is evidence of their halfhearted interest in carrying out any defense north of Corinth. To prevent the Persian fleet from attacking or bypassing the sea flank of the troops at Thermopylae, the Greek fleet of about 330 triremes was stationed off Artemisium, on the northeastern coast of Euboea. In nominal command was the Spartan **Eurybiades,** though Themistocles, with nearly two-thirds of the total Greek naval strength, exercised a major voice in the councils of war. As the Persian fleet approached, the forces of nature took a hand; severe storms inflicted great damage on the Persian fleet, which lost nearly half of its fighting strength. Apparently the Greeks did not suffer so seriously.

480, August (?). Battle of Artemisium. An indecisive naval conflict took place off Artemisium in two cautious engagements on successive days, with few losses on either side. The Greeks were prepared to continue the battle more decisively on the third day, but on hearing the news from Thermopylae they sailed for Athens.

480, August (?). Battle of Thermopylae. Leonidas had carefully and soundly prepared for defense. With his main body, about 6,000 strong, he held the Middle Gate. He had posted a force of 1,000 men high on the mountains to his left, to cover the one forest track which led around the defile. As expected, the Persians tried to force their way through the pass, but the Greek hoplites repulsed them. For three days the Persians vainly tried to break through; then a Greek traitor told Xerxes of the forest track across the mountain behind Thermopylae. Xerxes promptly dispatched along this trail the "Immortals" of his bodyguard, who quickly overwhelmed the Greek flank guard in a surprise attack. Though Leonidas sent about 4,500 men to block the Persian envelopment, they were too late, and were crushed by the Immortals. The Thebans, and perhaps some of the other Greeks with Leonidas, now surrendered. But the Spartan King and his bodyguard fought on courageously till all were killed.

480, August–September. Persian Advance on Athens. All the Peloponnesians retired behind the fortifications of the Isthmus of Corinth. Themistocles, however, refused to withdraw his fleet as the Spartans requested, but instead used the vessels to ferry the population of Athens to the nearby island of Salamis. The remainder of the Greek fleet reluctantly agreed to stay and fight.

480, September. Persian Occupation of Athens. Xerxes' army, which had suffered few casualties, had been augmented by contingents from Thebes and other northern Greek states. The Persian fleet probably still numbered more than 700 fighting vessels—about double the number of Greek triremes. Themistocles feared a Persian blockade of the Greek fleet, while a powerful Persian Army contingent was landed behind the defenses of the isthmus. He therefore sent a secret message to Xerxes, saying that if the Persian fleet attacked, the Athenians would join the Persians and the rest of the Greek fleet would flee. Xerxes ordered the Persian fleet to move out that very night. While the Egyptian contingent blocked the western exit south of Salamis, the main fleet, at least 500 strong, formed in line of battle opposite the eastern entrance of the strait. Before dawn a force of Persian infantry landed on the islet of Psyttaleia, at the entrance to the channel. On the mainland, overlooking the strait from a hilltop, Xerxes sat on his throne to observe the battle which would win Greece for his empire.

480, September 23 (?). Battle of Salamis. Part of the Greek fleet was sent to defend the narrow western strait, and the rest of the triremes were drawn up in a line, behind a bend in the eastern strait, waiting for the main Persian fleet. Where the Persians came around the bend, the channel narrowed somewhat, forcing the ships to crowd together, with resultant confusion. At this moment the Greeks attacked. Maneuver was now impossible, superior numbers to no avail. Advantage lay with the heavier, more solidly built Greek triremes, carrying the whole Athenian army of at least 6,000 men. Literally hundreds of small land battles took place across the decks of the jammed vessels. Man for man the Greek hoplite was far superior to his foes. The battle lasted for 7 or more hours. Half the Persian fleet was sunk or captured; the Greeks lost only 40 ships. The remaining Persians broke off the fight and fled back to Phalerum Bay. A contingent of Greeks—mostly Athenians—under Aristides, now landed on Psyttaleia, overwhelming the Persians who had been isolated there.

480, September–October. Persian Retreat. Xerxes' army, largely dependent upon supply by sea, could no longer hold

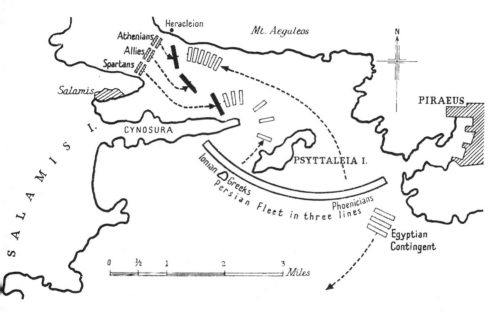

Battle of Salamis

Athens. With about half of his army, and the remnants of his fleet, he marched back to the Hellespont, leaving Mardonius with the remainder in northern Greece.

Campaigns of 480–479 B.C.

480–479. Operations of Mardonius. He restored Persian influence and prestige among the northern states, particularly Thebes, through combinations of threats and promises. In the spring, with perhaps 100,000 men, he marched south and captured Athens again. But upon the approach of the Spartan King **Pausanias,** with the main Greek Army from Corinth, Mardonius withdrew northward to Thebes, after destroying Athens (June). Pausanias followed cautiously, with less than 80,000 men, of whom about half were hoplites.

479, July (?). Campaign of Plataea. The Greeks found the Persian army holding the line of the Asopus River, about 5 miles south of Thebes. After a brief skirmish with the Persian cavalry, they advanced to a ridge running just south of the Asopus, Spartans on the right, Athenians on the left, and allied contingents in the center. Both sides held their positions for 8 days, each waiting for the other to attack. Finally Mardonius sent his cavalry raiding behind the Greek positions, destroying supply trains coming over the mountain passes from Athens, and polluting the springs from which the Greeks obtained water. Pausanias decided to withdraw that night to a new position at the base of the mountains, just east of Plataea. Here he could cover the 3 passes from Attica, and would have an assured supply of water.

Battle of Plataea. During the Greek withdrawal some units lost their way in the darkness. At dawn Mardonius discovered the Greeks stretched out in 3 uncoordinated groups. He ordered an immediate attack. The brunt of the first Persian cavalry and archery blows fell upon the Spartans. Thinking the Spartans were about to collapse, Mardonius led the Persian infantry in a charge. But he underestimated Spartan staunchness and discipline. They repulsed the charge, then counterattacked. A terrible struggle ensued, with neither side prevailing. Meanwhile the Athenians, to the left front of the Spartans, were engaged heavily by a mixed force of Persians, Thebans, and other pro-Persian Greeks. The allied contingents, formerly the Greek center, who had already reached Plataea, now marched promptly back to assist the Spartans and Athenians. Those going to help the Athenians were attacked by Persian and Theban cavalry. Though unable to make any progress, these Greeks indirectly saved the Athenians from an envelopment which would probably have been decisive. As a result the Athenians, no longer harassed by cavalry, began to gain the upper hand, and pushed the Thebans and Persians back toward the Asopus. Mardonius having been killed in the struggle against the Spartans, the Persians began to lose heart. As allied reinforcements arrived, the Spartans redoubled their efforts, and soon the Persians were fleeing back toward the river. The Greeks followed, driving them across the stream, inflicting terrible losses. Thebes was invested, and within a month surrendered. Greek losses were few, but probably more than the 1,360 reported by Plutarch. The Persians lost over 50,000. Victory was not due to superior Greek leadership; Mardonius appears to have outgeneraled Pausanias throughout the campaign. The battle was won by technical military superiority, in the first clear-cut example of the value of superior discipline and training.

479, August (?). Battle of Mycale. Meanwhile a Greek fleet under Spartan **Leotychidas** was operating off the Ionian coast. The Persian fleet withdrew to Mycale, near Samos, where Xerxes had left a strong army. Unable to entice the Persian fleet into a naval battle, Leotychidas landed his troops and attacked the Persian army—a foolhardy move, since the Greeks were greatly outnumbered. However, as the battle began, the contingent of Ionian Greeks in the Persian army changed sides. The Greeks won a complete victory, capturing Mycale and the Persian fleet.

Concluding Campaigns of the Persian War, 479–448 B.C.

479. Greek Capture of Cyprus and Byzantium. A fleet and army under Pausanias captured Cyprus, then returned through the Aegean and the Hellespont to seize Byzantium.

478–470. Athens Continues the War. Sparta and most of the other states of European Greece withdrew from the war, but Athens, becoming ever more dependent upon overseas commerce, particularly upon grain supplies from the Black Sea regions, continued to assist the Greek cities of Asia Minor to break away from Persia. This alliance was called the **Delian League.** Soon the alliance became a façade for virtual Athenian sovereignty over all member states.

466. Battle of Eurymedon. Cimon of Athens won a great naval battle against the Persians off the Eurymedon River in Asia Minor, ending the war in the Aegean area, though desultory fighting continued elsewhere.

460–454. Operations in Egypt. In response to an Egyptian appeal, a strong Athenian fleet sailed to Egypt, and helped rebels capture **Memphis,** the capital. The Persian garrison held out in the citadel, however, for nearly 4 years, until a new army from Persia drove off the Athenians (456). Athenians and rebels were now besieged for 2 years on an island in the Nile, to be finally annihilated when the Persians diverted the course of the river and attacked.

450. Battle of Salamis (in Cyprus). Cimon's Athenian fleet thoroughly defeated the Persians.

448. The Peace of Callias. The Greco-Persian War came to an end.

GREECE, 480–400 B.C.

Background of the Peloponnesian Wars, 480–460 B.C.

480–479. Themistocles Rebuilds Athens. The Spartans, secretly pleased by Mardonius' destruction of rival Athens (479), unsuccessfully opposed Themistocles' plans to reconstruct the city's walls. Themistocles also improved and fortified the harbor of the Piraeus, strengthening Athens' links with the sea, and in general stimulated the city's commercial greatness.

478–420. Growing Rivalry of Athens and Sparta. Sparta was jealous of Athens' growing prosperity and power. Like other Greeks, the Spartans also abhorred Athens' increasingly autocratic leadership of the Delian League. Athenian distaste for the military regimentation of Spartan society, and for ruthless Spartan suppression of the Messenian helots, was equally strong. Thus the paradox: a democratic state suppressing the freedom of its allies, while a militaristic oligarchy became the champion of self-determination.

The First Peloponnesian War, 460–445 B.C.

460. Athens' War with Corinth. Despite involvement in Egypt (see p. 29), economic rivalries caused Athens to go to war with Corinth and other Peloponnesian states. **Aegina** joined Corinth, but her fleet was soon overwhelmed by Athens (458), and the city was besieged and captured (457).

457. Sparta Joins the War. She denounced her alliance with Athens to enter the war, and a Spartan-led army defeated the Athenians at the **Battle of Tanagra,** near Thebes. After this, Spartan participation was only halfhearted, and soon afterward the Athenians crushed Thebes at the **Battle of Oenophyta.**

457–447. Athenian Successes. Despite some defeats, the Athenians under the military and political leadership of **Pericles** were generally successful in fighting on land and sea.

446. Change of the Tide. Athens was driven by Sparta and her allies from her conquests in mainland Greece, and threatened with revolts within her empire. The Athenian fleet was barely able to retain control of the seas.

445. Thirty Years' Peace. Concluded on the initiative of Pericles.

The Golden Age of Pericles, 445–432 B.C.

The fallacy of a policy of expansion in Greece proper was now obvious to Pericles; Athens lacked manpower and wealth to maintain both a large fleet and a large army. Like Themistocles he concluded that the glory and prosperity of Athens must be in trade and colonization overseas. The **Long Walls** he built connecting Athens with her seaport—the Piraeus—symbolized his strategic concept of a self-contained, invulnerable metropolis which could exist indefinitely, isolated from the rest of mainland Greece, so long as she retained command of overseas supply routes. Pericles hoped that his defensive policy on the mainland would eliminate the former causes of war between Athens and her neighbors. But Sparta was still jealous.

435. Naval War between Corinth and Corcyra. Corinth was a member of the Peloponnesian League; Corcyra (Corfu) was an ally of Athens.

433. Athenian Intervention. Athens threw her influence on the side of Corcyra and began economic reprisals against Corinth and her allies.

432. Sparta Declares War. She charged Athens with breach of the Thirty Years' Peace. The Peloponnesian and Boeotian Leagues joined Sparta.

The Second Peloponnesian War, 432–404 B.C.

431–430. Pericles' Strategy of Attrition. Athens defended on land, while taking the offensive at sea. Spartan armies invaded and ravaged Attica but were stopped by the Long Walls; command of the sea assured uninterrupted supplies to Athens. Athenian fleets ravaged the Peloponnesian coast.

430–429. Plague Strikes Athens. Brought by ship, the disease decimated the overcrowded populace. Pericles died (429); his place was taken by **Cleon,** who prosecuted the war with equal determination but less skill.

429. Battles of Chalcis and Naupactus (Lepanto). Athenian admiral **Phormio** won two great victories over superior Peloponnesian fleets to establish and maintain a blockade of the Gulf of Corinth. His death soon after was a blow to Athens no less severe than the loss of Pericles.

429–427. Siege of Plataea. A combined Spartan-Theban force invested Plataea, Athens' faithful ally. This siege saw the first known instance of besiegers establishing both lines of contravallation (facing inward, toward the city) and circumvallation (facing outward, to protect the besiegers from outside attack). When Plataea fell, the defenders were massacred and the city destroyed.

427. Revolts on Corcyra and Lesbos. Athens concentrated on suppression of the revolts. A Spartan expedition to help the rebels at Mitylene, capital of Lesbos, hastily withdrew upon the appearance of an Athenian fleet. The Athenians landed and speedily captured the city, suppressing the revolt.

426. Cleon Takes the Offensive on Land. He sent his most able general, **Demosthenes,** to Aetolia, preliminary to a projected two-front attack to crush Thebes and Boeotia. Demosthenes, due to insufficient force, was repulsed.

426. Battle of Tanagra. At the same time another Athenian general, **Nicias,** made a halfhearted invasion of Boeotia from the east, retiring to Attica after an inconclusive victory.

426. Battle of Olpae. Demosthenes retrieved his reputation by a brilliant victory, enticing the numerically superior Spartans into an ambush.

425. Battle of Pylos (Navarino). Demosthenes landed on the west coast of the Peloponnesus, and established a fortified base at Pylos. The Spartans reacted violently, but Demosthenes repulsed the land attacks and captured an entire Spartan fleet, leaving a Spartan contingent isolated on the island of Sphacteria, just off the coast.

425. Battle of Sphacteria. Cleon brought reinforcements, and the two Athenian generals overwhelmed the Spartans, capturing 292 survivors. Sparta, anxious to secure release of the prisoners, sued for peace, but Cleon foolishly refused.

424. Battle of Delium. The Athenians again planned convergent land attacks against Boeotia, but were frustrated when Theban general **Pagondas** defeated the main Athenian army under **Hippocrates,** who was killed.

424–423. Brasidas' Invasion of Thrace. Sparta's greatest general, **Brasidas,** probably following directives of the Spartan ephors (the body of magistrates responsible for Spartan policy and strategy), undertook a daring strategic diversion. The main base protecting the Athenian supply route to the Black Sea was a complex of colonies around the Chalcidice Peninsula. Brasidas, with less than 2,000 hoplites, plus auxiliary troops, marched north to threaten this base, defeating two Athenian armies en route (424). He captured Amphipolis, the most important Athenian colony in the Chalcidice. He was prevented from seizing the nearby port of Eion only by the timely arrival of the Athenian admiral **Thucydides** (historian of the war, who soon after was accused of negligence by Cleon and exiled for 20 years).

423. Truce. Largely because of Brasidas' threat to her supply route, Athens concluded a year's truce with Sparta. Brasidas, however, ignored the truce and continued to capture Athenian colonies in Thrace and Chalcidice.

422. Cleon and Nicias Rushed to Thrace. They forced Brasidas back to Amphipolis.

422. Battle of Amphipolis. Cleon advanced toward the city with inadequate security. Brasidas made a surprise attack, completely defeating the numerically superior Athenians. Cleon and Brasidas were both killed.

Peace of Nicias, 421–415 B.C.

421. Fifty Years' Peace. The treaty was intended to last for 50 years. However, Sparta's allies were generally dissatisfied with the terms, which restored the conquests of each side. This led to a shifting of alliances and the outbreak of numerous minor conflicts throughout Greece. Soon Athens' new allies—Argos, Mantinea, and Elis—were at war with Sparta.

418. Battle of Mantinea. Spartan King **Agis** invaded Argos and Mantinea. Athens sent a small force to assist her allies, but the allied army was decisively beaten by Agis. This, the largest land action of the Peloponnesian War, took place when the major antagonists were nominally at peace. The battle restored Sparta to unquestioned hegemony of the Peloponnesus.

417–416. Athenian Troops Assist Argos. Athens' relations with Sparta were strained, but both refrained from war.

416. Rise of Alcibiades. This brilliant young Athenian soldier and politician, portrayed by many historians as an evil, opportunistic villain, by others as a victimized hero, played the leading role in the last 11 years of the war. He turned his countrymen's attention toward Sicily, considered by many Greeks to be a land of opportunity and the gateway to Greek expansion. Syracuse, richest city of the island, was involved in a local quarrel with an Athenian ally. Alcibiades suggested that this was an opportunity to crush Syracuse, capture Sicily, and establish for Athens indisputable leadership of the Greek world.

The Sicilian Expedition, 415–413 B.C.

415. Athenians at Syracuse; Alcibiades Flees to Sparta. Against the advice of Nicias, the Athenian Assembly voted to send an expedition against Syracuse under the joint leadership of Nicias, Alcibiades, and the able general **Lamachus.** The expedition consisted of 136 triremes and an equal number of transports, carrying 5,000 hoplites and a somewhat smaller force of light troops. Before they reached Sicily, Alcibiades was recalled to stand trial on charges of religious sacrilege (possibly trumped up by political enemies). On the way back to Athens and certain execution, he escaped and fled to Sparta. Meanwhile Lamachus urged an immediate attack on Syracuse, before the city was alerted to danger. Cautious Nicias, however, so delayed the approach that the Syracusans were given ample notice. The Athenians won a battle outside the walls, but the strengthened defense of Syracuse defied them, and Lamachus was killed. Accordingly the Athenians encamped and began to build siege lines around the land side of the city.

414. Spartan Assistance to Syracuse. Upon the advice of Alcibiades, the Spartans sent their general **Gylippus** to assist the defenders. Under Gylippus' leadership the Syracusans prevented the Athenians from completing their planned wall of contravallation.

413. Athenian Disaster. The Athenian fleet, trying to operate in narrow waters close to Syracuse, was defeated by a combined Corinthian-Syracusan fleet. Soon after this, Demosthenes arrived from Athens with land and sea reinforcements. Realizing that Athenian morale and health were at low ebb, he urged immediate withdrawal. Nicias procrastinated as usual. While the two generals debated, the Syracusans and their allies blockaded and then annihilated the Athenian fleet. Nicias and Demosthenes now tried to escape overland, abandoning their sick and wounded. The victorious Syracusans pursued and captured the remnants of the Athenian army. Nicias and Demosthenes were executed; the survivors became slaves.

Final Phase, 414–404 B.C.

414. Sparta Declares War. She established a virtually permanent siege of Athens.

412. Naval Struggle for Ionia and the Aegean. A Spartan fleet sailed to Ionia, to lead a revolt against Athens. Alcibiades, now a trusted representative of Sparta, negotiated a treaty between Sparta and the Persian satrap of Sardis, **Tissaphernes,** recognizing Persian sovereignty over Athens' dependencies in Asia Minor. In return the Persians agreed to provide funds to support the Peloponnesian fleet. Amazingly, Athens replaced the fleet lost at Syracuse and was soon challenging the Peloponnesians in the Aegean Islands and off the coast of Asia Minor.

411. Alcibiades Rejoins Athens. Tissaphernes failed to provide the promised funds, making it difficult for Sparta to maintain her fleet. Alcibiades was secretly angling to rejoin Athens, and had suggested that Persia should stand aloof from the struggle. When an upstart Athenian government began to negotiate secretly with Sparta, patriotic Athenian citizens, and the strongly democratic fleet, overthrew the oligarchs, calling Alcibiades back to command the fleet. He at once sailed northward to counter Spartan efforts to incite rebellion in the Thracian colonies and along the Hellespont, threatening Athens' vital grain route from the Black Sea. Off **Cynossema** a victory was won over the Peloponnesian fleet, increasing the confidence of the newly raised Athenian crews and augmenting Alcibiades' prestige in Athens.

410. Battle of Cyzicus. Alcibiades won an overwhelming victory over the Peloponnesian fleet and a Persian army in a combined land-sea operation in the Sea of Marmora. Sparta now offered to make peace, on the basis of the *status quo,* but the demagogue **Cleophon,** who had just seized power in Athens, rejected the offer.

408. Alcibiades Recaptures Byzantium. Athens regained undisputed control of the Bosporus.

408–407. Cooperation of Sparta and Persia. They marshaled their forces in a major effort to humble resurgent Athens. A new Spartan fleet was built at Ephesus with funds and materials provided by Persia. Supervising the construction and training the crews was the Spartan general **Lysander.** The new satrap, **Cyrus,** lent him every support.

406. Battle of Ephesus. Alcibiades tried vainly to entice Lysander into combat. But when Alcibiades sailed off with part of his fleet to collect supplies, Lysander attacked and defeated the blockading Athenian squadron. Alcibiades rushed back, but Lysander again refused to fight. Word of this setback provided an opportunity for Alcibiades' personal enemies in Athens to persuade the amazingly fickle people to relieve him of command. **Conon** was appointed to command the Athenian fleet. Because Spartan law permitted an admiral to command a fleet for only one year, Lysander was replaced by **Callicratidas.**

406. Blockade of Mitylene. Callicratidas outmaneuvered Conon and blockaded the Athenian fleet in Mitylene Harbor. In a desperate and again amazing effort, impoverished Athens raised a new fleet, which was dispatched to raise the blockade of Mitylene.

406, August. Battle of Arginusae. The Athenians gained a great victory; Callicratidas was drowned. Once more Sparta offered to make peace, and once more Cleophon incredibly rejected the offer.

405. Return of Lysander to Command. When Cyrus demanded that Lysander be restored to command of the Persian-Peloponnesian fleet, he was permitted by Sparta to accompany the fleet, and in fact, if not in name, he commanded the fleet and the Persian army as well. Cautiously he sailed northward to the Hellespont, skillfully avoiding the Athenian fleet. Conon immediately sailed for the Hellespont to counter this new threat to Athens' grain supply route. Unable to entice Lysander into battle, Conon established a base at Aegospotami. In the following days he tried to force a battle, but Lysander refused. Soon, despite warnings from Alcibiades, Conon and his men relaxed their watchfulness.

405. Battle of Aegospotami. Lysander struck suddenly, while the Athenian fleet was moored for the night, with most of the crews ashore. This was the decisive action of the Peloponnesian War. The Athenian fleet of nearly 200 vessels was completely destroyed; most of the crews were captured and slaughtered. Lysander now sailed to blockade the Piraeus, while King **Pausanias** invested Athens by land.

404, April. Surrender of Athens. Forced by starvation after a six months' siege. Sparta was supreme in Greece.

The Anabasis, 401–400 B.C.

401. Revolt of Cyrus. Persian satrap of Lydia, **Cyrus** planned to overthrow his elder brother, Emperor Artaxerxes II. Cyrus marched on Susa with an army probably 50,000 strong, including some 13,000 Greek mercenaries, veterans from both sides of the Peloponnesian War, commanded by a Spartan general named **Clearchus** (see p. 221)

401. Battle of Cunaxa. At Cunaxa, near Babylon, Cyrus' army was met by Artaxerxes, with a Persian host numbering perhaps 100,000. The Greeks, on the right of Cyrus' army, utterly defeated the left wing of Artaxerxes' army. On the other side of the field, the struggle was prolonged. Then Cyrus was killed, and all the rebel army—except for the Greeks—fled. Changing front, Clearchus' phalanx now advanced against the victorious right wing of Artaxerxes' army and drove it from the field. This amazing battle was won by the Greeks—so Xenophon tells us—at the cost of only one hoplite wounded. Tissaphernes subsequently invited Clearchus and his senior officers to a feast, at which all the Greek leaders were treacherously seized. Clearchus was murdered and the others were sent to Artaxerxes, who had them beheaded.

401–400. "March of the 10,000." The younger officers—mostly Spartans and Athenians—took over, marching to the nearest friendly haven: the Greek Black Sea colony of Trapezus, over 1,000 miles away, across the wild mountains of Armenia. They lived off the country continuously fighting off the barbarian hill peoples, many subsidized by Persian agents and all resentful of the more than 12,000 plus men who requisitioned all available food. The superior energy and ability of **Xenophon,** a young Athenian officer, was soon evident.

400. Arrival at the Sea. After 5 months of fighting and marching, 6,000 survivors reached Trapezus. Xenophon was primarily responsible for the accomplishment. His later *Anabasis* ("Upcountry March") is one of the outstanding military histories of all time. In this book were fateful words: "Persia belongs to the man who has the courage to attack it."

ROME, 600–400 B.C.

The Kingdom, c. 600–509 B.C.

c. 600–509. Rome under the Tarquins. The city seems to have prospered under this line of Etruscan kings, achieving hegemony over most of Latium. The history of the period is most unreliable.

578–534. Reign of Servius Tullius. He was a man of plebeian birth who married into the royal family, then seized the throne. To him are attributed a number of the early laws and customs on which the subsequent military might of Rome was based. He is, however, a legendary figure, and it is possible that his supposed reforms were actually instituted about a century later, during the Republic.

The Republic, 509–400 B.C.

509. Republican Revolt. For several years the Tarquins, supported by their Etruscan relatives, endeavored unsuccessfully to regain the throne. It was during one of these struggles that legendary **Horatius Cocles** is reputed to have held the bridge over the Tiber River against an Etruscan host under **Lars Porsena** (508).

496. Battle of Lake Regillus. Another legendary encounter, this may have been fought against Latin foes rather than Etruscans. During the century there were frequent conflicts with neighboring Latin, Etruscan, or Sabine states, or with the Aequian and Volsci hill people to the northeast.

458. Dictatorship of Cincinnatus. With the Aequi threatening to overwhelm Rome, the Roman Senate called the respected warrior **L. Quinctius Cincinnatus** from his farm to take over the dictatorship (see p. 34). Cincinnatus decisively defeated the Aequi, gave up the dictatorship before it was due to end, and returned to his plow.

439. Cincinnatus Again Called to Dictatorship. This time he defeated the Volsci.

438–425. War with Veii. This Etruscan state was about 10 miles northwest of Rome, on the far bank of the Tiber. Rome was victorious in a drawn-out siege.

431. Defeat of the Aequians. By victories of dictator **A. Postumius Tubertus.**

405–396. Renewed War with Veii. The Romans besieged Veii for 9 years. Since an army was kept constantly in the field during this time, Rome began regular payments to the troops, inaugurating the concept of a regular, career service. When Veii fell (396), it was destroyed and its territory and people absorbed by Rome. The Roman Republic was now unquestionably the leading state of central Italy (see also p. 58).

ROMAN MILITARY SYSTEM, C. 400 B.C.

Servius Tullius—or some later organizer—divided the population for military purposes into six groups, in accordance with wealth, since soldiers furnished their own arms and equipment. The first class provided the cavalry and the best-armed heavy infantry, similar to the Greek hoplite. The next two classes provided slightly less elaborately equipped heavy infantry. The fourth and fifth classes furnished javelin men, slingers, and other unarmored auxiliaries. In the sixth class were those exempted from military service for physical, religious, or other reasons. Like the Greeks, Roman citizens served only when called upon, but frequent wars, a well-developed martial spirit, an inherent sense of discipline, and constant peacetime exercise and maneuvers made these part-time soldiers the terror of their enemies.

Each class was organized in units of 100 men, called **centuries.** In combat formation the heavy infantry was arranged like a phalanx, the better-armed men in front. The light troops functioned ahead of the main body and covered the flanks.

Under the Republic, executive and military authority were exercised by two coequal **consuls,** elected to office each year by popular vote. This system effectively ensured a balance of political power but had serious military drawbacks. The consuls shared responsibility for combat operations, usually exercising command on alternate days. Recognizing the military inefficiency of such an arrangement, Roman law provided that in time of emergency one individual—termed a **dictator**—could be called upon to exercise complete authority over the state and the armed forces, though for a limited time—usually 6 months—only.

CARTHAGE AND SICILY, 800–400 B.C.

c. 800. Carthage Founded. This was the most important colonial outpost established in the central Mediterranean by the Phoenicians. At this time, also, Greek seafarers began to penetrate into the same region, establishing colonies mainly in Cyrenaica, eastern Sicily, and southern Italy. Friction between Greeks and Phoenicians, and between their colonies, began early in the 8th century and continued for some 500 years. At the same time there was incessant conflict between colonizers and the barbarian peoples inhabiting the littoral.

c. 650–c. 500. Expansion of Carthage; Conflicts with Greek Colonies. Phoenician colonization dwindled, as Phoenicia was overrun by foreign conquerors. Carthage soon assumed the role of protector of the other Phoenician colonies, while aggressively founding colonies of her own in North Africa, Iberia, western Sicily, and other Mediterranean islands. With equal vigor, though less centralization, Greek colonization continued along the northern shores of the Mediterranean. By the 6th century there had been a number of violent clashes between Greeks and Carthaginians in Sicily, Corsica, Sardinia, southern Gaul, and eastern Iberia. The Carthaginians were successful in Corsica and Sardinia, while late in the 6th century the Greek colony of Massilia (Marseille) drove the Carthaginians from the coast of Gaul. Though the Greeks absorbed much of Sicily, Carthage established a firm foothold in the west.

c. 500. Rise of Syracuse. Under the wise rule of the tyrant **Gelo,** Syracuse began to rival Carthage, not only in Sicily but as a power in the central Mediterranean.

481. War of Carthage and Syracuse. The Carthaginians were easily persuaded by envoys from Xerxes of Persia to attack Syracuse (see p. 25). As a consequence, Gelo was forced to refuse an appeal for assistance from Greece, to devote all his attention to dealing with the Carthaginians.

480. Battle of Himera. Gelo, heading an

alliance of Greek Sicilian states, decisively defeated a large Carthaginian army under **Hamilcar,** who was killed. The Carthaginians, forced to pay an indemnity, temporarily abandoned their ambitions in Sicily.

480–410. Carthaginian Expansion Westward. They greatly augmented their sea power, gaining complete control of the western Mediterranean and contiguous regions farther west beyond the Straits of Gibraltar, with outposts down the African coast and possibly on the Madeira and Canary islands.

474. Battle of Cumae. Etruscan expansion into Campania was halted by the Syracusan fleet under **Hiero.**

409. Carthaginian Return to Sicily. An early **Hannibal*** gained revenge for the defeat of his grandfather, Hamilcar, at Himera by capturing that and other cities of northern and western Sicily. The Carthaginians pressed eastward, taking Agrigentum (406) and threatening to overwhelm Syracuse and the other Greek strongholds on the island (400).

---

* Note that the names Hamilcar, Hannibal, Mago, etc., were common among Carthaginians.

SOUTH ASIA

INDIA, 600–400 B.C.

c. 600–c. 500. Rise of Kosala. This Hindu kingdom became the leading power of northern India by defeating and absorbing Kasi.

c. 543–491. Rise of Magadha. Under King **Bimbisara,** this Hindu kingdom (modern Bihar) expanded greatly.

c. 537. Cyrus of Persia Reaches India. He campaigned across Bactria and Arachosia (modern Afghanistan and southern Soviet Turkestan) and turned south to the vicinity of modern Peshawar (see p. 20). He may have reached the Indus.

517–509. Darius Annexes the West Bank of the Indus. He also conquered part of the northwestern Punjab, east of the river. He sent the Greek admiral **Skylax** to explore the Indus as far as the Arabian Sea. These regions remained under Persian control until the beginning of the 4th century.

c. 490–c. 350. Magadha Predominant in Northwest India. Under **Ajatusatra,** Magadha began a series of successful wars with Kosala.

HINDU MILITARY SYSTEMS, C. 500 B.C.

The invasions of Cyrus and Darius seem to have stimulated the Hindus to develop cavalry, hitherto neglected in India. Hampered, however, by the difficulties of breeding good horses in the Indian climate, they continued to place primary reliance on the chariot, which had become the decisive element in Indian warfare. The best horses, therefore, were reserved for chariots. It was probably about the 6th century, also, that war elephants began to appear on Indian battlefields. By 400 B.C., it appears that the Hindu princes considered elephants equally important instruments of war as chariots.

The bow, the primary Hindu weapon, remained unchanged for approximately 2,200 years. It was usually 4 to 5 feet long. Though other materials, including metal, were tried, bamboo remained the preferred material. The arrows, made of bamboo or of cane, were 2 to 3 feet long, usually tipped with metal. The effective range of the bow was 100 to 120 yards, or slightly less when a heavy, iron antielephant arrow was used. Fire arrows were also used against elephants.

Bowmen did not usually carry shields, but were protected by a front rank of shield-bearing javelin throwers. Though hand-to-hand combat was avoided if possible, both archers and javelin men were also armed with a fairly long, broad-bladed sword. If a decision could not be reached by long-range fire, recourse was made to the sword in a confused melee.

CEYLON, 500–400 B.C.

A band of Hindu adventurers, under **Vijaya,** invaded successfully by sea from Gujarat, on the northwest coast of India (c. 483). Vijaya conquered the island with ease, but his centralized kingdom soon fell apart. In the following centuries Ceylon's history is one of resultant strife between minor chieftains, and of occasional invasions from the nearby Tamil (Dravidian) kingdoms of the mainland.

EAST ASIA
CHINA, 600–400 B.C.

c. **600–c. 500. Decline of Chou.** The emperors exercised only nominal sovereignty over some 10 or 12 feudal states, continuously warring with one another. Most important of these were (1) Ch'in, to the northwest, in the Wei Valley that had produced the Chous; (2) Ch'u, dominating the area from the Yangtze almost as far north as the Yellow River; and (3) the maritime state of Wu, holding the mouth of the Yangtze and the seacoast region almost up to Shantung.

c. **500. Sun Tzu.** This native of the state of Ch'i (modern Shantung) wrote *The Art of War,* the first known military treatise; its profound understanding of the philosophy of human conflict provides valuable lessons for military men even today. Apparently acknowledged as the leading military figure of his time, Sun Tzu moved to Wu, which he raised to a position of pre-eminence by brilliant victories over the principalities of Ch'u, Ch'i, and Ch'in (north-central China).

c. **473. Wu Overthrown by Yueh.** Yueh inherited both the coastal region and Wu's maritime tradition.

c. **450–221. The Era of Warring States.** This was merely an intensification of the existing feudal anarchy.

c. **400. Rise of Ch'in and Ch'u.** Although other states continued to participate in the multilateral struggle, these two emerged as the leading military powers of China.

III

THE ERA OF THE GIANTS:
400–200 B.C.

MILITARY TRENDS

The emergence of strategy, and of the tactical application of the combined arms—horse, foot, and artillery—highlighted this period, together with a dazzling display of military leadership. **Alexander the Great** and **Hannibal** were geniuses. But great generals in their own right also were **Philip of Macedon**—Alexander's father—and Alexander's successors, the **Diadochi.** To these we must add Hannibal's father—**Hamilcar**—and his pupils, the Romans **Scipio, Marcellus,** and **Nero;** also **Pyrrhus** of Epirus; **Epaminondas, Xanthippus,** and **Philopoemen** of Greece; **Dionysius** and **Agathocles** of Syracuse; the Indian **Chandragupta;** and many others. No other comparable period of history produced more capable military leaders.

THEORY OF WARFARE

Hannibal has been called the "father of strategy," although Alexander was no less aware of strategic fundamentals. Few other important leaders of the period demonstrated comparable strategic grasp, until the lessons learned from Hannibal were utilized to some extent by Nero in the Metaurus campaign, and by Scipio in Spain and Africa.

On the other hand, there was a general awareness of—and frequently an emphasis on—economic warfare. In consequence, save for the wars of Alexander, Hannibal, and the offensive-minded Romans, pitched battles were relatively infrequent. The opposing generals concentrated on raiding one another's resources while at the same time blockading towns and fortresses.

MILITARY ORGANIZATION

Another new development was the integration of basic military components into a combined fighting team. Asian leaders, particularly Persian, had understood how to employ cavalry, but they had never been able to coordinate this arm effectively with their infantry. In Europe Epaminondas at Leuctra showed how horsemen could be used for tactical screening and delaying purposes in coordination with his infantry. Dionysius of Syracuse was also apparently successful, about this same time, in creating a combined fighting force.

But the first scientifically organized military force of history was that of Philip II, of Macedon. His concept of the use of heavy missile engines in coordination with the field operations of infantry and cavalry was the genesis of field artillery. His son, Alexander, developed this concept further.

Philip also developed a new type of light infantry—his **hypaspists**—combining the discipline of the trained heavy **hoplite** with the speed and flexibility of the irregular **psiloi.** This development grew out of the Athenian **Iphicrates'** introduction of the lightly armed, disciplined **peltast**—usually a mercenary—into Greek warfare about half a century earlier.

WEAPONS

The **catapult** and **ballista** came into their own during the period. The catapult,* appearing first in Syria, was in essence a large, crew-served bow, using tension to propel large arrows—and later large rocks—up to 500 yards, with an accurate range of over 200 yards. The ballista,* similar in concept, was generally larger, and used torsion to hurl large rocks—and later, arrows—for comparable distances. These heavy

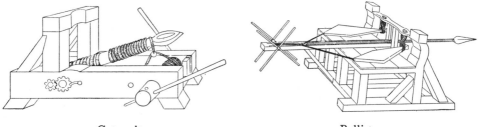

Catapult   Ballista

and cumbersome engines were usually used in siege operations—as well as in the defense of fortifications—but both Philip and Alexander also used light catapults and ballistae in field operations.

There were no important developments in small arms and armor, although there were some significant refinements: the **sarissa,** the long Macedonian pike; and the Roman **gladius** (short sword) and **pilum** (javelin). Also significant was the introduction of lightweight armor and equipment for Greek **peltasts** and Macedonian **hypaspists.**

SIEGE WARFARE

The basic siege weapons remained the battering ram and the movable tower. **Mantelets**—great wicker or wooden shields, sometimes mounted on wheels—were used to shelter outpost guards and operators of siege engines within range of weapons on the city walls. **Diades,** Alexander's engineer, invented a mural hook, or **crow,** consisting of a long, heavy bar or lever, suspended from a high vertical frame, to knock down the upper parapets of a wall. He also invented the **telenon,** a box or basket large enough to contain a number of armed men, slung

---

* There are some contradictions in nomenclature and identification of catapult and ballista among modern authorities.

from a boom. This boom was in turn suspended from a tall mast or vertical frame, on which it could be raised or lowered by tackle. By this elevator a group of infantrymen could be hoisted above parapet height, swung over any intervening obstacle, such as a moat, and deposited directly upon the enemy's battlements.

Archimedes, the great mathematician and scientist of his day, apparently created some other special engines for use in the defense of Syracuse (213–211) against the Romans. Unfortunately, no designs of these have come down to modern times. From the meager descriptions extant, these would appear to have been refinements on weapons already known and used (such as those of Diades). Archimedes was

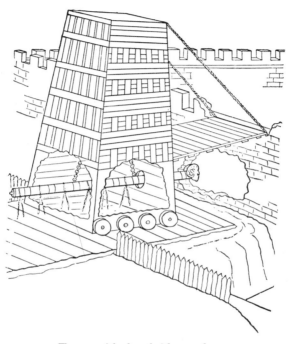

Tower with drawbridge and ram

partial to the use of huge grappling devices, or tongs, to be used against battering rams or to seize hostile warships approaching the sea wall of Syracuse.

TACTICS ON LAND

There were two major developments: the introduction of tactical maneuver by Epaminondas of Thebes and of tactical flexibility by the Romans.

In earlier periods there were crude, tentative—and usually fortuitous—attempts at tactical maneuver, the most notable being at Marathon. But at Leuctra, Epaminondas deliberately introduced the concepts of mass—or concentration—and of economy of force, in his oblique order of battle. His additional contribution was cavalry-infantry coordination in his plan of maneuver; a sharp departure from past reliance solely on cavalry shock action.

Tactical flexibility was introduced by the Romans in the cellular battle order of their legion, a drastic deviation from the solid mass of the Greek phalanx. The Roman formation was originally adopted to permit easier movement in combat

over uneven terrain. It took the Carthaginian Hannibal and the Greek Philopoemen to teach the Romans how this flexible formation could further tactical maneuver. Scipio, at Ilipa, in turn showed how well the Romans could take this lesson
to heart.

The tactical use of elephants, originating earlier in India, was brought forcibly
to the Western military mind at the Hydaspes, where both the potentialities and
the limitations of the war elephant were demonstrated. Alexander's horses refused
to face the beasts, yet his disciplined phalanx, despite initial surprise and dismay,
eventually turned the elephants back in panic-stricken flight. **Seleucus'** impressions,
however, were sufficiently favorable for him—20 years later—to cede substantial
territory to Chandragupta in exchange for 500 elephants, which he proceeded to
use to advantage in his victory at Ipsus. After that time the use of the war elephant spread rapidly to Greece and Carthage. That the beast was a valuable
weapon is clear from its use by such objective warriors as Hannibal and Pyrrhus
(the latter, in fact, owed to his elephants his hard-won victories over the Romans).

As proven at Beneventum and Heraclea, elephants were most successful when
used against troops unacquainted with them. Disciplined and resourceful opponents,

Mantelets   Telenon and mural hook

however, could stampede the elephants, which then became more dangerous to
friend than foe. For this reason, the war elephant's mahout (driver) carried a
steel spike to hammer into the beast's brain should he stampede.

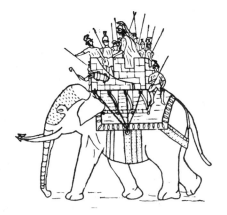

War elephant

Antielephant measures included the use of fire arrows, by the Indians, while some unidentified Greek genius evolved the prototype of an antitank mine field: iron spikes, chained and anchored in place, to rip the tender feet of the pachyderms. This last device was used effectively by **Ptolemy** at Gaza.

NAVAL WARFARE

Though navies declined in size during the 4th century, they increased greatly in the 3rd. During the First and Second Punic Wars the Romans and Carthaginians each frequently had at sea up to 500 war vessels, manned by as many as 150,-000 seamen and marines. Individual fleets ran as high as 350 ships. To control these vast maritime forces, Rome and Carthage had administrative organizations comparable to a modern admiralty or navy department.

The trireme was generally displaced by larger vessels during this period. Dionysius of Syracuse was apparently the first to build such vessels. By the time of the Punic Wars, the quinquireme had become the standard warship. The complement of these decked galleys consisted of up to 300 rowers and seamen, plus as many as 100 seagoing soldiers—equivalent of latter-day marines.

Naval tactics were unchanged until the middle of the 3rd century, when the Romans, recognizing both the inferiority of their relatively slower and clumsier ships and the superiority of Carthaginian seamanship, introduced a new concept: their combined grappling device and boarding bridge called the **corvus.** In order to come close enough to ram or to break the oars of the clumsier Roman ships, the Carthaginians had to risk being caught by the corvus, which was followed by an irresistible charge of Roman legionaries.

ADMINISTRATIVE AND LOGISTICAL SERVICES

We know little of the manner in which supply operations were organized in this period, and in most instances these were undoubtedly quite haphazard. There is, however, clear evidence of much advance planning and systematic organization of the supply service of the long-range (both in time and distance) operations of both Alexander and Hannibal.

Macedonians, Carthaginians, and Romans had also systematized their baggage trains with the emphasis on austerity in impedimenta. Essential equipment, weapons and the like were carried on pack animals, though wagons and hand carts were also used.

EURASIA–MIDDLE EAST

PERSIA, 400–338 B.C.

c. 400. Persistence of Persian Power. Largely by default, Persia remained the major power of the Middle East, the Greeks having exhausted themselves in the Peloponnesian War. Although royal authority had greatly declined, and outlying provinces were drifting away, most of the empire had peace, prosperity, and order.
386–358. Continuing Decline in Central Au- thority. The satraps of Asia Minor, in particular, became virtually independent.
358–338. Reign of Artaxerxes III. In large part due to the Greek general **Mentor,** imperial authority was temporarily reasserted over the satraps. Egypt was reconquered (342).

GREECE AND MACEDONIA, 400–336 B.C.

Spartan Period, 400–371 B.C.

400–371. Spartan Hegemony. By virtue of victory in the Peloponnesian War,

Sparta was supreme in Greece. This hegemony was briefly maintained by Lysander and kings Agis and **Agesilaus,** while simultaneously conducting successful operations against Persia in Asia Minor (see below).

400-387. War of Sparta and Persia. Sparta came to the aid of the Ionian cities when Tissaphernes, satrap of Lydia and Caria, began to punish them for their support of Cyrus' revolt against Artaxerxes II (see p. 32). After desultory operations and extended truces, Agesilaus II campaigned aggressively and victoriously across western Asia Minor (396-394) until recalled to Greece where war had spread (see p. 32).

395-387. Corinthian War. Resentful of Spartan arrogance, and taking advantage of the war in Asia Minor, Athens, Thebes, Corinth, Argos, and some smaller states allied themselves with Persia against Sparta. On land Lysander won some initial successes, before he was killed in an unsuccessful attack on the town of **Haliartus** (395). Agesilaus, returning from Asia Minor, avenged their defeat at **Coronea** (394).

394. Battle of Cnidus. The former Athenian admiral **Conon,** commanding the Athenian-Persian fleet, destroyed the Spartan fleet (commanded by Peisander, Lysander's brother-in-law, who was killed) off Cnidus, near Rhodes, ending Sparta's brief term as a maritime power, though the Spartan admiral **Antalcidas** had some later success against the Persians and the Athenians (388).

394. Siege of Corinth. Agesilaus besieged Corinth, but soon the war became a stalemate (393). Athens, seizing the opportunity to recover some of the strength lost in the Peloponnesian War, rebuilt the Long Walls, and began to re-establish control over some old colonies. An Athenian army under Iphicrates relieved Corinth (390). Persia, alarmed, gave surreptitious assistance to its enemy (Sparta) against its ally (Athens).

387. The Peace of Antalcidas (or **King's Peace.** A compromise settlement. Athens' partial recovery was acknowledged; Sparta's hegemony, though shaken, continued. The Greek states agreed to nominal Persian suzerainty over Greece in hopes this would reduce jealousies.

387-379. Spartan Supremacy Continues. Sparta vigorously crushed several challenges, maintaining garrisons and puppet rulers in a number of Greek cities, including Thebes.

379-371. War of Independence. Thebes revolted against Sparta. Athens soon joined her, and although the allies were unable to win a decisive victory, they maneuvered the Spartans out of central Greece. At the same time Athens had the best of war at sea, **Chabrias** winning a great naval victory off **Naxos** (376). Sparta, however, taking advantage of a split between Athens and Thebes, recovered some initial land losses (375-372).

371. Persia's Efforts Bring Peace Settlement. Sparta, however, refused to allow Thebes to represent the other members of the Boeotian League, upon which the Theban leader, **Epaminondas,** withdrew from the negotiations. Spartan King **Cleombrotus** immediately invaded southern Boeotia with an army of 11,000 men. Epaminondas could muster only 6,000.

371, July. Battle of Leuctra. The Spartans drew up for battle in the conventional phalangial line, the best troops on the

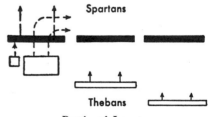

Battle of Leuctra

right, a few cavalrymen and light troops covering the flanks. They expected the Thebans to form in similar fashion. In such a battle the Spartans, superior both in numbers and in fighting quality, would unquestionably have been victorious. Epaminondas, however, refused to fight on Spartan terms. He quadrupled the depth of his left wing, forming a column 48 men deep, and 32 wide. The remainder of his army, covered by a cavalry screen, was echeloned to his right rear in thin lines facing the left and center of the Spartan army. This is the first known example in history of the deep **column of attack** and of a **refused flank,** prototype of the holding attack and main effort of more modern times. Epaminondas personally led his left-wing column in a vigorous charge against the Spartan right, while his cavalry and the infantry of the refused center and left advanced slowly, occupying the attention of the Spartans to their front, but without engaging them. The Spartans were hopelessly confused by these novel tactics. The weight of the Theban column soon crushed the Spartan right. Epaminondas completed the victory by wheeling against the exposed flank of the remaining Spartans, who promptly fled when simultaneously engaged by the Theban center and right. The Spartans lost over 2,000 men; Theban casualties were negligible. Spartan military prestige was shattered forever.

Theban Period, 371–355 B.C.

371–362. Theban Hegemony. The most startling event of a decade of desultory warfare was an alliance of Sparta and Athens to circumvent Theban supremacy (369). But the military and political genius of Epaminondas prevailed on land and sea. Thebes' most dangerous enemy was **Alexander** of Pherae, ruler of Thessaly, who at **Cynoscephalae** fought a drawn battle with Theban general **Pelopidas,** who was killed (364). The following year Epaminondas defeated Alexander.

362. Battle of Mantinea. The Arcadian League of the Peloponnesus—founded by Thebes (370) as a counterweight to Sparta—broke apart, a number of members joining Sparta and Athens. Epaminondas marched to the Peloponnesus, where his army was joined by some faithful allies. Near Mantinea he met an army composed of troops of Mantinea, Sparta, Athens, and dissident former members of the Arcadian League. Each army numbered about 25,000 men. By a combination of unexpected maneuvers and deception, Epaminondas completely surprised his enemies, then overwhelmed them with an oblique attack almost identical to that he had introduced at Leuctra. He, however, was killed in the moment of victory, and his followers were unable to take advantage of the success. Theban supremacy collapsed. In the words of Xenophon, Greece fell into "even greater confusion and indecision."

359–355. Rise of Macedon. Philip II began a new phase in the history of Greece. After securing his throne from a pretender supported by Athens, Philip began to reorganize his army, stabilizing the political and social conditions in his backward kingdom and expanding Macedonia's frontiers in all directions. He was undoubtedly inspired by the example of Epaminondas, whom he had known as a youth, while a hostage at Thebes. After successful campaigns in Illyria and against barbarian tribes between Macedonia and the Danube, Philip took advantage of Athens' disastrous involvement in the **Social War** (358–355) with her allies and colonies, to seize some Athenian possessions in Thrace.

Macedonian Period, 355–336 B.C.

355–346. Third Sacred War. The Amphictyonic Council of central Greece, supported by Thebes, declared war against Phocis (which had profaned the temple at Delphi) and against Phocian allies: Sparta, Athens, and Pherae (in Thessaly). Philip offered to aid the Amphictyonic Council, and seized Thessaly after a bitter two-year struggle against Thessalians, Phocians, and Athenians (355–353), climaxed by a victory at **Volo** in which Phocian general **Onomarchus** was killed. Blocked at Thermopylae by a combined Phocian, Spartan, Athenian, and Achaean force, Philip returned north to carry out a systematic conquest of Athenian colonies in Thrace and Chalcidice (352–346). When Athens sued for peace, Philip's terms were generous (346). He now turned against Phocis. Bribing his way through the pass at Thermopylae, he crushed the Phocians in a brief campaign and was elected chairman of the Amphictyonic Council.

345–339. Philip's Consolidation of Northern Conquests. Moving westward, Philip subdued all remaining opposition in Epirus, Thessaly, and southern Illyria (344–343). Next, moving north to the Danube, he brought all the wild tribes of that region under his sway. The following years were devoted to extending his domains eastward in Thrace, as far as the Black Sea. Here he met the only serious military failures of his career: after he had conquered Propontis, Athens supported uprisings in Perinthus and Byzantium. Philip was repulsed in efforts to capture these two fortified seaports (339).

339–338. Fourth Sacred War. Demosthenes of Athens, whose famed Philippic orations (351) had warned Greece to unite against the growing power of Macedon, again stirred Athens and Thebes to war against Philip and the Amphictyonic Council.

338. Battle of Chaeronea. Philip, with 32,-000 men, crushed an Athenian-Theban army of 50,000, which included the best mercenaries obtainable from other Greek states. Philip's young son, Alexander, distinguished himself in command of the cavalry of the Macedonian left flank. Greek casualties were about 20,000; those of the Macedonians are unrecorded, but must have been severe. Philip was now the unquestioned master of Greece.

337–336. The Hellenic League. Philip called a congress of Greek states at Corinth; all—except Sparta—participated, creating a **Hellenic League,** in perpetual alliance with Macedonia. Philip's plan for a war against Persia—for the ostensible purpose of freeing the Greek cities of Asia Minor—was approved; he was appointed chairman of the League for the duration of the war, and at the same time commanding general of the combined Graeco-Macedonian army. His trusted general **Parmenio** was then sent to Asia with an advance body, to carry out a reconnaissance in force (336).

336. Assassination of Philip. The murder was probably instigated by his divorced wife, **Olympias,** mother of Alexander. Historians agree that Alexander was not implicated in the plot.

MACEDONIAN MILITARY SYSTEM, 350–320 B.C.

Philip, as soon as he came to power, completely reorganized the Macedonian army (359). The result was the finest fighting force the world had yet seen: a national army, combining the disciplined skill of Greek mercenaries with the patriotic devotion of Greek citizen soldiers. For the first time in history, scientific design —based on exhaustive analysis of the capabilities and limitations of the men, weapons, and equipment of the time—evolved into a clear concept of the coordinated tactical action of the combined arms. Careful organization and training programs welded the mass into a military machine which under the personal command of Philip (or later Alexander) probably could have been successful against any other army raised during the next 18 centuries—in other words, until gunpowder weapons became predominant.

The backbone of the army was its infantry. The Macedonian phalanx was based on the Greek model, but 16 men deep, instead of 8 to 12, and with a small interval between men, instead of the shoulder-to-shoulder mass of the Greek phalanx. There were two types of hoplites: **pezetaeri** and **hypaspists.** The more numerous pezetaeri carried **sarissas,** or spears more than 13 feet long.* (For training purposes, a heavier, longer sarissa was used.) In addition, each man carried, slung over his shoulder, a shield large enough to cover his body when kneeling, with a short sword worn on a belt, plus helmet, breastplate, and greaves. The sarissa was held 3 to 6 feet from its butt, so that the points of the first 4 or 5 ranks protruded in front of the phalanx line in battle. Despite the heavier armament, constant training made pezetaeri units more maneuverable than the normal Greek phalanx. They were capable of performing a variety of movements and maneuvers in perfect formation.

More adaptable to any form of combat, however, was the hypaspist, cream of the Macedonian infantry. He was distinguished from the pezetaeri only by his

---

* Some authorities assert that the war sarissa was 21 feet long, the training sarissa 24 feet long. This is not totally unreasonable (as other authorities insist) since medieval Swiss pikemen wielded spears of comparable length.

shorter pike, probably 8 to 10 feet in length, and possibly by slightly lighter armor. Formations and evolutions of the hypaspist phalangial units were identical to those of the pezetaeri. The hypaspists were, if possible, better trained, more highly motivated, faster, and more agile. Since Alexander usually used an oblique order of battle, echeloned back from the right-flank cavalry spearhead, the hypaspists were usually on the right flank of the phalanx, to provide a flexible hinge between the fast-moving cavalry and the relatively slow pezetaeri.

Although Philip designed this heavy infantry formation as a base of maneuver for the shock action of his cavalry, the phalanx was a highly mobile base, which, completing a perfectly aligned charge at a dead run, would add its powerful impact upon an enemy not yet recovered from a cavalry blow. To exploit these tactics, Philip and Alexander tried to choose flat battlefields; but the concept was applicable, and was applied, on rough terrain.

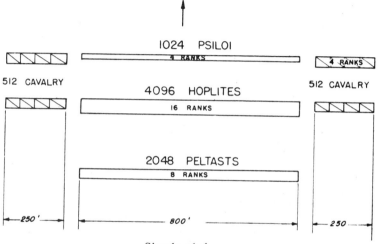

Simple phalanx

To protect flanks and rear, and to keep contact with the cavalry even on the most extended battlefields, there were two additional types of lighter infantry. For every four hoplites the organization called for two **peltasts** and one **psilos.** In normal prebattle formation, the peltasts—light pikemen—were drawn up in a line approximately 8 men deep, behind the phalanx. The psiloi—most of whom were servants and foragers for the heavy infantry—formed a skirmish line in front; their armament was the normal mixture of bows, javelins, darts, and slings.

The organization of the phalanx was remarkably like that of a modern army: a platoon (**tetrarchia**) of 64 hoplites; company (**taxiarchia**) of 128; battalion (**syntagma**) of 256; regiment (**chiliarchia**) of 1,024; division (**simple phalanx**) of 4,096 hoplites. Like the modern division, the simple phalanx was a self-contained fighting unit of combined arms; in addition to the heavy infantry, it included (at theoretical full strength) 2,048 peltasts, 1,024 psiloi, and a cavalry regiment (**epihipparchy**) of 1,024, for a total of 8,192 men. The grand phalanx, composed of four simple phalanxes, could be likened to a small modern field army, and had a strength of about 32,000 men.

Cavalry was a decisive arm of the Macedonian army, as well trained and as well equipped as the infantry. The elite were the Macedonian aristocrats of the

Companion cavalry, so called because Philip, and later Alexander, habitually led them personally in battle. Hardly less skilled, and also relying upon shock action, were the mercenary Thessalian horsemen. The Companions usually were on the right of the infantry phalanx, the Thessalians on the left. The principal weapon of these heavy cavalrymen was a pike, about 10 feet long, light enough to be thrown, heavy enough to be used as a lance to unhorse an opposing cavalryman, or to skewer an infantry foe. They were equally adept at using the short swords

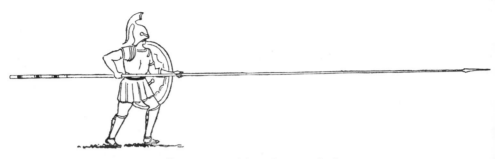

Pezetaerus, with sarissa couched

carried at their belts. They wore a scale-armor breastplate, plus shield, helmet, and greaves. Their horses also had scale-armor headpieces and breastplates.

There were other, intermediate, cavalry formations; some organized as lancers, others—prototypes of dragoons—capable of fighting on horse or on foot; both varieties carried lighter weapons and armor. Finally there were the light cavalrymen, mounted equivalents of the psiloi, who carried a variety of weapons: javelins, lances, bows. These light horsemen rarely wore armor, save for a helmet. Their functions were screening, reconnaissance, and flank protection.

The stirrup had not yet been invented; the horseman was seated on a pad, or saddle blanket of some sort (though the light cavalryman sometimes rode bareback), with bridle and headstall comparable to those of our own times. To become effective in combat, long training and practice were essential for both men and beasts.

The Macedonian army was the first to use prototypes of field artillery. Philip devised lightweight catapults and ballistae to accompany his siege train; it is not clear whether he actually used them in field operations. Alexander, however, habitually used these weapons in battle, particularly in mountain and river-crossing operations. Philip designed these engines so that the essential parts could be carried on a mule or pack horse; the bulky wooden elements would be hewn on the spot from tree trunks. This, of course, would delay their employment in field operations, so Alexander carried a number of the assembled weapons in wagons.

As noted earlier, Philip, Alexander, and their engineers introduced several innovations in siege warfare, and were far more successful in their sieges than their Greek predecessors. The highly organized Macedonian corps of engineers was responsible not only for the siege train but also for a bridge train for river crossing. As in the case of the artillery, the essential manufactured components of the specialized equipment were packed on animals or in wagons; these were then assembled with lumber hewn on the spot.

The details of the Macedonian staff system are not clear, though obviously well developed. Command was exercised by voice, by trumpet, and by spear movements. Long-range communication was accomplished by smoke signals in the daytime, by fire beacons at night. For battlefield messages Alexander used his seven aides-de-camp, or one of a more numerous corps of youthful pages. This latter corps was an officer-training unit, with programs of instruction and development comparable to those of modern military academies.

The most thorough administrative and logistical organization yet seen was developed by Philip of Macedon. Surgeons were attached to the Macedonian Army, and there is even some evidence of something like a medical field hospital service. There was also an efficient engineer corps, whose major function was to perform the technical tasks of siege operations and river crossings.

This was the compact, competent, smoothly organized, scientific instrument which Philip bequeathed to his son, Alexander the Great.

Macedonian cavalryman

CONQUESTS OF ALEXANDER, 336–323 B.C.

336–323. Reign of Alexander III (b. 356). The accession of this youth appeared to many Greeks to offer an opportunity to throw off Macedonian domination. Alexander, however, quickly marched to Greece at the head of an army; opposition disappeared. At Corinth he was elected captain general of the Hellenic League, in place of his father, for the projected operations against Persia (336).

335. Campaigns of Consolidation. The death of Philip had also caused the northern barbarian tribes to be restive. Alexander marched across the Danube, punishing recalcitrants firmly and re-establishing unquestioned Macedonian suzerainty over the region. Moving westward, he put down another uprising in southern Illyria, where he received word that Thebes and Athens had risen against Macedonian

leadership, and that most of Greece was wavering. **Darius III** of Persia had apparently been instrumental in arousing Greece against Macedonia. By forced marches Alexander arrived quickly in central Greece, captured Thebes by surprise, and virtually destroyed it. The lesson was salutary; Athens surrendered (and was treated generously); opposition ceased.

334. Invasion of Persia. Having assured the security of the Hellenic base, Alexander crossed the Hellespont into Asia with an army of 30,000 infantry and 5,000 cavalry. He had expanded his father's objective. He was determined to conquer Persia. He left **Antipater,** one of his most trusted generals, with an army of slightly more than 10,000 to hold Macedonia and Greece.

334, May. Battle of the Granicus. Alexander was met in western Asia Minor by a Persian army of about 40,000 men—about half Greek mercenaries. Alexander led an assault across the Granicus River, and was victorious in a short, sharp battle. He quickly liberated the Greek coastal cities of Asia Minor from Persian control, meeting little opposition, save at **Miletus,** which he captured after a brief siege.

334, July. Alexander's Strategy. Alexander now made the basic strategic decision for his subsequent campaigns against Persia. His only line of communications with Macedonia and Greece was overland, but across the Hellespont. The Persian fleet dominated the Aegean and eastern Mediterranean; not only could it cut his line of communications at the Straits; it could support dissident uprisings in Greece which could ruin his entire plan. He decided that before he could hope to conquer Persia, he must destroy Persian sea power. Lacking an adequate fleet, he would seize the entire Mediterranean seacoast of the Persian Empire; not only would this assure the security of his base, it would force the surrender of the Persian fleet. Then he could advance into Persia without fear for his communications.

334–333. Alexander conquered the coastal regions of Asia Minor, encountering difficulty only at **Halicarnassus,** captured after a hard siege. He went on to secure all important Persian strongholds in the interior, including Gordium, where occurred the famous incident of the Gordian knot.

333, October. Arrival of the Persian Army. Darius III, learning that Alexander was moving southward into Syria, hastened to place himself behind him and across the Macedonian line of communications, near Alexandretta (Iskendurun), with an army estimated at more than 100,000 men. Alexander, with some 30,000 men, turned to meet the threat.

333. Battle of Issus. Alexander found the Persians drawn up in a very deep formation on the narrow coastal plain, just north of the Pinarus River. Because of the tremendous discrepancy in numbers, Alexander decided to adopt the tactics of Epaminondas at Leuctra. With the Companion cavalry and the hypaspists he planned to attack the Persian left, with the remainder of the phalanx echeloned to his left rear. The Thessalian cavalry guarded the left flank of the phalanx from the dangerous Persian cavalry. In a preliminary action, he drove back a strong Persian covering force in the foothills south of the Pinarus. Then, leading the Companions, he put his plan into effect. The leading echelons of the phalanx were briefly in trouble when the Persian center counterattacked while they were crossing the stream. Meanwhile Alexander's cavalry assault had smashed the Persian left; with the hypaspists he wheeled westward into the exposed center of the Persian army. With this support, the Macedonian center recovered and renewed its attack. The Persian cavalry on Darius' right flank had meanwhile crossed the Pinarus to be repulsed by the left of the phalanx and the Thessalians. As his center crumbled under the combined Macedonian cavalry-infantry attack, Darius fled the field, amidst the panic-stricken survivors of his army. Persian losses were tremendous, probably more than 50,000. Macedonian casualties were 450 killed. The Macedonians captured, among others, the family of Darius, including his queen, children, and mother. Alexander pursued briefly, then returned to his original plan of securing the seacoast as a base.

332, January–August. Siege of Tyre. The principal Phoenician seaport of Tyre (Sur) was situated on an island less than half a mile off the mainland. The main base of the Persian navy, Tyre's capture was essential to Alexander's plan. To get at the city, Alexander built a mole 200 feet wide from the mainland out to the island. Tyrian opposition was vigorous. Using fire ships, they several times interrupted the work, burning down part of the mole, and the wooden besieging towers on it. Redoubling his efforts by land, Alexander also scraped up a naval force from other captured Phoenician towns. After winning a tough sea fight, he cooped up the Tyrian ships in their harbors. Finally as the mole approached the island city's walls, a breach was made by ship-borne engines, and the city was stormed. As an example to other towns on his route, Alexander treated the survivors harshly; the city was practically destroyed, and most of the inhabitants scattered as slaves.

332. Peace Overtures from Darius. The Persian ruler offered Alexander 10,000 gold talents ($300 million), all of the

Persian Empire west of the Euphrates, and his daughter in marriage. Alexander refused, replying that he intended to take all Persia, and that he could already marry Darius' captive daughter, if he wished, without Darius' consent.

332, September–November. Siege of Gaza. While besieging Tyre, Alexander had sent troops to seize the rest of Syria and Palestine. Gaza alone resisted. Alexander immediately marched there, and began another siege. The most memorable feature of the operation was Alexander's construction of a great earthen mound, 250 feet high and a quarter of a mile in circumference at its base, on which he mounted catapults and ballistae with which to bombard the defenders. After two months the city was stormed and sacked.

332–331, December–March. Occupation of Egypt. There was no significant opposition. Alexander's seacoast base was now secure. As in Asia Minor and Syria, Alexander established firm control with military garrisons in the chief cities. While in Egypt he founded the city of Alexandria —one of many of that name. He also made a journey to the Temple of Zeus Ammon, at the Siwa Oasis, some 200 miles west of Memphis in the Lybian Des-

ert, to be hailed by the priests as the son of Zeus.

332–331. Spartan Revolt. King **Agis II** of Sparta, with Persian financial support, had roused several Greek states to revolt against Macedonia while Alexander was away on his expedition. He was joined by most of the southern Greek states, and besieged **Megalopolis.** Antipater marched south and defeated the rebels outside Megalopolis (331). After this victory he sent a substantial reinforcement of infantry and cavalry to Alexander, which joined the king in Egypt.

331, April–September. Learning that Darius was assembling a vast army in Mesopotamia, Alexander rapidly marched to Tyre, then turned eastward to cross the Euphrates and Tigris rivers without opposition. He located the Persian host— probably about 200,000 strong—drawn up for battle on the Plain of Gaugamela, near ancient Nineveh, and about 70 miles west of Arbela (Erbil). Alexander, who now had about 47,000 men, halted seven miles from the Persian camp to reconnoiter and rest his troops. Another peace offer from Darius was refused; this time the Persian offered 30,000 gold talents ($900 million), half his kingdom, and his daughter's hand.

BATTLE OF ARBELA (OR GAUGAMELA), OCTOBER 1, 331 B.C.

Darius, whose best foot troops, the Greek mercenaries, had been almost destroyed at Issus, was relying mainly on his cavalry, chariots, and elephants. The Persians were in two long, deep lines, with cavalry on each flank. In the center were some remaining Greek mercenaries and the Persian Royal Guard cavalry. Numerous chariots lined the front of the entire army, with a clump of elephants in front of the center. Darius, expecting a night attack, had kept his tired troops in position all night.

As at Issus, Alexander advanced in echelon from the right, where his cavalry Companions, screened by light infantry, were to strike the hammer blow. Next came the hypaspists, with the main phalanx in the center of his line. The left was composed of the Greek and Thessalian horse, commanded by Parmenio.

Behind each flank of the Macedonian line moved a column of light horse and foot, prepared to protect them from envelopment by the long Persian line. Behind the center, and covering the camp, was a thin phalanx of Thessalian infantry. These last three elements comprised what was probably the first recorded battlefield use of a tactical reserve.

Apparently the Macedonian advance "drifted" obliquely to its right; the cumbersome Persian host endeavored to shift correspondingly to its left, the movement creating some gaps in the Persian line. As Alexander led his Companions forward in a charge, the Persian wings swept in to envelop the Macedonian flanks, but were met and repulsed by the flank reserve columns Alexander had disposed for that purpose. Alexander noticed a gap near the left-center of the Persian line, and led his charge there. Creating a giant wedge with his cavalry and the hypaspists, he smashed through completely; Darius, in the path of the onslaught, fled. Panic spread throughout the Persian center and left, and they crumpled and gave way. Alexander was forced to turn back to rectify conditions on his own left flank, which had been driven back by a determined Persian cavalry charge in great force. But the reserve had held, and Alexander's drive into the rear of the Persian attackers ended the threat, and concluded the battle as well. He now led his entire army in a vigorous pursuit of the fleeing Persians, scattering the defeated foe hopelessly. Alexander lost 500 men killed, and probably about 5,000 wounded. Persian casualties are unknown, but there were at least 50,000 slain.

331–330, October–July. Pursuit. Alexander marched into Babylon, which surrendered without a fight. Subduing wild mountain tribes as he advanced through the heart of the Persian Empire, he destroyed Persepolis, the ancient Persian capital, in somewhat delayed retribution for the burning of Athens in 480. Then he turned

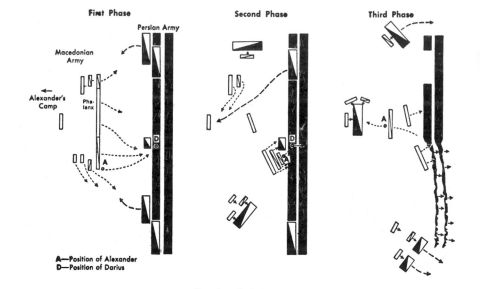

Battle of Arbela

northward to Ecbatana (Hamadan), where Darius had taken refuge, but on the approach of the Macedonians, Darius fled eastward through the Caspian Gates. Choosing 500 of his strongest men, Alexander dashed ahead of his army and, after marching 400 miles in eleven days, caught up with the fleeing Persians. As Alexander approached, only 60 men with him, the Persian nobles led by **Bessus,** satrap of Bactria, murdered Darius, then scattered. Alexander now was unquestioned ruler of the Persian Empire.

329. Consolidation and Advance into Central Asia. Alexander, pursuing the murderers of Darius, and at the same time consolidating his hold on the empire, marched eastward through Parthia into Bactria. Capturing and executing Bessus, he turned northward across the Oxus into Sogdiana in central Asia. He was forced to fight a number of bitter battles against the wild Scythian tribesmen in the mountain passes south and west of the Jaxartes, and was wounded—once seriously—in two of these. His crossing of the Jaxartes was brilliant. Rafts for the infantry were improvised by sewing up tents stuffed with hay. Scythian bowmen, lined up along the far river bank, were driven back by heavy missile fire covering the crossing. After inflicting a crushing defeat on the Scythians, he returned to Sogdiana, which had risen in revolt, under **Spitamenes,** former satrap of the province.

328–327. Advance to India. After a long,

hard campaign against the rebels, Alexander subdued Sogdiana, Spitamenes being murdered by his own adherents. Alexander married **Roxana,** daughter of **Oxyartes,** one of the Sogdianan chieftains who had fought most valiantly against him and who now became viceroy for the Macedonian emperor. He next prepared for a campaign into India, encouraged in this by the King of Taxala—at war with **Porus,** leading monarch of the Punjab—who thought Alexander would be a good ally. Despite bitter opposition from the natives of the Hindu Kush region, Alexander fought his way through passes north of the Kabul Valley (part of his army went through the Khyber Pass) to the Indus River (327). Crossing into India, he was welcomed by the King of Taxala (near Rawalpindi), who again asked Macedonian assistance against Porus.

326, March–May. March to the Hydaspes. Pleased to have an excuse to invade central India, Alexander marched eastward, until he was stopped at the unfordable Hydaspes (Jhelum) River, torrential and

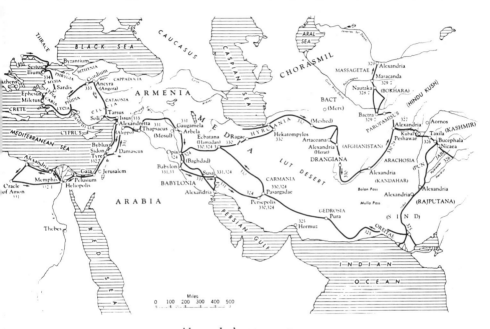

Alexander's conquests

swollen from rains. On the far bank lay the army of Porus, about 35,000 men. Alexander had about 20,000 with him. A crossing of the swollen river against opposition was out of the question; Alexander established a camp on the river bank, and endeavored to convince Porus that he would not attempt to cross before the river fell. To confuse the Indians, however, he undertook a series of feints up and down the river near the two opposing camps. Kept constantly on edge by this ceaseless activity, Indian reactions to the feints and alarms became perfunctory.

326, May. Battle of the Hydaspes. Sensing decreased Indian vigilance, Alexander moved rapidly. He had reconnoitered a crossing place 16 miles upstream from his camp. With about half his army, he marched to the selected point during a stormy night, leaving the remainder to continue the feints along the bank near his camp. Careful preparations had been made, boats were ready, and the crossing was completed shortly after dawn. Porus, bewildered by reports that Alexander was on his side of the river, drew up his army near his camp, with about 100 elephants lined up in front; he knew that the horses of Alexander's cavalry would not face the elephants. Alexander arrived in front of this formidable array with about 6,000 cavalry and 5,000 infantry. He promptly sent his general **Coenus** with half of his cavalry in a wide encirclement of the Indian right flank. The remainder of his small army he drew up beside the river, with his left refused, to prevent Porus from enveloping his open flank. His light infantry began to harass the elephants to his front. A number of the maddened beasts turned and dashed through their own lines, putting Porus' ranks into confusion. Just as the Indian right wing was advancing to envelop the open Macedonian flank, it was struck in the rear by Coenus, who then swept down the rear of the entire Indian line, adding to the existing confusion. At this moment Alexander led his Companions in a charge along the river bank, while the small phalanx smashed into the Indian left wing. For a while the Indians fought stoutly and casualties were severe on both sides. But, assailed from front, flank, and rear, Porus' men finally gave way and took to flight. Porus, badly wounded, was captured by Alexander.

326, July. Mutiny. Alexander now decided to continue into north-central India and planned to continue to the Ganges. He got as far as the Hyphasis (Beas) River when his exhausted, homesick Macedonians simply refused to go further. It was respectful but determined mutiny. Sadly Alexander gave in to their demands, and began the return.

326–324. Return to Persia. Alexander marched south down the Indus, meeting considerable resistance. In a battle with the Mallians near modern Multan he was seriously wounded. He recovered, and reached the mouth of the Indus, exploring the surrounding countryside. He built a fleet, and sent it westward under **Nearchus** across the Arabian Sea to the Persian Gulf, exploring a hitherto unknown sea route. A portion of his army under **Craterus** he sent back to Persepolis via the Bolan Pass and Kandahar. With the remainder Alexander marched across the mountains and deserts of Gedrosia, in one of the most grueling and difficult marches of military history. At two points en route he made contact with the fleet of Nearchus. Though we have no details, the administrative arrangement for this march must have been superb—evidence of a major factor in Alexander's invariable success.

324–323. Planned Union of East and West. Arriving back in Persia and Mesopotamia, Alexander discovered that his empire had become shaky while he was away campaigning. Promptly he restored order, and set in motion a grandiose plan for a melding of the best features of the cultures of Greece and Persia. How much further he would have changed the course of history can only be speculative; he died in Babylon of a fever (probably malaria).

COMMENT. *Of particular interest was Alexander's ability to adjust his tactics and tactical formations to fit conditions of the moment, as shown in his central Asian operations (329–327). Against guerrilla resistance he reorganized his army into light, mobile columns moving independently but in coordination. Much use was made of light cavalry bowmen. Exhaustive terrain reconnaissance assisted his supply needs. Military colonies, established at important road junctions, not only protected his communications, but these colonies, becoming cities, brought civilization to a large area of the Middle East. His accomplishments in mountain warfare and against irregular forces have never been equaled. No man in history has surpassed his intellectual, military, and administrative accomplishments; not more than two or three are worthy of comparison.*

THE DIADOCHI—SUCCESSORS OF ALEXANDER, 323–200 B.C.

Wars of the Diadochi, 323–281 B.C.

Upon the death of Alexander his leading generals (the Diadochi, or successors) immediately fell to wrangling over his empire in a multilateral conflict which lasted for more than 40 years.

The principal contestants were **Perdiccas** (d. 321), Alexander's prime minister or chief of staff, whom the dying king made his regent; **Antipater** (398?–319), able regent in Greece and Macedonia from 334 to 323; **Eumenes** (360?–316), staff secretary; **Ptolemy** (367?–283) and **Lysimachus** (361?–281), personal aides and principal staff officers; **Seleucus** (358–280), commanding the officers' training corps of pages; **Craterus** (d. 321, son-in-law of Antipater), **Polysperchon** (d. 310?), **Antigonus** (382–301), and **Cassander** (350–297, son of Antipater), all the equivalent of infantry division commanders; and **Demetrius** (d. 283, son of Antigonus), who had commanded a squadron of Companion cavalry.

These were the men Alexander had selected as his principal subordinates on the basis of combat performance; in addition to intrinsic toughness and ability, all had been trained by an unexcelled master of war. None of them, however, really understood Alexander's system or possessed his spark of genius. They were skilled professionals, but not great captains. Much of the struggle was waged by guile, treachery, and bribery. Their armies were completely mercenary, and would turn against their leaders if offered more money by the enemy.

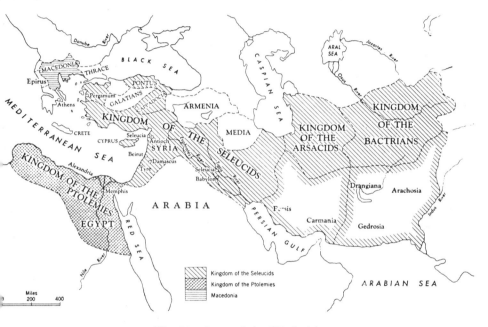

The kingdoms of the Diadochi

Between them, these men set Alexander's Macedonian Empire aflame from the Balkans to the Indus River and from the Caucasus to Egypt's southern border. The conflict consumed all of them and for the remainder of the 3rd century partitioned the empire loosely into three warring segments ruled by the descendents of Antigonus, Seleucus, and Ptolemy. A detailed recital of the military events of the Diadochian Wars is of no military interest. However, a few highlights merit attention.

322. Lamian War. Revolt by Athens and most of the Greek cities was crushed by Antipater and Craterus at the **Battle of Crannon.** The Macedonian fleet obliterated the Athenian navy forever at **Amorgos.** Demosthenes, leader of the revolt, took poison as the Macedonians occupied Athens.

321–319. Deaths of Perdiccas, Craterus, and Antipater. Perdiccas was killed by mutineers bribed by Ptolemy (321); Craterus, invading Cappadocia, was killed by Eumenes (320); Antipater died (319).

317. Battle of Paraetakena. This engagement, between Antigonus and Eumenes, in Iran, was indecisive. Next year, after another drawn battle, Eumenes was killed by his own men, who had been bribed by Antigonus.

311. Truce. Cassander was to hold Macedonia until Roxana's son, **Alexander IV,** came of age; Lysimachus was to keep Thrace and the Chersonese; Ptolemy held Egypt, Palestine and Cyprus; Antigonus retained Asia Minor and Greece; Seleucus kept the vast region east of the Euphrates as far as India.

310. Cassander's Assassination of Roxana and Alexander IV. The line of Alexander was extinguished. Again the surviving Diadochi clashed with one another (309).

308. Battle of Salamis (Cyprus). Decisive naval victory by Demetrius over Ptolemy's brother, **Menelaeus.** As a result Antigonus regained Cyprus (306).

307–306. Demetrius' Invasion of Greece and Palestine. He captured Athens and much of Greece, then marched to reconquer Palestine, but was repelled from Egypt by Ptolemy (305).

305–304. Siege of Rhodes. Demetrius attacked Ptolemy's garrison there. A two-year siege ensued. All the devices known to the times were tried by both sides: rams, attacking towers, liquid fire, mines and countermines, all the engines of attack and defense, raids and assaults in both directions. Ptolemy's sea power enabling adequate logistical support to the garrison, Demetrius withdrew and returned to Greece.

301. Battle of Ipsus. In Asia Minor, the aged Antigonus and Demetrius were defeated by Seleucus and Lysimachus, allies of Cassander, who made excellent use of war elephants, and who were aided by deserters from Antigonus' own forces. Antigonus was killed, but Demetrius escaped and established control over western Asia Minor. Cassander was recognized as king of Macedonia, but died soon after (300).

294. Demetrius Seizes Macedonia. He seized the throne after murdering the son of Cassander.

290–245. Rise of the Aetolian and Achaean Leagues in Greece. The Aetolian League, first organized in the 4th century in western Greece, became more active in this period, including central Greece. The Achaean League (280) covered most of the Peloponnesus. Athens and Sparta, generally independent, frequently became temporarily allied with one or the other of these leagues.

286. Downfall of Demetrius. King **Pyrrhus** of Epirus, allied with Ptolemy and Lysimachus, drove Demetrius from Macedonia. He retreated to Asia Minor, but his troops deserted him and he surrendered to Seleucus, dying in prison three years later (283).

283–280. End of the Diadochi. Ptolemy died (283). Seleucus and Lysimachus, last two surviving Diadochi, clashed. Aged Seleucus, aided by **Ptolemy Keraunos** (disinherited son of Ptolemy) defeated and killed Lysimachus in hand-to-hand combat at the **Battle of Corus** (Corupedion) (281). Seleucus, now ruling all of Alexander's Macedonian Empire except Egypt, was himself murdered (280) by Ptolemy Keraunos while en route to Macedonia.

Antigonid Macedonia, Seleucid Persian, Ptolemaic Egypt, 281–200 B.C.

279–275. Celtic Invasion. A migratory wave of Celts invaded Macedonia, Greece, and Thrace, then crossed to Asia Minor, where they established the kingdom of Galatia. Ptolemy Keraunos was killed in battle with the invaders (277). **Antigonus Gonatus** (son of Demetrius) then regained control of Macedonia, driving out the Celts (276). **Antiochus I** (son of Seleucus) finally subdued the Galatian-Celts (275).

280–279. Damascene War. The first of a series of wars between the Ptolemys and the Seleucids for the control of Syria and Palestine. **Ptolemy II,** second son of Ptolemy I, defeated Antiochus I.

276–272. First Syrian War. Ptolemy II again defeated Antiochus I, at the same time occupying Antiochus' ally, Antigonus, by subsidizing Pyrrhus' invasion of Macedonia (274–273).

266–255. Alliance of Antiochus I and Antigonus against Ptolemy II. Ptolemy subsidized invasions of Macedonia by Athens, Sparta, and Epirus. Sparta and Athens, led by Chremonides of Athens, were defeated by Antigonus in the **Chremonidean War.** Sparta was eliminated by defeat near **Corinth** (265); Athens was then invested, and surrendered after a siege of two years (262). **Alexander** of Epirus (son of Pyrrhus) was more successful, capturing most of Macedonia (263), but was finally driven out by Antigonus (255). To keep Antiochus busy in Asia Minor, Ptolemy subsidized **Eumenes I,** who successfully defended the independence of Pergamum from the Seleucid Empire (263). Antiochus invaded Syria, to initiate the **Second Syrian War** (260). Antigonus defeated Ptolemy in a naval battle off **Cos** (258). Ptolemy, admitting failure, made peace (255).

252–215. Turmoil in Greece. The principal events: War of Demetrius (238–229), in which **Demetrius II** of Macedon fought an inconclusive war against the Achaean and Aetolian leagues. **Cleomenes III** of Sparta defeated the Achaeans (228–227); **Antigonus III** of Macedon defeated Cleomenes at the **Battle of Sellasia** (222). In the **Social War** (219–217) **Philip V** of Macedonia crushed the Aetolians.

250–227. Decline of the Seleucid Empire. Bactria became an independent Macedonian kingdom (250) under **Diodotus I** (see p. 79). **Arsaces I,** Scythian nomad leader, controlled the province of Parthia (235), which he expanded at the expense of eastern portions of the Seleucid Empire. These losses were largely due to the preoccupation of **Seleucus II** (246–227) with the invasion of Syria by Ptolemy III (see below), and a civil war in Asia Minor (against his brother, **Antiochus Hierax**), in which the Galatians and Pergamum were also involved. Antiochus Hierax, aided by the Galatians, defeated Seleucus at **Ancyra** (Ankara; 236), but Antiochus and the Galatians were soon thereafter defeated in turn by **Attalus I** of Pergamum (230–229), leaving Seleucus secure on his throne, but with Pergamum dominant in western Asia Minor.

246–241. Third Syrian War. Ptolemy III conquered Syria and much of southern Asia Minor from Seleucus II, despite a defeat by Antigonus in the naval **Battle of Andros** (245).

224–221. War between Pergamum and the Seleucids. Attalus was at first successful, but then was defeated by the new Seleucid emperor, **Antiochus III (the Great),** who regained most of central Asia Minor from Pergamum.

223–200. Revival of the Seleucid Empire. After his victory over Pergamum, and

suppressing a revolt in Mesopotamia (221), Antiochus III became involved in the inconclusive **Fourth Syrian War** with **Ptolemy IV** (221–217); Antiochus was defeated at **Raphia** (Rafa; 217) after earlier victories, and left Palestine in Egyptian hands. He next subdued a serious revolt in Asia Minor (216–213). He then devoted his efforts, generally successfully, to restoring the vigor and domains of the empire. He defeated Armenia (212–211), which was forced to acknowledge Seleucid sovereignty. After re-establishing control over Media (210), he invaded Parthia (209) and quickly forced **Arsaces III** to become his vassal, as a result of a great victory at the **Battle of the Arius.** He continued on to Bactria (see p. 79), where, after a hard-fought campaign (208–206), he obtained the qualified submission of the Greek ruler, **Euthydemus.** He next marched down the Kabul River as far as the Indus and possibly into the Punjab (see p. 79). Returning to his capital, Seleucia, he then conducted a successful amphibious expedition down the Arabian coast of the Persian Gulf, to capture Gerrha (modern Bahrein, 205–204).

215–205. First Macedonian War. Philip V of Macedon made a treaty with **Hannibal** of Carthage against Rome, and threatened to invade Italy. Rome formed an alliance against Macedonia including the Aetolian League, Pergamum, Elis, Mantinea, and Sparta. Macedonia was joined by the Achaean League, under the inspired leadership of **Philopoemen,** last of the great Greek generals. Rome, fighting for her life against Hannibal, was able to contribute few ground forces, but aided with a sizable fleet which gave the allies naval superiority. Generally inconclusive, the most notable feature of this war was the brilliant leadership of Philopoemen, whose victory at **Mantinea** (207) crushed Sparta, whose able king and general, **Machanidas,** was killed.

203–195. Fifth Syrian War. Upon the accession of the infant **Ptolemy V** to the Egyptian throne (205), Antiochus III and Philip V made a secret agreement to strip the Ptolemaic Empire of all its holdings in Palestine, Syria, Asia Minor, and the Aegean Islands. In Palestine and Syria, Antiochus was successful, the crowning victory being that of the **Battle of Panium**

(198). He soon occupied all Palestine and other Ptolemaic possessions in Syria and southeast Asia Minor, save for Cyprus. Philip was less successful. In Asia Minor he was repulsed by Pergamum (under aged but still able Attalus I) and Rhodes, allies of Egypt, and in the Aegean he was defeated in the naval **Battle of Chios** (201). He was unable to redress these losses because he soon became engaged in the disastrous **Second Macedonian War** with Rome (200–196; see p. 85).

202–201. Rise of the Achaean League. Philopoemen defeated **Nabis,** tyrant of Sparta, at **Messene** and again in a naval battle off **Tegea.** By this time the military efficiency and skill of Philopoemen had brought the Achaean League to pre-eminence in Greece proper.

CENTRAL MEDITERRANEAN

CARTHAGE, 400–200 B.C.

400–264. Expansion Westward. Though Carthage was preoccupied with Sicily in the 4th and 3rd centuries B.C., she was simultaneously engaged in land operations and overseas expeditions along the Mediterranean coasts of Africa and Spain, and also along the Atlantic shores beyond the Pillars of Hercules (Straits of Gibraltar).

398–397. First War with Dionysius of Syracuse. A Carthaginian army under **Himilco** besieged Syracuse, but was repulsed with great losses. Carthage was forced to abandon its outposts in the eastern and central portion of Sicily.

392. Second War with Dionysius. Again the Syracusans were successful, and the war ended with Dionysius in control of most of the island; Carthage retained only a few footholds in the west.

385–376. Third War with Dionysius. The Carthaginians were successful and substantially increased their holdings in western and central Sicily.

368–367. Fourth War with Dionysius. This was inconclusive, and ended with the death of the Syracusan ruler.

347. Treaty with Rome. This, apparently, was a reaffirmation of an earlier treaty (509), in which Rome's trade was limited to Italy, while Carthage was to keep out of Italy entirely.

344–339. War with Timoleon of Syracuse. Initially successful, a Carthaginian army again besieged Syracuse, and actually occupied all the city except the citadel. But dissension and plague in Carthage weakened the armies in the field. **Timoleon** drove out the invaders, and then defeated them decisively at the **Battle of the Crimissus** (340). Peace terms were unfavorable to Carthage.

323–312. Expansion in Sicily. Again Carthage was able to profit from internal troubles in Syracuse to regain control of most of Sicily.

311–306. War with Agathocles. Hamilcar defeated Agathocles of Syracuse at **Himera** (311), and then laid siege to Syracuse (311–310). Agathocles led an army to Africa, and in turn besieged Carthage (310–307). The Carthaginians defeated the invaders outside the walls of their city, and Agathocles was forced to flee to Sicily, where his son had recently been defeated by a Carthaginian army. Despite these setbacks, peace terms were not unfavorable to Agathocles.

306. Treaty with Rome. Carthage and Rome limited their respective areas of Mediterranean commerce.

278–276. War with Pyrrhus. On the outbreak of another war, Syracuse called for the assistance of **Pyrrhus** of Epirus, who was in control of southern Italy after having defeated Rome (see p. 59). Pyrrhus drove the Carthaginians from their investment of Syracuse. He was generally victorious, but was unable to drive the Carthaginians from their strongholds in western and central Sicily. Carthage concluded a defensive-offensive alliance with Rome against Pyrrhus (277). Pyrrhus, who probably could have conquered Sicily, returned to Italy to meet a Roman threat (see p. 59).

264–241. First Punic War. (See p. 60.) Carthage lost Sicily to Rome.

241–237. Rise of Hamilcar. Political rivalry between Hamilcar Barca, hero of the First Punic War, and **Hanno,** renowned for victories against Numidians and Mauretanians in Africa. A revolt of unpaid mercenaries (inspired in part by Hanno's inept leadership) broke out under **Matho.** The rebels, 25,000 strong, laid siege to

Carthage (238). Hamilcar was called to command the Carthaginian Army. By a brilliant stratagem he got 10,000 men out of the city, and defeated the rebels at the **Battle of Utica.** Soon afterward, he ambushed and defeated another rebel army near **Tunes** (Tunis). This ended the mutiny. Hamilcar was now the acknowledged leader of Carthage.

238. Loss of Sardinia to Rome. (See p. 61.)

237–228. Conquest of Spain. To offset the loss of Sicily and Sardinia and to provide a base for renewed war with Rome, Hamilcar decided to conquer Spain. Raising an army largely with his own money, he expanded Carthaginian footholds in Iberia, conquering most of the peninsula below the Tagus and Ebro rivers before his death. Hanno, meanwhile, regained a position of political ascendancy in Carthage.

228–221. Hasdrubal Barca in Spain. Son-in-law of Hamilcar, Hasdrubal consolidated conquests and concluded a treaty with Rome which recognized Carthaginian sovereignty of all territories south of the Ebro.

221. Assassination of Hasdrubal. He was succeeded by **Hannibal Barca** (247–183), son of Hamilcar.

221–219. Hannibal Consolidates. After conducting two successful campaigns against barbarian tribes in outlying regions, and advancing his control northward to the Durius River, Hannibal attacked the seaport of Saguntum (Sagunto), an ally of Rome, the only territory south of the Ebro which rejected Carthaginian sovereignty. This precipitated the **Second Punic War** (see pp. 61–71).

MAGNA GRAECIA (SICILY AND SOUTH ITALY), 400–264 B.C.

405–367. Reign of Dionysius, Tyrant of Syracuse. After gaining power, Dionysius concluded a war with Carthage (404), then expanded Syracusan control over neighboring regions (403–400).

398–367. Wars with Carthage. (See p. 56.) Dionysius on balance was successful in these wars, and extended his control over most of Sicily.

390–379. Conquest of South Italy by Dionysius. Syracuse became the leading power

of Magna Graecia, and in fact of the entire central Mediterranean area. Dionysius crushed the Italiote League by his decisive victory at the **Battle of the Elleporus** (389).

366–344. Turmoil. For more than 20 years after the death of Dionysius there was constant turmoil in Syracuse and in the Greek states of Sicily. Carthage regained much of the areas lost to Dionysius. Order was re-established in Syracuse by the rise of another strong man, **Timoleon.**

344–339. Timoleon's War with Carthage. (See p. 56.)

338–330. Greek Intervention in Italy. War between the Italian Greeks and native Italians in southern Italy (Samnites, Lucanians, Umbrians) had been going on sporadically since the beginning of the century. The Greeks asked for and received the assistance of **Archimadus** of Sparta (338) and, after his death, that of Alexander of Epirus.

334–330. Campaigns of Alexander of Epirus. He came to Italy to assist the Tarentines against the Lucanians, Bruttians, and Samnites. He entered into an alliance with Rome against the Samnites, but was defeated and killed at the **Battle of Pandosia** (331). Alexander of Epirus was the uncle of Alexander of Macedon; before his death it is reported that when he received glowing reports of his nephew's victories against the Persians, he replied that his nephew fought women while he was fighting men.

317. Rise of Agathocles. He brought order to Syracuse, which had been in decline since the death of Timoleon (323).

311–306. War of Agathocles with Carthage. (See p. 56.)

302. Agathocles Invades Southern Italy. An expedition into southern Italy against the Italians, undertaken at the request of Tarentum, was indecisive.

282–275. Pyrrhus in Southern Italy and Sicily. (See above, p. 56, and below, p. 59.)

c. 275. The Mamertines. After the death of Agathocles, a group of Italian mercenaries revolted against his successor, **Hiero II** of Syracuse. These former mercenaries, called Mamertines, soon established themselves in Messana (Messina), which became a base for wholesale brigandage by land and sea. Carrying on more or less constant war with Syracuse, they eventually became hard-pressed by Hiero, and dissension broke out in Messina. One faction of Mamertines called on Rome for help; another asked for Carthaginian aid (265). Carthage immediately sent a garrison, which seized and held Messina; Rome had an expedition on the way. This was the basis of the First Punic War (see p. 60).

ROME, 400–200 B.C.

Conquest of Italy, 405–265 B.C.

405–396. War with Veii. The first of Rome's life-or-death contests, **Marcus Furius Camillus,** Rome's first great general, was appointed dictator (first of five times) after the besieging Roman army was defeated outside the walls of Veii. Camillus had a tunnel dug under the walls of Veii; he sent a party of picked men through to strike the defenders, while he attracted their attention by an external assault (see also p. 33). Complete victory ended the 9-year siege.

390. Sack of Rome by the Gauls. Celts, or Gauls, had migrated into the Po Valley (c. 400), spreading down the Adriatic coast as far south as the Aesis River. Invading central Italy (391), they laid waste much of Etruria, then decisively defeated a Roman army at the **Battle of the Allia** (390). They then swept into Rome itself, seizing all the city save for the citadel, on Capitoline Hill. Furius Camillus, again appointed dictator, raised an army in outlying districts, but got rid of the Gauls by paying a large tribute. Sporadic Celtic raids into central Italy continued for another 50 years.

389–343. Expansion in Latium. Quickly recovering from the Celtic raid, Rome expanded steadily in all directions in Latium and southern Etruria. Furius Camillus finally ended the threat of the Aequians and Volsci by defeating both tribes completely (389). Many conquered cities were accepted as allies, in a Latin confederacy under Rome's leadership.

367. Second Celtic Invasion. Furius Camillus, again called as dictator, drove the Gauls away. He reorganized the legion (see p. 72).

362–345. Latin Uprisings. Rome retained her leadership with great difficulty.

343–341. First Samnite War. The cities of Campania called on Rome for assistance against the warlike Samnite hill tribes. **Marcus Valerius Corvus** won a major victory at **Mount Gaurus** (342), but was unable to conquer the Samnites. Rome did however, establish a virtual protectorate over Campania.

340–338. Latin War. An uprising of the Latin allies and colonies, joined by the Campanians, for a time threatened to overthrow Rome. Fortunately for her, the Samnites were busy against the Italian Greeks (see p. 57). At the **Battle of Vesuvius** (339) the left wing of the Roman army, commanded by Consul **Publius Decius Mus,** was shattered; Decius, to permit the withdrawal of the remainder of the army, under his colleague **T. Manlius Torquatus,** deliberately sacrificed himself in a forlorn hope attack against the Latins; the result was a drawn battle. Manlius soon thereafter won the decisive **Battle of Trifanum** (338), crushing the revolt. Rome treated the defeated Latins with a mixture of firmness and leniency which thereafter assured their steadfast loyalty. Roman consolidation and slow expansion continued.

327–304. Second Samnite War. Initially successful (327–322), Rome was several times subsequently close to disaster. A Roman army, under the consuls **Spurius Postumius** and **T. Veturius Calvinus,** was decisively defeated by **Gavius Pontius** and forced to surrender at the **Battle of the Caudine Forks** (321). Rome agreed to a temporary peace or armistice under very unfavorable terms. A complete reorganization of the Roman military system resulted (see p. 72). Fighting broke out soon again, with Roman successes at first. Then they were defeated at **Lautulae** (316), but won an important battle a **Ciuna** (315). The construction of the Via Appia (312) gave Rome a logistical advantage which enabled her to drive the Samnites from Campania. This was soon offset by the entrance of the northern Etruscans into the war against Rome (311). The Etruscans were defeated a the **Battle of Lake Vadimo** (310) by **Q Fabius Rullianus,** and forced to make peace (308). Meanwhile **L. Papirius Cur**

sor had won a great victory over the Samnites in the mountains to the south (309). Then the Umbrians, Picentini, and Marsians (all Italian peoples inhabiting the southeast slopes of the Apennines) joined the Samnites (308). Rome sent land and sea expeditions against these peoples—the first use of naval force by the Romans in the Adriatic. The consuls **M. Fulvius** and **L. Postumius** defeated the Samnites in the decisive battle of the war at **Bovianum** (305). All of Rome's enemies were soon forced to make peace (304).

298–290. Third Samnite War. An early Samnite success at **Camerinum**, against **Lucius Scipio**, inspired the Etruscans to join another alliance against Rome. The Gauls and Umbrians also joined the Samnites. In the decisive **Battle of Sentinum** (295) the Romans under Fabius Rullianus and **Publius Decius Mus** (son of the hero of the Latin War) defeated a combined army of Etruscans, Gauls, and Samnites. Decius, like his father, deliberately sacrificed his life when the battle began to go against Rome; his men rallied to win an overwhelming victory. The Gauls, Umbrians, and Etruscans made peace, but the Samnites continued the war for a few years until crushed by **Manius Curius Dentatus** at the **Battle of Aquilonia** (293). In recognition of their gallantry, the Samnites were permitted to enter the Roman confederation as allies rather than as subjects of Rome.

285–282. Revolt of Etruscans and Gauls. A Roman army under **Lucius Caecilius** was annihilated by the Gauls at **Arretium** (285), but a combined invasion by Etruscans and Gauls was smashed by **P. Cornelius Dolabella** north of Rome at **Lake Vadimo** (283). Final Etruscan resistance was crushed at **Populonia** (282).

281–272. War with Pyrrhus. Roman expansion into southern Italy alarmed Tarentum, which declared war and asked **Pyrrhus,** king of Epirus, to come to her assistance. Pyrrhus arrived in southern Italy with an army of about 20,000 infantry, organized as a Macedonian-type phalanx, and more than 3,000 Thessalian and Epirote cavalry. He established himself as the virtual master of the Greek cities of southern Italy.

280. Battle of Heraclea (or of the Siris River). The Romans, under **Publius Valerius Laevinus,** numbered about 35,000; Pyrrhus had about 30,000. After a terrible struggle, Pyrrhus routed the Roman cavalry by judicious use of his elephants, which the Romans had never before encountered. He then drove the Roman infantry back across the Siris in great disorder. The Romans lost 7,000–15,000 killed; Pyrrhus had 4,000–11,000 dead. The Epirote king is reputed to have said: "One more such victory and I am lost." After advancing toward Rome, Pyrrhus gained further evidence of the toughness of his new foes and the loyalty of their allies when he learned that a Roman-allied army was marching to meet him. He retired to southern Italy, where he recruited a large army of about 70,000, including substantial contingents of Samnites and other southern Italians, as well as Greeks.

279. Battle of Asculum. The Roman consuls **Caius Fabricius** and **Quintus Aemilius,** with an allied-Roman army about the same size as that of Pyrrhus, marched south to Apulia, meeting Pyrrhus near Asculum (Ascoli). The first day of a two-day battle was indecisive. On the second day of fierce fighting Pyrrhus, badly wounded, again won by use of his elephants against the Roman cavalry. The Roman army, however, withdrew in good order. The losses on both sides were about 11,000 men; Pyrrhus lost particularly heavily in the contingents he had brought from Greece, and again was dissatisfied with the hard-won victory. From Heraclea and Asculum are derived the term "Pyrrhic victory."

278–276. Pyrrhus in Sicily. (See p. 56.)

275. Battle of Beneventum. Shortly after his return from Sicily, Pyrrhus met another Roman army, commanded by M. Curius Dentatus. In a seesaw battle, the Romans were again near defeat through Pyrrhus' judicious use of elephants. Driven back to the walls of their camp, they were joined by the camp garrison, and turned the elephants back into the phalanx, creating great confusion. A prompt Roman counterattack following, Pyrrhus was decisively defeated with great loss. Soon afterward he returned to Greece, reporting to have said on his departure: "What a fine field of battle I leave here for Rome and Carthage." Tarentum fell to the Romans the same year that Pyrrhus was killed in a street fight in Argos (272).

272–265. Consolidation of Italy. The capture of Rhegium (270) brought all southern Italy under Roman control. After defeating a Samnite uprising (269) Rome was unchallenged mistress of all Italy south of the Arnus River.

First Punic War, 264–241 B.C.

265. War Breaks Out at Messana. The leaders of the Mamertines of Messana, engaged in war with **Hiero II** of Syracuse, sent for assistance from Carthage; another faction sent to Rome for help (see p. 58). The Carthaginians arrived first and seized Messana. Driven out by the Romans, the Carthaginians, in alliance with Hiero, then besieged Messana, but were repelled (264) by a Roman army under Consul **Appius Claudius Caudex,** who then unsuccessfully besieged **Syracuse.** However, Roman successes under Consul **Marcus Valerius Maximus** in eastern Sicily caused Hiero to make peace with Rome, and to join an alliance against Carthage (263). The Romans then invaded western Sicily and laid siege to the Carthaginian stronghold of Agrigentum.

262. Siege and Battle of Agrigentum (Girgenti). The defenders under **Hannibal Gisco** put up a stout defense, and Carthage sent a relieving army under **Hanno** (one of several leaders of that name). In the ensuing battle Hanno was defeated, but Hannibal escaped the city with his army. This victory gave Rome control of most of Sicily, save for a few scattered Carthaginian fortresses along the western coast.

260. Battle of the Lipara Islands. A Roman naval squadron under **C. Cornelius Scipio** was defeated.

260. Battle of Mylae. **C. Duillius** commanded the Roman fleet, first revealing the new Roman methods of naval warfare (see p. 75) and winning a decisive victory. Control of the sea was wrested from the Carthaginians. Roman expeditionary forces invaded Corsica and Sardinia.

256. Battle of Cape Ecnomus. A fleet of 330 vessels under the consuls **M. Atilius Regulus** and **L. Manlius Volso** sailed from Sicily with a total force of about 150,000

soldiers and sailors to invade Africa. A Carthaginian fleet of 350 ships, commanded by **Hamilcar** and **Hanno** (common Carthaginian names), met the Romans off the coast of Sicily. In a hard-fought battle, the new Roman tactics again prevailed; 30 Carthaginian ships were sunk, and 64 captured, while only 24 Roman ships were lost.

256. Invasion of Africa. The Roman fleet continued to the coast of Africa near Carthage. An army of 20,000, under Regulus, was landed. Regulus won the decisive **Battle of Adys;** the Carthaginians sued for peace. The terms set by Regulus were so severe that the Carthaginians decided to continue the war; in desperation they asked for assistance from the Spartan soldier of fortune **Xanthippus,** who arrived at Carthage with a force of Greek mercenaries.

255. Battle of Tunes. Xanthippus, having reorganized, trained, and inspired the Carthaginian army, took the field against Regulus. The two armies were approximately equal in size—slightly less than 20,000 men each. Xanthippus, making good use of his cavalry, elephants, and his phalanx of Greek mercenaries, defeated Regulus, capturing him and about half of the Roman army. The remainder of the Romans—probably less than 5,000 men—entrenched themselves on an inaccessible promontory, and were later rescued by a Roman fleet. The fleet, however, was caught in a storm between Africa and Sicily, losing 284 ships out of 364—a disaster which cost Rome nearly 100,000 of her best soldiers, sailors, and marines.

254. Carthaginian Recovery. The loss of the Roman fleet, and elimination of the threat to their capital, permitted the Carthaginians to reinforce their besieged strongholds in Sicily and to recapture Agrigentum. The Romans responded with a successful amphibious assault on Panormus. A stalemate followed.

251. Battle of Panormus. In northwest Sicily the Carthaginian general **Hasdrubal** was defeated by Consul **L. Caecilius Metellus;** both armies were about 25,000 strong. The Carthaginians again made peace overtures. They sent the captured Roman general, Regulus, on parole, to Rome with the mission of at least negotiating an exchange of prisoners, if satisfactory peace terms could not be achieved. According to legend, Regulus advised his countrymen to reject both Carthaginian proposals; he then honored his parole by returning voluntarily to Carthage, where he was tortured to death.

249. Battle of Drepanum (Trapani). The Roman fleet blockading Lilybaeum, commanded by the Consul **P. Claudius Pulcher,** engaged a Carthaginian fleet under the admiral **Adherbal;** each fleet comprised about 200 warships. Just before the battle Claudius invoked the blessing of the gods by placing sacred chickens on the deck, where they were supposed to eat grain spread out before them and thus provide a favorable omen. The chickens refused to eat, so Claudius ordered them to be thrown overboard, with the words, "Then let them drink." The Romans were defeated with a loss of 93 ships; 8,000 Romans were killed, 20,000 captured. No Carthaginian ships were lost. Claudius survived the battle, was called back to Rome, and fined heavily by the Senate when he refused to appoint a suitable successor as dictator. This was a bad year for Rome. Land and sea attacks against a Carthaginian force commanded by **Hamilcar Barca** were repulsed at **Eryx.** Soon after this most of the remainder of the Roman fleet was lost at sea in a storm. This was the fourth time the Romans had suffered such a disaster, having lost more than 700 ships and 200,000 men in storms. Accepting this as a warning from the gods, for several years they refrained from major efforts at sea.

247–242. Hamilcar Barca Commands in Western Sicily. For five years he repulsed all Roman efforts to recapture the Carthaginian strongholds. The superiority of the legion was offset by the skill and ingenuity of Hamilcar. Without serious Roman opposition at sea, he sent his warships to harry the coast of Italy.

242. Conquest of Lilybaeum and Drepanum. Rebuilding their navy, the Romans sent a fleet of about 200 ships to western Sicily, under the command of **L. Lutatius Catulus.** By combined land and sea operations they captured the Carthaginian strongholds.

241. Battle of the Aegates Islands. The Carthaginians sent Hanno with a battle fleet of 200 ships to Sicilian waters. Catulus won a complete victory, 70 Carthaginian ships being captured, 50 more sunk. This disaster forced Carthage to make peace—after crucifying Hanno. They agreed to evacuate Sicily and to pay Rome 3,200 talents (about $95 million*) over ten years. Rome permitted Syracuse to retain control over eastern Sicily, but organized western Sicily as her first overseas province.

Between the Wars, 241–219 B.C.

238. Roman Seizure of Sardinia. Turmoil in Sardinia due to a mutiny of Carthaginian mercenaries (see p. 57) brought Roman intervention. For several years Roman troops were engaged in pacifying the wild tribes of Sardinia.

235. Peace. For the first time in recorded history the doors of the Temple of Janus —always open when Rome was at war— were closed.

229–228. First Illyrian War. The Greek states asked the assistance of Rome in suppressing Illyrian piracy in the Adriatic and Ionian seas. Roman ambassadors sent to the court of Queen **Teuta** of Illyria were murdered. A Roman army soon crushed the Illyrians.

225–222. Gallic Invasion of Central Italy. The Gauls won a victory at **Faesulae** (225). Then Roman armies under **Aemilius Papus** and **Caius Atilius Regulus** defeated them at the **Battle of Telamon,** though Regulus was killed (224). Forty thousand Gauls were slain, 10,000 captured, and 20,000 got away. The Romans pursued the remnants northward to the Po Valley, where **M. Claudius Marcellus** won the **Battle of Clastidium** (222).

219. Second Illyrian War. King **Scerdilaidas** provoked the Romans into another punitive expedition, which smashed the Illyrians.

Second Punic War, 219–202 B.C.

219. Siege of Saguntum. Hannibal, son of Hamilcar Barca, demanded the submission of Saguntum, a Greek city and Roman ally, the sole spot in Spain south of the Ebro not under Carthaginian control.

---

* Assuming these were gold talents; the usually quoted equivalent of $4 million seems relatively insignificant.

When Saguntum refused, Hannibal immediately invested it, realizing this would probably provoke war with Rome. He was following his father's plan of gaining revenge for the First Punic War. Rome demanded that Carthage halt the siege of Saguntum and surrender Hannibal. Carthage refused; Rome declared war. After a siege of 8 months, Hannibal captured Saguntum by storm. His Iberian base now secure, he was ready to carry out his carefully planned strategy.

218. Hannibal's Plan: To circumvent Roman control of the seas, he planned to take a large army overland from Spain, through southern Gaul, across the Alps to the Po Valley. He had already sent agents to secure allies in Transalpine and Cisalpine Gaul, thus assuring a line of communications back to Spain and a secure advanced base in northern Italy. He planned to recruit reinforcements from among the warlike Celtic tribes who hated Rome. He had also opened com-

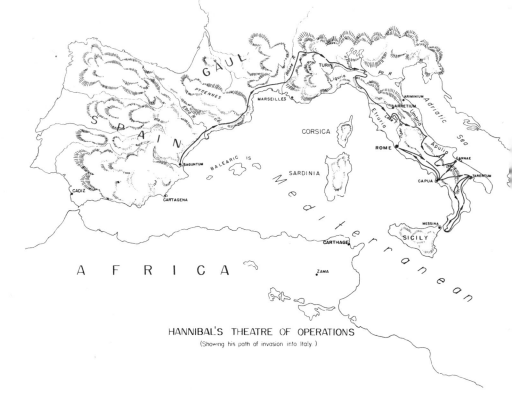

HANNIBAL'S THEATRE OF OPERATIONS
(Showing his path of invasion into Italy.)

munications with **Philip V** of Macedon with a view to forcing Rome into a two-front war. He planned to leave about 20,-000 men under his brother **Hasdrubal,** to hold Spain.

218. Roman Plans: Consul Titus Sempronius, with about 30,000 men, and a fleet of 160 warships were to invade Africa and attack Carthage; Consul **Publius Cornelius Scipio,** with his brother **Gnaeus Cornelius Scipio,** would invade Spain with an army of about 26,000 men and a fleet of 60 warships; Praetor **Lucius Manlius,** with about 22,000 men, would hold Cisal-

pine Gaul to keep the restless Celts in check while the consular armies were engaged with the Carthaginians. The Romans had no inkling of Hannibal's planned invasion.

218, March–June. Across the Pyrenees. Crossing the Ebro with about 90,000 men, Hannibal subdued the country south of the Pyrenees. He left a strong garrison in this region, and eliminated from his army all men unfit for the field. He entered Gaul with less than 50,000 infantry, 9,000 cavalry, and about 80 elephants.

218, July–October. Through Gaul. Though

he met some opposition on the march—
notably when crossing the Rhone River—
the passage through Gaul was generally
quick and easy, due to Hannibal's advance preparations. Scipio, learning of
this movement, landed with his army at
Massilia (Marseille) in hope of cutting
the Carthaginians off. But Hannibal, to
avoid interference, had already turned
north up the Rhone Valley, planning to
cross the Alps well inland—possibly at the
Traversette. Scipio, despairing of catching the Carthaginians, hastened along the
coast to north Italy with a small force; he
sent the bulk of his army to Spain under
his brother.

218, October. Passage of the Alps. The Alpine passes were already heavy with
snow, but Hannibal pressed on. Many of
his men and animals perished in the win-
try climate; many others were killed in
smashing through unexpectedly fierce resistance from mountain tribes. He reached
the Po Valley with 20,000 infantry, 6,000
cavalry, and a few elephants.

218, November. Battle of the Ticinus. Hannibal was as surprised by the presence of
Scipio as the Roman consul was by the
rapidity of the Carthaginian advance.
Scipio had taken command of Manlius'
army—shaken from a recent defeat by the
Gauls—and rushed to meet Hannibal at
the Ticinus River. In an engagement
mostly confined to cavalry, the Romans
were defeated and Scipio wounded.

218, December. Battle of the Trebia. Having learned of Hannibal's arrival, Sempronius took most of his army from Sicily by sea through the Adriatic to the Po
Valley, to join Scipio. Hannibal, who had
increased his army to over 30,000 by recruiting Gauls, enticed Sempronius to attack across the Trebia River (against
Scipio's advice). While Hannibal counterattacked the shivering Romans, a small
force of infantry and cavalry under his
brother **Mago,** concealed in a ravine upstream, struck the Roman flank and rear.
Of the Roman army of 40,000, only 10,-
000 escaped, cutting their way through
the Carthaginian center; the remainder
were slaughtered. Hannibal's loss probably exceeded 5,000.

218. Spain. Meanwhile, Gnaeus Scipio had
landed north of the Ebro River in Spain,

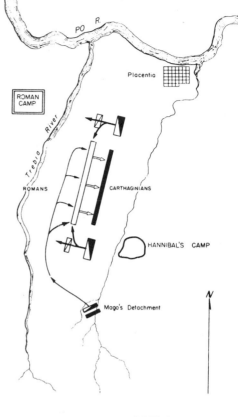

BATTLE OF THE TREBIA

and had defeated and captured Hanno,*
gaining control of the region between the
Ebro and Pyrenees.

**217, January–March. Winter Quarters in
the Po Valley.** Hannibal rested his men
and recruited Gauls, while collecting information from an efficient spy network
in Italy. He learned that the two new
consuls, who took office March 15, were
Gaius Flaminius, who had about 40,000
men at Arretium (Arezzo), and **Gnaeus
Servilius,** who had about 20,000 at Ar-
minium (Rimini). The consular armies
blocked the two main roads leading toward central Italy and Rome.

---

* Presumably this was Hannibal's third
brother, who apparently later escaped or was
released or exchanged. The name Hanno (like
Hamilcar, Hasdrubal, and Hannibal) was very
common among the Carthaginians, and it is
difficult to distinguish between several individuals bearing the same name.

217, March–April. Advance into Central Italy. In the first conscious turning movement of history, Hannibal with about 40,000 men made a surprise crossing of the snowy Apennine passes north of Genoa, marched south along the seacoast, and in 4 days struggled through the treacherous Arnus marshes—supposedly impassable during the spring floods. Pressing on, he soon reached the Rome-Arretium road, near Clusium (Chiusi), thus placing himself between the Roman armies and their capital. During this arduous march an eye infection caused Hannibal to lose the sight of one eye.

217, April. Battle of Lake Trasimene. Headstrong Flaminius, realizing too late that his line of communications had been

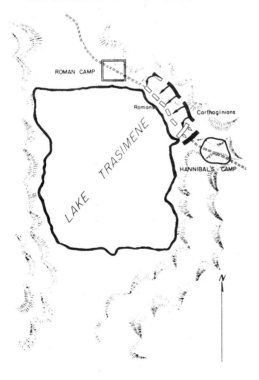

BATTLE OF LAKE TRASIMENE

cut, marched south rapidly to seek battle; security was sacrificed for speed. Hannibal, acquainted both with Roman practice and with the nature of his antagonist, set up an ambush by his entire army where the main road passed Lake Trasimene in a narrow defile under overhanging cliffs.

His light infantry was posted under cover on the mountainside, the cavalry concealed behind them. At the southern end of the defile he posted his heavy infantry, blocking the road. Upon reaching the southern end of the defile, the head of the Roman column was halted by Hannibal's infantry. Gradually the entire Roman army closed up into the 4-mile-long defile. Hannibal ordered his cavalry to close the northern end of the defile, then struck the east flank of the Roman column with his light infantry. The result was surprise, panic, and slaughter. About 30,000 Romans—including Flaminius—were killed or captured; another 10,000, in scattered groups, fled through the mountains to notify Rome of the terrible defeat. Hannibal then continued south, seeking a base in southern Italy, where he expected to be joined by the cities and tribes which were vassals of Rome.

217, May–October. Quintus Fabius Appointed Dictator by the Senate. Recognizing that he could not cope with Hannibal on the battlefield, Fabius wisely chose to avoid formal combat while conducting a campaign of delays and harassment. These "Fabian tactics" soon earned for Fabius the nickname of **Cunctator,** or "Delayer." Many Romans soon grew impatient; they knew only the tradition of offensive warfare. **M. Minucius Rufus,** his senior lieutenant, expressing scorn for Fabian tactics, was rewarded by the Senate with a command status coequal with the dictator. Hannibal had been doing everything he could to entice the Romans into combat, and suddenly his efforts were rewarded at **Geronium,** when Minucius accepted the challenge. Hannibal attacked at once. Minucius, on the verge of defeat, was saved by the timely arrival of Fabius, who threatened the Carthaginian flank. Hannibal prudently withdrew. Manfully, Minucius acknowledged his error and thereafter gave Fabius loyal support.

217–211. Spain and Africa. Meanwhile Publius Scipio had joined his brother in Spain, with 8,000 reinforcements. In the following years the two Scipios were generally successful, forcing Hasdrubal and Mago to withdraw from the Ebro line. They also induced **Syphax,** King of Numidia, to revolt against Carthage (213).

However, Hasdrubal returned to Africa, and with **Massinissa,** a Numidian prince, defeated Syphax. Hasdrubal then returned to Spain with reinforcements, including Massinissa's Numidian cavalry (212). At this time the Scipios recaptured Saguntum.

216, April–July. Thanks to the time gained by Fabius, Rome gathered an army of 8 Roman and 8 allied legions—80,000 infantry plus 7,000 cavalry—sending them south to Apulia under the two new consuls, **Aemilius Paulus** and **Terentius Varro,** to seek battle with Hannibal. Hannibal, who had about 40,000 infantry and 10,000

cavalry, sought favorable conditions for battle. Paulus, a cool, cautious leader, was careful to avoid presenting such an opportunity, and for a while was able to prevail upon his impetuous colleague, Varro, to follow the same policy. The two consuls alternated in command each day. In an effort to force the issue, Hannibal made a night march to Cannae, capturing a Roman supply depot, and gaining possession of the grain country of southern Apulia. The Roman army followed; both forces established fortified camps six miles apart on the south bank of the Aufidus River.

BATTLE OF CANNAE, AUGUST 2, 216 B.C.

Early in the morning on a day when he knew Varro would be in command, Hannibal drew up for battle near the Roman camp, with one flank on the stream, thus secured from envelopment by the more numerous Romans. He left about 8,000 troops to hold his camp. His center was composed of Spanish and Gallic infantry, spread out in a thin line. The wings each consisted of a deep phalanx of heavy, reliable African foot. On the left of his line were his 8,000 heavy Spanish and Gallic cavalrymen under Hasdrubal; on the right he posted his 2,000 Numidian light cavalry.

Varro accepted the challenge with most of his army; he sent 11,000 men to attack the Carthaginian camp. Perceiving that he could not envelop the well-protected flanks of the Carthaginian army, Varro decided to crush his opponent by weight of numbers. He doubled the depth of each maniple, the intervals also being greatly reduced so that his infantry front, comprising about 65,000 men, corresponded with that of Hannibal's 32,000. Varro placed 2,400 Roman cavalry on his right flank; on his left were 4,800 allied horsemen.

Under the cover of the preliminary skirmishing of light troops, Hannibal personally advanced the thin central portion of his line until it formed a salient toward the Romans; his heavy infantry wings stood fast.

The battle was opened on the left by a charge of the heavy Spanish and Gallic horse, who crushed the Roman cavalry, then swung completely around the rear of the Roman Army to smash the rear of the allied cavalry, engaged in indecisive combat with the Numidians. The allied horsemen were driven off the field, pursued by the Numidians. The heavy Carthaginian cavalry now turned to strike the rear of the Roman infantry.

The infantry combat, meanwhile, had gone according to Hannibal's plan. His central salient slowly withdrew under fierce Roman pressure. Varro sent the maniples of his second line into the intervals of his hastati; then ordered his triarii and even the velites to add their weight, in order to drive the Carthaginians into the river. Hannibal's line had now become concave, but was still intact. The Romans, in a dense phalangial mass, pressed ahead.

Suddenly Hannibal gave the signal to the commanders of his African wings, thus far hardly engaged. They advanced, wheeling inward against the Romans, who were already raising shouts of victory. At this time the Carthaginian cavalry struck the rear of the Roman line. Cries of victory turned to screams of consternation. The Romans became a herd of panic-stricken individuals, all cohesion and unity lost. There was only slight resistance offered by this hemmed-in mob during the following hour of grim butchery, though one contingent of about 10,000 fought free. At the close of the day about 60,000 Romans—including Paulus—lay dead on the field; with another 2,000 lost when they were repulsed from Hannibal's well-guarded camp. Ingloriously, Varro was among the handful of fugitives. Hannibal's losses were at least 6,000 men.

The Battle of Cannae was the high-water mark of Hannibal's career; it has also provided military theorists with a symbol of tactical perfection.

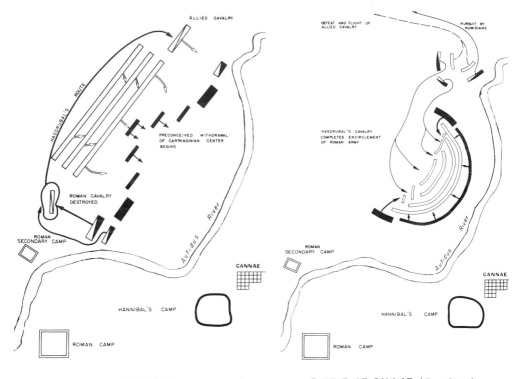

BATTLE OF CANNAE (Opening Phase)   BATTLE OF CANNAE (Final Phase)

216, August–December. Response of Rome. Never before nor since has a state survived after suffering such crushing defeats in close succession as those of Rome at the Trebia, Lake Trasimene, and Cannae. When the news of Cannae reached Rome, there were a few faint hearts, but as a group the Romans had but one thought: perseverance to victory. **M. Junius Pera** was appointed dictator by the Senate. All able-bodied men, regardless of age or occupation, were mobilized; the principal field commander was Proconsul **Marcus Claudius Marcellus,** who immediately marched south from Rome with two legions to maintain successfully the confidence of Rome's allies in ultimate victory.

If her allies had deserted her, Roman valor and determination could never have prevailed against the genius of Hannibal. But the majority remained loyal. Hannibal, without a siege train, was unable to seize Naples from a Roman garrison rushed there by Marcellus. Capua and a few other small towns of Campania joined Hannibal, as did some Samnites and Lucanians. But wavering Italian towns were impressed when Marcellus, taking advantage of the walls of Nola, repulsed the great Carthaginian in the **First Battle of Nola.** A few reinforcements from Carthage arrived late in the year, but lukewarm support from the Carthaginian Senate, then dominated by Hanno, his father's old political opponent, plus Roman naval superiority, prevented arrival of reinforcements in bulk, which might have tempted Hannibal to risk an attack on Rome itself. He has been criticized for not marching on Rome right after Cannae. But Hannibal rightly knew that without a siege train his own motley army had no chance of capturing the powerful fortress, garrisoned by 40,000 men. Accordingly, he concentrated upon the task of building a base in southern Italy, and in this he was relatively successful, despite the solidarity of the Italian cities with Rome.

215. Stalemate in Campania. Hannibal captured a number of towns and fortresses, but made no real gains. Rome had about 140,000 soldiers under arms, including detachments in Spain, Gaul, and Sicily; of these about 80,000 were concentrated against Hannibal's 40–50,000. The Romans, however, avoided battle, under the new policy established by the Senate. Marcellus, seizing another favorable opportunity, again repulsed Hannibal in the **Second Battle of Nola.**

215–205. First Macedonian War. Although Hannibal had succeeded in getting Philip of Macedon to join him in an alliance against Rome, the results were disappointing to him (see p. 55).

214–213. Inconclusive Campaigning. Rome now had more than 200,000 soldiers under arms, with 85,000–90,000 of these cautiously observing Hannibal, now able to maintain his army at 40,000 only by recruiting halfhearted Italians. He fought the indecisive **Third Battle of Nola** with Marcellus, then marched into Apulia, hoping to capture Tarentum as a seaport. His brother Hanno, with 18,000 men, was severely defeated at **Beneventum** (Benevento) by **Tiberius Gracchus** with 20,000. Marcellus went to Sicily, where he won some successes against the Syracusans (who had declared for Carthage) and Carthaginians. The following year Hannibal devoted himself to operations against Tarentum, while Hanno defeated Tiberius Gracchus in Bruttium (213).

213–211. Siege of Syracuse. For a year the assaults of Marcellus were frustrated by a number of brilliantly conceived defensive engines designed by **Archimedes.** The defense was skillfully conducted by the Syracusan general, **Hippocrates.** Finally (212)

Marcellus was able to force his way into the outer city, timing his assault with celebration of a local festival. Archimedes was killed. For 8 more months operations continued in Syracuse, as Marcellus nibbled away at the fortifications of the inner city and citadel, finally overwhelming the garrison by assault.

212. Tarentum and Capua. Hannibal captured Tarentum, but a Roman garrison held out in the citadel. Meanwhile, the Roman consuls **Quintus Fulvius Flaccus** and **Appius Claudius** invested Capua, which was already short of food. In response to Capuan pleas for help, Hannibal sent Hanno to relieve the city. Hanno gathered large quantities of food in a fortified camp at Beneventum, and then enticed the Roman armies away from Capua. He got some food to the beleaguered city, but the Capuans were slow in responding to Hanno's skillful arrangements, and while he was away on a foraging expedition, Fulvius made a successful night attack on Hanno's camp, capturing several thousand Capuan wagons and great quantities of supplies; 6,000 Carthaginians were killed and 7,000 captured. Hanno escaped back to Bruttium. The Romans resumed the siege of Capua. Hannibal now advanced from Tarentum with about 20,000 men, and though the Romans had more than 80,000 men in southern Italy, they were unable or unwilling to prevent him from marching into Capua.

212. The First Battle of Capua. Hannibal defeated the consuls in an indecisive battle outside the city. To lure him away from Capua, they marched off in different directions, threatening his strongholds in Campania and Lucania. Hannibal followed Appius into Lucania, but was unable to catch him. He did, however, meet and destroy the army of Praetor **M. Centenius Penula** in northwest Lucania probably near the **Silarus River.** Centenius had about 16,000 men, Hannibal about 20,000; Centenius was killed; only 1,000 of his men escaped slaughter or capture. A few days later Hannibal met the army of Praetor **Gnaeus Fulvius** (not the consul) and also destroyed it in another decisive victory at **Herdonia;** out of 18,-000 only 2,000 Romans (including Fulvius) escaped. Meanwhile the consuls had re-established the siege of Capua, but since the city was now well supplied, Hannibal returned to the south coast, where he was repulsed in an effort to capture Brundisium (Brindisi).

211. Spain. Hasdrubal's reinforced Carthaginian armies defeated the Scipio brothers in two separate battles in the **Upper Baetis** Valley, both Roman leaders being killed. Carthage again controlled all Spain south of the Ebro.

211. Siege and Second Battle of Capua. During the winter the Romans completed lines of circumvallation and contravallation around Capua. The new consuls, **Publius Sulpicius Galba** and **Gnaeus Fulvius Centumalus,** with more than 50,000 men, guarded against approach by Hannibal from the south, while the proconsuls Fulvius and Appius continued the siege with 60,000 more. Upon another appeal from Capua, Hannibal with 30,000 men marched north and again either eluded or overawed the Roman forces supposed to bar the way. While the garrison of Capua made a sortie, he attacked the Roman lines from the outside. He was repulsed by Fulvius, while Appius drove the Capuans back into their city.

211. The March on Rome. Hannibal decided to march on Rome itself, in hopes that the threat would cause all Roman forces to rush to the defense of their capital, and to abandon the siege of Capua. In fact, the two consuls hastened to Rome, and Fulvius took a small force from Capua, while Appius continued the siege. This must have brought the garrison of Rome to more than 50,000 men. Hannibal merely demonstrated, then marched slowly south again, harassed by the consuls, while Fulvius returned to command outside Capua. Now close to starvation, the city surrendered; the worst blow Hannibal had yet suffered in Italy.

210. Roman Offensives. Though still trying to avoid anything like an equal battle with Hannibal personally, the Romans now decided to attempt to destroy his base and sources of supply. Hannibal, however, destroyed the army of Proconsul **Fulvius Centumalus,** at the **Second Battle of Herdonia,** Centumalus being killed. Soon after this he defeated Marcellus in the **Battle of Numistro.**

210–209. Spain. After the death of Publius Scipio the Roman Senate sent his 25-year-old son **Publius Cornelius Scipio**—known to history as "Africanus"—to take command in Spain. He quickly re-established Roman control north of the Ebro. Then with 27,500 men he made a surprise march to the Carthaginian capital of New Carthage, while his fleet blockaded the town from the sea (209). He captured the town in a surprise assault.

209–208. Tarentum. Although Rome was near bankruptcy, and the people of Italy were close to starvation due to lack of men to till the fields, she again had 200,000 troops in the field. Hannibal could muster barely 40,000, mostly Italians, and save for a few veterans the quality of his army was much inferior to the legions. He was now holding on, awaiting reinforcements from his brother, Hasdrubal, in Spain. The Roman objective was Tarentum, which had become Hannibal's main base in Italy. Surprisingly the Roman garrison of the citadel was still holding out, supplied by sea. In a hard-fought two-day battle, Hannibal defeated Marcellus at **Asculum,** but again was unable to gain a decisive victory over his most persistent foe. Meanwhile Fabius Cunctator (consul for the fifth time) recaptured Tarentum, through the treachery of Hannibal's Italian allies. Amazingly, despite the loss of his base at Tarentum, Hannibal was able to carry on, and hold at bay the far more numerous and far more efficient Roman armies (208). Yet the Romans—and particularly Marcellus—were no longer afraid to try battle with him. Marcellus, however, was killed in an ambush this year.

208. Spain; Battle of Baecula. After extensive maneuvering and skirmishing, Scipio defeated Hasdrubal in an inconclusive battle near modern Cordova. Hasdrubal, whose losses had not been serious, now responded to Hannibal's orders to bring reinforcements to Italy, even though it might mean the abandonment of Spain to Scipio. He marched to Gaul, where he spent the winter, resting his men and recruiting reinforcements.

207. Hasdrubal in Italy. Early in the year Hasdrubal pushed over the Alps, arriving in the Po Valley with about 50,000 men, more than half Gauls. He sent a message to his brother, reporting his arrival, and began to advance slowly toward central Italy. Meanwhile Hannibal had been maneuvering against the efficient consul **Caius Claudius Nero.** At the **Battle of Grumentum** Nero, with 42,000 men, gained a slight advantage over Hannibal (who probably had about 30,000), but was unable to prevent the Carthaginian from marching north to Canusium (Canosa di Puglia) to await word from his brother. But Hasdrubal's messengers

missed him and were captured by Nero. The Roman consul now conceived a brilliant plan. Leaving most of his army facing Hannibal, he took 6,000 infantry and 1,000 cavalry—the best troops of his army —and marched north as quickly as possible to join his colleague, **M. Livius Salinator,** who was facing Hasdrubal in northeast Italy. He marched 250 miles in 7 days, joining Livius secretly south of the Metaurus River.

BATTLE OF THE METAURUS, 207 B.C.

Hasdrubal's patrols reported the arrival of Roman reinforcements, and he decided to make a night withdrawal north of the Metaurus to more favorable ground. He was deserted by his Italian guides, however, and his army got lost during the darkness. The Roman consuls caught up with him after dawn, just south of the river. Hasdrubal hastily prepared for battle, placing his least reliable troops on his left flank behind a deep ravine. His right was soon engaged heavily by Livius, but Nero on the Roman right was prevented by the ravine from reaching the Gauls to his front. Reasoning that the obstacle would be just as formidable to the Carthaginians, Nero pulled his troops out of line, and quickly marched behind the rest of the Roman army, swinging in behind the right rear of the Spanish infantry. The surprise rear attack completely demoralized the Spaniards, and despite valiant efforts of Hasdrubal, panic spread through his army. Hasdrubal, seeing that all was lost, deliberately rode into a Roman cohort, to die fighting. The Carthaginian Army was hopelessly smashed; more than 10,000 men were killed and the rest scattered; the Romans lost 2,000. Immediately after the battle Nero marched back to south Italy, in 6 days. According to legend, the first news Hannibal received of his brother's arrival in Italy was when Hasdrubal's head was catapulted into the Carthaginian camp. Sorrowfully he withdrew to Bruttium.

207–206. Spain. Despite determined opposition from Mago and Hasdrubal Gisco, Scipio rapidly spread his control over most of Spain. The climax came in the **Battle of Ilipa** (or Silpia), where Scipio with 48,000 men decisively defeated 70,000 Carthaginians in a battle of brilliant maneuver (206). Spreading out the center of his army in a manner somewhat reminiscent of Hannibal's formation at Cannae, Scipio employed it in an entirely different manner. The center was refused, while the Roman general undertook a successful double envelopment with his wings. This ended Carthaginian rule in Spain. Soon after this Scipio made a bold trip to North Africa, where he concluded an alliance with Massinissa, rival of Syphax for the throne of Numidia.
206–204. Hannibal at Bay. Incredibly, Hannibal maintained himself against tre-

mendous odds in Bruttium, despite the inferior quality of his troops. Although there were many skirmishes, the only important action was the drawn **Battle of Crotona** (204) against **Sempronius.** That same year his brother Mago landed in Liguria with a small army. Scipio, meanwhile, had been elected consul (205), and was in Sicily preparing an army to invade Africa.
204. Invasion of Africa. Scipio, as proconsul, sailed from Lilybaeum with a magnificently trained and equipped army of about 30,000 men. He landed near Utica, which he invested. Hannibal's brother Hanno was apparently killed in the preliminary skirmishing here. The arrival of a large Carthaginian army under Hasdrubal Gisco and Syphax forced Scipio to give up the siege, and to establish a fortified camp near the coast. An armistice was

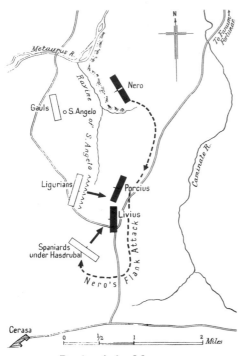

Battle of the Metaurus

attack on the Carthaginian camp, practically destroying the entire army. He immediately renewed the siege of Utica. Hasdrubal and Syphax soon raised a new army, and met Scipio at the **Battle of Bagbrades,** near Utica. Scipio won an overwhelming victory; Syphax was captured.

203. Return of Hannibal. The Carthaginian Senate, in desperation, sent for Hannibal and Mago; at the same time they sued for peace. During the ensuing armistice, Hannibal sailed from Italy with about 18,000 men, mostly Italians who remained loyal to their foreign leader. Mago, who had been defeated in Liguria, also returned with a few thousand men, but he died of wounds en route. Upon the return of Hannibal the Carthaginian Senate broke off negotiations, and helped Hannibal raise a fresh army around his nucleus of Italian veterans.

202. March to Zama. Hannibal marched inland from Carthage with an army of about 45,000 infantry and 3,000 cavalry. Apparently this was to draw Scipio away from the area around Carthage, which the Romans were systematically devastating. Scipio followed, with 34,000 infantry and 9,000 cavalry, having been joined by Massinissa and Numidian reinforcements.

arranged and the two armies went into winter quarters.

203. Battles Near Utica. Suddenly ending the armistice, Scipio made a surprise night

BATTLE OF ZAMA, 202 B.C.

With the two armies drawn up in battle formation, Hannibal met Scipio in an indecisive parley; then the battle began. Scipio's army was in the usual three lines, but with the distances between lines increased, and the maniples in column, rather than in the usual checkerboard formation. This was to create lanes through which the Carthaginian elephants could be herded. Hannibal's infantry was also in three lines—as early as Cannae he had begun to adopt much of the Roman formations and tactical system. But more than half of his infantry were raw recruits, the remainder being his Italian veterans and a few Ligurians and Gauls that had come back with Mago. He was particularly weak in cavalry, the arm on which he had depended in so many of his great victories. Consequently, he was unable to employ his favorite maneuvers.

The Carthaginian elephants attacked the legions, but were handled as Scipio had planned. At the same time the Roman and Numidian cavalry were driving Hannibal's horsemen off the field. The main infantry lines then clashed, and the Romans quickly disposed of the first two lines of Carthaginian infantry. The triarii then advanced against Hannibal's reserve, but under his inspiring leadership the veterans stood fast. Just as the remainder of the Roman infantry joined the attack, Massinissa and the Numidians returned from their pursuit of the Carthaginian cavalry and struck the rear of Hannibal's line. This ended the battle. Hannibal and a few survivors fled to Carthage. Left on the field were 20,000 Carthaginian dead and 15,000 prisoners. The Romans lost about 1,500 dead and probably another 4,000 wounded.

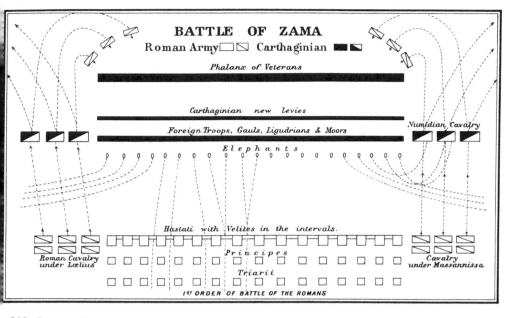

202. Peace. Carthage, suing for peace, accepted Scipio's terms: she handed over all warships and elephants; she agreed not to make war without the permission of Rome; Massinissa was reinstated as King of Numidia in place of Syphax; Carthage agreed to pay Rome 10,000 talents ($300 million) over the next 50 years.

202–186. The Tragedy of Hannibal. In the years immediately after the war Hannibal was so successful in reviving Carthaginian prosperity that the Romans accused him of planning to break the peace. He fled Carthage (196), and joined Antiochus III, but was forced to flee again when Antiochus was defeated by the Romans (see p. 86). Pursued by the Romans to Bithynia, he committed suicide (183).

COMMENT. *No other general in history faced such adversity or such formidable odds as Hannibal. His inspiring leadership, his consummate tactical and strategic skill, and his accomplishments with inferior material against the most dynamic and militarily efficient nation in the world have prompted many historians and military theorists to rank him as the greatest general of history. Objective assessment makes it impossible to rank him ahead of Alexander, Genghis Khan, or Napoleon; equally, it is impossible to rank them significantly ahead of him.*

ROMAN MILITARY SYSTEM, C. 220 B.C.

Army Organization and Tactics

The security of Rome depended upon a citizen army that was essentially professional. All able-bodied male Romans between 17 and 60 were obliged to serve (men over 47 were employed in garrisons only). In 220 B.C. the military manpower of Rome was about 750,000 men out of a total population of 3,750,000. Rome was frequently at war, so there was always a leaven of veterans. There were four major factors in the strength and success of Roman arms: (1) the moral strength of an army composed of free, intensely patriotic citizens; (2) the development of the legion—a new type of military organization superior to any previously seen on the battlefield; (3) maintenance of a high order of military competence, to some extent attributable to frequent combat experience, but resulting in particular from insistence on constant training and enforcement of severe discipline; (4) a traditional, intense, but intelligent reliance upon bold, aggressive doctrine, even in adversity. The wisdom of Rome's political system of confederation and colonization in Italy, including generous and magnanimous treatment of defeated Italian foes, was also an important element of Roman strength.

The evolution of the legion had begun with the legendary reforms of **Servius Tullius** (see p. 33). Many modifications were introduced by **Marcus Camillus**, including an organizational breakdown based primarily upon age and experience, rather than on wealth and quality of personally owned weapons. The individual was still expected to supply his own weapons, but frequently these were purchased from the state.

The lessons of mountain combat during the Samnite wars, particularly the disaster of the Caudine Forks (see p. 58), affected Roman doctrine. By about 300 the Roman legion had attained the cellular type of organization described below. It was this flexible, disciplined legion which acquitted itself so well against the Macedonian-Epirote phalanx of **Pyrrhus,** and which was employed also in the First and Second Punic Wars. During the last half of the 3rd century B.C. the Roman legion probably achieved its highest development and greatest competency.

There were four classes of soldiers. The youngest, most agile, and least trained men were the **velites,** or light infantry. Next in age and experience came the **hastati,** who comprised the first line of the legion heavy infantry. The **principes** were veterans, averaging about 30 years of age; the backbone of the army, mature, tough, and experienced, they made up the second line of the legion. The oldest group, the **triarii,** who contributed steadiness to offset the vigor of the more youthful classifications, comprised the third line of heavy infantry.

The basic tactical organization was the **maniple,** roughly the equivalent of a modern company. Each maniple was composed of two **centuries,** or platoons, of 60–80 men each, except that the maniple of the **triarii** was one century only. The **cohort,** comparable to a modern battalion, consisted of 450–570 men (120–160 **velites,** the same number of **hastati** and **principes,** 60–80 **triarii,** and a **turma** of 30 cavalrymen). The cavalry component of the cohort rarely fought with it; the horsemen were usually gathered together in larger cavalry formations.

The legion itself—the equivalent of a modern division—comprised some 4,500–5,000 men, including 300 cavalrymen. For each Roman legion, there was one allied legion, organized identically, except that its cavalry component was usually 600 men. (Some authorities suggest that allied contingents were not organized in this formal manner, but that it was merely Roman policy to support each legion with an approximately equal number of allied troops, whose largest formal organization was the cohort.)

A Roman legion, with its allied counterpart, was the equivalent of a modern army corps, a force of some 9,000–10,000 men, of whom about 900 were cavalry. Two Roman and two allied legions comprised a field army, known as a consular army, commanded by one of Rome's two consuls.

A consular army was usually 18,000–20,000 men, with a combat front of about one and a half miles. Often the two regular consular armies would be joined together, in which case the consuls would alternate in command, usually on a 24-hour basis. In times of war or great danger, however, Rome might have more than the 8 standard legions (4 Roman, 4 allied) under arms. In such cases, if a dictator had been appointed, he would directly command the largest field force, exercising over-all control over the others as best he could under the circumstances. Whether or not there was a dictator, additional armies were usually commanded by proconsuls (former consuls), appointed by the Senate, or praetors, elected officials.

Since consuls were elected executive officials, both military and political power lay in their hands; rarely were Roman commanders harassed by directives from home. On the other hand, this system often resulted in mediocre top military leader-

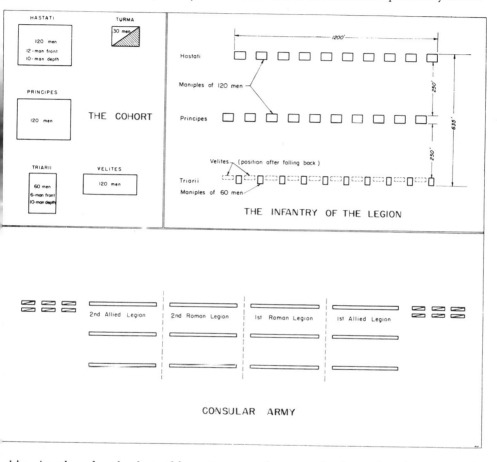

ship. Another drawback to this system was that consuls changed each year; yet in a long-drawn-out war, such as against Hannibal, Roman generals had to keep the field for years on end.

Under the consul or proconsul was a staff of senior officers or quaestors, who took care of administrative and planning tasks delegated by the army commander. The senior officers of the legion were the 6 tribunes—2 for each combat line. In a peculiar arrangement, the 6 tribunes rotated in command of the legion, though later a legate was frequently appointed over the tribunes as legion commander. Below the tribunes were 60 centurions, 2 for each maniple.

The flexibility of the legion lay in the tactical relationship of the maniples within each line, and between the lines of heavy infantry. Each maniple was like a tiny phalanx, with a front of about 20 men, 6 deep, but with the space between men somewhat greater than in the phalanx. Each man occupied space 5 feet square.

Between the maniples in each line were intervals of the same frontage as that of a maniple, about 20 yards. The maniples in each line were staggered, with those of the second and third lines each covering intervals in the line to their front. There were approximately 100 yards between each line of heavy infantry .

This cellular, checkerboard type formation had a number of inherent advantages over the phalanx: it could maneuver more easily in rough country, without fear of losing alignment, and without need for concern about gaps appearing in the line—the gaps were built in. If desired, the first line could withdraw through the second, or the second could advance through the first. With its triarii line, the legion had an organic reserve, whether or not the commander consciously used it as such. The intervals were, of course, a potential source of danger, but one that was kept limited by the stationing of other troops immediately behind those of the first two lines. In battle it appears that the lines would close up to form a virtual phalanx, but these could quickly resume their flexible relationship when maneuver became necessary once more.

The hastati and principes were each armed with two sturdy javelins, about 7 feet long, and with a broad-bladed short sword, about 2 feet long. The javelins were usually thrown at the enemy just before contact, with the sword (**gladius**) being wielded at close quarters. The tactical concept would be comparable to modern

Roman legionary

bayonet attacks preceded by rifle fire. The triarii each carried a 12-foot pike, as well as the gladius. The velites were armed with javelins and darts. To obtain greater diversity in range and effective missile weapons, the Romans sometimes employed foreign mercenaries, such as Balearic slingers and Aegean bowmen.

The Roman javelin, or **pilum,** was an ingeniously constructed weapon. Its head of soft iron was connected to the shaft by a slender neck. Once it had struck, the point became bent, and the head usually broke off from the shaft, thus making the weapon useless to the enemy. In addition, the soft iron head would frequently remain imbedded in the shields and armor of the enemy, adding to their discomfiture.

One of the great Roman military innovations was the practice of castrametation, or camp building. Every night during a campaign the Romans would build a fortified camp. Thus, no matter how far they might be from Rome, or from other friendly forces, the Roman troops always had a secure base, and the commander always had a choice of offensive or defensive combat. The construction of the camp was a relatively quick process, in which every man had a specific job, with which he was thoroughly familiar, due to constant practice. To build a palisade, each man carried two long stakes as part of his march equipment. A ditch was dug completely around the camp, with the earth thrown against the palisade to add thickness and sturdiness. Inside, the camp was laid out in a regular street pattern, each unit always occupying the same relative position.

Although the stakes and other equipment, as well as armor and weapons, gave each man a weight of 75–80 pounds on the march, the Romans marched quickly, and the legion was highly mobile. Surprisingly, there was no fixed march organization, which sometimes led to carelessness in reconnaissance and march security. This deficiency was corrected, however, during the Second Punic War, as a result of some costly lessons from Hannibal.

The other principal Roman military deficiency in this period was in siegecraft. They were far behind the Macedonians, for instance, and their sieges were usually drawn-out affairs of attrition. Again lessons of the Second Punic War brought improvements.

Naval Organization and Tactics

The Romans were not outstanding seamen. They relied largely upon allied and subject peoples—particularly the Greeks of southern Italy—to provide ships and seamen. Nevertheless, when necessary, the Romans applied characteristic efficiency and logic to maritime affairs.

Major developments in the Roman Navy came during the First Punic War. The Romans soon realized that neither they nor their allies possessed ships as maneuverable as those of the Carthaginians; they were also hopelessly outclassed in seamanship. Methodically, they attacked the problem. First, they began building vessels copied from the Carthaginian **quinquireme.**

Rightly confident of the superiority of the Roman legionary over the Carthaginian soldier and sailor in hand-to-hand fighting, the Romans then introduced two major modifications, permitting them to create conditions of land warfare at sea. The most important was the **corvus,** or "raven," which was a combined grappling device and gangway. This was, in fact, a narrow bridge, some 18 feet long. Mounted

Roman corvus

on a pivot near the bow of the galley, it was held in a near-vertical position by ropes and pulleys, and could be swung outboard in any direction. When an enemy ship approached, the corvus was let down with a crash on the opposing deck where it was held fast by a large spike attached under its outer end. Immediately a swarm of Roman soldiers dashed across this bridge to fight a land battle on the foe's decks. The Romans also installed fighting turrets fore and aft on their ships, from which additional soldiers supported the boarding party with missile weapons, and discouraged any enemy attempt at boarding.

These modified Roman warships were one of the first truly "secret" weapons of history. Unlike many later developers of technological innovations, the Romans waited until they had built a significant number of these new ships, then surprised the Carthaginians at the decisive Battle of Mylae (see p. 60).

Rome adapted castrametation to its naval tactics. As usual in ancient times, war fleets were beached on the shore every night. The Romans always entrenched the camp of rowers and marines, thus protecting men and vessels.

SOUTH ASIA

INDIA, 325–200 B.C.

The history of India remained virtually blank to about 325 B.C. It would appear that by the middle of the 4th century the Indian domains of the Persian Empire had achieved independence.

327–325. Alexander's Invasion of India. (See p. 51.)

c. 325. Magadha Dominant in Ganges Valley. She emerged from obscurity under a ruler named **Nanda,** who was, however, soon overthrown by the first great military figure of Indian history, **Chandragupta** (c. 323). As a young man Chandragupta had met Alexander, and had apparently spent some time with him while the Macedonian was in northern India, learning much about war and generalship.

323–297. Reign of Chandragupta. Chandragupta expanded his domains in all directions. He ejected the Macedonians from northwestern India during the early wars of the Diadochi.

305. Invasion of Seleucus Nicator. (See p. 54.) Details of Seleucus' campaign east of the Indus in an effort to re-establish Macedonian rule in India are unknown. It is doubtful if any great battles were fought with Chandragupta. Whatever the nature of the operations, Chandragupta evidently had the best of it. A treaty of alliance was drawn up in which Seleucus ceded to Chandragupta not only the provinces east of the Indus, but also substantial areas of Arachosia and Gedrosia west of the river, in return for 500 war elephants—which Seleucus used to advantage at Ipsus (see p. 54). Possibly the demands of the continuing Diadochian Wars caused Seleucus to leave India without attempting a decisive encounter with Chandragupta. Whatever the reasons, the result was to assure stability, and to increase the power of India's first great dynasty, known as the Maurya Empire.

297–274. Reign of Bindusara (Chandragupta's Son). He apparently expanded the empire considerably to the southward.

274–232. Reign of Asoka (Grandson of Chandragupta). He brought the Maurya Empire to the height of its power and grandeur. He apparently had to fight several claimants for the throne. After coming to power he undertook only one major campaign, in which he conquered the east coast of India between the Ganges and the Deccan. He was so saddened by the slaughter and misery of warfare that he forsook conquest, became a Buddhist, and devoted the rest of his life to good works and to the orderly, efficient administration of his vast empire. These domains included all India (save the southern tip, and Assam) plus Nepal and a substantial portion of Afghanistan. Most historians consider him to be the greatest and noblest ruler of Indian history.

232–180. Decline of the Mauryas. The later emperors lacked the zeal, energy, and organizing ability of the first three. Within 50 years the great empire had disappeared.

206. Antiochus III in the Kabul Valley. He possibly invaded the Punjab. He received the nominal vassalage of the Indian ruler **Sophagasenous,** apparently without fighting.

THE MILITARY SYSTEM OF THE MAURYAS

To rule his large dominions effectively, Chandragupta established at his capital of Pataliputra (Patna) an efficient governmental machinery which provided for complete control over national economy as well as over military affairs and admin-

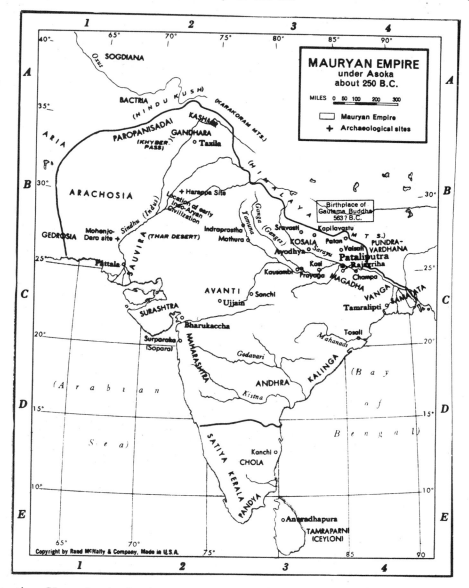

MAURYAN EMPIRE
under Asoka
about 250 B.C.

MILES 0 50 100   200   300

☐ Mauryan Empire
+ Archaeological sites

istration. He maintained a large permanent military establishment, which probably comprised one-quarter or one-third of the vast armies which he had raised for his victorious campaigns: 600,000 infantry, 30,000 cavalry, and 9,000 elephants. This possibly exaggerated report on the strength of Chandragupta's army comes from fragments remaining of the reports of the Seleucid Greek ambassador, **Megasthenes;** it is not clear whether he omits mention of chariots because of his contempt for such instruments of warfare or whether Chandragupta had learned from Alexander the uselessness of chariots.

It is interesting to note that in his highly organized military administration Chandragupta had an efficient secret service, and also a naval affairs office. His fleets operated on the Indus and Ganges, and probably along the coasts as well.

It was probably during the Maurya period that one of the most significant documents of Indian history—and of military history—was written. This was the *Arthasastra (Manual of Politics)*, which has been attributed to **Kautilya**, close friend and principal administrative assistant to Chandragupta. Whether or not the able and powerful Kautilya was the actual author or whether—more likely—the manual was prepared by an unknown writer a century or more later, it unquestionably reflects the ideas of Chandragupta and Kautilya, and is a remarkably clear portrayal of political, military, and social conditions during the 3rd century B.C. and later.

Essentially the *Arthasastra* was an exhaustive, thorough summation of early Hindu concepts of government, law and war. It has been compared with the writings of Machiavelli, while at the same time its military maxims have much in common with the earlier ideas of Sun Tzu. Its military sections include information on the composition of armies, the functions of the branches of service, duties of officers, rules of field operations, siegecraft, and fortification, plus a list of tactical and strategical maxims.

Standing armies had become normal in India by the 4th century, and a substantial portion of national revenues went to maintain such armies. In major campaigns, however, rulers usually found it necessary to expand their forces. One of the principal sources was from the so-called guild levies. These were members of the various trades or crafts, trained as soldiers, and mobilizable in time of war as a sort of militia. In addition to these part-time soldiers, there were a number of military guilds whose business was war; essentially military companies such as were seen in Europe in the Middle Ages, they sold their services to the various kings of India. The rulers apparently had some well-grounded suspicions of the guild levies, who had been known on occasion to usurp power during their term of military service.

It is clear that the importance of training and discipline was well known to the Hindus. They understood the theory, but apparently found it difficult to impose military fundamentals on their troops in practice.

It was much the same story with elephants and chariots. The unreliability of the one and the unwieldiness of the other, in the face of competent, trained infantry and cavalry, had been obvious at the Hydaspes. Chariots continued to be used in India for another 1,000 years, though their importance steadily declined. The post-Vedic chariots of India were usually rather large, drawn by 4 horses, and carrying 4 to 6 men.

Despite the constant danger that wounded elephants might do more harm to friends than to foe, they continued to be used by Indian warriors right up to the 19th century. In Maurya times they usually carried 3 or 4 men, including the driver. The principal weapon employed with elephants was the bow. The Hindus were able to make effective use of elephants in special circumstances. For instance, they were most useful in battering the gates of besieged forts or cities. And on some occasions they were used to bridge unfordable streams, infantrymen apparently making a precarious crossing on the backs of elephants lined side by side, facing the current.

From the *Arthasastra* we learn that the Maurya armies used entrenched camps, though apparently this was only when staying for a long period in one location. Such camps are clearly described by Kautilya, as well as the measures for defense, readiness, and alertness.

BACTRIA AND PARTHIA, 323–200 B.C.

323–311. **Decline of Macedonian Influence.** The eastern provinces of Alexander's old empire were under the successive nominal rule of **Perdiccas, Antipater, Eumenes,** and **Antigonus** (see pp. 52–54). In fact, however, these regions were gradually falling away from the empire under the rule of local princes and tribal leaders. At the same time, the Scythians began to move in from central Asia.

321–302. **Reconquest by Seleucus.** He carried out a systematic reconquest of the eastern provinces of the empire.

255. **Revolt of Diodotus.** Seleucid satrap of Bactria, he rebelled against **Antiochus II,** and established an independent kingdom. He conquered Sogdiana, and expanded also eastward toward the Indus and westward into Parthia.

250. **Arsaces in Parthia.** This Scythian tribal leader was driven by Diodotus into western Parthia, where he established an independent kingdom (249).

239–238. **Seleucid Setback.** Diodotus and Arsaces II (247–212) joined to repulse attempts of **Seleucus II** to reconquer the region. After initial success, Seleucus was forced to abandon his expedition in order to deal with a revolt by his brother, Antiochus Hierax, in Asia Minor (see p. 55).

230. **Rise of Euthydemus.** This Greco-Macedonian overthrew and slew Diodotus and made himself King of Bactria.

209–208. **Invasion of Antiochus III.** He defeated Arsaces III in Parthia (212–171). Arsaces appealed for help to Euthydemus, but Antiochus defeated the combined Bactrian-Parthian forces at the **Battle of the Arius** (208). Arsaces made peace and acknowledged the suzerainty of the Seleucids.

208–206. **War of Antiochus III and Euthydemus.** Although Antiochus won a number of minor successes, he was unable to conquer Bactria and Sogdiana. Finally he offered generous terms to Euthydemus, who acknowledged nominal Seleucid suzerainty.

EAST ASIA
CHINA, 400–200 B.C.

450–222. **Era of the Warring States. (See p. 36.)** To a degree this period of feudal anarchy became a duel between Ch'u and Ch'in, with first one, then the other, predominant. Shifting alliances among less powerful states preserved a balance of power. By the beginning of the 3rd century it appears that warfare had become less violent and more ritualistic.

c. 320. **Cavalry Appears in China.** The riding horse seems to have been introduced to war in China by King **Wu ling** of **Chao,** one of the Warring States.

247–222. **Reign of Cheng, Ruler of Ch'in.** One of the great figures of Chinese history, he undertook a systematic conquest of the other feudal states. He was not only a consummate politician, but an accomplished general. The backbone of his army was the powerful Ch'in cavalry, developed through extended combat with the warlike Hsiung-nu and Yueh Chih nomads of Mongolia.

222–210. **Reign of Shih Huang Ti.** Having overcome the last feudal opposition, Cheng declared himself Emperor of China, with title of Shih Huang Ti. This marked the beginning of the short-lived but memorable **Ch'in Dynasty,** from which the name "China" is derived. Shih Huang Ti now devoted his exceptional talents as a planner and organizer to the creation of the system of government which was to last in China for more than 2,100 years. In many respects this organization was comparable to that created by Cyrus and Darius in Persia, the most obvious similarities being in the creation of military satrapies and the construction of an excellent system of roads. After defeating the Hsiung-nu (later known to Europe as the Huns), Shih Huang Ti built the Great Wall along the northern border of his domains as a barrier to prevent further nomadic inroads. Internally he disarmed all the feudal armies; the confiscated weapons were melted down and used for statues and farm implements. His stern, ruthless, autocratic rule was efficient, but was resented by many Chinese.

221–214. **Expansion of China.** Shih Huang Ti undertook a series of great military expeditions south of the Yangtze, conquering the regions later known as Fukien, Kwantung, Kwangsi, and Tongking. He also conquered north Korea. Apparently most of these operations were under the immediate command of his generals **Ming T'ien** and **Chao T'o.**

210–207. Reign of Hu Hai. The weak son of Shih Huang Ti was soon beset by a combination of palace intrigue, a resurgence of the feudal lords, and widespread popular uprisings.

207–202. Anarchy. Hu Hai was killed by his courtiers. **Hsiang Yu,** a powerful and able general of the Ch'u principality, and **Liu Pang,** a popular revolutionary leader, joined to overthrow the Ch'in Dynasty. A great struggle between these two followed, with Liu Pang eventually triumphing. North Korea broke away from Chinese control during the struggle.

202. The Han Dynasty. Liu Pang, taking the imperial name of **Kao Tsu,** was the first emperor of the dynasty. His position was very shaky in the early years of his reign, due to the internal unrest which followed the violent collapse of the Ch'in Dynasty, and due also to inroads of the Hsiung-nu, who had gained supremacy in Mongolia by defeating the Yueh Chih tribes (see p. 120).

200. Defeat by the Hsiung-nu. Kao Tsu, apparently campaigning against a major Hsiung-nu invasion in northwest China, was surrounded for several days in a fortified border town, until he concluded a treaty with the Hsiung-nu chieftain, and gave him his daughter in marriage.

IV

THE RISE OF GREAT EMPIRES IN EAST AND WEST:
200–1 B.C.

MILITARY TRENDS

The most significant phenomenon of this period was the parallel growth of two great military powers: the Han Empire of China and the Roman Empire of the Mediterranean world. Standards of military leadership were generally lower than in the preceding period. **Caesar** alone is worthy of consideration with Alexander and Hannibal; even his illustrious predecessors, **Scipio Aemilianus, Sulla,** and **Lucullus,** were hardly up to the caliber of the Roman heroes of the Second Punic War, or to the competent professionals of the Diadochi.

MILITARY THEORY AND TACTICS

There were no major developments in theory, strategy, tactics, or weapons, but there were some important refinements, innovations, and modifications, particularly in Roman military organization. In Europe infantry remained the supreme arbiter of battles. In Asia cavalry predominated. The Macedonian phalanx and Roman legion met in two major battles—Cynoscephalae and Pydna; the legion was victorious.

The Romans employed field fortifications in battle to a degree hitherto unknown; a logical development of their earlier practice of using fortified camps as offensive and defensive bases. Following the initiative of Sulla at the Battle of Chaeronea, the Romans on numerous occasions were able to wield their shovels and axes in such a way as to integrate field fortifications into aggressive, offensive battle plans. They began also to use light missile engines as field artillery, in conjunction with their field fortifications.

CAVALRY

By the beginning of the Christian era the horse archer dominated warfare in Asia, save only in India. Though cavalry was the major arm in northern India, the principal weapons were lance and short sword; in central and southern India cavalry was less important than infantry, since geography and climate made it impossible to raise and support enough good horses for large cavalry units. Most of the good horses of southern India were used for chariots. (Chariots were still used elsewhere —notably by **Mithridates** of Pontus—but their importance had generally declined.)

The horse archer had been introduced into warfare by the nomadic barbarians of central Asia. Alexander encountered them as the major components of the Scythian tribes he defeated in Sogdiana and north of the Jaxartes. The Parthians, descendants of these Scythians, brought the horse archer to dramatic prominence in southwestern Asia in this period. Horse archers were the only type of warrior in the hordes of the fierce Mongoloid and Indo-European peoples who then dominated Mongolia and Turkestan: the Hsiung-nu and the Yueh Chih. Their depredations forced the Chinese to make cavalry their major arm.

One of the most significant portents of future military developments was the Battle of Carrhae, where the horse archers of the Parthian leader **Surenas** gained an overwhelming victory over the infantry legions of Roman **Crassus.** Alexander had had little trouble with similar foes, but no leader of genius comparable to Alexander appeared for centuries who could meet the horse archer with truly balanced forces of well-trained infantry and cavalry, working together as an integrated team.

The Parthians had little success, however, in their raids and invasions west of the Euphrates in the decades after Carrhae. They rightly were more fearful and respectful of the military power of Rome than vice versa. Nevertheless, Carrhae pointed to a trend. A few centuries later the horse archer would replace the legionary as the principal guardian of the eastern frontiers of Rome and Byzantium.

India was behind other civilized regions of the world in military developments, with one exception: the stirrup apparently was first used by Indian lancers as early as the 1st century B.C.

SIEGE WARFARE

Next to Alexander, Caesar was the outstanding director of siege operations of the ancient world. He, like other logical, methodical Romans, brought systematic procedure to siege operations. While the sequence of the details of operational and engineering actions naturally varied as required by local circumstances and the reactions of the besieged, an outline of a typical implementation of the system does give a clear picture of ancient siege operations:*

a. Reconnaissance of the fortifications, and of the surrounding region to note local resources in lumber, stones, animals, food, fodder.

b. Establishment of a fortified camp.

c. Collection of materials needed for construction and for siege engines.

d. Manufacture of mantelets and movable gallery sections. (These latter were like roofed huts, which, when placed together and the roofs covered with dampened skins, provided fireproof and missile-proof galleries through which troops and workmen could walk to the most advanced works and entrenchments.)

e. Building of redoubts around the circumference of the fortified place, then connecting these with lines of contravallation. (This would usually be begun at the same time as the two previous steps.) Sometimes a wall of circumvallation would also be built; Caesar almost invariably built double walls.

* With modifications, this is based upon the discussion in T. A. Dodge, *Julius Caesar,* Houghton Mifflin, 1892, 387–399.

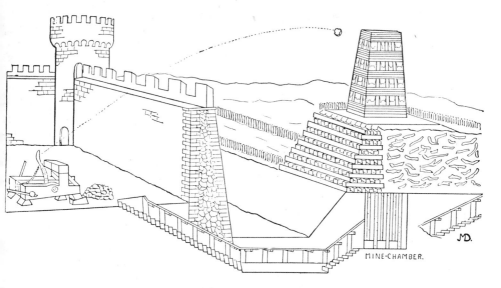

Fort, tower, mound, mantelets

f. By use of mantelets, galleries, and entrenchments, the preparation of covered ways toward the enemy walls; these would lead to mine heads, subterranean passages, and the advanced siege engines, which by now were beginning to harass the besieged troops and civilian population. Use of heavy and light machines became constant on both sides.

g. Building a terraced mound, raised one level at a time, and advanced gradually toward the walls, under the cover of a rampart of mantelets along its forward crest.

h. Erection of towers (usually on the terrace); these would be placed on great logs, then rolled gradually forward toward the besieged walls. The fronts of these towers were covered with dampened skins to prevent burning by incendiary arrows; their bases were well protected by infantry units, to prevent a destructive sortie by the defenders.

i. If the town or fort was surrounded by a moat, this would usually be filled

Penthouse and ram picked up by tongs

in ahead of the mound, and at any other point where a breach was desired. Breaches were achieved in two principal ways: (1) by use of rams, under protected galleries; or (2) by mine galleries under the walls, which when collapsed would cause the wall to crumple. If an alert defender built new interior walls, this breaching operation might have to be repeated several times. Alert defenders could also interfere with mining operations by construction of countermines.

j. The final assault; usually by charging through the breach made in the defending wall. Sometimes an assault would be attempted without a breach, the attackers rushing onto the ramparts from movable towers, up scaling ladders, or by telenons (see pp. 38–39). Sometimes an advance party would be sent secretly into the interior of the defended place through a mine shaft; thence to open the city gates and/or attack the defenders from the rear. One typically Roman innovation in the assault phase was the advance of a cohort to the walls under the protection of a **testudo** made by raising and interlocking their shields over their heads.

Testudo

NAVAL WARFARE

War at sea changed little. Triremes and quinquiremes remained the major combat vessels, though there were many other types, including special flat-bottomed craft (**pontones**) which the Romans used for their river flotillas. In battle the main objectives were still to run down the opponents, or to sink them by ramming, or to break their oars, or to board and capture, or to set them on fire. Cruise procedures such as camping along the shore at night whenever possible, were also unchanged.

The major innovation was introduced by **Octavian**'s admiral, **Agrippa: the harpax** or **harpago.** This was a pole, with a hook on its end, shot from a catapult into the side of an opposing ship, where the hook would hold it fast. Attached to the end of the harpago was a rope, which could be winched in to bring the two vessels together and facilitate boarding. This, the precursor of the whaling harpoon, was first used to good effect by Agrippa at the Battle of Naulochos and again at Actium.

EUROPE–MEDITERRA-NEAN

ROME, MACEDONIA, GREECE, AND PERGAMUM, 200–150 B.C.

200–191. Resubjugation of the Po Valley.
After the defeat of **Hannibal**, Rome began the pacification of Cisalpine Gaul. Major Roman victories were won at **Cremona** (200) and **Mutina** (Modena, 194).

Second Macedonian War, 200–196 B.C.

Philip V of Macedon, in alliance with **Antiochus III** of Seleucid Syria, after the indecisive First Macedonian War (see pp. 55 and 67), tried to dominate Greece, Thrace, and the Aegean coast of Asia Minor. Rome received appeals for help from Pergamum, Rhodes, and Athens.

200. Rome Declares War. Nabis, tyrant of Sparta, lined up with Philip. Two years of inconclusive minor operations followed.

198. Battle of the Aous. Titus Quinctius Flamininus, newly appointed Roman consul, drove Philip from a strong defensive position, while Roman diplomatic moves undermined his position in Greece. The Macedonian, taking the initiative, moved south from Larissa (197) as Flamininus advanced into Thessaly. Both armies were approximately equal in strength—about 26,000 each.

197. Battle of Cynoscephalae. They met unexpectedly in hill country, in a fog. Philip, encouraged by initial successes, brought on a general engagement on terrain unfavorable to the phalanx. His right wing drove back the Roman left; but while the Macedonian left was deploying from march column on uneven ground, it was struck by the Roman right, led by Flamininus, and routed. Part of the advancing Roman right now swung around —apparently without orders from Flamininus—hitting the Macedonian right and driving it from the field in confusion.

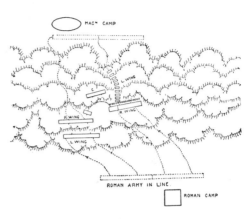

Battle of Cynoscephalae

Macedonian losses were about 13,000; Roman, a few hundred. This was the first battle in the open between the flexible Roman legion and the Macedonian phalanx.

196. Liberation of Greece. Philip was forced to give up all claim to Greece, as well as his possessions in Thrace, Asia Minor, and the Aegean.

195. Revolt in Spain. This was quelled by Consul **Marcus Porcius Cato.** Unrest was endemic on the peninsula until 155.

195–194. War between the Achaean League and Sparta. With some assistance from Flamininus, **Philopoemen** defeated Nabis, gaining an overwhelming victory at the **Battle of Gythium.** Flamininus, however, prevented Philopoemen from seizing Sparta.

194. Rome Declares Greece to Be Independent. Roman troops were withdrawn.

War with Antiochus III of Syria, 192–188 B.C.

Tensions between Rome and Seleucid Syria had mounted (see p. 56). Conciliation failed.

192. Rome Declares War. Antiochus, on invitation of the Aetolian League, invaded Greece, as a Roman army under **M. Acilius Glabrio** and Cato arrived in Epirus from Italy (early 191). Antiochus was driven from **Thermopylae** by the Romans. He evacuated Greece and sailed to Ephesus. Soon after, a Roman fleet commanded by **Gaius Livius** defeated a Syrian fleet between **Ionia** and **Chios** (191). Next year Roman admiral **Lucius Aemilius Regillus,** assisted by the Rhodians, defeated a Syrian fleet under **Hannibal** (taking part in his first and last naval battle) at **Eurymedon,** and then defeated a second Syrian fleet at **Myonnessus** (190). Meanwhile, a Roman army under **Lucius Cornelius Scipio** crossed the Hellespont to invade Asia. Lucius, a man of moderate ability, was accompanied by his brilliant brother, **Publius Cornelius Scipio Africanus,** victor of Zama, who actually planned the operations. But as the two armies approached each other, about 40 miles east of Smyrna, Scipio Africanus became ill and was unable to accompany the Roman army; tactical direction was assumed by **Cnaeus Domitius.** The Romans had been joined by **Eumenes II** of Pergamum, with a small army of about 10,000, mostly cavalry. The combined Roman-Pergamenian army was about 40,000 strong. Antiochus had about 75,000.

190, December. Battle of Magnesia. The Romans took the initiative, crossing the Hermus River to attack the Syrians, waiting behind a formidable line of war elephants. Eumenes, with the Pergamenian cavalry, was on the Roman right; Roman and allied cavalry were on the left of the legions and allied infantry. Antiochus had divided his cavalry into two elements, one on each flank of his phalanx; he commanded the right wing. At the outset the right flank cavalry contingents on each side won quick successes. Antiochus drove the Roman horsemen from the field, pursuing them across the river to the Roman camp, where he was barely repulsed by the Roman security detachment. Eumenes, however, halted his pursuit of the Syrian left wing cavalry, and turned to strike the exposed flank of the Syrian phalanx. Meanwhile, the legions had repulsed the elephants, a number of the maddened beasts being driven back through their own phalanx. While still in confusion, the Syrian infantry's left flank was struck by Eumenes and his cavalry. At the same time the legions pressed a vigorous frontal

assault. The Syrians broke and fled. The Romans—once again under the strategic and political direction of Scipio Africanus—followed up their victory to gain almost complete control over western Asia Minor (189).

188. Peace of Apameax. Antiochus was forced to give up his possessions in Greece and in Anatolia west of the Taurus Mountains. These lands were divided between Rome's allies, Rhodes and Pergamum, who were strengthened to offset Macedonia and Syria. Rome kept only the islands of Cephalonia and Zacynthus.

190. War between the Achaean League and Sparta. Complete victory of Philopoemen over Nabis, and the suppression of Nabis' social reforms. Philopoemen's ruthlessness caused him to be censured by Rome, which established a virtual protectorate over Sparta.

189. Galatian Invasion of Pergamum. A Roman army under **G. Manlius Volso** helped Eumenes to defeat and repel the Celts of Galatia.

189–179. Macedonia Prepares for War. Philip V of Macedon, who had assisted Rome in the war against Antiochus, was embittered by Roman failure to reward his services. After his death (179), his son **Perseus** continued quiet and efficient preparations for war.

186–179. Expansion of Pergamum. Eumenes greatly increased the power and influence of Pergamum in Asia Minor by victories over **Prusias I** of Bithynia (186) and **Pharnaces I** of Pontus (183–179). Rome was suspicious of his ambitions.

184. Death of Philopoemen. During a revolt of Messene against the Achaean League, Philopoemen was captured and executed by the rebels.

183. Deaths of Hannibal and Scipio. For the death of Hannibal in Bithynia, by his own hand, see p. 71. Scipio died at about the same time, in self-imposed exile in southern Italy, where he had retired after undergoing political attack, abuse, and trial in Rome on charges (probably false) of embezzlement.

Third Macedonian War, 172–167 B.C.

An unsuccessful attempt to murder Eumenes II of Pergamum, instigated by Per seus of Macedonia, led to war between those states.

172. Rome Enters the War. Almost equally suspicious of Perseus and Eumenes, Rome decided to support her old ally, sending an army against Macedonia, via Illyria, under **P. Licinius Crassus** (171). Perseus defeated Crassus at the **Battle of Callicinus** (near Larissa, 171). Perseus then repulsed **A. Hostilius Mancinus,** commanding another Roman army, in Thessaly (170). Still another Roman invasion attempt, under **Q. Marcius Philippus,** failed the following year. Perseus tried, unsuccessfully, to bribe Eumenes and the Rhodians—both Roman allies—to join him. **Genthius** of Illyria and **Clondicus,** chief of the Gallic tribes north of Macedonia, accepted Perseus' bribes, but their ardor waned when he failed to make promised payments.

168. Lucius Aemilius Paulus to Command in Greece. Son of the Roman consul at Cannae (see p. 65), Lucius arrived with reinforcements. At the same time Praetor **Lucius Anicus** took a small army to Illyria, and quickly overwhelmed Genthius. When Aemilius joined the dispirited Roman Army it was encamped on the south bank of the Enipeus River, beside the shore of the Gulf of Thessalonika; Perseus' army was camped to the northwest, on the far bank of the river. Aemilius used stern measures to restore traditional Roman discipline (April–May).

168. June. Aemilius Advances. He attempted a wide envelopment of the Macedonian army by sending a portion of his army around Mount Olympus. Perseus learned of the movement in time to withdraw to a position behind the Aeson River.

168, June 22. Battle of Pydna.* The action was started by accident during the afternoon while both sides were watering horses on opposite banks of the river. Perseus, seizing the initiative, formed his phalanx, and attacked across the Aeson. Despite the efforts of Aemilius to organize and rally his men, the phalanx swept forward irresistibly on the flat terrain near the river, but it was unable to keep alignment in the rolling ground farther south.

* The date is known from an eclipse of the moon the night before the battle, an omen the Romans considered favorable; it caused consternation among the Macedonians.

Aemilius counterattacked, taking advantage of gaps in the phalanx. Once the Romans penetrated, the phalanx fell apart; 20,000 Macedonians were killed, 11,000 captured; only a handful—including Perseus—escaped. Roman losses were less than 1,000. Perseus later surrendered, and died in captivity in Italy.

167. Rome Controls the Eastern Mediterranean. Macedonia was divided into 4 separate republics, under Roman protection. A virtual protectorate was established over Greece; **Antiochus IV,** who had conquered Egypt, had accepted Rome's demands that he withdraw and restore Egyptian sovereignty (168), thus acknowledging virtual Roman suzerainty. A protectorate was established over Anatolia; the power of Pergamum was cut sharply, since it was no longer needed by Rome to offset the power of Macedonia and Syria.

SELEUCID SYRIA AND PTOLEMAIC EGYPT, 200–50 B.C.

192–188. Seleucid War with Rome. (See p. 85.) Ptolemy V allied Egypt with Rome. A consequence of Antiochus' defeat was the defection of Armenia and Bactria from weakened Seleucid rule.

187. Death of Antiochus. This was in Luristan, while he was attempting to recover the lost eastern provinces.

171–168. Seleucid War with Egypt. Antiochus IV twice successfully invaded Egypt (171–170 and 168). His conquest of Egypt was almost complete when, while investing Alexandria, he was warned by Rome to restore Egypt to the Ptolemies. During his ignominious withdrawal from Egypt, he occupied Jerusalem, destroyed the city walls, and decreed the abolition of Judaism, causing a protracted Jewish revolt (168).

168–143. Wars of the Maccabees. (See p. 88.)

166–163. Seleucid Campaigns in the East. Antiochus IV recovered Armenia and other eastern provinces.

162–143. Dynastic Strife within the Seleucid Empire. Demetrius I and his son, **Demetrius II,** were opposed by **Alexander**

Balas. **Ptolemy VI** of Egypt supported the Demetrii, while Eumenes of Pergamum supported Balas. Crucial conflict of this struggle was the victory of Ptolemy over Alexander Balas at the **Battle of the Oenoparus** (145). Ptolemy died of wounds; Balas was soon thereafter murdered and succeeded by Demetrius II.

c. 161–159. Revolt of Timarchus. The governor of Babylonia, **Timarchus** of Miletus, threw off Seleucid rule, and conquered Media, taking the title of "Great King." Demetrius I defeated Timarchus, recovering Babylonia and Media for the empire (159).

150. Parthian Conquest of Media. Mithridates I took advantage of chaos in the Seleucid Empire.

141–139. Seleucid War with Parthia. Mithridates invaded Babylonia and captured Babylon (141). Demetrius II then drove the Parthians from Mesopotamia (130). Next year, however, he was captured through treachery.

145–51. Decline of Ptolemaic Egypt. Constant unrest and civil strife tore Egypt in an ugly succession of treachery, murder, and incest among the decaying Ptolemies. Frequent Roman intervention failed to bring lasting peace. **Cleopatra VII** and her brother **Ptolemy XII** jointly ascended the throne (51).

130–127. Renewed Seleucid War with Parthia. Antiochus VIII recovered Babylonia, forcing **Phraates II** of Parthia to release his brother, Demetrius II, from captivity. Continuing on into Media, Antiochus was defeated and killed at the **Battle of Ecbatana** by Phraates (129). This defeat cost the Seleucid Empire all of the region east of the Euphrates River.

125–64. Decline of Seleucid Syria. The dwindling Seleucid Empire was racked by dynastic disorders, while neighboring Parthia continued its encroachments in the east, and Armenia from the north. Finally Rome moved in to restore order and to prevent further Parthian and Armenian expansion (64); Syria, conquered·by Pompey, became a province of Rome (see p. 94).

JUDEA, 168–66 B.C.

168. Revolt of the Maccabees. Suppression of Judaism by Antiochus IV (see p. 87) ignited a Jewish revolt led by a priest, **Mattathias,** and his five sons, of whom the most prominent and most able was **Judas Maccabeus.**

166–165. Victories of Judas. Upon the death of Mattathias, Judas became leader of the rebellious Jews. In brilliant guerrilla actions, he defeated a succession of Syrian generals, his most renowned victories being at **Beth Horon** (166), **Emmaus** (166), and **Beth Zur,** near Hebron (165). After this latter victory he captured Jerusalem, liberating the temple, though a Seleucid garrison continued to hold out in the citadel.

165–164. Struggle for Jerusalem. Judas extended his control over much of Judea, while keeping a tight siege of Jerusalem's citadel. Antiochus being away on his successful campaign to the east, the Syrian regent **Lysias** led an invading army into Judea in an effort to recapture Jerusalem. He defeated the Jews at **Beth Zachariah,** but returned to Syria to suppress a revolt (164).

163–161. The Last Campaigns of Judas. Syrian general **Bacchides,** now commanding Seleucid forces in Judea, defeated Judas, and drove him from Jerusalem (162). Judas quickly resumed the offensive, defeating the Syrian general **Nicanor** at **Adasa,** near the site of his earlier victory of Beth Horon (161); Nicanor was killed. Later that same year, however, Judas was defeated and killed in battle by Bacchides at **Elasa.**

161–143. Leadership of Jonathan (Judas' Brother). He continued generally successful guerrilla warfare against the Syrians. Recognized as *de facto* ruler of Judea, he made his headquarters in Jerusalem (152). At **Ptolemais** (Acre) he was ambushed, captured, and later killed by the Syrians and dissident Jews (143).

143–66. Independence of Judea. **Simon,** another brother of Judas Maccabeus, was recognized as King of Judea by the Seleucids (143). The following decades were marked by internal violence, and frequent invasions by the Seleucids and neighboring Arab chieftains. The turmoil was brought to a close by Rome after Pompey captured Jerusalem (see p. 94); Judea was annexed by Rome, to round out her control over the eastern Mediterranean (64).

ROME AND THE MEDITERRA-
NEAN WORLD, 150–60 B.C.

152–146. Uprisings in Macedonia. (Sometimes called Fourth Macedonian War.) **Andriscus,** supposed son of Perseus, led an uprising which temporarily united Macedonia. Declaring himself king, Andriscus repelled initial Roman efforts to regain control. He was crushed by **Q. Caecilius Metellus** (148), who then suppressed subsequent outbreaks (148–146). Macedonia became a Roman province (146).

Third Punic War, 149–146 B.C.

BACKGROUND. Troubles long brewing between Carthage and aged **Massinissa** of Numidia broke out into open war (150). Carthage-haters in Rome—led by Marcus Porcius Cato—now acted against Carthage. Upon Roman demand Carthage ceased operations against Numidia, gave up 300 hostages to Rome, surrendered most of its weapons, and dismantled the battlements of the city. Carthage, however, refused the final crushing Roman demand to abandon the existing city and to move the populace inland.

149. Rome Declares War. Initial Roman land and sea efforts against Carthage were foiled by the vigorous defense of the hastily fortified city (148).

147. Scipio Aemilianus to Command. Son of L. Aemilius Paulus, victor of Pydna, and adopted grandson of Scipio Africanus, **Publius Scipio Aemilianus** bore his two names worthily. Upon arrival in Africa, he vigorously pressed the land and sea blockade of Carthage, whose population suffered terribly from starvation and disease.

146. Fall of Carthage. A determined assault by Scipio Aemilianus was followed by house-to-house conflict through the city. When it was over, nine-tenths of the population had perished by starvation, disease, or battle. By order of the Roman Senate, and despite Scipio's protests, the city was completely destroyed, and the survivors sold as slaves.

149–139. Lusitanian and Celtiberian Wars. Earlier disorders in Spain had been suppressed by **M. Claudius Marcellus,** who defeated the Lusitanians and Celtiberians

(154–151). The Lusitanians and Iberians took advantage of the Third Punic War, revolting under the leadership of **Viriathus,** who held Lusitania successfully against repeated Roman efforts. After Viriathus was assassinated by a traitor in Roman pay, the Lusitanians collapsed (139). The Celtiberians had already been crushed by Metellus, conqueror of Macedonia (144).

146. Achaean War. Hoping to take advantage of Roman preoccupation with Carthage, the Achaean League attacked Sparta, still under Roman protection. Consul **Lucius Mummius** led an army to Greece, and defeated the Achaean general **Critolaus** near Corinth. Mummius then captured and destroyed Corinth. The Achaean League was dissolved, and Rome subjugated all Greece.

137–133. Numantian War. Numantia, city of the upper Durius (Douro) River in Spain, became the center of revived Celtiberian independence efforts. The consuls **Quintus Pompeius** and **M. Papilius Laenas** were defeated and disgraced by the Numantians (137–132). Scipio Aemilianus, victor over Carthage, was appointed to command in Spain (134). He quickly reorganized the Roman armies, defeated and captured the city.

c. 135. Growing Internal Disorders in Rome. During the quarter-century beginning about 160 there had been a decline in Roman military capabilities reflecting serious political, economic, and social unrest. The Roman Senate was unequal to the task of governing the new empire; administration was inefficient, corruption rife. This deterioration had begun with the devastation and dislocation created by Hannibal and the Roman efforts to defeat him. The growth of large estates, operating with slave labor procured in overseas conquests, hastened the disappearance of the sturdy farm peasantry who had formed the backbone of the Roman militia army. These now pauperized peasants became the mobs of the city, or the permanent professional soldiery of the army. These soldiers lacked traditional Roman discipline. They owed allegiance only to generals, and were inspired by loot rather than patriotic ardor. The near-collapse of law and order was demonstrated in repeated uprisings of slaves, in the domination of the Mediterranean by pirates, and in recurrent civil strife. This state of affairs, gradually worsening, continued for a century. Yet, surprisingly, the essential vigor of Rome was demonstrated by a few military leaders of ability, like Scipio Aemilianus and Metellus, who inspired the degenerating army to fight worthily and to hold secure the far-flung Roman borders.

135–132. First Servile War. A slave uprising in Sicily, long defying repeated Roman efforts at suppression, was finally quelled by **Publius Rupilius.**

133. Assassination of Tiberius Gracchus. The violent death of the democratic tribune marked the beginning of endemic riot and bloodshed in the streets of Rome itself.

133–129. Conquest of Pergamum. **Attalus III** of Pergamum bequeathed his kingdom to Rome on his death. **Aristonicus,** pretender to the throne, defied Roman efforts to take over. He was finally defeated by Proconsul **P. Licinius Crassus,** with the assistance of Cappadocian forces. Pergamum became a Roman province of Asia.

125–121. Expansion into Transalpine Gaul. Consul **Marcus Fulvius Flaccus** commenced conquest of the region between the Alps, the Rhone, and the Mediterranean (125). Consul **Q. Fabius Maximus,** allied with the Aedui, defeated the Arverni and Allobroges tribes near the confluence of the Rhone and Isere rivers (121). The province of Transalpine Gaul (known as Provincia, or *the* Province) was established.

124. Revolt of Fregellae. Unrest among the Italian allies—partly due to their unsatisfied demands for the franchise, partly due to the extension of the democratic-conservative struggle in Rome—was evidenced by the revolt of Fregellae, in Latium, second largest city of Italy. Captured by ruse, the city was destroyed by the Romans.

115. Emergence of Caius Marius (155–86). As a praetor, he subdued Further Spain.

113. Appearance of the Cimbri. The Teutonic tribe of the Cimbri reached the Carnic Alps, defeated a Roman army under **G. Papirius Carbo** in the Drava Valley, then repulsed subsequent Roman punitive attempts.

Jugurthine War, 112–106 B.C.

BACKGROUND. A dynastic struggle in Numidia between descendants of Massinissa resulted in the victory of **Jugurtha** over **Adherbal** (119). Rome, however, divided the kingdom between the two contestants. Jugurtha refused to accept the Roman verdict, and intermittent fighting continued, marked by drawn-out negotiations and shameless bribery of leading Romans by the Numidian princes.

112. Jugurtha Declares War. After he won a few minor successes, a truce was reached (110), but fighting soon broke out again. Jugurtha began a systematic campaign to sweep the Romans from Numidia (109). **Caecilius Metellus** (nephew of Metellus Macedonicus) was then sent to take command in Africa. Reorganizing the shattered Roman forces, he invaded Numidia and defeated Jugurtha in the **Battle of the Muthul** (108). He then occupied most of the settled regions of Numidia. Jugurtha took refuge in the desert, and began a successful guerrilla campaign against the Romans. Uncouth and boorish Marius was a subordinate of Metellus in these operations.

106. Marius to Command. Elected consul, he superseded his former commander. His principal subordinate was a young quaestor, **Lucius Cornelius Sulla.**

106. Capture of Jugurtha. By a combination of his own energy and Numidian treachery, Sulla captured Jugurtha, bringing the war to a conclusion (106). Differing versions as to the respective roles of Marius and Sulla in this campaign gave rise to jealousy between them, heightening the bitterness of their later struggle as leaders respectively of the democratic and aristocratic factions of Rome.

109–104. Migrations of the Cimbri and Teutones. The Cimbri, accompanied by the related tribe of Teutones, migrated through what is now Switzerland to southern Gaul; near the Rhone River they defeated the army of **M. Junius Silanus.** After several futile efforts to subdue the barbarians, Consul **Mallius Maximus** led an army of 80,000 against them. The Roman army was defeated and virtually annihilated at the **Battle of Arausio** (Orange); 40,000 Roman noncombatants were also killed (105). This, one of the worst disasters ever to befall Roman arms, created consternation in Rome. The barbarians then moved toward Spain, but were repulsed in the Pyreneean passes by the Celtiberians. Returning to central Gaul, they clashed with the Belgae, then retired to southern Gaul.

105. Military Reforms in Rome. Marius, who had been re-elected consul, initiated sweeping reforms of the Roman military system, assisted by **P. Rutilius Rufus** (see p. 96).

104–101. War with the Cimbri and Teutones. Following the disaster of Arausio, Marius took command in Roman Gaul. At first he avoided battle, devoting efforts to training, rebuilding the discipline and confidence of his demoralized troops, and to the reorganization of the logistical system of the province. The Cimbri and Teutones now determined to invade Italy. Most of the Cimbri marched northeastward, through Switzerland, heading for the Brenner Pass. The Teutones, with some of the Cimbri, advanced toward the Little Saint Bernard Pass. Marius built a powerful fortified camp at the junction of the Rhone and Isere rivers, and repulsed repeated barbarian assaults (102). The Teutones then marched down the Rhone, heading for the passes over the Maritime Alps. Marius followed cautiously.

102. Battle of Aquae Sextae (Aix-en-Provence). Marius enticed the barbarians to attack him in a carefully selected hill position. At the height of the battle a small force of Romans in ambush attacked the rear of the Teutones, and threw them into confusion. In the ensuing slaughter 90,000 barbarians were killed, 20,000 captured.

102–101. Advance of the Cimbri. Traversing the Brenner Pass, the barbarians defeated Consul **Q. Lutatius Catulus** in the **Adige** Valley (102). They then wintered in the Po Valley. Marius hastened back to Italy, and joined forces with Catulus.

101. Battle of Vercellae. Marius literally annihilated the Cimbri; 140,000 barbarians (men, women, and children) were killed, 60,000 captured.

104–99. Second Servile War. The major uprising was in Sicily. After most of the island had been overrun by the slaves, the rebellion was suppressed by Consul **Manius Aquillius** (101–99).

100. Marius Elected Consul for the Sixth Time. This precipitated violence and bloodshed in a pitched battle in the streets of Rome. Marius, a good soldier, proved incompetent as a politician and statesman; the struggle between democrats and aristocrats was intensified by his misrule.

93–92. War with Tigranes of Armenia. Expanding the power of his kingdom, **Tigranes** invaded the Roman protectorate of Cappadocia. Sulla, then praetor of the Asian provinces, concluded an alliance against Tigranes with **Mithridates** of Parthia, but repulsed Tigranes without Parthian help.

91–88. Social War. Most of Rome's Italian allies rose in revolt because Rome refused to grant them citizenship. A new Italian republic was established, with capital at Corfinium. At first the rebels were generally successful. Rome made concessions by granting citizenship to those allies who remained loyal (mostly Latins, Etruscans, and Umbrians), and then offering it to rebels who laid down their arms to acknowledge Roman sovereignty. Consul **Lucius Porcius Cato** was defeated and killed at **Fucine Lake** (89), but his colleague **C. Pompeius Strabo** won a decisive victory at **Asculum** (89). Meanwhile, Sulla had besieged and captured **Pompeii.** Most of the rebels now accepted the Roman offer, and the revolt died out. The generally poor showing of Roman forces in the early stages of the war was due to a shocking deterioration of discipline in the Roman Army.

First Mithridatic War, 89–84 B.C.

BACKGROUND. **Mithridates VI** of Pontus, who had greatly expanded the power and prestige of his kingdom in Asia Minor and on the eastern and northern shores of the Black Sea, had had a long-standing dispute with **Nicomedes III** of Bithynia over the province of Cappadocia. Rome had previously intervened twice (95 and 92), and warned him to keep hands off Bithynia (89).

89. Mithridates Invades Bithynia and Cappadocia. Completely successful, he overran the Roman provinces in Asia Minor, then invaded Greece, where his successes fanned flickering flames of revolt against Rome. Sulla, placed in command of operations in the east, was en route to

Greece (88), when he was diverted by the outbreak of civil war in Rome (see below).

87. Arrival of Sulla. Having temporarily settled affairs in Rome, Sulla returned to Greece, where he promptly drove the two Mithridatic-Greek armies (commanded by **Archelaus** and **Aristion**) into the fortifications of Athens and the Piraeus, which he then invested. Sulla captured Athens by storm (86), and Archelaus escaped from the Piraeus by sea, landing in Boeotia. Meanwhile, Sulla's young subordinate, Lucius Licinius Lucullus, raised a fleet, and decisively defeated the fleet of Mithridates in a battle off **Tenedos** (86).

86. Battle of Chaeronea. Sulla, with about 30,000 men, moved to Boeotia, seeking battle with Archelaus, who had assembled an army of 110,000 men and 90 chariots. In the first known offensive use of field fortifications, Sulla built entrenchments

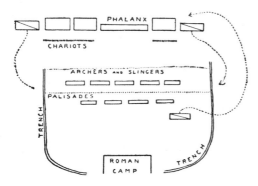

Battle of Chaeronea

to protect his flanks against envelopment by the Mithridatic-Greek cavalry, and erected palisades along the front of his position, to provide protection against the chariots. The battle opened with a charge by the Mithridatic cavalry, some of whom were able to avoid the entrenchments and the palisades. Sulla, his legions formed into squares, easily repulsed the charge. The chariot attack was handled according to plan; the maddened horses that survived the Roman arrows and javelins dashed back through the phalanx, throwing it into confusion. Sulla immediately launched a combined infantry and cavalry counterattack, and swept the foe from the field.

85. Battle of Orchomenus. Archelaus, who

had received reinforcements from Mithridates and from his Greek allies, again outnumbered Sulla, by about the same margin as at Chaeronea. Sulla, contemptuous of his adversaries, but exercising judicious care in his plans and preparations, again used field fortifications to assist him in advancing against the sluggish foes, defeating them by a decisive envelopment. Sulla now prepared to invade Asia.

85–84. Arrival of a New Roman Army. At this time the new democratic government in Rome under Marius and Cinna (see below), antagonistic to Sulla, sent another army to the east under **L. Valerius Flaccus,** who was to supplant Sulla. Sulla refused to acknowledge the authority of Flaccus, and continued his plans, assisted by Lucullus and his fleet. Flaccus was murdered by **Gaius Flavius Fimbria,** who then assumed command of the democratic Roman army in the east; apparently he tacitly supported Sulla's operations against Mithridates. The Pontine king, his territory threatened by two Roman armies, now made peace. When Sulla persuaded the army of Fimbria to join him, Fimbria committed suicide. Leaving this army in Asia under Lucullus, Sulla returned to Italy to intervene in the civil war there.

Roman Civil War, 88–82 B.C.

88. Democratic Uprising. Rebellious democrats, led by tribune **P. Sulpicius Rufus,** with the support of Marius, were crushed by conservative Sulla, who was called back while en route to Greece (see above). Marius and other rebels fled to Africa.

87. Renewed Uprising. After Sulla again left for Greece, the democrats rose again, now led by **Lucius Cornelius Cinna.** With the democrats in power, Marius returned to Rome and instituted a reign of terror, carried on by Cinna after Marius' death (86). Cinna was killed by a mutiny of his troops (84), but the despotic regime carried on for 2 more years.

83. Return of Sulla. After landing at Brundisium, Sulla defeated Consul **Caius Norbanus** at **Mount Tifata,** near Capua. He spent the winter in Capua. The 5-year reign of terror in Rome ended when Sulla, with his 40,000 veterans, marched up from southern Italy (82). Defeating the allied forces of the democrats and revolting Samnites in the **Battle of the Colline Gate,** Sulla seized Rome, made himself dictator, and restored law and order after slaying his political opponents. He sent **Cnaeus Pompeius** (Pompey), one of his subordinates, to Sicily and then to Africa to stamp out the embers of democratic dissension.

82–79. Sulla Dictator. He reformed the government and restored the authority of the Senate. He then permitted free elections and retired, dying the next year (78).

83–81. Second Mithridatic War. Essentially a local and apparently accidental clash between Mithridates and the Roman governor of Asia, **L. Licinius Murena.** Peace was re-established on the basis of the *status quo.*

80–72. Sertorian War. Quintus Sertorius, a democratic supporter of Marius, established an independent regime in Lusitania (Portugal and western Spain) after Sulla gained control of Rome. He raised an army of Lusitanians and defeated the legal governor, **Lucius Fufidias,** in the **Battle of the Baetis** (Guadalquivir) River (80). **Quintus Metellus Pius,** principal subordinate of Sulla, took the field, but Sertorius had the best of inconclusive maneuvering and skirmishing (80–78). Pompey arrived with an army from Italy, via the Pyrenees, to join Metellus (77), but Sertorius kept the two Sullan leaders at bay in a brilliant series of guerrilla and regular campaigns (76–73). Sertorius was assassinated in a plot directed by his principal subordinate, **Marcus Perperna,** who was then immediately defeated by Pompey, bringing the war to a close (72).

79–68. Operations against the Pirates. Sporadic punitive efforts to subdue or to limit the depredations of the Mediterranean pirates were generally unsuccessful.

78–77. Revolt of Lepidus. Marcus Aemilius Lepidus, leader of the democratic party, became consul, and attempted to overthrow the constitution of Sulla (78). Defeated in a battle outside Rome by **Q. Lutatius Catulus,** Lepidus and his supporters fled into Etruria, where they were wiped out by Pompey (77).

Third Mithridatic War, 75–65 B.C.

BACKGROUND. Nicomedes III of Bithynia, to thwart the ambitions of Mithridates, bequeathed his kingdom to Rome on

his death (75). Roman troops occupied Bithynia.

75. Mithridates Declares War. With 120,000 men, he invaded Cappadocia, Bithynia and Paphlagonia, at the same time encouraging revolt in the Roman provinces. The two consuls, **M. Aurelius Cotta** and L. L. Lucullus (former colleague of Sulla), led armies of about 30,000 each to Asia. While Lucullus re-established control in Roman possessions, Cotta and the fleet sailed to Chalcedon on the Bosporus. Mithridates moved against Cotta, defeated him outside Chalcedon, and drove him back into the city. The Mithridatic fleet at the same time defeated and destroyed the Roman fleet, cutting off Cotta.

74. Battle of Cyzicus. Lucullus marched to assist his colleague, defeating Mithridates' lieutenant **Marius** near Brusa. Mithridates, bottled up on the peninsula of Cyzicus between the two Roman armies, escaped by sea, while his army cut its way out overland, with terrible losses. Lucullus immediately pursued into Pontus.

72. Battle of Cabira (Sivas). Lucullus defeated Mithridates completely, after which he overran the entire kingdom. Mithridates fled to join his son-in-law and ally, Tigranes of Armenia, now the most powerful ruler of the Middle East. Tigranes refused Lucullus' demand to surrender Mithridates.

70–67. Lucullus Invades Armenia. With seeming reckless self-confidence, Lucullus, who had 10,000 men, attacked and defeated Tigranes, who had about 100,000, at the **Battle of Tigranocerta** (69). Advancing into northeastern Armenia and winning another victory at **Artaxata** (68), he returned to the Euphrates Valley when his worn-out troops refused to go farther (68–67). Mithridates meanwhile had invaded Pontus.

67. Pompey Given Command in the East. He reaped the fruits of the amazing victories of Lucullus. After being ambushed and utterly defeated by Pompey in the **Battle of the Lycus** (66), Mithridates escaped to the Crimea, where he committed suicide (64). Tigranes, defeated and captured, was forced to give up all his previous conquests (65; see p. 116).

73–71. Third Servile War. Led by the gladiator **Spartacus,** rebellious slaves established a base on the slopes of Mount Vesuvius, terrorizing southern Italy. Defeating the praetor **Varinius,** Spartacus with 40,000 men exercised virtual control over most of Campania. He defeated both Roman consuls, then ranged almost at will over most of Italy (72). Finally he was defeated by **M. Licinius Crassus** (71), and the revolt was stamped out completely by Pompey, just returned from the Sertorian War in Spain.

67. Pompey's War against the Pirates. The Senate now gave to Pompey (at his suggestion) unlimited authority over the Mediterranean Sea, and its littoral for 50 miles inland. In three months Pompey completely defeated the pirates of both western and eastern Mediterranean, conquering their bases and restoring relative tranquillity to that sea for the first time in more than half a century. Following this brilliant success, the Senate gave Pompey dictatorial powers in the east in order to bring to a conclusion the war against Mithridates (see above, p. 93).

65–61. Pompey in the East. Following his victories over Mithridates and Tigranes, Pompey swept through the Middle East. Reaching the Caspian Sea in Armenia (65), he annexed Syria (64), and when Palestine refused to accept Roman sovereignty, he captured Jerusalem, annexing Palestine as well (64). Then completely reorganizing the system of Roman provinces and protectorates in the east, he returned to Rome in triumph (61).

63–62. Insurrection of Catiline. A democratic conspiracy led by **Lucius Sergius Catiline,** to kill the consuls and seize power in Rome, was discovered and exposed by Consul **Marcus Tullius Cicero** in his famous orations. Some violence in Rome itself was quickly suppressed by the government, but Catiline fled to Etruria, where his adherents had raised an army. Pursued by Consul **Gaius Antonius,** Catiline was defeated and killed in a violent battle near **Pistoria** in Etruria (January, 62).

61–60. Caesar in Spain. Gaius Julius Caesar (102–44), a democratic politician of aristocratic birth, first gained military prominence as propraetor and governor of Further Spain. Prior to this he had been a staff officer under Sulla in the east (82–78) and had been a quaestor in Spain (69). Most of his adult life, however, had been devoted to politics. Now, exercising military command for the first time, he suppressed uprisings of unruly barbarians in his province, then conquered all of Lusitania for Rome.

THE FIRST TRIUMVIRATE,
60–50 B.C.

60. Establishment of the Triumvirate. An informal association of Pompey, Crassus (victor over Spartacus), and Caesar established political ascendancy in Rome. This was a period of violence and upheaval in Rome itself, with the triumvirs playing confused and intricate roles as each attempted to use the internal discord to his own advantage, while at the same time they divided responsibility for control of the colonial areas beyond Italy.

58–50. Caesar's Gallic Wars. (See p. 102.)

55–38. War with Parthia. (See p. 117.)

54–53. Campaign of Carrhae. In an effort to gain military renown comparable to his rivals and colleagues, Crassus had himself appointed proconsul for Syria. He then marched against the Parthians. He was defeated at Carrhae by the Parthian general **Surenas,** and was killed during the ensuing retreat (see p. 117).

52–50. Pompey Seizes Power. Partly because of anarchy in Rome, and partly because he was increasingly jealous of the growing fame of Caesar in Gaul, Pompey had himself elected sole consul and became virtual dictator. Relations between the two men grew more strained; the Senate, supporting Pompey, passed laws which would cause Caesar's political and military power to lapse on March 1, 49.

ROMAN MILITARY SYSTEM, C. 50 B.C.

In the century and a half following the Second Punic War the upheavals and disorders of the Roman state were mirrored in its armed forces. Yet despite individual incompetence, and a decline in the civic and military virtues of Rome, its mili-

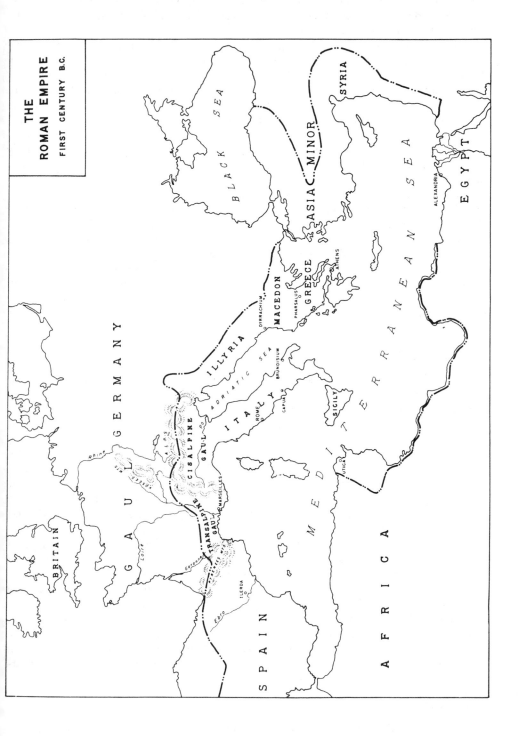

THE
ROMAN EMPIRE
FIRST CENTURY B.C.

BLACK SEA

ASIA MINOR

SYRIA

ALEXANDRIA

EGYPT

GREECE

ATHENS

PHARSALUS

MACEDON

DYRRACHIUM

ILLYRIA

ADRIATIC SEA

BRUNDISIUM

MEDITERRANEAN SEA

GERMANY

Rhine

CISALPINE GAUL

ALPS

PYRENEES

CAPUA

ITALY

PO

ROME

SICILY

UTICA

GAUL

Loire

TRANSALPINE GAUL

Garonne

MARSEILLES

ILERDA

EBRO

SPAIN

BRITAIN

AFRICA

tary system remained founded on the basic principles which had brought it to preeminence: regularity, discipline, training, flexibility, and unbounded faith in the efficacy of offensive action.

The decline in numbers and vigor of the sturdy Italian peasantry, and the tremendous expansion of year-round Roman military commitments due to the steady growth of imperial dominion, had seriously compromised the Roman militia concept of annual levies. Rome was now, in effect, maintaining a standing army of professional soldiers whose trade was fighting. This was particularly true in the overseas provinces, since the government could not afford to send out new armies each year.

The civil and military administrations of the Roman state remained essentially identical, and while this continued to have a number of advantages in the ability of the nation to prosecute war, the decline of the militia system had a serious impact on the level of competence and military leadership. Professional politicians, eschewing the hardships of campaign as legionaries and junior officers, were frequently thrust into positions of military command for which they had little background, experience, or inclination. The general lack of trustworthiness of troops recruited mostly from the less reliable elements of the society reduced discipline and training; increasing lack of confidence between commander and troops created a tendency to reduce the intervals between the maniples of the legion, which began to approach the old Greek phalanx in battle order. This in turn decreased the inherent superiority of the Roman formation over those of its enemies, and contributed to a number of Roman defeats.

The Reforms of Marius

The disaster of Arausio (see p. 90) was the death knell of the old militia system. The efforts to raise new armies caused the state to confirm the professionalization of the army by enlisting men for terms of up to 16 years. It also caused one tough-minded Roman, ignoring sentimental and theoretical attachment to old virtues, to adapt the military system to the realities of the time.

During his terms as consul, Marius established a new system of organization which would continue to be effective through the early years of the Christian era. Though Caesar, too, introduced a number of refinements and adaptations, the armies with which he fought were essentially modeled on those created by Marius about the time of Caesar's birth. Regardless of his political shortcomings, Marius' military reforms entitle him to a place of honor in Roman history.

The old aristocratic distinctions between militia classes were eliminated, as were also the distinctions of age and experience which had led to the creation of hastati, principes, and triarii (though these terms continued to be used). This permitted interchange of units and individual soldiers, greater operational flexibility and maneuverability, increased efficiency in recruitment and replacement.

A complete and revised manual of drill regulations was produced by Publius Rufus (105), a colleague of Marius. Though later refined, particularly by Sulla, these were the regulations in effect in Caesar's time. Thus in this respect, as in others, the trend to professionalism in the army tended to offset the decline in martial spirit and in civic responsibility to the state.

The Marian Legion

Accepting the trend toward a phalangial formation, Marius made the cohort his major tactical organization. The maniple remained merely an administrative element within the cohort. Ten cohorts, 400–500 men each, continued to comprise a legion.

The cohort formed for battle in a line of 10 or 8 ranks, with a frontage of about 50 men. In close order, which was used for maneuvering and for massed javelin launching—but rarely for hand-to-hand combat—there was an interval of about 3 feet between men. This did not leave adequate room for wielding a sword, so the open formation, with 6 feet between men, was used for close combat. To permit rapid extension from close to open formation, it was necessary to keep an

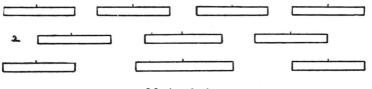

Marian legion

interval of one cohort's width between cohorts prior to actual engagement. Thus, with a legion formed in 2 or 3 lines, Marius was able (1) to retain the traditional flexibility and maneuverability of the legion by a cellular, checkerboard arrangement of cohorts (rather than maniples), (2) to keep the traditional sword-length interval between legionaries engaged in combat, and yet (3) at the same time to adapt this flexibility to the natural phalangial tendency by permitting a continuous front when engaged in close combat. It was a simple, brilliant, practical development, perpetuating the inherent virtues of the old legion.

The cohort formed battle line from marching column in 4's or 5's simply by closing up to massed double columns, then facing right or left. The marching evolutions to achieve this and various changes of front and direction were comparable to those of modern close-order drill.

The usual formation of the legion was 3 lines, with 4 cohorts in the first line, and 3 each in the second and third lines, alternatively covering the intervals of the lines to the front in the traditional **quincunx,** or checkerboard, concept. In 2-line formation, obviously, there were 5 cohorts to the line. On rare occasions the legion would be drawn up in one line and even more rarely in 4. The front of a cohort, about 120–150 feet, with an equal interval between cohorts, meant that in the normal 3-line formation the legion covered a front of about 1,000 feet. The distance between lines was usually about 150 feet, giving the legion in normal formation a depth of about 350 feet.

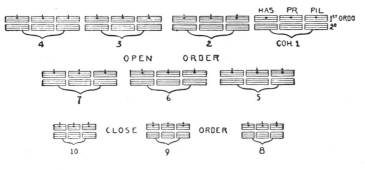

Caesar's legion

An army of 8 legions, then, with an average strength of 4,500 men per legion, would in the normal 3-line formation take up a front of about a mile and a half. The Marian legion, with some 13 men per yard of front, had about half the density of the Macedonian phalanx, which had had about 25 per yard.

The major defensive formations of the legion were the line, square, and circle. The line was usually a single line of 10 cohorts when formed behind fortifications or entrenchments. The square was formed from a normal 3-line formation by simple facing movements of 7 of the cohorts, leaving 3 facing front, while 3 faced the rear, and 2 to each flank. This, or its modification, the circle, was employed in defense against cavalry. Usually, however, if the flanks were protected by friendly horsemen or light auxiliary troops, the legion preferred to face the cavalry in its normal line formation; the combination of **pilum** (javelin), **scutum** (shield), and **gladius** (short sword) was usually too much for even the shock of the most desperate cavalry charge.

The standard of the legion was a silver replica of an eagle, wings outstretched, perhaps a foot in height, mounted on the top of a staff. The legion's eagle was revered perhaps even more than the colors of a modern military unit. Marius apparently regularized the system of legion insignia, which previously had included various other kinds of emblems. Each cohort had its own ensign, usually a device or a medallion of metal or wood, perhaps 6 inches in diameter, also carried on a staff or lance. Each maniple also had an ensign, to provide a rallying point like the modern company guidon. These were always a life-sized human fist, of wood or bronze, mounted on top of a lance, with other distinguishing symbols below it.

Light Infantry

A small but important component of the legion was its contingent of 10 scouts —**speculatores**. These formed, in effect, a kind of reconnaissance squad. The speculatores of several legions could be grouped for army reconnaissance missions.

Though not combined into legions, the light troops or auxiliaries of the Roman army were similarly organized in cohorts. Like the velites of old, these auxiliaries could operate in regular formation like the cohorts of the legion, as well as in their normal irregular skirmishing role to front and flank. Traditionally the best light infantry came from Liguria, in Cisalpine Gaul. As in centuries past, the best slingers came from the Balearic Islands, bowmen from Crete and other Aegean islands.

Cavalry

Under Marius the old Roman cavalry, made up of the **equites** or nobility, completely disappeared. The importance of cavalry, and its relative proportionate strength, increased however. Even more than formerly, therefore, the Romans relied upon allies and mercenaries to provide cavalry. In the time of Marius these came mostly from Thrace and Africa, and to a lesser extent from Spain. Caesar relied almost entirely upon Gallic and German mercenaries and allies to provide him with horsemen.

Naturally, therefore, the organization and discipline of the cavalry of the Roman Army were less formal and rigid than in the legion. The most forceful Roman commanders, however, were able to impose a substantial degree of regularity upon their horsemen. A **turma**, or troop, of cavalry consisted of 32 troopers under a **decurion** (sergeant), and was formed for battle in 4 ranks. Twelve turmae formed an **ala** (wing), the equivalent of a squadron, apparently commanded by an officer of rank equivalent to that of a tribune. The ala formed up in 2 or 3 lines, with intervals between the turmae, in a checkerboard formation similar to the cohorts of the legion.

The Legionary

The average soldier of the legion was an Italian peasant or lower-class city dweller. By Caesar's time all Italians were Roman citizens. The spread of the franchise throughout Italy was given much of its initial impetus by Marius, who, because of their conduct in action, gave Roman citizenship to allied cohorts at Vercellae (see p. 91), justifying this action to the Senate by saying that in the din of battle he could not distinguish the voice of the laws. But though the majority of the legionaries were still Italians in Caesar's day, there were growing numbers of other subject peoples and barbarians, some in separate legions, some intermingled with the Italians.

By the time of Marius the decline of the Roman military system had caused the loyalty of the soldier to be transferred from the state—as it had been in the days of the patriotic citizen militia—to the commanding general. The soldier swore allegiance to the general, who provided his daily pay—about 11 cents, the average wage of a day laborer in Rome. It was the general who gave the soldier opportunities for loot and plunder, and who obtained from the Senate, sometimes grudgingly, awards and retirement benefits (usually a plot of land) after the soldier had done with the campaigns. The average legionary was a tough, hard-bitten man, with values and interests—including a rough, heavy-handed sense of humor—comparable to those always found among professional private soldiers. Individually rarely more than 5'6" in height, robust and well muscled, the Italian legionary had a healthy respect for his huskier barbarian foes. In fact, until the time of Caesar, the almost unreasoning Roman fear of the Gauls and Germans—reinforced by the disaster of Arausio—was reflected in the individual emotions of even veteran soldiers. Yet they realized that regular formations and discipline made them militarily superior to the barbarians and, despite personal fears, under good leadership fought stanchly against Gauls and Germans.

Lacking the patriotic ardor of his militia predecessor, the professional Roman legionary under a leader like Marius, Sulla, or Caesar was at least equally tough in combat, and probably even more skillful in the essentials of drill and field campaigning.

Command and Administration

In the old militia army the centurions, tribunes, and staff officers were appointed to their positions each time a levy was made. A centurion one year might theoretically be a simple private the next time he was called to the ranks. With the professionalization of the army, a professional officer corps developed, divided into two main classes. The centurions, who still rose from the ranks, retained a permanent status as officers once they had proven their worth. But they rarely rose above the modern equivalent of company officer rank, though sometimes the senior centurion of the legion—the **primipilus**—would exercise command in battle. The primipilus normally carried the legion's revered eagle.

Officers of field rank—tribune and above—came from the aristocracy. The relationship between centurion and tribune was similar to that between sergeant and lieutenant in modern times.

Theoretically the command of the legion was still rotated among the 6 traditional tribunes, while each cohort was commanded by its senior centurion. It became common practice, however, to assign one officer—a legate—to command of a legion, with the tribunes acting as staff officers and commanding detached cohorts or task groups. Caesar made permanent assignments of legates to his legions.

As before, the general (**imperator**) was assisted by a small staff of quaestors, whose functions were primarily logistical and administrative. In addition, he was served by a group of volunteer aides—**comites praetori**—usually young aristocrats. To protect the general and his headquarters—the **praetorium**—there was now a special guard detachment, composed usually of veteran, trusted legionaries, called the **cohors praetorians.** Scipio Aemilianus had first created such a guard in the Numantian campaign (see p. 89). This was the origin of the famed Praetorian Guards of Imperial Rome.

The interrelationship of civil and military responsibilities exercised by the general and his staff facilitated administrative arrangements. The regimented, military nature of the early Republic had created in the Romans an almost inherent efficiency which was perpetuated, even if degraded, during the decline of the Republic. The combined civil-military organization of the outlying provinces greatly facilitated supply, logistics, and military administration in general. The ingrained efficiency of the Romans assured a smoothly functioning system of reporting, financial control, and the like.

Every army had an engineer detachment, skilled in the construction of bridges and the specialized structures of siege operations. They carried with them, on a special baggage train, tools and equipment needed for their missions, though their major reliance was on materials and lumber found on the scene of operations.

The Legion on Campaign

On the march a Roman army formed with advance, rear, and flank guards similar to those of modern armies. Each legion was usually accompanied by its baggage train of 500–550 mules. On these were carried skin tents—1 per 10 men—rations, the assigned ballistae and catapults, and miscellaneous equipment. In dangerous country the legion would often march in a square, with the train in the center. In flat, open country all the baggage trains could be assembled, with the entire army forming a large square as it advanced.

If action was likely, the soldier naturally wore his armor. To keep the size of baggage trains to a minimum, Marius insisted that the legionary carry his armor even on administrative marches. To make this easier, and also to help carry the normal 50-pound load of personal equipment and 15 days' rations, each man was given a forked stick—nicknamed "Marius' mule"—to permit him to hoist the load on his shoulder.

The practice of **castrametation**—preparing a fortified camp at the close of each day's march—was continued, and further developed by Caesar. Normally in a square or rectangle—with rounded corners for easier defense—the shape of the camp could vary with the details of terrain. A location next to a convenient source of water was important. It took 3 to 4 hours for the troops to dig the ditch, erect the rampart and palisade, lay out the streets, and pitch tents. The time was longer, of course, in hostile territory, when as much as a third or half of each legion mounted guard while the remainder made camp. If the encampment was prolonged, towers were usually built, the ditch deepened, and ramparts raised in the days subsequent to arrival. The only difference between the normal field camp and the camps for winter quarters was in the substitution of huts for the skin tents.

Traditionally, the camp was not only a measure of local security; it provided a Roman army with a base for offensive and defensive action wherever it might be, and was virtually a means for multiplying the combat value of the Roman soldier.

Battle Tactics

Whenever possible the Romans, like their enemies, tried to obtain the important advantage of being on higher ground than the foe. This added to the range of missiles, increased the shock effect of a charge while reducing the physical effort in making it, and even made it slightly easier to wield sword and spear. Usually—but not always—Caesar had his best cohorts in the first line, to get the maximum results from the initial shock of battle.

After the skirmishing and missile harassment by light troops had come to an end, the main battle lines approached each other. The legion deliberately advanced, or awaited the enemy, until the lines were about 20 yards apart. Then the first two ranks of the front lines hurled their javelins. Usually by this time the legion had adopted the open-order, semiphalangial formation, though sometimes this maneuver would be delayed until the javelins had been thrown.

Even on the defensive, for moral and physical effect, the legion almost always charged just before the actual hand-to-hand contact of the main battle lines. The first line—all 8 or 10 ranks—dashed violently against the foe, with the first 2 ranks only being able to employ their swords. The ranks behind would then throw their javelins over the heads of the melee. After a few minutes, the second set of 2 ranks would move forward to relieve the men already engaged, and so on, for as long as the fight lasted. Meanwhile, the rear-rank men would be resupplied with javelins by the light troops, who—in addition to protecting rear and flanks—had the mission of salvaging all usable javelins or darts they could find on the field.

Sometimes the initial clash of conflict would be delayed while all ranks of the first line threw their javelins, thus permitting 4 or 5 heavy volleys before the actual charge of the swordsmen.

If the first line was unable to prevail, or was hard-pressed, the second line would advance through the 6-foot intervals in the first line, and the first line would fall back to recuperate and reorganize. Finally, the third line was available, as the commander's reserve. Throughout the battle, therefore, there was incessant movement by ranks within lines, and between 2 or 3 main lines themselves. The discipline and organization which made this movement and replacement possible gave to the Romans a tremendous advantage over barbarian enemies, and is the main explanation why small Roman forces, under good leadership, were able consistently to defeat vastly larger aggregations of barbarians.

Even in drawn-out battles the casualties of a victorious army in antiquity were usually relatively light, while the losses of a defeated army were frequently catastrophic. This was particularly true of Roman battles. The large scutum (shaped like a segment of a cylinder) was probably the most efficient shield of antiquity, and its dexterous employment combined with helmet, breastplate, and greave (right leg only), gave the legionary excellent protection. But when ranks were broken, or an assault was received from flank or rear, the massed ranks of ancient armies were very vulnerable. It was rare that an army could be rallied after sustaining such a blow. Those who could escape, fled. The others were either slaughtered or captured. In a victorious army there were usually 3 to 10 times as many wounded as there were killed. In a defeated army few of the wounded survived.

There was growing use of small missile engines. By the time of Caesar each legion apparently had a complement of 30 small catapults and ballistae, each served by 10 men. These were primarily used in sieges, for defense of field fortifications, and to cover river crossings. Apparently they were also used on some open battlefields, during the preliminary phase and before the actual shock of heavy infantry lines.

THE GALLIC WARS, 58–51 B.C.

58. Caesar to Gaul. By agreement of the triumvirate, after he had served as consul Caesar was appointed governor of the Roman provinces of Gaul, as proconsul. His area of responsibility included Istria, Illyricum, Cisalpine Gaul (roughly the Po Valley of northern Italy), and the Province of Transalpine Gaul (roughly the French provinces of Provence, Dauphiné, and Languedoc).

58. Migration of the Helvetians. When Caesar took over his provinces at the beginning of the year, he discovered that the entire Helvetian people, a Gallic tribe inhabiting modern Switzerland, numbering 386,000, of whom more than 100,000 were warriors, were heading south for Gaul. Moving through the northern portion of the Province, they planned to concentrate on the Rhone by summer. Building a number of fortifications to block the main route of march of the Helvetians down the Rhone Valley, Caesar collected the scattered regular forces of the Province, and also accepted contingents from a number of Gallic tribes fearful of being overrun by the Helvetians (March–May). Finding their way blocked, the Helvetians continued their move westward, but across the wild Jura country north of the Rhone.

58, June. Battle of the Arar (Saône). Caesar with about 34,000 men caught the Helvetians in the process of crossing the Arar River. In a surprise attack, after a long night march, he overwhelmed and annihilated the 30,000-odd Helvetian warriors still on the east bank. The remainder of the horde continued west toward the Liger (Loire) River; Caesar followed cautiously.

58, July. Battle of Bibracte (Mount Beuvray.) Turning on Caesar, the Helvetians attacked. They still had about 70,000 warriors. Caesar had about 30,000 legionaries, about 20,000 Gallic auxiliaries, and 4,000 Gallic cavalry. Driving the Helvetians back to their camp, the Romans found the enemy's ranks swollen by women and children. In the violent struggle 130,000 Helvetians of all ages and sexes fell; Roman losses were heavy but are not known precisely. The remaining Helvetians submitted, and returned to their homes east of the Jura as demanded by Caesar.

58, August–September. Campaign against Ariovistus. A Germanic tribe, under the chieftain **Ariovistus,** had been terrorizing the Aedui, Sequani, and Arverni (Gallic tribes) in the region later comprising Alsace and Franche-Comté in France. The Gauls asked Caesar for assistance, and though the Romans were even more fearful and respectful of the Germans than of the Gauls, Caesar answered the call. Caesar and Ariovistus maneuvered cautiously in the region east of Vesontio (Besançon). Caesar had about 50,000 men; Ariovistus probably 75,000. Near modern Belfort, Mulhaus, or Cernay, Caesar found a favorable opportunity to attack (September 10). The Germans were completely routed; the remnants fled back across the Rhine, closely pursued by Caesar. Most of central Gaul now acknowledged Roman supremacy. Caesar went into winter quarters near Vesontio.

57. Campaign against the Belgae. The Belgae, collective name for the tough, Gallic-Germanic people of northeastern Gaul, were alarmed by Caesar's two successful campaigns along the southern fringes of their domains. They formed a coalition against the Romans, planning to march south with about 300,000 warriors. Caesar, learning of this, struck before they were ready. With about 40,000 legionaries and 20,000 Gallic auxiliaries, he invaded Belgica (probably April).

57, April–May. Battle of the Axona (Aisne). Hastily gathering a force of about 75–100,000, the Belgae, under **Galba,** King of Suessiones (Soissons), attempted to stop Caesar at the Axona. He defeated them, then pressed farther north into Belgica. A number of tribes submitted. But others, led by the Nervii, prepared for further conflict.

57, July. Battle of the Sabis (Sambre). Advancing with inadequate reconnaissance, Caesar was preparing to make camp on the banks of the Sabis when ambushed by an army of 75,000 Nervii. Fortunately the legions did not panic. The battle was desperate, Caesar going from legion to legion to fight in the front ranks and inspire his hard-pressed men. The Romans beat off the attacks, then seized the initiative. The Nervii suffered about 60,000 dead; Roman loss was also heavy.

57, September. Siege of Aduatuca (Tongres). Continuing into the country of the Aduatuci, Caesar besieged and captured their capital of Aduatuca. The Aduatuci treacherously attacked the Romans as they marched in the town. Caesar repelled the attacks, then overwhelmed the barbarians. Most of Belgica now submitted to the Romans. Caesar took up winter quarters along the line of the Loire, personally returning to Cisalpine Gaul to look after his political interests, as he did almost every winter he was in Gaul.

56. Campaign against the Veneti. During the winter the Veneti, inhabitants of Armorica (Brittany), seized some Roman ambassadors. At the same time scattered outbreaks against the Romans occurred throughout Gaul. Early in the spring Caesar, with three legions, advanced into Armorica, just north of the Loire. Another legion, under **Decimus Brutus,** manned a fleet hastily constructed near the mouth of the river. At the same time **Publius Crassus** (son of Caesar's triumvir partner), with a force slightly larger than a legion, invaded Aquitania (southwestern Gaul), which was becoming hostile to the Romans, while a small force under **Titus Labienus** patrolled the region near the Rhine, and another under **Q. Titurius Sabinus** was in modern Normandy. The campaign against the Veneti progressed slowly; a series of protracted sieges of small fortified towns. The decisive action was a naval battle in Quiberon Bay (or **Gulf of Morbihan**), under the eyes of Caesar and the Roman army. The light Roman galleys had difficulty coping with the powerful sailing vessels of the Veneti, but discovered they could disable the Gallic vessels by slashing the rigging with sickles tied on the ends of long poles. Suppression of the Veneti now proceeded rapidly, Caesar punishing the people severely for having mistreated his ambassadors. Meanwhile, Sabinus and Crassus had been successful against serious opposition in their respective areas of operations.

56, Fall. Campaign against Morini and Menapii. Caesar now moved to suppress dissident tribes in northwestern Belgica. He was frustrated by the Morini and Menapii tribes, most of whom sought refuge in the trackless seacoast marshes of the Low Countries; a few others escaped from the Romans in the wilderness of the Ardennes. Aside from these small areas of Belgica, all of Gaul was now under Roman domination.

55. Campaign Against the Germans. During the winter two Germanic tribes (Usipetes and Tencteri) crossed the Rhine into Gaul, establishing themselves on the lower Meuse, near modern Maastricht. Totaling about 430,000 souls in all, they had more than 100,000 warriors. Caesar marched to the Meuse and entered into negotiations with the Germans, with a view to persuading them to return to Germany (May). Discovering that they planned a treacherous attack under cover of the negotiations, Caesar decided to make an example of the invaders, to dissuade further German inroads. Using guile himself, he made a surprise attack during the negotiations, somewhere between the Meuse and Rhine rivers. He annihilated the Germanic armies, then massacred the women and children. There were no survivors. In Rome, Caesar's political enemies professed indignation at this cold-blooded act. Caesar, however, insisted that it had been necessary to prevent further Germanic inroads. He marched to the Rhine.

55, June. Crossing the Rhine. Near the site of modern Bonn, Caesar built a great bridge across the Rhine, in a memorable feat of engineering. He then marched into Germany, to further intimidate the German tribes. After receiving the submission of several tribes, he returned to Gaul, destroying his bridge.

55, August. First Invasion of Britain. With two legions, Caesar landed near **Dubra** (Dover), where he encountered serious opposition from the Britons on the beach; the landing was covered by catapults mounted on the ships. After some hard fighting, followed by a truce, Caesar returned to Gaul, having spent three weeks in Britain.

54, July. Second Invasion of Britain. With

Caesar's Rhine bridge

5 legions and 2,000 cavalry (about 22,-000 men), Caesar returned in a fleet of 800 small craft. He landed unopposed northeast of Dubra. After the debarkation a severe storm destroyed a number of vessels, and damaged others. A large force of Britons quickly gathered, under a chieftain named **Cassivellaunus.** Caesar marched inland, sweeping aside harassing Britons, crossing the Thames somewhere west of modern London. Cassivellaunus was unable to face the Romans in a major engagement. His diversionary attacks against the entrenched camp of the Roman fleet repulsed, he asked for peace near Verulamium (St. Albans). Caesar was apparently happy to halt the campaign and return to Gaul after receiving the nominal submission of the Britons.

54–53. Uprisings in Gaul. Unrest was seething throughout Gaul. The warlike tribes, who could probably muster more than 1,000,000 warriors, began to realize that they had been conquered by an army that rarely exceeded 50,000 men. The major uprising was led by **Ambiorix** of the Nervii. He seized the opportunity presented by the dispositions of small Roman detachments in 8 winter camps scattered across northern Gaul. Ambiorix first attacked Sabinus, near Aduatuca. He then offered Sabinus a safe-conduct to rejoin the other legions. When the Romans were on the march, they were attacked and annihilated. Ambiorix then attacked the fortified camp of **Quintus Cicero** near modern Binche. Repulsed, he tried to entice Cicero into the open, as he had with Sabinus; Cicero refused, so the siege continued. A messenger from Cicero reached Caesar in north-central Gaul. Gathering the nearest forces, totaling only 7,000 men, Caesar hastened to the rescue. Ambiorix with 60,000 men marched to meet him near the **Sabis,** leaving a strong force still besieging Cicero. Caesar, feigning indecision, enticed Ambiorix to undertake a careless attack, then counterattacked vigorously, driving the Gauls from the field. This exemplified Caesar's audacity and inspirational qualities. His never-failing luck was also working for him, but it was luck partly created by a restless energy and amazing vitality that always enabled him to seize the initiative from his foes, regardless of odds or circumstances. Marching on, Caesar relieved the hard-pressed forces of Cicero. Meanwhile, Labienus, who had also been under attack, had repelled his assailants and joined Caesar, who now consolidated his forces into more secure winter quarters.

53. Suppression of the Belgae. Caesar, who now had 10 legions, seized the initiative early in the spring, to crush the rebellions. In a systematic campaign, in which there was little fighting but considerable marching and pursuit, Caesar completely subdued Belgica. Since Ambiorix had been assisted by some Germans, Caesar again built a bridge and crossed the Rhine, to repeat his demonstrations in Germany. By the end of the summer the insurrection had been completely suppressed.

53–52. Revolt in Central Gaul. The conquered regions which Caesar considered most secure now revolted, under the leadership of Arverni chieftain **Vercingetorix,** by far the most able of Caesar's Gallic opponents. Raising an army in central Gaul, Vercingetorix trained and disciplined it in a manner hitherto unknown among the barbarians. Most of Caesar's legions were in northern Gaul, while Caesar himself was in Italy. Learning of the uprising, he hastened back to Gaul (January), to arrange for the protection of the Province, his main base in southern Gaul. Then, with a small force, he made a rapid, difficult march through the snow-covered Cevennes Mountains, evading Vercingetorix (February). Having reunited his forces north of the Loire, Caesar recaptured **Cenabum** (Orléans), where the rebellion originated, then turned to fight his way south to the heart of the rebellious territory, leaving Labienus to hold northern Gaul. As Caesar advanced, capturing town after town, Vercingetorix retreated in front of him, fighting a partisan war, destroying all food and supplies useful to the Romans.

52, March. Siege of Avaricum (Bourges). The Gallic defense was determined and skillful. Short of food, the Roman troops were in a serious situation. Vercingetorix, harassing the Romans constantly, tried to relieve the defenders. But Caesar, a master of the art of siegecraft, soon captured the town. He then marched rapidly south, hoping to capture Gergovia (Gergovie, near Puy-de-Dôme), capital of the Arverni, before it could be prepared for defense.

52, April–May. Siege of Gergovia. Vercingetorix, taking advantage of the natural strength of Gergovia, on a high, steep hill, was ready. Plentiful supplies had been gathered in the town, but the nearby country was denuded. The Roman situation became further complicated by the revolt of the remaining tribes of central and northern Gaul, including some who had been faithful Roman allies. Caesar sent for Labienus, before the Gauls could isolate and destroy his detachment. Endeavoring to obtain a quick solution at Gergovia, he tried an assault and was repulsed with heavy losses. Short of food, he now had no choice but to withdraw. He marched northward to meet Labienus, who had meanwhile won a battle at **Lutetia** (Paris), enabling him to march south without interference.

52, June (?). Retreat to the Province. Having united his army south of the Seine, and realizing that all his Gallic conquests were temporarily lost, Caesar now headed back to the Province, his main base, to refit and to get a new start. Furthermore, the seeds of rebellion were beginning to sprout even in that Romanized region of Gaul. Vercingetorix, with an army of 80,-000 infantry and 15,000 cavalry, probably the best Gallic army ever assembled, now attempted to intercept and to destroy Caesar in central Gaul. He took a position in the hills along the Vingeanne (a small tributary of the upper Saône) where he could block all possible routes by which Caesar could move from the Seine to the Saône Valley.

52, July (?). Battle of the Vingeanne. Caesar suddenly discovered the army of Vercingetorix in position on his line of march, but was alert and ready. After an indecisive cavalry skirmish, Vercingetorix retired without attempting to bring on a major engagement. Typically, Caesar grasped the initiative. He pursued.

52, July–October (?). Battle and Siege of Alesia. Vercingetorix retired to the strongly fortified mountaintop town of Alesia (Alise-Ste.-Reine, on Mount Auxois, near the source of the Seine River). He had over 90,000 men, Caesar had about 55,000, of whom approximately 40,000 were his legionaries, the remainder being auxiliaries, plus 5,000 faithful German-Gallic cavalry. Attacking vigorously, Caesar drove the Gauls inside the walls of Alesia. He built walls of contravallation and circumvallation, each about 14 miles in circumference. His wisdom in undertaking this formidable engineering feat was soon demonstrated. Responding to

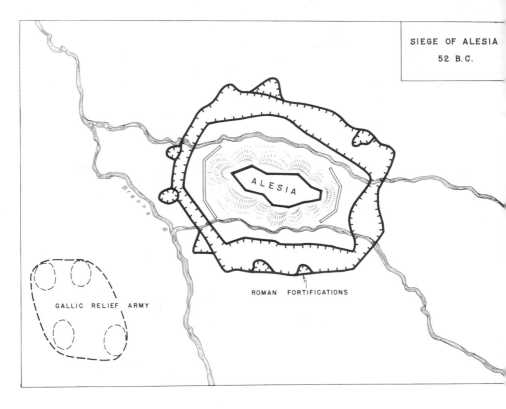

SIEGE OF ALESIA
52 B.C.

ALESIA

ROMAN FORTIFICATIONS

GALLIC RELIEF ARMY

Brienne R.

messages from Vercingetorix, a tremendous Gallic relief army, more than 240,000 in all, gathered around Alesia, besieging the besiegers. Caesar had collected large quantities of food, and had an assured water supply, so he calmly continued with his siege approaches to Alesia. He repulsed three relief attempts with heavy losses. To delay starvation, Vercingetorix tried to send out the women and children from Alesia, but Caesar refused to let them through his lines. The situation in Alesia was now hopeless. To save his people from further disasters Vercingetorix surrendered. (He was later taken to Rome for Caesar's triumph, then executed.) This defeat broke the back of the Gallic insurrection; most of the Gauls hastened to renew their fealty to Rome.

51. Final Pacification of Gaul. A few remaining embers of insurrection were squelched promptly and effectively. Caesar traversed the entire country, impressing indelibly on Gallic minds the power and glory of Rome, and his own skill and force of character. The Gallic Wars were

over, and Gaul would be an integral part of the Roman Empire for half a millennium to come.

THE GREAT ROMAN CIVIL WAR, 50–44 B.C.

50. Caesar Ordered to Return to Rome. Meanwhile Pompey, illegally appointed sole consul by the Senate (52), urged that body to order Caesar to give up his provinces, to disband his army, and to return to Rome, or else be declared a traitor. At this time Caesar, with one legion, was at Ravenna, in Cisalpine Gaul. Under Roman law, a general was forbidden to bring his forces into Italy proper without consent of the Senate. The southern boundary of Cisalpine Gaul on the Adriatic coast was the tiny Rubicon River, south of Ravenna.

49, January 11. Crossing of the Rubicon. Upon receipt of the Senate's order, Caesar immediately marched to the Rubicon. He made a night crossing, uttering his famous "The die is cast!" In addition to the one legion with him, he had 8 legions back in Transalpine Gaul, a total force of perhaps 40,000 first-rate veterans, plus about 20,000 auxiliaries and cavalry. Available to Pompey and the Senate were 2 legions in Italy, 7 in Spain, 8 more being raised in Italy, and at least nominal control of all Roman forces in Asia, Africa, and Greece, totaling perhaps 10 or more additional legions, plus an even larger number of auxiliary troops. Caesar hoped to make up for this great discrepancy in forces and resources by the energy which had brought him victory in Gaul. He marched rapidly southward along the Adriatic coast, collecting recruits and reinforcements en route. Pompey and most of the Senate abandoned Rome, seeking safety and adherents in the south. The only unfavorable news reaching Caesar was that his most able and trusted subordinate, Labienus, former lieutenant of Pompey, had defected to his old leader. All Caesar's other legates and all his legions remained steadfastly loyal.

49, January–February. Flight of Pompey. Not trusting the legions in Italy, and having been too slow in raising the forces he had ordered mobilized, Pompey fled to Epirus from Brundisium (Brindisi), taking 25,000 troops and much of the Senate with him. He retained control of the Roman navy. Caesar, in Rome, thereupon consolidated his position in Italy, and wrestled with his difficult strategic problem. Lacking control of the sea, he would have to go overland through Illyricum to get at Pompey in Greece. To do this would leave Gaul and his communications through Cisalpine Gaul exposed to the powerful Pompeian force in Spain. Boldly, he counted on Pompey's lethargy in Greece to give him time to dispose of the threat in Spain.

49, March 9. March to Spain. Caesar said, "I set forth to fight an army without a leader, so as later to fight a leader without an army." He left **Marcus Aemilius Lepidus** as prefect of Rome; the remainder of Italy was under **Marcus Antonius** (Mark Antony), Illyria under Gaius Antonius, Cisalpine Gaul under **Licinius Crassus**; **Gaius Curio** was sent to gain control of Sicily and Africa.

49, March–September. Siege and Battle of Massilia (Marseille). Lucius Domitius Ahenobarbus, a supporter of Pompey, arrived by sea at Massilia with a small force of troops, and persuaded the city to declare for Pompey. Caesar, who had sent most of his army ahead to seize the passes over the Pyrenees, quickly invested Massilia with 3 legions (April 19). Then he hastened off to Spain, leaving **Gaius Trebonius** to prosecute the siege. He also left Decimus Brutus to raise a naval force to blockade Massilia from the sea. The siege continued throughout Caesar's campaign in Spain, and was marked by Brutus' victory over the Pompeian-Massilian naval forces in a battle off the city.

49, June. Arrival in Spain. Caesar's troops meanwhile had seized the Pyrenees passes barely in time to forestall a Pompeian army of about 65,000 men under **L. Afranius** and **M. Petreius.** Frustrated in their plan to block the passes, Afranius and Petreius waited for Caesar at Ilerda (Lerida). Two more Pompeian legions, plus about 45,000 auxiliaries, held the rest of Spain, under **Vibellius Rufus** and **M. Varro.** Caesar advanced into northern Spain with about 37,000 men, confronting the Pompeian force at Ilerda.

49, July–Aug. Ilerda Campaign. Both sides were anxious to avoid battle; Caesar because of the preponderance of force against him, Afranius and Petreius because of their respect for Caesar's reputation. Gaining and keeping the initiative by maneuvering and skirmishing, Caesar decided to try to capture rather than destroy the Pompeian army. Thus he would not only avoid a major bloodletting among Romans, but also might be able to add recruits to his own army. Discouraged by Caesar's energy, Afranius and Petreius decided to withdraw, only to have their retreat cut off by Caesar's rapid movements. They returned to Ilerda, where Caesar surrounded them and cut off their water supply (July 30).

49, Aug. 2. Surrender at Ilerda. Afranius and Petreius surrendered; their legions were disbanded. Caesar, gaining some recruits, as he hoped, immediately marched south as far as Gades (Cádiz) to impress his authority on Spain. Then, leaving a small force to complete domination of the unruly province, he hastened back to Massilia.

49, Aug. 24. Defeat of Curio in Africa. Caesar's legate, Gaius Curio, had established Caesar's authority in Sicily without trouble. In Africa, however, he was opposed by a Pompeian force under **Attius Varus,** in alliance with **Juba,** King of Numidia. After defeating the allies near **Utica,** Curio was defeated at the **Bagradas River,** thus assuring Pompeian hold over Africa. Curio killed himself rather than surrender.

49, September 6. Surrender of Massilia. When Caesar arrived from Spain, Massilia surrendered, Domitius escaping by sea. Caesar hastened to Rome to discover that his small fleet in the Adriatic had been defeated near **Curicta** (Krk).

49, October (?). Caesar Appointed Dictator. That portion of the Senate remaining in Rome appointed him dictator. From that time on Caesar was a virtual monarch. This was the end of the Roman Republic. Finding Italy calm and peaceful, he prepared to move to Greece after Pompey. Despite Pompey's control of the sea, Caesar decided to risk the crossing over the Adriatic with 12 understrength legions.

48, January 4. Caesar Sails from Brundisium (Brindisi). Using every available vessel, Caesar was able to take with him only 7 legions and a few cavalry, about 25,000 men in all. His fabulous luck stayed with him, and he avoided Pompey's fleet, landing south of Pompey's base at Dyrrhachium (Durazzo). Caesar sent his vessels back to Brundisium to pick up Mark Antony, whom he had left in command of the 20,000 men remaining there. But Pompey's fleet, now alerted, blockaded Antony in Brundisium.

48, January – February. Maneuvering around Dyrrhachium. After Caesar landed, Pompey moved from eastern Epirus to Dyrrhachium, forestalling Caesar's plan to seize the town. By this time Pompey had raised an army of about 100,000 men, including a number of veterans, but the quality of his troops was inferior to Caesar's. Strangely, Pompey made no effort to take advantage of his 4-to-1 numerical superiority by forcing Caesar to battle. Caesar, in fact, seized the initiative in a series of bold but careful maneuvers south of Dyrrhachium.

48, March. Arrival of Antony. Sneaking out of Brundisium, Antony landed north of Dyrrhachium with the remainder of Caesar's army. Pompey moved promptly eastward, intending to defeat Caesar's divided forces in detail. But Caesar was even more prompt. He linked forces with Antony at Tirana, then cut Pompey off from his base at Dyrrhachium by a clever march through the mountains. This did not cause Pompey serious difficulty, since he still controlled the sea, and was able to maintain contact with his base on the coast a few miles south of Dyrrhachium.

48, April–July. Siege of Dyrrhachium. Pompey, realizing that the countryside was denuded of food, and having access by sea to plentiful supplies in Dyrrhachium, decided to avoid battle and to let Caesar's army starve. Caesar, however, was able to keep his army fed, and began a bold and amazing investment of an army more than twice the size of his own, building a chain of redoubts and ramparts around Pompey's beachhead. Pompey immediately built a similar line of fortifications, while skirmishing was conducted all along the line.

48, July 10. Battle of Dyrrhachium. Pompey, who had been cut off from water and fodder for his horses by Caesar's investment, now mounted simultaneous attacks on both ends of Caesar's wall of contravallation. With his great numerical superiority, and with the assistance of his fleet, he had no trouble breaking through. Faced with apparent disaster, Caesar rallied his men, collected his army, and withdrew successfully into Thessaly. His losses were more than 1,000 killed; Pompey's were much less. Pompey, failing to take advantage of his victory, followed cautiously, leaving a strong garrison in Dyrrhachium.

48, July–Aug. Caesar, obtaining supplies, regrouped in Thessaly. He now had about 30,000 infantry in his 12 thin legions, plus 1,000 cavalry. Pompey had about 60,000 infantry and 7,000 cavalry. The armies camped on opposite sides of the plain of Pharsalus. Caesar, typically, attempted to entice his enemy to battle. Pompey, typically, sat still.

BATTLE OF PHARSALUS, AUGUST 9, 48 B.C.

Finally Pompey decided to try to overwhelm Caesar's numerically inferior army. He formed a line of battle on the plain between the two opposing camps. Caesar at once advanced to fight. With his left flank resting securely on the steep bank of the Enipeus River, he realized that the chief danger lay on his right, where his cavalry was outnumbered 7 to 1 by Pompey's horsemen. He formed his legions in the customary 3 lines, but held out 6 cohorts—about 2,000 men—to cover his

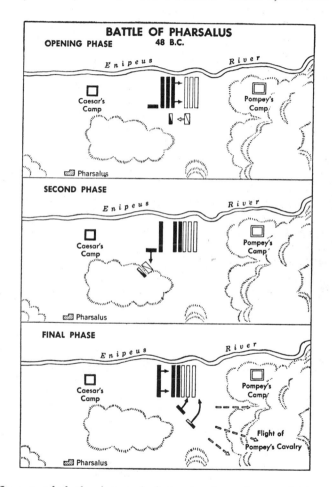

right rear. He extended the intervals between the cohorts of his main body, to match the frontage of Pompey's army, drawn up in normal formation. The 6 cohorts Caesar had held out were posted behind his right flank to support his cavalry (see diagram). The third line of his main body was, as usual, held out as a reserve to the first 2 lines. Caesar took his own post initially with the 6 cohorts—the so-called "Fourth Line"—on the right rear.

His dispositions completed, Caesar ordered his first 2 lines of infantry to attack the motionless army of Pompey. At the moment of impact, Pompey launched his cavalry, supported by archers and slingers, against Caesar's small contingent of horse. These fought stubbornly, but were forced back by weight of numbers. At the decisive moment, Caesar personally led his selected force of 6 cohorts against the flank of Pompey's advancing horsemen. Scattering the surprised cavalry, the small contingent pushed on, slaughtered the archers and slingers, then turned against the left flank of Pompey's main body. Caesar then galloped to join his third line, which he led through the intervals of the first 2 to smash into the front of the Pompeian legions. This charge, combined with the surprise envelopment by the 6 cohorts, broke Pompeian resistance. Pompey and his army fled to their camp. Without pause Caesar followed, stormed the camp, and, without letting his men stop to plunder, pursued the fugitives. Pompey fled in disguise; reaching the coast with only 30 horsemen, he embarked on a vessel and sailed to Egypt. In this decisive battle Caesar lost 230 killed and perhaps 2,000 wounded; Pompey lost 15,000 killed and wounded and 24,000 prisoners. The Roman provinces and protectorates of Greece and Asia immediately declared for Caesar. Only Juba and the Pompeians in Africa continued to defy him, while Egypt and seething Spain remained uncertain.

Operations in Egypt, 48–47 B.C.

48, August–September. Pursuit of Pompey. Caesar, with only 4,000 men, pursued Pompey to Egypt. At Alexandria he learned that Pompey had been assassinated by his associates (September 28). These former Pompeians, however, succeeded in arousing young **Ptolemy XII,** co-ruler with his sister **Cleopatra,** to defy Caesar. With his handful of men, Caesar was besieged in a corner of Alexandria by an army of 20,000, led by the young king and his Roman advisers.

48, August–47, January. Siege of Alexandria. Caesar held only a portion of Alexandria, and part of the eastern harbor. Disdaining flight, he sent for help while vigorously defending himself. Help was slow to arrive, however, since the former Pompeians still controlled the sea. Nevertheless, land and naval reinforcements trickled in, and Caesar was able to prevent a sea blockade by narrow victories in two desperate naval engagements just outside the harbor. Endeavoring to extend his control over the entire harbor, he was repulsed in a battle on the mole leading out to the harbor entrance. Then his ships were defeated in a third naval engagement nearby.

47, January. With his future bleak, Caesar learned of the arrival at the Nile River of a small army which had been led overland from Asia Minor by his ally, **Mithridates** of Pergamum (not to be confused with either Mithridates of Pontus or Mithridates of Parthia). Leaving a small garrison to hold his positions in Alexandria, Caesar slipped out of the city to join Mithridates. Ptolemy and the Roman-Egyptian army followed. The sizes of the opposing forces are unknown, but each probably totaled about 20,000 men.

47, February. Battle of the Nile. Caesar and Mithridates completely defeated Ptolemy, who was killed. Caesar then relieved his beleaguered forces in Alexandria.

47, February–March. Caesar established complete control over Egypt, placing on the throne with Cleopatra her still younger brother, **Ptolemy XIII.** For nearly two months Caesar lingered in Egypt, engaged in amorous dalliance with Cleopatra.

Pontic Campaign, 47 B.C.

BACKGROUND. Meanwhile in Asia Minor, **Pharnaces,** King of Bosporus Cimmerius (Crimean region), son of Mithridates of Pontus, had taken advantage of the Roman civil war to recreate his father's kingdom of Pontus. He extended his domains along the northern coast of Asia Minor and into Cappadocia, having defeated **Domitius Calvinus,** a subordinate of Caesar, in the **Battle of Nicopolis** (Nikopol) (October, 48).

47, April–May. Caesar Leaves for Pontus. Sailing from Alexandria to Syria with a portion of his army, Caesar collected reinforcements from the Roman garrison of Syria, then rapidly marched north through Asia Minor.

47, May. Battle of Zela. Caesar, met in Pontus by Pharnaces, in greater strength, was victorious. He sent to Rome his famous message: **"Veni, vidi, vici."** ("I came, I saw, I conquered.") He then reorganized the eastern dominions, giving to his ally Mithridates of Pergamum nominal rule over the kingdom of Pharnaces.

47, August. Mutiny. Caesar, back in Rome, was soon faced by mutiny of many of his veterans, who felt they should be discharged and rewarded for their efforts. He subdued the mutineers by personal leadership, then enlisted most to accompany him to Africa.

Operations in Africa, 47-46 B.C.

47, October. Invasion of Africa. Having concentrated an army of 25,000 in Sicily, Caesar sailed for Africa. There stood the remnants of the Pompeian forces defeated in Spain and Greece. In command was **Metellus Scipio**, assisted by—among others—Caesar's former lieutenant, Labienus. This army of more than 50,000 men was combined with a Numidian force of nearly equal size under Juba, and was supported by the formidable Pompeian fleet.

47, October–November. Operations around Ruspina. Though Caesar evaded the Pompeian fleet, his own squadron was scattered by a storm as it approached the eastern Tunisian coast, and he landed at Ruspina (Monastir) with a handful of troops. His opponents failed to seize this opportunity. By the time Labienus approached with a Roman-Numidian army of 60,000 men, most of Caesar's scattered units had joined him. Somewhat recklessly, Caesar with 12,000 men let himself be cut off from his base at Ruspina and completely surrounded by Labienus. His former lieutenant, however, was reluctant to press an all-out attack with light troops. Caesar, in a series of intricate maneuvers, followed by an attack against one portion of the encircling line, broke out and made his way back to Ruspina, where he was soon blockaded by the entire army of Scipio and Juba, more than 100,000 strong.

47, December–46, January. Maneuvers around Utica. Having collected all his scattered army, and having received reinforcements, Caesar again marched inland with 40,000 men, seizing the initiative in typical energetic maneuvers between Ruspina, Utica, and Thapsus. He laid siege to Thapsus, inviting an attack.

46, February. Battle of Thapsus. Desertions and illness had reduced the Pompeian-Numidian army to about 60,000. However, they attacked Caesar's positions outside of Thapsus, and were utterly defeated. Caesar's casualties were less than 1,000; Scipio and Juba lost more than 10,000 dead; at least as many more were wounded and captured. The remainder scattered, a few fleeing to Spain, where the Pompeian banner had been raised once more by Pompey's young sons. Having subdued Africa, Caesar returned to Rome (May).

Operations in Spain, 46-45 B.C.

46, December. Return to Spain. Caesar sailed to Spain with a small contingent of veterans. Upon arrival there he took command of the forces he had left after the Ilerda campaign. His total strength was about 40,000.

45, January–March. Corduba Campaign. Discovering that young **Gnaeus Pompey**, with 50–60,000 men, was in the neighborhood of Corduba (Cordova), Caesar marched there, and at once commenced his typical maneuvering and skirmishing. Apparently Labienus exercised field command of the Pompeian army, which retreated southward to the support of its fleet on the seacoast, meanwhile hoping to entice Caesar to battle on favorable terrain.

45, March 17. Battle of Munda. (Exact modern location unknown, probably the modern village of Montilla, north of the Singulis [Aguilar] River.) Finding Pompey and Labienus drawn up for battle on a formidable hill position, Caesar reluctantly decided to attack, impelled by his desire to prevent Pompey's escape, and by the aggressive confidence of his legions. Having halted Caesar's initial uphill attack, Pompey counterattacked and came very close to success. Caesar suppressed panic only by personally rushing into the center of the fight, first with one legion, then with another. The protracted struggle was perhaps the most bitterly contested of Caesar's battles. Finally, under his personal inspiration, his men began to forge ahead up the hill, breaking through the center of the Pompeian line. Resistance then collapsed, and the battle became a massacre, 30,000 Pompeians being killed, among them Labienus. Gnaeus Pompey was captured and executed; his younger brother, **Sextus**, escaped, to join the remnants of the Pompeian fleet, with which he conducted piratical operations for several years. Caesar lost more than 1,000 killed and at least 5,000 wounded.

45, March–July. From Spain to Rome. Caesar again marched through Spain, resubjugating the province, then returned to Rome, where he busied himself with the political, economic, and legal affairs of the Roman state, of which he was now the uncrowned but undisputed monarch.

44, March 15. Assassination of Caesar. Caesar was assassinated in the Senate by a group of conspirators including sincere democrats alarmed by his autocratic despotism, as well as former Pompeians and a number of his own disgruntled adherents. Among these latter were two of his favored subordinates, **Marcus Junius Brutus** and Caesar's distant kinsman, the naval leader, Decimus Brutus. (If he uttered his famous *"Et tu Brute!"* it was probably to the latter.)

COMMENT. *Probably lacking the superlative, balanced military genius of Alexander or Hannibal, Caesar was, nonetheless, one of the greatest generals of world history. His energy and audacity have never been excelled, and his charismatic leadership inspired the devotion of his soldiers to a degree matched by few other great leaders. His one serious military weakness was in carrying audacity to the extreme of recklessness, as at Dyrrhachium, Alexandria, and Ruspina. No general has ever been luckier, and this of course was because to a great extent he made his own luck by seizing and maintaining the initiative. No other man has ever matched his unique combination of talents: genius as a politician, statesman, lawgiver, and classic author, in addition to being a great captain.*

THE STRUGGLE FOR POWER, 44–43 B.C.

44, March–October. Confusion and Apathy. Despite severe denunciations by Mark Antony, the surviving consul and Caesar's most trusted subordinate, no punitive action was taken against the conspirators who had assassinated Caesar. Decimus Brutus went to Cisalpine Gaul to take over the governorship of the province, with Senatorial approval; Marcus Brutus became governor of Macedonia; **Gaius**

Cassius Longinus, the ringleader of the conspirators and an experienced soldier, took over the governorship of Syria. These conspirators, with some connivance from friends in the Senate, planned to raise sufficient forces in their provinces to be able to return to Rome to re-establish the Republic. During this period 18-year-old **Gaius Julius Caesar Octavianus** (or **Octavian**), nephew and civil heir of Julius Caesar, appeared on the scene. Mark Antony considered himself Caesar's successor, and refused to accept Octavian as Caesar's political heir. Antony, Octavian, and the Republicans maneuvered to gain political power and to raise forces for the violent struggle which was inevitable. Octavian increased his importance by raising a substantial force from among Caesar's veterans, whom the great general had settled in Campania.

44, November. Octavian Takes the Field. Though he despised Decimus Brutus as one of his uncle's assassins, young Octavian had apparently formulated a long-range plan to ally himself temporarily with Brutus in order to eliminate Antony and achieve complete control over Rome. With the force he had raised, he marched north to Cisalpine Gaul to join Brutus. Though he was only a mediocre soldier, he soon proved himself one of the ablest politicians of history.

44, December–43, April. Siege of Mutina. Antony marched north to Cisalpine Gaul, and besieged Brutus in Mutina (Modena). The new consuls, **Aulus Hirtius** and **C. Vibius Pansa,** Republicans, came to Cisalpine Gaul to support Brutus and Octavian. Joining forces with Octavian, the two consuls advanced toward Mutina.

43, April 14. Battle of Forum Gallorum. Leaving his brother **Lucius** to continue the siege of Mutina, Antony marched to meet the threat. A few miles east of Mutina he defeated Pansa, who was killed. But, while Antony's men were celebrating their victory, Hirtius came unexpectedly on the scene and routed them. Antony rallied the fugitives and withdrew to Mutina.

43, April 21. Battle of Mutina. Antony had the worst of another battle against Hirtius, though the consul was killed. Antony withdrew westward, crossing the Apennines into Liguria, and then going to the Province of Transalpine Gaul, to join Aemilius

Lepidus, one of Caesar's loyal adherents. Soon after this Decimus Brutus was killed by brigands.

43, August. Octavian Seizes Power. Returning to Rome, Octavian forced the Senate to declare him consul. He then made the Senate outlaw Caesar's assassins and acknowledge him as Caesar's heir under the terms of Caesar's will.

43, November. The Second Triumvirate. Octavian marched north again to Cisalpine Gaul with the intention of reaching an accommodation with Antony. At Bononia (Bologna) he reached an agreement with Antony and Lepidus to establish joint rule over the empire, and to punish the assassins of Caesar.

WARS OF THE SECOND TRIUMVIRATE, 43–34 B.C.

43–42. Brutus and Cassius in the East. Marcus Brutus and Cassius, establishing control over their provinces of Macedonia and Syria, seized the wealth of subject cities and protectorates to raise funds to support their armies. They met at Sardis (July, 42), their combined forces totaling about 80,000 infantry and 20,000 cavalry. They then returned across the Hellespont to Thrace (September).

42, September. Antony and Octavian to Greece. Antony and Octavian, with about 85,000 infantry and 13,000 cavalry, moved to Epirus from Brundisium. When their advance elements, moving northeastward, made contact with the Republicans near Philippi, Antony hastened ahead with most of the army, leaving ailing Octavian to follow more slowly. Throughout this entire campaign Antony was the principal triumvirate leader.

42, October 3. First Battle of Philippi. Discovering the Republicans in two fortified camps west of Philippi, Antony carefully planned a surprise attack through a swamp against the camp of Cassius, south of Brutus'. The attack was successful, but at the same time Brutus unexpectedly advanced against the left wing of the triumvirate army, smashing it, temporarily seizing its camp, and forcing Octavian to flee. Thus the honors and casualties were about even in this strange battle. But Cassius, the most able Republican leader, had committed suicide when he thought the Republican army had been defeated.

42, October 23. Second Battle of Philippi. The relative positions of the opposing armies were unchanged. Antony, hoping to cut the communications of the Republican army, again advanced secretly through the swamp, to envelop Brutus' left flank. At the same time Octavian, with the remainder of the army, attracted Brutus' attention to the front. In the ensuing battle south of Philippi, Antony routed the Republicans. Brutus escaped with about 4 legions, but committed suicide soon after, bringing the war to a close. The triumvirs now returned to their agreed areas of responsibility: Octavian and Lepidus in the west, Antony to the east. In Cilicia Antony met Cleopatra, Queen of Egypt, and followed her to Egypt, to begin one of the most famous and most fateful love affairs of history.

41. Perusian War. Lucius Antonius (brother of Mark Antony) who had become consul, clashed with Octavian. Civil war flared; Lucius was supported by **Fulvia,** wife of Mark Antony. Both were defeated and captured by Octavian at **Perusia** (Perugia). Fulvia soon died.

40–36. Octavian's War with Sextus Pompey. Sextus, younger son of Pompey the Great (see pp. 93 ff.), subjugated Sardinia, Sicily, Corsica, and the Peloponnese, threatening the vital grain route to Rome from Africa. This caused desultory hostilities between him and Octavian.

40. Treaty of Brundisium. Shortly after the Battles of Philippi, the conflict between Octavian and Antony's brother and wife brought the leaders to the brink of war. Allying himself briefly with Sextus Pompey, Antony landed near Brundisium with a small army. Octavian, however, negotiated an agreement whereby Antony agreed to support him against Pompey, in return for assistance in a proposed invasion of Parthia. A revised division of the empire was also agreed upon: Octavian to have Italy, Dalmatia, Sardinia, Spain, and Gaul; Lepidus to retain only Africa; Antony to have everything to the east. The agreement was cemented by Antony's marriage to **Octavia,** sister of Octavian.

38. Uprisings in Gaul and Germany. M. Vipsanius Agrippa, sent by Octavian, successfully put down disorders along the Rhine.

37. Treaty of Tarentum. The agreement of Brundisium (see above) was reaffirmed. Antony loaned 130 warships to Octavian to help against Sextus Pompey; Octavian in turn loaned Antony 1,000 men and promised 4 legions for the invasion of Parthia.

36, June–October. Antony's Invasion of Parthia. With an army of about 60,000 infantry and 10,000 cavalry, Antony moved via the Euphrates into Armenia, past Erzerum and Mount Ararat through Tabriz into Media Atropatene (Azerbaijan) southward as far as Phraaspa. There he encountered **Phraates IV** of Parthia. In an action reminiscent of Carrhae, Antony lost his siege train, and suffered heavy casualties, but repulsed the Parthian attacks, and extricated his army—losing 30,000 men in the process.

36, September 3. Battle of Naulochus (or Mylae). Octavian's fleet, commanded by his loyal lieutenant, M. V. Agrippa, defeated the fleet of Sextus Pompey, ending the war. In this victory the revolutionary new harpax played a major role (see p. 84). Meanwhile Lepidus had brought an army to Sicily, ostensibly to support Octavian but actually intending to seize the island himself. His army mutinied and surrendered to Octavian, who kept Lepidus in luxurious captivity in Rome until his death 23 years later.

34. Border Expeditions of Octavian and Antony. Octavian successfully pacified Dalmatia, Illyricum, and Pannonia. At the same time Antony, to punish the Parthians for repeated invasions of Syria, led another invasion. Though unable to win a clear-cut victory, he succeeded in regaining Armenia.

WAR OF OCTAVIAN AGAINST ANTONY, 33–30 B.C.

33. Rupture between Antony and Octavian. Antony's repudiation of his marriage to Octavia, and his subsequent marriage to Cleopatra—who had already borne him three children—hastened the inevitable break. Octavian aroused the people of Rome and of Italy against Antony and Cleopatra by a vicious propaganda attack against Cleopatra, pictured as seeking to gain dominion over Rome and its empire.

32. Declaration of War. The Senate declared war against Cleopatra and divested Antony of his triumviral title.

32, April–May. Antony and Cleopatra to Greece. Octavian convinced the Romans that this movement of an army and a powerful fleet to Greece was preparatory to an invasion of Italy. It seems clear, however, that Antony's objective was merely to discourage an Octavian invasion of the east. His army consisted of about 73,000 infantry and 12,000 cavalry. The fleet comprised about 480 vessels, with aggregate crews of nearly 150,000 men. They kept their fleet and army in winter quarters near Actium (Punta) on the west coast of Greece (32–31).

32–31. Octavian Prepares for Combat. He assembled a powerful army of 80,000 infantry and 12,000 cavalry at Brundisium. His fleet of more than 400 vessels, under Agrippa, was at Tarentum.

31. Octavian Crosses to Greece. Early in the year, while Agrippa demonstrated against Antony's and Cleopatra's supply line along the west coast of Greece, Octavian crossed the Adriatic to Illyricum and Epirus. With most of his army he marched south to seize and fortify a strong position 5 miles north of Actium. Meanwhile, by seizing islands and key points along the Greek coast, Agrippa had broken the Antonine supply line to Egypt and Asia (June). Antony and Cleopatra apparently decided that their best hope would be a naval battle, though doubtful of the loyalty of a substantial portion of their fleet. In any event, they felt that in the event of defeat they could outsail Agrippa's ships, leaving the army under **P. Crassus Canidus** to try to fight its way overland to Syria and Egypt.

31, September 2. Battle of Actium. The 2 fleets were almost equal in strength, each having more than 400 vessels. Agrippa's fleet was formed in 2 wings and a center, each about equal in strength. These were opposed by 3 similar, but smaller elements under Antony; Cleopatra commanded a reserve squadron of more than 60 vessels. Both Agrippa and Antony planned to envelop each other's north flank. The result was an immediate and violent struggle on that flank, in which Antony at first had

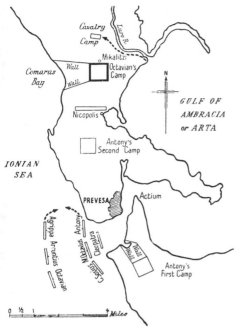

Battle of Actium

well as a profligate, fascinating woman. A measure of her stature is the fact that of all Rome's enemies only Hannibal had ever been more feared and hated in the city on the Tiber.

THE BEGINNINGS OF IMPERIAL ROME AND THE PAX ROMANA, 30–1 B.C.

29. Octavian's Triumphal Return to Rome. Granted the title of imperator which had been held by his uncle, Octavian dominated Rome. For the third time in Roman history the doors of the Temple of Janus were closed; Rome was at peace. Octavian began immediately to build up the imperial system of Rome, being careful, however, like Caesar before him, to retain the forms of republican democracy.

27. Octavian Becomes Augustus. The Senate conferred on Octavian the semigodly name of **Augustus**, by which he is known to history as the first emperor of Rome.

27–1 B.C. Military Reforms. Augustus reduced the army from an over-all strength of about 501,000 to about 300,000—25 legions, of 6,000 men each, and an approximately equal number of auxiliaries. Almost all of these were stationed to guard the frontiers of outlying provinces. In addition he created the Praetorian Guard—10 cohorts of 1,000 each—to give himself a private army to control Rome and Italy, without appearing to station regular troops near the capital. The soldiers of this new army were enlisted for terms of 20 years, and were promised bounties of land upon discharge. Noncitizens of the *auxilia* were also granted automatic citizenship for themselves and their families upon discharge.

20. Treaty with Parthia. By a policy of mixed conciliation and firmness, Augustus made a favorable treaty with Parthia. Phraates IV recognized Roman sovereignty over Armenia and Osroene (upper Mesopotamia), and also returned the eagles and other standards captured from Crassus and Antony.

20–1 B.C. Operations along the Northern Frontiers. Peace and prosperity settled over the Roman Empire, and existed along most of its frontiers. There were a few military operations, however. **Marcus**

slightly the better of the engagement. But almost at once the unfaithful center and left wings of the Antonine fleet either fled back into Actium or surrendered. Seeing that the situation was hopeless, Antony signaled to Cleopatra to escape, then tried to fight his own way clear to the open sea. Despite the odds, the fight was desperate. Antony's flagship being held by a harpax, he changed to another vessel. With a few of his ships he succeeded in breaking away, joining Cleopatra in flight to Egypt. On land Canidus tried to break out, according to plan, but almost all of his army mutinied and surrendered to Octavian, whose victory was complete and decisive.

0, July. Octavian Invades Egypt. Antony, in the depths of despondency since Actium, aroused himself to repulse Octavian's initial advance on Alexandria. Then, being misinformed that Cleopatra had committed suicide, he killed himself. Cleopatra surrendered, but upon learning that she would be led as a captive through the streets of Rome in Octavian's triumph, she too killed herself, probably by permitting herself to be bitten by a snake. Aged 39, she had proven herself a courageous, resourceful, and able national leader, as

Lollius, legate on the Rhine, was defeated by a horde of German invaders (16). Augustus himself went to Gaul, while sending his stepsons **Tiberius** and **Drusus** on successful punitive expeditions into Raetia and Pannonia. Drusus, after a hard-fought battle against great odds at the **Battle of the Lupia** (Lippe) **River** (11), continued to push Roman control toward the Elbe, until his death (9). Meanwhile, Tiberius and Drusus had also suppressed another revolt in Pannonia (12–9). Tiberius then completed the methodical advance to the Elbe (9–7).

SOUTHWEST ASIA

PARTHIA AND ARMENIA

188. Independence of Armenia. Following the defeat of Antiochus III by Rome (see p. 86), Armenia, nominally subject to the Seleucids, asserted her independence.

c. 175. Expansion of Parthia. Phraates I conquered the region along the south shores of the Caspian Sea, hitherto nominally owing allegiance to the Seleucid emperors.

c. 170–c. 160. War between Parthia and Bactria. A long and inconclusive war between Mithridates I of Parthia (171–138) and Eucratides of Bactria finally ended with the Parthians gaining control of some border regions of Turania.

166–163. Antiochus IV Reconquers Armenia. (See p. 87.)

163–150. Parthian Expansion. Mithridates I conquered Media. He continued to press west and southwest against the declining Seleucid Empire, as well as eastward against waning Bactrian power.

141–139. Struggle for Babylonia. (See p. 88.)

130–124. Scythian and Seleucid Alliance against Parthia. While **Phraates II** was engaged in the west against the Seleucids, the Tochari tribe of the Scythians mounted a major invasion from the northeast, defeating and killing Phraates in battle. Following this the Scythians overran and devastated most of the Parthian Empire. They defeated and killed **Artabanus I,** successor of Phraates (124).

123–88. Mithridates II Restores the Power of Parthia. In a series of successful campaigns in the east, Mithridates drove the Scythians from Parthian territory. He then turned westward to meet Armenian threats to the northwestern frontiers of the Parthian Empire, defeating **Artavasdes** of Armenia, who was forced to acknowledge Parthian suzerainty (c. 100). Less successful in dealing with Tigranes, successor of Artavasdes, Mithridates made a treaty with Rome against Armenia (92; see p. 91, and below).

95–70. Rise of Armenia under Tigranes. Early in his reign, Tigranes was repulsed from an invasion of Cappadocia (92) by Sulla (see p. 91). However, after the death of Mithridates II of Parthia (88), Tigranes conquered most of Media and northern Mesopotamia, and received the submission of the rulers of Atropatene, Gordyene, Adiabene (Assyria), and Osroene. He then invaded Syria, overrunning the vestiges of the Seleucid Empire (83). After the death of Sulla he again invaded Cappadocia, and annexed it (78). In the following years he consolidated his control over his conquests, and was generally acknowledged the most powerful ruler of southwest Asia.

89–70. Decline of Parthia. While Tigranes was conquering western Parthia, the Scythians were expanding again into Parthia from the east, and at one time actually dominated the country sufficiently to place a puppet ruler on the throne (77).

70–65. Tigranes Overthrown by Rome. (See p. 93.)

69–60. Initial Contacts between Parthia and Rome. **Phraates III** (70–57) of Parthia, endeavoring to restore the power and prestige of his empire, concluded an alliance with Lucullus against Tigranes (69). Later he supported **Tigranes the Younger** in a revolt against his father (65). Pompey defeated and captured the younger Tigranes; he refused to permit Parthia to annex the states of Gordyene and Osroene, instead annexing them to Rome. Fearful of Roman strength, Phraates grudgingly made peace with Pompey. Phraates was deposed and murdered by his sons, **Mithridates III** and **Orodes I** (57). Orodes then forced Mithridates to flee to Syria.

First War with Rome, 55–38 B.C.

BACKGROUND. **Aulus Gabinius,** Roman governor of Syria, supported the refugee Mithridates against Orodes, providing him with forces to invade Mesopotamia. **Surenas,** the great general of Orodes, met and defeated Mithridates at the **Battle of Seleucia** (55). Mithridates was then besieged in Babylon, where he was captured and killed (54).

54–53. Campaign of Carrhae. The Roman involvement in this campaign gave an excuse to Crassus for a campaign into Parthia (see p. 94). Shortly after crossing the Euphrates, Crassus and his army of 39,000 were surprised near Carrhae (Haran) by Surenas, with a cavalry army of unknown size. The Romans, surrounded in the semidesert plains, promptly formed a square against the Parthian cavalry. But Surenas made no effort to close, contenting himself with fire power—long-range harassment by a hail of arrows. As the bowmen of each contingent depleted their quivers, they were replaced by a new unit, then fell back to replenish their ammunition supply from a camel train loaded with arrows. The Romans, unable to come to grips with their foes, and suffering from the sun and lack of water, sustained great losses. Crassus sent his son, **Publius Crassus,** with a picked force of 6,000 legionaries, cavalry, and auxiliary bowmen, in an attack designed to pin down the elusive tormentors. The Parthian cavalry fell back, enticing the small column away from the main body, then, cutting it off, surrounded and annihilated the entire detachment. Meantime the harassment of the main body continued unabated. At nightfall Crassus withdrew westward, leaving 4,000 wounded to be massacred by the Parthians, but was brought to bay by Surenas again the next day. In negotiations following that fight, Crassus was treacherously killed. In subsequent days the Roman retreat continued and so did the Parthian harassment. Less than 5,000 Romans returned from the disastrous campaign; 10,000 were captured and enslaved by the Parthians; the remainder perished.

COMMENT. *Carrhae had both political and military significance. Politically the Roman invasion unnecessarily aroused the undying enmity of the Parthians. For the short term it gave Parthia control of Mesopotamia*

and Armenia. Militarily, it was a cavalry victory over the hitherto invincible infantry of Rome. An example of the superiority of mobility and firepower over shock action, it was the harbinger of eventual dominance of the Middle East by horse archers.

53–38. Sporadic and Inconclusive Warfare. Several subsequent Parthian invasion attempts into Syria were easily repulsed by the Romans. In the last of these, the able Parthian general **Pacorus** was killed at the **Battle of Gandarus** in northern Syria (38).

36–34. Antony's Invasions of Parthia. (See p. 114.)

32–31. Parthian Reconquest of Atropatene. Taking advantage of the civil war between Antony and Octavian, Phraates IV reconquered the region.

31–26. Dynastic War in Parthia. A revolt by **Tiridates** was put down with difficulty by Phraates IV.

20. Peace between Parthia and Rome. (See p. 115.)

BACTRIA AND THE HELLENIC STATES OF THE EAST

c. 200–c. 175. Bactrian-Hellenic Invasion of India. Euthydemus, now virtually independent of the Seleucid Empire (see p. 87), began to expand his dominions southeastward into Gandhara (northeastern Afghanistan) and the Punjab. After his death (c. 195), his son **Demetrius** apparently conquered at least the northern half of the Indus Valley, and then began to probe eastward. This was the height of Hellenic-Bactrian power and influence.

c. 175–c. 162. Revolt of Eucratides. A general of Demetrius, Eucratides took advantage of his master's adventures in India to seize control of Bactria proper. A violent civil war ensued, in which Eucratides conquered most of Gandhara and the western Punjab from Demetrius and his successors, who retained that portion of the Punjab east of the Jhelum River. At the same time Eucratides was engaged in a prolonged struggle with Mithridates of Parthia (see p. 116).

c. 162–c. 150. Continuing Civil Strife. Assassination of Eucratides caused renewal of struggle for control of the Bactrian kingdom. One of Demetrius' descendants,

Menander, seems to have been victorious, though the descendants of Eucratides retained some lands in the western Punjab and Kabul Valley.

c. 160. Scythian and Parthian Invasions of Bactria. The Scythians (mixed Indo-European and Mongoloid nomads) of central Asia, closely related to the Parthians, now pressed into Bactria from the north. (A major reason for this migration was pressure from the Indo-European Yueh Chih, who had been driven from Mongolia by the Hsiung-nu; see p. 120.) At the same time the Parthians, under Mithridates I, also began to expand into Bactria from the west and northwest. Thus, by the time Menander gained supremacy among the Hellenic Bactrians, their control was limited to southern Bactria, Gandhara, parts of Arachosia and the Punjab.

c. 150–c. 140. Expansion of Menander's Kingdom. Though unable to stop the progressive erosion of his Bactrian dominions, Menander appears to have been able to expand his control over north India as far as Pataliputra—former capital of the Mauryas. Known to Indian history as **Milinda,** he appears to have had more influence on India than any other Greek, save possibly Alexander himself.

c. 140–40. Decline of the Hellenic Kingdoms. Even during the time of Menander, the Greek kingdoms were breaking up from internal and external pressures. Crushed between the Hindus and the barbarians, they soon disappeared from India (c. 100). Their last strongholds in Gandhara were finally overwhelmed by the Scythians (c. 40).

140–100. Three-Way Struggle over Bactria. The situation in Bactria and neighboring regions of central and southwest Asia was extremely confused. The Scythians, under pressure from the Yueh Chih, tried to press southwestward into Parthia as well as southeastward into Gandhara. Temporarily repulsed by the Greeks from Gandhara, they found themselves engaged in a violent struggle with the Parthians, who were continuing their efforts to expand eastward. At the same time the first waves of the Yueh Chih appeared in northern Bactria.

100–1. Yueh Chih Absorption of Bactria. Gradually Yueh Chih domination over

Bactria checked Parthian expansion efforts, driving the Scythians farther south and southeast into Arachosia, Baluchistan, Gandhara, and the Punjab.

SOUTH ASIA

NORTH INDIA AND THE DECCAN

200–180. Decay of the Maurya Empire. As so often before and since, the decline of a strong regime in north India was an invitation to invasion from the northwest. This time it was begun by the Greek rulers of Bactria, who again brought Hellenic influence to India (see above).

c. 190–50. Confusion in North India. Three new dynasties, two of them short-lived, rose and struggled for supremacy during this era: the Kalinga, Sunga, and Andhra. Most of the petty Greek enclaves were absorbed in the struggle. By the end of the period Andhra had prevailed, only to face a new flux of invasion.

c. 80–c. 40. Scythians in the Punjab. Pushed by Yueh Chih pressure from Central Asia, and pulled by the attractions of India, the Scythians under a leader named **Maues** had meanwhile obtained a foothold in the Indus Valley (c. 80), finally overwhelming the last descendant of Eucratides at Kabul, ending the Greek episode in Southern and Central Asia (40). By the middle of the 1st century B.C. the Scythians (known to Indian history as Sakas) were in complete control of the Punjab. Successive waves of Saka nomads now poured through the Bolan and Khyber Passes, precipitating a sanguinary internecine struggle for the newly won land. These latest arrivals had become thoroughly mixed with the Parthians, and Indian history is unable to make a clear distinction between the Sakas and the Pahlavas (or Parthians). This influx of invaders into the Punjab caused the Saka-Pahlavas to push farther south and east, where they found resurgent Andhra prepared to dispute control of northern India.

50–1. Struggle of Andhra and the Sakas. The invaders were at first successful, but a semi-legendary Andhra king named **Vikramaditya** halted the nomads, and drove them back to the Punjab some time during this period. By the dawn of the Christian era Andhra had firmly established its supremacy in north-central and central India, while the Sakas retained their grasp over the Indus Valley. To the northwest, however, Yueh Chih pressure on the Sakas was increasing ominously.

26–20. Indian Embassy to Rome. An embassy from India arrived at the court of **Augustus,** apparently from Andhra.

SOUTH INDIA

Though Andhra apparently conducted a number of expeditions into the Tamil regions at the southern tip of the peninsula, they were either unwilling or unable to exert the effort required to overcome the three fiercely independent kingdoms of Chola (Coromandel Coast), Pandya (southern tip of India), and Kerala (Malabar). The fortunes varied among these three Tamil kingdoms, almost constantly at war with one another. A rough balance seems to have been maintained among them for many centuries, each retaining its independent integrity.

CEYLON

c. 200–c. 150. Constant Turmoil.
c. 160–c. 140. Tamil Conquest. The Chola leader **Elara** seems to have brought tem-

porary peace to the island through brief conquest. He and his adherents were finally defeated and ejected, however, by the Sinhalese national hero, Prince **Duttha-Gamani,** who reigned for 24 years (161–137).

c. 130–44. Anarchy. After the death of Duttha-Gamani, anarchy again pervaded Ceylon, in a welter of dynastic feuds and tribal wars.

44–29. New Tamil Invasion. The invaders from India, at first successful, were ejected by native uprisings (29). Chaos again ruled in Ceylon.

EAST ASIA*
CHINA

202–195. Rise of the Han Dynasty. Defeats at the hands of the Hsiung-nu and the loss of Korea (see p. 80) were not the only difficulties which Liu Pang (or **Kao Tsu;** first emperor of the Han Dynasty) encountered at the commencement of his reign. Other outlying regions had slipped away from central control during the collapse of the Ch'in Dynasty and in the en-

* The earliest historical information about Korea and Vietnam begins to emerge in this period. This information is so spotty and incomplete as not to warrant separate mention. See Chapter VIII.

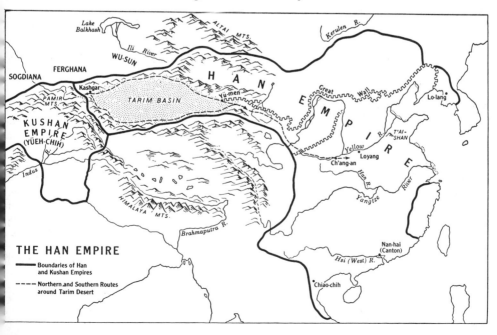

THE HAN EMPIRE
— Boundaries of Han and Kushan Empires
--- Northern and Southern Routes around Tarim Desert

suing civil war. Before his death (195), however, the new emperor established order and centralized control over most of the remainder of the former Ch'in Empire, save in the southeastern coastal region of Yueh (modern Chekiang and south to Tonkin).

196–181. Rise of the Kingdom of Yueh. Chao T'o, former general of Shih Huang Ti, was recognized by Kao Tsu as the autonomous king of Yueh (196). A subsequent imperial invasion was repulsed by Chao T'o (181).

c. 176–166. Supremacy of the Hsiung-nu in Mongolia. The Mongoloid Hsiung-nu people decisively defeated the Indo-European Yueh Chih tribes in the area of modern Kansu and western Mongolia, driving the survivors into Central Asia (see pp. 80 and 118). The victors then stepped up their depredations against the border regions of northwest China. One raid reached the vicinity of Loyang, the Han capital (166).

154. Feudal Revolt against the Han Dynasty. Seven feudal princes revolted against Emperor **Ching,** in an effort to overthrow the dynasty. Suppressing the rebellion with great difficulty, Ching began systematic measures to eradicate feudalism, a policy continued by his successors.

140–87. Expansion of China under Wu Ti. Known to history as the Martial Emperor, Wu Ti ascended the throne at the age of 16. His reign was one of the great periods of Chinese military glory. The young Emperor considered that the Hsiung-nu constituted the greatest threat to his realms, and undertook detailed, long-range plans to end this barbarian menace. He paid particular attention to improving the cavalry forces of his army, and to breeding good horses, so as to excel the frontier peoples at their forte.

138–126. Embassy of Chang Ch'ien. This envoy of the emperor undertook a dangerous mission to Central Asia to seek an alliance with the Yueh Chih against the Hsiung-nu. En route Chang was captured by the Hsiung-nu and imprisoned for several years. Escaping, he reached Central Asia, and went as far as Bactria, the new center of Yueh Chih power. Remembering their disastrous defeats at the hands

of the Hsiung-nu half a century earlier, and satisfied with their newly conquered lands in Central Asia, the Yueh Chih declined to join any such alliance.

127. Chinese Victory over the Hsiung-nu. Wu Ti invaded Hsiung-nu territory between the Great Wall and the northern bend of the Yellow River, defeating the barbarians disastrously.

121–119. Defeat of the Hsiung-nu. After further skirmishing along the frontier, Wu Ti sent his general **Ho Ch'u Ping,** hardly 20 years old, to invade the Hsiung-nu stronghold in modern Kansu with an army of 100,000 horsemen. In a series of resounding victories, the youthful cavalry general decisively defeated the Hsiung-nu and drove them north of the Gobi Desert. He died soon after this (117), reputedly being only 22 years old at the time. The significance of his victories was in the opening up of the invasion and trade routes to the west.

111–109. Wu Ti's Conquests in the South. Having consolidated the regions conquered from the Hsiung-nu, Wu Ti next turned his attention southward, to the upstart kingdom of Yueh (which now included Tonkin and Annam). He quickly defeated and reannexed Yueh to the empire. The chieftains of the mountain tribes of Yunnan also acknowledged Chinese sovereignty.

108. Expansion into Manchuria. The kingdom of Ch'ao Hsien—southern Manchuria and northern Korea—was next defeated and annexed.

105–102. Chinese Penetration into Central Asia. Li Kuang Li led a Chinese army into modern Sinkiang, and across the mountains into Ferghana, in the Jaxartes Valley. After winning a number of successes against the independent tribes of Central Asia, he was defeated by a coalition of nomadic tribesmen in Ferghana. Withdrawing into Sinkiang, he reorganized and again invaded Ferghana, this time successfully. Ferghana acknowledged Chinese suzerainty, but the cost had been high. Barely half of his army of 60,000 troops reached Ferghana and only 10,000 ever returned to China. Li returned, however, with 3,000 prize horses for breeding purposes.

100–80. **Consolidation of the Conquests of Wu Ti.** The final years of Wu Ti's reign were devoted to consolidation, and to undertaking economic measures to restore the imperial fortunes, which had been impoverished in constant wars.

80 B.C.–1 B.C. **Pax Sinica.** This was a period of substantial peace and prosperity in China, marked by a number of generally successful expeditions against the Hsiung-nu in Outer Mongolia.

73. **Hsiung-nu Invasion of Turkestan.** This was repelled by the Chinese and the Indo-European Wu Sun tribe (related to the Yueh Chih peoples) inhabiting the area northwest of the Jaxartes River.

54. **Renewed Hsiung-nu Invasion of Turkestan.** Again the invaders were repulsed by joint Chinese–Wu Sun efforts.

V

THE PAX ROMANA:

A.D. 1—200

MILITARY TRENDS

This, the era of the **Pax Romana,** was perhaps the least eventful period of military history. Not that there was any less strife outside of the relatively calm provinces of the Roman Empire. It was simply that the stability and overwhelming military strength of that empire were too solidly based to be seriously challenged either by external threats or by occasional internal discord. And, with possibly two exceptions, there were no military leaders of exceptional ability who could stand out above the level of their warrior contemporaries in the welter of conflicts across the continent of Asia. Possibly **Pan Ch'ao** of China and the dim figure of **Kanishka,** the Kushan emperor, can be compared with the four great soldier-emperors of Rome in this period: **Tiberius, Trajan, Marcus Aurelius,** and **Septimus Severus.** None of these was a military genius, but all were exceptionally energetic, all were sound, competent military professionals.

THE PAX ROMANA

The **Pax Romana** is generally considered to have begun in 29 B.C., when Octavian—Augustus—returned to Rome after his victory over Antony. It ended during the reign of Marcus Aurelius; probably the year 162 (beginning of the Eastern War) should be selected as the close of this golden age, even though the energy and skill of Marcus Aurelius were able to protect the interior of the empire from growing external challenges.

In 13 B.C. Augustus reduced the army of the Roman Empire to 25 legions. At this time total Roman armed strength, including auxiliaries and the Praetorian Guard, was probably not over 300,000. Gradually increasing barbarian pressure along the Rhine and Danube frontiers had raised this to somewhere between 350,000 and 400,000 by the time of Marcus Aurelius. The bases of the superiority of this relatively small army over the millions of the warrior races along the frontiers were the same as they had been for centuries: superior training, discipline, and organization.

Augustus showed no greater wisdom than in the policies he set to provide for

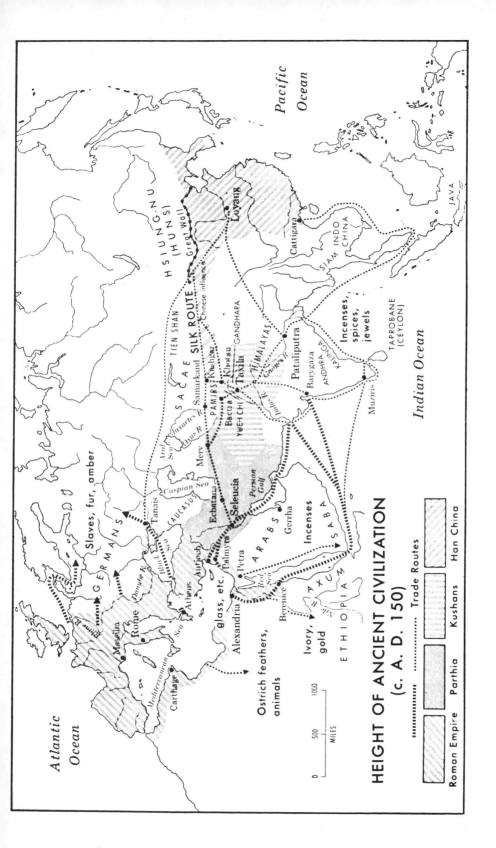

HEIGHT OF ANCIENT CIVILIZATION
(c. A.D. 150)

retired veterans. He established a permanent fund—the **aerarium militare**—from which assured retirement benefits were to be paid (A.D. 6). In addition, he apparently encouraged retired soldiers to settle in the frontier provinces, although this may have merely been the result of veterans settling down spontaneously near their old garrisons. In any event, as a result, in times of invasion or border squabbles substantial numbers of trained, steady soldiers were available to fight. In time these settlements became virtually a part of the over-all military defense system composed of the permanent camps of the legions and the small fortresses, or blockhouses (**castella**), strung along the length of the frontiers. From these settlements grew a sturdy race of frontier colonists—raised in tradition of military service, and loyal to a grateful and benevolent government—from whom more young soldiers could be continually recruited. Finally, this resulted in the development of a flourishing agricultural economy in these formerly barbarian regions; a matter of great importance in view of the steady deterioration of the farming population in southern Italy and other central regions of the empire. Thus the administration of veterans' affairs would become a vital aspect of the economic as well as the colonial and military policies of the empire.

During this period the Roman navy seems to have deteriorated to a police or coast guard status, utilized primarily for the suppression of piracy and smuggling rather than a fleet in being.

The least satisfactory aspect of Roman political and military policy during this period was in the control and status of the Praetorian Guard. There was no basis, constitutional, moral, or physical, for assuring the subserviency of the Guard to the state. They had little to occupy them, and so they were frequently idle, profligate, and vicious, at the same time possessing the means to influence policies and the succession to the throne. After the terrible events of A.D. 69—"the Year of the Four Emperors"—the Praetorians were brought under firm imperial control. A century later, however, the floodgates were again opened by the example of degeneracy given by **Commodus.** Again the Praetorians began to make and break emperors, and thereby ushered in the era of permanent military despotism which began with the reign of Septimus Severus.

WEAPONS, TACTICS, AND TECHNIQUES

There were no startling or significant developments in the design or employment of weapons, either on land or on sea. The Romans, with unchallengeable superiority in all aspects of warfare, had no incentive to modify or improve, though they were solicitous in maintaining the elements of their military superiority. In fact, for all practical purposes, the scientific knowledge and technology of the times had not advanced sufficiently in this period to provide a real basis for major changes.

EUROPE—MEDITERRANEAN

THE ROMAN WORLD

Early in his reign Augustus decided to establish the frontiers of Rome along clearly defined, easily defensible barriers. He created border provinces as military outposts and buffer regions to prevent incursions into the heart of the empire by the barbarian tribes of Eurasia. In the northwest and west, the English Channel and Atlantic Ocean simplified the defensive problem, as did the Sahara and Arabian deserts to the south. On the east the Euphrates and Lycus rivers—flowing through rugged mountains—and the Black Sea were natural frontiers, the potential threat from Parthia having diminished due to his diplomacy (see p. 115) and the internal weakness of the nomadic Parthian kingdom. The regions north and east of the Alps, however, posed military problems. These lands were populated by fierce, restless Teutonic tribes, one of which had penetrated into Gaul and Italy itself during the early years of Augustus' reign (see p. 116). Save for the Roman outposts on the Danube in Raetia and Pannonia, there was no clear barrier to barbarian migrations, no buffer region to provide maneuvering room for the legions protecting the frontier. The Rhine, Augustus felt, was too close to the rich province of Gaul; particularly dangerous was the deep salient between the upper Rhine and upper Danube, extending southwestward as far as modern Basel. Before the beginning of the Christian era Augustus had determined to establish the northern frontier of the empire along the Elbe and Danube rivers, and the campaigns of his adopted sons **Drusus** and **Tiberius** in Germany and Raetia (see p. 115) were the initial steps of this project.

A.D. 1–5. Revolts in Germany. Sporadic revolts (which had begun in 1 B.C.) spread throughout Germany, for a time threatening the earlier conquests. Augustus recalled his adopted son Tiberius from the east and sent him to Germany (A.D. 4). In two campaigns Tiberius skillfully suppressed the disorders; the second of these was a combined land and naval operation, with a flotilla operating along the north coast and up the rivers, in coordination with an overland expedition which swept as far as the Elbe (A.D. 5).

6–9. Revolts in Pannonia. Severe uprisings in Pannonia and Illyricum caused Tiberius to hasten to the Danube, leaving the consolidation of Germany to the legate **P. Quintilius Varus.** In a series of workmanlike, unspectacular operations, Tiberius pacified Pannonia. Moesia and upper Pannonia became frontier provinces (6 and 9).

9. Arminius and Varus in Germany. Varus commanded five legions in Germany, plus a number of auxiliaries. One auxiliary unit of the Cherusci tribe was commanded by **Arminius,** a young German chieftain, who had recently served under Tiberius in Pannonia. Varus, with 3 legions and Arminius' auxiliaries, was encamped in a summer garrison in central Germany east of the Visurgis (Weser) River, near modern Minden. As the end of the summer approached, Varus prepared to march back to his winter quarters camp at Aliso

(Haltern?) on the Lupia (Lippe) River. Arminius now set in motion well-laid plans for an uprising against Rome. At his command a small insurrection broke out in the region between the Visurgis and Aliso. Varus, warned of the conspiracy by friendly Germans, refused to believe that Arminius was unfaithful; he decided to suppress the uprising during the march back to Aliso.

9, September (October?). Battle of the Teutoberg Forest. With his 3 legions, plus the auxiliaries, Varus had perhaps 20,000 men. The force was accompanied by the families of the soldiers—at least 10,000 noncombatants—and a long baggage train. After crossing the Visurgis, the column entered the difficult, wooded, mountain region of the Teutoberger Wald. Heavy rains contributed to the difficulties the Romans began to encounter from harassing German guerrillas. Suddenly Arminius and his contingent deserted (not far from modern Detmold), annihilating a Roman detachment and creating havoc in the unsuspecting Roman column. Varus, rallying his troops, tried to press on to Aliso. Learning that his base had been invested by hordes of aroused Germans, he apparently decided to try to march northward along the Ems Valley to establish a base at one of the Roman outposts on the North Sea coast. But his advance was slowed by the encumbrance of his noncombatants, the baggage train, the terrible weather, and the lack of adequate forest trails. Constantly harassed by the barbarians, his men tried to hew new trails through the woods. Finally, after several days of a bitter, running fight, the Germans broke through the legions, and began to cut them to pieces. Varus and other surviving officers, all wounded, killed themselves. The few surviving legionaries, and nearly all of the women and children, were massacred. The exact location of the fight is unknown, but was somewhere between modern Detmold and Münster. Meanwhile the garrison of Aliso, better handled than Varus' legions, fought its way out to the Rhine. All of central Germany was lost to the Romans.

COMMENT. *The disaster of the Teutoberg Forest had far-reaching consequences. Augustus, grief-stricken, according to legend, during the remaining years of his life frequently burst into tears, crying: "Varus, give me back my legions!" Although he sent punitive expeditions into Germany during these years, the disaster of the Teutoberg Forest caused him to abandon his plans for the conquest and colonization of Germany; he settled for a boundary along the Rhine and the Danube. This decision, accepted by his successors, was of the utmost significance to the future of Europe. For this reason the victory of Arminius is generally considered one of the decisive battles of world history.*

9–13. Tiberius and Germanicus in Germany. Augustus sent Tiberius to avenge the Teutoberg disaster, and the Roman prince did his usual skillful job. Satisfied with this progress, Augustus again sent Tiberius to the east, replacing him with **Germanicus,** young son of Drusus (and adopted son of Tiberius), who led an expedition to the Elbe River (13).

14–37. Reign of Tiberius. Upon the death of Augustus, his selected heir, Tiberius, was invested by the Senate with the powers held by his adopted father. A forbidding and controversial figure, Tiberius was as able an administrator as he was a soldier, and followed the policies of his illustrious predecessor. The empire continued to prosper. Aside from continuing operations in Germany, there were few events of military significance in his reign. A brief revolt in Gaul (21) was promptly suppressed by **Gaius Silius.** There were nationalistic and religious disorders in

Judea attendant upon the crucifixion of **Jesus Christ** by Jewish leaders, with the authorization of **Pontius Pilate,** Roman governor (30). Tiberius foiled a conspiracy led by his chief minister and commander of the Praetorian Guard, **Lucius Aelius Sejanus,** who was executed (31). His troops defeated **Artabanus** of Parthia (35–36; see p. 130).

14–16. Operations against Arminius. Germanicus suppressed a mutiny by his Pannonian legions, then continued his successful campaigns in Germany. He fought a drawn battle with Arminius in the Teutoberg Forest (15). He finally defeated Arminius east of the Weser near **Minden** (16). The eagles of Varus' legions were recovered. But despite this, and despite the ability of the legions to march across Germany almost at will, there was no further effort to establish colonies or bases in Germany. Germanicus, whose relations with Tiberius became strained, was sent to the east, where he died under suspicious circumstances (19).

17–200. Internal Strife in Germany. The relaxation of Roman control led to widespread tribal warfare in Germany. **Marboduus,** leader of the Marcomanni tribe inhabiting modern Bohemia, began a fierce struggle with Arminius and other German leaders for the control of central Germany. Marboduus was eventually defeated, and forced to seek refuge in the empire (19). Violent internal disorders continued in Germany for several centuries.

21. Assassination of Arminius. This occurred during tribal warfare.

37–54. Reigns of Caligula and Claudius. Gaius Caesar Caligula, youngest son of Germanicus, and declared heir of Tiberius, soon became insane. He was assassinated by the Praetorian Guard, who replaced him with his uncle, **Tiberius Claudius Drusus Nero Germanicus,** son of Drusus (41). Roman forces patrolled successfully beyond the frontiers in Germany and Syria; Mauretania was occupied and incorporated into the empire (42), and the conquest of Britain began (see below).

43–60. Conquest of Britain. The invading forces—4 legions and auxiliaries, some 50,000 in all—were under the command of **Aulus Plautius.** The landing was made on the Kentish coast. Claudius personally led reinforcements, including some elephants (44). British chieftain **Caractacus,** of the Catuvellauni tribe, was finally defeated by Plautius (47) and driven into south Wales, from whence he led frequent forays into Roman-held territory to the east. He was defeated at **Caer Caradock** (in modern Shropshire) and captured by **Ostorius Scapula,** governor of Britain, and sent to captivity in Rome (50).

54–68. Reign of Nero. Claudius, poisoned by his wife **Agrippina,** was succeeded by his adopted stepson and Agrippina's son, **Nero Claudius Caesar Drusus Germanicus.** Despite his vicious, cruel, murderous nature, the empire continued to prosper.

56–63. War with Parthia. **Vologases** of Parthia invaded the Roman protectorate of Armenia, drove out the Roman-supported ruler, and placed his brother, **Tiridates,** on the throne. **Gnaeus Domitius Corbulo** was sent out to command in the east, where years of inaction had lowered the quality of Roman forces. After reorganizing the legions in Syria, Corbulo advanced into Armenia, capturing Artaxata (58). He invaded Mesopotamia, defeated the Parthians, and captured Tigranocerta (59). He then set up a new ruler, **Tigranes,** in Armenia. Vologases thereupon invaded Armenia, and in an inconclusive campaign forced Corbulo to withdraw (61). An armistice was negotiated; both sides agreed to evacuate Armenia. Nero then sent out **L. Caesennius Paetus** to replace Corbulo (who was reduced to command of a garrison of Syria). Paetus was defeated at the **Battle of Rhandeia** (62), by mixed Parthian-Armenian forces under Tiridates. Corbulo, restored to command, invaded Armenia again and defeated Tiridates, who accepted Roman sovereignty over Armenia (63). Parthia now withdrew from the war. Nero, jealous of the popularity and ability of Corbulo, accused him of treason and forced him to commit suicide (67).

61. Revolt in Britain. Boudicca (Boadicea), queen of the Iceni tribe of Britons in modern Norfolk and Suffolk, led a revolt against the Romans after **Suetonius Paulinus,** Roman governor, conquered the Druid center in Anglesea. After some initial success, she was joined by the Trinovantes of modern Essex. Paulinus suppressed the revolt in a victory near modern **Towcester.** Boadicea committed suicide.

68. Overthrow of Nero. Widespread disgust at the excesses of Nero led to a popular uprising. The Senate declared the emperor to be a public enemy. Nero, with some assistance from an eager slave, committed suicide.

66–73. Revolt in Judea. The Roman garrison was driven from Jerusalem with heavy losses. **Titus Flavius Vespasianus (Vespasian),** who had an excellent military and administrative record in Germany, Britain, and Africa, was sent to reconquer Judea (67). In a deliberate campaign, highlighted by the desperate defense of **Jotapata** by the Jews under historian **Josephus** (68), Vespasian overran the country and laid siege to Jerusalem (early 69). After Vespasian became emperor, the siege was brought to a successful conclusion by his son, **Titus Flavius Sabinus Vespasianus (Titus),** an able soldier. Roman forces consisted of 4 legions and perhaps 25,000 auxiliaries, plus a siege train of 340 catapults. The last Jewish stronghold, **Masada,** was beseiged by the Romans (72–73); when it fell **Eleazar ben Yair** and 900 men, women and children killed themselves rather than be Roman captives.

69. Year of the Four Emperors. Upon the death of Nero, **Servius Sulpicius Galba,** legate in Spain, was saluted as emperor by his legions, and then recognized by the Praetorian Guards and the Senate. In Germany, however, the legate **Aulus Vitellius** claimed the throne with the backing of his troops, and marched on Rome. Meanwhile, the fickle Praetorian Guards shifted their support to **Marcus Salvus Otho,** who had Galba murdered and seized the throne. Otho then marched north to meet Vitellius, but was defeated (April) in the **First Battle of Bedriacum** (near Cremona). Otho committed suicide, and Vitellius marched to Rome, where he was recognized as emperor by the Senate. Meanwhile **Antonius Primus,** legate of Pannonia, joined the legates of Egypt and Syria in nominating Vespasian as emperor. Antonius invaded Italy, and defeated Vitellius in the **Second Battle of Bedriacum** (October). Vitellius withdrew to Rome, where he was slain in street fighting (December). The Senate thereupon recognized Vespasian as emperor; he arrived in Rome about four months later.

69–71. Revolt in Batavia. Uprising of Batavian auxiliaries spread to legions and auxiliary units in northeastern Gaul and the Roman areas of Germany, under the leadership of **Claudius Civilis.** It was crushed near modern **Treves** by **Petillius Cerialis** (who, though one of the most popular generals of the army, had refused to take part in the earlier scramble for the throne). Vespasian disbanded 4 disloyal legions.

70–79. Reign of Vespasian. The new emperor was an enlightened and able ruler, who brought peace and prosperity back to the empire. The only important military operations were the gradual expansion of Roman control in Britain (72–84) and in the Agri Decumates region of Germany south of the Main River (73–74). In Britain the earlier conquests were consolidated, and Roman rule expanded into southern Scotland and Wales under the able leadership of **Gnaeus Julius Agricola** (77–84). Britain was peaceful for 3 centuries after his victory over the Caledonians at **Mons Graupius** (Mt. Kathecrankie?; 84).

79–81. Reign of Titus. Save for operations in Britain, there were no significant military events in this short reign. Titus died under suspicious circumstances.

81–96. Reign of Domitian. Titus Flavius Domitianus, younger son of Vespasian, succeeded his brother. He frequently took the field as emperor. To subdue the unruly Chatti tribe, he crossed the Rhine at Mainz, and continued the conquest and colonization of the Agri Decumates (83). He began the construction of a line of fortifications (the **Limes**) from the Rhine to the Danube, to protect this frontier region. He led Roman forces in repulsing a Dacian invasion of Moesia (85) under the Dacian King **Decebalus.** In a subsequent campaign north of the Danube in the area of modern Hungary, against the Dacians, Marcomanni and Quadi tribes, Domitian was defeated (89) and was forced to buy a humiliating peace from Decebalus (90). Jealous of the successes

of Agricola in Britain, he recalled him; probably was responsible for his death by poison. (85). A revolt of **Antonius Saturninus,** legate of upper Germany (88–89), was crushed, and as a result Domitian established a policy of keeping legions permanently quartered in separate camps, thus losing the military mobility and flexibility envisaged by Augustus in establishing his policy of frontier outpost provinces.

96–98. Reign of Nerva. Marcus Cocceius Nerva, a senator, was elected emperor upon the assassination of Domitian. His reign was militarily uneventful, save for a threatened military mutiny of the Praetorian Guard and other army units, which he averted by adopting the successful general, **Marcus Ulpius Traianus (Trajan)** as his successor (97).

98–117. Reign of Trajan. The first Roman emperor born outside of Italy (a native of Spain), Trajan was one of the most gifted militarily, and was an able, benevolent ruler.

101–107. Dacian Wars. The first of these (101–102) re-established clear Roman sovereignty over the arrogant Decebalus, nominally a vassal of Rome. When Decebalus rebelled, Trajan took the field, conquered Dacia, and defeated Decebalus, who was killed (103–107). Rome's frontier was advanced to the Carpathians and the Dniester.

107. Annexation of Arabia Petrea. Forces sent by Trajan rounded out the southeastern frontiers.

113–117. Eastern War. Osroes of Parthia violated the old treaty with Rome by installing a puppet ruler on the throne of Armenia (113). Trajan (then age 60) immediately marched east, repeatedly defeated the Parthians, and overran Armenia and northern Mesopotamia (114). He then invaded Assyria and southern Mesopotamia, capturing the Parthian capital at Ctesiphon and reaching the Persian Gulf. Roman fleets based on Egypt explored and raided along the Red Sea and Persian Gulf coasts of Arabia. Osroes raised a new army, and attacked the Roman forces scattered in the consolidation of Mesopotamia and Assyria; Trajan was cut off in southern Mesopotamia (115). Trajan united his scattered forces and, despite a setback at Hatra, reconquered most of Mesopotamia and Assyria (116). He subdued a Judean revolt (117) and planned to continue the operations in Mesopotamia the following year but, falling seriously ill, he started for Rome, leaving his able kinsman, **Publius Aelius Hadrianus (Hadrian),** in command in Syria and Mesopotamia; he died on the journey.

117–138. Reign of Hadrian. Knowing that he could not simultaneously conduct a major foreign war and establish control of the empire, Hadrian made peace with Parthia, abandoning Trajan's conquests east of the Euphrates, but retaining the nominal vassalage of Armenia. He then returned to Rome (via Dacia, where he suppressed a conspiracy of discontented generals). He spent most of his reign traveling to every corner of the empire, which, on the whole, he ruled wisely and well. On a visit to Britain (122), he supervised the construction of the great northern wall which bears his name. After personally suppressing an insurrection in Mauretania, he hastened to the east, where new war with Parthia threatened; this he averted by a personal meeting with Osroes (123). After other travels, he went to Judea to suppress another revolt under Jewish leader **Bar Kochba** (132–135). Apparently Hadrian assumed personal command of the operations which culminated in the crushing of the Jewish people and their dispersal throughout the world.

138–161. Reign of Antoninus Pius. The only important military events of this quiet reign were the suppression of a revolt of the Brigantes tribe of modern Yorkshire by **Q. Lollius Urbicus** (142–143), and a very brief, inconclusive border war with Parthia (155). Minor uprisings in Mauretania (152) and in Egypt (153) were easily suppressed.

161–180. Reign of Marcus Aurelius Antoninus. Last, and perhaps best, of the five "good" emperors, this scholar and philosopher was forced to devote most of his attention to repulsing almost incessant external threats to the empire.

162–165. Eastern War. Vologases III of Parthia invaded Syria and declared sovereignty over Armenia; Marcus Aurelius sent **Lucius Verus** (who was in effect "assistant emperor") to command Roman armies in the east. Verus remained in Antioch while **Avidius Cassius** led a successful counteroffensive against the Parthians, capturing Artaxata, Seleucia, and Ctesiphon, and occupying Armenia and Mesopotamia. The Parthians sued for peace. Troops returning from the campaign were infected with the plague; the result was a violent epidemic (166–167), depopulating vast areas of the empire.

166–179. Wars on the Danube Frontier. The Marcomanni, Langobardi, and Quadi tribes broke across the Danube in Pannonia and Noricum (Austria); some of the Teutons crossed the Alps into Italy to reach Verona, before being repulsed. Marcus Aurelius, accompanied by Verus, after severe fighting forced the Marcomanni to make peace (168). The following year the Marcomanni again burst across the Danube from Bohemia, and 3 years of bitter warfare followed, Marcus Aurelius remaining constantly in the field. He finally defeated the Marcomanni but permitted many of them to stay inside the empire and to settle on lands depopulated by the pestilence. The Quadi and other barbarians were finally crushed by Marcus (174). At about this same time the Sarmatians crossed the lower Danube into Moesia, while further unrest spread along the upper Danube in Germany. Sending subordinates to deal with the Sarmatians, Marcus marched to Germany, and then to Syria to suppress a revolt of the legate Avidus Cassius (175). After a brief respite, Marcus again took the field on the Danube frontier, accompanied by his son, **Lucius Aelius Aurelius Commodus** (179). Again success crowned the brilliant leadership of the emperor who hated war. Early the following year he became ill and died, probably at Vindobona (Vienna).

180–192. Reign of Commodus. A murderous nightmare, comparable to the terrible days of Caligula and Nero. Commodus was finally assassinated by the joint efforts of his favorite concubine and the leader of the Praetorian Guards. During this time Roman garrisons in Moesia repelled invasions by Scythians and Sarmatians.

193. Struggle for the Throne. Commodus was succeeded by elderly, noble **Publius Helvius Pertinax,** whose austere measures to restore the shattered economy of the empire led to his murder by the pleasure-loving Praetorians, after a reign of 3 months. The Praetorians then offered the throne to the highest bidder, profligate **M. Didius Severus Julianus.** Three rival claimants immediately arose: **D. Clodius Septimus Albinus,** legate of Britain; **Lucius Septimus Severus,** legate of Pannonia; and **C. Pescennius Niger Justus,** legate of Syria. Severus marched quickly to Rome (800 miles in 40 days), where he found that the Senate, in anticipation of his arrival, had executed Julianus. Severus disbanded the Praetorians, establishing a new guard from elements of the frontier armies. Gaining the support of one of his rivals, Albinus, by recognizing him as his successor, he then marched east to deal with the other rival, Niger.

193–211. Reign of Septimus Severus. In three battles—**Cyzicus, Nicaea,** and **Issus** (193–194)—Severus defeated Niger; after Issus, Niger tried to flee but was overtaken and killed outside the walls of Antioch. Severus then devoted himself to pacifying the frontier regions and to restoring order and imperial authority in the east. His only serious opposition was in the defiance of Byzantium, which he besieged, captured, and sacked (196). Returning to Rome, Severus, alleging that Albinus had revolted, marched to Gaul and defeated his rival (197) in the exceptionally bitter and hard-fought **Battle of Lugdunum** (Lyon). Returning to Rome, he established what was, in effect, a military government over the entire empire, ignoring and humiliating the Senate. A mean and petty man in many ways, he was vigorous and energetic, perhaps the most able Roman soldier since Caesar.

195–202. Parthian War. Mesopotamia, under nominal Roman rule since the time of Marcus Aurelius, was invaded by Parthian ruler **Vologases IV.** Severus reconquered Mesopotamia (197), then invaded Parthia in an inconclusive and unremunerative punitive expedition.

208–211. Campaigns in Britain. Revolts in northern Britain caused Severus to take personal command there. After mixed successes, he abandoned the region north of Hadrian's Wall. He died at Eboracum (York).

SOUTHWEST ASIA
PARTHIAN EMPIRE

BACKGROUND. This was a period of constant, violent internal strife in southwest Asia. The nomadic Parthians were never able to establish unchallenged control over the region; they clashed with other nomadic peoples to the north and northeast; they were frequently hard-pressed to retain control over their restless subjects; their royal princes were almost always intriguing or fighting against one another in fierce dynastic struggles. Despite their one great victory over the Romans at Carrhae (53 B.C.; see p. 94), and a few other scattered successes, they realized their military inferiority to Rome, and Parthian rulers generally acknowledged the supremacy of the Roman emperors. However, as a civilized and martial kingdom, they shared with Rome and China the responsibility of defending the heartland of civilization from the barbarians to the north.

2 B.C.–A.D. 35. Dynastic Struggles. Phraates V was succeeded by **Orodes II** (5), who, in turn, was overthrown by **Vonones I** (8), with Roman support. Vonones almost immediately became engaged in a prolonged and disastrous war against **Artabanus II** (11). Vonones fled to Armenia, then to Roman Syria, where he hoped to receive support from Augustus, his original sponsor. But Augustus died at about this time, and Tiberius refused to become embroiled in the internal Parthian struggle; he sent his heir and nephew, Germanicus, to make a treaty with Artabanus, in which the Parthian ruler recognized Roman sovereignty over Armenia (18). Though his control was shaky, intransigent Artabanus remained in power for nearly twenty years thereafter.

27–43. Revolt of Seleucia. Taking advantage of the internal breakdown of the Parthian Empire, the Hellenic city of Seleucia (on the Tigris) revolted, and maintained its independence until overthrown and destroyed by the Parthian emperor **Vardanes I.**

35–37. Invasion of Armenia. Artabanus' challenge to the Roman protectorate over Armenia caused Tiberius to sponsor a rival, **Tiridates III,** for the throne of Parthia, and to send a Roman army under **L. Vitellius** to Armenia. Artabanus was defeated (36), though he later temporarily deposed Tiridates (38–39).

38–42. Struggle of Vardanes and Gotarzes. In a three-way struggle for the throne, Vardanes deposed **Artabanus II** (39), but had more difficulty in dealing with his major rival, **Gotarzes.** Finally victorious (42), Vardanes drove Gotarzes into Hyrcania, then restored some of the lost power and prestige of the empire. He was assassinated, and Gotarzes returned to the throne (47).

51–77. Reign of Vologases I. Vologases was defeated by Corbulo in a war with Rome (see p. 127). However, his brother Tiridates became King of Armenia, as a vassal of Rome. At the outset of this war Vologases suppressed a revolt of his son, **Vardanes II** (54–55). At the same time he was hard-pressed by incursions of Scythians in the east. In Vespasian's war with Vitellius (see p. 127), Vologases offered Vespasian an army of 40,000 Parthian horse archers. Soon after, when the Alanis invaded Media and Armenia, Vologases vainly asked for help from Vespasian.

77–147. Chaos in Parthia. During this period of anarchy the only leader of importance was **Vologases II,** who maintained some control over major portions of the empire against a series of rival claimants (111–147).

148–192. Reign of Vologases III. Early in his reign Vologases reunited the troubled Parthian Empire. He was defeated in a disastrous war with Rome (see p. 129). He was overthrown by the successful revolt (191–192) of his son **Vologases IV.**

195–202. War with Rome. (See p. 130.)

SOUTH ASIA

NORTHERN INDIA

c. A.D. 1–50. Rise of the Kushans. The Kushans, apparently an offshoot of the Yueh Chih people who had conquered central Asia in the preceding century, began to follow the Sakas and Pahlavas they had driven into India. The Kushans soon held most of modern Afghanistan (25)

and completed the conquest of the Kabul Valley (50). Soon after this, under the leadership of **Vima Kadphises,** they reached the Punjab.

c. 78–c. 103. Reign of Kanishka. The greatest of the Kushan rulers, **Kanishka,** extended his rule to Pataliputra on the Ganges, and southward to include all of Rajputana. He established his capital on the site of modern Peshawar, from whence he vigorously controlled his vast empire, which included Bactria, at least a portion of Parthia, and most of modern Russian Turkestan. Much of his reign was taken up with a series of inconclusive wars with China for the control of central Asia. Dates are vague, but apparently Kanishka, or his subordinate general, **Hsieh,** were the principal opponents of the brilliant Chinese general **Pan Ch'ao** (see p. 132).

c. 103–200. The Successors of Kanishka. The direct successors of Kanishka allowed much of their authority to be usurped by satraps and feudal lords. One of the most renowned of these Saka satraps was **Rudradaman** (c. 150), who ruled much of northeastern India, was successful in subduing rebellious subjects, as well as in punishing wild tribes along the northern mountain frontiers. He also inflicted severe defeats on the Andhra kingdom to the south. The Hindus found it hard to distinguish between the Kushans and their Saka vassals; Kanishka's successors, as well as the surviving Saka chieftains, are all lumped together in Hindu history as "Sakas." The distinctions, in fact, soon disappeared, as both of the invader races rapidly became assimilated.

CENTRAL AND SOUTHERN INDIA

Barely maintaining its domains against the pressure of Sakas and Kushans, the Andhra kingdom rapidly declined in the years following its defeats at the hands of **Rudradaman** (see above). By the end of the period it had dwindled to its original area in the eastern Deccan.

The decline of Andhra encouraged the northward expansion of the Tamil states of Kerala and Chola. The interminable wars between these two states and neighboring

Pandya continued, punctuated by occasional overseas adventures against Ceylon.

TAMIL AND HINDU WARFARE, C. A.D. 200

The conflicts of the Dravidian Tamils were generally more ferocious than those of the Aryan Hindus farther north. Hindu warfare was conducted in accordance with formal, elaborate rules—not always adhered to, but nonetheless honored, even in the breach. War in the north was a sport of kings, and rarely took the form of a national struggle for existence—save when a new invader from the northwest rudely smashed the rules. Wars were usually limited in objectives, and conducted for the most part with far less savagery than elsewhere in the world. Provinces would change hands, but dynasties were rarel overthrown. Defeated foes were treated with chivalrous generosity; rarely did the Hindus indulge in mass slaughter after a victorious battle. This chivalrous, ritualistic conduct of war facilitated conquest by less punctilious invaders. It is interesting to note, however, that the invaders soon adopted the martial customs as well as the civilian culture of India, while Hindu kings and generals who violated the rules were looked upon contemptuously by their fellows.

No such inhibitions bothered the Tamils, whose conflicts were marked by copious bloodshed, violence and treachery.

CEYLON

The history of Ceylon was marked by endemic internal warfare, and by numerous raids and invasions from the neighboring Tamil kingdoms of the mainland.

EAST ASIA*

A.D. **1–23. Rule of Wang Mang.** First and only emperor of the Hsin (New) Dynasty, he seized the Chinese throne after first acting as a regent for child emperors of the decadent Han Dynasty. He invaded and announced the annexation of the Hsiung-nu

---

* For initial entries on Japan, Korea, and Southeast Asia, see Chapter VIII (A.D. 600–800).
lands (Mongolia and northern Turkestan).

Meanwhile the so-called "Red Eyebrow" rising, a peasant revolt at home, reached such proportions as to sap Wang's military strength and the invasion of Hsiung-nu territory failed. While he was occupied with successive revolts at home, China lost much of Turkestan. Wang Mang was killed during a revolt.

24–220. Re-establishment of the Han Dynasty. After a brief period of anarchy, **Kuang Wu Ti,** a warrior member of the former imperial family, seized control, restored internal order, and reasserted Chinese authority over most of the border regions.

40–43. Expansion in the South. Kuang Wu Ti sent his general **Ma Yuan** to crush a revolt in Tongking. Ma, an outstanding cavalry leader, also conquered Annam and Hainan.

c. 50–60. Operations against the Hsiung-nu. Renewed border raiding by the Hsiung-nu was met firmly and sternly, the nomads being driven from Kansu into the Altai Mountains and the area that is now northeastern Sinkiang (Chinese Turkestan).

73–102. Central Asian Campaigns of Pan Ch'ao. Soldier member of an exceptional and gifted family, **Pan Ch'ao** (32–102) was one of the great generals of Chinese history. After playing a subordinate role in a successful expedition against the Hsiung-nu, he was sent southwestward, in command of a small army. He conquered the Tarim Basin (eastern Turkestan). He next crossed the Tien Shan Mountains into western Turkestan, defeating the various nomadic tribes of the region between the Hindu Kush Mountains and the Aral Sea, and forcing them to accept Chinese sovereignty. Even the powerful Kushans (see p. 131) were forced to send tribute to China (c. 90). Possibly Pan Ch'ao's conquests extended as far as the Caspian Sea; Chinese reconnaissance elements under his command certainly reached the eastern shores of that sea.

89–91. Smashing the Hsiung-nu. A punitive expedition against the Hsiung-nu was led by **Tou Shien** (apparently a lieutenant of Pan Ch'ao), who overwhelmed the nomads and drove most of them westward. It was the final Chinese victory of this campaign—probably in the Kirghiz steppes—which apparently set in motion the great Hun migrations which swept into Europe a few centuries later. Replacing those Hsiung-nu who had departed (some remained in the northwestern fringes of Mongolia), the Mongol tribe of Hsien Pi moved into the desert-mountain region north and northwest of Kansu. In a few years (by 101) the Hsien Pi were raiding the Chinese frontiers just as their predecessors had done.

94–97. Expedition to Persia. **Kan Ying,** another lieutenant of Pan Ch'ao, led an expedition into Persia, reaching the Persian Gulf. This was apparently a form of ambassadorial mission, rather than a raid or invasion; it would never have been possible, however, had the Parthians not been fearful and respectful of Chinese power.

100–200. Decline of the Han Dynasty. All of the areas north and west of Kansu gradually fell away from Chinese control. The Hsien Pi, the revitalized Hsiung-nu, and the Ch'iang people of Tibet all proved particularly troublesome. The process was halted only temporarily by the victories of Chinese general **Chao Chung** over the Ch'iangs (141–144).

190–200. China under the Control of Military Dictators. Control of the empire became centered in the hands of powerful general **Tung Cho,** ruling in the name of a puppet Han emperor. The assassination of Tung Cho (192), however, was followed by a breakdown of central authority; regional war lords became practically autonomous. A civil war broke out between two rival generals, **Ts'ao Ts'ao** and **Liu Pei** (194). Ts'ao Ts'ao was successful, and became the new dictator of the empire (196). Though a weak Han emperor was still nominally on the throne at the close of the century, the dynasty was on the verge of collapse. The Hans, however, had brought a cultural and territorial unity to China which has persisted; to this day the Chinese refer to themselves as "sons of Han."

VI

THE DECLINE OF ROME AND THE RISE OF CAVALRY: 200–400

MILITARY TRENDS

In the Battle of Adrianople (378) we see the two most important trends of this period: (1) the impending collapse of history's greatest empire at the hands of Germanic barbarians, and (2) one of the momentous tactical revolutions of military history—the eclipse of the infantry by the cavalry. As in the era immediately preceding, there were no really great captains of the first rank, though there was perhaps a slightly higher over-all standard of professional competence—at least among the Roman leaders. The Roman emperors **Claudius II, Aurelian Probus, and Julian** were all capable, but all died before they had a chance to prove themselves great captains. Other generals of exceptional ability were the Romans **Carus, Constantine,** and **Theodosius;** the Romanized barbarian **Stilicho,** the Arab **Odenathus,** the Chinese **Ssu Ma Yen,** the Persians **Ardashir** and **Shapur I,** and possibly the Indian **Samudragupta.**

THE TEUTONIC BARBARIANS

The uncontrolled fury and bravery of the German tribes during most of this period could not compete successfully with Roman skill, discipline, and organization. Not until the middle of the 3rd century did they become a threat, when internal Roman disorders almost gave them the empire by default. But from that time on the barbarians became increasingly Romanized, and were able to compete with the Romans with increasing confidence and some success. Even so, and despite their victory at Adrianople, the Teutons could not take cities from the Roman legions, nor could they eject the Romans from imperial territory—save only in Dacia and (later) Britain, where Roman problems were more administrative than military. The Germans did not overthrow the Roman Empire; they merely inherited it —or its western portion—when the old Roman virtues finally died out.

There was no common pattern of barbarian military methods or tactics. The **Franks** of northwestern Germany were essentially foot soldiers, though they did make some use of cavalry. The **Alemanni** of southern Germany, like the **Quadi** farther east, were primarily horsemen, but they mixed light infantry in with their

134

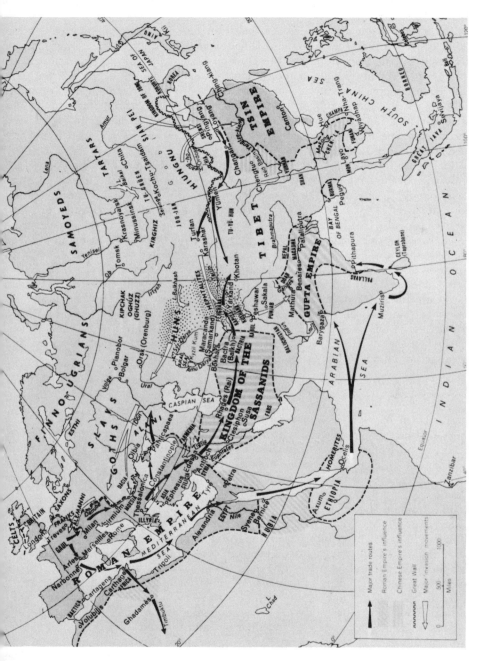

The ancient world, c. 400

mounted formations. The **Sarmatians** were also horsemen, more on the Asian model; apparently they were a mixed Scythian-Germanic people, closely related to the Turklike **Alans** farther east.

The **Goths** seem also to have been of mixed Scythian and German stock, though less Asian than the Sarmatians. They were divided into two main groupings: the **Ostrogoths,** or East Goths, of the Dnieper-Don steppes, were primarily horsemen; the military formations of the **Visigoths,** or West Goths, of the Carpathian-Transylvania region, were mixed horse and foot, with primary reliance on infantry. Like their cousins the **Heruli,** the Goths also became a seafaring people, and their most destructive raids into the Roman Empire were by water across the Black and Aegean seas. The **Saxons** of north Germany were also sea rovers, who frequently raided the coasts of Britain and Gaul.

The most interesting military innovation of the Germans was probably the Gothic wagon fort. When migrating, or when on campaigns, they moved in great wagon convoys. Every night they assembled the wagons in circular laagers, creating crude but effective forts. Not only were these useful for defense in hostile territory; they also provided ready-made bases for forage and plunder. The Germans were even known to bring their wagons together while on the march to create moving forts. Whether this was an original idea, or was inherited from Asia, or was an adaptation of the Roman system of castrametation is not clear.

As time went on, the barbarians played an ever-increasing role in the Roman army. **Constantine** made more use of barbarians in positions of authority and responsibility than had his predecessors. This trend continued in the reign of **Julian,** and reached its climax—so far as the unified empire was concerned—under **Theodosius,** when the barbarians were clearly the predominant element of the army, and most imperial military leaders were also barbarian in origin.

THE RISE OF CAVALRY

Horsemen had long dominated warfare in Asia, save only in India, but Asian cavalry had never been able consistently to defeat the disciplined infantry of Greece, Macedon, and Rome. However, in this era a number of factors brought cavalry to a position of gradually increasing importance in Europe until, at Adrianople, it became suddenly evident that horsemen were supreme in war in Europe as well as in Asia.

The Romans, never having had the balance of arms that had brought success to Alexander of Macedon, found that they needed greater mobility, speed, and maneuverability when operating over the great distances and flat spaces of eastern deserts and East European steppes. Hence they sought the capability to match and offset the principal and most effective methods of cavalry warfare of their Parthian, Persian, and Teutonic enemies. At the same time, the increased use of missile weapons created a tendency to extend and thin out the formations of the infantry, making them more vulnerable to cavalry charges, while at the same time reducing the occasions on which decisions were reached in hand-to-hand infantry fighting. Also, there was the natural human desire to win wars and campaigns by movement and maneuver, avoiding the risks and losses of pitched battle as much as possible. The Parthians had given the Romans a lesson in this kind of warfare by their tactics at Carrhae. Finally, the slow but perceptible weakening of Roman discipline made it more difficult for legionaries to stand up against the terror of a cavalry charge. Adrianople, then, was the culmination of a long, gradual evolution which had begun at least as early as Carrhae.

A great impetus to the employment of cavalry, particularly for shock action, came through Asian developments. First, the invention of the saddle, with stirrups, gave to the horse soldier a firm base from which a stout lance could brutally apply the force resulting from the speed of the horse multiplied by the weight of horse and rider. Second, in Persia and on the steppes of Central Asia new breeds of heavy horses appeared, particularly suitable for such shock action. These were soon adopted by the Romans, who—like the Persians—covered man and horse with coats of chain mail, to make them relatively invulnerable to small missiles and light hand weapons.

The Romans and their enemies discovered that these heavy lancers did not displace the light and heavy archers which the Parthian, Chinese, and Central Asian peoples had long used so effectively. These two major types of horsemen complemented one another: the horse archers preparing a foe for the charge of the lancers, while the threat of the lancers forced an enemy to remain in close order, thus becoming most vulnerable to the archers. Interestingly, in the Arabian and Nubian deserts, the Romans showed their adaptability by using light cavalry on the Arabian model, as well as a camel corps.

Rightly or wrongly, so far as the Romans were concerned, the lesson of Adrianople meant that the legion was finished as an offensive instrument. It was replaced by heavy cavalry—horse archers (cataphracts) and lancers—as the main reliance of the army. The heavy infantry was relegated to a purely secondary, passive, defensive role, in which it provided a base for maneuver by cavalry and light infantry. The phalanx had returned again, with all its vulnerability. The Romans, recognizing this vulnerability, generally kept the new phalangeal legion stationary.

MILITARY THEORY

During the latter part of this period, a shadowy aristocrat named **Flavius Vegetius Renatus** prepared a compilation of Roman military theory in a book called *De Re Militari* (*On Military Affairs,* commonly known as *The Military Institutions of the Romans*). Vegetius evidently wrote his work during the reign of **Valentinian II,** after the Battle of Adrianople, between 383 and 392.

Vegetius was not a great military leader; his work reveals that he had little practical military experience. But he was a student of military history, and he believed that Rome's past greatness could be restored by reviving the tactical and operational principles of the early Romans. His proposals for a return to the organization and doctrines of the early legion were impractical in the political, social, and cultural environment of the late 4th century, and were based upon an inadequate understanding of the effects of improved missile weapons and particularly of improvements in the armament and equipment of cavalry.

Vegetius' writings, therefore, did not greatly influence the practical Roman and East Roman soldiers of his own times and of the centuries immediately following. During the Middle Ages, however, his book was the principal reference work of military men, partly because it was the only compendium of sound military concepts available to educated soldiers of feudal Western Europe, and partly because his discussions of the developing cavalry tactics of his time were easily relatable to the crude military concepts of medieval Europeans. Vegetius became even more useful almost a millennium after he had written, when the combination of the crossbow (and longbow) plus heavier armor for cavalrymen reduced cavalry's shock capability, and led to the revival of the infantry. By the 14th century, *De Re Militare* had truly become the military bible of the Western world.

OTHER DEVELOPMENTS

Weapons

Weapons remained essentially unchanged. The Romans did refine and lighten ballistae and catapults, and used them in increasing numbers in their formations.

Fortifications and Siegecraft

There were no major innovations. Only the Chinese and the Romans had a real facility for siegecraft; while both made some refinements over methods of previous centuries, nothing startling appeared.

Naval Warfare

Here, too, there was nothing really new. In addition to river patrols, the Romans had standing fleets in the Adriatic and Tyrrhenian seas, and on the northern and western coasts of Gaul. But their functions were to prevent depredations by pirates, not to dispute command of the sea with a foreign power. The only important use of sea power in this period was in the campaign of **Constantine** and **Licinius,** in combination with their armies, during the struggle for control of the straits between Europe and Asia Minor. Like the Romans, the Chinese also employed naval power on the large rivers, and maintained fleets to protect their coasts. Apparently they did use sea power to further overseas trade to some extent, but little is known of this.

EUROPE–MEDITERRANEAN AREA

ROMAN EMPIRE, 200–235

193–211. Reign of Septimus Severus. (See p. 130.)

211–217. Reign of Caracalla (Bassianus Marcus Aurelius Antonius, Son of Severus). He and his brother **Geta** inherited the empire; Caracalla then murdered his brother, to become sole Augustus. Personally a vicious monster, he was a generally successful military leader and popular with the troops because he greatly increased their pay. He repelled an invasion of the Alemanni in southern Germany (213), the following year drove invading Goths back across the lower Danube. He reconquered Armenia, Osrhoene, and Mesopotamia from Parthia (216). While preparing to invade Parthia he was murdered at Carrhae by his officers, under the leadership of **Marcus Opelius Macrinus,** who became his successor (217).

217–218. Reign of Macrinus. He soon lost to Parthia most of the territory gained by Caracalla. An insurrection against his weak rule was led by Caracalla's young cousin **Varius Avitus,** who defeated Macrinus at the **Battle of Antioch** (218). Macrinus fled and was soon slain.

218–222. Reign of Elagabalus. Varius, recognized as emperor by the army and the Senate, assumed the name of **Elagabalus,** the Syrian sun god. A worthless ruler, he was murdered by the Praetorian Guards, who elevated his cousin **Alexander Severus** to the throne (222).

222–235. Reign of Alexander Severus. Potentially a good soldier and ruler, Alexander's greatest mistake was to reject the advice and support of the able Roman soldier-historian **Dio Cassius** (229). Alexander personally led a Roman army into Mesopotamia and Armenia (231–233) to repel an invasion by **Ardashir I,** founder of the new Sassanid Empire of Persia. Renewed Alemanni incursions across the upper Rhine brought Alexander to Gaul and Germany, where he combined a successful campaign with astute diplomacy. During this campaign he was murdered by a group of military conspirators, led by fierce tribune **C. Julius Verus Maximinus,** a gigantic, untutored Thracian peasant.

CHAOS IN THE EMPIRE, 235–268

This was a period of fierce but boresome strife between numerous rival claimants to the title of "Augustus." That the empire did not collapse is attributable to the fact that residual Roman military qualities—even though terribly debased and abused—remained superior to those of more vigorous, but less skillful, neighbors. The empire suffered severely during this period. As Gibbon wrote:

The discipline of the legions, which alone, after the extinction of every other virtue, had propped the greatness of the state, was corrupted by the ambition, or relaxed by the weakness, of the emperors. The strength of the frontiers, which had always consisted in arms rather than in fortifications, was insensibly undermined; and the fairest provinces were left exposed to the rapaciousness or ambition of the barbarians, who soon discovered the decline of the Roman empire.

Internal Turmoil

235–244. Maximinus and the Gordiani. The troops in Germany elected the crude Maximinus emperor. The Senate nominated two of its own members—**Maximus** and **Balbinus.** In Africa the legions proclaimed 80-year-old **Marcus Antonius Gordianus I** as emperor (238). A few weeks later his son, **Marcus A. Gordianus II** was defeated and killed in the **Battle of Carthage** by adherents of Maximinus, and the aged imperial aspirant committed suicide. His troops immediately proclaimed his grandson, **M. A. Gordianus III,** emperor. Maximinus meanwhile was killed by his own troops during the siege of Aquileia; the two Senatorial emperors were soon killed by the Praetorian Guards, and Gordianus became sole emperor (238). While engaged in war with the Persians (see p. 160), he was murdered by one of his officers, **M. Julius Philippus Arabus,** who seized the throne (244).

244–268. Philip, Decius, Gallus, Aemilianus, Valerian, and Gallienus. A period of incessant internal strife, intrigue, and murder as general displaced general as emperor. During the reign of Gallienus the competition became so widespread that it was called the "Age of Thirty Tyrants," though Gibbon comments that there were really only 19 (259–268).

259–274. Separation of Gaul from the Empire. M. Cassianus Postumus (one of the "Thirty Tyrants") first established control over Gaul, then over Britain and Spain. Momentarily attaining greater stability than the parent state, his provincial empire soon collapsed (274; see p. 140).

Wars with Persia; the Rise of Palmyra

241–244. First Persian Invasion. (See p. 160.)

258–261. Shapur and Valerian. At **Edessa** the Persian king defeated and captured the Roman emperor, then plundered Syria, Cilicia, and Cappadocia (see p. 160).

259–261. The Rise of Odenathus of Palmyra. Septimus Odainath, prince of Palmyra, was a Romanized Arab. Apparently he preferred to accept Roman authority rather than Persian. He may have tried to obtain Shapur's good will after the capture of Valerian; either his efforts were rebuffed or he was merely gaining time while raising a new Roman-Arab army to dispute Shapur's control of the Roman dominions of the East. The threat of Odenathus' small army seems to have caused Shapur to withdraw eastward from Cappadocia (261). West of the **Euphrates River,** Odenathus and his small army surprised and routed the Persians, who were carrying great quantities of booty from Antioch and Asia Minor. Abandoning most of their loot, the Persians fled across the river, harassed by Odenathus' light cavalry.

262. Odenathus and Gallienus. Odenathus then attacked, defeated, and executed **Quietus,** one of the "Thirty Tyrants," or usurpers, who was endeavoring to establish his rule in Syria. As a reward the then reigning emperor, Gallienus, appointed Odenathus as virtual coruler in the East, conferring on him the title of "Dux Orientis."

262–264. Odenathus Invades Persia. Having been substantially reinforced by Gallienus, Odenathus invaded the lost Roman provinces east of the Euphrates with a small army composed mainly of light foot archers, heavy cataphracts and lancers, and irregular light Arabian cavalry. He drove off a Persian army investing Edessa, and recaptured Nisibis and Carrhae (262). In the two following years he harassed Armenia and raided deep into Mesopotamia, consistently defeating Shapur and his lieutenants, and twice capturing Ctesiphon, the Sassanid capital. Apparently Odenathus was accompanied and assisted on his campaigns by his beautiful and able wife, **Zenobia.** Shapur sued for peace (264).

266. Odenathus against the Goths. Odenathus undertook a successful punitive expedition against the Goths, then ravaging Asia Minor. Soon after this he was murdered, and was succeeded as Prince of Palmyra by his son, **Vaballathus.** However, the virtual ruler of Palmyra—and thus of Rome's eastern dominions—was **Zenobia,** Odenathus' widow.

267. Independence of Zenobia. Not sure of Zenobia's loyalty, Gallienus sent an army to the East to reassert imperial control. Zenobia, assisted by her general, **Zobdas,** defeated the Romans, then confirmed her virtual independence by conquering Egypt.

Incursions of the Barbarians

The Germanic barbarians of central and southeastern Europe were not long in taking advantage of the internal wars of the Augusti. Prominent among the tribes taking part in the almost incessant raids across the frontiers were the Quadi, Sarmatians, Heruli, and (mostly by sea) Saxons. Three Germanic peoples, however, played the greatest roles in weakening the foundations of the empire at this time: Franks, Alemanni, and Goths.

236–258. Depredations of the Franks. Their raiding parties crossed the lower Rhine and ranged almost at will over Gaul; some penetrated the Pyrenees and plundered Spain, where many seized vessels, sailed across the Mediterranean, and continued their destructive activities in Mauretania. **Valerian** was defeated in Gaul in an unsuccessful attempt to subdue and punish the Franks (256). After the revolt of **Postumus** (see p. 139), who had established a Gallic empire (259–274), the Franks were limited to relatively minor border incursions (259–268).

236–268. Incursions of the Alemanni. Like the Franks to their north, the Alemanni penetrated Gaul with little difficulty. They also frequently crossed the Alps to raid Italy. On one of these raids they defeated Valerian north of the Po, overran Milan, and reached Ravenna (257). For years the interior cities of the empire had allowed their walls to decay; now old walls were hastily repaired and new walls built in northern Italy, Gaul, and Illyricum.

238–268. Raids of the Goths. Most devastating of all were the Goths, who began a reign of terror in Moesia and Thrace (238). However, when **Gaius Trajanus Decius** was legate of Dacia, he won a number of notable successes against the barbarians on both sides of the Danube (245–249).

250–252. First Gothic War. Taking advantage of Roman internal troubles, **Cuiva,** King of the Goths, crossed the Danube in great force, and defeated a Roman army at the **Battle of Philippopolis** (250). He continued on, penetrating as far as northern Greece. Decius, now emperor, marched against the invaders, and in two campaigns drove them back to the marshes south of the Danube mouth.

251. Battle of Forum Terebronii. Backed into a corner, the barbarians fought desperately. Early in the battle a son of Decius was killed, when one of the emperor's generals—**C. V. Tribonianus Gallus**—failed to push home an attack which could have assured Roman victory. The Goths counterattacked. Most of the Roman army—save for Gallus' legions—was shattered; Decius was killed while trying to rally his troops. Gallus, become emperor, then concluded a shameful peace, permitting the Goths to keep their booty and to withdraw peacefully across the Danube, while at the same time promising an annual tribute in return for Gothic agreement not to repeat the invasion (252).

252–268. Aemilianus and Claudius on the Danube. Although the Goths almost immediately broke this promise, they were promptly and decisively defeated by **Aemilianus,** the new legate of Moesia (252). When he left to seize the throne (see p. 139), his successor, **Marcus Aurelius Claudius,** retained command on the Danube frontier under emperors Valerian and Gallienus. His energy and skill discouraged the Goths from further attempts to cross the river.

253–268. Raids of Gothic Sea Rovers. The Goths now took to the Black Sea as an easy route to reach the defenseless coasts of Mocsia, Thrace, and northern Asia Minor. Valerian endeavored to halt these depredations, but had generally the worst of several inconclusive encounters along the Black Sea littoral (257–258). The Goths—joined by the kindred Heruli—expanded the scope of their raids, and penetrated still farther inland. Capturing bases along the coast, they ranged over Asia Minor, Caucasia, and Georgia, then forced their way through the Bosporus and Hellespont to reach the Aegean. They sacked the Ionian city of Ephesus, destroying the famed Temple of Diana, one of the Seven Wonders of the World (262). Pressing on to Greece, they captured and sacked Athens, Corinth, Sparta, Argos, and other cities (265–267). The only serious checks they encountered were at the hands of Odenathus (see p. 140) and in Greece, where Athenian general-historian **Publius Herennius Dexippus** drove them northward from central Greece (267). By the end of the reign of Gallienus, the Goths and Heruli were in effective control of most of the Aegean area, save for Greece (268).

REVIVAL UNDER THE ILLYRIAN EMPERORS, 268–305

268–270. Reign of Claudius II. Having loyally and effectively held the Danube frontier under three emperors, M. A. Claudius now came to the Roman throne by unanimous choice of army and people. He secured his position by defeating and executing his rival, **Aureolis** of Milan (268).

268. Battle of Lacus Benacus (Lake Garda). Almost immediately Claudius was faced with a new Alemanni incursion of Italy. These he apparently routed in the Alpine foothills, by the shores of Lake Garda. He then marched to Thrace to deal with the Gothic threat. Upon the approach of the emperor's army, the barbarians attempted to evade him and to march to Italy.

269. Battle of Naissus (Nish). Claudius pursued and decisively defeated the Goths in a major battle in the Morava Valley of the Balkan Mountains. He then marched south to capture and destroy the main Goth fleet at Thessalonika. These victories brought relative peace to Southeastern Europe for the first time in three decades, and won for Claudius the appellation of "Gothicus." He died in an epidemic of the plague (270).

270–275. Reign of Aurelian. Another able Illyrian general and trusted subordinate of Claudius, **Lucius Domitius Aurelianus,** was proclaimed emperor by the army.

270. Renewed War with the Goths. Learning of the death of Claudius, the Goths turned back across the Danube. Aurelian marched against them and drove them completely out of Moesia, and back across the Danube. He decided to abandon Dacia, which had been overrun by the barbarians for several decades. He resettled most of the surviving Roman colonists of Dacia in Moesia.

271. War with the Alemanni. The Alemanni made another raid across the upper Danube to ravage Pannonia and northern Italy. Aurelian defeated them just south of the Danube, only to have them escape due to the laxity of a legate. They headed for Italy, pursued by the emperor. Catching up, he was severely defeated at the **Battle of Placentia,** withdrawing in considerable disorder. The Alemanni then headed for Rome. Aurelian rallied, regrouped his troops, and continued the pursuit. He caught up with the barbarians at the Metaurus River, and defeated them at the **Battle of Fano.** The Alemanni now retreated northward, closely pursued by Aurelian, who practically annihilated them at the **Battle of Pavia.**

271–276. Reconstruction of the Walls of Rome. Aurelian wished to make sure that the heart of the empire would not again be defenseless against barbarian raids.

271–273. War against Zenobia. Most of the empire's eastern dominions—Syria, Egypt, Mesopotamia, and most of Asia Minor— were still ruled by the beautiful widow of **Odenathus** (see p. 140). Aurelian now marched east, and in the very bitterly contested **Battle of Immae,** near Antioch, defeated **Zenobia** and her general, **Zobdas** (271). The Palmyrans withdrew in good order, but Aurelian pursued and defeated them again in the decisive **Battle of Emesa** (272). Zenobia fled to her desert capital, Palmyra, where she was besieged by Aurelian. Despite harassment from nomadic guerrillas, and some interference from the Persians, Aurelian prosecuted the siege vigorously, feeding and supplying his army by means of excellent administrative arrangements. When Zenobia surrendered, Aurelian forgave her and left her in control of Palmyra and vicinity (272). But soon after the departure of the emperor and his army, Zenobia again declared her independence. Aurelian promptly returned, renewed the siege, and captured and sacked Palmyra. Zenobia, attempting to flee, was captured and taken back to Rome as a prisoner, to be led through the streets in chains during the emperor's triumph (274).

273. Revolt in Egypt. During the second siege of Palmyra, a pretender named **Firmus** proclaimed himself emperor in Egypt. Aurelian marched to the Nile Valley, suppressed the revolt, and executed Firmus.

273–274. War with Tetricus. Aurelian now turned to reunite with the empire the one remaining area of dissidence—the provincial empire of Gaul, Britain, and Spain, now ruled by **Tetricus.** He defeated his rival—whose resistance was only half-hearted—at **Châlons** (late 273), and within a few months had obtained the submission of all three provinces, thus restoring the unity of the empire.

274–275. Plans for War against Persia. The Sassanid Empire had given some assistance to Zenobia, and had taken advantage of Aurelian's internal preoccupations to annex Roman Mesopotamia and to strengthen its hold on Armenia. The emperor, preparing for war, began to march eastward. While in Thrace, near Byzantium, a cabal of officers, resenting his

stern discipline, assassinated him. Aurelian was a vigorous, able general, a wise and respected ruler, and a man of exemplary personal conduct. He well deserved his title "Restorer of the World."

275–276. Reign of Tacitus. An elderly, respected Italian statesman and soldier **Marcus Claudius Tacitus,** was chosen by Senate and army to succeed Aurelian. He marched to Asia Minor to deal with continuing depredations of the Goths and the Alans—a Scythian-type people. Despite his advanced years, he conducted a vigorous campaign and defeated the barbarians in Cilicia (276). He became ill and died (or was assassinated) after a reign of 6 months.

276–281. Reign of Probus. Another Illyrian general, **Marcus Aurelius Probus** proclaimed emperor by the army upon the death of Tacitus, promptly disposed of Florianus, younger brother of Tacitus who also claimed the throne. The death of Aurelian had encouraged the barbarians to renew their incursions into the empire. Probus, in a series of campaigns distinguished equally by his brilliant generalship and his legendary personal valor, inflicted crushing defeats on them. He expelled the Franks, Burgundians, and Lygians from Gaul (276); he then invaded Germany, marching without serious opposition as far as the Elbe (277). He rebuilt the old—and long-abandoned— **Limes,** with a permanent masonry wall from the Rhine to the Danube. He vigorously punished other barbarian raids across the Danube farther south, into Illyricum (278). His subordinate, **Saturninus,** commanding all Roman forces in the East while Probus attended to the Germans, revolted and declared himself emperor. Probus promptly marched to Asia Minor and defeated Saturninus, who was killed (279). It was possibly about this time that Probus crushed a long-standing revolt of the fierce Isaurian mountaineers in central Asia Minor. A new revolt in Gaul, however, called the warrior-emperor back to that province. He promptly defeated the leaders of the revolt—his legates **Bonosus** and **Proculus**—bringing complete peace to the empire for the first time in more than a century (280). To keep his soldiers busy, he put them to work on public projects: building roads, draining swamps, and the like. Resentful of this, and of his strict discipline, a group of soldiers killed him while he was inspecting their work (281).

281–283. Reign of Carus. The commander of the Praetorians, **Marcus Aurelius Carus** (another Illyrian), has sometimes been suspected (probably wrongly) of having instigated the death of Probus. Selected emperor by the army, he decided to invade Persia, to regain Mesopotamia and Armenia. Leaving his elder son, **Carinus,** to administer the western portions of the empire, Carus marched east via Illyria, defeating invading Quadi and Sarmatian tribes en route.

282–283. War with Persia. Carus defeated **Bahram I** of Persia in Mesopotamia. He then marched on to defeat the Persians again near their capital, Ctesiphon, which he captured. He then marched east of the Tigris—possibly intending to overrun the entire Sassanid Empire. Soon after this he died under mysterious circumstances, supposedly killed by lightning, but possibly murdered. The Romans, now led by Carus' younger son, **Numerianus,** withdrew behind the Tigris.

283–284. Carinus and Numerianus as Co-emperors. Near Chalcedon, while the army was marching back to Europe, Numerianus was murdered, evidently by **Arius Aper,** commander of the Praetorians (284). Meanwhile, in the west, Carinus assumed the throne on hearing of the death of his father.

284. Diocletian Chosen Emperor. Upon the death of Numerianus, the Illyrian commander of the imperial bodyguard, **Gaius Aurelius Valerius Diocletianus,** was chosen emperor by the army. Immediately he personally slew Aper, presumed assassin of Numerianus.

284–285. Civil War between Carinus and Diocletian. Carinus took the field against Diocletian. The armies met in Moesia, and Carinus had the better of the initial engagements. The climax came in the decisive **Battle of the Margus** (Morava). Again Carinus was having the better of the fight, when he was apparently murdered by one of his own officers. Diocletian became sole ruler of the empire (285).

284–305. Reign of Diocletian. Never known as an outstanding general, Diocletian is worthy of comparison with Augustus as an administrator and politician. His reign, bringing to fruition the military successes of his Illyrian predecessors Claudius, Aurelian, Probus, and Carus, was unquestionably the most important single factor in the survival of the Roman Empire for almost two more centuries. He instituted a number of major political, administrative, and military reforms. He completely separated military organization from governmental machinery; for the first time local military commanders were subordinate to regional officials of government. He reorganized the army completely, drastically reducing the size of the legion. At the same time he greatly strengthened the frontier defensive system, which had suffered seriously during the recent decades of barbarian invasions. By the end of his reign the barbarians found it practically impossible to penetrate the chain of forts, camps, and walled frontier colonies.

286–292. Reorganization of Imperial Administration. Diocletian believed that the size of the empire, combined with the threats of external enemies, constituted an administrative and military burden beyond the capacities of any single man. Accordingly he divided the empire into 2 major divisions—East and West—ruled by coequal emperors, or **Augusti.** Each of these, in turn, was assisted by a carefully selected imperial prince, or **Caesar,** who directly controlled about half of that portion of the empire ruled by his superior **Augustus.** This meant that the empire was divided into 4 major administrative regions, and had 4 principal armies to cope with external threats and to maintain internal order. The careful selection of the junior associates of the Augusti, furthermore, was intended to assure orderly and peaceful succession to imperial authority, in contrast to the violence and death which had characterized the rapid changes in rulers for the previous centuries. Diocletian put his new system into effect gradually, first choosing able general **M. A. Valerius Maximianus** (or Maximian) as co-Augustus, to rule over the West; Diocletian retaining the East, with his capital at Nicomedia, in Asia Minor (286). Then, a few years later, he and Maximian selected two more generals, **Gaius Galerius Valerius and Flavius Valerius Constantius,**

to be their assistant rulers, or Caesars (292). Each commanded one of the empire's four major armies. Diocletian was in direct control of Thrace, Egypt, and Asia; Galerius was administrator of Illyria and the Danubian frontiers from a capital at Sirmium (Mitrovica in Yugoslavia); Maximian directly controlled Italy and Africa from Mediolanum (Milan); Constantius ruled Gaul, Britain, and Spain from Augusta Trevirorum (Trier). By avoiding use of Rome as a capital, Diocletian reduced the importance of both the Praetorians and the Senate. Each of the four princes was practically sovereign in his own region, though sharing jointly over-all responsibility for the empire. Diocletian was acknowledged by his associates as first among equals; so long as he reigned there was no jealousy in this system of corporate, decentralized control. But, though it solved some of the empire's most pressing problems, the system had two major dangers: (1) Some discord would be inevitable among such a group of rulers. (2) The cost of four imperial courts would be likely to create a staggering economic burden. These dangers soon became facts.

286. Peasant Uprising in Gaul. This was suppressed promptly by **Marcus Aurelius Carausius,** commander of the Roman fleet at Gessariacum (Boulogne).

287–293. Revolt of Carausius. Carausius enriched himself by plundering the shores of Germany, when he was presumably protecting the northern coasts of the empire against Germanic pirates. Suddenly assuming the title of Augustus, he defied Maximian and Diocletian, and established firm control over northern Gaul and Roman Britain. The revolt was quelled by Constantius (294) after 5 years of indecisive fighting, and shortly after Carausius' murder by a subordinate, **Allectus.**

294–296. Disorders in Egypt. A usurper named **Achilleus** established himself as

emperor in Alexandria, controlling northern Egypt. Diocletian himself took the field, captured Alexandria after a siege of 8 months, and executed Achilleus (296). Southern, or Upper, Egypt was still in turmoil, however, due to incursions of a wild barbarian tribe—the Blemmyes—who apparently originated south of Nubia, and who had been terrorizing Upper Egypt for many years. Diocletian assisted the Upper Egyptians and Nubians in repelling the marauders and in establishing effective defenses.

295–297. Pacification of Mauretania (Morocco). The coastal regions of Mauretania were ravaged by an invasion of wild desert and mountain tribes of the interior. Maximian went to northwest Africa, and drove the invaders back into the desert and to their mountain strongholds. He then systematically pacified the mountain regions, capturing their strongholds, removing all their inhabitants, and resettling them in other parts of the empire.

298. Invasion of Gaul by the Alemanni. This major barbarian invasion was met promptly by Constantius, who defeated the Alemanni decisively at **Lingones** (Langres) and at **Vindonissa** (Windisch, Switzerland).

295–297. Persian War. (See p. 160.)

305. Abdication of Diocletian and Maximian. With the Roman Empire reorganized, law and order pervading its interior provinces, and the frontiers respected by chastened external foes, Diocletian abdicated, to facilitate the peaceful succession system he had planned. He persuaded his somewhat reluctant colleague, Maximian, to do likewise. Diocletian spent the last 8 years of his life as a gentleman farmer at Salona (near modern Split), on the Dalmatian coast of the Adriatic Sea; he lived long enough to realize that his hopes of orderly succession had been unduly optimistic.

ROMAN MILITARY SYSTEM, C. 300

From its earliest days the power and glory of Rome were derived from a superb military system unmatched in skill or efficiency by any potential enemy. There were many changes in the details of the system in the first 3½ centuries of the Roman Empire: some were normal and evolutionary; others were the result of internal

tresses and strains; some were inspired by the example of enemies. The supremacy
of the Roman military system—and thus the continued existence of the empire—
was in large part due to the continued pragmatic, logical approach of the Romans
o practical problems. They respected tradition, but they were not slaves to it, and
were extremely flexible in adapting themselves to military change. The fact that
here were no more fundamental changes in the Roman military system from about
0 B.C. to A.D. 300, therefore, reflects both the lack of technological change in these
centuries and the thoroughness with which the Republican Romans had adapted
existing technology to the art and science of warfare.

The Military Policy of Augustus

Augustus established certain fundamentals of military policy which could not
be improved by his successors. The most basic of these was relating the security of
he empire to economic soundness as well as to military excellence and adequacy.
The Roman Empire had become about as large as could be managed by one man
or one single administrative system. Armed forces were required only for the defense
of the frontiers and to maintain domestic tranquillity. Augustus wished to keep the
armies as small as possible, in order to place the least possible strain upon the economic fabric of the empire. By organization and skill, a small, efficient army could
perform the essential defensive missions. The force of 300,000 men under arms was
small, in the light of the size and the population of the empire (some 50 million)
and considering the number of warlike foes around the frontiers. Yet it was adequate.

Augustus well understood that aspect of economy of forces now often called
"cost effectiveness." His successors, almost without exception, adhered to this principle also. Even when the empire's frontiers seemed most seriously threatened, they
remained rightly confident that Roman military abilities would assure victory over
the greatest numerical odds without the need for raising vast levies of expensive,
and relatively inefficient, mass armies. As external pressures increased, so too did
the size of the standing army. But even in the middle of the 4th century the total
size of the Roman army would have been considered small by the standards of any
other age, before or since.

This policy of military economy permitted the empire to avoid an expensive
central reserve. Save for the 10,000 Praetorians—who were intended by Augustus
more to maintain internal tranquillity than as a personal bodyguard—all the armed
forces of the empire were scattered along the frontiers. A threat in any region would
be met by dispatching detachments from other portions of the frontiers. The superb
road network behind the frontiers, and connecting the provinces, was deliberately
built up as a substitute for a military reserve.

The Augustan Legion

Augustus standardized the size of the legion, setting it at 6,000 men, composed
of the traditional 10 cohorts. Apparently the first and tenth cohorts were 1,000 each
in strength; the other 8 were 500 strong. The reason for this is not clear, and it is
possible that the most common organization was 10 cohorts of 600 men each. Command arrangements were much as in Caesar's time. Augustus had 25 such legions
deployed along the frontiers of the empire.

With some exceptions, soldiers were enlisted for 20 years. There was apparently
no difficulty in obtaining recruits; most of them were the sons of veterans. Although
Augustus forbade his soldiers to marry, he did not intend that this should prevent

them from raising families. There were always arrangements for taking care of th
families of soldiers in or near the main camps of the legions, and the liaisons of so
diers and camp followers were always legalized upon the veteran's discharge. Pa
of the veteran's pension was usually a plot of farmland in the vicinity of his frontie
post, and the veteran's son more likely than not joined his father's old unit.

The morale of the legions was maintained by *esprit de corps,* by discipline, an
by rigorous training. It was no small contribution to unit *esprit* for the individua
to know that they belonged to an organization which had been in existence fc
centuries, with a proud record of almost uninterrupted victories, and whose heroe
more often than not were their own family ancestors.

As in the past, training and disciplinary measures were harsh, intensive, an
effective. Standards fluctuated over the centuries, and in later years unquestionab
declined. Nevertheless, even at their lowest, these disciplinary standards were neve
approached by Rome's foes, and they provided, to a greater degree than any othe
factor, the usually wide margin of Roman military superiority over all enemies.

Auxiliaries of the Imperial Army

To support his 25 legions scattered along the frontier, Augustus maintained a
approximately equal force of auxiliaries—about 150,000 in all: archers, slinger
light infantry, and cavalry; most were recruited from the barbarian or semibarbaria
tribes outside the empire.

The auxiliaries were paid less than the legionaries. Their terms of service we
usually for 25 years. They could then look forward to automatic citizenship and
sometimes—to veterans' compensation in land and money comparable to that of th
legionary veteran.

Initially most auxiliary units were permitted to retain their original tribal o
ganization and leadership. Save for special troops—such as archers and slingers, wh
usually came from the eastern regions of the empire—the auxiliaries at first serve
in the general area in which they were recruited. This sometimes led to revolts e
mutinies in which the auxiliaries joined forces with local fellow tribesmen. Thu
after the time of Augustus, barbarian auxiliary units were usually shifted from the
homelands to other frontier regions, where their homogeneous tribal organizatic
was deliberately diluted by reinforcements from other tribes.

By the time of Trajan this policy of discouraging revolt had been carried eve
further; tribes were completely mixed up in auxiliary units and officers were r
longer tribal chiefs. Consequently tribal enthusiasm had to be replaced by un
esprit de corps. This, in turn, led logically to the creation of certain regular standir
units of auxiliaries, comparable to the cohorts of the legions. These permanent uni
were given numerical identifications, and became known as **numeri.** This increase
permanence and regularity in auxiliary units lessened still further the diminishi
distinctions between the Romanized barbarians of the auxiliary units and the in
creasingly barbarian composition of the legions during the 3rd and 4th centuries.

As early as the time of Augustus the training and equipment provided the ba
barian auxiliaries by the Romans were sometimes used against Rome. Discharge
auxiliaries and deserters served in the barbarian ranks during raids across the fron
tier. At the same time the barbarians learned much by experience from their battl
against Roman formations. Certainly this continual improvement in barbarian met
ods of war contributed to the final overthrow of Rome. That this did not happe
earlier is a tribute to Roman political skill, and to the organizational and leadersh
abilities of the outstanding Roman generals.

nnovations of Hadrian, Marcus Aurelius, and Septimus Severus

Despite the essentially defensive military policy of Augustus and his successors, the mpire grew slightly in the century after his death. Hadrian, giving up some of the astern conquests of his predecessor, Trajan, decided that this expansion must stop; ie empire was already too vast to be effectively administered politically or con-·olled militarily. He modified the mobile defensive concept of Augustus to one of gid frontier defense. He had no intention that this should change the inherent 10bility of the legion, or its tactical flexibility. Rather he wanted to establish man-1ade obstacles which would supplement natural barriers—rivers and mountains. 'his would make it harder for barbarian raiders to cross the frontiers, and easier) cope with them if they did, without the necessity for shifting reinforcements from 1e frontier region to the other, or for conducting large-scale campaigns within or ·ithout the frontiers.

The **Limes** in Germany, and Hadrian's Wall in Britain were high mounds ' earth, topped by wooden palisades. These were not manned permanently by .oman troops—there were not enough soldiers in the army to do anything like 1at. Rather, the barriers provided protection and concealment for Roman border atrols, and made it more difficult for barbarian raiders to cross the frontier secretly. Iore important, they were obstacles to the easy escape of barbarian raiding parties, .any of whom were caught and slaughtered under the walls by pursuing imperial ·oops.

Hadrian made increasing use of river-boat patrols along the Danube and Rhine) make invasion more difficult. He also cultivated and expanded the already-exist-.g Roman intelligence network in barbarian areas beyond the imperial frontier.

Marcus Aurelius, exemplifying Roman imperial generalship and the intelli-2nt application of policy to strategy at their best, made few changes in organization. [e did, however, add 2 legions to the standing army, and an even greater propor-on of auxiliaries. In his time the Roman standing army probably numbered more 1an 350,000.

Septimus Severus added 3 more legions, one of these being stationed in Italy • provide the first mobile reserve of the imperial Roman army. The total strength ' the army probably reached 400,000 men in his time. Severus also improved the .t and comfort of the soldiers in a number of ways, including permission for legal 1arriage. He made some changes in command organization, the most important 2ing to split the major regional frontier commands, reducing the temptation and pportunity for regional commanders to revolt against central authority. He also 1anged Hadrian's Wall in northern Britain from a wooden palisade to a masonry all, 16′ high and 8′ thick.

It was about this time that cavalry began to assume a role of importance in the oman army. Related to this was the appearance of mounted infantry to provide :eater mobility to foot troops and to assure rapid, distant movements of com-ned arms.

?eforms of Diocletian and Constantine

During the chaotic times of the mid-3rd century, it became obvious that the lministrative, political, and military policies of Augustus, though modified and lapted by his successors, were in need of drastic revision. A frontier defensive sys-m without a central reserve was not readily adaptable to a situation in which the 1pire had to face increasingly dangerous raids by improved, Romanized barbarian forces, as well as the threats of a strengthened, militant Persia. Simply increasing the size of the forces, without changing their organization and operational concepts, was not sufficient.

This, however, was the only recourse of the early Illyrian emperors, who had no time for reorganization and who had to make do with the system and concepts they had inherited, beating back multiplying threats in whatever way they could. The over-all strength of the army grew to about 500,000 men. By stern and harsh measures Aurelian, Probus, and Carus restored training and discipline to standards at least approximating those of the early empire. With makeshift forces, they ejected the Germanic barbarians and chastened the Persians.

One of the major causes of disorganization in the Roman army had been the old system of sending units from one portion of the frontiers to reinforce armies engaged in major wars. Naturally, it was rarely possible to take a full legion, or even a major portion of a legion, from one area, since this would have left a dangerous gap in the frontier defenses. The logical solution was to take detachments from different cohorts, legions, and numeri, and to form these into temporary task forces, called **vexillations,** which then operated as tactical units attached to the army in the threatened area. It was discovered that the most manageable vexillations were units of about 1,000 infantry, or 500 cavalry.

The vexillation system had initially been satisfactory. As soon as the threat was taken care of, the task forces were dissolved, and the detachments returned to their parent organizations. But during the turbulent period from 235 to about 290, detachments and vexillations were shifted so rapidly from one frontier to another that units became hopelessly mixed up. The tradition of the legion, and its impact on *esprit de corps,* almost disappeared.

This was only one of the circumstances which caused Diocletian to make sweeping reforms in military policy and organization, reforms later carried on and brought to completion by Constantine.

To provide a mobile reserve, the army was divided into two major portions: frontier troops (known as **limitanei** or **riparienses**) and mobile field forces (composed of more mobile units) known variously as **palatini** and **comitatenses.** Approximately two-thirds of the army strength was in the frontier forces. The remainder was in the mobile units, which the emperors (Augusti and Caesars) kept centrally located in their respective domains. The mobile forces received slightly higher rates of pay than the frontier troops, later a cause of trouble.

Experience with the system of vexillations caused Diocletian to reduce the size of the legions of the field forces to about 1,000 men. This assured greater strategic and tactical flexibility, without need for detachments. The legions of the frontier forces were kept at 6,000-man strength. Auxiliary units were usually 1,000 each, in both mobile and frontier forces.

Diocletian also eliminated the position of praetorian prefect, a post which combined in one individual duties approximating those of an imperial chief of staff with direct command of the Praetorian Guard. The power of these prefects had too often been used to overthrow an emperor, or to win the throne. Instead, each Augustus and each Caesar had two major military subordinates: a master of foot and a master of cavalry. Not only did this divide military power and thus reduce political danger; it also indicated the increasingly important position of cavalry in the Roman army.

Constantine later abolished the Praetorian Guard; in its place each emperor had a personal bodyguard of about 4,000 men.

The New Formations

Save for the obvious change in size, there was little superficial change in the tactical organizations of the legions, or in their soldiers, as a result of the reforms of Diocletian and Constantine. On the whole these changes were good, and contributed to the extension of the life of the Roman Empire. There were, however, some unfortunate practical and psychological effects—unforeseen and probably unavoidable.

The infantry of the mobile field forces were generally more lightly equipped than the frontier units. This, combined with their greater pay, created jealousy in the frontier units. Since there was no longer much difference in the background or nature of the men in the legions and the auxiliary soldiers, service in the frontier legions became less popular than in the less heavily encumbered and less strictly disciplined auxiliaries, or in the better-paid field forces. The result was a decline in morale affecting much of the army. It also resulted in changes in equipment and training programs, reducing still further the distinction between legionaries and auxiliary soldiers.

The soldiers—legionaries and auxiliaries, field forces and frontier forces—were now mostly barbarians. The result of this, by 375, was to cause most barbarian warriors to be essentially Romanized in weapons and tactics. For the most part, barbarians in Roman service thought of themselves as Romans and generally maintained the full loyalty of professional soldiers to their units and to their commanders. Nevertheless, though barbarians seemed to have no objection to fighting their fellows when ordered to do so by their Roman commanders (who also were more often than not barbarians themselves), this did create a number of opportunities for collusion, mutiny, and mass desertion.

Two new types of soldier also appeared in the Roman army, contributing to the slowly declining standards of training and discipline.

First, the increasing numbers of barbarian tribes which had been permitted to settle within the empire resulted in a reversal of Trajan's trend away from tribal auxiliaries. Tribal units of auxiliaries, under their own chiefs and retaining their own weapons and methods of warfare, were incorporated into the army in increasing numbers. These were called **federati.** Due to the over-all Romanization of the barbarian warriors, this had little tactical impact. But it did create new opportunities for unrest and mutiny.

Second, a form of conscription appeared in some portions of the empire, when it was not possible to fill the ranks by volunteers. The large landholders were then required to provide new recruits, on a pro rata or on a rotational basis. Terms of service of these conscripts were less onerous than for the regulars. This did not happen often, but it was a step in decreasing the professionalization of the army. It was also a step toward later medieval feudalism.

Tactics of the Later Empire

Between the time of Julius Caesar and Julian, no leading soldier wrote about his experiences. Nor did any other first-class historian bother to describe the combat of his times. As a result, the tactical details of operations in the 4-century period from 50 B.C. to A.D. 350 are quite obscure.

So far as the basic formations of the legion are concerned, apparently there was increasing use of the 2-line formation, with 5 cohorts in each line. There are some indications that the formations became more dense and phalangeal as a result of the increasing importance of cavalry and the concurrent decline in disciplinary standards.

On the other hand, there are also indications that the fundamental facts of human combat which impelled Marius to adapt the ancient quincunx formation to the cohorts of his legion were as well known to later Romans as to the Republicans. It would appear from the records of Constantine's tactics at the Battle of Turin that well-trained, well-disciplined infantry of the later empire could in the traditional close formation face cavalry charges with as much confidence as Caesar's legions, and that they could extend their front and otherwise maneuver and fight in cellular formations with the same speed, flexibility, and decisiveness.

Nevertheless, granting that there had been no change in the basic fundamentals of close-order and open-order infantry tactics, the increasing role of cavalry in warfare undoubtedly had its effect. When standards of discipline were high, the formations probably were similar to the ancient quincunx; when discipline was low, generals probably kept their legions closed up in something resembling the even more ancient phalanx.

One indication of the effect of cavalry on the declining legion was the adaptation of the old pilum into a "throwing spear." Apparently the change was adopted reluctantly, since the new pike was light enough to be hurled, and this was always done, in order to get rid of the encumbrance, before the legion came to hand-to-hand combat with other infantry. Presumably, in order to obtain room to use the gladius, the front was extended to gain the old open formation of the early legion. Yet the very change in the pilum was indicative of the trend toward lessened flexibility and reduced offensive capability, and in turn showed that discipline was declining.

By the beginning of the 4th century, cavalry made up about one-fourth of the strength of the average Roman army; the percentage was much higher in the eastern deserts in combat with the Persians and Arabians. Cavalry had become the arm of decision.

Missile weapons, too, increased in importance in the Roman army. These combined developments posed a tactical dilemma. To face cavalry charges the infantry had to rely increasingly on close formations; yet the problems of using, and being subjected to, missile engines of war created a tendency toward a more extended order. Recognizing that this same dilemma faced their foes, the Romans simultaneously increased their proportion of missile weapons and added more and more horsemen to their armies. Quite naturally, they endeavored to retain their flexibility so that they could adapt themselves to whatever danger posed the greatest threat at any time.

By the beginning of the 4th century the Romans provided more than one ballista, catapult, or onager to every 100 men of the legion. In addition, possibly half of the foot auxiliaries were archers or slingers, and many of the cavalry were horse archers on the Asian model. One result of this great reliance on missiles of one sort or another was to reduce significantly the occasions when the legion engaged in hand-to-hand combat with the gladius.

ROME AND THE BARBARIANS,
305–400

305–306. Confusion in the Imperial Succession. Upon the abdication of Diocletian and Maximian, they were succeeded as Augusti by Constantius in the west and Galerius in the east. Two new Caesars appointed were **Flavius Valerius Severus** who took over control of Africa and Italy and **Galerius Valerius Maximinus Daia**

Ignored were two young men who had expected the honor: **Flavius Valerius Aurelius Constantinus** (Constantine), estranged son of Constantius, and **Marcus Aurelius Valerius Maxentius,** son of Maximian. When Constantius died, later in the year, the legions of Britain and Gaul declared Constantine his successor as Augustus. Galerius reluctantly accepted Constantine, but only as Caesar, insisting that Severus should become Augustus. At about this same time, in Rome, the Praetorian Guard acclaimed Maxentius as Augustus. Maxentius, however, would accept only the title of Caesar, calling his willing father, Maximian, back from retirement to resume his old title of Augustus.

306–307. Civil War; Severus against Maximian and Maxentius. A year of strife ended with the execution of Severus, the appointment of Constantine as junior Augustus, and the recognition of Maximian as the senior. Galerius, however, refused to accept either Maximian or Constantine as a fellow Augustus.

307. Invasion of Italy by Galerius. Maximian and Galerius now maneuvered cautiously against each other in stalemate. Galerius appointed **Valerius Licinianus Licinius** as Augustus in place of Severus; then when his nephew Daia complained, because he felt that as a Caesar he should have had precedence over Licinius to the title of Augustus, Galerius conferred the title on him as well (308). Thus there were five Augusti. Meanwhile Maxentius, with the support of the Praetorians, drove his father, Maximian, from the throne, and himself assumed the title of Augustus. Maximian fled to join Constantine in Gaul, refusing to relinquish his title.

308. Congress of Carnuntum (Hainburg in Modern Austria). Arbitration by Diocletian brought an accommodation among 5 of the 6 bickering Augusti. Maximian abdicated again (he remained at the court of Constantine). Maxentius was ignored in the Carnuntum agreements, but his control of Italy was not disputed by Licinius, who was content with Illyricum.

310. Revolt of Maximian. Taking advantage of the absence of Constantine on an expedition against the Franks, the old emperor again tried to seize active power. Constantine returned promptly, drove Maximian from Arelate (Arles) to Marseilles, where he captured his elderly rival and father-in-law, whom he permitted to commit suicide. Galerius died the following year (311). This left four Augusti: Constantine, Maxentius, Licinius, and Daia.

311–312. Civil War; Maxentius against Constantine. Maxentius, with the secret support of Daia, prepared to invade Gaul through Raetia with an army of 170,000. Constantine had about 100,000, of whom more than half were required to hold the Rhine and Caledonian frontiers. Learning of Maxentius' plans, he decided to seize the initiative. Before the snow had completely melted, Constantine marched over the Mount Cenis Pass with 40,000 men (312). He won successes at **Susa, Turin,** and **Milan** against superior forces under subordinates of Maxentius. Of these, the **Battle of Turin** was a major engagement, in which Constantine displayed great tactical skill. He was next met by **Ruricius Pompeianus,** the principal general of Maxentius. Constantine defeated him in the hard-fought battles of **Brescia** and **Verona.**

312. Battle of the Milvian Bridge. Gathering reinforcements as he went, Constantine marched rapidly south. By the time he reached the vicinity of Rome, he probably had about 50,000 men. Maxentius had about 75,000 to protect the capital. Here it was, legend has it, that Constantine saw a cross in the sky and heard the words: *"In hoc signo vinces!"* Vowing to become a Christian if he won, Constantine plunged into battle, gaining a decisive victory on the banks of the Tiber near the Milvian Bridge. Maxentius was drowned trying to escape. Constantine, entering the capital, first disbanded the remnants of the Praetorian Guard, then announced his conversion to Christianity. He recognized Licinius as Augustus of the East.

313. Civil War; Daia against Licinius. Daia, endeavoring to gain control of the entire eastern portion of the empire, marched from Syria, planning to invade Europe with an army of 70,000 men. Licinius, with 30,000 veterans of Danubian campaigns against the barbarians, met him near Heraclea Pontica, in western Asia Minor. In the **Battle of Tzirallum,** Licinius won a complete victory. Daia fled, but soon died. Licinius was now unchallenged ruler of the East.

313. Frank Incursion into Gaul. Constantine, marching from Italy, defeated the barbarians and ejected them from Gaul.

314. Civil War; Licinius against Constantine. Discovering that Licinius was inciting a conspiracy against him, Constantine suddenly marched with 20,000 men, to invade the eastern part of the empire. Licinius, hastily gathering 35,000, met the invaders in southeastern Pannonia.

314. Battle of Cibalae (Vinkovci?). Constantine, in a good defensive position, repulsed Licinius' attacks, then counterattacked. Licinius withdrew after losing more than half of his army as casualties in the violent, indecisive struggle. Constantine pursued into Thrace.

314. Battle of Mardia. Again the issue was hotly disputed. Constantine gained the victory by a surprise turning movement, but Licinius again withdrew in fair order. He sued for peace, and in the subsequent negotiations agreed to give up Illyricum and Greece to Constantine, retaining Asia, Egypt, and Thrace.

315. Operations against the Goths. Taking advantage of the civil war, the Goths crossed the Danube into Constantine's new dominions. He repelled them, then crossed the Danube to punish the barbarians in the old Roman province of Dacia.

323. Renewed War between Licinius and Constantine. After a smoldering dispute, war broke out again between the two emperors. Each assembled great armies and large fleets.

323, July 3. First Battle of Adrianople. Each army comprised 120,000 to 150,000 men. Again Constantine made use of a turning movement to win a great victory, which was distinguished by his own personal valor in leading the frontal attack. Licinius lost 35,000–50,000 casualties during and after the battle, when his fortified camp was taken by storm. He fled to Byzantium, which was besieged by Constantine.

323, July (?). Battle of the Hellespont. Crispus, elder son of Constantine, led his father's fleet of 200 vessels in a 2-day victorious naval battle against the 350 warships of Licinius, destroying 130 of the defending fleet and scattering the remainder. His line of retreat across the Bosporus thus threatened, Licinius fled to Chalcedon. Constantine followed with about 60,-000 men, leaving the remainder to pres the siege of Byzantium.

323, September 18. Battle of Chrysopoli (Scutari). Licinius had been able to gather an army of about 60,000. Again th fight was prolonged and bloody, but Constantine finally won a crushing victory Licinius, fleeing, later surrendered an was executed (324).

324–337. Constantine Sole Emperor. Mos of the declining years of this controversial flamboyant man were spent in the construction of a new imperial capital—Constantinople—on the site of Byzantium.

332–334. Intervention in War of Goths an Sarmatians. Constantine took the fiel to assist the Sarmatians (a Scythian-Germanic people). He decisively defeated **Araric,** King of the Goths, who ha crossed the Danube to invade Moesi (332). When the ungrateful Sarmatian began their own raids into the empire Constantine encouraged the Goths to re sume the war, and stood aside while **Geberic,** new Gothic ruler, crushed **Wisuman** King of the Sarmatians. Constantine the let the remnants of the Sarmatian tribe— some 300,000 people—settle in the empir (334).

337–340. The Successors of Constantine Constantine had divided the empire amon his three surviving sons, though he retaine supreme authority until his death (337 **Constantine II** held Britain, Gaul, an Spain; **Constans** had Illyricum, Italy, an Africa; **Constantius** ruled Thrace, Greec and the East. Almost immediately Constantine II invaded Italy. He was killed i ambush near Aquileia (340), and his do mains immediately seized by Constans Constantius, who had become engaged i a war with Persia, was not involved i this struggle.

337–350. Persian War of Constantius. (Se p. 161.)

343. Barbarian Raids in Britain. Incursion of Picts and Scots forced Constans to g to northern Britain to suppress the dis orders. About this same time he was als concerned with the depredations of Saxo sea rovers along the coasts of Britain an Gaul.

c. 350–376. Rise of Ostrogothic Kingdom c Ermanaric. The aged Ostrogothic rule **Ermanaric** (reputedly about 80 years ol in A.D. 350) united the Ostrogoths an

Visigoths in a powerful kingdom, and by conquest extended his rule from the Dnieper Valley to a vast empire extending from the Black Sea to the Baltic, an area comprising roughly the modern Ukraine, Poland, White Russia, Great Russia, Rumania, Slovakia, and Lithuania.

350. Revolt of Magnentius. In Gaul the general Magnentius led a successful revolt; Constans, attempting to flee to Spain, was murdered, and Magnentius declared himself emperor.

350–351. War of Magnentius and Constantius. Patching up a temporary peace with Shapur of Persia, Constantius marched west to deal with the usurper who had murdered his brother. He discovered that in Illyricum the aged general **Vetranio** had been crowned Augustus by **Constantina** (sister of Constantius) and had joined an alliance with Magnentius. In a dramatic confrontation between their two armies, Constantius persuaded Vetranio to resign and added the Illyrian army to his own. Meanwhile Magnentius gathered a large army and marched to meet Constantius in lower Pannonia. The armies were about equal in size, nearly 100,000 each. Magnentius had somewhat the best of the subsequent cautious maneuvering.

351. Battle of Mursa (Osijek, Yugoslavia). In a hard-fought battle, Constantius' more maneuverable army, with a superiority in auxiliary archers and in light and heavy cavalry, enveloped Magnentius' left flank; then his heavy cavalry drove through the harassed Gallic legions in a climactic charge. Both sides suffered enormous losses; Magnentius apparently lost about 30,000 dead, and Constantius nearly as many. Magnentius withdrew to Italy.

351. Battle of Pavia. Magnentius defeated the imprudently pursuing forces of Constantius. But the Italian population rose in favor of Constantius, and Magnentius retreated to Gaul. Here, too, the populace rose against him, as did his own soldiers. Magnentius committed suicide, leaving Constantius sole emperor (351).

351–355. Internal and Frontier Disorders. German barbarians were making serious inroads into Gaul, apparently bribed by Constantius himself during his civil war with Magnentius. The barbarians found the experience so pleasant that they were unwilling to stop when the civil war ended. The situation in Gaul was further complicated by the brief revolt of the general **Sylvanus** (355). During this same period Constantius was forced to deal with the gross misrule and conspiracy of his cousin **Gallus**, who had been left in command in the East. Gallus was relieved and executed.

355–358. Constantius along the Danube. Invasions of the Quadi and Sarmatians now occupied most of Constantius' attention, though he was able briefly to operate with **Julian** along the Rhine (358; see below). The emperor attacked the barbarian invaders along the upper and middle Danube, drove them back across the river, then conducted a successful punitive expedition into their homeland (357). Following this, he moved southward along the Danube, subduing other barbarian disorders.

355. Julian as Caesar. Somewhat reluctantly, Constantius appointed his scholarly cousin, **Flavius Claudius Julianus** (Julian), the only other surviving male member of the Constantine family, as Caesar of the West in Gaul. To the surprise—and alarm—of the emperor, the 24-year-old Julian proved to be an outstanding military leader.

356. Julian's First Campaign. This began inauspiciously with a defeat at the hands of the Alemanni at **Reims.** He recovered, defeated the raiders, and advanced to the Rhine at Cologne. Here he worked in cooperation with Constantius, who advanced from Raetia up the right bank of the Rhine, while Julian operated to the west. There were no large-scale battles, and Julian had an excellent opportunity to learn something about war from his enemies and from his experienced cousin. Late in the year, while in winter quarters at **Sens,** he survived and repulsed a violent Alemanni surprise attack.

357. Julian Takes the Offensive. A joint campaign had again been planned, with Constantius' general **Barbatio** operating from a base in Italy and Raetia. As Julian closed in on the Alemanni King **Chnodomar** in the area of modern Alsace, Barbatio approached from the East. But instead of assisting, Barbatio suddenly withdrew from the campaign, leaving Julian with 13,000 men, opposed to Chnodomar's 35,000, near Argentorate (Strasbourg).

357. Battle of Argentorate. Julian's heavy cavalry stampeded early in the battle, apparently because of the Alemanni tactic of sending lightly armed men to crawl under the armored horses and to stab their unprotected bellies. The legions stood firm, and Julian rallied the cavalry. After heavy losses, the Alemanni finally fled; Chnodomar was captured. Julian chased the survivors across the Rhine, and raided briefly across the river himself. He then moved northward against the Franks, and before winter had completely cleared the left bank of the Rhine of all barbarians.

357–359. Julian Consolidates Gaul. After repulsing one final Frank effort to cross the Rhine, Julian devoted himself to rebuilding frontier defenses, and to re-establishing Roman outposts east of the Rhine. Making his headquarters at Lutetia (Paris), he also encouraged the reconstruction of ravaged cities and towns, sending troops to assist whenever possible.

358–363. Renewed War with Shapur of Persia. A Persian invasion of Roman Mesopotamia forced Constantius to turn once more to the east (see pp. 161–162).

360–361. Civil War; Julian against Constantius. Constantius, jealous of the successes of Julian in Gaul, ordered him to send most of his best legions to the East for the war against Persia. Julian protested, but prepared to comply with the order. His legions, however, refused to leave their brilliant young leader and proclaimed him emperor. Julian's attempt to reach an accommodation with Constantius was rejected. In a surprise march of amazing rapidity, Julian took his army eastward through the Black Forest and Raetia, arriving in Illyricum so unexpectedly that he captured Constantius' legate, **Lucilian,** at Sirmium without a struggle. As he continued toward Constantinople, he received word that Constantius, marching back to oppose him, had died en route in Asia Minor (November, 361). Julian, meanwhile, had renounced Christianity and returned to paganism; thus he is known to history as "Julian the Apostate."

362–363. Julian Prepares for War with Persia. After a few months in Constantinople, where he cleaned up the dissolute court and established a regime of austerity, Julian marched to Antioch. There during the fall and early winter, he collected an army of 95,000 men, the largest expeditionary force Rome had ever assembled in the East.

363. Julian's Invasion of Persia. Early in the year Julian advanced to Carrhae where he detached a force of 30,000 men under generals **Procopius** and **Sebastian** to march northwestward into Armenia. In accordance with promises of King **Tiranus** of Armenia, Julian expected his two lieutenants would be joined by an Armenian army of 24,000, and that the combined force would then move down the east bank of the Tigris River, toward Ctesiphon the Persian capital. Julian, with the remainder of his army, accompanied by a fleet of 1,100 river supply ships and 50 armed galleys, marched down the east bank of the Euphrates at a pace of 20 miles per day. Reaching the point where the two rivers most closely approach each other, he besieged and captured two strong forts protecting the approach to Ctesiphon. He then set his men to widening the canal between the Euphrates and Tigris, so as to be able to bring his fleet to Ctesiphon.

363. Battle of Ctesiphon. Discovering that Shapur's army held the far bank of the Tigris in force, Julian, with the help of his fleet, undertook a successful river crossing and defeated Shapur in a violent battle under the walls of the capital. Shapur and part of his army retreated westward; the remainder took refuge behind the city walls. Julian was now disappointed by the nonarrival of Procopius, Sebastian, and Tiranus. (He did not know that the Armenian king would not cooperate as he had promised, and that the two Roman generals were unable to agree on a plan of action.) Julian decided not to try to besiege and capture Ctesiphon, but rather to pursue Shapur into the heart of Persia.

363. Julian's March from Ctesiphon. Destroying his fleet, and all supplies that could not be carried by his men and a small baggage train, Julian marched east. The Persians, however, had conducted a "scorched earth" policy, and Julian, deceived by the treachery of a Persian nobleman, was lost for several days. Realizing that his army was running dangerously short of supplies, the emperor decided to withdraw north, up the Tigris, to establish a new base in Armenia. As soon as the Romans changed direction, they were harassed by swarms of Persian light horsemen. Though supplies were getting low, the army moved rapidly, and Julian expected to reach Armenia in about two weeks. During a night attack on his camp, Julian led a counterattack, without waiting to put on his armor. He was mortally wounded and died a few hours later.

363–364. Disaster under Jovian. The army elected the general **Flavius Claudius Jovian** to succeed Julian. Alarmed by the shortage of supplies, weak and indecisive Jovian accepted Shapur's offer to negotiate, halting his army for several days. Finally, all food gone, Jovian had no choice but to accept harsh Persian terms: loss of all provinces east of the Tigris and of Nisibis and other Roman fortified towns in Mesopotamia, abandonment of suzerainty over Armenia and other Caucasian regions. With but the emaciated remnants of the great army led eastward by Julian, Jovian returned to Antioch. Early the next year, en route to Constantinople, he died under mysterious circumstances.

364–378. Reigns of Valentinian and Valens. An able soldier, **Flavius Valentinianus I,** was chosen by the army to replace Jovian. He immediately selected his brother **Valens** as coemperor in the East. Both Augusti were soon occupied with renewed, intensive barbarian incursions, and with some internal disorders.

365–367. War with the Alemanni. The violence of the barbarian onslaughts caused Valentinian to take the field in person in Gaul. Repulsing them at **Châlons,** he drove them back across the Rhine and won a great victory at **Solicinium** (Sulz) on the Neckar (367). He then devoted himself to strengthening the defenses along the Rhine.

366. Revolt of Procopius in the East. Gaining control of Constantinople and much surrounding territory, Procopius declared himself emperor. He was soon defeated, however, by Valens' generals **Arbetio** and **Lupicinus.** The usurper was captured and executed.

367–369. Gothic War. Valens and his generals imprisoned a force of Gothic mercenaries who had aided Procopius in the civil war. Ermanaric, ancient King of the Goths, protested and sent a Visigothic army, under **Athanaric,** across the Danube. During a period of confused fighting and negotiations, Valens released the prisoners. Finally repelling Athanaric, Valens and his generals **Victor** and **Arintheus** invaded Visigothic territory north of the Danube. Peace was restored by a treaty recognizing the Danube as the boundary between the Gothic and Roman empires.

368–369. Chaos in Britain. The inroads of Saxon sea rovers, combined with Scottish and Pict uprisings in the north, kept Britain in turmoil. Valentinian's general **Theodosius** restored order in 2 well-conducted campaigns.

371–372. Revolt of Firmus. This Moorish leader revolted against Roman rule, nearly driving the Romans from Mauretania. Theodosius, however, arrived and quickly defeated Firmus, who committed suicide to avoid capture.

372–374. Appearance of the Huns. The Hsiung-nu tribes driven from Mongolia by the Chinese 2 centuries earlier (see p. 132) were apparently the ancestors of a fierce Mongoloid people—the Huns—who now entered European history. They invaded the lands of the Scythian-Germanic Alans (cousins of the Sarmatians) in the region between the Volga and the Don. The Huns won a great victory at the **Battle of the Tanais River** (373?); in less than 2 years the kingdom of the Alans was overwhelmed. Some of the survivors were absorbed by the Huns; other refugees wandered through the lands of the Goths, and some reached the Roman Empire, where they joined the imperial cavalry.

373–377. War with Persia. (See p. 162.)

374–375. Wars with the Quadi and Sarmatians. While trying to settle a border dispute peacefully, **Gabinus,** King of the Quadi, was treacherously killed by the Roman general **Marcellinus.** The infuriated Quadi immediately invaded and laid waste to Pannonia; all the upper and central Danube region flamed. While young **Theodosius** (son of Firmus' conqueror) held Moesia against the Sarmatians, Valentinian marched from Gaul, defeating the Quadi and driving them back over the Danube. He died of apoplexy while planning a punitive expedition north of the river (375). He was succeeded as emperor in the West by his son, **Flavius Gratianus** (Gratian), a youth of sixteen.

376. Huns Invade Gothic Empire. While vainly attempting to repulse a major Hunnish invasion over the Dnieper, the ancient Ermanaric was killed, or committed suicide. His successor, **Withimer,** was soon after this also defeated and killed. The Ostrogoths—men, women and children—now led by **Alatheus** and **Saphrax,** began to stream across the Dniester, seeking refuge from the Huns. Athanaric, leader of the Visigoths, planned to stand and fight the invaders, but most of his people, infected by the panic of their Ostrogothic cousins, also began to migrate en masse toward the Danube, under the leadership of **Fritigern** and **Alavius.** There were between 700,000 and 1,000,000 refugees, of whom more than 200,000 were warriors. Athanaric and the remainder of his people then sought refuge in the Carpathian and Transylvanian forests.

376. Goths at the Danube. The panic-stricken Visigoths appealed to Valens to grant them refuge and protection. Valens reluctantly agreed, on condition that the warriors give up their arms, and that all male children under military age be surrendered as hostages. The frantic Goths agreed to the terms and began to cross the Danube. Most of the boys were surrendered and were scattered through Asia Minor, but the Visigoths were slower to give up their weapons, bribing venal Roman officers with gold and other treasures, including the favors of their wives and daughters. Meanwhile the remnants of the Ostrogoths reached the Danube, and appealed for refuge in the empire. When this was refused, they crossed the river anyway, since the Romans were too busy trying to look after the Visigoths—and their women—to pay much attention to the new arrivals.

377. Outbreak of War between Goths and Romans. Roman officials in Thrace, not knowing what to do with the great influx of barbarians, took advantage of every opportunity to exploit and mistreat them. Fritigern and Alavius apparently tried to cooperate with their presumed protectors, but soon lost patience and began to negotiate with the Ostrogoths to present a united front against the Romans. At about this time the Romans treacherously at-

tacked the Visigothic leaders at a parley. Alavius was killed, but Fritigern escaped and immediately led his men in a successful attack against the forces of Lupicinus at **Marianopolis** (Shumla, eastern Bulgaria). He then joined forces with Alatheus and Saphrax in the region between the lower Danube and Black Sea (modern Dobruja).

377. Battle of the Salices (Willows). Valens, making a hasty peace with the Persians, sent strong reinforcements to Thrace. His generals **Saturninus, Trajan,** and **Profuturus** drove the Goths northward, blockading them between sea and river in the marshy region just south of the Danube mouth. Here the Goths made a stand behind the protection of their wagon forts. A bloody, indecisive battle ensued. While the Romans were reorganizing to make another attack, Fritigern made a successful secret move through the marshes and escaped. Once free of the blockade, the Goths streamed through Thrace and Moesia, joined in their mad, destructive rampage by raiding parties of Sarmatian, Alan, and Hun horsemen. Valens rushed back to Thrace with reinforcements from the East, sending an appeal for help to Gratian, his youthful nephew and coemperor.

378. Alliance among the Barbarians. Either by coincidence or—more likely—some sort of informal alliance among the Germanic tribes, the entire European border of the empire now erupted from the mouth of the Rhine to the lower Danube.

378. Gratian Defeats the Alemanni. Gratian, gathering forces to assist Valens, was forced instead to march to Gaul to meet serious Frank and Alemanni incursions. He defeated and killed **Prianus,** ruler of the Alemanni, in the **Battle of Argentaria** (Colmar), nearly annihilating the 40,000 invaders. Boldly crossing the Rhine, Gratian seriously punished the barbarians, pacifying the northern frontier. He then marched southeastward to help Valens.

378, July–August. Campaign in Thrace. Meanwhile Valens' lieutenant, **Sebastian,** had slowly gained the upper hand in Thrace. Relying primarily on light, mobile task forces of well-trained infantry and cavalry, he inflicted a series of defeats on the Goths and their allies, of which the most important occurred at the **Maritza River.** By early August the bulk of the combined Visigoth-Ostrogoth forces of Fritigern, Alatheus, and Saphrax were brought to bay in an immense wagon-camp fort, or series of wagon forts, on a hill in a valley some 8 to 12 miles from Adrianople. Here they were joined by a force of Gothic mercenaries deserting from the Roman Army. The exact number of barbarian warriors present near Adrianople is not known, probably somewhere between 100,000 and 200,000, of which about half were infantry, mostly Visigoths, and about half were horsemen—Ostrogoths, Sarmatians, Alans, and possibly some Huns. Fritigern seems to have been in over-all command, but Alatheus and Saphrax apparently exercised considerable independent authority. The Goths, having ravaged Thrace for several months, were now having serious difficulties obtaining food for themselves and their families (numbering at least 200,000 women and children). While the Visigothic infantry held the wagon camp, the horsemen spent most of their time foraging and raiding in central Thrace. Fritigern, realizing the danger of his situation, tried to negotiate with Valens, who was marching from Constantinople to reinforce Sebastian. Valens, however, jealous of Sebastian's and Gratian's successes, saw an opportunity for a great victory before Gratian, approaching from the north, could arrive to share the glory.

SECOND BATTLE OF ADRIANOPLE, AUGUST 9, 378

As soon as he reached Adrianople, Valens moved on the Gothic camp with his combined army, some 60,000 men, of which about two-thirds were infantry, the remainder heavy and light cavalry. Fritigern's scouts learned of the advance, and he sent for Alatheus and Saphrax, who—as usual—were out with their horsemen on a foraging expedition. In order to gain time for the Gothic cavalry to return, he also sent a message to Valens, offering to negotiate. Valens, whose troops were tired and sluggish after a long morning's march in the midsummer sun, ostensibly entered into negotiations, but in fact used the time to deploy his exhausted troops for an attack on the Gothic camp. He apparently neglected proper security patrols to the flank and rear.

While this was going on, battle began prematurely, apparently by Roman auxiliaries opening fire on a Visigothic negotiating party. Though the legions were still only partially deployed from their march column, the Roman cavalry was ready on the flanks; so Valens ordered a general attack. Just at this moment, Alatheus and Saphrax arrived on high ground overlooking the valley, where the battle was just beginning. The Gothic horsemen fell like a thunderbolt on the Roman right-wing cavalry just as they were reaching the wagon camp, and swept them from the field. Some of the Gothic horsemen then streamed through the camp; others swept around behind the Roman army to attack the Roman left-flank cavalry, in coordination with Visigothic counterattacks from behind the wagon ramparts. The Roman cavalry was routed, leaving only the infantry on the field, still not completely deployed, and without maneuvering room. The Gothic cavalry now swarmed around the flanks and rear of the legions, while the Visigoths charged down from their camp on foot against the Roman front lines. The battle became a slaughter. Valens was soon wounded. He, Sebastian, Trajan, and 40,000 other Romans perished in this climactic defeat of the Roman legions. The Goths, unable to capture Adrianople or Constantinople, swarmed unchecked through Thrace.

379–395. Reign of Theodosius in the East. Gratian now called upon Theodosius, son of his father's great general and an able leader in his own right, to be Emperor of the East. The new emperor established himself at Thessalonika, built up the defenses of the principal cities of Greece and Thrace, and restored the morale and discipline of the dispirited army. With cooperation from Gratian, Theodosius sent small, mobile forces to punish Gothic detachments. Gradually (379–381) he built up the confidence of his troops, and in two campaigns re-established a measure of order in portions of Thrace. He then felt strong enough to conduct two major campaigns against the Goths. He defeated Fritigern in central Thrace; the Gothic leader apparently died or was killed in the operations (382–383). At the same time Theodosius' general, **Promotus,** cleared the region south of the Danube by a series of successes against the Ostrogoths under Alatheus and Saphrax. Combining skill, prudence, daring, and conciliation, Theodosius finally pacified Thrace and Moesia; large numbers of the Goths were driven north across the Danube and even more were permitted to settle as peaceful citizens of the empire.

383. Revolt of Maximus. In Britain the general **Magnus Clemens Maximus** assumed the title of emperor, then invaded Gaul. Gratian moved to meet the threat, but after some minor setbacks was murdered by adherents of Maximus at Lugdunum (Lyon). Maximus then gained control of Gaul and Spain, while the young brother of Gratian, **Valentinian II,** became the ruler in Italy under the regency of his mother.

387–388. Civil War; Maximus against Theodosius. Invading Italy, Maximus drove out Valentinian II. Theodosius, marching to the assistance of his young coemperor, met the usurper at the **Save,** in Illyricum, winning by a bold and unexpected river crossing (388). Maximus fled to Italy, closely pursued by Theodosius, who besieged the usurper at Aquileia (near Venice). Maximus was murdered by his followers, who then surrendered to Theodosius; Valentinian II was reinstated as Augustus of the West.

387. Renewed Gothic Inroads. Alatheus led a new invasion over the Danube. He was defeated and killed by Promotus. Theodosius then imposed easy terms on the Goths.

390. First Appearance of Alaric. The young Visigothic chieftain **Alaric** raided across the Danube into Thrace, but was soon subdued by Theodosius. Alaric was then permitted to join the Roman Army with most of his men, in a typical instance of Theodosius' mixture of firmness and conciliation.

392–394. Revolt of Arbogast and Eugenius. After the defeat of Maximus, the Frankish general **Arbogast** pacified Gaul at the behest of Theodosius (388–389). Having gained almost complete authority in Gaul, he resented the interference of the youthful Valentinian, and evidently instigated his murder (392). Arbogast then appointed his protégé **Eugenius** as emperor, and consolidated his position in Gaul by two successful campaigns against Frankish invaders along the Rhine. Theodosius, however, refused to accept the usurpers and, with an army composed mainly of Goths (including Alaric), marched to avenge the death of Valentinian II. Arbogast and Eugenius met Theodosius in northeastern Italy.

394, September 5–6. Battle of Aquileia or of the Frigidus (Vipacco, a tributary of the Isonzo). Theodosius recklessly attacked a position carefully chosen by Arbogast, and was repulsed with heavy losses. Rallying his troops, Theodosius spent the night alternately in prayer and in the reorganization of his shattered formations. Next day he attacked again, and apparently was aided by the effects of a violent windstorm. By evening of the second day of the battle Theodosius, thanks largely to the efforts of his brilliant Vandal general, **Stilicho,** had won a complete victory. Eugenius was killed; Arbogast committed suicide two days later. The Empire was reunited.

395–400. Renewed Chaos in the Empire. The death of Theodosius was a signal for a new rising of the barbarians against his relatively inept sons: **Arcadius** in the East and **Honorius** in the West.

395–396. Alaric against Stilicho. Alaric, marching and pillaging practically without opposition through Thrace and Greece, was only temporarily deterred by the genius of Stilicho, who had promptly marched with his army from Italy to Greece (396). But Arcadius, more jealous of his brother and his great Vandal general than he was fearful of the Goths, insisted that Stilicho leave the Eastern Empire. Reluctantly Stilicho obeyed the order, and Alaric resumed his plunders unhindered. At the same time two other rebellious Gothic leaders—an Ostrogoth, **Tribigild,** and **Gainas,** a former Visigothic general of the Roman Army—were terrorizing Asia Minor and the region around Constantinople and forced Arcadius to pardon them (399). Gainas, made master general of the armies, was soon overthrown by trickery, and was defeated by the loyal Gothic general **Fravitta** while trying to cross the Hellespont with a small army. With the remnants he fled north and was defeated and killed in Thrace by **Uldin,** King of the Huns (400).

395–400. The Rise of Stilicho. Only the strong character and ability of Stilicho kept the empire from collapse. In addition to his brief campaign against Alaric in Greece, Stilicho generally maintained the authority of Honorius in the West. One of his most brilliant victories was gained in Africa subduing a rebellion by the Moorish leader **Gildo** (396). By the end of the century Stilicho was the uncrowned ruler of the West.

SOUTHWEST ASIA

DECLINE OF PARTHIA, 200–226

Torn by a series of violent civil wars, the Parthian Empire's collapse was hastened through defeats by Roman emperors **Septimus Severus** (see p. 130) and **Caracalla** (see p. 138). **Artabanus V** rallied from this latter disaster to defeat weak and vacillating Roman emperor **Macrinus** at **Nisibis** (217), regaining all of the territory captured by Caracalla. Meanwhile Artabanus was engaged in a debilitating civil war with his brother, **Vologases V,** which he finally brought to a conclusion by defeating (and probably killing) Vologases in southern Babylonia (222). But the drain on Parthian strength caused by Artabanus' efforts to gain these victories facilitated the rise of an even greater threat to his throne.

SASSANID PERSIA, 226–400

c. 208–226. Rise of Ardashir of Sassan (Central Persia). Subduing his unruly neighbors in the region around Persepolis, Ardashir (or Artaxerxes), the Sassanid ruler, challenged the weakened authority of Ar-

tabanus (c. 220). A series of campaigns was climaxed by the bloody **Battle of Ormuz** (southern Iran, on the Persian Gulf), in which Artabanus was killed (226).

226. Establishment of the Sassanid Empire. Ardashir seized Ctesiphon, the Parthian capital, and declared himself the successor of the Achaemenid Dynasty of Cyrus and Darius. In a series of whirlwind campaigns he reasserted Persian supremacy over most of the former dominions of Darius. He defeated the Massagetae and other Scythians who had been harassing the northern boundaries of Parthia, to gain uncontested control over Hyrcania (south Caspian shore), Khorasan, and Kharesan (Oxus Valley). He also conquered Kushan dominions between the Oxus and Jaxartes rivers, as well as in the mountains of modern Afghanistan and Baluchistan. Only in the west were his ambitions balked by the wavering, but still formidable, power of Rome.

230–233. Ardashir's War with Rome. Ardashir demanded that Rome withdraw from all of her Asiatic provinces. When this demand was ignored, he invaded Syria and Armenia (ruled by **Chosroes,** Parthian-Arsacid vassal and ally of Rome). Some Persian scouting and raiding parties reached the Mediterranean near Antioch and pushed into the mountains of Cappadocia in Asia Minor (230–231). Alexander Severus responded to this threat by gathering a large army at Antioch, then marching eastward on a broad front. One Roman column went to the assistance of Chosroes in Armenia, another was sent toward Babylon, along the Euphrates River; the main force, under Alexander himself, reconquered Roman Mesopotamia, marching by way of Carrhae and Nisibis. Apparently, according to incomplete records, the coordination between the Roman columns was poor; the Romans seem to have won all of the major engagements, but to have lacked the ability to exploit success. Having reached the Tigris, but having also sustained heavy losses, Alexander withdrew to Roman Mesopotamia, and the war simply stopped by mutual consent (233). Desultory fighting continued for several years in Armenia, where Chosroes, with Roman assistance, repulsed sporadic Sassanid invasions.

241–244. Shapur's First War with Rome. Shortly before his death, Ardashir raised his son, **Shapur,** to be coruler. The Persians decided to exploit Rome's internal difficulties (see p. 139), and Shapur was leading an army into Mesopotamia when his father died. The new emperor continued his advance, capturing the Roman outposts of Nisibis (Nusaybin, southeastern Turkey) and Carrhae (Haran), then penetrated into Syria (242). **Gordianus III,** however, assisted by his father-in-law, **G. F. Sabinus Aquila Timesitheus,** inflicted a decisive defeat on Shapur at the **Battle of Resaena,** on the upper Araxes (Araks) River (243). Gordianus was planning to exploit this victory when he was murdered and succeeded by Philippus Arabus, who hastily concluded a peace generally favorable to Shapur, leaving the Roman-Sassanid boundaries essentially unchanged.

c. 250. War with the Kushans. Shapur defeated the Kushan ruler, **Vasuveda,** somewhere in Bactria or Gandhara, ending Kushan influence in Central or Southwestern Asia (see p. 162).

258–261. Shapur's Second War with Rome. Again Rome's internal decay invited attack. Chosroes of Armenia was murdered at the instigation of Shapur, who then overran and conquered Armenia (258). Continuing into Syria, he captured and plundered Antioch (258). Soon after this, however, **Valerian** arrived from the west and apparently defeated Shapur in a number of minor engagements in central and eastern Syria (259). He drove the Persians from Antioch and back across the Euphrates. Shapur, however, defeated Valerian at the **Battle of Edessa** (Urfa) and succeeded in blockading the Romans (260). His army surrounded and in dire straits, Valerian opened negotiations with Shapur, who treacherously captured the Roman emperor. The Roman army surrendered, and Valerian was sent to Persia, where he died in captivity. Shapur promptly marched back into Roman territory, devastating Syria, Cilicia, and Cappadocia. Delayed for a long time by the tenacious defense of Caesarea in Cappadocia by the general **Demosthenes,** Shapur's final capture and sack of that city appeared to assure the collapse of all Rome's dominions in Asia (261). But a new threat to his lines of communication caused Shapur to withdraw from Asia Minor.

261–266. Shapur's Wars with Odenathus of Palmyra. The Persians were driven from Rome's Asiatic provinces (see p. 139).

264–288. Persian Occupation of Armenia. Weakened by his defeats by Odenathus, and occupied with troubles elsewhere in his vast dominions, Shapur maintained only a tenuous hold over Armenia. He appointed as his satrap there the somewhat mysterious Chinese refugee prince, **Mamgo** (see p. 163), who with his army of Chinese cavalry for several years maintained nominal Persian control over the unruly Armenian nobility (c. 275–288).

282–283. Carus' Invasion of Mesopotamia. (See p. 143.) This was facilitated by a dynastic war between **Bahram I,** son of Shapur, and his brother, **Hormizd.**

288–314. Reign of Tiridates III of Armenia. Diocletian determined to re-establish Roman suzerainty over Armenia. **Tiridates,** son of Chosroes, had taken refuge in the Roman Empire. Diocletian sent the Armenian prince back to his homeland with the support of a small Roman force. At first opposed by Mamgo, Tiridates slowly gained ground as the Armenian nobility rose against the Persians and their Chinese mercenaries. Finding himself unsupported by the Persians, Mamgo changed sides and helped Tiridates regain control of Armenia and expel the remaining Persians. Tiridates now invaded Assyria (293).

294–295. Persian Conquest of Armenia. Having overthrown his nephew, **Bahram III,** the new Persian emperor, **Narses,** turned to punish Tiridates. Driving the Armenians from Assyria, Narses soon reconquered all of Armenia; Tiridates fled to refuge in the Roman Empire.

295–297. Persian War with Rome. The Persian invasion of Armenia and the expulsion of his protégé, Tiridates, caused Diocletian to declare war. He placed his colleague **Galerius** in charge of the campaign. Tiridates joined Galerius with a contingent of Armenian exiles. Narses, meanwhile, invaded Roman Mesopotamia. With a relatively small army, Galerius marched into Mesopotamia, gaining a number of minor successes against the wary Persians (296).

296. Battle of Callinicum. Near Carrhae, site of Crassus' defeat, Galerius undertook a rash piecemeal attack against Narses and the main Persian army. The Romans were decisively defeated; Galerius and Tiridates escaped with only a remnant of their forces. Diocletian publicly rebuked Galerius at Antioch, but did not relieve him from command. With a reinforced, reorganized army, Galerius marched back against the Persians, while Diocletian sent for more troops from the Danube frontier.

297. Victory of Galerius over Narses. Marching by way of southern Armenia, Galerius with about 25,000 men encountered Narses with 100,000 at an unidentified site, probably along the Tigris River between Amida and Nisibis. Galerius routed the Persians in a surprise attack, capturing much booty and many prisoners —including the family and harem of Narses. The Persian emperor sued for peace.

297. Peace of Nisibis. Diocletian and Galerius, their joint armies now assembled at Nisibis, dictated stiff terms. The Persians gave up their claim to Roman Mesopotamia; they ceded five provinces northeast of the Tigris River to Rome; they recognized Roman suzerainty over the entire Caucasus region, and recognized Tiridates as ruler of the Roman protectorate of Armenia. In return Narses got back his wives and concubines. This peace lasted for about 40 years, though intermittent bickering continued along the eastern borders of Armenia, largely inspired by religious differences between Christian Armenians (Tiridates III had been converted to Christianity about 300) and Zoroastrian Persians.

c. 320–328. Arab Wars. **Thair,** a king of Arabia (or Yemen), led a successful expedition into Persia. Eight years later **Shapur II** (then about 18) led a punitive expedition into Arabia, defeating Thair (328).

337–350. Wars of Constantius and Shapur II. Shapur II, probably provoked by religious differences, suddenly invaded Roman Mesopotamia (337). Constantine prepared for war, but died before he could take the field. His son, **Constantius,** continued the preparations, and marched to meet Shapur in Armenia. This was the beginning of a drawn-out war, very inadequately recorded. Apparently 9 major battles were fought. The most renowned was the inconclusive **Battle of Singara** (Sinjar, in Iraq), in which Constantius was at first successful, capturing the Persian camp, only to be driven out by a surprise night attack after Shapur rallied his troops (344—or 348?). Gibbon asserts that Constantius was invariably defeated by Shapur, but there is reason to believe that the honors were fairly evenly divided between two capable antagonists. (Since Singara was on the Persian side of the Mesopotamian frontier, this alone is evidence that the Romans had not seriously lost ground in the war up to that time.) The most notable feature of this war was the consistently successful defense of the Roman fortress of Nisibis in Mesopotamia. Shapur besieged the fortress 3 times (337, 344?, and 349), and was repulsed each time by Roman general **Lucilianus.** The war was concluded—or at least recessed—by a hasty truce patched up between the two emperors, who simultaneously were faced with severe threats in other regions of their respective domains (350).

349–358. Scythian Raids on Northeastern Persia. Destructive invasions by the Scythian Massagetae and other Central Asian tribes forced Shapur to hasten eastward to restore the northeastern borders of his empire. Most able and most persistent of his opponents was **Grumbates,** ruler of the Chionites (353–358). Finally defeating Grumbates, Shapur enlisted the barbarian leader and his light cavalrymen into the Persian Army.

358–363. Renewed War with Rome. Having restored order in his eastern dominions, Shapur returned to his struggle with Rome. With an army that included the Chionites of Grumbates, the Persian emperor invaded southern Armenia, but was held up by the valiant Roman defense of the fortress of Amida (Diyarbekir, in Turkey), which finally surrendered after a 73-day siege in which the Persian army suffered great losses (358). The delay forced Shapur to halt operations for the winter. Early the following year he continued his operations against the Roman fortresses, capturing Singara and Bezabde. (The fact that the Romans were still in possession of this town in northeastern

Assyria, east of the Tigris, is further evidence that Constantius had not been defeated in his earlier war with Shapur.) Constantius arrived from the west at this time, and unsuccessfully tried to recapture Bezabde. Finding his forces too weak to undertake a major counteroffensive, he sent to his cousin Julian for help. This led to civil war between Constantius and Julian, which was resolved (361) by the death of Constantius (see p. 154).

362–363. Julian's Invasion of Persia. (See p. 154.)

363. Shapur's Victory over Jovian. (See p. 155.)

364–373. Struggle over Armenia. By treachery, Shapur captured and imprisoned **Arsaces III** of Armenia, who soon committed suicide. He then endeavored to establish Persian control over the country. The Armenian nobles, however, led by **Olympias,** widow of Arsaces, resisted bitterly. Roman Emperor Valens then lent support to the Armenian cause, giving clandestine assistance to **Para** (or Pap), son of Arsaces, who established a "government in exile" in Roman Pontus.

373–377. Renewed War between Persia and Rome. Valens' support to Para, in violation of Jovian's treaty of 363, caused Shapur to declare war. While Valens remained in Antioch, his generals defeated the Persians in southern Armenia and again near Nisibis. The Roman-Armenian alliance was marked by intrigue and perfidy, however, and the Roman general **Trajan** had Para assassinated (374). Gradually Shapur gained the upper hand in Armenia. Valens now being forced to concentrate much of his attention on affairs along the Danube, the war trailed out inconclusively. Shapur, realizing he could never gain a major victory over the Romans, and satisfied with his conquest of Armenia, was happy to make peace when Valens had to hasten back to meet the Gothic threat in Thrace (377). Unrest and violence continued in Armenia, however, the Armenian nobles constantly endeavoring—with some success—to obtain Roman assistance against Persia.

390. Partition of Armenia. The prolonged wars of the Roman and Sassanid empires were brought to a conclusion by a treaty between **Theodosius** of Rome and **Bahram** IV of Persia, which divided Armenia between the two empires.

SOUTH ASIA

The 3rd century A.D. is another frustrating period of obscurity in the history of India, perhaps due to the fact that no major power appeared on the scene during that time.

200–250. Decline of the Kushans. The Kushan, or "Saka," Dynasty established by Kanishka lingered on into midcentury, to be crushed when the Sassanid Emperor **Shapur I** completely defeated the Kushan King **Vasuveda,** probably in Bactria or Gandhara (c. 250). However, Persian internal disorders, and the obsession of Shapur and his successors with the struggle against Rome, kept the Sassanids from seriously following up this success. Some Sassanid expeditions apparently reached the Indus River region in the latter quarter of the century. As a result of the expulsion of the Kushans from Central and Western Asia, Hindu India lost even nominal ties with those regions. Otherwise this defeat had little effect on affairs in Hindustan; the Saka kings and princes still dominated the Punjab, Rajputana, and Sind; the smaller Hindu states to the east and southeast continued their decentralized, warring existence.

c. 230. Fall of Andhra. Farther south, the old ruling dynasty of Andhra fell, to be replaced by the vigorous Pallava family. The new Pallava-Andhra regime began a tentative expansion of its influence in the eastern Deccan, and north toward the Ganges, as well as pressing south against the Tamil Cholas.

c. 300. Revival of Magadha. A new ruler of ancient Pataliputra began to raise Magahda once more to a position of ascendancy in the Ganges Valley comparable to that which it had held in the time of the Mauryas. **Chandragupta** of Pataliputra claimed to be descended from his great namesake, founder of the Maurya Dynasty. After a number of victories that brought most of the central Ganges region under his control, he had himself crowned "Chandragupta I, King of Kings," establishing the Gupta Dynasty (320).

330–375. Reign of Samudragupta (Son of Chandragupta). He was the greatest military leader of the Gupta line. Like his father, his aim was to re-establish the power, glory, and geographical area of the old Maurya Empire. He came close to his goal, conquering Rajputana, most of the northern Deccan, and the east coast region southwest of the Ganges mouths. In the process he subjugated the Pallava kings of Andhra. He also gained a more tenuous authority over Nepal, Assam, the Punjab, and neighboring Gandhara. He made at least one successful raid deep into south India. The area nominally under his control was not much smaller than that governed by Asoka; his actual authority, however, was substantially less extensive and less clear-cut.

c. 350. Temporary Eclipse of Pallava-Andhra Influence. Defeat at the hands of the Guptas seriously weakened the growing power of Pallava. As a result of lessened central power, the local principalities of the Deccan grew in strength. One of these —the warlike Vakataka Dynasty—which dominated the region south of Nagpur, appears to have been primarily responsible for limiting Gupta expansion farther south.

375–413. Reign of Chandragupta II. The son of Samudragupta, **Chandragupta II,** brought the Gupta Empire to its zenith. He defeated the Saka princes of the Punjab, establishing in fact the purely nominal sovereignty his father had exercised over that region. Symbolic of this victory was the addition to his name of that of **Vikramaditya,** legendary Andhra conqueror of the early Sakas. He also annexed Malwa, Saurashtra, and Gujarat. Under his wise and able administration, Hindustan experienced its "Golden Age" of art, literature, and learning.

EAST ASIA
CHINA

196–220. Last Years of the Han Dynasty. The actual ruler of China during the last quarter-century of nominal Han ascendancy was the war lord **Ts'ao Ts'ao** (see p. 133). Most of the regions south of the Yangtze River, however, refused to acknowledge his authority. In an effort to re-establish central control farther south, he sent a naval expedition up the river. This was defeated by the fleet of a coalition of southern war lords in the **Battle of the Red Cliff** (208).

220–280. The Era of the Three Kingdoms. Upon the death of Ts'ao Ts'ao, his son, **Ts'ao P'ei,** deposed the last of the Han emperors and established himself as the first ruler of the Wei Dynasty (220). Since the regions south of the Yangtze still refused to recognize the central authority of the Ts'ao Ts'ao family, the former Han Empire now fell apart into 3 major regions: Wei north of the Yangtze, Shu to the southwest, and Wu to the southeast. The constant strife among the trio offered increasing opportunities for barbarian raids along the outer fringes of Chinese civilization. This was the beginning of a period of anarchy in China that would last—with rare interludes of peace—for almost 4 centuries.

220–234. Rise of Shu. The Shu, or Shu Han, Dynasty of southwest China was established by Liu Pei, member of a collateral line of the Han family. His capital was at Ch'engtu. The period of greatest strength and prosperity of the Shu kingdom was under the leadership of its great general and prime minister, **Chu Ko Liang** (223–234).

222–280. The Kingdom of Wu. This kingdom, and dynasty, founded by **Sun Ch'uan,** was the first of the so-called "Six Dynasties" whose capital was Nanking (220–589). The kingdom extended along the seacoast from the lower Yangtze Valley to below Tongking. During its period of greatest power (c. 250), this maritime kingdom sent a naval-commercial reconnaissance mission into the Indian Ocean.

234–264. Decline of Shu. After the death of Chu Ko Liang, the Shu kingdom steadily lost strength. It was conquered by Wei general **Ssu Ma Yen.** After this defeat, the remnants of the Shu Army—apparently accompanied by their families— fled westward through Turkestan to Persia under the leadership of a Han prince, known to Persian history as **Mamgo.** Mamgo and his followers offered their services to Shapur I, who welcomed them. Some years later Ssu Ma Yen—by this time emperor of China—sent a demand to Shapur to surrender Mamgo and his

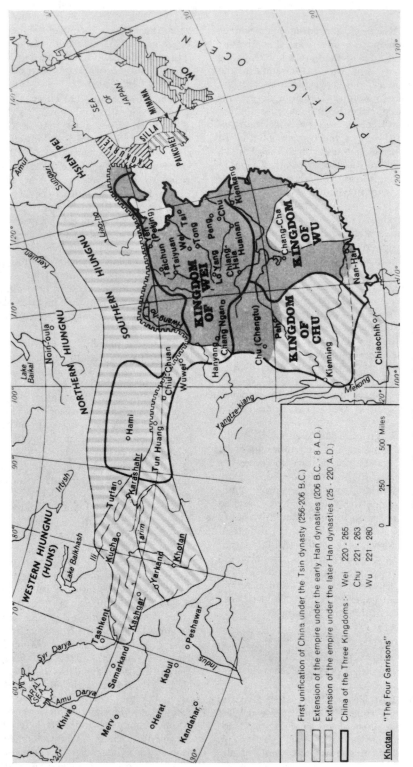

China under the Hans and the Three Kingdoms

adherents or else suffer a Chinese invasion. Shapur, facing war with Rome, wished to retain good relations with China; he simply sent Mamgo and his people to Armenia, then informed Ssu Ma Yen that they had been banished to "certain death" at "the ends of the earth." This apparently satisfied the Chinese emperor (see p. 160).

265. Appearance of the Chin Dynasty. Seizing the throne of Wei, Ssu Ma Yen established the Chin Dynasty, with himself as the first emperor, under the title of **Wu Ti.** He then conquered the kingdom of Wu, to reunite China temporarily and to end the Era of the Three Kingdoms (280).

290–316. Return to Chaos. The death of Wu Ti signaled a new outbreak of civil war. In the southwest, Szechwan established its independence (304). In the north, the Hsiung-nu and Hsien Pi (Hsien Pei) barbarians raided unopposed, and soon held most of the country north of the Yangtze Valley. The Hsiung-nus captured and killed two successive Chin emperors (311 and 316).

317–420. The Eastern Chin Dynasty. Driven from their northern capitals, the Chin emperors abandoned north China and reestablished themselves south of the Yangtze at Nanking, to continue as the Eastern Chin Dynasty, with their authority limited to South China.

317–589. Anarchy in North China. Northern China was now completely overrun and dominated by barbarians—or their direct descendants—for more than 2½ centuries. It was a period of utmost confusion: ceaseless fighting among the barbarians in the region, with an almost constant influx of new waves of barbarians, punctuated by frequent raids to the south, into the remaining dominions of the Chins. Initially the Hsiung-nu predominated. Later the Ch'iang tribe of Tibet became predominant (c. 350).

370. Reconquest of Szechwan. The beginning of a very slow and gradual rise of the Eastern Chins was marked by the reconquest of Szechwan by General **Huan Wen.**

383. Defeat of the Ch'iangs. A great invasion of Chin territory by Ch'iang ruler **Fu Chien** was decisively defeated by the Chinese at the **Battle of the Fei River.** Following this, the other barbarians in North China revolted against the Ch'iangs, bringing about the immediate collapse of their regime.

386–534. Rise of the To Pa. A branch of the Mongolian or Turkish Hsien Pi people, the To Pa (or T'u Pa, or Toba) tribe now established themselves as the dominant power in North China. Calling themselves the Northern Wei Dynasty, they held most of the region north of the Yangtze, including much of Mongolia and Turkestan.

VII

THE OPENING OF
THE MIDDLE AGES: 400–600

MILITARY TRENDS

This period witnessed one of the great turning points of world history: the dissolution of the decaying Western elements of the divided Roman Empire and the consequent emergence of the Empire of the East as the sole guardian of Western civilization. The decline of the old Empire was accompanied by a parallel decline in military leadership, ingenuity, and systematic study of war as an instrument of national policy. The crumbling of the West ushered in a new military era; armed force was applied vigorously and violently, but with little inspirational spark.

The Eastern Roman Empire was a partial exception, yet even there—with only slight modification during the reign of **Justinian**—national policy and military strategy were fundamentally defensive and passive in nature. (See Chapter VIII, p. 214, for discussion of the Byzantine military system.)

As might be expected under these circumstances, there were new military developments. The principal trend of the preceding era—predominance of cavalry—was accentuated in this, the opening phase of the so-called Middle Ages.

The one truly outstanding general during this early medieval period, **Belisarius,** was an exception to the trend and probably deserves consideration as one of the great captains of history. **Narses,** who had comparable skill in employment of combined arms, unquestionably learned the art of war from Belisarius (despite the parodox that he was nearly thirty years older). **Stilicho,** and possibly **Aetius,** were also professionals in the Roman tradition, far excelling their contemporaries and immediate opponents in skill, ingenuity, leadership, and the ability to integrate the efforts of infantry and cavalry in their battles. These four leaders were distinctly superior to **Attila,** who was an able tactician and an inspiring leader of light cavalry, but apparently unworthy of serious comparison with later outstanding Mongol, Turk, Tartar, or Arab leaders of light cavalry. **Alaric, Odoacer, Gaiseric, Theodoric,** and **Clovis** evidently owed their victories simply to superior vigor, craftiness, and charismatic inspirational ability in comparison to their foes. **Vitiges** and **Totila** were probably as able as any of these; they simply had the misfortune to be opposed by Belisarius and Narses.

166

THE BARBARIAN MERCENARIES

To an ever-increasing degree the East and West Roman empires made use of barbarian mercenaries in the early 5th century. These were enlisted in the dwindling number of regular units of the army, or more frequently were incorporated as **federati** in their respective national or tribal organizations under their own barbarian tribal leaders. Quite naturally, with the growing importance of cavalry, imperial generals favored the tribes who were natural horsemen. Thus the tribes of Asian origin—Huns, Alans, Avars, and Bulgars—were enlisted as light-cavalry bowmen. The German tribes inhabiting the plains between the Danube and Black Sea— mainly Goths, Heruli, Vandals, Gepidae, and Lombards—provided heavier cavalry who relied upon shock action with lance or pike.

The East Roman Army got many of its footmen from within its own provinces, particularly in Anatolia, though some barbarian foot soldiers—Germans and Slavs— were also enlisted. In the West, only a relatively small percentage of the armies were from the Roman provinces, and these mainly from Gaul. Thus foot soldiers as well as cavalrymen were obtained from the barbarian tribes, with the infantry coming mainly from the Franks and Burgundians.

The example of the fall of Rome undoubtedly influenced the East Roman Emperor **Leo I** and his successor **Zeno** to reduce their reliance upon federati. They vigorously endeavored to raise units from within the confines of their borders. The Isaurians, in particular, began to replace the hitherto preponderant foreign barbarians in the East Roman Army. By the time of Justinian the imperial armies were almost equally divided between federati and professional citizen troops.

CAVALRY TACTICS

In the early part of the 5th century, as the Romans were endeavoring to adjust their military system to the catastrophic lessons of the Battle of Adrianople, they particularly admired the effectiveness of Hun horse archers. This, combined with experience against the Persians, influenced the development of Roman cavalry. At first this new type of Roman cavalry was light and distinguished from the barbarian federati only by better organization and discipline. Gradually it became more heavily armored, and carried lance, sword, and shield as well as bow. Thus emerged (by the beginning of the 6th century) the **cataphract,** who, as the mainstay of the Byzantine Army of future centuries, would be the most reliable soldier of the Middle Ages. This heavy Roman horse archer combined fire power, discipline, mobility, and shock-action capability. He was the true descendant of the Roman legionary.

In his battles with Persians, Vandals, and Goths, Belisarius relied primarily upon his cavalry, which consisted of three main types: the heavy Roman horse archer, the light Hun federati horse archer, and the less important and less reliable Goth, Heruli, or Lombard heavy pike cavalrymen.

Only when combined with steadier organizations, and incorporated into a regular army organization with adequate logistical arrangements, could the Asiatic light cavalry conduct sustained operations. This was done successfully by the Romans and the Chinese. Otherwise, they were severely limited in their effectiveness. They could move only where they could find pasturage for their horses and (since they usually moved as tribes in great wagon trains) for the flocks of domestic animals that accompanied them. They were unable to campaign effectively in winter due to the lack of forage for horses. So, since they could only live off the country, and since they had so many animals foraging, they could never stay long in one spot, regardless of the requirements of the military situation.

In battle the Asian light cavalryman always avoided shock action against an organized foe. If long-range harassment with arrows was sufficiently effective, the Hun and his cousins would occasionally close to annihilate the enemy with sword and lasso. But if the foe could sustain punishment and return it, or if he was able to withdraw in good order, the Hun could not reach decisive conclusions and had to be satisfied with whatever raiding and looting he could accomplish.

INFANTRY TACTICS

By the end of the 5th century the legion had disappeared from the armies of the West and from the East Roman Empire. The frantic Roman search for a new answer to the combined threats of missile weapons and cavalry shock action had been relatively successful in the cavalry arm, but had failed utterly in the infantry. There was no infantry organization anywhere in the world that combined both the strength and the flexibility of the old legion. It was one extreme or the other—a relatively immobile mass of heavy infantry or swarms of lightly armed and armored missile-throwing skirmishers.

In consequence, with one significant but transitory exception, infantry became completely subsidiary to cavalry. The ponderous masses (sometimes combined with missile engines such as ballistae) could provide a base of maneuver for mobile cavalry. The light skirmishers—bowmen, javelin throwers, or both—could confuse, distract, and soften up a foe for the climactic shock of a cavalry charge. But (save for the East Romans and probably the Chinese) the military leaders of the age found it difficult to coordinate such combinations of missile and shock, steadiness and mobility. The result was stereotyped tactics and a general reversion to methods of warfare antedating the Battle of Marathon.

The one important exception to reliance upon cavalry was among the Franks. They had crudely combined infantry mass with mobility, missile power, and shock action. Lightly armored—or almost completely unarmored before the 6th century —the Franks rushed into action in dense, disorganized masses, comparable to the tactics their ancestors used against the early Romans. Just before contact with their enemy they would hurl a heavy throwing ax (**francisca** it was called by the Visigoths) or a javelin, then dash in with sword to take advantage of the confusion thus created. The fearless barbarians awaited cavalry charges in their dense masses, then swarmed around and under the stalled horsemen, cutting down mount and rider.

Oman* suggests that the Franks had learned nothing from their centuries of contact with the Romans so far as weapons, discipline, or tactics were concerned, and that their successes were due simply to their extraordinary vitality, and to the degeneration of the military art among their enemies. There is undoubtedly much to this; yet it cannot be the complete answer. There is evidence that Clovis was able to instill some discipline in his fierce warriors, and that he was an admirer of the Roman military system. His armies were small, and apparently he was outnumbered by his foes in many of his campaigns—particularly that against the heavy cavalry of the Visigoths. He could not, then, have been victorious without a greater degree of organization and tactical control than Oman would suggest.

Frankish experiences against Ostrogoths, Visigoths, Lombards, Avars, and East

---

* Charles Oman, *A History of the Art of War in the Middle Ages,* London, 1898, Book II, Chapter I.

Romans gave them a healthy respect for cavalry, and by the end of the 6th century they too had come to rely upon the shock action of heavy, lance-carrying horsemen.

The Angles, Saxons, and Jutes, in their invasion of Britain, employed the same kind of disorganized infantry tactics as the Franks. Infantry remained predominant in Britain simply because there was no challenge from an enemy possessing good cavalry.

NAVAL DEVELOPMENTS

If anything, war at sea had declined to an even greater degree than on land. The East Roman Navy showed flashes of effectiveness and retained a measure of control over the Black Sea and eastern Mediterranean. Yet Teutonic sea raiders consistently flouted the naval might of Constantinople, and the sailors of the East were not even able to prevent mass crossings of the Hellespont. **Gaiseric** the Vandal displayed considerable ingenuity and energy in organizing his long-range marauding expeditions and in dealing with threats to his own African coasts. But it seems doubtful that the Vandal fleets—or indeed those of any of their contemporaries— could have stood up to the navy of Themistocles, or to the Roman and Carthaginian fleets of the Punic Wars.

EUROPE-MEDITERRA-NEAN

ROME AND THE BARBARIANS, 400–450

The West

401. Alaric's First Invasion of Italy. With his Gothic-Roman army, **Alaric** marched from Thessalonika through Pannonia and across the Julian Alps (October). He besieged and captured Aquileia (at the head of the Adriatic), then overran Istria and Venetia. **Stilicho,** Patrician of the Empire and virtual ruler of the West for the incompetent Emperor **Honorius** (see p. 159), was taken by surprise. However, by harassing and delaying actions his outnumbered forces so hindered the Gothic advance that Alaric wintered in north Italy.

401–402. Stilicho Raises an Army. Stilicho personally crossed the snow-covered Alpine passes in midwinter to raise forces among German federati in Raetia and southern Germany. At the same time he ordered most of the Rhine garrisons and units in Gaul to join him in Italy.

402. February (?). Siege of Milan. Stili-

cho returned (probably via St. Gotthard or Splügen) with his German levies, an exceptional logistic feat in winter, particularly for his contingent of Alan cavalry. Joined by units from Gaul, he advanced rapidly toward Milan, which Alaric had invested. Alaric raised the siege and pressed southwestward after Honorius, who had fled to Asta (Asti). He apparently hoped to defeat the Romans in detail and to capture the emperor before Stilicho could interfere. (The exact sequence of events before April 6 is obscure.)

402, March (?). Battle of Asta. Stilicho pursued Alaric and seems to have had the better of an inconclusive battle outside Asta. Alaric withdrew up the Tanarus (Tanaro) River to the vicinity of Pollentia (Bra). Stilicho again pursued.

402, April 6. Battle of Pollentia. Early Easter morning, Stilicho attacked, surprising Alaric. The Goths rallied and Alaric's disciplined Gothic cavalry finally drove Stilicho's Alani federati off the field. Meanwhile, however, Stilicho's infantry had thrown back the Gothic foot troops and captured Alaric's camp. Alaric thereupon withdrew across the Apennines toward Tuscany, while opening negotiations with Stilicho and Honorius. A treaty followed: Alaric agreed to leave Italy, and retired to Istria for the winter.

403, June. Battle of Verona. Alaric, however, had no intention of giving up his invasion. He planned to advance through the Brenner Pass to Raetia as soon as the passes were clear of snow, thence to Gaul, now weakly garrisoned. Stilicho learned of the Gothic plan. Somewhere north of Verona in the narrow valley of the Athesis (Adige) River, the Goths were stopped by part of Stilicho's alerted army. Stilicho then attacked from the rear, inflicting a crushing defeat. Apparently Alaric was able to rally his troops sufficiently to withdraw eastward in good order—possibly via modern Trent or Bassano. Or, possibly, he made a deal with Stilicho. Honorius now moved his capital from Milan to heavily fortified Ravenna, inaccessible behind lagoons and marshes, save by two narrow, easily defensible spits of land.

404. Reconciliation of Alaric and Stilicho. Alaric renounced his adherence to the Eastern Emperor Arcadius, was appointed by Honorius (really by Stilicho) as master general of Illyricum, and subsidized to hold that province—which he had previously held for Constantinople—for Rome against barbarians and against the Eastern Empire.

405. Invasion of Radagaisus. Sweeping down from the Baltic area of modern Poland, Lithuania, and East Prussia came what was possibly the largest of all the barbarian migrations. The mixed Germanic peoples in that region, finding Hunnish pressures intolerable, banded together under a chieftain named **Radagaisus.** The exact numbers in this movement are unknown, probably nearly 500,000, of whom about one-third were warriors. Vandals, Suevi, and Burgundians predominated; there were also great numbers of Goths, Alans, and other smaller tribes. The invaders apparently crossed the Alps late in the year and spent the winter in the Po Valley, observed by Stilicho, who lacked sufficient strength to attack.

406. Radagaisus Moves South. With half to one-third of his warriors—approximately 70,000—Radagaisus advanced into central Italy, leaving the remainder of his army, and most of his noncombatants, in the north. Stilicho, who now had about 45,000 men—30,000 legionaries plus a sizable force of Huns under Uldin, as well as detachments of Alan and Gothic cavalry—moved to meet the barbarians.

406. Siege of Florence. Apparently while the poorly disciplined barbarians were settling themselves into an investment of Florence, Stilicho sent a heavily guarded convoy of provisions into the town. He then blockaded the barbarians, constructing a line of blockhouses, connected by trenches, after the fashion of Caesar. The barbarians were soon starved into submission. Radagaisus was executed; his surviving warriors were sold into slavery.

406–410. Barbarian Migration to Gaul. The remainder of Radagaisus' host now withdrew back over the Alps into south Germany, moving as separate tribes, of which the largest were the Germanic Suevi, Vandals, and Burgundians, and the Asian Alans. A portion of the Vandals were intercepted and seriously defeated by the Franks under **Marcomir;** the Vandal King **Godigisclus** was killed. In the following two or three years, all of the tribes, including the remnants of the Vandals, crossed the upper Rhine into Gaul to initiate the climactic Germanic invasion of that province.

407–408. Usurpation of Constantine. In Britain a simple soldier named **Constantine** had been elected emperor by his fellows (406?). To extend his dominion over Gaul and Spain, he took practically all the Roman garrisons from Britain and crossed the Channel. While he established tenuous authority over Gaul, sharing control with marauding barbarians, his son **Constans** and the general **Gerontius** conquered most of Spain in his name.

407–450. Roman Abandonment of Britain. Constantine's withdrawal meant the virtual abandonment of Britain, which became semi-independent under its local regional British-Roman leaders, who raised their own levies for defense against Saxon sea rovers.

408. Murder of Stilicho. At the instigation of Honorius, Stilicho was murdered. Mass murders of his adherents followed. Stilicho's barbarian auxiliaries thereupon turned against the emperor, urging Alaric to return to Italy to protect them and to avenge their murdered leader.

ALARIC'S OPERATIONS AGAINST
ROME, 409–410

409. Alaric's Second Invasion of Italy.
Crossing the Julian Alps by way of Aquileia again, Alaric marched into northern Italy, crossed the Po at Cremona, and advanced to invest Rome (409). Honorius, safe in inaccessible Ravenna, did nothing to aid the mother city of his empire, soon reduced to desperation by famine and pestilence. The Roman Senate agreed to pay Alaric a heavy tribute to raise the siege. The Goths then wintered in Tuscany, from whence Alaric opened negotiations with Honorius. Failing to obtain any satisfaction from the emperor, Alaric briefly blockaded Rome again, set up a puppet emperor, then marched on Ravenna. Unable to capture the city, he returned to the outskirts of Rome.

410, August 24. Capture and Sack of Rome.
After a short siege Rome was betrayed to Alaric, who turned the city over to his Gothic soldiers for 6 days of controlled looting. Rome had never before been captured by foreign invaders. He then marched through Campania to southern Italy. He was preparing to invade Sicily and Africa when he died (December). He was succeeded by his brother-in-law, **Athaulf** (Adolphus).

409–411. Chaos in Gaul and Spain. Meanwhile Honorius, unmindful of Italy's sufferings, set about recovering Gaul from Constantine and Constans. A three-cornered free-for-all followed between the usurper, his own general Gerontius—who had rebelled against him—and Honorius' general **Constantius.** After Gerontius defeated and killed Constans at Vienne (411), he lost most of his army by desertion to Constantius. With the remainder he returned to Spain, where he was halted by invading barbarians. Meanwhile Constantine was besieged at Arelate (Arles) by Constantius. After Constantius defeated a relief army under **Edobic,** Constantine surrendered and was put to death (411).

412–414. Visigothic Invasion of Gaul. Honorius' chicanery now resulted in another free-for-all, with four principal contenders again battling in Gaul: Athaulf and his Visigoths; **Jovinus,** a self-styled emperor supported by the Burgundians; Constantius; and the Roman-barbarian general **Bonifacius** (Count Boniface). The prize was control of Gaul. Also a prize was **Galla Placidia,** half-sister to Honorius, already promised by him to Constantius, but now promised to Athaulf if he would rid Gaul of the other barbarians. Jovinus was killed by Athaulf (412). The Visigoths then overran all southern Gaul save Massilia (Marseille), which was successfully defended in Honorius' name by Bonifacius (413). Constantius then defeated Athaulf, but was ordered back to Italy. Athaulf then announced Gaul had been returned to the empire, and married Placidia (414).

415–419. Visigothic Invasion of Spain. On Honorius' invitation Athaulf crossed the Pyrenees to reconquer Spain for the Empire (415), but was murdered (416). His successor **Wallia,** defeating the Alans, Suevi, and Vandals, drove them into Galicia (northwestern Spain). Having reestablished imperial control over Spain, Wallia was rewarded by Honorius with the region of Aquitaine, or Toulouse, the first barbarian kingdom within the old empire (419). Upon Wallia's death, **Theodoric I,** son of Alaric, became King of Toulouse (419–451). Meanwhile Placidia, Athaulf's widow, married Constantius (419).

420–428. Vandal Resurgence in Spain. Under their King **Gunderic,** the Vandals in Galicia quickly recovered from their defeat by the Visigoths. They defeated the Suevi, then defeated **Castinus,** the new Roman master general in eastern Spain (421), making themselves pre-eminent in the Iberian peninsula. Upon Gunderic's death (428), he was succeeded by his half-brother **Gaiseric** (Genseric). The Suevi under **Hermanric** now made one more effort to throw off the Vandal yoke, but Gaiseric crushed them on the Anas (Guadiana) River at the **Battle of Mérida** (428).

423–425. Usurpation of John. Upon the death of Constantius (421), his widow Placidia became estranged from her brother Honorius and, with her son **Valentinian,** sought refuge in Constantinople at the court of **Theodosius,** emperor of the East. Upon the death of Honorius, the West Roman throne at Ravenna was usurped by his prime minister, **John** (Johannes). Theodosius sent forces under the command of father-and-son generals, **Ardaburius** and **Aspar,** to depose the usurper. Ardaburius' fleet was scattered by a storm, and he was captured. Aspar, however, marched overland by way of Aquileia to the vicinity of Ravenna. Aided by confederates within the city, he captured it, deposing and killing John (425). Valentinian was enthroned, but Placidia became the virtual ruler of the Western empire. Illyricum was given to Theodosius in return for his aid.

424–430. Rise of Aetius. The usurper John had been supported by the Roman-barbarian general **Aetius** (390–454), who recruited a barbarian army (composed principally of Huns supplied by Aetius' friend **Ruas,** King of the Huns) which he brought to Italy from Pannonia (424). Arriving too late to rescue John, Aetius promptly made peace with Placidia and Valentinian and was placed in command of Gaul. He defeated Theodoric, King of Toulouse, at **Arles** (425), foiling a Visigothic attempt to conquer Provence. After making peace with Theodoric, Aetius in a series of campaigns subdued the Franks and other Germanic invaders of Gaul, re-establishing Roman control over all of Gaul save Visigothic Aquitaine (430).

428. Revolt of Bonifacius. During the usurpation of John, Bonifacius (see p. 171) remained loyal to Valentinian and Placidia, and was rewarded with the governorship of Africa. Feeling that his influence with Placidia had been undermined by Aetius, and disgusted with lack of imperial appreciation for his past services to the throne, Bonifacius revolted, calling for assistance from **Gaiseric,** the Vandal.

429–435. Vandal Invasion of Africa. Responding to Bonifacius' appeal, Gaiseric led an army (perhaps 50,000 men) of Vandals and Alans into Africa. Bonifacius, having meanwhile been reconciled to Placidia, attempted to call off the Vandal movement, but to no avail, and found himself at war with the barbarians he had invited into his province. Gaiseric twice defeated him (430) near **Hippo** (Bône, Algeria), then captured the city after a 14-month siege (431). (**St. Augustine,** Bishop of Hippo, died during the siege.) Taking advantage of internal religious dissensions, the Vandals soon held all

northwest Africa except eastern Numidia (modern Tunisia).

432. Battle of Ravenna. Placidia, fearful of the growing power of Aetius, called Bonifacius back from Africa during the siege of Hippo. Aetius, marching into Italy from Gaul, was decisively defeated by the imperial forces under Bonifacius. Aetius fled to Pannonia and refuge with his old friends the Huns. Bonifacius was mortally wounded in the battle (possibly by Aetius personally), and soon died.

433–450. Aetius Returns to Power. When Aetius returned from Pannonia with a large army of Huns, he was restored to favor and given the title of Patrician by Placidia. He became virtual ruler of the West. He made a treaty with Gaiseric, confirming Vandal control of northwestern Africa save the environs of Carthage (435). He spent most of his time in restoring and maintaining order in Gaul with an army composed mainly of Huns and Alans. He defeated a Burgundian uprising (435). He repulsed Theodoric at **Arles** in a new Visigothic effort to capture Provence, then defeated the Visigoths again at **Narbonne** (436). After desultory war, Aetius and Theodoric signed a treaty (442). To assure control of the Loire Valley from further Gothic encroachments, Aetius placed a colony of Alans at Orléans. For several years he campaigned against the Salian Franks under **Chlodian** (Chlodio). He defeated them repeatedly, but finally permitted the persistent barbarians to settle in the region north of the Somme River (c. 445). Aetius also subdued a number of peasant revolts, one of which briefly threatened his control of Gaul (437).

435–450. Expansion of Vandal Power under Gaiseric. After consolidating his hold on Mauretania and western Numidia, and building up a powerful fleet of sea rovers, Gaiseric seized Carthage and eastern Numidia (October, 439). Next year he raided Sicily, to begin a Vandal piratical career which would terrorize the Mediterranean for a century. Aetius, heavily involved in Gaul, asked help from the East Roman Empire. Theodosius sent a fleet to Sicily, intending an invasion of Africa, but Gaiseric, whose sea raiding had given him wealth, bribed his ally, Attila, ruler of the Huns, to attack Illyricum and Thrace;

the East Roman fleet was ordered back to Contantinople (see below).

439–450. Resurgence of the Suevi in Spain. The departure of the Vandals provided the Suevi, under their king **Rechila,** with an opportunity to overthrow weak Roman rule in Spain. He captured Mérida (439) and Seville (441), and had overrun all of Spain save Tarraconensis (modern Catalonia) before his death (447). His successor **Rechiari** endeavored to conquer northeastern Spain, but was repulsed when Aetius sent reinforcements.

The Eastern Empire and the Huns, 408–450

408. Death of Arcadius. Theodosius II was only 7 at the time of his father's death; the reins of government were assumed by his elder sister **Pulcheria** and the able praetorian prefect **Anthemius.**

409. Hun Invasion of Thrace. Uldin, king of the Huns, led his fierce horsemen into Thrace, but was defeated by Anthemius and forced to fall back across the Danube.

421–422. War with Persia. Persian persecution of Christians under **Bahram V** (see p. 192) led to war, quickly ended by a treaty after the East Roman general Ardaburius and his son Aspar won several minor successes in Mesopotamia. Persia agreed to allow freedom of worship to Christians, while Constantinople granted similar freedom to Zoroastrianism.

424–425. Expedition to Italy against John. (See p. 171.)

431. Expedition to Africa. At the request of Placidia, Theodosius and Pulcheria sent Aspar with a strong land-naval force to assist Bonifacius in the defense of Africa (see p. 172). Arriving at Hippo, the combined Roman-East Roman force, under the command of Bonifacius, marched out and was defeated by Gaiseric, who renewed the siege of Hippo. Presumably disgusted by the situation in Africa, Aspar and his force soon returned to Constantinople.

432. Treaty with Ruas, King of the Huns. The growing importance of the Huns in central Europe led Theodosius to pay tribute to Ruas, and to make him a general in the Roman Army. This in effect recognized the gradual extension of Hun sovereignty over Pannonia.

433–441. Conquests of Attila in the East. Upon the death of Ruas his nephews **Attila** and **Bleda** became joint rulers of the Huns. Renewing the treaty with Constantinople, the new Hun leaders undertook extensive conquests in Scythia (south Russia), Media, and Persia.

441. War with Persia. Another short religious war followed renewed persecution of Christians by Persian ruler **Yazdegird II.** Again Aspar was successful in a few minor conflicts, and peace was quickly restored on the basis of Persian promises to adhere to the earlier treaty (see p. 192).

441. Expedition against the Vandals. Upon the request of Aetius, Theodosius sent a large fleet and army to Sicily, with the intention of invading Africa. The East Romans were successful in several naval encounters with the Vandals, but the force was recalled to Constantinople when Attila invaded the East Roman Empire (see above and below).

441–443. Attila's First Invasion of the Eastern Empire. Bribed and encouraged by Gaiseric, Attila invaded Illyricum. A truce with the imperial court lasted for less than a year. Attila led his Huns into Moesia and Thrace to the very walls of Constantinople. He drove the main imperial army, under Aspar, into the **Chersonese** peninsula, where he practically annihilated it, only Aspar and a few survivors escaping by sea. Continuing to range over the Balkan peninsula at will, Attila suffered only one setback, being repulsed with heavy losses from the town of **Asemus** (or Azimus, modern Osma, 20 miles south of Sistova). Finally Theodosius made peace, promising an increased tribute (August, 443).

445. Murder of Bleda by Attila. Attila now became the sole ruler of a vast empire of undetermined extent, reaching roughly from southern Germany on the west to the Volga or Ural River in the east, and from the Baltic in the north to the Danube, Black Sea, and Caucasus in the south. He was a bold, fierce leader of light cavalry, an excellent tactician, and had some rudimentary strategic ability.

447. Attila's Second Invasion of the Eastern Empire. As the Huns advanced toward Thrace, panic broke out in Constantinople, where the walls had just been shattered by an earthquake. But the southward drive of Attila was checked briefly by the East Roman army in the indecisive **Battle of the Utus** (Vid). Though forced to withdraw, the imperial forces deflected the invaders from Constantinople toward Greece, where the Huns were finally halted by the fortifications at Thermopylae. Theodosius again sought terms. This time the annual tribute was trebled, and he was forced to cede the whole right bank of the Danube to Attila, from Singidunum (Belgrade) to Novae (Svistov, Bulgaria) for a depth of about 50 miles.

450. Death of Theodosius. Pulcheria, who had exercised virtual rule over the empire during the reign of Theodosius, married **Marcian,** who became the new Eastern emperor, and immediately stopped the tribute to the Huns. Attila was furious, but he had already made plans to invade the West, so decided to deal with Marcian later.

ROME AND THE BARBARIANS,
450–476

The West

450. Attila Decides to Invade the Western Empire. Because of a quarrel with Gaiseric, Theodoric of Toulouse prepared to invade North Africa. Gaiseric again called upon his friend Attila to make a diversion, suggesting that opportunities for rapine and loot were much greater in Gaul and Spain than in the devastated Balkan provinces of the East. At the same time a quarrel had broken out between the two sons of **Chlodian,** King of the Franks. One of these, **Meroveus,** asked Aetius for help; the other called on Attila. Another stimulus to Attila was his earlier rebuff when he called upon Valentinian, emperor of the West, for the hand of his sister **Honoria** and for half of the Western Empire.

451. Attila Crosses the Rhine. The Hun emperor led a great host which has been reported at 500,000 warriors (it was probably closer to 100,000), accompanied by a substantial wagon train of supplies and Hun families. He crossed the Rhine north of Moguntiacum (Mainz) in the territory of his Frank allies. The bulk of the army was Hunnish light cavalry, but there were substantial detachments of Ostrogoths,

Gepidae, Sciri, Rugi, Ripuarian Franks, Thuringi, and Bavarians. They advanced on a front of more than 100 miles, north and west of the Mosella (Moselle) River. Most of the towns of northern Gaul were sacked. Paris was saved, according to legend, by divine intervention besought by St. Geneviève. While advancing, Attila sent messages to Theodoric urging him to join in a campaign against Roman dominion in Gaul.

451. Aetius Raises an Army. Aetius raised a large army, his Gallo-Roman legions and Roman heavy cavalry forming the core, with substantial contingents of Franks under Meroveus, plus Burgundians and other German federati and Alan cavalry. Even with the unreliable and wavering Alans (kinsmen of the Huns), Aetius had a force probably no more than half the strength of Attila's. His personal appeal, however, persuaded Theodoric that the security of his Visigothic kingdom depended upon joining Aetius against the Huns.

451, May–June. Siege of Orléans. With more than half of his army Attila advanced through Metz (April 7) to the Loire Valley, where he laid siege to Orléans. The remainder of his forces devastated northern France. Starving Orléans was on the verge of surrender when the combined forces of Aetius and Theodoric approached. After some inconclusive skirmishing, Attila retreated precipitously, sending for the rest of his army. Aetius pursued closely. With his entire host assembled, the Hun king chose a position suitable for his cavalry army somewhere between Troyes and Châlons, and probably near Mery-sur-Seine. His wagon train was formed in a great laager behind the army, and was probably reinforced with entrenchments.

451, Mid–June. Battle of Châlons. Finding Attila thus prepared for battle, Aetius advanced cautiously, to be joined by a substantial number of Frank deserters from the Hun army. Attila drew his army up in three major divisions: he commanded the Huns in the center, the Ostrogoths were on his left, and most of his other German allies were on the right. Aetius placed Theodoric and the Visigoths (mostly heavy cavalry) on his right, and personally commanded the left, which

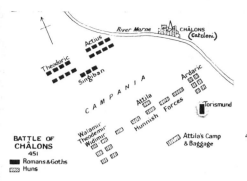

BATTLE OF
CHÂLONS
451
■ Romans & Goths
▨ Huns

consisted mainly of his legions, heavy cavalry, and the Frank infantry. The untrustworthy Alans were in the center, probably supported by a contingent of heavy Roman infantry or cavalry to dissuade them from deserting or changing sides. With Aetius was **Thorismund** (son of Theodoric) and a Visigothic contingent, possibly in the role of hostages. The battle was apparently opened when Aetius sent Thorismund's contingent to seize a commanding height overlooking the Huns' right flank. Attila replied with a general counterattack, which penetrated the allied center, as the Alans either deserted or fled. The Franks and Romans on the left and the main body of Visigoths on the right held firm, however, while fierce Hun attacks were unable to dislodge Thorismund from his isolated position. Theodoric now counterattacked the Ostrogoths to his front. The aged ruler was struck down in the confused fighting, but despite the death of their leader, the enraged Visigoths slowly forced their Ostrogothic kinsmen back. Meanwhile, on the Allied left, Aetius regained contact with Thorismund. Now, apparently in compliance with Aetius' preconceived battle plan, the Huns were threatened by a double envelopment. Realizing this, some of Attila's allies, and even his own Huns, began to waver. As darkness descended over the wild scene, Thorismund on the allied left, and the main Visigothic contingent on the right, apparently had routed the opponents to their immediate front; Thorismund himself actually reached the fortified Hun camp early in the evening, but was repulsed by Hun cavalry sent back by Attila. Realizing that the day had been lost, Attila had already ordered a general retirement. Fierce, confused fighting contin-

ued throughout the night as scattered Hun contingents tried to regain their camp. Aetius ordered his own wing of the army to stand fast under arms all night, while he tried to reorganize the shattered center. Apparently he was cut off by some of the retreating Huns and barely escaped to the bivouac fires of the main body of Visigoths, where he spent the night.

451. Aftermath of Châlons. Attila, expecting Aetius would attack his camp, prepared to fight to the end. Aetius, however, did not attack. It is not clear why he did not at least blockade Attila and starve the Huns to submission. Possibly he feared that complete annihilation of the common enemy would permit the Visigoths to take over all of Gaul. It has even been suggested that he entered into secret negotiations with Attila, promising no retribution if the Huns withdrew immediately from Gaul. In any event, he encouraged Thorismund, new King of the Visigoths, to return to Toulouse with most of his army to assure the security of his new crown. Attila quietly and quickly returned eastward across the Rhine. The casualties at Châlons are unknown; losses were apparently frightful, particularly among the Huns and their allies.

COMMENT: *Châlons is generally considered to have been one of the decisive battles of world history, since a victory by Attila would have meant the complete collapse of the remaining Roman civilization and Christian religion in Western Europe, and could even have meant domination of Europe by an Asian people.*

452. Attila Invades Italy. Having returned to Pannonia, Attila again demanded the hand of Honoria; when this was refused, he crossed the Julian Alps into northeastern Italy. Aquileia, traditional doormat of barbarian invaders, was completely destroyed. As the Hunnish horde advanced, the inhabitants of Venetia withdrew to islands off the coast, which resulted, according to tradition, in the founding of Venice, though fisher villages already existed on these islands. Destroying Padua, Attila advanced to the Mincio. Aetius, whose main army was still in Gaul, had rushed back to Italy, and apparently held the principal crossings over the Po, cautiously observing the Huns with a small force. At this time Attila apparently learned that one of his lieutenants had been defeated by an East Roman army in northeastern Illyricum. Famine and pestilence were raging in Italy, making it difficult for Attila to collect supplies for his men and horses, and already causing sickness in his army. At this time a Roman mission, led by Pope **Leo I,** visited Attila's camp. Whether they offered tribute to the Hunnish leader if he withdrew (which is likely), or whether he was miraculously awed by the demeanor of the Pontiff (according to tradition), or whether Attila was simply fearful for the security of his army and its line of communications (also likely), does not matter. He did withdraw, and Leo has received most of the credit in history.

453. Death of Attila. The vast Hun empire immediately fell apart as Attila's sons fought for the vacant throne and the Ostrogoths, Gepidae, and other German subject tribes revolted. **Ardaric,** King of the Gepidae, who had been Attila's right-hand man at Châlons, defeated and killed **Ellac,** son of Attila, at the **Battle of the Netad** in Pannonia (454). Dacia was occupied by the Gepidae, Pannonia by the Ostrogoths. The remnants of the Huns held on to their territory north and east of the Danube for a while under **Dengisich,** another son of Attila, but their dominions continued to dwindle as German tribes revolted and Dengisich was defeated and killed in south Germany (469). One contingent, under Attila's youngest son, **Irnac,** withdrew to the Volga-Ural region, but was soon overwhelmed and absorbed by the Avars (see p. 183). The Huns disappeared from European history.

454. Death of Aetius. Under circumstances remarkably similar to the end of Stilicho (see p. 170), Aetius was murdered personally by his jealous sovereign, Valentinian.

455. Death of Valentinian. Petronius Maximus, a protégé of Aetius, murdered the emperor, assumed the throne, and forced **Eudoxia,** widow of Valentinian, to marry him. Eudoxia thereupon appealed to Gaiseric, the Vandal, for aid.

455, June 2–16. Sack of Rome. Responding promptly to Eudoxia's plea, Gaiseric led a Vandal fleet to the mouth of the Tiber. Maximus was killed by his own people as he fled; the Vandals occupied and sacked Rome for two weeks. They

then sailed back to Carthage, taking Eudoxia with them as a hostage.

456. Rise of Ricimer. Upon the death of Maximus, the master general of Gaul, **Avitus,** briefly held the throne with the support of **Theodoric II** of Toulouse. But Duke **Ricimer** (of mixed Swabian and Visigothic royal blood) now became the major figure in Italy. He defeated the Vandals at sea near Corsica, then expelled them from a foothold in Sicily (456). He next overthrew Avitus at the **Battle of Piacenza** (October, 456). At about the same time the general **Marjorianus** (Marjorian), a former subordinate of Aetius, defeated an invading army of Alemanni at the **Battle of the Campi Cannini** (Valley of Bellinzona, southern Switzerland).

456. Visigothic Invasion of Spain. With the approval of Avitus, Theodoric II invaded Spain. He defeated Rechiari, King of the Suevi (see p. 173) at the **Battle of the Urbicus** (in Galicia), ending Suevi supremacy in Spain (456).

457–461. Reign of Marjorian. Set on the throne by Ricimer, Marjorian refused to play a puppet role. Defeating a Vandal force raiding near the mouth of the **Liri** (Garigliano) River, he decided that Vandal depredations could be ended only by destruction of the seat of Vandal power in Africa. First he determined to reunite the Western Empire. He led an invading army into Gaul (early 458) over snow-clogged Alpine passes. Marching westward near Toulouse, he met and defeated Theodoric II, who had hurried back from Spain to protect his capital. Marjorian granted magnanimous peace terms to Theodoric, facilitating his consolidation of renewed Roman control over the remainder of Gaul and Spain (458–460). He now bent every effort toward his main objective, invasion of Gaiseric's kingdom in Africa. He built up a large fleet in Cartagena. With Marjorian's preparations approaching completion, Gaiseric now began to sow treason among the Romans in Cartagena by bribery. Local treachery then permitted a Vandal fleet to surprise and destroy Marjorian's fleet shortly before he was ready to embark (461). Undaunted by this disaster, he began new preparations, but Ricimer now revolted in Italy. Refusing to rule an ungrateful nation, Marjorian abdicated, and shortly after ward was murdered at the instigation of Ricimer. Thus ended the last brief burst of glory of the Western Roman Empire.

461–467. Ricimer Uncrowned Ruler of Italy. Ricimer established dictatorial control over north Italy, while dominating the entire peninsula through a series of puppet emperors. A rival, **Marcellinus** (another former subordinate of Aetius), established himself as ruler of Dalmatia, and built up a fleet that controlled the Adriatic. Another rival, the general **Aegidus**, became virtual ruler of Gaul, and was accepted as such by both Visigoths and Franks. Meanwhile, continuing Vandal depredations along the coast of Italy caused Ricimer to request aid from Leo I, Eastern emperor. Marcellinus joined in the alliance against Gaiseric, driving the Vandals from Sardinia (468). East Roman expeditions against Africa were repulsed by Gaiseric (see p. 178), and Marcellinus withdrew from Africa to Sicily, where he was murdered by an agent of Ricimer (468). **Anthemius,** who had been installed as emperor by Ricimer (467), later quarreled with the kingmaker. Ricimer, his army reinforced by Suevi and Burgundian contingents, marched on Rome, which he captured by storm after a three-month siege; Anthemius was killed. Ricimer himself died soon afterward, leaving Italy in chaos.

461–476. Visigothic Expansion. After the death of Marjorian, Theodoric II of Toulouse rejected his alliance with Rome and quickly conquered Narbonne, thus bringing his dominions to the Mediterranean. He campaigned repeatedly, and generally successfully, against the Suevi in central and northwestern Spain. He invaded east and central Gaul, but was repulsed by Aegidus at **Arles,** and again at **Orléans.** Theodoric was assassinated soon after this and succeeded by his brother **Euric** (466). Euric continued Visigothic expansion in both Gaul and Spain. He defeated **Remismund,** King of the Suevi (468), extending control over all of Spain, with the Suevi, as vassals, confined to Galicia. In Gaul, Euric successfully carried the Visigothic frontiers to the Loire and Rhone rivers.

461–477. Continuing Success of Gaiseric. All coastal regions of the Western Mediterranean suffered from destructive Vandal raids, which extended as far east as

Thrace, Egypt, Greece, and Asia Minor. Gaiseric's greatest success was in repelling an invasion (468) by the combined forces of the Eastern and Western empires (see p. 178). Following this, he reconquered Tripoli and Sardinia (temporarily wrested from him by the allies; see above and p. 178), then conquered Sicily. At home in Africa, Gaiseric was plagued by constant religious unrest, and during most of his reign he and his Arian warriors cruelly persecuted the Catholic population. At the time of the death of Gaiseric (January, 477), Vandal sea power was virtually unchallenged in the Mediterranean.

475. Orestes Seizes Power in Italy. The master general in Italy, **Orestes,** seized power and deposed the emperor, **Julius Nepos.** He placed his own son, **Romulus Augustus** (or Augustulus), on the throne.

476. Uprising of Odoacer. A barbarian (part Hun) general named **Odoacer,** leading a mutiny by most of the barbarian mercenaries in Orestes' army, defeated him in the **Battle of Pavia** (August 23). After a brief siege Orestes was captured and killed.

476, September 4. Fall of the West Roman Empire. Odoacer deposed Romulus Augustulus and seized control of Italy. He did not assume the title of emperor. This date is usually accepted as the end of the Roman state established more than a millennium earlier.

The East

450–457. Reign of Marcian. After refusing to continue tribute to the Huns (see p. 174), Marcian evidently personally commanded expeditions to repel nomadic attacks on Syria and Egypt (452), and in Armenia (456). After the Ostrogoths threw off the Hun yoke, Marcian accepted them under their leaders **Walamir, Theodemir,** and **Widemir** (three brothers who had led the Ostrogoth contingent under Attila at Châlons) as subsidized federati in the East Roman Army (454). At about the same time a substantial contingent of Ostrogoths under **Theodoric Strabo** enlisted directly in the army under the master general Aspar (also of Gothic ancestry).

457–474. Reign of Leo I. Leo, who owed his throne to the support of Aspar, soon became estranged from his general. To reduce Aspar's influence, the emperor changed his bodyguard from Goths to Isaurians. Ending the subsidy to the Ostrogoths (461), Leo was forced to renew it the following year when Theodemir (now sole ruler of the Ostrogoths) ravaged Illyricum. An incursion of Huns over the Danube from Dacia was repelled by Leo's general Anthemius (466); a second Hun invasion was turned back by **Anagastus.** Meanwhile, following an agreement between Leo and Ricimer, in return for East Roman support against the Vandals, Anthemius had become emperor of the West (see p. 177).

468. War against the Vandals. Having entered an alliance against Gaiseric with Anthemius (and Ricimer) and with Marcellinus, Leo dispatched two invasion forces against Vandal territory. The smaller of these, under **Heraclius,** captured Tripoli and then prepared to march overland toward Carthage to join the main army. This, under **Basiliscus** (Leo's brother-in-law), was 100,000 strong (the figure probably includes the fleet strength). Sailing from Constantinople, Basiliscus, joined by Marcellinus, landed near Cape Bon. Gaiseric, after slight skirmishing, requested a truce, which Basiliscus unwisely granted. While this was in force, Gaiseric successfully attacked the allied fleet with fire ships and all of the fighting vessels he had; more than half of the allied fleet was destroyed. Basiliscus, embarking only about half of his army, fled back to Constantinople with the remnants of his expedition. Heraclius was able to withdraw successfully to Egypt, across the desert. Leo used this disaster as a pretext for charging Aspar with treason; the general and his son **Ardaburius** were both executed (471).

471–474. Ostrogothic Dispute. The death of Aspar caused great unrest among the Gothic soldiers of the East Roman army; Leo attempted to placate his Gothic troops by recognizing the claim of their leader— Theodoric Strabo—as King of the Goths. This in turn infuriated Theodemir, who began raiding into Illyricum and Thrace. This enmity between the rival Gothic houses of Strabo and Amal continued when the death of Theodemir brought his son **Theodoric** to the throne of the Goths in Pannonia (474). Leo died the same

year, and was succeeded by **Zeno,** who endeavored to continue the partially successful policy of playing the two rival Theodorics off against each other. Intermittent raiding and fighting continued.

THE BARBARIAN KINGDOMS, 476–600

Italy and the Ostrogoths, 476–553

476–493. Reign of Odoacer. After the fall of Rome, ex-Emperor **Nepos** established himself as ruler of Dalmatia. After Nepos' assassination (480), Odoacer sent forces to Dalmatia to punish the assassins and to annex the area (481). A few years later he led an army over the Alps into Noricum (Bavaria and Austria south of the Danube) to defeat and capture **Fava** (Feletheus), King of the Rugi (487). Th Rugi war was brought to a close th following year by the victory of **Onul** (Odoacer's brother) over **Frederick,** son of Fava. Odoacer annexed Noricum (488).

476–488. Rise of Theodoric the Ostrogoth The struggle between Theodoric Strabo and Theodoric Amal for recognition a King of the Ostrogoths was settled by th death of Strabo (481) and the treacher ous murder of his successor by Theodori Amal (484). The successful Theodori then quarreled with Zeno, whereupon h led his people and army into Thrace t ravage that province again (486). To ge rid of the troublesome Ostrogoths, and a the same time to reduce the dangerousl growing power of Odoacer, Zeno ap pointed Theodoric as Patrician of Italy and sent him off to try to seize Odoacer' kingdom.

488–489. Theodoric Invades Italy. Marching from Novae (Sistova), Theodoric too his entire kingdom, some 150,000–200,00 souls, of whom 50,000–75,000 were proba bly warriors. The Gepidae tried to ha the advance, but Theodoric defeated ther at the **Battle of Sirmium,** then continue on to cross the Julian Alps into Ital (August, 489).

489–493. War between Theodoric and Odo acer. Odoacer marched to meet the in vaders, but was defeated (August 28 489) at the **Battle of the Sontius** (Isonzo Falling back, he was defeated again at th

Battle of Verona (September 30). Odoacer withdrew to the impregnable defenses of Ravenna, where Theodoric blockaded him. Reinforcements arriving from the south, Odoacer sortied from Ravenna to defeat Theodoric at the **Battle of Faenza** (490). Theodoric fell back to Pavia, where he constructed a fortified camp, which was blockaded by Odoacer. At this time a force of Visigoths and Burgundians invaded Liguria, causing Odoacer to divide his forces. Taking advantage of this situation, Theodoric defeated Odoacer at the **Battle of the Adda** (August 11, 490), and Odoacer was again forced to flee to Ravenna.

490–493. Siege of Ravenna. For 3½ years Theodoric besieged Ravenna, until a naval blockade caused Odoacer to sue for peace. Theodoric, still uncertain of success, agreed to share the rule of Italy with Odoacer, bringing the war and the siege to an end (February 27, 493). Two weeks later Theodoric treacherously murdered his rival at a banquet, becoming undisputed ruler of Italy (March 15, 493).

493–526. Reign of Theodoric. He campaigned extensively beyond the borders of Italy, conquering Raetia, Noricum, and Dalmatia. After the defeat of the Visigoths by Clovis (see p. 181), Theodoric intervened in Gaul, seizing Provence, defeating the Burgundians, and blocking Frank expansion to the Mediterranean (507). Becoming involved in a war with the Eastern Empire, Theodoric defeated the general **Sabinian** at the **Battle of the Margus** (508). After some minor East Roman raids against the coasts of Italy, peace was concluded, confirming Ostrogothic control of Pannonia as far south as Sirmium. Soon after this, the declining Visigothic kingdom virtually recognized the sovereignty of Theodoric, who now came close to restoring the boundaries of the Western Empire in one great Gothic kingdom. This linking of the Gothic kingdoms, however, ended with his death (526).

534–553. Gothic War with Justinian. The power of the Ostrogoths was shattered by **Belisarius** and finally—after an exhausting war of nearly twenty years—destroyed completely by Narses at the **Battle of Monte Lacteria** (see pp. 188–189).

Britain; Angles, Saxons, and Jutes, 450–600

c. 450–500. Invasion by Angles, Saxons, and Jutes. The Saxons were the predominant element of the three related peoples gaining footholds in eastern Britain during this period. They had been raiding the coast of Britain for at least two centuries prior to actual invasion. Whether they actually settled on their own initiative or were invited by the Roman-Briton leader **Vortigern** to help repel the devastating raids of Picts and Scots is not clear. The most important early arrivals were the Saxon (or Jute (brothers **Hengist** and **Horsa,** who soon established themselves in Kent despite bitter resistance by Vortigern and later his son **Vortimer.** Horsa was slain at the **Battle of Aiglaesthrep** (c. 455). By the time of the death of Hengist, the barbarians were in complete control of Kent (488). Meanwhile other landings had taken place along the coast: the Saxons held the littoral around the mouth of the Thames and southeast Britain from Kent to the Isle of Wight; the Jutes held part of the Isle of Wight and the neighboring coastal regions; the Angles the coastal strip of modern Anglia and as far north as the mouth of the Humber.

500–534. Anglo-Saxon Conquest of Eastern Britain. In a century of almost constant, fierce warfare, the Germanic invaders gradually extended their hold over southeastern and central Britain. One outstanding early Saxon leader was **Cerdic,** who landed near Southampton (495) and was engaged in a series of violent but inconclusive conflicts by the Roman-Briton leader **Natanleod.**

c. 516–c. 537. Reign of Arthur. This semilegendary leader of the Roman-Briton peoples of southern Britain was the principal opponent of Cerdic and other Saxon invaders. For more than twenty years Arthur seems to have repulsed all or most of the Saxon efforts to penetrate central Britain. He may even have reconquered some of the territories seized by the Saxons to the south and the east. He probably commanded the Britons in a victory over Cerdic at **Mount Badon** (Badbury, Dorset, c. 517) and in another about ten years later. Nevertheless, by Cerdic's death (534), the Saxons controlled most of

Hampshire and (with the Jutes) had conquered the Isle of Wight.

534–600. Saxon Expansion in South Central Britain. Cynric, son of Cerdic, penetrated into Wiltshire, against fierce resistance, and **Ceawlin,** son of Cynric, advanced as far as the Severn, winning a major battle at **Dearham** (577). Attempting to push into Wales, however, Ceawlin was decisively defeated by the Britons west of the upper Severn at **Faddiley** (near Nantwich; 583). Further Saxon progress stopped, not only because of the increasingly effective resistance of the Britons but also due to internal strife among the petty Saxon kingdoms.

The Visigoths, 476–600

476–485. Continued Expansion under Euric. (See p. 177.) Euric consolidated Visigothic control over Spain, whose Catholic inhabitants were restive under their barbarian Arian conquerors. He also subdued the sturdy Gallo-Roman mountaineers of the upper Loire River. Defeating the Burgundians, he captured Arles, Marseille, and western Provence. This was the height of the power of the kingdom of Toulouse.

506–507. War with the Franks. Alaric II, who had been an ally of **Clovis,** King of the Salian Franks, later went to war and was defeated by Clovis (see p. 179). That the Visigothic kingdom survived at all, and that it retained this foothold in Gaul, was due to the intervention of Theodoric the Ostrogoth, father-in-law of Alaric (see p. 179).

526–600. Amalgamation of Visigoths and Romans in Spain. Subsequent, relatively ineffectual Visigothic rulers continued intermittent bickerings with the Suevi of northwestern Spain. A new Roman conquest under the resurgent East Roman Empire threatened temporarily (534–554), when Justinian sent small forces which—with the enthusiastic support of the populace—briefly conquered southern and southeastern Spain (see p. 190). The Byzantines made no real effort to retain their conquests, however, and the Visigoths soon retook all of the territory save a few coastal cities, which remained in East Roman hands at the end of the century. The Suevi were finally destroyed by Visigothic King **Leovigild** (585). Even more dangerous, and more persistent, was the

problem of subduing recalcitrant Catholic, Romanized Iberians, particularly in the mountainous regions. The constant small wars were only brought to a conclusion by the conversion of the Visigoths from Arianism to Catholicism (589).

Franks and Burgundians, 407–600

407–500. Consolidation of Burgundians in Rhone and Saône Valleys. After the expedition of Radagaisus (see p. 170), the Burgundians entered Gaul across the upper Rhine (407–413) and under their leader **Gundicar** established themselves in control of an indeterminate region astride the upper Rhine. They were pushed out of southwestern Germany, and Gundicar killed, by the Huns (436). His son, **Gunderic,** carved out a new kingdom in the Rhone and Saône valleys, and was involved in frequent wars with Visigoths and Romans. After a defeat at the hands of Aetius, however, Gunderic remained a fairly constant, though highly autonomous, ally of decaying Rome. The Burgundians became truly independent, and reached the height of their power under **Gundobad** (473–516), grandson of Gunderic, who for some time shared the kingship with his brother **Godegesil.**

c. 450–481. Consolidation of the Franks in Rhine Valley and North Gaul. One cause of Attila's invasion of the west had been a dynastic dispute among the Salian Franks (from the Somme River to the lower Rhine). The Battle of Châlons (see p. 174) virtually established the Merovingian dynasty of the Franks, under **Meroveus,** who had fought with Aetius. He and his son **Childeric** were faithful allies of the Romans, but slowly expanded the regions under their direct control. At the same time the Ripuarian Franks held the central Rhineland, striving to extend their influence southward against the Alemanni, who held the entire upper Rhine and southwest Germany. At the same time the Ripuarians were pushing up the Moselle Valley beyond Metz. Clashes were frequent between these two branches of the Frankish peoples, with the Meuse River the boundary between them.

481–511. Reign of Clovis. Upon the death of Childeric, his son **Clovis** (b. 466) became King of the Salian Franks. A gifted soldier, Clovis greatly admired the Roman military system and instilled a greater degree of order and discipline in his army than was common among the Franks. He soon came into conflict with **Syagrius,** a Roman general who had established himself as ruler of north Gaul west of the Somme and Meuse rivers, and north of the Loire. Clovis defeated Syagrius at the **Battle of Nogent** (or Soissons, 486). Syagrius fled to take refuge with Alaric II of Toulouse, but was surrendered to Clovis upon demand. Clovis gradually annexed the region north of the Loire, encountering considerable resistance from the local Gallo-Romans. He formed an alliance with Gundobar and Godegesil of Burgundy, marrying their niece **Clotilda.** At this time the Franks were still pagan, but the Burgundians had become Catholic Christians. Clovis noted that the relations between Burgundians and Gallo-Romans were eased by their common religion, while the Visigoths, Arian Christians, had constant religious trouble with their peoples. This undoubtedly facilitated his conversion to Catholic Christianity by Clotilda, a matter of great military and political importance, since it gave him popular support and facilitated his later conquests in Gaul.

96. War with the Alemanni. The Ripuarian Franks called upon Clovis for help against an Alemanni invasion of the Kingdom of Cologne. He broke the power of the Alemanni west of the Rhine by his decisive victory at the **Battle of Tolbiac** (Zulpich, southwest of Cologne). His actual conversion to Christianity is by legend attributable to his successfully calling for aid from Clotilda's God at a critical moment in this hard-fought conflict. This victory extended his domains to the upper Rhine and made him the virtual leader of the Ripuarian as well as the Salian Franks.

00. War of the Franks and Burgundians. A dispute between the brothers Gundobar and Godegesil caused Clovis to intervene on the latter's behalf. Clovis defeated Gundobar at the **Ouche,** and advanced down the Saône and Rhone valleys as far as Avignon. The continuing vigorous resistance of Gundobar, and his skillful, prolonged defense of besieged Avignon, caused Clovis to grant peace without conquest; the Burgundians became nominal vassals of the Franks. Almost immediately

Gundobar defeated and killed Godegesil in a successful assault of the stronghold of **Vienne.** Clovis did not intervene, possibly because he was again engaged against the Alemanni, eventually breaking their power east of the Rhine (506).

507. War with the Visigoths. Despite the mediation of Theodoric the Ostrogoth, war broke out between Clovis and Alaric II of Toulouse, ostensibly on religious grounds. The more numerous Visigoths lacked the enthusiasm, discipline, training, and leadership of the Franks. By his victory at **Vouillé** (see p. 180), where he defeated and personally killed Alaric, Clovis extended the Frankish kingdom to the Pyrenees, although the Visigothic foothold in **Septimania,** and that of the Ostrogoths in Provence, blocked him from the Mediterranean. This victory assured the triumph of Catholicism over Arianism in Western Europe. Soon thereafter Clovis was elected King of the Ripuarian Franks, which gave him personal rule over all northern Gaul and most of western Germany. His reign is generally accepted as the beginning of the French nation.

511–600. Expansion of the Franks. The amazing vigor and military prowess of the relatively few Franks, combined with the support of their fellow-Catholic Gallo-Romans, resulted in continual Frankish expansion in Gaul and Germany. It should be noted that these operations, unlike the migrations of most of the other barbarian peoples, were basically military expeditions, unencumbered by families and household possessions. Much energy was consumed, however, by violent dynastic wars, engendered by the Frankish custom of dividing the realm amongst all of the male survivors of a king. Thus, on the death of Clovis, his kingdom was shared by four sons. Nevertheless, Burgundy and Provence were conquered by the Franks (523–532), and Frankish armies frequently invaded Germany, Italy, and Spain. **Clotaire I,** longest-lived son of Clovis, briefly reunited the Frankish empire (558–561). In a series of great battles in central Germany (562), his sons halted the western migration of the Avars (see p. 183).

Vandals, 476–534

477. Death of Gaiseric. The great Vandal leader was succeeded by his son **Hunneric**

(477–484), who aroused animosity among the Catholic Afro-Roman population by his persecutions. This continued under his Arian successors **Gunthamund** (484–496) and **Thrasamund** (496–523). During this time Vandal possessions in Africa and the Mediterranean islands were somewhat extended and consolidated; piracy continued, but not so intensively as under Gaiseric.

531–532. Hilderic and Gelimer. Hilderic, son of Hunneric and the former empress Eudoxia (see p. 176), who was secretly a Catholic, ceased the persecutions of the Afro-Romans, but aroused the resentment of his Vandal people. His younger cousin, **Gelimer,** overthrew and imprisoned him (531) and began persecution of Catholics again. Imprisonment of the son of Eudoxia and the persecution led Justinian to send an expedition under Belisarius to invade Africa.

533–534. War with the Eastern Empire. The Vandal kingdom was destroyed (see p. 184).

Lombards, 500–600

c. 500–565. Lombard Domination of the Central Danube Valley. After the Rugi had been overwhelmed by Odoacer (see p. 178), the Lombards (or Langobardi, related to the Suevi) moved into the region just north of Pannonia and Noricum and began a struggle for control with the Heruli. **Tato** of the Lombards finally defeated **Rodulf** of the Heruli (508). In subsequent years the Lombards increased their dominions north of the Danube and began a series of violent wars with the Gepidae, as both peoples moved into Pannonia and Noricum after the collapse of the Ostrogothic kingdom in Italy. Playing the two tribes off against each other, Justinian gave nominal approval to Lombard expansion south of the Danube. The Lombard King **Audoin** (546–565) also fought under Narses in the Gothic War in Italy (see p. 188).

565–572. Reign of Alboin. The son of Audoin, **Alboin** precipitated a war with **Cunimund,** King of the Gepidae. At first defeated, he formed an alliance with the Avars (see p. 183) and again invaded Gepidae territory, defeating and killing Cunimund, and marrying the dead king's reluctant daughter, **Rosamond** (567).

Lombards and Avars then completely destroyed the Gepidae nation. Alboin, apparently somewhat fearful of the numbers and ferocity of his new allies, made an agreement with **Baian,** King of the Avars. He abandoned Pannonia and Noricum to the Avars in return for assistance in starting a migration southward (568).

568. Lombard Invasion of Italy. The entire Lombard nation (which probably included not more than 50,000 warriors), accompanied by 20,000 Saxons, invaded Italy by the traditional route across the Julian Alps. Alboin defeated imperial general **Longinus,** Exarch of Ravenna in northeast Italy (569), and quickly overran the Po Valley. Milan was soon captured; Pavia fell after a three-year siege (572). Settling in northern Italy (thereafter known as Lombardy), with their capital at Pavia, the Lombards soon drove imperial forces from most of Italy, save for a number of large coastal cities, which remained under Constantinople. Alboin was murdered by his vengeful wife (573), but the conquest of Italy continued unabated despite a lack of strong central authority. The Frankish King **Childebert** intervened briefly in the drawn-out war between Lombards and imperial forces in Italy (585). Subsidized by Constantinople, Childebert crossed the Alps three times to gain mixed success against **Autharis,** King of the Lombards. Failing to receive any cooperation from imperial forces, Childebert then withdrew. Anarchy pervaded Italy, with the semi-independent Lombard dukes constantly at war with each other.

Bulgars and Slavs, c. 530–600

c. 530. Appearance of Bulgars and Slavs. Two new barbarian peoples began to cross the Danube in great force. One group—the Bulgars—comprised fierce, nomadic Asian Turanian horsemen, related to Huns and Avars. The other group—the Slavs—were a blond Indo-European people, similar in appearance to the Germans. Avar pressure had driven the Bulgars into southeastern Europe (see p. 183). The Slavs, who seemingly lacked the inherent ferocity or aggressiveness of either the German or Mongoloid barbarians, had been slowly pushed southward from their homeland north of the Carpathians by successive tides of Asian invasions. Stolid foot soldiers, particularly reliable and effective on the defense, the Slavs were frequently incorporated into the fighting forces of the nomadic armies which swept through their lands. It was thus that they began to appear south of the Danube, first with the Huns, then with the Bulgars.

540–600. Bulgar and Slav Raids into the Balkans. Following time-honored invasion routes across the Danube, both Bulgars and Slavs—sometimes together, more often separately—ravaged the Balkans, and on occasion continued across the straits into Asia. One such invasion was stopped (550) by **Germanius,** nephew of Justinian, who won a great victory over the Slavs at **Sardica** (Sofia). A dangerous raid of Bulgars brought Belisarius out of retirement for his last victory under the walls of Constantinople (559; see p. 191). A few years later the Slav people began to settle in large numbers in depopulated regions of Thrace and Greece (c. 578).

Avars, 550–600

c. 555. Avars Driven into Europe. A Mongoloid people, akin to Tartars and Huns, the Avars of European history were probably basically a part of the Uighur people inhabiting the steppes lying generally between the Volga, Kama, and Ural rivers (c. 460–c. 555). When the Avar Empire of central Asia was overthrown by the Turks (see p. 197), the Avar-Uigurs were driven south into the northern Caucasus (c. 555). Obtaining a subsidy from Justinian, they appear to have migrated to the Danube Valley to assist the East Romans against Bulgars and Slavs. Like their kinsmen the Huns, Bulgars, and Turks, the Avars were essentially light cavalry, their principal weapon the bow.

562–600. Rise of the Avar Empire. Under their great chief, **Baian,** the Avars soon carved out a large empire. Invading Germany, they were repulsed in Thuringia by the Franks (562). After a raid into the Eastern Empire (564), the Avars allied themselves with the Lombards to destroy the power of the Gepidae (see p. 182) and to seize their lands in modern Transylvania (567). After the migration of the Lombards, the Avars moved into Pannonia and Noricum. Aside from the defeat by the Franks, Baian was for most of his reign universally victorious in his campaigns in central and southern Europe. He repeatedly invaded the Eastern Empire, capturing Sirmium (Sirmione, 580) and sweeping as far south as the Aegean (591 and 597). His successes, however, were finally halted by the emperor **Maurice** and his general **Priscus** in a series of victorious campaigns from the Black Sea to the Theiss River (595–601, culminating on the south bank of the Danube at the Battle of **Viminacium** (601). By the end of the century, nevertheless, Baian was nominal suzerain of an empire extending from the Julian Alps to the Volga, and from the Baltic to the Danube.

EAST ROMAN EMPIRE, 474–600

The Empire on the Defensive, 474–524

474–491. Reign of Zeno. A successful Isaurian general, **Zeno,** followed Leo I. A revolt by **Verina,** widow of Leo, and her brother **Basiliscus** (475) compelled Zeno to take refuge in Isauria, but within a year he had regained his throne and exiled the rebels (476). He handled the Ostrogothic threat by playing off Theodoric Strabo and Theodoric Amal against each other, and when the latter was successful, persuaded him to invade Italy (see p. 178).

491–518. Reign of Anastasius. A former civil official, **Anastasius** was an able and vigorous administrator. He soon faced a civil war started by **Longinus,** brother of Zeno.

492–496. Isaurian War. Though nominally an integral part of the empire, and though Isaurians comprised an important element in the East Roman Army, the mountain fastnesses of Isauria had long been semi-independent. Anastasius directed war vigorously against Longinus, with a view to subduing the wild Isaurians. His essentially Gothic army defeated them at the **Battle of Cotyaeum** (Kutahya, western Anatolia) and drove them back into their mountains in south central Anatolia (493). Continuing guerrilla resistance by the Isaurians was stamped out by systematic capture of their fortified towns.

502–506. War with Persia. Though essentially a war to prevent Persian expansion on the Black Sea through Colchis (or Lazica), most of the fighting took place along the Mesopotamian and Armenian frontiers of the two nations. The Persians succeeded in capturing Theodosiopolis (Erzerum) in Roman Armenia and—after a three-month siege—Amida in Roman Mesopotamia. They were repulsed from Edessa, however, and the remainder of the war consisted mainly of long-range raids by each side. After the East Romans recovered Amida, peace was restored on the basis of the *status quo ante.*

507–512. Anastasius' Fortifications. To offset the Persian fortress at Nisibis, Anastasius built a powerful fort at Daras (Dara), just west of Nisibis (507). Soon after this, alarmed by the depredations of Slavs and Bulgars in Thrace, he built the "Anastasian Wall" from the Black Sea to Propontis (Sea of Marmara), across the narrow peninsula a few miles from Constantinople (512).

514–527. Reign of Justin. A former general in the Isaurian and Persian wars, and probably of mixed Gothic-Slav ancestry, **Justin**'s reign is particularly noteworthy because of the important administrative role played by his nephew, **Justinian.** Just before Justin's death, another war broke out with Persia, partly on religious grounds and partly due to a dispute over the responsibility for protecting the Caucasus passes against barbarian inroads into both empires. In an earlier agreement the Romans had agreed to contribute to the support of Persian garrisons and fortifications at the Caspian (Albanian) Gate and the Caucasus (Iberian) Gate. Roman failure to keep up the payments had irritated the Persian emperor **Kavadh I.**

The Wars of Justinian, 527–565

527–565. Reign of Justinian (Nephew of Justin). He was the most illustrious ruler of the East Roman or Byzantine Empire.

JUSTINIAN'S FIRST PERSIAN WAR, 524–532

524–528. Persian Successes. At the outset Kavadh, assisted by his Arabian vassal, **Mondhir** of Hira, had the better of fighting in Mesopotamia. He was held up, however, by the successful defense of the

powerful Roman frontier fortresses. The Romans also repulsed Persian attacks into Lazica (Colchis or western Georgia).

529–531. Rise of Belisarius. The later years of the war were distinguished by the exploits of a young Thracian general, **Belisarius** (505–565). He led a successful long-range raid into Persian Armenia (529). As commander in the East, with 25,000 men he defeated a combined Persian-Arab army of 40,000 at **Dara** (530) by entrenching his infantry in a refused position in the center of his line, then carrying out a cavalry envelopment to culminate a classic defensive-offensive battle plan. The following year he repulsed several Persian efforts to invade Syria, but was defeated by greatly superior forces at **Callinicum.** Withdrawing to the islands of the Euphrates, at **Sura** he then repulsed all Persian efforts to overwhelm his shattered army, and so gained considerable glory despite the earlier defeat. The Persians, discouraged, withdrew and peace was soon made. As a result of this inconclusive war the East Romans strengthened their previously tenuous hold on Lazica, but agreed to make regular payment to subsidize the Persians' forts in the Caucasus passes.

532. Nika Uprising in Constantinople. Belisarius, withdrawn before the conclusion of the Persian War to command an expedition to Africa, was in Constantinople when an uprising almost overthrew Justinian. The firmness of the empress **Theodora** and the prompt military action of Belisarius and the generals **Narses** and **Mundas,** with 3,000 troops, saved the vacillating Justinian. Some 30,000 of the mob were killed and order restored.

THE VANDAL WAR IN AFRICA, 533–534

533. Belisarius' Expedition. For religious and political reasons, Justinian decided to reconquer Africa from the Vandals (see p. 182). Belisarius took a joint army-navy task force, consisting of 10,000 infantry and 5,000 cavalry, in 500 transports escorted by 92 war vessels manned by 20,000 seamen. He stopped at Sicily, which he used as a staging area, with the permission of **Amalasuntha,** daughter of Theodoric, and regent of Italy. At this time

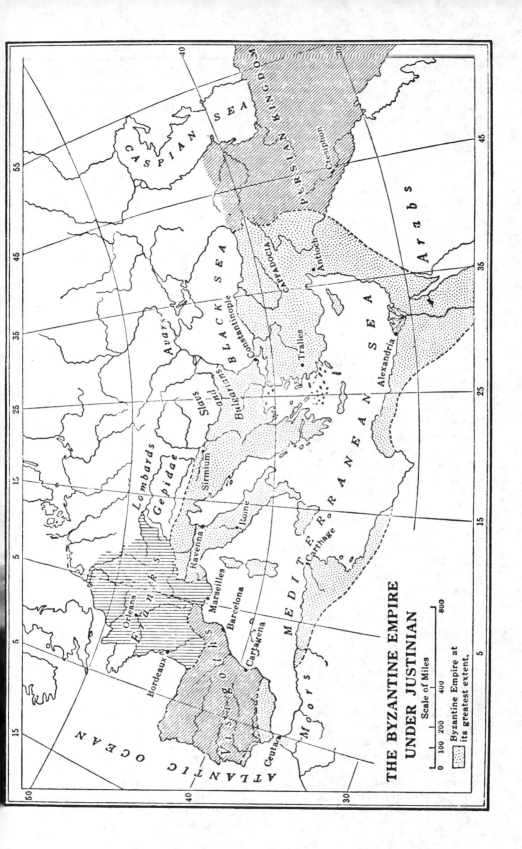

THE BYZANTINE EMPIRE
UNDER JUSTINIAN

Scale of Miles

0 100 200 400 800

▧ Byzantine Empire at
its greatest extent,

Tzazon (Zano), brother of the Vandal King **Gelimer,** led a force of 5,000 Vandal soldiers on an expedition to suppress an uprising in Sardinia which had been fomented by Justinian.

533, September 13. Battle of Ad Decimum. Belisarius landed (early September) at Cape Vada, and immediately marched north toward Carthage. Gelimer attempted an ambush in a defile at the 10th milestone from Carthage, but due to inadequate coordination and the alertness of Belisarius and his men, the attack was repulsed with heavy losses and the Vandals scattered into the desert. Belisarius promptly seized Carthage, which fell without further contest (September 15). Gelimer collected his shattered forces at Bulla Regia (Hamman Daradji) and sent urgently for Tzazon, who arrived a few weeks later.

533, December. Battle of Tricameron. With the arrival of Tzazon, Gelimer had assembled an army of about 50,000 men, mostly cavalry. He now advanced toward Carthage. Belisarius moved out to meet the Vandals. Leading the way with his cavalry, he discovered the Vandals, not fully prepared for battle, on the far side of a shallow stream. Without waiting for his infantry to come up, Belisarius charged, despite odds of almost 10–1, and threw the Vandals back in confusion. As soon as the infantry arrived, he captured the Vandal camp by storm. Tzazon was killed, the Vandal army shattered, and Gelimer forced to flee. He finally surrendered (March, 534), bringing the Vandal kingdom to an end; he and large numbers of his captured soldiers were carried back to Constantinople with Belisarius—who was recalled because Justinian was jealous of his successes (early 534). Belisarius left a small force in Africa under the general **Solomon** to continue the subjugation of the province. Initially successful in subduing the Vandals and pacifying the Moors and Numidians, Solomon was then plagued by a mutiny (536), which he suppressed only with the help of Belisarius (see below), and soon after was defeated and killed in a battle with the Moors. Justinian, however, sent reinforcements, and the gradual pacification of Africa continued (536–548).

THE ITALIAN (OR GOTHIC) WAR, 534–554

534. Justinian Declares War on the Ostrogoths. The Ostrogothic Queen Amalasuntha (who had acknowledged the sovereignty of Justinian) was murdered by her coruler, **Theodatus,** providing Justinian an excuse for intervention in Italy so as to reunite it with the Empire.

535. Expedition of Belisarius to Sicily and Italy. Justinian sent Belisarius with an expeditionary force of only 8,000 soldiers (about half were heavy East Roman cavalry) to begin the reconquest of Italy. Landing first in Sicily, Belisarius met little opposition, save for the Gothic garrison of Palermo. Laying siege to the citadel, he brought his ships into the harbor, then hoisted archers to the mastheads, from which they could shoot down over the walls at the garrison. The Goths quickly surrendered.

536. Mutiny in Africa. While preparing to invade Italy itself, Belisarius was forced to rush to Africa with 1,000 men to suppress a mutiny. With the addition of 2,000 loyal troops, he promptly defeated 8,000 mutineers, then hurried back to Sicily. About this time Theodatus offered to surrender Italy to imperial control.

536. Battle of Salona (Near Split). Meanwhile, the imperial general **Mundas,** who had invaded Dalmatia with only 4,000 men, was defeated by the far more numerous Gothic defenders of Dalmatia. This so encouraged vacillating Theodatus that he withdrew his offer of peace and prepared to defend Italy.

536. Belisarius Invades Italy. Crossing the Strait of Messina, Belisarius marched to Naples, which he captured after a month's siege by sending troops into the city through an abandoned aqueduct. Meanwhile a Frankish army, allied to Justinian, prepared to cross the Alps. The Goths, disgusted by the vacillation and inaction of Theodatus, deposed and killed him, electing the warrior **Vitiges** in his place. Vitiges immediately bought off the Franks by ceding Provence to them.

536, December 10. Capture of Rome. Upon the approach of Belisarius, the Gothic garrison of 4,000 fled Rome, permitting Belisarius to enter the city without a struggle. Since Vitiges was collecting a powerful army in north Italy, Belisarius decided not to risk further advance without more troops. He sent an urgent request for reinforcements to Justinian, meanwhile preparing Rome for a siege by bringing in great quantities of food and other supplies, and repairing the neglected walls of the city. With him he had only 5,000 men, of whom half were his personal bodyguard, probably the finest troops in the world at that time. He stretched chains across the Tiber to hold both parts of the city, and he recruited approximately 20,-000 young Romans to help man the long city walls.

37, March 2–538, March 12. Siege of Rome. Vitiges arrived with an army probably about one-third the strength of 150,000 attributed to it by the chroniclers, but at least ten times the size of Belisarius' field force. Conducting a delaying action outside the **Flaminian Gate,** Belisarius was almost cut off, but fought his way back to the city, inflicting numerous casualties on the Goths. Vitiges attempted an assault, but was repulsed with heavy losses from ballistae, catapults, and Belisarius' veteran archers (March 21). The Goths' ranks were so depleted that they were unable to keep a continuous ring around the city, Belisarius being able to send and receive messages, receive reinforcements, and even obtain supplies. One reinforcing body of 2,000 men was sent by Belisarius on a raid to the east coast of Italy under the command of **John "the Sanguinary."** When he realized that the people and garrison of Rome were not starving, Vitiges attempted another assault, but was repulsed again (early 538). The arrival of an East Roman fleet in the Tiber and of another 5,000 reinforcements forced Vitiges to raise the siege. He marched east in pursuit of John the Sanguinary, whom he besieged in Rimini.

538–539. Siege of Ravenna. The arrival of an army under Narses and pursuit by Belisarius across the Apennines forced Vitiges to raise the siege of Rimini and to retreat to Ravenna. There he was besieged by Belisarius, who was having difficulty in coordinating the operations of the numerous semi-independent imperial commands in Italy. Meanwhile **Theodebert,** Frankish King of Austrasia, sent a small force across the Alps to operate with Gothic forces against imperial troops near Milan (538), and the next spring led a much larger army into north Italy. Taking advantage of the confused fighting in the Po Valley, the Franks indiscriminately attacked both Goths and imperial troops, and ravaged north Italy. Belisarius, still besieging Ravenna, negotiated a treaty with Theodebert (whose forces were suffering from pestilence) and the Franks withdrew. Justinian now became alarmed by renewed barbarian (Bulgar and Slav) incursions across the Danube and the threat of renewed war with Chosroes of Persia (who was negotiating with Vitiges). Justinian offered to make peace with Vitiges, but Belisarius refused to transmit the message. The Goths then offered to support Belisarius as emperor of the West. The general pretended to agree, but when Vitiges surrendered Ravenna (late 539), Belisarius—ever faithful to Justinian— captured the Gothic king and sent him to Constantinople as a prisoner.

540–541. Belisarius Consolidates in Italy. The East Roman general now began mopping-up operations all over Italy. One by one the remaining Gothic fortifications were captured. Finally the only remaining Gothic strongholds of any importance were the besieged cities of Pavia and Verona. At this point Justinian, still jealous of Belisarius, and fearful that he might belatedly accept the proffered crown of emperor in the West, called his great general back to Constantinople (541). Imperial operations in Italy were now being directed, without central coordination or supervision, by eleven different imperial generals.

541–543. Resurgence of the Goths. Upon the departure of Belisarius, the Goths, under their new King **Ildibad,** broke out of Verona and defeated the uncoordinated imperialists at the **Battle of Treviso,** regaining control over all of the Po Valley (541). After some internal disputes and the death of Ildibad, **Totila** (Baduila), nephew of Vitiges, became King of the Goths. He immediately carried the Gothic offensive into central Italy, defeating the imperialists decisively at the **Battle of Faenza,** then at **Mugello** (542). He next marched south to besiege and capture Naples and to reconquer most of Italy, save for a handful of cities remaining under imperial control.

544–549. Return and Departure of Belisarius. Once more Justinian sent Belisarius —as usual with totally inadequate forces (4,000 men)—to retrieve the situation. After a year's siege, which Belisarius' harassment was unable to disrupt, Totila captured Rome (545). But when he moved to Lucania to attack imperial forces there, Belisarius promptly recaptured Rome. Totila hurried back, but was repulsed in three costly assaults (546). The four following years were reminiscent of the operations of Hannibal in Italy. The Goths were unable to oppose Belisarius in the field; he was able to march over the country at will, but he was unable to obtain sufficient forces from the jealous emperor to permit him to accomplish anything. Finally he was recalled to Constantinople (549). Totila, immediately besieging and recapturing Rome, not only re-established firm Gothic control over most of Italy but was able to reconquer Sicily, Sardinia, and Corsica as well. He tried to capture Ravenna by a combined land and sea blockade, but his naval force in the Adriatic was disastrously defeated and he was forced to give up the attempt (551). Soon afterward an imperial expedition under **Artaban** again wrested Sicily from the Goths.

551. Narses Commands Imperial Forces in Italy. Justinian now finally realized that he could not succeed in Italy without a major effort, in which an able general would have to be placed in command of adequate forces. Still jealous of Belisarius, he first selected his nephew **Germanius,** who had distinguished himself as a subordinate of Belisarius in Persia and who had recently won a substantial victory over the Slavs (see p. 183). Germanius, however, died near Sardica, so Justinian selected the aged eunuch **Narses** (478–573) for command in Italy. Narses refused to accept the post without adequate forces. When he marched north from Salona, later that year, he probably had a total force of 20,000–30,000 men. Arriving in Venetia, he discovered that a powerful Gothic-Frank army at least 50,-000 strong, under the Goth leader **Teias** and the Frank King **Theudibald,** blocked the principal route to the Po Valley. Not wishing to engage such a formidable force and confident that the Franks would soon tire of their alliance with the Goths, as they had in the past, Narses cleverly skirted the lagoons along the Adriatic shore by using his vessels to leapfrog his army from point to point along the coast, some going by ship, some marching, in a manner similar to a modern truck and foot march. In this way he arrived at Ravenna without encountering any opposition. Near Ravenna he attacked and crushed a small Gothic force at **Rimini.**

552. Battle of Taginae (Near Modern Gubbio). Narses now began an advance on Rome. Crossing the Apennines with nearly 20,000 men, he was met by Totila, who probably did not have more than 15,000. In a narrow mountain valley suitable for the shock tactics of his heavy-cavalry lancers, Totila had chosen a position which Narses could not bypass. The imperial general immediately deployed his army in a concave formation. He dismounted his Lombard and Heruli cavalry mercenaries, placing them as a phalanx in the center. His heavy Roman cavalry cataphracts were on each flank, reinforced with all his infantry—who were foot archers. On his left he sent out a mixed force of foot and horse archers to seize a dominant height. Totila's army was in two lines: the heavy cavalry lancers in the front, with his archers and a line of spear and axe-wielding infantry behind. The Goths opened the battle with a determined cavalry charge. As they swept down the valley they first came under the fire of the advanced force on Narses' left, then rode into the cross fire of the archers in his concave wings. Halted by the devastating fire, the attackers were then thrown back in confusion on the infantry advancing behind them. Efforts of the Gothic archers to support their cavalry were foiled by the more aggressive, more mobile imperial horse archers on the flanks. Covered by continued fire from the foot archers, these heavy cataphracts then swept into the milling mass of Goths in a double envelopment. More than 6,000 of them, including Totila, were killed. The remnants fled. Narses then continued on to Rome, which he captured after a brief siege.

553. Battle of Monte Lacteria (or of the

Samus, near Cumae). Teias was now elected King of the Goths. He had reassembled most of the remnants of Totila's army in the Po Valley, while his brother, **Aligern,** still retained some strongholds in Campania. In a secret, well-conducted march, Teias joined forces with his brother in Campania. Narses immediately followed, blockading the combined Gothic force west of Naples. The Goths were crushed in a hopeless last-ditch fight, and Teias was killed. Aligern escaped, but surrendered a few months later. Narses now divided his forces to besiege the remaining Gothic strongholds and fortresses scattered throughout Italy.

553–554. Frankish Invasion. Two Frankish-Alemanni dukes—the brothers **Lothaire** and **Buccelin**—now crossed the Alps from Germany with a force of 75,000 men, mostly Frankish infantry. In the Po Valley, they won an easy victory over a much smaller imperial force at **Parma,** and were then joined by remnants of the Gothic armies, bringing the total strength of the invaders to about 90,000. They began to march south. Narses, gathering his forces as quickly as possible, marched north to harass the Franks, but did not yet feel strong enough to engage them in battle. In Samnium (south-central Italy) the brothers divided their forces; Lothaire went down the east coast, then returned to the north, to winter in the Po Valley. Buccelin followed the west coast to the very toe of the boot, where he spent the winter—his army being seriously wasted by high living and disease.

554. Battle of Casilinum. In the spring Buccelin marched north, his army reduced to about 30,000 men. Narses with 18,000 men (including a contingent of Goths under Aligern) marched south to meet him at Casilinum (on the banks of the Volturno, near Capua). Outmaneuvering Buccelin, Narses forced the Franks to battle on ground of his own choosing. He took up a concave formation, similar to that he had used at Taginae. The Frankish infantry, in a wedgelike phalanx, advanced against the imperial center, much as the Romans had done at Cannae. The result was almost identical. The imperial foot archers engaged the flanks of the Frank phalanx, while the heavy Roman horse archers swung around behind them.

Pausing, the imperial horse and foot archers softened up the milling mass of Franks with volley after volley of arrows—then they charged. The Frankish army was annihilated. Meanwhile, in the north, Lothaire and his men had been struck by an epidemic which killed most of them. The Italian, or Gothic, War was over; Italy had been rewon for the Empire. But it was a prostrate, exhausted, depopulated Italy which, after a few years of corrupt imperial misrule, was ready to accept another barbarian migration (see p. 182).

JUSTINIAN'S SECOND PERSIAN WAR, 539–562

539. Chosroes Declares War. Partly because of unsatisfactory Roman performance in helping to pay for the garrisons in the Caucasus passes, partly for religious reasons, and partly because he feared imperial strength was growing too much from the victories in Africa and Italy, Chosroes declared war on the Empire.

540. Persian Invasion of Syria. Advancing up the Euphrates, Chosroes swept into the heart of Syria, capturing Antioch, plundering the region, and taking back with him vast numbers of captives.

541–542. Chosroes in Lazica. The Persian ruler now shifted his attention to the northern front, where he was generally successful. He captured Petra from the Romans (541), and in two campaigns succeeded in establishing firm Persian control over the country.

542–544. Belisarius in Mesopotamia. Recalled from Italy (see p. 187), Belisarius was sent by Justinian to take command in Syria and Mesopotamia. Driving the Persians out of the positions they had captured early in the war, Belisarius forced Chosroes to return from Lazica (543). In a campaign of maneuver, with no major battles, Belisarius recovered all of Roman Mesopotamia and raided deep into Persia. Persian efforts to take Dara and Edessa were repulsed, as was a Roman attempt to invade Armenia. Chosroes and Justinian then agreed to an armistice (545). Belisarius was thereupon sent back to Italy (see p. 188).

549. Resumption of War in Lazica. Upon appeals from the Christian population of Lazica, being cruelly oppressed by the Persians, Justinian sent an expedition of

8,000 troops under General **Dagisteus,** who laid siege to Petra. A Persian relieving force drove back the Romans, but reinforcements under **Besas** enabled imperial forces to renew the siege, which lasted for more than a year. After a heroic defense, the Persian garrison was finally overwhelmed (551). The war in Lazica dragged on for several years, but the climactic action was the **Battle of Phasis,** in which the imperial forces decisively defeated the Persian general **Nacoragan.**

562. Peace Restored. With both nations engaged in other wars, and both close to bankruptcy, the final years of the war had been desultory. The *status quo ante* was restored, with Lazica firmly in imperial hands, but with Justinian again agreeing to help pay for the Caucasus fortifications by an increased subsidy.

JUSTINIAN AND BELISARIUS

Justinian combined pettiness with great vision, parsimony with soaring ambition, timidity with vigor, brilliant organizational ability with inept administration, bellicosity with appeasement. It has been suggested that his reputation as the greatest of all East Roman emperors was due to three people: his steel-willed ex-prostitute wife, Theodora; the noble general, Belisarius; the crafty old eunuch-soldier, Narses. Yet though his debt to each of these was great, no man could stamp his imprint so forcibly on his own times, and on the future history of his nation, without exceptional natural ability. One explanation of the paradoxes of his nature and of his accomplishments is the fact that he had an unusual ability to recognize his own weaknesses, and relied upon able assistants to make amends for his deficiencies.

In addition to four major wars, Justinian's overextended, underpaid, and inadequate military forces were engaged in widespread operations in Spain, the Balkan-Danubian region, and elsewhere along the entire Mediterranean littoral. He built several tremendous systems of fortifications to protect vulnerable frontiers and to control unsettled and disputed regions—along the Danube; throughout Thrace, Epirus, Thessaly, and Macedonia; at the defiles of Thermopylae, Corinth, the Chersonese (Gallipoli) Peninsula, and the Tauric Chersonese (Crimean) Peninsula; along the eastern frontier with Persia—and he extended and reinforced the wall Anastasius had built across the peninsula approach to Constantinople. At the same time he subsidized and encouraged his Ghassanid and Abyssinian allies in Arabia to harass the southern fringes of the Persian Empire.

Justinian recognized the danger that incessant wars, and the expenses of widespread fortifications, could ruin the economy of the nation, and this recognition undoubtedly had much to do with his notorious and frequently shortsighted parsimony, reflected by the tiny forces he provided his commanders and by the delays in payment of troops that sometimes caused entire armies to melt away in desertion, or to turn against the empire in mutiny. The regular forces of his army never exceeded 150,000 men, scattered in Spain, Italy, Africa, Egypt, and along the Danube and Persian frontiers. Unquestionably, even his budgetary caution could not prevent serious straining of the economic fabric of the entire empire, and his parsimony contributed to the total collapse of the economy of Italy through unnecessary protraction of the war in that unfortunate country.

Yet on the whole, despite the strain on its economy, it is probable that the wars and conquests of Justinian halted the decline of the East Roman Empire. Even though most of these conquests were partial or temporary, the victories of the empire restored the prestige of Roman arms, and provided new and justified confidence to the rulers of Constantinople in the tremendous residual superiority of even their debased Roman military system over the military capabilities of their civilized and barbarian neighbors.

Most reprehensible—and probably most shortsighted—of all of Justinian's controversial conduct was his jealousy and mistreatment of Belisarius. No prince has ever been better served by a loyal subject than was the emperor by his great general. To prevent Belisarius (or any other general) from becoming too powerful, Justinian frequently hampered him by imposing divided command, and by sending him on vast projects with totally inadequate forces; more often than not Belisarius succeeded anyway. The inevitable result of such success was relief and insults at the hands of Justinian. Yet, in renewed crises, the noble soldier responded loyally and effectively to the desperate appeals of his emperor.

Having been relieved for the second time from his command in Italy (see p. 188), Belisarius lived quietly in Constantinople until Justinian called him out of retirement to complete the consolidation of reconquered regions of southern Spain (554). Again he was thrust back into retirement and obscurity. But the emperor had no hesitation in calling on Belisarius, and the soldier had no hesitation in responding, when a combined Bulgar-Slav invasion of Moesia and Thrace, under the Bulgarian leader **Zabergan,** reached to the outer defenses of Constantinople (559). All of the regular forces of the empire were scattered in fortifications or in campaigns against Persians or barbarians. With a force of 300 of his veteran cavalry, plus a few thousand hastily raised levies, Belisarius repulsed a Bulgarian attack near **Melanthius,** just outside the walls, then counterattacked to drive the barbarians away. Having saved Constantinople by his last victory, Belisarius, with little thanks from the emperor, returned to his retirement.

Soon after this the jealous emperor accused him of treason, disgraced and imprisoned him (562). Remorse and better judgment caused Justinian a year later to release Belisarius, to restore to him the properties and honors which he had stripped from him, and to permit the general to live in relative honor, if in obscurity, until his death shortly before that of the emperor himself (565).

After Justinian, 565–600

565–574. Reign of Justin II (Nephew of Justinian). He began his reign by refusing further subsidies to the Avars, who thereupon conducted several large-scale raids through the Balkan Peninsula. He responded favorably to an embassy from the Turks, who were at war with Persia in central Asia (see p. 192), and as a result of this, and the continuing Persian persecution of Christians, embarked on another war with Persia (572).

572–596. War with Persia. (See p. 192.)

574–582. Reign of Tiberius. Due to recurring seizures of insanity, Justin abdicated in favor of the general **Tiberius.** The war with Persia continued without important developments (see p. 193), while the Avars continued to raid at will over the European areas of the Empire (see p. 183).

582–602. Reign of Mauricius (Maurice). Having distinguished himself in the war with Persia, this general was selected as emperor by the dying Tiberius. Prior to ascending the throne, Maurice had written an encyclopedic work on the science of war (the *Strategikon*) which was to exercise a major influence on the military system of the Byzantine Empire for centuries to come (see p. 214). His personal attention to the military affairs of the empire resulted in solid imperial victories over both the Persians (591; see p. 193) and the Avars (598–601; see p. 183). His insistence on strict discipline as the basis of the old military virtues of the Romans, however, resulted in a mutiny in the Danube army, which spread to the populace of Constantinople. In an effort to restore peace, Maurice abdicated, only to be cruelly murdered by his successor, **Phocas** (602).

SOUTHWEST ASIA

SASSANID EMPIRE OF PERSIA

399–438. Reigns of Yazdegird I and Bahram V. Following the relatively peaceful, prosperous, and benevolent reign of **Yazdegird** (399–421), his son **Bahram V** provoked a brief, unsuccessful war with Rome (421–422) as a result of his violent persecutions of Christians (see p. 173). Bahram, too, was the first of the Sassanid kings to be subjected to the depredations of the White Huns, or Ephthalites—apparently related to the Kushans, and like them descended from the Aryan-Mongolian people known to the Chinese as the Yueh Chih (see p. 118). Bahram drove them back over the Oxus River.

438–459. Reigns of Yazdegird II and Hormizd III. Like his father, Bahram, Yazdegird II (438–457) provoked a brief, unsuccessful war with Rome (441); see p. 173). He also repulsed Ephthalite inroads with the help of subsidies from Constantinople (443–451). In a later war against the White Huns he was defeated near the Oxus (457). **Hormizd III** (457–459) succeeded his father Yazdegird to the throne, but was forced to fight continuously against his brothers, as well as the White Huns.

459–488. Reign of Peroz (Firuz) and Balash. Peroz (459–484), with the assistance of the White Huns, overthrew and killed his younger brother, Hormizd III. He was soon engaged in a series of disastrous wars with his former allies, who overran Bactria and other eastern regions of the Sassanid Empire (464–484). Seriously defeated by the Ephthalites, or their cousins the Kushans, east of the Caspian (481), he prepared a major expedition to recover his lost provinces. Advancing eastward with a large army, apparently he became lost in the desert and fell an easy prey to the White Huns; he and all his army perished (484). He was succeeded by another brother, **Balash** (484–488), who ended a revolt in Armenia (481–484) by agreeing to end persecutions of Christians. Balash spent most of his reign in a civil war with still another brother, **Zareh.** Because of his ineptitude and failure to deal with the dangerous Ephthalite threat to the kingdom, he was deposed.

488–531. Reign of Kavadh (Nephew of Balash). Initially he had no more success against the Ephthalites than his father or uncles. He was deposed briefly in favor of his brother **Jamasp** (496–499), and took refuge with the Ephthalites. When he re-turned to his throne, Kavadh was angered when the East Roman Emperor Anastasius refused his request for subsidies, so contracted an alliance with the Ephthalites and went to war with Rome (502–506; see p. 183): This inconclusive struggle was brought to an end by the invasion of the western Huns through the Caucasus (505), prompting the two empires to make common cause against the barbarians and to agree on joint responsibility for defense of the Caucasus passes.

524–531. Kavadh's Second War with Rome. (See p. 184.)

531–570. Reign of Chosroes I (Anushirvan). He concluded "eternal peace" with Justinian, but was forced to fight a bitter dynastic war before establishing firm control over the Sassanid Empire, of which he became the most illustrious ruler.

539–562. Chosroes' First War with Rome. (See p. 189.)

c. 554–c. 560. Persian and Turk Alliance against the Ephthalites. Chosroes entered an alliance with the newly risen Turkish people in Central Asia (see p. 197). The Ephthalites were crushed. Later Chosroes conducted a successful campaign in the steppes north of the Caucasus against the Khazars.

572–579. Chosroes' Second War with Rome. Justin, allied with the Turks, started a new war by supporting an uprising of the Christian Armenians (see p. 191). Chosroes, now an old man, immediately dispatched an expeditionary force into Roman Mesopotamia, while holding off the Turks in the east. His grandson, also named **Chosroes,** successfully besieged **Dara,** while the general **Adarman** raided effectively into Syria as far as Antioch. The Romans, dismayed by this unexpected result of a war they had initiated, sought a truce, which lasted three years (573–575). Both sides used the lull to prepare for a renewal of the struggle. Chosroes, again seizing the initiative, sent his grandson once more into Roman territory. The Persians were driven from Cappadocia (575) by the young general Mauricius (Maurice). The following year the Roman general Justinian (son of Germanius, see p. 188) defeated young Chosroes in the hard-fought **Battle of Melitene,** just west of the upper Euphrates, and drove the Persians westward. Justinian then invaded Persian Armenia, reaching the Caspian, where he established a base and constructed a fleet (577). The following year he invaded Assyria, causing the elder Chosroes to seek peace (see p. 191), which was being negotiated when he died (589).

579–590. Reign of Hormizd IV; Continued War with Rome and the Turks. The new king, son of Chosroes, refused to give up any territory, and so the war with Rome and the Turks continued, generally to the disadvantage of Persia. The East Romans cleared the Persians from much of Armenia and the Caucasus, capturing a number of fortresses along the Mesopotamian frontier. At the same time the Turks overran most of Khorasan, and reached Hyrcania on the shores of the Caspian. Meanwhile Hormizd's cruelty and misrule stimulated widespread rebellions within Persia, and alienated allies and vassals. With the Sassanid Empire on the verge of collapse, an able general, **Bahram Chobin,** appeared on the scene. With a small army he ambushed the Turks to win a great victory at the **Battle of the Hyrcanian Rock** (588). Pursuing vigorously, he regained much of the lost areas south of the Oxus. He then turned against the Romans (589), winning an initial victory at **Martyropolis** (near modern Mus, Turkey). Maurice defeated Bahram at **Nisibis,** and drove him back into Armenia. Attempting to invade Lazica, Bahram was defeated again at the **Battle of the Araxes** (589). Jealous Hormizd seized this opportunity to dismiss Bahram, but the general refused to be dismissed, and revolted. Hormizd was overthrown by other dissidents, who placed young Chosroes (son of Hormizd) on the throne, but Bahram also refused to accept him, defeating and deposing the new ruler and seizing the throne himself (590). Chosroes took refuge with Roman forces at Circesium (on the Euphrates).

590–596. Roman Intervention. Maurice, seeing an opportunity to end the prolonged war to the advantage of Constantinople, immediately supported Chosroes against Bahram. A Roman army, probably about 30,000 strong, under the general **Narses** (apparently unrelated to Justinian's great general) was sent into Persia through Assyria to restore Chosroes to the throne. At the same time Roman forces in Armenia advanced into Media. Bahram rushed west with an army of about 40,000, and attempted to halt the invasion at the Zab River. Narses, whose total strength, including Persians defecting to Chosroes, was about 60,000, decisively defeated Bahram at the **Battle of the Zab** and pursued him into Media, where the Romans won another victory, smashing Bahram's army (591). Bahram then fled east, to seek refuge with the Turks, but soon died or was killed. Chosroes, returned to the throne with Roman assistance, promptly made peace. Maurice, hoping to establish perpetual peace through magnanimity, merely insisted upon Persian recognition of the traditional frontiers and the cessation of subsidies for the Caucasus forts; Roman troops were withdrawn from the positions they held in Armenia.

591–628. Reign of Chosroes II. The only important military events in the early years of this reign were operations in Media to suppress a revolt by a Prince **Bistam** (591–596).

ARABIA AND ABYSSINIA,
400–600

c. 400. Rise of Hira. Located at the northeastern edge of the Arabian desert on the fringe of Mesopotamia, and about 100 miles south of the Persian capital of Ctesiphon, the principality of Hira had become prosperous as a vassal of Persia. The most renowned ruler of Hira was **al Mondhir,** an able warrior, whose support was decisive in Bahram V's gaining the throne of Persia (421) in the dynastic disputes following the death of Yazdegird I (see p. 192). Another **al Mondhir** was a leading Persian general under Chosroes I (see p. 184).

c. 400. Rise of Ghassan. A Christian tribe, apparently originating in Yemen, the Ghassanids established themselves in northwestern Arabia, just east of the Jordan (c. 200). Vassals of Rome, they gradually extended their control over most of the region between Palmyra and Petra. They clashed frequently with Hira.

c. 400–525. Struggle for Yemen. One of the three relatively fertile and prosperous regions of Arabia, Yemen had long figured in struggles between native Arabs (Sabaeans or Himyarites) and the Abyssinians of the African kingdom of Axum (Aksum, near modern Aduwa). The Christian Abyssinians (apparently of mixed Arabian-Ethiopian stock) had briefly conquered the region (c. 350), only to be ejected by the native Sabaeans (who adopted the Jewish religion) of southwest Arabia (c. 375). The Abyssinians retained several footholds, and obtained periodic support from the kings of Axum in the bitter Christian-Judaic struggle that raged for more than a century and a half in southwestern Arabia. Finally, an Abyssinian leader named **Abraha** (apparently with some assistance from **Kaleb** of Axum) succeeded in conquering Saba and re-establishing Abyssinian control over the region (525). Soon after this, Justinian concluded an alliance with Axum, and with Abraha (530).

c. 500–583. Wars of Ghassan and Hira. On the fringes of the two great empires, the two Arab kingdoms waged almost constant war on each other, largely at the behest of their suzerains (East Roman Empire for Ghassan, Persia for Hira). The Ghassanids had generally the best of these encounters, but the close proximity of the center of Persian power prevented them from fully exploiting their victories. The most outstanding warrior of the Ghassanids was **Harith Ibn Jabala,** who inflicted a crushing defeat on Hira (528). Harith led the highly effective Bedouin cavalry contingents that fought under Belisarius in his Mesopotamian campaigns (541–544). Dynastic troubles, combined with Persian intervention in northern Arabia, soon after brought about the collapse of Ghassan (583).

570. Abraha's Invasion of Hejaz. Having consolidated and expanded his control of southwestern Arabia, Abraha led an Abyssinian invasion of western Arabia. He was generally successful, until he suffered a setback near Mecca (570). He died soon after this and was succeeded by his son, **Taksoum.**

572–585. Persian Intervention in Western Arabia. When war broke out again between Persia and the East Roman Empire (see p. 192), Chosroes decided to intervene in Arabia against the Abyssinian allies of Constantinople. Despite some support (mostly moral) from the emperor Justin, the Abyssinians were defeated in a series of hard-fought struggles. Although their kingdom in Yemen was overrun and substantially conquered (579), the struggle continued for several years before the Abyssinians were completely ejected from Arabia (c. 585). Meanwhile Persian influence had become predominant in western and southwestern Arabia; Roman influence was eliminated.

SOUTH ASIA

NORTH INDIA

c. 400–c. 450. Ephthalite (Huna) Expansion into Gandhara. In the years following the reign of Chandragupta Vikramaditya (see p. 163), northwest India began to feel the pressure of another people migrating from central Asia. These were the Ephthalites, or White Huns (see p. 192), a people of mixed Indo-European and Mongoloid blood, evidently descended from the Hsiung-nu people of Mongolia, and closely related to the Yueh Chih and their offshoot, the Kushans. Pushing into the Sassanid Empire, the Ephthalites (known to Indian history as Hunas) became firmly established in Bactria (c. 420), and dominated all of modern Russian Turkestan southeast of the Aral Sea. From here they began to conduct raids into Gandhara and as far as the Punjab, while they gradually pressed their bases southward into the mountains.

c. 450–480. Clash of the Hunas and the Gupta Empire. At first successful in nibbling at the Punjab domains of **Kumaragupta** (413–455), the Ephthalites began a full-scale invasion of the Gupta Empire. They were decisively defeated (457) by **Skandagupta** (455–470), and made no further inroads during his lifetime. His successors, however, were helpless against the invaders, who soon brought about the complete collapse of the empire (480).

480–530. Rise and Fall of the Huna Empire. As the Gupta Empire dissolved, the Hunas carved out their own empire in the Punjab and Rajputana. Their ruler **Toramana** (500–510) conquered Malwa. His son,

Mihiragula (510–530), continued the expansion southward and eastward, only to be defeated (530) by a coalition of Hindu princes, of whom the most important were **Balditya** of Magadha and **Yasodharman** of Ujjain. The Huna Empire collapsed, and the Ephthalites, like their predecessors from central Asia, were soon absorbed by the Hindus. Northern India again became a collection of warring Hindu principalities.

SOUTH INDIA

c. 400–575. Resurgence of Pallava. In the eastern Deccan, Pallava steadily regained strength as Gupta power declined. Having established hegemony over most of the Deccan, Pallava King **Simhavishnu** drove Chola south of the Kaveri River valley (575).

550–600. Rise of Chalukya. A new power now appeared in the western Deccan, near Bijapur: the Chalukya Dynasty, established by **Pulakesin I** (550–566). Toward the close of the century, the Chalukya defeated Pallava in a series of violent wars, and established themselves in control of the central Deccan. Pallava was hard-pressed to hold the core lands on the east coast against the sons of Pulakesin: **Kirtivarman I** (566–597) and **Mangalesa** (597–608).

575–600. Resurgence of Pandya. The defeats suffered at the hands of the Pallava caused the Chola Dynasty to go into decline, and to lose most of its power in the southern tip of India. Its influence was replaced by that of the Pandya Dynasty.

HINDU MILITARY SYSTEM (c. 500)

It was sometime during the 5th or 6th centuries that one of the great military classics of India was written—or collected—by an unknown author or editor, possibly named **Siva**, or **Sadasiva**. This was the *Siva-Dhanur-veda*. Like other Dhanur-vedas that preceded and followed this, its central theme was archery and the employment of the bow as the main weapon of Hindu warfare. This pre-eminence of the bow, in fact, caused the Hindus to use the term Dhanur-veda—or archery manual —to apply to all writings on the art of warfare, and the *Siva-Dhanur-veda* dealt with the employment of other weapons, and with military science in general. Significantly, it repeated much that had appeared several centuries earlier in the *Arthasastra* of Kautilya (see p. 78).

During this period the only significant change in the art of warfare in south Asia had been the gradual disappearance of the chariot—which Kautilya had not much favored anyway. The growing importance of cavalry had posed a great challenge to the Hindus, who still had difficulty in raising horses of requisite quality and stamina. The Deccan, in particular, was unfavorable to horse raising, and the warrior dynasties of the south customarily imported horses from the north. As in the time of Kautilya, the Hindu princes placed much reliance upon their powerful hill forts to defend their lands from the raids of neighbors, and to provide bases for their own frequent raids.

Weapons and armor changed little. Mail armor had become the common raiment of the horsemen, whose principal weapons were the lance and the mace. Despite their reliance upon infantry bowmen, the Hindus never showed much interest or competence in use of the bow on horseback, even though mounted archers were usually the main components of the armies that had invaded from central Asia. The fact that the invaders soon adapted themselves to the Hindu form of cavalry employment would seem to indicate that Indian horses had neither the stamina nor agility necessary for mounted archery tactics.

There had been no increase in interest in naval warfare. Rulers along the sea-coast near the mouths of the Indus and Ganges usually had small naval forces, whose primary missions were to provide merchant shipping and coastal towns with some protection from the depredations of the pirates who based themselves in the river deltas. But the employment of warships as instruments of national power was practically unknown, save in the Tamil kingdoms of the extreme south, whose naval expeditions were almost exclusively raids against the island of Ceylon.

EAST AND CENTRAL ASIA

CHINA

400–589. Continuing Anarchy in China. This was a continuation of the period known as that of the "Six Dynasties," which had begun with the collapse of the Han Empire (see p. 163). China remained divided into two major portions, one generally north of the Yangtze River, the other to the south. This was China's "Dark Age," a time of incessant warfare between these two regions, and of almost constant internal strife within both.

South China, 400–589

420–549. Appearance of the Third, Fourth, and Fifth Dynasties. The Eastern Chin Dynasty was overthrown by general **Liu Yu,** who established the Liu Sung, or "Former" Sung Dynasty (420). This, in turn, was overthrown by general **Hsiao Tao-ch'eng,** who killed the last two Liu Sung emperors to establish himself as the first ruler of the Southern Ch'i Dynasty (479). This disappeared when general **Hsiao Yen** seized the throne to establish the Liang Dynasty (502). He took the imperial title of **Liang Wu Ti,** and during his reign of 47 years south China had a modicum of internal peace, regained some strength, and demonstrated some vigor. A revolt in Annam (541–547) was suppressed (see p. 272), and Liang Wu Ti then attempted an invasion north of the Yangtze. This quickly bogged down, however, through the protracted siege of Hsiangyang. Soon after the failure of this invasion, Liang Wu Ti died, and his dynasty disappeared with him.

557–589. Last of the Six Dynasties. After eight years of violent and confused civil war, the Ch'en Dynasty was established by **Ch'en Pa Hsien.** This disappeared under the impact of invasion from the north.

North China

400–500. Ascendancy of the Northern Wei Dynasty. The T'upa, or Northern Wei, Dynasty maintained its supremacy in the north. Though apparently originally a branch of the Turklike Hsien Pi people, the Northern Wei had become thoroughly Sinicized, but relied militarily almost completely on cavalry. One reason for the relative longevity of this dynasty was the attention lavished on horse units, particularly by utilizing much of the best of the northern farmlands for pasturage—an estimated 7 acres per horse. The Northern Wei probably introduced the stirrup into China (c. 477), possibly having adopted this valuable aid to horsemanship from the Hsiung-nu. Having achieved complete control of north China, the Northern Wei expanded their empire to include part of Sinkiang (c. 450).

500–534. Decline of the Northern Wei. A principal cause of the dynasty's collapse was a disastrous defeat suffered in an attempted invasion of south China (507). Violent civil war broke out in the north (529–534), leading to the split of the Wei Empire into two warring parts: Western Wei and Eastern Wei.

534–557. Internal and External Disorders. While Eastern and Western Wei kingdoms fought each other bitterly, both were troubled from within, and from barbarian pressures in the north. The Eastern Wei reconstructed damaged portions of the Great Wall in the face of Avar pressure (543), before the kingdom was overthrown in civil war and replaced by the Northern Ch'i Dynasty (550). The Turks soon replaced the Avars in the north (see p. 197), and again the Great Wall was strengthened (556). That same year the Western Wei Dynasty was overthrown and replaced by the Northern Chou Dynasty. Warfare between the two portions of north China continued, despite the changes in dynasties, with Northern Chou soon defeating and annexing the dominions of Northern Ch'i (557).

581–600. Rise of the Sui Dynasty. North China was unified by **Yang Chien,** who established a new and vigorous dynasty. Contemplating an invasion of the south, with a view to reuniting China, Yang renewed the work on the Great Wall so as to protect his base area from the barbarians. At the same time he completed plans for his expedition. The Sui invasion of the south was a complete success (589). The Ch'en Dynasty was overthrown, and China was reunited for the first time in almost four centuries.

INNER ASIA*

Throughout most of history the land which we here call Inner Asia has been inhabited by racially and linguistically varied, nomadic, warlike, restless peoples, usually at war with each other and with the more civilized peoples to the west, south, and east. These incessant conflicts and other migratory influences have stimulated almost constant centrifugal population pressures which have posed equally constant threats to the more civilized neighbors around the periphery. Since the dawn of history the tides of migration from Inner Asia have had periodically earth-shaking effects upon other regions of Europe and Asia.

c. 400–546. Ascendancy of the Avars. A Mongol people (also called the Juan Juan or Gougen), the Avars, under a leader named **Toulun,** had defeated the Hsiung-nu, or Huns, driving them south and west (c. 380). Toulun then established a powerful nomadic empire spreading out to the north of that of the Northern Wei. He took the title of Khan or Cagan (c. 400). The Avars then became engaged in almost constant border warfare with the Northern Wei.

546–553. Rise of the Turks. A peasant people, of mixed Indo-European and Mongol stock, the Turks were subject to, and serfs of, the Avars, most of them working in the iron mines of the Altai Mountains. Revolting, under a chieftain named **Tuman** (or **Tumere**) they soon overthrew the Avar Empire, to establish themselves as the most powerful force in northern and central Asia, and to begin a career of military conquest which would have a profound effect upon history for more than a thousand years. The Avars were completely shattered. Some of them slipped south into China, where they were absorbed. Most migrated west, reaching the Urals (558) and (in combination with other nomads, who adopted the Avar name; see p. 183) continuing on to the Danube (c. 565).

553–582. Expansion of the Turkish Empire. After consolidating the former Avar Empire, the Turks began to press southwestward. They defeated the White Huns in Transoxiana, then continued into Khorasan, conquering most of the territory between the Aral Sea and the Hindu Kush Mountains from the Sassanid Empire (see p. 192). They raided frequently and successfully into China. They also pushed after the Avars into the south Russian steppes, apparently reaching as far as the Black Sea. Tuman and his immediate successors, however, lacked the organization and ability to administer the vast empire which had been conquered so rapidly by their fierce mounted bowmen, and the first Turkish Empire soon collapsed into a number of squabbling principalities.

---

* For the purposes of this book, Inner Asia is that vast region of mountains, deserts, and steppes lying generally north and west of China, north of the Himalayas, north and east of Persia, east of the Volga River and Ural Mountains, and bounded on the north by Arctic Siberia. (For all practical purposes, it is the area which Mackinder has called the "Heartland.") Although this region has affected and been affected by the regions to the west, southwest, and south, its history has been more closely linked with that of China and East Asia. Accordingly, in this book it will normally be included in general sections dealing with East and Central Asia.

KOREA

c. 400. The Three Kingdoms. In prehistoric times (traditionally 2300 B.C.) Korea was occupied by a Mongoloid, or Tartar people; little is known of the country or people prior to the 1st century B.C. Off and on during the five centuries preceding A.D. 400, various Chinese dynasties had conquered north Korea, but had never been able to maintain a permanent foothold, or to penetrate substantially south of the Han River. Chinese influence and culture, however, pervaded the entire peninsula. During most of this time Korea was divided between three warring kingdoms: Kokuryo in northeast Korea (which also usually included northwest Korea, when that area was not under Chinese control), Paekche in the southwest, and Silla (oldest of the three) in the southeast. During this time there had been some contact with the Japanese, who apparently had colonies on the south coast, between Silla and Paekche, for much of the 4th century. Silla, fearful of the Japanese, traditionally sought an alliance with China. Paekche usually maintained connections with the Japanese.

c. 500–600. Expansion of Silla. Silla gradually achieved predominance in Korea, mainly at the expense of Paekche. Expanding to the west coast (554), Silla eliminated the last Japanese footholds in the south (562). The ascendancy of Silla was also favored by the rise of the strong Sui Dynasty in China (see p. 197), whose suzerainty was accepted by Kokuryo (589).

JAPAN

c. 400. The Clan Period. Like the Koreans, the original Japanese people probably migrated from northern Asia before 2000 B.C. They soon expelled the aboriginal Ainus from most of the three southern islands, establishing themselves in a number of cohesive tribes or clans. Japanese history traditionally begins with the accession of the first emperor, **Jimmu Tenno,** a legendary warrior from Kyushu, who supposedly united the country (600 B.C.). The clan structure of society continued, however, and unity was nominal, though the ascendancy of the imperial clan was recognized by the others. Fierce wars between the clans were frequent, as were overseas expeditions (some joint, some by clan) to Korea. A major invasion of Korea resulted in the establishment of colonies on the south coast of that peninsula (c. 360).

c. 500–600. Rise of the Soga Clan. By a combination of intrigue, martial prowess, and assassination, the leaders of the Soga Clan gradually achieved ascendancy in the imperial government. This resulted in relegation of the emperors to positions of nominal or symbolic power.

VIII

THE RISE AND CONTAINMENT
OF ISLAM: 600–800

MILITARY TRENDS

This was a period of dynamic change marked by the explosive rise of Islam and its sweep of conquest across nearly half of the civilized world. Equally remarkable was the resilience of the Byzantine Empire in sustaining and repelling the direct shock of the violent Moslem assault. This was far more significant than the eventual success of the Frankish and Chinese empires in snubbing the westward and eastern expansion of Mohammedanism, thousands of miles farther away from Mecca.

One general of the period is worthy of consideration as a great captain of history: the Byzantine Emperor **Heraclius.** There were a number of other capable, first-rate soldiers in this period: the Chinese **Li Shih-min** (Emperor **T'ai Tsung**), the Indians **Harsha** and **Pulakesin II,** the Moslems **Khalid ibn al-Walid** and **Harun al-Rashid,** the Byzantines **Leo III** and **Constantine V,** and the Frankish emperor **Charlemagne.**

Of these Charlemagne had the greatest impact on the history of his times and the greatest influence on future events. His military and political successes were due more to sound, deliberate organizational skill than to imaginative genius. He imparted to chaotic Western Europe an order, prosperity, and stability which had been missing since the collapse of the Roman system. Though much that he accomplished died with him, nevertheless enough survived to create a pattern for European development for several centuries to come.

THE IMPACT OF ISLAM ON WARFARE

The major cause of the meteoric expansion of Islam was the fanaticism engendered by the charismatic leadership of **Mohammed,** and by specific tenets of his teachings which promised everlasting pleasure in heaven to those who died in holy war against the infidel. No other religion has ever been able to inspire so many men, so consistently and so enthusiastically, to be completely heedless of death and of personal danger in battle.

Thus it was energy more than skill, religious fanaticism rather than a superior military system, and missionary zeal instead of an organized scheme of recruitment

199

which accounted for Moslem victories. It should be noted, furthermore, that these successes might never have been possible had it not been for unusual circumstances which existed in Southwest Asia at the moment Islam appeared as a major religious, political, and military force in the region. The Byzantine and Persian empires were both exhausted by prolonged wars. Both were plagued by serious internal political and religious unrest, leaving their outlying provinces rebellious and ripe for plucking. Without the impetus derived from their early, relatively easy victories over Byzantines and Persians, it is doubtful if the Moslems would have been able to expand so fast or so far.

Once their initial headlong rush had run its course, the Moslems began to realize that even their own religious fervor could not afford the appalling loss of life resulting from heedless light-cavalry charges—almost entirely by unarmored men wielding sword and lance—against the skilled bowmen of China and Byzantium, or the solid masses of the Franks. Having by this time come into contact with practically every important military system in the world, the Mohammedans sensibly adopted many Byzantine military practices (see p. 214). They were never so well disciplined as the East Romans, nor so well organized. They relied primarily upon tribal levies rather than upon a standing military force. Their original fanaticism, nevertheless, combined with astute adoption of Byzantine tactics and strategic methods, made them still the most formidable offensive force in the world at the close of this period.

By that time, however, dynastic and sectarian differences had caused the Moslems to turn more of their energies inward. By the end of the 8th century the perimeter of Islam was generally stabilized, but endemic warfare persisted—and would persist for centuries—along three flaming frontiers: the mountains of Andalusia, the mountains of Anatolia, and the mountains and deserts of central Asia.

WEAPONS

Only one major new weapon appeared during this period: Greek fire, decisive and history-making, introduced to warfare by the Byzantines during the first Moslem siege of Constantinople (see p. 223). The exact composition of this explosive-inflammatory material, a closely guarded secret, has not survived to modern times. But this prototype of the modern flame thrower apparently was based upon a mixture of sulphur, naphtha, and quicklime which burst explosively into flames when wetted.

The combustible mixture was evidently packed into brass-bound wooden tubes, or siphons. Water was then pumped from a hose at high pressure into the tube. The material burst into flames and was projected a considerable distance by its own explosion as well as by the force of water pressure. The deadly effect of this weapon upon wooden ships, and upon the flesh of opposing soldiers, can well be imagined. Greek fire retained Byzantine maritime supremacy against a strong Moslem challenge. It also helped to keep the walls of Constantinople inviolate.

There were the usual modifications and improvements of existing weapons, of which the development of the cavalry lance was perhaps the most important. This was becoming the principal weapon of Western Europe, and was an important secondary weapon of the Byzantine cataphract (see p. 217).

On a world-wide basis, however, the bow was by far the predominant weapon. Its almost universal use had caused the more highly developed armies (such as the Byzantine) to discard, for field operations, the heavier and clumsier catapult and ballista used so effectively by the Romans (though these weapons were used extensively by the Byzantines in the siege and defense of fortifications). The general effectiveness and utility of the bow were such that it was being adopted extensively by the

Moslems at the end of the period, and Charlemagne was making a determined but vain effort to introduce it to the armies of Western Europe (see p. 209).

TACTICS

The most important tactical developments of the period are discussed in some detail in connection with the military systems of Charlemagne and of the Byzantines (see pp. 208 and 214).

In general the most significant feature of tactics was the world-wide supremacy of cavalry. This, in combination with the almost equally prevalent reliance upon the bow as a missile weapon, meant that warfare throughout most of the world was one of fire and movement, with shock action relegated to a secondary role and used normally to confirm a decision already achieved with missile weapons. There were two important exceptions: the Moslems and the Western Europeans.

Only among the Byzantines did there seem to be any real effort or ability to establish coordination between the actions of infantry and cavalry. This required a high state of training, discipline, and control—conditions rarely found save among the East Romans.

WESTERN EUROPE

VISIGOTHIC SPAIN, 600–712

The Visigothic monarchy in Spain declined steadily during the 7th century. Internal dissension between the nobility and the inept kings, and between Visigoths and the Ibero-Roman population, had brought the kingdom to the verge of disintegration when **Roderick** ascended the throne (710). The suddenness and completeness of the collapse in the face of the Moslem invasion (711–712) was less a measure of the military capability of the Saracens than proof of the utter incompetence of a regime on the verge of collapse. Important events of the period were:

616–624. Elimination of the Last East Roman Footholds in Southern Spain. This occurred while the Byzantine Empire was fighting for its life against the Persians and Avars (see p. 211). During this period Ceuta (on the Moroccan shore of the Strait of Gibraltar) was also conquered from the Byzantines (618).

710. Moslems Reach the Strait of Gibraltar. Count **Julian** repulsed a Moslem attack on Ceuta led by **Musa ibn Nusair.** Julian, disloyal to King Roderick, then made an alliance with Musa, promising assistance in an Arab invasion of Spain. With his assistance a Moslem raiding party led by **Abu Zora Tarif** made a reconnaissance in force in the Algeciras area of southern Spain (July).

711. Moslem Invasion of Spain. Musa sent a force of 7,000 under **Tarik ibn Ziyad** across the strait. Landing at Gibraltar (whose name commemorates the incident: Gebel el Tarik) he proceeded northwest, seeking the Visigoths, finding them between the Barbate and Guadalete rivers.

711, July 19. Battle of the Guadalete (Near Medina Sidonia). Roderick, with 90,000, was completely defeated by Tarik, now reinforced to about 12,000. The Moslem victory was facilitated by Visigothic dissension, treachery, and wholesale defections during the battle. Roderick fled while the issue was still in doubt, and was drowned while trying to cross the river. Tarik swept through southern Spain to win another victory at the **Battle of Ecija,** then captured the Visigothic capital at Toledo without opposition.

712. Arrival of Musa. Taking the command from Tarik, Musa completed the conquest of Spain save for isolated regions in the Asturias Mountains.

LOMBARDY, 600–774

The Lombards never achieved unity among themselves; as a result they never succeeded in conquering all of Italy. Until overwhelmed by **Charlemagne,** the Lombard kings were constantly at war with the Byzantine Empire in vain efforts to absorb the remnants of the East Roman Empire in Italy. At the same time they had to contend not only with their own unruly nobility but with frequent inroads of Franks, Avars, and Slavs into north Italy. Kings **Liutprand** (712–744) and **Aistulf** (749–756) were the strongest of the Lombard rulers. Liutprand broke the power of the southern dukes of Benevento and Spoleto, and briefly captured Ravenna, capital of Byzantine holdings in Italy. Building on his accomplishments, Aistulf again captured Ravenna and twice came close to capturing Rome. These successes caused Pope **Stephen II** to appeal to **Pepin,** King of the Franks, for assistance. Pepin twice marched into Italy to defeat Aistulf, and by the "donation of Pepin" ceded to the Pope territory formerly belonging to the Byzantine emperors and to the Lombard kings, thus establishing the temporal powers of the papacy. Renewed Lombard threats against the new papal possessions caused Pope **Adrian I** to appeal for assistance to Charlemagne, son of Pepin. In two campaigns Charlemagne defeated and captured **Desiderius,** last King of the Lombards, took the Lombard crown himself, and annexed all of Lombardy to his empire. Important events of the period were:

728. Capture of Ravenna by Liutprand. Soon after, it was retaken by the Byzantine Exarch of Ravenna.

752. Capture of Ravenna by Aistulf.

754. Invasion of Italy and Recapture of Ravenna by Pepin. Aistulf sued for peace, agreeing to end attacks against Rome.

756. Pepin's Second Invasion. Upon renewed attacks against Rome by Aistulf, Pepin again invaded Italy, defeated Aistulf near **Ravenna,** and granted lands to Pope **Stephen II.**

773–774. Charlemagne Defeats Desiderius. After besieging and capturing Desiderius at Pavia, Charlemagne took the crown of Lombardy for himself.

BRITAIN

Early in the 7th century the Britons were eliminated from England proper—save for Cornwall, where they retained a foothold until the 9th century—and were driven into Wales. Subsequent violent struggles among the seven Anglo-Saxon kingdoms of England were not decisive; supremacy shifted from one to the other, with Northumbria and Mercia most often predominant. Nowhere in the Western world did the art of war sink lower than in Britain during this period. Savage ardor had overcome all vestiges of Roman system and discipline. Retaining little direct contact with continental affairs, Anglo-Saxon methods of warfare had probably regressed since the time of Hengist and Horsa. Strategy and discipline were unknown; tactics simply consisted of the disorderly alignment of opposing warriors in roughly parallel orders of battle followed by dull, uninspired butchery until one side or the other fled. Fortifications were crude and rudimentary palisades; armor was scarce and poor. In consequence warfare was, as Oman says, "spasmodic and inconsequent." Near the end of the 8th century, Norse raiders began to appear along the coasts of Britain and Ireland, to find lands ripe for conquest. The important events of the period were:

597–616. Supremacy of Kent.   King Aethelbert was ruler of Kent.

603. Scottish Invasion.   This was repelled by King Aethelfrith of Northumbria, who defeated King Aidan of the Dalriad Scots at the Battle of Daegsastan.

615. Battle of Chester.   Aethelfrith defeated the Britons, pushing on to reach the Irish Channel, separating the Britons in Wales from those of northwest England.

616. Battle of the Idle.   Raedwald, King of East Anglia, defeated and killed Aethelfrith to help Edwin become the first Christian King of Northumbria.

616. Supremacy of Northumbria.   Edwin defeated the Britons in north Wales and Anglesea. His principal rival was the Briton, Cadwallon, a king in north Wales. The supremacy of Northumbria continued under Oswald, successor of Edwin (632–641).

632. Battle of Hatfield Chase.   Edwin was defeated and killed by the alliance of the Christian Briton Cadwallon and the heathen Angle, Penda of Mercia.

633. Battle of Hefenfelth (Rowley Water).   Oswald defeated and killed Cadwallon to drive the Britons completely from northwest England.

641. Battle of Maserfeld (Oswestry, Shropshire).   Penda defeated and killed Os-

wald to establish Mercia temporarily as the leading Anglo-Saxon kingdom. He was defeated and killed at the Battle of Winwaed (655) by Oswy (641–670), younger brother of Oswald, who re-established Northumbria in a position of pre-eminence.

685. Battle of Dunnichen Moss (North of Tay River in Forfar, Scotland).   Egfrith, successor of Oswy, was defeated and killed by the Scots after he had overrun most of southern Scotland. This battle assured the independence of Scotland from Anglo-Saxon England.

716–796. Supremacy of Mercia.   This was under Kings Aethelbald (716–757) and Offa (757–769). Aethelbald successfully invaded Wessex (733) and Northumbria (744). His cousin Offa succeeded to the throne after a violent civil war. He re-established Mercian hegemony in a series of hard-fought campaigns which resulted in the first real unification of England. He was treated as an equal by his contemporary, Charlemagne.

789–795. Arrival of the Vikings.   The first recorded Viking raid on England was near Dorchester (789). The Danes raided Lindisfarne Island off the Northumbrian coast (793). The first recorded Viking raids against Scotland (794) and Ireland (795) soon followed.

KINGDOM OF THE FRANKS, 600–814

Decline of the Merovingians, 600–731

The vigor and bellicosity of the Franks were undiminished despite the decline and degeneracy of the ruling Merovingian family. A remarkable noble family seized the reins of leadership. Pepin I became mayor of the palace (prime minister) of Austrasia early in the 7th century. After an anarchic interval and a series of violent civil wars, he was succeeded by his son Pepin II, who expanded his authority over Neustria as well. He was succeeded as mayor of the palace early in the 8th century by his illegitimate son Charles Martel (Charles the Hammer).

In Aquitaine, Count Eudo (Eudes, or Odo) was emerging as Charles Martel's principal rival for Frankish supremacy. Most of Eudo's attention, however, was directed to repelling Moslem incursions across the Pyrenees, which began in 712 and which waxed in frequency and intensity in the following decade. At first successful, by 731 Eudo found himself unable to cope with nearly simultaneous invasions of his realm from the northeast by Charles Martel and from the south by the Moslems. The principal events were:

613. Temporary Reunification of the Principal Frankish Kingdoms.   Austrasia, Neustria, and Burgundy were united under Merovingian King Lothair II.

623–629. Pepin I Mayor of the Palace.   This was during the minority of Dagobert (last strong Merovingian king). After coming of age (628), Dagobert exiled

Pepin. After the death of Dagobert, Pepin again became mayor of the palace briefly before his own death (638–639).

c. 675–678. Rise of Pepin II. He led Austrasian nobles in civil war to overthrow **Ebroin,** whom he replaced as mayor of the palace.

687. Battle of Tertry (Near St. Quentin). Pepin conquered Neustria. In subsequent campaigns against Frisians, Alemanni, and Burgundians, he reunited the old Frankish kingdom of Clovis, save for Aquitaine.

712. Arrival of the Moslems. First raid north of the Pyrenees.

714. Rise of Charles Martel. The death of Pepin caused temporary anarchy, resolved in Austrasia by victories of Charles Martel over his rivals in the battles of **Amblève** (near Liége, 716) and **Vincy** (near Cambrai, 717).

c. 715. Rise of Eudo. He consolidated his control over Aquitaine. He soon made an alliance with **Ragenfrid,** mayor of the palace of Neustria and rival of Charles.

717–719. Moslem Raids into Aquitaine and Southern France. The Moslem leader **Hurr** captured Narbonne (719) to obtain a base in western Septimania (coastal strip along the Mediterranean between the Pyrenees and the Rhone River).

719. Battle of Soissons. Charles gained control over Neustria by victory over Ragenfrid and Eudo. Eudo made peace temporarily by surrendering Ragenfrid to Charles.

721. Battle of Toulouse. Eudo decisively defeated and killed **Samah,** Moslem governor of Spain, who had invaded Aquitaine and invested Toulouse; remnants of the Moslem Army were driven back into Spain and Septimania.

721–725. Appearance of Abd er-Rahman. The governor of Moslem Spain, he led repeated raids into Aquitaine and southern France.

725–726. Moslem Invasion of Southern France. Under the leadership of Anbaca (Anabasa), the Moslems captured Carcassonne and Nîmes, and conquered all Septimania. The expedition culminated in a raid up the Rhone Valley as far as Besançon and the Vosges.

726–732. Expeditions of Charles Martel into Germany. These resulted in the conquest of Bavaria, expansion of the kingdom into Thuringia and Frisia, and limited success against the Saxons.

731. Charles Martel Invades Northeastern Aquitaine. He annexed Berry (region around Bourges).

Campaign and Battle of Tours, 732

Abd er-Rahman led a Moslem army of unknown strength (probably about 50,000) into Aquitaine, slipping past the western flank of the Pyrenees at Irun. This army, almost entirely cavalry, was comprised mostly of Berbers and other Moors, with a leavening of Arab leadership. Abd defeated Eudo at the **Battle of Bordeaux.** With the remnants of his defeated army, Eudo fled to Austrasia to make peace and swear fealty to Charles Martel, who had hastily returned from a campaign along the upper Danube upon hearing of the Moslem invasion.

The Moslems, meanwhile, had been halted temporarily by the fortified city of Poitiers. Leaving a part of his army to invest the city, Abd advanced to the Loire, near Tours, plundering en route. The Moslems had just laid siege to Tours when they became aware of the secret and rapid approach of Charles and Eudo from the east, south of the Loire, threatening their lines of communication. Abd hastily dispatched his great train of booty to the south, following in a slow withdrawal toward Poitiers.

The Frank army evidently made contact with the foe somewhere south of Tours early in October, 732. From scanty records it appears that for the next six days Abd er-Rahman endeavored to cover the retreat of his train of booty in a classical delaying action marked by frequent but indecisive skirmishes. It would also seem that Charles maintained strong pressure on the Moslems and forced them back steadily toward Poitiers. Accordingly, Abd er-Rahman decided to fight a major battle somewhere between Tours and Poitiers, probably near Cenon, on the

Vienne River. The subsequent action, known usually as the Battle of Tours, is sometimes (and more appropriately) called the Battle of Poitiers.

Though the respective strengths are unknown, the Frank army was probably larger than that of the Moslems. Charles had both infantry and cavalry, probably in nearly equal proportions, consistent with the increasing trend toward cavalry. His rapid and secret march into Touraine, and the nature of the skirmishing during the week prior to the battle, support the assumption that Charles had a substantial cavalry contingent, which he used skillfully against the Moslem horsemen.

The Franks had engaged in more or less constant warfare against the Moslems for nearly two decades. Thus Charles was undoubtedly aware of the respective strengths and weaknesses of his own and Abd er-Rahman's forces. He evidently realized that the heavy Frank cavalry was undisciplined, sluggish in comparison with the mobile light Moslem cavalry, and extremely difficult to control in mounted combat. He also realized that the Moslems were effective only in attacking, that they were deadly in taking advantage of a gap in a battle line, but that they had no defensive staying power and that they lacked the weight to deliver an effective blow by shock action against a strong defensive force. These must have been the considerations which led him to dismount his cavalry when he saw the Moslems preparing for a decisive encounter. Apparently he formed his army into a solid phalanx of footmen, presumably on the most commanding terrain available in the rolling country of west-central France.

The classic and frequently quoted description of the battle is that of Isodorus Pacensis, as contained in Bouquet's *Recueil des Historiens des Gaules et de la France* and translated freely and dramatically by Oman:

> The men of the north stood as motionless as a wall; they were like a belt of ice frozen together, and not to be dissolved, as they slew the Arabs with the sword. The Austrasians, vast of limb, and iron of hand, hewed on bravely in the thick of the fight; it was they who found and cut down the Saracen king.

This and other accounts, including those of the Moslems, indicate that repeated and violent cavalry attacks were repulsed in desperate fighting that lasted till nightfall. One report implies that the Frank right wing, under Eudo, enveloped the Moslem left and forced them to withdraw to protect their threatened camp. At any rate, when night fell, the disheartened and exhausted Moslems had withdrawn to their camp, when they discovered that Abd er-Rahman had been killed during the fight. They then apparently panicked; abandoning their train, they fled south after nightfall.

At dawn next morning Charles formed his army again to meet a renewed assault. When cautious reconnaissance revealed the flight of the enemy, he rightly refused to pursue. In pursuit his own undisciplined troops were at their weakest, and not amenable to control. It was a favorite Arab tactic to entice the cumbersome Frankish cavalry to such pursuit, and then to turn and slaughter them when they were spread out. Furthermore, he did not wish to leave the great quantities of booty which he had recaptured. Finally, he possibly did not wish to eliminate completely Moslem opposition to his rival, Eudo.

The Battle of Tours is considered one of the decisive battles of history, complementing the even more decisive victory won by Leo III of Byzantium fourteen years earlier at Constantinople (see p. 224). Together these two victories stemmed the hitherto irresistible tide of Moslem expansion and assured Christian Europe of several centuries of growth and development before being faced with comparable pagan threats in the 13th and 15th centuries.

The Battle of Tours cemented the authority of Charles Martel (whose sobriquet was won there) over the Franks, laying the basis for the establishment of the Holy Roman Empire by his grandson Charlemagne.

Rise of the Carolingians, 732–814

Following the Battle of Tours, Charles and Eudo drove the Moslems from all of their conquests in France except for Septimania, where they held on for nearly three decades. There were a few more Arab raids to the north, but the Franks dealt with these readily. They aggressively whittled at Septimania, and **Pepin III,** son and successor of Charles Martel, finally drove the Moslems back over the Pyrenees.

After serving for ten years as the actual ruler of France in the pose of Mayor of the Palace, Pepin ended the mockery of the Merovingian Dynasty by deposing

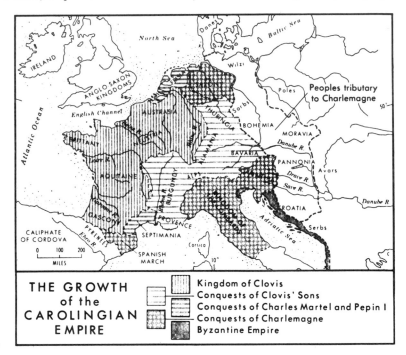

THE GROWTH of the CAROLINGIAN EMPIRE

Kingdom of Clovis
Conquests of Clovis' Sons
Conquests of Charles Martel and Pepin I
Conquests of Charlemagne
Byzantine Empire

Childeric III and, with the approval of Pope **Zacharias,** having himself crowned King of the Franks. In subsequent years (751–768), in addition to wars against the Moslems, Pepin campaigned aggressively in Germany, in Aquitaine, and in Italy. His campaigns in Germany expanded Frankish influence over Bavaria, but he was unable to subdue the stubborn Saxons. He defeated **Waifer,** Duke of Aquitaine and successor to Eudo, bringing that province firmly under central control. In Italy, at the request of Pope **Stephen** (see p. 202), he defeated the Lombards and established the temporal power of the papacy.

Upon the death of Pepin the kingdom was divided equally between his two sons, **Charles** (the elder) and **Carloman,** according to the Frankish custom of succession. Relations between the brothers were cool, but on the death of Carloman (771), Charles became sole ruler of the Franks, to commence the brilliant reign which caused him to be known to history as "the Great," or **Charlemagne.**

Charlemagne's principal attributes were vigor, brilliance, efficiency, and intel lectual curiosity. He stimulated and encouraged revivals of learning, art, and literature. Under his firm, benevolent rule most of the Christian nations of Western Europe enjoyed peace and prosperity to an extent unknown since the Antonine emperors of Rome. His cultural, economic, political, and judicial accomplishments were based upon a remarkably efficient military system which he devised in a series of aggressive campaigns around the frontiers of his realm. He kept his external enemies so busy that they had neither the time nor inclination to think of invading or harassing his territories. The principal events of the period were:

735. Rebellion in Aquitaine. After Eudo's death his sons rebelled against Charles Martel, who invaded Aquitaine and forced the rebels to pay homage.

734–739. Charles Martel's Rhone Valley Campaigns against the Moslems. During this time the Moslems attempted only two major raids into Frankish territory, which Charles repulsed after the Moslems reached Valence and Lyon (737 and 739).

741–747. Joint Rule of Carloman and Pepin III (Pepin the Short). Upon the death of Charles Martel, his sons ruled jointly as Mayors of the Palace.

743–759. Moslems Driven from France. Pepin drove the Moslems across the Pyrenees from Septimania, which he annexed to France.

747. Resignation of Carloman. Pepin became sole ruler of France.

751. Coronation of Pepin.

754–756. Campaigns of Pepin against the Lombards. (See p. 202.)

757–758. Pepin's Campaigns in Germany. He defeated **Tassilo III,** Duke of Bavaria, who had tried to assert his independence (757), and defeated the Saxons, requiring them to pay tribute (758).

760–768. Campaigns in Aquitaine. Pepin finally defeated **Waifer,** rebellious Duke of Aquitaine.

763. Revolt of Tassilo of Bavaria. Frankish control was eliminated from Bavaria for fifteen years.

768–771. Joint Rule of Charlemagne and Carloman. After the death of Pepin, his two sons divided the kingdom. During this period Charlemagne suppressed another insurrection in Aquitaine (769).

771–814. Reign of Charlemagne. The kingdom was reunited after the death of Carloman.

772–799. Charlemagne's Campaigns against the Saxons. Generally successful in these eighteen campaigns, Charlemagne was frequently frustrated by Saxon uprisings as soon as his main army withdrew. Minor setbacks were suffered by the Franks when the Saxons captured **Eresburg** by treachery (776) and took **Karlstadt** by storm (778). The back of Saxon resistance was broken by Charlemagne's vigorous winter campaign (785–786), although sporadic resistance continued for 13 more years.

773–774. Charlemagne Defeats Desiderius. Charlemagne besieged and captured Desiderius, last King of the Lombards, in **Pavia,** and took the Lombard crown himself (see p. 202). The following year he suppressed a Lombard revolt (775).

777–801. Frankish Conquest of Northern Spain. The first expedition against the Emir of Cordova was successful, but ended in a disaster when the Christian Basques of Pamplona joined the Moslems in ambushing and destroying the rearguard of the Frankish army under Charlemagne's nephew, **Roland,** in the **Pass of Roncesvalles** (778). (One result was the classic epic poem, *The Song of Roland.*) In subsequent campaigns Charlemagne subdued the Basques and drove the Moslems south of the Ebro River. These campaigns culminated in the successful siege of Barcelona (800–801).

780 and 787. Campaigns in South Italy. Charlemagne's successful punitive expeditions against the Duke of Benevento.

787–788. Reconquest of Bavaria. Charlemagne defeated Tassilo.

789. Occupation of Istria. Charlemagne ignored Byzantine objections.

791–796. Defeat and Conquest of the Avars. During these campaigns Frank armies under Charlemagne and his son **Pepin** operated in the central Danube Valley, and penetrated east of the Theiss River. The Franks also conquered parts of Croatia and Slovenia from the Slavs. Subsequent Avar revolts were suppressed (799, 803).

800, December 25. Charlemagne Holy Roman Emperor. He was crowned by Pope Leo III

803–810. Operations against Byzantines. These desultory campaigns were fought on land in Dalmatia and at sea on the Adriatic. Though generally successful, Charlemagne made a conciliatory peace with the Byzantines, surrendering most of his conquests in Dalmatia, but retaining Istria. In return Byzantine Emperor Nicephorus I recognized Charlemagne as Emperor of the West (see p. 263).

809–812. Arrival of the Norsemen. Charlemagne and his subordinates repelled Danish raids across the Elbe. His fleet, based on Boulogne, prevented harassment of the sea coast of the Frank Empire.

THE MILITARY SYSTEM OF CHARLEMAGNE, C. 800

Charlemagne's military system was crude in comparison with the organization of the Macedonians, Romans, and Byzantines. It was, however, a revolutionary departure from the military anarchy which had prevailed in Western Europe for four centuries, and which returned after his death. Furthermore, it provided a basis for the development of feudalism and the chivalry of the Middle Ages.

Prior to Charlemagne the principal military characteristics of the Franks were exceptional vigor and exceptional indiscipline. Even under such able warriors as Charles Martel and Pepin, Frank armies were unreliable, Frank conquests impermanent. The principal reason why opponents of Charlemagne were consistently outclassed was because he was able to harness Frankish vigor in a disciplined, efficient organization, while at the same time providing a high order of personal leadership.

One demonstration of the working of Charlemagne's military system was its adaptation to the Lombard heavy cavalry. He had relatively little trouble in defeating the Lombards in two brief campaigns, but recognized an intrinsic superiority of the Lombard cavalry to his own Frankish horsemen. While working successfully to improve his Frank cavalry, he henceforth made much use of the Lombards, who provided the major component of the Frank armies which defeated the Avars. Prior to their reorganization and disciplining under Charlemagne, these same Lombards had been relatively helpless against Avar raids into north Italy.

As in every successful military system, discipline was the prime ingredient. Cavalry and infantry were responsive to the commands of superior authority in a way unknown to the Teutons since they had overthrown the Roman legion. Charlemagne established a system of calling men to service through his noble vassals, which enabled him to maintain standing armies in the field indefinitely without placing an undue strain on the economy, without being forced to employ unreliable riffraff, and without denuding the provinces of local resources for preserving law and order.

One reason why the predecessors of Charlemagne had been unable to keep armies in the field for any length of time had been lack of logistical organization. Frankish armies had subsisted on foraging and plunder. In nominally friendly areas this soon antagonized the inhabitants and contributed to internal unrest. In hostile territory the dispersal of forces on plundering missions often led to disaster at the hands of an alert, concentrated foe. Supply shortages almost always caused the dissolution of Frankish armies after a few weeks in the field. Charlemagne established a logistical organization, including supply trains with food and equipment sufficient to maintain his troops for several weeks. Replenishment of supplies was done on an orderly basis, both by systematic foraging and by convoying additional supply trains to the armies in the field. This permitted Charlemagne to carry war a thousand miles from the heart of France and to maintain armies in the field on campaign, or in sieges, throughout the winter—something unknown in Western Europe since the time of the Romans.

Charlemagne also revived the Roman and Macedonian practice of maintaining a siege train. Thus he was never embarrassed by inability to deal with hostile fortifications. The supply and siege trains slowed down the advance of his main armies, but assured reliable progress. Furthermore, by increasing reliance upon cavalry, accompanied by mule pack trains, he was still able to project his strength quickly and forcefully.

A key element of Charlemagne's military system was his use of frontier fortified posts, or burgs. These were built along the frontiers of every conquered province, and were connected with each other by a road along the frontier. In addition, another road led directly back to the old frontier from each burg. Stocked with supplies, these forts became bases for the maneuver of the disciplined Frank cavalry, either to maintain order in the conquered territory or to project Frankish power forward in further operations.

Charlemagne also brought the bow back into the arsenals of Western Europe, probably as a result of experience against the Avars and Byzantines. For reasons that are not clear, this weapon was soon again discarded by most European armies after his death, although popular as a hunting weapon.

Another evidence of the efficacy of the system was uniform tactical doctrine. Indoctrination and training of subordinate commanders is only possible in a highly efficient military organization. The completeness and directness of Charlemagne's orders—some of which have been preserved—prove not only his own professional competence but also that this competence had created an effective staff system.

The main elements of Charlemagne's system are contained in a series of five imperial ordinances, issued between 803 and 813, which were a form of field-service regulations. In these he prescribed the duties of vassals in preparing forces to be raised on call; the property basis for military call-ups of individual soldiers; the organization of units; the weapons, armor, and equipment to be carried by each man and to be brought with each unit; lists of punishments for common offenses, and the like.

MOSLEM AND CHRISTIAN SPAIN, 712–800

Under Musa ibn Nusair the Moslem conquest of Spain was completed quickly, save for scattered resistance in the narrow strip of mountains of the northwest. He was delayed only by the fortifications of Seville and Mérida, which he took after protracted sieges. The Ibero-Roman inhabitants were glad to be rid of the Visigoths, and the Moslems were lenient in allowing Christians and Jews to continue the practice of their faiths. Moslem leadership had been Arab initially, and the core of the army had been Arab-Syrian. Most of the fighting men, however, had been Berber, and as more Berbers arrived from Morocco, the flavor of the occupation became essentially Moorish. The internal dissensions of Islam were reflected in the Moslem community in Spain, and additional discord was created by friction among Arabs, Syrians, and Berbers. The establishment of the independent Omayyad Dynasty in Spain by refugee Prince **Abd-er-Rahman ibn Mu'awiya** (see p. 210) eventually led to relative peace and centralized control. Meanwhile, the dissension among the Moslems had given the Visigothic refugees in the Asturias Mountains a breathing spell to organize their defenses and to begin tentative efforts to expand their tiny enclave of Christian freedom. By the end of the 8th century, Moslem-Christian warfare, which would be endemic in Spain for more than seven centuries, had begun. Principal events were:

712–720. Consolidation of the Moslem Conquest of Iberia. Raids were begun across the Pyrenees (see p. 204).

c. 718. Establishment of the Christian Kingdom of the Asturias. Visigothic Prince **Pelayo** (718–737) made his capital at Cangas de Onís. He repulsed the Moslems at the **Battle of Covadonga** (718).

732. Battle of Tours. (See p. 205.)

740. Berber Revolt. This created chaos in Morocco and Spain, and permitted the tiny kingdom of the Asturias to expand to the south and west, culminating in the Christian conquest of Galicia (750).

755–756. Establishment of the Omayyad Emirate of Cordova. Abd-er-Rahman ibn Mu'awiya, refugee from the Abbassid massacre of the Omayyads (see p. 233), founded the emirate.

756–786. Moslem Consolidation. Abd-er-Rahman suppressed internal disorders in Moslem Spain and halted Christian resurgence in the northwest.

777–801. Invasion of Spain by Charlemagne. (See p. 207.)

EURASIA AND THE MEDITERRANEAN

BYZANTINE EMPIRE, 602–642

Disaster under Phocas, 602–610

602. Overthrow and Murder of Maurice. **Phocas,** a centurion of the Byzantine army on the Danube, fomented a mutiny, displaced Priscus (see p. 183), and led the mutinous army back to Constantinople, forcing the abdication of Maurice, whom Phocas then cruelly murdered.

603–604. Resurgence of the Avars. Aided by the mutiny, Avar raiders swept through imperial lands south and west of the Danube. Phocas brought temporary peace by paying a large tribute (604).

603–610. War with Persia. Chosroes II of Persia, who owed his throne to Maurice (see p. 193), declared war on the murderer of his benefactor. Persian armies

were victorious in Mesopotamia and Syria, capturing the fortress towns of Dara, Amida Haran, Edessa, Hierapolis, and Aleppo, though they were repulsed from Antioch and Damascus. They then overran Byzantine Armenia and raided deep into Anatolia through the provinces of Cappadocia, Phrygia, Galatia, and Bithynia. Byzantine resistance collapsed; cowardly, inept Phocas did nothing to halt the invasion. A Persian army penetrated as far as the Bosporus (608).

610. Revolt of Heraclius (the Elder). The Exarch of Africa, **Heraclius,** a loyal subordinate of Maurice, had refused to accept the usurpation of Phocas. He now sent a fleet from Carthage to Constantinople, under the command of his son, also named **Heraclius.** Assisted by an uprising in the city, Heraclius overthrew Phocas, who was killed by the mob. Young Heraclius then accepted the throne thrust upon him by popular demand.

Heraclius and the Last Persian War, 610–628

610. Continuation of the War with Persia. The downfall of Phocas should have satisfied Chosroes, but the Persian ruler now had visions of re-establishing the empire of Darius, and intensified his war effort. The Byzantine Army, ruined by defeat, corruption, and misadministration, offered only halfhearted opposition.

611–620. Persian Victories in Syria and Anatolia. Antioch and most of the remaining Byzantine fortresses in Syria and Mesopotamia and Armenia were captured (611). After long sieges the invaders took Damascus (613) and Jerusalem (614). Chosroes then began a determined invasion of Anatolia (615). Persian forces under General **Shahen** captured Chalcedon on the Bosporus after a long siege (616). Here the Persians remained, within one mile of Constantinople, for more than 10 years. Meanwhile they captured Ancyra and Rhodes (620); remaining Byzantine fortresses in Armenia were captured; the Persian occupation cut off a principal Byzantine recruiting ground.

616–619. Persian Conquest of Egypt. After defeating Byzantine garrisons in the Nile Valley, Chosroes marched across the Libyan Desert as far as Cyrene. These victories cut off the usual grain supplies from Egypt to Constantinople.

617–619. Renewed Avar Invasions. Avar raiders swept the Balkan provinces, reaching the walls of Constantinople.

619–621. Heraclius and Sergius. Heraclius vainly attempted to reorganize the army. In despair, he prepared to leave Constantinople and to return to Africa. At this point **Sergius,** Patriarch of Constantinople, sparked a popular resurgence of patriotism in Constantinople. By entreaty and reproach he obtained from Heraclius an oath that he would never abandon the capital. Sergius promised to make available all of the resources of the Church. With renewed energy and confidence, Heraclius turned to the task of reorganization. With the somewhat reluctant approval of Sergius, he emptied the overcrowded monasteries to recruit monks into the army, and seized much of the wealth of the churches of Constantinople. He made peace with the Avar chagan (chieftain) just outside the walls of Constantinople by paying a large indemnity. Meanwhile, negotiating with Shahen, he pretended to consider unacceptable Persian terms (which would have recognized all of Chosroes' conquests), while preparing to take the field.

622, April. Heraclius Sails from Constantinople. Taking advantage of continuing Byzantine command of the sea, Heraclius sailed from Constantinople with an army of unknown size (probably less than 50,000). He landed a few days later at the junction of Cilicia and Syria, near Alexandretta and ancient Issus.

622–623. The Campaign of Issus.* The coastal plain of Issus, ringed by mountains, is accessible only through three passes, all of which Heraclius promptly seized. A much larger Persian army under the general **Shahr Baraz** probed cautiously at the passes, but was repulsed. To restore martial prowess in his army, Heraclius combined tough drill-field training with

carefully controlled engagements against the frustrated Persians encamped outside his enclave. Finally ready (probably October), Heraclius apparently pretended to march through the Amanic Gates as though striking toward Armenia. He enticed the Persians into battle on the heights overlooking Issus. Pretending flight, he apparently drew the Persians back toward the plain, while he sent the main body of his army eastward through another pass. Counterattacking with his rear guard, he halted the Persian advance in the pass, then hurried after the main body, leaving Shahr Baraz and his army far behind. The **Battle of Issus** was a minor engagement, but the emperor and his army were elated by the ease with which they had outmaneuvered and outwitted their enemy. After several days of indecision and countermarching, Shahr Baraz followed Heraclius into Pontus. At the end of the year the two armies were again facing each other, this time in the Anti-Taurus Mountains along the upper Halys River. After several weeks of skirmishing, Shahr Baraz attempted an ambush, but Byzantine reconnaissance discovered the Persian dispositions (January, 623). Heraclius pretended to fall into the trap while setting one of his own. As the concealed Persians burst out of their hiding place, Byzantine troops converged on them from the surrounding mountains. The entire Persian enveloping force was annihilated. Heraclius immediately turned to attack Shahr Baraz' main body, but the remaining Persians were so shaken by the unexpected turn of events that they soon fled in disorder. Following this decisive **Battle of the Halys,** Heraclius put his army into winter quarters, then personally returned to Constantinople to supervise defensive measures being taken against the continuing Avar threat.

623. Invasion of Media. Leaving his son **Constantine** to command the capital against the Avars and the Persians still at Chalcedon, Heraclius sailed with 5,000 reinforcements to join his army at Trapezus (Trebizond). Raising additional forces in Pontus, Heraclius struck quickly through the mountains of Armenia to northern Media, heading for the capital, Tauris (Tabriz). The strength of his army is not known, but was probably more than 50,-

---

* The details of this and the subsequent operations of Heraclius are inadequately recorded. What he accomplished is known; how he did it is often vague.

000. Chosroes, dashing to protect Media with about 40,000 men, declined battle and abandoned Tauris to Heraclius. The Byzantine emperor then advanced to Thebarma (Urmia, or Rizaiyeh), where he captured the shrine at the supposed birthplace of Zoroaster. He then withdrew northeastward from the mountains to winter in the fertile Araxes Valley of Albania (northern Azerbaijan).

624. Invasion of Central Persia. Heraclius apparently led his army southeastward along the shores of the Caspian, then turned south through the Hyrcanian (Elburz) Mountains into the heart of Persia, advancing as far as Ispahan—the farthest penetration into Persia ever made by a Roman or Byzantine army. Chosroes, withdrawing most of his troops from Chalcedon, assembled three great armies, converging on Heraclius in central Persia. Heraclius seems to have operated successfully on interior lines between the Persian armies, then withdrew to spend the winter in northwest Persia or Media. When the Persians went into winter quarters nearby, Heraclius made a surprise attack on Shahr Baraz, routing his army and successfully storming a walled city in which the Persian general had taken refuge. Shahr Baraz escaped, and the Byzantine army spent the winter in and around the captured Persian fortifications.

625, Spring. Campaigns in Corduene and Mesopotamia. Heraclius marched west through the mountains of Corduene (Kurdistan) and across the Tigris, accompanied by a great train of booty. The speed of his march seems to have surprised the Persians, and he recaptured the fortified towns of Amida and Martyropolis (Maipercat), apparently without a struggle. The Persian army in northern Mesopotamia withdrew westward across the Euphrates. Heraclius pursued into Cilicia, where he found the reinforced Persians, under his old foe Shahr Baraz, holding the line of the Sarus River.

625. Battle of the Sarus. Heraclius was victorious in an assault river crossing. Shahr Baraz withdrew northwestward, pursued by Heraclius. Clearing the Persians from Cappadocia and Pontus, Heraclius returned to spend the winter at Trapezus.

625–626. Alliance of Persia and the Avars. Learning of this alliance, Heraclius evidently made a sea voyage to Constantinople to organize the defense of the city against the double threat. Presumably while he was there, he made arrangement for a new army under his brother **Theodore** to operate against the Persians in western Anatolia while he returned to his own army in Pontus.

626. Persian Plans. During the winter Chosroes planned an all-out effort against Constantinople. He returned to Anatolia with three armies—of unknown size, presumably more than 50,000 men each. One of these (possibly commanded by Chosroes himself) was to contain Heraclius in Pontus; another, under Shahen, was to prevent any junction between the armies of Heraclius and Theodore; the third, evidently under Shahr Baraz, was to cooperate with the Avars in an attack against Constantinople.

626, June 29–August 10. The Defense of Constantinople. An Avar army about 100,000 strong (including large contingents of Slavs, Germans, and Bulgars) stormed the walls protecting the approach to the city and advanced to the city wall itself. Rejecting Byzantine bribes, the Avars closely invested the city. Heraclius himself hard-pressed in Pontus, rushed 12,000 of his best veterans by sea to bolster the defenders of the city, commanded by his son, **Constantine.** After careful coordination of plans between the Avar chagan and Shahr Baraz, the allies mounted a furious offensive (August 1). While the Avars stormed at the walls, the Persians attempted to cross the Bosporus by small boats and rafts above Constantinople, aided by a swarm of Slavic small craft. While Constantine and his soldiers repulsed every Avar assault, the Byzantine Navy smashed the Slavic and Persian flotillas on the Bosporus. The action continued incessantly for ten days until the allies admitted defeat (August 10). The Persians had been unable to effect a landing either at Constantinople itself or behind the Avar lines. The Avars, having suffered terrible losses, running short of food and supplies, were forced to withdraw. This was one of the great moments in the long history of Constantinople.

626, Summer. Operations in Anatolia. Meanwhile Heraclius, his army reduced by campaigning and detachments to lesser than 30,000 men, was on the defensive in Pontus. Apparently he left a strong garrison in Trapezus and withdrew slowly northeastward along the Black Sea into Colchis, where he halted the Persians by aggressive defensive-offensive operations along the Phasis River. By attracting the main Persian army in Anatolia, he provided his brother Theodore with the opportunity to defeat the one remaining Persian army somewhere in western Anatolia. By the end of the summer Theodore's army was probably in central Anatolia, threatening to cut off the Persian armies at Chalcedon and in Colchis. The defensive strategy of Heraclius—with the able assistance of his son and his brother —had proven as successful as his offensive operations.

26–627. Preparations for a Renewed Offensive. During the winter Heraclius made an alliance with **Ziebel,** Khan of the Khazars, for a joint invasion of Persia the following spring. The Khazars were to advance across the Oxus into eastern Persia, and to raid from the Caucasus into Armenia and Media; the Byzantines would meanwhile drive through Syria, Mesopotamia, and Assyria toward the Persian capital of Ctesiphon. In preparation Heraclius (reinforced by troops from Constantinople) marched southward to Edessa, either during the winter or (more likely) in the early spring.

27, Spring. Opening the Campaign. With 70,000 men Heraclius swept through Syria, Mesopotamia, and southern Armenia, recapturing most of the Byzantine fortresses lost to the Persians 10 and 15 years earlier. The army of Shahr Baraz, still at Chalcedon, was now cut off completely. The Persian general then learned that Chosroes, dissatisfied with his failure to capture Constantinople, was planning to have him executed. Accordingly, Shahr Baraz surrendered to Heraclius, although refusing to join the Byzantine army against his ungrateful sovereign. Anatolia was now free of the invaders.

27. Invasion of Assyria. Heraclius now marched from southern Armenia to the upper Tigris, then continued southward into Assyria. The hoped-for cooperation of the Khazars was not forthcoming; Ziebel had died unexpectedly, and his successor did not see fit to continue the alli-

ance. Heraclius, however, was determined to carry the war into Persia. A Persian army, under the general **Rhazates,** hovered to the eastward, but refused battle. The aged Chosroes ordered Rhazates to stand and fight near ancient Nineveh.

627, December. The Battle of Nineveh. On the same Assyrian plain where Alexander had won the climactic victory of Arbela, the decisive battle of the last war between the East Roman and Sassanid empires took place. The two armies were apparently about evenly matched; Rhazates probably had a substantial numerical superiority, but Heraclius had the moral ascendancy. The battle was hard-fought, and Heraclius —as usual—was in the thick of the fray. Although wounded, he refused to leave the field, and in a final charge personally killed the Persian general. By nightfall the Persian army was completely smashed.

627. Pursuit. No greater tribute to the leadership of Heraclius can be paid than by noting that, despite his wounds and his army's severe losses at Nineveh, he immediately pursued the remnants of the Persian Army. Within 48 hours of his great victory he had marched at least 40 miles to seize the bridges over the Great and Lesser Zab rivers. He continued on into Assyria, Chosroes fleeing ahead of him to. Ctesiphon. Arriving in front of the Persian capital, Heraclius evidently toyed with the idea of attempting an assault. But his army had suffered severely and he had been unable to bring a siege train with him in his rapid pursuit. Apparently remembering the fate of the army of Julian (see p. 155), Heraclius, after a brief demonstration, turned northeastward into the Persian highlands again, to rest his army and to recuperate in the familiar country around Tauris. He now sent an offer of peace to Chosroes.

628. The End of the Persian Wars. When stubborn Chosroes refused Heraclius' generous terms, he was overthrown by the war-weary Persians, who installed his son **Kavadh II** (Siroes) on the throne. Kavadh immediately accepted Heraclius' terms. These are not precisely known, but Heraclius apparently had no desire "to enlarge the weakness of the empire" (in Gibbon's words) and asked for no territorial cessions. The Persians were forced to relinquish all of their conquests and to give up all of the trophies they had captured, including the relic of the True Cross. Evidently there was also a large financial indemnity. Having dictated peace on his own terms in the capital of ancient Media, Heraclius returned in triumph to Constantinople.

COMMENT. *In six campaigns Heraclius had led his army from total disaster to glorious victory. Had he died at this moment, his name would be ranked in military history with those of Alexander, Hannibal, and Caesar—as it deserves to be. Later events have* *unfairly beclouded the reputation of this truly great captain. The fact remains that he inherited an empire on the verge of destruction, which unquestionably would have fallen early in the 7th century had it not been for his perseverance and military skill. At the end of his reign, admittedly, some of the frontier provinces he reconquered from Persia had been lost forever to a new enemy. But he had recovered, rebuilt, and bequeathed to his successors a cohesive core of empire which could and did survive this shock and which would shield Christendom for eight more centuries.*

HERACLIUS AND THE IMPACT OF ISLAM, 629–641

The long war with Persia had prostrated the Byzantine Empire. Some 200,000 men had been killed and untold riches destroyed or squandered. Hardly had Heraclius set himself to the task of recovery when a new foe appeared on the eastern frontiers of the empire (629). Islam—the religion and empire founded by Mohammed (see p. 230)—swept out of Arabia to strike the Persian and Byzantine empires when both were totally exhausted. Overwhelming Persia, the Moslems quickly conquered the eastern provinces of the Byzantine Empire (633–642), aided by the passive neutrality of the Syrian and Egyptian peoples, who had little loyalty to the Byzantines (see p. 230). Heraclius, ill and infirm, unpopular with his church and his people as a result of marriage to his niece, was unable to take the field himself. His subordinates were unable to cope with the fanatic onslaughts of the Moslems. When Heraclius died of the dropsy (641), all of the provinces east of the Taurus had been lost—most of them forever. But, thanks to his earlier accomplishments, the Anatolian and Thracian heart of the empire survived.

BYZANTINE MILITARY SYSTEM, C. 600–1071

The Theoretical Basis

The remarkable longevity of the Byzantine Empire was due primarily to the fact that, as Oman says, its army "was in its day the most efficient military body in the world." The system that produced this army was the result of superior discipline, organization, armament, and tactical methods, which in turn combined with treasured Roman traditions to generate an unsurpassed *esprit de corps*. The Byzantines were able to achieve and maintain these superiorities by their emphasis on analysis: analysis of themselves, of their enemies, and of the geophysical factors of combat.

The results of this analysis are evident in a number of military treatises, of which three are outstanding. The first of these was the *Strategikon* of Maurice, written about 580, just before he became emperor. The second is the *Tactica* of Leo the Wise, written about 900. The third is a small manual, apparently inspired by the warrior emperor **Nicephorus Phocas,** and probably written by a staff officer about 980. These three documents reveal that the fundamentals of the system changed very little in the half-millennium after Belisarius, despite many evolutionary changes in detail which would inevitably be found in a system based upon frequent, objective analysis.

The organization and doctrine herein discussed emerged in the century and more following the reign of Heraclius as his successors struggled to adapt their system to the challenge of Islam. During those years—as in the century preceding —the system was not universally successful. But despite some defeats, and occasional disaster, the superior bases on which the system rested reasserted themselves under thoughtful and energetic leadership. For five centuries such leadership always appeared in time to re-establish Byzantine military supremacy over its neighbors; and for almost four centuries after that, the vestiges of the system helped to postpone the final demise of the empire.

During most of this period the basic military textbook was the *Strategikon*. This was a comprehensive manual on all aspects of warfare and military leadership, not unlike the field-service regulations of modern armies. It covered training, tactical operations, administration, logistics, and discussions of the major military problems to be encountered in operations against any of the many foes of the empire.

Organization

The basic administrative and tactical unit of the Byzantine Army, for infantry as well as cavalry, was the **numerus,** or **banda,** of 300–400 men; the equivalent of a modern battalion. The numerus was commanded by a tribune, or count, or (later) a **drungarios**—the equivalent of a colonel. Five to eight numeri were combined to form a **turma**—or division—under a **turmarch,** or duke. Two or three turmae comprised a **thema**—or corps—under a **strategos.** A deliberate effort was made to keep units different in size, so as to make it difficult for opponents to estimate the exact strength of any Byzantine army.

All officers of the rank of drungarios and higher were appointed by the emperor and owed their allegiance to him. This method of encouraging allegiance to central national authority, rather than to army commanders as was the Roman practice, was apparently introduced by Maurice.

The field organization of the Byzantine Army, as outlined and largely introduced by Maurice, was integrated into a geographical, military district organization during the latter part of the reign of Heraclius and the reigns of his successors **Constans II** and **Constantine IV.** The inroads of Persians and Arabs had completely obliterated the old provincial organization of the empire. Thus, as the Anatolian provinces were reoccupied, local governmental authority was perforce exercised by the military commanders responsible for defense of each region. In the face of the continuing threat of Saracen raids, the emperors adopted this civil-military administrative system permanently. Each district was called a **theme,** under a strategos; his thema was the garrison of the district, which was broken down into smaller administrative districts under the turmarchs and drungarios. Some of the most critical frontier regions, especially around the key Taurus passes, were organized into smaller districts called **clissuras,** each under a **clissurarch,** where the garrisons were maintained in an especially high state of readiness against attack.

By the end of the 7th century there were 13 themes: 7 in Anatolia, 3 in the Balkans, and 3 in island and coastal possessions in the Mediterranean and Aegean seas. By the 10th century the number of themes had grown to about 30. The army had not grown comparably in those 300 years; there were simply fewer forces in each theme. During most of this period the standing army of the empire numbered about 120,000–150,000 men, proportionately half and half in horse and foot.

Apparently themes closer to the frontier had larger standing forces than those in the interior. On the average each strategos could take the field on short notice with two to four turmae of heavy cavalry. He also had available approximately an equal number of infantry. Depending upon the situation (the nature of the foe, the area of expected operations, etc.), he could leave some or all of his foot soldiers for local garrisons.

Man Power and Recruitment

Theoretically maintained by universal military service, in practice the standing forces of each theme were kept up by selective recruitment from the most promising of the local inhabitants. No longer was the empire dependent upon the barbarians for its soldiers, though some barbarian units were usually maintained in the army. For the most part the empire raised its own soldiers, and of these the best came from Armenia, Cappadocia, Isauria, and Thrace. The Greeks were deemed the least suitable military material.

The theme system included a militia concept of home-guard local defense. This was satisfactory where the local inhabitants were hardy and warlike, but was useless in regions like Greece. Where this concept worked, the guerrilla tactics of the local inhabitants greatly assisted the regular forces of the empire in repelling or destroying invading forces.

Byzantine Strategic Concepts

During most of its existence the Byzantine Empire had no incentive for conquest or aggression, once its people became reconciled to the losses of their extensive peripheral possessions. Living standards were high; the nation was the most prosperous in the world. Foreign conquests were expensive in lives and treasure in the first place, and merely resulted in increased costs for administration and defense. At the same time, they recognized that their wealth was a constant attraction to predatory barbarian neighbors.

The essentially defensive Byzantine military policy is thus easily understood. The objective was the preservation of territory and resources. Byzantine strategy was essentially a sophisticated medieval concept of deterrence, and was based upon the desire to avoid war if possible—but when necessary to fight, to do so by repelling, punishing, and harassing aggressors with the minimum possible expenditure of wealth and man power. Their method was usually that of elastic defensive-offensive, in which the Byzantines would endeavor to throw the invaders back against defended mountain passes or river crossings, then to destroy them in a coordinated concentric drive of two or more themas.

Economic, political, and psychological warfare assisted—and often obviated—the use of brute force. Dissension among troublesome neighbors was craftily fomented. Alliances were contracted from time to time to reduce danger from formidable foes. Subsidies to allies and to semi-independent barbarian chieftains along disputed frontiers also helped to reduce the burden on the armed forces. In all of this, imperial action was facilitated by an efficient, widespread intelligence network, comprised mainly of merchants and of trusted, well-paid agents in key positions in hostile and friendly courts.

The emperors were not above using religion for temporal ends. Sincerely anxious to spread Christianity to heathen peoples, they also found that missionaries could exert subtle and helpful influence at the courts of converted rulers—and that common adherence to the Christian faith automatically created a bond against pagan and Moslem.

Cavalry: Weapons, Equipment, and Uniforms

The basic military strength of the empire lay in its disciplined heavy cavalry. The cataphract of the Byzantine Empire symbolized the power of Constantinople in the same way that the legionary had represented the might of Rome.

The individual horseman wore a casque or conical helmet, topped with a colored tuft of horsehair. His chain-mail shirt covered him from neck to thighs. On his feet were steel shoes, usually topped with leather boots or greaves to protect the lower leg. Hands and wrists were protected by gauntlets. He carried a relatively small round shield strapped to his left arm, thus leaving both hands free to control the horse's reins and to use his weapons, yet available to provide protection to his vulnerable left side in hand-to-hand fighting. Over his armored shirt he wore a lightweight cotton cloak or surcoat, dyed a distinctive color for each unit; helmet tuft and shield also were of this same color for uniform purposes. A heavy cloak for cool weather, which served also as a blanket, was strapped to the saddle. Some horses—those normally deployed in front rank positions—wore armor on their heads, necks, and chests.

Byzantine cataphract

The cataphracts' weapons usually included bow, quiver of arrows, long lance, broadsword, dagger, and sometimes an ax strapped to the saddle. Apparently a proportion of the heavy cavalry were lancers only, but most seem to have carried both bow and lance. Presumably, when he was using the bow, the soldier's lance rested in a stirrup or saddle boot, like the carbine of more modern cavalrymen. In turn, the bow was evidently slung from the saddle when he was using lance, sword, or ax. Attached to the lance was a pennon of the same distinguishing color as helmet tuft, surcoat, and shield.

Men and horses were superbly trained and capable of complex evolutions on drillfield and battlefield. There was great emphasis on archery marksmanship and on constant practice in the use of other weapons.

Infantry: Weapons, Equipment, and Uniforms

The infantry was almost equally divided into two classes: heavy and light. The heavy infantrymen, known as **scutati** from the round shields they carried, were equipped much like the cataphracts. They wore helmet, mail shirts, gauntlets, greaves (or knee-length boots), and surcoats. They carried lance, shield, sword, and (sometimes) ax. Uniform appearance was achieved by color of surcoat, helmet tuft, and shield.

Most of the light infantrymen were archers, though some were javelin throwers. To permit maximum mobility they carried little in the way of armor or additional weapons, though apparently there was some leeway allowed to individual desires. Most wore leather jackets, some may have worn helmets, and apparently they usually carried a short sword in addition to bow and quiver (or javelins).

Battlefield Tactics

Although it was not at all unusual for Byzantine armies to be composed entirely of cavalry, more frequently the two arms were combined on campaign in about equal proportions. The infantry, in turn, was usually divided equally between heavy and light.

Byzantine tactics were based upon offensive, or defensive-offensive, action and envisaged a number of successive coordinated blows against the enemy. Their normal tactical formation, which could be varied greatly depending upon the circumstances, comprised five major elements. There were (1) a central front line; (2) a central second line; (3) a reserve/rear security, usually in two groups behind each flank; (4) close-in envelopment/security flank units; (5) distant envelopment/screening units. In a force of combined arms, with infantry and

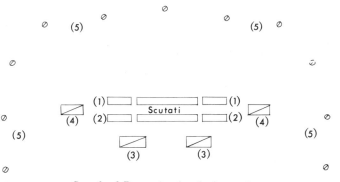

Standard Byzantine battle formation

cavalry present in about equal numbers, the first two of these elements were infantry, with the scutati in the center, the light troops to their flanks; the latter three were always cavalry. If the infantry contingent was small, it might compose only the central second line or be placed as an additional reserve behind two cavalry central lines.

When the opposing army was mainly cavalry, and their own army included substantial infantry, the infantry front line would await enemy attack. Byzantine scutati, confident of flank and rear protection by their cavalry, were as effective against horsemen as the Roman legionary had been. The enemy's first attack would be struck on the flanks by the close-in envelopment/security flank units. Soon thereafter would come a heavier blow to the hostile flank and rear from the distant envelopment/screening units. If these counterpunching tactics failed to achieve their objective, and if the Byzantine front line should be forced to fall back, it could do so through the intervals in the second line—left there in the traditional Roman manner for this purpose. The enveloping units would withdraw, regroup, and return to the attack. Finally, if the second Byzantine line should fail and the former front line had not yet had time to rally, the day could still be saved by a smashing coordinated counterattack by the fresh reserve units, almost always conducted as a double envelopment rather than a frontal attack.

Obviously there was room for many variants in such a set-piece battle, and many different combinations possible against different enemies and different kinds of forces. The important thing to note here is the existence of a standard tactical doctrine: the emphasis on envelopment, on coordinated action (including coordination between missiles and shock action, between the arms, and between all elements of the force) and on retaining a fresh reserve with which ultimately to gain the day in a hard-fought action.

Though subsidiary to the cavalry, Byzantine infantry doctrine was far from passive. Whenever opposed by infantry—either in a combined-arms battle or in essentially infantry operations in rough terrain—the scutati, in close coordination with archers and missile throwers, were wont to seize the initiative and to carry the attack to the foe. The normal formation of the scutati was 16 deep, and separate numeri were capable of individual evolutions, extending and closing the ranks like the old Roman cohort. In the attack they would rush on the foe, throwing their lances just before contact, again like the cohort of the legion. Thus the numerus of the scutati combined the attributes of legion and phalanx, though lacking the moral feeling of superiority which contributed so much to the success of the infantry of Alexander and Caesar.

The numeri of the cavalry usually formed in lines 8 to 10 horsemen in depth. The Byzantines acknowledged that this was perhaps more cumbersome than an optimum formation, but were willing to accept a slight decrease in flexibility in exchange for the greater feeling of security the men derived from the deep formation.

Adaptation to Hostile Characteristics

Byzantine military theoreticians spent as much time in study of the traits of their foe as they did in elaboration of their own tactical formations. Combining these different studies and analyses was an important aspect of their consistent superiority.

Maurice, for instance, suggested that whenever possible campaigns should be undertaken during seasons in which the various and diverse neighbors were least prepared to fight. The Huns and Scythians of Eastern Europe, for example, were in poorest condition in February and March, when their horses were suffering most from lack of forage. A little earlier—midwinter—was best against the Slavic marsh dwellers, since the Byzantine troops could cross the ice to their hideouts and the defenders would be unable to take refuge in water and reeds. Fall, winter, and spring were good against mountain tribes, since the snow would reveal their tracks and the lack of foliage would reduce their concealment. Any cold or rainy weather was good for campaigning against the Persians or Arabs, since they were depressed and less effective at such times.

Later, Leo the Wise had much similar advice for the officers of his time—then the main enemies were European Franks and wily Arab Moslems. Of the Franks, Leo had this to say (adapted from Oman's translation):

The Franks (and Lombards) are bold and daring to excess; they regard the smallest movement to the rear a disgrace, and they will fight whenever you offer them battle. So formidable is the charge of the Frankish chivalry with their broadsword, lance and shield, that it is best to decline a pitched battle with them till you have put all the chances on your own side. You should take advantage of their indiscipline and disorder; whether fighting on foot or on horseback, they charge in dense, unwieldy masses, which cannot maneuver because they have neither organization nor discipline. . . . Hence they readily fall into confusion if suddenly attacked in flank and rear—a thing easy to accomplish, as they are utterly careless and neglect the use of outposts and reconnaissance. They camp in confusion, without fortifying themselves, so that they can be easily cut up by a night attack. Nothing succeeds better against them than a feigned flight, which draws them into an ambush; for they follow hastily and invariably fall into the snare. But perhaps the best tactics of all are to protract the campaign, and lead them into hills and desolate regions, for they take no care of their supply, and when their stores run low their vigor melts away, and after a few days of hunger and thirst desert their standards and steal home as best they can. For they have no respect for authority—each noble thinks himself as good as the other—and will deliberately disobey when they are discontented. Nor are their chiefs above the temptation of taking bribes; a moderate outlay of cash will frustrate one of their expeditions. On the whole, therefore, it is easier and less costly to wear out a Frankish army by skirmishes, protracted operations in desolate districts, and the cutting off of its supplies, than to attempt to destroy it at a single blow.

Leo had much more respect for the Arab Moslems. As quoted by Oman, he says of the Saracens: "Of all the barbarous nations they are the best advised and most prudent in their military operations. . . . They have copied the [Byzantines] in most of their military practices, both in arms and strategy." Yet he noted that for all of their imitation the Arabs had failed to absorb the organizational and disciplinary basis of Byzantine success. Despite the superior numbers of the Moslems, their fanatic courage, and their willingness to learn from experience, Leo believed that Byzantine skill, discipline, and organization should prevail—and usually they did.

Administration on Campaign

Although each soldier carried his weapons, elementary necessities of life, and food for several days, each army was always accompanied by a supply and baggage train with sufficient additional supplies and equipment to permit sustained operations and to undertake siegework if necessary. This baggage train was composed partly of carts and partly of pack animals. Accompanying the baggage train were the camp followers: servants and foragers for the officers and men. Apparently female camp followers were discouraged.

Basic equipment included picks and shovels, necessary for the practice of castrametation, observed by the Byzantines as faithfully as by the early Romans. A camp site was selected and marked out in advance by the army's engineer unit. While part of the army deployed to provide security, the remainder took the picks and shovels from pack animals and quickly prepared entrenchment and palisade in the old Roman fashion.

Attached to each numerus was a medical detachment, usually consisting of a doctor and a surgeon, plus 8 to 10 stretcherbearers or medical aid men. As an incentive to their efficient performance of duty, aid men were given a substantial cash reward for each wounded soldier they rescued during battle.

A highly developed signal service existed. In addition to the expected corps of messengers, the Byzantines had developed a system of beacon signal fires whereby warning of attack could be sent from the frontiers to Constantinople in a matter of minutes.

Chaplains were always present with the army. As in Western Europe, priests and monks were able to take their place in the battle line, although the Orthodox Church was more strict than that of Rome in tempering crusading zeal by adherence to the Biblical injunction, "Thou shalt not kill."

Staff and Command

The training of an officer began when a youth—usually of noble family—enlisted in a cadet corps. The peacetime training of these youths was probably not much different in concept from a modern officer training program: emphasis on the basic tasks of the soldier, mastery of weapons and horses, study of the writings of military experts of the past and present, exercises in which the theoretical knowledge was put to practice. In addition, during wartime the cadet corps served on the staffs of the various strategi, acting as clerks and messengers—undoubtedly occasionally getting opportunities to assist staff officers in the simpler aspects of writing orders and preparing plans.

The advancement of the young officer through staff and command duties was apparently arranged to give him experience and to give his superiors an opportunity to observe him in action. The most promising turmarchs were given opportunity for independent command as clissurarchs; if successful, they could be assured of promotion to strategos. During these formative years conscious emphasis seems to have been given to encouragements of objective analysis, since the Byzantines were rightly convinced that this provided the basis of their success and that it was essential to the development of good commanders and staff men.

Evidently the strategi were rotated from one theme to another. This kept them from getting either too entrenched politically or too settled from the standpoint of personal attitude toward the rigors of combat. Furthermore, the senior strategi were assigned to the largest and most important themes—usually those on the frontiers, save for the Anatolian Theme of central Asia Minor. The army's senior strategos was usually the commander of the Anatolian Theme and (in the absence of the emperor) exercised over-all field command.

The Byzantine Navy

Only occasionally after the Punic Wars had the Romans—and later the Byzantines—given much thought to the concept of naval power and control of the sea. They took for granted their mastery of the Mediterranean, even when it was challenged by pirates, Gothic raiders, or Vandal sea rovers. But the development of Moslem sea power in the latter half of the 7th century stirred Constantinople to energetic reaction. By the early years of the 8th century, Byzantine supremacy had been re-established—as was demonstrated by Leo III in the siege of Constantinople. Though occasionally shaken or threatened, this supremacy was generally maintained for the next four centuries.

The principal base of Byzantine sea power was the Theme of Cibyrrhaeots, on the south coast of Anatolia, where a hardy race of sailors had descended from the pirates of Roman republican days. Ships and sailors were also supplied by the Aegean islands and other maritime regions of Anatolia. Cibyrrhaeots, however, was the one theme which supplied almost no soldiers to the Byzantine Army, yet maintained a standing fleet of nearly 100 vessels and more than 20,000 sailors, about half of the man power of the Byzantine navy.

The navy was made up of relatively small, light, fast galleys, most with two banks of oars (usually 30–40 on each side), two masts, and two lateen sails. In addition to the oarsmen—trained to fight hand-to-hand if necessary—there was a small force of marines on each vessel, which had a total complement of 200–300 men. The larger warships had revolving turrets, mounting war engines. But the most deadly weapons on these ships—beginning about 670—were the bow tubes from which the dreaded and deadly Greek fire was hurled with explosive force (see p. 223).

Byzantine Honor in War

Guile and fraud were admired by the Byzantines and used whenever possible. Scorning the often hypocritical honor of Western chivalry, their objective was to win with minimum losses and the least possible expenditure of resources—if possible without fighting. Bribery and trickery were common, and considered respectable. They were masters at forms of psychological warfare which caused dissension in hostile ranks; they did not hesitate to use false propaganda to raise the morale of their own men.

In the light of some modern practices of warfare one cannot be too critical of the Byzantines. They probably merit admiration for a practical, no-nonsense, alert attitude toward the basic issues of national survival. Furthermore, they *did* have a moral code of conduct for war. Signed treaties were inviolate. Ambassadors and negotiators were scrupulously protected. Captured male and female noncombatants were not mistreated. A brave defeated foe was treated with generosity and respect.

BYZANTINE EMPIRE, 642–800

The Successors of Heraclius, 642–717

The successors of Heraclius devoted most of their attention to defense against the Arabs, who had completely displaced the Persians on the empire's eastern boundaries. Frequently close to disaster, and subject to numerous Moslem raids deep into Anatolia, the Byzantines nevertheless maintained the frontier generally along the line of the Taurus Mountains. To the southwest, however, the Arabs soon conquered all Byzantine possessions on the shores of north Africa, aided by religious dissension between the provinces and Constantinople. They then began seriously to challenge Byzantine control of the sea, defeating the fleets of the emperor **Constans II** and capturing some islands in the eastern Mediterranean. They next undertook a determined effort to overthrow the empire, and for six years their fleets and armies literally hammered at the gates and walls of Constantinople in a protracted siege. Thanks to Greek fire, and to the efficiency of the Byzantine military system, **Constantine IV** repulsed the Moslems so violently that they sued for peace and paid tribute to the empire for several years.

Meanwhile the emperors also had to cope with nearly constant threats to their European dominions. The Avars and Slavs continued depredations south and west of the Danube. By the end of the 7th century a new Bulgar kingdom had established itself permanently in the eastern Balkans (see p. 226). Lombard pressure against Byzantine possessions in Italy was constant (see p. 202).

Though these external threats were unremitting, the inherent toughness and vigor of the empire and its military system were demonstrated by the repulse of all major invasions. Then, at the turn of the century, internal discord once again wracked Byzantium. Seizing the opportunity, the Arabs began a climactic effort to overthrow the empire. The major events were:

641–668. Reign of Constans II. This grandson of Heraclius established a new civil-military defensive organization based upon geographical military districts (themes).

645–659. Continued War with the Arabs. The Arabs repulsed a halfhearted Byzantine effort to recapture Alexandria (645). Pushing westward, they began their invasion of the province of Africa (647).

The Arabs also temporarily conquered Cyprus (647–653) and part of Byzantine Armenia (653). At sea they plundered Rhodes (654) and defeated a Byzantine fleet, commanded personally by Constans, in a great naval battle off the coast of Lycia (655). Because of other pressures, a temporary peace was negotiated between the Byzantine Empire and the Caliphate (659).

662–668. Operations in Italy. Constans personally campaigned against the Lombards in Italy with mixed success. He was killed during a mutiny in Italy, which was vigorously suppressed by his son, **Constantine IV.**

668–679. Renewed War with the Caliphate. An Arab invasion of Anatolia reached Chalcedon; the Moslems crossed the Bosporus to attack Constantinople, but were repulsed (669). The Arab army was then virtually destroyed at **Armorium.** An Arab naval attack on Constantinople was repulsed; the Arab fleet was destroyed in the **Battle of Cyzicus** (in the Sea of Marmara); Greek fire, apparently first used, contributed greatly to the victory (672). The Arabs returned to establish a land and sea blockade and intermittent siege of Constantinople (673–677). Greek fire continued to play a great part in destroying Moslem warships and in repulsing assaults against the city walls. The climax came when the Byzantines destroyed the Arab fleet at the **Battle of Syllaeum** (southern Asia Minor). These disasters led Caliph **Mu'awiya** to sue for peace; he agreed to evacuate Cyprus, to keep the peace for 30 years, and to pay an annual tribute to Constantinople.

675–681. Operations in the Balkans. Repeated Slav assaults on Thessalonika were repulsed. Constantine recognized the virtual independence of Bulgaria (680; see p. 226).

685–695. First Reign of Justinian II. He was defeated by the Bulgars, but gained a victory over the Slavs in Macedonia (689).

690–692. Arab War. A generally unsuccessful war with the Arabs was culminated by the **Battle of Sebastopolis** (Phasis), which resulted in Moslem conquest of Armenia, Iberia, and Colchis, last remaining Byzantine footholds east of the Taurus. Justinian was also forced to agree to joint Byzantine-Moslem control of Cyprus.

695–698. Usurpation by Leontius. Justinian was overthrown and banished to the Crimea.

697–698. Arab Conquest of Carthage. This eliminated Byzantine influence from north Africa.

698–705. Usurpation by Tiberius Absimarus. Overthrowing Leontius, he assumed the title of Tiberius III.

705. Restoration of Justinian. Assisted by Bulgar King **Terbelis,** Justinian captured Constantinople in a surprise attack.

705–711. Second Reign of Justinian II. He executed all of his former opponents (including Leontius and Tiberius) and their adherents in a 6-year reign of terror. At the same time he was defeated in intermittent wars with the Arabs and with Terbelis of Bulgaria.

711. Overthrow of Justinian. He sent an expedition to the Crimea to punish his subjects who had mistreated him during his exile. The troops mutinied under the leadership of **Bardanes Philippicus,** with the assistance of the Khazars; the mutineers returned to Constantinople; Philippicus defeated and killed Justinian in a battle in northwestern Anatolia and seized the throne.

711–717. Disaster and Anarchy. The frontiers collapsed during the reign of incompetent Philippicus (711–713). The Bulgars reached the walls of Constantinople (712). The Arabs overran Cilicia, then invaded Pontus to capture Amasia (Amasya). The Byzantine Army mutinied, overthrew Philippicus, and installed **Anastasius II** in his place (713). Anastasius restored internal order and began to rebuild the army. His harsh reforms were resented, however; part of the army mutinied and proclaimed **Theodosius III** as emperor (715). Theodosius captured Constantinople after a 6-month siege and banished Anastasius to a monastery. Meanwhile a major Moslem invasion reached Pergamum (716). Failure of Theodosius to take adequate action against the threat caused his leading general **Leo** ("the Isaurian") to overthrow the emperor and assume the throne himself as Leo III (717).

The Siege of Constantinople, 717–718

717, June. The Moslems Cross the Hellespont. The Moslem general **Maslama** led his army of 80,000 men from Pergamum to Abydos, where he crossed the Hellespont. To prevent interference by the Bulgars, or by any Byzantine forces in Thrace, he sent part of his army to a covering position near Adrianople; with his main body, Maslama laid siege to Constantinople (July).

717, August. The First Moslem Assault. Leo had been hurriedly preparing the city for siege. Maslama's assault was repulsed with heavy loss.

717, September. Arrival of Moslem Reinforcements. The Moslem general **Suleiman** led a great armada of 1,800 vessels and 80,000 additional troops through the Hellespont. After landing most of his men, Suleiman tried to take his fleet past the city to blockade the Bosporus. Leo led his own fleet in a successful attack, winning an overwhelming victory and driving the surviving Moslem vessels back into the Sea of Marmara. Greek fire played a great part in this victory, which assured a supply line from Constantinople through the Bosporus to Byzantine provinces on the Black Sea. The Moslems made no more direct attacks on the city during the remainder of the year, being mostly occupied in keeping themselves warm and alive during an exceptionally cold winter. Leo made a treaty with Terbelis, King of Bulgaria, who promised to join the war against the Arabs.

718, Spring. Renewed Moslem Pressure. Taking advantage of night and of stormy weather, Suleiman got part of his rebuilt fleet up the Bosporus to tighten the blockade of the city. At the same time approximately 50,000 more reinforcements arrived to swell the besieging forces on both sides of the straits. Leo repulsed several assaults.

718, June (?). Leo Counterattacks. Leo's fleet surprised and annihilated the Moslem blockading squadron in the Bosporus. He then landed an army on the far (Asiatic) shore of the Bosporus and defeated the Arab blockading army near Chalcedon.

718, July (?). Battle of Adrianople. Terbelis, King of Bulgaria, now honored his alliance by leading an army into Thrace. He attacked and defeated Maslama south of Adrianople.

718, August. Moslem Withdrawal. The appearance of the Bulgars, combined with the terrible losses which Leo had inflicted, caused Maslama and Suleiman to abandon the siege of Constantinople. Part of their army marched back through Anatolia, harassed by Leo's army. The remainder of the Moslem army embarked in Suleiman's fleet, which was destroyed in a storm; only 5 vessels are said to have survived. Of more than 200,000 Moslems committed to the siege of Constantinople, only 30,000 eventually returned across the Taurus Mountains.

COMMENT. *The successful defense of Constantinople saved Christian Europe from Moslem invasion. Its importance probably transcends even that of the later Battle of Tours (see p. 205), Islam's high-water mark in the West.*

Byzantine Empire, 717–802

Leo III consolidated his victory by sweeping reforms: administrative, economic, legal, social, military, and religious. Most controversial were his religious reforms—pertinent to this text because of direct military consequences. About 726 Leo began to issue a series of imperial edicts against both the veneration and worship of religious images, causing him to be known as the "Iconoclast." A major motive in his iconoclasm was evidently a belief that elimination of frills from Christian worship would restore to it a vigor which would enable it to compete more successfully with the simple and austere tenets of Islam. Most of the clergy—particularly in Italy and Greece—were violently opposed to these edicts, insisting that veneration was not image worship. The result was turbulence during much of his reign. Pope Gregory inspired the Italian provinces to revolt against Leo, and became the virtual temporal ruler of most Byzantine possessions in Italy. Although the religious disorders probably weakened imperial control over some possessions, Leo's iconoclasm seems eventually to have solidified popular support in Anatolia;

his other reforms were unquestionably beneficial. Two Arab invasions later in his reign were easily repulsed; long-term Byzantine stability was unquestionably enhanced.

Leo's policies were vigorously continued during the long and successful reign of his son, **Constantine V.** The empire regained the initiative in its struggles with the Arabs, Slavs, and Bulgars, and reoccupied some of the lands lost in Europe and Asia in the previous century. Internal religious disputes over the issue of the distinction of veneration and image worship continued to rage, however. These contributed to the only important military and territorial losses of the reign, in Italy, where the Lombards were able to take advantage of the disorders to conquer most of the Exarchate of Ravenna and to threaten Rome. The popes, seriously estranged from the emperor on religious grounds, then turned to the Franks for assistance, leading to the end of Byzantine control over Rome and the surrounding territories (see p. 207).

In the last quarter of the 7th century there was renewed dynastic and political disorder in the empire; again the Moslems were able to exploit these troubles by military victories. The dominant personage of these years was **Irene,** wife of feeble **Leo IV** and mother of **Constantine VI.** Young Constantine finally tried to throw off his mother's able but dictatorial dominance, but through intrigue she soon returned to power, had her son deposed and blinded, and seized the throne for herself. She contributed to internal peace by ending the iconoclastic policies of the empire. She bought peace temporarily from the Moslems. The major events were:

717–741. Reign of Leo III.

721. Revolt of Anastasius. This was suppressed by Leo, who had Anastasius executed.

726. Arab Invasion. The Arabs were repulsed in eastern Anatolia.

726–727. Revolt in Greece. Defiance of the first imperial edict against image worship was crushed by Leo after his fleet destroyed a rebel fleet sailing against Constantinople.

726–731. Revolt in Ravenna against Leo's Iconoclasm. This resulted in the virtual independence of the exarchate, after part of an imperial invasion fleet was lost in an Adriatic storm and the remainder of the invasion force repulsed from the city walls (731). The Lombards had earlier attempted to take advantage of the dispute and had temporarily captured part of the city, but were then repulsed (728; see p. 202).

739. Arab Invasion. After initial success, the invaders were repulsed by Leo at the **Battle of Akroinon** (Afyon Karahisar).

741–775. Reign of Constantine V.

741–752. Arab War. Constantine invaded Syria, but had to withdraw to deal with civil war at home (see below). Having reestablished control of his empire, he again

invaded Syria, reconquering a few ·small border regions (745). His fleet won a victory over the Arabs near Cyprus; the Moslems were eliminated from Cyprus (746). The war came to an indeterminate conclusion after Constantine defeated the Arabs in Armenia, regaining part of the province (751–752).

741–743. Civil War. While Constantine was campaigning against the Arabs, immediately after his accession, his brother-in-law, **Artavasdus,** led a religious revolt with the support of the image worshipers. Constantine successfully fought on two fronts and overcame the rebels.

752–754. Final Loss of Ravenna. First to Lombards, then to Franks (see p. 202).

755–772. Intermittent Campaigns in Thrace. Constantine fought wars against the Bulgars and the Slavs in Thrace. In the west he overwhelmed the Slavs (758). He defeated the Bulgars in eastern Thrace at the battles of **Marcellae** (759) and **Anchialus** (763). After a lull of several years, he again defeated the Bulgars (772).

775–780. Reign of Leo IV (Son of Constantine V).

778–783. Arab War. An invasion of Anatolia was repulsed by the Byzantine victory at the **Battle of Germanicopolis**

(Gangra, 778). Byzantine general **Michael** captured Mas'ash (in Cilicia, 778).

780–797. Reign of Constantine VI. Irene was regent for ten years (780–790). During this time an Arab invasion reached the Bosporus, where it was bought off by tribute (783). Wars with the Bulgars were intermittent. Byzantine general **Staurakios** defeated the Slavs in Macedonia and Greece (783). An army mutiny forced the retirement of Irene (790). Irene soon again became virtual co-ruler (792).

797–802. Usurpation of Irene. She had her son blinded. She was deposed by a revolt of Byzantine nobility.

797–798. Renewed Arab Invasion of Anatolia. Caliph Harun al-Rashid defeated Byzantine general **Nicephorus** at the **Battle of Heraclea.** The Moslems were again bought off by tribute.

SLAVS, AVARS, BULGARS, AND KHAZARS

By the beginning of the 7th century the Slavs had spread over much of Eastern Europe. There was no unity among their many tribes; those north of the Danube and Carpathians were involved in more or less constant conflict among themselves and with German neighbors, but otherwise played little part in the development of military history. The southern Slav tribes maintained a semi-independent status under the suzerainty of Avars or of the Eastern Empire. They soon drove out the remnants of the former inhabitants of the inland regions of Illyricum, Macedonia, and Greece; their frequent raids into Thrace and the coastal regions still under Byzantine control presented a constant military problem to the empire. As their strength grew, they eliminated Avar influence south of the Danube, thus ending the frequent wars between Avars and Byzantines.

By the middle of the 8th century, both Slavs and Avars found themselves under simultaneous pressure from Bulgars to the northeast and Franks to the northwest. By the end of the century, the Franks had destroyed the Avar empire (see p. 207), but their further advance into the Balkans ceased as a result of treaties between Franks and Byzantines (see p. 208).

The Bulgars were a Turanian people, related to the Avars and Huns, inhabiting the steppes north of the Caspian in the 5th and 6th centuries. Early in the 7th century, under a leader named **Kubrat** (or Kurt), they threw off Avar domination and established an independent kingdom in the area roughly bounded by the Volga and Don rivers and the Caucasus Mountains. Under pressure from the Avars and Khazars, they migrated southwestward in the middle of the 7th century, to reach the lower Danube Valley. Gaining ascendancy over the Slavs in this region, their leader **Isperich** (Asparukh) established an independent kingdom, centered between the Balkan Mountains and the lower Danube, but also extending north of that river into Wallachia, Moldavia, and Bessarabia. A slow process of intermingling and amalgamation with the Slavs began; a few centuries later Bulgaria was essentially Slavonic. During most of the 8th century, the Bulgars were at war with Byzantium, though **Terbelis** (Tervel) did form an alliance with Leo III against the Arabs during the great siege of Constantinople (see p. 224).

The Khazars were another Turanian people, possibly descended from the Huns, who became predominant in the steppes north of the Black and Caspian seas in the latter 6th century. They were probably part of the great Turkish empire which then flourished in Central Asia (see p. 238). With the collapse of central Turkish control, the Khazars created a powerful and extensive empire of their own, extending westward to frontiers with the Avars and Bulgars in the Carpathians and on the lower Danube, southward to the Caucasus, and eastward beyond the Caspian Sea. During much of the 7th and 8th centuries, they were engaged in fierce warfare with the expanding Moslem Caliphate on both sides of the Caspian. They were usually allied with the Byzantines, but had some wars with them. The principal events were:

601–602. Byzantine-Avar War. Byzantine general **Priscus** defeated the Avars south of the Danube (see p. 183).

603. Independence of the Slavs in Moravia. Avar rule was thrown off.

617–620. Avar Raids to the Walls of Constantinople. (See p. 211.)

619. Byzantine-Bulgar Alliance. Heraclius and Kubrat against the Avars.

626. Avar Siege of Constantinople. In alliance with the Persians (see p. 212).

627. Byzantine-Khazar Alliance. Heraclius and **Ziebel,** Khan of the Khazars, against the Persians (see p. 213).

c. 634. Independence of Bulgaria in the Volga Region.

640. Independence of the Slavonian Croats. Avar rule was thrown off.

643–701. Reign of Isperich. Successor to Kubrat as leader of the Bulgars. He led a migration from the Volga to the Danube (c. 650–c. 670). Later he led the Bulgars across the Danube in force, defeated the Byzantines, and forced Constantine to cede the province of Moesia (679–680; see p. 223).

661–790. Recurring Wars between Khazars and Moslems. Started by an Arab invasion north of the Caucasus which drove the Khazars from Derbent on the Caspian (661). Slowly the initiative passed to the Khazars, who invaded Armenia, Georgia, Albania, and Azerbaijan (685–722). The tide changed again with an Arab invasion of Khazar country, penetrating the Caucasus to capture Balanjar (near Daryal Pass, 727–731). In turn the Khazars struck south, reaching into Mesopotamia before being driven back to the Caucasus (731–733). Sporadic border warfare continued; the Khazars raided Arab-held Georgia (790).

701–718. Reign of Terbelis (Tervel) of the Bulgars. He defeated the Byzantines at the **Battle of Anchialus** (708). Following this, he raided through Thrace to the walls of Constantinople (712).

717–718. Alliance of Terbelis with Leo III. (See p. 224.)

755–772. Byzantine-Bulgar Wars. Marked by victories of Constantine V over **Telets** (see p. 225).

777–802. Reign of Kardam of the Bulgars. His frequent invasions of Thrace forced the Byzantines to pay tribute.

791–796. Overthrow of the Avars by Charlemagne. (See p. 207.)

SOUTHWEST ASIA

SASSANID PERSIA, 600–650

This was a half-century of violent vicissitudes in the ever-fluctuating fortunes of the Sassanids. Under **Chosroes II** the Persians virtually eliminated the Byzantines from all their Asiatic and Egyptian provinces, expanding Sassanid dominions practically to the extent of the empire of Darius. Then in six brilliant campaigns Heraclius gained complete victory over Persia (see pp. 210–214).

As the exhausted Byzantine and Persian empires endeavored to recover from this disastrous and costly quarter-century war, both were struck simultaneously by a new, vigorous, and fanatic power: Islam. The Sassanids, lacking the political and military stability of the East Roman Empire, completely succumbed to the Arab invaders in less than 20 years (see p. 230). The principal events were:

603–628. Persian War with Byzantine Empire. (See pp. 210–214.)

610. Battle of Dhu-Qar. An army of raiding Arab tribes defeated a small Persian force south of the Euphrates before being driven back into the Arabian Desert.

628–629. Reign of Kavadh II (Siroes). Son of Chosroes II, who was overthrown and killed by an army revolt under the leadership of the general **Gurdenaspa.** Kavadh made peace with Heraclius (see p. 213). His death (of plague) was followed by chaos in Persia.

633. Arab Invasion. Taking advantage of the disorders in Persia, the Arabs, under **Khalid ibn al-Walid,** invaded, capturing Hira and Oballa. They were checked temporarily at the **Battle of the Bridge** (see p. 230).

634–642. Reign of Yazdegird III (grandson of Chosroes II).

637–650. Arab Conquest of Persia. (See p. 230.)

640–651. Flight of Yazdegird. Driven from Persia to Media and to Balkh, Yazdegird appealed in vain to the emperor of China for assistance. He was later murdered near Merv (651).

THE RISE OF ISLAM, 622–800

The Early Caliphate, 622–750

Before Mohammed's death (632) and even before the complete consolidation of his control over Arabia, the new religious tide of Islam began to sweep northwestward and northeastward against the exhausted Byzantine and Persian empires. The eastern provinces of the Byzantine Empire—particularly Syria and Egypt—were estranged from Constantinople by a sectarian Christian dispute. So bitter was this that the Syrians and Egyptians for the most part welcomed the Moslems as deliverers from tyranny; they gave no support to the imperial armies, and in some instances actually aided the invaders. At the same time Persia, prostrated by defeat, had been thrown into anarchy by the untimely death of Kavadh II. In a little more than a decade the Byzantines were ejected from Syria and Egypt, to be thrown back across the Taurus Mountains of Anatolia. Simultaneously Sassanid power was completely destroyed, and the vast Persian Empire fell to the Arabs.

Internal disputes now caused a brief pause in Islamic expansion. But these were soon—though only temporarily—settled, and the amazing vitality of Islam was demonstrated by a centrifugal push in all directions. The main thrust was against the Byzantines in Anatolia, but simultaneous advances were made westward along the North African coast, eastward toward India, northward against the Khazars through the Caucasus, and northeastward across the Oxus into Central Asia.

Twice repulsed at Constantinople, the Arab caliphs finally were forced to recognize that the Byzantines had a vitality (if not an aggressiveness) to match their own. They were also stopped along the line of the Caucasus Mountains by the fierce resistance of the Khazars. But they continued a slow advance into South and Central Asia, while sweeping across North Africa and through Spain.

After more spectacular successes, the initial Moslem tide was halted early in the 8th century by several factors. Most important of these was the resilience of the Byzantine Empire. Next, perhaps, was the vitality of the Franks, demonstrated by Charles Martel at the Battle of Tours (see p. 204). Overextension unquestionably drained Moslem resources, despite remarkable ability to inspire converts to a religious zeal matching that of the original Arab disciples of Mohammed. Finally, renewal of internal disputes, in even more violent form, split the Caliphate and caused the Moslems to turn their still-fiery energy upon each other. The principal events were:

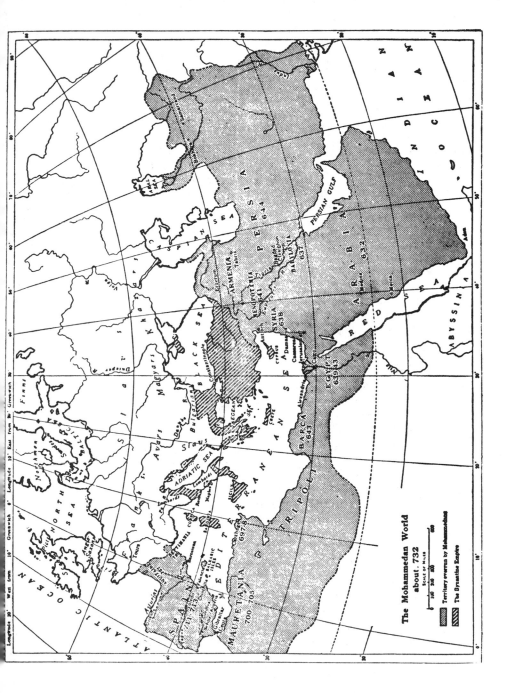

The Mohammedan World
about. 732

SCALE OF MILES

Territory overrun by Mohammedans

The Byzantine Empire

622. The Hegira. Mohammed's flight from Mecca to Medina.

624–630. War between the Arabs of Medina and Mecca. Mohammed was victorious at the **Battle of Badr** (624), defeated at the **Battle of Ohod** (625), repulsed a Meccan attack on Medina (627), and captured Mecca by assault (630). During this period he had also begun the conquest of nearby Arab tribes; this continued rapidly after the capture of Mecca.

629. Battle of Muta. Repulse of the first Moslem raid into Byzantine Palestine (see p. 214).

632–634. Reign of Abu Bekr. This loyal disciple of the prophet became the first caliph upon the death of Mohammed. He vigorously suppressed the revolts of "false prophets" **Tulayha** and **Musaylima;** the actual military operations against the rebels were undertaken (632–633) by **Khalid ibn al-Walid,** the first and one of the greatest Moslem generals. The final victory was won over Musaylima at the **Battle of Akraba** (633).

633. First Expansion of Islam. Khalid invaded Persian Mesopotamia (see p. 228). At the same time another Arab force under **Amr ibn al-As** invaded Palestine and Syria (see p. 214).

634–644. Reign of the Caliph Omar.

634–636. Operations in Syria and Palestine. A Byzantine counteroffensive threatened the forces of Amr and other Arab leaders in Palestine. Khalid made a forced march from Mesopotamia to join them and to defeat Theodore between Jerusalem and Gaza at the **Battle of Ajnadain** (July, 634). Pursuing relentlessly, Khalid defeated the Byzantines again at the **Battle of Fihl** (Pella or Gilead, near Baisan; January, 635). Continuing north, he defeated the Byzantine General **Baanes** at the **Battle of Marjal-Saffar** (near Damascus), then captured Damascus and Emesa (Homs). He abandoned these cities when threatened by a new Byzantine army under Theodore, and retired to the Yarmuk River (636). Here he repulsed a diversionary attack by the Sassanid allies of the Byzantines. Taking advantage of a mutiny in Theodore's army, Khalid attacked. After a bitter struggle, decided only when the Byzantines exhausted their supply of arrows, Khalid won a decisive victory in the **Battle of the Yarmuk** (Au-

gust, 636). He then recaptured Damascus and Emesa.

634–637. Operations in Persia. After Khalid left Mesopotamia for Palestine, the Persian general **Mihran** defeated the remaining Arabs at the **Battle of the Bridge,** on the Euphrates River, and drove them back to Hira (634). Arab reinforcements under **Muthanna** halted the Persian pursuit by a victory at the **Battle of Buwayb** (south of Kufa, 635). After Khalid's victory at the Yarmuk, Omar sent a new Arab army into Mesopotamia under the command of **Sa'd ibn-abi-Waqqas.** With 30,000 men, Sa'd defeated more than 50,000 under the Persian chancellor, **Rustam,** in the 3-day **Battle of the Qadisiya** (June, 637), then captured Ctesiphon (September ?). Pursuing, Sa'd defeated the Persians again at the **Battle of Jalula** (50 miles north of Madain, December, 637).

637–645. Completion of the Conquest of Syria. This included capture of Jerusalem and Antioch (638), Aleppo (639), Caesarea and Gaza (640), Ascalon (644), and Tripoli (645). Most of the fortified places, stoutly defended, were taken only after long sieges.

639–641. Completion of the Conquest of Byzantine Mesopotamia.

639–642. Invasion of Egypt. Amr ibn al-As defeated the Byzantines at the **Battle of Babylon** (near Heliopolis, July, 640). He next captured the fortress city of Babylon (April, 641), then Alexandria (September, 642), both after long sieges.

640–650. Invasion of Persian Highlands. The Arabs won decisive victories at the **Battles of Ram Hormuz** (near Shushtar, 640) and **Nahavend** (641). Organized resistance ended in Persia; consolidation took about a decade. The Oxus became the boundary between the Arabs and the Turks.

642–643. Expansion in North Africa. Cyrene and Tripoli were captured by **Abdulla ibn Zubayr,** who raided within 100 miles of Carthage.

644–656. Reign of the Caliph Othman.

645. Revolt in Alexandria. A Byzantine invasion fleet was repulsed and the uprising suppressed by Amr, who recaptured the city by assault.

649–654. Expansion at Sea. The growing Moslem navy demonstrated its prowess by capturing Cyprus (649), then the island of Aradus (off the coast of Syria); Moslem raiders next pillaged Sicily (652) and captured Rhodes (654).

652–664. Recurring Moslem Invasions of Afghanistan. Temporary capture of Kabul (664).

655. Naval Battle of Dhat al-Sawari (off Phoenix, Lycian Coast). Victory by Moslems over Byzantine fleet commanded by Emperor Constans.

656–661. Reign of Ali. Cousin, son-in-law, and adopted son of Mohammed, he succeeded Othman, who was murdered.

656–657. Revolt of Talha and Zubayr. The rebels were supported by **Ayesah,** widow of Mohammed. They were defeated by Ali in Mesopotamia near Basra in "**The Battle of the Camel.**"

657–661. Civil War. This was precipitated by the revolt of **Mu'awiya,** cousin of Othman, governor of Syria. Ali invaded Syria; he and Mu'awiya fought the drawn **Battle of Siffin** (657). After prolonged and inconclusive negotiations, Mu'awiya was proclaimed Caliph in Jerusalem (660). Ali was murdered soon thereafter; his first son, **Hassan,** after brief resistance, abdicated (661). This civil war led to the division of Islam into two major sects: the Shi'ites, or supporters of Ali, and the more orthodox Sunnites, who abhorred him.

659. Peace with Byzantine Empire. To permit him to devote full attention to the civil war, Mu'awiya concluded peace and agreed to pay an annual tribute to Constantinople.

660–680. Reign of Mu'awiya. First Omayyad caliph.

661–663. Arabs Reach India. Raid into Sind and lower Indus Valley by **Ziyad ibn Abihi.**

668–679. War with Byzantines. The Arabs were defeated (see p. 223).

674–676. Moslem Invasion of Transoxiana. Temporary capture of Bokhara (674) and Samarkand (676).

680–683. Reign of Yazid I (son of Mu'-awiya). Hussain, second son of Ali, revolted, was defeated at the **Battle of Kerbela** (on the Euphrates), and was cruelly murdered with most of his family (680). Another revolt in Arabia was led by **Abdulla ibn Zubayr** (son of the conqueror of Tripoli; see p. 230), who successfully conducted the defense of Mecca (682–683) against Yazid's army, which raised the siege upon news of the death of Yazid. Zubayr was recognized as caliph in Arabia, Iraq, and Egypt.

681–683. Invasion of Morocco. An Arab army from Egypt, led by **Okba ibn Nafi,** reached the Atlantic, but was then driven back to Cyrene by the Berbers, in alliance with the Byzantines based in Carthage. Okba was killed in the retreat.

683–684. Continued Civil War. Marwan **ibn Hakam** of the Omayyad family defeated adherents of Zubayr at the **Battle of Marj Rahit** (near Damascus) to affirm his claim to the Caliphate (684).

684–685. Reign of Marwan. He immediately reconquered Egypt for the Omayyad Caliphate. He died before he could attack Arabia or Iraq.

685–705. Reign of Abd ul-Malik (son of Marwan). Complicated religious strife continued throughout the Moslem world during the early years of this reign. At the same time Abd was occupied putting down Byzantine-inspired revolts in Syria (685–690).

690. Reconquest of Iraq. Abd ul-Malik defeated **Mus'ab ibn-Zubayr** (brother of Abdulla) on the Tigris River, near Basra.

691–692. Reconquest of Arabia. Al-Hajjaj **ibn Yusuf,** general of Abd ul-Malik, captured Medina (691) and Mecca (692). Abdulla was killed in al-Hajjaj's successful assault on Mecca, following a 6-month siege.

691–698. Continued Disorders in Iraq. The dissident Kharijite sect was suppressed by the generals Muhallab and al-Hajjaj. This left Abd ul-Malik the undisputed ruler of the Moslem world.

693–698. Conquest of Tunisia. Byzantine influence in north Africa was eliminated with the capture of Carthage (698).

699–701. Revolt in Afghanistan. An Arab army, commanded by **Ibn al-Ash'ath,** revolted against al-Hajjaj, over-all governor of the Eastern Moslem domains. Ibn al Ash'ath marched back to Iraq, where he occupied Basra, and marched against al-Hajjaj at Kufa. Al-Hajjaj was forced to withdraw into Kufa after losing the indecisive **Battle of Dair al-Jamajim.** Receiving reinforcements, al-Hajjaj finally defeated Ibn at the **Battle of Maskin** (on the Dujail River, 701) to suppress the revolt.

703. Repulse in Algeria. The Berbers defeated an Arab army under **Hassan ibn No'man** near Mount Aurasius (Aures Mountains). For reasons not quite clear the Berbers then entered into an alliance with the Arabs, facilitating their subsequent conquest of all North Africa (705).

705–715. Reign of Caliph Al-Walid (Son of Abd ul-Malik). Zenith of the Omayyad Dynasty, and greatest extent of a single Moslem empire. Continued expansion in the east under the over-all supervision of al-Hajjaj. **Qutayba ibn Muslim** reconquered Bokhara and Samarkand; he conquered Khwarizm, Ferghana, and Tashkent. He then raided into Sinkiang as far as Kashgar (713). After capturing Kabul (708), **Mohammed ibn al-Kassim** invaded and conquered Sind (708–712), after defeating the Indian King **Dahar** and capturing Multan after a long siege. He then raided the Punjab.

708–711. Conquest and Pacification of Northwest Africa. Musa ibn Nusair led the Arab forces.

710–714. Arab Invasion of Anatolia. The Byzantine province of Cilicia was conquered (711); the Arabs gained partial control of Galatia (714).

711–712. Conquest of Spain. (See p. 201.)

715–717. Reign of Caliph Sulaiman. Another son of Abd ul-Malik.

716–719. Invasions of Southern France. (See p. 204.)

716. Invasion of Transcaspian Region. The area between the Oxus and the Caspian Sea was conquered by Yemenite general **Yazid ibn Mohallib.**

717–718. Siege of Constantinople. (See p. 223.)

717–720. Reign of Omar II. There were no major military operations, other than frontier raids in France and Central Asia.

720–724. Reign of Caliph Yazid II. Another son of Abd ul-Malik. A revolt by Yazid ibn Mohallib was suppressed by Maslama at the **Battle of Akra** (on the Euphrates, 721). Internal disorders continued, however, with the southern Arabian, or Yemenite (or Kalb), faction generally opposed to the Caliphate, which was supported by the Qais (or Maadite, or northern Arabian) faction.

724–743. Reign of Caliph Hisham. Another son of Abd ul-Malik. He reorganized the administrative and military organizations of the empire. Recognizing that much greater expansion was undesirable, he established defensive regions to help stabilize the frontiers.

727–733. War with the Khazars in the Caucasus. Initially successful, the Moslems established a foothold north of the Daryal Pass, then were defeated and thrown back to Mesopotamia by the Khazars (see p. 227). Counterattacking, the Moslems reconquered Georgia, establishing their northern frontier on the Caucasus, with an outpost at Derbent.

730–737. War with the Turks in Transoxiana. After suffering a disastrous defeat at the hands of Chinese-led Turks near Samarkand (730), and again near Kashgar (736), the Arabs under **Nasr ibn Sayyar** rallied to defeat the Turks near Balkh (737). The Arab struggle against the Chinese and Turks continued without a decision for many more years (see pp. 233 and 240).

732. Battle of Tours. (See p. 205.)

739. Unsuccessful Invasion of Anatolia. (See p. 225.)

741–742. Revolt of Kharijites and Berbers. Omayyad troops were driven out of Morocco; they barely retained their control over their other North African provinces.

743–750. Turmoil in the Caliphate. Dynastic struggles, regional revolts, and religious disputes were interrelated in confusing abundance. The inept caliphs **Al-Walid II** (743–744) and **Yazid III** (744) were followed by the more able **Marwan II** (744–750). By hard fighting, Marwan restored order in Syria, Iraq, Arabia, and much of Persia (744–748).

Commencement of the Abbasid Caliphate, 750–800

The Abbasids—descendants of the Prophet's companion and first cousin, **Al-Abbas**—led a revolt which flamed from Khorasan through Persia into Mesopotamia. The violence of the internecine warfare impeded the expansion of Islam, providing a breathing spell for its enemies. By the end of the period, Abbasid caliphs were firmly on the throne in the new city of Baghdad, while in Morocco and Spain an independent Omayyad state had been established. The principal events of the period were:

747–749. Outbreak of Abbasid Rebellion in Khorasan. Leader was **Abu Muslim,** henchman of **Ibrahim** and **Abu'l Abbas,** grandsons of Al-Abbas. Despite the opposition of the governor of Khorasan, Nasr ibn Sayyar, Abu Muslim captured Merv (748). Ibrahim's general **Kahtaba** next defeated Nasr at the **Battle of Nishapur,** and again at the **Battles of Jurjan, Nehawand,** and **Kerbela.** A general rising in Persia and Mesopotamia permitted Abu'l Abbas (Ibrahim being dead) to proclaim himself caliph at Kufa (749).

750, January. Battle of the Greater Zab. Kahtaba decisively defeated Marwan, who fled to Egypt, where he was killed. This was followed by the systematic murder of most of the Omayyad family.

750–754. Reign of Abu'l-Abbas, First Abbassid Caliph. Recurring Omayyad revolts in Syria and Mesopotamia. Taking advantage of these disorders, the Byzantines raided deep into Moslem territory.

751. Battle of Talas. The Moslems finally drove the Chinese from Transoxiana (see p. 240).

754–775. Reign of Al-Mansur (brother of Abu'l Abbas). Al-Mansur's succession was challenged by other Abbasids. These revolts were suppressed with the assistance of Abu Muslim, who was now governor of Khorasan. Al-Mansur then had Abu Muslim assassinated, causing renewed revolts in Khorasan and elsewhere throughout the Caliphate. These and continuing Omayyad revolts were finally suppressed, but efforts to restore Abbasid control in Spain failed (see p. 210). Having firmly established the Abbasid dynasty, Al-Mansur established a new capital at Baghdad (762–766).

762. Shi'ite Rebellion. This was suppressed at the **Battle of Bakhamra** (48 miles from Kufa).

775–785. Reign of Al-Mahdi. Son of Al-Mansur. After suppressing several revolts, he renewed the war with the Byzantines (778; see p. 225).

779–783. Intensification of War with Byzantine Empire. After a number of successful penetrations of Anatolia by **Harun al-Rashid** (son of Al-Mahdi), Byzantine Empress Irene made peace and agreed to pay tribute (783; see p. 226).

786–809. Reign of Harun al-Rashid. The zenith of the power and prosperity of the Abbasid Caliphate. There were a number of continuing disorders in the empire, but the Moslems were generally successful in recurring wars with the Byzantine Empire (see pp. 226 and 265).

SOUTH ASIA, 600–800

Two leading figures of Hindu history dominated the subcontinent and vied for supremacy during the first half of the 7th century. The north was conquered by **Harsha,** who started his career as the ruler of the obscure kingdom of Thaneswar in the eastern Punjab. The Deccan was dominated by the greatest of the Chalukyas, **Pulakesin II.**

NORTH INDIA

Harsha was a conqueror in the tradition of the Chandraguptas; his empire approximated that of the earlier Maurya and Gupta dynasties. He subjugated most of north India in the first 15 years of his long reign. Turning southward, he invaded Chalukya territory, but was repulsed by Pulakesin. They concluded a treaty establishing a boundary along the Narbada River. During the remainder of his reign, Harsha devoted his energy and administrative skill to the consolidation

of his empire and to the inspiration of a cultural revival comparable to the Golden
Age of the Guptas.

Harsha's empire fell apart on his death. One of his ministers, an adventurer
named Arjuna, seized the eastern provinces—modern Bihar and Bengal. He then
made the mistake of molesting an embassy which the Chinese emperor had sent to
Harsha. The amazing Chinese ambassador raised a small Nepalese and Tibetan
army, then overthrew Arjuna.

The history of Hindustan in the centuries after Harsha is a drab and confusing story of endemic warfare between numerous rival dynasties. As in earlier
times, these wars were punctuated by the arrival of new invaders from the north
and west. The first of these was an obscure group of nomads—the Gurjaras—from
central Asia who arrived in Rajputana about the beginning of the 7th century.
By the middle of the century, they became the leading power of northwestern
India. They were followed by the Arabs, whose centrifugal drive reached Baluchistan late in the 7th century. A few years later the Arabs conquered Sind, but their
further advance was checked by the fierce resistance of the Gurjaras.

Farther north the brief resurgence of Kanauj was shattered by the rising
power of Kashmir, which, by the close of the 8th century, was engaged in a four-
way struggle for supremacy in north India with the Gurjaras, the new Pala Dynasty in Bengal, and the Rashtrakuta Dynasty which was pressing northward from
the Deccan. The principal events were:

606–648. Reign of Harsha.

**648–649. War between Arjuna and Wang
Hsuan Tze.** When his embassy was attacked in north India by Arjuna, Wang
—evidently a man of spirit and ability—
withdrew to Nepal where he collected
about 7,000 soldiers from the King of Nepal and another 1,200 from the King of
Tibet (both vassals of the Chinese emperor). Wang then marched back to the
Ganges, defeated Arjuna, and carried him
away to captivity in China. (If these
strength figures are correct, one must conclude that Wang was an exceptionally
gifted general, or that he was extremely
lucky, or that the strength figures usually
given for Indian armies were grossly exaggerated—or possibly all three.)

c. 650. Arrival of the Gurjaras. They established themselves in Rajputana.

c. 650–707. Arrival of the Moslems. Arab
conquest of Baluchistan.

708–712. Arab Conquest of Sind. Arab
general **Mohammed ibn Kasim** seized the
province. Subsequent Moslem raids into
Rajputana and Gujarat were repulsed by
the Gurjaras.

720–740. Resurgence and Fall of Kanauj.
Yasovarman, a collateral descendant of
Harsha, conquered Bengal (c. 730), bringing most of the Ganges Valley under his
control. While attempting to expand to
the northward, he was defeated in the
Punjab by **Lalitaditya,** King of Kashmir;
the new Kanauj Empire collapsed (740).

730–750. Rise of Kashmir. Under Lalitaditya, Kashmir became the leading power
of the Punjab. He campaigned against the
Gauda kings of Western Bengal, and evidently defeated an invading Tibetan army
in the awesome mountain regions near the
headwaters of the Indus. Like his Kashmiri
predecessors, Lalitaditya maintained close
relations with China and acknowledged
the suzerainty of the Chinese emperor.

740–750. Brief Rise of the Gauda Tribe.
They dominated western Bengal following
the collapse of Yasovarman's empire.

c. 740–c. 780. Rise of the Pratihara Dynasty.
Gurjara King **Nagabhata** decisively repulsed Moslem invasions of Rajputana
and Gujarat (740–760). In subsequent
years the Hinduized Gurjaras extended
and consolidated their control over all
Rajputana. Toward the end of the century they were being pressed from the
south by Rashtrakuta (see below).

750–770. Rise of the Pala Dynasty. Gopala
established the dynasty in eastern Bengal,
then extended his rule over all Bengal.

770–810. Reign of Dharmapala. This son
of Gopala continued expansion of Pala
dominions, reaching the edge of the Punjab by conquest of Kanauj (c. 800).

SOUTH INDIA

Early in his reign, Pulakesin II defeated the Pallavas and extended Chalukya rule to the east coast of the Deccan. This began an almost incessant series of wars between Pallava and Chalukya. For several years the great Pallava ruler **Mahendravarman** fought Pulakesin on almost equal terms. But after Mahendravarman's death the Chalukya king steadily compressed the Pallava kingdom to the coastal area near modern Madras. Before this he had repulsed Harsha's invasion of the Deccan (see p. 233). He also defeated the Chola, Pandya, and Kerala kingdoms. Having eliminated practically all rivals in south India, Pulakesin's power was jolted by a revolt led by his brother. Pallava seized this opportunity to rise in revolt, and Pulakesin was defeated and killed by Pallava King **Narasimharvarman I.**

The Chalukya-Pallava feud continued with varying fortunes until the middle of the 8th century. By that time Chalukya had again achieved ascendancy, when it was suddenly overthrown by the new Rashtrakuta Dynasty, which appeared in west-central Deccan. Rashtrakuta established a military state, comparable in concept and organization to that of ancient Assyria, which steadily expanded in all directions. Its principal thrust, however, was toward the Ganges Valley, at the expense of the Pratihara Dynasty of Rajputana. By the end of the century, under **Govinda III,** greatest Rashtrakuta, it had not only consolidated supremacy in the Deccan but had become one of the four major powers contending for hegemony in Hindustan. The principal events were:

600–625. Reign of Mahendravarman of Pallava.

608–642. Reign of Pulakesin II of Chalukya.

608–625. Wars between Pulakesin and Mahendravarman. Initially successful, Pulakesin's expansion in the northeast Deccan was halted after he pushed to the Bay of Bengal (609). Soon after this he undertook his victorious campaigns in the far south.

620. Pulakesin's War with Harsha. Harsha's attempt to invade the Deccan was repulsed.

625–630. Pulakesin's War with Pallava. This established Chalukya supremacy in south India.

630. Revolt of Kubja. The brother of Pulakesin, Viceroy of Vengi, declared his independence and established the Eastern Chalukya Dynasty.

630–642. Resurgence of Pallava. Narasimharvarman I defeated and killed Pulakesin in a battle outside Vatapi, capital of Chalukya (642). Pallava then pillaged Vatapi.

655. Chalukya Victory over Chola and Pandya. Vikramaditya, son of Pulakesin II, defeated Chola and Pandya to conclude a drawn-out war.

674. Chalukya Victory over Pallava. Vikramaditya destroyed the Pallava capital of Kanchi, revenging his father's defeat and death.

c. 730–740. Chalukya War with Pallava. Vikramaditya II, grandson of Vikramaditya I, smashed Pallava power, capturing Kanchi three times.

753. Rise of the Rashtrakuta Dynasty. Dantidurga, founder of the dynasty, defeated and overthrew **Kirtivarman II,** last Chalukya, to begin meteoric expansion of Rashtrakuta.

794–813. Reign of Govinda III of Rashtrakuta. He conquered Malwa and Gujarat, as well as defeating Pallava, which was attempting to rise after the downfall of Chalukya.

EAST AND CENTRAL ASIA

CHINA, THE TURKS, TIBET, AND NANCHAO

The resurgence of China during this period caused the military history of the Turks, Tibetans, and T'ais to be almost completely intermingled with that of their more powerful and more civilized neighbor.

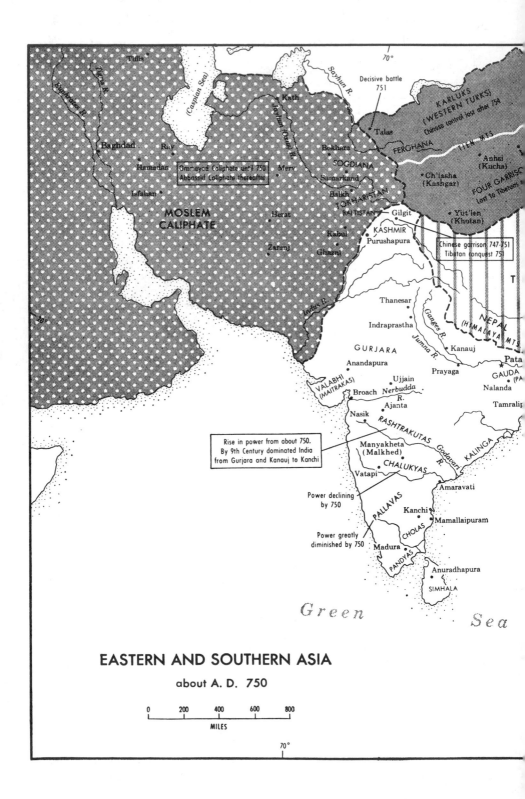

Tiflis

Tigris R.

Euphrates R.

Baghdad

Hamadan

Isfahan

Ray

(Caspian Sea)

Kath

Jaihun (Oxus) R.

Bokhara

SOGDIANA

Samarcand

Balkh

TOKHARISTAN

BALTISTAN

Merv

Seyhun R.

Talas

FERGHANA

Decisive battle
751

KARLUKS
(WESTERN TURKS)
Chinese control lost after 754

TIEN MTS

Anhsi
(Kucha)

Ch'iasha
(Kashgar)

FOUR GARRISO
Lost to Tibetans

Yut'ien
(Khotan)

MOSLEM
CALIPHATE

Ommayad Caliphate until 750
Abbassid Caliphate thereafter

Herat

Zaranj

Ghazni

Kabul

Gilgit

KASHMIR
Purushapura

Chinese garrison 747-751
Tibetan conquest 751

NEPAL
(HIMALAYA MTS

T

Hydaspes R.

Thanesar

Indraprastha

GURJARA

Anandapura

VALABHI
(MAITRAKAS)

Broach

Nasik

Ujjain

Nerbudda
R.

Ajanta

Ganges R.

Jumna R.

Kanauj

Prayaga

Pata

GAUDA (PA

Nalanda

Tamralip

Rise in power from about 750.
By 9th Century dominated India
from Gurjara and Kanauj to Kanchi

RASHTRAKUTAS

Manyakheta
(Malkhed)

CHALUKYAS

Vatapi

Godavari R.

KALINGA

Amaravati

Power declining
by 750

Power greatly
diminished by 750

PALLAVAS

CHOLAS

Kanchi

Mamallaipuram

Madura

PANDYAS

Anuradhapura

SIMHALA

Green   Sea

EASTERN AND SOUTHERN ASIA

about A. D. 750

0   200   400   600   800

MILES

70°

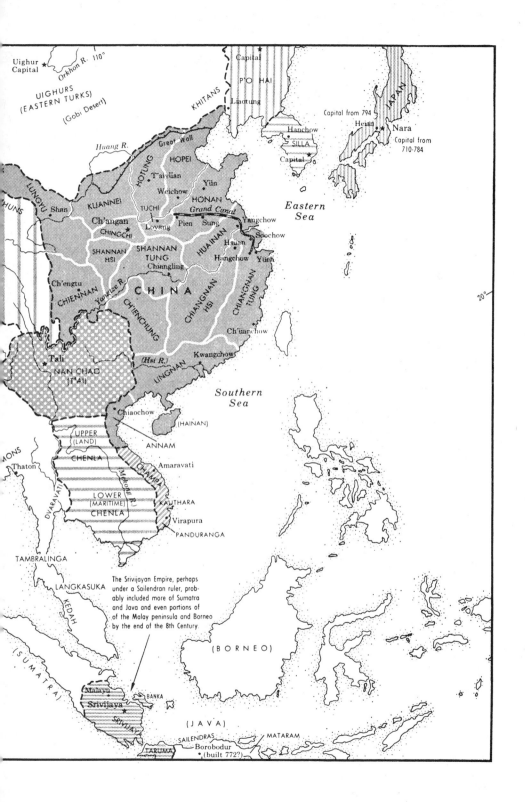

Uighur
Capital ★ Orkhon R. 110°

UIGHURS
(EASTERN TURKS)

(Gobi Desert)

Huang R.

LUNGYU

HUNS

KHITANS

Great Wall

HOTUNG

HOPEI

T'aiyüan

Weichow

Yün

HONAN

TUCHI

Grand Canal

KUANNEI

Shan

Ch'angan

CHINGCHI

Loyang Pien Sung Yangchow

Soochow

SHANNAN
HSI

SHANNAN
TUNG

Chiangling

HUAINAN

Hsüan

Hangchow Yüeh

Ch'engtu

CHIENNAN

Yangtze R.

CHINA

CHIANGNAN
HSI

CHIANGNAN
TUNG

CHIENCHUNG

Ch'üanchow

Tali

NAN CHAO
(T'AI)

(Hsi R.)

Kwangchow

LINGNAN

Chiaochow

(HAINAN)

P'O HAI

Capital

Laotung

Hanchow

SILLA

Capital

Eastern
Sea

JAPAN

Capital from 794
Heian Nara

Capital from
710-784

20°

Southern
Sea

MONS

Thaton

UPPER
(LAND)
CHENLA

DVARAVATI

MEKONG R.

ANNAM

Amaravati

CHAMPA

LOWER
(MARITIME)
CHENLA

KAUTHARA

Virapura

PANDURANGA

TAMBRALINGA

LANGKASUKA

KEDAH

The Srivijayan Empire, perhaps
under a Sailendran ruler, probably included more of Sumatra
and Java and even portions of
of the Malay peninsula and Borneo
by the end of the 8th Century.

(BORNEO)

(SUMATRA)

Malayu
Srivijaya

BANKA

(JAVA)

SAILENDRAS
Borobodur
(built 772?)

MATARAM

TARUMA

At the beginning of the 7th century, China was just emerging from four dismal centuries of chaos, to enter one of its great periods. The revival began under the short-lived Sui Dynasty. The T'ang Dynasty, which followed, made China the largest, most powerful, most prosperous, and (possibly) most cultured nation in the world of its time.

The man most responsible for this was a military genius named Li Shih-min, better known to history as the Emperor **T'ai Tsung,** whose reign combined almost universally successful external conquests with internal peace and prosperity. China's resurgence had begun when T'ai Tsung inherited a still-shaky kingdom from his father—the first of the T'ang Dynasty. The growing power of the Eastern Turks was menacing the northern and northwestern frontiers. Based upon extensive and successful combat experience against the Turks in his youth, the new emperor decided to reorganize Chinese military policy and doctrine. Concluding that the only sure way to prevent nomad invasions was to defeat them on their own grounds, he refused to strengthen the Great Wall, as his councilors advised. Instead, he fought delaying actions on the frontiers, while building up a new army—primarily cavalry—which he trained partly on the battlefield and partly in the interior.

When ready, T'ai Tsung began a series of punitive expeditions against the Eastern Turks. He destroyed that khanate in about 10 years of systematic campaigning. Simultaneously his diplomacy weaned the Uighur Turks from their allegiance to the khanate of the Western Turks. At about this time the Tufans (Tibetans) invaded western China. T'ai Tsung inflicted a crushing defeat on them and forced the Tibetan ruler to acknowledge Chinese suzerainty. With Uighur assistance, he then defeated and conquered the Western Turks, annexing all of modern Chinese Turkestan and most of the area between the Altai, the Pamirs, and the Aral Sea. His sovereignty was acknowledged by the tribes inhabiting most of modern Afghanistan; the kings of Kashmir were his vassals.

By the middle of the 7th century, China had no rival in northern, eastern, or central Asia. T'ai Tsung's death, however, was followed by a sharp decline, as many of the conquered peoples tried to throw off Chinese rule. But by the end of the century a revival of Chinese power took place under the Empress **Wu,** one of the great women of history. An able, unscrupulous monarch, she dispatched armies to the frontier regions which soon restored order and Chinese control.

The power of the T'ang Dynasty peaked just before the middle of the 8th century under **Hsuan Tsung,** who extended and consolidated Chinese control of the Oxus and Jaxartes valleys. He threw back Arab penetration into Central Asia —mostly by playing off the local rulers against the Moslems. At the same time, with Chinese blessing, the Uighurs extended their semi-independent dominions northeastward from the Altai over the remnants of the Eastern Turks in Mongolia.

The T'ang Dynasty declined in the last half of the 8th century. This was precipitated by Arab victories which expelled the Chinese from Transoxiana. Only the assistance of the loyal Uighurs enabled the Chinese to retain Sinkiang. The Khitan people of eastern Mongolia and Manchuria began raiding deep into north China; the Tufans of Tibet threw off Chinese rule, as did Korea and the T'ai Kingdom of Nanchao in Yunnan. At this time the general **An Lu-shan** started a revolt, which grew into one of the violent civil wars of Chinese history. The rebellion was finally quelled—with Uighur assistance—but its ravages hastened still further the political and military decline of the T'ang Dynasty. Another reason for the decline was the historical inability of the Chinese to develop horse-breeding competence, or to match the desert nomads either in horsemanship or in cavalry tactics.

This decline facilitated the rise of the powerful new T'ai Nanchao Kingdom in Yunnan. Having thrown off Chinese rule, Nanchao expanded steadily during the last half of the 8th century, to gain control over the northern Irrawaddy Valley in Burma. Nanchao raiding expeditions undoubtedly reached the Gulf of Martaban, and possibly even crossed over the mountains into India. The principal events were:

589–605. Reign of Yang Chien. Consolidation of the reunited Chinese empire under the first of the Sui Dynasty.

c. 600–603. Temporary Reunification of the Turk Empire. Under **Tardu,** a Western Turk chieftain, the Turks briefly threatened Ch'ang-an, the Chinese capital (601), but this menace disappeared with the collapse of Tardu's empire (603).

c. 600. Rise of the Tufan People of Tibet. Related to the earlier Ch'iang tribe, the Tufans controlled parts of Kansu, Sinkiang, and north India, under a north Indian ruling family.

602–605. Chinese Reconquest of Tongking and Annam. General **Liu Fang** subdued the rebellious provinces. He defeated the neighboring Chams, forcing them to pay tribute. Liu possibly marched across Cambodia to the Gulf of Siam; at any rate, the Khmer states of Cambodia began to pay tribute to China.

605–618. Reign of Emperor Yang Ti. He undertook aggressive expansion in all directions.

607–609. Chinese Advance into Sinkiang. General **P'ei Chu** defeated the Western Turks, driving them into Tibet and Sinkiang from footholds in Kansu and Kokonor. He occupied the oasis of Hami (Khamil, 608) and penetrated into Sinkiang (609). At the same time Yang Ti undertook a major reconstruction program on the Great Wall, to consolidate his northern conquests and to protect the left flank of a proposed invasion of Manchuria-Korea.

607–610. Conquest of Yunnan. Chinese forces subdued the barbarian T'ai inhabitants.

610. Conquest of Formosa. An overseas expedition under general **Ch'en Leng** conquered at least part of Formosa.

611–614. Operations in Manchuria and Korea. Yang Ti undertook a series of major campaigns against the Kokuryo State of southern Manchuria and northwestern Korea. These costly operations were generally unsuccessful and greatly weakened a nation already overextended militarily and economically.

613–618. Revolts against Yang Ti. Economic hardships and the losses of the disastrous Korean campaigns stimulated a rash of uprisings. The Eastern Turks resumed their raids against the northern frontiers. Yang Ti took the field personally; was defeated and surrounded in the fortified town of Yenmen (615). He was rescued by a daring attack led by young Li Shih-min, then about 20 years old. Three years later Yang Ti was murdered during internal disorders.

618–626. Reign of Kao Tsu. Li Yuan, a Wei nobleman, aided by his brilliant soldier-son, Li Shih-min, seized the throne and restored order. Li Yuan took the imperial name **Kao Tsu,** starting the T'ang Dynasty.

c. 620–650. Reign of Song-tsan Gampo of Tibet. He conducted many forays into neighboring countries, possibly including a brief conquest of Upper Burma. He established his capital at Lhasa.

c. 622. Rise of the Western Turks. They conquered the Oxus region and parts of Khorasan from Persia, cooperating with Byzantine Emperor Heraclius (see p. 213).

624–627. Eastern Turk Raids into China. These were repulsed at the gates of Ch'ang-an (Sian), the capital, by Li Shih-min, who combined force, threat, and diplomacy to establish a temporary peace with the Turks.

626–649. Reign of T'ai Tsung. Li Shih-min, under the title of T'ai Tsung, succeeded his father after a brief struggle with rival claimants.

629–641. Wars with the Eastern Turks. T'ai Tsung's punitive expeditions destroyed Eastern Turk power. By diplomacy he kept peace with the Western Turks and established an alliance with the semi-independent Uighur Turks. During this period the Khitan Mongols, east of the Gobi Desert, submitted to T'ai Tsung (c. 630).

641. War with Tibet. T'ai Tsung inflicted a crushing defeat on invading Tibetans under Song-tsan Gampo. To avoid a multifront war against barbarians, he concluded an easy peace, establishing an alliance which was sealed by giving his niece as wife to the Tibetan king, who acknowledged Chinese sovereignty. Nepal also began sending tribute about this time.

641–648. Wars with the Western Turks. T'ai Tsung defeated and conquered the Western Turks with the assistance of the Uighurs. He re-established Chinese sovereignty over Sinkiang, and received tribute from tribes and principalities west of the Pamirs.

645, 647. Chinese Expeditions into Korea. These had limited success, but failed to subdue the area.

646. War of Wang Hsuan-tsu and Arjuna in India. (See p. 234.)

649–683. Reign of Kao Tsung. The expansion of T'ang power continued in the early years of his reign, but declined near the end.

c. 650. Emergence of Nanchao. This T'ai state in western Yunnan was nominally subject to China.

657–659. Revolt of the Western Turks. This was crushed, the Khan being captured. Chinese control over the Oxus Valley was strengthened.

660–668. Conquest of Korea. This was accomplished in alliance with the Korean vassal state of Silla.

663–683. Military Disasters. The Tibetans revolted and seized portions of the Tarim Basin, cutting off China from its dominions farther west, which thereupon asserted their independence. Nanchao, Korea, and the Western and Eastern Turks all threw off the Chinese yoke.

684–704. Reign of Empress Wu. Chinese power revived. The Tibetans were driven from Sinkiang, and portions of the other outlying regions were recovered.

712–756. Reign of Hsuan Tsung. By a combination of force and diplomacy, Chinese control over the Oxus and Jaxartes valleys was re-established. Arab invaders were defeated in a series of hard-fought campaigns (730–737; see p. 232). The Tibetans were driven from the passes of the Nan Shan and Pamir mountains and forced again to acknowledge Chinese suzerainty. The Koreans resumed payment of tribute. A series of campaigns in Yunnan punished Nanchao, and forced the T'ais to reaccept Chinese sovereignty (730).

c. 745. Expansion of the Uighurs in Northern Mongolia. They conquered the remnants of the Eastern Turks, creating an empire—nominally subject to China— from Lake Balkash to Lake Baikal.

747–751. War with Arabs and Tibetans. After conclusion of an Arab-Tibetan alliance, general **Kao Hsien-chih** (of Korean descent) surprised and defeated both allies following an amazing march across the Pamirs and the Hindu Kush (747). Kao then engaged in some questionable, and probably treasonable, intrigues in the Oxus region, whereupon the Prince of Tashkent called upon the Arabs for assistance. Kao was decisively defeated (751) by the Arabs in the **Battle of Talas** (in Kirghiz SSR). This ended Chinese control in the areas west of the Pamirs and Tien Shan mountains. Further losses in Turkestan were prevented with the assistance of the Uighurs.

751–755. More Military Disasters. The Khitan Mongols (descendants of Hsien Pi) invaded North China, where they were barely held through the efforts of general An Lu-shan, a Turkish adventurer in the Chinese Army. Nanchao again rebelled, and decisively repulsed two Chinese invasion attempts (751, 754). Tibet and Korea again became independent.

755–763. Revolt of An Lu-shan. Declaring himself emperor, he quickly overran the Yellow River Valley, but was held up by the loyal garrison of Sui Yang. This delay permitted the T'ang Army, reinforced by Uighur allies, to reorganize, and to defeat him just after he captured Sui Yang (757). He was then killed by his son, who continued the revolt, which was not crushed until an Uighur force captured Loyang, the rebel capital (763).

755–797. Ascendancy of Tibet. The height of Tibetan power under **Khrisong Detsen.** Taking advantage of the civil war in China, he captured and sacked the Chinese capital, Ch'ang-an (763).

c. 760–800. Expansion of Nanchao. King Kolofeng (748–779) conquered the upper Irrawaddy Valley. Nanchao expansion was continued by I-mou-hsun, his grandson and successor.

760–800. Progressive Weakening of T'ang Authority. The seacoast was raided constantly by pirates, mostly Indonesian, but evidently including some Arab and Persian Moslems who had gained control of the Indian Ocean, and who had established themselves on the trade routes between the Indian Ocean and the China Sea.

KOREA, 600–800

The unceasing struggle between the three kingdoms of Kokuryo, Paekche, and Silla continued into the early years of the 7th century. At the same time Kokuryo was being subjected to increasing pressure from the expanding Chinese Empire of the Sui and T'ang Dynasties. Soon after the middle of the century, Silla, in alliance with the Chinese, overcame both of its rivals and accepted Chinese sovereignty. Apparently Paekche or Kokuryo received some assistance from Japanese allies, but to no avail. T'ang influence in Korea soon declined, but was reestablished in the early 8th century.

Important events of the period were:

611–647. Chinese Invasions. Kokuryo repulsed five major invasion efforts (611–614, 645, 647).

660–663. War of Paekche with Silla and China. The allies overthrew Paekche, defeating also a combined Japanese army and fleet sent to the assistance of Paekche (see p. 242). The enlarged Kingdom of Silla accepted Chinese suzerainty.

663–668. War of Kokuryo with Silla and China. The allies overthrew Kokuryo. All of Korea was united under one rule, subject to Chinese suzerainty.

c. 670–c. 740. Autonomy of Silla. During the decline of the T'angs, the Korean Kingdom of Silla became virtually independent. The Koreans began paying tribute again, however, with T'ang resurgence.

JAPAN, 600–800

The Soga clan, which had long dominated Japan, was eclipsed during the early years of the 7th century by brilliant Prince **Shotoku,** nephew and heir to the Empress **Suiko** (593–628). Acting as regent for the empress until his death (621), Shotoku introduced a constitution and created the basis for a centralized Japanese state. Like his successors, he was engaged in constant frontier war with the Ainu tribes in northern Honshu. Apparently he also planned an invasion of Korea, but abandoned the idea to meet pressing internal problems. After his death the Soga clan re-established its ascendancy over the imperial family, but was soon overthrown in a brief struggle by an imperial prince who took the imperial name **Kotoku.** He was aided by **Nakatomi-no-Kamatari,** who became the founder of the Fujiwara clan. These two instituted the Taika Reforms, carrying further the centralization of the government which had been begun by Shotoku. After one disastrous expedition to Korea, the Japanese devoted their attention to internal affairs and to the continuing war with the Ainu. By the end of the 8th century these wars were drawing to a close, with the Japanese consolidating the newly conquered regions in northern Honshu. The important events were:

593–621. Regency of Prince Shotoku. Promulgation of a constitution established the basis of a centralized state (604).

621–645. Resurgence of the Soga Clan. This renewed ascendancy was abruptly ended by the victory of Kotoku.

662–663. Japanese Land and Sea Expedition to Korea. (See p. 241.)

710–781. Period of Internal Unrest. This was marked by intrigue and frequent *coups d'état*. A decline in central authority resulted in several defeats at the hands of the Ainu.

781–806. Reign of the Emperor Kammu. He vigorously re-established a strong central government and revitalized the army. By the end of the century his general **Sakanoue Tamuramaro** had crushed most Ainu resistance in northern Honshu.

IX

THE DARK AGES—BATTLE-AX AND MACE: 800–1000

MILITARY TRENDS

This, the darkest period of the Middle Ages, was characterized by aimless and anarchic strife. Any effort to catalogue the multitudinous wars would be hopelessly confusing, dull—and relatively unimportant. Presented here are only those events which are most significant, as well as representative of the period as a whole.

There were no great captains. Among the Byzantines, however, there were a number of outstanding soldiers, including **Basil I, Nicephorus Phocas** (probably the best), **John Zimisces,** and **Basil II.**

In the welter of chaotic conflict, four significant historical and military trends stand out:

First, the rise of feudalism in Western Europe, in the Moslem world, and in Japan.

Second, the continued superiority of the Byzantine military system, permitting that empire to stand like a mighty rock amidst swirling tides and waves which buffeted it from all directions. The manner in which the Byzantine Empire withstood the first two centuries of Moslem assaults, and then was able to expand its power and influence in Asia and Europe during these two centuries, provides a useful object lesson for those impatient or fearful of the tide of modern events.

Third, the growing force of the Turkish migration, moving slowly but steadily from central Asia against the Moslem eastward current. This Turkish migratory process had two facets. There was, of course, the actual westward and southwestward movement of tribes and peoples from the area known today as Turkestan. At the same time, the martial prowess of the Turks was utilized increasingly by the Abbasid Caliphate in military units comprised of Turkish mercenaries or slaves. The most important of these was the large imperial guard, the only standing, professional force in the Caliphate. The Turkish generals commanding these units began to appear first as governors, then as independent princes, in provinces as far to the west as Egypt.

Fourth was the appearance of a number of states clearly identifiable as the precursors of modern nations. (Save for China, there had been little connection between the kingdoms and peoples of earlier periods and states of our modern world.) In some instances the link over the intervening millennium is tentative—as for Russia and Burma, for instance. In others, such as France and Japan, the relationship is clear and direct.

FEUDALISM

Western Europe

The trend toward feudalism in Western Europe had been evident in the tumultuous period following the fall of Rome, as barbarian tribal chieftains became the landowning nobles of the Teutonic kingdoms, providing protection to their people and receiving service and goods in return. This trend had been suspended by the stability of the centralized empire of Charlemagne. Yet Charlemagne's policies, demanding higher military standards of the contingents which the nobles furnished to his armies, provided a basis for subsequent acceleration of the feudalizing process.

The immediate stimuli for this acceleration in Western Europe were the Viking and Magyar invasions. Kings and nobles took frantic measures to protect their resources—people, livestock, and commercial centers. The chaotic dynastic disputes among the successors of Charlemagne precluded centralized effort against the devastations of the raiders; there was no leader with the ability to re-create his centralized military and administrative machinery. Consequently, defensive and protective measures had to be local, and largely uncoordinated. These measures took two principal forms: the construction of fortifications to protect rural populations as well as commercial and communications centers, and creation by each landowner of permanent military forces to man his fortifications and to harass the raiders whenever possible.

It was in this latter respect that the military standards of Charlemagne contributed to the establishment of excellent, even though small, professional units under the standards of the nobles. The trend toward cavalry continued; these standing forces were entirely mounted men—knights and men-at-arms. The nobles would, on rare occasions, call up levies of all their able-bodied men who had had some training as foot soldiers, but who were generally inadequately armed, protected, and organized; the role of such infantry was always passive and defensive.

From these developments emerged feudal society, based on the mounted knight and fortified castle, in which the strong protected the weak—and the weak had to pay a price. The independent middle class disappeared. Freemen of some wealth and property became vassals of the neighboring lord and, in return for his promise of protection, pledged themselves (and retainers, if any) to serve him as cavalry soldiers under certain clearly defined conditions. The poorer freemen simply became serfs of the gentry or nobility. Though liable to call-up for military service, they rarely were mobilized, save possibly to assist in the defense of the lord's castle. In return for tilling the soil or other menial service they, too, were given protection by their betters—and they found this to be a much more satisfactory arrangement than being left at the mercy of Vikings or Magyars.

Feudalism was based upon a military concept concerned primarily with local defense. Each great lord held his lands from the king. In return he was to be prepared to take his men out of his own local district on operations at the call of the king for a given period each year—usually 40 days. His primary responsibility, however, was for the local security of his own lands, 365 days a year. The military result of this system was that when royal armies were assembled and employed for offensive operations, they lacked homogeneity; there was no common loyalty to king and nation, they had no cohesive discipline based upon a common organization and integrated training, and there was no effective unity of command.

The one common social force was sincere devotion to Christendom. This provided a basis for the essentially moral concept of knightly honor which, in turn, was the principal ingredient of the chivalry of the Middle Ages, which created the romantic aura that tints our distant view of that essentially barbarous grim age and society.

The Viking raids provided the same impetus toward feudalism in Britain as on the Continent, but the standing forces of the Anglo-Saxons—and later the Danes—were almost entirely infantry. Otherwise, the feudalizing process was parallel on both sides of the English Channel, although the art of fortification was much less advanced in Britain, where simple ditches and wooden palisades substituted for the stone castles of Europe. The feudal lords and military leaders in England were known as thegns.

The local defensive measures which soon slowed, then halted, the Norse and Magyar depredations were found by the nobles to be equally useful in permitting defiance of the central authority of kings and emperors with relative impunity. The remainder of the medieval period in European history, therefore, was to be largely a struggle between central authority and the jealously guarded local power and privileges of nobles and of walled cities.

Islam

The rise of feudalism in Moslem lands had a somewhat different basis, at least initially. This was the pressure of the violent internal centrifugal religious and political forces which tore at the early Caliphate and its successors, forces which led to the rise of numerous, largely independent, great and small Moslem principalities and heretical religious communities. The rivalries among these independent Moslem groups, and between them and central authority, combined with raids by Byzantines, Khazars, Turks, and Spanish Christians, led to the same kind of local defensive and protective measures which appeared about the same time in Western Europe. As the local defensive capabilities were enhanced, this feudalizing process of course compounded the fragmentation of Islam.

Japan

Though feudalism appeared in Japan also at about this same time, it had a slightly different origin, and followed a somewhat different course than in the West. This is discussed elsewhere in this chapter (see p. 277).

WEAPONS AND ARMOR

There were no important innovations in weapons during this period, though there were some modifications, mainly in Europe. Swords became somewhat heavier and longer; no longer suitable for thrusting, they were used mainly as cutting weapons. The double-edged ax became more popular in Europe. These were indications of the greater emphasis on ponderous, brute force—rather than nimble skill—in West European warfare in the Middle Ages.

Charlemagne's efforts to introduce the bow into western Europe had failed completely. Aside from the Byzantines, the bow was used in Europe only by the Norsemen and the Turko-Scythian invaders from Asia (Bulgars, Magyars, and Pechenegs). One mark of their Norse background was the occasional use of the bow by the Normans—but usually for hunting rather than warfare.

Defensive armor became more common and more effective among Europeans and Moslems. For the most part Byzantine example was followed, and in some respects improved on. The ancient crested helmet disappeared, to be replaced by an iron conical headpiece, to which Europeans began to attach a nosepiece—precursor of the visor. The mail shirt was universally the basic item of armor, and was increased in length so that its flaps would cover the knees of a mounted man. One of the most important innovations of the Western Europeans was the evolution of the kite-shaped shield, which may have been the result of a conscious effort to combine the best features of the ancient Roman scutum and the more common round targe. This was a much more sensible item of equipment for mounted men, providing more protection, with less bulk, than a round shield. Another useful innovation was the hauberk, to protect the neck between helmet and mail shirt.

LAND TACTICS

General

There were no really important tactical innovations. Cavalry remained supreme throughout most of the world. Byzantine practices were much as they had been; their enemies tried to copy Byzantine tactics, but lacked the discipline, training, and organization to do so with full effectiveness.

The great revival of fortification throughout most of the world naturally put a premium on siegecraft. Again Byzantine example was copied, but neither they nor their enemies had improved upon the techniques of Julius Caesar—with the sole exception of Byzantine introduction of Greek fire (see p. 223). In Western Europe, both weapons and techniques were crude in comparison with those the Romans had employed a thousand years earlier. On the other hand, all of these techniques and weapons were well known and applied—even by the Vikings, as was demonstrated in the well-documented siege of Paris.

In siegecraft and in the defense of fortified places—and indeed in tactics in general—the Western Europeans tried to follow Roman example as best they could understand it and could adapt it to their own form of ponderous, heavy shock cavalry. The only important military manual to be found in the West was *De Re Militari* of Vegetius (see p. 137), which became required reading for those among the gentry who could read.

Viking Tactics

The Vikings were essentially raiders, more interested in plunder and the spoils of victory than in any kind of permanent conquest. On the other hand, they had a fierce love of combat, and though they rarely sought battle—and would wisely avoid it against odds—under most circumstances they were never averse to a good fight.

The Vikings, skillful warriors, initially had a higher standard of discipline—based on loyalty to their immediate chieftain—than was to be found in Western Europe. They were foot soldiers, usually armed with spears, swords, and axes—sometimes also carrying bows. Defensive armor consisted of helmet, round shield, and leather jacket. Later many adopted the mail shirt.

As European opposition to their inroads became more effective, the individual marauding Viking bands of 100 to 200 men would join together to form armies that sometimes were quite numerous. The Viking force besieging Paris in 885–886 must have been close to 30,000 men.

When fighting Western Europeans, the Vikings found defensive-offensive tactics to be effective against the more numerous, but poorly armed, poorly trained, poorly led militia levies with whom they first had to deal. The same tactics were obviously the best against the new professional class of cavalrymen developed in Europe to meet the Viking threat.

The Europeans, from their standpoint, found that this cavalry professionalization (combined with fortification) was an effective answer to the Norse raids. The heavy cavalrymen had greater shock power, and could fight the Vikings on equal terms or better if not outnumbered. And if the Vikings were too strong, then fast-moving, professional cavalrymen could operate from a secure, fortified base, keep up with the Viking foot columns, and frequently harass them effectively. They could also concentrate rapidly with other contingents to force battle on the raiders.

This led the Norsemen to two countermeasures. First, wherever they went ashore—on the coast, or on the river banks in inland waters—they would seize all horses in the vicinity, mounting as many men as possible to permit rapid movement. At first they used such horses only for transportation. Later, as their cavalry opposition became more formidable, they maintained large, permanent, well-defended bases on coastal or river peninsulas and islands, and developed their own cavalry units. To the end, however, the bulk of the Viking forces were infantry.

Magyar Tactics

The Magyars fought and raided as Scythians had since the dawn of history. They were light horsemen, usually unarmored, whose principal weapon was the bow and whose most important characteristic was mobility. They could not stand up and fight the heavy West European cavalry, and avoided hand-to-hand combat if it was at all possible. They fought as the Parthians had against the Romans at Carrhae (see p. 117). Using their superior mobility and exploiting their missile weapon—the bow—they would try to circle their more ponderous foes, harassing them for hours until the combination of casualties, exhaustion, and frustration led to gaps in the European formations. They would exploit such gaps—usually by attacking from the rear—endeavoring to cut off and overwhelm any isolated groups.

On their long raids the Magyars relied mainly on speed and rapid changes of direction to avoid large concentrations of West European cavalry. But though they were always more mobile than their principal enemies, the steady improvement in effectiveness and mobility of European heavy cavalry, combined with the growing number of fortifications, gradually reduced the returns from their raids.

NAVAL WARFARE

There were no important improvements in naval warfare. There was only one really effective navy: that of the Byzantine Empire, though its fleets were allowed to decline during the early part of this period. The principal employment of sea power—if it can be termed that—was by raiders and pirates: the Vikings against the coast of Western Europe, Moslem corsairs in the Mediterranean, Varangian (Scandinavian Russian) raiders in the Black Sea.

Thus naval engagements were rare, since a battle at sea was the last thing a raider wanted. In the 10th century, however, the revitalized Byzantine Navy systematically hunted down the Moslem corsair and pirate fleets, with the result that there were several spectacular sea battles in the Mediterranean.

Viking ships were considerably different than those earlier used for warlike purposes in the Mediterranean. Generally less than 100 feet in length, they had

10 to 16 oars to a side, plus a mast carrying a square sail when favored by a following wind. These vessels at first carried only 60 to 100 men. But during the latter years of the 9th century, some larger ships carried as many as 200. Viking seamanship was as admirable as their fighting abilities on land.

Much has been made of the fact that **Alfred the Great** of England built a navy with which to defend his coasts against the Viking raiders. This is a fact of considerable military and historical significance, as was the subsequent development of that navy by his successors **Edward** and **Aethelstan** into an instrument of offensive warfare against the Danes and Scots. It is a mistake, however, to consider Alfred as the father of the Royal Navy of today, since the Anglo-Saxon fleets of the 9th and 10th centuries soon thereafter disappeared completely, and new beginnings for Britain's sea power were made centuries later.

In the combined naval and land operations of Nicephorus Phocas against Crete (see p. 264), the Byzantines demonstrated a high order of skill and inventive-

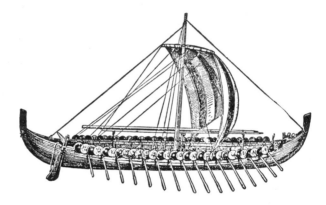

Viking ship

ness in amphibious warfare. His transport vessels were equipped with bridges, or ramps, whereby his mounted cavalrymen could charge ashore directly onto the beaches in opposed landings. These were the prototypes of the modern LST (landing ship, tank).

WESTERN EUROPE

THE VIKING INVASIONS AND SCANDINAVIA

The history of Scandinavia emerged from obscurity at the beginning of the 9th century, about the same time that Scandinavian raiders—known variously as Vikings, Norsemen, and Northmen—began their fierce raids against Western Europe and the British Isles. The three principal Scandinavian countries of Denmark, Norway, and Sweden were already separate entities, with Denmark the most advanced.

The reasons for the relatively sudden commencement of the great Viking raids of the 9th century have never been clear. With few exceptions, these were neither nationalistic nor even tribal invasions or migrations, but rather were independent forays for loot and plunder, led by Scandinavian nobles and adventurers.

For the most part the Norwegian and Danish Vikings sailed west and southwest, Swedes confining themselves mostly, but not exclusively, to the Baltic area. The Viking raids began late in the 8th century; within fifty years they achieved an amazing level of intensity and destructiveness, and did not begin to taper off until the latter years of the 9th century.

The most important result of the raids was the impetus given to the development of feudalism in Western Europe (see p. 244). At the same time, the course of events in France, the British Isles, and Russia was profoundly affected, with indirect results later evident in Southern Europe, the Mediterranean, and the Near East.

The Vikings in Ireland, 800–1000

Norse raids grew in intensity during the early years of the 9th century, during which they established numerous permanent posts in northern and eastern Ireland. In the vicissitudes of constant conflict over the next century and a half, the Norse were driven from their positions in the north, but established themselves firmly in eastern and central Ireland, Dublin, Waterford, and Limerick being their main centers of strength. They played a dominant role in Ireland during most of the 10th century, but by the end of the period their decline was hastened by repeated defeats at the hands of **Brian Boru**, King of Munster. The principal events were:

807–832. First Serious Viking Raids. Subsequently the raiders occupied islands off the coast and in the Irish Sea. The Norse chieftain **Thorgest** made the first deep overland peneration into the interior of Ireland (832).

841. Vikings Seize and Fortify Dublin and Annagassan. Thorgest sailed up the Bann River into Lough Neagh; later up the Shannon to Lough Ree. By this time he was the ruler of half of Ireland. He was killed in battle in the interior of Ireland by **Mael Sechnaill,** King of Mide (845).

853. Olaf the First Norse High King of Ireland.

862–879. Irish Resurgence in the North. Aed Findliath, Irish high king, drove the Vikings from northern Ireland, but was unable to prevent their expansion on the east coast.

914–920. Norse Expansion. The Vikings seized and fortified Waterford (914) and Limerick (920). **Niall Glundub,** Irish high king, was defeated and killed in an attack on Norse-held Dublin (919).

c. 965–975. Reign of Mathgamain, King of Munster. He defeated the Vikings at Limerick, capturing the city (968). He was defeated and killed by **Mael Muaid,** a rival Irish prince who seized the throne of Munster (975).

976. Rise of Brian Boru. The brother of Mathgamain, he defeated, killed, and succeeded Mael Muaid. He steadily increased his power and domains at the expense of Norse and Irish rivals.

999. Battle of Glen Mama. Brian defeated the Irish King of Leinster (who was allied with the Norse ruler of Dublin), forcing Leinster and Dublin to acknowledge his suzerainty. (For subsequent events in the career of Brian, see p. 291.)

The Vikings in Britain, 800–914

Beginning shortly after their inroads into Ireland, Norse raiders ranged along the coasts of Scotland and—somewhat later—England. By the middle of the 9th century they had seized many Scottish islands and had footholds in Scotland proper. After establishing bases on islands and peninsulas along the English coast, Danish rovers invaded and completely destroyed the kingdoms of Northumbria, Mercia, and East Anglia. In a few years they had seized and colonized all of Anglo-Saxon Britain except for Wessex. Alfred (the Great) of Wessex barely maintained his independence, and later drove the Vikings from Southern England. His victories over the

Danes were due to a high order of battlefield leadership and administrative ability. He and his successors encouraged the development of the feudal warrior class of thegns (see p. 245). They effectively utilized crude fortifications for defense and as bases for invasions of the Danish lands of northern England; they built up an effective navy to meet and repel the Vikings at sea. During the 10th century the Anglo-Saxon struggle with the Danes was no longer a matter of Viking raiders against local inhabitants, but rather a more or less constant war between Southern and Northern England. The principal events of the Viking invasions of Britain were:

802–835. Norse Depredations Begin. Frequent raids against the coasts of Scotland and England, seizure of many Scottish islands. Viking settlements were established on the Scottish mainland (c. 835).

838. Battle of Hingston Down. **Egbert** of Wessex defeated a combined Viking-Welsh invasion force.

850. Viking Raids in Southeast England. The raiders sacked London and Canterbury, but were defeated by **Aethelwulf** of Wessex at **Ockley.**

851. First Viking Settlement in England. This was on the island of Thanet (near Margate). Soon afterward they established a permanent base on Sheppy Island at the mouth of the Thames (853).

865–874. Danish Conquest of Northumbria, Mercia, and East Anglia. The Danes decisively defeated the Northumbrians at **York** (867). Under their leader **Halfdan** most of the Norsemen settled in the conquered regions. They repulsed **Aethelred** of Wessex and his brother Alfred in an effort to reconquer Mercia (868). **Edmund** (Saint) of East Anglia was defeated and killed at **Hoxne** (870).

870–871. Danish Invasion of Wessex. The English under Aethelred and Alfred won the first engagement at **Englefield** (December, 870), were badly defeated at **Reading** (January, 871), were victorious at **Ashdown** (January), defeated at **Basing** (January), fought two indecisive engagements (February), and were defeated again at **Marton** (March). After the death of Aethelred, Alfred was defeated at **Wilton** when retreating Danes turned upon disorganized English pursuers. A five-year peace ensued.

876–878. Renewed Invasion of Wessex. The Danes captured Wareham (876) and Exeter (877). Blockaded in Exeter by Alfred, they sought terms and withdrew to Mercia. Soon after, **Guthrum,** Danish leader, made a surprise attack on Alfred at **Chip-**

penham (January, 878), smashing his army and forcing him to flee with a few survivors to a fort at Athelney, where he gathered a new force while using guerrilla tactics to harass the Danes. Then Alfred attacked, winning a decisive victory at the **Battle of Edington** (May, 878). Guthrum sued for peace. The Danes agreed to abandon their efforts to conquer Wessex, but retained control of Northern England. It was during this war that Alfred began to build a navy.

884–885. Renewed War Between Alfred and Guthrum. This was started by a Danish raid on Kent, which was repulsed. Alfred captured London (885) and in the ensuing peace expanded his holdings north of the Thames.

893–896. Danish Invasions of Kent and Wessex. A large Danish expedition was blockaded by Alfred immediately after landing. Danes from North England simultaneously invaded Wessex by land. Part of the shipborne raiding force broke out from Alfred's blockade. In confused fighting that ranged all over southern and western England, Alfred, assisted by his son **Edward** and by his great vassals, defeated both invading forces (893, 894). The following year the Danes sailed up the Thames and Lea rivers, but Alfred cut off their escape by building two forts at the mouth of the Lea and blocking the stream by a great boom. The Danes abandoned their ships and marched north to join their countrymen in Danish England.

905. Renewed Danish Invasion. An overland expedition reached the Thames, where it was repulsed by Edward (who had succeeded Alfred). Edward retaliated by a successful and destructive raid through much of Danish England, culminating in a major victory at **Tetlenhall** (910).

914. Viking Invasion from Brittany. The invading fleet sailed up the Severn, but was blockaded by Edward and forced to withdraw. Though much border fighting continued against the Danes in northern and eastern England, the initiative now passed to the Anglo-Saxons. Final victory came when Edward captured **Tempsford,** killing **Guthrum II,** Danish King of East Anglia (918). The Viking era in Britain was ended—though the Danish era was not.

The Vikings in Western Europe, 800–929

During the reign of Charlemagne the few Viking raids on the coast of western Europe were dealt with effectively on land and sea (see p. 208). The depredations increased in intensity during the reign of **Louis the Pious** (son of Charlemagne), but burst like a storm over the Continent when the Vikings discovered that they could take advantage of the internal confusion caused by the dynastic struggles of the later Carolingians. For half a century they ranged over most of France, the Low Countries, and northern Germany, plundering, killing, and destroying, meeting little effective resistance save when the kings and great nobles temporarily halted their civil and dynastic wars to deal with the raiders. And though the Vikings preferred plunder to battle against organized opposition, they frequently and successfully engaged the best Frankish armies during the third quarter of the 9th century.

The height of Viking power and destructiveness came during the reign of inept Emperor **Charles the Fat,** during the darkest of the Dark Ages, and was marked by their vigorous and partially successful siege of Paris (885–886). But the forces they had set in motion among their victims—the development of effective feudal cavalry armies and the fortification of important places—now began to thwart the Norse raiders. In the latter years of the 9th century the cost of plundering often exceeded the rewards; Viking armies were as often defeated as they were victorious.

The last gasp of the Vikings was the invasion of northern France by **Rollo,** or Rolf, in the early years of the 10th century. Though generally successful, he found the opposition so strong that he was happy to accept an offer, from **Charles the Simple,** King of France, to settle in the region around Rouen in return for his promise to be a faithful vassal. Thus was Normandy created, with Rollo as its first duke. Only once, after the death of Charles the Simple, did the Normans return to their old ways, when they made an unsuccessful raid through western France. By the end of the 10th century they had become completely assimilated; though unruly, they were the most faithful and most vigorous vassals of the kings of France. The principal events were:

810. Invasion of Frisia. Danish King **Godfred** was repulsed by forces of Charlemagne, who later made a treaty with Godfred or his successor (811).

811–840. Increasing Viking Raids. Against outlying islands and coastal regions of Western Europe. Their most dramatic exploits were the plundering of Dorstadt and Utrecht (834).

c. 840–c. 890. Viking Conquest of Frisia. This included most of modern Holland, from Walcheren Island to the mouth of the Weser River.

843. First Viking Settlement at the Mouth of the Loire River. Viking raiders also ravaged the Mediterranean coasts of Spain and France.

845. First Viking Raid on Paris.

851, 880. Plundering of Hamburg. In both cases the raiders sailed up the Elbe River.

852–862. The Vikings against Charles the Bald. They first defeated him at **Givald's Foss** (exact location unknown, 852). A few years later he unsuccessfully besieged the Viking base on the island of Oiselle (in the Seine River, 10 miles above Rouen, 858). Charles was again repulsed in a similar attack three years later (861).

A peasant uprising in the Loire region failed in a vain effort to drive out the Vikings (859). A Viking raid through Paris and up the Marne River was frustrated by Charles, who blockaded the mouth of the Marne River, forcing the raiders to abandon their boats and to retreat overland to the sea (862).

863. Vikings Raid Deep up the Rhine Valley.

882. Battle of Ashloh (exact location unknown). After a setback at Saucourt (881) at the hands of **Louis III,** the Vikings defeated **Charles the Fat.**

885–886. Siege of Paris. The Viking army of about 30,000 was led by **Siegfried** and **Sinric.** This is generally considered the high point of Norse power in Western Europe. Using the fortifications begun by Charles the Bald, Count **Odo** (Eudes) of Paris, assisted by Bishop **Gozelin,** successfully defended the island city and its fortified bridgeheads for 11 months against fierce and skillful Viking assaults and siege operations. Unable to maintain a complete land and water investment of the city, which received a trickle of reinforcements and provisions by river and from relieving armies, the Vikings, however, were able to drive away relief armies led by Duke **Henry of Saxony** and by Charles the Fat. Although they were defeated near **Montfaucon** by Odo, they were still vigorously prosecuting the siege in September, 886, when Charles the Fat bought them off by paying a large ransom and permitting them to ravage Burgundy (which did not acknowledge his authority) without interference.

886–887. Six Months' Siege of Sens. The Vikings under Sinric were again unsuccessful.

891. Battle of Louvain. Arnulf, King of Germany, defeated the Vikings and captured their base fortifications by assault. There were no further deep Viking raids into Germany.

c. 896–911. Raids of Rollo in Northern France. These culminated in the Treaty of St. Clair-sur-Epte; Rollo accepted the region around Rouen as a fief from Charles the Simple to establish the Duchy of Normandy (911).

929. Norman Raid. The expedition through west-central France toward Aquitaine was defeated by King **Rudolph** at the **Battle of Limoges.**

The Vikings in Russia, c. 850–900

Origins of Norse influence in Russia are not clear. Apparently raiders from Sweden had penetrated far inland from the Baltic Sea by the middle of the 9th century. Soon after this, **Rurik,** a semilegendary leader of the Rus, or Varangian, tribe of Sweden, established himself as the ruler of Novgorod (c. 862), and a few years later Norse rule extended as far as Kiev (c. 865). By the end of the century (c. 880) Kiev was the capital of an extensive Varangian empire extending from the Gulf of Finland to the northern Ukraine and the Carpathians. Varangian raiders had already reached the Black Sea, and had made their first effort against Constantinople (865).

Denmark

The first historical King of Denmark was **Godfred,** whose military prowess and prestige were sufficient to warrant Charlemagne's recognition in a treaty (811). Apparently Godfred was suzerain of substantial regions of Norway. The Danish kingdom appears to have disintegrated after his death (c. 811), and the attention of the nobility seems to have been directed more at plunder of the British Islands and Western Europe than to achieving stability at home. Toward the beginning of the 10th century a new Danish dynasty was established by **Gorm,** who evidently reunited most of the region comprising modern Denmark. His son, **Harold Bluetooth** (c. 940–c. 985), appears to have completed national unification and to have begun the conquest of Norway. Harold's son, **Sweyn Forkbeard** (c. 985–1014), seized the kingdom by force from his father (who was killed in battle) and completed the conquest of Norway with Swedish assistance by his overwhelming victory over **Olaf I** of Norway at the naval **Battle of Svalde** (1000). Late in the 10th century he began a series of invasions of England, brought to a successful conclusion by his son **Canute** early in the next period (see p. 285). During one of his absences in England, Denmark was temporarily occupied by Swedish King **Eric Segersall** (992–994).

Norway

From the earliest period of its recorded history, Norway was subject to nominal or actual control from Denmark. This control seems to have slipped during the middle of the 9th century, when most Danes and Norwegians were occupied in Viking raids. Norwegian raiders discovered and settled Iceland (c. 850–c. 875). Taking advantage of the absence of many of the most powerful Norwegian nobles in Western Europe, Norway was conquered by **Harold Fairhair**—a process completed by his victory at the **Battle of Hafursfjorour** (c. 880). Harold extended his rule to the Shetland and Orkney Islands (c. 890). His sons, **Eric Bloody Ax** and **Haakon**, appear to have disputed the throne for several years (c. 930–c. 935). After a reign of five years, Eric seems to have been driven from the country by Haakon, and led some belated Viking raids in Britain, where he was killed (954). About this same time Haakon was killed at the **Battle of Fitjar** by Danish invaders (c. 960). The remainder of the century is a period of confused internal turmoil and progressive conquest of the country by the Danes and Swedes, culminating in the decisive sea **Battle of Svalde** (off the west coast of Rügen), in which Sweyn of Denmark and King **Olaf** of Sweden defeated and killed King **Olaf Trygvesson** of Norway (1000).

Sweden

A flourishing Swedish kingdom existed during the 9th century, with its capital at Uppsala. During this period the Swedes (and possibly Danes as well) seem to have conducted many expeditions to the eastern shores of the Baltic, where they established settlements. Most famous and most significant of these was the expedition of **Rurik** (c. 850) which led to the foundation of the Varangian, or Rus, dynasty in Novgorod and Kiev, to initiate the history of Russia (see p. 261). Late in the 10th century the Swedish king, **Olaf Skutkonung** (994–1021), joined in an alliance with Sweyn of Denmark to conquer Norway, which was temporarily divided between Sweden and Denmark (1000).

THE MAGYAR INVASIONS, C. 850–955

The Magyar tribe (related racially and linguistically to both Finns and Turks) inhabited the lower Don Basin in the early 9th century, where they were vassals of the Khazar Turks. Militarily they were typical Scythian light cavalry, with the bow their principal weapon. Soon after the middle of the century, the first recorded Magyar raid reached Frankish outposts in the middle Danube Valley. At this time the Magyars were under increasing pressure from the Pechenegs (or Patzinaks, a Turkish people living between the Volga and the Urals) who gradually drove them across the Dnieper and Dniester rivers to the lower Danube Valley. About 890, Magyar contingents were serving under Byzantine emperors in wars against the Bulgars, and under German King Arnulf against the Slavs of Moravia. After being badly defeated by a Pecheneg-Bulgar alliance, the Magyars, under their chieftain **Arpad,** migrated across the Carpathians into the middle Danube and Theiss valleys, driving out the Slavic and Avar inhabitants and establishing the Hungarian nation which has continued to the present.

From their new home the Magyars first began to raid their Slavic neighbors, then pushed farther into Germany and north Italy. As with the Vikings a few decades earlier, the Magyar raids were facilitated by the anarchy then existing in the Holy Roman Empire. The raids gave further impetus in eastern Germany to the process of feudalism already progressing rapidly farther west as a result of the Viking inroads.

During the early 10th century the Magyars ranged unchecked across Germany, Italy, and France. Their first setback came at the hands of German King **Henry the Fowler.** Their raids continued, but opposition became more effective because of the fortifications built by Henry and his son **Otto I,** and because of the steadily improving quality of the Holy Roman Empire's feudal cavalry. The last, most destructive, and most extensive Magyar raid came shortly after the middle of the 10th century, a national Hungarian effort to take advantage of civil war in Germany. Attempting to repeat this performance the following year, the Magyars were crushed by Otto in a fierce battle near Augsburg. From then on they were on the defensive against the Germans and never again threatened western Europe. The principal events were:

862. First Magyar Raid West of the Danube. Into the Frankish Ostmark.

862–889. Magyars Driven from Don Basin. They were pushed into Moldavia by the Pechenegs.

c. 895. Magyar Defeat by Pechenegs and Bulgars. Arpad led the Magyars and other future Hungarian tribes into the Middle Danube Valley (c. 896).

896–906. Establishment of Magyar Hungary. The Magyars drove the Slavs from the Danube and Theiss Valleys, destroying the Kingdom of Moravia (906).

899. First Magyar Raids into North Italy.

900. First Magyar Raids into Bavaria. These were followed by increasingly bold and destructive inroads (900–933).

910. Battle of Augsburg. The Magyars defeated the Germans (under the nominal leadership of King **Louis III,** The Child) by ambush after pretending to flee.

924. Raid through Germany and France. The Magyars swept through Bavaria, Swabia, Alsace, Lorraine, Champagne, back across the Rhine through Franconia to the Danube Valley.

926. Raid into North Italy and South France. The Magyars marched through Venetia and Lombardy, and were repulsed at the Pennine Alps (probably one of the St. Bernard passes) by **Rudolph** of Burgundy and **Hugh** of Vienne. Turning south, they crossed the Maritime Alps, raided across Provence and Septimania to the Pyrenees, then returned, after further inconclusive engagements in the Rhone Valley against Rodolf and Hugh.

933. Battle of Riade (or Merseberg). Henry the Fowler defeated the Magyars near Erfurt. The Magyars did not seriously contest the field, apparently being surprised by the determination and vigor of their foes.

933–954. Declining Intensity of Raids into Germany. The result of fortifications in East Germany built by Henry and Otto. During this period the Bavarians began to raid back into Hungary (950).

942. Raid to Constantinople. The Magyars were bought off by the Byzantines.

954. The Great Magyar Raid. A force between 50,000 and 100,000 swept through Bavaria and into Franconia. **Conrad** of Lorraine, then in revolt against Otto I, made a treaty with them, helped them to cross the Rhine at Worms, and facilitated their movement into Lorraine. They then crossed the Meuse to devastate northeastern France, through Rheims and Châlons into Burgundy, then to Italy via the Great St. Bernard Pass, through Lombardy, then across the Carnic Alps to the Drava and Danube valleys.

955, August. Battle of Lechfeld. A Magyar force of about 50,000 men invaded Bavaria. It was besieging Augsburg when Otto I arrived with an army of about 10,-000. Raising the siege, the Magyars accepted battle, making a surprise turning movement which captured the German camp, and drove one-third of Otto's army off the field. Assisted by his former enemy, Conrad of Lorraine, Otto repulsed the enveloping force, then charged the Magyar main body. He drove them off the field with heavy losses, captured their camp and its booty, then pursued vigorously for three days. Conrad was killed at the moment of victory. This ended Magyar depredations into Germany.

BRITAIN

During the early years of the 9th century, Wessex became the predominant kingdom of Anglo-Saxon England, under King **Egbert.** Shortly after the middle of the century Britain was struck by the Viking invasions (see p. 249). During the 10th century the successors of Alfred the Great slowly regained central and northern England from the Danes, and conquered Scotland by using their new navy. The end of the century, however, saw a new Danish invasion under King **Sweyn Forkbeard** (see p. 252). This was a Danish national effort, and thus not properly classifiable as a part of the Viking era.

802–839. Egbert of Wessex. He established supremacy in England following a crucial victory over **Beornwulf** of Mercia at **Ellandun** (825).

856–914. The Viking Invasions. (See p. 249.)

871–899. Reign of Alfred the Great. He established the basis of Anglo-Saxon feudalism.

899-924. Reign of Edward (the Elder, Son of Alfred). At the outset Edward was forced to fight a sanguinary civil war with his cousin, **Aethelwold,** who allied himself with the Danes (c. 900–905). After repelling the final Viking invasions of southern England (see p. 251), Edward devoted his reign to the conquest of Danish England, which was more than half completed at the time of his death.

924–939. Reign of Aethelstan (Son of Edward). He completed the conquest of remaining Danish holdings in northern England, and also received the homage of the Britons of Wales and of **Constantine III** of Scotland, thus unifying Britain under one ruler for the first time.

934–937. Invasion of Scotland. By land and sea Aethelstan subdued recalcitrant Constantine, who had formed an alliance with some resurgent Welsh leaders and with Norse chieftains based in Ireland. After three years of hard fighting, Aethelstan won a decisive victory over the allies at the **Battle of Brunanburgh** (southeast Dumfrieshire) to re-establish his control over all Britain (937).

954. Battle of Stanmore. Eric Bloody Ax (exiled King of Norway; see p. 253) was defeated and killed in an effort to seize northern England.

978–1016. Reign of Aethelred the Unready. In the early years of his reign, a revival of minor Norse raids (c. 980) soon led to full-scale Danish invasion under Sweyn Forkbeard (991). One of a number of Danish victories that year was the **Battle of Maldon** in Essex. Repeated Danish invasions resulted in the defeat and death of Aethelred and the conquest of England by Sweyn and his son Canute (see pp. 285 and 292).

CAROLINGIAN EMPIRE, 814–887

The decline of the Carolingian Empire began immediately after the death of Charlemagne. His son, Louis the Pious, was ineffectual as a ruler and as a soldier. Viking raiders became increasingly bold, and while Louis was alive his sons were engaged in civil war as they endeavored to stake out their inheritance claims. Immediately after his death the civil war became more violent as the two younger sons—**Louis the German** and **Charles the Bald**—combined to fight a bloody battle at **Fontenay** against their elder brother, **Lothair I.** A temporary settlement was achieved through the subsequent **Treaty of Verdun,** in which Lothair was recognized as emperor and as ruler of Italy, Burgundy, and Lotharingia (a strip of land extending north from the Jura Mountains through the Rhine and Meuse valleys to the North Sea), while Louis obtained the German lands to the east, and Charles held the future French kingdom to the west.

For nearly 50 years, near anarchy pervaded the Carolingian domains, resulting from the combination of continuing dynastic civil wars and the depredations of the Vikings. Lothair soon disappeared from the scene, and was succeeded as emperor first by his son **Louis II,** and then (briefly) by his brother Charles the Bald. Following Charles's death, anarchy became absolute, and the situation was hardly improved by the temporary unification of most of the Carolingian domains under **Charles the Fat**—who was deposed because of his ineptitude in dealing with internal problems and his timidity in the face of the Vikings at Paris (see p. 252).

For all practical purposes this ended the Carolingian Empire, though Carolingian descendants continued to reign for more than two decades in Germany and (nominally) for a century in France. As central authority declined, the power of the nobles increased. In Germany, in particular, the old tribal organizations became virtually independent duchies. Moslem raiders from North Africa took advantage of the situation to ravage and to occupy extensive regions of Sicily and south and central Italy. Rome was sacked (846; see p. 268). The principal events were:

814–840. Reign of Louis I the Pious.

840–855. Reign of Lothair I (as Emperor). A period of continual strife between Lothair and his brothers Louis and Charles.

841. Battle of Fontenay (Fontenat, Near Sens). Louis and Charles defeated Lothair, who was forced to sue for peace.

843. Treaty of Verdun. Charlemagne's empire was divided among his three grandsons.

843–876. Reign of Lewis the German (over the East Frankish Kingdom, Germany). During most of this period he was at war with his brothers (Lothair and Charles the Bald), with Lothair's sons (Louis II, Lothair, and Charles) and later with his own sons (Carloman, Louis, and Charles). He was possibly the most able ruler and soldier-descendant of Charlemagne.

843–877. Reign of Charles the Bald (over the West Frankish Kingdom, France). By his policy of building extensive fortifications, Charles laid the foundation for the eventual neutralization of the Vikings in France (see p. 252). In shifting alliances, Charles was almost constantly at war with his brothers and nephews. By clever diplomacy he outmaneuvered Carloman (son of his brother Louis) to become Emperor (875), in return for which the elderly Louis invaded and ravaged France. After Louis' death the

next year, Charles endeavored to annex Germany, but was decisively defeated by his brother's son (also named Louis) at the **Battle of Andernach** (October, 876).

855–875. Reign of Louis II (as Emperor). Son of Lothair, he participated in the confused Carolingian family wars with and against his uncles, brothers, and cousins. He was unable to recover Lotharingia, which his uncles Louis and Charles had seized and shared after the death of his father. He was successful in campaigns against the Moslem invaders of southern Italy (866–875). He made an alliance with Byzantine Emperor **Basil I** for joint land and sea operations against Bari (871–875; see p. 264).

870. Treaty of Mersen. Lotharingia was divided between Louis the German and Charles the Bald, thus bringing about a temporary settlement of their violent disputes. Central Lotharingia (or Lorraine) continued to be disputed between them, however, until the death of Louis.

879. Independence of Lower Burgundy (Provence). This was under **Boso** during the anarchic period which followed the death of Charles the Bald.

884–887. Reign of Charles the Fat (as Emperor). All of Charlemagne's empire save Burgundy was briefly united under him. He was deposed by an assembly of nobles after his shameful deal with the Vikings at Paris (see p. 252).

FRANCE, 888–1000

After the deposition of Charles the Fat, Count **Odo** (defender of Paris against the Vikings; see p. 252) was elected King of the West Franks. During the last five years of his reign he was engaged in a generally unsuccessful war against Charles III, "The Simple," nephew of Charles the Fat, who claimed the throne. Charles III finally became sole ruler on the death of Odo. A group of nobles later rebelled against Charles, electing Count **Robert** of Paris, brother of Odo, as king. Charles was defeated and deposed. Robert, killed during the war, was replaced by **Rudolph,** Duke of Burgundy (a Carolingian, not to be confused with Rodolph, founder of Upper Burgundy; see below). Following the reign of Rudolph, the Carolingians declined in authority, while the great vassals became practically independent.

After the death of the last Carolingian ruler of France, the nobles elected **Hugh Capet,** Count of Paris, as king. By the time of his death, he had established the basis for a strong monarchy. The important events were:

887–898. Reign of Odo.

893–923. Reign of Charles III. One of the most important events was the **Treaty of St. Clair-sur-Epte** (911) between Charles and Rollo, the Viking, which resulted in establishing the Duchy of Normandy. (See p. 252).

921–923. Robert's Revolt against Charles. Charles was defeated and deposed, but Robert, Count of Paris, was killed in the climactic **Battle of Soissons** (923).

923–936. Reign of Rudolph. Marked by his victory over the Normans and Aquitanians at the **Battle of Limoges** (see p. 252).

942. Franco-German War. Between **Louis IV** of France and **Otto I** of Germany (see p. 258).

947–948. Civil War. This was between Louis IV and **Hugh the Great,** Count of Paris. Initially successful, Hugh was forced by Otto I of Germany to make peace and to restore Louis to the throne (see p. 258).

987–996. Reign of Hugh Capet. It began with civil war between Hugh and his rival, **Charles of Lorraine,** in which Hugh was victorious.

HOLY ROMAN EMPIRE (GERMANY, ITALY, BURGUNDY), 887–1000

Arnulf, Carolingian King of Bavaria and Lombardy, ringleader of the uprising which deposed Charles the Fat, was elected King of the East Franks. His victory over the Vikings at the **Battle of Louvain** (see p. 252) signaled the decline of the Norsemen in Germany. For much of his reign Arnulf was engaged in a struggle with the Slavs of Moravia and Bohemia. He twice came to the assistance of the Pope against unruly Italian nobles, and in return was crowned Emperor. Central authority in Germany declined during the reigns of **Louis the Child** and **Conrad I,** but revived markedly under **Henry the Fowler,** able soldier, diplomat, and administrator. His son, **Otto I, the Great,** became virtual creator of a new Holy Roman Empire. The most important events were:

887–899. Reign of Arnulf.

888. Independence of Upper Burgundy. Established by Rodolph, who repulsed Arnulf's attempts to re-establish German control.

890–975. Moslem Footholds in Southern

France. Raiders seized and held the southern coast of Provence (Lower Burgundy).

891. Battle of Louvain. Arnulf's victory over the Vikings (see p. 252).

892–893. Slavic Invasion of Bavaria. With

Magyar assistance (see p. 254), Arnulf repulsed invaders under **Sviatopluk** of Moravia.

894–896. Arnulf's Successful Expedition to Italy. He was crowned Emperor (896).

899–911. Reign of Louis III, the Child.

900. First Magyar Raids into Germany. (See p. 254.)

911–918. Reign of Conrad I. (The former Duke of Franconia). Plagued by widespread civil war through Germany and Italy.

919–936. Reign of Henry I, the Fowler. (The former Duke of Saxony.) Henry waged successful war against **Arnulf**, Duke of Bavaria, claimant to the German throne (920–921).

924. Truce with the Magyars. This was in return for payment of tribute for 10 years. During that time Henry built up the defenses of Eastern Germany (see p. 254).

933. Battle of Riade. Victory of Henry over the Magyars (see p. 254).

936–973. Reign of Otto I, the Great. During the early years he successfully fought two civil wars to assure his succession: The first was against his half-brother **Thankmar** (938–939). The second was against a group of rebellious nobles (including his brother **Henry**), supported by **Louis IV** of France (939–941). Otto won the battles of **Xanten** (940) and of **Andernach** (941). His victories brought Lorraine definitely under German control and increased his central authority.

942. Invasion of France. Otto's purpose was to punish Louis IV for the support given the rebels. Peace was quickly made, and Otto withdrew.

944–947. Bavarian Revolt. Otto was defeated by **Bertold**, Duke of Bavaria, at the **Battle of Wels.** Later, combining diplomacy with military action, Otto gained control over Bavaria (947).

948. Invasion of France. Otto was supporting his brother-in-law, Louis IV, imprisoned by Hugh the Great, Count of Paris. Otto captured Rheims; Hugh submitted and restored Louis to the throne.

950. Invasion of Bohemia. Otto defeated Duke **Boleslav** and forced him to accept his suzerainty.

951–952. Otto's First Expedition to Italy. Upon request of **Adelaide**, widow of King **Lothair** of Italy, Otto defeated rival claimants, crowned himself King of the Lombards, and married Adelaide.

953–955. Rebellion in Germany. The revolt was led by Otto's son, **Ludolf**, assisted by **Conrad**, Duke of Lorraine, and **Frederick**, Bishop of Mainz. After initial defeat and capture by the rebels, Otto escaped, then defeated the rebels, his victory culminating with the capture of the rebel stronghold of Regensburg.

955. Victory over the Magyars at the Battle of Lechfeld. (See p. 254.)

955. Battle of the Recknitz. Otto defeated the Slavic Wends.

961–964. Otto's Second Expedition to Italy. Upon the appeal of Pope **John XII,** Otto led his second expedition to Italy against **Berengar II,** King of Italy. He defeated Berengar and forced him to vassalage (961). Otto was crowned as Holy Roman Emperor by Pope **John XII** (962). Soon after this he deposed John and appointed a new Pope, **Leo VIII** (963).

966–972. Otto's Third Expedition to Italy. He suppressed a revolt in Rome, where **Benedict V** had deposed Leo VIII. Since Leo had died, Otto appointed another new Pope, **John XIII.** He then marched to South Italy and operated successfully against the Saracens and Byzantines.

973–983. Reign of Otto II. This began with five years of violent civil wars, in which **Henry the Wrangler** of Bavaria and Boleslav of Bohemia were the main rebels (973–978).

978–980. War with France. A dispute over Lorraine led to an invasion of Germany by **Lothair** of France. The French were repulsed after briefly occupying Aachen. Otto invaded France and besieged Paris. Forced to withdraw due to an epidemic in his army, he was harassed severely by the French during the withdrawal. Lothair abandoned his claim to Lorraine.

981–983. Expedition to Italy. Otto was disastrously defeated by a Moslem-Byzantine alliance, being repulsed from **Crotona** while his fleet was crushed nearby at the **Battle of Stilo** (982), and barely escaped with his life.

983–1002. Reign of Otto III (Age 3). During his minority, his vigorous mother, **Theophano,** suppressed a number of revolts led by Henry the Wrangler and others.

996. Expedition to Italy. Otto appointed a new Pope, **Gregory V,** and was crowned emperor.

998. Expedition to Italy. Otto suppressed an antipapal revolt by **John Crescentius,** who was captured and killed in the castle of **St. Angelo** at Rome. Otto died unexpectedly, four years later, while attempting to suppress still another revolt in Rome (1002).

SPAIN

During the 9th century the Christian rulers of the Kingdom of the Asturias expanded their control over all Galicia (Northwest Spain). For most of the following century, however, the pendulum swung the other way, under pressure from the resurgent Omayyad caliphs of Cordova. Frontier warfare between Christians and Moslems was literally continuous. The principal events were:

796–822. Reign of al-Hakam I, Emir of Cordova. There were recurrent revolts, the most serious being in Cordova (805, 817) and Toledo (814).

792–842. Reign of Alfonso II of the Asturias. He began the advance of the Christians from the northern mountains toward the central plains of Spain, until stopped by **Abd-er-Rahman II** (see below).

801. Capture of Barcelona by Charlemagne. (See p. 207.)

822–852. Reign of Abd-er-Rahman II. He defeated Alfonso II and drove the Franks back in Catalonia. He suppressed a revolt of Christians and Jews in Toledo (837).

852–886. Reign of Mohammed I. He conducted successful expeditions into Galicia and Navarre.

866–910. Reign of Alfonso III. The greatest of the kings of Asturias. Before his death Alfonso had extended the southern frontier of Christian Spain to the Duero (Douro) River. His successor, **Garcia** (910–914), moved the capital to León, and the kingdom became known by that name.

903. Moslem Capture of the Balearic Islands. The Franks were defeated by **Isam-al-Khamlani.**

912–961. Reign of Abd-er-Rahman III. The greatest of the Omayyads of Spain, he reunited Moslem Spain and took the title of Caliph of Cordova (929). He was generally successful in wars with León and Navarre, forcing the Christian kings to pay tribute.

914–924. Reign of Ordono II of León. His occasional military successes prevented threatened Moslem conquest of the kingdom.

924–950. Reign of Ramiro II of León. He regained the initiative for the Christians by great victories over Abd-er-Rahman at **Simancas** (934) and at **Zamora** (939), where he drove off a besieging army. However, during the latter part of his reign the eastern provinces of the kingdom, known as Castile, under the Counts of Burgos, became virtually independent.

961–976. Reign of al-Hakam II (Son of Abd-er-Rahman). This able ruler continued to enjoy success over the Christians (thanks largely to his excellent general **Ghalib**). Morocco was conquered (973).

976–1013. Nominal Reign of Hisham II of Cordova. His weakness resulted in the establishment of a military dictatorship under the powerful palace chamberlain, **Ibn Abi Amir al-Mansour** (981–1002), who seized power by defeating and killing his father-in-law, Ghalib, in a brief civil war. Al-Mansour inflicted decisive defeats on León, Navarre, and Barcelona, capturing and sacking León (988) and ravaging most of the kingdom. He also suppressed rebellions in Morocco.

EASTERN EUROPE

BULGARIA

During the 9th century and first half of the 10th, Bulgarian power steadily increased, despite some setbacks at the hands of the Byzantines, and despite the loss of holdings north of the Danube to the Magyars and Pechenegs. After the middle of the 10th century, the Bulgars suffered crushing defeats by the Byzantines and Russians. Briefly resurgent under **Samuel,** the Bulgars were engaged in a disastrous war with Byzantium at the close of the century (see p. 302). The principal events were:

808–814. Reign of Krum. He fought successfully against the Byzantines (808–813; see p. 263).

817. Battle of Mesembria. Victory of **Leo V** over **Omortag,** son of Krum (see p. 263).

827–829. Bulgar Raids into Croatia and Pannonia.

852–889. Reign of Boris I. In the early years he failed in attempts to expand into Serbia and Croatia. Under Byzantine duress, he accepted Christianity (866). Bulgaria prospered under his rule. He abdicated to enter a monastery (889).

893. Return of Boris. Boris came out of retirement to subdue a revolt against his inept son, **Vladimir.** He deposed Vladimir in favor of his second son, **Symeon,** then returned to his monastery.

893–927. Reign of Symeon. Repeated and generally successful wars with the Byzantine Empire (894–897, 913–924). Preoccupied with ambitions to capture Constantinople, Symeon lost the outlying semiautonomous provinces of Transylvania and Pannonia to the Magyars, and Wallachia to the Pechenegs. Offsetting these losses were his conquest of Macedonia, Thessaly, and Albania from the Byzantines (c. 914) and of Serbia (918–926). The Byzantines paid him tribute.

927–969. Reign of Peter (Son of Symeon). He had to meet frequent Magyar and Pecheneg raids.

967–969. Byzantine and Russian Invasion. Nicephorus Phocas led a Byzantine army overland in an alliance with Prince **Sviatoslav,** who came by sea. The Russians captured the new Bulgarian King **Boris II.** Bulgaria was overrun.

969–972. Russian-Byzantine War over Bulgaria. The result of a dispute over division of Bulgaria (see p. 262). The victorious Byzantine Empire annexed all of Eastern Bulgaria up to the Danube.

976–1014. Reign of Samuel. A Bulgarian noble in the West, he re-established the Bulgarian state (976).

981–996. Resurgence of Bulgaria. Samuel defeated a Byzantine invading army under **Basil II** near Sofia (981). After periodic raids to the south, he invaded Thessaly to capture Larissa and Dyrrhachium (986–989). Taking advantage of internal discord in the Byzantine Empire, also involved in war with the Fatimids, Samuel began to extend his control over Eastern Bulgaria (989–996) and also northwestward into Serbia.

996–1014. Conquest of Bulgaria by Basil II (See p. 302.)

SERBIA

The Serb tribes coalesced as a kingdom toward the end of the 8th century. From its earliest years Serbia suffered constant internal turmoil, while at the same time fighting off incessant encroachments by the neighboring Bulgars. The Serbs allied themselves with the Byzantines against Bulgaria and acknowledged the suzerainty of Constantinople (c. 870). Despite this, practically all of Serbia was conquered by Symeon of Bulgaria (918–926; see p. 260). Part of Serbia regained its independence under Prince **Chaslav** (931), but he was unable to establish a truly unified state. Most of Serbia was again conquered by the Bulgars, under Tsar Samuel (c. 989; see above), and remained under Bulgarian control until early in the 11th century.

CROATIA

The various Croat and Slovene tribes had not yet coalesced into a state when they were conquered by Charlemagne, late in the 8th century (see p. 207). During the 9th and early 10th centuries Croatia was buffeted by tides of warfare and migration, and was at different times dominated by Franks, Moravians, Byzantines, Bulgars, and Magyars. A true Croatian state, under the nominal suzerainty of the Byzantine Empire, finally appeared under the leadership of King **Tomislav** (c. 925). **Drzislav** (969–997) assisted Byzantine Basil II in his wars against the Bulgars, and in return was granted recognition as an independent monarch.

BOHEMIA, C. 900–1000

Late in the 9th century the wild Slavonic tribes of Bohemia became Christianized, and coalesced into a state, initially subject to Moravia. After the destruction of Moravia by the Magyars, Bohemia became independent. After several decades of constant warfare, during the reign of **Boleslav I** (929–967) Bohemia was forced by Otto I to accept German suzerainty (950). Boleslav led a contingent in the German Army which defeated the Magyars at the **Battle of Lechfeld** (955; see p. 254). At the very end of the century Bohemia lost some of its territory to Poland (999–1000; see below).

POLAND, C. 960–1000

Poland was a unified, pagan Slavonic state when it first came into contact with the Germans (963). Its first historical ruler was **Mieszko I** (c. 960–992), who expanded his frontiers westward as far as the Oder River, thus arousing German alarm. After a decade of warfare, Mieszko voluntarily accepted German suzerainty (973) in order to accelerate the civilization of his country. His son **Boleslav the Brave** (992–1025) continued the process of organizing and modernizing the Polish state, and had ambitions of uniting all of the western Slavs. One of the leading soldiers of his time, Boleslav conquered east Pomerania (994), then defeated the Bohemians to conquer Silesia, Moravia, and Cracow (999). His military successes continued in the following century (see p. 300).

RUSSIA, C. 900–1000

Late in the 9th or early in the 10th century, the two Varangian states of Kiev and Novgorod were united into a single Russian state by Prince **Oleg,** who had probably led the original Norse expedition to Kiev. He obtained a commercial treaty with the Byzantine Empire (911), renewed by his son **Igor.** Igor's son, **Sviatoslav,** had ambitions which led him to foreign adventures that eventually cost his life. The son of Sviatoslav, **Vladimir the Saint,** was the last of the Vikings and the first of the Christian Russians. His early years were spent in civil and foreign wars; after his conversion to Christianity he appears to have become truly a man of peace—but he retained both the vigor and the will to protect his people from foreign invaders. The principal events were:

c. 880–912. Reign of Prince Oleg. Creator of the Russian state.

912–914. Reign of Prince Igor.

964–972. Reign of Prince Sviatoslav. He brought greater unity to the Russian state, and defeated the Khazars on the lower Volga (965).

967–972. Sviatoslav's Wars in Bulgaria. (See pp. 260 and 264.)

967–968. Pecheneg Invasion of Russia. The threat to Kiev forced Sviatoslav to return from Bulgaria. After repulsing the Pechenegs (968), he immediately returned to Bulgaria, where he fought successfully against the Bulgarians, but was disastrously defeated by the Byzantines.

972. Death of Sviatoslav. He was defeated and killed by the Pechenegs while returning to Kiev from Bulgaria.

972–980. Dynastic Struggle. The three sons of Sviatoslav—**Yaropolk, Oleg,** and **Vladimir**—vied for control. Vladimir went back to Scandinavia to attract Vikings to his cause (977–978). Returning, he subdued the principality of Polotsk, and regained control of Novgorod (978–979). He then defeated and killed his brother Yaropolk, captured Kiev, and established himself as the unquestioned ruler of all Russia (980).

981–985. Foreign Wars of Vladimir. He conquered Chervensk (modern Galicia, 981), then overran the heathen tribes between Poland and Lithuania (modern White Russia, 983). He conquered all or part of the Bulgar state on the Kama River, east of the Volga (985).

988. Conversion of Vladimir to Christianity.

EURASIA AND THE MIDDLE EAST

THE BYZANTINE EMPIRE

There was an amazing revival in the strength, stability, and prosperity of the Byzantine Empire. Byzantine generals were generally successful in repelling the frequent foreign inroads—the Caliphate remaining the most important and most dan-

Byzantine themes, *c.* 950

gerous foe. Border fighting was incessant on the eastern frontier. Toward the end of the period a series of outstanding soldier-emperors, and their able subordinates, deliberately expanded the imperial frontiers in the Balkans, Asia Minor, Syria, Armenia, Italy, and the Mediterranean islands. This was not a reversal of the traditionally defensive strategic policy of the empire, but was rather a logical implementation of that policy, in consonance with the growing strength of the empire in contrast to the gradual weakening of the Moslem threat. Expansion was limited to areas which, in previous centuries, had been traditionally Byzantine. The new frontiers were always carefully selected with two main considerations in mind: for their natural defensive strength (mountains, rivers, or deserts), and to protect by coverage and depth the vital regions of the empire and the traditional invasion routes.

Decline of the Byzantine Navy during the latter 8th and early 9th centuries was corrected by the energetic and gifted emperor **Basil I,** who also revitalized the army and began the trend of imperial expansion on land. A slight recession in the progress of imperial power about the beginning of the 10th century was reversed dramatically by the military brilliance of the emperors **Nicephorus Phocas, John Zimisces,** and **Basil II.** The principal events were:

802–811. Reign of Nicephorus I. He was engaged in almost constant war with the Caliph **Harun al-Rashid** (see p. 233). Able Nicephorus was handicapped in the prosecution of this war by various conspiracies and a revolt led by the general **Bardanes.** He made peace with Charlemagne—whom he recognized as Emperor of the West—by treaties delineating the frontiers between the two empires in Italy and Illyria (803, 810). After Harun's army captured **Heraclea Pontica** (Eregli) by assault (806), Nicephorus sued for peace.

809–817. War with Krum of Bulgaria. Nicephorus personally led his army into Bulgaria, with consistent success. After capturing Krum's capital, Pliska, he was defeated and killed in a surprise Bulgarian night attack in a nearby mountain pass (811).

811–820. Reigns of Stauracius, Michael I, and Leo V. The Bulgarians were generally successful in subsequent operations against weak Stauracius (811) and Michael I (811–813). Disgusted by the ineptitude of Michael, his general, **Leo the Armenian,** refused to support him in the **Battle of Versinikia** (813), won by the Bulgars. Krum took Adrianople and advanced to the walls of Constantinople. Leo revolted against Michael, usurped the throne as Leo V, and then was consistently victorious. He defeated **Omortag,** son of Krum, at the **Battle of Mesembria** (817), forcing the Bulgarians to agree to a 30-year peace.

820–829. Reign of Michael II. Called "The Stammerer," he was a general who had conspired against Leo, and who was made emperor after Leo was assassinated. His fellow general **Thomas** led a revolt which collapsed after two unsuccessful attempts to capture Constantinople (822–824). During his reign the Arabs took advantage of Byzantine naval decline by conquering Crete (825–826) and invading Sicily (827).

829–842. Reign of Theophilus. This was marked by intensified but inconclusive war against the Caliphate. Byzantine armies five times invaded the Abbasid dominions, but the Empire was also frequently ravaged by Moslem raids and invasions. In his most successful invasion, Theophilus reached the Euphrates in northeastern Syria, where he captured and sacked the towns of Samosata and Aibatra (837). Next year, however, the Caliph **al-Mu'tasim,** led a great force into Anatolia, defeating Theophilus in the **Battle of Dasymon** (or Anzen) on the Halys River. The Moslems then captured and sacked Amorium (after a long siege) and Ancyra before retiring to Syria (838).

842–867. Reign of Michael III (Age 3). Under the influence of his uncle, **Bardas,** who became virtual dictator, Michael successfully renewed the war against the Caliphate (851–863; see p. 266).

c. 850–1000. Periodic Paulician Revolts. This heretical Christian sect in northeastern Anatolia was sternly persecuted by the Orthodox Byzantine emperors.

865. Arrival of the Varangians (Russians). A pillaging expedition reached the Bosporus and threatened Constantinople.

866. Invasions of Bulgaria. Michael and Bardas forced the conversion of the Bulgarian King **Boris I** to Christianity.

867–886. Reign of Basil I. Known as "the Macedonian," he was a peasant by birth. He overthrew Michael to establish the most powerful dynasty of Byzantine history.

871–879. Renewed War with the Caliphate.
Basil was generally successful; he moved the frontiers eastward to the Euphrates after a decisive victory at **Samosata** (Samsat; 873).

875–885. Byzantine Expansion in South Italy. The Moslems were driven from **Bari** (875) and **Tarentum** (880), and Calabria was reconquered (885). Basil's simultaneous efforts to drive the Moslems from Sicily, however, were not successful. There was a rare instance of collaboration between the Byzantine and Holy Roman empires in the siege of Bari (871–875); the Byzantine fleet blockaded the port, while a land army, under Emperor Louis II, conducted the siege by land (see p. 256).

880–881. Eastern Mediterranean Secured.
Basil's reorganized navy smashed Moslem pirates.

886–912. Reign of Leo VI. Known as "the Wise," he was author of the *Tactica* (see p. 214). He continued Basil's wars against the Moslems in Sicily and South Italy.

889–897. Bulgarian Wars. Despite early success and an alliance with the Magyars, the Byzantines were generally unsuccessful (see p. 260).

912–959. Reign of Constantine VII (Age 7).
Real authority was exercised by his father-in-law, the admiral **Romanus,** at first regent, later coemperor (919–944).

913–924. Renewed Wars with Bulgaria.
Symeon repeatedly threatened Constantinople, temporarily captured Adrianople (914), and gained a major victory at the **Battle of Anchialus** (near Bargas, 917).

915. Battle of the Garigliano. The Byzantines crushed a Moslem threat to their hold on south Italy.

920–942. Northeastern Campaigns of John Kurkuas. This general captured Theodosiopolis (modern Erzerum), east of the upper Euphrates (928) and Melitene (Malatya, 934). He brought Byzantine authority once again to the upper Tigris.

924. Battle of Lemnos. The Byzantine Navy crushed the power of Moslem pirate **Leo** of Tripoli, who had threatened control of the eastern Mediterranean for 20 years.

941. Russian Raid to the Bosporus. Defeated by the Byzantine Navy.

956–963. Eastern Campaigns of Nicephorus Phocas. This general drove Moslem invaders from eastern Anatolia, then raided deep into Syria. He invaded and reconquered Crete (960–961). Following this he invaded Cilicia and Syria, temporarily capturing Aleppo, while his brother, **Leo Phocas,** repelled a Moslem invasion of Anatolia (963; see p. 266).

963–969. Reign of Nicephorus Phocas (Nicephorus II). He was coemperor with the infant sons of **Romanus II** (959–963): **Basil II** and **Constantine.**

964–969. Eastern Conquests. Nicephorus invaded Cilicia, captured **Adana** (964) and **Tarsus** (965), completing the conquest of the province the following year. Meanwhile his general **Nicetas** invaded and conquered **Cyprus** (965). Nicephorus then invaded Upper Mesopotamia and Syria, capturing **Antioch** and **Aleppo,** forcing the Caliphate to sue for peace (969).

966–969. War with Bulgaria. (See p. 260.)

966–967. Failure in Sicily. Nicetas was repulsed by the Fatimid Moslems.

967–969. War against Otto. Making peace with the Fatimids, Nicephorus entered an alliance with them against Otto I, who had been encroaching on Byzantine and Moslem territory in south Italy. Otto reduced both Moslem and Byzantine holdings in south Italy (see p. 258).

969–976. Reign of John Zimisces. He assassinated his uncle, Nicephorus, to become coemperor with Basil and Constantine, and maintained control by suppressing the insurrection of **Bardas Phocas** (971).

969–972. War with Russian Prince Sviatoslav in Bulgaria. John defeated the Russians near Adrianople at the **Battle of Arcadiopolis** (970). While the Byzantine Navy drove the Russian fleet away and blockaded the mouth of the Danube, John pursued Sviatoslav to the Danube, defeated him again in the **Battle of Dorostalon** (971), then invested the Russians on the land and river sides of Dristra with his army and navy. After a siege of two months Sviatoslav was forced to submit and to abandon Bulgaria (972; see p. 264).

973–976. War with the Moslems. John eliminated all Moslem holdings west of the middle Euphrates River, and extended Byzantine control south and east in Syria. After capturing **Damascus,** he advanced as far south as Jerusalem, where he was halted by Fatimid resistance (976). He died before he could resume the offensive.

976–1025. Reign of Basil II. Initially under the regent, **Basil Paracoemomenus,** until Basil seized full power (985).

976–979. Revolt of Bardas Skleros. This was suppressed mainly because of the victory of loyal general Bardas Phocas at the **Battle of Pankalia.**

981. Unsuccessful Invasion of Bulgaria. (See p. 260.)

987–989. Rebellion of Bardas Phocas and Bardas Skleros. The rebels briefly threatened Constantinople (988). Phocas was then defeated by Basil at the **Battle of Abydos** (989). Phocas died shortly thereafter, and the revolt collapsed.

995–996. War in Syria. The Fatimid Caliphate in Egypt began encroaching on Byzantine Syria. In two campaigns Basil brought all Syria under control.

996–1018. War with Bulgaria. (See p. 302.)

MOSLEM DOMINIONS

The Abbasid Caliphate and Syria

The Abbasid Caliphate reached the height of its glory in the first half of the 9th century. But by the end of the period the Abbasids had lost almost all of their temporal power through internal dynastic struggles, constant conflicts between the rival Moslem principalities, and innumerable foreign wars along the northern and eastern frontiers of Islam. They retained considerable religious prestige as the lineal successors of Mohammed—though even this was disputed by rival Caliphates at Cairo and Cordova. The principal events were:

786–809. Reign of Harun al-Rashid. (See p. 233.)

803–809. Renewed Byzantine War. Nicephorus I broke the treaty between al-Rashid and Irene (see p. 233). Al-Rashid led invading armies across the Taurus three times (803, 804, 805–807), defeating Nicephorus in several engagements, of which the most decisive was the **Battle of Crasus** (in Phrygia, west-central Anatolia, 805). While Harun was capturing numerous cities in Anatolia, his fleets ravaged Rhodes and captured Cyprus (805–807). Nicephorus, however, rallied, seized the offensive, and had recovered much lost territory when (808) Harun was forced to go to Khorasan (see below).

806–809. Rebellion in Khorasan. Harun died while leading his armies there.

809–813. Civil War. Between Harun's sons: **al-Amin,** the new caliph, and **al-Ma'mun.** The Khorasanian rebels, led by the general **Tahir ibn Husain,** sided with al-Ma'mun. Tahir defeated al-Amin's troops, marched to Mesopotamia, capturing Baghdad (811), after a siege of nearly two years. Al-Amin was killed while attempting to escape.

813–833. The Reign of Al-Ma'mun. Despite internal discord and revolt (814–819), al-Ma'mun restored relative stability. The remainder of his reign was one of the most splendid of the Abbasid Caliphate.

816–837. Khurramite Revolt. This sect in Azerbaijan, under their leader **Babek,** received considerable Byzantine support; they raided constantly into Persia and Mesopotamia. Babek was finally defeated by Abbasid general **Afshin** (835–837).

821. Autonomy of Khorasan. Under Tahir, who had been appointed governor.

825–826. Conquest of Crete. By Arab refugees expelled from Spain by the Omayyads. It became a Moslem pirate base.

829–833. Byzantine War. Al-Ma'mun repulsed Byzantine invasions of Syria, and in turn led successful expeditions into Anatolia (see p. 263). During this time he also crushed continuing disorders in Egypt (832).

833–842. Reign of Abu Ishak al-Mu'tasim. The last strong Abbasid caliph, he created a new imperial bodyguard composed mainly of Turkish slaves and mercenaries. He suppressed a revolt in southern Mesopotamia (834).

837–842. Renewal of the Byzantine War.

(See p. 263.) Al-Mu'tasim's plan to besiege Constantinople was frustrated by the destruction of his fleet in a storm (839).

842–847. Reign of Harun Al-Wathik. He sent the imperial guard, under Turkish general **Bogha,** to subdue an uprising in Arabia (844–847).

847–861. Reign of Ja-far Al-Mutawakkil. He was usually influenced by the Turkish guards, who eventually murdered him.

851–863. Renewal of the Byzantine War. A Byzantine amphibious force sacked **Damietta** in Egypt (853). The Moslems, augmented by Paulician refugees, gained a great victory over Michael III on the Euphrates in North Syria (860), following which there was a truce and exchange of prisoners. A powerful Moslem army under Abbasid general **Omar** invaded Anatolia (863). After sacking Amisus (Samsun) and ravaging Paphlagonia and Galatia, Omar withdrew eastward toward the Anti-Taurus Mountains, pursued by **Petronas,** uncle of Michael III. Petronas virtually annihilated Omar's army (863).

863–870. Anarchy in the Caliphate. The Turkish guards made and murdered caliphs. Central authority disappeared from the outlying provinces.

870–892. Reign of Ahmad Al-Mu'tamid. The real ruler was his soldier-brother, **Abu Ahmad al-Muwaffak,** who regained control of the Turkish guards and re-established order in Mesopotamia and Iraq (870–883). He also repulsed an attack on Baghdad (876) by the Saffarids of Khorasan (see p. 269). However, he lost most of Syria to the Egyptian Tulunids (see p. 267).

892–902. Reign of Ahmad Al-Mu'tadid. The son of al-Muwaffak, he somewhat strengthened central authority and regained partial control of Egypt, Syria, and Khorasan.

899–903. Carmathian Revolt. This Shi'ite sect was led by **Abu Sa'id al-Jannabi** in the Arabia-Mesopotamia border region south and west of the Euphrates. After overrunning Syria, al-Jannabi withdrew into northeastern Arabia to establish an independent state on the shores of the Persian Gulf. The remaining Carmathians in Syria were defeated by Abbasid general **Mohammed ibn Sulaiman** (901–903).

902–932. Decline of the Caliphate. There were further Carmathian uprisings in Syria and Arabia, including the sacking of **Basra** (923), **Kufa** (925), and **Mecca** (929). The Caliphate survived mainly because of the ability of the general **Mu'nis,** who held the resurgent Byzantines at bay, repulsed early Fatimid attempts to conquer Egypt (915–921; see p. 267), and was able to limit (but not stop) the depredations of the Carmathians.

c. 929. Rise of the Hamdanid Dynasty. Autonomous princes in northeastern Syria and Kurdistan.

932–946. Impotence of the Caliphate. Mu'nis was executed by the ungrateful Caliph **al-Kahir** (932–934). The Buyid dynasty of Persia (see p. 269) captured Baghdad (946). Succeeding caliphs were merely Buyid puppets.

936–944. Anarchy in Syria. Control was seized by an adventurer, **Ibn Raik,** who repulsed feeble Abbasid attempts to reconquer the country. In the drawn **Battle of Lojun,** he also repulsed **Ibn Tughj,** Ikhshid ruler) of Egypt (see p. 267), who attempted to conquer Syria. After the death of Ibn Raik, the Ikhshidites quickly overran Syria (941). The Hamdanid prince, **Saif al-Dawla,** entered the struggle and captured **Aleppo** and much of northern Syria from the Ikhshidites (944).

945–948. Byzantine - Hamdanid - Ikhshidite Struggle for Syria. At first Saif al-Dawla defeated Ikhshid general **Kafur,** but then had to deal with Byzantine inroads. Kafur then regained southern and central Syria. Al-Dawla, retaining northern Syria, held the Byzantines at bay by skillful defensive tactics and counterraids into Anatolia.

956–969. Campaigns of Nicephorus Phocas in Syria. (See p. 264.)

963. Hamdanid Invasion of Anatolia. Saif al-Dawla was defeated by **Leo Phocas,** brother of Nicephorus, in the **Battle of Maghar-Alcohl,** a pass in the Anti-Taurus Mountains of Charisiana, near the headwaters of the Halys River.

969. Battle of Ramleh. Fatimid general **Ja'far** defeated the Ikhshidite forces in Syria and Palestine between Jerusalem and Jaffa.

970–971. Carmathian Invasions of Palestine and Egypt. After defeating and killing Ja'far (970), they were repulsed from Fatimid Egypt by **Jauhar** (see p. 267).

974–975. Renewed Carmathian Invasions

They were repulsed from Egypt by Fatimid Caliph **Mu'izz** (see below), who then drove them out of Palestine and Syria.

974–977. Turmoil in Syria. This was largely stirred up by Byzantine intrigue and invasions. Hamdanid general **Aftakin** (a Turk), in alliance with the Carmathians, drove the Fatimids under Jauhar from central and southern Syria (976). Rein-

forced from Egypt, Jauhar and Fatimid Caliph **Aziz Billah** defeated Aftakin and the Carmathians at another **Battle of Ramleh** (977). Aziz, however, was unable to recover all of the lost territory since the Byzantines and Hamdanids had moved in.

980–1000. Fatimid-Byzantine Struggle for Syria. (See p. 265.)

NORTH AFRICA

Egypt and Cyrenaica

Eastern North Africa was the scene of almost constant war and revolt until the last quarter of the 10th century. Intermittently and sporadically Egypt was under the direct control of the Abbasid caliphs at Baghdad. More frequently, it was ruled by independent princes, only nominally vassals of the caliph. Most important among these were the Tulinids, during the latter 9th century, and the Ikhshidite dynasty, during the middle of the 10th. The Ikhshidites were then overthrown by the Fatimids from Tunisia (see below). By the end of the 10th century the Fatimid caliphs, who had moved their capital to Cairo, controlled all of North Africa and much of Arabia, and were engaged in a struggle for Syria. The principal events were:

817–827. Piratical Refugees from Spain Occupy Alexandria. Recaptured for the Abbasids by general **Abdullah ibn Tahir** (827).

828–832. Uprising of Arabs and Christian Copts in Egypt. Cruelly suppressed by Caliph al-Ma'mun after his general Afshin defeated the rebels at the **Battle of Basharud** in the Nile Delta.

868–876. Rise of the Tulunid Dynasty. **Ahmed ibn Tulun,** Turkish governor of Egypt, became virtually independent. He later conquered most of Syria (878–884; see p. 266).

904–905. Abbasid Authority Re-established. Abbasid general **Mohammed ibn Sulaiman** defeated and overthrew the Tulinids in a combined land and sea invasion of Egypt.

914–915. Fatimid Invasion of Egypt. Abu'l Kasim al-Kaim (son of 'Obaidallah; see p. 268) briefly occupied Alexandria, but was repulsed by Abbasid general Mu'nis.

919–921. Second Fatimid Invasion of Egypt. Al-Kaim again occupied Alexandria, but once more Mu'nis repulsed the Fatimids, on sea as well as on land.

922–935. Chaos in Egypt. Finally ended by Abbasid general **Mohammed ibn Tughj,** appointed by the Caliph to be semi-inde-

pendent governor with title of **Ikhshid** (ruler), beginning the Ikhshidite Dynasty (935), which controlled Egypt for 30 years.

969. Fatimid Conquest of Egypt. The general Jauhur conquered Egypt and overthrew the Ikhshidites at the **Battle of Gizeh,** then sent part of his army to Syria to defeat Ikhshidite forces there (see p. 266).

970–971. Carmathian Invasions. (See p. 266.) Jauhur, on the verge of disaster, rallied and defeated the invaders at the **Battle of Cairo** (971). He then continued construction of the new city of Cairo (meaning "Victory") near the site of ancient Memphis. This became the capital of his master, Fatimid Caliph **Mu'izz li-Din allah** (973).

974–975. Renewed Carmathian Invasion. Fatimid Caliph Mu'izz was briefly besieged in Cairo, but rallied to crush the invaders, then reconquered Syria. This was the height of the power of the Fatimid Caliphate, which was recognized in all North Africa, Syria, western Arabia, and much of the western Mediterranean.

982. Byzantine Invasion of Sicily. Repulsed by the Fatimids.

Tunisia, Tripolitania, Eastern Algeria

At the outset of the 9th century, central north Africa came under the contro of the vigorous Aghlabid family, who devoted most of their attention to invasion of Sicily and south Italy, and to extensive piratical raids of western Mediterranean islands and coasts. Shortly after the beginning of the 10th century the Aghlabid were overthrown by 'Obaidallah al-Mahdi, who claimed descent from the union o Fatima, daughter of Mohammed, and the controversial Caliph Ali (see p. 231) 'Obaidallah founded the Shi'ite Fatimid Dynasty. He and his successors continue Moslem incursions into Southern Europe. The important events were:

801. Rise of Aghlabid Dynasty. Ibrahim ibn Aghlab, Abbasid governor of Africa, established a virtually independent emirate at Kairouan (Tunisia).

827–831. Aghlabid Invasion of Sicily. The Byzantines were driven from all of the island except Syracuse and Taormina.

836–909. Aghlabid Intrusions in Southern and Central Italy. Extensive areas were seized. Part of Rome was sacked (846; see p. 256).

878. Aghlabid Capture of Syracuse.

902. Aghlabid Capture of Taormina. This ended the last Byzantine foothold in Sicily.

902–909. Revolt of Fatimid Shi'ites. Ab Abdullah al-Husain (known as al-Shi'i) overthrew the Aghlabids. 'Obaidallah a Mahdi was declared Caliph, to establis the Fatimid Dynasty at Kairouan.

934. Fatimid Capture of Genoa. A Mosler fleet seized and sacked the city.

934–947. Kharijite Rebellion. A religiou sect under Abu Yazid Makhlad was finall overcome by Fatimid Caliph al-Mansur.

965. Byzantine Recapture of Taormina.

975. Fatimid Conquest of Egypt. (Se above.)

Morocco and Western Algeria

In the extreme northwest of Africa, Idris ibn Abdulla, a descendant of Moham med, had established an independent emirate late in the 8th century, and his suc cessors reigned for most of the two following centuries, rarely acknowledging eve the nominal sovereignty of the Caliphs of Baghdad. During the 10th century, how ever, the Idrisids were forced to submit first to the Fatimids, then to the Omayyads o Spain, then again to the Fatimids, before finally succumbing to a native Berber tribe The principal events were:

c. 800–922. Idrisid Independence. Morocco and Western Algeria were controlled by the Arab-Berber dynasty.

922. Fatimid Conquest of Morocco. 'Obaidallah defeated the Idrisids, who accepted Fatimid suzerainty.

973. Omayyad Conquest of Morocco. By

Caliph al-Hakam II of Spain (see 259). The Fatimids temporarily regaine control two years later (975).

975–1000. Turmoil in Morocco. Authorit and control were disputed between Omay yads of Spain, the Fatimids, the decayin Idrisids, and various Berber factions.

PERSIA AND SOUTH-CENTRAL ASIA, 821–1000

When Abbasid Caliph al-Ma'mun appointed Tahir as viceroy of Khorasan an the eastern provinces early in the 9th century (see p. 265), Persia became virtuall independent. The Tahirid Dynasty retained control of most of Persia and much o Transoxiana for more than half a century, but minorities refused to acknowledg either the authority of the Caliph or of the Tahirids; principal among these was heretical Shi'ite community in the region around Dailam in the Elburz Mountains.

Shortly after the middle of the century a revolt broke out among the frontier warriors of Seistan (southwestern Afghanistan and Baluchistan). Known as the Saffarids, they were led by **Yakub ibn Laith.** They soon conquered most of Persia and Khorasan from the Tahirids, and even made a vain attempt to capture Baghdad. Meanwhile the Persian Samanid family had long reigned as governors of Transoxiana under the caliphs and the Tahirids. In the inevitable clash between Saffarids and Samanids, at the beginning of the 10th century, Samanid leader **Isma'il** was successful. The Samanids held Transoxiana and most of eastern Persia until the end of the century.

Western expansion of the Samanids was blocked by the Shi'ites of Dailam. During the third decade of the 10th century, under the leadership of **Merdawj ibn Ziyar,** these Shi'ites had just begun to expand southward into the plains of Persia when three brothers of the Buyid family suddenly seized power in Dailam. The Ziyarids were forced back into the Caucasus Mountains. The Buyid Shi'ites spread over southwestern Persia and shortly before the middle of the century they occupied Baghdad (see p. 266).

Late in the 10th century, Samanid control over Transoxiana and eastern Persia was challenged by the rising Turkish Ghaznevids (of modern Afghanistan) and by the Ilak Turks, pressing down from central Asia. By the end of the century the Ghaznevids had occupied much of Khorasan. At the same time the Ilak khans had begun to move into Transoxiana. The principal events were:

821. Tahir Appointed Viceroy of Khorasan and the East.

c. 860. Growing Importance of Dailam. It became the Persian center of Shi'ism.

866–900. Rise of the Saffarids. Under **Yakub ibn Laith,** who overthrew the Tahirids (872).

876. Saffarid Attempt to Capture Baghdad. Repulsed by al-Muwaffak (see p. 266).

903. Overthrow of the Saffarids. Samanid leader **Isma'il** defeated **Amron ibn Laith,** brother and successor of Yakub.

c. 925. Shi'ite Expansion. From Dailam, under the Ziyarids.

932. Emergence of the Buyid Dynasty of Dailam. The brothers **Imad al-Dawla, Rukn al-Dawla,** and **Mu'izz al-Dawla** succeeded to Shi'ite leadership, driving the Ziyarids into the Caucasus.

946. Conquest of Baghdad. Buyid Mu'izz al-Dawla captured Baghdad and the caliph, who became a Buyid puppet.

c. 962. Beginning of Ghaznevid Dynasty. Turkish slave **Alptagin,** fleeing from the Samanid court at Bokhara, established a semi-independent state in the mountains of Ghazni.

977–997. Reign of Sabuktagin of Ghazni. The son-in-law of Alptagin, he gained control of much of Khorasan, and began to expand into Northern India (see p. 270).

c. 990–999. The Ilak Turks Conquer Transoxiana. The Samanids were expelled.

1000. Mahmud of Ghazni Conquers Khorasan from the Samanids. He left control of the frontier north of the Oxus to a vassal Turkish tribe under the leadership of **Seljuk** (see pp. 310 and 321).

SOUTH ASIA

NORTH INDIA

During the 9th century there was a drawn-out but fierce three-way struggle between the Pratihara (or Gurjara) dynasty of Rajputana, Pala of Bengal, and the Rashtrakuta kings from the Deccan. Rashtrakuta, under their king **Govinda III,** drove Pratihara from the Malwa plateau and southwestern Ganges Valley, while the

Pratihara King **Nagabhata II** was ejecting Pala from the recently conquered province of Kanauj. Pratihara then moved the capital to the city of Kanauj from whence, by the end of the century, the dynasty gradually gained ascendancy in north India under Kings **Bhoja I** and **Mahendrapala.** They pressed Rashtrakuta back from the Ganges Valley, and drove Pala back into native Bengal. In the early years of the 10th century, Pratihara held all of north India save for Moslem Sind, Pala Bengal, and a Kashmiri foothold in the northern Punjab. The unsuccessful Pratihara attempts to eject the Kashmiris, combined with persistent Rashtrakuta attacks from the south, contributed to a rapid decline in Pratihara power. By the middle of the 10th century, north India reverted to its usual condition as a cockpit of war between minor dynasties. Rashtrakuta, whose unremitting efforts had created this situation, was unable to take advantage of it because of interference from two resurgent powers in the south (see below).

But a new force was ready to exploit the near anarchy existing in the Indus and Ganges valleys. Early in the 10th century the Turks from Central Asia, like so many nomads before them, had begun to move into modern Afghanistan. This became the Moslem emirate of Ghazni, feudatory to the Samanids of Bokhara (see p. 269). The Ghazni Emir **Sabuktagin** began to raid into the northern Punjab late in the century. Finding relatively slight resistance, he seized Peshawar, in a repetition of the old familiar pattern of invasion of India. The principal events were:

790–815. Reign of Govinda III of Rashtrakuta. (See p. 235.)

800–840. Reign of Nagabhata II of Pratihara. He conquered Kanauj from Pala (c. 830).

890–910. Reign of Mahendrapala of Pratihara. Pratihara became predominant in North India.

c. 916. Temporary Occupation of Kanauj by Rashtrakuta.

c. 962. Establishment of Ghazni by Alptagin. (See p. 269.)

977–997. Reign of Sabuktagin of Ghazni. He began expansion into India by the seizure of Peshawar (c. 990).

SOUTH INDIA

After the collapse of the Chalukya Dynasty in the middle of the 8th century, its old rival, Pallava, recovered some of its former power on the east coast of the Deccan. During most of the 9th century resurgent Pallava engaged in more or less constant warfare with its immediate neighbors: to the north the offshoot Chalukya Dynasty of Vengi and the Ganga Dynasty of Kalinga; to the south Chola and Pandya. During most of this time Pallava was favored by the benevolent neutrality —or outright assistance—of more powerful Rashtrakuta.

Farther south, by the middle of the 9th century, Chola under King Vijayala (836–870) had become the dominant Tamil state, ruling over the Coromandel coast and much of the Eastern Deccan. Late in the century, in alliance with Chalukya of Vengi, Chola King Aditya I (c. 870–906) defeated and annexed the Pallava kingdom of Kanchi (Conjeeveram, 888). Early in the 10th century, Aditya's son, **Parantaka I** (906–953), extended Chola control southward to Cape Comorin, at the expense of the Pandya kings of Madura. But growing Chola power now attracted the jealous attention of **Krishna III** (939–968) of Rashtrakuta, who consequently shifted his interest from north to south India. In a series of campaigns around the middle of the century, Rashtrakuta overwhelmed Chola. King Parantaka was killed in battle (953).

Rashtrakuta's old enemy, the Chalukya—which had continued to exist as a minor vassal principality—suddenly rose under **Taila II** (973–995), overthrowing and completely destroying the Rashtrakuta Dynasty (973). Taila and his successors are known as the Later Chalukya Dynasty, or as Chalukya of Kalyani.

The disappearance of Rashtrakuta permitted Chola to re-establish itself as a major power of southern India under **Rajaraja I** (985–1014). This led to a struggle between resurgent Chola and resurgent Chalukya. Though Chola had somewhat the best of these conflicts, Rajaraja was unable to conquer Chalukya. However, he did conquer Pandya, Kerala (or Chera), Vengi, and Kalinga on the mainland, while overseas his fleets and armies annexed Ceylon and the Maldive Islands.

SOUTHEAST ASIA (to A.D. 1000)

BACKGROUND OF MILITARY HISTORY OF SOUTHEAST ASIA

The early history of Southeast Asia is vague and spotty, the origins of its people indefinite. The entire region has from the earliest recorded times been strongly influenced by its two powerful neighboring civilizations, India and China.

Chinese mercantile and military contacts came earliest, particularly along the east coast. But Indian cultural influence began to affect the region beginning about the 1st century A.D., becoming significant about the 5th century. This Indian influence was expressed in literature, art and architecture, court ceremonials, religions and other customs, and is particularly noticeable in the names and titles of rulers and military leaders.

CHAMPA AND VIETNAM

The area of Tonkin and northern Annam had been strongly influenced by China as early as the 9th century B.C. The people were of mixed Mongoloid-Indonesian stock. Late in the 3rd century B.C. the area was conquered by Chinese general **Chao T'o** and combined by him in a rebellious regime he established in South China (c. 208) at the time of the fall of the Ch'in Dynasty (see p. 80). The name Nam-viet, which was at first applied to Chao T'o's entire Canton kingdom, soon was limited to the Tonkin and northern Annam provinces. When the Canton kingdom was overthrown and reannexed by the powerful Han emperor, Wu Ti (111 B.C.), he also annexed the provinces of Nam-viet, which remained under Chinese rule until A.D. 939.

Sometime after the Chinese conquest of Nam-viet, in southern Annam, south of modern Hué, an Indonesian people, known to history as the Chams, had established an independent kingdom (c. A.D. 200). In due course the Chams adopted a form of Indian culture. Military contacts with China were sporadic, the semibarbaric Chams raiding by land and sea into the civilized area to the north, and being subjected to occasional Chinese punitive expeditions.

During the 5th and early 6th centuries, a period of weakness and anarchy in China, the Chams made numerous raids into Nam-viet. One of the leading Cham warriors and rulers who conducted such expeditions was King **Bhadravarman** (c. 400). A Chinese naval punitive expedition against Champa was repulsed (431). At this time the Cham King **Yang Mah** unsuccessfully sought the aid of Funan (see below) in a major expedition into Tonkin. An overland Chinese punitive expedition some years later led by **T'an Ho-ch'u,** governor of Tonkin, was successful and sacked the Cham capital (446). This apparently greatly reduced Cham interest in raiding into Nam-viet. About a century later, however, Cham King **Rudravarman** sought to take advantage of local disorders in Nam-viet (now also known as Vietnam) and led an unsuccessful raiding expedition to the north.

Under the leadership of **Li-Bon,** the Vietnamese rebelled and temporarily expelled the Chinese (541). Li-Bon then repulsed a raiding expedition from Champa (543) under King Rudravarman (see above). The Chinese soon defeated Li-Bon and suppressed the revolt (547). Internal weaknesses in China encouraged Vietnamese patriots to rise and again temporarily throw off the Chinese yoke. The Su Emperor **Yang Chien,** however, soon sent forces which re-established Chinese control over the rebellious provinces of Tonkin and Annam. Farther south the independent Chams remained relatively peaceful, having been severely punished (605) by an aggressively conducted Chinese expedition under General Liu Fang (see p. 239). During the latter half of the 8th century the coasts of Champa and of Chinese Vietnam were constantly harassed by Indonesian raiders—probably mostly from Srivijaya.

In the early years of the 9th century, King **Harivarman I** renewed Cham harassment of Chinese Annam, and apparently also did some raiding against the Khmer Kingdom of Cambodia. But from the middle of that century until the middle of the next (when King **Indravarman III** repulsed a Khmer invasion; see p. 273) Champa was relatively peaceful. Chinese Vietnam, meanwhile, had sustained an invasion by Nanchao (862–863; see p. 274). Some time after this the Annamese took advantage of the chaos in China after the fall of the T'ang Dynasty (907; see p. 275) to begin a struggle for independence that was finally successful (939).

The latter years of the 10th century saw almost incessant war between Champa and newly independent Annam. The conflict was begun by an invasion of Annam by Cham King **Paramesvaravarman** (979). He was repulsed, and the Annamese King **Le Hoan** led a destructive raid into Champa that resulted in the sacking of the Cham capital and the death of the Cham king (982). At this time a revolt in Annam created chaos in that country from which a new dynasty, founded by King **Harivarman II,** emerged (989). The war between Champa and Annam was soon renewed and continued far into the next century (p. 324).

FUNAN AND CHENLA (CAMBODIA)

During the 1st and 2nd centuries A.D. an Indonesian people in the lower Mekong Valley coalesced into a Kingdom of Funan. The first ruler of importance was a conqueror known as **Fan Shih-man,** who extended his domains to the sea in modern Cochin-China, and who apparently also controlled all of modern Cambodia and possibly much of modern Thailand (c. 200). The Kingdom of Funan prospered continued to grow, and had extensive contacts with both China and India. One of its most illustrious early rulers was **Chandan,** who may have been an exile from India, of Hindu-Kushan descent (c. 350).

Under King **Jayavarman** (c. 480–514), the Empire of Funan reached its greatest extent and the height of its prosperity. It is possible that military expedition from Funan actually reached and conquered parts of the lower Irrawaddy Valley. During the reign of **Rudravarman,** an uprising (apparently starting as a dynastic dispute) broke out in the province of Chenla (northern Cambodia, along the middle Mekong from the Mun River to Bassak), led by the brothers **Bhavavarman** and **Chitrasena** (c. 550). Rudravarman was deposed and driven into southern Cambodia where a remnant of the Funan Kingdom continued to exist for a few more decades

Bhavavarman assumed the throne of Chenla and, with the help of his warrior brother, absorbed much of the former Funan Empire (c. 550–c. 600).

After the death of Bhavavarman his brother, Chitrasena, took the throne with the royal name of **Mahendravarman** (c. 600–c. 611). The great conqueror was followed by his son, **Isanavarman I** (c. 611–635), who completed the conquest of Funan (c. 627), and who extended the boundaries of Chenla steadily westward to include most of modern Cambodia. This expansion was continued under **Jayavarman I** (c. 655–695), who overran southern and central Laos to establish a common frontier with Nanchao. Apparently Chenla became overextended during this reign, since there was much unrest, and the empire was crumbling at Jayavarman's death. A few years later (c. 706) Chenla broke apart into regions known as Upper and Lower Chenla. We know little of what happened in Upper Chenla, save for some fighting against the Chinese in Tonkin. Lower Chenla apparently was in turmoil during the remainder of the period. This was intensified in the latter half of the 8th century by frequent raids from the Indonesian islands of Sumatra and (possibly) Java. For part of the time Lower Chenla was apparently tributary to the Sumatran Kingdom of Srivijaya (see below).

During the first half of the 9th century the Khmer Kingdom of Lower Chenla revived under **Jayavarman II** (802–850). Throwing off Indonesian suzerainty (see below), he in effect was the founder of the magnificent Angkor monarchy. The actual construction of the temples and palaces of Angkor was begun under his successor, **Indravarman I** (877–889). The Angkor Kingdom expanded steadily, and reached its first peak under King **Yasovarman** (889–900), who ruled an empire which probably included Cambodia, Southwestern Vietnam, most of Laos and Thailand, and Southern Burma. There was a decline in the Khmer Kingdom under the usurper **Jayavarman IV** (928–942) and his son, **Harshavarman II** (942–944), who moved the capital from Angkor. Harshavarman was overthrown by a revolt which placed **Ravendravarman II** on the throne, and which brought the capital back to Angkor. Though Ravendravarman was repulsed in an attack on Champa (945–946), the fortunes of the Khmer Kingdom again rose under him and his successors.

MALAYSIA (INDONESIA AND MALAYA)

In the 2nd and 1st centuries B.C. the islands of Indonesia and the Malay Peninsula had some contacts with Chinese seafarers and traders. However, Indian influence became more significant in the early centuries of the Christian era. By the beginning of the 5th century there were a number of independent, relatively civilized principalities, Hindu in nature, on the peninsula as well as in the neighboring large islands. The records are very sketchy. It is clear, however, that by the end of the 7th century the powerful Kingdom of Srivijaya had grown up in southern Sumatra, with its capital at Palembang. This kingdom conquered at least the western portion of Java, and raided frequently along the mainland coasts to the north, exacting tribute. Srivijaya dominated Western Indonesia and the South China Sea for several centuries.

Though the power of Srivijaya appears to have declined somewhat by the early 9th century, it retained its ascendancy in Indonesia throughout this period. Its position in Java was challenged by the states of Sailendra and Sanjaya, which in turn were engaged in a bitter struggle for supremacy in central Java. This was won by Sanjaya after a final clash around the Sailendra fortified stronghold on the Ratubaka Plain (856). **Balaputra,** the last Sailendra to rule in Java, married a Srivijayan princess and eventually succeeded to the throne. Since Balaputra brought with him his claim to Central Java, Srivijayan pressure apparently caused the removal of the Sanjaya capital to East Java (early 10th century). Javanese tradition has it that during subsequent warfare, **Dharmauamsa** (c. 958–c. 1000), King of East Java, attacked Sumatra but was repelled by Srivijaya, which counterattacked (1016–1017) and destroyed the East Javanese capital.

THE THAIS AND SHANS

The early inhabitants of the lower Menam River Valley of modern Thailand were the Mons, whose principalities also controlled Lower Burma. By the 8th century, extensive migrations from the northwest had brought a Mongoloid people related to the Chinese, into the mountainous region between the upper Salween and Mekong Rivers in modern Yunnan. These people, known as the Nanchao, were the ancestors of the modern Shans (of Burma), Thais, and Laotians. For several centuries, however, the history of Nanchao was inextricably bound with that of China

Late in the 8th century a powerful independent Nanchao Kingdom was established by **Kolofeng** in Yunnan, Laos, and northeast Burma (see p. 241). Nanchao prospered and expanded under his grandson and successor, **I-mou-hsun**, early in the 9th century. Central and southern Burma were overrun (832) and the Pyu Kingdom destroyed (see below). The Nanchao then invaded south China and Tonkin (858–863), and sacked Hanoi (863). They were finally repelled from Tonkin by Chinese General **Kao P'ien**. Turning to the northwest, they invaded Szechuan and laid siege to the Chinese city of Ch'engtu, where once again they were repulsed by Kao P'ien (874). A long period of relative peace seems to have followed, though Tai mercenary contingents played an active part in other wars in Southeast Asia Late in the 10th century the Chinese Sungs made tentative attempts to reconquer Yunnan, but evidently gave it up in the face of determined Nanchao resistance. (All during this period the Thai, or Shan, people seem to have been slowly shifting southward through Yunnan into the regions they had conquered in eastern Burma, northern Siam, and Laos.)

BURMA

As early as the 2nd century B.C., Chinese traders were using an overland route from the area of modern Yunnan, through Upper Burma, and into India through Assam. Despite the ferocity of wild tribes in this region, the route was apparently used extensively for about 500 years, and was traversed by embassies between China and India, as well as by embassies from Rome and Constantinople to the courts of China. Apparently the use of this route was discontinued for several centuries, some time around the middle of the 4th century A.D. Meanwhile in the south, in the Irrawaddy Valley, a people known as Pyus had established a civilized society strongly influenced by Hindu culture.

By the beginning of the 9th century the Kingdom of Nanchao held the northern portion of what is modern Burma (see above), while a Pyu kingdom (evidently subject to Nanchao) flourished in central Burma, with its capital at Srikshetra (Hmawza, near Prome). Southern Burma and central Thailand contained a number of small states inhabited by the Mon (Talaing) people. The principal center of Mon culture was in Siam, where their Buddhist Kingdom of Dvaravati flourished from the 6th century onward. Nanchao armies destroyed the Pyu Kingdom, and two of the Mon principalities in Lower Burma also fell. However, the Mons were finally able to repulse the invaders (935). Some time after this, the Mons appear to have

xpanded northward into the remnants of the old Pyu Kingdom and, in collabora-
ion with Pyu refugees, established a new capital for Central Burma at Pagan (c.
)50).

Meanwhile, shortly after the middle of the 9th century a new people, related
o the Pyus, had begun to migrate into central Burma around the region of Kyaukse,
vhere Mons and Pyus had established a highly developed irrigation system. These
iew people were evidently an offshoot of the old Ch'iang Tibetan tribes (see p. 133)
.nd over a period of centuries had moved slowly, under pressure from Chinese and
Nanchao, from Kansu to eastern Tibet, to western Yunnan, to central Burma. These
varlike invaders, ancestors of the modern Burmans, began to drive the Mons south-
vard. Spreading out over the central Irrawaddy Valley, by the end of the 10th cen-
ury they firmly held the region from Shwebo south to Prome.

EAST AND CENTRAL ASIA

CHINA

The T'ang Dynasty gradually declined in the 9th century. As central authority
:ssened, the power of semiautonomous war lords increased. During much of this
.me the T'ang were engaged in inconclusive war with their nominal vassals, the
Nanchao kings of Yunnan. During the growing lawlessness of the latter part of the
entury, a popular leader named **Huang Ch'ao** set himself up as a sort of Robin
lood, taking goods of the wealthy and of government officials to distribute to starv-
ig peasants. As Huang's strength grew, so did his ambition; he started a revolt,
onquered much of the country, and declared himself emperor. Eventually, however,
ie T'ang defeated him, and he committed suicide. This prolonged civil war ex-
austed the country and accelerated the T'ang decline.

Early in the 10th century the T'ang Dynasty was overthrown by a war lord,
nd there followed a period of anarchy called the Era of Five Dynasties. Toward
ie end of the century, however, most of the country was reunited under a general
f one of these dynasties—**Chao K'uang-yin**—who inaugurated the stable Sung Dy-
asty. He reduced the power of the war lords, centralizing military control. The
orthern areas of China had been absorbed by barbarians, however, and resisted
:hao's unification efforts. These regions included the best horse-breeding and graz-
ig grounds of the Far East, thus embarrassing Chao and later Sung emperors, who
ere unable to create worthwhile cavalry. This contributed largely to the fact that
ie Sung were constantly on the defensive against the barbarians of the north for
vo and a half centuries. The most important events were:

29–874. **Intermittent War between the T'ang and Nanchao.** The T'ang repulsed three major Nanchao invasions against Ch'engtu (829 and 874) and Hanoi (863).

18. **Reconquest of Kansu.** The Tibetans—who had gradually worked their way back into Kansu—were driven out by T'ang forces.

'5–884. **Revolt of Huang Ch'ao.** He conquered the capital cities (Loyang and Ch'ang-an) and declared himself emperor (880). T'ang Emperor **Hsi Tsung** fled to the southwest and raised a new army, which he put under the command of General **Li K'o-yung** (of Turkish stock). Li defeated Huang (882), who fled and later committed suicide (884).

907. **End of the T'ang.** General **Chu Wen** seized control of China, murdering the last T'ang emperor.

907–959. **The Era of Five Dynasties.** An

anarchic period during which five successive families sought to maintain imperial authority.

960–976. Establishment of Sung Dynasty. **Chao K'uang-yin** (general of the Later Chou Dynasty) established the Sung Dynasty, after being declared emperor by his soldiers, taking the name **T'ai Tsung.**

976–997. Reign of T'ai Tsung. He completed the reunion of China (essentially modern China proper), less Kansu, Inner Mongolia, and northeast China.

979–1004. War with the Khitans. T'ai Tsung was repulsed in efforts to capture Peking (986). The Khitans then began a slow advance into north China.

INNER ASIA

Toward the middle of the 9th century the Uighur Turk Empire was overthrown by the Kirghiz and Karluk Turks—apparently with some assistance from the Chinese T'ang, who had been frequently embarrassed by the power of their nominal vassals and allies (see p. 240). The Uighurs migrated southward into the Tarim Basin, where they established a new kingdom and eliminated the last remaining traces of earlier Indo-European influence (c. 846). Early in the 10th century, however, they were forced to submit to the khans of the Ilak Turks, who began to dominate Central Asia.

Early in the 10th century, **Ye-lu A-pao-chi,** chieftain of the Khitan Mongol people of eastern Mongolia, conquered all of Inner Mongolia, southern Manchuria, and much of north China (907–926). He received tribute from the Uighurs of Sinkiang. His successor, **Ye-lu Te-kuang** (927–947), strengthened the Khitan Empire, which he designated as the Liao Dynasty. Playing an important role in Chinese affairs during the anarchic Five Dynasties period, Te-kuang helped to establish the Later Chin Dynasty (936), only to overthrow it later (946).

Meanwhile the Tangut tribe—a Tibetan people—again established themselves in Kansu (c. 990), where they created the Western Hsia Kingdom, with Ninghsia as their capital. They were almost constantly at war with Uighurs, Khitans, and Chinese.

KOREA

Most of the 9th century in Korea was peaceful. Silla, under strong influence from the Chinese T'ang, was prosperous; the country became homogeneous. Toward the end of the century, however, there were several revolts. Early in the 10th century the general **Wanggun** rebelled to establish the new Kingdom of Koryo in West-Central Korea, with the capital at Kaesong (918). Soon after this the last king of Silla abdicated, and the Wang Dynasty of Koryo peacefully absorbed Silla. Paekche, however, attempted to re-establish its independence (935). The Wang immediately invaded Paekche, destroying it and annexing it to a reunified Korea (936).

Earlier, when the T'ang Dynasty of China had collapsed (907), the kings of Silla had voluntarily submitted to the nominal suzerainty of the Khitan Mongols of North China and Manchuria (see above). The Wang Dynasty, however, ignored this Khitan suzerainty and established an alliance with the Sung emperors (c. 960). The Khitan Liao Dynasty resented this and late in the century forced the Wang to renounce their alliance with the Sung (985), and to submit once more to Khitan suzerainty (996).

JAPAN

Aside from sporadic warfare with the Ainu in the north and some inroads by Korean pirates (c. 869), the 9th century was generally peaceful in Japan. The period aw two developments of great significance to the future history of the country. The irst was the growing power and influence of the Fujiwara clan, which gained virtual control over the country by its complete domination of the imperial family; **Fujiwara Yoshifusa** was the first to achieve this power (858) and soon thereafter he took the itle of regent.

The second development was the trend toward feudalism. This was the result of the growing professionalism of the retainers of the great nobles—partly due to the military reforms of **Sakanoue Tamuramaro** (see p. 242), and partly to the accumulation of wealth and power by the nobles in a prospering nation. This trend to feudalism obviously had something in common with the feudal trend in Europe, but had one unique aspect. This was the appearance of two warrior leagues, each affiliated with a great family of imperial origins: the Taira and Minamato. Evidently, in addition to their fealty to their own feudal lords, all Japanese warriors affiliated themselves with one or the other of these warrior clans. There seems to have been no particular system or pattern of such relationships.

Though there was some growing internal unrest, stimulated partly by clan rivalries, the 10th century was almost as peaceful as the 9th—save for one short period of intense civil strife (935–941). The warrior leagues were involved in this, but not in a formal or unified way. One of the most serious uprisings was led by **Taira Masakado** (of the warrior league family) in eastern Japan, and was finally suppressed 940). Another, led by **Fujiwara Sumitomo** (of the ruling clan) established piratical control over the Inland Sea, but was crushed with the assistance of the Taira League 941).

X

THE RETURN OF SKILL
TO WARFARE: 1000–1200

MILITARY TRENDS

Savage strife continued to rock all corners of the so-called civilized world, but political aims—some vague, others more definite—were emerging. At the same time there was a noticeable rise in the level of military skill, particularly in Western Europe and among the Moslem Turks.

Although no true military genius emerged during this period, there were a few outstanding soldiers: **Mahmud** of Ghazni; **Richard the Lionhearted** of England; **Alexius** of Byzantium; the Seljuk Turk, **Alp Arslan; Saladin** of Egypt and Syria; and the Sicilian Norman, **Robert Guiscard.** All six demonstrated characteristics of leadership higher than heretofore seen outside the Byzantine Empire, and all six played a part in one or more of the four major historical developments of this period.

The first of these was a continuation of an earlier trend: the westward progression of the Turks north and south of the Black and Caspian seas. The northern current—that of the Pechenegs and Cumans—would be halted, after a bitter struggle, by the combined forces of the Byzantine Empire and its Slavic neighbors. But the southern surge—probably because of the interaction of Turkish vigor and Moslem fanaticism—was more significant. It swept away most of Byzantium's Asian holdings, pervaded the entire Middle East, and, although checked by the Crusades, was continuing as the period ended.

The second trend was in part contributory to, and in part a result of, the first. This was the decline of the Byzantine Empire. Despite erosion of energy and of military competence, Constantinople was still unsurpassed in theoretical mastery of the art of war, and this, together with amazing resiliency, would prolong the life of the empire for several more centuries. However, as the Battle of Adrianople had clearly foreshadowed the fall of Rome, so the Battle of Manzikert sounded the knell for Byzantium.

The third trend was the growing centralization of power in the kingdoms of Europe. Despite the inhibiting effects of the still flourishing feudal system, a kind of nationalistic coagulation was in process. This was particularly true in England and France; less so in Germany, Spain, and Poland.

The fourth and most momentous of these trends, from the standpoint of military, religious, and cultural history, was that of the Crusades.

WEAPONS AND ARMOR

One important new weapon appeared: the crossbow. This was literally a hand ballista, somewhat more clumsy and with a slower rate of fire than the traditional bows of military history. But the metal bolts or arrows fired from these machines flew farther, faster, and generally more accurately than the lighter arrows of conventional archers. Most important, they could penetrate armor impervious to other missiles. Apparently the Chinese and the Romans had experimented with hand ballistae, but the concept was forgotten in the West after the fall of Rome. It was revived, however, in the 11th century; crossbows made their first unmistakable appearance in action in Europe with the Norman Army at the Battle of Hastings.

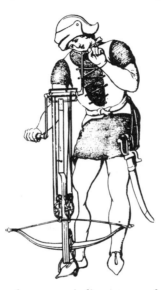

Crossbowman winding up crossbow

The crossbow was the West European answer to Turkish horse archery. Usually European crossbowmen were on foot. The Crusaders experimented with mounted crossbowmen, but discovered that the added mobility was more than offset by the decrease in accuracy and in rate of fire. Interestingly, the Chams of Southeast Asia apparently used mounted crossbowmen about this same time (see p. 324).

Another new weapon in Western Europe was the infantry halberd. This modified the pike by the addition of an axhead near the point to permit the weapon to be used for cutting as well as thrusting. More important than the weapon itself was the fact that West Europeans were devoting attention and ingenuity to improving the fighting capabilities of the once-despised foot soldier. Thus the halberd, like the crossbow, was an early indication of the revival of infantry.

One other example of weapons improvement was the perfection of the Moslem scimitar. The significance of this curve-bladed sword lay in quality of metallurgy rather than in any radical change of design. The craftsmen of Damascus and Toledo, particularly, became known for the magnificent steel blades they created: amazingly supple, yet tough and sturdy and capable of being honed to razor keenness.

In Europe, defensive armor continued to improve. It also became increasingly heavy. The mail shirt was shortened, its long skirts replaced by mail breeches. Sleeve were lengthened to the wrists and a coif, or mailed hood, was often added, replacing a helmet. Such a suit of chain mail weighed between 30 and 50 pounds. To enhance protection and to prevent bruises from blows against its hard surface, mail armor was worn over a coat of heavy leather or felt. Such leather or felt jackets were usually the only body protection of the foot soldier. But even this was enough to stop most arrows; Turkish chroniclers describe unharmed Crusader infantrymen in battle as often looking like pincushions.

The fit of the helmet was improved. The nosepiece was lengthened and strength ened. In fact, complete facial coverage was provided by many armorers, who pro duced flat-topped casques covering the entire head and neck, with slits in the front for vision and breathing. Helmets of this sort, however, were so heavy and so suffo cating that they were usually carried on the saddle pommel until action was about to begin. The most common pot helmets of the period weighed 15 or 20 pounds. By the end of the period armorers were experimenting with pointed helmet fronts to deflect frontal blows and to reduce the unpleasant possibility of having the helme smashed back into the wearer's face.

These improvements in armor kept casualties low in European battles. They also made for great disproportion in the losses of Crusaders and Moslems in their battles in the East. When the Crusaders won, their casualties were always relatively light; when they were defeated, they suffered heavily in the final phases of the battle since they were unable to escape from their more mobile foes.

FORTIFICATION AND SIEGECRAFT

There were no new developments in fortification. However, the Crusaders learned lessons from the Byzantines that completely changed West European con cepts of fortification and of the defense of cities (see p. 320). But in one important respect the Europeans differed from the Byzantines in their application of these

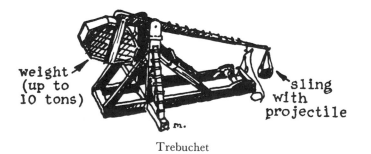

weight (up to 10 tons)   sling with projectile

Trebuchet

lessons. To the Byzantines, fortresses were essentially bases for defensive-offensive operations in the field, and thus they were usually located on commanding, but accessible, ground. The Europeans, more defensive-minded, and still limited by their feudal concepts of short-time, small-scale military operations, sited their new forts or castles in the most inaccessible spots possible. Thus it was extremely difficult for an attacker to reach and to assault such forts. But it was almost as difficult for the defenders to debouch rapidly, and so they had little opportunity to seize the initiative from a besieging or blockading force.

In siege operations, one new weapon was introduced. This was the **trebuchet,** or **mangonel,** a missile-hurling machine for battering fortifications, or for throwing rocks or other projectiles over walls. Unlike the ballista and catapult, which obtained their power from tension or torsion (see p. 38), the propelling force of the trebuchet was provided by a counterweight.

Siege methods were unchanged. Human ingenuity had long before devised practically every possible way of battering down, climbing over, or tunneling under walls. European medieval siegecraft, however, rarely visualized employment of the favorite, and effective, siege technique of the Macedonians and Romans. This was the **agger,** or mound, which could be built up to dominate the defending fortifications. In the first place, man-power shortages (discussed elsewhere) kept European armies relatively small, and the construction of a great siege mound required tremendous man power. Second, the usual location of European castles on inaccessible rocky promontories precluded employment of mounds.

Thus, to a greater extent than ever, the principal siege weapon was starvation. Since it was very difficult and expensive for feudal monarchs and nobles to keep armies in the field indefinitely, a well-provisioned castle had a very good chance to survive siege.

TACTICS OF LAND WARFARE

General

Cavalry remained the dominant arm. But infantry was reviving in importance. Even prior to the Crusades the Western Europeans had discovered that—all things being equal—an army which included a reliable foot element had an advantage over a completely cavalry force. This was because the infantry provided a base of maneuver for the cavalry, and because the infantry could seize and hold commanding or vital ground. For this reason, many European leaders would habitually dismount a portion of their knights and men-at-arms, to obtain a reliable nucleus for the less trustworthy footmen of the feudal levies. Sometimes the only foot element of an army would be its dismounted knights. The reason for this was that the knights, with their heavier armor, better weapons, and a code of honor which gave them a kind of discipline, could stand firm against a cavalry attack that would scatter the fyrd or militia. Because this was obviously an uneconomical use of expensive cavalry, a kind of medieval intuitive cost effectiveness led to development of standing forces of well-equipped, disciplined infantry.

This phenomenon was accelerated by Crusade experience. In fighting the mobile Moslems, the Crusaders found it essential to maintain a solid infantry base from which to launch their overwhelming cavalry charges. The significance of this was soon realized by the Moslems, who then made it one of their important objectives to separate the Crusader cavalry from the infantry, then to defeat each in detail. This is how Saladin won his decisive victory at Hattin (see p. 317). This Moslem tactic, in turn, taught the Crusaders to devote more attention to close coordination of the actions and movements of both infantry and cavalry, leading to some really effective operations of the combined arms, as in Richard's great victory over Saladin at Arsouf (see p. 318).

Part of this coordination of foot and horse elements was centered around the related concept of fire and movement. Reliance upon crossbows was greatly accelerated by the Crusaders' experience, and by their realization that they needed fire power to offset that of the Turkish horse archers. Whenever possible, the Crusaders would launch their battle-winning heavy cavalry charges immediately after a cross-bow volley had shaken the opposing force.

The Turks, in turn, found that they needed combined arms against the formidable Crusaders. Saladin was apparently the first who effectively combined fanatic Arab and Egyptian foot soldiers with Mameluke (Turkish slaves) horse archers. But in such a contest the more lightly armed Moslems had no hope of success against well-coordinated European combined arms.

Infantry Tactics

Even by the end of this period, the foot soldier was still decidedly inferior to the cavalryman in prestige and effectiveness. There was little infantry maneuver in battle. Its purpose was to stand firm as the base for battle-winning cavalry maneuvers. An additional purpose, as discussed above, was to provide fire power which would enhance the chances of success of cavalry charges.

Cavalry Tactics

There were three distinct cavalry types during this period. First was the horse archer of the Byzantine and Turkish armies, with the Byzantine being far better disciplined, more heavily armored, and capable of functioning also as the second type: heavy shock-action cavalry. The West Europeans were supreme in this type; no other military force in the world could stand up against equal numbers of the mailed knights and men-at-arms of the Franks (as Moslems and Byzantines called all West Europeans). The third type was light cavalry, usually lightly armored and equipped with lance and sword. Only the Arabs, Egyptians, and North Africans attempted shock tactics with such horsemen; this accounts for the ability of the Crusaders—prior to the time of Saladin—to operate so successfully against much more numerous Egyptians.

The Crusaders, however, learning from Byzantines and Moslems, did make use of light cavalry themselves for screening and reconnaissance purposes. They also used light horse archers. Later, in addition to using Moslem mercenaries in these light-cavalry roles, they also had units of what were known as **Turcopoles**: lightly armed European horse bowmen who were usually second-generation Europeans born in Syria.* The Christian Spanish also developed a similar light cavalry—known as **Genitours**—armed with light lance or javelin, for reconnaissance and screening, and for skirmishing with their Moorish opponents.

Efforts to introduce horse archers in Western Europe were unsuccessful. However, Hungarian or Turkish mercenary horse archers sometimes appeared on European battlefields.

THE SOLDIERY OF MEDIEVAL EUROPE

As we have seen, heavy armored cavalry, designed for shock action, was the central feature of the feudal military forces of Western Europe. Because the weapons and armor were expensive, at first only the wealthy members of the aristocracy could afford so to equip themselves. Only to them was the old Roman term *miles* (soldier) originally applied, and thus the elite of the heavy cavalry were also the knights of medieval chivalry.

---

* J. F. C. Fuller is in error when he applies the term Turcopole to the bastard offspring of Crusaders and Syrian women.

Two factors caused a change in this situation. First, the nobles and kings found that their offensive or defensive needs required more numerous forces than they could raise among the feudal gentry who owed them allegiance. Furthermore, the short terms of service which a vassal owed his liege lord for offensive military operations seriously inhibited the military ambitions of the many feudal lords. An obvious solution was to provide the horses and heavy equipment necessary to arm and train more promising commoners, who would then ride and fight beside the knights, and who would be available for operations all year round—if the liege lord had the wherewithal to pay and feed them. These were called men-at-arms, and the term *miles* gradually began to be applied to them as to the knights. To help support these standing forces, the king or noble would accept money instead of service from his feudal vassals, an arrangement satisfactory to all.

We have seen how the unreliability of the medieval militia foot levies first led commanders to dismount their knights and men-at-arms, which in turn led to the more economical measure of raising dependable standing formations of foot soldiers, well-armed and well-equipped, though not so lavishly as the mounted soldiers. Most of these were pikemen, whose main role in battle was to stand solidly in a heavy phalanx as a firm base for the fire power of crossbowmen and the ponderous maneuvers of the heavy cavalry. It was such footmen as these who repulsed the German knights and provided the base for the Milanese cavalry charge that defeated Frederick Barbarossa at the Battle of Legnano (see p. 295). Perhaps the best pike units of the 12th century were raised in the Netherlands.

Earlier, in England, the unreliability of the fyrd, or militia, had caused Canute to create a large standing force of bodyguards, or **housecarls,** who became the nucleus of his feudal armies. The housecarls remained the mainstay of English military forces until they were annihilated at the Battle of Hastings (see p. 286).

Some noble adventurers hit upon the scheme of raising mercenary forces which they would then hire out to other nobles or kings who could not afford to maintain full-time standing armies, or who had special requirements which could not be met by their regular standing forces. Such mercenary units made up a substantial portion of the army of Duke **William** of Normandy when he invaded England.

NAVAL WARFARE

The most important naval development was the rise of the maritime states of Italy, particularly Venice, Pisa, and Genoa. The Norman Kingdom of Sicily also developed a substantial naval capability. By the close of the 12th century the navies of these four states dominated most of the Mediterranean. The Byzantine Navy declined markedly during this period, in large part due to the devastation of the maritime regions of Anatolia after the Battle of Manzikert.

Sea power was a decisive element in the Crusades. Thus, during the 12th century the maritime states of Italy and Sicily were able to make healthy profits by ferrying Crusader armies to the Holy Land, and then by providing them with logistical support. Had the Moslems not been driven from the Mediterranean during the early 11th century, even a partial Christian success would have been impossible.

The principal fighting vessels of the era were—as they had been for centuries—long, low galleys, whose oarsmen were usually slaves. Methods of naval warfare were unchanged. The objective of a naval fight was to ram the opposing vessel, or to capture it by boarding.

THE CHURCH AND MILITARY AFFAIRS

The Western Church

In theory the Catholic Church was consistently opposed to the warlike brutality of the age in Western Europe. Yet in practice the Church realistically accepted its bellicose environment, and not infrequently leading churchmen—popes and bishops —employed force to obtain both spiritual and temporal objectives of the Church. This was particularly true during the prolonged struggle between the popes and the German emperors.

One of the paradoxes of the time, in fact, was the personal participation of some priests in the actual business of battle. Many of these were hardly a credit to their calling; they were generally members of the nobility who had entered the Church to enjoy its temporal benefits, rather than because of any religious vocation. On the other hand, many warrior priests were devout men of God, meticulous in eschewing combat for any cause that they could not sincerely reconcile with the teachings of the Church. Such men as Bishop **Adhemar du Puy,** for instance, believed that fighting the infidel Moslems was a direct contribution to Christianity and to the glory of God.

The first attempts to control or to limit war were made by the Church during these centuries. There were at least three manifestations of this.

First was the "Peace of God." Late in the 10th century (c. 990), the Church in France had begun to propagate the understandable maxim that priests, monks, and nuns must not be harmed during military operations. This was later extended to cover shepherds, schoolchildren, merchants, and travelers. A further extension applied the Peace of God to churches, and to people going to or from church on Sundays. From this grew almost universal acceptance of church buildings as sanctuaries. The provisions of the Peace of God were fairly faithfully adhered to in most of Europe, possibly because they did not interfere greatly with actual military operations.

More sweeping—and thus less effective—was the "Truce of God." This Church precept, which apparently first appeared in Aquitaine early in the 11th century, forbade fighting on Sundays. At first the teaching was observed; but as bishops extended the Truce, first to cover the entire week end and later to last from Vespers on Wednesday to sunrise on Monday, as well as all of Lent, Advent, and Holy Days, it was generally ignored.

The third Church ruling affecting the warfare of the period was a direct measure of arms control. It was also an indirect testimonial to the effectiveness of the crossbow. This weapon was outlawed by a Vatican edict in 1139 as being too barbarous for use in warfare between Christians; its employment against Moslems, or other infidels was, however, deemed perfectly appropriate.

The Eastern Church

The Orthodox Church of the Byzantine Empire was somewhat less compromising in its attitude toward war and slaughter than was the Roman Church—as might be expected in a more cultured and less aggressive society. But Orthodox religious leaders recognized and granted absolution for killing in self-defense—both individual and that of the state.

WESTERN EUROPE

ENGLAND

Dynastic Struggles of Saxons, Danes, and Normans, 1000–1066

Soon after the beginning of the century, able Danish King **Sweyn Forkbeard** took advantage of the ineptitude of the Saxon King **Aethelred** ("the Unready") to begin the conquest of England, completed by his brilliant son, **Canute** (after the death of Aethelred's eldest son, **Edmund Ironside**). England enjoyed a period of unprecedented peace and prosperity under Canute, who at the same time extended his empire by conquest of Norway, Scotland, and part of Sweden.

The basis for a complicated and momentous series of dynastic wars was Canute's marriage to Aethelred's widow, **Emma,** daughter of **Richard I,** Duke of Normandy. By an earlier liaison Canute had a son of questionable legitimacy, **Harold Harefoot.** By Emma he had a son **Harthacanute.** Meanwhile **Edward** and **Alfred,** two sons of Aethelred and Emma (brothers of Edmund Ironside), were residing in exile at the court of their kinsmen, the Dukes of Normandy. The election of Harold to succeed Canute resulted in a three-way war between Harold, Harthacanute, and Alfred. Harold captured and killed Alfred, and repulsed the efforts of Harthacanute (supported by his mother, Emma) to gain the throne. Upon the death of Harold, Harthacanute finally achieved his objective, but died after reigning two years. He selected his elder half-brother, Edward, to be his successor.

Edward, a deeply religious man, known to history as "the Confessor," created dissension in England by bringing many Norman advisers with him. This led to an abortive civil war in which **Godwine**, Earl of Wessex, and his son, **Harold,** tried to end Norman influence. After a brief exile, Godwine became the closest and most trusted adviser of Edward, a relationship continued by Harold after Godwine's death. This ended Norman influence at Edward's court. Apparently Edward had earlier selected his cousin **William**, Duke of Normandy, as his heir. At the time of his death, however, Edward chose Earl Harold (son of Godwine) as his successor, and Harold was elected king by the Witan (council of nobles). William of Normandy, considering himself the rightful heir to the throne, immediately prepared to invade England. But before William's fleet could sail from Normandy, Harold's brother, **Tostig,** with **Harold Hardraade,** King of Norway, led another invasion to Northumbria. Harold defeated and killed these two invaders at the **Battle of Stamford Bridge,** just before William landed on the south coast of England. The principal events were:

968–1016. Reign of Aethelred the Unready.

1003–1013. Danish Conquest of England. By Sweyn, with the assistance of his son, Canute. Aethelred took refuge in Normandy.

1014–1016. War between Aethelred and Canute. Aethelred, unsuccessful in an invasion attempt, died in London while Canute was approaching with a victorious army.

1016. War between Canute and Edmund (Son of Aethelred). Edmund was victorious at the **Battle of Pen** in Somersetshire. The **Battle of Sherston** in Wiltshire was indecisive. Edmund drove Canute from his siege of London, but was badly defeated by Canute at the **Battle of Assandun** (Ashington) in Essex, thanks in part to treachery in the Saxon Army. Canute and Edmund then agreed to divide England, Canute reigning in the north, Edmund in the south. Edmund died soon afterward, and Canute was elected king of the entire country by the Witan.

1016–1035. Reign of Canute.

1035–1040. Reign of Harold Harefoot.

1040–1042. Reign of Harthacanute.

1042–1066. Reign of Edward the Confessor.

1051. Revolt of Godwine and Harold. They were restored to favor the next year.

1053. Death of Godwine. Harold became Earl of Wessex.

1055–1057. Civil War. Harold's influence was challenged by **Aelfgar,** Earl of Mercia and East Anglia. Aelfgar was assisted in this inconclusive struggle by **Gruffyd,** Prince of North Wales.

1063. Invasion of North Wales. Harold, assisted by his brother **Tostig,** Earl of Northumbria, defeated Gruffyd.

1064. Harold's Oath. Shipwrecked off the coast of Normandy, Harold was forced by Duke William to swear to support his claim to the throne of England as heir of Edward the Confessor.

1065. Revolt in Northumbria. Tostig was ejected in favor of **Morkere,** son of Aelfgar, and brother of **Edwin,** Aelfgar's successor as Earl of Mercia. Harold recognized the new earl, gaining the undying enmity of his brother, Tostig.

1066, January 6. Death of Edward. Harold was elected king by the Witan. William of Normandy prepared to invade South England. During the spring and summer Harold repelled several raids of Norse adventurers under his brother Tostig.

1066, September. Norwegian Invasion. Harold Hardraade, with Tostig, brought an army by ship up the Humber River. Harold agreed that Tostig would be made Earl of Northumbria if he helped the Norwegians to conquer the rest of England.

1066, September 20. Battle of Fulford. Harold and Tostig defeated Edwin and Morkere, Earls of Mercia and Northumbria, then occupied York. Meanwhile Harold had collected an army and started north from London (September 16).

1066, September 25. Battle of Stamford Bridge. Harold defeated the invaders in an exceedingly hard-fought battle, the decisive blow being struck by the cavalry contingent of Harold's housecarls. Both Tostig and Harold Hardraade were killed. Casualties were heavy among the housecarls, the only regular standing force in England. The Northumbrian and Mercian levies were also decimated.

1066, September 28. Norman Invasion. Landing of William at Pevensey in Sussex.

1066, October 2. Harold Marches South. As soon as he learned of William's landing, Harold started marching south with his housecarls.

THE BATTLE OF HASTINGS (OR SENLAC), OCTOBER 14, 1066

As soon as Harold ascended the throne of England, William of Normandy began to raise an army to fight for what he considered his rightful inheritance. He could not use his feudal levies for such a large-scale protracted operation outside of their own localities. Accordingly, most of his men were mercenaries, or were feudal contingents attracted to his standard by the promise of lands and wealth in England. The exact size of his army is unknown. Estimates of reliable military historians vary from 7,000 to 50,000. Oman suggests that his total strength might have been as much as 12,000 cavalry and 20,000 infantry.

William was ready to sail for England in a great armada by midsummer, but was long delayed by unfavorable winds. Finally (September 27) the wind changed; the next day the Norman army began to debark at Pevensey. William certainly knew of the invasion of Tostig and Harold Hardraade. (They may even have been secret allies.) He decided to let the Norse and Anglo-Saxon armies punish each other, and remained on the defensive near the south coast. Building a powerful wooden fortification as a base near the coast at Pevensey, he sent his cavalry ravaging the Sussex countryside to gather supplies and to force Harold to act.

Harold covered the 200 miles between York and London in less than 5 days. He waited a few days at London, from October 6 to 11, to gather up all available militia and to rest his exhausted housecarls briefly. He then marched to Senlac,

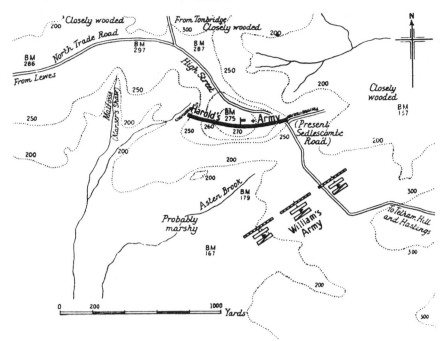

Battle of Hastings

arriving the afternoon of the 13th—about 56 miles in 48 hours. Choosing a ridge about 8 miles northwest of Hastings, Harold organized his army for defense since he felt certain that William would attack as soon as possible. As with the Norman Army, we have no accurate figures for Harold's strength. But on the basis of the description of the battle, and the known frontage of the Anglo-Saxon Army, it would appear that he must have had at least 20,000 men. Accordingly, Oman's tentative suggestion of 25,000 seems reasonable. It has been suggested that if Harold had waited a few days, he would have been joined by the Northumbrian and Mercian levies, and that he would have been able to gather more south Englishmen as well. There is some doubt whether the northern levies ever started out, or indeed if they were in any condition to. Whether he could have raised more men in the south or not, Harold apparently felt his political and military situations were sufficiently insecure to make it essential to seek a decision as soon as possible.

Believing (probably correctly) that he was outnumbered, and that—save for his depleted housecarls—his troops were neither so well trained nor so well armed as the Norman mercenaries, Harold decided to fight on the defensive. He dismounted his cavalry housecarls, and these, with the infantry housecarls, formed the center of his line at the highest point on the ridge. The remainder of his army—men of the fyrd, or militia—were stretched out along the ridge on each side, some 300–400 yards, in a dense infantry mass, probably about 20 men deep. Harold's army awaited the Norman attack early on October 14. Possibly during the afternoon of the 13th, the Anglo-Saxons hastily erected a rough hedge, or abatis, in front of their line; there is dispute about this among scholars.

The Normans advanced soon after dawn in three lines. In the front were William's archers, including a number of crossbowmen (first recorded appearance of the medieval crossbow in battle). In the second line were William's infantry pikemen. The third line contained the cavalry knights.

The battle was opened by the Norman archers, firing from less than 100 yards. But since they had to fire uphill, most of the arrows and bolts were either deflected by Anglo-Saxon shields or flew harmlessly overhead. The archers then evidently fell back through intervals in the line of Norman pikemen. The pikemen rushed up the slope, but were met by a shower of javelins and rocks—some thrown by hand, some hurled from slings—and were thrown back by the Anglo-Saxons, who were wielding swords, pikes, and great two-handed, double-bladed battleaxes.

With his infantry discomfited, William led his cavalry in a charge up the slope, with no better results. The Norman left wing was so roughly handled, in fact, that it fell back in panic. The elated Anglo-Saxon militiamen on the right immediately dashed down the hill in pursuit. Panic began to spread through the rest of the Norman army as the rumor of William's death passed like wildfire through the ranks.

Hastings from Bayeux tapestry

Throwing off his helmet so the men could see his face, William galloped along the line of his retreating center, which quickly rallied. He then led a charge against the Anglo-Saxon right wing, which had become scattered in premature, heedless pursuit. The Norman cavalry quickly overwhelmed the surprised pursuers.

William now led his cavalry once more against the Anglo-Saxon center, and again was repulsed. Hoping to lure more of the English to leave their solid defensive position, William ordered his men to feign flight. Despite Harold's efforts to hold his men fast, a number of them fell into the Norman trap, and were cut down in the open at the base of the hill when William led another cavalry counterattack. But the main Anglo-Saxon line still stood firm and impervious to repeated assaults.

For several hours the Normans alternated harassment by bowmen with renewed infantry and cavalry assaults. William ordered his archers to use high-angle fire, so that the arrows and bolts would plunge down on the Anglo-Saxon line. Though many were killed this way, Harold's men were still unshaken by midafternoon, but, having had no respite from alternating Norman fire and movement, were close to exhaustion.

At this time a chance arrow struck Harold in the eye, mortally wounding him.

Encouraged, the Normans renewed their assaults, and now the leaderless English line began to collapse. The fyrd gave way, and soon only the housecarls were left, at the top of the ridge, around the body of their dying king. But their fight was now hopeless; completely surrounded, their line began to break. By dark the Normans held the crest. William led a pursuit into the woods behind the ridge, and was almost killed when a few housecarls rallied to renew the fight. But these brave men were soon overwhelmed. The Battle of Hastings was over.

No battle was ever more hard-fought than Hastings; no battle has had more momentous results. In one respect this was merely the conclusion of a dynastic war establishing the succession to the crown of a small island kingdom. But in fact this battle was a turning point in history: the initiation of a series of events which would lead a revitalized Anglo-Saxon-Norman people to a world leadership more extensive even than that of ancient Rome.

Following the battle, William seized Dover, then advanced on London. At first the capital rejected his demand for its surrender. William thereupon began to devastate the surrounding countryside, and London quickly capitulated. William's claim to the throne was acknowledged, and on Christmas Day, 1066, in Westminster Abbey, he was crowned William I, King of England.

The Early Norman Kingdom, 1067–1200

Within four years William had completely consolidated his control over England. He broke the power of the great Anglo-Saxon earldoms. His was still a feudal kingdom, but with a far greater degree of centralized authority than would exist in any other European nation for several centuries. For instance, no baron could build a stone castle without royal authority; when feudal levies were called to his service, they had to swear allegiance to the king.

Under subsequent rulers in the following century, there was some decline in the centralized authority of the king; but despite the feudal pressures of the time, and despite a number of civil wars, the nation remained unified.

During the remainder of this period, the rulers of England were also the greatest landowners of France. Thus the dynastic succession to the Duchy of Normandy was as important to them as the crown of England. Their French possessions involved them in frequent armed conflicts with other feudal lords in France, and not infrequently with the French kings.

The last king of England during this period was **Richard I,** known as "the Lionhearted." Possibly the greatest European soldier of the Middle Ages (though opinions differ widely), he spent most of his time in foreign wars, and was a poor king. Ironically, the campaigns in which he won his military reputation (the Third Crusade, see p. 318) were failures, politically and strategically. The principal events were:

1067–1071. Consolidation of England by William I. The most serious of his several campaigns of pacification was in suppressing the rebellion led by **Hereward the Wake,** the "great uprising of the north" (1069–1071). The rebels, aided by a Danish force under **Jarl Osbiorn** sent by King **Sweyn Estrithson,** captured York. William defeated the joint force, recaptured York, and drove the Danes back to their ships. The revolt ended with William's successful assault on Hereward's island stronghold of Ely.

1072. Invasion of Scotland. King **Malcolm** was forced to pay homage.

1073. William's Reconquest of Maine. This French province had revolted from his feudal control while he was busy in England (1069).

1075. Revolt of the Earls of Hereford and Norfolk. Suppressed by William.

1076. Invasion of Brittany. The Duke of

Brittany was sheltering the fugitive Earl of Norfolk. William abandoned the campaign under pressure from **Philip I,** King of France.

1077–1082. Dynastic Unrest. This was marked in Normandy by sporadic revolts of **Robert,** eldest son of William.

1087. War with Philip of France. During this campaign William died as a result of an accident.

1087–1100. Reign of William II (Second Son of William I). He was almost constantly at war with his elder brother Robert, who had become Duke of Normandy, over succession to the throne of England and over control of family holdings in France.

1100–1135. Reign of Henry I (Fourth Son of William I). He continued the conflict with Robert of Normandy, culminating in the **Battle of Tinchebrai.** Henry defeated and captured Robert, and declared himself Duke of Normandy as well as King of England. A series of wars with **Louis VI** of France, who assisted Norman rebels, ended with the defeat of Louis at the **Battle of Bermule** (1119).

1135–1154. Reign of Stephen (Nephew of Henry). For 18 years (1135–1153) Stephen was engaged in a seesaw, unimaginative, exhausting, and inconclusive dynastic war with his cousin **Matilda** (daughter of Henry) and her son, also named **Henry.** Stephen's principal opponent in this warfare was **Robert,** Earl of Gloucester, half-brother of Matilda. The "Anarchy" was ended by a truce concluded after the drawn **Battle of Wallingford** (1154).

1154–1189. Reign of Henry II (Son of Matilda). He founded the Plantagenet dynasty. An able ruler and general, Henry restored general peace and prosperity to England. His marriage (1152) to **Eleanor** of Aquitaine, divorced wife of **Louis VII** of France, made him the Lord of Poitou, Guienne, and Gascony, and thus the largest landholder in France, laying the basis for the later Hundred Years' War (see p. 353). Henry was sporadically at war with his suzerain, Louis (1157–1180). He invaded and subdued Wales in a series of campaigns (1158–1165). He sent his vassals to invade Ireland (1169–1175; see p. 291), participating there briefly himself (1171). He vigorously suppressed the last important feudal revolt of the Anglo-Saxons (1173–1174). The murder of Saint **Thomas à Becket,** Archbishop of Canterbury and enemy of Henry, by Norman knights (December, 1070) may have led to that revolt, which was also sponsored in part by at least two of Henry's sons. This was the beginning of sporadic intrigue and frequent open warfare in England and in his French domains between Henry and his sons, **Henry, Richard, Geoffrey** and **John,** with constantly shifting alliances between sons and father (1173–1189). At the time of his death Henry was engaged in an unsuccessful war against Richard and King **Philip II Augustus** of France, the victorious allies having just been joined by Henry's youngest son, John.

1189–1199. Reign of Richard I (Son of Henry II). He was the very epitome of the chivalrous knight, performing well-documented prodigies of valor and strength. During the Third Crusade he also proved himself one of the few brilliant generals of the Middle Ages (see p. 318). He was a poor ruler, spending very little time in England because of his occupation with the Crusades (1190–1191), a period of captivity in Austria (1192–1194), and his protracted war with Philip of France (1194–1199; see p. 294). Richard won the only important battle of this war of sieges at **Gisors** (near Paris; 1197). He died of a wound received at the siege of **Châlus** near Limoges. He was succeeded by his brother **John** (1199–1216).

SCOTLAND

At the outset of the 11th century, Scotland comprised four principal communities or kingdoms: Scots, Picts, Britons, and Angles, upon whom were superimposed a number of independent Norse settlements, particularly in the islands off the coast. These separate entities coalesced into a single kingdom of Scotland under Scottish Kings **Malcolm II** (1005–1034) and **Duncan** (1034–1040), though the islands still remained Norse. But despite this apparent unification, and the general acceptance of the suzerainty of a single Scottish king, the nation was in a state of anarchy during this period. In addition to almost constant internal wars and feuds, the Scots raided frequently into the northern provinces of England, and in turn were subjected to a number of English punitive expeditions. The principal events were:

1009–1010. Danish Invasions. Malcolm was defeated by Sweyn Forkbeard at **Nairn** (1009), but the Danes withdrew. Returning the following summer, Sweyn was repulsed by Malcolm in a desperate battle at **Mortlack.**

1018. Battle of Carham. Malcolm invaded Northumbria, defeated the Northumbrians on the Tweed River and annexed the region between the Tweed and the Firth of Forth.

1040–1057. Reign of Macbeth. A usurper who seized the throne, probably after killing Duncan. He was defeated by Duncan's son **Malcolm** at the **Battle of Dunsinane** (1054), which led to his overthrow and death three years later.

1057–1093. Reign of Malcolm III. He engaged in sporadic border wars with the English. William the Conqueror invaded Scotland and forced Malcolm to acknowledge his suzerainty (1072). Full-scale war with the Anglo-Normans broke out again (1077–1080), and Malcolm finally was killed in his last invasion of England at the **First Battle of Alnwick** (1093).

1124–1153. Reign of David I. Supporting Matilda (mother of Henry II) in her wars against Stephen of England (see p. 290), David conquered most of the English provinces of Northumberland and Cumberland, despite a defeat by the local English nobles and militia at the **Battle of the Standard,** or of Northallerton (1138). He was later repulsed by Stephen when making further inroads into England (1149).

1153–1165. Reign of Malcolm IV (Grandson of David). He was forced to surrender Cumberland and Northumberland to Henry II of England.

1165–1214. Reign of William the Lion (Brother of Malcolm IV). He supported the feudal rebels and sons of Henry II in the Great Rebellion (1173–1174); he was defeated and captured by Henry at the **Second Battle of Alnwick,** and forced to pay ransom to the English king (1174).

IRELAND

As the 11th century opened, **Brian Boru** was consolidating his position as the leading king of the several Irish kingdoms (see p. 249). In the following decade, he drove out the Danes to gain unchallenged sovereignty over the entire island. One further Danish effort to re-establish themselves in Ireland was smashed by Brian at the **Battle of Clontarf** (just north of Dublin), but Brian was killed during the battle. There was no successor who could hold the turbulent Irish in check; the following century and a half were chaotic. Early in the 12th century **Magnus,** King of Norway, led the final Norse invasion of Ireland, but was killed in Ulster, and his men withdrew. Just after the middle of the century, a number of Norman-English adventurers invaded Ireland with the approval of Henry II and under the leadership of **Richard of Clare.** After they established themselves on the east coast of Ireland, Henry himself came with a substantial army and with papal authority to rule Ireland. There was little further fighting. The Irish, awed by the Norman strength and respectful of Henry's church support, submitted. The island was relatively peaceful for the rest of the century. The principal events were:

1002. Brian Boru High King. He defeated **Mael Sechnaill II,** former high king, who recognized Brian as his successor.

1014. Danish Invasion. Danes from the Orkney Islands were joined by an uprising of Danes around Dublin. Brian defeated the invaders and suppressed the insurrection by his last great victory at **Clontarf.**

1014–1167. Chaotic Internal Squabbling.

1167–1171. Norman Conquest.

SCANDINAVIA

Denmark

This period opened and closed with Denmark one of the leading powers of Northern and Western Europe. But for much of the intervening time the country had been relatively weak, and at one point was on the verge of disintegration. The important events were:

985–1014. Reign of Sweyn I, Forkbeard. He made Denmark predominant in Scandinavia, and conquered most of England (see pp. 252 and 285). He left his English dominions to his son **Canute** and his Danish kingdom to another son, **Harold** (1014–1018). When Harold died, Canute also inherited the Danish throne.

1018–1035. Reign of Canute II. He completed the conquest of England (see p. 285).

1026–1030. War with Norway and Sweden. Canute defeated **Olaf Haraldson** of Norway and **Anund Jakub** of Sweden. There were two great Danish naval victories: the **Battle of Stangebjerg** against the Swedes (1026) and the **Battle of Helgeaa** in which he smashed the combined Swedish-Norwegian fleets (1028). Following this Canute overran Norway and established control over most of the south coast of the Baltic.

1035. Death of Canute. The empire was divided between his sons **Harold Harefoot** (England), **Harthacanute** (Denmark), and **Sweyn** (Norway).

1035–1042. Reign of Harthacanute. He was more interested in England than in Denmark (see p. 286).

1042–1047. Reign of Magnus, King of Norway. (See below.) He repulsed a Slav invasion of Jutland at the **Battle of Lysborg** (c. 1045).

1047–1050. Revolt of Sweyn Estrithson (Nephew of Canute). Magnus died during the campaign. Sweyn seized the throne, preventing **Harold III Hardraade** of Norway from reimposing Norwegian rule over Denmark.

1050–1134. Reigns of Sweyn II and His Five Sons. Denmark was relatively quiet.

1134–1157. Dynastic Struggles and Chaos. Ended by the victory of **Waldemar** over **Sweyn III** at **Viborg** in Jutland.

1157–1182. Reign of Waldemar I, the Great. Assisted by the remarkable soldier-statesman-bishop, **Absalon,** Waldemar restored internal order and expanded Danish influence in the Baltic at the expense of Swedes, Wends, and Germans.

1160–1169. War with the Wend Pirates. Absalon eventually conquered the Wend island stronghold of Rügen.

1170–1182. Danish Expansion. Absalon extended Danish control over the coast of Mecklenberg, with expeditions establishing outposts in Estonia.

1182–1202. Reign of Canute VI. Danish power and prestige continued to expand, with Absalon continuing as the principal royal adviser. He repulsed a German invasion (1182), and smashed a Pomeranian effort to challenge Danish supremacy on the Baltic in an overwhelming victory at the naval **Battle of Strela** (Stralsund, 1184).

Norway

Norway, conquered by Sweyn Forkbeard at the end of the 10th century, was briefly resurgent about 20 years later under **Olaf II Haraldson,** while Canute was engaged in completing the conquest of England. A few years later, however, Canute reconquered the country (see above). After Canute's death Norway regained its independence. The principal events were:

1015–1028. Reign of Olaf II Haraldson. Expelled by Canute (1028), he tried to come back, and was defeated and killed at the **Battle of Stiklestad** (1030).

1035. Reign of Sweyn (Son of Canute). He was soon expelled in favor of **Magnus,** son of Olaf II.

1035–1047. Reign of Magnus I. Upon the

death of Harthacanute, he also became King of Denmark (see p. 292).

1047–1066. Reign of Harold Hardraade. He had earlier served in the Varangian Guard at Constantinople. He was unsuccessful in his efforts to reconquer Denmark (1047–1050). He invaded and seized a portion of southeastern Sweden (c. 1063). Allied with Tostig and (probably) William of Normandy, he invaded England and was killed at the **Battle of Stamford Bridge** (see p. 286).

1066–1093. Reign of Olaf III, the Quiet. He was never involved in war.

1093–1103. Reign of Magnus III, Barefoot. He conducted several expeditions to Scotland, where he re-established Norse control over the Orkney and Hebrides Islands. He was killed while invading Ireland.

1103–1130. Reigns of the Sons of Magnus III. Of these the most renowned was **Sigurd I,** the Crusader (see p. 316).

1130–1217. Dynastic Wars.

Sweden

These two centuries in Sweden, less civilized and less Christianized than either Norway or Denmark, can be divided into three equal subperiods. In the first, Sweden was involved continuously in the wars of Norway and Denmark. In the second, the country was in a state of anarchy. In the third, peace was restored under a strong central monarchy. The principal events were:

994–1021. Reign of Olaf Skutkonung. After conquering southeastern Norway (1000), he was driven out by Olaf II of Norway (1015).

1021–1050. Reign of Anund Jakub. Anund and Olaf II of Norway formed an alliance against Canute of Denmark, but were decisively defeated (1026–1030; see above).

1050–1066. Reign of Steinkel. He was de-feated by Harold Hardraade of Norway, and by Sweyn II of Denmark (see above and p. 292).

1066–1134. Civil War and Chaos.

1134–1200. Restoration of Order. Beginning with the reign of **Sverker** (1134–1155) Sweden became relatively peaceful under a strong, centralized monarchy.

FRANCE

A period of gradual expansion of the authority and the domains of the kings of France, the successors of Hugh Capet (see p. 257). Royal authority and the very existence of the kingdom were seriously threatened when **Henry of Anjou** married **Eleanor of Aquitaine** (former wife of Louis VII of France) to become feudal lord of all of Southwestern France in addition to the Norman dominions of Northern and Northwestern France, followed by his coronation as Henry II of England. But Louis VII and his son and successor, **Philip Augustus,** encouraged and profited from the revolts of Henry's sons, thus preventing the English king from taking over all of France. During the last two decades of the 12th century, Philip Augustus began military and diplomatic successes which brought him unquestioned supremacy. The principal events were:

1031–1060. Reign of Henry I. He defeated a rebellion of his brother **Robert** (1032). He then was engaged in a series of wars against the counts of Blois, of Champagne, and of other great fiefs of northern France (1033–1043). In the opening campaigns he was greatly assisted by **Robert,** Duke of Normandy.

1035. Accession of William I as Duke of Normandy. Because of his illegitimate birth, many Norman nobles revolted against him (1035–1047). The revolt was finally suppressed, with the assistance of Henry I of France, by victory at the **Battle of Val-des-Dunes,** near Caen. Two years later William and Henry were at war, and the Normans repulsed a French invasion (1049). They fought another prolonged, inconclusive war (1035–1058).

1060–1108. Reign of Philip I. He accomplished little save to gain a victory over William the Conquerer (1079).

1108–1137. Reign of Louis VI. He fought two inconclusive wars with Henry I of England (1109–1112, 1116–1120). He repulsed a German invasion (1124), and generally expanded the power of the monarchy at the expense of the great nobles.

1137–1180. Reign of Louis VII. He inspired and participated in the Second Crusade (see p. 316). The most important events of his reign were the annulment of his marriage to Eleanor of Aquitaine and her subsequent marriage to Henry II of England. As a result, the power and prestige of the French monarchy were greatly diminished.

1180–1223. Reign of Philip II, Augustus. Early in his reign he subdued the great lords of the north and northeast (1180–1186). He allied himself with the rebellious sons of Henry II of England in order to reduce Plantagenet power in France (1187–1190). Save for a brief and stormy alliance in the Third Crusade (see p. 318), Philip was almost constantly at war with Richard I of England (see p. 290). By the end of the century he had gotten off to a good start in his efforts to restore and enhance the power and prestige of the French monarchy.

GERMANY

In the early 11th century there was a gradual rise in imperial power and prestige under three able emperors. Then complicated and intermingled political and religious strife rocked Germany. The power of the emperors (Holy Roman Empire) declined steadily, despite some restoration of imperial prestige under **Frederick I** in the latter part of the 12th century. Yet the basic vigor and vitality of the German people were demonstrated by steady expansion eastward, at the expense of neighboring Slavs.

Germany's internal troubles stemmed mostly from a prolonged struggle between the emperors and the popes in both spiritual and temporal affairs. A reform movement in the Church caused a line of vigorous 11th-century popes (**Gregory VII** being outstanding) to insist upon the right of appointing bishops, and of eliminating the graft and corruption which had stemmed largely from imperial control over the clergy in Germany. German nobles took advantage of the dispute to increase their power at the expense of the emperors, while the popes also exploited Germany's internal political troubles to gain their ends. For their part, the German emperors (**Henry IV** and Frederick I being most renowned) conducted frequent military expeditions into Italy for the purpose of controlling the papacy.

Early in the 11th century, the Hohenstauffen family of Swabia and the so-called Welf family of Saxony and Bavaria became engaged in a bitter struggle for the imperial succession. The resultant civil wars became involved with the concurrent church-state disputes. Because of the Hohenstauffen estates near Waiblingen, this civil war became known as that of the Welfs and Waiblingens. In Italy these same names, with some linguistic modifications, were applied to the participants in the church-state struggle: Guelphs for adherents of the papal party, Ghibellines for supporters of the emperor. The principal events were:

1002–1024. Reign of Henry II. During the early years he conducted a series of wars against **Ardoin,** King of Lombardy, whom he finally defeated and deposed (1002–1014). He was less successful in his wars against **Boleslav** of Poland, who conquered Lusatia and Silesia from the Germans (1003–1017). He suppressed a revolt by **Baldwin,** Count of Flanders (1006–1007).

1024–1039. Reign of Conrad II. A vigorous, capable soldier and administrator, he asserted his authority over the unruly

German nobles and in Italy as well. He was repulsed in an attempted invasion of Hungary by (Saint) **Stephen I** (1030). He defeated the Poles and temporarily recovered Lusatia for Germany (1031).

1039–1056. Reign of Henry III. He centralized authority and expanded the empire by foreign conquests. He defeated **Bratislav** of Bohemia (1041). He was involved in a number of conflicts with his vassals, **Baldwin V** of Flanders and **Godfrey** of Lorraine, suppressing their most serious combined revolt (1047). He was repulsed in repeated invasions of Hungary by **Andrew I** (1049–1052).

1056–1106. Reign of Henry IV (Aged 6). When he came of age, Henry was forced to exert great efforts to recover central power lost during a weak regency. He suppressed a particularly violent Saxon revolt (1173–1175). His struggle with the papacy (1073–1077) ruined his reign and seriously weakened the empire. The real victor in this struggle was the Bishop **Hildebrand**, later Pope Gregory VII, before whom Henry finally abased himself at Canossa.

1077–1106. Civil War in Germany. Rebellious nobles elected **Rudolph** of Swabia to replace Henry. Though the emperor soon defeated and killed Rudolph (1080), the revolt continued. Henry finally defeated another rival, **Herman** of Luxembourg (1086–1088). The revolt continued sporadically to the end of the reign.

1081–1085, 1090–1095. Henry's Expeditions to Italy. He briefly captured Rome (1083), but Gregory took refuge with the Norman duke, **Robert Guiscard,** of southern Italy, who recaptured the city (1084).

1093–1106. Revolt of Henry's Sons. Henry (later **Henry V**) and **Conrad** joined German and Italian rebels. The emperor was captured, but escaped (1105), and died while raising a new army (1106).

1106–1125. Reign of Henry V. The political-religious-military struggle between emperor and popes continued. Much of this reign was occupied with domestic and foreign wars: Henry campaigned successfully in Bohemia (1107–1110), but was repulsed in invasions of Hungary (1108) and Poland (1109). An expedition to Italy (1110–1111) forced the temporary submission of Pope **Paschal.** He was only partially successful in dealing with a series of revolts in Lorraine and other German provinces (1112–1115). He campaigned repeatedly and with mixed success in Holland (1120–1124). He was repulsed by Louis VI in an invasion of France (1124; see p. 294).

1125–1137. Reign of Lothair II. He was elected by the German nobles over a rival, **Frederick Hohenstaufen,** Duke of Swabia. The rivalry erupted into civil war (1125–1135) to initiate the struggle of Welf (Guelph) and Waiblingen (Ghibelline). After defeating the Hohenstaufens, Lothair led an unsuccessful expedition against **Roger II,** King of Sicily (1136–1137).

1138–1152. Reign of Conrad III (First of Hohenstaufen Dynasty). The Welfs, under Dukes of Saxony **Henry the Proud** and his son, **Henry the Lion,** rebelled. Henry the Lion (1142–1180) became a virtually independent king, expanding his dominions eastward against the Slavs, while successfully defying the emperor. Conrad, accompanied by his able warrior nephew, **Frederick,** participated in the disastrous Second Crusade (1146–1148; see p. 316).

1152–1190. Reign of Frederick I, "Barbarossa." The greatest of the Hohenstaufens. Sporadic war against Henry the Lion continued, but Frederick eventually defeated and deposed the Welf duke (1182). He was victorious in a number of campaigns in Poland, Bohemia, and Hungary (in intervals between his campaigns in Italy, 1156–1173).

1154–1186. Frederick's Six Expeditions to Italy. Frederick had mixed success in the imperial struggle with the papacy. Though he captured Rome on his fourth expedition (1166–1168), he was forced to leave Italy by a pestilence which destroyed his army. His fifth (1174–1177) ended in disaster at the **Battle of Legnano** (May 29, 1176), when, with a force consisting only of cavalry, he rashly accepted battle with a much larger infantry and cavalry army of the Lombard League. The steady Italian pikemen repulsed Frederick's attacks; the Lombard cavalry then routed the Germans by an envelopment. (This battle has sometimes been incorrectly cited as the first medieval victory of infantry over cavalry; the Lombard victory was due to the coordinated use of both arms.)

1189–1190. The Third Crusade. Frederick was drowned in Cilicia (1190; see p. 318).

1190–1197. Reign of Henry VI. Welf revolt erupted again under aged, but still vigorous, Henry the Lion, composed by the **Peace of Fulda** (1190). The emperor campaigned inconclusively in southern Italy against **Tancred** of Sicily (1191–

1193); he returned to conquer Sicily and be crowned king (1194–1195). He died in south Italy while suppressing a rebellion (1197). This premature death caused chaos in Germany, where two antikings (**Rudolph** of Swabia and **Otto** of Saxony) were elected as rivals to each other and to Henry's young son, **Frederick II.**

THE MARITIME STATES OF NORTH ITALY

Genoa

At the beginning of the 11th century, Genoa, which had suffered severely from Moslem piratical raids in previous centuries, had begun to gain wealth and power as an independent maritime city-state. In conjunction with the Pisans, Genoese warships ended the naval dominance of the Moslems in the northern Mediterranean, a process climaxed by a joint naval expedition which drove the Moslem pirate **Mogahid** from his bases in Sardinia (1005–1016). The two republics also collaborated in a number of raiding expeditions against Moslem cities in North Africa. The joint capture of Mahadia (1087) gave the Genoese and Pisans effective control of the western Mediterranean. Genoese power and prosperity waxed, and early in the 12th century Genoa challenged Pisan pre-eminence in the northern Mediterranean and on the islands of Corsica and Sardinia (1118–1132). That conflict was a standoff, but warfare became endemic between the two city republics. Genoa gained its first actual foothold on Corsica by the capture of Bonifacio (1195).

Pisa

Despite the persistent challenges of Genoa, Pisa was the predominant maritime power of western Italy during this period. After defeating Lucca (1003), Pisa was sacked in the last major Moslem raid against Italy (1011). Recovering rapidly, Pisa joined Genoa in operations against the Moslems (see above). One noteworthy success was the capture and sack of Palermo by a Pisan fleet (1062). With papal approval, Pisa obtained virtual sovereignty over Corsica (1077). Pisan warships, joining the First Crusade, provided decisive logistical support in the operations around Antioch (1098) and in the advance on Jerusalem (1099; see p. 314). Pisan expeditions in the western Mediterranean were marked by two particularly successful and profitable raids on the Balearic Islands (1113, 1115). Despite almost continuous warfare with Genoa, Pisa was at the height of its prosperity and power.

Venice

The independence of Venice was recognized by the Byzantines in 584. The Venetians successfully defied combined land and sea attacks by Pepin against their island stronghold (774). In the following centuries Venice became a wealthy trading center. Depredations of Dalmatian pirates, who dominated the Adriatic in the late 10th century, forced the Venetians to build a fleet to protect their commerce. Under Doge **Pietro Orseolo II,** the Venetian fleet defeated the pirates and captured their strongholds of **Curzola** and **Lagosta,** assuring Venetian predominance in the Adriatic. Soon after this the Venetians captured Bari from the Moslems (1002). Later Venice lost most of the Dalmatian coast in a war with King **Calomar I** of Hungary (1097–1102). King **Bela III** of Hungary repulsed Venetian efforts to reconquer

Dalmatia (1172–1196). During most of this period Venice was allied with Byzantium, and Venetian fleets played an important role in the struggles between the Byzantines and the Normans. A dispute with Byzantium over trading concessions, however, led to war (1171) in which an attempted Venetian invasion was repulsed and the Venetians were defeated at sea (see p. 306).

NORMAN STATES IN SOUTH ITALY AND
SICILY, 1016–1200

Norman involvement in South Italy and Sicily was apparently accidental, resulting from the presence of a group of Norman pilgrims, returning from the Holy Land, who helped defend Salerno from a raiding Moslem fleet (1016). Soon more adventurers arrived from Normandy, and some of them established a permanent stronghold at Aversa, near Naples. In subsequent years Norman control spread over south Italy. The most important Norman leader, flourishing in the middle and latter portion of the 11th century, was **Robert Guiscard,** who expelled the Byzantines and Moslems from Southern Italy and conquered most of Sicily from the Moslems. He then attempted to invade the Byzantine Empire via Epirus, Thessaly, and Macedonia, but was eventually repulsed. During the next century the Normans consolidated their positions in southern Italy and Sicily, and played an important role in the struggles between the German emperors and the popes, while continuing to be involved in Mediterranean affairs and in the Crusades. The principal events were:

1027. First Permanent Norman Settlement in Italy. Established by **Rainulf** in the fortress of Aversa.

1030–1059. Extension of Norman Possessions in Apulia and Calabria.

1038. Byzantine Invasion of Eastern Sicily. The Byzantine Army, under **George Maniakes,** included many Normans. When Maniakes was recalled to Constantinople, the Moslems rallied and drove the Byzantines out.

1053. Battle of Civitella (Civitate, North-western Apulia). Normans, led by **Humphrey Guiscard** and his brother Robert, defeated the army of Pope **Leo IX,** which was attempting to relieve the region of Norman depredations. The Pope was captured.

1059. Rise of Robert Guiscard. In return for assistance against German Emperor **Henry IV,** Pope **Nicholas II** appointed Robert Duke of Calabria and Apulia, and authorized him to conquer Sicily.

1060–1091. Norman Conquest of Sicily.

1071. Capture of Bari. Robert eliminated the last Byzantine foothold in Italy.

1081–1085. Invasion of Byzantine Empire. Robert, aspiring to the imperial throne, led a Norman fleet and army across the Adriatic to capture Corfu (1081) and laid siege to Durazzo, defended by **George Palaeologus.** Despite defeat in the naval **Battle of Durazzo** (1081) by a combined Byzantine-Venetian fleet, Robert, who had less than 20,000 men, maintained his position around Durazzo during the winter, but was forced to lift the siege upon the arrival of a relieving army of some 50,000 led by Byzantine Emperor **Alexius Comnenus.**

1082. (Land) Battle of Durazzo* (or Dyrrhachium). Robert, assisted by his son, **Bohemund,** converted defeat to victory by a desperate surprise cavalry attack, smashing and routing Alexius' famed Varangian Guard. Robert's wife, **Sicelgaeta,** apparently participated actively and helped her husband rally his troops before the final decisive charge. In this battle the Norman cavalrymen were faced by Anglo-Saxon axmen, some of them veterans of Hastings, who had taken service with the Byzantines after the Norman conquest of Britain. (Comparison of the two battles is interesting; in both cases the tough, courageous Anglo-Saxons, in their monolithic phalanxes, advanced prematurely, without orders, and were eventually overwhelmed by

---

* Erroneously called the Battle of Pharsalus by some historians who have misread Gibbon's cryptic comments.

the combined efforts of bowmen and a furious Norman heavy-cavalry charge.) Robert reinvested Durazzo, which soon surrendered. The Normans now advanced into Thessaly. Soon after this Robert returned to Italy in response to an appeal from Pope Gregory VII for assistance against Emperor Henry IV, leaving Bohemund in command in Greece. Bohemund advanced to the Vardar River, but while besieging **Larissa** was defeated by Alexius, who drove him back into Epirus.

1083–1084. Relief of Rome. While Henry IV was besieging Gregory VII in Castel San Angelo, in Rome, Robert collected an army of Normans, Lombards, and Moslems, then marched north. Henry retired into north Italy, without risking a major battle (May, 1084). The Norman soldiers then sacked Rome, causing the local population to rise against their deliverers and against the pope who had called them. Robert escorted Gregory to Salerno, then rejoined Bohemund in Epirus.

1084. Battle off Corfu. The Norman Fleet fought an indecisive battle with the Byzantines and Venetians.

1085. Death of Robert. Bohemund was forced to return to Italy.

1096–1104. Participation of Bohemund and Tancred in the Crusades. (See p. 312.)

1104–1108. Bohemund's Operations in Epirus. (See p. 305.)

1105–1150. Reign of Roger II of Sicily. A period of confused warfare against **Rainulf** of Apulia; Roger was eventually successful, establishing sovereignty over all southern Italy as well as Sicily (1137–1139). During this conflict he was at one time or another at war with the Pope, Emperor Lothair of Germany, Pisa, Genoa, Venice, and the Byzantines; he repulsed all invasions, and eventually (1139) obtained papal sanction for his earlier claim to the title of king (1130). Meanwhile he had been engaged in frequent overseas wars against the Moslem rulers of North Africa. His admiral, **George of Antioch,** captured Malta, Tripoli, Mahadia, and other North African coastal cities to establish a Norman colony extending from Barca to Kairouan (1146–1152). During this time also George's fleet operated successfully along the European coast of the Byzantine Empire, capturing Corfu and sacking Athens, Thebes, and Corinth (1147–1149). George actually brought his fleet within bowshot of the imperial palace at Constantinople (1149), but sailed away when Emperor **Manuel** returned to his capital with a large army.

1154–1166. Reign of William I of Sicily. His fleets were defeated by the Byzantines under Palaeologus, who invaded Apulia (1155; see pp. 305–306). William won an overwhelming land victory at the **Battle of Brindisi** (1156), driving the Byzantines from Italy. He could not prevent the steady conquest of his North African dominions by the Almohads (1147–1160; see p. 308).

1166–1189. Reign of William II of Sicily. Despite energetic efforts, William was generally unsuccessful militarily. He failed in several efforts to reconquer the lost North African colonies and was repulsed at Alexandria (1174). He invaded the Byzantine Empire, and captured Durazzo and Thessalonika (1185). Advancing on Constantinople, he was decisively defeated by the Emperor **Isaac II Angelus** at the **Battle of the Strymon** (September 7, 1185), and was forced to make peace and to abandon his conquests (1189).

1190–1194. Reign of Tancred (Illegitimate Grandson of Roger II). His rule was disputed by Emperor **Henry VI,** husband of Roger's legitimate daughter, **Constance.** Tancred repulsed one invasion by Henry (1191) and subdued baronial revolts (1192–1193).

1194. Hohenstaufen Usurpation. Upon Tancred's early death, Henry seized the throne and was succeeded by his son, **Frederick II,** under the regency of Constance (1198–1208).

SPAIN

The slow process of Christian reconquest continued, despite a number of setbacks at the hands of periodically resurgent Moslem leaders. While constant warfare occurred along the shifting Moslem-Christian frontiers, violent internal struggles took place on both sides of the border, resulting in the establishment of a number of virtually independent principalities, kingdoms, and emirates, only occasionally subject to central authority. The principal events were:

1000–1035. Reign of Sancho III, the Great, of Navarre. He had also inherited Aragon, and in a series of wars against his neighbors conquered Castile, León, and Barcelona. As a result he became ruler of all Christian Spain (1027). Upon his death he divided his kingdom among his sons.

1002–1086. Decline of Moslem Spain. After the death of Al-Mansour (see p. 259), his son, **Abdulmalik-al-Mozaffar** briefly maintained Moslem ascendancy in Spain, but his early death led to a succession of disputes and widespread civil war. The caliphate collapsed completely (1031), breaking into a number of minor principalities. The most important was the Abbasid Dynasty of Seville, acknowledged as suzerain by many of the others. During this period of decline, most of the Moslem dynasties, including the Abbasids, became tributary to the aggressive successors of Sancho.

1035–1065. Reign of Ferdinand I, the Great, of Castile (Son of Sancho). After seizing León from one brother (1037), he reconquered former Castilian territory inherited by another brother, **Garcia** of Navarre. He won numerous victories over the Moslems, forcing the emirs of Saragossa, Toledo, and Seville to become tributaries.

1035–1065. Reign of Ramiro I of Aragon. Another son of Sancho, Ramiro was the first king of independent Aragon, and expanded his small country at the expense of Christian and Moslem neighbors.

1065–1072. Dynastic Civil War in Castile and León. Sancho, eldest son of Ferdinand I, was at first successful, thanks largely to the inspired generalship of **Rodrigo Díaz de Bivar.** When Sancho was killed in a siege, his younger brother, **Alfonso,** became unchallenged ruler of Castile.

1072–1109. Reign of Alfonso VI of Castile. He was successful in his early wars against the Moslems, his armies being led to victory by Rodrigo Díaz, who soon became known to the Moslems as "sidi" (lord), known in history as **El Cid Campeador.** Ordered into exile by the jealous king (1081), the Cid offered his services to the Moorish emir of Saragossa, winning consistent victories over the Christian rulers of Aragon and Barcelona.

c. 1074–1104. Reign of Pedro I of Aragon. Aragon continued to grow and prosper. He captured the fortified town of **Huesca** by assault (1096) and made it his capital.

1085. Castilian Conquest of Toledo. Mohammed al-Motamid, Emir of Seville, was so alarmed by the loss of Toledo that he called for assistance from the Almoravids of Morocco. **Yusuf ibn Tashfin** thereupon brought a Moorish army to Spain (see p. 308).

1088, October 23. Battle of Zallaka (Near Badajoz). Yusuf decisively defeated Alphonso VI. The Castilian king pardoned the Cid, who returned to reorganize the shattered armies of Castile. After another dispute with the king, however, the Cid was banished again (1089).

1086–1091. Almoravid Conquest of Moslem Spain. On the verge of defeat by his erstwhile allies, al-Motamid endeavored to ally himself with Alfonso, but was soon overwhelmed and imprisoned by the Almoravids (1091), who had overrun all of Moslem Spain except Saragossa.

1089–1094. Conquest of Valencia by the Cid. Raising a private army of Christians and Moslems, Diaz made himself virtually an independent monarch. He repulsed invasions by the Almoravids at the **Battle of Cuarte** (1094) and again at the **Battle of Bairen** (1097). After his death (1099), the Almoravids reconquered Valencia (1102).

1104–1134. Reign of Alfonso I, the Warrior, of Aragon. His brief marriage with **Urraca,** Queen of Castile, involved him in Castilian affairs. Quarreling with his wife, he defeated her adherents at the **Battle of Sepulveda** (1111). He expanded Aragon below the Ebro, capturing Saragossa (1118).

1126–1157. Reign of Alfonso VII of Castile and León (Son of Urraca). He was generally successful in wars against Christian and Moslem neighbors, and forced Aragon and Navarre to accept his sovereignty. However, his cousin, **Alfonso (Affonso) Henriques,** asserted the independence of Portugal (1140; see p. 300).

To suppress Moslem resurgence under the Almohads (see below), Alfonso of Castile invaded southern Spain, but was repulsed, and died in the **Battle of Muradel** during the withdrawal (1157).

1145–1150. Almohad Conquest of Moslem Spain. The Moorish Almohads (see p. 308), under **'Abd al-Mu'min al-Kumi,** overwhelmed the Almoravids.

1158–1214. Reign of Alfonso VIII of Castile (Grandson of Alfonso VII). An infant at accession, Alfonso as a young man had to fight refractory nobles to establish his authority. He then undertook several successful campaigns against the Moslems until he was overwhelmingly defeated by Almohad Caliph **Abu-Yusuf Ya'qub al-Mansour** at the **Battle of Alarcos** (near Ciudad Real, 1195). Following this disaster, Castile was invaded by León and Navarre, as well as by the Moslems, but Alfonso repulsed the invaders.

PORTUGAL, C. 1100–1200

The County of Portugal came into existence on the north bank of the Douro River in the 10th century as the Kingdom of León pressed the Moslems southward on the west coast of the Iberian peninsula. Separatist tendencies appeared early in the 12th century during the stormy reign of Queen Urraca of Castile and León (see p. 299). The strong Count **Alfonso Henriques** (1112–1185) won numerous victories over the Moslems, culminating (1139) at the **Battle of Ourique** (location uncertain, probably not modern Ourique). Alfonso then declared his independence from his cousin, Alfonso VII of Castile and León, who reluctantly recognized him as King of Portugal (1140). Alfonso continued to press the Moslems southward, capturing Lisbon and establishing the Tagus as the southern boundary of Portugal (1147). In his operations against Lisbon he was assisted by Crusader contingents from England and the Low Countries, en route to the Holy Land for the Second Crusade (see p. 316). In the latter years of his reign, Alfonso repelled repeated Almohad invasions. He also raided frequently into Moslem territory; in one of these he was captured at Badajoz (1169), but was later released. He captured **Santarem** (1171) and repulsed a Moorish effort to recapture the city (1184).

EASTERN EUROPE*

POLAND

During the first century and a half of the period, Poland gradually expanded under a number of able and martial rulers. During the latter part of the 13th century, however, the country suffered from internal discord, dynastic disputes, and weak leadership. The principal events were:

992–1025. Reign of Boleslav I, the Brave. (See p. 261.) This great king continued the process of centralization and expansion. He fought a series of wars against **Henry II of Germany (1002–1019)** in

---

* Bohemia, Hungary, Moravia, and Bulgaria are omitted as separate sections during this period, save as they appear in the sections of other nations. The many wars of these small states had little lasting military or historical significance.

---

which he was generally successful, conquering the province of Lusatia and displacing the German emperor as the suzerain of Bohemia. He then turned eastward, defeated **Yaroslav,** Prince of Kiev, in the **Battle of the Bug** (1020), and temporarily occupied Kiev. At his death Poland extended from the Elbe to the Bug, and from the Baltic to the Danube.

1025–1034. Reign of Mieszko II (Son of Boleslav). A period of decline. Slovakia and Moravia broke away (1027, 1031). Ruthenia was reconquered by Yaroslav of Kiev, and Pomerania was lost to Canute of Denmark (1031).

1034–1040. Dynastic Struggles. Silesia was lost to **Bratislav I** of Bohemia (1038), who also temporarily occupied Cracow (1039).

1038–1058. Reign of Casimir I, the Restorer (Son of Mieszko). After re-establishing order in Poland, Casimir reconquered Silesia (1054).

1058–1079. Reign of Boleslav II, the Bold (Son of Casimir). A strong and vigorous ruler, Boleslav failed in two attempts to reconquer Bohemia, though he did reconquer Upper Slovakia (1061–1063). He twice occupied Kiev (1069, 1078), and regained Ruthenia for Poland. He was overthrown by a rebellion of nobles.

1079–1102. Period of Decline.

1102–1138. Reign of Boleslav III. A strong ruler and good soldier, he repulsed an invasion of Silesia by German Emperor Henry V at the **Battle of Glogau** or **Hundsfeld,** near Breslau (1109). He reconquered Pomerania by a great victory over the Pomeranians at the **Battle of Naklo** (1109). He subdued a Pomeranian revolt under Prince **Warcislaw** of Sczecin (1119–1124). He failed in invasions of Bohemia and Hungary (1132–1135).

1138–1200. Decline of Poland. The German nobles **Albert the Bear,** Margrave of Brandenburg, and **Henry the Lion,** Duke of Saxony, steadily drove the Poles east of the Vistula, while the Danes, under Waldemar and Absalon, seized the Baltic coastal region (see pp. 292 and 295).

RUSSIA

The history of Russia during this period was dominated by the presence or by the memory of two great princes of Kiev: **Vladimir the Saint** (see p. 261) and his son **Yaroslav.** They and their direct descendants ruled Russia for nearly three centuries. The principal events were:

978–1015. Reign of Vladimir the Saint.

1015–1019. Dynastic War between the Sons of Vladimir. Yaroslav was eventually successful, defeating **Sviatopolk,** and driving **Mstislav** east of the Dnieper, where he remained semi-independent until his death (1036).

1019–1054. Reign of Yaroslav the Wise. He defended his domains successfully against the Poles (despite some setbacks; see p. 300), as well as against the Pechenegs.

1054–1136. Arrival of the Cumans. This Turkish tribe, even more ferocious than the Pechenegs, contributed to the decline of Kiev. At the same time the principalities of Novgorod and Suzdal, nominally subject to Kiev, prospered. The rulers of all three states were descendants of Yaroslav.

1113–1125. Reign of Vladimir II, Monomakh. The last great ruler of Kiev, he was engaged in almost ceaseless war against the Cumans.

1157–1174. Reign of Andrei Bogoliubski of Suzdal. He conquered Kiev from his cousin, **Mstislav II, the Daring.**

EURASIA AND THE MIDDLE EAST

BYZANTINE EMPIRE

During the first part of this period the Byzantine Empire continued to demonstrate the remarkable vigor which had returned it to pre-eminence in the Middle East in the preceding two centuries. This was brought to a sudden and catastrophic conclusion by the appearance of the Seljuk Turks under **Alp Arslan,** who inflicted the disastrous defeat of **Manzikert** on the Emperor **Romanus.** Almost overnight practically all of the Asiatic dominions of the empire were lost to the Turks, the Byzantines retaining only a handful of fortified seaports on the coast of Anatolia. With considerable assistance (as well as some opposition) from the First Crusaders (see p. 313), the able soldier-emperor Alexius Comnenus began a slow and painful process of resurgence, fighting more or less successfully against Normans, Bulgars, Turks, and occasionally Crusaders. Despite the amazing vitality and resilience demonstrated under Alexius and his successors, the empire never fully recovered from Manzikert. Yet at the end of this period it was still the wealthiest and most powerful single nation of Eastern Europe and Southwestern Asia. The principal events were:

Continued Byzantine Revival, 1000–1067

976–1025. Reign of Basil II. (See p. 265.)

996–1018. Conquest of Bulgaria. Basil defeated Bulgarian Tsar **Samuel** at the **Battle of the Spercheios** (996), and reconquered Greece and Macedonia from the Bulgarians. Soon after this Samuel invaded Macedonia again, capturing and sacking Adrianople (1003). Resuming the offensive, Basil finally ejected the Bulgarians from Thrace and Macedonia (1007); his advance into Bulgaria culminated at the decisive **Battle of Balathista** (1014). Basil blinded his 15,000 Bulgarian captives, then sent them back to Samuel, who died of shock. After this, Bulgarian resistance crumbled; Basil soon conquered the entire country (1018).

1018. Battle of Cannae. Byzantine victory over Lombards and Normans attempting to invade south Italy.

1020. Annexation of Armenia. The Armenians asked protection against the Seljuk Turks (see p. 310).

1025–1028. Reign of Constantine VIII. This was marked by a Pecheneg invasion across the Danube. The barbarians were defeated and driven back across the river by **Constantine Diogenes** (1027).

1028–1050. Reign of the Empress Zoë. Her husband, **Romanus,** was defeated by the Moslems in Syria (1030). The precarious situation in Syria was soon restored, however, by a series of victories won by the great general, **George Maniakes** (1031).

1032–1035. Naval Wars against Moslem Pirates. In combination with the Ragusans, a Byzantine fleet defeated Moslem pirates in the Adriatic (1032), completing the work begun earlier by the Venetians (see p. 296). A Byzantine fleet, largely manned by Norse mercenaries under Harold Hardraade (see pp. 286 and 293), swept Moslem pirates from much of the Mediterranean, and harassed North Africa.

1038–1040. Invasion of Sicily by George Maniakes. His army included Harald Hardraade's mercenaries and Normans from south Italy. Maniakes captured Messina (1038) and won important victories at the battles of **Rametta** (1038) and **Dragina** (1040). When he was called back to Constantinople to deal with a Bulgarian revolt, the invasion collapsed; the Moslems recovered the island (1040).

1040–1041. Unsuccessful Revolt in Bulgaria. Rebellion, led by **Peter Deljan,** was suppressed by Maniakes.

1041–1042. Revolt of Michael V. After temporarily usurping the throne from Zoë, he was overthrown by the Byzantine nobility.

1042. Battle of Monopoli. Maniakes decisively defeated Norman invaders of Byzantine southern Italy.

1042–1059. Decline. During the reigns of Constantine IX (1042–1054), second husband of Zoë), **Theodora** (1054–1056, Zoë's sister), **Michael VI** (1056–1057), and **Isaac I Comnenus** (1057–1059), the army and fleet were seriously neglected and allowed to deteriorate.

1043. Revolt of Maniakes. He crossed the Adriatic from Italy, but died in an accident while marching on Constantinople.

1048–1049. Appearance of the Seljuk Turks. They defeated the Armenians at **Kars** and occupied Ardzen, west of Lake Van. They fought a drawn battle with the Byzantines at **Kapitron,** but were defeated at **Stragna** and repulsed at **Manzikert** (Malazgirt).

1048–1054. Pecheneg Raids. Repeated forays across the Danube.

1059–1067. Reign of Constantine X. Continuing neglect of the military resulted in a series of defeats. In Italy, the Normans captured Rhegium, and completed the conquest of Calabria (1060). The Seljuks under **Alp Arslan,** overran most of Armenia (1064) and began raiding deep into Anatolia (1065–1067). A Cuman raid across the Danube reached Thessalonika (1064–1065).

Romanus and Manzikert, 1067–1071

1067–1071. Reign of Romanus Diogenes. An able general, Romanus was married by the Empress **Eudocia,** widow of Constantine X, apparently under pressure from the Byzantine aristocracy, who wanted a strong military ruler to meet the mounting foreign threats to the Empire.

1068–1069. Early Campaigns of Romanus. After spending nearly a year in rebuilding the army, Romanus conducted a successful winter campaign against the Turks, who had boldly taken up winter quarters in Phrygia and Pontus. He defeated Alp Arslan at the **Battle of Sebastia** (Sivas), forcing him to withdraw to Armenia and Mesopotamia. Romanus then conducted a successful lightning campaign into Syria, where the Arabs had taken advantage of the Seljuk success to rise against the Byzantines. After subduing a mutiny among his mercenaries, Romanus marched back to Cappadocia, where the Turks had again begun raiding. Driving them off, he marched eastward to the Turkish stronghold of Akhlat (Ahlat) on Lake Van, which he besieged. He sent part of his army on a raid farther east, into Media, where it was defeated by Alp Arslan. Romanus abandoned the siege, and Alp raided into Anatolia toward Iconium. Romanus cleverly moved behind the Turks and defeated them at the **Battle of Heraclea** (Eregli). Alp withdrew to Aleppo. Save for a few fortresses in Armenia, Romanus had now driven the Turks completely out of the empire.

1068–1071. Operations in Italy. Taking advantage of Romanus' occupation with the Turks, the Normans renewed their attacks against Byzantine outposts in southern Italy, capturing Otranto (1068), and threatening Bari. Romanus hastened to Italy (1070), where he had mixed success against the Normans. But events in Anatolia soon forced him to return there. After his departure the Normans captured Bari, driving the Byzantines completely from Italy (1071).

1070. Renewed Turk Invasion. Two Turkish armies invaded the empire while Romanus was in Italy. One, under **Arisiaghi,** brother-in-law of Alp Arslan, defeated the main Byzantine army under **Manuel Comnenus** near **Sebastia.** Meanwhile, Alp captured the fortress of Manzikert, but was repulsed from Edessa (Urfa).

1071. Campaign of Manzikert. Early in the spring Romanus advanced east from Sebastia, via Theodosiopolis (Erzerum), with an army of 40,000–50,000 men. He sent part of his army ahead to the vicinity of Lake Van, under the general **Basilacius,** to ravage the country around Akhlat and to screen the main body. Romanus besieged and captured Manzikert. He then advanced to lay siege to Akhlat, while his covering force advanced toward Khoi, in Media, where Alp Arslan was gathering an army. Late in July or early August, Alp advanced with 50,000 or more men. He brushed aside Basilacius' covering force (probably 10,000–15,000 strong), which apparently withdrew to the southwest without informing Romanus. Since Basilacius' mission was to screen the main Byzantine army, he evidently was involved in a widespread treasonous conspiracy which pervaded it. (The conspirators' leader was the emperor's principal lieutenant, **Andronicus Ducas,** and Empress Eudocia was probably behind the plot.) In any event, Romanus was surprised, in mid-August, by the sudden appearance of Alp's army, which ambushed and annihilated a Byzantine force near Akhlat. Romanus hastily fell back toward Manzikert, and prepared to give battle between that fortress and Akhlat. During this withdrawal his mercenary Kipchak and Pecheneg light cavalry deserted, bringing his strength down to less than 35,000 men.

1071, August 19 (?). Battle of Manzikert. Romanus formed his army up in a typical Byzantine formation of two lines, in open, rolling country. He personally commanded the first line. Andronicus Ducas commanded the second. While the opposing light-cavalry units were skirmishing and the main Turkish army was forming, Alp sent a messenger offering peace. Considering this a ruse—which it probably was—Romanus refused to consider any terms save an immediate Turkish withdrawal from Byzantine territory. Soon after this the Turkish horse archers opened the battle at long range. Judiciously combining the fire of his own archers with the advance of his heavy cavalry, Romanus tried in vain to pin the Turks down. He did, however, drive his elusive foe back so far that in the late afternoon the Byzantines captured the Turkish camp. With dusk approaching and no decision reached, his army in an exposed position, several miles from his own lightly guarded camp, Romanus decided to withdraw. The Turks immediately turned to harass the retiring Byzantines, causing some disorder among the mercenaries. To prevent the confusion from spreading, Romanus ordered a halt and turned against the Turks with his first line. It is not clear whether he intended to bivouac under arms for the night or merely wanted to drive off the Turks before continuing the withdrawal. Despite the order to halt, Andronicus Ducas continued the retirement with the second line and the flank outpost units. The Turks immediately seized the opportunity and swarmed around Romanus, who had no time to reorganize his remaining troops for all-around defense. The two wings of the front line were quickly overwhelmed. As darkness fell the Turks closed in around the small body remaining with Romanus. Every man was killed or captured, the emperor himself being taken a prisoner to Alp Arslan.

1071, August–September. Outbreak of Civil War. In Constantinople, upon word of the defeat at Manzikert, **John Ducas** seized power and established his nephew, **Michael VII**, son of Constantine X, on the throne. Romanus, soon released by Alp Arslan upon promise to pay ransom, endeavored to regain his throne, but was defeated by his enemies, captured, and blinded by Andronicus Ducas; he died soon after. Pathethically, the last act of this tragic, noble figure was to gather all of the money he could raise to send to Alp Arslan in proof of his good faith in paying his ransom.

COMMENT. *Neither inferior combat capability nor poor generalship lost the Battle of Manzikert; the one real cause of defeat was treason. The consequences were stupendous. While rival claimants struggled for the Byzantine throne, the victorious Turks overran practically all of Anatolia, wiping out the heart of the empire. The Turks ravaged the country mercilessly, partly from barbarism, partly from policy. Anatolia became a virtual desert. A great proportion of the population perished; the survivors fled. When parts of Anatolia were later reconquered by the Byzantines, they were unable to raise any significant forces from the region. The most important single military result of Manzikert, then, was to eliminate the principal native recruiting ground of the empire, a region from which it had habitually raised armies of 120,000 men and more. Thenceforward the empire was forced to rely upon mercenaries for the bulk of its armed forces. Principal among them were West Europeans for heavy cavalry, Russians and Norsemen for infantry, Pechenegs and Cumans for light cavalry. The most important permanent component of the imperial armies became the Varangian Guard—the name revealing the Norse-Russian origin of most of its members. Yet, surprisingly, the empire survived for almost four more centuries, its continuing existence almost entirely due to the legacy of doctrine and professional skill of its amazing military system.*

Byzantium Struggles for Survival, 1071–1200

1071–1081. Internal Chaos. The Seljuk Turks overran all of Anatolia save for a few isolated coastal cities. The downfall of Michael came with the simultaneous revolts of generals **Nicephorus Bryennius** in Epirus and **Nicephorus Botaniates** in the dwindling Anatolian provinces (1078) Botaniates, with Turk help, was successful, and became Nicephorus III. He was immediately faced with more insurrections. His general, Alexius Comnenus, subdued Nicephorus Briennus in the hardfought cavalry **Battle of Calavryta,** in eastern Thessaly, in which a high order of leadership and professional skill was displayed on both sides (1079). Soon after this, however, the emperor's jealousy led Alexius to revolt and seize the throne (1081). Meanwhile, taking advantage of the inner turmoil of the empire, the Turks captured Nicaea (1080).

1081–1118. Reign of Alexius Comnenus One of the most astute diplomats and resourceful rulers of history. With meager resources, with the empire falling apart from internal dissension, he was faced with external threats from all directions The Turks were hammering at the Asiatic gates of Constantinople, the Pechenegs and Cumans were ranging south of the Danube, Bulgaria was in revolt, and the Normans under **Robert Guiscard** and **Bohemund** were driving toward Constantinople through Epirus and Thessaly. Yet surprisingly, despite many defeats and heartbreaking setbacks, he met these terrible dangers with a fortitude and skill worthy of a successor of Heraclius. He was particularly adroit at turning his enemies—internal and external—against each other. By the end of his reign the European boundaries of the empire had been restored nearly to their pre-Manzikert positions, while more than one-third of Anatolia—including the entire coast line—had been recovered, thanks in large part to the unintended and somewhat reluctant assistance of West European Crusaders (see p. 313).

1081–1085. War against the Normans. (See p. 297.) In order to meet this threat Alexius was forced to make peace with the Seljuks, temporarily recognizing their conquests in Anatolia. He then employed a number of Turk mercenaries in his battles against the Normans.

1084. Fall of Antioch. The Seljuks captured the last Byzantine foothold in Syria.

1086–1091. Revolt of the Bogomils. This Christian heretical sect of Bulgaria formed an alliance with the Pechenegs and Cumans. The allies defeated Alexius at the **Battle of Dorostorum** (Silistra, 1086). Eventually Alexius suppressed the revolt, then defeated the Pechenegs at the **Battle of Leburnion** and drove them back across the Danube (1091).

1094. Revolt of Constantine Diogenes. He led a Cuman army across the Danube into Thrace, where he besieged Adrianople. Alexius defeated the pretender in the **Battle of Taurocomon.**

1098–1102. The First Crusade. (See p. 312.) This enabled Alexius to recover almost half of Anatolia from the Turks.

1098–1108. Renewed Norman War. The cause was Bohemund's refusal to return Antioch to the Empire in accordance with the Crusaders' promise (see p. 314). The Byzantines, supported by **Raymond** of Toulouse and Tripoli, fought a desultory war against Bohemund and his nephew **Tancred** in northern Syria (1099–1104). Bohemund then returned to Italy, raised a polyglot army of West European volunteers (mostly Normans), and crossed the Adriatic. He besieged Durazzo, but was repulsed (1106). Alexius then defeated Bohemund in a number of minor engagements, finally forcing him to make peace and to give up his claim to Antioch (1108). This was meaningless, however, because Tancred refused to honor Bohemund's signature; sporadic fighting continued between Byzantines and Normans in northern Syria.

1110–1117. Renewed War with the Seljuks. The Turks were initially victorious, and again ravaged Byzantine Anatolia, raiding as far as the Bosporus. Alexius, however, waging war in typical, calculating manner, repulsed them, gaining a great victory at the **Battle of Philomelion** (Akshehr, 1116). The Turks sued for peace, and agreed to abandon the entire coast of Anatolia to the Byzantines.

1118–1143. Reign of John II Comnenus (Son of Alexius). He defeated the Seljuks, recovering most of Anatolia (1120–1121). He crushed a Pecheneg invasion of Bulgaria so thoroughly that they were never again a threat to the Empire (1121–1122). He was unsuccessful in a prolonged naval war with Venice (1122–1126). He intervened in Hungary to settle a dynastic war, forcing the Hungarians to accept Byzantine suzerainty (1124–1126). He reconquered southeastern Cilicia (1134–1137), where the Armenians had maintained their independence against both Turks and Byzantines since Manzikert. He defeated Raymond of Antioch (who had assisted the Armenians) and was preparing to invade the Principality of Antioch when he died (1143).

1143–1180. Reign of Manuel Comnenus (Son of John). Continuing his father's campaign in Syria, he defeated Raymond and forced him to swear allegiance to the empire (1144). He then drove the Turks from their mountain strongholds in Isauria (1145).

1147–1149. The Second Crusade. (See p. 316.)

1147–1158. War with Roger of Sicily. The Norman fleet captured Corfu (1147) and ravaged the coast of Greece. Manuel reestablished the old alliance with Venice, and the combined Byzantine-Venetian fleets defeated the Normans (1148) and reconquered Corfu (1149). Manuel then invaded Italy and seized Ancona (1151), which he held, despite Norman repulse of his further invasion attempts (1155–1156; see p. 298).

1150–1152. Serb Rebellion. Subdued by Manuel.

1151–1155, and 1153–1168. Byzantine Invasions of Hungary. Manuel's victory in the **Battle of Semlin** (Zemun, northeast Yugoslavia) forced Hungary to make peace and to cede Dalmatia and other territories to him (1168).

1158–1177. Renewed Wars with the Seljuks and Raynald of Antioch. Manuel forced **Kilij Arslan IV** to recognize Byzantine suzerainty (1161). Manuel was badly defeated in the **Battle of Myriocephalum** (1176), but recouped his losses with the assistance of **John Vatatzes** the following year in Bithynia and in the Meander Valley.

1169. Expedition to Egypt. A joint Byzantine-Crusader force under King **Amalric** of Jerusalem was repulsed at **Damietta** (see p. 309).

1170–1177. War with Venice and the Normans. The Venetians were driven completely from the Aegean (1170). However, with Norman assistance, the Venetians captured Chios and Ragusa (1171), but were repulsed at Ancona (1173). The war was a draw.

1180–1185. Regency and Reign of Andronicus Comnenus. This brilliant soldier and dissolute prince seized power from the child Emperor **Alexius II,** whom he soon put to death (1183). His strong rule an-

tagonized the nobility, who invited **William of Sicily** to assist them (1184). William, decisively defeated by Andronicus, was forced to return to Sicily (1185; see p. 298). Andronicus was overthrown and brutally killed in an uprising in Constantinople.

1180–1196. Serb Independence. A successful rebellion under **Stephen Nemanya.**

1185–1195. First Reign of Isaac Angelus. A new war against the Normans resulted in the temporary loss of Durazzo and Corfu. Byzantine Admiral-General **Alexius Branas** won a decisive victory off the Greek coast at the **Battle of Demetritsa** (1185). The Normans were finally driven from their conquests (1191). Meanwhile, the Bulgarians, under **John** and **Peter Asen,** successfully revolted (1186–1187) and began to raid periodically into Thrace. They defeated Isaac at **Berrhoe** (1189) and retained their conquests despite a Byzantine success at **Arcadiopolis** (1194).

1186–1195. Internal Discord. Imperial power declined as Isaac was forced to defend his throne against numerous rival claimants, the first being Branas, who was defeated and killed by the emperor near Constantinople (1186). Isaac was overthrown, blinded, and imprisoned by his brother, **Alexius.**

1195–1203. Reign of Alexius III. The empire began to disintegrate; Turks raided at will through Byzantine Anatolia, while the Bulgars ravaged the European provinces.

MOSLEM DOMINIONS

The Middle East (Syria, Arabia, Mesopotamia, Anatolia)

There was utmost confusion and turmoil in the Moslem Middle East, with almost incessant warfare among minor Moslem potentates. Three major historical trends emerge from the bloody welter of minor wars. First was the overrunning of most of the Middle East by the Seljuk Turks during the latter half of the 11th century. Next was the appearance of the Crusaders, whose presence shaped events in the region during the entire 12th century. Finally, there was the temporary unification of Arab, Egyptian, and Turkish Moslems of the Middle East—a reaction to the Crusades—under the leadership of **Nur-ed-din** and his renowned successor, **Saladin.** The principal events were:

1000–1098. Chaos in Mesopotamia and Syria. Among the many contenders for supremacy were the Byzantines, who held the north and northwest, centered around

Antioch (until 1087), the Buyids of Baghdad (until 1055), and the Fatimids around Damascus (until 1079).

1043–1055. Seljuk Conquest of Mesopo-

tamia. (See p. 310.) Capture of Baghdad by Tughril Beg ended the Buyid Dynasty.

1055–1060. Revolt in Mesopotamia. This was led by **Al-Basasiri,** Turk general formerly under the Buyids, and supported by the Fatimids. While Tughril was putting down a mutiny in his own army, Al-Basasiri temporarily occupied Baghdad (1058), but Tughril soon crushed the revolt.

1063–1092. Seljuk Conquest of Syria and Anatolia. (See p. 310.)

1092–1098. Breakup of the Seljuk Empire. Taking advantage of a dynastic civil war in the heart of the Seljuk Empire (see p. 311), Kilij Arslan, son of Sulaiman ibn Kutalmish (see p. 310), re-established his father's domain in Anatolia: the Sultanate of Roum or Rum, with its capital at Iconium. A rival regime was set up at Sivas under the Turk atabeg (general or prince) **Danishmend.** In Syria and northern Mesopotamia, **Ridwan,** son of Tutush, was Emir of Aleppo.

1097–1102. The First Crusade. (See p. 312.)

1102–1144. Many-Sided Struggle for Control of Mesopotamia. The Crusaders held the northwestern portion around Edessa (until 1144). Ridwan and his successors were predominant, but their supremacy was disputed by the Seljuks of Rum and several other Moslem principalities. Kilij Arslan of Rum captured Mosul (1102), but was defeated and killed by Ridwan at the **Battle of the Khabur River** (1107).

1102–1127. Struggle for Syria. The Crusaders held the entire coastal region, and consolidated their control, but they never had the numerical strength to expand far beyond the coast. After Ridwan's death (1117), the Seljuks of Aleppo were overthrown by the Burid atabegs of Damascus, whose principal rivals were the Urtuqids of northeastern Syria. Throughout this period and the remainder of the century, the Assassins held a mountain stronghold northeast of Tripoli against all efforts, Christian and Moslem.

1127–1146. Reign of Imad-al-Din Zangi, Atabeg of Mosul. He extended his rule over all of northern Mesopotamia and northern Syria, capturing Edessa from the Crusaders (1144).

1146–1174. Reign of Nur-ed-din. (Son of Zangi). He conquered all of Moslem Syria and defeated **Raymond** of Antioch (1149–1150). Later his general **Shirkuh** conquered Egypt (1163–1169; see p. 309).

1147–1149. The Second Crusade. (See p. 316.)

1155–1194. Resurgence of the Abbasids. The Caliphs gained control of southern and central Mesopotamia, despite continued opposition from the declining Seljuk Dynasty.

1174–1186. Rise of Saladin. (See p. 309.) Expanding from Egypt into Syria and northern Mesopotamia, he conquered the entire empire formerly held by Nur-ed-din.

1187–1189. Saladin's Jihad (Holy War) against the Crusaders. This resulted in the conquest of Jerusalem and most of the Crusader kingdom.

1189–1192. The Third Crusade. (See p. 318.)

North Africa

MOROCCO AND WESTERN ALGERIA

Northwest Africa was fragmented under local Berber chieftains until veiled Tuareg tribesmen erupted from the Sahara in the mid-11th century to establish the vigorous Almoravid (or Murabit) Dynasty. They swept through Morocco and western Algeria, while simultaneously conquering the Negro kingdom of Ghana. They next conquered Moslem Spain and reconquered part of central Spain recently captured by the Christians. Slightly less than a century after their appearance, the Almoravids were swept from power, as abruptly as they had seized it, by a mountain Berber tribe which established the Almohad (Muwahhid) Dynasty in control of the same territory. The Almohads then expanded eastward. The principal events were:

1053–1056. Rise of the Touaregs. This Berber people inhabiting the Sahara gained control of most of the Western Sahara oases under **Yana ibn Omar,** a natural military genius, who established the Almoravid Dynasty and organized his people for war.

1054–1076. Almoravid Conquest of West Africa. The first penetration of Islam south of the Sahara.

1056–1080. Almoravid Conquest of Morocco, and Western and Central Algeria. This was under the leadership of **abu-Bakr ibn-'Umar** and his brilliant soldier cousin, Yusuf ibn Tashfin.

1086–1092. Almoravid Conquest of Moslem Spain. (See p. 299.)

c. 1120–1130. Rise of the Almohads. A militant Berber religious confederation was established in the Atlas Mountains by **Mohammed ibn-Tumart.**

1130–1147. Overthrow of the Almoravids. The Almohad leader was **'Abd Al-Mu'min ibn-'Ali (al-Kumi),** a follower of ibn-Tumart and a great soldier.

1145–1150. Almohad Conquest of Moslem Spain. (See p. 300.)

1147–1160. Almohad Conquest of Algeria, Tunisia, and Western Tripolitania. Following his victories, al-Mu'min took the title of caliph.

EASTERN ALGERIA, TUNISIA, AND TRIPOLITANIA

Central North Africa remained under the nominal rule of the Fatimid caliphs of Cairo until the middle of the 11th century, when the local Zirid Dynasty declared its independence. In retaliation the Fatimids sent a number of wild Arab nomadic tribes to devastate the region. The Pisans, Genoese, and Normans raided the coast frequently; the Normans held much of the littoral for several years. Zirids, Arabs, and Christians, however, were all overwhelmed by the violent Almohad expansion shortly after the middle of the 12th century. The principal events were:

1015–1016. Zirid Corsairs Driven from Sardinia. (See p. 296.)

1049. Zirid Independence. Emir Mu'izz ibn Badir declared independence from the Fatimids and abjured the Shi'ite faith, returning to Sunni teachings.

1058–1060. Fatimid Retaliation. Arab nomads were sent to ravage Zirid territory by Fatimid Caliph **al-Mustansir.** They overran most Zirid territory save the immediate vicinity of the capital, Mahadia (Mahdia).

1060–1091. Zirids Driven from Sicily. (See p. 297.)

1087. Temporary Conquest of Mahadia by Genoese and Pisans. (See p. 296.)

1135–1160. Norman Invasions of North Africa. (See p. 298.)

1147–1160. Almohad Conquest. (See above.)

EGYPT AND CYRENAICA

Eastern North Africa was held by the Fatimid caliphs for most of this period, though during the 12th century actual power was usually exercised by the caliphs' viziers. In the middle of the 12th century a complicated struggle for control of Egypt took place between the Crusader King Amalric of Jerusalem and the Zangid Turkish armies of **Nur-ed-din** of Aleppo and Mosul. Eventually the Turkish general, **Saladin,** founder of the Ayyubid Dynasty, became the virtual ruler of Egypt, though still nominally subject to Nur-ed-din. Upon the death of Nur-ed-din, Saladin asserted his independence and conquered the former Zangid domains of Syria, Kurdistan, and Mesopotamia. He then captured Jerusalem and most of Palestine from the Crusaders, to precipitate the Third Crusade. He repulsed the Crusaders' efforts to retake Jerusalem, and negotiated a compromise peace with **Richard I** of England. The principal events were:

996–1020. Reign of al-Hakim. A brutal and oppressive tyrant, he founded the religious sect of Druses.

1020–1035. Reign of al-Zhir. This was the beginning of Fatimid decline. Egypt was raided by various Syrian insurgents, including **Salih ibn Mirdas** of Aleppo. Tenuous Fatimid control of Syria was re-established by the victory of **Anushtakin al Dizbiri** over Mirdas at the **Battle of Ukhuwanah** (1029).

1035–1094. Reign of al-Mustansir. Continued Fatimid decline. Mirdas established his independent Mirdasid Dynasty at Aleppo (c. 1040). Mecca and Medina became independent (1047). The Zirids of Tunisia defected (1049; see p. 308). Much of Syria and Palestine was overrun by the Seljuks (1060–1071). Egypt was wracked by uprisings and revolts of Turkish elements of the army (1060–1074). Order was gradually established in Egypt and parts of southern Syria by the Armenian general and vizier, **Badr al-Jamali** (1074–1094).

1094–1101. Reign of al-Musta'li (Son of al-Mustansir). He was supported in a successful dynastic war against his brother by **al-Afdal Shahinshah,** son of Badr, who then recaptured Jerusalem and other cities of Palestine and southern Syria (1098). The Crusaders soon took Jerusalem, however, and decisively defeated al-Afdal at the **Battle of Askalon** (1099; see p. 314).

1101–1121. Rule of al-Afdal. He exercised control in the name of puppet caliphs. His attempts to reconquer Palestine were repulsed by the Crusaders (see p. 316).

1121–1163. Civil War and Dissensions. Ascalon, last Egyptian foothold in Syria, was lost to the Crusaders (1153).

1163–1169. Crusader and Zangid Struggle for Egypt. A Turkish-Syrian army under Nur-ed-din's general **Asad ud-Din Shirkuh** arrived in Egypt to assist the Egyptian vizier, **Shawar ibn Mujir,** suppress an insurrection (1163). At the same time the Crusaders from Jerusalem were raiding the Nile Delta. Discovering that Shirkuh intended to seize control of Egypt for Nur-ed-din, Shawar asked for help from King Amalric I of Jerusalem. The Crusaders helped Shawar defeat Shirkuh near Cairo (1167, April 11). Shirkuh's nephew, Saladin, distinguished himself in the battle. The Crusaders established themselves firmly in Cairo, which was repeatedly threatened by Shirkuh, but were unsuccessful in besieging Saladin at Alexandria. After negotiations, both antagonists agreed to evacuate Egypt, save for the Christian garrison of Cairo. Moslem disorders in Cairo caused Amalric to return to Egypt (1168). Shirkuh immediately returned also, and forced the Crusaders to withdraw (January, 1169). Shirkuh, although still subject to Nur-ed-din, became vizier to the Fatimid caliph, but died two months later. He was succeeded by Saladin, who became virtual ruler of Egypt.

1169–1193. Regency and Reign of Salah-al-din Yusuf ibn-Ayyub (Saladin). A Kurd of Turkish descent, he founded the Ayyubid Dynasty. He deposed the Fatimid Caliph and restored the Sunnite Moslem faith in Egypt (1171). He conquered Tripolitania from the Almohads (1172). Though nominally loyal to Nur-ed-din, he was virtually independent, and a coolness arose between them before Nur-ed-din's death (1174). Saladin then asserted his claim to all of the Zangid dominions, and gradually made this good in a series of campaigns against a number of other claimants (1174–1183). His successes were due primarily to his well-trained regular army of Turkish slaves (Mamelukes), primarily horse archers, but also including shock-action lancers. During this time he had had frequent minor conflicts with the Crusaders; as his power increased, and completely encircled the Latin states, these wars grew in intensity (1183–1187).

1187–1192. Saladin's Jihad (Holy War). Saladin conquered Jerusalem and most of Palestine, and caused the Third Crusade (see p. 318). Despite some defeats, Saladin retained Jerusalem and most of his Palestine conquests; but in a treaty with Richard I of England, granted the Christians special rights in Jerusalem (1192).

1193. Death of Saladin. The kingdom was divided between his sons: **al-Aziz** became ruler of Egypt; **al-Afdal** became ruler of Syria.

1196–1200. Dynastic War between Saladin's Successors. The brothers' uncle, **Abul Bakr Malik al-Adil,** fought on both sides and eventually gained full control of Saladin's empire as a result of a victory over al-Afdal at the **Battle of Bilbeis** (Egypt, January, 1200).

Persia and South-Central Asia

Under **Mahmud** of Ghazni, the Ghaznevids expanded their control from Khorasan southward, to include all of eastern Persia, and northward to gain undisputed control of Khwarezm (Khiva) and much of Turkestan between the Oxus and Syr Darya rivers. His most important campaigns, however, were in India (see p. 321). After his death the Ghaznevids declined and soon lost their western dominions to the Seljuks, under **Tughril Beg** and **Chaghrai Beg**. Tughril then went on to conquer western Persia and Mesopotamia from the Buyids, and to begin Turkish penetration of Anatolia (see pp. 303 and 307). The Seljuk practice of assigning semiautonomous control of provinces to their generals, or atabegs, soon resulted in the disintegration of the Seljuk Empire (save for Khorasan) into a number of warring principalities. During this time the small Shi'ite sect of Assassins prospered at Dailam, on the heights of Mt. Alamut in the Elburz range. Shortly after the middle of the 12th century, migrations of Turkish tribes from Turkestan overthrew **Sanjar**, Sultan of Khorasan and last of the direct Seljuk line. Following this, the Turkish shahs of Khwarezm (Khiva) conquered Khorasan and Isfahan to establish a new and powerful Persian empire. The principal events were:

PERIOD OF GHAZNEVID ASCENDANCY, 1000–1040

1006–1007. Ilak Invasion of Khorasan. Ilak Khan **Nasr I** from Transoxiana was repulsed by Mahmud, who defeated the invaders near Balkh.

1011–1016. Uprisings in Ghor and Khwarezm. Mahmud suppressed these and strengthened his control.

1029. Expedition into Persia. Mahmud defeated the Buyids and annexed their eastern territories.

PERIOD OF SELJUK ASCENDANCY, 1040–1150

1034–1055. Rise of the Seljuk Turks. Tughril Beg and Chaghrai Beg, grandsons of Seljuk (see p. 269), rose against the Ghaznevids. Crossing the Oxus, they occupied most of Khorasan, decisively defeating **Mas'ud**, son of Mahmud, at **Nishapur** (1038) and near **Merv** (1040). Chaghrai and the main body of Turks remained in Khorasan, operating successfully against the Ghaznevids until his death (1063). Tughril formed a standing army of Mamelukes and began moving westward against the Buyids and Byzantines.

1043–1055. Seljuk Conquest of Mesopotamia. Tughril conquered the Buyid regions of eastern Persia and northern Mesopotamia, and began raiding into Armenia and Byzantine Anatolia (1048). He captured Baghdad, ending the Buyid Dynasty (1055).

1063–1072. Reign of Alp Arslan (Son of Chaghrai Beg). He invaded Armenia, capturing Ani, the capital (1064). He began a determined invasion of the Byzantine Empire (see p. 302), while at the same time expanding into northern Syria (1068–1071). He defeated the Byzantine Emperor Romanus in the decisive **Battle of Manzikert** (1071; see p. 303). Jerusalem was captured from the Fatimids that same year.

1072. Khwarezmian Invasion. Alp defeated **Yakub** of Khwarezm at the **Battle of Berzem.** Yakub was captured, but he assassinated Alp in an interview after the battle.

1072–1092. Reign of Sultan Malik-shah (Son of Alp Arslan). Malik continued the conquest of Anatolia (1072–1081; see p. 304). Despite numerous revolts, he held his empire together and even expanded it in Central Asia (see p. 327) with the assistance of his able vizier, **Nizam-al-Mulk,** who conquered Transoxiana and advanced as far as Kashgar. Malik's principal rival was **Sulaiman ibn Kutalmish,** who briefly held most of Anatolia (1080–1086), and who captured Antioch from the Byzantines (1084). Sulaiman was defeated and killed near **Aleppo** by **Tutush,** Malik's brother (1086). **Atsiz** the Khwarezmian led one of Malik's armies through Syria, capturing Damascus (1086), and then on to the Nile, where he was repulsed by the Fatimids.

1092–1117. Decline of the Seljuk Empire.
While the sons of Malik (**Sanjar, Barki-yarok,** and **Mohammed**) fought over the succession in the heart of the empire (Iraq and Persia), outlying provinces fell away.

1117–1157. Reign of Sanjar, Seljuk Sultan of Khorasan (Son of Malik-shah). He occupied Ghazni (1117) and later returned to put down a revolt there (1134). He had earlier suppressed a revolt of the Turk Khan of Transoxiana (1130). Sanjar's principal rival was **Atsiz,** his viceroy in Khwarezm, who repeatedly revolted against Sanjar, with mixed success (1138–1152). During this period an invasion of Kara-Khitai Tartars was joined by local tribes; the combined forces decisively defeated Sanjar near **Samarkand** (1141), forcing him to abandon Transoxiana. He defeated and temporarily captured **Ala-ud-din Jihansuz** of Ghor (1150). The continuing influx of Turkoman into Khorasan led to widespread revolts, which caused the collapse of Sanjar's kingdom (1153–1157).

1148–1152. War between Ghor and Ghazni. The initial successes of **Saif ud-din Suir** and Ala-ud-din of Ghor over **Bahram Shah** of Ghazni were temporarily offset by the capture of Ghor by Sanjar (1150; see above). Bahram recaptured Ghazni from Saif ud-din, who was made prisoner and killed. Ala-ud-din then invaded Ghazni again, destroying the city completely and wrecking the remaining power of Ghazni (1152). This set the stage for a rapid expansion of Ghori power into India (see p. 321) and Khorasan.

PERIOD OF KHWAREZMIAN ASCENDANCY, 1150–1200

1172–1199. Reign of Takash, Shah of Khwarezm. A period of steady Khwarezmian expansion through Khorasan and Isfahan, culminating in the conquest of Mesopotamia (1194). Throughout this period, however, Khwarezm's control over southern and eastern Khorasan was constantly challenged by Ghor.

1173–1203. Reign of Ghiyas-ud-Din of Ghor. He had established himself as unquestioned master of all modern Afghanistan. He then devoted himself to constant inconclusive warfare against Khwarezm in Khorasan, appointing his brother **Muizz ad-Din Mohammed**—known to history as Muhammad of Ghor—as governor of Ghazni with the mission of extending Ghori rule into India (see p. 321).

THE CRUSADES

The Crusades were military expeditions undertaken by West Europeans for purposes primarily religious, but in which political considerations frequently played an important part. The immediate, direct, or ostensible object of the Crusades was the liberation or preservation of the Holy Land (and particularly the Holy Places in Jerusalem) from Moslem control. It should be noted, however, that during the Middle Ages the term "crusade" was frequently applied to other military expeditions against non-Christian foes who were pagans (as the German eastward expansion into Slavic territory; see p. 295) or Moslems (as the wars of reconquest in Spain; see p. 298) or heretics (as the Albigensian Crusade; see p. 367).

The forces which brought about the Crusades were really set in motion by the victory of the Moslem Seljuk Turks over the Byzantines at Manzikert (see p. 303), and Seljuk conquest of Jerusalem that same year from the more tolerant Fatimid caliphs of Cairo (1071). The subsequent Seljuk conquest of practically all of Anatolia from the Byzantines, combined with persecution of Christian pilgrims to Jerusalem, aroused Christendom. After several vain appeals for help from Byzantine emperors to popes and to West European monarchs, Pope **Urban II** eloquently called for action at the Synod of Clermont (1095). This evoked from his listeners spontaneous cries of "God wills it!"—which became the watchword of the Crusaders.

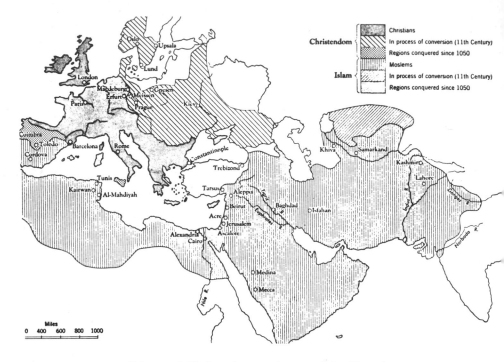

Christendom		Christians
		In process of conversion (11th Century)
		Regions conquered since 1050
Islam		Moslems
		In process of conversion (11th Century)
		Regions conquered since 1050

Islam and Christendom on the eve of the Crusades

The First Crusade, 1096–1099

1095–1096. The Leaders. The most prominent were French Bishop Adhemar du Puy, a courageous, wise soldier-priest who was appointed papal legate and was the mediator in the many disputes among his belligerent fellow leaders, Norman Duke **Bohemund** of Taranto (son of Robert Guiscard; see p. 297), his nephew **Tancred,** Count **Raymond** of Toulouse, Duke **Godfrey** de Bouillon of Lorraine, his brother **Baldwin,** Duke **Hugh** of Vermandois (brother of the King of France), Duke **Robert** of Normandy, Count **Stephen** of Blois, and Count **Robert** of Flanders.

1096, April–October. The People's Crusade. A crowd of unarmed pilgrims under **Peter the Hermit** marched overland toward the Holy Land. Many died of starvation; most of the remainder were massacred by the Turks in Anatolia.

1096–1097. The Assembly of Forces. The various contingents moved toward the agreed rallying point of Constantinople in four main groups. Godfrey and Baldwin, with their own and other German units, followed the Danube Valley through Hungary, Serbia, and Bulgaria, thence over the Balkan mountains, having several armed brushes with local forces en route. This was the first contingent to reach Constantinople; they camped outside the city through the winter. Bishop Adhemar, Count Raymond, and others from southern France proceeded through north Italy, continued down the barren Dalmatian coast to Durazzo in a grueling march, thence east to Constantinople. Hugh, the two Roberts, and Stephen, with contingents from England and northern France, marched across the Alps, and then down the Italian peninsula. While his companions wintered in south Italy, Hugh took ship to Constantinople, was shipwrecked, but was rescued by the Byzantines and taken to Constantinople, where he became a virtual hostage to Emperor Alexius Comnenus. The following spring the two Roberts and Stephen crossed the Adriatic to Durazzo, and then marched east to Constantinople. This was also the route followed by the Sicilian Normans of Bohemund and Tancred.

1096–1097. Byzantine-Crusader Friction.

Alexius had hoped his appeal for help would net him a few thousand mercenaries for his depleted armies. He neither expected nor desired an independent and unruly army of upward of 50,000 men to collect at his capital. Long-standing religious and political differences between Byzantines and West Europeans made him suspicious of Crusader motives and intentions, particularly since Bohemund had recently been an active and exceedingly dangerous enemy (see p. 297). Alexius, desirous only of regaining his Asiatic dominions from the Turks, had little interest in the Crusader objective of capturing Jerusalem. The Crusaders were equally suspicious of the Byzantines and their wily diplomacy. They had no desire to serve as pawns of Alexius in the reconquest of his empire from the Turks. These mutual suspicions seriously affected the outcome of this and most subsequent Crusades. The first manifestation was in intermittent skirmishing which went on between Crusaders and watchful Byzantine guards on the outskirts of Constantinople during the winter.

1097, Spring. Agreements between Alexius and the Crusaders. By a combination of firmness and diplomacy, Alexius avoided serious disturbances. In return for his assurance of assistance, he obtained oaths of fealty from the Crusader leaders, and their promise that they would help him to recapture Nicaea (Iznik) from the Turks and return to him any other former Byzantine possessions which they conquered. Alexius then transported them across the Bosporus—being careful not to allow any large gathering of Crusader contingents inside the walls of his capital. He also provided them with food and with an escort of Byzantine troops to guide them toward their objectives (and incidentally to prevent Crusader plundering).

1097, May 14–June 19. Siege of Nicaea. Accompanied by Alexius and his main army, the Crusaders invested Nicaea. By a combination of skillful fighting and skillful diplomacy, Alexius arranged for the surrender of the city to him, following a successful Crusader-Byzantine assault on the outer walls. The Crusaders were affronted by Alexius' refusal to grant them permission to sack the city. They then continued the advance southeastward,

marching in two parallel columns. There was no single commander; decisions were reached by council of war, with Bishop Adhemar serving as mediator.

1097, July 1. Battle of Dorylaeum (Eskisehir). The left-hand column, which was led by Bohemund, was suddenly attacked by a Turkish cavalry army under the personal command of Kilij Arslan, Seljuk Sultan of Rum (see p. 307). Using their traditional mounted-archer tactics, the Turks (probably more than 50,000 strong) severely punished the outnumbered Crusaders, who were unable to come to grips with their elusive, mobile foes. Bohemund's contingent was close to disintegration when the heavy cavalry of the right-hand column, under Godfrey and Raymond, smashed into the Turkish left rear. Kilij Arslan had failed to secure the approach from the south. Caught in a vise, about 3,000 Turks were killed and the rest scattered in rout. Total Crusader losses were about 4,000.

1097, July–November. Advance to Syria. The Crusaders resumed their advance and captured Iconium (Konya), Kilij Arslan's capital. (Meanwhile, behind them, Alexius and his Byzantine Army were reoccupying the western portions of Anatolia from the shaken Turks). After one more battle, near **Heraclea** (Eregli), the Crusaders continued on through the Taurus Mountains toward Antioch. During this advance a detachment under Tancred and Baldwin had a hard fight at **Tarsus.** Then Baldwin left the main column to embark on a private career of conquest, crossing the Euphrates and seizing Edessa, which became the center of an independent Christian domain.

1097–1098, October 21–June 3. The Crusader Siege of Antioch. The city was held by Emir **Yagi Siyan,** who conducted a skillful, energetic defense. Soon after the investment began, the Turks made a successful sortie, causing heavy casualties among the uncoordinated Christian contingents. Skirmishing outside the walls was frequent. Two Syrian relieving armies were driven off in the **Battles of Harenc** (December 31, 1097; February 9, 1098). For a while the Crusaders were close to starvation, since they had no logistical organization and had made no arrangements for supply. They were saved, however, by the fortuitous arrival of small English and Pisan flotillas, which seized the ports of Laodicea (Latakia) and St. Simeon (Samandag) and brought provisions. During the 7 months of the siege, the bickering among the leaders became more intense, particularly between Bohemund and Raymond. Finally, due mainly to the initiative of Bohemund and the treachery of a Turkish officer, Antioch was captured (June 3). It was none too soon; a relieving army at least 75,000 strong, commanded by Emir **Kerboga** of Mosul, was only two days' march distant. Stephen of Blois, feeling the situation was hopeless, fled from Antioch.

1098, June 5–28. Kerboga's Siege of Antioch. The Crusaders were now besieged and cut off from their seaports. Yagi Siyan still held the citadel. The Crusaders were again on the verge of starvation; the misery of the population of Antioch was intense. Alexius, who had been leading his army through the Taurus Mountains to occupy Antioch in accordance with his agreement with the Crusaders, met Stephen of Blois, who assured him the Crusaders were doomed. The Byzantine Army accordingly withdrew into Anatolia. Despair in the city was suddenly dissipated by the discovery of the supposed Holy Lance (the weapon which had pierced Jesus' side during the Crucifixion). Few historians or theologians believe that this supposedly miraculous discovery was valid (in fact there were doubts among many of the Crusaders), but it nonetheless had a truly miraculous effect. Confident of victory, the Crusaders sallied out.

1098, June 28. Battle of the Orontes. The starving Crusaders were able to muster only 15,000 men fit for combat, with less than 1,000 of these mounted as cavalry. Under the coordinating direction of Bohemund, they crossed the Orontes under the eyes of the surprised Moslems. Then, repulsing Kerboga's attacks, the Christians counterattacked. Hemmed in between the river and nearby mountains, the Turks were unable to maneuver, and they could not stand against the determined Crusader charges. The Moslem army fled, after suffering heavy casualties.

1098, July–August. Pestilence in Antioch. One of the victims was Bishop Adhemar.

After his death the disputes among the Christian leaders became more acute, particularly between Bohemund (who was determined to keep control of Antioch) and Raymond (who insisted that the Crusaders should return the city to Byzantium in accord with their oath to Alexius).

1099, January–June. Advance to Jerusalem. After much bickering, all the Crusaders except Bohemund and his Normans agreed to continue on to Jerusalem. (Bohemund stayed in Antioch, where he established an independent principality.) With the logistical support of the Pisan fleet, the Crusaders—now about 12,000 strong—advanced slowly down the coast to Jaffa, then turned inland to Jerusalem.

1099, June 9–July 18. Siege of Jerusalem. The city was defended by a strong force of Fatimid Moslems considerably more numerous than the besiegers. By this time Godfrey was generally accepted as the principal leader, assisted by Raymond and Tancred. The Crusaders were not numerous enough to blockade the city completely, and so they could not hope to starve it into submission. Despite a severe water shortage, they grimly prepared to assault the powerful fortifications, building a large wooden siege tower and a battering ram. Under heavy missile fire from the walls, the Crusaders pushed the tower against the city wall and Godfrey led the assault over a wooden drawbridge, while other Crusaders scaled the wall with ladders. This was apparently the only fully coordinated operation of the entire 2-year campaign. Fighting their way into the city, the Crusaders brutally massacred the garrison and the Moslem and Jewish population. Godfrey was elected Guardian of Jerusalem. (He refused the title of king.)

1099, August 12. Battle of Ascalon. Learning of the approach of a relieving army of 50,000 men from Egypt under Emir al-Afdal, Godfrey led his remaining 10,000 Crusaders out to meet them. Unlike the Turks, who were mainly mounted archers, the Fatimids relied upon the combination of fanaticism and shock action which had been so successful in Islam's earliest days. They were at a hopeless disadvantage against the heavily armored and armed Crusaders. Godfrey won an overwhelming victory, culminating in a crushing cavalry charge.

The Crusader States, 1099–1148

Most of the Crusaders returned home, but a handful remained in Jerusalem with Godfrey; a few others joined the banners of the three other leaders remaining in Syria: Baldwin in the County of Edessa, Bohemund in the Principality of Antioch, Raymond in the County of Tripoli (so called, even though the Moslems still held

Tripoli itself, which Raymond besieged). Godfrey died less than a year after his great victories (July, 1100). He was succeeded by his brother Baldwin, who assumed the title of King of Jerusalem. The other three Crusader states, nominally subject to his feudal authority, actually were completely independent. All occupied themselves at once in consolidating their positions by besieging the remaining Moslem towns and fortifications in the coastal regions, and by constant fighting with the neighboring Moslem principalities. Successive tides of Crusaders set out from

Europe to help in this activity. The first of these, an expedition almost as large as that of the First Crusade, met disaster in Anatolia. But many others came in smaller groups, by sea, and gave some help before returning to their homes. The Crusaders won most of the pitched battles, which were not frequent, but they lacked the man-power to exploit success, and were never able to cut Moslem communications be-tween Syria and Egypt. Their ability to maintain themselves was simply due to the lack of unity among the bickering Moslem principalities. After three decades, how-ever, **Imad-al-Din-Zangi** unified the Moslems of northeastern Syria and Northwest-ern Mesopotamia, and captured Edessa from the Crusaders (see p. 307). The princi-pal events were:

1100. Capture of Bohemund. He was am-bushed and captured by the Turks near Aleppo, remaining a prisoner at Sivas for 3 years.

1101–1102. Crusader Disasters in Anatolia. Three expeditions started across Anatolia under the leadership of **William** of Poi-tiers, Raymond of Toulouse, Stephen of Blois, and Hugh of Vermandois. The first, attempting to rescue Bohemund, was smashed at **Mersevan** by Turks under **Mo-hammed ibn Danishmend** (1101). Only a few survivors, including Raymond, es-caped. The second group was overwhelmed at **Heraclea** (1101). The third was almost wiped out a few months later, also at Heraclea (1102).

1101. First Battle of Ramleh. Baldwin, with 1,100 men, defeated 32,000 Egyptians un-der **Saad el-Dawleh** at Ramleh, an impor-tant road junction west of Jerusalem.

1102. Second Battle of Ramleh. Overcon-fident, Baldwin with 200 men attacked an Egyptian army of 30,000, and was crushed. He escaped, collected another army of 8,000, and defeated the Egyptians at the **Battle of Jaffa,** then pursued them to As-calon.

1102–1103. Danish Crusade. Eric I, the Good, of Denmark marched overland to Constantinople through Russia, then went by sea to Cyprus, where he died. His wife, **Bothilda,** then took command of the little expedition and continued to Jaffa.

1104. Battle of Carrhae. Bohemund, re-cently released from prison, was defeated in a battle reminiscent of the defeat of Crassus (see p. 117).

1107–1109. Norwegian Crusade. Sigurd I of Norway led an expedition by sea, har-assing Moorish Spain en route. He was the first European king to reach the Holy Land. With the Venetians he helped Bald-win capture Sidon; they were repulsed at Tyre (1109).

1116–1117. Expedition to the Red Sea. Baldwin led an expedition to the Gulf of Aqaba, where he built the fortress of Ai-lath (Eilat).

1118. Invasion of Egypt. Baldwin, with less than 1,000 men, crossed the Sinai Desert, but he died during the campaign. His little army returned to Palestine, accomplish-ing nothing.

1119. Battle of Antioch. A force under Count **Roger** at Salerno, marching to meet an invading army under **Ilghazi** at Aleppo, was surprised and wiped out.

1124. Attack on Jerusalem. The Crusaders repulsed an Egyptian raid.

1144. Fall of Edessa. Zangi captured Edessa from Count **Joscelin II.** This Cru-sader disaster led to a papal call for an-other Crusade.

1146. Expedition into Arabia. Successful Crusader raid on Bosra, 100 miles east of the Jordan.

The Second Crusade, 1147–1149

The principal leaders were Emperor **Conrad III** of Germany and King Louis VII of France. Both set out from Constantinople by separate routes (1147). The Germans followed the same general route as the First Crusade, but ran out of food near **Dorylaeum.** There the starving Crusaders were overwhelmed by a Turk attack. Conrad and a handful of survivors got back to Nicaea, then went by sea to Pal-estine. The French had taken a longer route, closer to the coast so as to remain in Byzantine territory as long as possible. Checked by the Turks in an indecisive battle east of **Laodicea,** Louis embarked his cavalry and went by sea to Palestine. The infantry continued eastward on foot and were annihilated by the Turks. Upon arrival in Palestine, Conrad and Louis joined **Baldwin III** of Jerusalem in an expedition against Damascus (1148). After investing the city, the Crusader army soon fell apart due to dissension among the three leaders. This ended the ill-starred Second Crusade.

The Crusader States, 1149–1189

Following the death of Zangi, the Crusader states were subjected to ever-increasing pressure from his son, **Nur-ed-Din** (see p. 307). To prevent his armies from conquering Egypt, King Amalric I of Jerusalem campaigned repeatedly in the Nile Valley, but was eventually repulsed. Soon after this, the Moslems of Syria and Egypt were united under the strong rule of **Saladin,** who after some preliminary campaigns declared a holy war against the Christians. He won a great victory over King **Guy** (of Lusignan) of Jerusalem at the **Battle of Hattin,** then captured Jerusalem and most of the Christian towns and forts of Palestine. Tyre was the only important seaport remaining in Christian hands, thanks to the fortuitous arrival by sea of Marquis **Conrad** of Montferrat and a small contingent of new Crusaders. While the pope issued a call for a new Crusade, Conrad and Guy continued to fight against Saladin. The principal events were:

1146–1174. Consolidation of Moslem Syria by Nur-ed-Din. (See p. 307.)

1153. Capture of Ascalon. Baldwin III gained control of the entire Palestine coast.

1156. Battle of Jacob's Ford (Near Sea of Galilee). The Moslems defeated separated Crusader infantry and cavalry contingents while crossing the Jordan.

1163–1169. Struggle for Egypt. (See pp. 306 and 309.)

1169–1193. Reign of Saladin. (See p. 309.)

1174–1187. Crusader Dissension. The leprosy of childless King **Baldwin IV** caused a struggle for succession. Saladin profited from this by completing his conquest of Syria, while constantly harassing the Crusaders, although he was defeated at **Ramleh** (1177). Count **Raymond** of Tripoli was the most able Crusader leader, but his enemy, Guy of Lusignan, became king by marrying Baldwin's sister. Meanwhile, unscrupulous **Reginald** of Châtillon and Kerak twice broke Crusader truces with Saladin, provoking him into declaring a holy war.

1187, June. Saladin's Invasion of Palestine. He besieged Tiberias with an army of about 20,000. Guy gathered all available Crusader manpower, raising an army of almost equal size, and advanced against Saladin. Ignoring Raymond's advice, Guy led the army into a waterless area, where he was attacked and surrounded by the Moslems.

1187, July 4. Battle of Hattin. Saladin separated the Crusader infantry from the cavalry, then overwhelmed the detachments. Raymond and a small force of cavalry cut their way through the Moslems; the remainder of the Crusaders were killed or captured. Saladin later released Guy on parole not to fight again. Meanwhile Raymond died of wounds.

1187, July–September. Saladin's Conquest of Palestine. He captured Tiberias, Acre, Ascalon, and other cities. The garrisons of these places had been captured at Hattin. Saladin was advancing on Tyre when **Conrad** of Montferrat and a body of Crusaders fortunately arrived by sea, providing a garrison. Saladin was repulsed.

1187, September 20–October 2. Saladin's Capture of Jerusalem. He then turned against the Crusaders around Tyre. There was cautious skirmishing for more than a year.

1189, August. Investment of Acre. Guy of Lusignan boldly led a small Crusader force to besiege Acre. He was joined by Conrad and other Crusaders recently arrived from Europe, driving off relieving forces sent by Saladin.

1189–1191. Battles around Acre. Nine major engagements and innumerable minor skirmishes were fought between the Crusader besiegers and Saladin, whose army surrounded the Crusaders by land. The Genoese and Pisan fleets controlled the sea, assuring an uninterrupted flow of supplies and reinforcements to the Crusaders.

The Third Crusade, 1189–1192

Responding to the appeal of Pope Clement III for a new Crusade were the three most powerful rulers of Europe: Emperor **Frederick I**, Barbarossa, of Germany; King **Philip II**, Augustus, of France; and King **Richard I**, the Lionhearted, of England. All were able and experienced soldiers. The principal events were:

1189–1190. Frederick's March. Departing Germany in the spring, Frederick marched overland to Constantinople. While spending the winter there (1189–1190), he became involved in a dispute with Byzantine Emperor **Isaac Angelus.** Their troubles were patched up, and Frederick continued across Anatolia. His force of 30,000 was better organized than his predecessors on this route, and he repulsed all Turk attacks. His crossbowmen were particularly effective against the horse archers. He captured Iconium by storm, after which the Sultan of Rum made peace and offered no further resistance to the German advance. Late in the summer, in Cilicia, the old emperor was drowned, either in a river crossing or while bathing in a river at the end of a hot march. His son, **Frederick** of Swabia, continued, but, lacking his father's ability, he lost most of his men through starvation, disease, and local Moslem harassment. With little more than 1,000 men he joined the Crusader army besieging Acre late in the year.

1190–1191. Voyages of Richard and Philip. A year after Frederick started, Philip and Richard went by sea to Sicily, where they spent the winter quarrelling continuously. Next spring Philip sailed directly to Acre. Richard stopped en route to conquer Cyprus, which he wisely wanted as a base. He then sailed to Acre.

1191, July 12. The Fall of Acre. Upon Richard's arrival (June 8), his leadership was tacitly accepted by all Crusaders. He drove off Saladin's relieving army, then pressed the siege with such vigor that the Moslem garrison surrendered, ending a defense of 2 years. Soon after this increasing dissension between Richard and Philip resulted in the return of the French king to France. Considerable bickering continued among the Crusaders, particularly between Richard and Conrad.

1191, August–September. The March to Ascalon. Richard was determined to press on to Jerusalem. He organized the polyglot Crusader force (probably about 50,000 strong) into a unified army and started out on a march in which he demonstrated exceptional strategic and tactical ability, as well as the effect of his dominant personality in enforcing responsiveness from unruly knights and barons of many lands. His staff and logistics work was far superior to that normally found in West European medieval armies. He even had a laundry corps to keep clothes clean to prevent disease. In short daily marches to avoid fatigue, he marched slowly down the coast, accompanied by his fleet offshore. Saladin's army hung on the inland flank, harassing the Crusaders, and seeking opportunities to cut off stragglers or to break into the Christian formation as they had at Hattin. But Richard's carefully planned and organized march column offered no such opportunities. He forbade his knights to respond to the Turkish harassment; all of Saladin's efforts to entice them to break ranks proved unavailing. Richard kept the Turkish horse archers at a distance by disposing crossbowmen throughout the column.

1191, September 7. Battle of Arsouf. Saladin set an ambush near the coast at Arsouf, then launched a strong attack at the rear of Richard's column to try to force the knights of the rear guard to charge against their tormentors. Richard at first refused permission, and the column continued its dogged march. Then as the Turks grew bolder, and the pressure on the rear guard became more than his knights could bear,

Richard gave the prearranged trumpet signal for attack. The astonished and unsuspecting Turks were taken completely by surprise by the overwhelming coordinated charge. In a few minutes the battle was over. Following Richard's orders, the Crusaders overcame the temptation to scatter in pursuit of the defeated foe. About 7,000 Turks were cut down, and the remainder were scattered in flight. The Crusaders lost 700 men. Saladin never again attempted a battle in the open against Richard.

1192. Advance on Jerusalem. While the Crusader army wintered at Ascalon, Conrad was murdered by one of the Assassins. Soon after this Richard advanced on Jerusalem. Saladin retired before him, carrying out a "scorched earth" policy, destroying all crops and grazing land and poisoning all wells. The lack of water, absence of fodder for the horses, and growing dissension within his multinational army forced Richard to the reluctant conclusion that he could not besiege Jerusalem without risking almost certain destruction of his army. Reluctantly he withdrew to the coast. There were numerous minor engagements during the remainder of the year, Richard distinguishing himself as a heroic knight as well as a tactical leader.

1192. Treaty with Saladin. Abandoning hope of capturing Jerusalem, Richard concluded a treaty with Saladin in which special rights and privileges were granted to Christian pilgrims to Jerusalem.

1193. Death of Saladin. The breakup of Saladin's empire (see p. 309) gave the Crusader states a brief respite.

MILITARY SIGNIFICANCE OF THE CRUSADES

For centuries Western Europe survived the collapse of Rome only because it was shielded from the assaults of Islam by the sturdy Byzantine Empire. During those centuries a vigorous new Germano-Latin society had risen and begun to flourish. The Crusades were a natural reaction of this society to protect Europe from a renewed western thrust of Islam when Byzantium was faltering.

At this time the relative crudity of western military methods was such that the First Crusade would almost certainly have failed had the Moslems of the Middle East not been hopelessly divided by internal squabbling. That initial success, however, and the consequent creation of the Kingdom of Jerusalem and the other Crusader Latin states of the East had far-reaching results. There, to an extent not matched either in Spain or Sicily, took place a meeting and mingling of three distinct civilizations. The sophisticated, cultured, cynical, and resilient Byzantine civilization had already had fruitful interactions with the equally cultured and intellectual civilization of the Moslem East. Both eastern societies looked with a mixture of awe, amusement, and disgust at the rough, brutal, crude European society whose military spearhead literally bludgeoned its way into their midst.

Though there was never real peace among these three societies during the two centuries of the Crusading era, nonetheless there was considerable social contact, facilitated by frequently shifting alliances in their wars against one another and in the inevitable meddling of neighbors in the incessant internal disorders of each.

From these contacts the Crusaders profited most—since they had the most to learn. In the process, they became fatally enervated by their contacts with the more subtle civilizations in which they had placed themselves. But, fortunately for the future of Western Europe, this enervation in Syria and Palestine did not affect the basic, vigorous home societies which became the beneficiaries of the lessons learned in the East, brought to Europe by returning Crusaders. The military lessons were as important to the West as were those in culture, science, and economics.

Among the tactical lessons learned by the Crusaders were the use of maneuver in the form of envelopment and ambuscade, the employment of light cavalry for reconnaissance and for screening, the use of mounted fire power in the form of horse archers, and, above all, the importance of the coordinated employment of the combined arms of infantry and cavalry, and of missiles and shock action, when dealing with a resourceful, mobile foe.

The most obvious military effect of the Crusaders' eastern experience was seen in European fortifications. The Westerners were particularly impressed with the powerful Byzantine walled cities and fortresses, with double or triple concentric lines of massive turreted walls. There was nothing like this in the West at the time. The result was a complete revolution in castle construction and city defense in Western Europe in the 12th century. The most impressive single manifestation was Château Gaillard, built by Richard the Lionhearted in Normandy after his return from the Third Crusade. This was a tribute not only to his powers of observation but to his ingenuity and competence as a military engineer, since he improved on eastern fortresses.

The Crusaders learned little new about siegecraft, but improved the methods and machines which they already used. Nor did they learn much about weapons, save for increased emphasis on archery. The one aspect of military activity in which they probably taught more than they learned was in arms and armor. Yet even here they profited, learning better methods of manufacture and construction so as to obtain comparable protection, or equal striking power, with lighter equipment.

One of the important lessons was the importance of logistics, an art which had practically disappeared in the West after the fall of Rome. European armies lived off the countryside, or they evaporated. Because of the limited time of obligatory feudal service, campaigns were rarely long, save for sieges and for the operations of the relatively small mercenary standing forces of kings and nobles. But in protracted campaigns in the East, with long marches over barren country, the Crusaders had to learn logistical organization or perish. In the First and Second Crusades, in fact, more perished from starvation, or from lack of fodder for their horses, than from any other single cause—including Turkish swords and arrows. Richard, in particular, showed how well he had learned this lesson by the establishment of an intermediate supply base at Cyprus, by exploiting the logistical potentialities of sea power, by the excellent logistical arrangements of his march from Acre to Ascalon, and by his refusal to embark on a protracted siege of Jerusalem with inadequate logistical facilities.

There were several unrelated military implications in the role of the Church in the Crusades. In the first place, many churchmen considered the Crusades as a means of diverting the inherent bellicosity and brutality of the feudal gentry from private and domestic wars to the more laudable purposes of supporting religious objectives. As one historian has observed, in reference to the unkept "Truce of God" (see p. 284), it was "easier to consecrate the fighting instinct than to curb it."

One other religious-military development was the appearance of military orders of monks: the Knights Templars, the Knights of St. John (or Knights Hospitalers), and the Teutonic Knights. This last order, although established in the Holy Land (1190), soon moved to Prussia, where it did its crusading against heathen Slavs (see p. 371). The Templars and Hospitalers, however, maintained themselves in the Holy Land and provided the nucleus of the regular fighting forces of the Kings of Jerusalem; their fortresses long stemmed the resurgent tide of Islam under Zangi, Nur-ed-din, and Saladin. By the end of the 12th century these two orders probably had the most efficient military establishments in the world. Their members were highly valued as military advisers and staff officers to rulers and generals of West European armies.

The other important religious development with military implications was the increasing friction between the Roman Catholic Church and the Greek Orthodox Church of Constantinople. The suspicions and fighting between Crusaders and Byzantines inflamed the long-smoldering disputes between the two churches. The consequences would be momentous and tragic early in the following century (see pp. 380–382).

SOUTH ASIA

NORTH INDIA

During the early years of the 11th century, North India was dominated in repeated campaigns by one of the most able warriors of Asiatic history, Mahmud of Ghazni, son of Sabuktagin (see p. 270). But although he forced the Hindu princes of the Punjab to swear allegiance, Mahmud made no effort to annex the regions he overran there and elsewhere in India. He did, however, weaken the power of the Hindu states of the north, and completely wrecked the Pratihara Dynasty of Kanauj, which had so long held off the threat of Islam (see p. 270). For more than a century after the death of Mahmud, there were no more major incursions from the northwest, where the various Turk tribes and dynasties were struggling for control of Persia and Central Asia. Late in the 12th century, **Muizz ad-Din Mohammed** (Muhammad of Ghor) undertook a series of invasions which led to a complete Moslem conquest of north India by the end of the century. The principal events were:

977–1030. Reign of Mahmud of Ghazni. He made 17 or more invasions of India (beginning 1000). Although he extended his father's foothold in the Punjab, Mahmud's principal interest was not conquest but rather plunder and—incidentally—gaining religious merit. Nevertheless, at his death his suzerainty included all of modern Afghanistan, eastern Persia, and Transoxiana, as well as the Punjab. He invariably defeated the much more numerous Hindu armies with more mobile forces, primarily cavalry horse archers, which he directed with great skill, courage, and vigor.

1001. Victory over Jaipal, Raja of Lahore. In subsequent years Mahmud ranged east and south over the Punjab.

1009. Battle of Peshawar. Mahmud was opposed by a coalition of north Indian Hindu princes under the leadership of **Anang-pal,** son of Jaipal. Mahmud's victory was reminiscent of Alexander's at the nearby Hydaspes, since he created panic among the Hindus' elephants. In this and the following years Mahmud marched far and wide over north India, fighting, killing, looting, and destroying Hindu temples. Particularly notable were the sack

of Thaneswar (1014) and of Kanauj (1018).

1025. Raid to the Coast of Gujarat. Mahmud's major purpose of this expedition across the desert from Multan was to destroy the phallic idol of a famed Hindu temple at Somnath. He also killed perhaps 50,000 Hindus.

1030–1175. Internal Wars of North India. The numerous north Indian princes continued their interminable wars with each other, employing the same unwieldy armies that Mahmud had consistently cut to ribbons. They had learned nothing from their defeats.

1175. First Indian Expedition of Muhammad of Ghor. He overcame the Ghaznevid rulers of the Punjab. Soon after this he sought to emulate Mahmud by expeditions farther afield.

1178. Defeat in Gujarat. Following the route taken by Mahmud, Muhammad was decisively defeated by the Hindu Raja of Gujarat and forced to retire.

1179–1191. Muhammad's Consolidation of the Punjab. He prepared for a renewed invasion. He began more cautiously with raids into the upper Ganges Valley (1187–1190).

1191. First Battle of Tarain (Tirawari). Muhammad, leading an expedition to Thaneswar, was badly defeated by **Prithviraja,** Raja of Delhi and Ajmer. Badly wounded, Muhammad returned to Ghazni, where he made great preparations for another expedition to Thaneswar.

1192. Second Battle of Tarain. On almost exactly the same battleground as that of the year before, Muhammad decisively defeated the Hindu allies, capturing Prithviraja, whom he had killed. In this battle Muhammad exploited to the utmost the superior mobility of his Turkish horse archers. North India was now at the mercy of the Moslems.

1192–1199. Muhammad's Conquest of North India. He seized Delhi (1192), Kanauj (1194), Bihar (1197), and Bengal (1199).

SOUTH INDIA

During the first half of the 11th century, Chola expanded its already substantial influence by land and sea to dominate the entire Deccan. In the middle of the century, the Chola were forced on the defense by a coalition of Hindu states, led by the Chalukya. Chola resurgence in the latter part of the century was perpetuated into the next by the emergence of a Chalukya-Chola dynasty as the result of a marriage alliance. At the same time, the Chalukya Dynasty of Kalyani returned to a position of predominance in the northwestern Deccan. Both of these dynasties declined rapidly, however. The principal events were:

985–1014. Reign of Rajaraja I of Chola. Continued expansion of Chola power in the Deccan and along the shores of the Bay of Bengal.

1014–1042. Reign of Rajendra I (Son of Rajaraja). This was the height of Chola power. Rajendra suppressed a revolt in Ceylon. His armies dominated the Deccan. In a combined land and sea expedition he defeated the Pala King of Bengal on the banks of the lower Ganges. His overseas expeditions may have brought tribute from the Mon kings of Pegu (Burma), but it is more likely that Chola merely established trading settlements on the Burmese coast. His fleets harried the west coast of the Malay Peninsula and southeast Sumatra, including Srivijaya (1025).

1042–1052. Reign of Rajadahira I (Son of Rajendra). He spent most of his reign fighting a coalition of Hindu princes eager to gain revenge for their earlier humiliations. The principal leader of this alliance was the Chalukya ruler, **Somesvara I** (1040–1068). Another was the Chalukya Princess **Akkadevi,** one of the few female generals of history, who participated in a number of battles and sieges. Somesvara defeated and killed Rajadahira at the **Battle of Koppan** (1052).

1062–1070. Reign of Virarajendra of Chola. He defeated Chalukya, and re-established Tamil supremacy in south India. An overseas expedition assisted Kedah (in Malaya) against Srivijaya. Upon his death his two sons killed each other off in a struggle for supremacy.

1070–1122. Reign of Rajendra Chola Kullotunga. This eastern Chalukya prince had married the daughter of Virarajendra, and established the Chalukya-Chola Dynasty controlling the eastern and southern Deccan.

1076–1127. Reign of Vikramaditya VI. He began the rise of Chalukya of Kalyani in the northwestern Deccan.

1076–1147. Reign of Anantavarman Choda Ganga of Kalinga (or Orissa). He raised his country to a position of leadership on the east coast between the Godavari and Ganges rivers.

c. 1100–1150. Rise of the Hoysala Dynasty (Modern Mysore). They began to challenge the hegemony of Chalukya and Chalukya-Chola.

1050–1200. Resurgence of Pandya. They gained independence from Chola.

1156–1183. Religious Civil War in the Chalukya Dominions. This weakened the dynasty's power; during most of this time, the rebels held Kalyani.

1172–1210. Reign of Vira Bellala II of Hoysala. In alliance with other Hindu neigh-

bors, he overthrew the Chalukya of Kalyani (1190). During this war the Hoysala
king was assisted by his warrior-queen
Umadevi, who apparently exercised command in at least 2 campaigns against the
Chalukya and their allies.

CEYLON

During the 11th and 12th centuries Ceylon was invaded frequently by the
Tamil kingdoms of the southern tip of India. From about 1001 to about 1070 the
Chola dominated the island, but were plagued by frequent uprisings. **Vijaya Bahu**
(1065–1120) finally expelled the Chola; and brought prosperity to a united, inde-
pendent kingdom. The zenith of Sinhalese glory was under the great King **Parakram
Bahu** (1164–1197), who repelled a Tamil invasion (1168) and in turn invaded
Madura on the mainland, taking advantage of the struggle between Pandya and
Chola.

SOUTHEAST ASIA, 1000–1200

THE TAI

The Kingdom of Nanchao was relatively quiescent during this period. It remained independent of China, but evidently attempted few foreign adventures. Tai
mercenary soldiers were common in the armies of the Khmer, Mon, and Burmese;
most of these probably came from Nanchao. The gradual southern migration of the

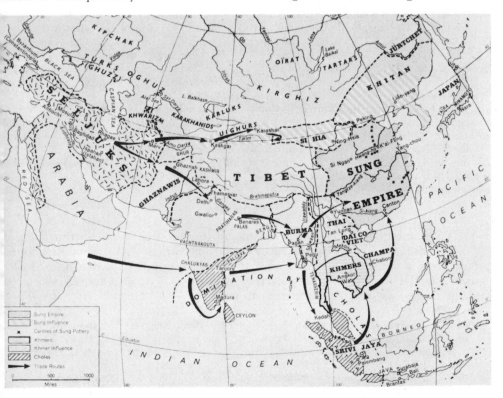

Asia, *c.* 1030

Tai people continued as they inched their way into the regions that their descendants now occupy in Thailand, eastern Burma, and Laos. A number of small independent Tai states began to appear in these areas late in the 11th century, the first being Raheng (1096) at the junction of the Mep'ing and Mewang rivers (northwestern Thailand).

VIETNAMESE REGION

During most of the 11th century, Champa and Annam were at war with each other, a continuation of the disputes arising from conflicting claims to three border provinces which had been seized by Champa in the preceding century (see p. 272). The Annamese generally had the best of these wars. Even more bitter was the warfare between Champa and the Khmer kings of Angkor which raged during most of the following century and continued through the close of the period. The principal events were:

1000–1044. Intermittent War between Champa and Annam. The Annamese usually held the initiative, finally capturing Vijaya (Binh Dinh), the Cham capital. They killed the King of Champa and evidently reannexed the disputed provinces (1044).

1068–1069. Cham Counterinvasion of Annam. This was eventually repulsed.

1074–c. 1100. Reign of Harivarman IV of Champa. He repulsed Annamese and Khmer attacks (1070–1076), and later raided successfully into Cambodia.

1103. Cham Defeat. The Annamese repulsed an attempt to recover the disputed provinces.

c. 1130–1132. Khmer Invasion of Champa. Suryavarman II of Angkor forced the Cham (probably not unwillingly) to assist him in his concurrent unsuccessful invasion of Annam.

1145–1149. War between Champa and Ang- kor. Suryavarman conquered Champa, but was then expelled by a Cham uprising.

1149–1160. Rebellion and Disorder in Champa.

1150. Khmer Invasion of Annam. The Khmer were disastrously defeated near Tonkin.

1167–1190. Constant Warfare between Champa and Angkor. A Cham invasion of Cambodia was initially successful, thanks largely to the effective use of mounted crossbowmen. The Khmer rallied under **Jayavarman VII,** who repulsed the Cham, then conquered Champa, which he divided into two puppet vassal regimes (1190).

1191–1192. Civil War in Champa. Suryavarman, one of the puppet rulers, united the country, then expelled Khmer occupation forces.

1192–1203. Continued War between Cambodia and Champa.

CAMBODIA

This period of Khmer history was dominated by three great warrior kings of Angkor—**Suryavarman I, Suryavarman II,** and **Jayavarman VII**—who distinguished themselves as much by their magnificent construction programs at Angkor as by their extensive foreign conquests. Each of these glorious reigns, however, exhausted and weakened the country. The principal events were:

1002–1050. Reign of Suryavarman I. He consolidated his initially tenuous control over the country by victories in civil wars during the first 10 years of his reign. He then expanded his domain northward by conquering the Mekong Valley as far north as Luang Prabang.

1050–1066. Reign of Udayadityavarman II. Plagued by constant revolts, some of which were inspired by neighboring Champa. The revolts were suppressed by the brilliant Khmer general, **Sangrama.**

1066–1113. Internal Disorder.

1113–1150. Reign of Suryavarman II. Despite repeated victories over Champa, he was unsuccessful in attempts to conquer Annam, and was eventually repelled from Champa as well (see above). He was more successful in his campaigns to the west, apparently overrunning all of the small Tai states between Cambodia and the plains of Burma. His embassies to China were received with respect and honor.

1150–1177. Internal Turmoil. Champa exploited this by capturing and sacking Angkor (1177; see p. 324).

1177–1218. Reign of Jayavarman VII. He unified his discouraged people, then de-

feated the Chams in a great naval river battle, probably on the Mekong River or Tonle Sap Lake (1178?). He restored internal order (1178–1181) and suppressed a revolt of the vassal Kingdom of Malyang (Battambang). He made good use of the military skill of refugee Cham Prince **Sri Vidyananda,** who also played an important part in the subsequent conquest of Champa (1190). Jayavarman expanded Khmer control of the Mekong Valley northward to Vientiane and to the south, down the Kra Isthmus. He built the powerful fortified city of Ankor Thom.

1192. Renewed War with Champa. (See p. 324.)

BURMA

A Burmese nation, covering much of the area of modern Burma, first emerged in the middle of the 11th century under the great ruler and conqueror, **Anawrahta.** His successors were able to maintain the kingdom more or less intact, despite considerable internal disorder and the revolts of subject peoples. The principal events were:

1044–1077. Reign of Anawrahta. After annexing Arakan and Lower Burma, he conquered the Mon Kingdom of Thaton in the lower Irrawaddy and Salween Valleys (1057), checking Khmer probes. He established his capital at Pagan. He conducted a number of punitive expeditions in the Shan (Tai) states to the east, and may have raided eastward as far as the Chao Phraya Valley of modern Thailand. He built a number of fortifications along his eastern frontier to prevent Shan depredations.

1077–1084. Reign of Sawlu (Son of Anawrahta). A prolonged Mon rebellion was initially successful, resulting in the temporary capture and sacking of Pagan and the overthrow of Sawlu.

1084–1112. Reign of Kyanzittha (Another Son of Anawrahta). He repulsed the Mons and eventually suppressed their rebellion.

1112–1173. Internal Disorder.

1173–1210. Reign of Narapatisittu. Order and peace were restored.

EAST AND CENTRAL ASIA

CHINA

At the outset of the 11th century, the Sung Dynasty of China was involved in unsuccessful wars with neighbors to the north and northwest: the Liao Dynasty of the Khitan Mongols of Manchuria and the newly established Western Hsia Kingdom in Kansu. Fortunately for the Sung, these northern barbarian kingdoms were also engaged in more or less continuous warfare with each other. The latter part of the century was relatively peaceful, thanks to annual tribute paid to the northern barbarian kingdoms. Early in the 12th century, the Sung joined with the Juchen Mongols to overwhelm the Khitan. Almost immediately, however, the Juchen (later known as the Chin Dynasty) turned against the Sung and drove them from northern China. During the remainder of the century, the Sung and Chin were engaged in several wars; the Sung were unable to reconquer north China, but kept the Chin from penetrating south of the Yangtze. The principal events were:

1000–1004. Khitan Invasion. This culminated a long-drawn-out war between the Khitan and Sung dynasties. The Khitan drove to the Yellow River near the Sung capital of Pien Liang (modern Kaifeng). The Sung sued for peace, agreeing to pay a large annual tribute.

1001–1003. War with the Western Hsia Kingdom. This was inconclusive.

1038–1043. Renewed War between Sung and Hsia. With the assistance of the Uighurs of Sinkiang, the Sung achieved a face-saving peace whereby the Hsia agreed to continue nominal vassalage to China in return for annual tribute.

1070. Military Reorganization. This was part of a sweeping program of reform of the entire governmental and financial systems by **Wang An-shih,** Sung prime minister. Due to constant external threats and frontier incidents with Khitans and Hsia, the Sung standing army had grown to about 1,100,000 men. This, combined with the tribute to the northern neighbors, was an economic burden that was bankrupting the country. Wang created a conscript militia system designed to provide for more effective border defense and more effective internal and local security, while permitting a reduction of the standing army to about 500,000. Within 6 years the militia force numbered 7,000,000.

1115–1122. Sung Alliance with the Juchen Mongols. The allies destroyed the Khitan Liao Kingdom.

1123–1127. Juchen Mongol Invasion. They reached Pien Liang, but were repulsed (1126). The following year, however, they stormed the Sung capital and captured the emperor, **Hui Tsung,** and his eldest son, **Ch'in Tsung.** A younger son, **Kao Tsung,** escaped and fled south to the Yangtze River to establish the Southern Sung Dynasty, with its capital at Nanking. The Juchen (now the Chin Dynasty) pursued, crossed the Yangtze to capture Nanking, and drove Kao Tsung to Hangchow (1127).

1128–1140. Yangtze Campaigns. Sung General **Yueh Fei,** with the cooperation of the Sung fleet in the Yangtze River, defeated the Chin (Juchen) Army, and drove it north of the river. In a series of campaigns, Yueh Fei and other Chinese generals pushed the Chin north to the vicinity of Pien Liang. A palace intrigue then resulted in the recall of Yueh Fei, who was executed by Kao Tsung (1141).

1141. Uneasy Peace. The boundary between the Southern Sung and the Chin was established along the Hwai and upper Han rivers.

1161. Chin Invasion of Southern China. This was led by Chin Emperor **Liang.** He was halted by the Sung army and fleet at the Yangtze River. Sung General **Yu Yun-wen** employed explosives, apparently for the first time in warfare, in defeating the Chin at the **Battle of Ts'ai-shih** (near Nanking).

INNER ASIA

The nomadic barbarians of North and Central Asia inhabited a great arc of land extending generally from the Sea of Japan, Korea, and the Yellow Sea in the east, across modern Manchuria, Mongolia, Sinkiang, and Russian Turkestan roughly to the line of the Syr Darya River. This had been an area of constant ferment, and the origin of numberless migrations and invasions to the southeast (into China), to the southwest (into Transoxiana, Persia, and India), and west (across Scythia toward Europe) since the dawn of history. In the earliest days the inhabitants of the western portion of this region had evidently been mainly Aryans; the inhabitants of the eastern regions had been primarily Mongoloid in their ethnologic characteristics. As the centuries passed, and as the tribes roamed and fought over the vast area, there was considerable mixing of the races. The principal Aryan group, the Yueh Chih, had earlier migrated toward Europe, Persia, and India (see p. 120).

Thus, by the beginning of the 11th century, this vast arc of deserts, mountains, and pastureland was inhabited by swarthy or yellow-skinned people resembling each other in racial, cultural, and linguistic characteristics, and ethnologically more Mongoloid than Aryan. This similarity among the Mongols, Turks, Tartars (Tatars), and Tanguts who inhabited the vast region makes for considerable ethnic and historical confusion. Generally speaking, the Mongols and Tartars inhabited the northern and eastern areas; the Turks (who had already begun to spread over Western Asia and Southeastern Europe) were in the southwest; the Tanguts, who were more closely related to the Tibetans than were the other nomads, were generally in eastern Sinkiang and Kansu.

The Khitan Mongols of Manchuria comprised a homogeneous nation, and were beginning to lose their nomadic characteristics. To their west and northwest were many other Mongol tribes, linked together in various amorphous alliances and groupings, but with little national cohesiveness. In Kansu and Eastern Sinkiang the Tanguts had recently formed a nation—the Western Hsia—still nominally under Chinese rule. In Sinkiang were the Uighur Turks, who were still loosely allied with the Chinese. Farther west, between the Tien Shan Mountains and the Aral Sea, were the so-called Guzz Turks, comprising many independent tribes and tribal groups, including those of the Seljuks and the Ilak khans. (Farther north and west were the Kipchak Turks—or Cumans—of the steppes of Western Asia and Caucasia, and to their west were the Pechenegs of the South Russian steppes; these Turkish peoples, however, were by this time more involved in Eurasian history.)

During much of the 11th and 12th centuries the Khitan and Western Hsia were frequently at war with each other and with the Sung Dynasty of China. The Uighurs were often involved in these wars, aiding their Chinese allies against the Hsia. Early in the 12th century a new Mongol people—the Juchen—moved southeastward from Mongolia to clash with the Khitan, whom they soon overthrew with Chinese assistance. The Juchen did not pause, however, and immediately invaded the territory of their former allies, the Sung Chinese, to precipitate a series of wars that continued through the rest of the century. Toward the end of the century, in central Mongolia, another new Mongol kingdom was coalescing around the tribe of a brilliant young chieftain named **Temujin**. The principal events were:

1000–1038. Intermittent Wars of the Khitan and the Tangut of Kansu.

1038–1043. Revolt of Western Hsia. They obtained complete independence from China, under **Yuan Ho** as emperor. Despite Uighur assistance, the Chinese were unable to suppress the revolt. In return for Chinese payment of tribute, Yuan Ho agreed to consider himself a Sung vassal.

1044. Renewed War between Khitan and Western Hsia. This was precipitated by Tangut invasion of Manchuria, repulsed by the Khitan Liao Dynasty.

1080–1090. Seljuk Expansion. (See p. 310.)

1115–1123. Juchen Mongol Conquest of Khitan. Accomplished with Chinese assistance. The Liao ruler, **Ye-lu Ta-shih**, fled with the small remnant of his army to the Tarim Basin, where he allied himself to the Uighurs to establish the Kingdom of Kara Khitai.

1122. Proclamation of the Chin Dynasty. The Juchen leader **Tsu** took the imperial name **T'ien Fu.** He then began an invasion of China (1123; see p. 326).

1126–1141. Expansion of the Kara Khitai. The former Khitans, now also called the Western Liao, controlled both sides of the Pamirs. Ye-lu Ta-shih defeated Sanjar, Seljuk Sultan of Persia, and drove him from Transoxiana (1141; see p. 311).

1135. Mongol Invasion of Chin. The Mongol Khan **Kabul** led this, the first of a series of Mongol raids into the new empire.

1161. Chin Invasion of Sung China. Chin Emperor Liang was defeated near Nanking (see p. 326). When he ordered his defeated troops to renew the attack, they mutinied and hanged him, then withdrew across the Yangtze.

1162. Birth of Temujin. He was the son of Mongol chieftain **Yesugai,** in the region southeast of Lake Baikal.

1180–1190. Rise of Temujin's New Mongol Kingdom. Created by a combination of alliances and conquests of neighboring tribes.

1194. Temujin Campaigns against the Tartars. In alliance with the Chin and with the Kerait Mongols, he conducted a successful campaign southwest of the Gobi.

KOREA

The Wang Dynasty (see p. 276) continued to rule Koryo throughout this period. They had several wars with the Khitan Liao Kingdom of Manchuria during the 11th century. An effort to prevent Khitan depredations by construction of a great wall across the narrow neck of the peninsula (1044) was only partially successful; the Wang paid tribute to the Khitan until Liao was overwhelmed by the Juchen (1123; see p. 326). The Wang immediately acknowledged Juchen suzerainty. The regime barely survived military revolt late in the 12th century (1170).

JAPAN

The Fujiwara clan continued to dominate Japan during the first half of the 11th century. Although this was a period of relative peace and prosperity for the country as a whole, the two warrior clans of Taira and Minamoto (see p. 277) clashed in many small conflicts between feudal lords. Both clans were also called upon frequently by the Fujiwara regent-dictators to deal with an unusual class of lawbreakers. These were Buddhist monks, who had become increasingly secular and arrogant, and who were wont to achieve their demands by force of arms if necessary. The increasing reliance of the Fujiwaras upon the warrior clans impaired their own prestige, permitting the imperial family to regain its power. From the middle of the 11th century until the middle of the 12th, the emperors ruled as well as reigned. This period was ended by two civil wars resulting from a dynastic dispute between rival emperors. The Taira clan emerged predominant from these wars. Their long-standing rivalry with the Minamoto soon became bitter and acute. The result was further civil war in which the Minamoto clan virtually annihilated the Taira and seized power. By the end of the century Japan was under a feudal military dictatorship. The principal events were:

1000–1068. Zenith and Decline of the Fujiwara Clan.

1051–1062. The Earlier Nine Years' War. This was an uprising of the Abe clan of northern Japan, suppressed by the Minamoto.

1068–1156. Period of Direct Imperial Rule. Actual power was usually exercised by an abdicated or retired emperor.

1083–1087. The Later Three Years' War. The Minamoto clan destroyed the dissident Kiyowara clan of northern Japan.

1156. The Hogen War. This was the result of a complicated dispute over imperial power between two brothers, **Goshirakawa II** and **Sokotu,** who had formerly reigned as emperor. Members of the Taira, Minamoto, and Fujiwara clans fought on both sides of this war. Mainly through Taira assistance, Goshirakawa was successful and Sokotu was exiled.

1159–1160. The Heiji War. The Minamoto clan temporarily seized power in a surprise coup, but were then decisively defeated by the Taira.

1160–1181. Predominance of Taira Kiyomori. He was practically a dictator.

1180–1184. War of the Taira and Minamoto. Under the leadership of **Minamoto Yoritomo** the Minamoto clan rose against the Tairas. A prolonged and bitter war ensued. At first the Taira were successful, but their arrogant rule alienated some of their feudal vassals, who joined the Minamoto. The Taira were driven from Kyoto (1183). The Minamoto won an important victory at the **Battle of Yashima** on Shikoku. The climax of the war came in the naval **Battle of Dannoura,** at the western exit of the Inland Sea; a land battle took place simultaneously on the adjacent shore. The Minamoto, under the command of Yoritomo's brother, **Yoshitsune,** were victorious, and the Taira virtually annihilated. Also distinguishing themselves in the war were Yorimoto's uncle, **Yoshiie,** and his cousin, **Yoshinaka.**

1185–1199. Military Dictatorship of Minamoto Yoritomo. Jealous and suspicious of the military successes of his relatives—Yoshitsune, Yoshiie, and Yoshinaka—Yorimoto had them all assassinated (1189). He then accused the Fujiwaras (whose power was increasing) of responsibility for the crimes, and took this opportunity to destroy the Fujiwara clan. He was the first Japanese dictator to hold the title of **Shogun** (generalissimo).

XI

THE AGE OF
THE MONGOLS: 1200–1400

MILITARY TRENDS

During most of these two centuries the military and political history of mankind was dominated by one power. The Mongols—or their Tartar vassals—conquered or ravaged every major region of the known world save Western Europe. It was caused by the unique military and political genius of an illiterate Mongol chieftain, **Genghis** (or **Jenghiz**) **Khan,** one of the greatest military geniuses the world has seen. No other leader of this period can be ranked with the great Khakhan of the Mongols, though comparable strategical and tactical skill was demonstrated by subordinates and successors such as **Subotai, Chepe, Mangu,** and **Kublai.** There were, of course, other able generals, of whom **Edward I** of England, **Du Guesclin** of France, **Tamerlane** the Tartar, **Baibars** the Mameluke, and **Murad** the Ottoman were outstanding. Although he was short on strategic ability, the tactical skill and success of English King **Edward III** probably warrant his inclusion with this group.

The continuing importance of the Turks in warfare during this period is demonstrated by the fact that three of the generals mentioned above were Turanians or Turks. By the same token, the inclusion of two English names is also significant.

Although cavalry domination of warfare reached its zenith in the Mongol conquests, this period also saw the return of the infantry soldier to predominance on the battlefield. The Battle of Crécy is generally accepted as the symbol of this return, just as the Battle of Adrianople marked the earlier ascendancy of cavalry over footmen. Edward III, building on a tactical system created by his grandfather Edward I, accomplished this by combining the staunch defensive capability of heavily armored pikemen with the maneuverability and fire power of light archers wielding the formidable English longbow. This, plus his use of cavalry for counterattack, demonstrated once more that military success is most likely to crown the efforts of those who employ the capabilities of combined arms to their maximum.

Although it did not have a significant effect on military operations during this period, the appearance of gunpowder weapons on the battlefield marked the beginning of one of the most momentous military trends of history.

This period also saw the conclusion of two great eras of military history. The

330

Byzantine Empire, once a bastion of Christian Europe, had virtually disappeared by the close of the 14th century. Even earlier, the fall of the last Christian footholds in Palestine and Syria to the Mamelukes closed the age of the Crusades.

ARMOR

The steadily improving metallurgical skill of medieval European armorers permitted the introduction of plate armor in the 13th century. At first these iron plates—covering vital and vulnerable areas such as shoulders and thighs—were worn under chain mail. By the middle of the century they were being worn over the mail, or in its place, covering shoulders, elbows, kneecaps, shins, and thighs. Late in the 13th century plate cuirasses or breastplates began to replace chain shirts.

Early combinations of plate and mail sometimes resulted in inadequate protection at the junction of the two, and on the inside of elbow, shoulder, and knee joints. This led armorers in the 14th century to develop cleverly constructed complete suits of plate armor that began to replace mail.

Skillful European smiths introduced mail mittens early in the 13th century, soon followed by mail gloves.

As plate armor made the knight or man-at-arms increasingly impervious to the weapons of the day, the shield became reduced in size to a relatively small triangle on which were emblazoned armorial bearings. Heraldry was becoming important to medieval nobility and gentry, and armorial bearings were also often embroidered on surcoats, decorative as well as useful for identification.

Most knights adopted the pot helmet with its eyeholes and breathing holes, though a number were still satisfied with the lighter and more comfortable simple casque worn over a mail coif. During the 14th century movable visors began to appear on the pot helmets.

These innovations still further increased the weight of the knight's armor. If knocked down, or unhorsed, he could rarely rise without assistance; this put a premium upon disabling heavy mounts, which in turn led to increasing the armor protection of horses. By the end of the 14th century, then, the heavy cavalry horse was usually carrying a total weight of at least 150 pounds of armor and equipment—its own and its rider's- -in addition to the man's basic weight. This meant that only ponderous, slow horses could be used for heavy-cavalry work, and even these could charge only at a trot or a slow canter.

One effect of these improvements and additions to armor was to reduce greatly the over-all numbers of combat casualties, but it sometimes led to massacres of defeated armies. (One important mitigation of this latter effect, however, was in the handsome ransoms which could be obtained for titled prisoners.) Another effect was to sacrifice mobility for protection—and mobility was the essential characteristic of cavalry. This sacrifice was not serious so long as a relative superiority of mobility could be combined with relative invulnerability. But events of the 14th century foretold the knell of armored heavy cavalry. Crécy and the subsequent introduction of gunpowder weapons showed that neither superior mobility nor invulnerability could be maintained by increasingly ponderous armored horsemen.

WEAPONS

Pre-Gunpowder Weapons

One important new weapon appeared shortly before the introduction of gunpowder: the English longbow. Originally a Welsh weapon, introduced in England in the 12th century, its potentialities were first fully appreciated by Edward I in his campaigns in Wales (see p. 364). He adopted it as the basic arm of the English yeoman infantry—both militia and professional—and employed it successfully against the Scots. Methods for tactical employment of the longbow were perfected in the Scottish campaigns of Edward III, who then used it with such stunning effect at Crécy.

The longbow not only had twice the range of the crossbow—up to 400 yards maximum, and an effective range approaching 250 yards—but also a far more rapid rate of fire. In the hands of English professional soldiers it was more accurate than, and apparently had penetrating power comparable to, the crossbow. It was lighter, more easily handled, and adaptable for skirmishing or for volley fire. It was the most effective and most versatile individual weapon yet to appear on the battlefield.

English longbowman

There were no other significant developments or improvements in individual weapons or war machines.

The Advent of Gunpowder

The origin of gunpowder weapons is obscure. Apparently the Chinese had been using some kind of explosives as early as 1161, but mostly as a noisemaker. There is some evidence that the Chinese had developed rudimentary rockets in their long wars against the Mongols in the 13th century, and that these were employed at least experimentally by some of the successors of Genghis Khan. There seems to be little doubt, however, that the first serious and effective use of gunpowder as a missile propellant was in Europe in the mid-14th century. Both the Englishman Roger Bacon and German monk Berthold Schwarz have been credited with the discovery of gunpowder in Europe.

It is commonly accepted that the first use of gunpowder weapons in battle in Europe was by the English at the Battle of Crécy (1346), although guns may have been used at Metz (1324) or at Algeciras (1342). Edward is reported to have had three or five **roundelades** or *pots de fer* (iron jugs), so called because of their shape, like round iron bottles. Soon after this, crude cannon were being used in the Hundred Years' War by both English and French on the battlefield and in siege warfare. They appeared in Germany and Italy about the same time.

The first gunpowder weapons were small metal pots or tubes inaccurately propelling arrowlike bolts. Because of the problems of weight, size, and the difficulties of holding such weapons while firing with a match or fuse, the first crude handguns —really small cannon—were unsuccessful. There were rapid and dramatic improvements in larger artillery pieces, however. As a result, by the end of the century artillery had become a permanent element of all European armies, and had even appeared in battles between the Lithuanians and the "Golden Horde" in Russia.

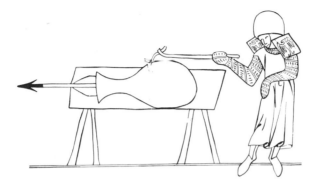

Early cannon

FORTIFICATION AND SIEGECRAFT

There were no basic improvements either in fortification or siegecraft in this period. Powerful castles appeared in increasing numbers throughout Europe patterned after the Byzantine fortifications of Anatolia and the magnificent castles which the Crusaders continued to build in Syria and Palestine.

The technique of siegecraft lagged far behind the art of fortification. Human ingenuity and mechanical skill had seemingly exhausted themselves. No important new machines or siege weapons could be devised until the human brain found some means for propulsion more powerful than the forces of torsion, tension, and counterpoise, or more destructive than fire.

The capture of Château Gaillard by Philip II proved that a powerful and wealthy monarch who was able and willing to devote sufficient resources to the task could in time overcome even the most powerful defenses. But such patience, wealth, determination, and skill were rare in the Middle Ages. Feudal armies could rarely be maintained long enough to undertake the prolonged sieges necessary to capture such powerful forts; feudal levies could be called to action for only a few weeks of the year, and mercenary armies were extremely expensive to maintain in the field indefinitely.

As a result, defensive strategy could usually be counted upon to offset offensive capabilities. Accordingly, this period probably had relatively fewer pitched battles in the open field than any era before or since. The weaker side could usually count on being able to retire behind fortifications to win—or at least not to lose. In gen-

Twelfth-century castle

eral, only the foolhardy or inept, or unlucky, would risk a battle when not completely confident of superior combat power.

TACTICS OF LAND WARFARE

The return of infantry to predominance in warfare as the principal element of a balanced combined-arms infantry-cavalry team—a trend evident in previous centuries—reached its climax at the Battle of Crécy only because of a new and improved firepower weapon—the longbow—supporting disciplined armored pikemen.

The full significance of this was not appreciated even by the English. As for other 14th century leaders, they sought in vain for the elusive key to victory by following the English example of dismounting their heavy cavalry in battle. They failed to realize that the secret of English success was not merely their dismounted knights and their archers, but the judicious combination of these two with one another and with mounted cavalrymen to obtain a flexible combination of missile fire power, defensive staying power, and mobile shock action.

The successes of the English, as well as those of Flemish and Swiss pikemen, resulted in giving to the defense a substantial tactical superiority over the offense in European warfare. This complemented and reinforced the strategic superiority of the defense resulting from the power of fortifications noted above.

It is interesting to speculate on what might have occurred if the 14th century combined-arms defensive tactics of Edward III had ever been opposed by the 13th century cavalry-offensive tactics of Genghis Khan.

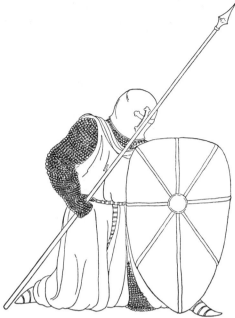

English dismounted man-at-arms   Swiss halbardier

WESTERN SOLDIERY IN THE LATER MIDDLE AGES*

Reliance upon the ill-trained, hastily raised feudal levies continued to decline while mercenary forces waxed in numbers, size, and influence. In England, however, and later in France, there was a partial reconciliation of these two inconsistent systems.

The Plantagenet kings introduced the method of "indenture" as a means of combining the militia and mercenary systems. They encouraged their vassals to provide standing contingents of troops for wars and for garrisoning royal fortifications in return for set payments and allowances. Although nominally this had no connection with the vassal's feudal obligation, the English kings rarely called out the militia.

These standing contingents were, in effect, the genesis of a permanent royal English Army. The system avoided compulsion, since the barons were paid for the forces they raised. These were professional soldiers, in both the Roman and modern sense of the term; they bore allegiance to the king, even though commanded and raised by the nobles, and they thought of themselves as English soldiers. They were, however, also mercenaries, who were not easily controlled or utilized in times of peace, when they often turned their unruly natures and military skills to plundering and terrorizing the civil populace. Since English standing units were usually quartered in the French domains of the Plantagenets, this aspect of the indenture system had less impact on England than it did on France and those other European countries using the method.

It is perhaps a paradox that every soldier in the English armies, which dominated European warfare by virtue of their infantry superiority, was a horseman.

* A discussion of the Mongol military system appears elsewhere in this chapter (see p. 340).

This explains the ability of Edward III and his son, the Black Prince, to raid fast and far through France, and to more than match the mobility of the French cavalry armies.

EAST AND CENTRAL ASIA

MONGOLIA AND THE MONGOL EMPIRE

The Early Conquests of Genghis Khan, 1190-1217

1190-1206. Unification of Mongolia. By conquest of neighboring tribes, and by adroit diplomacy, **Temujin** (see p. 328) created a large and homogeneous Mongol empire in East-Central Asia, around the Gobi Desert. Establishing his capital at Karakorum, he proclaimed himself **Genghis** (Jenghiz) **Khan** (meaning "Perfect War Emperor," or "Supreme Emperor").

1206-1209. First Wars against the Western Hsia Empire. Genghis began his conquest of China in a series of campaigns against the Western Hsia (1205, 1207, 1209). The Western Hsia emperor, with reduced dominion, acknowledged the suzerainty of Genghis Khan.

1208. Battle of the Irtysh. Genghis overcame the last resistance in Mongolia by defeating **Kushluk** (Guchluk), leader of the Naiman tribe, who fled to seek refuge with the Kara-Khitai Tartars.

1211-1215. First War against the Chin Empire. At first frustrated by the strong fortifications of the northern Chinese cities, and by his own lack of siegecraft, Genghis gradually built up a siege train and conquered Chin territory as far as the Great Wall (1213). He then advanced with three armies into the heart of Chin territory, between the Wall and the Yellow River. He completely defeated the Chin field forces, spread fire and sword through North China, captured numerous cities, and finally besieged, captured, and sacked Peking (1215). The Chin emperor was forced to recognize the suzerainty of the Mongol conqueror. **Yeh-lu Ch'u-ta'ai,** a Khitan official in Chin service, was taken into Mongol service. Apparently his expertise in administering sedentary populations was utilized by Genghis in later conquests.

1209-1216. Kushluk and the Kara-Khitai. The fugitive Kushluk, supported by **Mohammed Shah** of Khwarezm, treacherously overthrew the Khan of Kara-Khitai and seized the throne. He prepared for war with Genghis, whose spies kept him informed of these events.

1217. Conquest of Kara-Khitai. The Mongol army was exhausted by 10 years of continuous campaigning. So Genghis sent only two **toumans** (20,000 men) under brilliant young general **Chepe** (Jebei) against Kushluk. A Tartar revolt was incited, then Chepe overran the country. Kushluk's forces were defeated west of Kashgar; he was captured and executed. Kara-Khitai was annexed by Genghis.

Campaigns against Khwarezmian Empire, 1218-1224

1218. Outbreak of War. Following mistreatment of Mongol ambassadors by **Ala-ud-Din Mohammed** (Mohammed Shah) Khwarezmian-Turkish ruler of Persia Genghis gathered a force of more than 200,000 men (including auxiliaries), divided into 4 main armies commanded respectively by himself and his sons **Juji, Jagatai,** and **Ogatai.** He planned to advance into Persia from the northeast, while Chepe also moved in from Kara-Khitai with a small force.

1219. Battle of Jand. Juji and Chepe, with not more than 30,000 men between them, fought a drawn battle in the Ferghana Valley against Mohammed's vastly superior forces (perhaps 200,000).

1220. The Mongol Advance. The Mongols moved on a broad front. Juji, reinforced to about 50,000, advanced down the Ferghana Valley to besiege Khojend. Jagatai and Ogatai, with about 50,000 men each, marched in parallel columns past Lake Balkash to invest Otrar on the Syr Darya (Jaxartes) River. Genghis, with an army of similar size, swinging wide to the north of Lake Balkash, approached the Syr

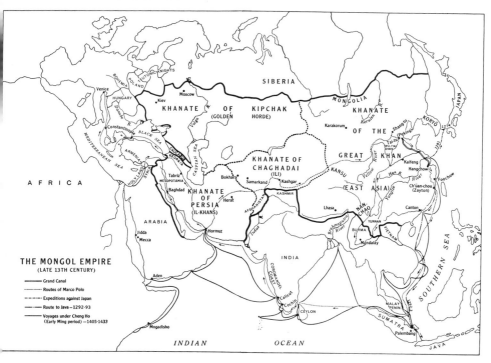

THE MONGOL EMPIRE
(LATE 13TH CENTURY)

━━━━━ Grand Canal
━━━━━ Routes of Marco Polo
━ ━ ━ Expeditions against Japan
━ ･ ━ Route to Java—1292-93
━━━━━ Voyages under Cheng Ho
(Early Ming period)—1405-1433

Darya near its Aral Sea mouth. Chepe, with 20,000 men, moving south through the Pamirs to the headwaters of the Amu Darya (Oxus) River, followed it into the heart of Transoxiana.

220. Flight of Mohammed. The shah, near Samarkand, learned of the investments of Khojend and Otrar, then got alarming reports of Chepe's advance. As he shifted a large force (possibly 100,000 men) to the southeast to protect his lines of communication to Khorasan and Ghazni, the stunning news came that Genghis Khan himself was advancing against Bokhara from the west—a direction totally unexpected. The rapid Mongol movements and the utter devastation they spread for miles on each side of their lines of march caused the Khwarezmians greatly to exaggerate their strength. Mohammed wrongly believed the forces in the encircling armies outnumbered his own 500,000 men. In panic he threw most of the remainder of his great host into Bokhara, Samarkand, and other fortresses and fled south with his family and a small bodyguard.

220. Conquest of Transoxiana. As Genghis was reaching Bokhara, his sons sacked and destroyed Khojend and Otrar. In the upper Amu Darya Valley, Chepe defeated the Turk force which Mohammed had sent against him and advanced toward Samarkand, pillaging, killing, and destroying. Bokhara surrendered to Genghis, who forced the population to raze the city's walls. Hastening onward, he joined his other forces outside Samarkand, garrisoned by 100,000 men. Despite desperate resistance, it was quickly stormed, cruelly sacked, and destroyed; the garrison and much of the population were massacred.

1220–1221. Pursuit. A force of about 30,000 men under generals Chepe and **Subotai** chased the Turkish emperor relentlessly for five months through his vast empire to the shore of the Caspian. On an islet off the coast, Mohammed died (it is said) of a broken heart (February, 1221).

1220–1221. Consolidation. Genghis supervised the conquest of Khwarezm by Ogatai, Juji, and Jagatai, and of Khorasan by his youngest son, **Tuli.** Moslem resistance was prolonged but ineffective at **Herat, Merv** and **Bamian.** Meanwhile Genghis' scouts and spies discovered that **Jellalud-**

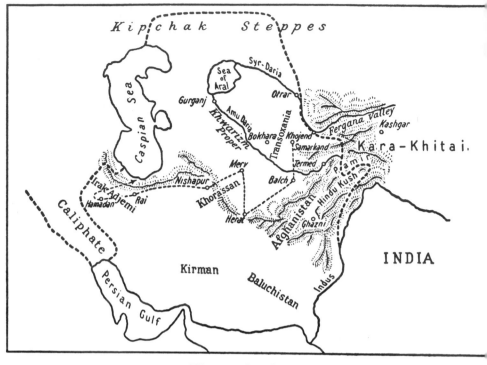

Khwarezmian Empire
Chepe's and Subotai's pursuit of Shah Mohammed

din, son of Mohammed Shah, was raising a new army in Ghazni.

1221. Battle of Pirvan. While Genghis was gathering his sons' contingents together for another campaign, Jellaluddin with 120,000 men defeated an advance Mongol force of three toumans (30,000 men) in the Hindu Kush Mountains northwest of Ghazni. Genghis moved swiftly to avenge the defeat, and the Turkish prince, deserted by his Afghan allies, withdrew into the northern Punjab with about 30,000 men. Genghis followed with more than 50,000.

1221. Battle of the Indus. The Turks took up an excellent defensive position beside the Indus, their flanks protected by mountains and a bend of the river. A violent Turkish counterattack almost broke the center of the Mongol army, but Genghis rallied his men and sent a touman over apparently impassable mountains against Jellaluddin's flank. Struck from two directions, the Turkish defense collapsed. Jellaluddin himself rode his horse over the edge of a cliff to plunge into the river, escaping to the far bank under

Genghis' admiring eyes. The Mongol sent a few toumans in pursuit; these ravaged the Lahore, Peshawar, and Multan districts of the Punjab, but did not find the Turkish prince. Later, learning that Jellaluddin had been refused asylum by the Sultan of Delhi, Genghis wisely avoided overextending his resources by an invasion of India. He called back the pursuers and withdrew from the Punjab to consolidate his conquest of Ghazni (1222–1224).

The Expedition of Chepe and Subotai, 1221–1224

1221. Advance into the Caucasus. After the death of Mohammed Shah, Chepe and Subotai received permission from Genghis to make a reconnaissance in force through the Caucasus into Southern Europe. Reinforcements probably brought their total strength close to 40,000. Apparently Chepe was in command. After advancing through Azerbaijan, they probably spent the winter on the pleasant banks of the Araxes in eastern Armenia.

1222. Invasion of Russia. The Mongols decisively defeated a large Georgian army which had been gathered to join the Fifth Crusade, then continued northward into the steppes of Russia, smashing mountain tribes that endeavored to interfere with their passage. The Cumans briefly halted the invaders in a drawn battle in the foothills east of the Kuban River. Combining rapid movement with guile, the Mongols defeated them in detail, captured Astrakhan, then pursued across the Don. Penetrating into the Crimea, they stormed the Genoese fortress of Sudak on the southeast coast, then turned north into the Ukraine.

1222–1223. Winter by the Black Sea. The Mongol leaders now felt they had accomplished their mission. Before returning to Mongolia, however, they decided to rest their toumans and to gain more information about the lands to their north and west. Their spies were soon scattered all over Eastern and Central Europe.

1223. Battle of the Kalka River. Under the leadership of **Mstislav,** Prince of Kiev, a mixed Russian-Cuman army of 80,000 marched against the Mongols near the mouth of the Dnieper River. Chepe and Subotai sought peace, but when their envoys were brutally killed, they attacked and practically annihilated the Russians. After raiding a few hundred miles to the north, the Mongols turned eastward in compliance with a courier message from Genghis. As they were marching north of the Caspian Sea, Chepe sickened and died. Subotai brought the expedition back after a trek of 4,000 miles to a rendezvous with the main Mongol armies, now returning from their victories over the Khwarezmians (1224).

The Final Campaigns of Genghis Khan, 1225–1227

1224–1226. Resurgence of the Hsia and Chin Empires. The vassal Tangut emperor of the Western Hsia had refused to take part in the war against Mohammed Shah. The Hsia and Chin Empires now formed an alliance against the Mongols.

1225–1226. Mongol Preparations. Feeling his age, Genghis selected Ogatai as successor to his throne, established the method of selection of subsequent Khakhans, studied intelligence reports from Hsia and Chin, and readied a force of 180,000 men for a new campaign.

1226. Invasion of Western Hsia. Late in the year, when the rivers were frozen, the Mongols struck southward with their customary speed and vigor. The Tanguts, well acquainted with Mongol methods, were ready, and the two armies met by the banks of the frozen Yellow River. The Hsia army numbered something more than 300,000 men.

1226. Battle of the Yellow River. Genghis enticed the Tangut cavalry to attack over the ice. As they crossed, his dismounted archers harassed them. The Tangut horsemen, soon thrown into confusion, were now charged by mounted and dismounted Mongols. At the same time several toumans swept past the struggle on the ice to attack the Hsia infantry on the far bank. The battle was soon over. The Mongols counted 300,000 dead; it is not known how many Tanguts escaped.

1227. Victory over Hsia and Chin. Pursuing with customary vigor, the Mongols killed the Hsia emperor in a mountain fortress. His son took refuge in the great walled city of Ninghsia, which the Mongols had vainly besieged in earlier wars. Leaving a third of his army to invest the Hsia capital, Genghis sent Ogatai eastward, across the great bend of the Yellow River, to drive the Chin from their last footholds north of the river. With the remainder, he marched southeast (evidently to eastern Szechwan), taking a position in the mountains where the Hsia, Chin, and Sung empires met, to prevent Sung reinforcements from reaching Ninghsia. Here he accepted the surrender of the new Hsia emperor, but rejected peace overtures from the Chin.

1227. The Death of Genghis Khan. A premonition of death caused the Khakhan (or Great Khan) to start back to Mongolia, but he died en route. On his deathbed he outlined to his son Tuli the plans which would later be used by his successors to complete the destruction of the Chin Empire.

THE MONGOL MILITARY SYSTEM, c. 1225

The Mongol "Hordes"

The word "horde," denoting a Mongol tribe or a field army, has become synony-mous with vast numbers because the Mongols' Western foes refused to believe that they had been overwhelmed by small forces. Half to excuse their defeats, half be-cause they never had the opportunity to understand the marvelous system that per-mitted the Mongols to strike with the speed and force of a hurricane, 13th-century Europeans sincerely but wrongly believed the Mongol armies to be tremendous, rel-atively undisciplined mobs that achieved their objectives solely by superior numbers.

Genghis Khan and his armies accomplished feats that would be hard, if not impossible, for modern armies to duplicate, principally because he had one of the best-organized, best-trained, and most thoroughly disciplined armies ever created. The Mongol Army was usually much smaller than those of its principal opponents. The largest force Genghis Khan ever assembled was that with which he conquered Persia: less than 240,000 men. The Mongol armies which later conquered Russia and all of Eastern and Central Europe never exceeded 150,000 men.

Mongol Organization

Quality, not quantity, was the basis of Mongol success. The simplicity of their organization was its chief characteristic. Consisting entirely of cavalry—with the exception of some auxiliary elements—it was homogeneous. The organization was based on the decimal system. The largest independent unit was the *touman*, consist-ing of 10,000 men, corresponding roughly to a modern cavalry division. Three tou-mans normally constituted an army, or an army corps. The touman, in turn, was composed of 10 regiments of 1,000 men each. The regiments consisted of 10 squad-rons, each comprising 10 troops of 10 men.

About 40 per cent of a typical Mongol army consisted of heavy cavalry, for shock action. These men wore complete armor, usually of leather, or mail armor secured from defeated enemies. They wore a simple casque helmet such as was nor-mally used by contemporary Chinese and Byzantines. The heavy cavalry horses also usually carried some leather armor protection. The main heavy-cavalry weapon was the lance.

Light-cavalry troopers, comprising about 60 per cent of the army, wore no armor, save usually a helmet. Their chief battle weapons were the Asiatic bow, the javelin, and the lasso. The fire power of the Mongol reflex bows—only a little shorter than the English longbow—was particularly devastating, in the Scythian-Turkish tradition. Each light cavalryman carried two quivers of arrows and there were addi-tional arrows in a supply train. The mission of the light cavalry was reconnaissance, screening, provision of fire-power support to the heavy cavalry, mopping-up opera-tions, and pursuit.

To assure and to enhance mobility, each Mongol trooper had one or more spare horses. These were herded along behind the columns, and were available for quick change of mounts on the march, or even during battle. Changes were made in relays to maintain security and to assure minimum interference with accomplish-ment of assigned missions.

Both light and heavy cavalrymen carried either a scimitar or a battleax. Each man also had a shirt of strong raw silk to be donned just before action. Genghis found that an arrow would rarely penetrate such silk, but rather would drive it into the wound. Thus the conscript Chinese surgeons were able to extract arrow heads from wounded soldiers merely by pulling out the silk.

Training and Discipline

The individual Mongol troopers were the best-trained soldiers of the time. Hardened veterans of Spartan endurance and fortitude, highly skilled in the use of weapons, they had been riders from early youth, brought up in the harsh school of the Gobi Desert. Inured to hardships and extremes of weather, lacking luxuries and rich food, these men had strong bodies and needed little or no medical attention to keep fit for operations.

The commander of each unit was selected on the basis of individual ability and valor on the field of battle. He exercised absolute authority over his unit, subject to equally strict control and supervision from his superior. Instant obedience to orders was demanded and received. Discipline was of an order unknown elsewhere during the medieval period.

We know little of the details of the training system of Genghis Khan. We do know that each troop, squadron, and regiment was capable of precise performance of a kind of battle drill that formed the basis of Mongol small-unit tactics. Such precision required constant practice under close and demanding supervision. The battlefield coordination of units within the toumans, and between toumans and the larger hordes, is evidence of painstaking practice in precombat maneuvers by forces of all sizes.

Doctrine and Tactics

The mobility of Genghis Khan's troops has never been matched by other ground soldiery. He seems to have had an instinctive understanding that force is the product of mass and the square of velocity. No other commander in history has been more aware of the fundamental importance of seizing and maintaining the initiative—of always attacking, even when the strategic mission was defensive.

At the outset of a campaign, the Mongol toumans usually advanced rapidly on an extremely broad front, maintaining only courier contact between major elements. When an enemy force was found, it became the objective of all nearby Mongol units. Complete information regarding enemy location, strength, and direction of movement was immediately transmitted to central headquarters, and in turn disseminated to all field units. If the enemy force was small, it was dealt with promptly by the local commanders. If it was too large to be disposed of so readily, the main Mongol army would rapidly concentrate behind an active cavalry screen. Frequently a rapid advance would overwhelm separate sections of an enemy army before its concentration was complete.

Genghis and his able subordinates avoided stereotyped patterns of moving to combat. If the enemy's location was definitely determined, they might lead the bulk of their forces to strike him in the rear, or to turn his flank. Sometimes they would feign a retreat, only to return at the charge on fresh horses.

Most frequently, however, the Mongols would advance behind their screen of light horsemen in several roughly parallel columns, spread across a wide front. This permitted flexibility, particularly if the enemy was formidable, or if his exact location was not firmly determined. The column encountering the enemy's main force would then hold or retire, depending upon the situation. Meanwhile the others would continue to advance, occupying the country to the enemy's flank and rear. This would usually force him to fall back to protect his lines of communication. The Mongols would then close in to take advantage of any confusion or disorder in the enemy's retirement. This was usually followed by his eventual encirclement and destruction.

The cavalry squadrons, because of their precision, their concerted action, and their amazing mobility, were easily superior to all troops they encountered, even when these were more heavily or better armed, or more numerous. The rapidity of the Mongol movements invariably gave them superiority of force at the decisive point, the ultimate aim of all battle tactics. By seizing the initiative and exploiting their mobility to the utmost, the Mongol commanders, rather than their foes, almost always selected the point and time of decision.

The battle formation was composed of five lines, each of a single rank, with large intervals between lines. Heavy cavalry comprised the first two lines; the other three were light horsemen. Reconnaissance and screening were carried out in front of these lines by other light-cavalry units. As the opposing forces drew nearer to each other, the three rear ranks of light cavalry advanced through intervals in the two heavy lines to shower the enemy with a withering fire of well-aimed javelins and deadly arrows.

The intensive fire-power preparation would shake even the staunchest of foes. Sometimes this harassment would scatter the enemy without need for shock action. When the touman commander felt that the enemy had been sufficiently confused by the preparation, the light horsemen would be ordered to retire, and synchronized signals would start the heavy cavalry on its charge.

In addition to combining fire and movement—and missile action with shock action—the Mongols also emphasized maneuver and diversions at all tactical levels and in all phases of combat. During the main engagement, a portion of the force usually held the enemy's attention by frontal attack. While the opposing commander was thus diverted, the main body would deliver a decisive blow on the flank or rear.

Siegecraft and Attack of Fortifications

In his early campaigns, Genghis Khan's cavalry armies were frequently frustrated by the strong walls of Chinese cities. After intensive analytical study—plus the adoption of Chinese weapons, equipment, and techniques, and considerable empirical experience—the Mongol leader in a few years developed a system for assaulting fortifications which was well-nigh irresistible. An important component of this system was a large, but mobile, siege train, with missile engines and other equipment carried on wagons and pack animals. Genghis conscripted the best Chinese engineers to comprise the manpower of his siege train. Combining generous terms of service with the compulsion of force, he created an engineer corps at least as efficient as those of Alexander and Caesar.

In Genghis' later campaigns, and in those of his brilliant subordinate Subotai, no fortification could long stop the march of a Mongol army. Those of importance, and those which contained large garrisons, would usually be invested by a touman —supported by all or part of the engineer train—while the main force marched onward. Sometimes by stratagem, ruse, or audacious assault, the town would be quickly stormed. If this proved impossible, the besieging touman and the engineers began regular siege operations, while the main army sought out the principal field forces of the enemy. Once the inevitable victory had been achieved in the field, besieged towns and cities usually surrendered without further resistance. In such cases, the inhabitants were treated with only moderate severity.

But if the defenders of a city or fort were foolish enough to attempt to defy the besiegers, Genghis' amazingly efficient engineers would soon create a breach in the walls, or prepare other methods for a successful assault by the dismounted toumans. Then the conquered city, its garrison, and its inhabitants would be subjected to the pillaging and destruction which have made the name of Genghis Khan one of the most feared in history.

Sometimes even the strongest cities were overwhelmed and captured before they were fully aware that any large force of Mongols was in their vicinity. The leading Mongol light horsemen always attempted to pursue defeated enemies so closely and so vigorously as to ride through the gates before they could be closed. Even if the enemy was sufficiently alert to prevent this, he rarely anticipated the speed, efficiency, and vigor with which the Mongol engines of war—ballista and catapult—were put into action within a few minutes of the arrival of the leading cavalry units. The Mongols discovered that a prompt and vigorous assault, covered by a hail of fire from these machines, would often permit them to scale the walls and to seize a portion of the defenses before the surprised enemy was prepared to resist.

If the initial assaults were repulsed and regular siege operations were required, the ballistae and catapults provided fire cover for battering rams, siege towers, and all of the normal methods of siegecraft. When the Mongols were prepared to make their final major assault through a breach, or over the opposing fortifications, they frequently made use of a ruthless, heartless, but usually effective method of approach. Herding great numbers of helpless captives in front of them, the dismounted Mongol troopers would advance to the walls, forcing the defenders to kill their own countrymen in order to be able to bring fire against the attackers.

To add to the confusion and difficulties of the enemy, the Mongols often preceded their assaults by firing flaming arrows into besieged camps and cities to start fires. These arrows were fired by light cavalrymen dashing in front of the walls, as well as by catapults from farther away.

Staff and Command

We know little of the staff system of Genghis Khan, probably because the history of his operations was mostly written by his enemies, who rarely understood how he accomplished his victories. He seems to have been his own operations officer, although later he evidently made considerable use of the skill and genius of able subordinates like Subotai and Chepe. Strategy and tactics for every campaign were obviously prepared in painstaking detail in advance.

An essential element of Mongol planning was its intelligence system. Operations plans were always based on thorough study and evaluation of amazingly complete and accurate information. The Mongol intelligence network spread throughout the world; its thoroughness excelled all others of the Middle Ages. Spies generally operated under the guise of merchants or traders.

Once the intelligence had been evaluated, lines of operation were decided upon in advance for the entire campaign, and toumans were assigned to follow these lines, each with its own objective. Nevertheless, the widest latitude was given to each subordinate commander in accomplishing the specific objective assigned to him. Prior to a general engagement a touman commander was at liberty to maneuver and to meet the enemy at his discretion, and was required only to maintain general conformance with the over-all plan. Orders and the exchange of combat intelligence information passed rapidly between the Khan's headquarters and his subordinate units by swift mounted couriers. Thus Genghis, to an extent rarely matched in history, was able to assure complete unity of command at all levels and yet retain close personal control over the most extensive operations.

The Mongols were particularly adept at psychological warfare. Tales of their ruthlessness, barbarity, and slaughter of recalcitrant foes were widely disseminated in a deliberate propaganda campaign to discourage resistance by the next intended victim. As a matter of fact, while there was considerable truth in this propaganda, it was equally true that the Mongols were most solicitous in their treatment of any foe who gave evidence of willingness to cooperate, particularly those who had skills which the great Khan thought might be operationally or administratively useful.

One evidence of the existence of a general staff is the way in which the Mongols responded to the lessons of their campaigns. They not only promptly analyzed each of their major actions; they put the results of this analysis to work immediately in a systematic training program which must have been directed by an alert, smoothly-functioning staff.

Administration

The gathering of supplies on campaign was apparently left to individual subordinate commanders. The Mongol toumans lived off the country through the most ruthless requisitioning practices. That this was done efficiently, however, and in a systematic and coordinated manner, is clearly evidenced by uniform success of the Mongols in maintaining their forces, even when operating in desert and mountain regions. The administrative staff of the great Khan apparently consisted largely of captured Chinese scholars, officials, and surgeons.

The food supply problem was facilitated by the Mongol practice of drinking mare's milk; most of their horses were mares.

A somewhat gruesome evidence of the thoroughness and efficiency of the Mongol administrative and staff operations is the manner in which they kept a record of enemy casualties. (Their own losses, of course, were easily determined by a roll

call.) After a battle, specified units were responsible for cutting off the right ear of each enemy corpse on the battlefield. These were thrown into sacks so as to obtain at leisure an accurate count of enemy dead.

Communications

We have already noted the extensive use of couriers for long-range communications purposes. Tactical movements were controlled by black and white signal flags under the direction of squadron and regimental commanders. Thus there were no delays caused by poorly written orders or messages. (Probably few of the Mongol commanders could read or write.) The signal flags were particularly useful for coordinating the movements of units beyond the range of voice control.

When signal flags could not be seen, either because of darkness or intervening terrain features, the Mongols used flaming arrows.

Stratagems and Ruses

Unlike the sometimes foolishly chivalrous knights of Western Europe, the Mongols disdained no trickery which might give them an advantage, or which would reduce their own losses or increase those of their foes. Some of their tricks were obviously the result of inspiration of the moment—encouraged by the latitude of initiative which Genghis Khan inculcated among his subordinates. Most, however, were apparently included in a kind of repertoire of stratagems, with which all commanders were acquainted. Two examples are worth noting.

The Mongols liked to operate in the winter, when their mobility was enhanced by frozen marshes and ice-covered rivers. A favorite way of finding out when the river ice would be thick enough to support the weight of their horses was to encourage the local population to test it for them. In late 1241, in Hungary, Mongols left untended cattle on the east bank of the Danube, in sight of the famished refugees they had driven across the river earlier in the year. When the Hungarians were able to cross the river and bring the cattle back with them, the Mongols decided to start their next advance.

Another stratagem, which might more properly be called a tactical technique, was their use of smoke screens. It was common practice to send out small detachments to start great prairie fires, or fires in inhabited regions, both to deceive the enemy as to their intentions and to hide movements.

Military Government

Once armed resistance ceased in a conquered territory, the Mongols changed immediately from apparently wanton destruction to carefully calculated reconstruction. Genghis created what was probably the most carefully planned military government system to appear before the 20th century. The civil administration was usually left under a local leader satisfactory to the Mongols, who was supported, and closely supervised, by a Mongol occupation force. A census was taken, and efficient tax-collection machinery immediately established. Genghis Khan had no intention of allowing conquered territories to be a burden on his economy. On the contrary, the funds collected in this fashion not only maintained the local government, and its occupation troops, but also were used to pay tribute to Karakorum.

The Mongols absolutely forbade any continuation of local and internal squabbles in their conquered territory. Law and order were rigidly and ruthlessly maintained. As a consequence, regimented conquered regions were usually far more peaceful under the Mongol occupation than they had been before the invasion.

The Successors of Genghis Khan, 1227–1388

1227–1241. Reign of Ogatai Khan. The new ruler completed the conquest of the outlying territories of the Western Hsia. The expansion of the Mongol Empire continued in all directions. The first new victim was Korea (1231; see p. 352).

1231–1234. Conquest of the Chin Empire. Forming an alliance with the Sung, the Mongols undertook the final destruction of Chin. Tuli led a great army south, through Hsia territory, into the Sung province of Szechwan, then turned east through Hanchung (Nancheng) into Chin territory. In the middle of the campaign Tuli died, and Subotai took command (1232). He continued on to besiege the great city of Pien Liang (Kaifeng), Chin capital. Despite skillful use of explosives by the defenders, the city finally fell to Mongol assault after a year's siege (1233). Subotai then completed the conquest of the Chin Empire. Ogatai refused to divide the conquered region with the Sung, who then attempted to seize the former Chin province of Honan. This was the signal for war.

1234–1279. War with the Sung Empire. This prolonged conflict was brought to a conclusion by Ogatai's nephews and successors, **Mangu** and **Kublai.** Operating under Mangu, Kublai conquered Yunnan from the Nanchao, vassals of the Sung (1252–1253). A subordinate then overran Tonkin, capturing Hanoi (1257). Sung resistance was based upon determined defense of their well-fortified, well-provisioned cities. The Chinese Empire crumbled, however, under the impact of a series of brilliant campaigns personally directed by Mangu (1257–1259). His sudden death from dysentery caused a lull in the war during a Mongol dynastic dispute (see below); the Sung revived, and the war dragged on. Finally, Kublai could turn his full attention to the war in China (1268).

A series of campaigns, distinguished by the skill of the general **Bayan** (grandson of Subotai) were culminated by the capture of the capital city of Hangchow (1276). It took three more years to subdue the outlying provinces. The last action of the war was a naval battle in the Bay of Canton (1279). The Sung ships were all destroyed by a Mongol fleet. The Chinese admiral jumped into the waves, carrying the Sung boy emperor in his arms. Refugees on coastal islands were rounded up and slaughtered.

1237–1241. Mongol Conquests in East and Central Europe. (See p. 347.)

1239. Mongol Conquest of Tibet. This was done by **Godan,** son of Ogatai.

1243. Battle of Kosedagh. The Mongols, after overrunning the remnants of the Khwarezmian Empire, defeated the Seljuk Turks and established suzerainty over Anatolia.

c. 1250. Politico-Military Organization of the Empire. Ogatai and his successors adhered to the system of territorial viceroyalties established by Genghis before his death. Batu, son of Juji, was confirmed as ruler of the steppes of Northwestern Asia and Eastern Europe. First khan of the Golden Horde (1243–1256), Batu established his capital at Sarai on the Volga (see p. 351). Jagatai and his successors ruled the vast intermediate region roughly corresponding to modern Turkestan and Central Siberia. They were known as khans of the Jagatai (Chagatai) Mongols. Farther south, Transoxiana, Khorasan, and modern Afghanistan became the realm of Tuli. One branch of Tuli's family, through Kublai, became the direct imperial line of khakhans and Yuan emperors of China. Another branch under Hulagu and his progeny completed the conquest of Southwest Asia and became the Ilkhans of Persia. The khans of the Golden Horde, the Jagatai, and the Ilkhans remained vassals and viceroys of the khakhans of Karakorum and Peking until the decline of the Yuan Dynasty in the mid-14th century (see p. 351).

1251–1259. Reign of Mangu (Son of Tuli). He was an able warrior and administrator. Though he devoted most of his attention to prosecution of the war against China, he also sent his brother Hulagu to carry out the conquest of Southwest Asia.

1252–1287. Mongol Conquests of Nanchao and Annam. (See p. 397.)

1255–1260. Hulagu's Conquests in Southwest Asia. (See p. 390.)

1260–1294. Reign of Kublai Khan. Selection of Kublai as khakhan was violently opposed by his younger brother, **Arik-Buka,** precipitating a civil war, which Kublai won by vigorous action (1260–1261). Upon the overthrow of the Sung Dynasty, he declared himself emperor, and established the Yuan Dynasty (see p. 351). One of the ablest of all the rulers of China, he reunited the country, which has ever since remained at least nominally unified (despite subsequent civil wars).

1261–1262. Civil War between the Ilkhans and the Golden Horde. (See p. 391.)

1274. First Mongol Invasion of Japan. (See p. 352.)

1281. Second Mongol Invasion of Japan. (See p. 352.)

1281. Battle of Homs. An Ilkhan Mongol army invading Syria was defeated and repulsed by Mameluke Sultan Kala'un (see p. 390).

1281–1287. Invasions of Annam and Champa. (See p. 397.)

1287–1300. Invasions of Burma. (See p. 398.)

1292–1293. Invasion of Java. (See p. 399.)

1294–1307. Reign of Timur. The grandson of Kublai, Timur (not to be confused with Timur the Lame, or Tamerlane) was the last recognized khakhan of the entire Mongol Empire.

1299–1300. Invasion of Syria. Ilkhan **Ghazan Mahmud** captured Damascus and overran most of Syria, then withdrew.

1303, April 20. Battle of Marj-as-Suffar. In their last important invasion of Syria, a Mongol Ilkhan army was defeated and repulsed by the Mamelukes.

1307–1388. Decline of the Yuan Dynasty. The Mongol Empire gradually fell apart. Ilkhans, Jagatais, and the Golden Horde became independent khanates; other Mongol princes became independent or were overthrown by the subject peoples.

1356–1388. Overthrow of the Mongols by the Chinese Ming Dynasty. (See p. 352.)

Mongol Campaigns in Europe, 1237–1242

INVASION OF EASTERN EUROPE, 1237–1240

In 1237 Ogatai sent an army of 150,000 men to invade Eastern Europe. Nominally in command was Batu, son of Juji, but the real commander was Subotai, who led his troops westward over the frozen Volga River in December, 1237. As a result of his initial reconnaissance in 1223 (see p. 339), and subsequent accumulation of intelligence information about Russia, this invasion had been prepared with the same care that had characterized all the campaigns of his mentor, Genghis Khan. Sweeping over the frozen countryside like a whirlwind, the Mongols advanced through Moscow and Kaluga and completely destroyed the north Russian princi-

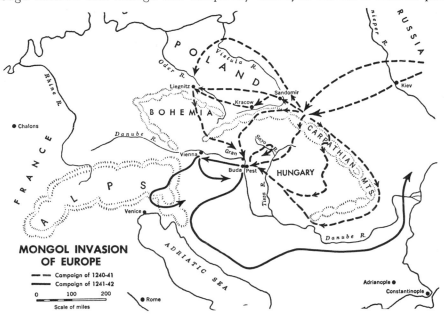

MONGOL INVASION
OF EUROPE
— — Campaign of 1240-41
——— Campaign of 1241-42
0   100   200
Scale of miles

palities in a few months. When the thaws began in March, Subotai turned south to the steppes of the Don River basin to rest his army, to regain strength, and to prepare for new advances.

During the next two years Subotai consolidated control over eastern and southern Russia, at the same time accumulating detailed information about Europe to his west. Only the vaguest rumors of the Mongol conquest of southern and eastern Russia—largely carried by Cuman refugees—had reached the kingdoms of Central and Western Europe. Subotai, on the other hand, knew the political, economic, and social conditions in Europe in detail. Again moving in winter, to assure full mobility over the great rivers of the Ukraine, 150,000 Mongols crossed the frozen Dnieper at the end of November, 1240. When the Prince of Kiev rejected the Mongol demand for surrender, Subotai assaulted, captured the city, then destroyed it (December 6). Overrunning all of the regions southeast of the Carpathians and northwest of the Black Sea, Subotai was now ready to start his next campaign.

INVASION OF CENTRAL EUROPE, 1241

Subotai left 30,000 men to control the conquered regions and to protect his lines of communication, leaving about 120,000 men to invade Central Europe. He realized that Hungary, Poland, Bohemia, and Silesia could each raise forces larger than his own, and he was equally aware that an invasion of any one of these countries would bring him into immediate conflict with the other three, and with the Holy Roman Empire. His knowledge of European politics, however, made him confident that he could count on jealous bickering between the pope, the German emperor, and the kings of France and England to keep these more powerful nations from involvement until he had secured Central Europe. He then intended to deal with them one at a time.

Subotai divided his army into four principal columns, or field armies, each of three toumans. One of these, under **Kaidu,** grandson of Ogatai, was to protect the northern flank. Another flank force, under **Kadan,** son of Ogatai, was to protect the southern flank while invading Hungary from the south, through Transylvania and the Danube Valley. The two remaining hordes, apparently advancing in parallel columns, under Batu and Subotai, were to force the passes over the central Carpathians. These two columns would meet on the Hungarian plains in front of the city of Pest, on the east bank of the Danube opposite the capital, Buda.

Kaidu, to attract the attention of the Poles, Bohemians, and Silesians from the main objective, moved out in early March, somewhat ahead of the other three columns. He swept through Poland and into Silesia, defeating three larger Polish armies as he went. A detached touman protected his right flank, swinging north through Lithuania, then west through East Prussia and along the Baltic coast into Pomerania. With the other two, Kaidu smashed the army of **Boleslav V** of Poland at **Cracow** (March 3).

As the toumans carried fire and sword through northeastern Europe, panic spread across the countryside. Terror-stricken refugees fled westward. As town after town was seized, destroyed, and burned, the swarm of refugees was augmented and the tale of horror was repeated and amplified. By the time Kaidu's two toumans of 20,000 men had reached Silesia in early April, the Europeans believed that his force was upward of 200,000 men.

THE BATTLE OF LIEGNITZ, APRIL 9, 1241

Despite their belief in these wild exaggerations, the chivalry of North-Central Europe was prepared to fight desperately. Prince **Henry** (the Pious) of Silesia gathered a mixed army of some 40,000 Germans, Poles, and Teutonic Knights, and took up a defensive position at Liegnitz in the path of Kaidu's horde. King **Wenceslas** of Bohemia marched northward hastily with an army of 50,000 men to join Henry.

Kaidu struck while the Bohemians were still two days' march away. The Europeans fought bravely and stubbornly, but Henry's army was smashed; its broken remnants fled westward. Because the Mongols did not pursue, some European historians have incorrectly inferred that the **Battle of Liegnitz** (or Wahlstatt) was a drawn fight and that the Mongols had suffered so severely at the hands of their Western opponents that they decided not to press further into Germany.

Kaidu had no reason to pursue. He had accomplished his mission. All North-Central Europe from the Baltic to the Carpathians had been devastated. All possible danger to the right flank of Subotai's army had been eliminated. The one remaining effective army of the region—the Bohemians of Wenceslaus—was withdrawing to the northwest to join the hastily gathered forces of other German nobles. Having so brilliantly carried out his part of Subotai's plan, Kaidu called in his detached touman from the Baltic coast and turned south to join the main body in Hungary, laying Moravia waste as he advanced.

ADVANCE INTO HUNGARY

The southern column had been equally effective, although thawing snows and flooding rivers held up the advance. After three pitched battles, all resistance collapsed in Transylvania by April 11. Passing between the Danube and the Carpathians at the Iron Gates, Kadan drove northward into the Hungarian plain to meet Subotai.

Meanwhile, on March 12, the columns of the main body had broken through the Hungarian defenses at the Carpathian passes. King Bela of Hungary, receiving word of the Mongol advance through the passes, called a council of war in Buda, 200 miles away, to consider how to prevent the Mongols from continuing their invasion. While this council was in progress, on March 15, he received word that the Mongol advance guard had already arrived at the opposite bank of the river.

Bela did not panic. Within two weeks he had gathered nearly 100,000 men, while the Mongol advance was held up by the broad Danube River and the formidable fortifications of the city of Pest.

At the beginning of April, Bela marched eastward from Pest with his army, confident of repelling the invaders. As he advanced, the Mongols withdrew. After several days of cautious pursuit, he made contact with them late on April 10, near the Sajo River, almost 100 miles northeast of Budapest. Bela surprised Subotai by promptly and vigorously seizing a bridge over the Sajo from a weak Mongolian detachment. He established a strong bridgehead beyond the river, and encamped with the remainder of his army in a fortified camp of wagons chained together on the west bank. He had received accurate and complete information regarding the Mongol strength from loyal subjects, and knew that his army was considerably more numerous than the Mongols.

BATTLE OF THE SAJO RIVER, APRIL 11, 1241

Just before dawn the Hungarian bridgehead defenders found themselves under a hail of stones and arrows, "to the accompaniment of a thunderous noise and flashes of fire." That the Mongols were actually using the first cannon of European military history is doubtful. More likely, it was their normal employment of catapults and ballistae with terror-inspiring sound effects from early forms of Chinese firecrackers. In any event, this was a 13th-century version of a modern artillery preparation. It was followed closely, as in modern tactics, by fierce assault.

The defenders, stupefied by noise, death, and destruction, were quickly overwhelmed, and the Mongols streamed across the bridge. Bela's main army, aroused by the commotion, hastily sallied out of their fortified camp. A bitter battle ensued. Suddenly it became evident, however, that this was only a Mongol holding attack.

The main effort was made by three toumans, some 30,000 men, under the personal command of Subotai. In the predawn darkness he had led his troops through the cold waters of the Sajo River, south of the bridgehead, then turned northward to strike the Hungarians' right flank and rear. Unable to resist this devastating charge, the Europeans hastily fell back into their camp. By 7 A.M. it was completely invested by the Mongols. For several hours they bombarded it with stones, arrows, and burning naphtha.

It appeared to some desperate Hungarians that there was a gap to the west. A few men galloped out safely. As the intensity of the Mongol assault mounted elsewhere, more and more men slipped out. Soon a stream of men was pouring westward through the gap. As the defense collapsed, the survivors rushed to join those who had already escaped. Lacking all semblance of military formation, many of the fugitives threw away weapons and armor in order to flee better. Suddenly they discovered that they had fallen into a Mongol trap. Mounted on swift fresh horses, the Mongols appeared on all sides, cutting down the exhausted men, hunting them into marshes, storming the villages in which some of them attempted to take refuge. In a few hours of horrible butchery the Hungarian army was completely destroyed, losing between 40,000 and 70,000 dead. More serious, the defeat assured Mongol control of all Eastern Europe from the Dnieper to the Oder and from the Baltic Sea to the Danube. In four months they had overwhelmed Christian armies totaling five times their own strength.

WITHDRAWAL OF THE MONGOLS, 1242

During the summer of 1241, Subotai consolidated control of eastern Hungary, and made plans to invade Italy, Austria, and Germany the following winter. Frantic efforts of panic-stricken West Europeans were poorly coordinated, and little was accomplished to prepare an effective defense. Only chance—or Divine Providence—saved the remainder of Europe.

Just after Christmas of 1241, the Mongols started westward across the frozen Danube. Spearheads crossed the Julian Alps into North Italy, while scouts approached Vienna through the Danube Valley. Then came a message from Karakorum, 6,000 miles to the east. Ogatai, the son and successor of Genghis Khan, was dead.

The law of Genghis Khan explicitly provided that "after the death of the ruler all offspring of the house of Genghis Khan, wherever they might be, must return to Mongolia to take part in the election of the new Khakhan." Reluctantly Subotai reminded his three princes of their dynastic duty. From the outskirts of trembling Vienna and Venice, the toumans countermarched, never to return. Their ebb went through Dalmatia and Serbia, then eastward across northern Bulgaria, virtually destroying the kingdoms of Serbia and Bulgaria before they vanished across the lower Danube (see pp. 379 and 380).

Khanate of the Golden Horde, 1243–1400

Under the Mongol system of administrative decentralization, **Batu,** grandson of Genghis Khan, reigned as the first khan of the Golden Horde, ruling most of Western Asia and practically all of Europe east of the Carpathians. By a combination of military superiority, wise diplomacy, and cunning intrigue, Batu and his Mongol or Tartar successors retained almost uninterrupted authority over Russia for a century and a half (see p. 435). They were unquestionably the most powerful rulers in Europe during this period. Dynastic troubles toward the end of the 14th century almost tore their empire apart. The White Horde, in the region extending northward from the Aral Sea, became practically independent, and the Russian principalities attempted to follow this example, at first successfully. After two decades of civil war and decay, however, the Khan **Toktamish,** with the help of **Tamerlane** of the Jagatai Mongols (see p. 391), established himself first as the leader of the White Horde, then by conquest reunited the White and Golden Hordes. He ruthlessly suppressed the tentative independence of the Russian principalities. He made the mistake, however, of provoking a war with his benefactor Tamerlane. After conflicts lasting ten years, Toktamish was defeated and overthrown. This defeat contributed to the lingering decline of the Horde in subsequent centuries. The principal events were:

1242–1256. Reign of Batu. He established his capital at Sarai (Zarev) on the lower Volga. He accepted the vassalage of **Alexander Nevski,** Prince of Novgorod, who assisted in the establishment of Mongol suzerainty over all of Russia (see p. 378). In return, Alexander was treated with courtesy and respect by the Mongols.

1256–1263. Reign of Bereke (Batu's Brother). The first descendant of Genghis Khan to become a Moslem, he sent armies raiding deep into the Balkans, Hungary, and Poland. One of these raids, led by his generals **Tulubaga** and **Nogai,** reached as far as Silesia; the cities of Cracow, Sandomir, and Bythom were all captured and sacked (1259).

c. 1270–1296. Autonomy of Nogai. As governor of the south Ukrainian region, he became virtually independent. The rulers of Bulgaria and Serbia paid him tribute.

1290–1313. Reign of Toktu. For several years Toktu was engaged in a bitter war to establish central authority over Nogai. After one serious defeat near the Dnieper River, Toktu finally overwhelmed Nogai, who died in battle (1296). Toktu revitalized the Golden Horde.

1314–1340. Reign of Uzberg. He was the last great khan of the Golden Horde. On his orders, a revolt of the Prince of Tver (Kalinin) was suppressed by Prince **Ivan** of Moscow (see p. 378) with a mixed Russian-Mongol army. Ivan's success established the princes of Moscow as the principal vassals and administrators for the Mongols in northern and central Russia.

1359–1379. Dynastic Civil War. During this period **Urus,** Khan of the White Horde, became virtually independent, and also took part in the continuing confused struggle for the khanate of the Golden Horde. One of the claimants, a chieftain named **Toktamish,** defeated by his rival **Mamai,** fled to seek safety and assistance from Tamerlane, by that time ruler of the Jagatai Tartars (see p. 391).

1378. Rise of Toktamish. With Tamerlane's assistance, Toktamish became the Khan of the White Horde.

1380. Battle of Kulikovo. Mamai, allied with the Lithuanians, attempted to reconquer the rebellious Russian principalities. He was defeated by **Dmitri** of Moscow, leader of the Russian princes, before the arrival of the Lithuanians, who then retreated.

1380. Battle of the Kalka River. Near the site of Subotai's great victory (see p. 339), Toktamish defeated Mamai to become Khan of the Golden Horde.

1381–1382. Russian Rebellion Suppressed. Toktamish campaigned across northern and central Russia, completely subduing the rebellion. He captured Moscow (August 23, 1382), massacring many inhabitants.

1385–1395. Wars between Toktamish and Tamerlane. (See p. 391.) Toktamish was defeated in three great battles: on the Syr Darya River (1389), at Kandurcha (1391), and at the Terek River (1395).

1396. War with Lithuania. In alliance with the fugitive Toktamish, **Vitov,** grand prince of Lithuania, supported by both Poles and the Teutonic Knights, invaded the Khanate of the Golden Horde. Vitov's army had a substantial number of artillery pieces. Despite the superiority in weapons of the invaders, they were decisively defeated by the Mongols at the **Battle of the Vorskla,** a tributary of the Dnieper.

CHINA

The history of China during these two centuries is essentially the record of the conquest of the country by Genghis Khan and his successors, of their establishment of the Mongol (Yuan) Dynasty, and of the eventual overthrow of that dynasty by the new Ming Dynasty of native Chinese. Important events were:

1205–1279. Mongol Conquest of China. (See pp. 336 and 345.)

1279. Kublai Khan Establishes the Yuan Dynasty. (See p. 346.)

1307–1388. Decline of Yuan Dynasty. (See p. 346.)

1356–1368. Rise of the Ming. Chu Yuan-Chang, a Buddhist monk, led a popular uprising. He captured **Nanking** (1356), where he established a native Chinese government. He slowly expanded his control over most of China. For a while his efforts were hampered by rival Chinese rebels, whom he defeated at the **Battle of Lake Po-yang** (1360?). Having driven the Mongols completely from most of China, Chu later proclaimed himself to be the first emperor of the Ming Dynasty (1368).

1368–1388. Continuing Ming War against the Mongols. Yunnan was the last province of China to be reconquered (1382). The Chinese then invaded Mongolia, driving the Mongols from their capital of Karakorum, winning a great victory in the **Battle of the Kerulen River** (1388).

1398–1402. Civil War. A struggle for succession after the death of Chu Yuan-Chang.

c. 1400. Ming Maritime Power. Chinese merchant vessels and warships dominated the South China Sea, and extended Chinese maritime influence to the Indian Ocean. An indication of the extent of this maritime power was payment of tribute by Ceylon.

KOREA

For more than half of this period Korea was a dependency of the Mongol Empire (1231–1356). The Wang Dynasty finally regained its independence after an eight-year war in which General **Li Taijo** finally ejected the Mongols (1364). This was followed by a period of internal violence which was ended only when Li deposed the last Wang emperor to establish his own dynasty (1392). He continued to recognize the suzerainty of the Ming, which the Wang had accepted (1369). During most of these two centuries Japanese pirates and adventurers conducted constant depredations against the Korean coast.

JAPAN

During the early years of the 13th century the Hojo family gradually replaced their kinsmen, the Minamotos, in control of the Kamakura Shogunate (1199–1219). The Hojos ruled over a generally peaceful and prosperous country. Toward the end of the century, however, Japan was constantly threatened by Mongol invasion. Two actual invasion attempts were made, but neither succeeded. The Kamakura Shogunate was overthrown in a two-year civil war which left the nation and the imperial family hopelessly split. For more than half a century Japan was divided between two emperors, and the country was plagued by constant civil war. Peace was finally established by the strong Shogun **Yoshimitsu** of the Ashikaga family. The principal events were:

1221. Uprising against the Hojos. Several members of the imperial family, including retired emperor **Gotoba II,** were defeated.

1274. First Mongol Expedition to Japan. This was apparently only a reconnaissance in force. Using Korean ships, the Mongols captured the islands of Tsushima and Iki. They landed at Hakata Bay (Ajkozaki) in northern Kyushu. Japanese forces were hastily assembled, and attacked the invaders near the beaches. The Mongols easily defeated the numerically superior Japanese. Part of the invasion fleet was wrecked in a storm, and as more Japanese gathered, the Mongols embarked to return to Korea.

1281. Second Mongol Expedition. The Japanese refusing to recognize Mongol suzerainty, and having mistreated and killed Mongol ambassadors, Kublai prepared a major expedition. In Mongol and Korean ships, the army sailed in two divisions from north China and Korea. Again the islands of Tsushima and Iki were captured to provide a base for operations. The invading army was probably less than 50,000. The Japanese were waiting, and a series of violent land and sea engagements took place in and off north Kyushu. The Japanese carried out a number of daring raids against the larger Mongol fleets. On land the Japanese were unable to drive the invaders into the sea, but by superior numbers and fanatic defense were able to limit their advance inland. A few days after the landing, a violent storm wrecked most of the invasion fleets. The Mongols, their supplies cut off, were soon defeated and only a few survived and escaped. Kublai planned another expedition, but never got around to it.

1331–1333. Civil War. Emperor **Go Daigo II** led a revolt against Hojo rule. He was assisted by the great samurais **Kitabatake, Chikafusa,** and **Kusoniki Masashige.** At first defeated and captured (1332), Go Daigo escaped and continued his revolt. He was finally successful when several Hojo generals, including **Ashikaga Takauji,** deserted to join his cause, permit-

ting him to capture **Kamakura,** the Hojo capital.

1335. Revolt of Takauji. Expecting to be shogun, the general revolted when the emperor insisted upon personal imperial rule.

1336–1392. Civil Wars of the Yoshino Period. Takauji expelled Go Daigo from the capital of Kyoto, set up another member of the imperial family on the throne, and established himself as military dictator and shogun (1338). Go Daigo, in the mountainous Yoshino region south of Nara, continued the war. It was prosecuted bitterly and vigorously on both sides for 56 years.

1392. Peace was established through the diplomacy of **Yoshimitsu.** The successor of Go Daigo agreed to abdicate.

WESTERN EUROPE

THE HUNDRED YEARS' WAR—PHASE ONE, 1337–1396

Actually this was a series of eight major periods of conflict between the royal houses of England and France, lasting nearly 120 years (1337–1453). Four of these periods of military activity took place in the 14th century, four in the 15th century (see p. 409).

Although this war, or series of wars, started out as a typical feudal dispute, it had from the outset nationalistic aspects unseen in Europe since the fall of Rome, growing into an Anglo-French military-political rivalry which persisted for more than five and a half centuries. There were three principal causes of the war:

1. The feudal relationship of the kings of France and of England. As dukes of Aquitaine and barons of other French lands, the kings of England were vassals; as rulers of England, they were sovereign. The French kings rightly feared that the English rulers would endeavor to consolidate their French lands with their English dominions; the English kings disliked their partially subordinate position.

2. Growing English commercial dominance in the wealthy industrial County of Flanders. The French kings had eliminated German influence from Flanders in the 13th century only to discover that their hegemony was becoming increasingly threatened by growing English commercial relationships with the burghers and weavers of Flemish towns.

3. French influence in Scotland and the assistance and support the French rendered to the Scots in their almost continuous wars with England.

The Sluys Period, 1337–1343

Philip VI of France announced the forfeiture of English fiefs south of the Loire River, then halfheartedly invaded them (1337). In response, **Edward III** of England sent raiding parties into northern and northeastern France from England and Flanders (1337–1338). There was only one decisive action: a great English naval victory over the French fleet at the **Battle of Sluys.** After that battle, the war petered out and was suspended by a two years' truce. The principal events were:

1337–1338. English Bases Established in Flanders. These were provided by Flemish weavers under **Jacques van Artevelde,** who had revolted against Count **Louis** of Flanders.

1338. Edward Proclaims Himself King of France. His claim of direct succession, through the daughter of Philip IV, was recognized by Emperor **Louis IV** of Germany.

1339. Edward in Northern France. Raiding from Flanders, he withdrew upon the approach of Philip's much larger army.

1340, June 24. Battle of Sluys. Edward, with an English fleet of about 150 vessels, engaged a French fleet of some 190 ships at the entrance of Sluys harbor. English archers and war engines placed a devastating fire on the French fleet, which was virtually annihilated, 166 French vessels being captured or sunk. Edward landed, besieged Tournai, but later was forced to raise the siege and make a truce with Philip.

1341–1343. Dynastic War in Brittany. Philip supported **Charles of Blois,** Edward assisted **John de Montfort.** Inconclusive operations ended in another truce (1343).

The Crécy Period, 1345–1347

1345. Renewal of War in Brittany. Pro-English forces gained minor advantages. Edward began to raise a large expeditionary force in England.

1346. French Invasion of Gascony. A French army under Philip's son, **Duke John of Normandy,** invaded Gascony. The French were held up by the stubborn defense of the castle of Aiguillon, at the junction of the Lot and Garonne Rivers (April–August).

EDWARD'S EXPEDITION TO FRANCE, 1346

Learning of the siege of Aiguillon, Edward sailed from Portsmouth for northern France (July 11?) to relieve pressure in Gascony, and to assist his hard-pressed allies in Flanders and Brittany. Edward's army probably comprised about 3,000 knights and men-at-arms (heavy cavalry), 10,000 English archers, and 4,000 Welsh light infantry, of whom half may have been archers. The squires and retainers of the knights and men-at-arms probably numbered an additional 3,000 men, serving as light cavalry for reconnaissance, screening, and combat. This was no feudal levy. Raised under the indenture system (see p. 335), these were experienced soldiers, veterans of the Scottish wars. While owing allegiance to the king through his vassals, they were paid fighting men whose term of service was for the "duration." This was probably the best-organized, most-experienced, and best-disciplined force gathered in Western Europe since the days of the Roman legion.

Edward landed at La Hogue, near Cherbourg (probably July 12). For reasons not clear, his fleet sailed back to England shortly after the army was disembarked, leaving the small English army on its own in hostile country.

Edward marched inland via Carentan and St. Lô (July 18). After a sharp engagement, he captured Caen (July 27). The army continued slowly toward the Seine, pillaging as it went. Edward learned that John of Normandy had raised the siege of Aiguillon and was marching north from Gascony, while Philip was collecting a large army near Paris. Edward therefore decided to cross north of the Seine, so as to have a free line of retreat to Flanders if need be.

Reaching the Seine near Rouen, Edward discovered that the French had destroyed all bridges across the lower river save for one in strongly defended Rouen. Increasing his pace, he marched rapidly upriver toward Paris, seeking a crossing. Evidently he was becoming nervous, since if Philip came out from Paris he would be forced to fight south of the river. At Poissy, only a few miles from Paris, he found a repairable bridge. While Philip and his army unaccountably sat idle at St. Denis, the English crossed the Seine (August 16).

Only then, too late to strike the English astride the river, did Philip begin to move. Edward, still in danger of being cut off, began forced marches northward. About one day ahead of the pursuing French, he reached the Somme River (August 22) to find that its bridges (save in fortified towns) had also been destroyed. While the English sought a crossing, the French reached Amiens to the east. Finally English scouts discovered a ford near the mouth of the river, passable only at low tide. The English army forced its way across against light opposition just as the tide was rising and as the French army appeared on the south shore (August 24).

THE BATTLE OF CRÉCY, AUGUST 26, 1346

Having passed the last major obstacle to a further retreat into Flanders, Edward decided to fight. While the French army crossed the Somme at Abbeville, he discovered a suitable battleground a few miles farther north near the village of Crécy-en-Ponthieu (August 25). Here a gentle slope overlooked the route which the French Army would have to take.

During the next day the English organized their position carefully. The right flank, near Crécy, was protected by a river. The left flank, in front of the village of Wadicourt, was covered by trees and by ditches dug by the English infantry. The army was formed in three main divisions, or "battles," each of about equal strength. English strength was probably about 20,000.

The division on the right was nominally commanded by 17-year-old **Edward, Prince of Wales**, later known as the "**Black Prince**"; actual command was evidently exercised by the veteran Earl Marshal **Warwick**. About 300 yards to the northeast, and echeloned slightly to the rear, was the left division, commanded by the Earls of **Arundel** and **Northampton**. A few hundred yards to the rear and covering the gap between the two front rank divisions was the third "battle," under Edward's personal command. The king took a position in a windmill midway between his division and that of the Prince of Wales, from which he could observe all of the action and send orders to his subordinate commanders.

The core of each division was a solid phalanx of some 1,000 dismounted men-at-arms, probably 6 ranks deep and about 250 yards long. The archers were ranged on the outer flanks of each division and echeloned forward so as to obtain clear, converging fields of fire. In front of the center of the army, the flank archers of the two front divisions met in an inverted V pointed toward the enemy. It is not clear whether the Welsh light infantry were interspersed with the archers or were ranged in the central phalanx with the dismounted men-at-arms. Behind the center of each division was a small reserve of mounted heavy cavalry prepared to counterattack if any French assault should break through the front lines. During the day it appears that the English and Welsh infantrymen dug a number of small holes in the rolling fields to their immediate front as traps for the French cavalry horses. Crécy was probably the first European battle in which gunpowder weapons were employed (see p. 332), but they had no influence on the outcome of the battle.

The French army, estimated at nearly 60,000 fighting men, was composed of approximately 12,000 heavy cavalry—knights and men-at-arms—the flower of French chivalry, about 6,000 Genoese mercenary crossbowmen, some 17,000 additional light cavalry (the retainers of the chivalry), and more than 25,000 communal levies—an undisciplined rabble of footmen straggling along in the rear.

This force, strung in an interminably long march column without any reconnoitering screen, bumped unexpectedly into the English line of battle about 6 o'clock

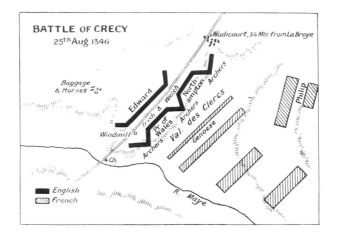

in the late afternoon. Philip endeavored to halt the mass and concentrate. He was apparently able to get his crossbowmen into the lead, but the impetuous knights, filled with pride and the valor of ignorance, could not be controlled; so the French vanguard began to pile forward in a confused mass behind the Genoese.

A quick shower and thunderstorm momentarily swept the field, making the footing slippery. Then the sinking sun shone out again as the disciplined Genoese, deployed in firm alignment, crossed the valley and started up the slope. Halting about 150 yards from the English front, they fired their bolts, most of which fell short. Then they moved on again to meet the full blast of cloth-yard English arrows sheeting like a snowstorm on their line.

Shattered, the Genoese reeled away from this devastating fire. The French van, impatient, put spurs to their mounts and rolled through and over them, a ponderous, disorganized avalanche. In a moment the slippery slope was covered by a churning mass of mailed men and horses, pounding and stumbling through the unfortunate Genoese, while English arrows rained down on all. The impetus of the assault carried some of the French as far as the English line, where a sharp fight developed for a few moments. Then, repulsed by the stout English line, French survivors were driven back by Prince Edward's mounted detachment.

Without rhyme or reason, each successive element of the French column came rushing into this horrible welter, to be caught in turn by the devastating arrows. Apparently Edward had made excellent arrangements for a resupply of arrows, and evidently as each French charge ebbed away scuttling archers would rush across the field to collect arrows for reuse.

The slaughter continued into the night; some 15 or 16 separate French waves dashed themselves to fragments in that ghastly valley. Then the French gave up. The English stood in their formations until dawn.

In dreadful piles across the little valley lay 1,542 dead lords and knights (including King John of Bohemia; see p. 377); between 10,000 and 20,000 men-at-arms, crossbowmen, and infantrymen; and thousands of horses. The French king and many others of his lords and knights were wounded; there is no accurate total. The English loss was probably about 200 dead and wounded; the killed included 2 English knights, 40 men-at-arms and archers, and "a few dozen" Welsh infantrymen. Again we have no accurate figures.

COMMENT. *Europe was stunned by the English victory over a French force nearly three times its size. Continentals, knowing nothing of the fierce wars with the Welsh and the Scots, were unaware of English tactical, technical, and organizational developments. In a few earlier European battles, as at Legnano (see p. 295), Courtrai (see p. 369), and in the conflicts between the Austrians and the Swiss (see p. 376), infantry had gained some successes against feudal heavy cavalry. In each of these earlier battles, however, some special circumstances contributed to the outcome. Crécy was different. Here was a clear-cut victory in the open field of steady, disciplined infantrymen over the finest cavalry in Europe—even though atrociously led. Edward, who had scant strategical skill, proved himself the master tactician of his time. Understanding the value of disciplined infantry against cavalry, and aware of the devastating fire power of his longbowmen, he made the optimum use of the force at his disposal. Within a century the political significance of Crécy would be negated by other factors (see p. 417). In a purely military sense, however, this was one of the most decisive battles of world history. After almost a millennium in which cavalry had dominated warfare, the verdict of Adrianople had been reversed. Since the time of Crécy, infantry has remained the primary element of ground combat forces.*

AFTER CRÉCY, 1346–1354

1346–1347. Siege and Capture of Calais. Resuming a leisurely march northward, Edward reached Calais (September 4, 1346), which he invested and captured after nearly a year's siege (August 4, 1347). This was followed by a truce (September 28).

1347–1354. Truce. Both sides were prostrated by the ravages of the Black Death.

The Poitiers Period, 1355–1360

1355. Resumption of the War. Negotiations for a permanent peace having failed, Edward crossed the Channel and led an army in devastating raids across northern France. At the same time, the Black Prince raided deep into Languedoc from Bordeaux, causing great damage and collecting much booty. Edward's second son, **John of Gaunt** (and of Lancaster) raided into Normandy from Brittany (1356).

1356, August–September. Raid by the Black Prince. Starting from Bergerac (August 4), young Edward conducted a deliberate and devastating raid into Central France. His army consisted of about 4,000 heavy cavalry, probably another 4,000 light cavalry, some 3,000 English archers, and another 1,000 light infantry. All were professional indentured troops, but (save for the archers) most were French Aquitanians, vassals of the English royal family. The prince avoided fortified places and concentrated on plundering as far as Tours (September 3).

1356, September 11–17. French Pursuit; English Retreat. Learning that King John (former Duke of Normandy) had crossed the Loire at Blois (September 8), the Prince started south as rapidly as his great train of booty could move. Unencumbered, the French moved more rapidly, converging to intercept the English at Poitiers. Apparently neither side conducted adequate reconnaissance, and neither had any idea of the other's location. By-passing Poitiers, the English advance guard unexpectedly ran into the French rear guard less than three miles east of the city (late afternoon, September 17). Edward, realizing that his tired and burdened army could no longer elude the French, spent the evening and next morning locating a good defensive position.

1356, September 18. Preparation for Battle. While their armies rested and prepared for battle, the French king and English prince conducted fruitless negotiations through intermediaries. Edward had found an excellent position overlooking a gently sloping vineyard facing north. His left flank was protected by a marsh and creek; his front of 1,000 yards was covered by a hedge traversed only by a few narrow sunken lanes. His exposed right flank was protected by a wagon park. The hedge, the sunken lanes, and wagon park were lined with archers; other archers were extended forward as skirmishers in the vineyard and in the marsh to the left. As at Crécy, Edward's men-at-arms were dismounted behind the hedge, save for a small mounted reserve which he posted near his exposed right flank. The French army consisted of about 8,000 men-at-arms, 8,000 light cavalry, 4,500 professional mercenary infantry (including 2,000 crossbowmen), and possibly 15,000 unreliable militia infantry. This mass was organized into four divisions or "battles," each comprising nearly 10,000 men. Save only for about 3,000 heavy and light cavalrymen in the first battle, all of the French horsemen were dismounted, on the supposition that this was the only way to beat the dismounted Englishmen. John did

not understand that the secret of the English success at Crécy had been the use of dismounted men-at-arms only as a solid defensive base for the devastating fire power of the English archers. By dismounting his knights he deprived them of their principal assets for offensive action: mobility and shock. Because of the narrow English front, he planned to attack in a column of divisions, one behind the other. Apparently he gave no consideration to any kind of maneuver, to envelop, or to turn the outnumbered English from their exposed position.

BATTLE OF POITIERS, SEPTEMBER 19, 1356

Early in the morning Prince Edward sent much of his booty train across the creek, accompanied by about two-thirds of his army. Possibly he hoped to withdraw without a fight. He left one "battle" to hold the previously selected position. The French advance, however, caused him to hasten back to the scene with his two other battles. The first French division attacked prematurely, with typical feudal lack of coordination. The crossbowmen, lined up behind the French mounted cavalry, had no chance to engage the English archers. The first mad mounted dash was broken by the English archers just as at Crécy. In renewed assaults a few of the horsemen and some of the infantry reached the English line, to be thrown back by the stout dismounted defenders and by enfilading fire from the English archers in the marsh.

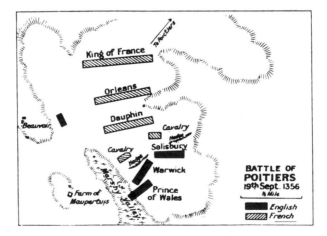

Some time later, the second French battle, under the Dauphin, approached the English line. Their armor clanking loudly, the French knights trudged up the gentle vineyard slope, to be met by a hail of English arrows. Despite heavy losses, the gallant French closed grimly against the English line. There was a prolonged, desperate struggle. The French came very near to breaking through, and the English line was re-established only when Edward put his third division into the front line, holding out only a 400-man reserve. The French-English men-at-arms, aided by continuing harassment from the archers on the flank, finally repulsed the attackers. Both sides had suffered severely. If the remainder of the French had advanced promptly, or if they had enveloped the exposed English right, the Black Prince would have been decisively defeated. However, the sight of the disaster suffered by the Dauphin's division caused the third division, commanded by the **Duke of Orléans,** brother of the king, to lose heart and to flee before getting in range.

Next the fourth and largest French division, under John himself, approached. Although the French were exhausted by marching more than a mile in their heavy armor, the English were at least equally exhausted from the prolonged combat. Fearful that his outnumbered men could not sustain a determined French attack, the Prince seized the initiative. Putting his 400 fresh men-at-arms in front, he ordered the entire army to charge. He also sent about 200 mounted men, probably light cavalry, to attack the French left rear. The two advancing lines met with terrific impact in the vineyard. The English archers, having used up all of their arrows, joined in the vicious hand-to-hand combat. The issue was in doubt until the small English enveloping force suddenly struck the French rear. This was too much for the French, who began to flee. John, surrounded by the flower of French chivalry, fought on until he was overpowered and captured. The exhausted English did not pursue, but they captured thousands of prisoners who were too tired and encumbered to escape. In this bitterly contested battle, the French lost 2,500 dead and 2,600 prisoners, most of the casualties being knights and men-at-arms. English losses are unknown; they were probably over 1,000 killed and at least an equal number wounded.

1356, September–October. English Withdrawal. Making no effort to exploit his great victory, the Black Prince retired to Bordeaux with his booty and his prisoners.

1356–1360. English Raids. Recognizing their inability to meet the English in the open field, the French remained in their castles and fortified towns while the English ranged all over France. King Edward himself made a final raid to the walls of Paris (1360).

1360, October 24. Peace of Bretigny. English holdings in southwestern France were augmented and France recognized English possession of Calais and Ponthieu. Edward gave up his claims to Normandy and to the French crown, while John was ransomed for 3 million gold crowns.

1360–1367. Nominal Peace. The war of succession in Brittany continued and one major battle was fought: an English army besieging **Auray** defeated a French relieving army and took the town (1364). **Charles the Bad** of Navarre attempted to take advantage of French troubles by inroads into Southern France. Disbanded French and English mercenaries participated in both of these wars. Still others took part in a civil war in Castile (see p. 375), where the French and English continued the Hundred Years' War by proxy. Still others of the disbanded mercenary companies ranged over France, ravaging the countryside.

The Du Guesclin Period, 1368–1396

A revolt of Gascon nobles against the Black Prince (who was also Duke of Aquitaine) provided French King **Charles V** with an excuse to intervene with a new, improved French military force (see p. 369). Leading the French armies was Bertrand Du Guesclin, Constable of France and one of the great soldiers of the age, who was able to reconcile chivalry with common sense. Recognizing the superiority of English archery fire power, Du Guesclin avoided attacks against the English in prepared positions. He seized all possible opportunities to force the English to fight at a disadvantage. He excelled particularly in night attacks, despite English objections that these were "unknightly." Determined and skillful in siegecraft, he captured the English towns and castles in Poitou and Aquitaine one after another, reducing English holdings in France to small regions around Bordeaux, Bayonne, Brest, Calais, and Cherbourg. Desultory, truce-studded warfare continued for 16 years after his death. The French retained what he had gained; France, however, was in ruins. The important events were:

1368. Noble Revolt in Gascony. In reponse to Du Guesclin's assistance to the rebels, Edward III reclaimed the throne of France.

1370. Massacre of Limoges. The Black Prince captured and sacked Limoges, slaughtering many of the inhabitants. Soon afterward he returned to England (1371).

1372. Battle of La Rochelle. With Castilian assistance, the French fleet defeated an English fleet, regaining control of the western and northern coasts of France.

1375–1383. Truce. Spasmodic fighting continued between French and English adherents.

1376. Death of the Black Prince.

1377. Death of Edward III.

1380. Death of Du Guesclin and Charles V.

1386. French-Planned Invasion of England. Never too serious, the plan was abandoned after the combined French-Castilian fleet was defeated off **Margate** by the English (1387).

1389–1396. Period of Truces. These were interspersed with fighting.

1396. Peace of Paris. Richard II of England and **Charles VI** of France agreed to peace for 30 years; England retained only Calais and that part of Gascony between Bordeaux and Bayonne.

THE BRITISH ISLES

England

During these two centuries of violence, unrest, and endemic civil war, there were two relatively long periods of peace and prosperity under two of England's greatest monarchs—**Edward I** and **Edward III**—who were able to divert the energies of their vigorous brawling barons into highly successful foreign wars. Edward I —who proved his tactical and strategic brilliance by defeating the nobles who had overthrown his father—later conquered Wales and Scotland. To him must go the credit for starting the tactical system with which his grandson revolutionized warfare in the Hundred Years' War (see p. 357). **Edward II,** an inept ruler, was driven from Scotland by Robert Bruce (see p. 366), and was later defeated and deposed by rebellious nobles. His young son, Edward III, made common cause with the barons, then gained ascendancy over them. In the Hundred Years' War, Edward proved himself the leading tactician of his age and made his country the most powerful in Europe. In his declining years, French resurgency reduced England's power on the Continent. Predeceased by his eldest son, the famous Black Prince, Edward was succeeded by his grandson, **Richard II,** whose reign was another period of foreign defeats and internal unrest. At the close of the century, Richard was defeated and deposed by his successor, **Henry IV.** The principal events were:

1199–1216. Reign of John I (Brother of Richard I). John was constantly, and generally unsuccessfully, at war with his barons at home and with Philip II of France abroad. His reluctant signature of the Magna Carta was the most important result of his wars with the barons.

1202–1204. War with Philip of France. John lost Anjou, Brittany, Maine, Normandy, and Touraine. With the assistance of his vassals in Aquitaine, he repulsed Philip's efforts to seize his possessions southwest of the Loire.

1213–1214. Renewed War with France. In

an effort to regain his lands north of the Loire, John made an alliance with **Otto IV** of Germany and Count **Ferdinand** of Flanders. By invading West-Central France from Aquitaine, John hoped to so distract Philip as to permit a successful invasion of northeastern France by his allies. He failed, and his allies were crushed at the **Battle of Bouvines** (1214; see p. 368).

1215–1217. Intensified Civil War in England. **Louis,** Dauphin of France, was invited by a faction of English barons to replace John. Outnumbered, most of his kingdom in the hands of his enemies, and his own forces close to dissolution, John revealed a vigor and ability worthy of comparison with his great brother, Richard I. His determination and skill rallied to him the support of most of the people in England in opposition to the baronial party. Avoiding major battles, John consolidated control of western and central England, repulsed an invasion by King **Alexander** of Scotland (see p. 365), and forced Louis and the barons to the defensive in southeastern England. John died (1216), but his followers completed his victory on land at **Lincoln** and at sea off **Sandwich** (1217).

1216–1272. Reign of Henry III. A period of inept rule both before and after Henry came of age (1227). England lost control of most of Aquitaine and Poitou; Henry was repulsed in efforts to re-establish his authority. Meanwhile bickering in England flared into revolt.

1263–1265. Civil War. The rebels were led by Earl Simon de Montfort.*

1264, May 14. Battle of Lewes. Simon and the other barons were besieging Rochester when Henry, who had just captured Northampton, arrived with a relieving army. In a cavalry battle, Henry was decisively defeated, though his young son Prince Edward (later Edward I) drove a portion of the baronial army off the field. Henry became a prisoner and puppet of Simon, who became virtual ruler of England. Prince Edward escaped to raise an army in Western England. Simon made an alliance with **Llewellyn,** Prince of Wales, and marched against the royal insurgents.

1265, July 8. Battle of Newport. Culminat-

---

* Son of the leader of the Albigensian Crusade; see p. 367.

ing several minor setbacks, Simon was defeated by Edward's larger army. Simon retreated into Wales; his efforts to evade the royal army and to return to Central England were blocked by Edward's skillful defense of the Severn River.

1265, July–August. Campaign of Evesham. Simon de Montfort the younger, son of Earl Simon, marched west from London with about 30,000 men to the relief of his father. Edward, with 20,000, now found himself caught between the two converging Montfort armies, whose combined strengths were approximately twice his own. Edward marched eastward from Worcester (July 31) by forced marches, making a surprise dawn attack on young Simon and practically annihilating his larger army in the brief **Battle of Kenilworth** (August 2). He immediately returned to Worcester (August 3). Meanwhile Earl Simon had taken advantage of Edward's move by promptly throwing his army across the Severn, marching toward Stratford to join his son by way of Evesham (August 3). Edward at once left Worcester, driving his exhausted men to march southeastward through the night (August 3–4), planning to interpose himself between Simon and his line of retreat to the east. By dawn two-thirds of Edward's army had reached the Stratford-Evesham Road, just northeast of Evesham. The remainder approached Evesham from the west.

1265, August 4. Battle of Evesham. Simon, with only 7,000 men against Edward's 20,-000, was cooped in a bend of the Avon River, and in a hopeless position. Nevertheless, he attempted a desperate charge against the central column of Edward's converging army. Despite exhaustion, Edward and his men were full of fight. Simon's army was annihilated. Edward became the virtual ruler of England, his father king in name only. Edward stamped out the embers of revolt. His forces crushed the remaining rebel barons at **Chesterfield** (1266) and in their refuges in fens or marshes at **Axholme** (1265) and **Ely** (1267).

COMMENT. *The Evesham campaign was one of the most brilliant operations of the Middle Ages—truly Napoleonic in concept, vigorous execution, and personal exercise of leadership. It alone is sufficient to in-*

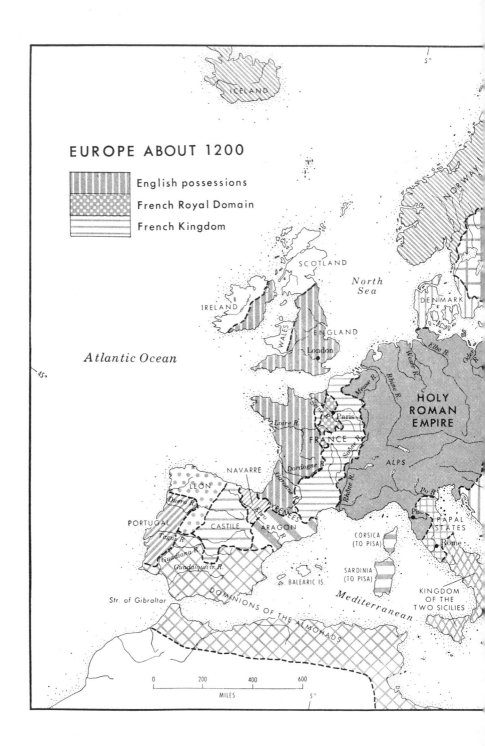

EUROPE ABOUT 1200

English possessions
French Royal Domain
French Kingdom

ICELAND

NORWAY

SCOTLAND

IRELAND

North Sea

DENMARK

WALES

ENGLAND

London

Atlantic Ocean

45°

5°

HOLY ROMAN EMPIRE

Elbe R.

Weser R.

Oder R.

Rhine R.

Meuse R.

Seine R.

Paris

FRANCE

Loire R.

Dordogne R.

Garonne R.

Saône R.

ALPS

Rhône R.

NAVARRE

PYRENEES

LEÓN

Duero R.

PORTUGAL

CASTILE

ARAGON

Tagus R.

Ebro R.

Guadiana R.

Guadalquivir R.

Str. of Gibraltar

DOMINIONS OF THE ALMOHADS

BALEARIC IS.

CORSICA
(TO PISA)

SARDINIA
(TO PISA)

Po R.

Pisa

PAPAL STATES

Rome

KINGDOM
OF THE
TWO SICILIES

Mediterranean

5°

0   200   400   600

MILES

5°

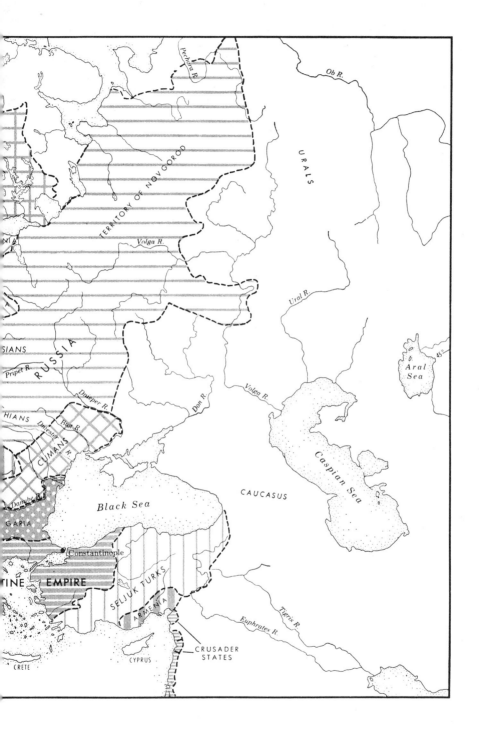

clude Edward I among the very greatest of English generals.

1270–1272. Edward in the Crusades. He left England in the hands of trusted subordinates (see p. 386).

1272–1307. Reign of Edward I. As a ruler and soldier, he fulfilled the promise revealed at Evesham.

1278. Reorganization of England's Militia System. Edward increased centralized control.

1282–1284. Conquest of Wales. Wales had become virtually independent of England under able Prince Llewellyn. After Welsh incursions into England, Edward conquered and pacified the country, Llewellyn having been killed at **Radnor** (1282). During these campaigns Edward became familiar with the Welsh longbow and adopted it as a basic English weapon.

1293–1303. War with France. In an inconclusive struggle, Philip IV of France annexed Gascony and repulsed Edward's expeditions to reconquer the province (1294, 1296, 1297). The war was settled by negotiation, however, and Gascony was returned to Edward.

1295–1307. Scottish Wars. Border disputes and internal difficulties in Scotland led to war (see p. 365). Edward invaded, stormed and sacked Berwick-upon-Tweed, defeated King **John Baliol** at the **Battle of Dunbar,** and declared himself King of Scotland (1296). The Scots rose, under Sir **William Wallace,** who was decisively defeated by Edward at the **Battle of Falkirk** (1298; see page 365). In subsequent operations Wallace was captured and executed (1305), and Scotland again annexed to England. Scottish resistance continued, however, under the leadership of **Robert Bruce** (see p. 366).

1307–1327. Reign of Edward II. A weak ruler. Scotland virtually re-established its independence. Attempting to reconquer the country, Edward was decisively defeated by Robert Bruce in the **Battle of Bannockburn** (1314; see p. 366). England was forced to recognize Scottish independence. Continuing disorders in England broke into violent civil war in which Edward and his adherents defeated the **Duke of Lancaster** at the **Battle of Boroughbridge** (1322). Edward was a puppet in the hands of his favorites, **Hugh le Despenser,** Earl of Winchester, and his son,

Hugh; they were defeated and overthrown by a revolutionary party led by Queen **Isabella** and her lover, **Roger Mortimer.** Edward was forced to abdicate, and was murdered (1327). Isabella and Mortimer became regents for her son, Edward.

1327–1377. Reign of Edward III. Fifteen years old when his father was deposed, Edward seized power by leading the barons in a revolt against Mortimer and Isabella (1330). His was one of the most momentous reigns of England, militarily and politically.

1332. Battle of Dupplin Muir. Under **Edward Baliol,** a mixed group of noble Scottish exiles ("the Disinherited") and English adventurers invaded Scotland, then technically at peace with England. The expedition consisted of about 1,000 knights and men-at-arms and 1,500 archers. They were opposed by about 2,000 Scottish heavy cavalry and 20,000 infantry under the Earl of Mar. The invaders made a daring and successful night attack across the Earn River. The Scots rallied and at dawn counterattacked in overwhelming force. The invading men-at-arms dismounted to form a small phalanx on a hilltop. The archers, probably echeloned forward in an irregular line, covered the flanks. The Scots were halted by the stout phalanx, then suffered so heavily from the archery fire on their flanks that they broke and fled. This battle provided Edward III with an excuse to invade Scotland, as well as a model for his tactics in subsequent battles.

1333. Battle of Halidon Hill. Edward, in a defensive position, formed his army into three battles or divisions; he dismounted his men-at-arms and covered the flanks of each division with archers. The attacking Scots were repulsed by the archers and the men-at-arms, then smashed by a counterattack. Edward had discovered the effective infantry tactics which would, a few years later, make England supreme in European warfare (see p. 357).

1337–1396. First Phase of the Hundred Years' War. (See p. 353.)

1350–1367. English Involvement with Spain. This began with a Spanish naval expedition into the English Channel, during a lull in the Hundred Years' War. Edward led his fleet to victory in a hard-fought battle off **Winchelsea,** protecting his communications to Calais (1350). This undeclared war culminated in the great victory of the Black Prince at the **Battle of Navarrette** (see p. 375).

1377–1399. Reign of Richard II (Aged 10 at Accession). At the outset England was ruled by a regency in which his uncle **John of Gaunt,** Duke of Lancaster, was dominant (1377–1385). The government was nearly overthrown by a **Peasants' Revolt** (1381); London was seized and terrorized by a mob of 100,000 under **Jack Straw** and **Wat Tyler.** The youthful king negotiated with the rebels and granted most peasant demands, though harsh reprisals were later taken. Richard led a futile expedition to Scotland (1385). A brief revolt was led by **Thomas, Duke of Gloucester** who defeated the Royalists at **Radcot Bridge** and forced Richard to submit to the barons (1387). After a few years of relative calm, another dispute with his leading nobles led Richard to seize absolute power in defiance of Parliament (1397). This resulted in rebellion, in which he was at first supported, then opposed, by his cousin **Henry of Bolingbroke,** son of John of Gaunt. Richard's supporters deserted him; he was forced to abdicate. Henry of Bolingbroke ascended the throne as King **Henry IV** (1399).

Scotland

The 13th century was relatively peaceful. This was suddenly changed by a dynastic dispute, leading to English intervention and the outbreak of almost incessant war. This began with a prolonged struggle for independence, during which Scotland was twice conquered by Edward I, despite the gallant resistance of **William Wallace.** Later **Robert Bruce** led the Scots in a successful uprising which culminated in his great victory of Bannockburn and independence. Renewed outbreak of war after the death of Robert prompted French support, which in turn was one of the causes of the Hundred Years' War. For the remainder of the century there was continuous conflict with England. The English were generally on the defensive, since their major efforts were devoted to the struggle against France. The principal events were:

1214–1249. Reign of Alexander II. Hoping to take advantage of the barons' revolt against John of England, Alexander invaded England and attempted to seize Northumberland, but was repulsed near London by John (1216; see p. 361).

1249–1286. Reign of Alexander III. He drove the Norwegians from the islands of western Scotland by his victory in the **Battle of Largs** (1263).

1290. Dispute Succession. The death of Alexander (1286) and of his only direct descendant, **Margaret,** "Maid of Norway" (1290), resulted in claims to the throne by 12 different Scottish nobles. Edward I of England, asked to mediate, gained recognition of English overlordship, then chose John Baliol as king.

1295. Alliance with France. John entered this as a result of a dispute with Edward, who thereupon declared John's right forfeited and claimed the throne of Scotland for himself.

1296. English Invasion and Conquest. Edward defeated John at the **Battle of Dunbar** (April) and annexed the kingdom.

1297. Scottish Uprising. Sir William Wallace, the leader, defeated the **Earl of Warenne** in the **Battle of Cambuskenneth Bridge.** He then raided into Northumberland and Durham.

1298. English Invasion. Edward led an army of about 7,000 heavy cavalry, 3,000 light cavalry, and 15,000 infantry. Despite Wallace's efforts to avoid a major battle, Edward's aggressive advance forced the Scots to fight.

1298, July 22. Battle of Falkirk. Wallace had approximately 1,000 heavy cavalry, 2,500 light cavalry, and about 25,000 infantry. The steady Scottish pikemen, in four "schiltrouns" (circular phalanxes), repulsed English attacks. Driving the Scottish cavalry off the field, Edward brought up his archers to riddle the pikemen. After the Scots had suffered heavy losses, the English cavalry charged and broke the schiltrouns, annihilating Wallace's army. This was the first significant English use of the longbow. Edward reannexed Scotland, and in subsequent operations captured and executed Wallace (1305).

1306. Rebellion of Robert Bruce. He was a grandson of one of the earlier claimants to the throne, and had fought under Edward against Wallace at Falkirk. After some minor successes he was defeated by the **Earl of Pembroke** at **Methven** (1306, June 19), and **Dalry** (1306, Aug. 11). He won his first major victory over the Earl of Pembroke in the **Battle of Loudoun Hill** (1307, May).

1307–1314. Scottish Revival. Bruce, now King **Robert I** (1306–1329), gradually cleared the English from Scotland by energetic and resourceful operations, combining ambush with raids into northern England and against English strongholds in Scotland. As a result of these brilliant operations, only Stirling, Dunbar, and Berwick remained under English control (1314).

CAMPAIGN OF BANNOCKBURN

1314. Siege of Stirling. To rescue his garrison, Edward II finally took the field against Robert. The English army consisted of at least 60,000 men, including nearly 5,000 heavy cavalry, 10,000 light cavalry, some 20,000 archers, and about 25,000 other infantry. Investing Stirling, Robert had an army of about 1,500 heavy cavalry and 40,000 infantry.

1314, June 23. Scottish Preparations for Battle. Robert carefully selected a position a few miles south of Stirling, placing his army on a slope behind Bannockburn. This sluggish, fordable stream passed through a marshy valley with only one old road affording a good passage. The battlefield was restricted by an impassable morass on the Scottish left, and by a forest to their right. The front was about a mile long, on a slope overlooking the stream. In front of his position Robert had had his men dig numerous small holes, covered with branches and grass, intended as traps for the English horses. Before the arrival of the English, he had his troops stake out their battle positions. The main army then withdrew behind the next hill to avoid harassment by English archers before the battle began. A line of skirmishers was left along the banks of the stream.

1314, June 24. Battle of Bannockburn.

When the English began to cross the stream, the Scots resumed their positions. The English archers, crowded behind several contingents of cavalry, never had a chance to employ their weapons properly. A series of English cavalry charges were thrown back by the Scottish pikemen. As more and more English tried to crowd forward into the narrow battle area, they became hopelessly confused. The archers, attempting overhead fire, hit more of their own men in the back than they did Scots in the front. Efforts of the archers to deploy in the woods to their left flank were smashed by Bruce's reserve. While the armies were locked in combat on the slope above the stream, the Scottish camp followers (probably not upon orders from Robert) decided to pretend an attack through the woods against the English left flank. Blowing horns, waving banners, and simulating a large combat force, they approached the English left, which began to crumble. Edward himself decided to leave the battlefield, and his craven example was soon followed by most of his army. The Scots pursued, slaughtering thousands of Englishmen trying to struggle back across the stream and the marsh. English losses were at least 15,000, those of the Scots probably about 4,000. "So ended," says Oman, "the most lamentable defeat which an English army ever suffered."

1314–1328. Scottish Victory. The Scots raided frequently and far into England, **James Douglas** winning a victory at Myton (1319). However, Robert was careful to avoid a major battle. When Edward attempted another invasion, Robert defeated him in a surprise dawn attack at the **Battle of Byland,** and the English king again fled the battlefield (1322). The war ended with the **Peace of Northampton** (1328). Scottish independence was recognized. The following year Robert died (1329).

1329–1371. Reign of David II (Bruce).

1332. Battle of Dupplin Muir. (See p. 364.)

1333. English Invasion. Supporting Edward Baliol's claim to the throne, Edward III invaded Scotland and won the **Battle of Halidon Hill** (see p. 364). David fled to France. The outbreak of the Hundred Years' War in France forced the English to the defensive in Scotland, and permitted David to regain his throne.

1346. Battle of Neville's Cross. David invaded England, but was defeated and captured.

1350–1400. Desultory Warfare. A kind of sideshow to the Hundred Years' War. The most important episode was a Scottish-French invasion of northern England by Earl **James Douglas.** He defeated an English army under Sir **Henry Percy** at **Otterburn** (1388), where Douglas was killed.

Ireland

English colonial control of Ireland was shaken by a Scottish invasion under **Edward Bruce,** brother of Robert. Edward was crowned king (1316), but English rule was re-established when Edward was defeated and killed at **Faughart** (1318). In following years English control weakened as the strength of the Irish chieftains increased. Richard II led an expedition to Ireland to pacify the country (1398–1399). This had no permanent results, and by the close of the century English control had become nominal.

FRANCE

During the 13th and early part of the 14th centuries, the power of the French kings steadily increased. This process was accomplished by rulers such as **Philip II** (Augustus), **Philip IV,** and to a lesser extent **Louis IX,** despite the frequently vigorous and violent opposition of the kings of England, who were the principal feudal landholders in France. One of the most important events of the early 13th century was the so-called Albigensian Crusade against heretical communities of southern France. The French kings exploited this "crusade" by greatly expanding their control and power in southern France at the expense of local barons. These royal gains were all undone in the early years of the Hundred Years' War during the latter part of the 14th century. The French monarchy was almost destroyed by the great victories of English King **Edward III.** The tide had turned by the end of the century as the result of the brilliant leadership of Bertrand Du Guesclin, but France had been ruined and impoverished. The principal events were:

1180–1223. Reign of Philip II, Augustus. (See p. 294.)

1202–1204. War with John I of England. Philip conquered English fiefs north of the Loire (1202–1204). The outstanding event of this war was Philip's siege and capture of Château Gaillard (see p. 333) and Rouen in Normandy (1203–1204). During this and subsequent wars Philip established a semipermanent royal army, using the mercenary-indenture system (see p. 335).

THE ALBIGENSIAN CRUSADE, 1203–1226

1208–1213. First Phase. At the beginning of the 13th century the Catharist and Waldensian heresies flourished in southern France. The principal heretical centers were Toulouse and the Catharist stronghold of Albi. Efforts of the Catholic clergy to eliminate the heresies having failed, Pope **Innocent III** proclaimed a crusade against them. Philip II took no personal part in the crusade, but, with royal urging, the barons of northern France raised substantial forces. The principal leader of the crusading armies was half-English **Simon de Montfort.** Methodically and ably Simon campaigned across western Languedoc, destroying most of the military forces of the southern French barons and capturing most of their strongholds. Albi and most of the other heretical centers were captured and their inhabitants ruthlessly slaughtered by the crusaders. Only the cities of Toulouse and Montauban still held out. The counts of Toulouse, Foix, and Comminges were the only southern nobles still daring to resist. Most of the northern nobles had returned to their homes, leaving Simon with relatively small forces to complete the task of conquest and religious conversion.

1213. Intervention of Pedro of Aragon. Fearful of the increase in French royal power in southern France, and anxious to protect his own feudal holdings north of the Pyrenees, Pedro, despite his own staunch Catholicism, led a Spanish army into Languedoc to join the heretics. Joining forces with Count **Raymond** of Toulouse, he captured several of Montfort's fortified posts. With a combined army of about 4,000 heavy cavalry and 30,000 infantry, Pedro and Raymond invested Muret, one of the most important of Simon's strongholds, garrisoned by 700 men. Just as Pedro and Raymond were arriving to besiege the town, Montfort and about 900 heavy cavalry joined the defenders.

1213, September 12. Battle of Muret. Simon discovered that Muret was low on provisions. He could not expect reinforcements to arrive from northern France before the garrison would be forced by starvation to surrender. He seized the initiative with a brilliant, daring plan. He enticed part of the besieging army to attack an apparently poorly defended gate on the southeastern side of the city. As the attackers rushed in, Montfort and his cavalry ambushed them just inside the gate and drove them back with heavy casualties. Then, while the attention of the enemy was attracted to this side of Muret, Montfort and his 900 cavalrymen dashed out of the city through the southwestern gate, causing the besiegers to think he was endeavoring to escape. In fact, riding around some low hills to the west of the city, Montfort and his cavalrymen turned north and crossed the Longe, which flowed north of Muret, dispersing a small force which was protecting the far bank. Montfort next surprised and smashed a far larger force under the Count of Foix. This brief action provided warning to Pedro and his Aragonese troops. They barely had time to form line when two-thirds of Montfort's force hit them in a violent frontal charge. Outnumbering the attackers by more than 30 to 1, the Aragonese quickly engulfed them. But while their attention was devoted to this attack, Montfort and his 300 remaining men completed a wide envelopment and came charging in behind the Aragonese army. The Spanish broke and fled, suffering

heavy losses, including the death of King Pedro. After a very short pursuit, the Crusaders turned to strike the force of Count Raymond of Toulouse, the one remaining portion of the besieging army not yet engaged. Dismayed by what had happened, the Toulousans were quickly overwhelmed and almost annihilated.

1213–1226. Conclusion of the Crusade. Muret was the last important engagement of the crusade, but the heresies persisted for more than a decade while the crusaders systematically seized one fortified stronghold after another and ruthlessly put most of the heretics to the sword. Simon was killed during the siege of a stronghold near Toulouse (1222). But his successors carried on; the last embers of the heresy were stamped out (1226).

1213–1214. War against England, Germany, and Flanders. (See pp. 360 and 371.) Philip was foiled in his efforts to conquer Flanders by an English naval victory at **Damme** (1213). However, he displayed his military ability by repulsing English King John I's diversion in western France and then turning to meet the main allied invasion of northeastern France under **Otto IV** of Germany.

1214, March–July. Campaign of Bouvines. Philip (with 11,000 heavy cavalry and 25,000 infantry) slightly outmaneuvered Otto (who had 11,000 heavy cavalry and 60,000 infantry). With German and Flemish reinforcements about to arrive, Otto endeavored to cut Philip's communications between Tournai and Paris. Pretending panic, Philip enticed a rash German attack on the good cavalry terrain east of Bouvines, where superior French cavalry would have an advantage. Otto, unexpectedly finding himself faced by Philip's army in order of battle, hastily formed his own.

1214, July 26. Battle of Bouvines. A French infantry attack was repulsed by Flemish and German pikemen. While part of his cavalry engaged the main imperial cavalry forces on the flanks, Philip led the remainder of his knights in determined converging attacks which finally smashed the center of Otto's army. At the same time his right flank cavalry, under **Garin** the Hospitaler, drove off superior imperial forces facing them. While the battle was still in doubt, Otto fled the field, permitting Philip to concentrate against the imperial right (where a small English contingent particularly distinguished itself), which was soon overwhelmed.

1223–1226. Reign of Louis VIII. Most of this short reign was devoted to a war with England over the lands southwest of the Loire. After some initial successes, Louis lost most of his conquests in Aquitaine, but retained Poitou, Limousin, and Périgord.

1226–1270. Reign of Louis IX (St. Louis). During Louis's minority (1226–1234), his mother, **Blanche of Castile,** was regent. She suppressed several feudal rebellions (1226–1231). Particularly renowned for his participation in two crusades (see pp. 384 and 385), Louis was the epitome of chivalric valor and knightly prowess. He was an able ruler, as well as an essentially holy man who deserved subsequent canonization. He was partially successful in outlawing private warfare in France.

1242–1243. War with England. By a victory at **Saintes** (1242) Louis defeated an invasion by **Henry III,** and conquered most of Aquitaine and Toulouse.

1270–1285. Reign of Philip III. With papal support Philip invaded Aragon in an effort to dethrone excommunicated Pedro III, and to give the crown of Aragon to his son, Charles (1284). Disastrously repulsed, Philip died soon afterward.

1285–1314. Reign of Philip IV (the Fair). He greatly extended royal power and royal domains.

1294–1298. Inconclusive War with Edward I of England. This was over the province of Guienne in Aquitaine. Philip began the French alliance with Scotland (1295), with its far-reaching effects on France, Scotland, and England (see pp. 364 and 365). The French repulsed Edward's invasion of northern France.

1300–1302. Renewed War against England and Flanders. The culmination of this otherwise indecisive war was a disastrous defeat of the French heavy cavalry by Flemish infantry at the **Battle of Courtrai** (July 11, 1302). The Flemish pikemen had taken up a position in a boggy area, cut up by canals and traversed by a few bridges. When an initial infantry and crossbow attack failed to shake the Flemish, the French knights charged recklessly over their own infantry, but were repulsed by a combination of the staunchness of the Flemish pikemen and the difficulty of horse movements over the marshy terrain. Caught in the morass, great numbers of the French men-at-arms were massacred. This was the first important victory of an essentially infantry army over cavalry in the Middle Ages, but its significance is diminished because of the special conditions. Two years later the French knights gained revenge at **Mons-en-Pévèle** (1304).

1328–1350. Reign of Philip VI. He was the first ruler of the House of Valois. His victory at **Cassel** (1328) brought Flanders again under French control.

1337–1453. Hundred Years' War. (See pp. 353 and 409.)

1358. The Jacquerie. A bloody peasant uprising, centering in the Oise Valley north of Paris, was suppressed by nobles led by **Charles the Bad** of Navarre.

1364–1380. Reign of Charles V (the Wise). Thanks to his own sagacity, and with the aid of his great Constable of France **Bertrand Du Guesclin,** Charles saved his country from collapse after his predecessors Philip VI and John II (1350–1364) had suffered a series of stunning defeats. Drastic and far-reaching measures improved the military organization of France. Charles and Du Guesclin created new regular units of a permanent army, including the formation of artillery units. A new, permanent military staff was established; the French Navy was reorganized. New walls were built around Paris.

1364–1367. Intervention in Civil War in Castile. This culminated in the **Battle of Navarrette** (1367; see p. 375).

1380–1422. Reign of Charles VI. The ineptitude of this partially insane king, as well as the continuing English pressure in the Hundred Years' War, made this a period of violence, unrest, and frequent revolts.

1382. Flemish Revolt. The rebels, led by **Philip van Artevelde,** were crushed by the French at the **Battle of Roosebeke.**

SCANDINAVIA

These were violent centuries in Scandinavia. Three Danish rulers warrant particular attention. **Waldemar II** (the Conqueror) undertook numerous crusading expeditions to conquer the eastern shores of the Baltic Sea from pagan Slavs. After a century of decline and anarchy, the glory and power of Denmark were re-established by **Waldemar IV**. Although successful in most of his wars, Waldemar was fought to a standstill by the fleets and armies of the rising towns of the Hanseatic League. The century closed with Denmark under the firm and able rule of Queen **Margaret** (1387–1412), one of the greatest of Scandinavian rulers, who temporarily united the crowns of Denmark, Norway, and Sweden. The principal events were:

1202–1241. Reign of Waldemar II of Denmark. He sent successful crusading expeditions to Livonia, Estonia, and Finland, winning his most important victory at **Revel** (Tallin; 1219). However, his defeat at **Bornhöved** (1227) by Germans led by his vassal Count **Henry of Schwerin** lost Schleswig-Holstein and ended Danish domination of the Baltic.

1223–1250. Reign of Eric Laispe of Sweden. The country was dominated by his able soldier-statesman brother-in-law, **Birger Magnusson**.

1223–1263. Reign of Haakon IV of Norway. He was unsuccessful in his attempted invasion of Scotland (1263; see p. 365).

1319–1363. Reign of Magnus II of Sweden (Nephew of Birger Magnusson). He was also King of Norway. He was unsuccessful in wars against Denmark, and was deposed by the Swedish nobles.

1340–1375. Reign of Waldemar IV of Denmark. In wars with Sweden, Holstein, and Schleswig, he regained control of the regions of Zealand (1346), Fyn and Jutland (1348), and Skåne (1360).

1361–1363. Waldemar's First War with the Hanseatic League and Sweden. This was precipitated by Danish capture of Wisby, a main center of the League on Gotland. The allies captured and sacked Copenhagen, but Waldemar then defeated the Hanseatic fleets at the **Battle of Helsingborg** (1362), forcing his enemies to make peace.

1368–1370. Waldemar's Second War with the Hanseatic League. This was complicated by a civil war in Denmark forcing Waldemar to flee the country briefly. Taking advantage of this internal trouble, the Hanseatic League, supported by Sweden, Norway, Holstein, and Mecklenberg, defeated Waldemar. The **Peace of Stralsund** brought the Hanseatic League to a position of ascendancy in the Baltic Sea region.

1397. Union of Kalmar. Union of Denmark, Norway and Sweden.

GERMANY

As previously, developments within Germany were still greatly affected by the obsession of the emperors with Italy, and their constant power struggle against the popes. The first half of the 13th century was dominated by brilliant, able, and cruel **Frederick II,** who combined the good and bad qualities of his Hohenstaufen and Italian Norman ancestors. Soon after his death Germany descended into the chaos of the "Great Interregnum," finally ended by the election of **Rudolph I,** first Hapsburg emperor. The 14th century was marked by almost incessant dynastic disputes between the houses of Hapsburg, Wittelsbach, and Luxembourg.

During these two turbulent centuries two strong, semiautonomous forces rose within Germany. Early in the 13th century, under the leadership of **Hermann von**

Salza, the knights of the Teutonic Order began to expand Christianity and their own power through the heathen lands of Prussia and Lithuania. Farther west, the growing wealth and power of German cities—particularly those bordering the North and Baltic seas—were enhanced by banding together into the loosely organized Hanseatic League. Victories over German barons and against the Scandinavians brought the League to a position of pre-eminence in North Germany and the Baltic Sea by the middle of the 14th century. The principal events were:

1197–1214. Rival Emperors. **Otto IV** of Brunswick (Welf) and Philip II of Swabia (Waiblingen) were rivals until the assassination of Philip (1208). Frederick II then became Otto's rival. He allied himself with Philip II of France against Otto and John of England in the war which culminated in Otto's downfall at the **Battle of Bouvines** (see p. 368).

1210–1239. Rise of the Teutonic Knights.

1211–1250. Reign of Frederick II. He spent most of his reign in Italy opposing the popes. He also became King of Jerusalem (see p. 383). A high point in his many Italian wars was his victory over the Lombard League at the **Battle of Cortenuova** (1237). Frederick also twice fought the armies of Pope **Gregory IX** (1229–1230, and 1240–1241). His successful war against Pope **Innocent IV** (1244–1247) led the Pope to support antikings **Henry of Thuringia** and **William of Holland** (1247–1256) in civil war against Frederick and his son **Conrad IV** in Germany (1246–1256).

1211–1224. The Teutonic Knights in Hungary. They operated against the Cuman Turks at the request of **Andrew** of Hungary. Alarmed by the growing strength of the Knights, Andrew later expelled them.

1226–1285. Crusade and Conquest of Prussia by the Teutonic Knights.

1241. Battle of Liegnitz (or Wahlstatt). Mongol victory over **Henry the Pious** of Silesia (see p. 348).

1250–1254. Reign of Conrad IV. This was marked by continuing civil war in Germany and struggles against the Pope and other independent states of Italy.

1254–1273. The Great Interregnum. Germany was in utter chaos.

1260. Battle of Durben. The Teutonic Knights were disastrously defeated by the Lithuanians.

1273–1291. Reign of Rudolph I (of Hapsburg). It began with wars against **Ottocar II** of Bohemia, who was defeated and killed at the **Battle of Marchfeld** (or Durnkrut, 1278; see p. 377 and 379).

1314–1347. Reign of Louis IV (of Wittelsbach). Civil war raged between Louis and **Frederick** of Hapsburg during the early years of his reign (1314–1325). Louis defeated and captured Frederick at **Mühldorf** (1322). He was deposed in a civil war against **Charles** of Bohemia and Luxembourg (1346–1347).

1347–1378. Reign of Charles IV (of Luxembourg). Internal unrest and anarchy continued in Germany.

1387–1389. The "Town War." This resulted from the jealousy of the German nobility over the rising wealth and power of the cities. The strength of the cities was impaired in this indecisive conflict.

ITALY

North and Central Italy

The interminable struggles among the petty states of Northern and Central Italy had two major unifying themes: the continuing struggle between Guelph and Ghibelline (papal party versus imperial party) and the commercial rivalry of the great maritime states of Venice and Genoa. The principal events were:

1204. Participation of Venice in the Fourth Crusade. (See pp. 381–382.)

1237. Battle of Cortenuova. Victory of Frederick II over Guelph army of Milan and the Lombard League.

1242. Mongol Raids. (See p. 350.)

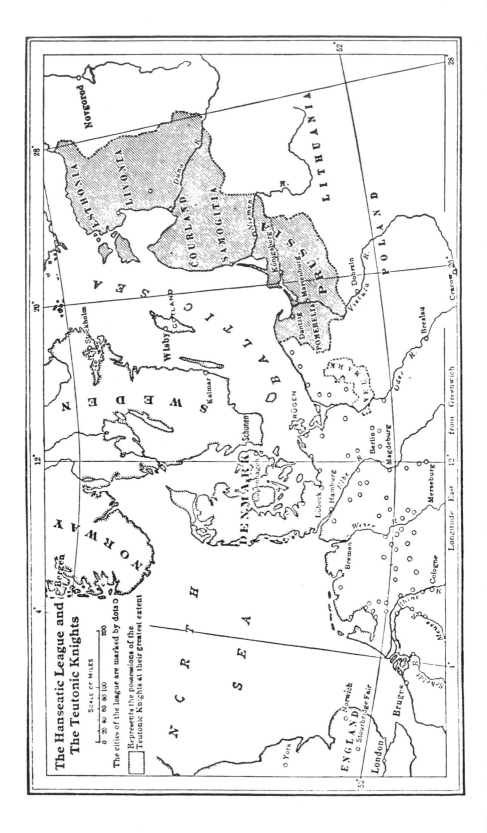

The Hanseatic League and
The Teutonic Knights

Scale of Miles

0 20 40 60 80 100   200

Represents the possessions of the
league are marked by dots ○

The cities of the league are marked by dots ○

Teutonic Knights at their greatest extent

1253–1299. **Wars between Venice and Genoa.** These were caused by a commercial dispute over trading concessions at Acre in Palestine. After early Venetian successes, Genoa recovered by assisting the Byzantines in recapturing Constantinople from the Latin emperors (1261; see p. 387). By a naval victory in the **Battle of Trepani** near Sicily (1264), Venice regained ascendancy and re-established trading rights in Constantinople. A Genoese victory at **Alexandretta** (1294) was offset that same year when a Venetian fleet under Admiral **Morosini** forced the passage of the Dardanelles and sacked **Galata,** the Genoese trading post at Constantinople. Peace was finally negotiated after a Genoese victory in the Adriatic at the **Battle of Curzola** (1299).

1312–1400. **Growth of Milan.** Led by the Visconti family, Milan conquered Verona, Vicenza, and Padua (1386–1388), and Pisa and Siena (1399).

1320–1323. **War between Florence and Lucca.** Lucca was victorious.

1351. **War between Florence and Milan.** Neither succeeded in gaining control of Tuscany.

1375–1378. **Alliance of Florence and Milan.** They opposed papal efforts to annex Tuscany.

1397–1398. **Renewed War between Florence and Milan.** Again the issue was control of Tuscany.

1353–1355. **Renewed War between Venice and Genoa.** Genoa won the decisive **Battle of Sapienza** (1354), in which most of the Venetian fleet was destroyed.

1378–1381. **The War of Chiogga (between Venice and Genoa).** Genoese Admiral **Luciano Doria** defeated the Venetians under **Vittorio Pisani** at **Pola,** but was killed. His brother **Pietro Doria** seized Chiogga, and blockaded Venice. Pisani in turn blockaded and captured the Genoese fleet (1380). Genoa, forced to make peace, never again seriously threatened Venetian maritime supremacy.

South Italy and Sicily, 1200–1400

During most of the 13th century, South Italy was the main Hohenstaufen base in the imperial-papal struggles. The papacy finally prevailed, through the instrumentality of **Charles** of Anjou. Like his Norman predecessors, Charles was then attracted toward the glittering prize of Constantinople, but during the last years of the century he and his Angevin successors were defeated and overthrown by the allied forces of decaying Byzantium and expanding Aragon. During the 14th century the Aragonese consolidated their control over southern Italy. The principal events were:

1221–1231. **Frederick II Consolidates South Italy.**

1228–1241. **Wars of Gregory IX and Frederick II.** Papal mercenary armies devastated Apulia (1228). Frederick, returning from his crusade, expelled the invaders, and forced the pope to make peace (1229). When war broke out again (1240), Frederick threatened Rome and annexed Tuscany (1241).

1244–1250. **War between Frederick and Pope Innocent IV.** Frederick successfully invaded Campagna (1244). The struggle spread throughout Italy. Although Frederick was repulsed after a long siege of Parma (1248), he was generally successful until his sudden death. His son, **Conrad IV,** continued the struggle (1250–1254).

1255–1265. **Ascendancy of Manfred (Half-Brother of Conrad).** He gained control of southern Italy (1255) and of Sicily (1256). In subsequent campaigns he established his control over most of Italy. Pope **Urban IV** offered the crown of Sicily to Prince **Charles** of Anjou, brother of Louis IX of France, and provided funds to assist Charles to raise an army against Manfred (1265).

ANGEVIN-HOHENSTAUFEN STRUGGLE, 1266–1268

1266, January. **Angevin Invasion.** Despite winter weather, Charles invaded Naples and crossed the Apennines to avoid Manfred's army holding the line of the Volturno River. Manfred pursued to Benevento. The two armies were closely matched, Manfred probably having a slight numerical superiority.

1266, February 26. Battle of Benevento. Manfred's failure to coordinate the operations of his archers and light and heavy cavalry permitted Charles's heavy cavalry to defeat the German and Neapolitan army in detail. Manfred was killed, and Charles established himself as King of Naples.

1268, July–August. Hohenstaufen Invasion. A Ghibelline army under **Conradin,** 15-year-old son of Conrad IV, invaded Southern Italy after seizing Rome (July). The autocratic rule of Charles had already led to widespread revolt in Southern Italy and Sicily. Conradin led his German army of 6,000 men across the Apennines into Apulia (August 18).

1268, August 25. Battle of Tagliacozzo. Charles, who had less than 5,000 men, took a defensive position near the Salto River, holding out approximately one-third of his army in reserve, hidden behind a hill. With more imagination than usual in medieval battles, Conradin enveloped the smaller Angevin army and dispersed all except the hidden reserve. After most of the German army had scattered in pursuit of the fleeing Angevins, Charles led his reserve against the victors, defeating each of its contingents in detail as they returned from their pursuit. Charles's victory was complete; Conradin

was captured and executed, thus ending the Hohenstauffen line.

1266–1285. Reign of Charles I of the Two Sicilies (Naples and Sicily). Charles participated in his brother's crusade to Tunis (1270; see p. 385). In a subsequent expedition to Tunisia, Charles won the hard-fought **Battle of Carthage,** defeating the Moors in a brilliant cavalry maneuver after pretending flight (1280). He made repeated expeditions to the west coast of the Balkans, establishing bases in anticipation of a major effort to overthrow the Byzantine Empire.

1282–1302. War of the Sicilian Vespers. A bloody uprising against Charles in Sicily was incited by the Byzantines, who also encouraged **Pedro** of Aragon to lead an expedition to the island. Charles had been assembling an army in Calabria, preparatory to an expedition against Constantinople. With this he rushed to Sicily, where he engaged in a war of maneuver with Pedro near Messina. At the same time Aragonese Admiral **Roger de Loria,** with a Catalan fleet, defeated the Angevin fleet in the naval **Battle of Messina** (1283). Loria defeated the Angevins again in the naval **Battle of Naples,** capturing **Charles,** son of the king (1284). The war dragged on for 20 years, Aragon finally conquering Sicily. French intervention on the side of Charles was abortive (1284–1285; see p. 375).

THE IBERIAN PENINSULA

Spain

Christian expansion on the Iberian peninsula continued, the Moors being reduced to the small enclave of Granada in southeastern Spain. After a half-century of glory, Castile declined under mediocre rulers, while the power and influence of smaller Aragon grew steadily. Having no remaining frontier with the Moslems, vital Aragon began an eastward maritime expansion. Conquering the islands of the western Mediterranean plus Sicily and southern Italy, by the close of this period Aragon had become the most powerful state in the Mediterranean area. The principal events were:

1158–1214. Reign of Alfonso VIII of Castile. (See p. 300.) Continuing his earlier successes, Alfonso led a series of coordinated Christian offensives against the Almohads, culminating in his great vic-

tory at the **Battle of Las Navas de Tolosa** (1212), which gave Castile control of central Spain.

1196–1213. Reign of Pedro II of Aragon. His defeat and death at the **Battle of**

Muret (1213; see p. 368) ended Spanish interests and influence north of the Pyrenees.

1213–1276. Reign of James I (the Conqueror) of Aragon. One of the great soldiers of Spanish history, he conquered the Balearic Islands (1229–1235) and Valencia (1233–1245) from the Moors. He took a leading part in the campaign which recovered Murcia from the Moslems for Castile (1266; see below).

1217–1252. Reign of Ferdinand III of Castile. He gained the throne after a prolonged dynastic war (1214–1217). He won a series of great victories over the Moors, capturing Cordova (1236), Seville (1248), Jaén (1246). By the close of his reign the Moors had been reduced to the small Emirate of Granada, acknowledging his suzertainty. Intermittent warfare with Granada continued for a century and a half.

1252–1284. Reign of Alfonso X of Castile. Generally unsuccessful in frequent wars with Granada, France, and Portugal, he regained his losses to the Moslems with the aid of James I of Aragon (see above).

1276–1285. Reign of Pedro III of Aragon. Forming an alliance with the Byzantine Empire, Pedro, pretending to sail on a crusade to Africa, actually landed at Sicily to begin the War of the Sicilian Vespers (1282; see p. 374). He was excommunicated by Pope Martin IV, who offered the crown of Aragon to Charles of Valois, son of Philip III of France. Philip, allying himself with his uncle, Charles of Anjou, invaded Aragon, but was decisively repulsed by Pedro (1284).

1312–1350. Reign of Alfonso XI of Castile. He consolidated royal control of Castile. With the assistance of **Alfonso IV** of Portugal he decisively defeated a combined army of Spanish and Moroccan Moslems at **Rio Salado** (1340, October 30), ending the last serious Moslem threat to Spain. He besieged and captured **Algeciras** (1344) to gain control of the north shore of the Strait of Gibraltar.

1323–1324. Aragonese Conquest of Sardinia. Captured from Genoa and Pisa.

1336–1387. Reign of Pedro IV of Aragon. Prolonged difficulties with his barons culminated in a violent civil war in which Pedro won a great victory at the **Battle of Eppila** (1348). He conquered Sardinia from Genoa (1353).

1350–1369. Reign of Pedro the Cruel of Castile. He was constantly engaged in a dynastic civil war with his brother **Henry of Trastamara,** who held the throne on several occasions in this seesaw war. Pedro was assisted by the English, under **Edward** the Black Prince, while Henry was allied with the French, whose contingent was led by Du Guesclin. This, despite a truce in France, was really an episode of the Hundred Years' War (see p. 359).

CAMPAIGN AND BATTLE OF NAVARRETTE, 1367

The Black Prince led an army across the Pyrenees (February, 1367) to restore Pedro to his throne. Demonstrating greater strategical skill than in previous campaigns, the prince outmaneuvered the French and Castilian army which attempted to block his advance through the Pass of Roncesvalles into the Ebro Valley. Rapidly marching around the Castilians, Edward crossed the Ebro and forced Henry and Du Guesclin to retreat hastily south of the river. The Castilian army consisted of about 2,000 French heavy cavalry, 5,500 Castilian heavy cavalry, 4,000 light cavalry, 6,000 crossbowmen, and about 20,000 unreliable infantry. The Black Prince's army comprised probably about 10,000 heavy and light cavalry, plus 10,000 mercenary infantrymen, of whom perhaps half were English archers, the remainder being mixed crossbowmen and javelin men.

Facing each other near Nájera (Navarrette) south of the Ebro (April 3), each army formed in three lines and advanced, with no attempt to maneuver. Leading the Castilian vanguard were the dismounted French heavy cavalry under Du Guesclin. The English archers took a heavy toll of the Castilian cavalry, driving them off the field, but were unable to do serious damage to the heavily armored French contingent. Though the French fought staunchly and gallantly, their Spanish allies were soon dispersed. After a ferocious fight the French surrendered. The Castilian army lost 7,000 dead, including 400 French and 700 Spanish heavy cavalry, and about 6,000 of the fleeing infantry; they probably had an equal number of wounded. The English army probably lost no more than 100 dead and perhaps a few hundred wounded.

1369. Battle of Moutiel. A quarrel with Pedro caused Edward to leave Spain. Henry, again supported by Du Guesclin, rebelled. In a violent battle near Ciudad Real, Henry personally killed Pedro and gained the throne.

1369–1379. Reign of Henry II of Castile (and Trastamara). He fought several inconclusive wars with Portugal and Aragon. The Castilian fleet aided the French in their victory over the English at the **Battle of La Rochelle** (1372; see p. 360).

Portugal

During these centuries, the Portuguese continued incessant warfare with the Moors, sometimes alone, sometimes in coordination with Castile and Aragon. **Alfonso II** supported the Castilians at Las Navas de Tolosa, and with Crusader assistance expanded southward as a result of a victory at **Alcácer do Sol** (1217). Wars against Castile were also frequent. Toward the end of the 14th century, when it seemed likely that Portugal would succumb to Castile, English support resulted in victory in the **Battle of Aljubarrota** (1385) by **John I** of Aviz. This was followed by the **Treaty of Windsor** (May 9, 1386), establishing an alliance between Portugal and England which has continued to this day.

SWITZERLAND

During the latter part of the 13th century, the mountainous region that is now the heart of Switzerland became relatively autonomous, though nominally under the Hapsburg family of Swabia and Austria. Early in the 14th century, the Swiss opposed the Hapsburgs in the Welf-Waiblingen disputes. The Hapsburgs sent punitive expeditions into the mountains, and precipitated nearly a century of warfare which eventually brought complete independence to the mountain cantons. The principal events were:

1315, November 15. Battle of Morgarten. An Austrian army of about 8,000 men, at least one-third heavy cavalry, under **Leopold** of Austria, invaded Switzerland. A Swiss force of about 1,500 pikemen and archers ambushed the Austrians in a defile between a lake and a mountain. The Austrians were thrown into confusion by boulders and trees hurled down the mountainside; the Swiss then practically annihilated the invaders with arrows and halberds.

1339. Battle of Laupen. Here the Swiss pikemen met a Burgundian invasion and first displayed their prowess and steadiness. Despite uneven terrain, the pikemen, supported by archers, drove the Burgundian infantry from the field, then repulsed a heavy-cavalry charge.

1386, July 9. Battle of Sempach. Some 1,600 Swiss pikemen were faced by approximately 6,000 Austrians under **Leopold III** of Swabia. Remembering the lessons of their previous defeats at the hands of the Swiss infantry, and influenced by English example in the Hundred Years' War, the Austrian heavy cavalry dismounted. Advancing across broken mountain fields as a line of heavily armored pikemen, they were at first successful in pushing back the less numerous and more lightly armored Swiss. The encumbered Austrians became exhausted, however, and some gaps appeared in their line.* The Swiss counterattacked, broke the Austrian

---

* Swiss legend says that the first gap was created by the self-sacrifice of **Arnold Winkelried,** who grasped a number of Austrian pikes, to plunge them into his own breast; his countrymen then exploited the gap thus made.

line, and smashed Leopold's army. This was the decisive battle of the Swiss-Hapsburg war, although the Swiss won the subsequent **Battle of Näfels** (1388).

1394. Truce with the Hapsburgs. This in effect recognized the complete independence of the Swiss confederation within the German (or Holy Roman) Empire.

EASTERN EUROPE

BOHEMIA AND MORAVIA

Under the great rulers **Ottocar I** and **Ottocar II,** Bohemia in the 13th century was briefly the most powerful nation of Central Europe. Ottocar II was defeated, humbled, and finally killed in a series of wars against **Rudolph** of Hapsburg. Bohemia revived under **Wenceslas II,** who also became King of Poland. Under the rule of the House of Luxembourg, Bohemia again became a major European power. The principal events were:

1253–1278. Reign of Ottocar II (the Great). Ottocar joined the Teutonic Knights in a successful campaign against the Prussians (1255). He next conquered Styria from Hungary by a victory over Bela IV at **Kressenbrunn** (1260). He was unsuccessful in his efforts to establish domination over Poland and Lithuania. Following this, he took advantage of the Interregnum in Germany to annex Carinthia, Carniola, and Istria.

1274–1278. Wars against Rudolph of Hapsburg. After several defeats, Ottocar was forced to abandon his conquests between the Danube and the Adriatic, and to acknowledge the suzerainty of Rudolph over Bohemia and Moravia (1275). In a renewal of the war, Ottocar was defeated and killed in the **Battle of Marchfeld** (August 26, 1278; see above and p. 379).

1278–1305. Reign of Wenceslas II. He also became King of Poland (1290) and was briefly King of Hungary (1301–1304).

After his death Poland re-established its independence (see p. 378).

1310–1346. Reign of John of Luxembourg (Son of Henry VII of Germany). A typical valiant, foolhardy medieval warrior, John sought all opportunities to fight. Blinded in the process, he was generally successful, and greatly increased his own prestige as well as that of his nation. He frequently fought with the Teutonic Knights against the Lithuanians (1328–1345). He allied himself with Philip VI of France against Edward III, and was killed leading a contingent of French and Bohemian knights at the Battle of Crécy (see p. 356).

1347–1378. Reign of Charles I (Also Charles IV of Germany, Son of John). A time of great prosperity and expansion for Bohemia, which became the most powerful state within the Holy Roman Empire.

1378–1419. Reign of Wenceslas IV (Son of Charles). As a result of internal conflicts, Bohemia began to decline.

POLAND

During much of the 13th century, Poland, weak, disunited, and frequently in a state of anarchy, was exploited by her neighbors, particularly the Teutonic Knights and Bohemia. Despite this, and despite internal difficulties due principally to an inadequate system of royal succession, she regained strength in the 14th century. By the end of the century, union with Lithuania established a basis for Poland's subsequent emergence as a great power. The principal events were:

1200–1279. Decline of Poland.
1228. Appearance of the Teutonic Knights in Prussia.
1241. The Mongol Invasion. (See p. 348.)
1242–1253. Wars with the Teutonic Knights. Their continued expansion eventually cut off Poland from access to the Baltic Sea (1280).
1290–1305. Bohemian Domination. (See p. 377.)
1305–1333. Reign of Ladislas IV. Poland regained its independence from Bohemia.

During this reign the Teutonic Knights raided frequently into Poland.
1333–1370. Reign of Casimir (the Great). A competent soldier, who waged war successfully with most of his neighbors.
1370–1382. Reign of Louis of Anjou. His daughter **Jadwiga** (Hedwig) succeeded to the throne after a bitter civil war over the succession (1382–1384).
1384–1399. Reign of Jadwiga. She married **Jagiello,** Grand Duke of Lithuania, to unite the two countries.

LITHUANIA, 1300–1400

Largely as a result of pressure and influence by the Teutonic Knights, Lithuania emerged as a state early in the 14th century, and under Grand Duke **Gedymin** (1316–1341) expanded rapidly to the east and south at the expense of Russia. His successors warred successfully against the Russians and against the Cuman Tartars, extending their domains as far as the Black Sea between the Bug and the Dnieper rivers. Under Jagiello, who also became King of Poland upon the death of his wife Jadwiga, Lithuanian expansion and prosperity continued.

RUSSIA

These were dark centuries of decline for Russia. This was due in large part to the Mongol conquest. The principal events were:

1223. Battle of the Kalka River. First appearance of the Mongols (see p. 339).
1236–1263. Reign of Alexander Nevski of Novgorod. He was a vassal of the Mongols (1240–1263). He defeated the Swedes under **Birger Magnusson** (see p. 370), at the **Battle of the Neva River,** ending Swedish attempts to conquer Northern Novgorod (1240). He defeated the Teutonic Knights in the **Battle of Lake Peipus** (1242).

1325–1353. Rise of Moscow. Princes **Ivan I** and **Simeon I** became the principal vassals of the Tartars.
1359–1389. Reign of Dmitri Donskoi of Moscow. His victory in the **Battle of Kulikovo** on the upper Don was the first important Russian victory over the Tartars (1380). He and his successors also fought a series of generally unsuccessful wars against the Lithuanians, who were sometimes allied with the Tartars.

HUNGARY

Hungary played a leading military and political role in Eastern Europe. Despite his disastrous defeat by the Mongols, King **Bela IV** later restored and enhanced his country's greatness. A prolonged dynastic war at the beginning of the 14th century was finally ended by the selection of **Charles I** (of Anjou) as king. He and his son **Louis** still further increased the power and prosperity of the country. The principal events were:

1206–1270. Reign of Bela IV. Decisively defeated by the Mongols at the **Battle of the Sajo River** (1241; see p. 349), Bela was ruthlessly pursued and finally found safety in the islands of Dalmatia. Following the withdrawal of the Mongols, Bela restored central authority and repulsed an invasion by **Frederick** of Austria (1246). He repulsed a second Mongol invasion (1261). Bela was less successful in his prolonged, indecisive wars with Ottocar II of Bohemia. His last years were plagued by disputes with his son, **Stephen.**

1272–1290. Reign of Ladislas IV. He allied himself with **Rudolph** of Hapsburg, helping to win a decisive victory over Ottocar at the **Battle of Marchfeld** or **Durnkrut** (1278; see p. 377).

1301–1308. Civil War over the Succession.

1308–1342. Reign of Charles I (of Anjou). He was forced to fight continuously during the first part of his reign to subdue unruly nobles (1308–1323).

1342–1382. Reign of Louis (the Great, Son of Charles). He led a successful expedition to Italy to solidify Angevin control over Naples (1347). Allied with Genoa against Venice in prolonged wars, he forced Venice to cede Dalmatia and to pay tribute (1381). He temporarily stopped Turkish penetration into the Balkans in northern Bulgaria (1356). When selected King of Poland, during his final years Louis was the most powerful ruler in Eastern Europe (1370–1382).

1387–1437. Reign of Sigismund. Decline of the kingdom. During this reign occurred the disastrous Crusade of Nicopolis (1396; see p. 386).

SERBIA

During the 13th century, Serbia barely maintained itself against pressures from Hungary, Bulgaria, and the Byzantine Empire. During much of the 14th century, however, Serbia prospered under three great soldier kings. Then, by the end of the century, a series of crushing defeats at the hands of the Ottoman Turks, and the loss of the outlying regions to other neighbors, reduced Serbia to a vassal of the Ottoman Empire. The important events were:

1254. Defeat by Hungary. Loss of Bosnia and Herzegovina.

1281. Defeat by Byzantines. King **Dragutin** abdicated.

1281–1321. Reign of Milvutin (Brother of Dragutin). He extended Serbian domains into Macedonia, at the expense of the declining Byzantines (see p. 387).

1321–1331. Reign of Stephen Dechanski. He gained control of most of the Vardar Valley through his decisive victory over a combined Byzantine-Bulgarian army at the **Battle of Kustendil,** or Velbuzhde (1330; see p. 388).

1331–1355. Reign of Stephen Dushan (Stephen Urosh IV). The son of Stephen Dechanski, whom he deposed and killed, Dushan was the greatest of Serbian medieval monarchs. Taking advantage of the continuing weakness of Byzantium, he subjected all of Macedonia, Albania, Thessaly, and Epirus and conquered Bulgaria. He invaded and annexed part of Bosnia (1349–1352). Victories over Louis of Hungary permitted Serbia to annex much of the western bank of the Danube River, including the site of modern Belgrade. Dushan, intending to seize the Byzantine throne, captured **Adrianople** and was advancing against Constantinople when he died (1355).

1371. Battle of Cernomen (or Maritza River). The Turks defeated **Lazar I** (1371–1389).

1376. Bosnian Aggression. Tvrtko I, ruler of Bosnia, proclaimed himself King of Serbia and Bosnia, annexing all of western Serbia including much of the Adriatic coast.

1389, June 20. Battle of Kossovo. (See p. 389.) Serbia became subject to the Turks.

1389–1427. Reign of Stephen Lazarevich (Son of Lazar). He fought loyally under the Turks at the **Battle of Nicopolis** (1396; see p. 386) and the **Battle of Angora** (1402; see p. 392).

BULGARIA

Bulgarian expansion during the early years of the 13th century was brought to a halt by crushing defeat at the hands of the Mongols (1241). For the remainder of this period Bulgaria played a minor role in the Balkans, a satellite in turn of the Byzantine Empire, Serbia, and the Turks. The principal events were:

1197–1207. Reign of Kaloyan. He expanded his nation as a result of victories over the Serbs, Hungarians, Byzantines, and the Latin Crusader States. At the **Battle of Adrianople** he captured Latin Emperor **Baldwin I** (1205; see p. 387).

1207–1217. Reign of Boril. He was defeated by the Crusaders, under **Henry I,** at the **Battle of Philippopolis** (Plovdiv; 1208). He was later besieged, captured and overthrown at **Trnovo** by **Ivan Asan** (1217–1218).

1218–1241. Reign of Ivan Asan II. He defeated **Theodore** of Epirus at the **Battle of Klokonitsa** on the Maritza River (1230); see p. 387). Later, in an alliance with the Empire of Nicaea against the Crusaders, Ivan unsuccessfully besieged Constantinople.

1241. Mongol Invasion. Bulgaria was crushed (see p. 350).

EURASIA AND THE MIDDLE EAST

THE LATER CRUSADES, 1200–1396

The Fourth Crusade, 1202–1204

BACKGROUND, 1195–1200

1195. Hohenstaufen Ambitions. Henry VI, German (Holy Roman) Emperor, and King of Sicily, inherited the Norman-Sicilian ambition to overthrow the Byzantine Empire and established a tenuous Hohenstaufen claim to the Byzantine succession. He also desired to emulate the exploits of his father, Frederick Barbarossa, as a Crusader (see p. 318).

1197–1198. Preliminary Moves. Henry sent an advanced party of German Crusaders to the Holy Land; they captured Beirut and other coastal towns (1198). Meanwhile Henry died (1197); plans for the Crusade were suspended.

1199. Renewed Papal Appeal. Pope Innocent III called upon Christendom to undertake a new effort to regain Jerusalem from the Moslems.

PRELIMINARIES, 1200–1203

1200. The Leaders. Responding to the papal appeal were **Theobald III,** Count of Champagne, Count **Louis** of Blois, Count **Baldwin** of Flanders and his brother **Henry,** Count **Boniface** of Montferrat, and the renowned French-English warrior **Simon de Montfort.** Theobald was the main leader. Philip of France and John of England ignored the appeal.

1201. Negotiations with Venice. Theobald, Louis, and Baldwin, agreeing with the pope that the Crusade should go by way of Egypt, negotiated with aged Venetian doge **Enrico Dandolo** to transport 25,000 Crusaders to Egypt, and to maintain them there for three years, in return for 85,000 marks and half of the Crusader conquests.

1201, May. Death of Theobald. Boniface of Montferrat was selected as the new Crusader leader. A cousin of Philip of Swabia, he was a strong Hohenstaufen supporter.

1201, December. Meeting at Hagenau. Philip persuaded Boniface to lead the Crusade to the Holy Land by way of Constantinople, in accordance with the plans of Henry VI. **Alexius,** son of deposed Isaac II of Constantinople and brother-in-law of Philip, was evidently at the conference, plus possibly a representative of Venice. (The idea of the expedition to Constantinople did not originate with the

Venetians, even though they adopted it eagerly.)

1202. Assembly at Venice. During the summer and early fall, the Crusaders gathered. When they were unable to raise 85,-000 marks, the Venetians agreed to transport them anyhow, in return for assistance in reconquering Zara, a former Venetian dependency now belonging to Hungary. The pope angrily denounced the deal, and threatened to excommunicate Crusaders who shed the blood of other Christians instead of going on to the Holy Land.

1202. Capture of Zara. Despite papal objections, the Crusader-Venetian expeditions captured and sacked Zara. Innocent excommunicated them.

EXPEDITION TO CONSTANTINOPLE, 1203–1204

1202–1203. The Final Decision. While at Zara the Crusader leaders negotiated with Dandolo about continuing on to Constantinople. Alexius joined the expedition and promised that in return for assistance in overthrowing Alexius III, he and his father would bring the Greek Church back into union with the Roman Church; that they would pay the Crusaders and Venetians 200,000 marks; and that they would

provide active support for the expedition to the Holy Land. Ignoring papal demurrer, the Crusader and Venetian leaders agreed to go to Constantinople. Simon de Montfort and some other Crusaders refused to participate in the expedition and sailed directly to Palestine.

1203, June 23. Arrival at Constantinople. Sailing into the Bosporus, the Crusaders landed near Chalcedon, on the Asiatic shore. They then crossed to Galata, where, despite Byzantine efforts, they established a fortified camp. Soon after this the Venetian fleet forced its way into the Golden Horn.

1203, July 17. The First Assault. While the Crusader army attacked the land defenses of the city from the west, the Venetian fleet assaulted the sea wall. The Byzantines, led by **Theodore Lascaris,** repulsed the Crusaders, but the Venetians, inspired by the personal courageous leadership of their venerable Doge (95 years old), finally gained a foothold on the sea wall. Against vigorous opposition, by dark they captured several towers and held a portion of the city. During the night Alexius III fled the city. Next morning the Byzantine nobles released Isaac II from prison and replaced him on the throne.

Young Alexius was elected coemperor as Alexius IV.

1203–1204. Delay at Constantinople. The Crusaders returned to their camp at Galata and the Venetians to their ships on the Golden Horn to await payment of the promised 200,000 marks. Isaac and Alexius had difficulty in raising the sum. Meanwhile they asked the Crusaders to help them consolidate their shaky control of the Empire.

1204, January. Byzantine Revolt. Increasing resentment of the Byzantine nobles against the Crusaders and against their puppets, Isaac and Alexius, resulted in an insurrection led by **Alexius Ducas Mourtzouphlous,** son-in-law of Alexius III. Isaac was imprisoned, Alexius IV executed. Alexius Ducas seized the throne as Alexius V. The Crusaders now had an excuse for attacking Constantinople. Investing the city, the Crusaders and Venetians planned an assault (March–April).

1204, April 11–13. Conquest of Constantinople. For two days violent land and sea attacks were skillfully resisted by the Byzantine army. The Varangian Guard, composed primarily of English and Danish mercenaries, particularly distinguished itself. Catapults on the Venetian ships flung incendiaries into the town, starting a violent conflagration. Assisted by this diversion, Crusaders and Venetians gained footholds on both the land and sea walls. An unaccountable panic seized part of the defending forces. The attackers redoubled their efforts and forced their way into the city, annihilating the Varangian Guard. For 3 days Constantinople was sacked in an orgy of violence, slaughter, loot, and rape.

COMMENT. *This, the first successful assault of Constantinople, was for all practical purposes the end of the Byzantine Empire. Remnants persisted, scattered along the coasts of Anatolia and Greece, and after 57 years even re-established themselves in Constantinople. (See p. 387 for the Latin Empire of Constantinople and its struggles with the Byzantines.) Even though these last fragments would persist for almost 2½ centuries, it would be only as pale shadows of the once-great Byzantine Empire. The Fourth Crusade smashed the bulwark of Christendom in the East.*

The Fifth Crusade, 1218–1221

Innocent III preached another Crusade in 1215, again urging that the expedition go by way of Egypt. To gain papal support in his struggle with **Otto IV** for the imperial throne in Germany (see p. 371), **Frederick II** promised to lead. Crusader contingents arrived in Acre from Hungary, Scandinavia, Austria, and Holland, where they joined **John of Brienne,** King of Jerusalem, and the Hospitalers, Templars, and feudal levies of the Crusader States (1217–1218). Landing near Damietta, they were vigorously opposed by a Moslem army under **Malik al-Kamil,** son of the Sultan, **al-Adil.** While the Genoese fleet defeated an Egyptian fleet in the mouth of the river, the Crusaders invested Damietta. The siege lasted for almost a year and a half before Damietta fell (November, 1219).

Meanwhile Cardinal **Pelagius,** papal legate, joined the crusading army and insisted upon assuming command. Somewhat reluctantly, King John acceded, but retained operational control. For more than a year, rejecting Egyptian peace overtures, the Crusaders waited in Damietta, momentarily expecting the arrival of Frederick II and reinforcements. Frederick never came, but early in 1221 **Hermann von Salza,** Grand Master of the Teutonic Order, and **Louis,** Duke of Bavaria, arrived with reinforcements. This brought the Crusader army to a total of about 46,000 men, of whom perhaps 10,000 were cavalry. Al-Kamil, who had become sultan upon the death of his father, had about 70,000. In June—despite intense heat and the flooded condition of the Delta—Pelagius ordered a march on Cairo. The advance was painfully slow, but by July the army had reached an Egyptian fortress overlooking the fork of the Damietta branch of the Nile, near the site of Mansura. Al-Kamil again offered peace, proposing to cede Jerusalem and other areas of the Holy Land to the Crusaders in return for Crusader evacuation of Damietta. John urged acceptance, but Pelagius demanded an additional indemnity and the cession of the fortresses of Kerak and Monreal. Negotiations broke down. The Crusaders attempted to cross the Ashmoun Canal and were decisively repulsed. At the same time the Moslem fleet seized control of the river between the Crusaders and Damietta, cutting their supply line. Facing starvation, Pelagius now agreed to give up Damietta in return for a free retreat and the face-saving cession of some holy relics by the Egyptians. An 8-year peace was agreed upon. The Fifth Crusade had been an abject failure.

The Sixth Crusade, 1228–1229

Shortly after this failure, Frederick II married **Yolande,** daughter of John of Brienne and heiress to the Kingdom of Jerusalem. Frederick, taking the title of King of Jerusalem, then began preparations for a Crusade. He was under considerable pressure from Rome, since the pope believed with some cause that the Fifth Crusade would have succeeded if he had participated as promised. Finally he sailed from Sicily in 1227. But when the fleet was at sea many of the Crusaders, including Frederick, were stricken with fever. He returned to Sicily to recuperate. Pope **Gregory IX,** assuming this was only more procrastination, excommunicated Frederick. Relations between Pope and emperor were already strained as a result of Frederick's attempts to incorporate his Kingdom of South Italy into the Holy Roman Empire. Without bothering to ask the Pope's forgiveness, Frederick started again for the Holy Land in 1228. Considering that the emperor was being insolent, Gregory renewed the excommunication, declared Frederick's lands in south Italy forfeited, and proclaimed a Crusade against the Crusader. Papal troops invaded Naples.

Frederick meanwhile arrived in the Holy Land, where his excommunicated status caused most other Crusaders to refuse cooperation. His orders were accepted only by his own troops and by Hermann von Salza's Teutonic Knights. Frederick opened negotiations with Al-Kamil. Through able and adroit diplomacy, Frederick obtained Jerusalem, Nazareth, and Bethlehem, with a land corridor connecting Jerusalem to the coast. Going to Jerusalem, he crowned himself king (February 18, 1229). Returning to Italy (May), he drove the papal armies from South Italy, then made peace with the Pope (August).

Because it culminated merely in a deal between two sharp traders, some historians refuse to recognize Frederick's expedition as a true Crusade. Nonetheless, he accomplished more in his few months in the Holy Land than any other Crusader leader since Godfrey de Bouillon.

The Crusader States, 1229–1247

Fifteen years after Frederick had regained Jerusalem, and while the local Crusaders were preoccupied with petty bickerings, Jerusalem fell unexpectedly to a new Moslem tide from the East. The Crusader States were also pressed from the south by resurgent Egyptian power. The important events were:

1229–1243. Discord. Constant bickering between Frederick (who never returned to the Holy Land) and the local Crusader barons, who became increasingly independent. Frederick's position was further undermined when he was again excommunicated in another quarrel with the Pope (see p. 373).

1239–1241. Reinforcements. Count **Theobald IV** of Champagne (and King of Navarre) sailed to Acre, despite papal prohibition (1239). (The Pope felt that the arrival of new Crusader strength in the Holy Land would strengthen Frederick's position; he preferred to have Jerusalem fall to the Moslems rather than to have Frederick keep it.) **Richard** of Cornwall, brother of Henry III, also defied the prohibition and sailed to the Holy Land (1240). He joined Theobald in fortifying Ascalon and in conducting a few unimportant raids against Moslem territory. Nothing else was accomplished.

1244. Fall of Jerusalem. Khwarezmians, fleeing from the Mongol conquerors of Persia (see p. 346), captured and sacked Jerusalem, and allied themselves with Egypt. The local Crusaders, allied with the Emir of Damascus, were decisively defeated by the Egyptians and Khwarezmians at the **Battle of Gaza.** An important part in the victory was played by the young Tartar Mameluke leader, Baibars.

1247. Mameluke Capture of Ascalon.

The Seventh Crusade, 1248–1254

Christian reaction to the Moslem capture of Jerusalem led King Louis IX (later St. Louis) of France to lead still another Crusade, moving again by way of Egypt. After occupying Damietta, Louis was repulsed in an effort against Cairo; his army was routed and he was captured. Later ransomed, Louis went to Acre, where he tried in vain to re-establish the power of the Kingdom of Jerusalem. The principal events were:

King Louis IX (later St. Louis)

1245. Papal Appeals for Crusades. Innocent **IV** preached a Crusade to recapture Jerusalem, and simultaneously preached another Crusade against excommunicated Frederick. Louis IX tried in vain to mediate between pope and emperor.

1248. Louis Sails for the East. His fleet of 1,800 ships carried 20,000 cavalry and 40,000 infantry, mostly French. He spent the winter in Cyprus.

1249. Occupation of Damietta. Louis landed against slight opposition. The garrison abandoned the city in panic (June 6). Possibly remembering the difficulties encountered by the Fifth Crusade in attempting to advance on Cairo in midsummer, Louis waited until fall. This delay,

however, permitted Sultan **Malik-al-Salih,** despite severe illness, to restore confidence in his panic-stricken troops and to prepare opposition.

1249, November 20. Advance toward Cairo. The Crusaders traveled only 50 miles in 4 weeks. They were stopped in front of the Ashmoun Canal, at the same point where the Fifth Crusade had been halted. The Moslem army, probably about 70,000 men, under Emir **Fakr-ed-din,** held the line of the canal. The core of that army was a force of 10,000 Mamelukes (see p. 389). The Sultan died, but this was kept secret, and one of his wives, **Shajar-ud-Durr,** ruled in his name.

1249–1250, December–January. Operations along the Canal. When Louis endeavored to build a causeway, the Moslems harassed the French with war engines, at the same time widening the canal by digging away the opposite bank. A surprise Egyptian attack was repulsed on Christmas.

1250, February 8, Battle of Mansura.* During the night Louis secretly took his cavalry across a ford which had been discovered about 4 miles from the causeway. The Moslems were completely surprised; Fakr-ed-din was killed. Louis's brother, **Robert** of Artois, leading the advanced guard, was supposed to seize the canal bank, opposite the causeway, to await the

---

* Actually the village where this action took place was named Mansura—Victory—after the battle.

arrival of the main body of the cavalry and to cover a river crossing by the waiting infantry. He disobeyed orders. Rashly attempting to win the battle by himself, he pursued the Moslems into Mansura, where the effectiveness of his heavy cavalry was limited in street fighting. The Moslems rallied, annihilated Robert's division, and almost overwhelmed the remainder of the French cavalry. Louis was saved only by the timely arrival of his infantry over a bridge hastily constructed from the end of the causeway.

1250, February 11. Egyptian Counterattack. The exhausted Crusaders, hemmed in their bridgehead, barely held their position, making effective use of Greek fire.

1250, March–April. Retreat. His line of communications cut, his army wracked by disease, Louis retreated toward Damietta, harassed by the Moslems.

1250, April 6. Battle of Fariskur. Attacked by their pursuers, the French infantry broke into panic. The Moslems closed in, annihilating most of the army, and capturing Louis.

1250–1254. Failure. Louis agreed to pay 800,000 gold livres in ransom and to abandon Damietta (May). Sending most of the survivors back to France, he sailed to Acre. His further efforts, including attempts to negotiate with the Mongols, accomplished nothing (1250–1254).

The Crusader States, 1254–1270

The Crusader States became pawns in a great struggle between the new Mameluke Empire of Egypt and the Mongol conquerors of Persia. When the Mongol tide receded from Syria, Baibars, now Sultan of Egypt (see p. 389), began a systematic conquest of the remaining Crusader footholds in the Holy Land. The principal events were:

1258–1260. Mongol Conquest of North Syria. Ilkhan Hulagu (see p. 390) was preparing to move south when the death of Khakhan Mangu caused him to return to Karakorum, in accordance with the law of Genghis Khan (see pp. 390 and 350). He left a detachment, under the general Kitboga, to hold the conquered area. Apparently he also directed Kitboga to assist the Crusaders against the Mamelukes. Bohemund VI of Antioch allied himself with Kitbogha. The other Crusaders held aloof, finding it difficult to choose between the Moslem Mamelukes and the pagan Mongols.

1260. Battle of Ain Jalut. Kitboga, supported by a few Crusaders, was decisively defeated by a much larger Mameluke

army under Kotuz near Nazareth. This was the high-water mark of Mongol expansion.

1260–1268. Mameluke Conquests. Under Baibars the Mamelukes expanded steadily, aided by bickering among the Crusader barons and the wars between Genoa and Venice, and between Venice and the Latin Empire of Constantinople. After the fall of Antioch (1268) only Acre, Tripoli, and a few scattered castles remained in Christian hands.

1269. Aragonese Crusade. James the Conqueror, responding reluctantly to papal pressure, led a futile expedition to Asia Minor. Deterred by storms, he abandoned the effort.

The Eighth Crusade, 1270

The disasters in the Holy Land inspired Louis IX to take the cross again. Baibars' intrigues led the French king to believe that the Bey of Tunis could be converted to Christianity; he decided to go to the Holy Land via Tunis and Egypt. His brother, Charles of Anjou, newly established king of Sicily, reluctantly agreed to join. The Tunisians resisted, and Louis besieged Tunis. Soon after, this expedition was swept by an epidemic, in which Louis died. Charles took command. Entering negotiations with the Bey of Tunis, Charles obtained tribute for himself and for France. Prince Edward of England (later Edward I) arrived, to discover that the Crusade had ended without further hostilities.

The Crusader States, 1271–1291

The Moslem reconquest of the Crusader lands was completed. Although there was some later sporadic activity, the fall of Acre ended the real Crusader era after two momentous centuries. The principal events were:

1271. Capture of Krak. After a long siege, Baibars captured the Knights Hospitalers' castle near Tripoli, probably the most powerful fortification in the world.

1271–1272. Arrival of Edward of England. With 1,000 men, he made some raids against the Moslems—once reaching Nazareth—and attempted negotiations with the Mongols. He was almost a victim of the Assassins. Edward, virtually the last of the great Crusaders, accomplished little.

1281. Battle of Homs. A Mongol raiding army, 30,000–50,000 strong, swept into Syria, where it was joined by a substantial force of Crusaders. Sultan **Kala'un,** successor of Baibars, led an army probably 100,000 strong to meet the invaders in an indecisive battle. Soon afterward the Mongols withdrew.

1289. Fall of Tripoli. Captured by Kala'un.

1291. Fall of Acre. Sultan **Khalil,** son of Kala'un, captured Acre after a long siege and a gallant defense. This ended the Crusader dominions of the East.

Aftermath of the Crusades, 1291–1396

During the century after the fall of Acre, the crusading spirit died a lingering death. The most important events were:

1299–1301. Mongol Invasion of Syria. They apparently expected Crusader cooperation and intended to reinstall the Christians in Jerusalem (see p. 390). When Christian help was not forthcoming, they withdrew, never to return to Syria.

1310. Knights Hospitalers Capture Rhodes. The island would become for more than two centuries the strongest bulwark of Christendom against the Turks.

1311. Suppression of the Knights Templars. Its members were exterminated by Philip IV of France.

1344. Capture of Smyrna. A crusading expedition of Knights Hospitalers, Cypriots, and Venetians captured Smyrna from the Ottoman Turks. It remained in Christian hands until it was captured and sacked by the Tartars of Timur (1402; see p. 392).

1365–1369. Crusade of Peter I of Cyprus. He sacked Alexandria (1365) and continuously ravaged the coasts of Syria and Egypt. His project ended with his assassination (1369).

1396. Crusade of Nicopolis. Pope **Boniface IX** preached a crusade against the Ottoman expansion in the Balkans. Duke **John the Fearless** of Burgundy, **Jean Bouciquaut** (Marshal of France), and a number of other nobles (mostly French) advanced into the Danube Valley. They were decisively defeated by the Turks at the **Battle of Nicopolis** (Nikopol, Bulgaria; see p. 380).

THE BYZANTINE EMPIRE

Wrecked and fragmented by the Fourth Crusade (see p. 382), the Byzantine Empire was reunited in reduced and weakened form in the latter half of the 13th century. The declining empire was shaken by ever-weakening, dying convulsions during the remainder of the period, while its territory was slowly absorbed by the Ottoman Empire. Important events were:

1202–1204. Fall of Constantinople to the Fourth Crusade. (See p. 382.)

1204. Establishment of the Latin Empire. Count **Baldwin** of Flanders became Emperor Baldwin I of Constantinople (1204–1205). **Theodore Lascaris** established himself as Emperor of Nicaea, the largest remnant of the Byzantine Empire (1206–

1222). **Alexius Comnenus** established the Empire of Trebizond; his brother **David Comnenus** established a short-lived empire on the northern shores of Bithynia and Paphlagonia.

1205. Battle of Adrianople. The Bulgarians under **Kaloyan** defeated Baldwin and Doge Dandolo (see p. 381). Baldwin, captured, died in captivity.

1207–1211. Byzantine Internecine War. Theodore Lascaris defeated David and Alexius Comnenus. The Seljuk Turks of Rum were first allied with Theodore, and later with the Comneni.

1214–1230. Reign of Theodore Ducas Angelus of Epirus. In a series of wars with his Latin, Byzantine, and Slavic neighbors, Ducas extended his control over most of Macedonia and Thrace.

1222–1254. Reign of John III, Ducas Vatatzes of Nicaea. He was an able ruler and excellent soldier in the Byzantine tradition. In successful wars against all of his neighbors, he made Nicaea a powerful, prosperous country.

1224. Three-Way War. Theodore of Epirus, John of Nicaea, and **Robert** of Courtenay, Emperor of Constantinople, fought a confused struggle. John defeated the Crusaders at the **Battle of Poimanenon.** He then sent an army across the straits to seize Thrace from Theodore. Meanwhile Theodore had defeated the Crusaders at the **Battle of Serres.** In Thrace he then repulsed the Nicaean effort to capture Adrianople.

1229–1237. Regency of John of Brienne. The former King of Jerusalem (see p. 382) became regent for the boy emperor **Baldwin II.** The ablest of all the Crusader leaders, John restored Latin control over the approaches to Constantinople, and became coemperor (1231).

1230. Battle of Klokonitsa. Ivan Asen of Bulgaria defeated and captured Theodore of Epirus (see p. 380).

1236. Alliance of John of Nicaea and Ivan of Bulgaria. Their plan to attack Constantinople was thwarted by the arrival of a Venetian fleet and a Latin army from Achaia.

1244. Seljuk Pressure Relaxed. The Nicaean Empire was relieved as a result of Mongol victories over the Seljuks (see p. 346).

1246. Nicaean Conquest of Macedonia and Thrace. John of Nicaea led an expedition across the straits.

1254–1258. Reign of Theodore II Lascaris of Nicaea. Michael Asen of Bulgaria, hoping to take advantage of the death of John III, occupied much of Thrace and Macedonia. Theodore defeated Michael at **Adrianople** (1255) and, despite ill health, in two brilliant campaigns reconquered the lost territories.

1259–1282. Reign of Michael VIII Paleologus of Nicaea. An able general, he seized the throne from the child emperor John Lascaris.

1259. Battle of Pelagonia. The Nicaeans defeated an alliance of the Byzantines of Epirus with Manfred of Sicily and the Latin prince of Achaia.

1261. Byzantine Seizure of Constantinople. A small Nicaean army under General **Alexius Stragopulos** captured Constantinople from the Latins by surprise, and almost without opposition, during the absence of the Venetian fleet. Michael reestablished the Byzantine Empire with its capital in Constantinople, and formed an alliance with Genoa against Venice (see p. 373).

1261–1265. Byzantine Successes. Campaigns against the Latins in Greece, the Bulgarians in Thrace and Macedonia, and Epirus.

1267–1281. Wars with Sicily. Charles of Anjou attempted to expand into the Balkans, with the intention of capturing Constantinople (see p. 374). Michael won a great victory over the Angevins at the **Battle of Berat,** Albania (1281). Charles made an alliance with Venice, the Pope, the Serbs, and the Bulgars for the final overthrow of the Byzantine Empire. Michael formed an alliance with Pedro of Aragon, supporting him in the War of the Sicilian Vespers, thus relieving Angevin pressure against the Byzantine Empire (see pp. 374 and 375).

1282–1328. Reign of Andronicus II. Renewed Angevin and Turkish threats against Byzantium caused Andronicus to hire a small army of Catalan mercenaries under **Roger de Flor** (1302). Although the Catalans repulsed Turkish attacks, they terrorized Constantinople and other Byzantine territories. After the murder of Roger de Flor (1305), his troops became the scourge of Thrace and Macedonia, later seizing Athens and setting up an independent state (1311).

1317–1326. Siege of Bursa. (See below.)

1321–1328. Civil War. This was between Andronicus and his grandson, also named **Andronicus.** Much of the empire was devastated. Young Andronicus established himself as coemperor (1325), and finally deposed his grandfather (1328).

1325–1341. Reign of Andronicus III. After an initial defeat by Serbia (1330; see p. 379) he was generally successful against European neighbors and in the Aegean. Andronicus lost most of his remaining Anatolian possessions to the Ottoman Turks.

1341–1347. Civil War. This was between the supporters of **John V,** son of Andronicus (under the regency of his mother **Anna** of Savoy), and **John Cantacuzene,** rival claimant to the throne. Thrace and Macedonia were ravaged. Both sides called in Serbs and Turks in complex shifting alliances. The result was the loss of most of the dwindling possessions of the empire and the devastation of that which remained under Byzantine control.

1347–1354. Reign of John VI (Cantacuzene). He captured Constantinople through treachery. He called for Turkish assistance against Stephen Dushan of Serbia. The Ottomans repulsed the Serbs and at the same time established a foothold on the European shore at Gallipoli.

1355–1391. Second Reign of John V. He recaptured Constantinople and forced Cantacuzene to abdicate. A weak ruler, he lost Adrianople to the Turks (1365) and was captured by Czar **Shishman** of Bulgaria (1366).

1376–1392. Confused Dynastic Struggle. The participants were John V, his sons **Andronicus IV** (1376–1379) and **Manuel II,** and grandson, **John VII** (1390–1391, 1399–1402). The Turks took advantage of the chaos to overrun most remaining Byzantine territory.

1391–1425. Reign of Manuel II. An able ruler, he inherited an empire consisting only of Constantinople, Thessalonika, and the Morean Peninsula.

1391–1399. Ottoman Siege of Constantinople. French Marshal **Jean Bouciquaut,** leader of a small force of volunteer soldiers and sailors, gained a respite by repulsing repeated attacks of Ottoman Emperor **Bayazid I** on land and sea (1398–1399).

THE OTTOMAN EMPIRE, 1290–1402

Near the middle of the 13th century, the Seljuk Turks were overwhelmed by the Mongols, and Turkish Anatolia disintegrated into chaos. Soon afterward, a new Turkish tribe, under Osman I (Othman), emerged into prominence in Anatolia. After establishing their supremacy over neighboring Turkish tribes, the Ottomans steadily whittled away at the declining Byzantine power and territory, taking advantage of incessant internal discord and intrigue within Constantinople. Near the middle of the 14th century, the Ottomans established a foothold in Europe, then rapidly overran Thrace, Macedonia, Bulgaria, and much of Serbia. However, they continued to be frustrated by the powerful defenses of Constantinople, where the Byzantine Empire was eking out a few years of miserable existence. Just as Constantinople was on the verge of surrender, the Ottomans were smashed, apparently beyond hope of recovery, by the Tartar conqueror **Tamerlane** (1402; see p. 392). The principal events were:

1230. Battle of Erzinjan. Seljuk Sultan of Rum, **Ala ud-Din Kaikobad,** defeated Khwarezmian Shah Jellaluddin, who had retained the western remnant of his empire after his defeat at the Indus (see p. 338). This defeat facilitated the Mongol advance through western Persia and into Anatolia in the next 7 years (see p. 390).

1243. Battle of Kosedagh. The Mongols defeated the Seljuk Turks, and established suzerainty over Anatolia (see p. 346).

1290–1326. Reign of Osman I. He culminated his successes against the Byzantines by besieging Bursa (1317), which fell shortly after his death (1326).

1326–1359. Reign of Orkhan I. He made

Bursa his capital. He was the real organizer of the Ottoman Empire. The first of his many victories over the Byzantines was over Andronicus III at the **Battle of Maltepe** (1329). In the following years the Byzantines were eliminated from most of their remaining footholds in Anatolia by the capture of Nicaea (1331) and Nicomedia (1337). While assisting John Cantacuzene, the Ottomans conducted their first expeditions into Europe (1345) and established their first permanent European settlement at Gallipoli (1354). In subsequent years they expanded rapidly in Thrace. The Byzantine Empire became a virtual Ottoman fief.

1359–1389. Reign of Murad I. Capturing Adrianople (1365), Murad made this his capital.

1366. Crusader Interference. A Crusade led by **Amadeus** of Savoy and Louis of Hungary was initially successful. Amadeus captured Gallipoli, but was later driven out. Louis defeated the Turks near **Vidin,** but was later forced to withdraw.

1369–1372. Ottoman Conquest of Bulgaria.

c. 1370. Establishment of the Janissary Corps. Murad created this elite body of soldiery, at first almost entirely infantry archers, and consisting of former Christians captured in childhood and brought up as fanatic Moslems. For more than 500 years the Janissaries would play a leading role in Ottoman history.[*]

1371. Battle of Cernomen. Turkish victory over the Serbs on the Maritza River resulted in the conquest of Macedonia (see p. 379).

1389, June 20. Battle of Kossovo. Victory of Murad and his son Bayazid over a coalition of Serbs, Bulgars, Bosnians, Wallachians, and Albanians under the leadership of Lazar of Serbia, who was killed in the battle. Murad was later assassinated by a Serbian prisoner.

1389–1402. Reign of Bayazid I.

1391–1399. First Ottoman Siege of Constantinople. (See p. 388.)

1396. Crusade of Nicopolis. (See pp. 380 and 386.)

1397. Turkish Invasion of Greece.

1402. Battle of Angora. (See p. 392.)

---

[*] Oman suggests that Orkhan, rather than Murad, established the Janissaries.

EGYPT, SYRIA, AND THE MAMELUKES

The Ayyubid successors of Saladin briefly expanded his empire, then quickly declined, to be overthrown and replaced by their Mameluke slave-soldiers. During the latter part of the 13th century, the Mamelukes were engaged in a desperate struggle against the Mongols. Through a combination of luck, able leadership, and adoption of Mongol military practices, the Mamelukes halted the invaders at the gates of Egypt, and retained possession of most of Syria. During lulls in this struggle, they evicted the Crusaders from Syria and Palestine. For most of the following century they prospered in Egypt and Syria, expanding their control southward up the Nile Valley into Nubia. At the very end of the century, however, Tamerlane inflicted a crushing defeat on the Mamelukes and drove them from Syria. The important events were:

1200–1238. Ayyubid Expansion. Military success, expansion, and prosperity under sultans Abul Bakr Malik al-Adil and his son Malik al-Kamil.

1218–1221. The Fifth Crusade. (See p. 382.)

1231–1232. Ayyubid Invasion of Anatolia. This was repulsed by the Seljuk Turks.

1238–1240. Dynastic Struggle.

1240–1249. Reign of Malik-al-Salih. He devoted himself to the reconquest of Syria.

1249–1250. The Seventh Crusade. (See p. 384.)

1250. Mameluke Revolt. Turanshah, son of al-Salih, was overthrown during the Seventh Crusade by a conspiracy of Mameluke leaders and Queen **Shajar ud-Durr,** al-Salih's widow. Shajar married the Mameluke leader **Aidik,** the first Mameluke sultan. She later murdered Aidik, but was in turn killed by his adherents (1257).

1257–1260. Reign of Kotuz. Assisted by his lieutenant, **Baibars,** Kotuz defeated the Mongol general, **Kitboga,** at the **Battle of Ain Jalut** (see p. 385). Kotuz was then murdered by Baibars.

1260–1277. Reign of Baibars. The greatest

of the Mameluke sultans. Of Tartar origin, he had served in the Mongol armies in his youth, and recognized the deadly threat the Mongols posed to his empire. He formed an alliance with **Bereke,** Mongol Khan of the Golden Horde, who had become a Moslem (see p. 351). From Bereke he obtained Mongol instructors for his army. This permitted Baibars and his successors to fight on even terms with the Mongols in Syria. Baibars' efforts to restore the Abbasid Caliphate in Baghdad were repulsed by the Mongols. In a series of deliberate campaigns he recovered most of the Crusader territory in Palestine and Syria (see p. 385). All of the North African Moslem states were tributary to him.

1277–1290. Reign of Kala'un (Father-in-law of Baibars' Son). He repulsed a Mongol invasion of Syria by his victory at the **Battle of Homs** (1281). He continued the recovery of Crusader territory.

1290–1293. Reign of Khalil Malik al-Ashraf (Son of Kala'un). He completed the eviction of the Crusaders from the Levant.

1294–1341. Reign of Malik al-Nasir. Twice deposed from the throne during his childhood and youth, Malik eventually established himself firmly (1310) and under his rule the Mameluke domains expanded. He made peace with the Mongol Ilkhans (1322). By frequent raids up the Nile Valley, he strengthened Mameluke influence in Nubia. There was a decline after his death.

1381–1399. Revival of the Mamelukes. This was under warrior-Sultan **Bartuk Malik-al-Zahir.**

1400–1402. Tamerlane's Conquest of Syria. This began with his overwhelming victory at the **Battle of Aleppo** (October 30, 1400). Syria never recovered from Tamerlane's devastation.

PERSIA AND TURKESTAN, 1200–1405

Khwarezmian and Mongol Periods, 1200–1381

The conquests of the Khwarezmian Turks, begun by Takash (see p. 311), were continued by his son, **Ala-ud-Din Mohammed,** who expanded from Khorasan and Khwarezm to create a vast empire by conquering all of Persia, Transoxiana, and Afghanistan. Mohammed's glory was smashed by the Mongols under Genghis Khan. Mohammed's son, **Jellaluddin,** was defeated by the Mongols in two vain efforts to re-establish the Khwarezmian Empire. The Mongols held Persia and Turkestan for a century and a quarter, the powerful, autonomous Ilkhan dynasty being formally established by **Hulagu,** grandson of Genghis. The Ilkhans expanded westward to conquer Mesopotamia, Transcaucasia, most of Anatolia, and much of Syria, but failed in repeated efforts to destroy the Mameluke sultans of Egypt. They were occasionally involved in fierce but indecisive struggles with their cousins, the khans of the Golden Horde and of the Jagatai Mongols. During the last four decades of the Ilkhan period, central authority declined, and their empire became a collection of virtually independent Turkish and Tartar principalities. The principal events were:

1199–1220. Reign of Ala ud-Din Mohammed, Shah of Khwarezm.

1205. Battle of Andkhui (South of the Oxus). Mohammed defeated **Muhammad of Ghor** to begin Khwarezmian expansion into modern Afghanistan (see p. 395) and thence to take all of Persia.

1220–1221. Mongol Conquest of Khwarezm. (See p. 336.)

1221. Battle of the Indus. Genghis defeated Jellaluddin (see p. 338). Jellal fled into India, then returned to southern Persia, where he was later defeated by Mongol troops of **Ogatai Khan.** Next defeated by the Seljuks (1230; see p. 388), he soon after was assassinated (1231).

1231–1236. Mongol Conquest of the Remainder of Persia. To include Northern Mesopotamia, Azerbaijan, Georgia, and Armenia.

1243. Mongol Conquest of Anatolia. (See p. 346.)

1255–1260. Conquests of Hulagu. He was the first of the Ilkhans, subject to the loose suzerainty of his brother Mangu, in Karakorum (see p. 346). He conquered Southern Mesopotamia, where he stormed **Baghdad** and extinguished the Abbasid Caliphate (1258). He had begun the conquest of Syria when he was recalled to Karakorum at the death of Mangu (1260).

1260. Battle of Ain Jalut. Hulagu left his general Kitboga (Ket-Buka) in command west of the Euphrates. Learning of Hulagu's departure, the Mameluke leader Kotuz hastily gathered an army of 120,000 men at Cairo and invaded Palestine. Kitboga moved with two or three toumans (20–30,000 men) to meet the Egyptians near Goliath Wells. The Mongols were close to victory, and pursuing the fleeing Egyptians, when they were ambushed by Baibars and the Mamelukes. Kitboga was killed and the Mongols routed. The Mongol army was small, but this Moslem victory had great psychological significance.

1260–1304. Mongol Raids into Syria. (See pp. 386 and 390.)

1261–1262. Civil War between Golden Horde and Ilkhans. Bereke, supporting the Mamelukes (see p. 390), marched south against Hulagu. Bereke withdrew, after inconclusive skirmishes in the Caucasus, when threatened by Kublai (see p. 346).

c. 1294. Conversion of the Ilkhans to Islam.

1335–1381. Decline of the Ilkhans.

The Period of Tamerlane, 1381–1405

Timur (Timur the Lame, or Tamerlane) was born at Kesh (Shahr-i-sabz) near Samarkand (1336). His claim of descent from Genghis Khan is doubtful; he was apparently a Tartar, not a Mongol. By fighting and intrigue, at the age of 28 Tamerlane became vizier, or prime minister, of the khan of the Jagatai Mongols (see p. 346). He then overthrew the khan (1369). During the next ten years he fought wars with Khwarezm and Jatah (Eastern Turkestan). The capture of Kashgar gave Tamerlane control of Jatah (1380), and was the beginning of a quarter of century of ruthless conquest. The principal events were:

1381–1387. Conquest of Persia. Beginning with the capture of Herat (1381), Tamerlane continued with the conquest of Khorasan (1382–1385). He later overran Fars, Iraq, Azerbaijan, and Armenia (1386–1387). He massacred ruthlessly.

1385–1386. First War with Toktamish. A former protégé of Tamerlane, Toktamish, now Khan of the Golden Horde (see p. 351), invaded Azerbaijan and defeated one of Tamerlane's armies in that area (1385). Tamerlane repulsed the northern Mongols, but did not pursue.

1388–1395. Second War with Toktamish. Taking advantage of Tamerlane's absence in Persia, Toktamish raided into Transoxiana, defeated one of Tamerlane's lieutenants, and advanced against Tamerlane's capital of Samarkand. By forced marches exceeding 50 miles a day, Tamerlane returned to Transoxania; Toktamish and his allies hastily retreated northward.

1389. Battle of the Syr-Darya. Toktamish returned during the winter with a larger army, but was outmaneuvered and decisively defeated by Tamerlane. Toktamish retreated with the remnants of his army.

Tamerlane prepared to invade the Khanate of the Golden Horde (1389–1390).

1390–1391. Tamerlane's Invasion of Russia. With an army that probably exceeded 100,000 men, Tamerlane marched northward. He had no political or strategic objective such as always characterized the operations of Genghis Khan. His intention was merely to seek and to destroy Toktamish. He was relying upon his own tactical ability, and upon the superb fighting qualities of his mercenary—but completely devoted—army. Toktamish apparently deliberately lured Tamerlane west of the Ural River to exhaust and discourage the invaders. His strength is not known, but it was undoubtedly substantially larger than that of Tamerlane.

1391. Battle of Kandurcha (or of the Steppes). The two armies met somewhere east of the Volga and south of the Kama rivers. The battle lasted for 3 days, with Tamerlane often close to defeat. By the third day Toktamish had destroyed Tamerlane's left wing and personally led an enveloping force to attack from the rear. Tamerlane seems to have gained the victory eventually by a ruse, causing Tok-tamish's army to believe that their khan was dead when in fact he was on the verge of victory. Discouraged, the north-ern Mongols and Tartars scattered into the steppes. Casualties are unknown; based upon one chronicle, it may be estimated that Toktamish lost more than 70,000, Tamerlane more than 30,000. Probably realizing that he was dangerously overex-tended, Tamerlane made no effort to con-tinue into Russia, but returned to Persia to deal with trouble there.

1392. Revolt in Persia. Tamerlane defeated and killed rebel Shah **Mansur** in the **Battle of Shiraz.**

1393–1394. Conquest of Mesopotamia and Georgia. He captured Baghdad (1393). While in Georgia, Tamerlane was at-tacked by Toktamish, but drove him back north of the Caucasus Mountains. Tamer-lane pursued.

1395. Battle of the Terek. Again on the verge of defeat, Tamerlane rallied his troops and finally drove Toktamish from the field. Tamerlane pursued relentlessly, up to the Volga Valley, westward to the Ukraine, and across much of Central Rus-sia, south of Moscow. Defeating all Mon-gol detachments that he found, he mas-sacred and ravaged ruthlessly. He de-stroyed the cities of Astrakhan and Sarai (capital of the Golden Horde). He estab-lished a vassal khan to replace the fleeing Toktamish; the Golden Horde never re-covered.

1398–1399. Invasion of India. Tamerlane's advance guard and right wing, under his grandson **Pir-Mohammed,** debouched into the Punjab to seize Multan (spring, 1398). The left wing, under another grandson, **Mohammed Sultan,** marched by way of Lahore. Tamerlane himself, with a small picked force, traversed the highest regions of the Hindu Kush before turning south to join his main body east of the Indus (September). Killing and plundering, he marched against Delhi. He destroyed the army of **Mahmud Tughluk** in the **Battle of Panipat** (December 17; see p. 396). After massacring 100,000 captive Indian soldiers, he stormed Delhi. After several horrible days of slaughter, rape, plunder, and destruction, Tamerlane marched north into the Himalayan foothills, storm-ing supposedly impregnable **Meerut,** then westward back to the Punjab, destroying everything in his path, then disappeared from India as suddenly as he came (March, 1399). Probably no more sense-less, bloody, or devastating campaign has ever been fought.

1400. Invasion of Syria. Tamerlane de-stroyed the Mameluke army at the **Battle of Aleppo** (see p. 390). He captured both Aleppo and Damascus, slaughtering many of the inhabitants.

1401. Capture of Baghdad. Another horri-ble massacre, punishment for the city's uprising after its previous capture (see above).

1402. Invasion of Anatolia. He defeated the Sultan Bayazid of the Ottoman Turks in the **Battle of Angora** (July 20; see p. 389). He then captured Smyrna from the Knights Hospitalers (see p. 386). After overrunning all of Anatolia, and having received tribute from the Sultan of Egypt and the Byzantine emperor, he returned to Samarkand (1404).

1405. Death of Tamerlane. Hoping to con-quer an empire even larger than that of Genghis Khan, Tamerlane started for China, but died en route at Otrar.

AFRICA

NORTH AFRICA

Morocco

Early in the 13th century, the Almohad Dynasty began to break up, the prin-cipal cause being the rise of the Berber tribe of Beni Marin, which became the Mari-nid Dynasty, with capital at Fez. After consolidating control of Morocco, the Mari-nids began to expand eastward, while also sending numerous expeditions to Spain, where they temporarily halted the advance of Christianity. After a prolonged struggle they conquered the Ziyanids of western Algeria and briefly overran the Hafsid dominions of western Algeria and Tunis. Overextended, they soon lost their conquests to the resurgent Hafsids and Ziyanids, barely retaining control of their own turbulent kingdom of Morocco. The principal events were:

1201. Almohad Conquest of the Balearic Islands.

1215-1258. Breakup of the Almohad Empire.

1217-1258. Marinid Conquest of Morocco.

1229-1233. Aragonese Reconquest of the Balearic Islands.

1258-1286. Reign of Yakub II. Greatest of the Marinids, he campaigned against the Ziyanids of Algeria (1270-1286) and also in Spain (1261, 1275, 1277-1279, 1284). In the latter campaigns he was allied with Alfonso X of Castile and León against Alfonso's insurgent son **Sancho.** The death of Alfonso left Yakub temporarily in control of most of Spain, but he was soon driven out by Sancho.

1286-1307. Reign of Yusuf IV. He was constantly at war with the Ziyanids of Tlemcen. During a siege of Tlemcen (1300-1307) he was assassinated, and the siege was raised.

1335-1337. Siege of Tlemcen. The Ziyanid capital was captured by **Ali V,** son and successor of Yusuf.

1347. Invasion of Tunisia. Repulsed by the Hafsids.

1351. Dynastic Civil War. Ali was defeated and overthrown by his son **Faris I.**

1351-1359. Conquest and Loss of Algeria and Tunisia. Faris conquered the remaining Ziyanid dominions (1351-1357), then overran much of the Hafsid lands, including Tunis itself (1357). The defeated dynasties made common cause, drove out the invaders, and recaptured Tlemcen (1359).

1359-1400. Decline of the Marinids. Morocco was wracked by internal violence.

1399. Sack of Tetuán. This Castilian raid was linked with operations against Granada (see p. 375).

Western Algeria

The Zenata tribe, under **Abu Yahia Yarmorasen,** drove out the Almohads. Abu established the Abd-el-Wahid or Ziyanid Dynasty, which retained control of the region for the remainder of the period, save for two decades of Marinid occupation. The principal events were:

1236-1248. Rise of the Ziyanids. Almohad resistance collapsed with the fall of Tlemcen (1248).

1248-1282. Reign of Abu.

1270-1359. Wars with the Marinids. (See above.)

Tunisia and Eastern Algeria

The Prince of Tunis, **Abu Zakariya,** established the Hafsid Dynasty by ejecting the Almohads. The Hafsids retained control of the region (which included Tripolitania) despite frequent internal uprisings, and numerous land and sea invasions. The principal events were:

1236. Ejection of the Almohads.

1270. French Invasion. The short-lived Eighth Crusade of Louis IX (see p. 385).

1280. Angevin Invasion. (See p. 374.)

1347-1359. Wars with the Marinids. (See above.)

1390. Siege of Mahdia. During a truce in the Hundred Years' War, a joint Franco-English force, under Prince **Louis** of Bourbon, invaded by sea and besieged Mahdia unsuccessfully for 61 days.

WEST AFRICA

The once-flourishing Empire of Ghana never recovered from an Almoravid invasion which had sacked its capital of Kumbi (1076). The breakup of Ghana into several smaller states was soon followed by the coalescence of power in three of these —Mandingo (or Mali), Soso, and Songhoi—by the beginning of the 13th century. By this time Mandingo and Songhoi had been converted to Islam. During the 13th century, after some setbacks, Mandingo gradually established virtually complete control over most of West Africa, and the culture of its capital of Timbuktu became known even in Europe and the Middle East. The principal events were:

c. 1200–c. 1230. Ascendancy of Soso. This was largely attributable to its warrior king, **Sumanguru,** who sacked the ancient Ghanaian capital of Kumbi (1203) and temporarily conquered Mandingo (1224).

1235. Revival of Mandingo. King **Sun Diata** overthrew Soso control, and in following years steadily expanded his territory at the expense of Soso, Songhoi, and other neighboring kingdoms.

1307–1332. Reign of Gongo Musa of Mandingo. The height of Mandingo's power and expansion.

1325. Mandingo Conquest of the Songhoi Empire.

EAST AFRICA

In the 10th century, Moslem Arabs from Yemen had crossed the Strait of Bab el Mandeb and begun to conquer most of the coastal regions of Christian Ethiopia (including modern Eritrea, French Somaliland, and northwestern Somalia). This conquest was consolidated in the 11th and 12th centuries. In the 12th century, also, they conquered the Red Sea pagan state of Bega (roughly, the modern Sudanese coast). At the same time, repulsed from Ethiopia, they had begun to push into Nubia and the Nile Valley, and around the Horn of Africa along the Somalian East African coast, with some expeditions apparently reaching as far as modern Zanzibar by the 13th century. During that century the Mamelukes of Egypt took over the Arab conquests along the Nile, and pushed farther up the Nile Valley into Nubia. The displaced Arabs, joining with others from the Red Sea coast and from the Sahara, during the late 13th and the 14th centuries conquered the upper Nile Valley—save for that part in Ethiopia which they were still unable to penetrate. Thus all of modern Sudan was now in Moslem hands. Farther east, however, the Arabs suffered a setback at the hands of the pagan Somalis, who reconquered the entire East African coast, and also seized part of eastern Ethiopia.

SOUTH ASIA

NORTH INDIA

By the beginning of the 13th century, Muhammad of Ghor had conquered most of Hindustan. Soon after this, however, his empire was shaken by his defeat in Northern Khorasan by Ala-ud-Din Mohammed, Shah of Khwarezm (see p. 390). While restoring order in Ghazni and India, he was assassinated and the Ghuri Empire collapsed. The northwestern regions were absorbed by Mohammed Shah, who installed his son Jellaluddin as Viceroy of Ghazni. In Hindustan, after a period of turmoil,

Moslem control was perpetuated by the so-called Slave Dynasty of the Sultanate of Delhi. During the remainder of the century, periods of stability in North India were punctuated by anarchic dynastic changes, Mongol raids, Hindu uprisings, and endemic civil war among the Turkish nobility. At the turn of the century, under able Turkish Sultan **Ala-ud-Din,** they conquered the Deccan, to unite most of the subcontinent under one rule. During the subsequent reign of **Mohammed bin Tughluk,** this great empire began to fall apart. At the very end of the century a strong man appeared on the scene, but not to restore order. In six months **Tamerlane** inflicted on India more misery than had been caused by any other conquerer, and destroyed the Sultanate of Delhi. The principal events were:

1203. Muhammad Became Emperor of Ghor. He succeeded his elder brother **Ghiyas ud-din.** His empire extended from the Caspian and Aral seas to the Arabian Sea and the Bay of Bengal.

1205. Battle of Andkhui. Muhammad was defeated south of the Oxus River by Mohammed Shah of Khwarezm. Later in the year Muhammad of Ghor marched to India, suppressing uprisings en route and defeating the rebellious Rajput Hindus (November).

1206. Assassination of Muhammad. This was followed by anarchy.

1207–1210. Establishment of Sultanate of Delhi. This was by **Qutb ud-Din Aibak,** a general who had been a right-hand man of Muhammad of Ghor. He was the first of the so-called Slave Dynasty. His death in a polo accident was followed by turmoil.

1210–1236. Reign of Iltutmish. After restoring order and reconquering rebellious provinces, this Turkish general gained control of all North India as far south as the Narbada River.

1216. Battle of Tarain. In the Punjab, Iltutmish defeated the invading army of **Taj-ud-din** of Ghor and Ghazni (who had been driven from his kingdom by the Khwarezmians; see p. 390).

1221. Flight of Jellaluddin. Driven from Ghazni by Genghis Kahn (see p. 338), the Khwarezmian prince fled into the Punjab with the remnants of his army. Iltutmish refused him asylum and pursued Jellaluddin southward through the Indus Valley, then westward into Persia. After a few raids into the Punjab, Genghis Khan withdrew without further action.

1236–1240. Reign of Raziya (Daughter of Iltutmish). She was nominated for succession because of the Sultan's dissatisfaction with his sons. She ruled firmly and vigorously, but was doomed to failure as a

leader of a Moslem hierarchy. Beset by constant revolts, she was eventually captured and killed by rebellious Turkish nobles, and was succeeded by an incompetent brother.

1238–1264. Reign of Naruseinha I of Orissa. He established the only Hindu dynasty which successfully resisted later Turkish invasions of east and south India.

1241. Mongol Raid into the Punjab. Taking advantage of turmoil in North India, the raiders captured Lahore.

1245–1266. Reign of Nasir-ud-din. He restored order in North India, largely through the ability of his chief minister, **Ghiyas ud din Balban.** Balban repulsed several Mongol raids and suppressed a number of rebellions.

1266–1287. Reign of Balban. He revitalized the Sultanate, reducing the power of the nobles. His reign was beset by a number of Mongol raids. Upon his death North India reverted to anarchy as the Turkish nobility struggled for power, and Hindu princes of Malwa and Gujarat, among others, threw off the hated Moslem yoke.

1290–1296. Reign of Jalal-ud-din Firuz. He was founder of the Khalji, or Afghan, Dynasty. He repelled another Mongol invasion (1292). His nephew and son-in-law, **Ala-ud-din Khalji,** led the first Moslem expedition south of the Narbada River, capturing and plundering Devagiri, the capital of Yadava (1294). Firuz heaped honors on Ala-ud-din, who demonstrated his gratitude by murdering the Sultan and seizing the throne.

1296–1316. Reign of Ala-ud-din. A ruthless, bloodthirsty monarch.

1299–1308. Mongol Invasion. The invaders swept through the Punjab to the gates of Delhi, where Ala-ud-din defeated them. He finally expelled them from India (1308).

1300–1305. Reconquest of Malwa and Gujerat. Noted for the hard-fought sieges of the Hindu fortresses Ranthanbor and Chitor. Ala-ud-din finally captured Chitor after the hopeless defenders performed the rite of *jauhar*, casting their wives and children on a great funeral pyre, then sallying from the fortress to die in a suicidal attack on the besiegers.

1307–1311. Moslem Conquest of the Deccan. General **Malik Kafur** took Devagiri (1307), Warangal (1309–1310), Hoysala (1310), and Pandya (1311). Only Orissa remained independent of the Moslem Sultan of Delhi.

1316–1317. Reign of Kafur. He had become virtual dictator during the declining years of Ala-ud-din, and probably hastened his master's death by poison. His death soon after was followed by 3 years of anarchy.

1320–1325. Reign of Ghiyas-ud-din Tughluk. Accepted by the warring Turkish nobles, this strong general restored order, suppressing rebellions in Warangal and Bengal. He was killed in an accident, reputedly engineered by his son, Mohammed.

1325–1351. Reign of Mohammed bin Tughluk. Early in his reign this ruthless, impractical intellectual defeated a Jagatai Mongol invasion under **Tarmashirin,** Khan of Transoxiana, which penetrated nearly to Delhi. Mohammed then planned to conquer Persia, but was unable to cope with the logistical problems of moving a great army across the intervening deserts and mountains. Later he sent another large army into the mountains between India and Tibet, forcing the hill tribes there to acknowledge his suzerainty, but losing nearly 100,000 men in the process (1337). Meanwhile his dominions in the Deccan began to break away (1331–1347). Mohammed died while battling a revolt in Sind (1351).

1351–1378. Decline of the Sultanate of Delhi.

1398–1399. Tamerlane's Invasion. (See p. 392.) North India, never so thoroughly devastated before or since, was in utter chaos. Delhi did not rise from its ruins for more than a century.

SOUTH INDIA

The old multipartite conflicts continued between the various Hindu and Hindu-Dravidian dynasties of the Deccan. All of the competing Hindu dynasties disappeared, however, following the conquests of Ala-ud-din and his general Kafur at the beginning of the 14th century. The Moslem tide was reversed by the rise of the new Hindu Kingdom of Vijayanagar, continually at war during the latter part of the 14th century with the new Moslem Sultanate of Bahmani. These conflicts were typical of Moslem-Hindu warfare; the Bahmanis were essentially cavalrymen, while Vijayanagar, suffering from the historical difficulties of raising horses in the Southern Deccan, relied primarily upon infantry. The principal events were:

1200–1294. Incessant Wars. Participants were the Yadava, Kakatiya, Hoysala, and Pandya; the Hoysala were the most successful.

1294–1306. Moslem Expeditions into the Northern Deccan.

1307–1311. Conquest of the Deccan. By Malik Kafur (see above).

1311. Revolt of Madura. The Moslem governor established an independent sultanate in southern Deccan.

1336. Establishment of Vijayanagar (Modern Mysore). The first ruler was **Bakku Rai** (or Raya).

1344. Independence of the Central Deccan. The result of a rebellion of a confederacy of Hindu princes.

1347. Independence of the Bahmani Sultanate. This drove the Delhi Turks from the northern Deccan.

1350–1400. Wars between Vijayanagar and the Bahmani. Though the Moslems won several notable victories (1367, 1377, 1398), the Hindu kingdom maintained its independence and prospered.

1378. Vijayanagar's Conquest of Madura. This gained Hindu control of the entire southern Deccan.

SOUTHEAST ASIA

THE TAI

The slow and gradual migration of the Tai into Southeast Asia was accelerated by the overthrow of the Nanchao (Tai) Kingdom in Yunnan by Kublai Khan (1252–1253; see p. 346). Pressing into the Irrawaddy and Menam valleys, the Tai (or Shan) pushed back Burmese, Mon, and Khmer. By the end of the 13th century, the many small Tai states in the Menam and Mekong valleys began to coalesce into larger states. The city and kingdom of Ayuthia were established in the middle of the 14th century, the genesis of modern Thailand. The latter part of the century was a period of continuous wars between Ayuthia and its neighbors, particularly against the Tai state of Chiengmai and the Khmer Kingdom of Angkor (see p. 324). The principal events were:

1283–1317. Reign of Rama Khamheng, of Sukhot'ai (in the Upper Menam Valley). This conqueror expanded to the southwest far down the Malay Peninsula (c. 1295) and northeast to the Mekong River near Luang Prabang. He was a loyal ally of Mongol China. His kingdom declined rapidly under his successors.

1350–1369. Reign of Ramadhipati. He founded the city and kingdom of Ayuthia. He expanded rapidly in all directions, and conquered Sukhot'ai. He also warred frequently with the Tai state of Chiengmai and with the Khmer of Cambodia. He is considered the first King of Siam or Thailand.

1369–1388. Reign of Boromoraja I. He suppressed a rebellion of Sukhot'ai (1371–1378). His forces invading Chiengmai were defeated and repulsed at the **Battle of Sen Sanuk,** near Chiengmai.

VIETNAMESE REGION

The old and bitter conflict between Champa and Annam, quiescent for a century, was renewed and prosecuted bitterly on both sides. In a brief hiatus in the struggles late in the 13th century, the two small nations united to oppose successfully a series of Mongol invasions. The principal events were:

1203–1330. Khmer Occupation of Champa. This ended with the voluntary withdrawal of the Khmer, probably because they found themselves overextended in their struggles with the Tai (see above).

1220–1252. Reign of Jaya Parmesvaravarman II of Champa. He renewed the old war with Annam over the still-disputed frontier provinces (see p. 324). The conflict was drawn out and indecisive. He was killed during an Annamese invasion by King **Tran Thai-ton.** Both sides made peace.

1257. Mongol Invasion of Annam. Kublai sent his general **Sogatu** to conquer Champa. Apparently Sogatu was able to advance through Annam without serious opposition, but was unable to overcome the Cham, who retired into the mountains to carry out a prolonged guerrilla war.

1285. Mongol Disasters. Togan, son of Kublai, led an army into Annam to assist Sogatu. He captured Hanoi, but then was defeated and repulsed by the Annamese. Meanwhile Sogatu, attempting to join Togan, was frustrated by the Cham and Annamese. Driven back to Champa, he was defeated and killed by the Cham.

1287. Final Mongol Invasion. The invaders captured Hanoi, but were unable to progress farther in the face of determined Annamese resistance under King **Tran Nhon-Ton** (1278–1293). Both sides agreed to a face-saving solution. The kings of

Champa and Annam acknowledged the suzerainty of the emperor; Kublai was happy to stop the costly invasions.

1312–1326. Renewed War between Champa and Annam. Champa was defeated and annexed by Annam (1312). Combined Cham-Annamese forces then repulsed an invasion by the Tai of **Rama Khamheng** (1313). This was followed immediately by Cham rebellions against the Annamese. Finally **Che Anan** drove out the Annamese and became king. There was a quarter-century of peace between the two exhausted countries.

1353. Cham Invasion. The Annamese repulsed them from the disputed province of Hué.

1360–1390. Reign of Che Bong Nga of Champa. A great soldier, he was incessantly at war against Annam. He captured and sacked Hanoi (1371). The Annamese continued guerrilla resistance, and at one point King **Tran Due-Ton** attempted a counteroffensive into Champa, only to be defeated, killed, and his army annihilated by Che at the **Battle of Vijaya** (1377). Despite his many victories, Che never completely pacified Annam. He was killed in a sea battle off the coast against Annamese and Chinese pirates.

CAMBODIA

At the beginning of the century the great King of Angkor, **Jayavarman VII,** conquered Champa (see p. 325). A few years later, he was compelled to withdraw to meet the increasing pressure of the Tai from the west. During the remainder of these two centuries the kings of Angkor were constantly on the defensive against the Tai, losing their outlying provinces in the Mekong and Menam valleys, and hard-pressed to maintain themselves in their home territories (see p. 397).

BURMA

The first half of the 13th century was relatively uneventful. Then the accelerated Tai (Shan) migration from the north (see p. 397) brought increasing friction between Burmese and Shan. Soon after this the King of Pagān refused to acknowledge the suzerainty of Kublai Khan. Almost simultaneously with an outbreak of internal war between Burmese and Shan, a Mongol invasion swept through Burma to capture Pagān and topple the Burmese dynasty. During the remainder of the period Burma was wracked by constant internal warfare. The principal events were:

1271. Burmese Refusal of Tribute to Kublai Khan. Two years later King **Narathihapate** executed a Mongol ambassador repeating Kubai's demands (1273). Kublai, occupied with other affairs in his vast empire, took no immediate punitive action.

1277. Burmese Raid into Kanngai. This was a border state owing allegiance to China. The Governor of Yunnan sent 12,-000 Mongol troops, who decisively defeated 40,000 Burmese invaders at the **Battle of Ngasaunggyan.** Their horses frightened by Burmese elephants, the Mongol archers dismounted to fight on foot. After dispersing the elephants, they remounted to make a decisive charge. The Mongols raided into Burma as far as Bhamo.

1283. Battle of Kaungsin. Repulsing another Burmese border raid, the Mongols again invaded and defeated the Burmese near Bhamo, and established outposts along the upper Irrawaddy.

1287. Mongol Invasion. Prince **Ye-su Timur,** grandson of Kublai, swept through Burma to capture Pagan and establish a puppet regime.

1299. Shan Revolt. The Burmese puppet of the Mongols was overthrown.

1300. Last Mongol Invasion. Planning to re-establish control, the small invading army was held up by the stubborn defense of the fortified Shan town of **Myinsaing.** Accepting a large Shan bribe, the Mongol commander withdrew. He was executed by the governor of Yunnan, but the Mongols did not return.

365. Capital at Ava. The principal Shan chieftain, **Thadominbva,** established the new capital of a mixed Shan-Burmese kingdom on the middle Irrawaddy River. This became the true successor of the Kingdom of Pagān.

1368–1401. Reign of Mingyi Swasawke. Ava was almost constantly at war with Pegu, with its Shan neighbors, with a new Burmese kingdom at Toungoo, and with the Arakanese states on the western sea-coast.

INDONESIA

During the 13th century the power of Srivijaya was reduced in the Malay Peninsula and in the islands partly by the Tai and partly due to revolts and encroachments of Indonesian neighbors. Of these, the Kingdom of Singosari of Java expanded over much of Indonesia in the late 13th century. Almost simultaneously with a Javanese revolt which overthrew this kingdom came a Mongol invasion. The Mongols, in alliance with the heir of the overthrown Singosari Kingdom, soon conquered Java, but then encountered such serious guerrilla opposition from their former allies that they finally withdrew to China. During the middle of the following century, under the great minister **Gaja Mada,** the Singosari-Majapahit Kingdom again established control over most of Indonesia. By the close of the century this empire was seriously threatened by the growing strength of Islam in the Malay Peninsula and western Indonesia. The principal events were:

1222. Rise of Singosari. It overthrew the Kediri Kingdom of western Java.

c. 1230–1270. Reign of Dharmaraja Chandrabam of Ligor (in Malaya). He evidently threw off domination by Srivijaya, and established a powerful maritime kingdom. He sent expeditions to Ceylon (1247 and 1270). His successors succumbed to the Tai conqueror Rama Khamheng of Sukhot'ai (c. 1290; see p. 397).

1275–1292. Reign of Kertanagara of Singosari. He evidently began a plan to conquer the island possessions of decaying Srivijaya.

1292. Kediri Revolt. Kertanagara was killed by Kediris under **Jayakatwang.**

1292–1293. Mongol Invasion of Java. Prince **Vijaya,** son-in-law of Kertanagara, formed an alliance with Mongol Admiral **Yi-k'o-mu-su** which overthrew Jayakatwang and conquered Java. Vijaya then turned against the Mongols, defeating several detachments in a guerrilla war. The Mongols finally withdrew after Vijaya recognized Mongol suzerainty. He established his capital at Majapahit.

1295–1328. Series of Rebellions. These were against Vijaya and his son **Jayanagara.** They were finally suppressed by the young officer **Gaja Mada** (1319).

1330–1364. Ascendancy of Gaja Mada. As prime minister, he was actual ruler of the kingdom. This was a period of conquest and expansion in neighboring islands of Indonesia and on the Malay Peninsula. By the time of his death, West Java, Madura, and Bali were firmly held, and a large number of coastal city states throughout Indonesia paid tribute.

XII

THE END OF
THE MIDDLE AGES: 1400–1500

MILITARY TRENDS

GENERAL

The 15th century was an epoch of change. The same scientific, cultural, economic and social forces that inspired the Renaissance, the sudden initiation of oversea exploration and colonialism, and changing political patterns throughout the world—particularly in Europe—also definitely affected warfare. The result was an era o military uncertainty and of blundering experimentation.

No single nation or military leader dominated the world. There were, however a number of competent soldiers, such as **Henry V** of England, **John Ziska** of Bo hemia, **John Hunyadi** of Hungary, and the Ottoman Sultans **Murad II** and **Mo hammed II. Joan of Arc** of France was not really a military person and—save fo her ability to use the moral factor in war—lacked any real understanding of mili tary affairs.

Historians generally agree that the Middle Ages ended with the close of thi century. This was no abrupt change, however, and was symbolized by the following primarily military, events: the fall of Constantinople, the end of the Hundred Years War, the end of the Wars of the Roses, and Charles VIII's invasion of Italy.

Each of these climactic events was greatly influenced by gunpowder weapons— the Wars of the Roses less than the others. This growing effectiveness of gunpowde weapons was the main theme of the century's military history, although there wer two others of importance: the reappearance of military professionalism in Wester warfare after an absence of more than a millennium, and the growing importanc of infantry. By the end of the period these three themes foretold the subsequent com bined-arms concept of the cavalry-infantry-artillery team.

One example of the appearance of professionalism was the resumption of the oretical studies of warfare, almost unknown since the time of Vegetius. Representa tive of this new intellectual approach to military affairs were treatises on war an on chivalry by **Christine de Pisan.**

In the politico-military sphere, ancient Byzantium finally succumbed to revital ized Islam, opening Southern and Eastern Europe to the Moslems. But the breach was blocked for a century by the Hungarian descendants of the Magyars.

ARMOR

Personal armor reached the height of development at the very time when the three major military trends of the period were assuring its obsolescence. The still-increasing weight of the armor made the knight (or man-at-arms, or heavy cavalry-man) ever more ponderous; yet after midcentury the tempered steel plates of even the finest German and Italian armor could no longer stop the new and increasingly powerful missile weapons of gunner and foot soldier. Furthermore, the frustrated, encumbered cavalryman needed more—not less—mobility and flexibility in dealing with dangerous hostile infantry formations, or working in cooperation with his own infantryman.

As a result of these imperatives, by the end of the century plate armor had become important more as a prestige symbol than for defense or protection. There can be no better example of the flux or confusion in military art than what was then happening to armor. It was at its very heaviest, in a vain effort to protect from small-arms fire, while it was being lightened or discarded by realistic cavalrymen seeking mobility. The polished plates of tempered steel were shaped to assure the greatest protection by providing a glancing surface, while (sometimes on the very same suit of armor) they were also being embossed and etched with magnificent designs, which necessarily reduced tensile strength and impaired the tangential characteristics.

WEAPONS

General

By the beginning of the century, the practice of the heavy cavalry of fighting on foot had caused some modification and diversity in the weapons used by men-at-arms when dismounted. The sword was generally left sheathed, and the scabbard was now often strapped to the saddle instead of on the knight's belt. Because of the greater protection of armor, the men-at-arms usually carried battering weapons com-bining great weight with a sharp cutting edge. Although the spiked mace was still used, even more popular was some kind of poleax, with the glaive—a sort of cleaver or broad-bladed ax—and the halberd among the most favored.

But fearsome though these implements of slaughter were, the new gunpowder weapons were rapidly proving to be even more effective in smashing through armor plate. By the end of the century even the most conservative knights had to admit that commoners serving gunpowder weapons had become the arbiters of the battle-field. The pre-eminence of the aristocracy, shaken by English yeomen at Crécy and by Swiss mountaineers at Sempach, was now ended forever. The power and poten-tialities of these new weapons were so obvious that they were generally adopted throughout Europe, despite the problems imposed by powder that had to be pro-tected from the weather, by clumsy and cumbersome methods of combustion, and by the dangers of explosion posed to those who handled the weapons.

Strangely enough, the two military systems most responsible for restoring the ascendancy of the infantry were the slowest to adopt the new gunpowder weapons which reinforced that ascendancy. These were the English, satisfied with their still-efficient longbow; and the Swiss, who relied primarily upon their deadly pikes. The French, who developed the finest artillery and artillerymen of the era, were strangely slow in adopting gunpowder small arms; it would take a disaster at Pavia in the following century (see p. 474) to make them realize the dangers of their almost total dedication to cannon. The Spanish seem to have done more than other nationalities to exploit both cannon and small arms, while minimizing the limitations of these weapons by continued utilization of pike and sword, and by skillful employment of field fortifications. As a result, at the close of the century Spain had the finest and best-balanced military force in the world.

Small Arms

At the outset of the century there was no real distinction between artillery pieces and small arms, other than size and portability. Those iron tubes small enough to be carried onto the battlefield by an infantry soldier were called "fire sticks" or "hand cannon." They were usually about 2 or 3 feet in length, with a bore of a half inch, or greater, and frequently the tubes were strapped to a pike handle. Later, for convenience the butt ends of these hand cannon were often fitted with short wooden sleeves, or cases, which could be held under the armpit or, more usually, rested on the ground or on objects of convenient height, such as a rock, a window, a wagon,

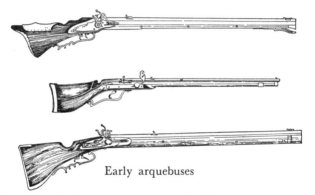

Early arquebuses

or a forked stick. The Hussites were apparently the first to attempt to aim such pieces from the shoulder.

Powder, poured into the tube, was held in place by cloth or paper tamping, as was the projectile (an iron or leaden ball or slug), pushed in on top of the powder. At the beginning of the century, this powder charge was ignited, as in the case of larger artillery pieces, by means of a slow-burning "match": a cord or tightly twisted rag which had been soaked in saltpeter and then dried out. Like the "punk" of a modern Fourth of July, this would smolder (unless extinguished by rain) and would ignite priming powder sprinkled in the "pan" (a slight depression on top of the tube); the pan was connected to the powder charge inside by a touchhole, also filled with priming powder. The difficulties of loading, aiming, and firing such a weapon are self-evident. Accuracy in range and in direction was impossible. Thus these weapons had little direct effect on tactics or the conduct of war. They could supplement, but not replace, the more manageable longbow and crossbow.

Sometime before mid-15th century these crude noisemakers were transformed into weapons of significance by development of the matchlock. An S-shaped mechanism attached to the side of the gun, referred to as a "serpentine," held a burning match, usually of cord, which could be applied to the priming powder of the pan and touchhole (moved to the side of the gun for convenience and also for protection from rain) by means of a trigger. Thus the operator of the gun could hold the wooden butt piece against his shoulder, while aiming and firing the weapon in much the same manner as a modern shoulder gun. Sometime after midcentury this led to another improvement, in which the butt piece became a curved or bent stock, which could be held against the shoulder more conveniently and more comfortably. Because of this crooked stock, the modified weapon was called a "hackbut" (in German) or "arquebus" (in French)—literally meaning "hookgun." Here, for the first time, was a truly usable small-arms gunpowder weapon, as manageable as crossbow or longbow, and with substantially greater destructive power than either—although its effective range of barely 100 yards was less than that of the bows. This remained the standard infantry weapon for the next century.

Artillery

By the beginning of the century practically every European army had some artillery weapons, and cannon had been introduced into Asia by the Turks. These simple tubes—mostly cast iron or wrought iron, but sometimes built up from iron bars encased with hoops—were almost exclusively used for seige operations, or for the defense of fortifications. Moved from place to place on ox-drawn sledges, these bombards, as they were mostly called, had to be emplaced on mounds of earth or on locally constructed log platforms. Thus they were totally unsuited for mobile warfare and could not be considered as prototypes of field artillery. Projectiles were either iron or stone. The art of cutting stone cannon balls was well developed by midcentury.

As the techniques of casting and gunmaking improved and the methods of handling the crude and unstable powder mixture were perfected among "master gunners," bombards became increasingly effective in the attack and defense of fortified places. They grew in size so that the Turkish bombards at the siege of Constantinople included 70 heavy pieces, of which 12 were particularly large, including one 19-ton monster, firing stone balls up to 1,500 pounds in weight for a distance of more than a mile. Because of the effects of recoil, and the need to replace the cannon in position after each shot, these weapons could fire only about 7 rounds per day.

Most cannon were muzzle-loaders, but breechloading bombards were not uncommon. The breechloaders were prone to accident, however, due to lack of adequate sealing (or obturation, as modern artillerymen call it) to prevent explosive gases from escaping to the rear, and thus soon became unpopular. All weapons were smoothbore, although the first experiments with rifling may have begun in Germany at the end of the century.

The greatest advances in gunmaking and in gunnery throughout the century were made in France. French artillery ascendancy was begun about 1440 by the Bureau brothers (see p. 425), and was a major factor in the sudden and overwhelming French victory in the Hundred Years' War. The Bureaus used their cannon to batter down the walls of English-held castles with amazing rapidity. The improvement in siege artillery during the early 15th century is demonstrated by the contrast of the length of the sieges in Henry V's campaigns in Normandy (exemplified by the 5- and 6-month investments of Rouen and Cherbourg in 1418 and 1419) with the brief sieges which marked the speedy French reconquest of the province in 1449–1450. By the end of the century, artillery had made medieval fortification obsolete—this, to a degree, was because castles and walled cities had found no way to emplace large cannon suitable for counterbattery.

Artillery also played a significant part in the two most important field battles of the concluding phase of the Hundred Years' War: Formigny and Castillon (see pp. 417 and 418). It should be noted, however, that the culverins (relatively light long-range cannon) and bombards which facilitated these French victories had in each instance been previously emplaced for siege operations, and were merely shifted in direction to repulse English relieving armies.

The one approach to the concept of field artillery in the first part of the century was in the wagon forts of John Ziska in the Hussite wars (see p. 432). He put bombards in the intervals between his wagons. The fire of these cannon, combined with that of infantrymen armed with handguns, invariably repulsed the attacks of

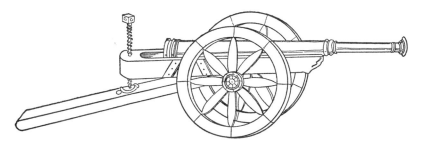

Fifteenth-century culverin

German, Hungarian, and Polish cavalrymen and infantrymen, setting the stage for Ziska's typical climactic counterattack. But these guns were always emplaced in the *wagenburg* prior to battle, on ground selected in advance by Ziska; they were useless if the enemy did not attack.

True field artillery made a sudden and dramatic appearance in the final decade of the century when the French—still pre-eminent artillerists—mounted new and relatively light cast-bronze cannon on two-wheeled carriages pulled by horses. The new mobile French field artillery could be quickly unharnessed and unlimbered on the battlefield and, by going promptly into action from a march column, played an important part of the significant French victory of Fornovo.

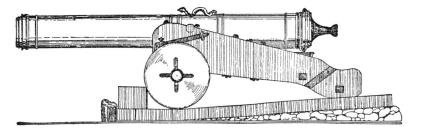

Medium bombard

It was during this decade that the French also introduced the concept of the trunnion, which facilitated both the mounting of cannon on permanent wheeled carriages and relatively accurate aiming and ranging—in sharp distinction to the earlier awkward methods of raising and lowering the weapon's bore. Some, but certainly not all, of the French cannon at Fornova probably had trunnions, and could be elevated or depressed for ranging without the need for digging holes under the trail or putting the wheels on blocks.

FORTIFICATION AND SIEGECRAFT

There were no real developments in fortifications in this century. A refinement of some importance was the general adoption of stone machicolation on the upper ramparts of the permanent walls of castles and fortified towns. Extending out over the tops of the walls, these permitted the defenders to fire down (or pour boiling oil, or the like) through narrow slits directly on attackers at the base of a wall or tower without incurring much danger in the process. Prior to this, machicolation had been in the form of wooden galleries or "hoardings" hung over the tops of walls; these had been vulnerable to incendiary missiles and to pulverizing blows from siege machines or early bombards.

All existing fortifications were rendered obsolete in this century by the growing strength of siege artillery (see p. 403). Another important use of gunpowder was in mining operations, which thus became even more formidable than in earlier times. The most dramatic demonstration of the effectiveness of these new gunpowder techniques in siegecraft (particularly artillery bombardment) occurred at the siege of Constantinople. The walls had unquestionably fallen into some decay, but they were still fundamentally the same massive fortifications which had defied so many attacks for so many centuries. The effective artillery of Mohammed II, assisted by mining operations, battered down these walls and brought the siege to a successful conclusion in a mere 55 days.

TACTICS OF LAND WARFARE

General

The importance and value of well-trained, well-disciplined infantry continued to grow in this century, to the degree that infantry could undertake successful offensive action against cavalry, as well as against other infantry, either on its own or in combination with cavalry. In the case of the superbly disciplined and trained Swiss pikemen—and their German imitators, the **landsknechts**—successful infantry offensive tactics were not in the slightest dependent upon missile weapons—bows, handguns or artillery. They were virtually a reincarnation of the Macedonian phalanx. By the close of the century, however, both Swiss and landsknechts were enhancing the morale and momentum effects of their terrifying, inexorable charges by the use of arquebusiers. The employers of these mercenary pikemen obtained the maximum value from them by fitting them into a combined-arms team with heavy and light cavalry. By the end of the century the French had made this into the prototype of the infantry-cavalry-artillery team which dominated land warfare tactics for more than four centuries.

English and French Infantry Tactics

The actual and moral ascendancy of the English infantry defensive tactics over Continental chivalry was reaffirmed early in the century by the almost unbroken string of successes won by Henry V and his brother **John of Bedford.** Joan of Arc's subsequent inspirational success did not change the fundamental technical superiority of disciplined, heavily armored pikemen, flexibly supported by powerful missile weapons, in defensive formation against medieval heavy cavalry, on horse or on foot.

The final French successes of the Hundred Years' War, in fact, substantiated the superiority of good infantry on the defense, when well supported by missiles. The Bureau brothers merely added to the power of the missiles by substituting their new artillery weapons for longbows and crossbows.

The Hussite Tactical System

This same lesson was also being given to the chivalry of Germany and Eastern Europe by John Ziska and his Hussites. Ziska had apparently noted the effectiveness of Russian and Lithuanian wagon laagers in defense against Tartar, Polish, and Teutonic Knight cavalry. He also noted that the wagon defenders were lost if a combined cavalry and infantry attack could penetrate the laager. From this lesson he developed one of the simplest and most effective tactical systems in history.

The Hussites moved in columns of horse-drawn carts or wagons, most of which were armor-plated, the sides pierced with loopholes. Inside these protected wagons, or on other open four-wheeled carts, he carried a number of small bombards. His troops were mostly footmen, highly disciplined by the intensive training and control methods established by Ziska in his Mount Tabor stronghold; a number of these were armed with handguns; most were pikemen. In addition he had a small force of lightly armored cavalrymen, probably lancers on the Polish model, used for reconnaisssance and for counterattack. Although good at siegecraft, Ziska always avoided an offensive battle in the open. His strategy was to penetrate as far as possible into enemy territory and then to select a good defensive position upon which to establish a wagon fort. Hussite raids from the wagon base inevitably forced the foe to disastrous attack.

The wagons were formed into a laager and linked together by chains. In front of this wall of wagons a ditch was dug by camp followers—who were also ammunition carriers. In the intervals between wagons he placed his bombards—possibly on their four-wheeled carts, but more likely on earthen mounds or heavy wooden platforms. Also in these intervals, and firing from the wagon loopholes, were his handgun operators and crossbowmen. Pikemen were available to protect the bombards and to prevent enemy infantry from cutting the chains holding the wagons together. They rarely had to perform these missions, however, since the attackers were more often than not repulsed by the firepower of the *wagenburg*. As soon as an attack was repulsed, Ziska's pikemen and cavalry charged to counterattack, sealing the victory.

Though Ziska did not introduce true field artillery, and did not use gunpowder weapons in a tactically offensive role, his was a most imaginative and offensive-minded use of field fortifications, and his battles were classics of defensive-offensive tactics. The *wagenburg,* however, could not be properly established if the enemy army was alert and aggressive. After the death of Ziska, his successors were unable to seize and maintain his strategic initiative. Furthermore, the wagon fort was extremely vulnerable to true field artillery and to efficient small arms; thus it was soon outmoded.

The Swiss Tactical System

It was the Swiss who really brought infantry back into offensive warfare for the first time since the decline of the Roman legion. A relatively poor mountain people, without horses, the lightly armed, lightly armored Swiss foot soldiers had been forced to fight their wars for independence against the Hapsburgs by making the best possible use of their local resources and of the difficulties of their mountain terrain. In the process they had discovered the benefits of mobility which they gained through lack of encumbrances, and had also rediscovered the ancient Greek concept of the massed shock of a body of pikemen charging downhill. Like the Greeks and Macedonians, they had also learned that this same principle would work on level ground if the pikemen could maintain their massed formation without gaps and without faltering in the face of a cavalry charge. If they could press their own attack home with speed and vigor, the massed pikes could be more terrifying to horse and rider than the cavalryman was to the pikeman.

To exploit this lesson required excellent organization, rigorous training, and iron discipline of a sort unseen since Roman times. The determined Swiss met these challenges, and produced forces comparable to the Macedonian phalanxes in maneuverability, cohesiveness, and shock power. As a result, by midcentury they were universally recognized as incomparably the finest troops in the world.

As with the Macedonians, the principal Swiss weapon was a 21-foot pike, consisting of an 18-foot wooden shaft topped by a 3-foot iron shank which defied desperate slashes of attacking cavalry swords. They marched in cadence, often to music, the first to do so since the Romans. Again like the Macedonians, they had a variety of formations—such as line, wedge, square—which they could adopt in prompt, systematic, orderly fashion. For the most part, however, they marched and fought in heavy columns, with a frontage rarely exceeding 30 men, but often 50 to 100 men deep.

In addition to the basic pikemen, Swiss formations included a few crossbowmen —later handgunmen and arquebusiers—as skirmishers, and a number of halberdiers in the interior files of the column or phalanx. The principal task of the halberdiers was to cut down individual horsemen in a melee, when the pikemen had stopped or repulsed a cavalry charge.

Whenever possible, the Swiss marched directly and rapidly into combat from march column. There was no deploying, no delay of any sort in going through the formality of establishing a battle line. They usually fought in 3 columns, or phalanxes, echeloned to the left or right rear. If the countryside would permit, the individual columns would march on parallel roads, or across country, in the same relationship as they planned for action. If only one route was available, the first group would march directly ahead into the fight, the others peeling off to the left or right, as the case might be, then hurrying up on the flank of the first column.

The Swiss scorned cannon, and during the 15th century did not fully understand the vulnerability of their own massed columns to effective artillery fire— mainly because up to that time there had been no real field artillery. Charles the Bold of Burgundy recognized this Swiss vulnerability to cannon and small-arms fire, but his own rashness prevented him from exploiting his relatively advanced tactical ideas (see pp. 428–429).

No other infantry in Europe could stand up to the Swiss, and by the end of the century their moral as well as tactical ascendancy was complete. Although they hired themselves out as mercenaries indiscriminately, more often than not they provided the principal infantry component of the French armies of the late 15th century. Maximilian of Hapsburg, plagued by this as much as by his wars with Switzerland, tried to offset the Swiss infantry advantages by creating a German counterpart: the landsknechts. Organized, trained, and equipped just like their model, the landsknecht mercenaries were soon nearly as sought after as the Swiss themselves. Strangely, however, whenever Swiss and landsknechts were pitted against each other, although the struggle was always fierce and bloody, the Swiss were invariably victorious. They seem to have been even more ferocious and bloodthirsty against their German imitators than against any other foe.

Cavalry Tactics

The frustration experienced by Western European heavy cavalry in action against English infantry in the 14th century was intensified by the appearance of the Swiss tactical system and the advent of firearms. No real solution to this problem had been found by the end of this century. Heavy cavalry lingered on as a major element of all of the West European armies, since in conjunction with other arms it was still effective in a climactic charge or counterattack against an enemy thrown into confusion by artillery fire, or by a prior infantry encounter. The disciplined French **gendarmes** were the best European heavy cavalry.

As a compromise, however, more lightly armed and armored horsemen began to appear in Western Europe. Some Westerners who had participated in the Turkish wars of Eastern Europe had noted the effectiveness of the relatively lightly armed and armored Hungarian, Turkish, and Albanian cavalry, who combined discipline and some shock power, on the one hand, with the mobility and flexibility of unarmored light cavalry, on the other. These were mixed horse archers and lancers, quite similar in organization, armament, and tactics to the old Byzantine cataphract, though less heavily armored. The Venetians seem to have introduced Albanian cavalry of this variety, called **stradiots,** into their wars in north Italy at the end of the century, and their example was quickly followed by the French. The term stradiot began to be used in Western Europe for any cavalry of this intermediate genre, whether or not they were actually Albanians. The similar Spanish **genitours** (see p. 282) also began to appear in Italy about the same time.

This was the first step in a series of major transformations in European cavalry, which did not really regain effectiveness until the next century.

MILITARY ORGANIZATION

At the beginning of the century only the English and the Ottoman Turks had armies which approximated regular standing forces. Both accomplished this by modifying, without eliminating, the traditional pattern of feudal levies.

English armies were raised by contract, along the lines established by Edward III (see p. 335). Each knight or noble who had the influence, wealth, or ability contracted with the king to raise a force of given size for foreign operations. In addition to the funds disbursed by the royal treasury for such contracts, the leaders and their men were also attracted by prospects of loot. The English kings and great nobles usually had a substantial number of English fighting men engaged in local conflicts in France, as well as along the Scottish border. This led to the growth of a reserve of battle-experienced men in England who would flock to the king's colors for any major expedition to the north or across the Channel.

The Ottoman sultans avoided any hereditary feudal relationship insofar as possible. In particular, they made a point of bestowing newly conquered land in Europe or Asia to the most deserving of their warriors. Thus a noble who raised a large effective force for the sultan's wars could hope to share in the distribution of lands gained by that war. Similarly, young, impecunious soldiers could gain lands and riches by performing well in combat. The result was that the sultans had no difficulty in raising excellent enthusiastic forces, with war naturally feeding upon conquest.

The Turkish armies were composed mostly of cavalry, the feudal levies being lightly armored horse archers or lancers of the stradiot variety. Constant experience in warfare assured competence, and although these feudal levies could not stand up against the heavily armored Western men-at-arms, their lesser shock capability was somewhat offset by greater mobility and maneuverability. The nuclei of the Turkish armies were the highly trained and disciplined Janissary infantry units—never more than 10,000 strong in this century—and the sultan's horse guards. These cavalry guardsmen, called **spahis,** were lancers somewhat more heavily armored than the feudal cavalry. Turkish armies also included large numbers of irregular light horse and light infantry, useful for reconnaissance and pursuit but of little use in pitched battles.

In Western Europe—and particularly in war-torn France—nobles and kings relied extensively upon mercenary contingents to provide the continuity and professional competence and experience missing from their short-term feudal levies. In time of peace, however, these free companies, as they were called, were deadly menaces, pillaging, looting, and murdering indiscriminately. They were too strong to be dealt with by the feudal levies, and so rulers tried to entice them out of the country or to hire them for foreign expeditions which hopefully would provide enough loot to pay their wages.

The French solution to the problem of the free companies, apparently recommended to Charles VII by Constable **Arthur de Richemont,** was to establish a standing army. Fifteen, later 20, **compagnies d'ordonnance** were established, each under the command of a reliable noble captain. Each company consisted of 100 "lances" of 6 men each: a knight or man-at-arms (now known as a gendarme), a squire, two archers, a valet, and a page. All were mounted; the man-at-arms and squire were typical heavy cavalrymen of the era; the two "archers" were sometimes mounted infantrymen, who might or might not be archers and sometimes were additional gendarmes; the valet and page were scarcely soldiers, although they were foragers and sometimes acted as light cavalry for reconnaissance purposes. The men were well paid and were provided liberal rations. Thus there was no need to pillage. Their only loyalty was to the king.

These companies were quartered in various regions of France, and absorbed a number of the free companies, both en masse and individually. Quickly they established law and order, the remaining mercenaries soon going elsewhere—mainly to the **condottiere** companies in Italy.

Establishment of the *compagnies d'ordonnance* was the death knell of feudalism as a military and social system, and the true beginning of standing armies and professionalism in modern warfare.

Less successful was the simultaneous French effort to set up a centralized semipermanent militia force of some 16,000 men (1448). They were called "free archers," since they were armed with bows, and were exempted from taxes. This was another step away from feudalism, but due to shortcomings in training and administration the "free archers" proved ineffective and soon disappeared.

WESTERN EUROPE

THE HUNDRED YEARS' WAR—PHASE TWO, 1396–1457

The Uneasy Truce, 1396–1413

The 30-year Truce of Paris (1396) was intended by the rival monarchs—**Richard II** of England and **Charles VI** of France—to terminate the war. Internal instability in both countries, however, contributed to continuing small-scale violence,

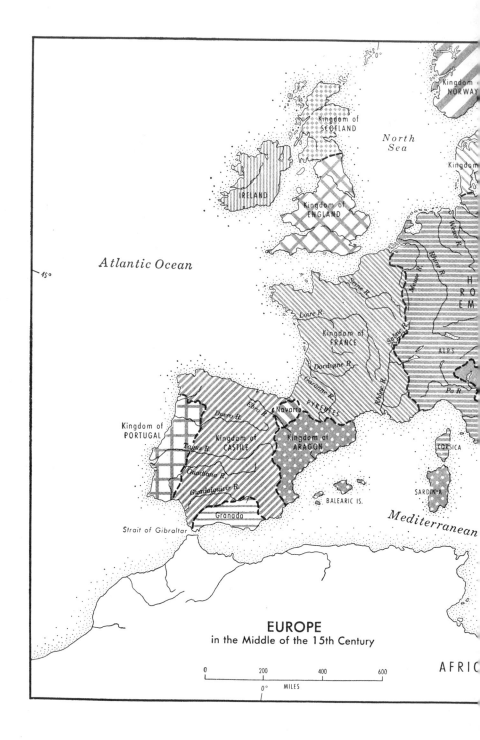

EUROPE
in the Middle of the 15th Century

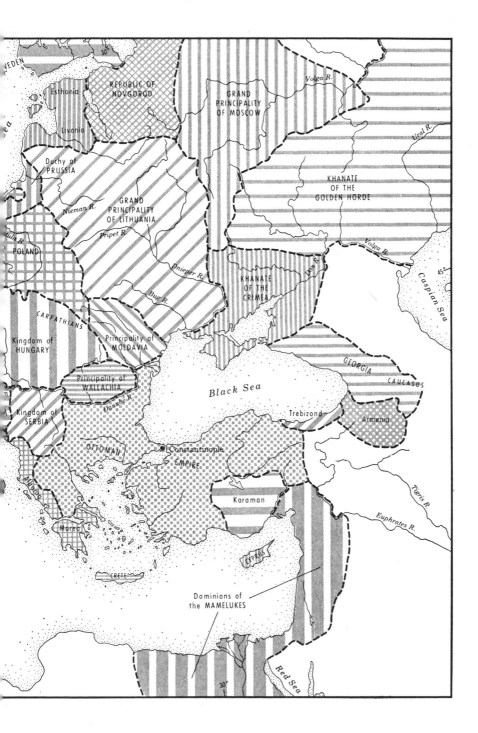

each ruler implicitly encouraging raids and revolts. In England central authority was soon re-established under strong kings **Henry IV** and **Henry V** (see pp. 418–419). In France, however, the intermittent insanity of Charles VI prompted a power struggle between the rival dukedoms of Orléans and Burgundy which soon grew to full-scale civil war. The principal events were:

1402. French Support to Scotland. French troops (primarily Orléanist) assisted a Scottish invasion of England (see p. 419).

1403. French Raids on the English Coast. Plymouth and other English Channel ports were ravaged while Henry IV was preoccupied with scattered revolts (see p. 419).

1405. French Support to Wales. French troops assisted Welsh rebel **Owen Glendower** (see p. 419).

1406. French Attacks on English Possessions in France. The Burgundians and Or-

léanists temporarily collaborated in operations in Vienne and against Calais.

1407, November 24. Burgundian Assassination of Duke Louis of Orléans. This led to full-scale war between the Burgundians and Orléanists. An important anti-Burgundian role was played by Count **Bernard of Armagnac;** thus the royal (or Valois, or Orléanist) faction was also called Armagnac.

1411. French Appeals to England. Both Orléanists and Burgundians sought aid from Henry IV.

The Period of Henry V, 1413–1428

Young King Henry V, one of the strongest and most vigorous rulers of English history, seized the opportunity created by anarchy in France to attempt ending the war on the basis envisaged by his great-grandfather (Edward III). After adroit diplomacy assured the neutrality of **John the Fearless,** Duke of Burgundy, Henry invaded France and won an overwhelming victory against a far larger French army at Agincourt, a battle in the Crécy and Poitiers pattern. Most Orléanist leaders were killed in the disaster, permitting the Burgundians to gain ascendancy in strife-torn France. During the 4½ years following Agincourt, Henry systematically conquered Normandy, then advanced on Paris. The French government, then dominated by John of Burgundy, submitted to Henry in the Treaty of Troyes, in which Charles VI disinherited his son, the Dauphin **Charles,** declared Henry his heir, and gave Henry his daughter **Catherine** in marriage. Henry spent the following 2 years consolidating northern France, but died suddenly as he was preparing to move into south-central France, where the Dauphin still had some following. Charles VI died soon after; infant **Henry VI** was declared King of France as well as of England, and John, Duke of Bedford, younger brother of Henry V, acting as regent in France, continued consolidation of English authority. The Dauphin set up a rival court in the city of Bourges, and delayed English conquest of France with Breton assistance. Bedford defeated the combined armies of the Dauphin and the Duke of Brittany at Avranches, thus finally eliminating all opposition to English control in northern and western France. He then renewed preparations for an invasion of the province of Berry, south of the Loire, in order to overthrow the last center of Valois resistance. The principal events were:

1413, May. Alliance of Henry V with John of Burgundy. John promised neutrality in return for increased territory as Henry's vassal. Henry began preparations for an invasion of France.

1415, April. Henry's Declaration of War on Charles VI of France. He sailed for Nor-

mandy with an army of 12,000 men (August 10).

1415, August 13–September 22. Siege of Harfleur. Henry finally captured the city after his army had been depleted by casualties and disease.

THE CAMPAIGN OF AGINCOURT, OCTOBER 10–24, 1415

For obscure reasons, Henry decided to march overland from Harfleur to Calais (October 10). He may have hoped to entice the French into a battle, although—considering the circumstances of his army (now about 9,000 men), his selected line of march, the fact that he took no artillery or heavy baggage, and the speed with which he moved—this is very doubtful. On the other hand, the apparent rashness of the move is hard to reconcile with Henry's normally deliberate nature. Moving more than 14 miles a day, despite torrential rains, he headed directly for the Ford of Blanchetaque, where Edward III had crossed in the Crécy campaign. Finding this blocked by local feudal levies, he headed eastward, up the Somme River, seeking an undefended crossing. All the bridges were down, or strongly defended, and the fords were either defended or impassable due to high waters. Finally at Athies, 10 miles southeast of Péronne, he found an undefended crossing (October 19). Meanwhile, a French army of more than 30,000 men, under the Constable of France, Charles d'Albret, had pursued from Rouen in two divisions. Barely failing to intercept the English, the French crossed the Somme at Abbéville and Amiens, joined at Corbie, and then moved northeast via Péronne and Bapaume. Apparently well informed of Henry's advance, d'Albret took a blocking position on the main road north toward Calais near the castle of Agincourt. Here the French were found by the English on the afternoon of October 24. Henry was apparently ready to negotiate. His army was isolated, its line of retreat blocked by the French. The English had been short of food, and had barely subsisted by plundering the countryside. In turn the local inhabitants had harassed the English column, killing many stragglers and pillagers. There was some inconclusive parleying, but the French, confident of victory, were in no mood to offer concessions, and Henry would not give up his claim to the French throne.

It has been suggested that d'Albret should have attacked as soon as the English army appeared. Save for a few hours' rest which this gave the English, it is doubtful if the delay contributed to the factors which determined the outcome the following day. D'Albret, a disciple of Du Guesclin, had planned a defensive battle. During the evening, however, the more impetuous French nobility pleaded with him to attack, confident of their more than 3–1 superiority and aware of the generally low physical condition of the English army.

BATTLE OF AGINCOURT, OCTOBER 25, 1415

At daybreak the English army was in position at the southern end of a defile—slightly over 1,000 yards in width—formed by heavy woods flanking the main road north to Calais. The open fields, between road and woods, were freshly plowed and sodden from recent heavy rains. The English—some 900 men-at-arms and 8,000 archers—were drawn up in three "battles" in the tactical formation proved so effective by Edward III at Crécy. The French army was also deployed in three main battles, one behind the other, due to the narrowness of the defile. The first two French battles consisted primarily of dismounted men-at-arms, and the third of mounted men. A few crossbowmen were uselessly placed behind each division. In the rear was the infantry. For some three hours the two armies faced each other at opposite ends of the wooded defile, probably a little more than a mile apart. D'Albret, apparently relying on Henry's unfounded reputation for youthful recklessness, seems still to have hoped for an English attack. Henry, deciding late in the morning to entice a French assault, ordered a cautious advance of approximately half a mile. Coming to a halt, the English resumed their usual formation, archers echeloned for-

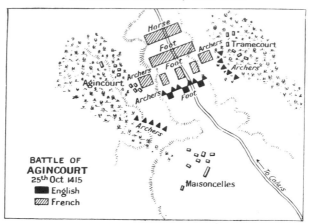

ward in V's in the intervals between the battles of dismounted men-at-arms and pikemen. Archers on the flanks evidently infiltrated forward for 100 yards or more in the edges of the woods. Those in the two V's in the center of the line quickly pounded stakes into the ground to form a palisade to impede a mounted attack.

The English advance had the desired effect. Unable to control his eager and undisciplined fellow nobles, who had "forgotten nothing and learned nothing," the French constable reluctantly ordered an advance. As the first battle of dismounted men-at-arms moved ponderously forward in their heavy armor, mounted contingents on each flank galloped past them toward the English lines. The experience of Crécy and Poitiers was repeated. A large proportion of these men, or their horses, was cut down by English arrows. The remainder, thrown into confusion by the hail of arrows, and moving slowly because of the soggy ground, were thrown back with heavy loss when they reached the thin but solid English line.

The cavalry attack had been completely repulsed before the first French battle, led by d'Albret himself, labored ponderously within range of the archers. The combination of the weight of their armor—even heavier than at the time of Poitiers—and the very difficult movement over the wet plowed fields had exhausted the French knights before they came within range of the English archers. French losses were heavy as they struggled through the mud for the last 100 yards, but nevertheless most of them reached the English line, and sheer weight of numbers bore the defenders back. But now the English archers, wielding swords and hatchets and axes, came out from behind their palisades and from the edges of the woods into gaps in the French line from the flank and rear, causing fearful destruction among the weary, terribly immobile French knights and men-at-arms. Within a few minutes every man in the first French battle had been cut down or captured.

Now, completely uncoordinated with their predecessors, the French second battle surged forward. This attack, however, was apparently not pushed with the same vigor or determination, and although losses were heavy the French knights fell back to re-form. Apparently joined by some of the mounted men of the third battle, they prepared for one final effort. At this moment Henry received a report that the French had attacked his camp, a mile to the rear. He ordered the slaughter of his prisoners, since he did not think his army was strong enough both to guard the prisoners and to meet attacks from front and rear. It turned out, however, that the feared envelopment had been only a rabble of French peasants seeking plunder. The third assault, furthermore, was halfhearted and was easily thrown back. The climax of this final phase of the battle was a charge by a few hundred English mounted men under Henry personally, completely dispersing the remnants of the French army.

French losses were at least 5,000 men of noble or gentle birth killed and another 1,000 captured. D'Albret was among the killed; the **Duke of Orléans** and the famed Marshal **Jean Bouciquaut** (see p. 386) were among the captured. Most of the important leaders of the Orléans-Armagnac faction were killed. Thus an important result of the Battle of Agincourt was to assure the ascendancy of the Burgundians in France. English losses were reportedly only 13 men-at-arms and about 100 footmen killed; it is likely that casualties were substantially greater than this.

1415, November. Return to England. Henry, taking no strategic advantage of his overwhelming tactical victory, marched to Calais and shortly thereafter returned to England. It is not clear whether this was due to a lack of strategic competence or to other factors. Evidently he was concerned by a threat to control the English Channel posed by a Genoese fleet, allies of the French. Also he seems to have developed considerable respect for the guerrilla fighting capabilities of the French peasants, who had caused him so much trouble on the march from Harfleur to Agincourt.

1416. A Year of Preparation. Henry built up a powerful fleet and drove the Genoese from the Channel. His recognition of the importance of control of the sea and his actions to secure it have led some historians to suggest him as the founder of the Royal Navy. He proved his skill and ability as a diplomat by obtaining the neutrality of the Emperor **Sigismund,** formerly an ally of France.

1417–1419. Return to France. Henry systematically conquered Normandy in 3 well-planned campaigns, notably different from the uncoordinated raids of Edward III three-quarters of a century earlier. The principal feature in these otherwise uneventful campaigns was the 5 months' siege of Rouen (September 1418–January 1419). In the following 6 months Henry completed consolidation of his conquest of Normandy save for the coastal fortress of Mont-Saint-Michel. He was now ready to move inland.

1418, May 29. Burgundian Capture of Paris. John of Burgundy, after taking the capital, massacred most of the remaining Armagnac and Orléanist leaders, with the notable exception of the Dauphin, Charles, who escaped to the south.

1419, September 10. Assassination of John of Burgundy. This took place during a truce, while he was in conference with the Dauphin on a bridge at Montereau. As a consequence, the Burgundians—now led by **Philip the Good** and sustained by Queen **Isabella,** wife of insane Charles VI —were confirmed in their support of the English alliance against the Dauphin and the Orléans-Armagnac faction.

1420, May. Henry Marches on Paris. He took advantage of the renewed bitterness in the French civil war.

1420, May 21. Treaty of Troyes. Henry became heir of Charles VI and virtual ruler of France.

1420–1422. Henry's Consolidation of Northern France. He intended to eliminate systematically all remaining Valois opposition north of the Loire before moving directly against the Dauphin. This culminated in the successful siege of Meaux (October, 1421–May, 1422), where Henry became ill.

1421, March 21. Battle of Baugé. A French raiding force surprised and defeated a small body of English under **Thomas, Duke of Clarence** (Henry's brother) in southern Normandy. Clarence was killed.

1422, August 31. Death of Henry V. His 9-month-old son, **Henry VI,** became King of England and heir of France.

1422, October 21. Death of Charles VI. Henry VI was declared King of France; John, Duke of Bedford was regent.

1422, October 31. The Dauphin Proclaimed Charles VII at Bourges. He made no other immediate effort to regain his birthright.

1422–1428. Bedford's Consolidation of Northern France. While John pursued his brother's strategy, Burgundian enthusiasm in support of English objectives waned.

1423, July 21. Battle of Cravant. A small

English and Burgundian army was victorious over a slightly larger French force, which included a Scottish contingent.

1424, August 17. Battle of Verneuil. Bedford defeated a larger French army in a battle fought in the Crécy-Agincourt pattern, although the French did attempt an envelopment, which was repulsed by archers of the English baggage guard. The principal French leaders were the **Duke of Alençon** and the Scots **John Stuart** and the **Earl Archibald of Douglas.** Alençon was captured and Douglas was killed.

1426, March 6. Battle of St. James (near Avranches). Bedford defeated **Arthur de Richemont,** Constable of France, forcing de Richemont's brother, the **Duke of Brittany,** to submit to the English.

1426–1428. Bedford Completes Consolidation of Northern France.

1428, September. English Advance to the South. The **Earl of Salisbury** moved from Paris with about 5,000 men to seize the Loire River crossing at Orléans as a preliminary to invasion of Berry, the principal stronghold of the Dauphin.

1428–1429. Siege of Orléans. Salisbury commenced operations (October 12) by eliminating the fortified French bridgehead south of the Loire. Mortally wounded by a cannon shot from across the river in the culmination of these assaults (October 24), he was succeeded by the **Earl of Suffolk.** In subsequent months Suffolk constructed a line of redoubts (**bastilles**) around the city on the north bank of the river. The English were so weak numerically that the blockade was incomplete, permitting a trickle of supplies and reinforcements to get into the beleaguered city, mainly via the river. The defenders, under **Jean, Count of Dunois** (the "Bastard of Orléans"), considerably outnumbered the besiegers, but French morale was so low, and the terror inspired by English victories so effective, that the French made no serious offensive effort.

1429, February 12. Battle of Rouvray (or "of the Herrings"). Sir **John Fastolf** (model for Shakespeare's Falstaff) successfully defended a supply convoy carrying Lenten rations to Suffolk's army from a French attack under the **Count of Clermont** and John Stuart. Fastolf formed his wagons, filled with salted herrings, into a laager and beat off the attackers.

Revival under Joan of Arc, 1429–1444

A deeply religious peasant girl from Champagne, 17-year-old **Joan of Arc,** partially convinced the Dauphin that she had a divinely inspired mission to help him to expel the English from France and to have him crowned as rightful king. Despite his doubts and the intense jealousy of most of his court, Charles put Joan in command of an army to relieve Orléans. Her inspirational, if untutored, leadership drove the English from their siege lines in defeat, and ended the myth of English invincibility. Joan won numerous subsequent victories, and engineered the triumphant coronation of the Dauphin as Charles VII, although she was subsequently repulsed in a rash attack on Paris. The following year she was captured by the Burgundians near Compiègne. Turned over to the English by the Burgundians, she was tried by a religious court on the orders of Bedford, who thus hoped to discredit Charles' coronation. Charles, who could have bargained for her release, made no effort to help her, and Joan was convicted and burned at the stake as a heretic. Her spirit, however, continued to inspire French fighting men. English morale, in turn, was shaken by the fear that they had killed a saint. Within 5 years of Joan's death, the Burgundians and Orléanists had ended their civil war, and the French had recaptured Paris. In the following 8 years the French were generally successful in small actions and sieges in northern France, causing the English to agree to a 5-year truce. The principal events were:

1429, February–April. The Emergence of Joan of Arc. She inspired new hope and determination in the Dauphin.

1429, April 27–29. Joan Reaches Orléans. Accompanied by the **Duke of Alençon,** she led a relief army of 3,000–4,000 men, plus supplies, from Blois, slipping past the British siege lines by boat along the river.

1429, May 5. The First Sortie. Joan led a successful attack on a British bastille north of the river.

1429, May 7. Relief of Orléans. Joan led an attack against the British-held fortified bridgehead on the south bank of the Loire. Despite a serious arrow wound, she remained in the forefront of desperate assaults, and was successful by nightfall. The British blockade was broken. Suffolk withdrew the next morning. Mistakenly, he divided his army into garrisons to retain English-held towns in the Loire Valley. In subsequent weeks Joan retook most of these towns.

1429, June 19. Battle of Patay. In a surprise attack, Joan's army smashed the forces of Lord **John Talbot,** culminating efforts to drive the English from the Loire Valley. Talbot was captured.

1429, June–July. French Resurgence. Under Joan's inspiration French morale soared, while that of the English plummeted. The peasants rose in guerrilla war against the English, despite Charles' lethargy and inaction. This unprecedented popular resistance marked the beginning of French nationalism. Joan captured Troyes, Châlons, and Rheims (July).

1429, July 16. Coronation of Charles VII at Rheims. This followed Joan's bold invasion of territory formerly dominated by the English. Henceforward Charles and his jealous court did everything in their power to hamper Joan and to restrict her influence.

1429, August. Arrival of English Reinforcements at Paris.

1429, September 8. Attack on Paris. Despite lack of royal support, Joan with a small force made an unsuccessful attack, in which she was wounded.

1430, May 23. Capture of Joan. She led a small relief force to Compiègne, which the English and Burgundians were besieging as part of Bedford's efforts to re-establish English control of the central Seine Valley. Leading a sortie that same day, she was captured by the Burgundians.

1431, May 30. Execution of Joan of Arc.

1431–1444. Continued Effect of Joan's Inspiration. Nobles and peasants continued to wage a partisan war against the English despite the apparent indifference and lethargy of Charles VII. Bedford manfully and skillfully opposed the French resurgence until his death (1435).

1435, September 21. Peace of Arras. This ended the Burgundian-Armagnac civil war, disrupting the Burgundian-English alliance.

1436, April. Recapture of Paris. The English garrison took refuge in the Bastille, but was starved into surrender.

1444, April 16. Truce of Tours. A 5-year peace.

The Triumph of Professionalism, 1444–1453

The end of the Burgundian-Armagnac civil war in France foreshadowed French victory, since England's population of 2½ million could scarcely hope to overcome a united nation of 15 million. The slight continuing English tactical advantage conferred by the longbow was offset by the higher morale and greater numbers of the French. Only a condition of internal anarchy in France—the result of depredations of thousands of soldiers demobilized at the end of the civil war—gave the English any hope of salvaging a substantial remnant of their former vast holdings in the north and west. But this was speedily dashed when otherwise inept Charles VII followed wise military advice to establish the basis of a disciplined standing army, leading to the emergence of history's first efficient and scientific artillery organization. When the 5-year Truce of Tours expired, the new French military organization had not only enforced internal peace and stability but had achieved a substantial technical and tactical superiority over the English. It took this revitalized, professional French army only 4 years to sweep the English completely out of France, save for one tiny foothold at Calais. The principal events were:

1444–1449. Reorganization of the French Army. (See p. 425.)

1449–1450. French Reconquest of Normandy. The **Duke of Somerset,** incompetent English commander in Normandy, surrendered **Rouen** (1449) and soon after was besieged in Caen (March, 1450).

1450, April 15. Battle of Formigny (near

Bailleul). Constable de Richemont, learning of the advance of an English relieving army of some 4,500 men toward Caen under Sir **Thomas Kyriel** and Sir **Matthew Gough,** sent the **Count of Clermont** with about 5,000 men to block the English advance. The English formed up in typical defensive formation, but the French, refusing to follow the Crécy-Agincourt pattern, moved up 2 culverins beyond each flank of the waiting English army. Out of longbow range, the cannon began a deliberate enfilade bombardment of the English line, causing considerable damage. Spontaneously the English archers on both flanks charged against the guns, which they briefly seized. At this point the French dismounted men-at-arms and infantry counterattacked to recapture the cannon, bringing on a general engagement. While the issue was still in doubt, French reinforcements struck the English flank. In the resulting rout, Gough and a few survivors fought their way to safety; most of the English, nearly 4,000 men, were killed.

1450, July 6. Surrender of Caen. De Richemont immediately advanced to invest Cherbourg.

1450, August 12. Surrender of Cherbourg. English rule in Normandy was ended.

1451. French Invasion of Guyenne. The Count of Dunois, with 6,000 men, made efficient use of an excellent artillery siege train, and soon captured Bordeaux (June 30) and Bayonne (August 20). Considerable overt and underground resistance continued, however, on the part of the nobles of Aquitaine, still loyal to the kings of England and feeling little identity with their French cousins.

1452, October. English Resurgence. In response to Aquitanian appeals, John Talbot, now **Earl of Shrewsbury,** landed near the mouth of the Garonne with 3,000 men. Much of the countryside rose to meet him and support him. Bordeaux opened its gates to the English.

1453, July 17. Battle of Castillon. Shrewsbury led an army to raise the siege of Castillon, then being attacked by **Jean Bureau,** French master of artillery. The well-entrenched French refused to fight in the open. In an effort to break through, Shrewsbury formed his army into a powerful attacking column, and dashed at what appeared to be the weakest point in the French lines. Accurate French artillery fire halted the English column. The French immediately counterattacked, smashing the English army. Shrewsbury was killed. This was Crécy, Poitiers, and Agincourt in reverse.

1453, October 19. Fall of Bordeaux. This virtually ended the Hundred Years' War, although there was some minor coastal activity, particularly French raids on the English coast, for the next 4 years. England retained only Calais on the coast of northern France.

THE BRITISH ISLES

England

THE LANCASTRIAN ERA, 1400–1455

Henry IV, who had seized the shaky throne of Richard II (see p. 365), dealt firmly and vigorously with continuing unrest. His brilliant son, **Henry V,** brought England to the pinnacle of power and prestige in the Middle Ages. His great victory at Agincourt (see p. 413), followed by a cautious and sound campaign of conquest, made him virtual ruler of northern and western France, and recognized heir to the French throne. His early death, however, caused a sudden reversal in the fortunes of his nation and his family. Infant **Henry VI** grew up a pious, weak, and mentally unbalanced ruler. At home the country was racked with anarchy, while abroad the Hundred Years' War was lost. Strong-willed Queen **Margaret** seized the reins of government during her husband's fits of insanity, but she and her favorites were unpopular with most English nobles, who turned to the leadership of **Richard, Duke of York,** the king's cousin. The principal events were:

1399–1413. Reign of Henry IV. He soon suppressed a revolt of adherents of Richard II (1400).

1402, September 14. Battle of Homildon Hill. The northern nobles, under the leadership of Lord **Henry** (Harry "Hotspur") **Percy,** overwhelmingly repulsed a Scottish raiding army under the Earl of Douglas in a typical English longbow defensive battle.

1402–1409. Revolt of Owen Glendower in Wales. A master of ambush and surprise, Glendower made use of his knowledge of the Welsh hills to fight a highly successful partisan war.

1402. Battle of Pilleth. One of Glendower's rare battles, in which he surprised and routed an English force under Sir **Edmund Mortimer** in a mountain defile,

1403–1408. Revolt of the Percys. Northern rebels, under "Hotspur" Percy, advanced deep into southwest England with some 4,000 men, planning to join Glendower. Henry interposed his army of 5,000 between the two rebellious allies, and at the **Battle of Shrewsbury** (July 21, 1403) defeated the Percys before Glendower could come up. Hotspur was killed. His father submitted, then rebelled again, and was defeated and killed at **Brahmam Moor** (1408).

1405. French Landing in Wales. Little was accomplished by this expedition in support of Glendower, and the disappointed French returned home toward the close of the year.

1405. Rebellion of Archbishop Scrope of York. This was promptly subdued by Henry.

1409. Defeat of Glendower. The English captured his stronghold of Harlech. Glendower disappeared, and Henry's troops gradually pacified Wales.

1413–1422. Reign of Henry V. A brave, resourceful, and calculating soldier and king. At the outset of the reign he suppressed a Lollard (heretical) uprising (1413–1414).

1413–1457. Conclusion of the Hundred Years' War. (See p. 418.)

1422–1461. Reign of Henry VI. This began under the regency of Duke **Humphrey of Gloucester** in England and John, Duke of Bedford in France, the infant king's uncles. Gloucester's rashness and ineptitude contributed greatly to the unrest which plagued the reign.

1437–1450. A Period of Growing Disorder.

1450. Cade's Rebellion in Kent and Sussex. **Jack Cade,** an ex-soldier, briefly occupied and pillaged London after defeating royalists in an ambush at the **Battle of Seven Oaks** (June 18). The rebels were driven from London by troops from the Tower, assisted by aroused London militiamen. A royal general pardon brought about collapse of the rebellion; Cade was later captured and executed for treason. **Richard, Duke of York,** governor of Ireland, returned to protect himself against accusations that he had inspired the rebellion.

1454, March 27. Richard Elected Protector by Parliament. This was during Henry VI's first fit of insanity.

1454, December. Richard Dismissed. The king having regained his sanity, he was persuaded by Queen Margaret to dismiss Richard from the government.

THE WARS OF THE ROSES, 1455–1485

The dismissal of Richard of York from the King's Council, and the assumption of dictatorial powers by Queen Margaret and the **Duke of Somerset,** prompted a revolt by Richard and his adherents, who included wealthy, powerful **Richard Neville, Earl of Warwick.** Five years of alternate violent conflict and political maneuvering followed, marked by treachery, murder, and wildly fluctuating fortunes. Richard was killed in battle, but his son Edward proclaimed himself **Edward IV,** and then crushed the Lancastrians in the sanguinary Battle of Towton. After nearly 10 years of relative peace, Edward and Warwick fell out due to Warwick's efforts to assume dictatorial powers. Edward cleverly outmaneuvered Warwick politically and militarily; the earl thereupon joined forces with Margaret to lead an invasion army from France, and temporarily replaced Henry VI on the throne. Warwick ("the kingmaker") was killed in the decisive Battle of Barnet. Edward reigned for 12 more peaceful and prosperous years, succeeded upon his death by his 13-year-old son, **Edward V. Richard, Duke of Gloucester,** younger brother of Edward IV, then usurped the throne. The House of York, left securely in control of England by Edward IV, was now threatened by a series of uprisings, which culminated in an invasion led by **Henry Tudor, Earl of Richmond,** leader of the revived Lancastrians. Richard, an able warrior, was defeated and killed by Tudor at the Battle of Bosworth because of the defection of most of his army. Henry Tudor ascended the throne as Henry VII.

Edward IV and his brother Richard were the best generals in this generally dull, sanguinary series of wars. Both sides adhered to the policy of "slay the nobles, spare the commons," which resulted in exceptionally high loss of life among the leaders. Both sides generally avoided pillage and massacre of civilians. The principal events were:

1455, May 22. First Battle of St. Albans. Richard of York and Warwick, marching on London with 3,000 men, defeated and killed Somerset, leading 2,000 Lancastrians. Richard seized Henry VI, had himself appointed Constable of England, and assumed almost dictatorial power.

1456–1459. Political Maneuvering. Mainly a power struggle between Queen Margaret and Richard. Henry, intermittently sane, was a pawn. Margaret and her adherents regained control of the king; York and his supporters were again dismissed from the government.

1459, September 3. Battle of Blore Heath. The **Earl of Salisbury** (father-in-law of Richard and father of Warwick) defeated and practically destroyed a Lancastrian force near Market Drayton.

1459, October. Flight of Richard and Warwick. A royal army under Henry and Margaret approached Richard's stronghold of Ludlow Castle; a number of his adherents treacherously abandoned him, forcing Richard to flee to Ireland (October 12); Warwick fled to Calais.

1460, June. Return of Warwick. Warwick and **Edward, Earl of March** (second son of Richard and later Edward IV) landed at Sandridge with a small army, then marched triumphantly to London, where the townspeople favored the Yorkists.

1460, July 18. Battle of Northampton. Warwick and Edward, aided by treachery and by a rainstorm which drenched the Lancastrians' gunpowder, defeated a royal army marching on London, and recaptured King Henry. Richard returned from Ireland, somewhat hesitantly claiming the crown. In a compromise, Parliament proclaimed him heir to the throne, which Henry was to retain during his life. This

disinherited **Edward,** Prince of Wales, the infant son of Margaret and Henry. Margaret, having fled to Wales, went to northern England and raised a new Lancastrian army. Richard and his eldest son **Edmund** led an army north to deal with the main Lancastrian threat, while his second son, Edward, took another force to subdue uprisings in the west.

1460, December. Battle of Wakefield. The Lancastrians, inspired by Margaret, ambushed the Yorkists, Richard and Edmund both being killed. The Lancastrian army moved slowly south toward London, pillaging freely in areas suspected of Yorkist sympathies. As a result much of southern England was alienated against the Lancastrian cause.

1461, February 2. Battle of Mortimer's Cross (near Leominster). Edward, now Duke of York as the result of the death of his father and brother, defeated a Lancastrian army under the **Earl of Pembroke** and pursued the fugitives into the mountains. A number of captured Lancastrian nobles were summarily executed, initiating the brutality which marked the remainder of this war.

1461, February 17. Second Battle of St. Albans. Warwick's Yorkist army intercepted Margaret's troops advancing toward London. Warwick was defeated, and King Henry recaptured by the Lancastrians. Warwick withdrew to the southwest, where he joined young Edward, returning hastily toward London (February 22). While the Lancastrians continued a slow, triumphant advance toward London, Edward and Warwick rushed to the capital, where Edward proclaimed himself King (March 4). In the face of this unexpected development, Margaret and the

Lancastrian army withdrew to Yorkshire. Edward pursued (March 19), defeating a delaying force at **Ferrybridge** on the Aire River (March 28).

1461, March 29. Battle of Towton. Fought in a blinding blizzard, this was probably the most sanguinary battle ever fought on English soil. The exact sizes of the two armies are not known, but Edward apparently had more than 15,000 men, and was opposed by about 20,000 Lancastrians. Edward took advantage of the poor visibility to send out a skirmish line of archers under Lord **Thomas Fauconberg** (Thomas the Bastard) to contact the Lancastrians. The Yorkist archers fired a few volleys and hastily fell back. The Lancastrian archers, replying blindly to this fire, used up most of their arrows in a barrage that fell on empty ground. Edward then attacked, his own vigor and inspirational qualities finally assuring victory. Exact casualties are unknown, but conservative estimates suggest approximately 9,000 men dead on both sides, and presumably at least an equal number wounded—more than 50% casualties. Henry VI, Margaret, and Prince Edward fled to Scotland.

1461–1471. Sporadic Lancastrian Uprisings. All were suppressed by Edward and Warwick.

1464, April 25. Battle of Hedgeley Moore (near Wooler). Lord Montague (Warwick's brother) defeated Sir **Ralph Percy,** who was killed.

1464, May 15. Battle of Hexham. Montague defeated another Lancastrian army, accompanied by both Henry VI and Queen Margaret. Following this battle, widespread executions crushed the Lancastrian cause. Margaret and Prince Edward fled to France; Henry went into hiding in a monastery in northern England, where he was found a year later, and imprisoned in the Tower of London.

1469. Rebellion of Robin of Redesdale. This Lancastrian rising in the north was really inspired by Warwick, who, with Edward's younger brother, **George, Duke of Clarence,** was plotting to seize power. Edward left London, planning to join a hurriedly raised army in the north, assembling under the **Earl of Pembroke.** Before Edward arrived, however, the rebels had defeated Pembroke and the **Earl of Devon** at the **Battle of Edgecote,** near Banbury.

Edward, joined by Warwick and Clarence, who had followed him north with a large army, now became a virtual prisoner of the plotters. During subsequent months, however, Edward made skillful political use of his influence with the Yorkist nobility to re-establish power. As a result Warwick began to negotiate secretly with the Lancastrians.

1470, March. Lancastrian Uprising in the North. This was defeated near Empington, Rutlandshire, by a royal army at the **Battle of "Lose-Coat" Field.** The rebel leader, Sir **Robert Welles,** was captured and confessed that the rising had been provoked by Warwick, with the intention of making Clarence the king. Warwick and Clarence fled to France. There, through the mediation of King **Louis XI,** Warwick was reconciled with Margaret and plans were made for a new Lancastrian effort with French support.

1470, September–October. Uprising in Yorkshire. This was inspired by Warwick, to attract Edward away from London. With the king in the north, Warwick and Clarence landed at Dartmouth and marched rapidly to London. Warwick released Henry VI from prison in the Tower and restored him to the throne. Edward, finding himself caught between the northern rebels and Warwick's growing army in the south, fled to Flanders to seek support from his brother-in-law, **Charles the Bold** of Burgundy.

1471, March. Return of Edward. Sailing from Flushing with about 1,500 men—mostly German and Flemish mercenaries—he eluded a Lancastrian fleet and landed at Ravenspur (in the Humber estuary). He marched quickly south, evading an army under the **Earl of Northumberland** (one of Warwick's many brothers), to Nottingham (March 23), where he learned that Warwick was assembling an army at Coventry. The **Earl of Oxford** was to his left at Newark with another Lancastrian army. Feinting toward Newark, then toward Coventry (March 29), Edward slipped south, gathering adherents as he went. Of these the most important was his brother, the Duke of Clarence, who changed sides to rejoin him (April 3). Continuing southward, Edward entered London (April 11). Warwick, whose army was now combined with those of Northumberland and Oxford, followed, and Edward marched out to meet him (April 12).

1471, April 14. Battle of Barnet. Edward had approximately 9,000 troops, Warwick about 12,000. The battle began in the early morning, in a heavy fog. As the two armies groped for each other blindly, the right wing of each overlapped the left flank of the other. The Lancastrian right, under Oxford, defeated the Yorkist left, under **Lord Hastings,** while the Yorkist right under Richard of Gloucester (Edward's younger brother) was having comparable success in enveloping the Lancastrian left. Oxford's men pursued Hastings' routed wing. With considerable difficulty Oxford reassembled some of his men and attempted to rejoin the battle. Because of the mutual envelopments of the opposing left flanks, both armies had swung about at almost a right angle to their original front. In the fog Oxford's men blundered into the rear of his own center, under the **Earl of Somerset,** causing most of the Lancastrians to assume that they had been betrayed by treachery within their own ranks. In the ensuing rout, Warwick was cut down and killed. Margaret and Prince Edward landed in southwestern England that same day.

1471, April–May. Tewkesbury Campaign. Learning of the Barnet disaster and joining forces with the remnants of Warwick's army, now under Somerset, Margaret and Prince Edward attempted to reach Lancastrian strongholds in Wales. Edward hastily remobilized his army and marched rapidly from London, hoping to prevent the Lancastrian army from reaching Wales. He caught up with them near Tewkesbury (May 3) after both armies had made a series of grueling forced marches.

1471, May 4. Battle of Tewkesbury. The outnumbered Lancastrians took up a strong position on a slope, between two brooks, and awaited attack. Edward opened the battle by sending some archers and bombards forward to harass the Lancastrians. Somerset, commanding the Lancastrian right, replied vigorously, and when the Yorkist skirmishers fell back, thought he saw an opportunity for a successful charge. He was repulsed by Edward, who had placed an ambushing force

of some 1,000 men on his left flank to meet such an attack. On being driven back to the main battle line, Somerset personally killed **Lord Wenlock,** commanding the Lancastrian center, for having failed to support his charge. This did nothing to steady the shaken Lancastrians. The Yorkists, closely following Somerset's withdrawal, gained a complete victory. Prince Edward was killed, Margaret was captured, and most of the Lancastrian nobles were captured and slaughtered. Soon afterward Henry VI was murdered in the Tower, apparently on orders of Edward, and possibly under the supervision of Edward's brother, Richard, Duke of Gloucester (May 21).

1475. Edward Declares War against France. Allied with Charles the Bold of Burgundy, Edward led an invading army across the Channel. Following negotiations with adroit Louis XI, however, he abandoned the expedition in return for a substantial cash payment.

1483, April 9. Death of Edward. He was succeeded by his 13-year-old son, **Edward V.** Richard of Gloucester became regent.

1483, June 26. Richard III's Usurpation of the Throne. He was evidently supported by most English nobles, who did not wish to be ruled by a child king.

1483, October. Revolt by the Duke of Buckingham. This was apparently in conspiracy with **Henry Tudor,** Earl of Richmond (now head of the House of Lancaster), and was promptly and efficiently crushed by Richard.

1483–1485. Growing Unrest. Widespread unpopularity of Richard, suspected of having murdered Edward V and his young brother, **Richard,** Duke of York, in the Tower.

1485, August. Invasion by Henry Tudor. With approximately 3,000 French mercenaries, he landed at Milford Haven. Picking up considerable support in Wales and western England, Henry marched into central England, avoiding interception by royalist (Yorkist) forces under the brothers Lord **Thomas** and Sir **William Stanley.** By the time Henry reached the vicinity of Bosworth, his army had grown to about 5,000 men. Richard, with about 10,000, marched rapidly northwest from London to meet him. Unknown to Richard, the

Stanleys were in communication with Henry, and were merely waiting a suitable opportunity to betray the king.

1485, August 22. Battle of Bosworth. With the army of Sir William Stanley standing strangely aloof on high ground to the northwest, while that of Lord Stanley hovered to the southeast, the armies of Richard and Henry Tudor deployed in the open area between Sutton Cheney and Stanton. When Richard ordered an advance, his entire left wing, under the **Earl of Northumberland,** refused to move. Simultaneously the Stanleys moved in to join the Lancastrian army. With only a portion of his army remaining loyal, Richard led a handful of adherents in a vigorous charge into the center of the Lancastrian army, apparently hoping either to reach Henry and to win the battle single-handed or to die like a king. Despite his gallantry, Richard was soon overwhelmed by superior numbers and killed. His death ended the Wars of the Roses.

THE BEGINNING OF THE TUDOR ERA, 1485–1500

Henry Tudor, crowned as **Henry VII,** re-established peace in England and laid the foundations for four centuries of English glory. For more than a decade there were periodic instances of Yorkist insurgency, but these were mainly led by impostors, who were unable to obtain any substantial support. The principal events were:

1487. Uprising of Lambert Simnel. Pretending to be **Edward, Earl of Warwick** (son of the Duke of Clarence), Simnel was supported by Margaret of Burgundy, sister of Edward IV and Richard III. Simnel landed in Ireland with about 2,000 German landsknecht mercenaries, then crossed to England, where he was defeated and captured by royal troops in the hard-fought **Battle of Stokes** (June 16).

1488–1499. Insurrections of Perkin Warbeck. He impersonated Richard, younger of the murdered sons of Edward IV. He too was supported by the Dowager Duchess Margaret. With considerable foreign recognition and support, Perkin made several unsuccessful efforts to land in England and Ireland. After participating in an unsuccessful revolt in Cornwall (1497), he was captured and later executed 1499).

Scotland

As in past centuries, border warfare against England was more or less continuous during this period, but was less intense than in previous centuries. The entire period was marked by frequent struggles between the kings and recalcitrant nobles, led mostly by the House of Douglas. The principal events were:

1390–1406. Reign of Robert III.

1406. Capture of Prince James. The heir to the throne was captured by the English at sea on his way to school in France, just before the death of his father.

1406–1424. Imprisonment of James I in England. During most of this time Scotland was under the regency of the **Duke of Albany,** the young king's uncle. Albany, taking advantage of English occupation in the renewed activity of the Hundred Years' War in France, succeeded in recovering important areas of southern Scotland from the English. He also sent substantial contingents of Scottish soldiers to assist the French in the war against the English.

1411. Battle of Harlaw (near Inverurie). Donald, Lord of the Isles, invading Aberdeenshire, in an alliance with northern English nobles, was defeated by the **Earl of Mar.**

1424–1437. Effective Reign of James I. Having been ransomed (1423), for several years James maintained peace with England. Finally renewing the war, during the regency of Humphrey of Gloucester, James besieged Roxburgh, but was repulsed (1436).

1437–1460. Reign of James II. Constant bickering along the English border. James raided Northumberland (1456), and later successfully besieged Roxburgh, which surrendered shortly after the king was killed by explosion of a siege cannon (1460).

1460–1488. Reign of James III. During this time the Scots took advantage of the Wars of the Roses to recover all remaining areas of southern Scotland still in English hands.

1464–1482. Truce with England.

1482. Renewal of the War against England. Edward IV supported the king's younger brother, **Alexander, Duke of Albany.** Richard, Duke of Gloucester (Richard III), accompanied Albany with an army to invade southern Scotland, recapturing Berwick from the Scots. James's efforts to defend his country were frustrated by a noble revolt, permitting Albany and Gloucester to capture Edinburgh and seize control of the country. Albany was later forced to flee.

1484. English Invasion. Albany and the 9th **Earl of Douglas** invaded Scotland with a small English force, but were repulsed.

1488. Death of James III. He was killed at the **Battle of Sauchieburn,** near Stirling, in an effort to suppress a noble's revolt.

FRANCE

The Crisis of the French Monarchy, 1400–1444

The reign of intermittently insane Charles VI brought France to the verge of dissolution. While the nation was being torn to pieces by violent civil war between two major factions of the nobility, Henry V of England established himself as the legally recognized heir to the French crown, and was on the verge of bringing the entire nation under English control (see p. 415). The trend of history in all Western Europe would have been vastly different had it not been for two events: the early and unexpected death of Henry, closely followed by the meteoric appearance of Joan of Arc, who ignited the spark of French nationalism. The Dauphin, who became Charles VII, was a weak, unenterprising prince, totally incapable of rallying his people to stop the steady, systematic English conquests. Despite himself, however, Charles was carried along to victory and the consolidation of the French monarchy by Joan of Arc and the French nationalism which she inspired. The principal events were:

1380–1422. Reign of Charles VI. An era of chaos and economic distress.

1411–1435. Civil War between Burgundians and the Armagnacs. (See p. 412.)

1413–1414. Cabochian Revolt in Paris. (So-called from **Simon Caboch,** leader of the Parisian butchers.) This was connected with the great civil war raging between the noble factions. Paris and the French court were terrorized.

1413–1453. Conclusion of the Hundred Years' War. (See p. 409.)

1420. Treaty of Troyes. Henry V became virtual ruler of France (see p. 415).

1422. Deaths of Henry V and Charles VI.

1422–1429. Disintegration of France. The English and their Burgundian allies continued a slow and systematic conquest, without effective opposition from the uncrowned Dauphin.

1429. Spiritual and Nationalistic Revival of France. This was initiated by Joan of Arc (see p. 416).

1440. The Praguerie. A noble revolt which followed the pattern of a previous similar uprising in Prague, Bohemia. The rebels, who included the Dauphin, later Louis XI, were defeated in a campaign of maneuver in Poitou by Charles' able constable, Arthur de Richemont, but were then pardoned by the king.

1443. Revolt of Count of Armagnac. This was suppressed by Dauphin Louis.

1444. Expedition against Switzerland. (See p. 428.)

The Rise of Military Professionalism, 1445–1500

The anarchy created by the disbanded companies of mercenary soldiers threatened the recovery of France brought about by the victories of Joan of Arc. This led

Charles VII and his advisers to undertake a series of military reform measures of the utmost significance. Fifteen (later 20) **compagnies d'ordonnance,** consisting of approximately 600 men each (see p. 409), were created as a permanent military establishment to maintain order in France. These companies, which included the most reliable of the officers and men of the disbanded companies roaming the country, soon restored order. At the same time two of the king's ablest military advisers, **Jean** and **Gaspard Bureau,** established a permanent artillery organization, which their energy, scientific interests, and military skill soon made into an organization which was technically and organizationally far superior to any artillery elsewhere in the world. The creation of a French standing army, combined with this development of a superb—for that period—artillery organization within that army, enabled the French to eject the English from their country with ease when the war was resumed (see p. 417). Upon the death of Charles VII his son Louis XI, one of the ablest kings in French history, continued the military and political reforms initiated in the previous reign, to consolidate royal power and to return the nation to peace and prosperity.

Louis's measures to increase central control were opposed by most of the great nobles, particularly the Dukes of Burgundy, whose realm extended from the Swiss Alps to Flanders on the North Sea. Charles the Bold (or the Rash) of Burgundy seemed to be on the verge of establishing a new and independent West European kingdom, rivaling in wealth and power both France and the Empire. He was frustrated, however, by Louis's diplomatic skill and by the military prowess of the Swiss (see p. 428). The power of the French monarchy continued to increase during the subsequent reign of Charles VIII, culminating in a French expedition to Italy, which for the first time revealed to the rest of Europe the efficiency of the new French Army. This, the first appearance of what was essentially a modern-type professional army, marked the end of the Middle Ages and the dawn of the modern era. The principal events were:

1445–1449. Military Reforms. The establishment of the first standing army in Europe since the days of the Romans.

1449–1453. Expulsion of the English from France. (See p. 418.)

1461–1483. Reign of Louis XI. Feudal anarchy ended in France.

1465, July 13. Battle of Montlhéry. A drawn battle between Louis and a league of great nobles, led by Charles the Bold of Burgundy and the Dukes of Alençon, Berry, Bourbon, and Lorraine. This was primarily a cavalry battle, which ended with both armies in great confusion. Louis was forced to sign the unfavorable **Treaty of Conflans,** which he then evaded, splitting the noble league by adroit diplomacy.

1467–1477. Reign of Charles the Bold, Duke of Burgundy. He married Margaret of York (1468) to establish a new Anglo-Burgundian alliance with Edward IV of England, then treacherously captured Louis XI at a conference at Péronne. To regain his freedom Louis was forced to

submit temporarily to the demands of Charles.

1471–1472. Charles the Bold's Invasion of Normandy and Île de France. He was repulsed at **Beauvais.**

1472–1475. Intermittent Warfare with Aragon. Operations in the Pyrenees region ended with French conquest of Roussillon, but their repulse from Catalonia.

1474–1477. War of Charles the Bold with the Swiss. The Swiss received diplomatic support from Louis XI. This resulted in the defeat, humiliation, and death of Charles the Bold (see p. 429).

1475. Invasion of France by Edward IV. This ended without conflict by the **Treaty of Picquigny** (August 29), in which Louis XI bought off the English king.

1479, August 7. Battle of Guinegate. Louis, hoping to take advantage of the death of Charles, sent an army to invade the Netherlands, but the French were defeated by **Maximilian** of Hapsburg, son-in-law of Charles. French cavalry defeated the imperial horse, but Flemish infantry held the field, Maximilian fighting on foot in their midst. The French "free archers" (a new militia force) fled.

1483–1498. Reign of Charles VIII.

1488–1491. The "Mad War." A revolt of the Dukes of Orléans and Brittany supported by Henry VII of England and German Archduke Maximilian. Royal forces defeated the rebels at **St.-Aubin-du-Cormier** (1488), which settled the war, though inconclusive skirmishing continued for more than 2 years.

1493. Treaty of Barcelona. Charles obtained Spanish neutrality in preparation for his planned invasion of Italy.

1494–1496. Expedition to Italy. Charles conquered Naples as the first step in a contemplated crusade to recapture Constantinople or Jerusalem from the Moslems. His army of more than 25,000 men included 8,000 Swiss mercenaries. Most of the remainder of Europe, alarmed by the French success, formed a "Holy League" including Emperor Maximilian, Pope Alexander VI, Spain, England, Venice, and Milan. With his line of communications to France threatened, Charles left half of his army to hold Naples while he marched to northern Italy to make a junction with a small army under **Louis, Duke of Orléans** in Piedmont. Italian condottiere **Giovanni Francesco Gonzaga** of Mantua, commanding a combined mercenary army of Milan

and Venice, moved to intercept the French retreat in the Apennines (July, 1495).

1495, July 6. Battle of Fornovo. Gonzaga, who had approximately 2,400 men-at-arms, 2,000 light cavalry, and 10,000 infantry (mostly crossbowmen) and some artillery, blocked the northern side of the Pass of Pontremoli, where there was adequate room for his condottiere cavalry to maneuver. The French army consisted of approximately 900 men-at-arms and 8,000 infantry, plus the highly efficient field artillery corps. The French, realizing that the Italians would attempt to interfere with their passage, marched through the pass prepared for battle. When the Italians attempted a flank attack in the defile, the alert French unlimbered their artillery and counterattacked vigorously. The Italians, used to a highly formalized and relatively apathetic form of combat (see p. 429), were dismayed by the violence of the French onslaught and were quickly routed. Total French losses were 200 killed and possibly an equal number wounded. The Italians lost 3,350 men killed, most of their wounded being cut down by the vigorously attacking French. Charles failed to exploit his victory, and marched on into northern Italy and back to France.

1495–1498. Franco-Spanish Conflict for Control of Naples. (See p. 469.)

1498–1515. Reign of Louis XII.

1499. Invasion of Naples by Louis XII. (See p. 470.)

SCANDINAVIA

The Union of Kalmar of the three Scandinavian countries (see p. 370) prospered under the strong rule of Regent Margaret of Denmark. The Union persisted through the remainder of the century, with numerous vicissitudes, including a generally unsatisfactory, drawn-out war with the Hanseatic League and frequent revolts in Sweden. The principal events were:

1397–1412. Reign of Margaret over United Scandinavia. (See p. 370.)

1412–1439. Reign of Eric VII.

1422–1435. War with Holstein and the Hanseatic League. The Scandinavians were generally superior at sea, but unsuccessful on land. Internal revolts forced Eric to make an unfavorable peace, Schleswig being surrendered to Holstein.

1434–1439. Revolts throughout Scandinavia. Started by **Engelbrecht Engelbrechtson** in Sweden, these spread to Norway and then to Denmark as a result of general dissatisfaction with the burden of war. Eric was deposed and the Union reestablished.

1440–1448. Reign of Christopher III. Scandinavia was largely dominated by the Hanseatic League.

1448–1481. Reign of Christian I. This was marked by prolonged civil war in Sweden and Norway against rival Swedish King **Charles VIII** (1448–1470), who was finally ousted. Christian then started an invasion of Sweden but was decisively defeated by the Swedes at **Brunkeberg** in Norway (1471).

GERMANY

During this century the power and importance of the Holy Roman Emperors declined markedly. There were several reasons, not least being generally inept leadership, permitting the usually unruly German nobility to exercise even more independence than usual. The wealth and power of the towns increased, at the expense of both emperors and nobles. The Hanseatic League remained influential, although its strength declined in the face of growing Scandinavian power in the Baltic. Germany was also overshadowed during much of the century by the resurgency of neighboring countries under strong leadership. Bohemia reasserted its independence, while the increasingly warlike Swiss smashed every effort to re-establish imperial control over their cantons. The principal events were:

1400–1410. Four-Sided Civil War. There were four rival emperors: **Wenceslas, Rupert III, Sigismund,** and **Jobst.** Sigismund of Luxembourg, King of Hungary, was eventually triumphant.

1410, July 10. Battle of Tannenberg. The Teutonic Knights were decisively defeated by a Polish-Lithuanian army, starting the decline of the order (see p. 434).

1410–1437. Reign of Sigismund. He was also King of Hungary, and (nominally) of Bohemia.

1420–1431. Hussite Wars in Bohemia. (See p. 432.)

1438–1439. Reign of Albert II (Son-in-Law of Sigismund). This began the Hapsburg line of emperors. An able soldier, he spent most of his brief reign defending Hungary against the Turks.

1440–1493. Reign of Frederick III.

1451. Revolts in Austria and Hungary. These were suppressed by Frederick's subordinates.

1463–1485. Bohemian and Hungarian Raids on Austria. George of Podebrad, King of Bohemia, and **Mathias Corvinus,** King of Hungary, ravaged Austria, culminating in the expulsion of Frederick from Vienna by the Hungarians (see pp. 433 and 436). Archduke **Maximilian,** Frederick's son, elected King of the Romans (1486), assumed most of the imperial authority from his inept father.

1479. Battle of Guinegate. (See p. 425.) This was the beginning of the protracted Valois-Hapsburg struggle (see p. 469).

1486–1489. Renewed War with France. Maximilian supported the revolt of **Francis II,** Duke of Brittany (see p. 426). Maximilian, preparing to operate against France from the Netherlands, was forced to spend most of his time suppressing opponents of this unpopular war in the Low Countries.

c. 1486. Creation of the Landsknechts in Germany. This followed the Swiss example (see p. 407). It was the beginning of an imperial standing army.

1491. Maximilian's Reconquest of Vienna. He drove the Hungarians from Austria.

1492. Battle of Villach. Maximilian repulsed an invading Turk army.

1493–1519. Reign of Maximilian I.

1494. Rebellion in the Netherlands. Suppressed by Maximilian.

1499. Maximilian's Invasion of Switzerland (See p. 429.)

SWITZERLAND

During the early part of this century the Swiss so perfected their infantry organization of pikemen, halberdiers, and crossbowmen that Switzerland became the leading military power of Europe. The ascendancy of infantry over cavalry, begun by the defensive tactics of Edward III at Crécy, were brought to culmination by the offensive capability of the highly disciplined, well-trained, maneuverable Swiss columns. That the Swiss did not utilize this tremendous military superiority for wars of foreign conquest was not due to lack of ambition, or any early tendency toward neutrality. It was, rather, a reflection of the imperfect Swiss federal system, which did not permit any unified national foreign policy, or even the development of a consistent and cohesive military strategy. Tactically, during the 15th century the Swiss were practically invincible. Strategically most Swiss operations, other than in defense of their homeland, were usually abortive. As a result this nation of warriors had little influence on the over-all history of Europe during this century, save to the extent that more able politicians and strategists of other nations were able to use Swiss mercenaries to further their own ambitions. The Swiss reputation of invincibility, combined with their ruthless slaughter of foes, inspired such terror that by the end of the 15th century Swiss battles were usually won before the engagement began. The principal events were:

1403–1416. War with Savoy. The Swiss gained control of the southern Alpine passes into northern Italy.

1415. Conquest of the Aargau Region. The Swiss defeated Austria, with the support of Emperor Sigismund.

1422–1426. Intermittent Warfare with Milan. Duke **Filippo Maria Visconti** intrigued to prevent the Swiss cantons from acting in concert. The result was the temporary loss of Bellinzona to Milan after the drawn **Battle of Arbedo** (June 30, 1422).

1436–1450. Civil War. Zurich fought neighboring cantons, with frequent intervention and participation by Germans and French.

1444, August 24. Battle of St. Jakob (near Basle). Frederick III, hoping to take advantage of the civil war to re-establish Hapsburg control over Switzerland, obtained assistance from Charles VII of France, who was desperately seeking employment for troops disbanded during a long truce in the Hundred Years' War (see p. 417). The Dauphin Louis later Louis XI) collected an army of 30,000 and invaded Switzerland. Near Basel the French veterans were met and attacked by approximately 1,500 Swiss. In the ensuing battle, the Swiss force was annihilated, but they killed approximately 3,000 French attackers. The determination and efficiency of the Swiss infantry so discouraged the French that they withdrew, and turned instead to harass Frederick's domains in Alsace. This defeat made the reputation of the Swiss as Europe's finest soldiers.

1460. Renewed War with Austria. The Swiss conquered Thurgau.

1468. Renewed Civil War. The Austrians again attempted to exploit the situation. Patching up internal peace, the Swiss again repulsed the Austrians.

1474–1477. War with Charles the Bold of Burgundy. The Swiss were allied with the south German cities and the Hapsburgs (who were fearful of Charles' ambitions of conquest in Alsace), and were supported by subsidies from Louis XI of France, bitter enemy of Charles the Bold. After repulsing Charles at **Héricourt** (1474, November 13), the Swiss and their allies occupied Burgundian territories on the borders of Switzerland and Alsace (1474–1475). Charles recaptured Granson (February, 1476) and hanged the entire Swiss garrison.

1476, March 2. Battle of Granson. A Swiss army of 18,000 men, without artillery, attacked the Burgundian army of 15,000. The Swiss, eager to avenge their slaughtered countrymen, advanced in 3 heavy columns, echeloned to the left rear, moving directly into combat without deploying, in typical Swiss fashion (see p. 407). The speed of the Swiss advance did not give the Burgundians time to make much use of their numerous artillery and missile units. Charles attempted a double envelopment of the leading Swiss column before the other 2 arrived, but as his troops were shifting to make this attack, they caught sight of the other Swiss columns and retreated in panic. The Burgundians lost about 1,000 men, the Swiss only 200.

1476, June 22. Battle of Morat. Charles, having rallied and reorganized his army, moved to drive the Swiss from the Burgundian territory they had occupied. With

20,000 men he besieged Morat, near Bern and Fribourg, establishing a heavily entrenched and palisaded defensive position to cover his besieging troops. Inexplicably, he established no outposts or patrols. The weather being rainy, only about 1/5 of the Burgundians were in the entrenchments; the remainder were in their nearby camp. Moving with typical rapidity, a Swiss army of 25,000 infantry, plus about 1,000 Austrian and German allied cavalry, advanced unexpectedly against the Burgundian entrenchments, again moving directly into battle without taking time to deploy. The few Burgundians holding the entrenchments were driven out in confusion, just as the remainder of the Burgundian army, belatedly alerted, was rushing to join in the defense. The Swiss simply overran the confused Burgundians. About 1/3 of Charles' army, with their backs to the lake, were cut off by the Swiss advance and were slaughtered to a man. Burgundian losses were between 7,000 and 10,000 men killed; Swiss losses were negligible.

1477, January 5. Battle of Nancy. The Swiss and their allies advanced into Burgundian territory, where Charles met them with a new and reorganized army. Again the vigorous Swiss infantry assault, combined with an envelopment of the Burgundian left flank, resulted in a complete victory. Charles was killed as he fought bravely to try to cover his army's retreat.

1478. War with Milan. This ended with a Swiss victory at the **Battle of Giornico** (December 28).

1499. War with Emperor Maximilian. This was the result of a boundary dispute on the Austrian border. The emperor was supported by the south German cities; the Swiss were allied with the French. For a few months fighting raged all along the northern and eastern frontier, the principal battles being fought at **Hard, Bruderholz, Schwaderloh, Frastenz,** and **Calven.** The decisive battle was fought at **Dornach** (July 22), when the Swiss defeated Maximilian himself, who was forced by the **Treaty of Basel** (September 22) to grant to Switzerland virtual independence from the Empire.

ITALY

This century in Italy was perhaps the most sterile in military history. The many small states of Italy were almost incessantly at war with each other, and in this respect the century has been compared with the 2nd and 3rd centuries B.C. in Greece. Politically, the comparison is apt, in that the wars were senseless and accomplished little, either at the time or in lasting results. Militarily, however, there is no comparison. The conflicts in Greece had been fiercely contested. Those in Italy in the 15th century were *opéra bouffe*. This was the heyday of the mercenary **condottieri,** whose companies were always for sale to the highest bidder, even on the eve of combat or during battle. No soldier, from lowest private to highest general, felt the slightest stirrings of patriotism or personal interest in success or victory other than as a contribution to personal profit. The condottiere forces were built around contingents of heavy cavalry, since this was the safest and most comfortable way to fight. Much of Italy is totally unfitted for cavalry operations, either because of mountains or the extensive marshlands of the lower Po Valley; thus battles could only take place in relatively limited areas. Neither the generals nor the cynical soldiers were eager to risk heavy losses in fighting for their employers. This, combined with the limitations on suitable operational ground for cavalry, meant that the wars were for the most part intricate maneuvers, sometimes concluded when one army found itself in such an unfavorable situation that victory would be extremely unlikely. On those occasions when two armies finally ended up face to face on suitable terrain for battle, the engagements were like a chess match, fought either to a cautious draw or only up to that point at which it became obvious that one side or the other had gained a clear-cut advantage. The other would then resign, conceding the victory. The heavy cavalrymen, who bore the brunt of the actions, were so thoroughly protected by their armor that bloodshed was relatively slight and loss of life insignificant. Casualties were largely limited to prisoners of war, since few soldiers saw any reason for continuing resistance in desperate situations. An important aspect of condottiere business was the ransoming of prisoners after a battle. As a means of settling otherwise insoluble disputes between nations, this cynical, bloodless *kriegspiel* was senseless. The Italian soldiers and their employers were living in a fool's paradise which was bound to come to a violent and unpleasant end. As a result, for three subsequent centuries, Italy was to become the battle-ground of the great European powers. The condottieri's house of cards collapsed when Charles VIII of France led a hard-fighting, professional army into Italy toward the close of the century (see p. 469). The principal events were:

1402–1454. Series of Wars between Milan, Venice, and Florence.

1402–1405. Fragmentation of Milan. This followed the death of **Gian Galeazzo Visconti.** Venice seized the former Milanese possessions of Padua, Bassano, Vicenza, and Verona to control most of northeast Italy.

1405–1406. Conquest of Pisa by Florence.

1414–1435. Reign of Joanna II of Naples. This was a period of incessant conflict between Joanna and her favorites, on the one hand, and the barons, on the other, with frequent intervention by Aragon and the papacy.

1416–1453. Intermittent Turkish-Venetian Naval Warfare. The goal was domination of the Aegean area.

1420. Venetian Conquest of Fruili (from the Emperor Sigismund).

1423–1454. Wars of Milan against Florence and Venice. The result of this intermittent warfare was to the general advantage of Venice and Florence.

1435–1442. Conquest of Naples by Alfonso V of Aragon.

1447–1450. Civil War in Milan. This ended in the victory of former condottiere **Francisco Sforza,** originally of Naples.

1463–1479. War between Venice and Tur- key. The Turks were victorious; beginning of the decline of Venice (see p. 438).

1482–1484. Ferrarese War. Milan, Florence (under **Lorenzo de' Medici**), and Naples combined to prevent Venice from seizing Ferrara; Pope **Sixtus IV** was allied with Venice.

1485–1486. Neapolitan Revolt. The Neapolitan barons, supported by Pope **Innocent VIII,** rose against King **Ferdinand I.** Ferdinand was supported successfully by Florence.

1494–1495. French Invasion of Naples. Charles VIII led the invaders, following the death of Ferdinand I (see p. 469).

1492–1503. Reign of Pope Alexander VI. This was marked by pacification of Romagna by his son, **Cesare Borgia,** breaking the power of the great Roman families (1492).

1495–1498. Spanish Intervention in Naples. Spanish forces were led by **Gonzalo de Cordova** (see p. 469), who was defeated by **Gilbert, Duke of Montpensier** at the **Battle of Seminara** (1495). Cordova's subsequent cautious defensive-offensive tactics were successful against Montpensier at **Atella** (July, 1496).

1499. Renewed French Invasion of Naples. (See p. 470.)

IBERIAN PENINSULA

During the first three-quarters of the 15th century, Castile was wracked by anarchy, while Aragon, despite some internal disturbances, maintained its position as the principal maritime power of the western Mediterranean. During much of this time Aragon was involved in a series of struggles for the control of Naples (see above). The last quarter of the century witnessed the beginning of an amazing new era in a united and revitalized country, which in a few years would lead Spain to a pre-eminent global position of power and wealth. This was the result of the marriage of **Ferdinand II** of Aragon with Queen **Isabella** of Castile, followed by their joint conquest of Granada, completing the expulsion of the Moslem Moors from Spain. This, in turn, was followed immediately by a period of vigorous overseas exploration and expansion, initiated by the earth-shaking voyage of Columbus to discover the Western Hemisphere. The principal events were:

1406–1474. Decline of Castile. The country came close to disintegration in repeated civil wars, in which Aragon and Navarre frequently intervened; royal power was tenuously preserved only by the support of the towns against the rebellious nobility.

1409–1442. Aragon's Involvement in Naples. Intermittent warfare, at first unsuccessful, finally ended in conquest by **Alfonso V** (see p. 430).

1458–1479. Unrest and Intermittent Revolt in Catalonia. This was during the reign of **John II** of Aragon.

1474–1479. Civil War of Succession in Castile. After the death of Henry IV, rival claimants were his sister, **Isabella,** wife of Prince **Ferdinand of Aragon,** and **Joan,** Henry's doubtfully legitimate daughter, who was wife of **Alfonso V** of Portugal. Portuguese intervention was ended by Ferdinand's victory at the **Battle of Toro** (1476). Ferdinand and Isabella then triumphed over Joan's adherents in Castile.

1479–1504. Joint Reigns of Isabella of Castile (1474–1504) and Ferdinand of Aragon (1479–1516). Pope Innocent VIII gave them the title of "Catholic Kings."

Final Christian-Moslem War in Spain, 1481–1492

This was begun by the raid of **Muley Abu'l Hassan,** bellicose King of Granada, to capture Zahara, near Ronda (December 26, 1481). Marquis **Rodrigo Ponce de León** of Cadiz raided back to seize Alhama, 25 miles from Granada (February 28, 1482). When Hassan invested Alhama, Ferdinand and Isabella came to the assistance of Ponce de León, forcing the Moslems to raise the siege (May). Incessant war continued for 10 years. Christian successes were facilitated by protracted internal civil war between Hassan and two rivals for the throne of Granada: his brother, **Abdullah el Zagal,** and his son, **Abu Abdulla Mohammed Boabdil.** The principal events were:

1482, July 1. Battle of Loja. Ferdinand was ambushed and defeated.

1483. Capture of Boabdil. Captured by the Christians at **Lucena,** he obtained his release by acknowledging complete suzerainty of Ferdinand and Isabella over Granada. This was not accepted, however, by Hassan or Zagal.

1483–1487. Spanish Military Reorganization. Centered around a permanent constabulary, loosely modeled on the French **compagnies d'ordonnance** (see p. 409). A contingent of Swiss mercenaries became a model for the new constabulary infantry. Constant campaigning against the Moors, and the strict discipline demanded by the sovereigns, resulted in the emergence of one of the finest armies in Europe. The Spanish fleet was also built up, preventing intervention from Morocco.

1485–1487. Campaigns against Málaga. Following the capture of Loja (1486) and

systematic Spanish conquest of the surrounding region, Málaga was besieged and captured (May–August, 1487).

1488–1490. Approach to Granada. The surrounding mountain regions were systematically conquered and Granada isolated by the capture of the fortresses of **Baza** and **Almería** (1489).

1491, April–1492, January 2. The Siege of Granada. The Christians, in overwhelming force, repulsed all desperate Moorish sorties. The final surrender of the city by Boabdil concluded 8 centuries of Moslem-Christian struggle for control of Spain.

1492–1502. The Four Voyages of Columbus. He began the colonization of America on the island of Hispaniola (1493). Following a revolt against the authority of Columbus there (1498), royal authority of the Indies was established under the first governor, **Francisco de Bobadilla** (1499).

Portugal

The conclusion of long-drawn-out wars with the Moslem Moors and with Castile late in the 14th century brought unexpected and unwanted inactivity to the warlike, vigorous Portuguese. An outlet for this energy was soon found in a series of overseas expeditions of conquest and exploration which made Portugal the leading maritime nation of the world at the close of the 15th century. The principal events were:

1385–1433. Reign of John I. The first ruler of the House of Avis, which brought Portugal to glory.

1415. Conquest of Ceuta from the Moors. Prince **Henry,** third son of John, later renowned as "the Navigator," particularly distinguished himself.

1418–1460. Beginning of Portuguese Explorations. Africa and the South Atlantic were explored under the sponsorship of Henry the Navigator.

1433–1438. Reign of Edward I.

1437. Repulse at Tangier. An invasion expedition was disastrously repulsed by the Moors.

1438–1481. Reign of Afonso V (Infant Son of Edward). During his minority there was a three-way struggle for power and the regency between Alfonso's mother, **Eleanora;** his uncle, **Peter;** and the powerful family of Braganza. This culminated in Alfonso's seizing power himself and turning against the able Peter, who was defeated and killed at the **Battle of Alfarrobeira** (May, 1449).

1463–1476. War with Morocco. The Portuguese captured Tangier and Casablanca.

1474–1476. Intervention in Castile. (See p. 431.)

1481–1495. Reign of John II. He energetically revived the program of exploration which had lagged following the death of Henry (1469).

1481–1483. Noble Revolt. Ferdinand of Braganza, the rebel leader, was decisively defeated by John.

EASTERN EUROPE

BOHEMIA

A period of turmoil and civil war in Bohemia, the fierce Hussite Wars foreshadowing the violent religious struggles of the Reformation. The early years of these wars were dominated by the military genius of John Ziska. The principal events were:

1378–1419. Reign of Wenceslas IV. This was marked by almost continuous conflicts with the barons. For much of his reign **Sigismund** (stepbrother of Wenceslas and later emperor) actually ruled the country.

1419–1437. Reign of Sigismund. He was not recognized by the Bohemians for 17 years (1436).

1419–1436. Hussite Wars. These resulted from the persecution of the religious followers of **John Huss,** executed by Sigismund (1415). The Hussites were considered heretics by the majority of the Catholic population of Bohemia. Under the leadership of **John Ziska,** an able soldier with much experience as a mercenary in Poland's wars against the Teutonic Knights, they established a fortified mountain community at Tabor, near Usti, which served as a base of operations. Ziska developed a new and effective defensive-offensive tactical system, built around a **wagenburg,** or wagon fortress, equipped with artillery (see p. 406). When not on campaign, Ziska drilled his soldiers endlessly.

1419. Battle of Sudoner. Ziska, leading the Hussites on their exodus from Prague to Tabor, repulsed pursuing Catholics. Soon after, Pope **Martin V** declared a Bohemian Crusade against the Hussites (March 17, 1420).

1419, June 30–July 20. Siege of Prague. Sigismund, asserting his claim to the throne of Bohemia, invested Prague. The citizens appealed to the Hussites for assistance.

1419, July 30. Battle of Prague. Ziska led an army to Prague, taking up a *wagenburg* position on Vitkov Hill, where he decisively repulsed an attack by Sigismund, who was forced to withdraw from Bohemia. The continuing religious struggle between Catholics and Hussites now became inextricably involved with the political struggle between the Bohemians and the unwanted ruler Sigismund.

1421. Return of Sigismund. He was defeated by Ziska and the wagon defenses at the **Battles of Lutitz** and **Kuttenberg.** During this campaign Ziska lost his remaining eye in the Siege of Rabi. (He had lost his other eye in the earlier civil wars against Wenceslas.) Despite total blindness, Ziska retained control of the Hussites.

1422, January. Sigismund Returns Again. And again was severely defeated by Ziska in the **Battles of Nebovid** (January 6) and of **Nemeclsybrod** (January 10).

1423. Civil War among the Hussites. The Utraquist sect and the citizens of Prague opposed the Taborites. Ziska re-established Taborite supremacy by victories at the **Battles of Horid** (April 27) and **Strachov** (August 4).

1423, September–October. Ziska's Invasion of Hungary. This failed, despite initial success.

1424. Renewal of Hussite Civil War. Ziska re-established peace by decisive victories over Utraquists and Praguers at the **Battles of Skalic** (January 6) and **Malesov** (June 7). Ziska then planned an invasion of Moravia, but died before it could be undertaken. Military command of the Hussites was assumed by **Prokop "the Great,"** a priest and former Utraquist.

1426–1427. Renewed German Invasions.

The Germans were decisively defeated by Prokop at the **Battles of Aussig** (1426) and **Tachau** (1427).

1427–1432. Hussite Raids. Repeated expeditions went into Germany, Hungary, Misnia, and Silesia, and ranged as far as the Baltic.

1433–1434. Renewed Civil War. The Taborites opposed the combined forces of nobles and Utraquists. The Taborite leaders, Prokop the Great and unrelated **Prokop the Less,** were decisively defeated and killed at the **Battle of Lipan** (June 16).

1436. Peace in Bohemia. All factions accepted Sigismund as king.

1437–1439. Reign of Albert of Austria. He died during a war with Ladislas of Poland (see p. 434).

1439–1457. Reign of Ladislas Posthumous (Son of Albert, Born after His Father's Death). Bohemia was racked by civil wars during a period of ineffectual guardianship by Emperor Frederick III.

1448. Emergence of George of Podebrad. He seized power and proclaimed himself regent; recognized as such by Frederick III. Podebrad captured Gabor, to assure the ascendancy of the Utraquist faction of the Hussite religion as the official religion of Bohemia (1452).

1459–1471. Reign of George of Podebrad. He took the crown after the death of Ladislas.

1462–1471. Renewed Civil War in Bohemia. Pope **Paul II** excommunicated George and all Hussites as heretics (1465). King **Mathias** of Hungary supported the Catholic rebels and had himself proclaimed King of Bohemia (1469).

1471–1516. Reign of Ladislas II (Son of Casimir of Poland). This began with continuing war against Mathias of Hungary, was ended by the **Treaty of Olomouc;** Mathias recognized Ladislas as King of Bohemia, but received Moravia, Silesia, and Licesia in compensation (1478). During the remainder of this reign the power of the nobility grew greatly at the expense of the authority of the weak king.

POLAND

This was a century of transition for Poland, during which the crude, semibarbarous society matured and foreign threats from the northeast and south were repelled. The century ended with Poland emerging as a leading power in Europe. The principal events were:

1386–1434. Reign of Jagiello (Ladislas II).* The former Grand Duke of Lithuania, he had become King of Poland by marriage (see p. 378). During his long reign Jagiello had to contend with three formidable antagonistic forces: the turbulence of the unruly Polish nobles; the separatist tendencies of Lithuania under his cousin **Witowt,** who succeeded him as grand duke; and the ruthless aggression of the Order of Teutonic Knights. By a combination of diplomacy and generalship Jagiello maintained ascendancy over each of these forces, although he could not eliminate any of them.

1410, July 15. Battle of Tannenberg. The combined Polish and Lithuanian forces of Jagiello and Witowt decisively defeated the Teutonic Knights. Included in the Polish army was a force of Bohemian mercenaries under John Ziska (see p. 432) and some Russian and Tartar contingents. Following the victory the Poles and Lithuanians devastated the holdings of the Teutonic Order in Prussia, but, lacking support from his unruly Polish nobles, Jagiello concluded the **First Peace of Thorn** with the Knights, permitting them to retain most of their lands. Nonetheless, the terrible losses suffered at Tannenberg, combined with the disastrous blow to prestige, marked the beginning of the order's decline.

1434–1444. Reign of Ladislas III (Son of Jagiello). The first years were under the regency of Cardinal **Olesnicki,** a great diplomat and administrator.

1435. Lithuanian Revolt. Despite support from the Teutonic Knights, the rebels were subdued by a Polish army under Olesnicki.

1444. Death of Ladislas. He was defeated and killed at the **Battle of Varna** against the Turks (see p. 435).

---

* Some authorities give him the title of Ladislas V.

1447–1492. Reign of Casimir IV (Younger Brother of Ladislas).

1454–1466. War with the Teutonic Order. The Poles supported a Prussian revolt. After desultory campaigns, Casimir won a decisive victory at the **Battle of Puck** (September 17, 1462). The war was concluded by the **Second Peace of Thorn,** which gave Poland an outlet to the Baltic by cession of the province of Pomerania and the region around the mouth of the Vistula. The Teutonic Knights, retaining Prussia, acknowledged the suzerainty of Poland.

1471–1478. War with Hungary. This resulted from the election of **Ladislas,** son of Casimir, as King of Bohemia, in opposition to the claims of Mathias of Hungary (see pp. 433 and 436).

1478–1493. Semiwar with Hungary. This followed Mathias' efforts to stir up border troubles, to encourage the Teutonic Order to rebel against Poland, and to incite the Tartars to ravage Lithuania.

1475–1476. Turkish Invasion of Moldavia. This was repelled by **Stephen,** Voivode of Moldavia, a vassal of Poland.

1484–1485. Expedition to Moldavia. A new Turkish invasion caused Casimir to lead an army to assist Stephen in expelling the Turks. Casimir was leading an army of 20,000 men to cross the Pruth River into Turkish territory when Ottoman Emperor **Bayazid II,** then engaged in war in Egypt, made a truce (see p. 439).

1492–1501. Reign of John Albert (Son of Casimir). He increased the authority of the monarchy by reducing the power of the great nobles in the cities.

1497–1498. Renewed Struggle with the Turks in Moldavia. Stephen played the Turks off against the Poles, who were repulsed from Moldavia. Turkish forces raided deep into Poland. The independence of Moldavia was recognized by both Poles and Turks (1499).

RUSSIA

During this century the Grand Dukes of Moscow struggled to obtain increasing independence from the suzerainty of the Tartars of the Golden Horde. At the same time they were engaged in a continuing series of frontier struggles with the Lithuanians and Poles. Shortly before the end of the century, **Ivan III** (the Great) of Moscow threw off the Tartar yoke. The principal events were:

1389–1425. Reign of Basil I of Moscow. He annexed Nijni-Novgorod, and was engaged in practically continuous warfare with both Tartars and Lithuanians.

1425–1462. Reign of Basil II. This was marked by anarchy and civil war against rival princes **Yuri** and **Shemyaka.**

1451. Tartar Invasion. This reached the walls of Moscow.

1462–1505. Reign of Ivan III. He was the first national sovereign of Russia. He defeated and then conquered Novgorod (1471–1478), later annexing Tver (1485).

By his marriage to **Zoë,** only niece of the last Byzantine Emperor, he established a claim for himself and subsequent Russian monarchs as the successors of the Byzantine emperors.

1480. Independence from the Tartars. Ivan refused to pay tribute; he then repulsed Tartar efforts to re-establish their sovereignty.

1492–1503. Intermittent War with Lithuania. Ivan, generally successful, was supported by **Mengli Girai,** Tartar Khan of the Crimea.

HUNGARY

Hungary succeeded the Byzantine Empire as the bulwark of Christendom against the rising tide of the Moslem Turks. Although their kings were constantly distracted by feudal claims and dynastic adventures elsewhere in Central and Eastern Europe, the Hungarians fought the Turks to a standstill. This was due primarily to two great soldiers: **John Hunyadi,** the national hero of Hungary, and his son **Mathias Corvinus,** who reigned as King of Hungary for nearly a third of a century. The principal events were:

1387–1437. Reign of Sigismund of Luxembourg. He was also German Emperor and King of Bohemia. Despite the distraction of his responsibilities and struggles in Germany, and his protracted efforts to subdue the Hussites in Bohemia, Sigismund devoted himself energetically to defending Hungary, and all of Christendom, against the Turkish threat, which he perceived better than most of his contemporaries. He was unable, however, to prevent the Turkish conquest of most of Serbia. He also failed to suppress revolts of the former Hungarian provinces of Bosnia, Wallachia, and Moldavia. These setbacks, and the loss of Dalmatia to Venice, were the result of Sigismund's prolonged absences from his country.

1437–1439. Reign of Albert of Hapsburg. An able warrior, his short tenure was plagued by increasing troubles with the Hungarian nobles.

1437. Emergence of John Hunyadi. A Transylvanian nobleman, he had served under Sigismund in his wars in Central Europe and against the Turks. In the first of many victories, he evicted the Turks from **Semendria** (Smederevo).

1439–1440. Civil War in Hungary. **Ladislas I** (Ladislas III of Poland; see p. 434) was successful, due largely to Hunyadi's support.

1440–1444. Reign of Ladislas. This was marked by Hunyadi's victorious campaigns against the Turks (1441–1443). He won the **Battles of Semendria** (1441), **Hermannstadt** (1442), and the **Iron Gates** (1442). In Turkish Europe he captured Nish and Sofia, finally—in combination with King Ladislas—winning a major victory against Sultan Murad II at the **Battle of Snaim** (or Kustinitza, 1443). Turkish power was temporarily smashed in the Balkans. Murad agreed to a 10-year truce (1443).

1444. Ladislas' Crusade. In alliance with Venice, Ladislas broke the truce, invading Bulgaria (July). The Venetian fleet failed in its mission to prevent Murad from crossing back into Europe from Asia with his army (see p. 438).

1444, November 10. Battle of Varna. The

Hungarians were completely routed, Ladislas was killed, and Hunyadi escaped with the remnants of the Hungarian army (see p. 438). This ended the last real Crusade.

1444–1457. Reign of Ladislas V (Son of Albert). This began under the regency of Hunyadi (till 1452). Hunyadi invaded Austria to force German Emperor Frederick III, protector of Ladislas as King of Bohemia, to permit the young king to come to Hungary (1446). The ungrateful and jealous monarch spent most of the next decade hampering Hunyadi's efforts to defend Hungary against the Turks.

1448, October 17. Second Battle of Kossovo. Hunyadi, with 25,000 men, was defeated by Turkish Sultan Murad II, with 100,000 men, in a 2-day battle due to the treachery of **Dan,** ruler of Wallachia, and Hunyadi's traditional enemy, Prince **George Brankovic** of Serbia. Hunyadi made excellent use of German and Bohemian mercenary infantry, armed with handguns, who were opposed by Janissary archers. Infantry on both sides used palisades to protect themselves in prolonged exchange of missile fire at a range of about 100 yards. Casualties were enormous, the Hungarians losing half their army, the Turks one-third.

1449. Invasion of Serbia. Hunyadi led a successful punitive expedition against Brankovic.

1445–1456. Turkish Invasion. Hunyadi sent a force to hold Belgrade, while raising a relief army and river flotilla in Hungary.

1456, July 14. Naval Battle of Belgrade. Hunyadi defeated the Turkish fleet on the Danube.

1456, July 21–22. Battle of Belgrade. Hunyadi routed the investing Turkish army, forcing Sultan **Mohammed** to withdraw to Constantinople. He was planning to carry the war back into Turkey when he died (August 11). Ladislas died the following year.

1458–1490. Reign of Mathias Corvinus (Son of Hunyadi). He spent more time warring in Central Europe than in taking advantage of his father's victories over the Turks. He did undertake 2 limited invasions of Turkey (1463 and 1475).

1468–1478. War in Bohemia. (See p. 433.)

1477–1485. Wars against the Emperor Frederick III. (See p. 427.) Following an unsuccessful siege of Vienna (1477), Mathias eventually captured the city (1485), at the same time annexing Austria, Styria, and Carinthia. Hungary now dominated Central and Southeastern Europe.

1490–1516. Reign of Ladislas VI (Ladislas II of Bohemia). A weak ruler; Hungary's power declined rapidly.

SERBIA

Although the rulers of Serbia were vassals of the Turkish sultans at the outset of this century, with Hungarian assistance Serbia briefly re-established its independence in midcentury. This was followed by Turkish reconquest; Serbia again was completely submerged. The principal events were:

1389–1427. Reign of Stephen Lazarevich. As a vassal of the Turks, he fought against Tamerlane at the Battle of Angora (1402; see p. 392).

1427–1456. Reign of George Brankovic (Despot of Serbia). Reasserting independence, Brankovic was driven from his fortress capital of Semendria by the Turks (1439). Despite a personal feud with John Hunyadi of Hungary, Brankovic was restored to his dominions by the victories of Hunyadi and Ladislas over the Turks, 1443 (see p. 435).

1459. Turkish Conquest. End of Serbia's tenuous independence.

1463. Turkish Conquest of Bosnia.

1483. Turkish Conquest of Herzegovina.

1499. Turkish Conquest of Montenegro.

EURASIA, THE MIDDLE EAST, AND AFRICA

THE BYZANTINE EMPIRE, 1400–1461

Although the Byzantine Empire had declined to insignificance in size and power due to internal decay and the steady encroachments of the Ottoman Turks, even in its dying years it demonstrated some flashes of its ancient vitality. But the old, crumbling fortifications of Constantinople, which had defied assault for so many centuries, could not stand up against the bombardment of the massive siege artillery of **Mohammed II.** The last Emperor, **Constantine XI,** died a hero's death in a vain but gallant defense of the breach pounded in the walls by the Turkish guns. The principal events were:

1391–1425. Reign of Manuel II. An able ruler, but his domains were limited to the cities of Constantinople and Thessalonika, and part of the Morean Peninsula in southern Greece.

1422. Turkish Attack on Constantinople. Repulsed by Manuel.

1425–1448. Reign of John VIII (Son of Manuel). His younger brother, **Constantine** (later Constantine XI), and **Thomas Palaeologus** conquered Frankish Morea (1428).

1446. Byzantine Invasions of Central Greece. Constantine Palaeologus was repulsed by Sultan Murad II.

1448–1453. Reign of Constantine XI.

1453, April–May. Siege and Capture of Constantinople. (See p. 438.)

1460. Turkish Conquest of Morea.

1461. Turkish Conquest of Trebizond. This ended the last vestiges of the Roman and Byzantine empires.

THE OTTOMAN EMPIRE

Despite the catastrophic defeat of Bayazid by Timur (see p. 388), the Ottoman Empire made a remarkably quick recovery during the early years of the 15th century. This was principally due to the skill and vigor of **Mohammed I,** son of Bayazid. His son **Murad II** resumed the Turkish career of conquest in Southern Europe interrupted by the Tartar invasion. This was brought to an abrupt halt, however, by stubborn and vigorous Hungarian resistance. Their northern advance being thus checked, the Turks now tried to consolidate their control over areas of southern Europe and the Levant which they had originally by-passed. First and foremost was Constantinople. The remaining fragments of the once-great Byzantine Empire were absorbed, while the growing Turkish fleet gradually gained ascendancy over the Venetians and Genoese in the Aegean, plucking off their island and coastal colonies one by one. By the end of the century, steady Turkish expansion had conquered all the Balkans save for Hungary. The principal events were:

1400–1403. Tamerlane's Invasion of Anatolia. (See p. 392.)

1403–1413. Three-Way Civil War. The sons of Bayazid fought for succession to the Ottoman throne. Mohammed defeated and killed in turn his brothers **Suleiman** (1411) and **Musa** (1413). While this was going on, Ottoman holdings in Europe shrank to Thrace, around Adrianople.

1413–1421. Reign of Mohammed I ("the Restorer"). He re-established central authority. He expanded his dominions in Asia Minor and in Europe, notably by the conquest of Wallachia (1415).

1416. Naval War with Venice. The Doge

Loredano defeated and destroyed a Turkish fleet off **Gallipoli,** causing Mohammed to sue for peace.

1421–1451. Reign of Murad II. He briefly besieged Constantine unsuccessfully (1422) in reprisal for aid the Byzantines had given to an unsuccessful rival.

1425–1430. War with Venice. Turkish fleets captured Thessalonika and Venetian possessions along the coasts of Albania and Epirus. Venice, also engaged in a war with Milan, made an unfavorable peace with the Turks.

1441–1442. Turkish Invasions of Serbia and Hungary. They were repulsed by Hunyadi (see p. 435).

1443–1444. The Last Crusade. This was led by Ladislas of Poland and Hungary and his brilliant general, Hunyadi. Most of the Crusaders came from Hungary, Poland, Bosnia, Wallachia, and Serbia. After Hunyadi captured Nish and Sofia, Murad made peace, abandoning his suzerainty over Serbia and Wallachia (1443). Murad then abdicated. When the Hungarians broke the truce and renewed their invasion by an advance to Varna, Murad resumed the throne. A Venetian fleet was supposed to meet the Crusader army at Varna and to convoy it to Constantinople, meanwhile keeping the principal Ottoman armies from crossing the Straits from Anatolia to Europe. The Venetians failed to carry out their part of the campaign, and Murad with a great army marched to Varna, where he decisively defeated the Crusaders (November 10; see p. 435).

1443–1468. Albanian Wars of Independence. Their leader, **Skanderbeg (George Castricata),** had risen to prominence as a soldier (probably a Janissary) in the Turkish army in the wars against Serbia and Hungary. Skanderbeg established Albania's virtual independence and, with occasional and sporadic assistance from Venice and Naples, repulsed all Turkish invasions. Upon his death, however, the country was quickly reconquered by the Turks.

1448, October 17. Second Battle of Kossovo. (See p. 436.) Largely because of the experience of this hard-won victory over Hunyadi, the Janissaries began to adopt handguns to replace bow and crossbow.

1451–1481. Reign of Mohammed II ("the Conqueror").

1453, February–May. The Siege of Constantinople. Mohammed led an army of more than 80,000 men, with a siege train of **70** heavy cannon, commanded by **Urban,** a Hungarian renegade. To defend the city Constantine XI had less than 10,000 men, including some Genoese mercenaries under gallant **John Giustiniani.** A Venetian fleet provided some initial assistance, but was driven off by the Turkish navy, which completed the blockade of the city. The great siege batteries, including 12 superbombards, were then established and began to hammer against the more vulnerable parts of the ancient city wall from the west (April 2). Several breaches were made both by artillery and mining, and a number of unsuccessful assaults attempted, but the defenders, under the energetic and gallant leadership of Constantine, built palisades behind each breach, and vigorously counterattacked to drive off each Turkish assault. Most of the Turkish mines were detected and blocked before they reached the walls. A final and intensive bombardment leveled a great portion of the wall, which the defenders were unable to block off completely (May 29). Nevertheless, Constantine's gallant defense for several hours stopped a massive Turkish assault through the breach, until another Turkish force, gaining entrance through an unguarded section of the thinly manned wall, attacked the defenders in flank and rear. Disdaining to flee, Constantine fought on in the breach until he was overwhelmed and killed. The victorious Turks then pillaged the city for 3 days.

1456. Mohammed's Siege of Belgrade. He was driven off by Hunyadi (see p. 436).

1459–1483. Turkish Conquest of Serbia, Bosnia, and Herzegovina.

1461. Conquest of Greece and the Aegean. A Turkish fleet drove the Genoese from the Aegean, while at the same time Turkish land and sea forces conquered Morea.

1463–1479. War with Venice. The Turks raided Dalmatia and Croatia (1468), while a Turkish fleet and army invaded and conquered Negroponte (Euboea, 1470). Venetian diplomacy brought Persia into the war, but invading Persians were defeated at the **Battle of Erzinjan** (see p. 440). Having reconquered Albania after the death of Skanderbeg (see above), the Turks then captured most of the

Venetian coastal posts in Albania, while Turk cavalry raiders crossed the Alps from Croatia into Venetia, terrorizing northeastern Italy. Thoroughly defeated, the Venetians made peace, recognizing the loss of all of the regions conquered by the Turks (1479). **Scutari,** whose Venetian garrison had repulsed repeated Turkish attacks (1478–1479), was ceded to the Ottomans.

1480. Turkish Expedition to Italy. They crossed the Adriatic to seize Otranto.

1480–1481. First Siege of Rhodes. Mohammed II besieged Rhodes, but was repulsed with heavy loss due to the gallant resistance and effective defense of the Knights of St. John.

1481–1512. Reign of Bayazid II. This started with a civil war of succession against his younger brother **Djem,** who also claimed the throne. Djem was defeated and took refuge on Rhodes. Essentially a peaceful man, Bayazid ordered the abandonment of the Turkish outpost in Otranto (1481), and generally relaxed pressure against Turkey's European neighbors.

1492–1494. Turkish Invasion of Carniola and Styria. This was repulsed by the Emperor Maximilian.

1495–1500. Inconclusive War against the Poles in Moldavia.

1499, July 28. First Battle of Lepanto. The Turkish navy won its greatest naval victory over the Venetians. It then captured several Venetian island and coastal possessions in the Aegean and Ionian seas (1499–1502).

EGYPT AND SYRIA

During this turbulent century the Mamelukes retained control over Egypt and Syria, but were generally unsuccessful in efforts to expand into Asia Minor and the Kurdistan highlands. The principal events were:

1400–1403. Tamerlane's Invasion of Syria. (See p. 392.)

1412–1421. Reign of Sultan Sheikh Mahmudi. This was a period of internal anarchy and turbulence, during which Sheikh Mahmudi established tenuous suzerainty over the Turkoman principalities in the mountainous regions of eastern Asia Minor and Armenia.

1422–1438. Reign of Sultan Barsbai. He continued Mameluke efforts to subdue the Turkoman states. These brought him into inconclusive conflict with **Shah Rukh** of Persia, son of Tamerlane.

1424–1426. Mameluke Invasions of Cyprus. These were repulsed after initial success and conquest.

1442–1444. Attacks on Rhodes. Repeated invasions by the Sultan **Malik al-Zahir** were repulsed by the Knights of St. John.

1468–1496. Reign of the Sultan Kaietbai. He re-established order in the Mameluke domains after a long period of internal violence. His efforts to expand in eastern Asia Minor brought him into conflict with Ottoman Sultan Bayazid II.

1487–1491. War with the Ottomans. The Mamelukes were at first successful, then were repelled by the Turks from Adana and Tarsus.

1496–1501. Anarchy. A succession of rival sultans.

PERSIA AND TURKESTAN

After the death of Tamerlane (1405), much of his empire was split up among several sons and grandsons, while other portions seized the opportunity to reassert independence. Timurids (successors of Tamerlane) ruled at Herat, Fars, Tabriz, and Transoxiana, frequently in conflict with each other and with the Turkoman tribes of Armenia and Azerbaijan. **Shah Rukh,** a son of Tamerlane and ruler of Herat, established control over much of his father's empire near the middle of the century. Soon after this, however, the Turkomans began to spread across most of northern Persia and into Transoxiana. These Turkoman tribes were organized into two rival confederacies, the "Black Sheep" and "White Sheep" Turkomans. A three-way struggle ensued between the Timurids, the Black Sheep, and the White Sheep. The White Sheep, ultimately successful, quickly declined after a series of unsuccessful wars with the Ottoman Turks. The principal events were:

1390–1420. Rise of the Black Sheep Turkomans. They were led by **Kara Usuf,** who ruled most of Azerbaijan and Armenia.

1404–1447. Reign of Shah Rukh of Herat. He defeated his brothers and nephews in a series of wars to unify most of the southern dominions of Tamerlane. He also defeated Kara Usuf to re-establish Timurid control of Azerbaijan and Armenia.

1420–1467. Black Sheep Expansion. Kara Iskandar, son of Kara Usuf, repelled the Timurids from Armenia and extended his power into Azerbaijan and north Persia (1420–1435). His successor, **Jehan Shah** (1435–1467), conquered north Persia as far as Herat (1448).

1452–1469. Reign of Abu Said (Nephew of Shah Rukh). He controlled eastern Persia and Transoxiana.

1453–1478. Rise of the White Sheep Confederacy. They were led by **Uzun Hasan.** He was defeated by the Ottomans in his efforts to expand westward into Anatolia (1461).

1460–1488. Rise of the Turkoman Safawid Dynasty. The Safawids inhabited the mountainous region southwest of the Caspian Sea around Ardabil in northeastern Azerbaijan. Under their leader **Haidar,** they were intermittently in conflict with both Black and White Sheep confederacies. Haidar was defeated and killed by the White Sheep confederacy and the Georgians of Shirvan (1488).

1467–1469. Struggle for Persia. Jehan Shah was defeated and killed by Uzun Hasan (1467). Abu Said then invaded Azerbaijan, and was also defeated and killed (1469). Uzun Hasan and his White Sheep confederacy thus controlled Persia, Armenia, and Azerbaijan, the Timurids retaining only Transoxiana and Herat.

1473. War with Turkey. Uzun Hasan invaded Anatolia, in an alliance with the Venetians against the Ottomans. He was defeated and repulsed by Mohammed II in the **Battle of Erzinjan.**

1478–1500. Decline of the White Sheep Confederacy. It began to break up into a number of petty states.

1499–1500. Revival of the Safawids. Ismail, son of Haidar, conquered Shirvan, captured Baku, and renewed the war with the White Sheep (1500).

c. 1500. Ascendancy of the Kazakhs in Turkestan. A pagan tribe of Tartar-Turkish origin, the Kazakhs, part of the Golden Horde, occupied the area south and east of the Urals. As the Golden Horde and the Timurids declined in the mid-15th century, the Kazakhs, without any over-all central authority, became the virtually independent rulers of western Turkestan and of the Kirghiz steppes.

SOUTH ASIA

NORTH INDIA

Tamerlane's invasion and the consequent collapse of the Sultanate of Delhi completely and hopelessly fragmented north India for more than a half-century. A new Delhi sultanate, nominally subject to the Timurids of Persia, maintained tenuous control over the turbulent Moslem nobles of northwestern India. In the central Ganges Valley, between Delhi and the Sultanate of Bengal, was the Moslem Kingdom of Jaunpur, almost constantly at war with both of its neighbors. Hindu Orissa, which had successfully defied the Delhi sultans at the height of their power, and which had now become one of the leading states of India, expanded far southward along the east coast of the Deccan. In south-central and southwestern Hindustan were a number of small Moslem states, of which the most important were the kingdoms of

Malwa and Gujarat. In the Rajputana Desert of west-central Hindustan, the Hindu princes who had been driven into this area by Muhammad of Ghor took advantage of Delhi's weakness to regain some of their old power and influence. The most important of these Rajput states was the Kingdom of Mewar. The principal events were:

1414. Establishment of the Sayyid Dynasty. This was by **Khizar Khan,** Tamerlane's governor of the Punjab, who seized Delhi, but remained nominally subject to Shah Rukh of Persia.

1414–1450. Intermittent Wars between Delhi and Jaunpur. A struggle for control of the central Ganges Valley.

1451–1489. Establishment of the Lodi Dynasty. Bulal Lodi overthrew the Sayyid Dynasty. Most of his reign was spent in a drawn-out struggle with Jaunpur, which the Lodis finally conquered (1487).

1458–1511. Reign of Mahmud Shah Begarha of Gujerat. He was an able soldier and magnificent builder, who brought his state to the pinnacle of its wealth and power.

1489–1517. Reign of Sikandar (Son of Bulal). He added further to the revived power and prestige of the new Delhi Sultanate.

SOUTH INDIA

The central feature of the history of the Deccan in the 15th century was a continuation of the struggle between the Moslem sultans of Bahmani and the Hindu kings of Vijayanagar. During most of the century Bahmani was also engaged in frequent wars with its Moslem neighbors of Malwa and Gujerat to the north and northwest, and Hindu Orissa to the northeast. The Carnatic coast was also the scene of frequent contention between Vijayanagar and Orissa, with outcomes generally in favor of Vijayanagar. The principal events were:

1397–1422. Reign of Firuz Shah of Bahmani. He obtained regular tribute from Vijayanagar as a result of his victories in the early wars of his reign (1398–1406). Firuz was defeated, however, by a resurgent Vijayanagar at the **Battle of Pangul** (1420).

1408–1440. Chinese Conquest of Ceylon. An amphibious Chinese expedition conquered the island, which remained tributary to China for more than 30 years (see p. 442).

1422–1435. Reign of Ahmad Shah of Bahmani. He restored Bahmani superiority in the Deccan by capturing Vijayanagar and again imposing annual tribute (1423). He next defeated and annexed Warangal (1425). During the remainder of his reign he was engaged in wars against Malwa, in which he was successful, and against Gujerat, which repulsed the Bahmani armies.

1435–1457. Reign of Ala-ud-din of Bahmani. He again defeated Vijayanagar (1443).

1436–1469. Reign of Mahmud I of Malwa. This warrior king consistently defeated Bahmani and annexed its northern provinces (1457–1469). Had it not been for the intervention of Mahmud Shah Begarha of Gujerat, who wished to preserve a balance of power, Mahmud of Malwa might have succeeded in completely overthrowing Bahmani during this period of weak rule.

1463–1482. Reign of Mohammed III of Bahmani. Bahmani power reached its height, due almost entirely to the military and administrative genius of Bahmani's chief minister, **Mahmud Gawan.** Gawan conquered and annexed to Bahmani the Hindu principalities of the Konkan coast, between Gujerat and Goa (1469). He next invaded and defeated Vijayanagar, annexing Goa (1475). Gawan then turned to the northeast, defeating Orissa and annexing much of the coastline northeast of the Godavari River (1478). He was next victorious in another war with Vijayanagar (1481), following which he was executed by his ungrateful, jealous master.

1481–1500. Decline and Collapse of Bahmani. This was caused by attacks from resurgent Vijayanagar and Orissa. As a result, by the end of the century, the frontiers of these two Hindu states met along the Krishna River.

EAST ASIA

CHINA

During the first half of this century the Ming Dynasty reached the height of its power. This was due primarily to the Emperor **Yung-lo** (or **Ch'eng Tsu**), who conducted an aggressive and uniformly successful foreign policy supported by excellent land and sea forces. A series of punitive expeditions kept the Mongols in check, while Chinese armies re-established imperial authority in Upper Burma and in Annam. The great admiral **Cheng Ho** led a series of naval expeditions which gave China unchallenged control of Indonesian waters and of the Indian Ocean. This Chinese naval ascendancy was due in part to research and development of improved seagoing junks with watertight compartmented hulls. By the middle of the century, however, decline had set in. The outlying provinces in Southeast Asia were lost. By the end of the century the Mongols were again a serious menace in the north. Control of the sea was lost, and the coasts of China were at the mercy of ruthless Japanese pirates. The principal events were:

1398–1403. Dynastic Struggle. Chu Ti was finally successful, taking the royal name of **Ch'eng Tsu,** but is more commonly known by the name of his reign, **Yung-lo.** This civil war laid waste much of the land between the Yellow and the Yangtze rivers.

1403–1424. Reign of Yung-lo.

1405–1407. Early Naval Expeditions of Cheng Ho. This Moslem eunuch seaman invaded Sumatra, conquered Palembang, and forced most of the Malay and Indonesian states to pay tribute to the emperor.

1408–1411. Invasion of Ceylon. Following an insult to a Chinese ambassador, Cheng Ho led a combined land and naval force which conquered Ceylon. The king and royal family were taken to Peking.

1410–1424. Punitive Expeditions into Outer Mongolia. These operations prevented incipient coalescence of Mongol power.

1412–1415. Indian Ocean Expedition. Cheng Ho led a naval expedition as far as Hormuz.

1416–1424. Further Expeditions of Cheng Ho. He extracted tribute from most of the important nations on the shores of the Indian Ocean.

1427. Revolt in Annam. This resulted in the loss of that province (1431; see p. 444).

1431–1433. Cheng Ho's Final Expedition. It included a cruise up the Red Sea, where he obtained tribute from Mecca.

1436–1449. Reign of Ying Tsung. This began the decline of the Ming Dynasty. The emperor was defeated and captured in a battle on the northern frontier by a Mongol Oirat army (1449).

1449–1457. Reign of Ching Ti (Brother of Ying Tsung). He seized the throne during the captivity of his brother. When Ying Tsung was released by the Mongols (1450), a prolonged dynastic war followed.

1457–1464. Second Reign of Ying Tsung.

c. 1470–1543. Resurgence of Mongol Power under Dayan. (See p. 511.)

KOREA

This century was the golden age of Korea and probably the most peaceful epoch in the history of that strife-torn peninsula. A strong and enlightened central monarchy, nominally subject to the Ming emperors, maintained internal peace and protected the coasts against Japanese pirate depredations which had plagued the country in previous centuries, and which would soon recur. An important factor in this success against the pirates was Korean seizure of the Tsushima Islands (1460).

JAPAN

The first half of this century in Japan was relatively quiet, though growing political unrest was a harbinger of violence to come. Internal wars for more than a century were precipitated by a struggle for succession to the Shogunate in the Ashikaga family. The principal events were:

1465. War of the Monks. Conflict between the monks of Enryakui and those of Hongaji, the latter being defeated and their monastery destroyed.

1467–1477. Onin War. This raged primarily in the region immediately around the capital city of Kyoto. Nominally a war of succession in the Ashikaga family, in reality this was a struggle between two great warlords of western Japan: **Yamana Mochitoyo** and his son-in-law **Hosokawa Katsumoto.** Both died during the war (1473), but a senseless struggle continued between their adherents.

1477–1490. Continuing Unrest. Though relative peace returned to the Kyoto area after the return to power of former Shogun **Yoshimasa** (1449–1467, 1474–1490), violence spread through the provinces.

1493. Renewed Civil War. Hosokawa Masamoto led a revolt to drive Shogun **Yoshitame** from Kyoto. Masamoto then set up a puppet shogun; civil strife lasted intermittently through the end of the century.

SOUTHEAST ASIA

THE TAI

During this century there were two principal centers of power among the Tai peoples who inhabited what is now Thailand. In frequent wars the larger Kingdom of Ayuthia was unable to establish ascendancy over the smaller, vital Kingdom of Chiengmai in the jungled mountain ranges of northwestern Thailand. Even more intensive were fierce conflicts between Ayuthia and the Khmer of Angkor. Also during this century, the Tai consolidated control over most of the Malayan Peninsula, with the notable exception of the region around Malacca, where a new and vigorous kingdom fought the Tai to a standstill. The principal events were:

1408–1424. Reign of Int'araja. He intervened successfully in a succession dispute in Sukhot'ai (1410) to reassert the suzerainty of Ayuthia. He was also partially successful in an invasion of Chiengmai, capturing the town of Chiengrai, but being repulsed from the towns of P'ayao and Chiengmai itself (1411). Accounts of the battle near **P'ayao** have been interpreted (probably incorrectly) to imply that both sides used cannon.

1424–1448. Reign of Boromoraja II. He continued the wars with the Khmer. He captured Angkor after a long siege, but was then driven out (1430–1432; see p. 444). He twice tried and failed to conquer Chiengmai (1442, 1448).

1448–1488. Reign of Boromo Trailokanat. He strengthened and centralized control of the Kingdom of Ayuthia, establishing an organized military administration, which was by far the most advanced in Southeast Asia. He was involved in practically incessant war with Chiengmai. At one time the Ayuthians captured Chiengmai (1452), but were later forced to withdraw because of the intervention of Luang Prabang. A few years later, after several Chiengmai invasions, Ayuthian forces again advanced toward Chiengmai. This

campaign came to a conclusion in a moon-
light **Battle of Doi Ba,** near Chiengmai,
where Chiengmai forces repulsed the Ayuthians (1463).

**1455. Unsuccessful Siamese Attack on Ma-
lacca.**
**1494–1520. Renewed Intermittent War be-
tween Chiengmai and Ayuthia.**

VIETNAMESE REGION

The continuing fierce struggle between Champa and Annam was interrupted
early in the century by the temporary (20-year) conquest of Annam by the Chinese.
A successful struggle for independence against China, however, by Annamese leader
Le Loi was a signal for the resumption of the Cham-Annamese conflict, which continued without interruption until Annam finally conquered Champa late in the century. The principal events were:

1400–1407. Civil War in Annam. Despite
this internal struggle, Annamese forces
conquered the northern province of
Champa.
1407. Chinese Conquest of Annam. The
pretext was to restore order following internal unrest.
**1418–1427. Guerrilla War against the Chi-
nese.** This was led by Le Loi.
**1427–1428. Siege of the Chinese Garrison in
Hanoi.** Upon the surrender and withdrawal of the Chinese, Le Loi made himself king, then concluded peace with the
Ming Dynasty, agreeing to nominal submission to the emperor.

1441–1446. Civil War in Champa. Frequent Cham raids into Annam were repulsed.
1446–1471. Annamese Invasion of Champa.
After initial success, and capture of the
Cham capital of Vijaya, the Annamese
were temporarily driven out, but returned
to complete a systematic conquest of
Champa as far south as Cape Varella.
This ended the centuries-old war. An insignificant Cham kingdom persisted farther south as a buffer between the Annamese and the Khmer.
1460–1497. Reign of Le Thanh Ton. He
was the conqueror of Champa.

CAMBODIA

This century was marked by almost continuous war between the Khmer and the
Tai of Ayuthia. Though the Tai won the most spectacular success by capturing Angkor, they were subsequently driven out by the Khmer, and the war continued to rage
throughout the century, with raids and invasions continuing on both sides, the
Khmer frequently threatening Ayuthia. The principal events were:

1394–1401. Tai Invasions. They conquered
much of western Cambodia, but were
eventually repulsed.

**1421–1426. Cham Invasion of the Mekong
Delta.** Despite the strain of the continuing war between Ayuthia and Angkor, the
hard-pressed Khmer repulsed the Chams.

1430–1431. Siege of Angkor. Boromoraja
II of Ayuthia captured the city by treachery after 7 months.
1432. Khmer Counteroffensive. The Tai
were expelled from Cambodia. The Khmer
abandoned Angkor as a capital and re-
established their kingdom on a much reduced scale with Pnom Penh as capital.

BURMA

During this confused century of Burmese history, war was endemic between 6
major rival powers. Within Burma itself, the most important of these were the Burman Kingdom of Ava and the Mon Kingdom of Pegu, both of which were embroiled
almost constantly with each other, with the smaller Burman Kingdom of Toungoo,

and with the Shan (Tai) tribes of northeast Burma. Despite relative isolation by the coastal mountain ranges, the Arakanese were also frequently at war with both Ava and Pegu. During most of this century there were numerous Chinese interventions in the affairs of northern Burma, as the Ming attempted to pacify China's frontiers. For much of the time Ava and the Shan states were subject to the real or nominal authority of Ming governors. The principal events were:

1401–1422. Reign of Minhkaung of Ava. He had numerous desperate struggles with the Mons and Arakanese. He was repulsed in efforts to conquer Pegu.

1385–1423. Reign of Razadarit of Pegu. He was an excellent soldier and administrator, as well as an adroit diplomat. The early years of his reign were devoted to desperate defensive wars against Ava, Chiengmai, Ayuthia, and various smaller Tai and Shan principalities. The most dangerous threat to his embattled nation was that of the Burmans of Ava, whom he eventually repulsed with Arakanese assistance. After repulsing a final Burman invasion (1417), Razadarit initiated a long period of relative peace and prosperity for his country.

1404–1430. Conflicts of Ava and Arakan. This series of violent raids and counterraids was inspired by the intrigues of Razadarit.

1406. War of Ava and Mohnyin. Minhkaung sent a punitive expedition against the Shans of Mohnyin under his able general **Nawrahta**. Threat of Chinese intervention caused the Burmans to withdraw.

1413. Shan Invasion of Ava. The Sawba (lord) of Shenwi raided deep into Ava territory, reaching modern Maymyo, where he was defeated and repulsed by the Burmans.

1414–1415. Ava Invasion of Pegu. Under Prince **Minrekyawswa**, this brought the Mon Kingdom to the verge of disaster.

1415. Shan Raids into Ava. Inspired by the diplomacy of Razadarit, these raids threatened Ava, forcing Minhkaung to recall his son from his invasion of Pegu.

1416–1417. Renewed Ava Invasion of Pegu. This ended with the death of Minrekyawswa in the Irrawaddy Delta. The Ava army again withdrew to meet renewed Shan threats, ending, for the time being, the struggle between Ava and Pegu.

1422–1426. Reign of Hsinbyushin Thihatu of Ava (Son of Minhkaung). Leading a punitive expedition against the Shans, he was killed due to the treachery of his Shan wife.

1426–1440. Anarchy in Upper Burma. The Shans dominated the country.

1438–1465. Chinese Intervention. The Ming, wishing to stabilize their frontiers, re-established order in Upper Burma. General **Wang Chi** conquered and subdued the Shan states.

1445. Chinese Invasion of Ava. They were defeated at **Tagaung** and Wang Chi was killed.

1446. Renewed Chinese Invasion. A large punitive expedition reached Ava, forcing King **Narapati** (1443–1469) to submit to Ming suzerainty. The Chinese then helped him restore order and suppress rebellions. Thirty-five years of relative peace followed.

1481–1500. Unrest and Violence in the North. There were frequent Shan raids into Upper Burma, as Chinese control in the Shan states weakened.

INDONESIA

The Majapahit Dynasty of Java declined and disappeared into obscurity about the end of the century. Early in the period some of the Indonesian states, including Majapahit, were forced to acknowledge the suzerainty of China, and to pay tribute, as a result of the naval expeditions of Chinese Admiral Cheng Ho (see p. 442).

MALAYA

During the first half of this century, practically all of the states of the Malayan Peninsula were under the domination of the Tai Kingdom of Ayuthia, which ejected remaining vestiges of Majapahit authority. By the middle of the century, however, the rapid expansion of Malacca, under its great leader **Tun Perak,** began to drive the Siamese from southwestern and southern Malaya, repulsing repeated Tai efforts to re-establish control. The principal events were:

c. 1402–1424. Reign of Paramesvara. A prince of Palembang, he was a fugitive of civil war in Majapahit who established himself at Malacca. Creating essentially a pirate kingdom, he established control of the Straits of Malacca and extracted tolls from ships passing through, obtaining recognition by the Ming emperors as a ruler independent of Siam (1405).

1409. Chinese Visit to Malacca. A show of force by the war fleet of Cheng Ho.

c. 1414. Paramesvara's Conversion to Islam.

He took the name of **Megat Iskandar Shah.** Malacca continued to expand and prosper until his death (1424).

c. 1450–c. 1498. Virtual Dictatorship of Tun Perak. This prime minister overshadowed 4 sultans, and by combined military and political genius greatly expanded Malacca's power at the expense of other neighbors in Malaya and Sumatra.

c. 1490. Conversion of Java to Islam. Begun by Malaccan traders.

AFRICA

NORTH AFRICA

Save for the beginnings of European colonialism along the Moroccan coast, this was a period of anarchy and of little military significance in North Africa. Petty squabbles between the minor dynasties continued, with the Marinids of Morocco being replaced by the Wattasids through a palace revolution shortly after the middle of the century. Farther east the Hafsids were slowly being expelled from Algeria by the rising Ziyanids, while their hold on Tunisia and Tripolitania was being constantly menaced by the Arab nomads of the desert to the south and east. Meanwhile, the Portuguese and Spanish took advantage of these internal squabbles to seize a number of coastal footholds. The principal events were:

1415. Capture of Ceuta by the Portuguese. (See p. 432.)

1437. Portuguese repulsed at Tangier. (See p. 432.)

1468. Sack of Casablanca by the Portuguese.

This temporarily destroyed the pirate base at Casablanca.

1470. Capture of Melilla by the Spanish.

1471. Capture of Tangier by the Portuguese.

WEST AFRICA

This region began to emerge from obscurity primarily because of the expansion of Portuguese maritime power southward down the Atlantic coast throughout this entire century. The Portuguese were unsuccessful, however, in eliminating a Spanish foothold off West Africa in the Canary Islands. During this century, the great Negro empire of the Songhoi, with capital at Timbuktu, achieved considerable power and splendor. The Songhoi, who had apparently originated in the Nile Valley, dominated the central Niger region from the 8th century on. They were converted to Islam in the 11th century. During the 15th century, under the great Kings **Sunni Ali** and **Askia Mohammed,** the Songhoi Empire dominated most of the western bulge of Africa. The principal events were:

1402–1404. **Spanish Conquest of the Canary Islands.**

1425. **Portuguese Expedition to the Canaries.** The Portuguese, sent by Prince Henry, were repulsed by the Castilians.

1433. **Tuareg Raid to Timbuktu.** The city was captured and sacked by the nomads.

1434–1498. **Portuguese Explorations.** These went along the coast of Africa south of Cape Bojador.

1450–1453. **Renewed Portuguese Attacks on the Canaries.** They were all repulsed.

1469. **Songhoi Capture of Timbuktu.** King Sunni Ali made this the capital of the Songhoi Empire.

1493–1529. **Reign of Askia Mohammed.** The great period of the Songhoi Empire.

XIII

SPANISH SQUARE AND
SHIP-OF-THE-LINE: 1500–1600

MILITARY TRENDS

This was a crucial century of world history, marking the beginning of the Reformation and of a period of bitter religious struggle which had lasting political, military, and cultural effects on the entire world. The tactical-technical flux caused by the introduction of gunpowder continued.

The most remarkable operational development of the century was the relatively abrupt change in the strategy and tactics of naval warfare, both of which had been relatively static for approximately 2,000 years. During those millennia, control of the seas had been exercised near the coastlines by war fleets of short-ranged row galleys. By the end of this century the row galley had been displaced in most parts of the world by the sailing warship, with its heavy broadsides of long-range cannon.

It is not surprising, therefore, that this century was more notable for its admirals than its generals—though standards of military competence on land were substantially higher than in previous centuries. Outstanding were two of the most farsighted innovators of naval warfare, who can be ranked among the handful of great admirals of history, though neither participated in the great naval tactical revolution in Western Europe: Portugal's Dom **Affonso de Albuquerque,** the father of modern naval strategy, and Korea's **Yi Sung Sin,** inventor and successful commander of the world's first armored warships. Hardly less capable were **Khair ed-Din** of Algiers, one of the last and greatest of galley admirals, and Britain's Sir **Francis Drake,** the man most responsible for introducing long-range naval gunnery tactics. Three Spanish admirals rank close behind: Italian-born **Andrea Doria,** the great rival of Khair ed-Din; **Don Juan** of Austria, who won the last great fleet engagement of war galleys; and the Marquis **Álvaro of Santa Cruz,** who distinguished himself in both galley and sailing warfare.

The honors in land generalship during this century were shared by Turks and Spaniards. The most outstanding Turks were the Ottoman Sultans **Selim** and his son **Suleiman,** and the Mogul conquerors of India, **Babur** and his grandson **Akbar.** Italian-born Duke **Alexander Farnese** of Parma was the outstanding European soldier of the century, though his Spanish predecessors **Hernández Gonzalo de Córdoba** and conquistador **Hernando Cortez** were probably equally able. Parma's su-

448

periority among Europeans is based mainly upon his ability to outmaneuver and dominate two almost equally great opponents: French King **Henry IV** and Dutch Stadholder **Maurice** of Nassau. **Bayinnaung** of Burma and **Hideyoshi** of Japan deserve mention in the company of these other leading generals of the era.

During this century, gunpowder domination of the battlefield became complete in Europe, and was almost equally pronounced in Asia. Armor, of little use against either small arms or artillery fire, was fast disappearing. The great nobles continued to wear light armor, more for prestige reasons than anything else; many cavalrymen retained helmet and breastplate, useful in hand-to-hand combat; some infantry, particularly in the pike formations, also retained helmet and breastplate for the same reason.

SMALL-ARMS WEAPONS

Throughout this century the Spanish were consistently ahead of other nations in the development and employment of infantry small arms. This ascendancy began with the Italian campaigns of Gonzalo de Córdoba (El Gran Capitán) at the turn

European arquebusier

of the century. Recognizing the tactical importance of small-arms fire, the Spanish strove constantly to perfect and improve their weapons. By the close of the century the French, learning the lesson as a result of disastrous defeats at Spanish hands, were fast catching up.

Shortly before midcentury, both Spanish and French began to standardize the calibers and mechanisms of their weapons in order to simplify ammunition supply and training procedures. The newly standardized arquebuses were often termed "calivers"—an English corruption of the word "caliber." This development was largely the result of efforts of the Florentine **Filippo Strozzi.**

During the latter part of the century the Spanish, endeavoring to enhance the solidarity of their infantry tactics, began to introduce a heavier small arm, called the musket, with a range up to 300 yards. (This was developed from the so-called *arquebus à croc,* really a light artillery weapon generally mounted on walls or ramparts for defensive fire. Count **Pedro Navarro** introduced the *arquebus à croc* into mobile warfare at the Battle of Ravenna by mounting some 30 of them on hand-carts, which he fitted into Spanish field fortifications.) Appearance of the musket, which had to be fired from a fork rest, and which took longer than the arquebus to load and fire, added complexity to already complicated maneuver and loading drills. The sacrifice was accepted, however, because of greater range and striking power. By the end of the century it had largely replaced the old arquebus as the basic infantry weapon of Europe.

The English were the last important European nation to adopt officially gunpowder small arms. After prolonged debate, a Royal Ordinance of 1595 banned the longbow as the basic weapon of the militia train bands. Each soldier now had to supply himself with an arquebus, caliver, or musket. This did not end the debate in England, however, since archers frequently proved that they could shoot faster, farther, and more accurately than most musketeers (Benjamin Franklin would seriously urge adoption of the longbow as the basic American infantry weapon almost two centuries later).

Efforts to adapt gunpowder weapons to cavalry had resulted in the development of the small, light, horse arquebus early in the century. This prototype of the pistol was theoretically a one-hand weapon, but because of the complexities of handling the clumsy matchlock, two hands were really necessary. Thus horse arquebusiers usually had to choose between fire power and horsemanship; both were usually inadequate and chaotic.

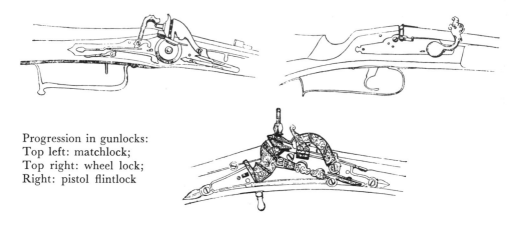

Progression in gunlocks:
Top left: matchlock;
Top right: wheel lock;
Right: pistol flintlock

Shortly before the middle of the century, however, the invention of the wheel lock brought about the development of the first true pistols. Possibly invented by the German **Johann Kiefuss,** this mechanism operated much like a modern cigarette lighter: a rough wheel rotated against a piece of iron pyrite to generate a spark which ignited the powder in the weapon's flash pan. The wheel rotated when a heavy spring was released by pulling a trigger. To assure a modicum of sustained fire power, the horse pistoleer carried three weapons: two in holsters and one in the right boot. After all three pistols had been fired, the cavalryman either had to drop the last pistol and draw his sword or else retire to reload the pistols—an operation requiring both hands.

Because the wheel lock was more expensive and more delicate, it did not replace the rugged, reliable matchlock on infantry weapons during this century.

ARTILLERY

Development of artillery weapons in this century failed to keep up with the progress of small arms mainly because artillerymen were unable to solve the problem of combining mobility with reliable long-range fire power. It had long been realized that long range, accuracy, and destructiveness were best achieved by guns that were

20 or more calibers in length (bore length 20 times the bore diameter), and with thick walls, which could withstand the pressures built up by detonation of a large powder charge. Pieces with thinner walls and lighter powder charges could fire equally heavy projectiles, but with significant reduction in accuracy and range. And even the lightest of these weapons was still clumsy, difficult to move, and took a long time to prepare for action.

Because of these limitations, the artillery supremacy achieved by the French at the end of the previous century was soon reversed by the dramatic Spanish improvements in infantry small arms and the tactics of their employment. As a result, artillery declined in importance during this century, save in the attack and defense of fortifications and in naval warfare. Few major battles were fought without artillery being employed, but in general, after the bloody Battle of Ravenna, small arms were more decisive.

At about the same time the French lost their superiority in artillery construction and techniques to more imaginative German gunmakers. These in turn were soon excelled by the Spanish, who enjoyed a clear-cut superiority in this, as in most other aspects of military science, for most of the century.

An interesting commentary on the status of artillery tactics and techniques during this century is contained in Manucy's *Artillery through the Ages*:

> Although artillery had achieved some mobility, carriages were still cumbrous. To move a heavy English cannon, even over good ground, it took 23 horses; a culverin needed nine beasts.* Ammunition—mainly cast-iron round shot, the bomb (an iron shell filled with gunpowder),† canister (a can filled with small projectiles), and grape shot (cluster of iron balls)—was carried the primitive way, in wheelbarrows and carts or on a man's back. The gunner's pace was the measure of field artillery's speed: the gunner *walked* beside his gun! Furthermore, some of these experts were getting along in years. During Elizabeth's reign several of the gunners at the Tower of London were over 90 years old.
>
> Lacking mobility, guns were captured and recaptured with every changing sweep of the battle; so for the artillerist generally, this was a difficult period. The actual commander of artillery was usually a soldier; but transport and drivers were still hired, and the drivers naturally had a layman's attitude toward battle. Even the gunners, those civilian artists who owed no special duty to the prince, were concerned mainly over the safety of their pieces— and their hides, since artillerists who stuck with their guns were apt to be picked off by an enemy musketeer. Fusilier companies were organized as artillery guards, but their job was as much to keep the gun crew from running away as to protect them from the enemy.‡

Gunmakers experimented constantly with new designs and combinations of bore diameter, wall thickness, powder charges, and projectile weights. As a result there were almost as many types of artillery pieces as there were weapons. Ammunition supply became an impossible task, contributing to the decline of artillery's importance in field operations. To correct this situation, shortly before midcentury Emperor Charles V ordered standardization of all artillery weapons into 7 types. Soon afterward Henry II of France followed suit by establishing 6 standard models for French artillery. Experimentation continued, and many additional types were added to these basic standard models, but in a more orderly and systematic manner than previously. There were no fixed standards among the weapons of different nations, though in general Spanish leadership resulted in imitation by other nations.

By the end of the century the art of gunmaking had progressed to the point where the range, power, and major types of guns were to change little for nearly

---

* More than 60 horses were required to move some basilisks.
† These first crude efforts to create explosive shell were not very successful.
‡ Manucy, Albert, *Artillery Through the Ages,* Washington, 1949.

three centuries. Artillery modifications would be mainly limited to improved mobility, organization, tactics, and field-gunnery techniques.

The distinctions between the three major types of weapons as they existed at the end of the century were fundamentally the same as those that exist today. The first class comprised long-barreled (about 30 calibers), thick-walled pieces designed to fire accurately and at long range. This was the **culverin** type of weapon, roughly comparable to the modern **gun.**

The second class consisted of lighter, shorter pieces designed to fire relatively heavier projectiles shorter distances, sacrificing range and accuracy in order to achieve more mobility without loss of smashing power. This was the so-called **cannon** type of weapon, about 20 calibers in length and roughly comparable to the modern **howitzer.**

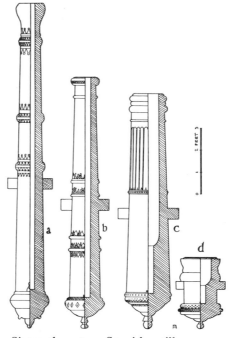

Sixteenth-century Spanish artillery:
(a) culverin; (b) cannon; (c) pedrero;
(d) mortar

The third class comprised short-barreled, thin-walled weapons, firing relatively heavy projectiles for shorter ranges. Within this class were two subcategories. First of these was the **pedrero,** so called because it fired a projectile of stone, which was much lighter than an iron projectile of the same diameter. Thus the pedrero (10 to 15 calibers in length) could have quite thin walls and still fire a rather large stone cannon ball almost as far as a cannon. The other subcategory was that of the **mortar,** identical in concept to the weapons class of the same name today. Mortars were and are short (10 calibers or less) weapons, firing relatively large projectiles for relatively short distances in a high, parabolic trajectory.

Bearing in mind the fact that even within nations standard types varied greatly, the table shows typical characteristics of the most common artillery weapons within each of the three above classes.

16th-Century Artillery Pieces

(Characteristics are indicative and approximate; records are
incomplete, confusing, and contradictory)

Name	Piece Weight (lbs.)	Pro-jectile Weight (lbs.)	Bore (in.)	Length (ft.)	Point-blank or Effective Range (yds.)	Maxi-mum Range (yds.)
Class I: Culverin Types (25–44 calibers in length)						
Esmeril (or rabinet)	200	.3	1.0	2.5	200	750
Serpentine	400	.5	1.5	3.0	250	1,000
Falconet	500	1.0	2.0	3.7	280	1,500
Falcon	800	3.0	2.5	6.0	400	2,500
Minion (or demi-saker)	1,000	6.0	3.3	6.5	450	3,500
Pasavolante	3,000	6.0	3.3	10.0	1,000	4,500
Saker	1,600	9.0	4.0	6.9	500	4,000
Culverin bastard	3,000	12.0	4.6	8.5	600	4,000
Demiculverin	3,400	10.0	4.2	8.5	850	5,000
Culverin	4,800	18.0	5.2	11.0	1,700	6,700
Culverin royal	7,000	32.0	6.5	16.0	2,000	7,000
Class II: Cannon Types (15–28 calibers in length)						
Quarto-cannon	2,000	12.0	4.6	7.0	400	2,000
Demicannon	4,000	32.0	6.5	11.0	450	2,500
Bastard cannon	4,500	42.0	7.0	10.0	400	2,000
Cannon serpentine	6,000	42.0	7.0	12.0	500	3,000
Cannon	7,000	50.0	8.0	13.0	600	3,500
Cannon royal	8,000	60.0	8.5	12.0	750	4,000
Basilisk	12,000	90.0	10.0	10.0	750	4,000
*Class III: Pedrero and Mortar Types**						
Pedrero (medium)	3,000	30.0	10.0	9.0	500	2,500
Mortar (medium)	1,500	30.0	6.3	2.0	300	750
Mortar (heavy)	10,000	200.0	15.0	6.0	1,000	2,000

* Though variations were great, pedreros were usually 10–15 calibers in length, and fired projectiles up to 50 pounds in weight. Mortars were 3 to 5 calibers in length, and fired projectiles up to 200 pounds.

FORTIFICATION AND SIEGECRAFT

A revolution in fortification was in progress at the beginning of the century. The high masonry walls of even the most massive medieval fortifications had been rendered obsolete by the smashing power of heavy siege guns. Use of cannon by the defenders did little to rectify this situation; light guns mounted on the high walls could not reach long-range attacking guns. Heavier weapons—when they could be laboriously lifted to the tops of the ramparts—soon became counterproductive; the force of recoil shook the foundations, dangerously weakening the walls and making them easier to breach.

Consequently, walls became lower and thicker—as much to provide adequate emplacements for defending artillery as to make the breaching process more difficult for attacking siege guns. New fortifications were built with broad, low walls from which triangular bastions extended to permit defending artillery to sweep all approaches to the fort. Existing fortifications were modernized by the erection of new walls and bastions of this type; older walls were lowered and broadened where possible.

The remainder of the century saw an intensive struggle between the rapidly improving science of fortification and the equally rapid increase in power and range of siege artillery. The great basilisks and cannon royal could still breach the new walls by prolonged, concentrated fire. To make this more difficult, and to foil exploitation by besieging infantry, the ditches around fortifications were widened, and in turn protected by a counterscarp wall, where light artillery pieces could be emplaced beyond the ditch to keep the great siege guns at a distance. To provide clear fields of fire for the artillery and small-arms weapons of the counterscarp defenders, earth excavated from the ditch was spread in front of the counterscarp wall to create a gradually sloping terrace, or **glacis.** This open slope, descending from the counterscarp, added to the strength of that low wall, and at the same time complicated the task of the attackers in bringing effective fire to bear on counterscarp defenders.

Mining became difficult since tunnels now had to be too long to permit fresh air to reach the diggers. Another deterrent to mining was the costliness of gunpowder; when an opportunity for mining could be exploited, it was almost always

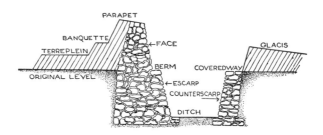

Elements of fortification

by collapse rather than explosion, a reversion to the ancient technique of burning the tunnel support timbers.

The new scientific methods of fortification having outstripped gunnery development, sieges again became lengthy, difficult affairs. This, in turn, caused warfare once more to become a series of sieges, punctuated by battles only when some combination of maneuvering skill, confidence, or logistical pressures brought two armies face to face in the open.

This led to serious efforts to improve siegecraft by adapting it to the new problems posed by the new fortifications. The obvious solution to the problem posed by the counterscarp and the power of defensive artillery was to find a relatively safe method of getting attacking artillery and small arms close enough to the defenses to bring effective fire to bear. The old apparatus of mantelets, siege towers, and the like were totally ineffective against defending gunpowder weapons. Attackers, accordingly, resorted to digging. Before the end of the century the concept of approach entrenchments was quite well developed—though crude in comparison with the refinements that would be introduced by Vauban in the following century.

Under the cover of long-range culverin-type guns, attacking engineers and infantry dug trenches toward a presumably vulnerable point in the defenses. When these trenches were within easy artillery battering range of the fortification's counterscarp—or other outworks—thick earthen walls were thrown up in front of wide, shallow trenches to create protected emplacements for siege guns. Under the cover of darkness the heavy weapons would be trundled into their emplacements, and would then begin the painstaking battering process. Under the cover of this fire, trenches would again be pushed forward until a combined artillery and infantry attack could overwhelm the counterscarp defenders. Again the big guns would be moved forward, this time to concentrate against the main fortifications.

It was a long, laborious, costly, and bloody process—almost prohibitive against active and alert defenders. A 16th-century fortress, if provided with adequate stocks of food and ammunition, was as impregnable as the 13th-century castle had been in its day.

The new fortifications, and the siege process to deal with them, greatly stimulated the long-lost art of field fortifications, largely dormant in Europe since Roman times. The principal stimulus, however, had already been provided by farsighted Spanish soldiers, led by Gonzalo de Córdoba, who was apparently the first to realize the potentialities of field fortifications in combination with the new fire power of gunpowder small arms. Following his example, Pedro Navarro and Alexander of Parma kept Spanish engineering and field fortification techniques pre-eminent, a major element of Spanish military supremacy.

TACTICS OF LAND WARFARE

General

Tactical experimentation continued as military men strove to adapt changing and improving gunpowder weapons to problems of combat. The result was a variety of organizational and tactical patterns, which began to crystallize by the close of the century. During most of this time Spanish military men were generally more imaginative and farsighted than those of other nations. By the close of the century, however, the French under Henry IV and the Dutch under Maurice of Nassau—both following Spanish precedents—began to wrest tactical superiority from the overextended Spanish.

As pointed out above, the increasing effectiveness of firearms, combined with the growing strength of fortifications, impelled generals to avoid battle unless success seemed to be assured. This practice, particularly evident after the hitherto aggressive French learned their lesson at the disastrous Battle of Pavia (see p. 474), was also due in part to the increased logistics problems posed by ammunition supply.

The effectiveness of small-arms fire, combined with the vulnerability of arquebusiers and musketeers when reloading their clumsy weapons, kept coordination of combined arms an ever-present challenge to 16th-century generals. Differing methods of employing cavalry shock action, cavalry small-arms attacks, artillery fire, pike assaults, and field fortifications were usually results of the experimental efforts to get the maximum advantage from infantry small-arms fire.

Infantry Tactics

In his campaigns in Naples at the turn of the century, Gonzalo de Córdoba led the way in recognizing and exploiting the potentialities of small-arms fire. He discovered that extensive frontages could be held by arquebusiers behind entrenchments, thus permitting him to meet, and to outmaneuver, much larger French forces. He also recognized the basic infantry problem that was to govern tactics for the remainder of the century: the need to protect arquebusiers in the open while they were reloading. His solution was to use pikemen to provide steadiness in the defense, and to exploit small-arms fire power by offensive shock action.

Córdoba's Spanish successors followed his example and improved on it. Arquebusiers were employed as skirmishers in front and on the flanks of pike and halberdier columns. The skirmishers—called *enfants perdus* by the French—were particularly important during the slow and painful process of forming up a conglomerate 16th-century army for battle.

As the century continued, the Spanish steadily increased the proportion of small-arms men to pikemen, and began to employ them in solid formations of several ranks, intermixed with pike units. A steady volume of fire could be maintained by having

Spanish pikeman

front-rank men retire to reload, while those behind moved up to the firing line. The pikes continued to bear the brunt of both offensive and defensive shock action in this heavy kind of formation, sometimes called the "Spanish Square." The mutually supporting roles of highly disciplined Spanish arquebusiers and pikemen frustrated their enemies during much of the century.

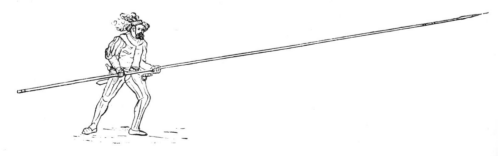

Swiss pikeman

Toward the close of the century the fire power of these heavy-infantry formations was still further increased by introduction of the musket. The lighter, more maneuverable arquebusiers were now almost completely relegated to skirmishing roles. This change seems to have been initiated almost simultaneously by Alexander of Parma and Maurice of Nassau. About the same time Henry of Navarre (at the Battle of Coutras) initiated the practice of having front-rank arquebusiers kneel in front of a standing second rank, so as to increase the steadiness of the formation and to double its fire power.

Cavalry Tactics

During the first portion of the century, French heavy cavalry (mainly built around the **gendarmerie** of old **compagnies d'ordonnance;** see p. 409) remained pre-eminent among European horsemen. The disaster of Pavia, however, impressed upon the French the obsolescence of these successors to the medieval knights. Like other European soldiers they began experimenting with greater proportions of light horsemen and attempting to find ways of adapting gunpowder firearms to cavalry.

During this period of experimentation the Germans developed a new species of heavy cavalry armed with the new wheel-lock pistols. These were organized into mercenary units, the men usually wearing black armor and accouterments, causing them to be called **reiters**—contraction of Schwartzreiter, or "black rider." The reiters were a kind of mounted counterpart of the famed Landsknechts. At first the reiter wore mail armor; later this became open helmet, breastplate, and heavy thigh-length leather boots. The reiters "charged" at a trot in a line of small, dense columns, each several ranks deep. As they approached a foe, the front-rank horsemen each emptied their three pistols, then swung away to flanks and rear in a tactic called the "caracole." While these men were reloading and joining the rear of their respective columns, the succeeding ranks continued the process of deliberate advance, pistol fire, and peeling off. Usually the caracole tactic was employed against pike elements of the opposing infantry for the purpose of knocking gaps in the line prior to a general advance. The caracole was a very difficult operation to carry out smoothly, and could easily be disrupted by a cavalry countercharge. The fact that it was used throughout the century, however, combined with the great demand for German mercenary reiters, is clear proof that the tactic was relatively effective.

During the latter part of the century, however, French cavalry regained its pre-eminence in Europe. Charging at the gallop in long lines two or three ranks deep, the French heavy cavalry fired their pistols as a prelude to shock action with the sword. The French discarded the lance completely. By the end of the century all European cavalry was armed with the pistol, or pistol and sword, save for a few Spanish and Polish lancers.

European cavalry tactics and organization were greatly influenced by the Turks, who in turn borrowed much from their Christian enemies. Save for the relatively small force of Janissaries, Turk armies were composed almost entirely of cavalry fairly equally divided between light, irregular skirmishers—armed mostly with the bow—and the heavier, lightly armored, well disciplined **timariot** (horsemen), feudal cavalry units in which lancers and horse archers were equally divided. At the beginning of the century this Turk feudal cavalry was capable of effective shock action against almost any cavalry opponent save for the French-type gendarmerie. The Turks, satisfied with the effectiveness of their archers, were slower than Western Europeans in adopting cavalry firearms.

The best Turkish cavalry were the **spahis** of the sultan's guard, more heavily armed and armored than the timariots, and capable of meeting the very best European infantry and cavalry. These, like the Janissaries, were permanent standing military formations.

The Turkish cavalry armies had two major weaknesses. In the first place, such an army had to move constantly in order to find enough forage for great numbers of horses. This made it most difficult for them to carry on sustained operations in any one region, and put them at a disadvantage when their conquests brought them up against the cavalry and infantry armies of Central Europe, who could base themselves on powerful fortifications such as Vienna. Another weakness was the lack of steadiness of a fluid cavalry army in fighting a prolonged and hard-fought battle against a balanced professional infantry and cavalry force. The Turks got around this, to some extent, by steadily augmenting their small, well-disciplined corps of infantry Janissaries, and by using field entrenchments so that the Janissaries could provide a base of maneuver for the cavalry elements. The results were sufficiently effective as to pose a mortal threat to Central Europe for most of the century.

Envying, and baffled by, the Turkish light and intermediate cavalry, Germans and Hungarians put increasing emphasis on the development of **hussars**—effective light cavalry of the Turkish type—for screening, reconnaissance, and raiding. This trend—already started in Western Europe by the Spanish **genitours** and French and Venetian **stradiots**—resulted in the development of two clearly distinct types of European cavalry by the end of the century: helmeted, breastplated, pistol-carrying heavy cavalry of the reiter or French heavy-cavalry type, designed primarily for battlefield combat; and lighter, unarmored horsemen, armed with one or two pistols and a light sword, to undertake the other kinds of cavalry tasks.

MILITARY ORGANIZATION

Combat Formations

Though outmoded and inadequate, the medieval combat formation of three massive "battles"—dense blocks of mounted men and infantry—lingered on into the early years of the century. These unwieldy masses were particularly vulnerable to firearms and artillery.

The Spanish took the lead in efforts to solve the problem by thoughtful experimentation and improvisation. Based upon the experience of Córdoba (and possibly at his suggestion or instigation), in 1505 King Ferdinand created twenty units called **colunelas** (columns) each consisting of some 1,000–1,250 men: mixed pikemen, halberdiers, arquebusiers, and sword-and-buckler men, organized as five companies. This was the first clear-cut tactical formation based upon a coherent theory of weapons employment to be seen in Western Europe since the decline of the Roman cohort. The colunela was, for all practical purposes, the genesis of the modern battalion and regiment. It was commanded by a *cabo de colunela* (chief of column), or **colonel.**

Interestingly, this title soon became corrupted in the land of its origin. The colunelas, standing formations of the permanent Spanish royal army, or "crown" troops, were frequently called *coronelia*. Through inaccurate usage (similar to the corruption of the word "shrapnel" in our own time) colunelas were frequently called *coronelias*, and their commanders became commonly known as *coronels*.

The French soon copied the successful colunela concept, and also adopted the military title of rank which—uncorrupted—persists to this day in the French and English languages. For reasons quite unaccountable, the English language retains the uncorrupted Spanish word, as received through the French, but has adopted the Spanish pronunciation.

Over the next 30 years the Spanish gradually developed a larger organization called a **tercio,** which consisted of several colunelas—finally standardized at three—giving the tercio a total strength of slightly more than 3,000 men. It is not clear whether the term tercio came from this triangular formation or (more likely) originated because it comprised about one-third of the infantry component of the average Spanish army. By the time this formation became standardized the Spanish had eliminated the sword-and-buckler soldiers and halberdiers, leaving pikemen and arquebusiers as the components of a tercio, or "Spanish Square." This organization, like the ancient Roman legion and the modern division, became the basic combat unit of its army—a permanent formation, with a fixed chain of command, large and diverse enough to fight independent actions on its own.

The French, again following Spanish lead, soon organized permanent regional units at first called legions, and later regiments. These were somewhat smaller than the Spanish tercios, and not so well organized. This was the origin, however, of the famous French regional regiments of the 17th and 18th centuries.

Command Procedures and Military Rank

Following tradition tracing back to the Roman title of **imperator,** a European monarch was always the general of his country's army. His principal military assistant, in peace and war, was usually called a **constable,** a member of the nobility renowned for military prowess. Other outstanding noble warriors, particularly in France, frequently carried the honorific title of marshal. When the ruler was present in the field, he automatically exercised command as general. His second in command, who might or might not be the constable or one of the marshals, exercised his military functions as the **lieutenant general.** In the absence of the monarch, the lieutenant general commanded in the king's name.

Under the operational command of the monarch or his lieutenant general was a senior administrative officer known as **sergeant major general.** An experienced soldier, not necessarily a nobleman, the sergeant major general was in effect the chief of staff. He was responsible for supply, for organization, and for forming up the heterogeneous units of a 16th-century army for battle—a long, complicated process, with much shouting and confusion, considerably helped if the sergeant major general had a stentorian voice. In his administrative functions he was assisted in the subordinate units—national or mercenary—by administrative officers known as sergeants major and sergeants.

There was no permanent military hierarchy or chain of command below king and constable. Lieutenant generals and sergeant major generals were appointed for a campaign only.

The Composition of Armies

By the beginning of this century most monarchs had a number of permanent standing units to provide a nucleus for armies raised in war. The officers of these permanent professional units were almost always noblemen, though outstanding commoners could rise from the ranks, and some even became sergeant major generals.

The expense of maintaining a large, balanced standing army, however, was still prohibitive to the national economies of the time. Thus in wartime rulers relied primarily upon temporarily hired mercenaries to augment their relatively small permanent forces. The French permanent units, for instance, were mostly cavalry; they relied for infantry upon Swiss mercenaries or (on the few occasions when the Swiss were hostile) German landsknechts and reiters, and Italian infantry and cavalry condottiere companies.

Rulers relying so heavily on mercenaries had many headaches. Though usually well-disciplined and perfectly willing to fight (particularly the Swiss and Germans), the mercenaries had no patriotic feelings and were frequently untrustworthy. It was not uncommon for them to ask for bonuses on the eve of battle—threatening to abandon the army, or to join the enemy, if the demand was not met. This unreliability of mercenaries was one reason why generals were reluctant to risk a major battle. And the expense of paying the mercenaries was a primary factor in keeping armies small.

For foreign operations, an army would consist only of a relatively few national and mercenary professional units. The undisciplined, poorly organized feudal militia would have been a detriment rather than a help in any offensive operations, aside from the expense of paying them and of supporting them logistically. The feudal obligations of the nobility and the towns persisted, however, and the militia were levied, if necessary, in times of foreign invasion; in a defensive role, they could provide some support to the professional units.

There were three important European exceptions to the operational pattern discussed above. One of these, the Turkish, has been discussed in a previous chapter (see p. 408).

Another exception was the appearance of a national regular army in Sweden in the latter part of the century, as the Vasa kings lifted their country to great power status. The Swedish rulers used no mercenaries. The nucleus of their armies was relatively numerous regular units, paid by the state, augmented in wartime as necessary by levies from a well-trained militia.

Maurice of Nassau raised a similar regular army in the Netherlands in the final years of the century. The ever-present Spanish threat enabled him to insist upon long-term enlistment of regular soldiers, and to impose the strictest discipline seen on the Continent since Roman times. Thanks to the sudden expansion of Dutch commerce, he was able to pay his soldiers well, and punctually. The result was a highly disciplined, homogeneous, responsive professional army, at least a match for the finest Spanish troops, and far superior to most of the Spanish mercenaries.

MILITARY THEORY

The increasing complexity of combat with gunpowder weapons, and the growing significance of economic and political considerations of waging war, attracted the attention of more and more men of intellectual bent. All aspects of military affairs were subjected to analysis in this revival of interest in the theory of warfare: strategy, tactics, organization, gunnery and ballistics, fortification.

Most important of the military theorists was **Niccolò Machiavelli** (1469–1527), Florentine statesman and political philosopher. Inactive most of the last 15 years of his life, because out of favor with the ruling Medici family of Florence, he devoted himself to study and writing. From a military point of view his masterpieces, *The Prince* and *The Art of War*, are the most important of his writings. His concepts were based upon his own experience, combined with intense study of classical military history. He was contemptuous of the *opéra bouffe* Italian wars of the 15th century and of the mercenaries who fought them. But he did counsel against taking unnecessary battle risks. He came to the conclusion that the old Roman legion should be the model for the military forces of his time—a conclusion which the Spanish and French were approaching more slowly and more pragmatically. He erred, however, in underrating the effectiveness of both firearms and cavalry. He devised a militia system for Florence, under procedures designed to assure the retention of civilian control, which was later largely adopted by the Medicis. The system's failure was due more to the inherent weakness of Florence than to Machiavelli's theoretical shortcomings.

More specialized theoretical contemporaries of Machiavelli included the famous German artist, **Albrecht Dürer** (1471–1528), who wrote on the theory of fortifications, and **Niccolò Tartaglia** (1500–1557), who published a number of works on the science of gunnery.

The French Huguenot **François de la Noue** (1531–1591) was an intellectual successor to Machiavelli. Like the Florentine, de la Noue combined a brilliant mind with extensive practical experience and an intense interest in military history. He was a principal Protestant leader in the early French Wars of Religion. His clear insight on strategy and tactics was reflected in his writings (mostly done while a prisoner of war), of which the most important was *Political and Military Discourses*.

DEVELOPMENTS IN NAVAL WARFARE

The Revolution in Tactics

This century witnessed an unprecedented revolution in naval warfare. The era of the galley, which had lasted for more than 2,100 years, ended shortly after it had reached its climax under three of the most able galley admirals of history: Khair ed-Din, Andrea Doria, and Don Juan of Austria. War galleys continued to operate

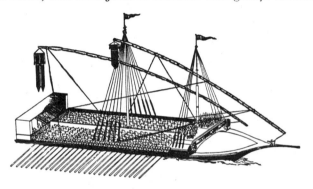

Mediterranean galley

in the Mediterranean for more than a century, but they were merely auxiliaries to the broadside battery sailing ship whose era began as the potentialities of naval gunfire were realized and exploited by such Spaniards as the Marquis of Santa Cruz. He died before he could meet Sir Francis Drake, who probably recognized the new developments in naval warfare even more clearly.

Naval tactics had changed little between the Battles of Salamis and Lepanto. The objective of combat was either to ram or to board an opponent. The fragile galleys were not much different than those which the Romans had used in the Punic Wars. They were long, narrow, single-decked vessels, about 150 feet long and 20 feet in beam, propelled by about 54 oars, 27 to a side. In addition they had two or three lateen-rigged masts, useful to rest the oarsmen and to give added speed when the wind was favorable. There were 4 to 6 oarsmen—usually slaves—on each oar. In Christian vessels they were usually protected by mantelets; the Turks did not bother with such a consideration for galley slaves. The total crew consisted of some 400 men, including oarsmen, sailors, and a contingent of soldiers. Most Christian galleys at Lepanto had 5 small cannon mounted in the bow; the slightly smaller Turkish galleys had only 3 guns. Projecting forward from the bow, just above the water line, was a metal beak, some 10 to 20 feet long, for the purpose of ramming.

There were two important variants of these galleys at the time of Lepanto. The first was the Turkish **galiot,** a smaller, faster vessel, modeled after an earlier Byzan-

tine type, with 18 to 24 oars and a crew of about 100. The other variant, in the
other direction, was the **galleass,** introduced by the Venetians. This was a double-
sized galley, slower but stronger, more seaworthy, and carrying more soldiers. It
was a not very successful effort to reach a compromise between the fast Mediterranean war galley and the new multicannoned sailing vessels of Northern Europe. The
galleass carried 50 to 70 guns, but most of these were falcons or smaller, designed for
man-killing rather than ship-smashing.

Up until the beginning of this century, the Northern European sailing warship,
like the Mediterranean galley, had been considered primarily as a floating fort or
platform, carrying soldiers who were to engage other soldiers on hostile ships. Naval
battles were essentially fought like ground combat as soon as the vessels came within
archery, or light cannon, range of each other, the conflict culminating in the boarding and capturing of one ship by the soldiers of the opponent. The vessels were still

Spanish galleon

essentially transformed merchant "round" ships, barely twice as long as they were
wide. The advent of gunpowder had merely added to the range of the fighting by
the incorporation of small cannon on the fore and after castles, and along the railings
of the upper deck. Heavy cannon could not be mounted on the castles or upper
decks without risk of capsizing the vessel.

But at the beginning of the 16th century, someone—credit is sometimes given
to one **Descharges,** a shipwright of Brest, France—invented the "port": an opening
in the ship's side with a hinged cover facilitating the stowage of cargo in the hull
without hoisting overside. English shipbuilders, spurred by Henry VIII's determination to mount heavy guns in his newly planned warships, seized on the idea as
a way to permit a cannon to be fired from the lower decks of a ship. Thus the
broadside battery came into existence—its weight safely distributed below the center
of gravity. The Spanish soon followed this example. The resulting warship, barely
100 feet long and about 30 feet in beam, was called a galleon—probably because,
like the galley, it was a vessel designed specifically for war, because of the trend
toward a slimmer shape, and because it had a low beak, just above the water line,
which facilitated ramming. This three-masted, square-rigged sailing ship still carried castles fore and aft, with large numbers of small cannon mounted on the upper

works. But its row of larger cannon in the main hull gave the galleon the ability to fight effectively at long range without necessarily closing for the traditional hand-to-hand climax of earlier naval engagements.

The principal shortcoming of the galleon, as compared with the galley, was that it was largely at the mercy of the wind. This was only partly offset by the fact that newer vessels were more maneuverable than the old round ships and, thanks to improved sails and rigging, were able to "beat" against the wind. Unlike the galley, the galleon had the seaworthiness to make long-range ocean voyages.

English sailors, as early as the time of Henry VIII—who greatly encouraged and stimulated the development of English warships—seem to have had a glimmering of the tactical change made possible by the introduction of broadside guns. Though boarding was still considered the main aim of battle, the English tended to put more and more emphasis on designing their ships for long-range gunnery. As a result, the fore and aft castles became lower and lower, and the beaks soon disappeared from English galleons. The proportion of big guns to small guns steadily increased. The Spanish, however, kept the galleon beak, and maintained a balance between man-killing and ship-smashing guns. They followed the English example of lowering the forecastle, but retained a towering aftercastle, on which was mounted a formidable array of small guns.

The Spanish still considered their ships primarily as floating fortresses, carrying garrisons of land soldiers. The English, on the other hand, emphasized seamanship, and their officers and sailors became more skillful than the Spanish. Rather than wasting space and man power by carrying a garrison of landlubber soldiers, the individual English sailor was trained to leave his gun, or to scramble down the rigging, to pick up pike or cutlass when the time came to board an enemy ship or to repel boarders.

These were the differences in naval tactical theory which led to the decisive Battle of the English Channel (see p. 466) in which the English repelled the Spanish Armada, and introduced the new era of the broadside, sailing warship in naval warfare—while at the same time staking out their claim to mastery of the seas.

The Emergence of Naval Strategy

Prior to this century naval strategy was largely an adjunct of land strategy. It is possible that the Chinese Admiral Cheng Ho had had some glimmering of the use of sea power as an instrument supporting national political and economic interests across wide expanses of ocean (see p. 447). There can be no question, however, that this concept of the employment of naval forces in support of national objectives was clearly in the mind of Portuguese Affonso de Albuquerque when he established a network of bases around the Indian Ocean which gave Portugal virtual control of its sea routes and coast lines (see p. 509).

The Spanish probably did not understand sea power quite so clearly as the Portuguese. They employed it successfully, nonetheless, throughout most of this century, in consolidating their control of much of the Western Hemisphere, and in dominating the sea routes of the Atlantic and the eastern Pacific Oceans.

The significance of Spanish bases, and their control of major sea routes, was certainly evident to English seamen like Drake. Confident that the new tactics of broadside sailing ships gave him and his compatriots a clear-cut naval advantage over the Spanish, Drake was probably more responsible than any other Englishman for deliberately initiating the chain of events that were to lead to the supremacy of British sea power.

The First Ironclad Warships

Few men of relative obscurity have so directly influenced the course of history as did Admiral Yi Sung Sin of the semi-independent Korean state of Cholla. His two great victories over the Japanese fleets of Hideyoshi are all that saved Korea—and possibly China—from Japanese conquest at the close of the 16th century. The principal instruments of these victories were two or more ironclad warships which Yi himself had designed and built, and which he employed in battle with courage, skill, and determination.

Yi's "tortoise ships" were low-decked ironclad galleys, with a complete overhead covering of iron plates, ringed with spikes to prevent boarding. Since galleys were uncommon in the Far East, his use of oars, and oarsmen protected by armor plate, reveals the imaginative genius of a man who realized that his concept required a motive power other than the wind. The vessels were equipped with heavy iron rams, and were armed with two or more cannon that fired from gun ports in the armor plate. Other embrasures were used by archers who fired incendiary arrows at the sails, rigging, and wooden hulls of enemy warships.

Yi died in the moment of his final victory. With his death disappeared the imaginative concept of using heavily gunned armored warships. Not until more than 2½ centuries later, after the Industrial Revolution had provided a new kind of motive power, did Yi's idea emerge again. It might be said that Yi was a visionary, like **Leonardo da Vinci,** whose imaginative ideas were unrealistically centuries ahead of his time. The difference is that Yi actually converted imaginative designs into successful instruments of war that changed the course of history.

WESTERN EUROPE

BRITISH ISLES

England

This was the century of the Tudors, dominated by lusty **Henry VIII** and his amazing daughter **Elizabeth I.** Between them they established the foundation for the great maritime British Empire, already in the making before Elizabeth's death. Endemic border warfare with Scotland persisted, though the potential Scottish threat did not seriously inhibit English overseas activities after their great victory at the Battle of Flodden early in the century. Sporadic warfare with France continued during the century, but with little important result, and largely incidental to France's greater external and internal conflicts (see p. 469 and 477). With the growth of English overseas commerce and the beginnings of the Royal Navy, insular Britain's obvious enemy was the nation then dominating the seas and monopolizing the most lucrative colonial trade: Spain. Efforts to avert this rivalry brought about the marriage of Queen **Mary I** with **Philip II** of Spain, but to no avail; in fact, it possibly hastened the crisis. Under Elizabeth there was a decade of undeclared war—on the high seas, in the Americas, and in the Netherlands—before the outbreak of formal hostilities led to the famed Spanish expedition of the Great Armada. Repulsed from England's shores in a series of tactically significant, but indecisive, combats, the Armada was destroyed by the elements—not by the English Navy. But this heralded the decline of the Spanish Empire in Europe and in the Americas, and portended England's future mastery of the waves. The principal events were:

1485–1509. Reign of Henry VII. Central royal authority was strengthened and private feudal armies suppressed (see p. 423).

1509–1547. Reign of Henry VIII.

1511–1514. Wars with France and Scotland. (See pp. 471 and 468.)

1520, June 7. Field of the Cloth of Gold (near Calais). Establishment of a short-lived alliance between Henry VIII and **Francis I** of France.

1522–1523. English Invasions of France. (See p. 474.) These were abortive.

1530–1534. Break with the Papacy. Henry established the independent Church of England, creating a basis for future internal and external conflicts. He was soon forced to suppress the first of several Catholic rebellions (1536).

1542–1550. Wars with France and Scotland. (See pp. 476 and 468.) French landings on the English coast (1545–1546) led Henry to commence an intensive naval construction program, the true beginning of the modern Royal Navy. He also began a great coast-defense construction program.

1547–1553. Reign of Edward VI. He died before reaching his majority. The warrior **Edward Seymour, Duke of Somerset** was Lord Protector at the beginning of the reign.

1549. Internal Unrest. A Catholic revolt in Devonshire was suppressed by Somerset. A peasant revolt in Norfolk, under **Robert Ket,** was also suppressed by royal forces led by **John Dudley, Earl of Warwick.**

1549–1550. Renewed War with France and Scotland. French successes outside Boulogne and Scottish recapture of Haddington, combined with internal religious and social unrest and noble dissatisfaction with Somerset's liberal ideas, permitted Warwick to force Somerset out of power (September, 1549). Warwick (who became **Duke of Northumberland**) made peace with France, surrendering Boulogne in return for a cash payment.

1553, July 6–19. Insurrection of Northumberland (Warwick). Upon the death of Edward VI, he attempted to place his daughter-in-law, Lady **Jane Grey,** on the throne instead of the rightful successor, Edward's sister, **Mary.** Most of the nation rallied to Mary; Northumberland was captured, and Jane was deposed and executed after a reign of nine days.

1553–1558. Reign of Mary I. She re-established Catholicism. Her marriage to Philip of Spain added to religious unrest, many English Catholics joining the Protestants in distrust of Spain and Spanish Catholicism.

1554. Insurrection in Kent. Led by Sir **Thomas Wyatt,** Sir **Thomas Carew,** and the **Duke of Suffolk,** this was to prevent Mary's marriage to Philip. Wyatt was defeated and overpowered while trying to take London; the rebellion collapsed and the leaders were executed.

1557–1559. War with France. Mary's marriage led to English involvement in Spain's endemic wars with France (see p. 477).

1558–1603. Reign of Elizabeth I (Sister of Edward VI and Mary). Return of England to Protestantism. She followed a general policy of avoiding involvement in major continental wars, though she intrigued constantly and sent several small expeditions to the Continent.

1559–1560. Intervention in Scotland. (See p. 468.)

1562. English Expeditions to France. These were to aid Huguenots (see p. 478).

1568–1572. Growing Hostility between England and Spain.

1573. Temporary Rapprochement with Spain. This was due to the ascendancy of the Guises in France (see p. 479).

1577. Alliance with the Netherlands Republic. The Netherlands was in rebellion against Spain (see p. 484), but Elizabeth refrained from outright war against Spain.

1577–1580. Sir Francis Drake Circumnavigates the Globe. He raided Spanish and Portuguese colonies and shipping en route.

1585. English Military Assistance to the Netherlands. (See p. 485.)

1585–1586. Drake's Expedition to the Caribbean. (See p. 518.)

THE SPANISH ARMADA, 1586–1588

1586, March. Spain Plans a Naval Expedition against England. This was recommended by Admiral Marquis de **Santa Cruz.** Philip II directed the Duke of **Parma,** Spanish commander in the Netherlands, to prepare to take his army to England under convoy by Santa Cruz's fleet.

1587, April–June. Drake's Expedition to

Cádiz. He was aware of Spanish naval preparations, and sailed into Cádiz with a fleet of 23 ships, destroying 33 Spanish vessels of all sizes, "singeing the beard of the King of Spain" (April 19). On his return Drake harassed Spanish shipping off Cape St. Vincent, sacked Lisbon harbor, then captured a Spanish treasure galleon in the Azores (May–June).

1587–1588. Spanish Preparations. Santa Cruz diligently repaired the damage done by Drake, but died (January 30, 1588) before the expedition was ready. His death was probably the most important single factor in saving England from Spanish invasion. **Alonzo Pérez de Guzmán, Duke of Medina Sidonia,** replacing Santa Cruz, was a man of courage and ability, but without either naval or army experience. Admiral **Diego de Valdéz** was second in command. The Duke of Parma was to assume over-all command when the expedition reached the Netherlands.

1587–1588. English Preparations. Elizabeth selected Lord **Howard of Effingham** as the commander in chief of her fleet (December 21, 1578). Commoner Drake was appointed vice admiral. Howard had little naval experience, but relied upon good seamen serving under him, particularly Drake. Drake and Howard urged another expedition against Spanish ports to prevent the sailing of the Spanish Armada. Elizabeth overruled them (March). She did, however, raise a force of about 60,000 men to meet the threatened invasion (June).

1588, July 12. The Armada Leaves Corunna. The fleet, which had started from Lisbon (May 20), had stopped at Corunna to take refuge from a storm and to repair a number of unseaworthy vessels. It comprised 20 great galleons, 44 armed merchant ships, 23 transports, 35 smaller vessels, 4 galleasses, and 4 galleys. The fleet was manned by 8,500 seamen and galley slaves, and 19,000 troops; the warships mounted 2,431 guns. Of these 1,100 were heavy guns, including about 600 culverins; over half of the cannon mounted on Spanish ships were light antipersonnel weapons, based on age-old naval tactics of reaching decision by grappling and hand-to-hand fighting.

1588, July 19. Appearance of the Armada.

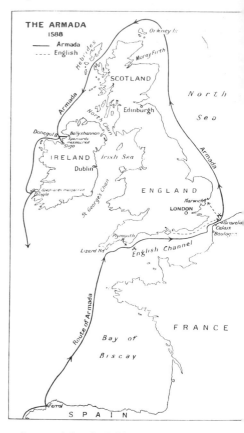

THE ARMADA 1588
—— Armada
---- English

It was sighted off Lizard Head by English scout vessels.*

1588, July 20. Howard Sails from Plymouth. Naval forces available for the defense of England, under his over-all command, consisted of his own fleet of 34 ships, Drake's squadron of 34 (also based on Plymouth), a London squadron of 30 ships, and another squadron of 23 vessels under Lord **Henry Seymour** off the Downs in the eastern English Channel. There were some 50 additional vessels of varying types, carrying a few guns, mostly transports and supply ships that took little part in the subsequent action. The principal warships of the English fleet carried a total of approximately 1,800 heavy cannon, mostly long-range culverins.

1588, July 21. Engagement off Plymouth. The English outsailed and outshot the Spanish, who lost one ship sunk, and suf-

* Dates are given here in Old Style, thus differ by 10 days from those in the best-known account: Garrett Mattingly, *The Armada,* New York, 1959.

fered heavy losses and damage from English long-range fire.

1588, July 23. Action off the Devon Coast. This all-day engagement followed a day of protracted calm and aimless maneuvering. There was no coordination between vessels on either side, much ammunition was consumed, no vital damage was done.

1588, July 25. Battle off Dorset. The English had replenished their ammunition; the Spanish had had no such opportunity. Medina Sidonia, abandoning his plan of landing on the Isle of Wight, headed for Calais, hoping to be able to replenish his empty ammunition magazines from Parma's supply depots.

1588, July 26–27. Cannonade off Calais. The Spanish fleet, now 124 vessels, anchored off Calais, unable to renew action without ammunition. Howard now had 136 ships of all types, organized into 4 squadrons under himself, Drake, Sir **John Hawkins,** and Sir **Martin Frobisher.** He contented himself with long-range fire, but anchored most of his fleet out of range. He knew that he could do no serious damage to the Spanish ships without coming so close as to be in danger of boarding by the Spanish soldiers. Medina Sidonia requested Parma to come to his assistance, but Parma was unable to leave Bruges, which was being closely blockaded by a Dutch fleet under **Justinian of Nassau.**

1588, July 28. Battle off the Flanders Coast. Before dawn the English sent several fire ships into the Spanish fleet. To avoid the fire ships, Medina Sidonia ordered anchor cables cut. He planned to return to the anchorage after the danger was past, but his subordinates panicked in predawn darkness. Due to unfavorable winds, the Spanish, unable to concentrate, drifted northward in a straggling formation. The English pursued and closed in, to begin an all-day running fight at very close range, with Spanish small guns and arquebuses trying vainly to reply to the English culverins and other heavy cannon. The English kept to windward, with several ships concentrating against individual Spanish vessels, firing alternate broadsides. The Spaniards fought heroically but were unable to reply effectively, since they had no heavy ammunition. Despite severe damage and heavy loss of life on the Spanish ships, none was sunk, but the English were closing in toward the end of the day to cut off and capture 16 of the hardest hit. The Spanish vessels were saved by a sudden squall.

1588, July 29–30. Unfavorable Winds. The Spanish fleet was unable to approach Dunkirk or Bruges, where Medina Sidonia had planned to refit, obtain new ammunition, and to join Parma. After the fleet almost went aground on Zeeland, and with no change in wind, the Spanish lost all chance of reaching any Netherlands port. Medina Sidonia decided to return to Spain via the North Sea, completely encircling the British Isles.

1588, August 2. Past the Firth of Forth. The Spanish fleet was now fairly well concentrated. The English fleet, which had been following, ran short of provisions and returned to home ports.

1588, August–September. The Ordeal of the Armada. Terrible hardships and losses were suffered by the Spanish, partly due to storms, but even more to starvation and thirst. Thousands of men died. Out of 130 ships that started, 63 were known to be lost, the survivors straggling into Spanish ports in September. The English sank or captured about 15. Nineteen were wrecked on the Scottish or Irish coast. The fate of the remaining 33 vessels is unknown.

1589–1596. Small Expeditions to the Continent. Lord **Peregrine Bertie Willoughby** led an expedition of 4,000 men to Normandy to aid **Henry of Navarre** (1589). Small forces were landed at St.-Malo and Rouen (1591). Troops were landed during a raid on Cádiz (1596).

1594–1603. Tyrone Rebellion in Ireland. Endemic rebellion in Ireland erupted into full-scale war under the leadership of **Hugh O'Neil, Earl of Tyrone,** who joined already rebellious **"Red" Hugh O'Donnell.** O'Neil defeated the English at **Yellow Ford** on the Blackwater River (1598, August), and outmaneuvered Queen Elizabeth's favorite, the **Earl of Essex** (1599–1600). In response to Irish appeals for help, a Spanish army of 4,000 men under Don **Juan D'Aquila** arrived in Ireland and captured **Kinsale** (1601). A few weeks later, **Charles Blount, Lord Mountjoy** defeated the Irish-Spanish army at the **Battle of Kinsale.** The rebellion soon was suppressed. O'Neil surrendered and was pardoned by James I (1603).

Scotland

Fierce, incessant conflicts with England persisted through this century. The Scots continued to seek French assistance whenever possible, and to exploit all English preoccupation on the Continent. This was, however, the last century in which the armed forces of the two nations were ranged against each other in formal battle. The principal events were:

1488–1513. Reign of James IV. He greatly increased central authority.

1513. War with England. When Henry VIII led an invasion of Scotland's traditional ally, France, James promptly declared war (August 11) and invaded England.

1513, September 9. Battle of Flodden. Thomas Howard, **Earl of Surrey** hastily raised an army to defend England, aided by James's slow advance. Finding the Scottish army drawn up in an extremely strong defensive position on a hill known as Flodden Edge, Surrey boldly and rapidly moved his entire army around the Scottish position, and forced James to face to the rear. Surrey covered the deployment of his army and the arrival of his rearmost contingents by a long-range artillery bombardment and archery harassment of the Scottish position. Though James had planned to fight a defensive battle, this harassment caused the impatient Scots (mostly in masses of pikemen) to charge violently down the hill. The battle began in late afternoon and lasted till darkness. The English repulsed repeated Scottish charges and gradually gained ascendancy in a violent melee. Ten thousand Scots were killed, including James and most of his leading nobles. English losses were also heavy.

1513–1542. Reign of James V. During most of his reign there was indecisive border warfare with England (1513–1534).

1542–1550. Renewed War with England. This was due mainly to religious differences between James and Henry VIII, who renewed old claims of English suzerainty.

1542, November 25. Battle of Solway Moss. An English invading army inflicted a crushing defeat on weak and disorganized Scottish forces. The English failed to exploit.

1544–1547. Reign of Mary, "Queen of Scots" (one week old when her father died). English forces under **Edward Seymour,**

Earl of Hertford inflicted much damage in southern Scotland (1544–1545). The Scots renewed their alliance with France, and French expeditionary forces soon arrived in Scotland. The Scots rejected the demand of Seymour (now Duke of Somerset and Lord Protector of England; see p. 465) to establish an English-Scottish alliance by the marriage of Edward VI (age 9) to Mary (age 5).

1547, September 10. Battle of Pinkie. An English army of 16,000 under Somerset invaded Scotland. A Scottish army of 23,-000 under Earl **James Hamilton of Arran,** Regent of Scotland, met the English at the River Esk, on the Firth of Forth. Each side attempted to turn the other's left, but Somerset's superiority in cavalry, artillery, and arquebusiers gave him a decisive victory with the offshore assistance of an English fleet under Lord **Edward Clinton.** Scottish casualties exceeded 5,000, plus 1,500 captured; the English lost about 500. This was the last formal battle fought between the national armies of Scotland and England. The English occupied Edinburgh.

1547–1550. Guerrilla Warfare and Small-Unit Raids. The Scots with French assistance regained the territories captured earlier by the English, who abandoned Edinburgh (1550).

1550–1559. Growing French Influence. Many Scots became resentful of "foreign occupation."

1559–1560. Rising against the French. The Scots, assisted by English forces sent by Elizabeth, besieged the French contingents and forced them to surrender at Leith (February, 1560).

1560, July 6. Treaty of Edinburgh (between England, France, and Scotland). The French agreed to end their intervention.

1567, June. Noble Revolt. Mary's adherents were defeated at the **Battle of Carberry Hill** (June). She was imprisoned and forced to abdicate; her half-brother,

James, Earl of Moray, became regent for her infant son, **James VI.**

1567–1625. Reign of James VI (Who Became James I of England and Scotland). His minority was a period of turmoil, during which his mother's adherents, led by Arran initially (1567–1573), attempted to overthrow the regency.

1568, May. Battle of Langside. Mary escaped from prison; her adherents rose to support her, but were defeated by Moray.

Mary fled to England, where she was imprisoned by Elizabeth in the Tower of London.

1582–1583. Edinburgh Raid. Adherents of Mary captured James VI, who was held prisoner for 10 months.

1585. James's Alliance with Elizabeth. This ended the national wars between England and Scotland.

1587, February 8. Execution of Mary. This was ordered by Elizabeth.

FRANCE, 1495–1600

During the first half of this century, France vainly attempted repeatedly to gain ascendancy in Italy and to become the principal power of Western Europe. It is not surprising that the Valois kings were unable to achieve their objectives against the united power of the Empire and Spain, with England and most of the Italian states also being generally allied against them; it is remarkable that they frequently came close to success, and that their determination never faltered, despite numerous defeats. There were several victories, as well. On balance, the French national spirit, created by Joan of Arc during the adversity of the Hundred Years' War, was strengthened and tempered in the constant struggle of the Valois-Hapsburg wars. French national territory actually grew slightly during this period at the expense of less united neighbors. The principal feature of the Valois-Hapsburg Wars was the intense personal feud of Francis I and Emperor Charles V.

These wars had barely ended, just after midcentury, when France was plunged into nearly four decades of bitter religious civil strife. Despite her neighbors' efforts to take advantage of this violent, divisive struggle, France emerged without serious or lasting effects. In part, this was due to the fact that the neighbors were also suffering from conflicts spawned by the Reformation; in part, it was because the French, so violently divided against each other religiously, and eager to accept foreign aid from those of like religious faith, nevertheless closed ranks periodically to prevent foreign political domination; finally, it was due to the genius of **Henry of Navarre,** who gained decisive military victories as a Protestant leader, but who brought political as well as military unity and peace to France by embracing the Catholic religion as King Henry IV. The principal events were:

Wars with Spain and the Empire, 1495–1559

ITALIAN WARS OF CHARLES VIII AND LOUIS XII, 1495–1515

Failures in Naples against the "Gran Capitán," 1495–1504

1495. Charles VIII's Invasion of Italy. (See p. 426.) A Spanish expedition of some 2,100 men was sent to support Aragonese King Ferrante of Naples. The Spanish commander, **Hernández Gonzalo de Córdoba,** landed in Calabria (May 26), one of the few parts of Naples still unsubdued

by the French, whose over-all commander was **Gilbert, Duke of Montpensier.**

1495, June 28. Battle of Seminara. Córdoba and Ferrante, with a combined force of about 8,000 men, were defeated by a somewhat smaller French army under Marshal **Everard d'Aubigny** (a member of the Scottish Stewart family). This was Córdoba's first and last defeat.

1495–1498. Victories of Córdoba. Adapting the Spanish-Moorish methods of operations to the French and Swiss military systems as he found them in Italy, and refusing to fight any large-scale engagements, Córdoba slowly reconquered most of Naples. He was assisted greatly by the length of the insecure French line of communications through northern Italy. His principal success was the siege and capture of Montpensier at Atella (July, 1496). During this time Córdoba intensively trained a portion of his infantry in Swiss pike tactics.

1498. Departure of Córdoba. Upon the withdrawal of the French, he returned to Spain. Civil war broke out in Naples. Taking advantage of this, the French again invaded (1499).

1498–1515. Reign of Louis XII.

1500, November 11. Treaty of Granada. The French and Spanish agreed to divide Naples between them.

1500–1502. Louis XII Invades Italy. The French easily conquered Milan, then advanced south to overrun Naples. At the same time a Spanish fleet seized Taranto (March, 1502).

1502. Renewal of Franco-Spanish War in Naples. Córdoba with about 4,000 men was opposed by the **Duke of Nemours** with approximately 10,000. Córdoba was forced to withdraw into Apulia, to the seaport of Barletta, leaving most of Naples in the hands of the French.

1502, August–1503, April. Blockade of Barletta. The loosely maintained French investment was enlivened by frequent duels and tournaments. Seigneur **Pierre de Bayard** was the principal French champion.

1503, April 26. Battle of Cerignola. Reinforced by sea to 6,000 men, Córdoba marched out of Barletta and took a position on a hillside, behind a ditch and a staked palisade. The French attacked. At the outset, the Spanish artillery became useless due to the explosion of its powder supply. Supported by effective artillery fire, French heavy cavalry and Swiss pikemen attacked, but were disastrously repulsed by the effective fire of Spanish arquebusiers behind the ditch and palisade. With the attackers in confusion, the Spanish infantry counterattacked to drive them off the field. Nemours was killed. This was probably the first battle in history won by gunpowder small arms.

1503, May 13. Fall of Naples. After taking the city, Córdoba advanced to Gaeta.

1503, June–October. Siege of Gaeta. Arrival of French and Italian allied reinforcements caused Córdoba to fall back to the line of the Garigliano River.

1503, August–December. French Probes in the Pyrenees. These were repulsed by the Spanish.

1503, October–December. Stalemate on the Garigliano. Because of illness of Marshal **Louis de La Trémoille,** command of the French army passed to Italian condottiere allies: first was **Gonzago, Marquis of Mantua** (who had opposed the French at Fornovo; see p. 426), until he was in turn replaced due to illness by **Ludovico, Marquis of Saluzzo.** Neither of these Italians was trusted or respected by their French subordinates. Córdoba conducted frequent raids along the river, but avoided any general attacks.

1503, December 29. Battle of the Garigliano. When Córdoba's army was reinforced to about 15,000 men, he decided to attack the French-Italian army of some 23,000. Taking advantage of bad weather, his skillful engineers used secretly assembled bridging materials to make a surprise crossing of the swollen river immediately opposite the French winter cantonments. The Franco-Italian forces were driven in confusion into Gaeta with heavy losses in killed and captured.

1504, January 1. Fall of Gaeta. The terms permitted the French army to evacuate by sea.

1504–1507. Córdoba Viceroy of Naples.

1505. Treaty of Blois. Louis XII gave up his claims to Naples and made peace with Spain, which now controlled all of Naples.

1507. Córdoba's Recall to Spain. Due to the jealousy of Ferdinand, he was never given another opportunity to command. His death (December 1, 1515) preceded that of Ferdinand by 3 months.

Later Italian Wars of Louis XII, 1508–1514

1508–1510. War of the League of Cambrai. Urged by Emperor Maximilian, France joined the Empire, the Papal States, and Spain in an alliance to break the power of Venice. Because of mutual jealousies the League did not prosecute the war intensively; there was no coordination of allied activities. The only important battle was a French victory at the **Battle of Agnadello** (May 14, 1509). Imperial, French, and Papal forces, acting separately, occupied most of Venetian territory in northern Italy. At the same time

Spanish troops captured the Venetian Apulian towns, including Brindisi and Taranto. Taking advantage of allied disunity, the Venetians recaptured Padua and Vicenza (July). After a brief and unsuccessful siege of Padua by Maximilian, the war became a stalemate, due to allied mutual jealousies.

1510–1514. War of the Holy League. Pope **Julius II,** fearful of both French and Germans, joined Venice in a new alliance, later called the Holy League. Ferdinand of Spain, at first neutral, joined Venice before the end of the year, as did Henry VIII of England. Desultory military operations were almost entirely between French forces and those of the Holy League allies dominated by Spanish leaders.

Campaigns of Gaston of Foix, 1511–1512

1511. Arrival of a New French Commander. This was Count **Gaston of Foix,** age 21, the new Duke of Nemours. The war was electrified by his energy.

1511–1512. Campaign of Bologna and Brescia. The French had captured Bologna (May 13, 1511), but a combined Papal and Spanish force under **Raymond of Cardona,** Viceroy of Naples, had laid siege to the city. Gaston marched to Bologna, where he drove the allied army off. He then turned north to defeat the Venetians near Brescia, which he then invested and captured by storm (February, 1512).

1512, March–April. Campaign of Ravenna. With most of north Italy under his control, Gaston now marched boldly south to besiege Ravenna, hoping to entice the Spanish into battle. A combined Spanish-Papal army under Cardona moved cautiously toward Ravenna, to establish a strong defensive position nearby, threatening the French siege lines. Cardona had approximately 16,000 men; Foix had 23,000, including 8,500 German landsknechts. The garrison of Ravenna was probably about 5,000 men. Foix sent a formal invitation to battle to Cardona, who accepted with equal formality.

1512, April 11. The Battle of Ravenna. The Spanish position was selected with its back against the unfordable Ronco River, and its front protected by strong entrenchments and obstacles prepared by the excellent Spanish engineer, **Pedro Navarro,** who also commanded the Spanish infantry. Gaston had 54 artillery pieces; Cardona probably had about 30. The French army moved from the siege of Ravenna, leaving only 2,000 men to guard against a sortie by the garrison. They crossed the stream between Ravenna and the Spanish camp without interference, and drew up in a semicircle facing the Spanish trenches. The French artillery on the flanks began an intensive bombardment; the Spanish artillery returned the fire. This bombardment lasted for several hours, extremely heavy casualties being suffered by both sides. Navarro's infantry was protected by its entrenchments. The Spanish cavalry, less protected, finally could endure the bombardment no longer, and attacked without orders. These attacks, poorly coordinated, were repulsed by the French, and Gaston promptly counterattacked. The struggle between the landsknechts and the Spanish infantry at the entrenchments was particularly bloody and indecisive, lasting for perhaps an hour. At this point two French cannon which Gaston had sent back across the river behind the Spanish camp opened fire from the rear, creating panic among the defenders. In the ensuing rout, the Spanish, endeavoring to cut their way out to the south, suffered great losses. Gaston, taking part in the pursuit, was killed in a minor skirmish with one stubbornly withdrawing unit of Spanish infantry. French losses were about 4,500 killed and at least an equal number wounded, the majority of these being among the landsknechts. Spanish losses were 9,000 killed and an unknown number wounded. Navarro was captured. (When the Spanish government later did not ransom him, in disgust he renounced his allegiance to Spain and entered the French service, performing with distinction.)

COMMENT: *The death of Gaston of Foix, as the result of his own impetuous participation in the pursuit, was a real disaster to the French. In the previous six months of campaigning he had demonstrated a potentiality of becoming one of the great captains of history.*

1512, May–July. The French Situation Becomes Desperate. The Emperor Maximilian and Switzerland both joined the Holy League. (This was the real beginning of the Valois-Hapsburg wars.) As a result, the German landsknechts withdrew from the French army and joined imperial forces advancing across the Alps into north Italy. At the same time Swiss troops occupied Lombardy. Marshal **Jacques de la Palice** raised the siege of Ravenna and withdrew behind the Alps. The Swiss established a virtual protectorate over the Duchy of Milan.

1512. English Invasion of Guyenne. An expedition under Marquis **Thomas of Dorset** ended in mutiny and failure.

1513, May–June. French Invasion of Italy. An army of 12,000 under Prince **Louis de La Trémoille** crossed the Alps into Italy and captured Milan. He then besieged a Swiss garrison at Novara. Threatened by a Swiss relief army of some 5,000 men, La Trémoille withdrew from his investment lines and prepared for battle.

1513, June 6. Battle of Novara. The Swiss, sleeping only 3 hours, marched all during the night to join the garrison of Novara and to make a surprise dawn attack upon the unsuspecting French. Attacking in typical echelon form, in 3 heavy columns, the Swiss first struck the French left flank and smashed through to the center of the French camps, cutting the infantry to pieces, though most of the cavalry escaped. La Trémoille withdrew the remnants of his shattered army back behind the Alps into southern France.

1513, June. English Invasion of France. Henry VIII, with an army of about 28,000 English and continental mercenary troops, invaded France from Calais. A hastily assembled French army of approximately 15,000 men, under la Palice, endeavored to harass the English besieging Thérouanne, but avoided battle.

1513, August 16. Battle of Guinegate (Battle of the Spurs). A French effort to harass the English siege lines at Thérouanne was anticipated by the English, and the French, expecting to achieve surprise, were the ones who were surprised by fierce opposition. The French cavalry fled from the field in confusion. Casualties were slight; the battle received its nickname from the fact that many of the French knights lost their spurs during the flight, and these were later picked up by local townspeople. Among the prisoners captured by the English were la Palice and the Chevalier **Pierre Terrail de Bayard,** one of the few Frenchmen who had fought bravely, and who had attempted to rally his panic-stricken comrades. Bayard, who had distinguished himself in the sanguinary combat of Ravenna, is known to history as "the knight without fear or reproach."

1513, August 22. Surrender of Thérouanne to the English.

1513, September. Swiss Invasion of France. At Dijon the Swiss accepted a French indemnity and made peace, thus letting down their English and German allies.

1513, October 7. Battle of La Motta. Cardona, Viceroy of Naples, defeated the Venetians, largely due to the superior performance of the Spanish infantrymen—pikemen and arquebusiers—under **Fernando F. de Avalos, Marquis of Pescara.**

1513–1514. Allied Indecision. Despite victories at Novara and Guinegate, the allies could not agree upon a common strategy. Discouraged by the defection of the Swiss, one by one they made peace with France, first the Pope and Spain (December, 1513) and then the Empire and England (March, July, 1514).

THE REIGN AND WARS OF FRANCIS I, 1515–1547

1515, June. Invasion of Italy. Francis, inheriting his predecessor's obsession with Italy, formed an alliance with Henry VIII and with Venice against the Emperor, the Pope, Spain, Milan, Florence, and Switzerland. Leading an army of about 30,000 men, he suddenly invaded Italy by the high and difficult Argentière Pass; the difficult passage was facilitated by the skill of turncoat Spanish engineer Pedro Navarro (see p. 471).

1515, June–September. Advance on Milan. Francis at the same time attempted to bribe the Swiss to make peace. Nearly 10,000 of the Swiss in Lombardy accepted the bribe and marched off to Switzerland. This left approximately 15,000 Swiss in and around Milan, still faithful to their allies. Meanwhile a Venetian army of about 12,000 was facing a Spanish army of comparable size near Lodi.

1515, September 13–14. Battle of Marignano. The French were in an entrenched camp about 10 miles from Milan. Francis had called on **Bartolomeo de Alviano,** the Venetian commander, to join him as soon as possible. The Swiss, after a typical rapid advance, launched a surprise attack in midafternoon. The rapidity of the Swiss advance gave the French no opportunity to use their artillery. Repulsing a French cavalry attack, the Swiss smashed their way across the entrenchments, but were finally halted by a counterattack led by Francis himself, with Bayard at his side. A fierce fight raged at the edge of the French camp for some five hours, when both sides pulled back by mutual consent at about 10 P.M. By dawn both sides had reorganized; the battle was resumed by a violent Swiss attack. This time the French artillery was ready, but despite heavy casualties the Swiss pressed forward so rapidly that again an inconclusive, sanguinary hand-to-hand combat ensued. About 8 A.M. Alviano's Venetian army neared the Swiss rear after a forced march. The Swiss, sending a small force to delay the Venetians, undertook a deliberate and remarkable withdrawal from contact with the French. Total Swiss losses were about 6,000 killed as against 5,000 French dead. Francis immediately occupied Milan, and Switzerland negotiated peace—which would endure until the French Revolution. The Pope soon sued for peace, and the anti-French alliance collapsed, leaving most of Lombardy in French hands.

1516, August 13. Treaty of Noyon. Charles I, newly crowned King of Spain (later Emperor Charles V), also made peace, recognizing French control of Milan in return for Francis' renunciation of his claim to Naples. Charles' grandfather, the Emperor Maximilian, after an abortive attempt to invade Lombardy, also made peace at the **Treaty of Brussels** (December 4).

First War between Charles V and Francis, 1521–1526

The new German Emperor (also the King of Spain) claimed Milan and Burgundy, while Francis claimed Navarre and Naples. Italy was again the principal battleground, although considerable fighting took place in the Pyrenees, particularly in Navarre. The principal events were:

1521. French Invasion of Luxembourg. This invasion, led by **Robert de la Marck, Duke of Bouillon,** precipitated undeclared border war between the Rhone and the North Sea.

1521, May–June. French Invasion of Navarre. André de Foix conquered part of Navarre, **Ignatius de Loyola** being wounded in the unsuccessful defense of Pamplona. The invading army had barely installed the exiled king, Frenchman **Henri d'Albret,** on the throne when they were surprised and defeated by a Spanish force at the **Battle of Esquiroz,** near Pamplona (June 30), and driven out of the country.

1521, November 23. French Loss of Milan. Italian condottiere General **Prosper Colonna,** commanding the combined Spanish-German-Papal Army, outmaneuvered Marshal **Odet de Lautrec** and captured Milan in a surprise attack.

1522, April. Operations near Milan. Lautrec, with Swiss and French reinforcements bringing his strength to about 25,-000 men, plus 10,000 allied Venetians, advanced on Milan. Colonna, with less than 20,000, took up a strong defensive position at Bicocca, near Milan. Lautrec's 8,000 Swiss troops, their pay in arrears, threatened departure unless paid immediately, then agreed to fight one battle before leaving. Lautrec, therefore, decided to attack.

1522, April 27. Battle of Bicocca. Lautrec carefully prepared a plan to make the maximum use of his artillery. The impatient Swiss, refusing to wait for the French artillery to get in position, attacked without orders. Held up at the entrenchments, they suffered heavy casualties from the Spanish arquebusiers and were repulsed with severe losses. In half an hour 3,000 Swiss were killed. French heavy cavalry attempted a diversion by striking at the rear of the allied position, but were driven off. Lautrec withdrew eastward into Venetian territory. Allied losses were merely a few hundred men. This battle struck a terrible blow at Swiss morale, and they never again attacked arquebusiers in their old confident fashion. The battle was a clear demonstration of the predominance of gunpowder small arms.

1522–1523. English Raids in Picardy. The English, based on Calais, were first under the **Earl of Surrey,** later under the **Duke of Suffolk.**

1523. Venice Makes Peace. The remnants of the French army were forced to withdraw to France. Francis planned to invade Italy again, but the treason of Prince **Charles of Bourbon,** Constable of France, interfered. Bourbon fled to Germany to join Charles V. Francis then sent the army to Italy under **William de Bonnivet,** Admiral of France, who had recently conquered Fontarabia, on the Spanish frontier. Bonnivet captured Novara, but was held there by Colonna's skillful maneuvering.

1524, March. Imperial Spring Offensive. A reinforced imperial army under **Charles de Lannoy,** Viceroy of Naples, surprised the dispersed French forces in their winter cantonments in northwestern Italy; Bonnivet withdrew in confusion.

1524, April 30. Battle of the Sesia. The French were routed by Lannoy, Bayard being killed in a vain effort to lead a counterattack. Bonnivet, wounded, was replaced by Count **François de St. Pol,** who retreated back across the Alps.

1524, July–October. Imperial Invasion of Southern France. An imperial army of 20,000 men invaded Provence through the Tenda Pass. While a Genoese fleet blockaded the sea approaches to Marseille, the imperials invested the city (August–September). They withdrew on the approach of a French relieving army of about 40,000 men under Francis moving down the Rhone Valley. The imperials hastily retreated eastward through the then-trackless Maritime Alps, suffering severely.

1524, October. French Invasion of Italy. Francis immediately marched into Italy, crossing by the Argentière Pass. Due to a plague in Milan, Lannoy withdrew to Pavia. The French, leaving a small force to observe Milan, followed (October 24).

Campaign of Pavia, 1524–1525

1524, October 28–1525, February 24. Siege of Pavia. Lannoy, who felt that his army was in no shape for battle, left a garrison in Pavia and retreated to the southeast to recruit. The French, unable to capture Pavia by storm, invested the city. Francis stupidly divided his forces, sending an army of 15,000 men under Scottish **John Stuart, Duke of Albany** on an abortive expedition to conquer Naples. This left barely 25,000 French troops before Pavia.

1525, January–February. Approach of Imperial Army. Lannoy, with a reorganized and reinforced army of approximately 20,000 men, approached Pavia from the east (January 25). Though Lannoy was the nominal commander, the Marquis of Pescara appears to have exercised actual command. Francis shifted part of his army to face the imperial forces, building trenches to block the most likely route of advance, meanwhile continuing the investment of Pavia. The two armies, both entrenched, faced one another across a narrow, unfordable brook, harassing one another with intermittent artillery fire. During this period approximately 6,000 Swiss mercenaries departed from the French army to reopen lines of communication to Switzerland, now harassed by imperial detachments. Approximately 4,000 Swiss remained with Francis, whose army was now reduced to less than 20,000 men.

1525, February 23–24. Imperial Maneuver. On a stormy night, and under the cover of night bombardment, the imperial army marched to its right, crossed the brook 2 miles above the opposing lines of entrenchments, turning the French left. A few companies were left in the trenches to demonstrate, so as to fool the French. Breaking through an old park wall, on which Francis had counted to protect his left flank, by dawn the imperials were in order of battle about 1 mile north of the main French camp.

1525, February 24. Battle of Pavia. Francis, completely surprised, endeavored to reorganize his army to meet the threat. He personally led a cavalry charge against the imperial left center for the purpose of providing his army time to shift 90° to face to the north. The vigor and gallantry of the French charge surprised the attackers and temporarily halted them. If the French infantry, which straggled up slowly, had taken advantage of this momentary success, French victory might have been possible. As it was, the imperial troops rallied, drove the French cavalry back, then overwhelmed the still-confused French infantry in a 2-hour battle. About a third of the French army, under Duke **Charles of Alençon**, was never engaged. Francis fought gallantly, leading his dwindling heavy-cavalry detachment in charge after charge until his horse was killed under him, and he was badly wounded and captured. La Trémoille was killed. Alençon led the remnants of the French army in a withdrawal to the west; he was thereafter treated with contempt by his countrymen. French losses in killed and wounded were about 8,000 men. Imperial losses were probably no more than 1,000. Artillery took little part in this fight, partly because Francis had charged so impetuously at the outset as to block the field of fire of the few French guns that were in position. Most French casualties came from Spanish arquebusiers. The French, who had very few arquebusiers or crossbowmen, were unable adequately to return the imperial small-arms fire.

1526, January 14. Treaty of Madrid. To obtain his freedom, Francis, a prisoner in Madrid, signed a treaty giving up all of his claims in Italy, and surrendering Burgundy, Artois, and Flanders to Charles V.

Second War of Francis and Charles V, 1526–1530

1526, May 22. Francis Repudiates the Treaty of Madrid. He claimed it had been made under duress. He formed the **League of Cognac** with the Pope, Milan, Venice, and Florence against Charles V.
1526, July 24. Fall of Milan. It was captured by Lannoy's Spanish army.
1527. Inconclusive Maneuvering by Lautrec and Lannoy. The French had the worst of a war of attrition. Spanish and German mercenaries sacked Rome, committing horrible atrocities (May 6).
1528. French Disasters. A revolt in Genoa, led by Andrea Doria, lost the most important French base in Italy. A French army under St. Pol was decisively defeated at the **Battle of Londriano.**
1529. Treaty of Cambrai. Known as the "Ladies' Peace," reached through the instrumentality of Charles' aunt and Francis' mother. Charles V, alarmed by a Turkish threat (see p. 497), was anxious for peace, as was Francis. The *status quo* was restored with Francis agreeing to pay a nominal indemnity and again renouncing his claims in Italy, while Charles withdrew his claims to Burgundy.
1530. Defeat of Florence. Though abandoned by Francis' unexpected treaty, the Florentines continued an unequal contest with the Empire. They were led by an exceptionally able soldier, **Francisco Ferrucio;** the imperial forces by Prince **Philibert of Orange.** Both leaders were killed at the **Battle of Gavinana** (August 2). Florence soon surrendered (August 12).
1531. French Reorganization. Francis established infantry legions, standing units of 6,000 mixed pikemen and arquebusiers, of Picardy, Languedoc, Normandy, and Champagne.

Third and Fourth Wars of Francis and Charles V, 1536–1544

1536–1538. The Third War. A large French army unexpectedly invaded Italy, capturing Turin, but was unable to reach Milan. Charles V attempted two attacks against France, personally leading one through Provence and sending the other through Picardy. The northern invasion soon bogged down. Charles advanced as far as Aix, but when he discovered that Francis was prepared to fight at Avignon, the emperor declined the challenge and returned to Italy. A temporary peace was patched up by the **Truce of Nice,** intended to restore the *status quo* for 10 years. The French retained their foothold in northwest Italy.
1542–1544. The Fourth War. Taking advantage of a number of imperial setbacks, Francis concluded an alliance with Ottoman Sultan **Suleiman the Magnificent,** to the horror of many Christians in his own country and elsewhere in Europe. **Henry VIII** of England allied himself with Charles. For the first 2 years, fighting was inconclusive and centered mostly in north Italy and Roussillon.
1543. Sack of Nice. A combined Franco-Turkish fleet under Turkish Admiral **Khair ed-Din** (Barbarossa; see p. 500) bombarded, besieged, and sacked the imperial town of Nice.
1543, September–October. Charles Invades

Picardy. He besieged Landrecies (September). Francis approached with a large army (October). After some inconclusive maneuvering, both sides retired to winter quarters.

1543–1544. English-Imperial Plan to Invade France. Henry and Charles agreed that the English would advance from Calais, while imperial forces invaded through Lorraine and Champagne.

1544, April 14. Battle of Ceresole. French forces under **Francis of Bourbon (Prince of Enghien)** were maneuvering against imperial forces under Spanish **Marqués del Vasto** south of Turin. The French army was approximately 15,000 strong, including 4,000 Swiss infantry, 7,000 French infantry, 2,000 Italian infantry, and 1,500 French and Italian heavy and light cavalry. The imperial army consisted of 7,000 landsknechts, 6,000 Italian infantry, 5,000 Spanish infantry, and approximately 1,000 cavalry. Each side had about 20 guns. After a prolonged arquebus skirmish and a long-range artillery duel, the principal infantry contingents became locked in a sanguinary conflict; the landsknechts were almost completely wiped out by the Swiss infantry and French cavalry. The French infantry, on Enghien's left, was simultaneously being overwhelmed by the Spanish and German veterans, but Enghien retrieved the situation there by an enveloping cavalry charge. Del Vasto was forced to retreat, having lost more than 6,000 dead and 3,200 prisoners. The French lost approximately 2,000 dead. The battle reaffirmed the lesson that infantry of the day— whether arquebusiers or Swiss and landsknechts pikemen—could repulse any cavalry attack; but that the employment of cavalry against the flank of infantry engaged against other infantry was likely to be decisive.

1544, May–August. Imperial Invasion. In accordance with the allied plan, Charles invaded eastern France. He was delayed by the gallant defense of St.-Dizier (June 19–August 18), giving Francis time to call back his army from Italy and to collect other forces to defend Paris. The imperial army halted after seizing Épernay, Château-Thierry, Soissons, and Meaux.

1544, July. English Invasion. This followed Henry's leisurely crossing to Calais, which gave Francis adequate warning. The English army, about 40,000 men, included many foreign mercenaries.

1544, July 19–September 14. English Siege of Boulogne. Henry captured the city but made no attempt to coordinate actions with the Germans.

1544, September 18. Peace of Crépy. Charles, discouraged, was eager to accept Francis' offers of peace. The *status quo* was re-established, with the French retaining northwest Italy. The English thus suddenly found themselves without allies. Henry returned to England, leaving a garrison in Boulogne.

1544, October 9. "Camisade of Boulogne." French troops under the Dauphin Prince **Henry** (later Henry II) assaulted Boulogne, and were almost successful, but were driven out by rallying English.

1545–1546. Continuing War Between France and England. The French held the initiative, but operations were limited to the Boulogne-Calais area and to coastal raids on both shores of the English Channel. After failure of a planned French invasion of the Isle of Wight, peace was concluded, the French recognizing English conquest of Boulogne (1546).

THE LAST VALOIS-HAPSBURG WAR, 1547–1559

1547–1559. Reign of Henry II (Son of Francis). He formed an alliance with Prince **Maurice of Saxony** to take advantage of Charles V's preoccupation with the Turks and the German Protestants (1551).

1552, April. French Invasion of Lorraine. They captured Metz, Toul, and Verdun.

1552, October–December. Seige of Metz. Charles, having patched up a peace with the Protestants, attempted to reconquer Lorraine, but was repulsed at Metz.

1552–1555. French Invasion of Tuscany. This was a failure. Marshal **Blaise de Montluc** was defeated by an imperial army under the **Marquis of Marignano** at the **Battle of Marciano** (August 2, 1553). He was cooped up in Siena, where he was forced to surrender after a long siege (1553–1554).

1553–1556. Inconclusive Maneuvering in Flanders. Charles personally led one invasion of Picardy which was ended by French success in a small cavalry fight in the **Battle of Renty,** where **Francis, Duke of Guise** distinguished himself (August 12, 1554).

1556, February–November. Truce of Vaucelles. This was marked by the abdication of Charles V (October), broken in spirit by his failures. He was succeeded in Spain by his son **Philip II,** and in the Empire by his brother **Ferdinand** (see pp. 488 and 482). The truce soon collapsed.

1556–1557. French Invasion of Southern Italy. Despite severe losses and hardships, the French, under Guise, established a foothold in northern Naples. They were forced to withdraw upon word of French disasters elsewhere (1557). The French retained northwestern Italy around Turin.

1557, June. England Joins the War. Mary of England, wife of Philip II, brought her country into the war against France.

1557, July–August. Philip's Invasion of Northern France. He had an army of 50,000, including an English contingent of 7,000 men. The senior commander was Duke **Emmanuel Philibert of Savoy.** Since the flower of the French army was engaged in Italy, the Constable, Duke **Anne of Montmorency,** was able to raise a conglomerate force of only about 26,000 to oppose this invasion threat. Foolishly, the Spanish army paused to besiege St.-Quentin, where Admiral **Gaspard de Coligny** organized a small force for defense.

1557, August 10. Battle of St.-Quentin. Montmorency attempted to cross the Somme River to attack a detached portion of the Spanish army and to relieve St.-Quentin. While the French were crossing, Savoy ordered a counterattack by imperial cavalry. The French were disastrously routed; about half their army escaped; 6,000 were killed and about 6,000 captured, including Montmorency. Northern France was now completely defenseless. Savoy wished to march on Paris, but cautious Philip refused to by-pass St.-Quentin.

1557, August 27. Fall of St.-Quentin. It was taken by storm in a hard fight.

1557, September. Philip Orders Withdrawal to the Netherlands. Savoy was disgusted. Meanwhile Henry had called Guise back from Italy, and had begun desperate efforts to rebuild the French army.

1557, November–December. Guise Seizes the Initiative. Taking advantage of allied vacillation and overcaution, Guise boldly sent raiding expeditions into Champagne and along the Netherlands frontier. Meanwhile, he assembled an army of 25,000 men at Abbeville.

1558, January 2–7. Fall of Calais. Guise undertook a bold and well-calculated assault against weakly held Calais, first storming the outworks, then capturing one fort after the other until the small garrison under Lord **Thomas Wentworth** capitulated. Calais, England's last foothold in France, was lost forever.

1558, May–June. The French Maintain the Initiative. Guise led a small army into northern Champagne to capture Thionville. At the same time Marshal **Paul des Thermes,** with about 10,500 men, raided from Calais into Spanish Flanders to capture Dunkirk (June 30). After gathering much loot, the French withdrew toward Calais, closely followed by **Lamoral, Count of Egmont,** commanding Spanish forces in Flanders.

1558, July 13. Battle of Gravelines. Egmont, catching up with the withdrawing French on the sand dunes near Gravelines, promptly attacked. At the same time an English fleet just offshore opened fire on the French army. The combination routed the French and their landsknechts mercenaries; they lost about 5,000 dead and 5,000 prisoners. Only a handful escaped.

1558, July–August. Guise Rushes to Picardy. He retrieved the disaster by putting on such a bold front that the Spanish failed to exploit.

1559, April 3. Peace of Catteau-Cambresis. This ended the Hapsburg-Valois Wars and a projected attack on Spain by Admiral Coligny. France gave up all of its holdings and claims in Italy (save for the border region of Saluzzo) and the other frontier conquests made by Guise in the latter days of the war (save for the cities of Metz, Toul, Verdun, and Calais).

The Wars of Religion, 1560–1598

THE PERIOD OF CONDE, COLIGNY, AND CATHERINE DE' MEDICI, 1560–1574

1559–1560. Reign of Francis II. National policy was dominated by the towering figure of Francis of Guise, now the leading personality in France. Because of their suspicions of Guise, and his sponsorship of French meddling in Scotland, Philip of Spain and Elizabeth of England were temporarily united in opposition to him and to Mary of Scotland (see pp. 465 and 469). Within France the political and religious policies of the ardently Catholic Guise family were firmly opposed by Protestant Prince **Louis of Bourbon and**

Condé and other Protestant nobles. Religious unrest in France became acute.

1560–1574. Reign of Charles IX (10-Year-Old Younger Brother of Francis II). This began under the guardianship of his mother, **Catherine de' Medici,** widow of Henry II and rival of Guise.

1560. Conspiracy of Amboise. This attempt of a group of the minor nobility (many of them Protestant) to overthrow Guise's government was brutally suppressed.

First War of Religion, 1562–1563

The principal Protestant (Huguenot) leaders were Prince Louis of Bourbon and Condé and Count Gaspard of Coligny, Admiral of France. The principal Catholic leaders were Guise, Constable Montmorency, and vacillating ex-Protestant Prince **Antoine of Bourbon and Navarre** (brother of Condé, father of Henry of Navarre). Because of the recent peace with Spain and the Empire, France was full of unemployed soldiers, ready and eager for fighting and loot.

1562, March 1. Massacre of Vassy. A number of Protestants were massacred by Guise troops.

1562, April–November. Huguenot Rising. Condé and Coligny seized Orléans and called for a national rising of Protestants. Irregular skirmishing and atrocities spread throughout France.

1562, September 20. English Intervention. A force under **John, Earl of Warwick,** sent by Queen Elizabeth to assist the Huguenots, landed to capture Le Havre.

1562, October 26. Fall of Rouen. The Catholics stormed this Protestant center, Antoine of Bourbon being killed in the attack.

1562, December 19. Battle of Dreux. A Huguenot army of nearly 15,000 men, under Condé and Coligny, marching north to make contact with the English at Le Havre, unexpectedly ran into a Catholic army of about 19,000, nominally under Montmorency, actually under Guise. The Catholic army included about 5,000 Swiss mercenary pikemen; the Protestants had about an equal number of landsknechts. A hard-fought, confused, and indecisive battle ensued, in which gallant leadership by Guise saved the Catholics from disaster and held the field. A unique aspect of the battle was that the two opposing commanders, Condé and Montmorency, were each captured. Losses on each side were about 4,000.

1563, February 18. Assassination of Guise. He had been besieging Orléans.

1563, March. Peace of Amboise. This was negotiated between the two prisoners, Montmorency and Condé, at the instigation of Queen Catherine. The Catholics and Huguenots then immediately marched jointly against the English at Le Havre.

1563, July 28. Fall of Le Havre. Warwick's English army surrendered.

Second War of Religion, 1567–1568

1567, September 29. Huguenot Uprising. Condé and Coligny and 500 Huguenot gentlemen failed in an attempt to seize the royal family at Meaux. Other Protestant bands, however, seized Orléans (captured by **François de La Noue** and 15 other Huguenot cavaliers), Auxerre, Vienne, Valence, Nîmes, Montpellier, and Montauban. Condé immediately gathered the scattered Protestant forces to threaten Paris (October–November).

1567, November 10. Battle of St.-Denis. Montmorency, then aged 74, took advantage of Huguenot dispersion. With 16,000 men he moved against Condé, who had only 3,500 at St.-Denis. Condé rashly stood to fight, and amazingly the Huguenots held the field for several hours before finally being driven off by sheer weight of numbers. Montmorency was killed. The moral effect of Condé's magnificent defense was demonstrated by the fact that the following day, when he scraped together almost 6,000 troops, he again offered battle, which the Catholics declined.

1568, March 23. Peace of Longjumeau. Substantial concessions were made to the Huguenots by Catherine.

Third War of Religion, 1568–1570

1568, August 18. Royalist Treachery. An attempt to capture Condé and Coligny by treachery failed, but precipitated war. During the remainder of the year there was considerable indecisive maneuvering in the Loire Valley.

1569, March. Royalist Initiative. Marshal **Gaspard de Tavannes** outmanuevered Condé in the region between Angoulême and Cognac.

1569, March 13. Battle of Jarnac. Precipitated by Tavanne's surprise crossing of the Charente River near Châteauneuf. The Huguenot army, unprepared, was badly defeated; Condé was captured and murdered. Coligny succeeded in withdrawing a substantial portion of the Protestant army in good order.

1569, June 10. Arrival of German Protestant Reinforcements. Some 13,000 reiters and landsknechts joined Coligny near Limoges.

1569, July–September. Protestant Siege of Poitiers. Prince **Henry of Navarre,** then 15, Protestant son of Antoine of Bourbon, was with Coligny at this siege.

1569, August 24. Battle of Orthez. Count **Gabriel of Montgomery,** detached by Coligny, repulsed a Royalist invasion of French Navarre, defeating Royalist General **Terride.**

1569, September. Relief of Poitiers. Tavanne, resuming the offensive, forced Coligny to raise the siege. A campaign of maneuver followed in the vicinity of Loudun.

1569, October 3. Battle of Moncontour. Tavanne's army consisted of 7,000 cavalry, 18,000 infantry, and 15 guns; Coligny had about 6,000 cavalry, 14,000 infantry, and 11 guns. The Royalist army included a substantial Swiss contingent. A combined attack by Catholic cavalry and the Swiss infantry put the Huguenot cavalry to flight. The Catholics then crushed the Huguenot infantry, the Swiss being particularly ruthless in slaughtering the landsknechts. Huguenot losses were

nearly 8,000, Royalist losses probably no more than 1,000. Coligny was wounded; La Noue was captured.

1570, April–June. Protestant Initiative. Coligny, recovered from his wound, boldly marched through central France with 3,000 cavalry and 3,000 mounted infantry, threatening Paris in late June.

1570, August 8. Peace of St.-Germain. The Huguenots again were promised wide religious freedom and considerable military and political autonomy.

The Fourth War of Religion, 1572–1573

1572, August 23–24. Massacre of St. Bartholomew's Eve. Coligny and thousands of other Protestants were murdered in Paris. Young Prince Henry of Navarre succeeded Coligny as the nominal Huguenot leader. Save for a prolonged siege of La Rochelle by a Royalist army under Prince **Henry,** younger brother of Charles IX, there was little military action. During this war the Protestants established political and military control over most of southwest France, which became virtually autonomous. A new political party emerged, the "Politiques," moderate Catholics anxious to make concessions to the Protestants in order to restore national peace and unity. The royal princes, **Henry** (later Henry III) and **Francis of Alençon,** were leaders of the Politiques.

THE PERIOD OF THE THREE HENRYS, 1574–1589

1574–1589. Reign of Henry III. He was the third son of Henry II and Catherine de' Medici to become King of France. Since he was childless, as was his youngest brother, **Francis of Alençon,** the question of royal succession became mixed up in the Religious Wars, Henry of Navarre being next in line of succession to the throne of France. Henry of Navarre, not a very religious man, was largely motivated by natural political ambitions during this period. The principal Catholic leader was now **Henry, Duke of Guise,** son of Francis.

Fifth War of Religion, 1575–1576

1575. Outbreak of War. This followed widespread disorders. The Protestants had generally the best of scattered fighting throughout the country, though Guise was victorious in the one important action in the **Battle of Dormans** (October 10, 1575). Participation of Catholic Politiques on the Protestant side led King Henry, whose support of Guise was reluctant, to make peace and to renew pledges of religious freedom to the Protestants at the **Peace of Beaulieu** (May 5, 1576).

1576. The Holy League. Established by Guise, who refused to accept the Peace of Beaulieu, to take advantage of widespread Catholic resentment of favors granted the Protestants. He entered into conspiratorial negotiations with Philip of Spain, who agreed to intervene and place Guise on the throne.

Sixth and Seventh Wars of Religion, 1576–1580

1576–1577. The Sixth War. This included only one brief, inconclusive campaign, and was ended by the **Peace of Bergerac** (1577, reaffirming the Peace of Beaulieu).

1580. The Seventh War. This was called the "Lovers' War" because of indiscretions of Margaret, wife of Henry of Navarre. No important military actions took place.

1580–1585. Increasing Intrigue. Catholics, Protestants, and Politiques were all involved, due to the question of succession, with Henry of Navarre now the direct hereditary successor to the throne of France. Philip of Spain and the Guise family again reached an understanding (December, 1584) to support Henry of Guise to be the successor of aged Cardinal **Charles of Bourbon,** who was to be proposed as the immediate successor of Henry III.

Eighth War of Religion, 1585–1589

This was also known as the "War of the Three Henrys": Henry III, Henry of Navarre, and Henry of Guise.

1585. Royal Vacillation Precipitates War. Henry III, still partly under the influence of his scheming mother, nominally supported the Catholic League and withdrew religious freedom for Protestants. The Huguenots rose in revolt. In the subsequent confused and complicated struggle, the king endeavored to steer a middle course, undercutting the Catholic League

whenever possible in order to reduce Guise influence.

1587, October 20. Battle of Coutras. A Catholic army of 10,000 men, under **Anne, Duke of Joyeuse,** endeavoring to link up with Catholics in Bordeaux, was intercepted by Henry of Navarre with 6,500 men. Henry, awaiting a charge, prepared a coordinated arquebus-cavalry counterattack. The overconfident Royalist cavalry was smashed, following which the combined Protestant infantry and cavalry cut the Royalist infantry to pieces. More than 3,000 Royalists were killed; Henry lost less than 500 dead. Henry was in the forefront of the Huguenot countercharge, fighting boldly and well. He did not, however, exploit his victory.

1587, October–November. Catholic Successes. Guise, by victories at **Vimory** and **Auneau,** was able to turn back a force of German auxiliaries which had marched to the Loire Valley to make contact with the Huguenots.

1588, May 9–11. Guise Seizes Paris. King Henry fled, then later capitulated to Guise and the League (July).

1588, December 23. Murder of Guise. Inspired by King Henry. Two days later he also instigated the murder of Guise's brother, Cardinal **Louis of Guise.** This aroused the Catholic League against the king, who fled to refuge with Henry of Navarre.

ASCENDANCY OF HENRY OF NAVARRE, 1589–1598

1589, August 2. Assassination of Henry III. The murderer was a Catholic monk, avenging the Guise brothers. The dying king designated Henry of Navarre as his successor. The formerly 3-way conflict now became simplified, though its intensity and ferocity in no way abated. It was now the Catholic League, probably supported by less than half the population of France, against Henry of Navarre, supported by Protestants and Catholic Politiques. Cardinal Charles of Bourbon, proclaimed king by the Catholic League, was actually a prisoner of Henry of Navarre and acknowledged him as king. Spanish forces moved into France to support the League against Henry. The new leader of the League, was **Charles, Duke of Mayenne,** younger brother of Henry of Guise.

1589, September 21. Battle of Arques. Near Dieppe, Henry, with 8,000 troops, lured Mayenne with 24,000 French Catholics and Spanish (from Flanders) into a defile of the Bethune River, which he had prepared with trenches and gun emplacements. The ambush, combined with superb tactics and excellent employment of his artillery, gave Henry a tremendous victory over great odds; Mayenne was driven off the field. He retreated to Amiens, to await Spanish reinforcements from the Duke of Parma in Flanders. Henry, with about 20,000 men, then dashed toward Paris (October 31).

1589, November 1. Repulse at Paris. Henry was repulsed by the Catholic garrison. Proclaiming himself Henry IV, he established a temporary capital at Tours. Civil war raged all over France.

1590, February–March. Siege of Dreux. Upon the approach of Mayenne's army, Henry raised the siege and prepared for battle near Evreux.

1590, March 14. Battle of Ivry. Henry had 11,000 men, Mayenne about 16,000. As at Coutras, Henry mixed his cavalry and arquebusiers to obtain the maximum advantage of the capabilities of each. In an extremely confused and hard-fought battle, the Huguenot arquebusiers and better artillery repelled Catholic cavalry charges, while Henry himself led a successful cavalry counterattack into the Catholic center. The entire Catholic army fled in confusion, save for the Swiss contingent, which stood in good order, threatening to fight to the death if quarter was not granted. Upon receiving honorable terms, they surrendered. Catholic losses were nearly 4,000 killed; the Huguenot-Royalist army lost only about 500 killed. Henry was slow in exploiting his victory, permitting the Catholics to rally and to prepare for the defense of Paris.

1590, May–August. Siege of Paris. The city was reduced to semistarvation. Henry was forced to raise the siege when the Duke of Parma joined Mayenne at Meaux. This gave Parma a combined Catholic army of some 26,000 men. Henry's army was about the same size.

1590, September–October. Inconclusive Maneuvering. After sending a relief force and substantial supplies into Paris, Parma withdrew to winter quarters (October).

1591–1592. War of Maneuver in Northern France. The opposing leaders were two of the outstanding soldiers of the western world: Henry of Navarre and Alexander, Duke of Parma. Parma, the abler strategist, was forced to divide his attention between the war in France, and a desperate struggle in the Netherlands (see p. 486). Henry succeeded in penning Parma's army up in a loop of the Seine River, only to have Parma's superb Spanish engineers bridge the river overnight, permitting 15,000 men to get across before dawn (May, 1592).

1593, July. Henry Formally Returns to the Catholic Faith. He thus reunited most of the nation against the threat of a full-scale Spanish invasion planned by Philip and the Catholic League.

1594, March 21. Henry's Triumphal Entry into Paris.

1595–1597. Inconclusive Warfare. Henry won the closely contested **Battle of Fontaine-Française** over the Spanish, but was almost killed due to his own rash gallantry (June 9, 1595). Next year the Spanish captured Calais by surprise (April 9, 1596). Taking advantage of Henry's internal preoccupations, the Spanish next captured Amiens (September 17). There was no more major campaigning.

1598, April 13. Edict of Nantes. Henry granted religious freedom to the Protestants, ending the Wars of Religion.

1598, May 2. Treaty of Vervins. End of the war with Spain, following secret negotiations in which Henry apparently double-crossed his English and Dutch allies.

GERMANY

During this century the Holy Roman Empire was involved not only with steadily increasing internal violence resulting from the religious Reformation, but also—later—with the personal enmity of Francis I of France and Charles V, which kept Western Europe constantly at war for more than a third of a century (see p. 473).

At the same time, the Ottoman Turks were overrunning the Balkans and hammering at the gates of Central Europe, making Vienna a frontier town. The principal events were:

1493–1519. Reign of Maximilian I. Almost continuous war with France, opposing the ambitions of Charles VIII and Louis XII in Italy. At the same time, in the complicated Italian wars, Maximilian also unsuccessfully endeavored to break the power of Venice (see p. 470).

1517, October 31. Luther's 95 Theses. His action at Wittenberg is generally considered the beginning of the Reformation, resulting in the most violent and implacable hostilities in European history.

1519. Rivalry for the Imperial Throne. Upon the death of Maximilian, the German electors chose the Spanish-German Hapsburg Charles I of Spain in preference to Francis I of France, precipitating a lifelong enmity.

1519–1556. Reign of Charles V. He was ruler of the combined lands of Castile, Aragon, Naples, Burgundy, the Hapsburg lands in Germany, and the tremendous new colonial empire of Spain in the Americas.

1521–1544. Wars between Charles and Francis. (See pp. 473–476.)

1522. The Knights' War. Minor nobles, sympathetic with the Reformation, attempted to overthrow the power of the church principalities in Germany; they were crushed by imperial and church forces.

1524–1525. The Peasants' War. This was an uprising in Swabia and Franconia by adherents of Luther, who repudiated them. The rebels were defeated at **Frankenhausen** (1525) and cruelly suppressed by the nobility.

1526. Collapse of the Teutonic Knights. The order, restricted to eastern Prussia as vassals of Poland since 1466, was evicted when its Grand Master, **Albert of Brandenburg-Anspach,** turned Protestant and secularized his territories. (Its remnants lingered in Germany proper until the French Revolution, when its Rhenish estates were absorbed; in 1809 the order was suppressed.)

1526–1534. War against the Turks. This was marked by the successful defense of Vienna against the Ottoman armies (see p. 497).

1535. Charles's Expedition to Tunis. (See p. 499.)

1541. Charles's Expedition against Algiers. (See pp. 499–500.)

1546–1547. Schmalkaldic War. This was a revolt of Protestant nobles. Charles, having made a truce with the Turks, won a decisive victory over the Elector of Saxony and other Protestant nobles at the **Battle of Mühlberg** (1547, April 24).

1547–1556. Charles's War with Henry II of France and Maurice of Saxony. (See p. 476.)

1553. Battle of Sievershausen. In a primarily cavalry battle, Maurice defeated Catholic forces under **Albert of Hohenzollern-Kulmbach.** Maurice, victorious, died of wounds.

1556, October. Abdication of Charles. (See p. 477.) Spain, Naples, Milan, Franche-Comté, and the Netherlands were inherited by his son, Philip II of Spain. The German Hapsburg lands were ceded to his brother, Ferdinand, who was elected emperor.

1556–1564. Reign of Ferdinand I. There was constant warfare over succession to the throne of Hungary, and against the Ottomans (see p. 500).

1564–1612. Reigns of Maximilian II and Rudolph II. There was continuing warfare against the Turks in Southeastern Europe.

SCANDINAVIA

Denmark

The uneasy Union of Kalmar fell apart early in the century when the Swedes established their independence under **Gustavus Vasa.** A decade of civil war in Denmark followed, more or less mixed up with sporadic warfare against Lübeck and other Hanseatic towns. **Christian III,** after settling the civil war, further reduced dwindling Hanseatic power by a series of successes against Lübeck. Around the middle of the century he involved Denmark in the early religious wars in Germany, lending assistance to the Protestants. During the remainder of the century royal authority was strengthened at the expense of the nobility and of the towns. The principal events were:

1513–1532. Reign of Christian II.

1520–1523. Successful Revolt of Sweden.

1523–1537. Internal and External War. Intermittent warfare with Lübeck was complicated by civil wars in Denmark. **Frederick, Duke of Holstein** seized the throne (1523). Christian, endeavoring to recover it, was captured in Norway and spent the rest of his life in captivity (1532). Frederick, due largely to the ability of his general **Johann Rantzau,** defeated the Hanseatic League.

1533–1536. The "Counts' War." The nobles were opposed by burghers and peasants after the death of Frederick. **Christopher, Count of Oldenberg** led the popular forces with Hanseatic support, while **Christän of Holstein,** son of Frederick, was selected by the Rigsraad to succeed his father. Johann Rantzau swept Jutland with Holstein and German troops. A Danish fleet under **Peder Skram** defeated Lübeck, and then conveyed the Holstein army to Zealand (July, 1535). Malmö and Copenhagen were besieged, and finally surrendered (April and July, 1536). This ended the civil war.

1534–1558. Reign of Christian III.

1563–1570. War with Sweden. (See below.)

1588–1648. Reign of Christian IV. He expanded Danish power and possessions in the Baltic.

Sweden, 1520–1600

Gustavus Vasa re-established the identity of the Swedish state, which began to expand on the eastern shores of the Baltic Sea, and by the end of the century was the leading state of Northern Europe. The principal events were:

1520–1523. Civil War within the Union of Kalmar. Gustavus Vasa, with the assistance of Lübeck (enemy of Denmark), threw off Swedish domination and was elected King of Sweden (June, 1523).

1523–1560. Reign of Gustavus I.

1531–1536. Alliance of Denmark and Sweden against Lübeck. With the assistance of its Hanseatic allies and Danish rebels (see above) Lübeck captured Copenhagen and Malmö. The Swedes assisted the Holstein army in ejecting Hanseatic forces and in re-establishing peace in Denmark.

1543. Revolt in Smaland. This was led by peasant **Nils Dacke.**

1561. Expansion in the Baltic. Upon the collapse of the Teutonic Knights (1526), Revel and neighboring regions in Estonia and Livonia joined Sweden, causing strained relations with Russia, Denmark and Poland, each of which also coveted this territory, and each of which had also gobbled up some of the Teutonic Knights' territory (see p. 490).

1562. Inconclusive Civil War. This was due partially to the intermittent insanity of **Eric XIV** and to Polish and Russian meddling in Swedish affairs.

1563–1570. War with Denmark, Lübeck and Poland. Neither side gained a clear-cut advantage.

1570–1595. War with Russia. Desultory operations resulted in Sweden's slow conquest of all of Estonia and Livonia.

1592–1598. Polish Invasion. Following the death of **John III,** political and religious differences between **Sigismund** (son and heir of John) and **Charles** (John's brother) broke out. Sigismund, who had earlier been elected King of Poland, invaded Sweden with a Polish army, but was defeated at **Stängebro** (1598, September 25), driven back, and dethroned by the Swedish Riksdag.

THE NETHERLANDS, 1566–1609

The Netherlands (including most of modern Netherlands, Belgium, Luxembourg, and the French provinces of Flanders and Artois), under domination of Spain since the days of Charles the Bold of Burgundy (see p. 426), boiled during this period. Arrogant Spanish misrule combined with religious differences caused open rebellion, led first by **William "the Silent,"** Prince of Orange and Count of Nassau and (after his assassination) his son **Maurice of Nassau.** Opposing the rebels were two exceptional soldiers: **Fernando Álvarez de Toledo, Duke of Alva** and **Alexander Farnese, Duke of Parma.** Against these two and their disciplined Spanish forces, the determination of William and the later display of military genius by Maurice finally brought freedom to the stout Protestant burghers of Holland. Spain retained the largely Catholic area of the southern Netherlands. Spain's preoccupation elsewhere, particularly in England and France, played some part in the Dutch victory, but the most important single factor in the eventual outcome was the Dutch ability to create a small fleet at the outset of the war and maintain command of the coastal waters despite Spain's naval might. Like the English, the Dutch grasped the significance of the large ship-killing gun which revolutionized naval warfare in the period. The Spanish did not. Of military interest, too, was the diversity of terrain. In Holland itself the dikes, rivers, canals, marshes, and inlets lent themselves to partisan warfare. The more open country farther south could be more easily dominated by regular troops. The principal events were:

1566. Political and Religious Riots. These spread throughout the northern and southern Netherlands; William of Orange unsuccessfully tried to mediate between the government and the people. Philip sent the Duke of Alva and a Spanish army from Italy to the Netherlands to restore order.

1567. William of Orange Outlawed. He fled to Germany.

1568, January–April. William Raises an Army. He sent this into northern Netherlands under his brother **Louis of Nassau.**

1568, May 23. Battle of Heiligerlee. Louis, who had about 3,000 men, defeated a small German-Spanish force under **John, Duke of Aremberg.**

1568, July 21. Battle of Jemmingen. Alva moved into northern Netherlands, enticed Louis to attack, and overwhelmed him with superior fire power and a crushing counterattack from front and flanks. Forces were equal—about 15,000 each. The Dutch loss was between 6,000 and 7,000 killed; Spanish losses were 100 dead. The rebel cause was completely crushed in the northeastern Netherlands for several years.

1568, October 5. William Invades the Southeastern Netherlands. With an army of 25,000 men, he forded the Meuse River at Stochen. In Brabant, Alva, with about 16,000 men, outmaneuvered him, destroying his rear guard in a skirmish near **Jodoigne** (October 20). Alva had so effectively terrorized the population that few Netherlanders rose to join William's dwindling army. He retreated southward into France, then back to Germany by way of Strasbourg (November).

1569–1572. The Netherlands Seethe under Alva's Stern Rule. The "Sea Beggars," Dutch privateers with commissions from William of Orange, began to prey on Spanish commerce, and raided the Netherlands' seacoast from bases in England and Friesland.

1572, April 1. The Sea Beggars Capture Bril. This precipitated renewed strife.

1572, April–July. Uprisings Sweep Low Countries. Save for Amsterdam and Middelburg, all of the provinces of Holland and Zeeland were swept clear of the Spanish. William and his brother Louis again invaded the southern provinces. Alva, besieging Louis in Mons, repulsed William's efforts to relieve the city.

1572–1573. Alva's Terrorism. Combining skillful military action with horrible atrocities, Alva slowly re-established Spanish control in the southern and eastern provinces, besieging and capturing city after city, massacring captured garrisons and many civilians. William retreated to Delft, where he organized desperate resistance of the Maritime Provinces. Alva captured **Haarlem,** which had resisted heroically in a 7-month siege (December–July), and the Spanish slaughtered the garrison to a man. Alva was repulsed in his siege of **Alkmaar** (August–October) when he discovered that the Dutch were prepared to cut the dikes rather than submit. A Dutch fleet defeated a Spanish squadron on the **Zuyder Zee** (October, 1573). Because of these setbacks, Alva resigned, and was replaced as viceroy by **Luis de Requesens** (November, 1573). Early the following year the Sea Beggars smashed another Spanish fleet off **Walcheren** in the Schelde estuary (1574, January).

1573, October–1574, October. Spanish Siege of Leyden. Various relief efforts by William and Louis failed.

1573, April 14. Battle of Mookerheyde. Louis' army was routed, and he was killed by a Spanish veteran army of 6,000 men under **Sancho de Avila.**

1573, September–October. Relief of Leyden. With the city on the verge of starvation, William cut the dikes, flooding the Spanish from their trenches and camps. Admiral **Louis Boisot**'s Sea Beggar fleet sailed across the inundated countryside to relieve the starving city (October 31).

1575–1576. The Revolt Spreads. Ineffective de Requescens could not halt the spread from the north through most of the southern provinces. The only important Spanish success was the capture of **Zierikzee,** an island off Zeeland; Boisot was killed in a vain attempt to block a bold Spanish crossing from the mainland at low tide.

1576, October 3. "The Spanish Terror." Mutinous Spanish troops, whose pay was in arrears, captured and sacked **Antwerp** with terrible ferocity. This atrocity temporarily united all of the Netherlands, whose provincial representatives signed the **Pacification of Ghent** (November 8).

1577. Complicated Negotiations. These involved the States General (civil government of the rebellious Netherlands provinces), William of Orange, and Don **Juan of Austria,** the new Spanish viceroy. William stepped down from leadership as a gesture to the Catholics. The States General raised an army of 20,000 men under Sieur **Antoine de Goignies** when negotiations broke down and Don Juan prepared to reconquer the provinces.

1578, January 31. Battle of Gemblours. Juan, reinforced by additional Spanish troops under Alexander Farnese (later Duke of Parma), moved against the Dutch army at Gemblours (Gembloux) with some 20,000 men. As the Dutch fell back toward Brussels, Farnese enveloped their cavalry rear guard, then pursued the routed Dutch horsemen through the columns of retreating Dutch infantry. In the ensuing slaughter, the Dutch lost about 6,000 men dead, to about 20 Spanish killed.

1578, February–September. Juan Recovers Control of the South. Internal jealousies and bickering on both sides then brought operations to a halt.

1578, October 1. Death of Don Juan. He was succeeded by Farnese as the Spanish viceroy.

1579, January 29. The Union of Utrecht. The northern Netherlands provinces established a confederation, the beginning of the modern history of Holland, or of the Netherlands. William was appointed stadholder by the States General.

1579–1589. Farnese's Campaigns of Pacification. Ignoring the complicated political maneuvering which involved his own sovereign (Philip), King Henry of France, and **Francis, Duke of Anjou,** on the one side, and the quarreling Catholic and Protestant Netherlanders, on the other, Farnese systematically conquered city after city of the southern Netherlands, beginning with **Maastricht** (1579, March) and culminating with the prolonged siege and capture of **Antwerp** (August 17, 1585). Soon after this he became the Duke of Parma (1586).

1584, July 10. Assassination of William of Orange. He was succeeded as stadholder by his 17-year-old son, **Maurice of Nassau.**

1585–1587. English Intervention. Robert **Dudley, Earl of Leicester,** brought 6,000 English troops to Holland, where the Dutch granted him almost dictatorial powers. However, he was inept, notably in his vain siege of Zutphen (1586). After the death of Sir **Philip Sidney,** Leicester's most able lieutenant (1586), the English withdrew (1587); Maurice was appointed by the States General as captain and admiral-general of the union (1588).

1587–1588. Parma Prepares to Invade England. The expedition of 25,000 men never got started, however, due to the disaster to the great Armada (see p. 467).

1589. Parma to France. Philip was confident that the reconquest of the Netherlands was close to completion (the Dutch held only the islands of Zeeland, the area north of the Waal in Holland, plus Utrecht and a few isolated towns farther east). Parma was ordered to take most of his army to assist the French Catholics against Henry of Navarre (see p. 481).

1589–1590. Maurice Takes the Offensive. Aided by the absence of Parma, his principal exploit was the surprise capture of **Breda,** the assault force hidden in barges which moored at the town wharves. At the same time the Dutch fleet, aided greatly by the English victory over the Spanish Armada, now held unchallenged control of the Netherlands' seacoasts.

1591, June–July. Maurice Expands Control. By rapidity of movement and concentration of greatly superior artillery fire, he captured **Zutphen** in a siege of 7 days (June) and **Deventer** after 11 days (July).

1591, August–September. Maurice vs. Parma. Parma, who had returned from France, threatened Utrecht. The two armies maneuvered cautiously on opposite banks of the Waal River near Arnhem. Parma was then ordered by Philip to return to France to relieve Rouen, being besieged by Henry of Navarre (see p. 481).

1591, September–October. Maurice Resumes the Offensive. Again taking advantage of Parma's absence, Maurice conducted another lightning campaign of movement by water and road, and brief sieges, marked by superb use of artillery. He captured **Hulst** (September 14) and **Nijmegen** (October 21).

1592–1594. Maurice Continues His Campaign of Conquest. Parma died of wounds in France (December, 1592). The next Spanish viceroy, **Peter of Mansfeldt,** was unable to offer effective interference to Maurice.

1594–1596. Maurice Consolidates the Northern Netherlands. He conducted sporadic border raids and expeditions, and devoted all possible attention to training and improving his army for operations in the southern Netherlands.

1597, January 24. Battle of Turnhout. Maurice, with approximately 7,000 troops, marched suddenly, taking advantage of bad weather, to attack and rout an isolated Spanish force of 6,000 troops, under Count **Jean de Rie of Varas,** at Turnhout. Spanish losses were 2,000 (including Varas) killed and 500 made prisoner. The Dutch lost about 100 killed.

1597–1599. Military and Political Consolidation. Archduke **Albert of Austria,** Philip's son-in-law, became the Spanish viceroy (1599), but was unable to interfere with Maurice.

1600. Maurice Invades Flanders. The States General ordered Maurice, despite his objections, to complete the conquest of the coastal strip of Flanders as far as Nieuport and Dunkirk. Maurice crossed the Scheldt River (June 21–22) and drove off Spanish forces blockading Ostend. He then crossed the Yser and immediately prepared to besiege Nieuport (July 1).

1600, July 2. Battle of Nieuport (Battle of the Dunes). Maurice, learning of the approach of Albert's Spanish army, sent a detachment to delay it at the Leffingham Bridge over the Yser, since his main army could not cross the river estuary until low tide. The Spanish won the race for the bridge, destroying the Dutch detachment. Maurice forded the Yser estuary at low tide (8 A.M.), marching rapidly northeast along the exposed beach toward the Spanish. The armies met about noon, at the turn of the tide. At the same time Dutch warships opened long-range fire with little effect. Driven by the rising waters, both armies shifted into the sand dunes farther inland. A Dutch cavalry charge was repulsed and Albert threw in his reserve, forcing the Dutch back. Effective Dutch artillery fire and a charge by Maurice's reserve cavalry checked the Spanish advance. Then Maurice made a general counterattack. The Spaniards, exhausted by several days of hard marching, collapsed. Their losses were about 3,500 men, Dutch casualties some 2,000. Maurice, with his lines of communication still vulnerable to Spanish attack, made no attempt at pursuit. Raising the siege of Nieuport, he withdrew into Dutch Flanders.

1601–1604. Spanish Siege of Ostend. The Dutch lost about 30,000 men in this long siege, but were able to prevent starvation by sending in reinforcements and supplies by sea. Albert's investing Spanish army lost perhaps 60,000 men by casualty or disease. Meanwhile, both England and France had made peace with Spain, leaving the Dutch without allies. Though Maurice had numerous successes elsewhere, the drain of defending Ostend, and at the same time meeting generally increasing Spanish pressure, caused the States General to order its surrender after a siege of 3 years and 71 days (September 20, 1604).

1604–1607. Desultory Warfare in the Netherlands. The Dutch were able to hold their own only because of control of the sea. A series of Dutch naval successes, culminated by the victory of Admiral **Jacob van Heenskerk** in the **Battle of Gibraltar** (1607), caused the Spanish to agree to a temporary truce during peace negotiations.

SWITZERLAND

During this century Swiss infantry lost its pre-eminence in Europe, due to the vulnerability of the pike phalanxes to the growing strength of artillery and small arms. The Swiss belatedly modified their tactics, increasing the percentage of arquebusiers and musketeers. Despite disasters early in the century, Swiss mercenary pike columns were still much sought by other European armies, though their callous avarice led to the common saying: "When the money runs out, so do the Swiss." The Swiss had their own strong national discipline, but refused to be disciplined by their employers. Nor did they allow sentiment to affect business; Protestant Swiss fought against French Huguenots. Within Switzerland itself, civil strife resulting from the imperfect federal union continued sporadically, complicated and intensified by the interjection of the religion issue in midcentury, by which time most of the northern and western cantons were Protestant. Despite civil war at home, Swiss mercenaries refused to fight one another. The principal events were:

1510. Switzerland Joins the Holy League against France. The Swiss Confederation restored Count **Maximilian Sforza** to control in Milan, annexing Locarno, Lugano, and Ossola (1512).

1513, June 6. Battle of Novara. Swiss victory over the French (see p. 472).

1513–1515. Swiss Protectorate over the Duchy of Milan. They thus obtained the duchy's rich revenues.

1515, September 13–14. Battle of Marignano. French victory over the Swiss (see p. 472).

1531. War between Zurich and the Catholic Cantons. This was culminated by Zurich's defeat in the **Battle of Kappel** (October 11).

1536. Expansion of Bern. Vaud, Chablais, Lausanne, and other territories of Savoy were subdued and annexed.

1541–1555. Sporadic Religious Civil War.

1564–1602. Intermittent War between the Protestant Cantons and Savoy. Bern, Geneva, and Zurich formed an alliance against Savoy and the Catholic cantons (1584). Spain intervened on the side of the Catholics (1587). This drawn-out war was inconclusive.

ITALY

Italy—weak, fragmented, and wealthy—was the principal battleground of the great wars between France, Spain, and the Hapsburgs during the first half of this century. The almost continuous minor wars between the petty Italian states were merely incidents in these larger struggles, described elsewhere (see pp. 469–477). Venice, despite the decline of her maritime empire, barely maintained her position as the most important independent state in Italy.

THE IBERIAN PENINSULA

Spain

Within the century Spain reached, then passed, the apogee of world power. The highly efficient military force created for the expulsion of the Moslems (1492; see p. 431) was further improved by the organizational and tactical genius of Gonzalo de Córdoba, "El Gran Capitán," the first important European soldier to fully understand, and to utilize, small-arms fire power. For the remainder of the century the Spanish were the pre-eminent soldiers of Europe. In addition to Córdoba, Spain provided three more of the finest military leaders of the century: **Hernando Cortez,** conqueror of Mexico, Álvarez de Toledo, Duke of Alva, and Italian-born **Alexander Farnese, Duke of Parma.** The ambitions of Spanish monarchs in exploring, conquering, and settling most of the Western Hemisphere, endeavoring to establish command of the seas, fighting interminable wars against France and Turkey, and in supporting the cause of the imperial Hapsburgs elsewhere in Europe all constituted an intolerable strain on Spain's slender man-power resources. Yet this relatively small nation had an impact on the rest of the world, in a similarly short period of time, comparable to earlier Macedonia and Mongolia. The result was the same. A brilliant burst of glory, lasting less than a century, followed by a long, slow decline. The principal events were:

1474–1516. Reigns of Ferdinand and Isabella. After the death of Isabella (1504), Ferdinand retained control of united Spain despite the legal claim of his daughter, **Joanna,** to Castile.

1495–1559. Wars with France. These were mostly in Italy, but also along the Pyrenees and the Franco-Netherlands and Rhine frontiers (see p. 469).

1509–1511. North African Expeditions. Cardinal **Jiménez de Cisneros,** an able statesman and general as well as churchman, commanded these amphibious operations. He captured Oran, Bougie, and Tripoli; all Moslem rulers of Northwest Africa were forced to pay tribute to Spain.

1516–1556. Reign of Charles I. He was the son of Philip of Hapsburg and of Joanna, daughter of Ferdinand and Isabella, and thus sole heir of the houses of Hapsburg, Burgundy, Castile, and Aragon. Elected Holy Roman Emperor, as Charles V (1519), he became the most powerful ruler in Europe. His reign was notable militarily for almost continuous wars with Francis I of France and Suleiman of Turkey.

1521–1523. Uprising of the Comuneros. This was an urban bourgeois movement, covertly supported by France. This, combined with personal rivalry, led to Charles's first war against Francis (1521–1529; see p. 473). The rebels were finally crushed at the **Battle of Villalors** (April, 1523).

1533. Exile of the Moriscos. Many Moslem Moors, refusing to become Christians, were exiled. The fleets of **Khair ed-Din** of Algiers ferried most of them to Morocco.

1535. Charles's Successful Expedition against Tunis. (See p. 497.)

1541. Charles's Disastrous Expedition against Algiers. (See p. 499.)

1556–1598. Reign of Philip II (Son of Charles, after Charles's Abdication). This meant the separation of Spain and the Holy Roman Empire. During this reign Spanish influence, prestige, and capability reached their apex, and began to decline.

1567–1609. Rebellion in the Netherlands. (See p. 484.)

1568–1571. Revolt of the Moriscos. These were converted Moslems who were still persecuted by Spanish Christians.

1571, October 7. Battle of Lepanto. (See p. 502.)

1580. Philip II Becomes King of Portugal. This followed the victory of the Duke of Alva at the **Battle of Alcántara** (August 25; see p. 489).

1582. **Naval Battle of Terceira.** (See below.)
1583. **Naval Battle of San Miguel.** (See below.)
1587. **Drake's Raid on Cádiz.** (See p. 465.)

1588. **The Great Armada.** (See p. 466.)
1589–1598. **War with France.** Philip's intervention in French civil war (see p. 480).

Portugal, 1500–1589

Portugal's maritime glory, initiated by Henry the Navigator (see p. 432), reached its zenith in the early years of this century, when the Portuguese established the oldest and the most enduring of all European colonial systems on the shores of the Indian Ocean. Pre-eminent among Portuguese sailors was Affonso de Albuquerque, one of the great admirals of history, who employed sea power with an understanding, determination, and energy unmatched until the time of Nelson. Like more populous Spain, Portugal, too, was soon overextended by colonial and maritime endeavors; ambitions exceeded capabilities. The collapse of Portuguese maritime supremacy began with the defeat and death of King **Sebastian I** in an effort to conquer Morocco. Civil war broke out between 7 rival claimants to the throne. Philip II of Spain was successful, thanks to the military ability of the Duke of Alva. Spain and Portugal were combined, a union that lasted for more than half a century, with evil effects from which Portugal never fully recovered. The principal events were:

1495–1521. **Reign of Manuel I, the Great.** The height of Portuguese greatness and glory.
1500–1513. **Almeida and Albuquerque in the Indies.** (See p. 509.) These two viceroys established Portuguese ascendancy in the entire Indian Ocean.
1557–1578. **Reign of Sebastian I.**
1578. **Battle of Al Kasr al Kebir.** Sebastian, personally leading an expedition of conquest to Morocco, was disastrously defeated. Three kings died in the battle: Sebastian, the King of Fez, and the pretender to the throne of Fez (allied with Sebastian).
1578–1580. **Civil War of Succession.** Philip II of Spain was successful, due to the victory of his general, the Duke of Alva, over Don **Antonio de Crato of Beja** at the **Battle of Alcántara** (August 25, 1580). Antonio fled to England, then to France.
1580–1598. **Reign of Philip.**

1582. **Naval Battle of Terceira (Azores).** Spanish Marquis **Álvaro de Bazán of Santa Cruz** defeated a French fleet under **Filippo Strozzi,** which was attempting to seize the Azores for Antonio de Crato.
1583. **Naval Battle of San Miguel** (or 2nd Terceira). Crato again tried to seize the Azores with French support, intending to reconquer the throne. The Franco-Portuguese fleet, under **Aymard de Chaste,** was again defeated by Santa Cruz. Spanish superiority in the Atlantic was reaffirmed.
1589. **English Intervention.** Crato again attempted to reconquer Portugal, landing in his native land with English amphibious support, led respectively by Sir Francis Drake and Sir **John Norris.** There was disagreement among the leaders; the population failed to rise as expected, alienated by English plundering. Crato was disastrously defeated, and fled to France. The English returned home.

EASTERN EUROPE

POLAND

Poland became firmly united with Lithuania, and the combined monarchy, after a series of fierce struggles with the princes of Moscow, repulsed Russian and Tartar threats, pushing Poland's eastern frontier well beyond the Dnieper River in

White Russia and the Ukraine, and establishing Poland as one of the great powers of Europe. The principal events were:

1501–1506. Reign of Alexander I. The union of Poland and Lithuania was broken, permitting **Ivan III** of Russia to conquer all the left bank of the Dnieper River (1503).

1506–1548. Reign of Sigismund I. This able and farsighted king reunited Lithuania with Poland. Sigismund labored intensively to build up the military strength and political unity of his weakened nation, but was defeated in a long war with **Basil III** of Russia, losing Smolensk (1514). Later, after creating an outstanding army, he fought a more successful, though inconclusive, war with Russia (1534–1536).

1548–1572. Reign of Sigismund II. Another able king. During his reign Lithuania and the Ukraine were permanently united with Poland.

1557–1571. Livonian War. Poland, Russia, Sweden, and Denmark had rival claims and aspirations in Livonia (modern Estonia, Latvia, and part of Lithuania). The war was precipitated by a Russian invasion after the collapse of the Teutonic Order (see p. 482). A confused 4-way war followed. The Russians were at first repulsed, with the Swedes occupying Estonia and Poland taking most of the remainder of Livonia, save for Kurland, which was seized by Denmark (1561). Poland's war with Russia continued

fiercely for nearly 10 more years, with Poland losing part of its Livonian conquests to **Ivan the Terrible** (1563–1571).

1573–1574. Reign of Henry of Galois (Later Henry III of France). A period of turmoil; weak Henry was unable to control the unruly Polish nobles. He left Poland to become King of France (see p. 479).

1575–1586. Reign of Stephen Bathory. A strong ruler and a capable warrior. Although plagued by the lack of discipline and unity amongst the great nobles, he won a series of substantial victories over Ivan the Terrible.

1579–1582. Renewed Livonian War. Stephen repulsed the Russians who were endeavoring to exploit internal unrest in Poland, recaptured Polotsk from Russia, and pressed the boundary of Livonia as far east as Pskov.

1582–1586. Reorganization of the Polish Military System. Stephen incorporated into it the fierce Ukrainian Cossacks. He made plans for a joint Polish-Russian crusade against the Turks to expel them from their footholds along the northern coast of the Black Sea, but died before anything came of the plans.

1587–1632. Reign of Sigismund III. He was the first Polish ruler from the Swedish Vasa family. He involved Poland in endless wars with Sweden, most of which took place in Livonia (see p. 483).

HUNGARY AND BOHEMIA

Bohemia and Hungary were combined under a single ruler for most of this period, and both were jointly incorporated into the Hapsburg dominions. Weak leadership resulted in disaster early in the century, when **Louis II** was defeated and killed by the Turks under Suleiman in the decisive **Battle of Mohacs.** This led to the collapse of Hungary, which for more than a century had barred Turkish aspirations to penetrate north up the Danube Valley into Central Europe. Suleiman, taking advantage of dissension, overran and annexed most of the country, while **Ferdinand of Hapsburg,** brother of Charles V, established tenuous control of a strip of northern and western Hungary, for which he paid tribute to the Turkish sultan. During the last three-quarters of the century, warfare was endemic along this entire border between the Ottoman and Hapsburg portions of Hungary. The principal events were:

1471–1516. Reign of Ladislas II of Bohemia (Ladislas VI of Hungary after 1490). A weak ruler, both of his kingdoms declined

while internal dissension arose. The Turks took advantage of this to encroach on Hungarian borders.

1514. Peasant Revolt in Hungary. This was led by **George Dozsa.** It was suppressed by the noble leader **John Zapolya** of Transylvania, after atrocities on both sides.

1516–1562. Reign of Louis II (Son of Ladislas II). Another weakling.

1521. Turkish Capture of Belgrade. (See p. 495.)

1526, August 29. Battle of Mohacs. Louis was killed and the Hungarian army smashed (see p. 497).

1526–1538. Civil War of Succession. This was between Ferdinand of Hapsburg and John Zapolya, who was supported by Suleiman (see p. 497).

1529. Siege of Vienna. (See p. 497.)

1538. Revolt in Moldavia. **Peter Rarish,** Prince of Moldavia and vassal of Turkey, allied himself with Ferdinand. Suleiman, aided by Krim Tartar vassals, suppressed the revolt brutally; Peter fled to exile.

1538. Treaty of Nagyvarad. Ferdinand recognized Zapolya as King of Hungary, while retaining the northern and western regions. The treaty recognized Ferdinand as the successor of Zapolya.

1540. Death of Zapolya. His adherents ignored the Treaty of Nagyvarad and elected Zapolya's son **John II** (1540–1571).

1540–1547. Renewed Civil War in Hungary. This caused Suleiman to invade and to annex all of Zapolya's former territories (see p. 501). Ferdinand agreed to pay tribute for the strip of northern and western Hungary which he retained.

1547–1568. Intermittent Ottoman-Hapsburg Warfare. The war was officially ended by the **Truce of Adrianople** (see p. 501), but frontier warfare continued.

1593–1606. The "Long War." Sigismund **Bathory,** Prince of Transylvania (1581–1602), in alliance with the Hapsburgs, conquered Wallachia by defeating Turk General **Sinan Pasha** at the **Battle of Guirgevo** (October 28, 1595). Internal warfare broke out in Transylvania, however, and Bathory was defeated by Voivode **Michael of Moldavia** at the **Battle of Suceava** (1600). An imperial army under **George Basta** then occupied Transylvania and began intense persecution of Transylvanian Catholics. Under the leadership of **Stephen Bocskay,** the Transylvanians formed an alliance with the Turks (1602). The war ended in a stalemate (see p. 584), with the **Treaty of Zsitva-Torok** (November 11, 1606). The independence of Transylvania was recognized by both sides.

RUSSIA

In this century the Grand Duchy of Moscow was transformed into the Russian Empire. Under **Basil III** and **Ivan IV** (the Terrible), this great new Slavic empire was almost constantly at war with its neighbors to the west, east, and south. These wars were caused partly by the lack of natural geographical frontiers on the vast flatlands of East Europe, and partly by the early manifestations of the landlocked Russians' insatiable desire for an outlet on the sea. At first they had more than their share of successes against the Poles and Lithuanians to the west; but as the century ended, Russian westward expansion had been halted by both the Poles and the Swedes, who now began to push the frontiers eastward. Russian expansion to the east was dramatic as they established loose authority over much of Siberia at the expense of the disorganized Mongols. To the south, the Russians were also successful in their struggles against the Tartars, gaining control of the entire Volga and Don river valleys. The principal events were:

1501–1503. War with Lithuania. The Russians conquered parts of White Russia and Little Russia.

1502. End of the Golden Horde. The Muscovites and Krim Tartars combined to defeat and kill **Ahmed Khan,** last ruler of the Golden Horde.

1505–1533. Reign of Basil III (Son of Ivan III and Zoë; see p. 435.) He not only consolidated the vast conquests of his father but also annexed the only 2 remaining independent Russian states: Pskov (1510) and Riazan (1517). He conquered Smolensk from the Lithuanians (1514).

1521. Tartar Invasion. Mohammed Girai, Khan of the Krim Tartars, invaded as far as Moscow. Basil agreed to pay perpetual tribute.

1533–1584. Reign of Ivan IV, "the Terrible" (Son of Basil). He ascended the throne at age 3. During his minority (1533–1547) the nobles (boyars) became dominant in Russia.

1547–1564. Subjugation of the Nobles. This culminated in Ivan's cruel suppression of a boyar revolt (1564).

1552–1557. Conquest of Kazan and Astrakhan. Russia gained control of the entire Volga Valley from the Tartars. **Devlet Girai,** Khan of the Crimea, instigated by Suleiman, invaded as far as Moscow. He captured the city, but was repelled from the Kremlin (1555).

1557–1582. Livonian Wars. (See p. 490.) Russian efforts to obtain an outlet on the Baltic were successful, but with Polish resurgence all these conquests were lost.

1569. War with Turkey. The Russians repulsed Turkish efforts to take **Astrakhan.**

1570. Sack of Novgorod. Ivan suspected the people of pro-Polish sympathies.

1571–1572. War with the Krim Tartars. A Tartar raid briefly captured and sacked Moscow. They were defeated by the Russians at the **Battle of Molodi,** 30 miles from Moscow.

1572. Revolt of the Volga Tartars. This was cruelly suppressed.

1578. Battle of Wenden. The Russians were defeated by the Swedes, resulting in the loss of Polotsk (1579).

c. 1580. Expansion East of the Urals. Russian traders, led by the merchant-noble family of **Strogonov,** began to expand eastward, establishing posts as far as the Amur.

1582. Revolt of the Volga Tartars. This was suppressed.

1584–1598. Reign of Theodore I (Son of Ivan). He was a weak ruler. The boyars again became dominant, the principal noble leaders being **Nikita Romanov** and **Boris Godunov.**

1598–1605. Reign of Boris Godunov. He was elected czar by the nobles after the death of Theodore.

EURASIA AND THE MIDDLE EAST

THE OTTOMAN EMPIRE, 1500–1606

This was the era of Turkey's greatest glory and power. In a brief reign, Sultan **Selim I** nearly doubled its size as the result of decisive victories over the Persians and the Egyptian Mamelukes. Selim's better-known son, **Suleiman the Magnificent,** inherited much of his father's military and administrative genius, though without the same grim, flinty character.

Probably the most powerful ruler of the century, Suleiman's long reign roughly coincided with those of Francis I of France, Charles V of the Empire, and Henry VIII of England. Suleiman conquered most of Hungary, but his ambitions to extend Ottoman control into Central Europe were dashed by the staunch defense of Vienna and of other fortifications along the Austro-Hungarian border. With the assistance of his great admiral, **Khair ed-Din Barbarossa,** Suleiman extended Ottoman suzerainty along most of the coast of North Africa. Other naval expeditions established Turkish pre-eminence in the Red Sea, but the Portuguese repulsed all efforts to gain control of the Arabian Sea (see p. 510). Victories over Persia resulted in Turkish conquest of Mesopotamia and much of Armenia. The Black Sea became a Turkish lake. The frequent diversions of Turkish strength to wars against Persia during the reign of Suleiman may have been the decisive factor in saving divided Europe from Ottoman domination. Charles V and Ferdinand wisely encouraged and fomented Persian opposition to Suleiman.

Six years after the death of Suleiman, the long, slow decline of the Ottoman

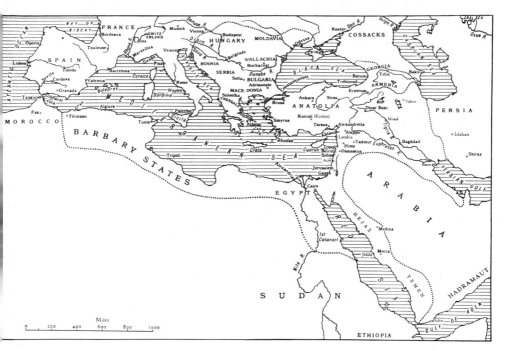

Ottoman Empire, *c.* 1550

Empire was initiated by a decisive naval defeat at the Battle of Lepanto by Don Juan of Austria. This decline is evident in retrospect; at the time it was less clear, since in the final years of the century the Turks decisively defeated the Persians, extending their conquests in the Caucasus, and also won slightly less conclusive victories over the Austrians in Transylvania and northern Hungary. The principal events were:

The Era of Selim, 1500–1520

1481–1512. Reign of Bayazid II. (See p. 439.)

1499–1503. War with Venice. The Turkish fleet under Admiral **Kemal Re'is** defeated the Venetian fleet in the **Second Battle of Lepanto,** or of Modon (1500). The Turks captured Modon (Methone), Lepanto, and Koron, though they lost Cephalonia. Turkish cavalry raided across the Julian Alps into Italy as far as Vicenza.

1501. Persian Raids. These were repulsed by the Bayazid's warlike son, Selim.

1502–1515. Undeclared Border War with the Mamelukes. Mameluke armies several times raided into Adana.

1509–1513. Civil War among the Sons of Bayazid. These were **Ahmed, Kortud,** and **Selim.** Selim was successful; he forced his father to abdicate, and seized the throne (1512).

1513–1520. Reign of Selim I. He was the greatest soldier of the Ottoman sultans. His concentration on Asiatic campaigns, however, lost Turkey the chance to capitalize on the divisions of Europe, which were partly healed by accession of Charles V (see p. 482).

1514–1516. War with Persia. Selim provoked this war partly because the Persians had supported his brother Ahmed, partly because Shah **Ismail** (see p. 505) had raided into Ottoman territory in previous years, and partly because of his implacable hatred, as a devout Sunni Moslem, of the Shi'ite sect of Persia.

1515, June–August. Invasion of Persia. Selim marched from Sivas, then the easternmost Ottoman city, with an army of more than 60,000 men, via Erzerum to the upper Euphrates. Despite the Persian "scorched earth" policy, Selim's logistical foresight permitted him to advance through the rugged mountains to Khoi, where the shah had assembled an army, probably less than 50,000 men, entirely cavalry—typical horse archers and lancers of Southwest Asia, based generally on the old Mongol system. Turkish food supplies were consumed on the march.

1515, August 23. Battle of Chaldiran. Selim deployed his army on the Plains of Chaldiran in front of the Persians, protected by a screen of irregular cavalry and infantry. Behind this screen the infantry Janissaries (mixed archers and arquebusiers) formed behind a hastily dug trench. The flanks were protected by carts chained together, and in front of these carts, to the right and left front of the Janissaries, was the Turkish artillery, roped together wheel to wheel. On either side of this semifortified position were the royal cavalry guards (spahis), with the feudal Ottoman light cavalry (timariot) units extending the line farther to the flanks. The Persians attacked, drove off the screen of irregular cavalry, routed the European timariots on the Turkish right, but were repulsed in a hard fight by the Asiatic timariots of the left. The spahis and Janissaries stood fast, repulsing repeated attacks by the Persian left. The Turkish left then swung around to engage the remainder of the Persian army in a violent struggle in which Ismail was wounded and his army routed. The Persians fled to Khoi, abandoning their camp and its provisions to the starving Turks. Casualties are unreported, but it is doubtful if the Persians lost more heavily than the Turks, since they were able to retreat rapidly and without effective Turkish pursuit.

1515, September 5. Capture of Tabriz. Selim took Ismail's capital without resistance. Soon after this, the Janissaries mutinied, refusing to advance farther into Persia. The timariots also wished to go home, so Selim reluctantly marched back by way of Erivan and Kars. The Persians reoccupied Tabriz. The Turks, however, kept their foothold on the upper Euphrates.

1515. Conquest of the Middle Euphrates. Selim's operations in this area, nominally subject to the Mamelukes, indicated contempt for both Persians and Mamelukes by thus engaging in war against both simultaneously. He then marched into Kurdistan, driving the Persians back into the Iranian highlands.

1516, July. Invasion of Syria. Selim, preparing for another invasion of Persia, learned that Mameluke Sultan **Kansu al-Gauri** had formed an alliance with Persia and was preparing to invade Turkey from Aleppo. Selim immediately turned south into Syria via the Euphrates Valley, bypassing the Taurus Mountains and surprising the Mamelukes (August). Kansu assembled his army, about 30,000 cavalrymen, at Merj-Dabik, 10 miles north of Aleppo. About half of these were Mameluke cavalry, mixed lancers, and bowmen, similar to the Persians, save that they wore turbans instead of helmets. The remainder were Arabic levies, unarmored, and less disciplined and less well organized than the Mamelukes. Kansu had neither infantry nor artillery. Selim had approximately 40,000 men, of whom 15,000 were timariot feudal levies, 8,000 Janissaries, 3,000 spahis, and perhaps 15,000 irregulars.

1516, August 24. Battle of Merj-Dabik. Selim drew up his army in the same formation as at Chaldiran. The Mamelukes attacked in a half-moon formation. Action on both flanks was indecisive, but the central and heaviest Mameluke attack was thrown back in rout by the Turkish artillery in the center. Kansu was killed, and the Mameluke wings then fled. The battle was over so quickly that casualties were relatively light on both sides. The Mamelukes abandoned Syria and fell back to Egypt.

1516, August–October. Occupation of Syria. Selim prepared to invade Egypt. Meanwhile the Mamelukes elected **Touman Bey,** Kansu's nephew, as their sultan.

1516, October 28. Battle of Yaunis Khan. The Turkish advance guard under Grand Vizier **Sinan** Pasha defeated a Mameluke force near Gaza.

1517, January. Invasion of Egypt. Selim marched across the Gaza Desert, via Salihia (January 16), and advanced on Cairo. At El-Kankah, Touman blocked the road to Cairo, emplacing some artillery hastily created by buying guns from Venetian ships at Alexandria and by stripping seacoast defenses. Selim decided to envelop these fortifications. In a night march, the Turkish army shifted to the left, forming before dawn in battle order at Ridanieh, on the edge of the desert.

1517, January 22. Battle of Ridanieh. Touman hastily shifted his army over 90° to its right, trying to drag his wheelless guns to new positions. Selim gave him no time to complete this movement, commencing an artillery bombardment for the purpose of provoking the Mamelukes to attack. As he intended, the Mamelukes charged the center of the Ottoman army, while light Arab auxiliaries harassed the flanks. The desperate charge broke one wing of the Turkish army, but the reserve under Sinan Pasha plugged the hole, though Sinan was killed in the resulting struggle. The Mamelukes were driven off, having lost about 7,000 dead. The Turks lost about 6,000. Selim immediately marched into Cairo.

1517, January–February. Conquest of Egypt. Touman continued desperate resistance, including several days of bloody street fighting in Cairo (January 29–February 3) in a surprise effort to recapture the Egyptian capital. Selim proclaimed himself Sultan of Egypt, and then Caliph— this supreme Moslem title ostensibly conferred by the last of the Abbasids. He left the Mamelukes as nominal rulers of Egypt, but under a Turkish governor general.

1517. Occupation of Mecca and the West Arabian Coast.

1518–1519. Religious Outbreaks in Anatolia and Syria. These were suppressed by Selim.

1519. Alliance with Algiers. Khair ed-Din, Dey of Algiers, paid homage to Selim, and offered a fleet to the Ottoman Empire, in return for support against Spain.

1520, September 22. Death of Selim. He was preparing an expedition against Rhodes.

The Era of Suleiman, 1520–1566

1520–1566. Reign of Suleiman I, the Magnificent (Son of Selim). During the early part of his reign, Suleiman was assisted greatly by his loyal vizier **Ibrahim** Pasha, who administered the empire, permitting Suleiman to devote himself almost exclusively to military conquest (1523–1536).

SULEIMAN'S EARLY WARS IN THE WEST, 1521–1544

1521, May–September. Invasion of Hungary. Suleiman advanced northward, ostensibly to redress pretended Hungarian slights. He captured **Shabotz** by assault (July 8), then besieged **Belgrade**; its small garrison surrendered after gallant defense (August 29). He sent raiding forces northward to terrorize Hungary and Central Europe. Finding that sea communications in his empire were hampered by the Christian fortresses of Rhodes, Crete, and Cyprus, he planned to seize them.

THE SIEGE OF RHODES, 1522

Suleiman continued his father's preparations against Rhodes, eastern Mediterranean stronghold of the Knights Hospitalers of St. John, and probably the most strongly fortified place in the world at that time. It was one of the earliest of the new bastion fortresses, with a broad ditch and a glacis, and (in some places) two interior walls. The port was protected by powerful tower forts at the entrance of the harbor, which was also blocked by massive bronze chains. Grand Master **Philip Villiers de L'Isle Adam** had 700 knights, plus 6,000 light local auxiliaries, including some cavalry, marines, pikemen, and arquebusiers. Artillery in substantial numbers was well emplaced. No reinforcements were available. Provisions and ammunition were plentiful, but no resupply could be expected. As Turkish preparations became obvious, Villiers had all available foodstuff collected from the remainder of the island within the fortified city, and gave refuge to the farm peasants.

1522, June 25. Turkish Landings. A beachhead was established without opposition. The Turkish army, approximately 100,000 men, was well trained, confident, and in-

cluded an excellent engineer corps, as well as a powerful train of siege artillery.

1522, July 28. The Siege Begins. A contest of artillery fire and mining operations, conducted with great skill, determination, and energy on both sides. Defending artillery fire was devastatingly accurate, since the knights had exact ranges to all key points. Though the knights destroyed most Turkish mines, some reached the walls to blow great breaches (August).

1522, September–November. Repeated Turkish Assaults. All were repulsed with shocking slaughter. Nonetheless, the losses among the garrison were heavy under the Turkish bombardment and in the hand-to-hand fighting in the breaches and along the walls. The garrison dwindled to a strength inadequate to man the walls properly, while gunpowder was almost exhausted. Turkish casualties were replaced by reinforcements from the mainland.

1522, December 1–15. Negotiations. Suleiman realized the difficulties of the defenders, but was horrified by the terrible losses his own army had suffered. He offered honorable terms of surrender, guaranteeing that the population could leave or stay and that their religion would be respected. The negotiations broke down, however, and fighting renewed.

1522, December 17–18. Turkish Penetration into the City. The knights counterattacked vigorously and blocked the streets to contain the Turkish lodgement.

1522, December 20. Negotiations Reopened. Suleiman did not relish the thought of more costly street fighting. Hostages were exchanged; the Turks pulled out of their lodgement in the city and withdrew one mile from the walls. Suleiman's personal conduct in the negotiations, and in living up to the terms of the treaty, was exemplary.

1522, December 21–1523, January 1. Evacuation of Rhodes. Only 180 knights, plus 1,500 other troops, were left alive, and most of these were wounded. Turkish losses in the siege of Rhodes were at least 50,000 dead, and may have been as high as 100,000, out of a total force of almost 200,000 engaged. The tragedy of the siege, from the Christian standpoint, was the fact that Rhodes could probably have been held indefinitely had the knights received some reinforcements and supplies. Venice and Spain could have provided such assistance. Possibly it was contrition which caused Charles V later to give Tripoli, and then the island of Malta, to the Hospitalers, where they began to establish a new island fortress.

1522–1525. Intermittent Border Warfare with the Hungarians. This was particularly intense in Wallachia.

1524. Neutrality Treaty with Poland. This freed Suleiman's hands for an invasion of Hungary.

The Campaign of Mohacs, 1526

1526, April 23. Advance from Constantinople. Suleiman's army was 70,000–80,000 strong.

1526, May–July. Hungarian Preparations. King Louis, aware of the danger, was unable to arouse interest among other European nations. He was slow in organizing his nation for defense, but was given additional time by the 2-week siege of **Peterwardein** (July 12–27). Slowly gathering troops, Louis moved south to Mohacs, where his army grew to about 12,000 cavalry and 13,000 infantry (August 15). At this point, rumors that Suleiman had 300,000 men caused Louis and some of his advisers to waver. He was persuaded to stand firm by the confident arguments of Archbishop **Tomori,** a formidable warrior, who correctly estimated Turkish strength and discounted their capabilities.

1526, August 28. Arrival of the Turks. Suleiman reached the southern edge of the Plain of Mohacs. His light reconnaissance cavalry discovered the Hungarian army prepared for battle in the center of the plain southwest of Mohacs. It was an area ideal for cavalry combat, the principal arm on both sides.

1526, August 28–29. Hungarian Dispositions. The infantry, about half German and other foreign mercenary contingents, the remainder Hungarian, was formed in 3 large phalanxes in front of Mohacs, the left flank covered by marshes along the Danube River, the right flank in the air. The infantry included a substantial percentage of arquebusiers. Louis's artillery (about 20 cannon) was in front of the central square. Large cavalry detachments were placed in the intervals between the 3 squares; the remainder of the cavalry was drawn up into reserve lines to the rear.

1526, August 28–29. Turkish Dispositions. Suleiman formed his army in 3 lines, the first 2 consisting of feudal timariots. Behind them, providing a base of maneuver for the cavalry, Suleiman deployed Janissaries, with artillery in front and the spahis on their flanks. A detachment of 6,000 timariots was sent by a circuitous route to the west, taking advantage of undulations of the ground, to launch a surprise attack on the Hungarian right after the armies were fully engaged.

1526, August 29. Battle of Mohacs. The advancing Turks were met by a cannonade. The Hungarian first-line heavy cavalry then charged to drive the Turkish first line back. The remainder of the Hungarian army advanced, following this initial success, but the guns could not keep up. Just as the Hungarian cavalry charged Suleiman's second line, the Turkish enveloping force hit them on the right flank and threw them into considerable confusion. However, this flank attack was driven off by the second line of Hungarian cavalry. Both Hungarian cavalry lines joined in smashing the Turkish second line. The Hungarians then charged against the center of the third and final Turkish line, but suffered heavy casualties from the Turkish artillery, which they could not penetrate because the cannon were chained together. When the Janissaries and spahis counterattacked, the exhausted Hungarians broke and fled. Suleiman's army, which had suffered severely, attempted no organized pursuit; a few timariot units, rallied from their earlier defeat, harassed the fleeing Hungarians, whose losses were enormous: 10,000 infantry and 5,000 cavalry killed. The few prisoners captured by the Turks were beheaded. Louis, Tomori, and most of the other Hungarian leaders were killed. Without leadership, the fleeing remnants of the Hungarian army simply scattered. Turkish losses are unknown, but they were probably at least as heavy as those of the Hungarians. Suleiman spent three days on the battlefield reorganizing his army.

1526, September 10. Occupation of Buda. This was unopposed. Deciding not to annex Hungary, Suleiman made it a tributary kingdom under **John Zapolya** of Transylvania (see p. 491), who had traitorously absented himself from Mohacs.

1526–1528. Civil War in Hungary. Zapolya, with Turkish assistance, established effective control over all of Hungary except a fringe to the north and west, which remained under the control of **Ferdinand of Hapsburg** (brother-in-law of Louis, brother of Charles V, and later emperor; see p. 482). Ferdinand, bringing a German contingent to form the core of a new Hungarian army, captured Raab, Gran, and Buda, pursuing John and defeating him at the **Battle of Tokay** (1527). John appealed to Suleiman for help.

1528. Suleiman Prepares Another Expedition into Hungary. His preparations included a secret alliance with France against the Hapsburgs (see p. 475).

The Vienna Campaign, 1529

1529, May 10–August 6. Turkish Invasion. With an army exceeding 80,000 men, Suleiman advanced to Essek, being joined en route by Zapolya with 6,000 Hungarians.

1529, September 3–8. Siege and Capture of Buda. Most of the garrison was massacred.

1529, September 10–23. Advance on Vienna. Accompanying Suleiman's army up the Danube was a Turkish flotilla. All of Lower Austria was ravaged by the Turkish light cavalry. Vienna was garrisoned by a force of 17,000 men commanded by **Philip, Count Palatine of Austria,** but the real leaders were aged **Nicholas, Count of Salm** and Marshal **William von Roggendorf.** While the Turks were advancing, these men were energetically and effectively preparing the city for defense. Vienna had an ancient medieval wall, to which a few bastions for artillery had been added. The defenders hastily leveled all of the area around the walls in order to prepare a field of fire. Interior lines of entrenchments were dug within the walls to bolster the areas most vulnerable to artillery bombardment and mining. All wooden and thatched roofs in the city were ripped away.

1529, September 23. Land Investment of Vienna. There was skirmishing between cavalry patrols.

1529, September 27. Investment Completed on the Danube. The Turkish river flotilla sailed past the city to cut the line of communications to Bohemia.

1529, September 27–October 15. Siege of Vienna. Fought vigorously on both sides, incessant Turkish artillery bombardments and mining activities were punctuated by assault attempts (particularly October 9–15). The defenders, who discovered underground activity by observing agitation in bowls of water placed on the walls and outworks, energetically countermined. At the same time they conducted numerous sorties, severely damaging the Turkish entrenchments, mineheads, and artillery positions (September 29, October 2, October 6). With cold weather coming on, it became obvious to Suleiman that success was impossible. He withdrew, after killing all adult male prisoners (October 14–15).

1529, October–November. Austrian Pursuit. The Turks were vigorously harassed. Adding to the Turkish difficulties were premature snowstorms, making the roads so muddy that all wagons and carts had to be abandoned. The flotilla, carrying the Turkish siege artillery, suffered severe damage as it passed by the guns of Pressburg (Bratislava).

1530. Austro-Hungarian Initiative. They captured Gran, and raided as far as Buda-Pest.

1531. Austro-Hungarian Siege of Buda. This was unsuccessful. Widespread fighting along the frontier was generally inconclusive.

1532. Renewed Turkish Invasion. Suleiman led another large expedition north from Belgrade (June 25). Charles V moved to defend Vienna with a large army, but Suleiman avoided a direct conclusion, turning into southwest Austria by way of the Mur-Drava Valley. While Turkish light cavalry was demonstrating against Vienna and ravaging Lower Austria, Suleiman besieged **Guns** (Koszeg), and was repulsed. After a feint toward Vienna and further demonstrations in Styria (avoiding both Graz and Marburg), Suleiman withdrew down the Drava River, the expedition a dismal failure.

1533. Peace between Suleiman and Ferdinand. The Turks were anxious to devote full attention to war with Persia (see below). The "eternal" peace conceded to Ferdinand control of the northern and western strip, about 1/3 of Hungary. Ferdinand and John Zapolya both paid tribute to Suleiman. This treaty did not affect Charles V; the Empire continued at war with Turkey in the Mediterranean (see p. 499).

SULEIMAN'S WARS IN ASIA, 1523–1559

1523–1525. Revolts in Egypt. These were suppressed by Ibrahim Pasha.

1525. Janissary Mutiny in Constantinople. Suppressed by Suleiman.

1526–1527. Insurrections in Anatolia. These were largely inspired by religious friction between the Sunni and Shi'ite sects. They were suppressed with difficulty, and forced Suleiman to hasten back to Turkey from Hungary.

1526–1555. War with Persia. Shah **Tahmasp** of Persia took advantage of Suleiman's European wars and of the Shi'ite uprisings (which he probably stimulated) to invade Turkish Armenia and to recapture Baghdad, Van, and other areas conquered by Selim (1526).

1533–1534. Invasion of Azerbaijan. Ibrahim Pasha captured Tabriz (July 13, 1534) against light opposition.

1534, December. Invasion of Mesopotamia. Suleiman joined Ibrahim at Tabriz and led the Turkish army into Mesopotamia via Hamadan to recapture Baghdad against light opposition. His army suffered heavy losses at the hands of Persian and Kurd guerrillas in its march.

1535, January 1. Persian Recapture of Tabriz. Tahmasp took advantage of Suleiman's absence in Mesopotamia.

1535, April–June. Turkish Recapture of Tabriz. Suleiman returned by forced marches from Baghdad. Tahmasp again retired without fighting.

1535, July–August. Invasion of Northern Persia. Suleiman pursued Tahmasp, but the shah avoided battle. Logistical difficulties caused Suleiman to return to Tabriz, which he destroyed (August), and then marched back to Constantinople by way of the Euphrates Valley and Aleppo.

1536, March 30. Assassination of Ibrahim Pasha. Suleiman ordered this, apparently upon the instigation of his Russian-born wife, **Roxelana,** who exercised great political influence over the Sultan.

1538. Suleiman Raids into Persia. Again he temporarily occupied Tabriz. In following years there was continuous border skirmishing.

1545–1549. Suleiman Renews Activity against Persia. Taking the field personally, he recaptured Van and Tabriz, the Persians again refusing to fight (1548). When the Turkish army went into winter quarters in Anatolia, the Persians once more reoccupied Tabriz, leaving the Turks with only minor gains (1548–1549).

1552–1555. Final Phase of the Persian War. This was initiated by a Persian offensive which captured Erzerum (1552). Suleiman took the field to recapture Erzerum. He then advanced into western Persia, which he ravaged (1553–1554). This time he established firm control over Erzerum, Erivan, Van, Tabriz, and Georgia, and established a tenuous Turkish foothold on the Caspian Sea. The war ended with the **Treaty of Amasia** (1555).

1553. Brief Janissary Revolt.

1559. Civil War between the Sons of Suleiman. Selim, with the support of his father, defeated his brother **Bayazid** at the **Battle of Konya.** Bayazid fled to Persia, but was executed by orders of the shah, who received a substantial payment from Suleiman.

STRUGGLES IN THE MEDITERRANEAN, 1532–1565

1532. Andrea Doria Raids Morea. His imperial fleet captured Coron (Karoni), installing a Spanish garrison. This precipitated a prolonged Turkish-Christian struggle for control of the Mediterranean.

1533. Operations of Khair ed-Din. The Dey of Algiers, a vassal of the Ottoman Empire (see pp. 517 and 475), was appointed by Suleiman as Admiral (Kapitan Pasha) of the Turkish fleet. He recaptured Coron and Patras.

1534. Khair ed-Din Seizes Tunis. The former sultan, **Mulai-Hassan,** fled to Europe, where he offered to become a vassal of Charles V in return for aid against the Turks and South Italy.

1535, June–July. Charles V's Amphibious Expedition to Tunisia. The emperor's army was protected by Andrea Doria's fleet. Doria decisively defeated Khair ed-Din in a battle off the coast. The imperial-Spanish army landed and quickly captured Tunis, Bey Mulai-Hassan being reinstated. A Spanish protectorate controlled Tunis for nearly 40 years (1535–1574).

1536. Alliance of Francis I and Suleiman (March; see p. 475.) The renewal of war in Western Europe forced Charles to abandon a plan to attack Algiers. Khair ed-Din, after rebuilding his fleet at Algiers, raided and devastated Minorca.

1537. Suleiman Declares War against Venice. This resulted from a presumed Venetian insult. He ordered Khair ed-Din to ravage Venetian territory. The admiral harried Apulia, Turkish forces raiding inland around Taranto (July), while Suleiman led an army to the Albanian coast opposite the Venetian island of Corfu.

1537, August 18–September 6. Siege of Corfu. Turkish land and naval forces received some French naval assistance. The approach of a combined imperial-Venetian fleet under Andrea Doria and Ferdinand's declaration of war against the Ottomans in Hungary, in compliance with orders from Charles, caused Suleiman to abandon the siege.

1538. Khair ed-Din Intensifies Naval Operations. He swept the Aegean and Adriatic, and raided the coasts of Sicily and south Italy. He rejected an effort by Charles V to bribe him from the service of Suleiman. Although the Venetian garrisons of Nauplia and Monenvasia in the Morea repulsed Turkish attacks, Khair ed-Din captured all other Venetian island and mainland Aegean outposts, and raided Crete. He engaged in prolonged and inconclusive maneuvers against Doria and a combined imperial-Venetian fleet off the west coast of Greece and Albania (August–December).

1538, September 27. Battle of Preveza. Khair ed-Din had the best of an indecisive fleet action against Doria.

1539. Venice Makes Peace. She acknowledged her Aegean losses, giving up her two remaining footholds in the Morea and promising neutrality for 30 years. The only remaining important Venetian possessions outside of the Adriatic were Corfu, Zante, Crete, and Cyprus.

1541, September–October. Charles V's Expedition to Algiers. The Emperor embarked despite Doria's warnings of seasonal storms. The force of 21,000 men was landed 12 miles east of Algiers (October 20). Just as the investment of the city was beginning, a great storm wrecked most of the imperial fleet. The Moslem defenders of the city took advantage of the storm to conduct a sortie which caused heavy casualties (October 24–26). Charles and 14,000 survivors embarked on the remaining galleys and transports to return to Europe (October 27).

1542–1544. Khair ed-Din Terrorizes the Western Mediterranean. Part of the time he was accompanied by a French fleet under **Francis, Prince of Enghien** (see p. 499). Doria took refuge in Genoa. The French and Turks ravaged the coast of Catalonia, then besieged and sacked Nice (see p. 475). After wintering on the coast of Provence, Khair ed-Din continued his bold raids along the coast of Italy. When Francis suddenly concluded the Peace of Crépy, Khair ed-Din, losing his base in the western Mediterranean, returned to Constantinople, died 2 years later (1546).

1546. Truce between Suleiman and Charles V.

1551. Capture of Tripoli. Turkish land and naval forces ejected the Knights of St. John, after a gallant defense.

1551–1553. Turkish Fleet Sweeps the Western Mediterranean. Again, French forces cooperated. The Turks captured Bastia in Corsica.

1554–1556. Turkish Expansion in North Africa. This was led by Admiral **Torghoud,** successor to Khair ed-Din. Most North African Moslem potentates acknowledged Ottoman suzerainty.

1555. Torghoud Captures Bugia (Bougie). The Spanish were ejected.

1558. Torghoud Captures Jerba Island. This brought the Turks close to Spanish-controlled Tunis. Turkish warships and corsairs terrorized the western Mediterranean; **Port Mahon,** Minorca, was seized and sacked.

1560. Doria Recaptures Jerba. He was then driven off by the Turkish fleet; Doria's garrison surrendered after a siege of 3 months (March–June).

1561. Turkish Naval Raids against Sicily.

1563. Assault on Oran. The Spanish repelled the Turks.

1565, May–September. Siege of Malta. The Turkish army was under **Mustafa** Pasha. The defending Knights of St. John were commanded by Grand Master **Jean de la Valette.** The Turkish army was initially

30,000; approximately an equal number of reinforcements arrived during the siege. De la Valette had 500 knights and about 8,500 other troops, including mercenaries and 4,000 Maltese levies. Reinforcements consisted of 80 knights and 600 other troops who slipped in during the siege. The struggle was fought with the same skill and intensity on both sides as the siege of Rhodes 43 years earlier. Turkish bombardment was almost continuous, assaults were frequent, but the defenses remained firm and the defenders fought boldly and well under a magnificent leader. The Turks abandoned the siege upon the arrival of a relieving Spanish fleet and army under **García of Toledo,** Viceroy of Naples. The Spanish did not interfere with the Turkish embarkation and withdrawal. Turkish losses were probably 24,000 killed. The defenders lost 240 knights and 5,000 other troops killed.

SULEIMAN'S LATER WARS IN EUROPE, 1537–1566

1537, September–December. Austro-Hungarian Invasion of Turkish Hungary. Ferdinand, ordered by Charles, joined the Empire, Venice, and Papal States against Turkey and France (see p. 475). He was repulsed at **Essek.** The Austrians, commanded by **John Katvianer,** withdrew into Austrian territory, harassed by the Turks and suffering severe losses from cold and snowy weather and from desertion as well. The Turks practically annihilated the remaining Austrians in a number of scattered engagements near **Valpo** (December 2). Approximately 20,000 Austrians were killed, the army entirely dispersed. Turkish forces raided the coast of Apulia.

1538, July–September. Operations in Moldavia. Suleiman, assisted by his Krim Tartar vassals, suppressed a revolt in Moldavia, which had allied itself with Ferdinand.

1540. Death of John Zapolya. Ferdinand invaded Turkish Hungary, but was repulsed at **Buda.** He sent an envoy to Persia urging the shah to attack Turkey (see p. 491).

1541. Suleiman Pacifies Hungary. He annexed the country to the Ottoman Empire.

1532. Ferdinand Invades Hungary. He was

repulsed after a vain siege of **Pest.** Suleiman, preparing for another expedition up the Danube, renewed the Franco-Turkish alliance.

1543, April–September. Suleiman Invades Austria. He marched up the Danube and then up the Drava, capturing Gran (August) and Stuhlweissenberg (September). He made no effort to engage the principal Austrian army which Ferdinand held to protect Vienna.

1544. Suleiman Makes Peace with Ferdinand. He gave up plans to invade Austria after being abandoned by his French ally (see p. 476). The situation in Hungary returned to the *status quo,* with Ferdinand agreeing to continue his tribute for his portion of Hungary (1545). This permitted Suleiman to renew his war with Persia (see p. 499).

1551–1553. Ferdinand Renews the Turkish War. He invaded Transylvania (see p. 491). The Austrians were repulsed, but stopped Turkish counterinvasion by successful defense of border fortresses. Intermittent border war continued (1553–1562).

1562. Peace of Prague. Ferdinand and Suleiman made peace, with no substantial changes in the *status quo;* Ferdinand continued to pay tribute. The Mediterranean war between the Ottoman and Holy Roman Empires continued (see p. 482).

1566, January. Renewed War in Hungary. This was precipitated by raids ordered by the new Emperor **Maximilian.**

1566, July–August. Invasion of Austria. Suleiman, despite his age (72 years) and suffering from gout, led an army of more than 100,000 men.

1566, August 5–September 8. Siege of Szigeth (Szigetvar). The fortress was gallantly defended by Count **Miklos Zrinyi.** When the walls had been battered to rubble and further resistance was useless, Zrinyi ignited time fuses to his powder magazine and led the survivors of his garrison in a desperate sortie, in which all were killed (September 8). Hundreds of Turks, rushing into the fortress, were killed when the magazine exploded. Suleiman had died 2 days earlier. The Turkish grand vizier, pretending Suleiman was still alive, marched the army back to Constantinople.

The Crest of the Ottoman Flood, 1566–1600

1566–1574. Reign of Selim II ("the Sot").

1568, February. Treaty of Adrianople. Peace with the Hapsburgs (see p. 491).

1569. Revolt in Turkish Arabia. This was suppressed by local Ottoman governors.

1569. Capture of Tunis. Ouloudj Ali, Bey of Algiers, drove out the Spanish.

1569. War with Russia. The Turks and Krim Tartars failed in efforts to conquer Astrakhan.

1570, January. War with Venice. The republic had refused to cede Cyprus to Turkey. Selim sent a fleet under Admiral **Piale** Pasha and an army of 50,000 men under General **Lala Mustafa** to seize Cyprus. The garrison of 10,000 was commanded by Governor **Nicolo Dandolo,** who divided his forces between the two cities of Nicosia and Famagusta.

1570, July 22–September 9. Siege of Nicosia. The garrison was not strong enough to man the modern defenses of the city, which were taken by storm. Most of the population and the entire garrison were massacred.

1570, September 18–1571, August 1. Siege of Famagusta. There was little activity other than blockade during the winter. Some reinforcements and supplies of munitions slipped past the Turkish blockading fleet (January). The governor, **Marcantonio Brigadino,** made good use of the time to strengthen the antiquated defenses, manned by a total force of 5,400 men. Fighting was fierce during the spring and summer; Brigadino's defense was masterly. After all his ammunition was consumed and his garrison reduced to 2,000, Brigadino accepted terms offered by Mustafa, who then treacherously massacred the defenders (August 4).

1570–1571. Pope Pius V Establishes the Holy League. Its purpose was to conduct a crusade against the Turks for the relief of Famagusta, but the forces were slow in gathering, due to mutual suspicions of Spain and Venice. Famagusta fell while Christian forces gathered at Messina.

1571, August–September. Turkish Naval Operations. Admiral Pasha **Ali Monizindade** ravaged Venetian possessions in the Aegean and Ionian seas, then sailed into the Adriatic to within sight of Venice. Learning of Christian naval preparations at Messina, Ali rushed back to the Ionian Sea.

1571, September 22. Formation of the Allied

Christian Fleet. This consisted of some 300 ships of all types, gathered at Messina, under the command of Don Juan of Austria. Next day they sailed for the Gulf of Corinth to seek the Turkish fleet.

THE BATTLE OF LEPANTO, OCTOBER 7, 1571

When the Turkish fleet was discovered at Lepanto, early on October 7, Juan's fleet available for battle was 108 Venetian galleys, 81 Spanish galleys, and 32 other provided by the pope and other small states. He also had 6 giant Venetian galleasses.

The Turkish fleet immediately moved out from Lepanto. Ali had 270 galleys, on the average somewhat smaller than the Christians'. The crews were probably not so experienced as those of the Christian ships.

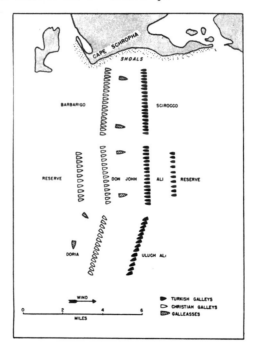

Battle of Lepanto

The two fleets formed up in a traditional battle formation which had varied little since the Battle of Actium: each in a long line of 3 divisions, with a reserve in the rear. Save that the Turkish left wing was larger than the right wing, thus indicating a planned envelopment, neither side had any real tactical plan other than a crude melee, to be won by ramming and boarding. For this latter purpose there were 20,000 soldiers (out of a total strength of 84,000) on board the Christian fleet, and about 16,000 Turkish soldiers (of a total of 88,000). The only real difference between these two fleets and those which had fought in the Punic Wars, nearly 2,000 years earlier, was that a few small cannon were mounted in the bows of the galleys, and in the broadsides of the galleasses. The Christian marines, who included a number of arquebusiers, wore light armor. Few of the Turks had armor, and most were armed with bows or crossbows.

The fleets, each stretched out over a 5-mile front, met in a series of great clashes, beginning about 10:30 A.M. By noon the main bodies of both sides were completely engaged. The galleasses broke the Turkish line, but this was not decisive. Confused fighting raged for about 3 hours, during which the superior skill of the Christian sailors, and the superior armament of the Christian soldiers, gradually asserted themselves. An additional advantage, though not of great significance, was that the wind was favorable to the Christians.

The Turkish right flank, which had not been able to get very far from land, was driven back against the shore and exterminated. The fight in the center lasted somewhat longer, but here too the Christian superiority finally overwhelmed the defending line. The Turkish left, which was far more numerous and led by **Ouloudj Ali**, Dey of Algiers, the best of the Moslem commanders, did better. The fight to the southwest was quite even until Ouloudj Ali discovered what had happened to the remainder of the Turkish fleet. He disengaged and escaped with 47 of his 95 vessels, plus one captured Venetian galley. These were the only Turkish survivors of the battle. Sixty other galleys had gone aground, 53 had been sunk, and 117 had been captured. Fifteen thousand Christian rower slaves were freed from captured or sunken Turkish vessels, though at least 10,000 more must have gone down with their ships. At least 15,000–20,000 Turkish sailors and soldiers were killed or drowned. Only 300 prisoners were taken. The Christians lost 13 galleys, 7,566 dead, and nearly 8,000 wounded (among these was **Miguel Cervantes,** who lost his left hand).

Because of the lateness of the season and the likelihood of seasonal tempests, the Christian fleet returned to Italy to await good weather the following spring before trying to exploit the great victory. Lepanto was one of the world's decisive battles. This success of temporarily united Christendom ended the growing Turkish domination of the central and western Mediterranean, and marked the high tide of Islam's second great threat against Christian Europe.

1571–1572. Turkish Shipbuilding Effort. This was inspired by Grand Vizier **Mohammed Sakalli,** who dominated the government of the inept Sultan Selim. Nearly 200 new Turkish vessels were built during the winter. Though many of these were poorly constructed and crews were inexperienced, nevertheless Ouloudj Ali, now the senior Turkish admiral, sailed from the Dardanelles with 160 galleys in the spring (June).

1572, June–August. Allied Indecision and Lack of Coordination. Philip of Spain, expecting war with France, refused to permit Juan to take his fleet into the Aegean. Finally Venetian Admiral **Jacopo Fascarini** sailed with about 150 ships, only 20 of which were Spanish (August). Off Cape Matapan he sighted the new Turkish fleet and, amazed at its size, fell back to Corfu to await reinforcements.

1572, August. Spanish Recapture of Tunis. Don Juan restored the Hafsid beys to the throne.

1572, September–October. Renewed Christian Naval Operations. Juan, finally gaining Philip's permission to operate against the Turks, joined Fascarini at Corfu with about 60 ships. The combined fleet then sailed to meet the Turks. Ouloudj, knowing that his new fleet had no hope of success against the veteran Christians, took refuge in the fortified harbor of Modar, where Juan refused to risk battle. He landed his troops under Alexander Farnese of Parma to attack the port from land, while the Christian fleet blockaded the harbor. Farnese's landing force was held off by the Turkish garrison, which was reinforced from central Greece. Juan re-embarked his troops and sailed for Italy.

1573, March. Venetians Make Peace. Disgusted by Philip's vacillation, the Venetians abandoned Cyprus. The treaty was not signed for almost a year (February, 1574).

1574–1595. Reign of Murad III.

1574, August–September. Moslem Recapture of Tunis. Ouloudj Ali again, and finally, captured Tunis and Galeta. Juan sailed to do battle, but was forced to abandon the enterprise when his fleet was badly damaged by a storm en route (September).

1574–1581. Inconclusive Naval War. There were no major actions, and peace was established.

1577–1590. Renewed War with Persia. This was initiated by Murad. The Turks conquered Shirvan, Tiflis, Daghestan, and Luristan. The principal Turkish leader was Lala Mustafa, the conqueror of Cyprus.

1590. Land War Renewed with the Hapsburgs. Emperor Rudolph refused tribute for the Austrian-controlled strip of Hungary. No major operations were conducted by either side, though border activity was incessant.

1593, June 20. Battle of Sissek. An Austrian army defeated and annihilated the army of **Hassan,** Ottoman governor of Bosnia. This infuriated **Sinan** Pasha, grand vizier under weak Sultan Murad III, who led an army to invade Austria and Hungary.

1593, October 13. Capture of Vesprism (Beszprem). Apparently Sinan planned to continue on toward Vienna, but the Janissaries refused further operations during the winter, and he was forced to return to Belgrade.

1593–1594. Austrian Raids into Turkish Hungary. They captured Neograd and other frontier places.

1594. Sinan Invades Northern Hungary. He forced the Austrians to raise their siege of Gran (June 1). He then captured Raab and some other border towns. He was repulsed in a long siege of Komorn (Komarno), an important Danube fortification.

1595. Revolts in Transylvania, Moldavia, and Wallachia. The Turks were temporarily driven out. **Charles of Mansfeldt** took advantage of this situation to lead an Austrian army in invasion of Hungary, defeating local Turkish forces in the **Battle of Gran** (August 4). The entire northern frontier of the Ottoman Empire was crumbling. Wallachian raiders crossed the Danube to sack Silistria and Varna.

1596. The Turks Regain Control of Hungary. New Sultan **Mohammed III** and his Vizier **Ibrahim** Pasha led a Turkish army north and repelled the Austrian invasions. They invaded Austrian Hungary to capture Erlau (September). An Austrian army of nearly 40,000 men under the Archduke **Maximilian** marched to recapture Erlau. Included in the army was **Sigismund Bathory** (nephew of the great Stephen) and a Transylvanian contingent (see p. 491). The Turk army, approximately 80,000 strong, met them 12 miles southeast of Erlau.

1596, October 24–26. Battle of Kerestes. The Austrians, entrenched behind a brook, repulsed strong Turkish attacks on the first day of the battle. After a day's lull, the Turkish attack was renewed at dawn. The Austrians repulsed the Turks and counterattacked to drive them back to their camp. At this moment an encircling detachment of Turkish cavalry under **Cicala** Pasha struck the Austrian rear. The Austrians broke in panic, abandoning their 97 cannon. The Turks rallied to pursue and inflicted great slaughter upon the retreating Austrians. Austrian casualties were about 23,000; Turk losses were probably nearly as great. The disorganized and badly punished Turkish army made no effort to pursue.

1597–1598. Renewed Austrian Invasions. They captured Raab and Vesprism. They were repulsed, however, by Turkish defenders of Buda (1598, October).

1598. Revolt in Iraq. Suppressed by the Ottomans.

PERSIA

At the outset of this century Shah **Ismail I,** the founder of the Safawid Dynasty, established himself as the ruler of Azerbaijan and western Persia. In following years he expanded his authority over all of Persia, but in the process came in conflict with the powerful Ottomans to the west and the Uzbek Tartars to the northeast. The remainder of the century was devoted to recurring wars against both foes, with the Persians generally defeated by the more powerful and more modern Turkish army, but more successful in repelling Uzbek incursions into Khorasan. As the century ended, Persia, under the leadership of her greatest Moslem ruler, Shah **Abbas I,** was building up a modern army, balanced between cavalry, infantry, and artillery and ready to seek vengeance against the Turks. The principal events were:

1500–1524. Reign of Ismail I. At the outset he attacked Shirvan and captured Baku from the Tartars (1500).

1500–1507. Uzbek Expansion. The Turkomans conquered Transoxiana, Khurasan, and Herat under the leadership of **Shaibani Khan,** a descendant of Genghis.

1501. Battle of Shurer. Ismail defeated **Alwand** of the White Sheep Confederacy. He then captured Tabriz and established himself in control of Azerbaijan and northwestern Persia (1502).

1502–1510. Safawid Expansion. Ismail consolidated control over western and central Persia.

1510, December. War with the Uzbeks. Ismail was victorious in a battle near **Merv,** Shaibani being killed. The Uzbeks were driven from Herat and Khorasan, but retained control of Transoxiana.

1514–1555. War with Turkey. (See p. 493.)

1587–1629. Reign of Abbas I. He soon established order in Persia. He quickly made peace with Turkey in order to consolidate his position, and to deal with an Uzbek invasion of Khorasan.

1590–1598. War with the Uzbeks. Under the leadership of **Abdullah II** the Turkomans had captured Herat, Meshed, and much of Khorasan. Abbas slowly drove the Uzbeks from most of Khorasan. He was severely defeated, however, near **Balkh** (1598). Both sides were exhausted, and so peace was made, with the Uzbeks retaining a small foothold in Khorasan around Balkh.

1598–1600. Reorganization of the Persian Army. Abbas, who wanted to build up a military force comparable to that of the Turks, was assisted by the English adventurers Sir **Anthony Shirley,** his brother **Robert,** and 26 other Europeans, sent on an unofficial mission to induce Persia to combine with the Christian nations of Europe against Turkey. Evidently the most useful of these foreign advisers was Robert Shirley, an artillery expert. In a short time an excellent artillery organization was created, and also a strong contingent of musket-armed infantry who comprised a regular standing force. At the same time, to reduce the power of the tribal chiefs who had contributed so much to Persia's past weakness, Abbas created a new tribe for the sole purpose of establishing a semipermanent cavalry force directly responsible to him. The best cavalry warriors of the nation flocked to join the new tribe and to pledge allegiance to the Shah. As a result, by the end of the century, a new and formidable military power was growing in Western Asia, anxious to settle old scores with the Ottoman Turks.

SOUTH ASIA

NORTH INDIA

In the early years of the century the Rajput revival continued, threatening Moslem hegemony of north India. Leader of this revival was **Rana Sanga,** King of Mewar (or Chitor), who took advantage of squabbles amongst the Afghan and Turkish nobility of the Delhi Sultanate. The anarchy in the Moslem states of north India also attracted the attention of **Babur,** King of Kabul, a descendant of Genghis Khan and Tamerlane. After some exploratory raids, Babur invaded and conquered north India to establish the Mogul Empire (so named because of his Mongol ancestry). Babur died soon after. His son, **Humayun,** was overthrown by **Sher Shah,** an elderly military genius; but, after the death of Sher Shah, Humayun reconquered north India and re-established the Mogul Dynasty. His son, Akbar, actually carried out the conquests planned by Babur and Sher Shah. Though perhaps not so brilliant a soldier as either of these predecessors, he was nevertheless one of the great warriors in Indian history. The principal events were:

1488–1517. Reign of Sikandar, Sultan of Delhi. His persecution of the Hindus led to frequent conflicts with the Rajput Hindu principalities, which, combined with internal dissension in the Sultanate, contributed to the steady decline of the Lodi Dynasty.

1509–1529. Reign of Rana Sanga, King of Mewar. He increased Rajput power by victories over the Lodi sultans of Delhi and the Moslem kings of Malwa and Gujerat.

1515–1523. Babur Raids into the Punjab. These were reconnaissances in force.

1517–1526. Reign of Ibrahim, Sultan of Delhi.

1524. Babur's Lahore Campaign. Taking advantage of an uprising in the Punjab, he seized Lahore, but was driven out by the Lodi governor of the Punjab.

1525–1526. Babur Invades North India. He conquered the Punjab (1525). Then he advanced on Delhi (March–April, 1526). He had about 10,000 men, allegedly including an Ottoman Turkish contingent of artillery* and musketeers. The remainder of his army consisted of the veteran Central Asiatic cavalrymen who had fought with him against the Uzbeks (see p. 511). Arriving at Panipat, about 30 miles north of Delhi, Babur learned that Ibrahim's army (probably 30,000–40,000 men) was just ahead. Babur immediately prepared a defensive position with his infantry and artillery sheltered behind a line of baggage carts tied together. In gaps purposely left in the line of carts, he placed his Turkish guns, tied together by chains in the typical Ottoman fashion. Other gaps were left for counterattacks by reserve cavalry. The Mogul army had been reinforced by a few thousand Hindu and Moslem Indians anxious to assist in overthrowing the Delhi Sultanate. Babur's total strength was probably about 15,000.

1526, April 20. Battle of Panipat. After several days of indecision, Ibrahim attacked. The attackers were held up by the protected infantry and artillery. Babur then sent his own cavalry to drive in the flanks of the Delhi army. Fighting in 3 directions, the Delhi troops soon broke and fled, suffering severe casualties. Ibrahim and 15,000 of his men were killed.

1526, April 27. Babur Occupies Delhi. This began the Mogul Empire.

1526–1537. Reign of Bahadur Shah of Gujerat.

1527, March 16. Battle of Khanua (or Fatehpur Sikri). Rana Sanga led a confederated Rajput army of nearly 100,000 men against Babur. The Mogul, with less than 20,000 men, marched to meet the Rajputs 40 miles west of Agra. Again Babur used his artillery and musketeers as a base of maneuver for his mobile cavalrymen. Rana Sanga was seriously wounded. A violent Mogul counterattack broke the Rajput army, which fled in panic, suffering heavy casualties.

1528–1529. Conquest of Bihar and Bengal. Babur's operations against the Turko-Afghans was culminated by victory in the 3-day **Battle of the Gogra River** (1529) near Patna. The Mogul Empire now stretched from the Oxus to the Brahmaputra. Babur died before he could expand further (1530).

COMMENT. *The hardships, disappointments, and defeats of his early years had taught the Mogul chieftain many lessons, and had made him cautious without dampening his ardor or love of adventure. His three great victories in North India, each against excellent armies greatly outnumbering his own, established him as one of the greatest warriors of his times. He was also a man of great literary skill, as proven by his admirable memoirs and a number of outstanding poems.*

1530–1540. First Reign of Humayun (son of Babur).

1531–1536. Mogul War against Gujerat. Humayun defeated Bahadur Shah at Chitor, and then captured Mandu and Chanpanir. But Bahadur energetically collected another army and drove the Moguls off.

1537–1539. Revolt of Sher Khan. This 65-year-old Afghan-Turk, of relatively humble origin, had risen through luck and ability to the position of governor of Bihar. He annexed Bengal to his own prov-

---

* Some authorities doubt whether Babur had any artillery.

ince, and became a rallying point for the Afghan-Turk nobles who opposed the Moguls. Humayun invaded Bihar, but Sher Khan avoided battle, while constantly harassing the Mogul line of communications. As more and more of the north Indian Moslem dissidents were attracted to his banner, Sher Khan finally felt strong enough to meet Humayun in battle, defeating him at the **Battle of Chaunsha** (or Buxar). Sher Khan then pursued the defeated Moguls up the Ganges Valley, winning another great victory at the **Battle of Kanauj.** Humayun fled to asylum in Persia. Sher Khan seized the imperial throne as **Sher Shah.**

1539–1545. Reign of Sher Shah. He quickly and firmly established control over all of northern Hindustan, including the Punjab. Sher Shah extended the Delhi dominions southward, conquering Malwa and Marwar (1541–1545). He was killed by an accidental gunpowder explosion at the **Siege of Kaninjar** (1545). During his brief reign he created an efficient standing army based on sound military policy, and had time to institute far-reaching governmental reforms. His tremendous military and administrative accomplishments as emperor were achieved between the ages of 68 and 73.

1545–1555. North India in Anarchy. The Hindu General **Hemu** became virtual dictator in Delhi (1552–1555).

1555. Return of Humayun. He had become ruler of Afghanistan (see p. 511). Seeing an opportunity to regain his old empire, he marched through the Punjab and recaptured Delhi. He died soon after in an accident (1556).

1556–1557. Turmoil in the Mogul Empire. The oldest legitimate son of Humayun, 14-year-old Akbar, was in the Punjab with his able adviser **Bairam.** In the Ganges Valley the Afghan-Turks had united under the leadership of Hemu, who again seized power in Delhi. In Afghanistan, Akbar's older half-brother **Mizar Mohammed Hakim** was virtually independent. Akbar and Bairam collected an army in the Punjab, then marched toward Delhi (October, 1556).

1556, November 5. Second Battle of Panipat. In a bitterly contested battle, Hemu's numerically superior army was close to victory, but was thrown into confusion when he was wounded by a chance arrow. Bairam and young Akbar counterattacked, to win the battle and to reinstate the Mogul Empire.

1556–1605. Reign of Akbar. This began with a 4-year regency of Bairam, during which Mogul control over northern Hindustan was firmly consolidated. Akbar then dismissed the regent and began to govern for himself (1560).

1561–1562. Conquest of Malwa.

1562–1567. Conquest of Rajputana. This culminated in Akbar's capture of Chitor (1567). He now conciliated the Rajput princes, confirming them on their thrones, repealing the discriminatory laws which had favored Moslems over Hindus under the old Delhi Sultanate. Save for the Mewar hero, **Pratap,** who continued resistance in the desert and mountain fastnesses of Rajputana, the Rajput princes soon became the most loyal supporters of the Moguls.

1566. Afghan Raid. Akbar's half-brother, Mohammed Hakim, raided into the Punjab, but withdrew in the face of Akbar's threats.

1573. Conquest of Gujerat. Akbar first came in contact with the Portuguese.

1574–1576. Conquest of Bihar and Bengal.

1576. Expedition into the Deccan. This was under Akbar's son **Murad.** The Moslem sultans of the northern Deccan banded together and drove the Mogul invaders out. In subsequent years Akbar campaigned almost constantly to gain control of all Hindustan.

1581. Hakim Again Raids into the Punjab. Akbar immediately marched to meet the threat, drove the Afghans out, invaded and conquered Afghanistan.

1586–1595. Conquest of Kashmir, Sind, Orissa, Baluchistan.

1596–1600. Operations in the Deccan. Akbar conquered Berar, Ahmadnagar, and Kandesh.

1601–1603. Revolt of Akbar's Son Salim. The old emperor returned to the Ganges Valley, defeated and captured Salim, and then pardoned him. When Akbar died 2 years later, it is likely that he was poisoned by this ingrate son (1605).

COMMENT. *The main characteristics of the reign of Akbar were conquest, justice, and tolerance. He built on the military and administrative foundations established by*

Sher Shah, and owed much to the accomplishments of his father's great rival. Akbar's standing army was organized on the same line as Sher Shah's, with loyal, well-paid garrisons to hold the key hill forts. Like his grandfather, Babur, Akbar favored the use of artillery and a corps of 12,000 musketeers as the central components of his field forces. Most of the remainder of his army was highly mobile cavalry, the major portion of which, paradoxically, consisted of Rajput lancers. His most able general was an exceptional Hindu, Raja Todar Malla, who was also his chief minister and financial expert.

SOUTH INDIA

During the first part of this century, while the Bahmani Sultanate collapsed and disappeared, the Hindu Kingdom of Vijayanagar achieved its greatest glory during the reign of **Krishna Deva,** who consistently defeated the neighboring Moslem kingdoms to the north, greatly expanding his dominions. The kingdom declined rapidly under his successor, but by midcentury King **Rama Raya** restored order to some extent, and revived Vijayanagar's waning power by taking advantage of the almost incessant wars between the Moslem Sultanates of Berar, Bijapur, Bidar, Golconda, and Ahmadnagar (the successors of the Bahmani Sultanate). The Moslems, however, finally composed their quarrels and temporarily united to overthrow Rama Raya and to smash the power of the Hindu kingdom. Vijayanagar, with diminished territory, prestige, and prosperity, continued to exist for nearly a century. The principal events were:

1509–1530. Reign of Krishna Deva of Vijayanagar. He defeated Bijapur, annexing much of the region between the Tungabedra and Krishna rivers (1512).

1512. Golconda Independent of Bahmani.

1513–1515. Expansion of Vijayanagar. Krishna Deva defeated Orissa, Golconda, and Bidar, extending his empire up the east coast of the Deccan as far as Vizagapatam.

1520. Vijayanagar Victory over Bijapur. Krishna Deva's boundary now reached the Portuguese colony of Goa. He was friendly with the Portuguese, who were also frequently at war with Bijapur. The Europeans imported horses for the Hindu cavalry, since Vijayanagar was poor horse-raising country (see p. 396).

1542–1565. Reign of Rama Raya of Vijayanagar. He restored order after a period of turmoil, and revived Vijayanagar's influence among its neighbors. He was involved in a bewildering series of alliances and wars with the northern sultanates, and became something of an arbiter in their disputes.

1565. Moslem Alliance against Rama Raya. His arrogance and power led the sultans of Bijapur, Bidar, Golconda, and Ahmadnagar to unite temporarily against him. Rama Raya was defeated and killed at the **Battle of Talikot.** The victors then sacked the capital city of Vijayanagar, which was never rebuilt.

1576. First Mogul Expedition into the Northern Deccan. (See p. 507.)

1596–1603. Akbar's Conquest of the Northern Deccan. (See p. 507.)

PORTUGUESE EMPIRE OF THE INDIAN OCEAN

The Indian Ocean had long been an important avenue of commerce between India and lands farther east and west. To a lesser extent it had also on occasion been a route of conquest for the maritime-minded Cholas of southeast India. To the east the major sea routes led from the Coromandel coast and from Bengal to Malaya, the Straits of Malacca, and the South China Sea. To the west the routes extended from Gujerat and the Malabar coast to the Red Sea and the Persian Gulf, thence overland through Egypt and Persia to the Mediterranean and Europe.

The arrival on the Malabar coast in 1498 of a small squadron of Portuguese vessels which **Vasco da Gama** had brought around the Cape of Good Hope shattered the old patterns of trade and piracy. By the beginning of the century, regular trade had been established between western India and Portugal, and the Portuguese had begun to assert themselves as a force along the entire coast from the mouth of the Indus to Cape Comorin.

Rarely in history have so few men been able to affect so profoundly the fortunes of millions, and to change so completely the course of history. The principal Portuguese objective was trade, particularly in pepper and other spices, which were literally worth their weight in gold in 16th-century Europe. Next in importance was missionary zeal in spreading the Christian faith. Hardly less significant was the fierce pride of these Portuguese in carrying the power and prestige of their tiny kingdom to the furthest corners of the earth.

In a very few years a number of Portuguese trading posts—known as factories —had been established either with the permission of the local Hindu or Moslem rulers or by force.

Outstanding among the adventurous Portuguese who established these outposts were **Francisco de Almeida** and Affonso de Albuquerque, who soon became rivals. When Almeida finally accepted the orders of the Portuguese king to turn over his post as Viceroy of Portuguese India to Albuquerque, he had, with Albuquerque's help, established complete Portuguese dominance over the west coast of India.

Albuquerque realized the significance of sea power, and was the first man to apply it systematically. Though his appointment as Viceroy of Portuguese India lasted only 6 years, in that short time he established complete maritime dominance over the Indian Ocean. This supremacy on the ocean, and along the west coast of India, continued through the century, though Portuguese vigor declined rapidly in subsequent years. The principal events were:

1500. Appearance of a Portuguese Fleet at Calicut.

1500–1505. Establishment of Portuguese Trading Posts. These were along the west coast of India; the most important was at Cochin (1503).

1505. Almeida Appointed First Viceroy of Portuguese India. He established bases along the east coast of Africa, then brought a large fleet to the Malabar coast, where he established several small forts. One of his principal assistants was Albuquerque, who returned to Portugal (1506). Almeida's son, **Lorenzo,** established a settlement on Ceylon and negotiated a commercial treaty with Malacca in the name of his father (1507).

1507. Albuquerque Appointed Viceroy of India. Almeida knew nothing of this appointment. Albuquerque sailed from Lisbon with a small squadron, en route capturing the island of Socotra near the entrance to the Red Sea. He then seized the island of Ormuz, commanding the entrance to the Persian Gulf and then one of the main trade centers of the East (1508). Lacking sufficient force to hold this vital point, however, he then sailed on to Cochin.

1508. Gujerat-Egyptian Alliance. Sultan **Mahmud Begarha** of Gujerat formed an alliance with **Kansu al-Gauri** of Egypt (see p. 494) in an attempt to eliminate arrogant Portuguese interference with Moslem trade between India and the Red Sea.

1508. Naval Battle of Dabul. The combined Mameluke-Gujerat fleet attacked Lorenzo Almeida's small Portuguese squadron near Chaul; Lorenzo was killed in the inconclusive engagement.

1508, December. Arrival of Albuquerque. He reached Cochin while Almeida was in the midst of plans to avenge the death of his son. Almeida refused to recognize Albuquerque's orders, imprisoned his rival, and sailed north.

1509, January–February. Almeida's Vengeance. He captured and burned a number of Moslem ports along the coast, including Goa and Dabul.

1509, February. Battle of Diu.   Almeida discovered the allied fleet near Diu. He attacked vigorously, completely destroying the Moslem fleet, then captured and sacked Diu. He returned to Cochin. Not until a new fleet arrived from Lisbon did he accept the Portuguese king's decree to turn his post over to Albuquerque.

1509. Expedition to Malaya.   Albuquerque sent **Diego Lopez de Siquiera** to establish a factory at Malacca.

1510. Albuquerque Captures Goa.   Seized from the Sultan of Bijapur in a bold, vigorous attack.

1511. Albuquerque Captures Malacca.   He stayed there for a year to consolidate this vital outpost controlling the main eastern approach to the Indian Ocean. From Malacca, he later sent expeditions to the Moluccas (1512–1514).

1512, September. Revolt at Goa.   Suppressed by Albuquerque upon his return from Malacca.

1513. Expedition to Aden.   Albuquerque besieged the port, but was unable to capture it.

1515. Albuquerque Recaptures Ormuz.   It remained in Portuguese hands for a century and a half.

1515. Recall of Albuquerque.   Unjustly deposed from his post, he died on the way home.

COMMENT. *Albuquerque was apparently the first man to realize that sea power is founded upon bases and upon merchant shipping as much as it is upon the fighting capabilities of a fleet of warships. From the outset he was obsessed with the need for gaining control of all of the major entrances into the Indian Ocean in order to be able to dominate shipping in the broad waters of that ocean. Only at Aden was he foiled in this effort, but he was nevertheless able to control trade between India and the Red Sea from Socotra and his many other bases along the coast of the Arabian Sea. Goa was the key to maintenance of this chain of bases, which were scattered along the coast in such a way as to dominate all the major seaports of western India.*

1519. Portuguese in Burma.   A trading station was opened at Martaban.

1528. Conquest of Diu.   Captured by **Nunho da Cunha,** Portuguese viceroy.

1536–1537. Gujerat-Ottoman Alliance.   Sultan Bahadur of Gujerat established an alliance with the Ottoman Turks to eliminate Portuguese control over trade between India and the West. Da Cunha, alarmed by the appearance of a large and powerful Ottoman fleet, entered into negotiations with Bahadur. The Sultan, relying upon the Portuguese reputation for integrity established by Albuquerque, visited da Cunha's flagship, where he and his entourage were seized and treacherously murdered.

1538. Siege of Diu.   The Ottoman fleet and a Gujerat army blockaded and besieged Diu, but were repulsed by the Portuguese.

1546. Indian-Ottoman Alliance.   Again the rulers of western India and of the Ottomans failed in attempts to capture Diu and other Portuguese posts in India.

1559. Seizure of Daman.   This port, on the east side of the Gulf of Cambay, was taken by **Constantine de Braganza.** Opposite Diu, it ensured Portuguese control of the Gulf.

CENTRAL AND EAST ASIA

INNER ASIA

At the outset of this century, Inner Asia was still in a state of flux. In the extreme west the tiny remnant of the Khanate of the Golden Horde in the middle Volga Valley was about to succumb finally to the onslaughts of its former vassals: the Christian principality of Moscow and the Moslem-Tartar khanates of Crimea, Astrakhan, and Kazan. In the vast central and eastern region, between the Ural Mountains and Lake Baikal, the Kalmuk, or Oirat, Mongols were linked together in a loose confederation of four tribes, dominated by the Oirat chieftain **Dayan Khan.** To the south the Kirghiz maintained themselves in the mountains of the Tien Shan, surrounded by the Turkic descendants of the Chagatai Mongols who occupied the lowlands to the east and west in the three independent sultanates of Yarkand (modern Chinese Turkestan), tiny Ferghana, and Khwarezm (or Khiva, or Transoxiana) with capital at Samarkand.

The most vigorous of the nomadic peoples of Inner Asia at this time were the Uzbek Tartars, who had broken loose from the authority of the Golden Horde in the previous century, and who had been slowly gathering strength in the steppes southeast of the Volga and between the Aral and Caspian seas. At the beginning of the century, under their great leader **Mohammed Esh Shaibani Khan,** the Uzbeks swept south and east to overrun the three independent Chagatai khanates. They continued southwest across the Oxus into Persian Khorasan, but Shaibani was defeated and killed by Shah Ismail of Persia in a great battle near **Merv** (see p. 505). The Uzbeks were forced to withdraw from Khorasan, but firmly consolidated their control over the regions now known as Chinese and Russian Turkestan. In a series of bitterly contested wars they repulsed efforts of Babur, former Sultan of Ferghana, to recover his kingdom. Babur conquered a new domain in the Hindu Kush, around Kabul (eastern Afghanistan), from which he later continued southeast to conquer north India and to establish the Mogul Empire (see p. 506).

During the remainder of the century only the Uzbek khanate remained relatively stable in Central Asia. The eastern Kalmuck Mongols disintegrated into insignificant tribal groupings, though the western Kalmucks retained considerable vitality and raided frequently across the Urals into the Volga Valley, which by now had been completely conquered by the new Russian Empire (see p. 492). The principal events were:

1494–1509. Uzbek Conquest of Western and Eastern Turkestan. Principal opponent among the Chagatai Tartars of Turkestan was Babur, Sultan of Ferghana. His ambitions of expanding from Ferghana into Transoxiana precipitated a series of violent clashes for control of Samarkand.

1497. Babur Captures and Loses Samarkand. He was driven out by Shaibani.

1500–1501. Babur Again Captures Samarkand. Shaibani defeated Babur in the **Battle of Sar-i-pul,** then conquered Ferghana, driving Babur south into the Hindu Kush mountains.

c. 1500–1543. Unification of Mongolia under Dayan Khan. He was a descendant of Genghis.

1502. Collapse of the Golden Horde. The Horde was defeated by the allied forces of the Krim Tartars and Muscovites.

1509–1510. Uzbek Invasion of Khorasan. This culminated in the **Battle of Merv;** Ismail of Persia was victorious; Shaibani was killed (see p. 505). The Uzbeks were driven from all of Khorasan, save for the region immediately around Balkh, where Ismail was repulsed.

1511–1512. Babur's Invasion of Transoxiana. Now based in his new kingdom of Kabul, Babur entered an alliance with Ismail of Persia. He quickly captured Samarkand, but the Uzbeks, already rallying from their disaster in Persia, defeated him in the **Battle of Ghazdivan,** driving him back to Kabul (1512).

1526. Babur's Invasion and Conquest of Northern India. (See p. 506.)

c. 1540. Humayun's Conquest of Afghanistan. He took the region from his brother, Komran, after his expulsion from India by Sher Shah (see p. 506).

c. 1550–1597. Reign of Uzbek Abdullah Khan. He revitalized his declining nation to create a strong centralized state in western Turkestan.

1555. Humayun's Reconquest of North India. (See p. 507.)

1597–1600. Breakup of the Uzbek State.

CHINA AND MANCHURIA

The Ming Dynasty, declining politically and militarily, was constantly on the defensive against Mongols and Tartars to the north and west, Manchus to the northeast, and Japanese pirates along the east coast. The century closed just after partial Chinese victories repulsed Japanese invasions of Korea. This success, however, was due primarily to Korean prowess at sea and to Japanese overextension on land. During this century, Europeans first appeared in force in East Asia: the Portuguese obtained a settlement on the coast of China, while Russian adventurers penetrated across the Amur River before being driven back by the Manchus. The principal events were:

c. 1514. Portuguese Appearance at Canton. Apparently there had been previous coastal contacts (c. 1411).

1520–1522. First Portuguese Mission to Peking. The Portuguese were expelled from the Chinese capital due to depredations of some of their ships along the coast of China.

1522–1566. Reign of Shih Tsung. China was plagued by pirate raids along the seacoast. The greatest threat was posed by the Mongols of **Altan Khan,** Prince of Ordos, within the great bend of the Hwang Ho (Yellow River; particularly in 1542 and 1550).

1525. Russian Adventurers Cross the Amur. They were repulsed by the Manchus.

1555. Siege of Nanking by Japanese Pirates.

1557. The Portuguese Establish a Base at Macao.

1567–1620. Reign of Shen Tsung. This was a period of considerable cultural development in China, but of accelerated military decline. China's borders were steadily eroded to the west and north.

c. 1560–1626. Rise and Consolidation of the Manchus. They were the descendants of the Juchen or Chin People (see p. 326), whose home was in the valley of the Sungari, in present central Manchuria. By the end of the century their leader, **Nurhachi,** had begun expansion of his territory to the Yellow Sea and to the Amur.

1592–1598. Japanese Invasions of Korea. The Chinese assisted the Koreans in repelling the invaders (see p. 513).

KOREA

During most of this century Korea was plagued by persistent coastal raids of Japanese pirates. Internally there were a number of minor disturbances; central authority declined steadily. With little central direction or coordination of defensive efforts against the Japanese, the military and naval contingents of the various provinces became almost autonomous and developed considerable combat skill. This stood the nation in good stead when Japanese dictator Hideyoshi decided to invade and conquer China by way of Korea. With some Chinese assistance, but particularly due to their superiority at sea and the genius of Admiral Yi Sung Sin, the Koreans repelled two Japanese invasions. The principal events were:

1592. Japanese Conquest of South and Central Korea. The Koreans, faithful vassals of the Ming Dynasty, refused free Japanese passage to China; Hideyoshi sent an army across the Straits of Tsushima to assault and capture Pusan (May, 1592). Advancing north, the Japanese captured Seoul and Pyongyang (June–July).

1592, July. Battle of the Yellow Sea. Yi Sung Sin, commanding the Cholla provincial navy, probably assisted by other provincial flotillas, met a Japanese fleet carrying reinforcements to the Japanese army at Pyongyang. Yi's fleet included at least two "tortoise ships," low-decked ironclad galleys of his own design. Apparently almost singlehanded these novel war-ships, the first ironclad vessels in history, won a smashing victory over the Japanese fleet, at least 59 Japanese ships being sunk or burned. The reinforcement convoy was scattered and destroyed.

1592–1593. Chinese Intervention. This was at the request of the Korean government (October, 1592). As the Chinese advanced south, the Japanese, short of supplies, without reinforcements, and constantly harassed by Korean guerrillas, withdrew slowly. After a long, dull campaign, the Japanese entrenched themselves in a rela-tively small beachhead perimeter around Pusan (October, 1593).

1594–1596. Inconclusive Peace Negotiations. The Chinese evacuated Korea, leaving the Koreans to observe the Japanese Pusan perimeter. There were a number of minor skirmishes. Breakdown of negotiations led

Hideyoshi to send reinforcements to Ko-rea.

1597–1598. Japanese Offensive. They broke out of their perimeter to advance north-ward. The Chinese sent another army to the assistance of the Koreans, but the al-lies, defeated in a number of battles, were unable to halt the steady Japanese ad-vance through south Korea.

1598, November. Naval Battle of Chinhae Bay. Admiral Yi Sung Sin attacked the Japanese fleet and won another great vic-tory, in which he himself was killed. Nearly half of the Japanese fleet of 400 ships was sunk; the survivors fled to Kyu-shu.

1598, December. Armistice. With their line of communications to Japan again cut, and Hideyoshi having died in Japan, the Japanese made peace and evacuated Ko-rea.

JAPAN

The violence which had split Japan into a land of independent warring feudal nobles continued into the early part of this century. Reunification began, however, shortly after the middle of the century with the emergence of the strong warrior Oda Nobunaga. Systematically, he began the unification of Honshu by force. With the support of the emperor, he overthrew the shogun and made himself dictator. He was assisted in his unification efforts by the young **Tokugawa Ieyasu** and his principal subordinate, **General Toyotomi Hideyoshi,** a commoner. Nobunaga died during the revolt of a vassal, and was succeeded by Hideyoshi, who—assisted by Ieyasu—completed the unification and pacification of Japan. Hideyoshi then initi-ated a grandiose plan for the conquest of Korea, China, and most of Asia. He was frustrated, however, by the unexpected vigor of Korean resistance, particularly at sea, combined with the support of a large Chinese army. The principal events were:

c. 1542. Arrival of the Portuguese in Kyu-shu. The Portuguese introduced the musket, which soon modified Japanese warfare.

1549–1587. Expansion of Christianity in Ja-pan. This was stimulated by Portuguese missionaries, of whom **St. Francis Xavier** was the first.

1560–1568. Nobunaga Begins the Reunifica-tion of Japan. He established himself in control of most of Honshu. He installed **Ashikaga Yashiaki** as shogun.

1571–1580. Overthrow of the Buddhist Mon-asteries. These had become militarily powerful. Nobunaga systematically de-feated and destroyed them.

1573. Overthrow of Yashiaki. With secret support from the emperor, Nobunaga de-posed the shogun, who was plotting against him.

1576. Nobunaga Begins Era of Castle Build-ing.

1577–1582. Rise of Hideyoshi. As Nobu-naga's principal general, he conquered most of western Japan from the Mori family.

1582–1584. Civil War. This was provoked by the revolt of General **Akechi Mitsuhibi.** Nobunaga, surprised and surrounded in his capital, Kyoto, committed suicide (1582). Hideyoshi defeated and killed Mitsuhibi (1582). With the assistance of

Tokugawa Ieyasu, he defeated the Oda family to gain control of all central Japan.

1585–1590. Hideyoshi Unifies Japan.

1592. Hideyoshi's Plan of Conquest. He planned to take over all of East Asia. China was to be invaded through Korea and conquered in two years, at which

time the Japanese court would move to Peking.

1592–1598. Korean War. (See p. 513.)

1598, August. Death of Hideyoshi.

1598–1600. Power Struggle. The leading vassals of Hideyoshi contended for control. Ieyasu was successful (see p. 594).

SOUTHEAST ASIA

BURMA

During the first half of this century, the long warfare between the Shan and Burman states came to a climax in the conquest and sack of Ava by the ruler of the Shan state of Mohnyin (1527). While the Shans gained control of northern and central Burma, the Burman rulers of Toungoo made a bid for the over-all leadership of Burma. The first attempt to reunite Burma was made by **Tabinshwehti** (1531–1550), who planned to deal with the Shans only after he had conquered the rich Mon Kingdom of Pegu. He was successful in this (1535–1541), but then dissipated his efforts in fruitless attempts to conquer Arakan and Siam (1547–1548). A Mon revolt brought his reign to an end (1550). Burma was only rescued from chaos by his foster brother, **Bayinnaung** (1551–1581), whom one historian has called "the greatest explosion of human energy ever seen in Burma." A special feature of Bayinnaung's wars was the participation of Portuguese mercenaries. In a period of 30 years Bayinnaung reunited Burma, destroyed the power of the Shans, expanded Burma to approximately its modern frontiers, and conquered the three Tai states of Chiengmai, Ayuthia, and Laos. His son **Nanda Bayin** had to face a strong movement of Siamese national independence led by **Pra Naret,** who threw off the Burmese yoke (1587) and became King **Naresuen** (1590–1605). Nanda Bayin repeatedly invaded Siam, but failed to re-establish control. Naresuen's counterattacks upon Burma caused Nanda Bayin's downfall and murder (1600). The Arakanese invaded Lower Burma, and the Upper Burma principalities threw off their allegiance. Burma relapsed into chaos for some years.

SIAM

During the first half of this century the two principal Tai kingdoms—Ayuthia (or Siam) and Chiengmai—were almost constantly at war with each other, save for one brief respite of about 5 years. In the second half of the century these internal Tai struggles were merged into, and overshadowed by, the Burmese wars of conquest. Both countries, as well as the related Tai peoples of Laos, were conquered by Burmese king Bayinnaung. After his death, however, first Laos, then Ayuthia, and finally Chiengmai broke loose from Burmese control. By the end of the century the Siamese, under strong and able King Naresuen, had conquered substantial portions of southeast Burma, and had gained unchallenged suzerainty over Chiengmai. The principal events were:

1491–1529. Reign of Rama T'ibodi II. He received the first Portuguese envoy to Siam, **Duarte Fernandez,** conqueror of Malacca. He signed treaties with Fernandez, giving the Portuguese certain commercial rights in Siamese ports.

1500–1530. War with Chiengmai. Smaller Chiengmai maintained the initiative, making repeated raids and invasions of Ayuthian territory, particularly against Sukhot'ai. Ayuthia undertook repeated punitive expeditions against Chiengmai. Because of this constant warfare, Rama T'ibodi created a comprehensive military system based on compulsory military service and regional military areas. The most important single action of this prolonged war was his victory in the **Battle of the Mewang River,** near Nakhon Lamp'ang. T'ibodi then ejected Chiengmai troops from Sukhot'ai.

1548. Burmese Invasion of Siam Repulsed.

1563–1584. Burmese Invasions, Conquest, and Occupation of Siam. (See p. 514.)

1571. Return of Prince Pra Naret to Siam. A hostage in Burma, Bayinnaung sent him back to serve as a puppet in Burmese-occupied Siam.

1584–1587. Revolt of Pra Naret. The Burmese were expelled from Siam (see p. 514).

1587. Invasion by King Satt'a of Cambodia. This diversion permitted the defeated Burmese army to escape pursuit at the hands of Pra Naret. He drove the Cambodians out, and pursued as far as their capital, Lovek.

1590. Pra Naret Ascends Throne as Naresuen.

1590–1600. Continuous War between Siam and Burma. Naresuen repelled invasions of his country by Nanda Bayin of Burma, then turned to invade Burma, capturing Tavoy and Tenasserim (1593), and then Moulmein and Martaban (1594).

1593–1594. Invasion of Cambodia. Naresuen captured Lovek after a desperate struggle, and established Tai overlordship.

1595. Laotian Invasion of Chiengmai. Tharrawaddy, son of Bayinnaung, who had installed him as ruler of Chiengmai, became a vassal of Naresuen in return for Siamese help in driving out Laotian invaders.

1595. Naresuen Invades Burma. He was repulsed from Pegu.

1599–1600. Naresuen Again Invades Burma. He took advantage of the collapse of Nanda Bayin's kingdom. The Siamese occupied Pegu, which had earlier been destroyed during the civil war in Burma, but were repulsed from Toungoo when the Burmese rebels, having overthrown Nanda Bayin, closed ranks against the Siamese invaders (see p. 514).

LAOS

During the first half of the century Laos had on occasion become involved in the disputes between her sister Tai states of Ayuthia and Chiengmai. A few years later, when the able Laotian ruler Sett'at'irat (1547–1571) unsuccessfully attempted to eject the Burmese forces of Bayinnaung from Chiengmai (1558), he gained the implacable enmity of the great Burmese conqueror. Twice Burmese armies overran Laos (1564–1565 and 1572–1573), the first time capturing the capital of Vien Chang. Determined Laotian guerrilla resistance each time forced the Burmese to withdraw. But Sett'at'irat's frequent efforts to assist Ayuthia against the Burmese, and to try to drive the Burmese from the Tai and Shan states, were invariably crushed by Bayinnaung. Sett'at'irat died during the prolonged war (1571) and Bayinnaung finally conquered the country (1575). But after his death Laos threw off the Burmese yoke and established its independence (1592). Later Laotian efforts to recapture Chiengmai were repulsed by the Siamese (1594).

VIETNAMESE REGION

This was a period of general decline in Annam, the result of weak rulers and endemic civil wars. Before the middle of the century Tonkin and Annam had broken apart, though Tonkin was still nominally subject to the impotent rulers of Annam. Soon after the middle of the century the southern provinces—former

Champa—had also become virtually independent. Late in the century the dictator **Trinh Tong** of central Annam conquered most of Tonkin, to reunite more than two-thirds of the country under the strongest and most stable rule Vietnam had during this century (1592).

MALAYA AND INDONESIA

The principal feature of the history of Malaysia during this century was the Portuguese capture of Malacca, and their subsequent establishment of fortified bases in the Spice Islands and intermediate islands of Indonesia, in the early part of the century. The remainder of the century was a constant and unsuccessful struggle on the part of the predominantly Moslem rulers of Malaya and Indonesia to eject the Portuguese. Subsidiary to this primary struggle was the continuing expansion of Islam in the archipelago. The principal events were:

1511. Conquest of Malacca by Albuquerque. (See p. 510). Sultan **Mahmud** of Malacca escaped and set up a new capital on the island of Bintang, from which he incessantly endeavored to regain Malacca.

1513–1521. Portuguese Bases in the Spice Islands. This was facilitated by intermittent warfare between the sultans of Ternate and Tidor.

1517–1520. Alliance of Acheh and Bintang. The Sumatran Sultanate of Acheh assisted Mahmud of Bintang in unsuccessful efforts to recapture Malacca.

c. 1520. Final Collapse of Majapahit. It fell under attacks from a coalition of Moslem states: Madura, Tuban, Surabaya, and Demak. Demak became the most important of the many small states on Java.

1521. Magellan Claims the Philippines for Spain. He was killed in a battle with the natives on the island of Mactan.

1521–1530. Portuguese-Spanish Friction. This came from conflicting claims to the Spice Islands.

1525–1526. Rise of the Moslem Sultanate of Bantam. Bantam conquered Sunda Kalapa, where the Portuguese had obtained trading rights, and renamed the city Jacatra (Djakarta). The hostile Moslems refused the Portuguese permission to establish a factory.

1526. Portuguese Capture of Bintang. Acheh became the leading state among the Portuguese enemies around Malacca.

1529–1587. Repeated Achenese Attacks on Malacca.

1535–1600. Portuguese Wars in Northern Java. The small Moslem states were steadily weakened by consistent defeats at the hands of the Portuguese.

1550–1587. War with Ternate. The Portuguese murdered their archenemy Sultan **Hairun** of Ternate (1570), causing the war to intensify under his successor **Baabullah,** who sought revenge. Baabullah captured the Portuguese fort on Ternate and massacred the garrison after a long siege (1570–1574). The Portuguese on Malacca were unable to send assistance, since they were at this time subjected to intensive attacks by the Achenese and the Moslems of Java.

1558. Achenese Siege of Malacca. A force of 15,000 Achenese, supported by 400 Turk artillerymen, were repulsed by the Portuguese after a siege of a month.

1568–1595. Expansion of Bantam. The Sultanate controlled all of western Java.

1570. Spain Begins to Colonize the Philippines. Miguel López de Legaspi began the conquest. He established the Spanish headquarters at Manila (1571).

1570–1580. Intermittent Spanish-Portuguese Warfare. This was for control of the Philippines and neighboring Indonesian islands. It was concluded by Spanish annexation of Portugal (see p. 489), though the two colonial systems remained separate.

1574. Javanese Attack on Malacca. The Moslem attackers were driven off only by the arrival of reinforcements from Goa.

1595. Arrival of a Dutch Fleet in the Spice Islands. This was the beginning of colonial rivalry with the Portuguese.

AFRICA

NORTH AFRICA

During the early part of this century, Portuguese and Spanish influence became widespread over North Africa. Both nations soon found themselves directly challenged, however, by the expanding power of the Ottoman Empire, spearheaded by **Khair ed-Din** (Barbarossa), Dey of Algiers. The struggle between Suleiman and Charles V for control of the Mediterranean was largely centered on the coast of North Africa. The Ottomans were successful, and by the end of the century most of the Iberian footholds in North Africa had been eliminated. The principal events were:

1509. Spanish Capture of Oran and Mers El Kebir.

1510. Pedro Navarro Captures Tripoli for Spain.

1517. Ottoman Conquest of Egypt. (See p. 494.)

1518. Rise of Khair ed-Din. He and his brother **Harush,** Moslem Greeks, became leaders of a North African pirate group; they defeated and expelled the Spanish from Algiers, Harush being killed in the battle for the city.

1518–1546. Reign of Khair ed-Din, Dey of Algiers. (See p. 499.)

1533. Khair ed-Din Ravages Sicilian and Italian Coasts.

1534. Ottoman Capture of Tunis. Khair ed-Din, acting as admiral of the Ottoman navy, captured Tunis from **Mulai-Hassan** of the decadent Hafsid Dynasty.

1535. Charles V Conquers Tunis. (See p. 499.)

1541. Charles V Repulsed from Algiers. (See p. 499.)

1574. Expulsion of the Spanish from Tunis. (See p. 504.)

1578. Battle of Al Kasr al Kebir. King Sebastian of Portugal was defeated and killed while intervening in a Moroccan dynastic dispute (see p. 489).

1580. Spanish Occupation of Ceuta.

1590. Janissary Revolt in Tunis. They seized power, while retaining nominal allegiance to Constantinople.

1591. Moroccan Expedition to West Africa. The force, composed predominantly of Spanish and Portuguese mercenaries, crossed the western Sahara to inflict a crushing defeat on the Songhoi Empire. Gao was destroyed, Timbuktu temporarily occupied, and the country generally devastated.

EAST AFRICA

The history of East Africa during this century was primarily a struggle between the Coptic Christians of Ethiopia and the Moslem coastal tribes of Somalia. Portuguese intervention on the side of Ethiopia in this struggle, under **Christopher da Gama,** at the request of the Negus, swung the scales toward the Ethiopians (1541). **Ahmed Gran,** who had invaded and occupied a substantial portion of eastern Ethiopia, was expelled by the Portuguese, who continued to exert great influence in Ethiopia until the end of the century.

WEST AFRICA

Three principal Negro empires flourished in West Africa during this century. The Songhoi Empire was still powerful, though declining, largely due to defeat by the Hausa Confederation, under **Kebbi.** The Hausas became dominant east of the

Niger River. To the northeast the empire of Kanen, or Bornu, expanded around Lake Chad. During the latter part of the century it flourished under Emperor **Idris III** (1571-1603). The slow decline of the Songhoi Empire was hastened by the crushing defeat inflicted upon it by the European mercenaries of Morocco toward the end of the century (1591; see p. 517).

THE AMERICAS, 1492-1600

This was the century of the **conquistadores,** following the discovery of America by Columbus. Towering over all of the others as a military man was **Hernando Cortez,** who conquered Mexico for Spain. Equally bold, perhaps, but an unprincipled adventurer who lacked the military and administrative genius of Cortez, was **Francisco Pizarro,** who conquered the Inca Empire of Peru. Struggles among the Spanish were almost as frequent as were their wars of conquest against the Indians. The principal events were:

CARIBBEAN REGION

1492, October 12. Discovery of America by Christopher Columbus. He explored numerous Caribbean islands, including Hispaniola (Santo Domingo), all of which he claimed for Spain.

1493. Columbus' Second Voyage. He established a permanent colony on Hispaniola, as the first Spanish Viceroy of the New Indies.

1493-1502. Explorations, Discoveries, and Colonization by Columbus. He discovered many more islands, the coast of South America, and Central America, all of which were claimed for Spain. Spanish adventurers rushed to the New World.

1494, June 7. Treaty of Tordesillas. This pact between Spain and Portugal established a line of demarcation 370 leagues west of the Cape Verde Islands; Spain was to have exclusive rights of exploration and colonization west of the line, Portugal exclusive rights east of the line. This modified Pope Alexander VI's original line, 100 leagues west of the islands (1493).

1508-1511. Conquest of Puerto Rico. A Spanish expedition from Hispaniola defeated the Carib Indians.

1511-1515. Conquest of Cuba. The leader was **Diego de Velázquez,** governor of Hispaniola.

1521-1535. Colonization of South America. The Spanish gained footholds along the coast of Venezuela and New Granada (Colombia).

1522-1523. Conquest of Nicaragua. The leaders were **Gíl González Dávila** and **Alonzo Niño.**

1523-1530. Spanish Squabbles. Conflict between Dávila and **Francisco Hernandez de Córdoba,** a subordinate of **Pedro Arias de Ávila,** the governor of Darien. Dávila defeated Córdoba, but in turn was defeated by another subordinate of Ávila's, **Cristobal de Olid,** thus permitting Ávila to gain control of Nicaragua.

1536-1538. Conquest of the Chibcha Indian Empire. Gonzalo Jiménez de Quesada took this region centered around modern Bogotá.

1585-1586. Drake's Raids. An English expedition under Sir Francis Drake sacked Santo Domingo, Cartagena, and St. Augustine (see p. 465), and generally terrorized the West Indies.

MEXICO

1500-1518. Height of the Aztec Empire. A period of expansion; they controlled all central and southern Mexico and northern Central America.

1518-1519. Expedition of Hernando Cortez. He was nominally under the command of Diego de Velázquez. In defiance of Velázquez' orders he led an expedition of 600 men, 17 horses, and 10 cannon from Hispaniola. He established Veracruz, subjugated the independent Mexican Indian state of Tabasco, and opened negotiations with **Montezuma,** Emperor of the Aztecs.

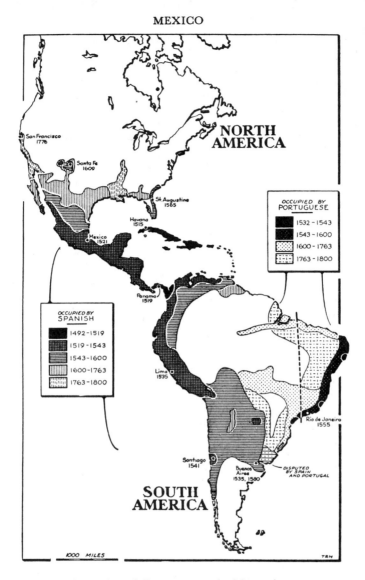

OCCUPIED BY
PORTUGUESE
■ 1532 - 1543
▨ 1543 - 1600
⬚ 1600 - 1763
⬚ 1763 - 1800

OCCUPIED BY
SPANISH
■ 1492 - 1519
▨ 1519 - 1543
⬚ 1543 - 1600
⬚ 1600 - 1763
⬚ 1763 - 1800

Spanish and Portuguese colonial empires

After establishing an alliance with the Totonac tribe, Cortez invaded the interior of Mexico, where he overcame the independent state of Tlaxcala, which then allied itself with him against the Aztecs. From Tlaxcala he marched on Tenochtitlán (near modern Mexico City). Despite a few skirmishes en route, the Spanish were permitted by Montezuma to enter the city as friends (November 8, 1519).

1519, December. Cortez Seizes Montezuma. This gave him virtual control of Tenochtitlán.

1520. Expedition of Pánfilo de Narváez. He was sent by Velázquez with a force of 1,500 men to subdue and punish Cortez for disobedience of orders. Cortez, learning of the arrival of this expedition at Veracruz, left **Pedro de Alvarado** in command at Tenochtitlán, marched to the coast with part of his force, defeated Narváez, and enlisted the survivors of Narváez' command. Cortez then marched back to Tenochtitlán, where Alvarado's excessive harshness had caused an Aztec revolt against the Spanish.

1520, June 30. Evacuation of Tenochtitlán. After hard fighting Cortez withdrew, suffering heavy losses in the process. During the confusion Montezuma was murdered by the Spanish. Cortez retreated to the north end of Lake Texcoco.

1520, July 7. Battle of Otumba. A desperate fight, which Cortez finally won decisively, though suffering heavy losses. Because of this, and the continuing threats of the Aztecs, he withdrew to Tlaxcala, where he reorganized his small army. While awaiting reinforcements, he conquered Topeaca, and other neighboring regions.

1521. Return to Central Mexico. Cortez established a base at Texcoco, then advanced on Tenochtitlán.

1521, May 26–August 13. Siege of Tenochtitlán. The Aztecs resisted desperately, but a Spanish assault was successful. Cortez captured the new emperor, **Cuauhtemoc,** and through him established firm control over the Aztecs. He then destroyed Tenochtitlán and established Mexico City nearby.

1522–1539. Conquest of South Mexico and of Northern Central America. Cortez advanced as far as Salvador. Mayan resistance was particularly violent in Honduras.

1524–1526. Expedition into Honduras. Cortez failed to achieve lasting results.

1524–1555. Conquest of North Mexico.

1529. Revolt of Tabasco. This was suppressed by **Francisco de Montejo,** successor of Cortez.

1539. Subjection of the Mayans. Montejo was successful after repeated campaigns.

1546. Mayan Revolt. This was cruelly suppressed.

1550–1600. Extensive Exploration and Conquest. Expeditions ranged along the Gulf and Pacific coasts to California and to Florida.

1565. Founding of St. Augustine. It was established by **Pedro Menéndez de Avilés** as a base of operations against the recently established French colony on the St. Johns River (see p. 521). He then captured the French post, massacring the garrison. The French threat to Spanish Florida was eliminated.

PERU AND THE WEST COAST

1500–1530. Power and Prosperity of the Inca Empire.

1531. Expedition of Francisco Pizarro. He had earlier explored along the northwest coast of South America. He now sailed south from Darien with an expedition of 180 men, 27 horses, and 2 cannon. He landed at Tumbes (San Miguel). Here he waited for reinforcements. He then advanced inland with a force of 62 cavalry and 102 infantry.

1532, November 16. Seizure of Atahualpa. Pizarro seized the Inca emperor by treachery at Cajamarca.

1533, August 29. Murder of Atahualpa. Despite payment of a ransom for his release, Atahualpa was murdered by the Spanish, who then established control over the territory of the Inca Empire.

1535–1536. Inca Revolt. During the absence of Pizarro, the Inca leader **Manco** revolted. The Incas besieged the Spanish in Cuzco, but were repulsed.

1537–1548. Civil Wars among the Spanish. These began with a revolt of **Diego del Amagro** against Pizarro. After some initial success, Amagro was defeated and executed (1538). In subsequent unrest and violence Pizarro was also killed (June 26, 1541).

1540–1561. Conquest of Chile. This was begun by **Pedro de Valdivia,** and was marked by a succession of wars against the warlike Aracanian Indians. After Valdivia was killed in battle (1553), the conquest was continued by **García Hurtado de Mendoza.**

1546. Royal Intervention. Charles V appointed **Pedro de la Gasca** as his viceroy in Peru. Gasca, assisted by Valdivia, defeated **González Pizarro** (younger brother of Francisco) in the **Battle of Xaquixaguana** (1548), which resulted in partial restoration of royal authority in Peru. The younger Pizarro was executed.

1557–1569. Continued Violence among the Spanish in Peru.

1569–1581. Royal Authority Re-established. Violence was suppressed by Viceroy **Francisco de Toledo.**

1579. Drake's Raids along the Peruvian Coast.

1587–1588. Cruise of Thomas Cavendish. His squadron of three English ships captured 20 Spanish galleons in the eastern Pacific.

PORTUGUESE AMERICA,
1494–1600

1494, June 7. Treaty of Tordesillas. This established Portuguese rights to the eastern tip of modern Brazil (see p. 518).

1500–1520. French and Portuguese Rivalry. Their expeditions explored the coast of northeast South America, with several armed clashes.

1521–1555. Portuguese Expansion. The coast of modern Brazil was systematically colonized.

1555. French Colony. This was established at Rio de Janeiro.

1556–1557. Portuguese on Rio de Janeiro. **Mem De Sa** destroyed the French colony (see below).

FRENCH AMERICA

1555–1557. Colony in Brazil. (See above.)

1564. Colony in Florida. **Jean de Ribaut** and **René de Laudonnière** established Fort Caroline at the mouth of the St. John's River.

1565. Spanish Destruction of Fort Caroline. The Spanish were led by Avilés (see p. 520).

1567. Raid on Fort Caroline. **Chevalier de Gourgues** temporarily seized the fort, massacring the Spanish garrison in revenge for Avilés' massacre two years earlier. Realizing their inability to cope with the Spanish in Florida, the French then abandoned the fort.

XIV

THE BEGINNING OF
MODERN WARFARE: 1600–1700

MILITARY TRENDS

In the 17th century the transition from the Middle Ages to the Modern Era was completed insofar as military weaponry, tactics, and organization were concerned. As the period opened, the musket and the pike were complementary rivals in land warfare, basic battle formations differed little from the Greek phalanx of two millennia earlier, the armored horsemen of the gentry had still not accepted the fact that gunpowder had destroyed chivalry, and artillery was essentially immobile. At the close of the period, the pike had practically disappeared, infantry was fighting in the linear formations which would persist into the 20th century, and mobile artillery had become a major combat arm in coordination with infantry and cavalry. Furthermore, standing armies in the modern sense of the term had come into being, with organizations and hierarchical ranks comparable to today's tables of organization.

One individual—**Gustavus Adolphus** of Sweden—was responsible for most of these changes. Their acceptance throughout Europe was facilitated by a series of wars—the Thirty Years' War, the War of the Grand Alliance, and the Dutch War—which transformed Europe into a vast, bloody proving ground.

On the high seas also, tactical concepts crystallized—to change relatively little in technical detail for two centuries to come. England's **Robert Blake** deserves most of the credit.

MILITARY LEADERSHIP

Gustavus Adolphus was the one great captain of this century. There was, however, a host of eminent leaders, of whom perhaps the best were Holland's **Maurice of Nassau,** France's exceptionally gifted **Henri de La Tour d'Auvergne de Turenne,** the Indian conqueror **Aurangzeb,** and the brilliant Manchu Emperor **K'ang-hsi.** Although the strategical genius of France, Cardinal Duke **Armand J. P. de Richelieu,** was not a soldier, his understanding and use of military strategy were unexcelled.

522

Among other outstanding soldiers of the century were Germany's Count **Johan T. Tilly** and Count **Albrecht von Wallenstein;** France's Prince **Louis II of Condé, Duke d'Enghien,** Duke **François Henri de Luxembourg,** Duke **Henry of Montmorency,** and the great engineer Marquis **Sebastien LeP. Vauban;** England's **Oliver Cromwell,** Italy's Count **Raimondo Montecuccoli,** the Maratha **Sivaji,** the Manchu **Nurhachi,** and Japan's **Ieyasu.**

At sea England's Blake was outstanding, though rivaled by such men as **George Monck** (soldier turned sailor) and **William Penn.** But Holland's **Maarten H. Tromp,** his son **Cornelis,** and **Michael A. de Ruyter,** and France's **Jean Bart** and **Anne Hilarion Tourville** were worthy opponents of England's best.

SMALL ARMS

The transformation of the musket was significant. Gustavus Adolphus found it a clumsy weapon weighing from 15 to 25 pounds, and fired from a forked rest. He trimmed the weight to 11 pounds. He also adopted, if he did not invent, the cartridge—a fixed charge, with powder carefully measured (affording ballistic uniformity) and the ball attached. The result was a lighter, handier weapon, easier to load, with rate of fire doubled to one round per minute.

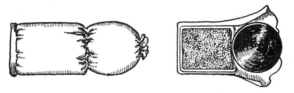

Early cartridge

The snaphance (or snaphaunce) lock, deriving a spark from flint on steel, had been introduced during the 16th century. The true **fusil,** or flintlock musket, invented by French gunsmith **Le Bourgeoys** in 1615, was perfected as a sporting weapon about 1630. However, adoption as a military weapon was slow, partly because of increased cost of manufacture, and partly because of traditional conservatism of military leaders satisfied with the matchlock. France armed one regiment entirely with the flintlock musket in 1670; by 1699, it was standard in European armies.

A plug bayonet, inserted into the muzzle of the musket, was widely in use by midcentury as partial replacement of the pike. However, since it rendered the weapon inoperable as a firearm, the pikeman was still a necessary adjunct to the infantry formation to ensure continued fire power. But about 1680, someone—possibly Vauban—invented the ring bayonet, which left the bore clear for firing. This was soon improved by a socket in the handle which firmly locked the bayonet to a stud on the musket barrel. By the end of the century this had been adopted by all European armies. The musketeer became his own pikeman; the pikeman himself was fading from the scene.

ARTILLERY

Gustavus Adolphus was the father of modern field artillery and of the concept of massed, mobile artillery fire. Deploring the fact that artillery's heavy fire-power potential could not support infantry and cavalry maneuver, Gustavus devoted much time and effort to solving the problem.

He reduced weight by decreasing the amount of metal in the barrel: shortening the tube and reducing its thickness. Then he introduced improved, standardized gunpowder, permitting greater accuracy despite the shortened barrel, and also restoring ballistic power lost by lightening of the tube.

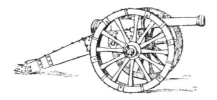

Swedish three-pounder regimental gun

He allowed only three standard calibers: a 24-pounder, a 12-pounder, and the light, sturdy 3-pounder regimental gun. Then, to ensure command control over the weapons, he abandoned the old system of hiring civilian contract gunners and established military units of cannoneers, as responsive to discipline and to training as were his infantry and cavalry.

SIEGECRAFT AND FORTIFICATION

One man—Vauban—dominated the culminating developments of the two opposed functions of siegecraft and fortification. Through him these approached the ultimate capabilities for military forces limited to muzzle-loading weapons and black powder. This was extremely important in a century in which sieges were the most common combat activity.

The Vauban system of siegecraft* provided for systematic approach of the attackers and their artillery to a fortification by means of entrenchments. The ultimate objective was to permit the attacking siege artillery to blast a breach in the defensive wall and the covering obstacles through which an infantry column could make an assault. Sometimes a successful assault could be made under the cover of fire from the approach trenches without waiting for the siege artillery to breach the walls. The attackers would then have to be prepared to cut their way through the defending obstacles across the moat (if there was one), and climb the wall, under the cover of artillery and small-arms fire from the approach trenches. Fascines (bundles of twigs or brushwood) were usually used to fill up ditches and the moat before such an assault.

The method of approach was standardized. A **first parallel** was dug some 600–700 yards from the fortification. This was a trench parallel to the line of defenses at the selected point of assault. This precluded enfilade fire by the defenders down the length of the trench. The distance was fixed because it was close to the maximum effective range of defending and attacking artillery of the age. When the parallel was dug, additional earthworks were thrown up in front of it as protection for siege-artillery emplacements. To expedite construction, fascines were used as the basis of the earthworks. Under the cover of fire from these guns the attacking

* The remaining paragraphs of this section are based upon Appendix IV, "Fortifications and Siegecraft," from *The Compact History of the Revolutionary War*, New York, 1963, with the permission of the publishers, Hawthorn Books, Inc.

engineers began to dig "saps," or approach trenches, toward the fort (thus the origin of the word "sapper" for engineer). These were dug at an angle, and zig-zagged back and forth, again to reduce the defender's opportunity for enfilade fire. The sappers were protected from direct fire by shelters called gabions: wicker baskets filled with earth and frequently put on wheels so that they could be pushed in front of the sap.

When the approaches progressed to a point about 300 yards from the defenses, a **second parallel** was dug, and new artillery emplacements prepared. From these positions the siege guns could begin an intensified bombardment to drive the defenders from the ramparts, to silence their artillery, and to begin to batter a breach. The defenders would, if possible, sortie in limited counterattacks to prevent the completion of the second parallel and to try to destroy or to "spike" the attacking guns. (Guns were "spiked" by driving spikes, nails, or bayonets down their touch-holes, thus rendering them useless until the spike could be removed.) The attackers had to be ready for such sorties, and strong forces of infantry were maintained constantly in the parallels to protect the guns and the cannoneers.

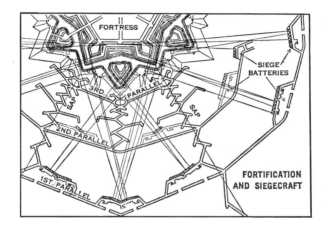

If the defenders persisted, and if the attackers did not believe they could assault successfully from the second parallel, approach saps were again pushed forward, this time in the face of small-arms fire from the defenders, to within a few yards of the ditch or moat at the base of the walls. Here a **third parallel** was constructed. While fire from attacking infantry prevented the defenders from manning the ramparts, the breaching batteries were emplaced to batter the walls at point-blank range. Sometimes improved mining techniques (based fundamentally on the old principles) were also employed, either to help knock down the wall or to permit small groups of attackers to debouch inside the fortification. The defenders, of course, would normally drive countermines.

A day or two of siege-gun pounding from the third parallel would usually knock a breach in the wall. The assault then followed, if the garrison had not already surrendered.

TACTICS OF LAND WARFARE

At the outset of the century the "Spanish square" dominated the battlefields of Europe. Actually, as we have seen (p. 456), these squares were broad columns of pikemen and musketeers, several usually arrayed abreast in a line of battle. The relatively immobile artillery was usually lined up in front of the columns, generally protected by cavalry. More cavalry protected the flanks of the ponderous "squares."

This columnar concept of infantry combat was changed completely and forever by Gustavus. Thanks to increased fire power and rate of fire, he arranged his musketeers and his reduced number of pikemen in relatively thin lines, no more than 6 men deep. A number of individual units, deployed abreast in such lines, with intervals between units, formed a longer line. Undoubtedly following the example of the Roman legion, the Swedish army usually comprised two such lines of infantry, with a third line in reserve. Gustavus usually had some cavalry and artillery deployed in the intervals in these infantry lines. For flank protection, there was usually cavalry on the flanks, but the small, mobile infantry units were also perfectly capable of protecting their own flanks when the need arose.

This was the genesis of modern linear tactics, which remained basically unchanged—though constantly modified—until World War I. Even today, despite

Swedish musketeer

drastic tactical changes of two world wars and the advent of nuclear weapons, vestiges of Gustavus' linear concept remain in modern infantry doctrine.

Gustavus also modified cavalry tactics, combining the best features of the cumbersome German "caracole" and the traditional French saber charge, so that his cavalry had both fire power and shock capability. And he trained his infantry, artillery, and cavalry to work closely together. This concept of tactical teamwork among the three combat arms was Gustavus' greatest tactical contribution to warfare.

MILITARY ORGANIZATION AND THEORY

Combat Formations

The Thirty Years' War marked a major turning point in methods of warfare and military organization. This undoubtedly would have occurred without the impact of a Gustavus Adolphus, but he sparked not only the tactical changes; he also transformed organization. His was the first true professional standing army. The internal structure within that army established prototypes for small-sized military units today. (For the larger units—divisions and corps—see p. 736).

Gustavus' infantry squadron, consisting of approximately 500 men, was called a battalion by the French, and this designation has persisted to this day for the basic combat command. The battalion usually consisted of four companies. Three battalions were combined into brigades (equivalent of modern regiments or brigades) for combat. This was not an entirely new concept—what was new was Gustavus' decision to make the brigade a permanent unit with a permanent command hierarchy, the origin of the modern regimental officer system. The regiment or brigade was commanded by a colonel, the battalion by a lieutenant colonel, and the companies—whose origin was the free companies of earlier centuries—by captains. Subordinate officers were lieutenants.

The Regimental Proprietary System

The establishment of permanent units hastened the almost universal adoption of the proprietary system, which had already begun to replace the vestiges of feudalism and of free companies. The permanent colonel was the proprietor of his regiment, accepted by the king as a permanent officer and authorized (personally, and through him his captains) to raise men. Initially, with armies being raised only for a campaign and disbanded afterward, the troops raised by the proprietary system were volunteers, more or less carefully selected from the available and willing man power. But as the armies became permanent, the standing units were not disbanded and were kept up to strength by regular influx of recruits, usually provided by the crown. This, combined with the financial considerations in maintaining year-round units, gave the crown increasing rights of supervision over the administration and training of the regiments, and thus somewhat restricted the proprietary rights previously exercised by colonels and captains.

This proprietary system could be profitable. A commander was paid for the number of men he mustered, as well as for their weapons, equipment, and subsistence. In addition to the profit to be derived from economical exercise of his proprietorship (to say nothing of the possibilities offered by parsimony and fraud), an officer could sell his proprietary interest when he retired. Thus officers' commissions were valuable, and could be purchased. This custom of purchase of commissions continued in some armies—notably that of England—long after the proprietary system itself had disappeared.

The Hierarchy of Command

Later in the century the French—who adopted the Swedish system almost in its entirety—extended the concept of a permanent combat military hierarchy upward from the regiment to the army commander. Hitherto the king or a prince of the realm was usually the titular "general" of an army. The second in command—and often the actual field commander—was the lieutenant general, almost invariably a nobleman, who usually exercised direct command over the aristocratic cavalry. The infantry was usually commanded by a senior professional soldier, who was not necessarily a nobleman and was usually called the sergeant major general, or major general. He was charged with the responsibility for forming up the army for battle and with care of the various administrative duties of command. When the army was disbanded at the end of a campaign, as was usually the case until the very end of this century, the lieutenant general and major general lost both command and rank. Usually they reverted to their proprietary positions as colonels of permanent regiments.

By the end of the century, however, the old title of marshal became a permanent rank in the French army for a commander of a field army in the absence of the king. Since **Louis XIV** usually had several armies in the field at once, this resulted in the establishment of a permanent list of officers, each with sufficient experience and distinction to warrant him to serve as major general, lieutenant general, or marshal of an army. In time the relative position of officers on this list established precedence for command. Thus, for the first time since the fall of Rome, one of the most significant aspects of modern military professionalism appeared: the permanent classification of an officer by rank, and not by the temporary command which he happened to be exercising. In due course the national general army lists were extended to the grades of colonel and below, eventually undermining the proprietary system of independent regiments, which mostly disappeared in the 18th century.

Supporting Services

This century also saw the real beginning of the militarization of the supporting arms and services. This was to some extent a natural concomitant of the emergence of the standing army. To Gustavus Adolphus' militarization of artillery personnel was later added the militarization of the teamsters who hauled the army's supplies. This was carried further, throughout the military supply system, by Marquis **François M. T. Louvois** of France, Minister of War of Louis XIV.

Vauban was responsible for carrying to fruition the systematization of the engineering tasks of an army begun by Gustavus. He consolidated the responsibility for these tasks under specially trained engineer officers and men, rather than leaving such things to individual line units and to civilian contractors. Similar militarization occurred in military medicine and military law.

Armies and Society*

This was an age of absolute monarchy—though absolutism was rejected in England—and war was indeed "the trade of kings," as Dryden, a product of the age, well put it. A military system based on strict discipline, centralized administration, and long-term, highly trained troops was particularly congenial to such form of government. Even the civilian economy was being centralized, since war's cost created the crown's need for money. The trend, which included higher taxation, was begun in France by Louis's great ministers Louvois and **Jean B. Colbert.**

The effect on society was profound, since the steady procession of wars created new demands for man power. War ceased to be of concern to the upper classes only. The cavalry, once the exclusive domain of aristocracy, opened its ranks to all who could ride a horse. Mercenary regiments drew heavily on the lower classes; the press gang and universal service were just around the corner.

Science and technology were increasingly being put to the service of war, particularly in the newly militarized artillery and the engineers. Maurice and Gustavus used portable telescopes; cartography for military purposes became essential. Soldiering, particularly for the officer, was becoming a profession; systematized instruction increased in importance. The first military academy of modern times was established in 1617 by **John of Nassau.**

There was a marked increase in the size of armies and the scope of warfare. Gustavus had about 30,000 men in 1631; his opponents had more in their pay, but rarely employed all of them in battle. Richelieu had more than 200,000 men under

---

* This section is adapted, with permission, from an unpublished study, "Historical Trends Related to Weapon Lethality," made for the U.S. Army by the Historical Evaluation and Research Organization, 1964.

arms before his death, and Louis XIV maintained a military establishment of 400,-000, with field armies sometimes approaching 100,000 men. It was estimated that a country could support an army of about 1 percent of its population, approximately the ratio in France at the end of the century.

THE MILITARY SYSTEM OF GUSTAVUS ADOLPHUS, C. 1631*

At the time Gustavus Adolphus assumed the Swedish crown in 1611, the Swedish army was poorly equipped, poorly organized, under strength, and badly led. Gustavus' first task was to rebuild his army. He provided for continuous training from the moment a recruit entered the ranks. There were frequent maneuvers for small and large units. Discipline was strict; every regimental commander read the Articles of War to his troops once a month. Punishment for infractions was heavy, and Gustavus' soldiers had a reputation for good behavior unusual for troops of that day.

Infantry

Gustavus' basic tactical unit was the squadron, consisting of 408 men—216 pikemen and the remainder musketeers. The pikes were formed in a central block, 6 deep, and the musketeers in 2 wings of 96 men, also 6 deep, on each side of the pikemen. Attached to each squadron was an additional element of 96 musketeers. He grouped 3 or 4 squadrons to form a brigade. Since the attached musketeers were employed frequently for outpost, reconnaissance, etc., they were often not available to the squadron.

In combining fire power with the pike, and missile with shock, Gustavus put principal emphasis on fire power. He employed the "countermarch" concept introduced by the Spanish, in which front-rank musketeers moved to the rear to reload after firing; but since he had speeded the loading process, he was able not only to reduce the number of ranks to 6 but to have 2 ranks of musketeers fire simultaneously before countermarching. Further, the countermarch was so executed that the formation moved forward; the fire was, in effect, a small-arms rolling barrage. During this movement, the musketeers were protected by the pikes while they reloaded. Later, Gustavus introduced the salve, or salvo, to increase further the fire power of his line. In the salvo, 3 ranks fired simultaneously.

Since salvo fire rendered the musketeers impotent while they reloaded, the role of the pike was enhanced in the Gustavian system. But the pike had a broader mission. It was to deliver the decisive blow, the salvo itself being but the prelude to the pike assault, as it was to the cavalry charge. And the best protection for the musket was the offensive action by the pike. Gustavus had his pikemen wear light armor, which was on the way out in other countries. He shortened the pike from 16 to 11 feet and sheathed its foremost part with iron so that it could not be severed by a sword blow. Thus the obsolescent pike became in Gustavus' hands an offensive weapon, combined with missile power.

Cavalry

Gustavus' cavalry, armed with pistol and saber, formed in 6 ranks (later in 3). The pistol was a gesture; the real effect came from the saber charge. The first rank fired when it was close to the enemy, the other 2 held fire, retaining the pistol for emergency use. Detached musketeers stationed between cavalry squadrons provided

---

* *Ibid.*

the fire power that shook the enemy line. While the cavalry charged, the musketeers would reload, to be ready to fire another volley for a second charge or to cover a retreat. To this was added the fire from the regimental cannon.

There was an obvious disadvantage to this system; by tying the cavalry to the infantry and artillery, Gustavus sacrificed the speed and momentum of the horse except for the final distance of the charge. But it was better than anything yet devised, and it was successful. As a result, it was imitated widely.

Artillery

Over-all artillery direction was provided by 27-year-old **Lennart Torstensson,** the best artilleryman of his time. The artillery was organized into permanent regiments of 6 companies. Of the 6 companies, 4 consisted of gunners, 1 of sappers, and 1 of men with special exploding devices. Thus the artillery was organized as a distinct and regular branch of the army, manned almost entirely by Swedish troops. After some experimentation Gustavus adopted the 3-pounder "regimental gun," which revolutionized the role of artillery; each regiment of foot and horse in Gustavus' army had 1 (later 2) of these cannon. The enormous advantage which this provided in battle was soon imitated in other armies.

Summation

Most of Gustavus' innovations were adapted from others, and he was not the only one to improve the military system. But no one else so surely bridged the gap between conception and achievement; no other fitted his innovations into a completely integrated system with its own set of unifying principles. His accomplishments were many: he gave to infantry and cavalry the capacity for the offense, he increased fire power and made it the preliminary for shock, he made artillery mobile, he made linear formations more flexible and responsive to the commander's will, he solved the problem of combined arms, and he made the small-unit commander the key to action. In him, the military revolution that began in the middle of the 16th century was most completely realized, although it did not find fullest expression until the time of Louis XIV.

THE FRENCH SYSTEM OF LOUIS XIV, C. 1695*

Under Richelieu and Louis XIV, the French army adopted from the Swedes the basic infantry formation—a battalion (or regiment) of 600–800 men. This unit was usually organized in 1 line, 6 deep, with the pikes in the center and the muskets on the flank, and occupied a front of about 100 yards. In battle, several lines were formed, with the battalions in checkerboard fashion. Two-thirds of the men were musketeers, and from this group a detachment supported the cavalry. The interval between battalions was supposed to be equal to their front, so that the second line, usually 300 to 400 paces behind, could pass through. The reserve was kept twice that distance behind the second line.

On his accession, Louis XIV possessed an army of 139 regiments, 20 of which were foreign; about 30 were cavalry. But they were far from disciplined, and administration was poor. The task of reorganizing and training the army was the work of Louvois. He hampered field commanders with deadening restrictions, but his talents paid off in other ways: his improved administration and the fortifications he

---

* *Ibid.*

built. Administrative reforms included control of the proprietary system (see p. 527) and frequent reviews and inspections.

A chain of fortresses, fully equipped and stored with all the supplies needed by an army, was constructed. An army on the march could base at any one of these posts, certain of finding there everything it needed, including heavy artillery. At the same time, an enemy army would find the task of breaching these forts, one after the other, an overwhelming job. Fortress construction was largely the work of Vauban (see p. 524). Altogether, Vauban built 33 new fortresses and remodeled 3,000 others.

Louis's cavalry consisted of **gendarmerie** (heavy cavalry), carabineers, light cavalry, and dragoons. The carabineers, numbering at the turn of the century about 3,000 men, were armed with rifled carbines and swords; the dragoons used the musket with the newly developed bayonet and carried an entrenching tool on their saddles. They combined the advantages of infantry and cavalry, and, being very mobile, proved very useful. From one regiment in 1650, the number of dragoons increased until, by 1690, there were 43 such regiments in the French army.

DEVELOPMENTS IN NAVAL WARFARE

Because of their revolutionary concepts of naval fire power, so strikingly demonstrated in the wars against Spain at the end of the previous century (see p. 463), English sailors at the beginning of the century were tactically far ahead of all

Early ship-of-the-line

possible rivals. Surprisingly, none of these rivals, not even the Spanish victims or the aggressive and imaginative Dutch, seem to have grasped the secret of English success: broadside fire power. And, with no major naval wars in the first half of the century, there was no opportunity for the others to learn, or for the English to improve.

The one important development of the early part of the century, apparently another English discovery, was how to harness a gun's recoil with ropes in such a way that it would be brought to rest far enough inboard from the gunport to permit easy reloading. Hitherto guns had been tightly bound to bulkheads to inhibit recoil. This had made loading very difficult—almost impossible in the heat of action. Thus evolved the English practice, followed in the Armada battle, of a small group of about 5 ships following each other in a circle, only one at a time firing its broadsides at the enemy. Harnessing the recoil, therefore, not only greatly increased the rate of fire of each ship; for all practical purposes it potentially multiplied this increased fire power by a factor of about 5.

From this development, and from experience in the First Dutch War, England's great Blake seems to have formalized the concept of the line-ahead formation —all ships in single column, at regular intervals, so as to achieve maximum fire power by broadside fire and, at the same time, maximum control in an orderly formation responsive to the admiral's will.

The difficulty of controlling a great number of ships, stretched across several miles of sea, created massive combined problems of naval tactics and seamanship. Rudimentary flag signals had been devised, but even when these reached the peak of sophistication more than a century later, they were totally inadequate for an admiral to communicate precise orders to his subordinates. Even if the flags could have transmitted exactly what he wanted, and transmitted it quickly (neither of which was possible), distance, fog, gunsmoke, and confusion of battle all made this a most uncertain means of communication at best. So the English Navy developed its system of "Fighting Instructions," which tried to establish a common, understood doctrinal procedure for dealing with every contingency. These instructions were augmented by further detailed orders given by an admiral to his subordinates before they put to sea, and (usually) before a battle was expected. But since no two battles could ever be exactly alike, and no two enemies would react in exactly the same way, contingencies constantly arose which the "Fighting Instructions" did not cover.

This led to the emergence in England, between the First and Second Dutch Wars, of two tactical schools of thought. Both agreed on entering battle with the line-ahead formation, endeavoring to be to the windward of the enemy so as to have the choice of closing or pulling away, as the circumstances of the battle might dictate. But once the battle was joined, the two schools differed on how it should be fought. Somewhat oversimplified, the differences were as follows:

The "formal" school believed in adhering to the line-ahead formation at practically any cost, until or unless complete victory was achieved. Each ship would engage with its guns the enemy closest to it, but would at the same time follow the course of the preceding vessel. Thus the admiral would always know where his ships were, could be assured that they were hammering away at their nearest opponent, and could pull them all out together, if necessary.

Those of the "melee" school, however, believed that if an opportunity arose the admiral should be able to release individual squadron and ship commanders to move out of the line in mass attacks against the enemy. They counted on the judgment and experience of subordinate commanders, and the traditional fighting spirit of the Royal Navy, to make the most of such opportunities, since it was impossible to give adequate orders on the spur of the moment.

By the end of the century both systems had been tested, each with mixed success and failure. For a variety of reasons, the formalists were in the ascendancy as the period ended, and they remained ascendant for more than a century.

The fighting Dutch admirals—even the two Tromps and de Ruyter—were always behind the British tactically. Although they adopted the British line-ahead fire-power system in the Second and Third Anglo-Dutch Wars, they always preferred to board and fight hand to hand. In sheer seamanship these three Dutchmen were equal to the very best English admiral, and perhaps better. Their challenge to English sea power was vigorous and nearly successful. But the English refused to be outfought, and their margin of victory was the clear gunnery superiority they maintained.

By the 1680's the French were prepared to challenge the British at sea. The British Navy had been administratively reorganized by **James II,** with the very able assistance of efficient **Samuel Pepys** as Secretary of the Admiralty. Between them they established methods for the direction, administration, and organization of the Royal Navy whose principles have, in large measure, persisted to this day.

But Louis XIV had in **Jean Colbert** a minister at least equally efficient. Colbert, furthermore, had been given a free hand by Louis in developing French sea power and finance, while James, before ascending the throne, had seen much of his work wasted due to the frivolous policies of his elder brother, **Charles II.** On top of this, Colbert had encouraged the development of scientific ship design and shipbuilding in French shipyards. The French adopted the best the English had done, and then improved on it. Ship for ship, the vessels of the French Navy were faster and better than those of the Royal Navy. When the War of the Grand Alliance began, the French Navy was the best in the world, and was numerically equal to the combined fleets of England and Holland. The senior French Admiral **de Tourville** was at least as courageous and probably more able than his mentor and counterpart, the English **Arthur Herbert, Earl of Torrington.**

By all logic, French sea power should have swept the British fleet from the Channel in the War of the Grand Alliance. That this did not occur was due primarily to the failure of Louis XIV to recognize the opportunity, and his refusal to let Tourville fight the war as he wished. France never again had a comparable opportunity.

By the end of the century France was able to threaten or annoy England at sea only by a *guerre de course* (destruction of commerce by attacks on merchant shipping). **Jean Bart,** the fighting French sailor who terrorized England's coasts in the War of the Grand Alliance, at least gave his successors a gallant example of an inherently defeatist method of naval war.

MAJOR WARS

THE THIRTY YEARS' WAR, 1618-1648

The Thirty Years' War started as a religious war, a product of the struggle between Roman Catholics and Protestants in Germany. Although the religious problem was always present, the war became increasingly a political struggle, with the Hapsburg Dynasty attempting to control as much as possible of Europe while other powers—particularly the Bourbon Dynasty of France—determined to contain the Hapsburgs. On the Catholic-Hapsburg side of the conflict were Austria, or the Holy Roman Empire, most of the German Catholic princes, and (intermittently) Spain. The Protestant princes of Germany and the kingdoms of Denmark, Sweden, and Catholic France were in opposition. The line-up changed from time to time; many German princes moved from one side to another, or attempted to stay out of the quarrel altogether. The separate wars—the Empire with Transylvania, Spain with France, Spain with Holland, Sweden with Poland, and Sweden with Denmark—all became involved in the great struggle. The fighting ranged all over Germany and into France, Spain, Italy, and the Netherlands. Much of the area—particularly Germany—was plundered and replundered by undisciplined and motley armies, whose major source of supply was the land over which they fought. The physical devastation of this war, and the loss of life among civilians, were the most severe in Europe since the Mongol invasion.

GERMANY DURING THE THIRTY YEARS' WAR.

Route of Gustavus Adolphus →

Background

1608. Evangelical Union. The Protestant princes of Germany, led by **Frederick IV,** Elector Palatine, and **Christian** of Anhalt, combined in protest against the occupation by **Maximilian** of Bavaria of the free city of Donauwörth.

1609. Holy Catholic League. Created by Maximilian and the other Catholic princes to offset the Evangelical Union.

1609. Freedom of Religion in Bohemia. King **Rudolph** guaranteed religious freedom to his Protestant subjects; it was to be safeguarded by a body of men known as "the Defenders." As a result, Rudolph was deposed by his brother **Matthias** (1611), who disapproved of religious freedom.

1612. Matthias Elected Emperor.

1617, June 17. Bohemian Succession Election. Because he was childless, Matthias' Catholic councilors elected his cousin Archduke **Ferdinand** of Styria as heir to the throne. The Protestants, led by Count **Matthias of Thurn,** refused to recognize Ferdinand.

1618, May 22. Defenestration of Prague. A Diet summoned by the Defenders met at Prague. Two of the king's most trusted councilors, **Martinitz** and **Slawata,** were thrown out of the windows of the Castle

of Hradschin. The Bohemians then established a rebellious provisional government and proceeded to raise an army under Count Thurn.

The Bohemian Period, 1618–1625

1618, July. Hostilities Begin. Thurn attacked and captured Krummau.

1618, November 21. Capture of Pilsen. Taken by Protestant Count **Ernst von Mansfeld,** with 20,000 mercenaries, in a desperate struggle.

1618–1619. Catholic Reinforcements. One army came from Flanders, supported by Spanish money; a second came from Austria. In the following winter months, native Bohemian troops under Count Thurn and Count **Andreas Schlick** kept the Flemish army shut up in Budweis and laid waste the Austrian border.

1619, March 20. Death of Matthias. The imperial and Bohemian thrones were vacant.

1619, May–June. Invasion of Austria. Thurn marched on Vienna, where he was joined by a Transylvanian army under Bethlen Gabor (see p. 581).

1619, June 10. Battle of Sablat. Mansfeld was badly defeated in Bohemia by imperial forces under Count **Charles B. de L. Bucquoi.** Thurn was recalled from Austria; Gabor returned to Hungary.

1619, August 26. Bohemian Protestants Elect

a New King. They chose **Frederick** Elector Palatine. They had already declared Ferdinand's election invalid. Bohemia was supported by Lusatia, Silesia, and Moravia.

1619, August 29. Ferdinand II Elected Emperor. This was by the Imperial Electoral College, at Frankfurt. In following months Ferdinand's efforts to eject Frederick from the throne in Bohemia were supported by Maximilian of Bavaria, **John George** of Saxony, and **Philip III** of Spain.

1620, April 30. Imperial Mandate Directs Frederick to Withdraw. His disregard of this mandate amounted to a declaration of war.

1620, July 3. Treaty of Ulm. Princes of the Evangelical Union, as jealous of fellow-Protestant Frederick as they were fearful of the emperor, declared neutrality. Meanwhile Bohemian troops had entered Austria, aided by an uprising of Austrian nobles.

1620, July 23. Intervention of Maximilian of Bavaria. With the army of the Catholic League, 25,000 men under the General **Johan Tserclaes, Count Tilly,** Maximilian crossed the Austrian frontier to support the emperor against the Bohemians and his unruly nobles.

1620, July–August. Spanish Intervention. Marquis **Ambrogio di Spinola** set out from Flanders for Bohemia, crossing the Rhine at Coblenz. Turning back into the Palatinate, he occupied Mainz, Kreuznach, and Oppenheim.

1620, August 4. Maximilian Victorious in Austria. He forced submission of the Austrian Estates at Linz.

1620, November 8. Battle of the Weisser Berg (White Hill). Maximilian and Tilly, coming from Linz, joined an imperial army under Bucquoi and entered Bohemia. Near Prague they were opposed by a Bohemian army, 15,000 strong, under Prince **Christian of Anhalt-Bernberg,** drawn up on the Weisser Berg. The Catholics, about 20,000, attacked at dawn. The Bohemians were routed. Frederick fled to Breslau; Maximilian entered Prague, which was sacked by imperial soldiers.

1621, January 29. Frederick Banned. His lands were confiscated. This action was protested by the princes of the Evangelical Union. Ferdinand rejected the protest. Meanwhile Mansfeld rallied an army of Bohemian refugees and mercenaries in the Palatinate, and declared allegiance to Frederick. Penniless, Mansfeld supported his army by pillaging the Rhine Valley. Thus began the depredations of the war.

1621, April 27. Frederick's Alliance with Holland. The Dutch agreed to support his efforts to reconquer his lands on the Rhine. Both Frederick and Ferdinand refused to accept Spanish and English mediation efforts.

1622. Protestant Reinforcements. Duke **Christian** of Brunswick and Margrave **George Frederick** of Baden-Durlach supported Frederick and Mansfeld.

1622, April 27. Battle of Mingolsheim. Mansfeld defeated Tilly and delayed his union with a Spanish force from the Netherlands under General **Gonzales de Córdoba.**

1622, May 6. Battle of Wimpfen. George Frederick, after initial success, was defeated by the combined forces of Tilly and Córdoba. Córdoba then pursued Mansfeld into Alsace; Tilly marched north to oppose Christian on the Main.

1622, June 20. Battle of Höchst. Christian, attempting to join Mansfeld, was intercepted by Tilly and Córdoba while crossing the Main River. Despite severe losses, Christian succeeded in joining Mansfeld with the remnants of his army.

1622, July–August. Protestant Withdrawal. Mansfeld, Christian, and Frederick retreated into Alsace, and then into Lorraine, living off the land, destroying towns and villages as they went. Frederick, after a dispute with his two army commanders, revoked their commissions, then retired to Sedan, leaving them with armies but without active employment for them. They decided to join the Dutch.

1622, August 29. Battle of Fleurus. The Spanish under Spinola had invaded Holland and laid siege to Bergen-op-Zoom. Mansfeld and Christian, marching to its rescue, were intercepted at Fleurus by Córdoba. Five desperate charges led by Christian broke the Spanish line. The Protestant army pushed on to raise the siege. It soon moved to East Friesland, where foraging was good.

1622, September 19. Tilly Takes Heidelberg. This followed a siege of 11 weeks. He had already conquered most of the Palatinate.

1623, February 23. Frederick Deposed as

Elector Palatine. This was by the Electoral College, at Ferdinand's behest. The title was given to Maximilian of Bavaria. The electors of Saxony and Brandenburg refused to recognize Maximilian.

1623, August 6. Battle of Stadtlohn. Christian, having left Friesland, was defeated by Tilly near the Dutch border, losing 6,000 dead and 4,000 prisoners. He fled into Holland with 2,000 survivors.

1623, August 27. Armistice. Frederick, after English urging, sought peace with Ferdinand. Mansfeld, however, as well as other Protestant princes, refused to make peace.

1624, January. France Enters the War. Already at war with Spain, Cardinal Richelieu brought his nation into the war against the Hapsburgs.

1624, June 10. Treaty of Compiègne. Alliance between France and Holland against the Hapsburgs. They were soon joined by England (June 15), Sweden and Denmark (July 9), and Savoy and Venice (July 11). France, Savoy, and Venice agreed on joint operations against the Valtelline, Alpine pass on the Spanish line of communications from Italy to the Netherlands, in order to prevent effective Spanish-Hapsburg cooperation.

1624, August 28–1625, June 5. Siege of Breda. This key fortress guarding the roads to Utrecht and Amsterdam was captured by Spinola.

The Danish Period, 1625–1629

1625, April. Wallenstein. Ferdinand hired mercenary general Count **Albrecht von Wallenstein,** who agreed to raise and quarter 20,000 men, to defend the Hapsburg lands. In June Wallenstein was charged with covering the whole empire.

1625, Summer. Danish Invasion of Germany. **Christian IV** of Denmark advanced down the Weser and tried to gather support from the Protestant German princes, from the Dutch, and from England, with limited success. Wallenstein moved north to join Tilly to oppose Christian.

1626, March 26. The Peace of Monzon. France withdrew from the war; a Huguenot revolt required Richelieu to recall French troops from operations against Spain.

1626, April 25. Battle of Dessau. Mansfeld, heading for Magdeburg, attempted to

cross the Elbe with 12,000 men. He was repulsed with heavy losses by Wallenstein, who pursued Mansfeld into Silesia. Mansfeld died soon afterward.

1626, August 24–27. Battle of Lutter. Christian of Denmark was badly defeated by Tilly. Christian, having lost about half his army, fled. Many Protestant princes made peace. The fortunes of the Protestant or anti-Hapsburg cause were at a low ebb.

1626–1627. Ordeal of Germany. The harvest had failed, famine, plague, and other diseases were widespread, violence was everywhere, as the various armies lived off the land where they were.

1627. Catholic King of Bohemia. The Archduke **Ferdinand,** Emperor Ferdinand's son, was crowned the first hereditary King of Bohemia.

1627. Peace between France and Spain. They formed an alliance against England.

1627, September and October. Repulse of the Danes. Tilly and Wallenstein marched down the Elbe and drove Christian over the frontiers of Holstein.

1628. Honors to Wallenstein. Ferdinand gave his successful general the duchies of Mecklenburg and Pomerania. This exercise of illegal imperial authority alarmed the German princes. The electors failed in attempts to get Wallenstein removed from command of the imperial armies.

1628, February–July. Siege of Stralsund. Wallenstein attempted to gain control of the Baltic coast, but the defense was vigorous and, in face of Swedish threats, Wallenstein withdrew.

1628, September 2. Battle of Wolgast. Wallenstein badly defeated Christian of Denmark.

1629, March 6. Edict of Restitution. Ferdinand ordered the restoration of all church lands which had been seized or acquired by Protestants.

1629, June 7. Peace of Lübeck. Denmark withdrew from the war, giving up the north German bishoprics of Holstein, Stormarn, and Ditmarschen, and agreeing not to meddle in the territorial arrangements of Lower Saxony.

1629, October 5. Truce of Altmark. Richelieu, alarmed by imperial victories, arranged a truce between Poland and Sweden to release Gustavus Adolphus to enter the war in Germany.

The Swedish Period, 1630–1634

1630, July 4. Arrival of Gustavus Adolphus. He landed at Usedom with 13,000 men and advanced on Stettin and into Mecklenburg. His army grew to 40,000.

1630, August 24. Dismissal of Wallenstein. Under pressure from the Protestant electors, meeting at Regensburg, Ferdinand, alarmed by the Swedish invasion, agreed to dismiss his favorite general in order to achieve German unity.

1630, November–1631, May. Siege of Magdeburg. This had been planned by Wallenstein, and was carried out by Count **Gottfried H. zu Pappenheim** and Tilly. The garrison was strong and well supplied, repulsing repeated attacks. The besiegers, finding it difficult to get food from the denuded countryside, suffered more than the besieged.

1631, January 23. Treaty of Bärwalde. Alliance of Gustavus with France, which was to provide financial support. He guaranteed freedom of worship for Catholics in Germany and to make no separate peace for 5 years.

1631, March 28. Leipzig Manifesto. Encouraged by the Swedish entry into the war, the Protestant princes, led by John George of Saxony, demanded that Ferdinand take steps to remedy many evils: the Edict of Restitution, depredations of imperial and Catholic armies, the decay of the rights of the German princes, disregard of the constitution, and the dreadful situation in the country. Ferdinand ignored the protests. The Protestant princes established an army under **Hans Georg von Arnim** (May 14).

1631, April 13. Capture of Frankfurt. Gustavus, after a brilliant surprise march, stormed Frankfurt on the Oder. He hoped this would cause Tilly to raise the siege of Magdeburg. When Tilly hung on grimly, Gustavus prepared to move directly to Magdeburg. Because of the alliance between Maximilian of Bavaria and France, Tilly renounced his allegiance to Maximilian and gave his loyalty to the emperor (May).

1631, May 20. Sack of Magdeburg. Tilly and Pappenheim stormed the city, which was thoroughly sacked by the enraged and hungry troops. Only about 5,000 of 30,000 inhabitants survived the holocaust.

1631, July–August. Gustavus vs. Tilly. The Swedish Army, dangerously weakened by lack of supplies, entrenched at Werben. Tilly attacked twice and was repulsed with heavy losses. Tilly then marched into Saxony, laying it waste. In an effort to save Saxony from Tilly, John George placed his troops under Gustavus (September 11).

1631, September 15. Tilly Takes Leipzig. He had been reinforced to about 36,000 men. The Swedish and Saxon armies, respectively 26,000 and 16,000 strong, joined at Düben, 25 miles to the north.

THE BATTLE OF BREITENFELD, SEPTEMBER 17, 1631

Tilly, influenced by Pappenheim, took a stand at Breitenfeld, 4 miles north of Leipzig. Drawing up his army with the infantry in the center and the cavalry on the wings, Tilly commanded the center and right, Pappenheim the left. Gustavus, under harassing fire from the imperialists, drew up his lines with the Saxons, under John George, on the left, Swedish infantry and other German infantry in the center and on the right, and Gustavus' cavalry on the right wing.

Pappenheim opened the battle, sweeping around behind the main body of the Swedish cavalry and attacking Gustavus' reserve. The maneuverable Swedish horse wheeled and pinned Pappenheim between them and the reserves, forcing him to flee in disorder. Tilly's right wing meanwhile attacked the Saxons, driving them from the field. Tilly now attempted to swing against the exposed Swedish left flank. The Swedes, shifting to the left with agility, countered the movement, repulsing the imperial attack. Gustavus then personally led his right-wing cavalry, followed closely by infantry, around Tilly's left flank, recapturing the Saxon guns as well as the unwieldy imperial artillery, which had been left behind when Tilly attacked. Cut off from their communications to Leipzig, and under fire from their own and the quick-firing Swedish artillery, the imperial army broke and fled when Gustavus pressed home his attack.

The Swedes pursued till nightfall, when the remnants halted under the cover of Pappenheim's rallied cavalry. Tilly's army lost 7,000 dead and 6,000 prisoners. He was badly wounded. The remnants of the imperial army retreated from Leipzig next day, and Gustavus entered the city. His army had lost 2,100 killed and wounded.

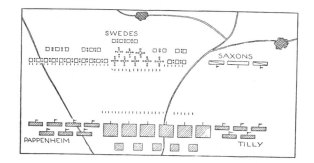

Battle of Breitenfeld

1631, September–December. Gustavus Adolphus Moves into the Rhineland. Because of the insecurity of the Protestant alliance, and thus of his base and his line of communications, Gustavus rejected suggestions that he advance on Vienna. Within 3 months he controlled all northwest Germany. Saxon troops had seized Prague. By Christmas, Gustavus and his allies had nearly 80,000 men within the shaking empire. He captured **Mainz** (December 22) and spent the rest of the winter there.

1632, April. Ferdinand Recalls Wallenstein to Command. Wallenstein's terms made him a virtual viceroy. He quickly began to raise a new army.

1632, April 7. Gustavus Advances into South Germany. He crossed the Danube at Donauwörth and marched eastward into Bavaria, where the reorganized imperial army waited, under Tilly and Maximilian of Bavaria.

1632, April 15–16. Battle of the Lech. Gustavus sent his army across the river on a bridge of boats and quickly attacked Tilly's entrenched camp. Tilly was mortally wounded, and Maximilian led the rest of the army in retreat, leaving most of the artillery and baggage on the field. Gustavus occupied Augsburg, Munich, and all southern Bavaria.

1632, July 11. Wallenstein Joins Maximilian

at Schwabach. He entrenched his imperial army of 60,000 near Fürth and the castle of Alte Veste (August). Gustavus, with 20,000, was entrenched near Nuremberg and sent for reinforcements. Their arrival brought his strength to 45,000.

1632, August 31–September 4. Battle of Alte Veste. Gustavus repeatedly attacked Wallenstein's entrenchments. The rough ground and heavy scrub of Wallenstein's well-chosen position made it impossible to bring either the redoubtable Swedish cavalry or artillery into action, and Gustavus withdrew with a heavy loss. The region around Nuremberg being denuded of food, both armies withdrew, Gustavus to the northwest, Wallenstein to the north.

1632, September–October. Wallenstein's Invasion of Saxony. Gustavus, responding to this threat to his communications, marched north at once. Wallenstein, who now had about 30,000 men, occupied the region around Leipzig. He vainly attempted to block Gustavus' crossing of the Saale with about 20,000 men (November 9).

1632, November 9–15. Gustavus Entrenches at Naumburg. He awaited reinforcements. Unaccountably, Wallenstein sent Pappenheim and a large detachment to Halle. Hearing of this, Gustavus marched rapidly to attack.

BATTLE OF LÜTZEN, NOVEMBER 16, 1632

As Gustavus approached (late November 15), Wallenstein sent an urgent summons to Pappenheim. He drew up his remaining forces, about 20,000 strong, in a defensive formation east of Lützen, facing south across a ditched road. The armies spent the night in battle formation.

Next morning Gustavus, held up by fog, was not able to attack until 11 A.M. He formed up his 18,000 troops south of the road, his right wing against a small treed area, with both wings composed, as at Breitenfeld, of interspersed cavalry and infantry units, **Bernard** of Saxe-Weimar commanding on the left wing, and Gustavus himself on the right, facing Count **Heinrich Holk.**

Gustavus charged Holk's cavalry, drove the musketeers from the ditch, and pushed the cavalry back upon the artillery. Wallenstein set fire to Lützen. The smoke blew into the faces of the Swedish center, which was then shaken by Wal-

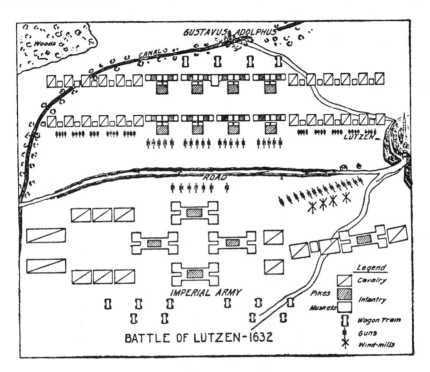

BATTLE OF LÜTZEN—1632

lenstein's surprise cavalry charge. It held, however, and Gustavus galloped to help rally the troops. In a confused cavalry engagement Gustavus was killed. Bernard took command.

At this juncture Pappenheim and his 8,000 men arrived, counterattacked, and again forced the Swedes back across the ditch. In the fray, Pappenheim was fatally wounded. Bernard drove Wallenstein's men back on Lützen, seizing the imperial artillery, clearing the ditch again, and drove Pappenheim's cavalry off. Wallenstein withdrew to Halle, leaving artillery and baggage behind. Wallenstein had about 12,000 casualties; the Swedes about 10,000.

1632, November 29. Death of Frederick. He died of the plague.

1633, March–April. The League of Heilbronn. This was established to defend the Protestant cause under the direction of Count **Axel Oxenstierna,** Chancellor of

Sweden, who had succeeded Gustavus in directing Swedish policy in Germany. He also renewed the Franco-Swedish alliance.

1633, September–December. Wallenstein's Bid for Power. Wallenstein, in Bohemia after futile overtures for peace to Arnim and to Bernard, defeated Thurn and conquered all of Silesia (October). While Bernard took Regensburg and occupied Bavaria, Wallenstein set up winter quarters in Bohemia, where he conspired to be King of Bohemia. Ferdinand, meanwhile, had again agreed to dismiss him.

1634, February 24. End of Wallenstein. His *coup d'état* failing, he fled with a few followers. Cornered at Eger, he was assassinated by his own officers, led by **Matthias Gallas.** King **Ferdinand** of Hungary (son of the emperor) was named to the nominal chief command of the imperial forces, with Gallas as field general.

1634, July. Campaign in Bavaria. Bernard and Swedish General **Gustavus Horn,** with about 20,000 men between them, moved from Augsburg toward the Bavarian-Bohemian border, hoping to divert Ferdinand and Gallas, who were moving toward Regensburg. The Protestant commanders took Landshut, but lost Regensburg and Donauwörth to Ferdinand and Gallas, who laid siege to Nördlingen.

1634. Appearance of the Cardinal-Infante. Youthful Prince **Ferdinand** of Spain, brother of **Philip IV,** was leading an army of 20,000 from Italy to Spain. Having been appointed a cardinal, Ferdinand was called the cardinal-infante (Cardinal-prince). He was ordered by Madrid to join the imperial army in Bavaria.

1634, September 2. Junction of the Cardinal-Infante and Ferdinand at Nördlingen. The combined army of these young royal cousins—both named Ferdinand—was 35,-000 strong. Horn and Bernard had arrived near Nördlingen with about 16,000 foot and 9,000 horse.

1634, September 6. Battle of Nördlingen. The Swedish-Protestant plan was poorly conceived and poorly executed. Horn, on the left, was to attack the imperial right, under King Ferdinand, entrenched on a commanding hill. Bernard, in the plain, was to contain the imperial left flank, comprising the Spanish contingent. Horn was at first successful, his veteran Swedes storming the entrenchments and capturing the imperial batteries. They fell into confusion, however, which was heightened when the captured powder magazine exploded. The unoccupied cardinal-infante turned most of his command to counter-

attack the hill. As the Swedes prepared to fire a volley, the alert Spanish infantry knelt and let the bullets pass over them, rising to fire themselves before the Swedes could reload. The Swedes were driven from the hill, Horn sending word to Bernard to cover his retirement across the valley. The Spanish and imperialists now charged Bernard's troops, who broke and fled. The Swedes were overwhelmed and almost annihilated; Horn was taken prisoner. The Protestant losses were 17,000 dead and wounded and 4,000 prisoners. The battle was a catastrophe for Sweden. Politically it forced Catholic Cardinal Richelieu to assume direction of the Protestant cause, bringing the struggle between Bourbon and Hapsburg into the open.

French Period, 1634–1648

1634, November 1. Treaty of Paris. France offered the German Protestants 12,000 men and half a million livres, in return for which Bernard and the Heilbronn League guaranteed the Catholic faith in Germany and ceded some lands in Alsace. France was not bound to enter the war openly, but no truce or peace was to be made without her.

1635, April 30. Treaty of Compiègne. Signed by Oxenstierna and Richelieu, Sweden recognized French ownership of the left bank of the Rhine from Breisach to Strasbourg. In return France accepted Sweden as an equal ally, and recognized Swedish control of Worms, Mainz, and Benfeld. France agreed to declare war on Spain and to make no separate peace.

1635, May 21. France Declares War on Spain. Meanwhile much of Sweden's forces were engaged in a war with Poland.

1635, May 30. Peace of Prague. A partial reconciliation between the Protestants and the Catholic-imperialists. From this point on, the war was primarily political rather than religious in nature.

1635, June–October. Richelieu's Strategy. His basic aim was to separate the Spanish Netherlands from Spanish Lombardy, with the related aim of eliminating all Spanish footholds in the intermediate areas of what is now eastern France and western Germany. French forces, totaling some 130,000 men, were divided into five main armies, having the following missions: (1) from Upper Alsace to invade and seize most of Spanish-controlled Franche-Comté; (2) to occupy Lorraine and repel Spanish invasion; (3) march across Switzerland to seize the key Valtelline Pass; (4) in alliance with Duke **Victor Amadeus of Savoy,** to invade Milan; (5) in alliance with Dutch **Frederick Henry of Orange,** to invade the Spanish Netherlands. The first 3 missions were successfully accomplished by French armies; the 2 allied efforts were failures. At the end of the year Bernard and his Protestant "Weimar Army," after vague maneuvering in the Rhine and Main valleys, were incorporated into the French armed forces.

1635, August–November. Swedish Operations in East Germany. The Saxons and other signatories of the Peace of Prague turned against the small Swedish army under **Johan Baner,** who completely outgeneraled his much more numerous opponents. Receiving reinforcements from Poland, he seized Domitz on the Elbe, then defeated the Saxons at the **Battle of Goldberg** (November).

1636. Invasions of France. Taking advantage of Richelieu's risky strategy of divergent forces and of the retreat of Frederick Henry back to Holland, and with western and central Germany relatively peaceful for the first time, the imperialists and Spanish decided to invade France. A Spanish and Bavarian army under the cardinal-infante drove through the scattered and outnumbered French forces in the northeast, while Gallas and the main imperial army marched westward into Burgundy. The Spanish captured Corbie, crossed the Somme, and advanced on Compiègne. Despite initial panic in Paris, Richelieu and **Louis XIII** raised a new—largely militia—army of 50,000 and rushed with it to Compiègne. The Spanish and Bavarians withdrew to the Netherlands, where Frederick Henry had resumed the offensive. Meanwhile Bernard's Weimar Army entrenched at Dijon and blocked the advance of Gallas, who, after attempting to go into winter quarters in Burgundy, was forced by desertions and French pressure to withdraw.

1636. Operations in Italy. A combined French-Savoyard army under Victor Amadeus and Marshal **Charles de Créqui** defeated the Spanish in the hard-fought **Battle of Tornavento** (June 22). But the duke refused to advance beyond the Ticino against Milan.

1636, October 4. Battle of Wittstock. Baner, with the assistance of Swedish Count Lennart Torstensson and some Scottish adventurers, decisively defeated the Saxons and their Protestant-Catholic imperialist allies in eastern Germany.

1637. Operations on the French Frontiers. A Spanish invading army crossed the Pyrenees from Catalonia into Languedoc, but was halted at the rugged fortress of **Leucate,** and then badly defeated and driven back into Spain by a relieving French army under Duke **Friedrich Hermann of Schomberg,** soldier of fortune. On the Netherlands frontier the French captured several important fortresses, largely because the Spanish were giving primary attention to Frederick Henry of Orange and attempting to relieve their beleaguered garrison of Breda. In the east, Bernard defeated Duke **Charles of Lorraine** on the Saône River (June) and advanced into Alsace, still held by imperial forces under Duke **Ottavio Piccolomini.** Piccolomini, however, was joined by a Bavarian army under **Johann von Werth,** who had cleared French detachments out of the Rhine Valley, and Bernard withdrew.

1637, February 15. Death of Ferdinand II. He was succeeded by his son and heir, Ferdinand III, King of Hungary.

1637, May. Swedish Advance in Germany. Armies under Baner and Torstensson reoccupied Brandenburg and threatened Leipzig and Thuringia. Their advance was halted by the arrival of Gallas' imperial army in Saxony.

1637, October 10. Fall of Breda. Frederick Henry, after a year-long siege, regained the city, which had been held by the Spanish for 12 years.

1638. French Frontier Operations. These were generally unsuccessful, save in Alsace (see below). The French were driven back in Italy and repulsed in the Netherlands; a large army under inept Prince **Henry II of Condé** advanced from Bayonne with Madrid as its objective, but was halted and repulsed at the small frontier fortress of **Fuenterrabia.**

1638. Swedish Operations in Eastern Germany. Imperial forces under Bavarian

General **Godfroid von Geleen** forced Baner's outnumbered Swedish army to withdraw from the Elbe to the Oder, where he expected reinforcements under Count **Karl Gustav Wrangel.** Instead, he was cut off by the main imperial army under Gallas. Barely escaping the trap, he joined Wrangel in Pomerania, where he spent a cold, miserable winter, which seriously reduced the strength of his army.

1638, February 28–March 1. Operations in Alsace; Battle of Rheinfelden. Bernard with his Weimar Army moved to cross the Rhine at Rheinfelden, near Basel. He and his advanced guard were cut off from their main army, west of the river, by a surprise attack of imperialists under Count **Savelli** and Werth. Bernard withdrew, crossed back at Laufenburg, and joined the rest of his army. Then he marched on Rheinfelden, breaking up and defeating Savelli's forces, which were attempting to defend it. Werth was captured.

1638, June–December. Siege of Breisach. Bernard, joined by a force under **Henri de La Tour d'Auvergne de Turenne,** invested the city and drove off imperial attempts to relieve it. After eating all dogs, cats, and rats, the city surrendered (December 17), giving to the French the key to the Rhine.

1639. French Frontier Operations. On the Netherlands frontier the French captured the fortress of Hesdin, but a French army investing **Thionville** was smashed by Piccolomini (June 7). Condé was again unable to make any progress into Spain, but an invasion of Roussillon made some progress. French forces in north Italy, under the Duke of **Harcourt** (Cadet la Perle), were more successful. Although Savoy had now joined the imperialists, Harcourt defeated an imperial-Savoyard army at the **Battle of the Route de Quiers.** Turenne served under Harcourt in this campaign.

1639. Swedish Operations in Eastern Germany. Baner, reinforced, advanced into Saxony, Gallas retiring in front of him. The Swedes crossed the Elbe, defeated John George with a Saxon-imperial army at the **Battle of Chemnitz** (April 14), and overran western Saxony. Baner then invaded Bohemia, but was repulsed in an effort to capture Prague. He lived off the countryside, further devastating the re-gion, retiring into the Erz Gebirge Mountains for the winter.

1639, February–July. Operations in Alsace. Bernard, having conquered Alsace, demanded possession with the title of Duke of Alsace. Richelieu refused. Bernard died of a fever as he was preparing to march to join Baner. His army was then commanded by Count **Jean de Guébriant.**

1639, October 21. Battle of the Downs. A strong Spanish fleet under **António de Oquendo** was destroyed by a Dutch squadron under **Maarten Tromp** (see p. 570).

1640. Minor Operations. Louis XIII captured Arras (August 8). In Italy, Harcourt with 10,000 men defeated 20,000 under Spanish General **Leganez** at the **Battle of Casale** (April 29). He then besieged another Spanish army in Turin, which was besieging the French garrison of the citadel. Leganez's reinforced army in turn tried to invest Harcourt, resulting in a situation unique in military history. Harcourt repulsed Leganez (July 11), then relieved the citadel and captured the city. In Germany, Baner was relatively inactive. Spain was in serious straits due to revolts in Catalonia and in Portugal (see p. 572).

1640, September 13–1641, October 10. Diet of Regensburg. Ferdinand, anxious for peace without concessions, tried to line up support from all the German princes. It was agreed that representatives should be chosen to negotiate on the basis of the Peace of Prague and a general amnesty.

1641. Revolts in Spain and France. These prevented major operations, though Harcourt continued to be successful in Italy. French troops in Catalonia assisted the rebels.

1641, May 20. Death of Baner. Lennart Torstensson took command of the Swedish army in Germany (November).

1642. French Operations. Unrest and revolt in France and Spain still handicapped the principal contestants. The Spanish had slightly the best of the continued frontier fortress sieges and countersieges on the Flemish border. The French had a similar advantage in northern Italy. Louis XIII led an army which conquered Roussillon on the Spanish frontier. Richelieu crushed a Spanish-inspired conspiracy in Paris, while the French· in Catalonia under Marshal **de la Motte Houden-court** helped the insurgents hold the province in a successful campaign culminated by a victory over Leganez at **Lérida.**

1642. Swedish Operations. In the spring Torstensson crossed the Elbe and besieged Leipzig, at the same time overrunning much of Saxony. An imperial army under Archduke **Leopold William** (brother of Ferdinand III) and Piccolomini approached, forcing Torstensson to raise the siege and retire northward toward Breitenfeld (November 1).

1642, November 2. Second Battle of Breitenfeld. While the imperial army was forming up under the cover of a cannonade (featuring one of the first uses of chain shot), Torstensson led a cavalry charge against the imperial left, which was smashed before it could form. The remainder of the Swedish army had meanwhile advanced, but was unable to gain any success until Torstensson and his cavalry hit the exposed left flank of the infantry of the imperial center. The imperial infantry was soon driven off the field, leaving isolated the cavalry of their right wing, initially successful against the Swedish left. Many of these were surrounded and captured; the remainder fled.

1642–1643. Deaths of Richelieu and Louis XIII. (See p. 560.) Before he died, Richelieu appointed the 21-year-old Duc **Louis d'Enghien,** son of the Prince of Condé, commander of the northeastern armies.

1643, May. Invasion of France. A Spanish-imperial army from the Netherlands advanced through the Ardennes toward Paris. The invaders, some 27,000 strong, under **Francisco de Mello,** stopped to besiege Rocroi. Enghien, now barely 22, advanced with his army of 23,000 to defend the line of the Meuse. Finding the Spanish besieging Rocroi, and knowing that Spanish reinforcements of some 6,000 were en route to join them, Enghien decided to attack at once (May 18). The only approach to the town was through a defile between woods and marshes, which the Spanish had failed to block. Against the advice of elderly subordinates, Enghien marched through the defile and in the late afternoon took up position on a ridge overlooking the besieged city. The Spanish immediately formed up between the French and Rocroi. The armies bivouacked in their lines through the night.

1643, May 19. Battle of Rocroi. Shortly after dawn Enghien attacked, personally leading a successful cavalry charge against the Spanish left. Sending some squadrons in pursuit, Enghien led the remainder of the cavalry against the exposed left flank of the Spanish infantry. Meanwhile, the cavalry of the French left flank, against Enghien's orders, attacked the Spanish right, and were repulsed. Counterattacking Spanish cavalry scattered the French horse, but were halted by the French reserve. Enghien, learning of the disaster on his left, swung behind the Spanish lines, then cut his way directly through the rear center of the Spanish infantry to attack the rear of the Spanish cavalry facing his reserve. These horsemen also scattered, leaving the 18,000 Spanish infantry on the field, somewhat shaken from the unexpected developments, but still the most formidable foot troops in the world. Twice the French attacked the Spanish squares and twice were repulsed. Enghien now assembled all of his guns and the captured Spanish guns, and began to hammer the Spanish infantry mercilessly. The outcome inevitable, the Spanish asked for quarter; Enghien and his staff advanced between the lines to receive their surrender. But some of the Spanish infantry, thinking this was the beginning of another charge, opened fire at him. Enraged at this apparent treachery, the French army hurled itself at the squares, completely overwhelming the defenders and cutting down all whom they encountered. The Spanish army was virtually annihilated; 8,000 were killed, 7,000 captured. French casualties were about 4,000.

1643, June 18–23. Capture of Thionville. Enghien, anxious to secure Lorraine and the Rhine Valley, besieged and captured this important fortress. Ferdinand began to explore peace possibilities.

1643, August–November. Operations in Swabia. The Weimar army, under Marshal Guébriant, crossed the Rhine and advanced through the Black Forest into Württemburg. Guébriant was killed in the successful siege of **Rattweil** (October). He was succeeded by General **Josias von**

Rantzau, who was defeated and captured by an imperial army under Baron **Franz von Mercy** and General von Werth on the upper Danube at the **Battle of Tuttlingen** (November 24). Turenne succeeded to command of the army and retreated to Alsace.

1643. Swedish Operations. Torstensson ravaged Bohemia and Moravia without any effective interference from the imperial army under Gallas. On outbreak of war between Denmark and Sweden, Torstensson hastily retreated to the Baltic, and spent the winter in Holstein.

1644. Early French Operations. Save for some fighting around Dunkirk, there was little activity on the northern frontier. Italy was also quiet. In Spain the French were driven from Lérida. Along the Rhine, Turenne, commanding the old Weimar Army, crossed the Rhine (May) and advanced into the Black Forest, where he was opposed by a numerically superior Bavarian army under von Mercy. He withdrew to Breisach, leaving a garrison in Freiburg, which was besieged by Mercy (June). Turenne awaited reinforcements under Enghien.

1644, August 2. Junction of Enghien and Turenne. Enghien assumed command over the combined army of 17,000 men at Breisach. Mercy also had 17,000. Meanwhile Freiburg had surrendered.

1644, August 3. First Battle of Freiburg. Enghien attempted a double envelopment of Mercy's entrenchments, Turenne making a long march to hit the Bavarian rear. In a bitterly contested fight, the stubborn Bavarians were finally forced out of their entrenchments, leaving the field to the exhausted and severely depleted French. Mercy, having suffered fewer casualties, immediately entrenched again.

1644, August 5. Second Battle of Freiburg. In an equally bitterly contested struggle, the Bavarians repulsed the French. Both sides suffered heavy losses, those of the French again being greater.

1644, August 10. Third Battle of Freiburg. Enghein attempted a turning movement, sending Turenne and most of the army by mountain paths to get behind Mercy. Suspecting the French intention, Mercy withdrew from his entrenchments just before Turenne arrived. Covered by a sharp rear-guard action, the Bavarians retreated in good order, leaving the Rhine Valley to the French. Despite loss of half of his army, Enghien (with excellent help from Turenne) had gained another great victory. Leaving Turenne and the Weimar Army at Speyer, Enghien methodically captured the fortresses of the middle Rhine Valley.

1644. Swedish Operations. Torstensson completely outmaneuvered the Danish and imperial armies under Gallas. The discouraged Gallas retreated into Bohemia, closely followed by Torstensson.

1644. Congress of Münster. Representatives of the warring powers met in an effort to achieve peace on the basis of preliminary diplomatic arrangements begun by Ferdinand.

1645. Swedish Operations. Torstensson, advancing toward Prague, was intercepted by a force of imperialists and Bavarians under von Werth, which he decisively defeated in the **Battle of Jankau** (March 6). But the invaders (under Wrangel, who relieved Torstensson) were held up by a 5-month-long siege at Brünn and, unable to support themselves in impoverished Bohemia, they finally withdrew to Hesse, followed by Archduke Leopold.

1645, May 2. Battle of Mergentheim. Turenne, invading central Germany, was surprised and badly defeated by Mercy. He withdrew toward the Rhine, as Enghien and a Swedish contingent rushed to reinforce him.

1645, August 3. Battle of Nördlingen (or Allerheim). The combined armies of Turenne and Enghien, invading Bavaria, won a costly victory from Mercy, who was killed in the desperate struggle.

1646, January–July. Preliminary Maneuvering. In Hesse the rival armies of Wrangel and Leopold cautiously maneuvered around each other, most of their energies spent in search for food and forage for men and horses from the desolate, denuded countryside. Meanwhile Turenne, not wishing to risk further losses, decided on a war of maneuver.

1646, August. Turenne and Wrangel Meet. Leopold's movement to the southwest in the Rhine-Main Valley, to seek food for the imperial army, gave Turenne an opportunity. Secretly and rapidly he marched down the Rhine to Wesel, then southeast to join Wrangel near Giessen

(August 10). Leopold, fearful that the larger allied army, 19,000 strong, would cut him off from central Germany, fell back to Fulda.

1646, September–November. Invasion of Bavaria. The Franco-Swedish army bypassed Leopold, marching southeast into Bavaria and on to Munich, laying waste the countryside. Bavaria, which had recovered from the devastation suffered early in the war, was again ravaged mercilessly until Maximilian, disgusted by lack of imperial support, sued for an armistice, resulting in the **Truce of Ulm** (signed March, 1647).

1646. Other Operations. In Flanders, the French, under **Gaston of Orléans** and Enghien, took several frontier fortresses, including Dunkirk. In Italy, the French attempted to advance into Tuscany with little success. In Spain, Harcourt was outmaneuvered by Leganez in efforts to take Lérida and by the end of the year was replaced by Enghien, who had succeeded to the title of **Prince of Condé,** or "the Great Condé."

1647. Operations in Germany. The increasing barrenness of the country made it more difficult for the armies to survive. Wrangel returned to Hesse, raided unsuccessfully into Bohemia, and retired to the Baltic coast. Turenne, ordered to Luxembourg to help repel a Spanish invasion from the Netherlands, was faced with a mutiny in the Weimar Army, which he suppressed after a brief fight; he disbanded the army, then moved to Luxembourg with his French troops. Late in the year Maximilian again made peace with the emperor and put his armies in the field against the French and Swedes, but too late for any action before winter.

1647. Other Operations. In the Flanders-Meuse area, save for one abortive Spanish attempt at invasion, the war of sieges continued. French forces in Italy, under Marshal **du Plessis-Praslin** (Duke César de Choiseul), won the **Battle of the Oglio** against the Spanish (July 4), but gained little from the victory. In Spain, Condé besieged Lérida, but was repulsed and had to withdraw toward the coast. Disgusted by lack of support from home and from the Catalonians, he resigned his command and returned to France.

1648, January 30. The Peace of Münster. End of the war between Spain and Holland (see p. 570), first result of the drawn-out negotiations begun in 1643. The other negotiations continued while the war went on in Germany.

1648, May. Invasion of Bavaria. Turenne and Wrangel again joined in Hesse and marched on into Bavaria, the imperial-Bavarian army of 30,000 under Marshal **Peter Melander** retreating before them to the Danube. The allies destroyed and burned as they advanced.

1648, May 17. Battle of Zusmarshausen. The allies caught up with the imperial rear guard and virtually destroyed it. 14 miles west of Augsburg. Melander was killed and the remainder of his army retreated in confusion. The allies continued on to the Inn, where they were halted by the reorganized imperialists, now under able Piccolomini. A flood of the Inn halted operations for several weeks.

1648, June–October. Swedish Invasion of Bohemia. Count **Hans Cristoph Königsmarck** led an army into Bohemia and besieged Prague. Piccolomini was withdrawn from Bavaria to protect imperial lands from this more immediate threat. Königsmarck continued the siege, driving off imperial relief efforts, and was preparing to assault the city in late October.

1648, July–September. Advance to Munich. The withdrawal of Piccolomini permitted Turenne and Wrangel to invest the Bavarian capital. But with peace negotiations close to culmination, Cardinal **Giulio Mazarin** of France (Richelieu's successor) ordered the allied army to withdraw into Swabia.

1648, August 10. Battle of Lens. Condé again commanded the northern army. He decisively defeated Archduke Leopold William in a final Hapsburg-Spanish attempt to invade France through Artois. Spanish military ascendancy was ended north of the Pyrenees.

1648, October 24. Peace of Westphalia. The Empire and France signed the **Treaty of Münster;** the Empire, Sweden, and the German Protestants signed the **Treaty of Osnabrück.** (The war between France and Spain continued; see p. 561.) Sweden received an indemnity and substantial Baltic coastal territories. France received

Alsace, most of Lorraine, and the right to garrison Philippsburg on the east bank of the Rhine. In addition to minor territorial changes among the German principalities, there was a general amnesty, and the sovereign rights of the German princes were recognized by the empire. Catholic and Protestant states were given complete equality in the Empire, with ownership of ecclesiastical states set as of 1624. Both treaties were guaranteed by France and Sweden.

WAR OF THE GRAND ALLIANCE, OR
WAR OF THE LEAGUE OF AUGSBURG, 1688–1697

By 1680, France under Louis XIV threatened to secure hegemony over the continent. Her population, approaching 19 million, was 3 times that of England or of Spain and nearly 8 times that of the United Provinces. The organizational reforms of Louvois, Minister of War, had created the most powerful army in Europe. Under the administrative and financial genius of Colbert (see p. 533), the navy was one of the three major powers in the Atlantic and, after the withdrawal of the English from Tangier (1684), was supreme in the Mediterranean. Unlike Holland and Spain, France's economy was not dependent upon overseas commerce. Thus, Anglo-Dutch efforts to apply economic pressures on France failed.

Louis's obviously expansionist objectives, particularly his efforts to gain influence over Spain, had aroused widespread fears. The Emperor **Leopold,** completing a successful war against Turkey, was strengthening the imperial position in Central Europe to prevent French encroachment. The Protestant princes of Germany (notably **Frederick William** of Brandenburg) had begun aligning themselves with **William of Orange** of Holland in opposition to Louis. And in England, William's supporters were maneuvering to overthrow **James II,** a friend of Louis's.

Louis's revocation of the Edict of Nantes had made it easy for William to establish an anti-French coalition (League of Augsburg; July 9, 1686). Two years later, Louis provoked the League into preparation for war by claiming the Palatinate and meddling in the election of the Bishop of Cologne. Almost simultaneously, a revolution in England brought William of Orange to the English throne.

The war was fought mostly in the Netherlands, and was distinguished by the military incompetence of William of Orange and the naval myopia of Louis. Combat on land generally assumed the form of siege warfare. Naval engagements and maritime policy were essentially reflexes of the campaigns on land. After 9 years of inconclusive combat, economic and political pressures led the antagonists to conclude peace. Though French influence had increased on land, and English at sea, the basic struggles of Bourbon vs. Hapsburg and England vs. France were still undecided. The principal events were:

1688, September 25. Invasion of Germany. Louis, to encourage Turkey to continue its war with Leopold, sent a French army under the Dauphin into Germany before the German princes could be united in an effective anti-French coalition. Employing Vauban's techniques (see pp. 524–525), the French besieged and captured Philippsburg (October 29). This aggressive thrust, and subsequent devastation of the Rhine territory, consolidated German support of the Emperor.

1688, November–December. Revolution in England. (See p. 558.) The accession of William III immediately reversed England's pro-French foreign policy.

1688–1689. Devastation of the Palatinate. To economize forces, Louis evacuated the Palatinate; to prevent the region being used as a base of operations against France, he ordered it devastated. Heidelberg, Mannheim, Speyer, and Worms were destroyed.

1689, April. Louis Declares War on Spain.

1689, May 1. Anglo-French Naval Skirmish at Bantry Bay. Thirty-nine French men-of-war, under Marquis **François de Châteaurenault,** clashed inconclusively with Admiral Earl **Arthur Herbert of Torrington's** 22 sail at Bantry Bay (Ireland).

1689, May 7. England and France Declare War.

1689, May 12. Treaty of Vienna. Alliance between Holland and the Empire against France. England, Spain, Savoy, Brandenburg, Saxony, Hanover, and Bavaria soon subscribed to the provisions, to establish the "Grand Alliance."

1689, August 25. Battle of Walcourt. In Flanders, Prince **George Frederick of Waldeck,** commanding an army of 35,000 (including an English contingent of 8,000 led by **John Churchill, Earl of Marlborough**), defeated a French army under Duke **Louis de C. d'Humières** and Duke **Claude de Villars.** D'Humières was soon replaced by Marshal François de Luxembourg.

1690, July 1. Battle of Fleurus. In a bold double envelopment, using his cavalry superbly, Luxembourg with 45,000 men defeated Waldeck's English, Spanish, and German force of 37,000. The French lost 2,500 killed; the allies lost 6,000 dead and 8,000 prisoners. Luxembourg wished to exploit the victory by striking deep into Holland and Germany, but Louis ordered him to keep abreast of other French armies maneuvering on the Meuse and Moselle.

1690, July 10. Naval Battle of Beachy Head. Admiral de Tourville with 75 ships decisively defeated Torrington's Anglo-Dutch fleet of 59 sail. Torrington, who had wished to avoid battle against a superior force in order to maintain a "fleet in being," had been ordered to fight by the Admiralty. The allies lost 12 warships. Subsequently, Torrington was tried; he was unanimously acquitted, but was dismissed from his command. Louis rejected recommendations that he should exploit the victory by sending a powerful army to Ireland and by pressing vigorously at sea for control of the Channel. This was the worst military decision he ever made. Britain and Holland feverishly built up naval strength unhindered.

1690, August–September. French Advance in Savoy. At the **Battle of Staffarda**

(Piedmont), Duke **Victor Amadeus II** of Savoy was defeated by a French army commanded by **Nicolas de Catinat** (August 18). The French advanced through Savoy with little resistance.

1690, October. Recapture of Belgrade by the Turks. (See p. 583.) This eliminated the possibility of an early peace on the eastern front; Leopold's main army remained tied down on the Danube.

1691, April 8. Capture of Mons. In Louis's presence, Luxembourg stormed Mons. William, operating ineptly from Brussels, failed to interfere. Luxembourg soon took Hal (June).

1691, July. Death of Louvois.

1691, September 20. Battle of Leuze. After a rapid night march, Luxembourg's cavalry routed Waldeck's army as it prepared to retire to winter quarters.

1691. Other Operations. In Piedmont, Catinat continued to progress. In Spain, the French Army of Catalonia, commanded by Duke **Jules de Noailles,** captured Ripoli and Urgel (September).

1692, May 25–June 5. Siege of Namur. It was taken by Vauban, under Louis's direct command, and supported by Luxembourg. William, attempting to relieve the besieged Dutch-Spanish-German garrison, was hampered by persistent rains and the flooding of the Mehaigne (a tributary of the Meuse).

1692, May 29–June 3. Naval Battle of La Hogue (Barfleur). De Tourville's fleet of 44 men-of-war and 38 fireboats, mounting 3,240 guns, engaged an allied force of 63 English and 36 Dutch warships and 38 fireboats, mounting 6,736 guns, under the command of Admirals **Edward Russell** and **George Rooke.** Unfavorable winds had prevented the French Toulon fleet from making a planned juncture with de Tourville. Despite inferiority in numbers, the French attacked and were decisively defeated, losing 15 men-of-war. This was the decisive battle of the war. Louis abandoned plans for an invasion of England by 30,000 troops under Marshal **Marquis B. C. de Bellefonds.** Henceforth, England dominated the Channel—although French privateers, like **Jean Bart,** inflicted severe losses on English shipping.

1692, July 24–August 3. Battle of Steenkerke. After unsuccessful attempts to engage Luxembourg throughout June and

July, William attacked the main French force entrenched at Steenkerke. The allies, after initial success, were beaten back by French counterattacks. William ordered withdrawal under cover provided by the British Guards. Each army lost about 3,000 men.

1693, June 27–28. Naval Battle of Lagos. Off Lagos, de Tourville intercepted an Anglo-Dutch convoy proceeding toward Smyrna. He defeated Rooke's protective squadron, then destroyed nearly 100 of the 400 allied vessels.

1693, July 29. Battle of Neerwinden (Landen). William, entrenched near Landen with 70,000 troops, dispatched 20,000 to support Liége, which was threatened by de Noailles. Luxembourg with 80,000 men attacked the allied position. After 3 unsuccessful assaults, the French cavalry penetrated the defenses; William's army was routed. The French suffered 9,000 casualties, the allies 19,000. Again Luxembourg failed to pursue, or William might have been forced to sue for peace.

1693, October 4. Battle of Marsaglia. Catinat's French army again decisively defeated the Duke of Savoy. He advanced into Piedmont.

1693, October 11. Capture of Charleroi. The French consolidated control over the Sambre southwest of Namur.

1693. Other Operations. In Catalonia the French took Rosas. The allied cause suffered another setback when an Austrian attack on Belgrade was repulsed (October; see p. 586).

1694, May–August. Operations in Catalonia. De Noailles captured Palomas, Gerona, Ostabich, and Castel-Follit. Supported by de Tourville's fleet, he besieged Barcelona.

1694, June–November. The English Fleet in the Mediterranean. In order to cut the French interior lines by land and sea, Russell, reappointed commander after an Admiralty purge, sailed for the Mediterranean (June). The arrival of the English fleet caused the French navy to withdraw to Toulon harbor; the army raised its siege of Barcelona.

1694, July. The English Bombard Dieppe and Le Havre.

1695, January. Death of Luxembourg. The undefeated French general was succeeded by the incompetent Duke François de N. de Villeroi.

1695, June–September. William's First Successful Campaign. He captured Dixmude and Huy (June). He then besieged Namur, manned by 14,000 troops under Duke **Louis de Boufflers.** After 2 months the French surrendered (September 1). The economics of the campaign were more significant than its uninspired military character; it was financed by the proceeds of the newly established Bank of England (1694).

1696, Spring. French Invasion Threat. The Mediterranean fleet, under Sir George Rooke (he succeeded Russell, September, 1695), was recalled to England early in the year when the appearance of Marquis François L. R. de Châteaurenault's fleet near Brest stimulated fears of invasion. This diversion enabled de Tourville to proceed from Toulon to Brest, increasing the apparent threat to England.

1696, June. Amphibious Failure at Camaret Bay. A landing near Brest, under English General **Thomas Talmash,** found the French prepared, and failed completely.

1696, June. Treaty of Turin. The Duke of Savoy reached an accord with Louis, who returned all conquests. This neutralized Italy and enabled Catinat to proceed to the northern front with his 30,000 soldiers.

1696, Summer–Fall. William Immobilized in Flanders. The French, reinforced by troops from Savoy, thwarted William's inept offensive efforts. Discouraged, he began secret peace negotiations with Louis (1696–1697).

1697, May–August. French Successes in the Mediterranean. With the English fleet gone, the French navy raided Cartagena (May) and seized Barcelona (August). Leopold decided to seek peace.

1697, September 20–October 30. Treaty of Ryswick. France, Spain, England, Holland, and the German principalities agreed to restore all territories acquired since 1679 (**Treaties of Nijmegen,** see pp. 566–567). Significantly—in anticipation of his Spanish ambitions—Louis surrendered fortifications at Mons, Luxembourg, and Courtrai to Spain and permitted Holland to assume control of vital strongholds in the Spanish Netherlands (for example, Namur and Ypres). In the following month, Leopold and Louis arrived at a similar accord (October 30).

WESTERN EUROPE

ENGLAND, SCOTLAND, AND IRELAND

The Early Stuarts, 1603–1642

1603–1625. Reign of James I. James VI of Scotland, son of Mary Queen of Scots.

1604, October 24. Unification of Britain. The union of the crowns of England and Scotland eliminated internal frontiers and, consequently, a primary need for a standing army; this reduction of the crown's forces augmented Parliamentary power at the expense of royal authority.

1624–1625. English Participation in Thirty Years' War. James decided to assist Frederick in the Thirty Years' War (see p. 536). James also agreed to provide financial support to the operations of Christian IV of Denmark in Germany. Ernst Mansfeld, a German mercenary, led a small English force of 1,200 men to Holland. There the expedition collapsed, suffering severe hardships as a result of inadequate training, supplies, and equipment. Spain considered dispatch of this expedition as an act of war.

1625–1649. Reign of Charles I.

1625, October 8. Failure at Cádiz. An ill-equipped force of 8,000, under Viscount **Edward Cecil of Wimbledon,** was repulsed.

1626–1630, April 24. Anglo-French War. The **Duke of Buckingham's** expedition to the **Isle of Ré,** near La Rochelle, to support Huguenot forces besieged by Richelieu was a fiasco (1627). Since Parliament refused to appropriate funds, Charles secured a forced loan to finance the French campaigns and to satisfy his debt to Christian IV. Buckingham was assassinated while preparing a second expedition against the French (1628).

1628, May. Petition of Right. A parliamentary list of demands and grievances, including protests against royal taxation without Parliamentary assent, the imposition of martial law during times of peace, and the mandatory billeting of troops in private homes.

1630, November 5. Peace with France and Spain.

1639. First Bishops' War. Scottish unrest, stemming from the restoration of church lands (1625) and efforts to introduce an Anglican liturgy into Scottish Presbyterian services, erupted in rioting. Insurgents seized Edinburgh Castle. Charles led an army to the vicinity of Berwick; however, continuing lack of funds, and Scottish military competence (many had fought under Gustavus Adolphus), compelled Charles to agree to a compromise settlement in **Pacification of Dunse** (June 18).

1640. Second Bishops' War. With hostilities renewed in Scotland, Charles convened the "Short Parliament" (April–May, 1640) to secure financial support. When the Commons refused, Charles dissolved Parliament. The Scots defeated Charles's troops at **Newburn** (August 28), then penetrated Northumberland and seized Durham. The **Treaty of Ripon** brought hostilities to a halt (November).

1640–1660. The Long Parliament. Charles, again in need of funds to pay his own army and the Scots, reassembled Parliament (November 3). The presence of Scottish forces in northern England, the crown's pressing monetary needs, and riots in London enhanced the power of Commons. Charles acquiesced in the execution of his Lord Lieutenant of Ireland, the **Earl of Strafford** (see below), and passage of the Triennial Act (May, 1641) permitting Parliament to assemble every 3 years without royal initiative.

1641, October. Outbreak of the Irish War. Irish opposition to Strafford's policies and those of his successors culminated in confused armed rebellion which continued intermittently for nearly a decade (see p. 553).

1641–1642. Prelude to the Great Rebellion. The crown, in desperate financial straits, required forces to cope with the Irish rising. Puritan dissidents in Parliament, like **John Pym** and **John Hampden,** feared the likely consequences of rejuvenated royal power in the form of a standing army. They secured passage of the **Grand Remonstrance** (December 1), a compilation of grievances spanning Charles's reign. Charles's inept attempt to arrest 5 leaders of Commons (January 3) prompted legislation providing for Parliamentary control of the armed forces and the ouster of ecclesiastics from the Lords. Charles, who had hastily established a military base of operations at York, rejected the bills (March). Parliament reiterated its earlier demands and also demanded Parliamentary consent to the appointment of officers commanding fortifications (June 2). Parliament established a force of 20,000 infantrymen and 4,000 cavalrymen under Earl **Robert Devereux of Essex** (July). Charles began to raise an army at Nottingham (August 22).

The First Civil War, 1642–1646

Royalist and Parliamentary partisanship in the Great Rebellion cut across social, economic, religious, and family lines. The aristocracy, the peasants, and the Anglican establishment in general supported Charles; the emergent middle and commercial classes and the navy supported Parliament. The north and west tended to be Royalists; the south, the Midlands, and London inclined toward Parliament. At the commencement of the war, Parliament's army was somewhat larger and better equipped and organized. Both forces suffered from the lack of experienced troops (however, both possessed experienced officers, many of whom had served in the continental war); they were plagued by the reluctance of local militia to leave their home grounds; most critically, both suffered from a dearth of weapons and material. (The navy's allegiance to Parliament prevented Queen **Henrietta Maria** from shipping supplies for the Royalists from the Continent.) On both sides, superfluous garrisons proliferated; supplies proved inadequate, pay tardy, and recruiting (from 1643, impressment) insufficient. The principal events were:

1642, October. Emergence of Oliver Cromwell. Parliament appointed him to command a military association of 6 counties.

1642, October 23. Battle of Edgehill. Charles with 11,000 men clashed with Essex, who had about 13,000. Prince **Rupert,** son of the Elector Palatine, beginning his dashing career as a leader of the superior Royalist cavalry, drove the Parliamentary cavalry off the field, then pursued. Essex, rallying his forces, counterattacked successfully, but was forced to withdraw when Rupert and the Royalist horse finally returned to the field at nightfall. Essex then fell back toward London. Charles moved his headquarters to Oxford.

1642, October 29. Charles Marches on London.

1642, November 13. Battle of Turnham Green. Following a skirmish at Brentford (November 12), Essex, reinforced by London militia to about 20,000, faced the king. After a brief skirmish Charles withdrew to Oxford.

1643, March–September. Widespread Inconsequential Strife. Oliver Cromwell had the best of a cavalry engagement at **Grantham,** east of Nottingham (March). The Cavaliers were successful in Yorkshire under Duke **William Cavendish of Newcastle** (April–July). Royalists under **Sir Ralph Hopton** were successful against **Sir William Waller** at **Stratton** in Cornwall (May), at **Lansdowne** near Bath (July 5), and **Roundway Down,** near Devizes (July 13). Rupert won a victory at **Chalgrove Field** near Oxford (June 18), and captured Bristol (July 26). Charles was repulsed from Gloucester (August 5–September 10).

1643, August 10. Conscription. Parliament empowered local authorities to impress troops. The Royalists followed suit.

1643, September 20. First Battle of Newbury. Charles, having retreated from Gloucester to Newbury in the face of Essex's advance, turned to fight an inconclusive engagement. He then returned to Oxford.

1643, September 25. The Solemn League and Covenant. To enlist Scottish military support, Parliament agreed to protect Presbyterianism in Scotland, with virtual establishment of Presbyterianism throughout Britain.

1644, January. Participation of Scottish Rebels. A Scottish army (18,000 infantrymen and 3,000 cavalrymen) under Earl

Alexander Leslie of Leven crossed the River Tweed.

1644, January. "The Cessation" in Ireland. Charles concluded a temporary peace. with the Irish confederation, permitting him to withdraw his troops from Ireland and to recruit Irish Royalists as reinforcements for his cause in England.

1644, January 25. Battle of Nantwich. Irish Royalists and local troops laid siege to Nantwich, Parliament's only stronghold in Cheshire. Parliamentary reinforcements, led by Sir **Thomas Fairfax,** routed the Irish, almost half of whom joined the victorious force.

1644, February–April. Operations in the North. The Scottish army advanced into northern England, ending Cavalier supremacy in Yorkshire. Newcastle marched to stop them (February). Taking advantage of Newcastle's move to the north, Fairfax defeated his lieutenant, Lord **Bellasis,** at the **Battle of Selby,** thus threatening Newcastle's rear (April 11).

1644, March–June. Operations in the South. Waller finally defeated his rival Hopton at the **Battle of Cheriton** (March 29) near Dover. Charles outmaneuvered Essex and Waller, inflicting a sharp defeat on Waller at **Cropredy Bridge,** north of Oxford (June 6).

1644, April–June. Siege of York. Newcastle moved from Durham to York (April 18), where he was besieged by the Scots and Fairfax. Charles ordered Rupert to proceed from Shrewsbury with reinforcements (May 16). Rupert's advance caused the Parliamentarians to abandon the siege and to march to the vicinity of Long Marston in an attempt to head off the Royalists. There they were joined by a Roundhead army under Earl **Edward Montagu of Manchester,** with Cromwell second in command. Newcastle joined Rupert and the joint force (under Rupert's command) proceeded to Marston Moor, 7 miles west of York.

1644, July 2. Battle of Marston Moor. Both armies had approximately 7,000 cavalry; however, Parliament had about 20,000 infantry to the Royalist 11,000. Manchester, Fairfax, and Leven jointly commanded the Parliamentary-Scottish army, with Manchester evidently "first among equals." Cromwell, commanding his "Ironsides" and a Scottish force, defeated part of Rupert's cavalry on the Royalist right. On the left, however, Lord **George Goring's** horse turned back Fairfax and smashed the Scottish infantry, but became disordered in the process. Cromwell, swinging his disciplined Ironsides to their right, routed Goring, then helped the remaining Parliamentary infantry crush the Royalist center. The Royalists lost nearly 3,000 dead, the Roundheads nearly 2,000. The defeat led to the capitulation of Royalist northern strongholds like York (July 16) and Newcastle (October 16). Rupert, with 6,000 survivors, escaped through Lancashire to rejoin Charles in the south.

1644, July–September. Charles's Successes in the South. After Cropredy Bridge, Charles took the initiative from his opponents. He suddenly turned southwest, where Essex was attempting to consolidate Parliamentary control. Essex, trapped at **Lostwithiel** in Cornwall, escaped with his cavalry, leaving 8,000 infantry and his artillery to surrender (September 2). Southwest England was held for the Royalists. However, Manchester and Cromwell now joined Waller to threaten Charles's hold on south-central England (September–October).

1644, September 1–1645, September 13. Operations in Scotland. Royalist Marquis **James Graham of Montrose** led several highland clans in a series of successful actions (**Tippermuir,** September 1; **Inverlochy,** February 2; **Auldearn,** May 9; **Alford,** July 2; and **Kilsyth,** August 15), eventually securing most of Scotland for Charles. However, following Naseby (see below), a Parliamentary expedition under General **David Leslie** crushed the Stuarts at **Philiphaugh** (September 13, 1645). Montrose fled the country and the Royalist cause collapsed.

1644, October 27. Second Battle of Newbury. Charles, with about 10,000 men, met Manchester, Waller, and Cromwell, with about 22,000. The inability of the numerically superior Parliamentary forces to coordinate their attacks allowed Charles to retreat to Oxford after an inconclusive battle. Manchester refused to pursue.

1645, January–February. Treaty of Uxbridge. A brief truce, terminated when

Charles rejected a set of Parliamentary proposals.

1645, January–March. The New Model Army. Meanwhile Cromwell, who had long felt the need for major military reform, had urged Parliament to adopt a "frame or model of the whole militia," a proposal accepted by the Commons (January) and the Lords (February) which provided for a standing army of 22,000. The force was to be raised by impressment and supported by regularized taxation. The infantry, 12 regiments, totaled about 14,000 men; the cavalry's 11 regiments totaled 6,600 men, plus 1,000 dragoons (mounted infantrymen). Artillery, a stepchild of the British weapons family, underwent some reorganization and expansion, largely on the basis of the continental experience. Modeled loosely after Cromwell's Ironsides, the new scheme introduced several innovations as well as vastly improved organizational principles. For the first time, red garb became the general uniform for a British army. Most significantly, the traditional aversion of the local militia to campaigns beyond their home territories was overcome in the creation of this mobile professional force.

1645, April 3. The Self-Denying Ordinance. It required members of Parliament to relinquish their civil and military commands. Fairfax succeeded Essex as captain general; Cromwell was granted a dispensation and became lieutenant general while still a member of Commons.

1647, May 7. Royalist Dissension. Charles resolved the growing rivalry between Rupert and Goring by splitting his 11,000-man army, sending Rupert to the north and Goring to the west. Parliament sent Fairfax to besiege Oxford.

1645, May 31. Battle of Leicester. Despite severe losses, the Royalists carried Leicester by storm in an effort to divert Fairfax from Oxford. Charles then proceeded toward Oxford. Parliament ordered Fairfax to raise the siege of Oxford and to "march to defend the association." Fairfax was reinforced by a cavalry contingent under Cromwell (June 13). Charles, surprised by the approach of the Roundheads, elected to fight.

1645, June 14. Battle of Naseby. Charles had about 7,500 men; the Parliamentary strength was 13,500. Rupert's Royalist cavalry defeated the Parliamentary left and charged off the battlefield in pursuit. Cromwell, whose mounted charge had defeated the cavalry on the Royalist left, exploited the prince's reckless pursuit and smashed the Royalist infantry, most of whom surrendered. Upon their return to the melee, Rupert's men refused to engage the Ironsides. Charles fled to Leicester. The victory at Naseby contributed decisively not only to Charles's eventual defeat but also to the ascendancy of Cromwell and the Independents within the Parliamentary party.

1645, June–1646, May 5. Royalist Collapse. In the southwest Fairfax and Cromwell overwhelmed Goring at **Langport** (July 10). Royalist strongholds (Leicester, Bristol, Bridgewater, Winchester) yielded one by one. After his final field force was crushed at **Stow-on-the-Wald,** west of Oxford, Charles surrendered to a Scottish, in preference to a Parliamentary, force (May 5, 1646).

Interlude between Civil Wars, 1646–1648

Charles's Scottish captors turned him over to Parliament for £400,000, about one-third of the amount owed the Scottish army (January, 1647). Meanwhile, tension between Presbyterians in Parliament and Puritan Independents in the army became an overt schism. Parliament voted virtual disbandment of the army, which was owed several months' pay. The army refused to disband (March). Under Cromwell's virtual leadership, the army seized Charles and occupied London. Cromwell pressed the King to accept the army's proposals; Charles meanwhile conducted clandestine negotiations with the Scottish Presbyterians (August–October). The King escaped to the Isle of Wight (November). He concluded an **Engagement** with the Scots, promising to impose Presbyterianism for a 3-year period in return for military support in a campaign to regain his kingdom (December 26). Parliament renounced allegiance to the King (January 15, 1648).

The Second Civil War, 1648–1651

OVERTHROW OF THE MONARCHY

Churchill has written: "The story of the Second Civil War is short and simple. King, Lords and Commons, landlords and merchants, the City and the countryside, bishops and presbyters, the Scottish army, the Welsh people, and the English Fleet, all now turned against the New Model Army. The Army beat the lot."* The principal events were:

1648, March–August. Uprisings in Wales and South England. Dissident Welsh Parliamentarians proclaimed allegiance to the King. Cromwell besieged and captured their stronghold at Pembroke Castle (July). A simultaneous revolt in Kent and Essex was suppressed by Fairfax; the insurgents took refuge at Colchester, but eventually capitulated (August).

1648, July–August. Scottish Invasion. James, Duke of Hamilton led 24,000 Scots into England. From south Wales, Cromwell marched with 8,500 men toward Wigan and Preston. He moved too fast for his artillery to keep up; the Scots had no artillery. Although numerically superior, the Royalists were poorly equipped (they were compelled to gather horses en route to serve as ammunition carriers); moreover, Hamilton permitted his units to straggle for nearly 50 miles.

1648, August 17–19. Battle of Preston. Cromwell attacked Hamilton's advance guard at Preston, defeating the Scottish-Royalist contingents in detail in 2 days of hand-to-hand combat, in which the main reliance of each side was on its pikemen. The Royalist survivors were split into disorganized bands; the army was supreme in England.

1648, August–December. Army against Parliament. Learning that Parliament reopened negotiations with Charles (July), the army occupied London and seized the king in order to bring him to trial. When Parliament defied the military, Colonel **Thomas Pride**'s troops prevented the entry of over 100 members of the Commons ("Pride's Purge," December 6–7). Those members permitted to sit (the "Rump Parliament") instituted a High Court which tried the king for treason.

1649, January 30. Execution of Charles. After a summary trial by the army-dominated Rump Parliament, the King was beheaded. The crown was abolished and a Commonwealth established under military control.

* *History of the English Speaking People,* Vol. 2, p. 274.

THE IRISH CAMPAIGN, 1649–1650

From 1641 to 1649, against the background of Royalist-Roundhead conflict in the south, Ireland was subject to incessant strife between the English Protestant Royalists, who held Dublin under Earl **James Butler of Ormonde,** and Irish dissidents. In turn, the Irish rebels were split into factions—a Catholic confederacy, led by Papal Nuncio Archbishop **John Rinuccini,** and the established Anglo-Irish gentry —reflected in the schism between **Owen Roe O'Neill**'s Ulster army and Earl **Richard Preston of Desmond**'s Leinster forces. O'Neill defeated a Roundhead force under Sir **George Monroe** at the **Battle of Benburb** (1647) while Ormonde surrendered Dublin to the Parliamentarians commanded by Colonel **Michael Jones.** Subsequent events were:

1649, August. Royalist-Catholic Alliance. Ormonde, leading the coalition, established tenuous control of Ireland in behalf of the crown. This was disputed by the Roundheads under Michael Jones.

1649, September. Cromwell to Ireland. Parliament ordered Cromwell to re-establish Commonwealth authority. After quelling a mutiny, Cromwell embarked.

1649, September. Battle of Rathmines.

Jones's Roundhead army defeated the Royalists under Ormonde. Thus, when Cromwell arrived, the Catholic-Royalists had taken refuge in fortified towns.

1649, September–1650, May. Cromwell's Reign of Terror. Immediately initiating systematic siege warfare, Cromwell captured the principal Catholic-Royalist strongholds: Drogheda (September), Wexford (October), Clonmel (May, 1650). He ruthlessly massacred the defenders of every captured fortress, the most horrible atrocities in British history.

1650, May. Cromwell's Return to England. He entrusted the continuation of the campaign to **Henry Ireton, Edmond Ludlow,** and **Charles Fleetwood.** Two years later the last Royalist stronghold at Galway surrendered (May, 1652).

UPRISING IN SCOTLAND,
1650–1651

1650–1651. King and Covenant. Upon the execution of Charles I, Scottish Presbyterians proclaimed his son, **Charles II,** King of Great Britain. But before accepting Charles, they demanded that he accept the Solemn League and Covenant (see p. 550). Montrose had meanwhile brought a Royalist mercenary force from France. Suspected of being a Royalist without being a Covenanter, he was defeated by the Scots at **Carbiesdale** (April 27, 1650), captured, and executed. Charles, however, after entering into an agreement with the Presbyterians and agreeing to accept the Solemn League and Covenant, was invited to Scotland and crowned (January 1, 1651).

1650, July–September. Cromwell's Invasion of Scotland. Fairfax refused to lead a Scottish expedition. Cromwell was installed as commander in chief and crossed the border with a force of 16,000, including nearly 6,000 cavalry, and proceeded toward Edinburgh. David Leslie, commanding 18,000 Scottish infantrymen and 8,000 cavalrymen, maneuvered cautiously and defensively, his scorched-earch strategy forcing the Roundheads to rely on supply by naval transport. Cromwell vainly sought a decision. Disease and exposure reduced Cromwell's army to about 11,000; the Roundheads pulled back to Musselburgh and then to Dunbar, the

Scottish army ringing the surrounding hills. The Scots then moved at night down from the hills in expectation of an attempted evacuation by sea (September 2–3).

1650, September 3. Battle of Dunbar. Cromwell gathered the cavalry on his left and struck at dawn. The surprise charge, led by **John Lambert,** overwhelmed the Scottish right wing. (At midnight, in the mistaken belief that no action was imminent, Leslie had ordered 5 of every 6 Royalist musketeers to extinguish their matches.) The victory was total: the Scots suffered 3,000 killed, while the Roundheads had less than 30 dead and captured 9,000 prisoners. Leslie retreated to Stirling, leaving Cromwell in control of southern Scotland and the route to Edinburgh.

1650–1651. Interlude. The illness of Cromwell, combined with discord between Scottish factions, caused a hiatus.

1651, June–September. Stirling-Worcester Campaign. Upon Cromwell's recovery, and following unsuccessful overtures to the Scots for a pacific settlement, Cromwell led his forces to Perth, threatening Royalist supply lines to Stirling, but also leaving the road to London deliberately unobstructed. Charles, thinking he could regain his throne in a bold move, fell into Cromwell's trap. With Leslie's army he marched southward, proceeding along the west coast (July 31). Cromwell instructed Lambert and his horse to follow the Royalists, ordered another force to move from Newcastle to Warrington, and ordered the Midlands militia northward. Then, after capturing **Perth** (August 2), at the rate of 20 miles a day, Cromwell led the main Roundhead force down the east coast, collecting volunteer militiamen en route. The four English contingents converged on the Scots at Worcester, Cromwell's engineers erecting bridges across the Teame and Severn.

1651, September 3. Battle of Worcester. Outnumbered, but not outfought, 16,000 Scots struggled hopelessly against 30,000 English, of whom 20,000 were the New Model Army. Few survivors reached Scotland, among them Charles II, who had fought with distinction. But he was soon forced to flee to France. Scattered Royalist strongholds held out until the capitulation of Dunettar Castle in May, 1652. The Civil Wars were ended.

The Commonwealth, 1649–1660

1649–1652. Naval Reform. Under Cromwell, zeal for military reform found expression in the navy as well as the New Model militia. During the life of the Commonwealth, 207 ships were added to the navy (40 between 1649 and 1651). The Royalist office of Lord High Admiral and the wartime Parliamentary Navy Board were replaced by the Committee of Admirals (1649). The committee improved food and instituted regularized wages and an incentive system of "prize money" for the capture or destruction of enemy vessels. It appointed three "Generals at Sea," former land commanders during the Civil War—**Edward Popham, Richard Deane,** and **Robert Blake**—the most important being Blake. The committee was transformed into the Commissioners of the Admiralty (1652); this body produced the original Articles of War.

1651, October 9. First Navigation Act. This anti-Dutch legislation forbade importation of goods transported by ships other than those of England or the vendor country.

FIRST ANGLO-DUTCH WAR, 1652–1654

The essentially naval conflict arose primarily from maritime competition, particularly in respect to the East Indies trade.

1652, May 19. Action off Dover (or Goodwin Sands). War began when Blake, patrolling the Channel with 20 ships (later reinforced to over 40) engaged a Dutch fleet under **Maarten Tromp** after he was refused permission to search a Dutch East Indies convoy. The Dutch withdrew after the loss of two vessels.

1652, July. Declarations of War.

1652, September 28. Battle of Kentish Knock. Blake with 60 English ships defeated an equal number of Dutch; personal antagonism of Dutch **Cornelius de Witt**'s subordinates impeded his efforts.

1652, November 30. Battle of Dungeness. Maarten Tromp, restored to command, led a reinforced Dutch fleet of 80 vessels, twice the size of Blake's fleet, in a decisive victory off England's south coast.

1653, February 18. Action off Portland. Blake, with 70 English ships, stalked a Dutch merchant convoy escorted by Tromp's men-of-war. Blake's squadron, separated from the main fleet by a dense fog, was engaged by 80 Dutch sail off Portland, the Dutch retreating upon the appearance of the main English force (February 18).

1653, February 20. Battle of Beachy Head. A 2-day running fight culminated in a bitter battle. Tromp escaped with difficulty after losing 17 men-of-war and over 50 merchant vessels. The English lost about 10 warships. Blake was badly wounded.

1653, March. First Issuance of the Fighting Instructions. This officially provided for line-ahead formations to make optimal use of the broadside.

1653, June 2–3. Battle of the Gabbard Bank. An English fleet, commanded by Deane and **George Monck** (another general turned admiral), followed the Fighting Instructions in an engagement with Tromp. The arrival of Blake with 13 ships and their subsequent loss of 20 vessels caused the Dutch to withdraw. The English pursued to the Dutch coast.

1653, June–July. Blockade of Holland. Finally Tromp managed to engage Monck in a diversionary action, slipped away, and joined Cornelius de Witt at sea (July 25).

1653, July 31. Battle of Scheveningen (or Texel). The combined Dutch fleet of 100 ships attempted to shatter the blockade. After a preliminary inconclusive engagement (July 30), the English fleet under Monck, about equal in strength, won a bitter 12-hour contest. Tromp and 1,600 other Dutch sailors were killed and the Dutch lost 30 men-of-war. English losses were less than half as great. There were no other operations of significance.

1654, April 5. The Treaty of Westminster. Holland indemnified England and agreed to respect the Navigation Act.

COMMENT. *This conflict was of particular interest not only because of the official introduction of line-ahead, close-hauled for-*

mations with 100-yard intervals separating ships but also in light of the English government's use of propaganda to consolidate public support.

STRUGGLE BETWEEN ARMY AND PARLIAMENT, 1653–1660

1653, April 20. Dissolution of the Rump. The growing schism between the army and the Rump—culminating in Parliamentary proposals to drastically reduce the military establishment—led Cromwell to dissolve the assembly and the council of state, and to establish a new Council and the Little, or "Barebones," Parliament.

1654–1655. Operations against the Tunisian Corsairs. Blake, with 24 ships, was ordered to the Mediterranean (November). After securing an indemnity from the Grand Duke of Tuscany, Blake engaged the corsairs, winning a brilliant victory at **Porto Farina.**

1655, March–May. Penruddock's Revolt. Colonel **John Penrudock** led a short-lived Royalist revolt in Wiltshire.

1655. Military Reorganization. Cromwell organized England and Wales into 11 military districts, each supporting an armed force (financed by 10 per cent taxes on Royalist property) and commanded by a major general.

1655. Capture of Jamaica. During undeclared hostilities with Spain, an expedition of 2,500 soldiers, ill equipped, poorly disciplined, and afflicted with dysentery, commanded by Admiral William Penn and General **Robert Venables,** earlier dispatched to Barbados (December, 1654), seized Jamaica (May). This led Spain to declare war.

1656–1659. Anglo-Spanish War. England joined France in an attempt to challenge Spanish hegemony over the Indies (see p. 561).

1656, September 9. Capture of Spanish

Treasure Fleet. Seized by Captain **Richard Stayner** off Cádiz.

1656–1657. Blake's Last Victories. During the winter Blake successfully imposed one of the first extensive naval blockades in history on the Spanish coast. In the spring, in the most effective action of the war, he took his fleet into **Santa Cruz** harbor (Tenerife, Canary Islands) and destroyed 6 treasure transports, 10 escorts, and 6 forts (April 20, 1657). He died on the return voyage to England. (For land operations, see p. 561).

1658, September 3. Accession of Richard Cromwell. Upon the death of Oliver Cromwell, his son was proclaimed Lord Protector. Relations between the army and the Parliament (convened in January, 1650) deteriorated. After a military show of force, Cromwell dissolved the Short Parliament (April 22).

1659, May 7. The Rump (Long) Parliament Reconvenes. Richard Cromwell, unable to control either army or Parliament, resigned. The army, suppressing Royalist uprisings, seized control and dismissed Parliament (October).

1659, November 7. Treaty of the Pyrenees. (See p. 562.)

1660, February 3. Monck Assumes Control. In response to popular dissatisfaction with the extramilitary activities of the army, Monck seized power. He restored the Rump Parliament and the ascendancy of civil over military authority (February–March, 1660).

The Later Stuarts, 1660–1700

1660, May. The Restoration of Charles II. Charles II returned to the throne, thanks to the support of Monck. Prince James, Duke of York, was appointed lord high admiral (later assisted by efficient Samuel Pepys) and Monck captain general. The army was reduced to 5,000 men (October). A Covenanters' revolt in Scotland was easily suppressed a few years later (1666).

SECOND ANGLO-DUTCH WAR, 1665–1667

Again commercial competition fostered Anglo-Dutch conflict. In 1663, the English had attacked the source of the Dutch slave trade, the West African ports (October), and the following year seized New Amsterdam (see p. 606).

1665, May. Declaration of War. This followed Dutch recapture of the African ports and Michael de Ruyter's attack on Barbados.

1665, June 3. Battle of Lowestoft. Lord Jacob Opdam led a Dutch fleet of over 100 ships in the seizure of English supply vessels returning from Hamburg. A powerful English fleet of 150 ships, commanded by Prince James (assisted by Prince Rupert, Sir William Penn, and Earl **Edward Montagu of Sandwich**), defeated Opdam in a sanguinary battle, in which Opdam, Dutch Admiral **Koetenaer,** and English Admiral **John Lawson** were killed. Over 30 Dutch vessels were sunk. **Cornelis van Tromp** (son of Maarten Tromp) skillfully covered the Dutch retreat. James's refusal to pursue the survivors led to his ouster from command; he was succeeded by Sandwich.

1665, August. Battle of Bergen. Sandwich, pursuing a valuable Dutch merchant convoy from the Indies into Bergen harbor, was repulsed by Danish shore batteries. England declared war on Denmark. Ruyter arrived soon thereafter and escorted the convoy to Texel.

1666, January. France Enters the War against England. (See p. 563.)

1666, June 1–4. Four Days' Battle. Monck, commanding 80 sail, detached Prince Rupert's squadron of 25 ships to intercept a French force mistakenly believed to be arriving from the Mediterranean (late May). De Ruyter sailed against Monck with 80 ships. The Four Days' Battle commenced off the North Foreland with an English attack (June 1); the arrival of Dutch reinforcements caused Monck to begin withdrawal (June 2). Rupert's squadron after being delayed by adverse winds returned (June 3, evening). Following a fierce engagement, in which 20 English ships were lost, Monck and Rupert retreated to the Thames (June 4), which de Ruyter blockaded.

1666, July 25. Battle of the North Foreland.* Having repaired and refitted, Monck attacked, broke the blockade, and defeated de Ruyter, who lost about 20 ships. Monck proceeded to the coast of Holland and attacked Vlie Channel, destroying 160 anchored merchantmen.

1666, August–1667, June. Peace Negotiations. The Dutch were now as ready for peace as were the British, still suffering from the Great Plague (1665–1666). While negotiations were in progress, Charles, responding to the effects of the Plague and the Great London Fire (September 2–9, 1666) and against Monck's adamant advice, moored the fleet and disbanded the crews. The Dutch made a token gesture at disarmament.

1667, June. De Ruyter's Raid in the Medway. The Dutch fleet, in a surprise raid into the Thames estuary, advanced up the Medway to within 20 miles of London, devastating shipping and several men-of-war en route. This highly effective strike and the ravages of the domestic catastrophes led England to seek peace in earnest.

1667, July 21. Treaty of Breda. The terms were a standoff, slightly in favor of the Dutch, who did, however, acknowledge English possession of New Amsterdam. England received some West Indies islands from France; France received Acadia from England (see p. 604).

1668, January 13. The Triple Alliance. (See p. 563.) Prompted by English, Swedish, and Dutch fears of French aspirations in the Spanish Netherlands.

1670, May. Treaty of Dover. Charles executed an about-face and concluded a secret treaty with Louis XIV. This provided for English naval support of proposed French operations against Holland (and the establishment of Roman Catholicism in Britain) in return for £200,000 per annum. The ships of the Royal Navy were hurriedly put back in commission.

THE THIRD ANGLO-DUTCH WAR, 1672–1674

This was a deliberately provoked war of aggression by England and France. Holland had no desire to fight either nation, and certainly not both simultaneously.

1672, March 13. English Attack on Dutch Smyrna Convoy. Sir **Robert Holmes** attacked Dutch craft in the Channel, but the convoy escaped.

1672, March–May. Preparations for War.

(For land operations, see p. 563.) While de Ruyter organized his fleet, British and French fleets, totaling 98 warships, con-

---

* Sometimes called St. James' Day Battle.

centrated in the Channel under the command of Prince James and completed their preparations off Sole Bay, Suffolk.

1672, May 28. Battle of Sole Bay. De Ruyter with 75 ships surprised the French and English. The rapid withdrawal of the 35 French vessels under Admiral Count **Jean d'Estrées** enabled de Ruyter to mass his ships against the slightly smaller English fleet. The arrival of English reinforcements forced the Dutch to retire, but only after they had badly mauled the English. The Duke of York was twice forced to abandon his flagship. Lord Sandwich was killed.

1672–1673. Lull in Naval Actions. Parliament opposed a war of aggression in alliance with France. During an internal political debate the Duke of York was forced to resign as High Admiral because of his conversion to Catholicism. Prince Rupert replaced him.

1673, May 28. Battle of Schoonveldt Channel. In preparation for an English invasion of Holland, Rupert attacked de Ruyter's fleet in its coastal anchorage. The Dutch were ready. De Ruyter counterattacked, driving off the British with heavy loss.

1673, June–August. De Ruyter Takes the Offensive. In a series of minor engagements he forced the English fleet to retire to the Thames. His attempt to impose a blockade was frustrated by the outbreak of plague on his ships. An allied fleet then blockaded Holland while the French prepared to invade by land.

1673, August 11. Battle of Texel. William of Orange ordered de Ruyter to sortie to protect an East Indies convoy. The French contingent, after a sharp fight, retired; following a more effective English defensive action, the French returned and the Dutch retreated. De Ruyter, however, had gained a clear-cut victory. He brought the convoy in, and he frustrated allied plans for a seaborne invasion.

1674, February 19. Treaty of Westminster. Due to growing public opposition to the war, the English government made peace.

The war between Holland and France continued (see p. 564).

1679. Covenanter Rebellion. A Scottish rebel force defeated a Royalist force under **John Graham, Viscount Dundee** at **Drumclog**, south-central Scotland (June 1). Duke **James Scott of Monmouth** (illegitimate son of Charles II) led a Royalist army that crushed the rebels at **Bothwell Bridge** (June 22). Monmouth then treated the rebels leniently.

JAMES II AND THE GLORIOUS REVOLUTION, 1685–1689

1685, February 6. Accession of James II. Upon his death (February 6), Charles achieved a final political victory—the accession of his brother, James II, a Catholic and former lord high admiral.

1685, July 6. Monmouth's Rebellion. The Duke of Monmouth, leading a Protestant revolt as pretender to the English throne, landed in Dorsetshire with 82 men. After recruiting considerable local support, he led a desperate attack at **Sedgemoor** (July 6), was repulsed and the rebellion crushed. Monmouth was captured and beheaded.

1685–1688. Unrest in England. English Protestants resented James's efforts to restore Catholicism to equality.

1688, November–1689, February. Accession of William III. Seven Tory and Anglican leaders solicited the assistance of William of Orange, Stadholder of the Netherlands (see p. 570; married to **Mary,** daughter of James II) and his army in countering James's efforts to assert royal authority over the Church of England. William accepted the invitation, with the intention of leading England into the anti-French League of Augsburg (see p. 546). He landed in November and advanced on London. James fled to France (December 11). William and Mary were proclaimed joint sovereigns of England (February 13, 1689).

1689, April 3. Mutiny Act. This provided a formal disciplinary code for the standing army in peace and war.

THE IRISH WAR, 1689–1691

This war, the British phase of the continental War of the Grand Alliance (see p. 546), was the product of disparate motives united by common opposition to William III: James's desire to regain the English throne, Louis's desire to divert

William from operations in Flanders in order to secure unopposed access to the Netherlands, and Irish support for a Catholic king against the hated Protestant English.

1689, March–April. James II in Ireland. James, accompanied by a small French force, landed at Kinsale. With the exception of several Protestant strongholds in the north, a Jacobite army of 40,000, under Earl **Richard Talbot of Tyrconnel,** held Ireland. Protestants in Enniskillen and Londonderry immediately affirmed their allegiance to William. James and Tyrconnel proceeded northward.

1689, April–August. Sieges of Enniskillen and Londonderry. Initial English efforts to raise the Irish-French investment failed. Later Captain **John Leake** led a naval convoy with reinforcements through the Londonderry blockade and terminated the siege (August 9–10). Soon after, local militia, commanded by Colonel **William Wolseley,** compelled the Jacobites to raise the siege of Enniskillen.

1689, June–July. Jacobite Rising in Scotland. While the joint Irish-French forces besieged Enniskillen and Londonderry, Viscount **John Graham of Claverhouse** and **Dundee,** James's leading Scottish partisan, attempted to foment a Jacobite rising in the Highlands. While defeating a Williamite army under Major General **Hugh Mackay** at the **Battle of Killiecrankie** (July 17), Dundee was killed. Despite the victory, after Dundee's death the revolt collapsed.

1689, September–November. English Offensives. English troops advanced into Ulster. Meanwhile, under orders from William, a small force led by Duke Friedrich Hermann of **Schomberg** landed near Belfast, but was repulsed at **Dundalk.**

1690, March–July. William in Ireland. William personally led an army of 35,000–40,000, including continental mercenaries, toward Dublin (June). Meanwhile, to the north, James's army—raised to 21,000 by the arrival of a relatively small contingent of French troops under Comte **Antonin Nompar de C. de Lauzun** (March)—encamped near the Boyne River.

1690, July 11. Battle of the Boyne. While the central infantry contingents of the 2 armies were engaged indecisively, the much more numerous English cavalry began an envelopment. James, competent and intrepid as an admiral, was unable to shift his Irish horse to block the English envelopment. He fled the field, and to France. His army fought well, and despite severe losses withdrew in good order to continue the war for another year.

1690–1691. William Consolidates. With the exception of western and southwestern Ireland, the island fell before William's advance. On the west coast, the Jacobite stronghold at Limerick, commanded by Earl **Patrick Sarsfield of Lucan,** resisted an English siege throughout the summer and autumn. However, Cork and Kinsale readily yielded to the Earl of Marlborough (September–October). Louis denied James's request for support in a proposed invasion of England.

1691, July 12. Battle of Aughrim. Godert de **Ginkel** led a Williamite army against an Irish-French force of 25,000 under the Marquis de **Saint-Ruth,** who was killed. The allied effort collapsed. The English suffered some 700 casualties, while the allied army lost 7,000. This defeat ended James's Irish aspirations and the war, save for the continuing siege of Limerick.

1691, October 13. The Pacification of Limerick. The terms of the surrender of Limerick provided for the voluntary transport of Irish soldiers to France, freedom of religious (Catholic) belief in Ireland, and an amnesty. It was ratified by the English Parliament; however, the predominantly Protestant Irish assembly rejected the liberal terms and enacted a harshly anti-Catholic Penal Code.

COMMENT. *Had Louis XIV fully exploited his command of the sea prior to 1692, and sent an adequate force to Ireland, English and Irish history would have followed a far different course, and France might have achieved military hegemony on the Continent by the end of the century.*

FRANCE

The Age of Richelieu, 1610–1642

1610, May 14. Assassination of Henry IV. He had been preparing for war against the Hapsburgs on the Rhine to settle a succession dispute in Jülich-Cleves.

1610–1643. Reign of Louis XIII (9 Years Old). The queen mother, **Marie de Medici,** was regent during his minority.

1619–1624. Rise of Richelieu. The Cardinal Duke **Armand Jean du Plessis** became virtual dictator of France after political triumphs over the queen mother.

1625. Protestant Revolt. The Huguenots rose under the leadership of Duke **Henri of Rohan** and his brother **Benjamin of Rohan and Soubise.** Based upon La Rochelle, the revolt seemed destined to tear France apart, as had occurred in the previous century. Duke **Henry of Montmorency,** High Admiral of France, defeated a Protestant fleet under Soubise off **La Rochelle,** to begin a partial blockade of that Protestant stronghold (September).

1626–1630. English Intervention. (See p. 549.)

1627–1628. Siege of La Rochelle. Richelieu personally supervised the 14-month siege. After 3 months' blockade, a land investment was begun (November). Duke **Henry II of Lorraine and Guise,** with the royal fleet, carried out a maritime blockade while stone dikes were built to close the port. By spring the dikes and sunken hulks blocked the channel. Two English relief fleets were repulsed (May, September). After heroic resistance the garrison capitulated (October 29), and the Protestant city lost all of its former privileges.

1628–1629. Defeat of the Huguenots. With the defeat of the Duke of Rohan by Montmorency in Languedoc, the Huguenots were crushed as a major and semi-independent political-military force in France.

1628–1630. War with Savoy. Richelieu indirectly attacked Spanish power by conquering Savoy and re-establishing control of the Valtelline Valley of the upper Adda River, above Lake Como, leading to the Stelvio Pass, linking the Hapsburg possessions of Milan and the Tyrol, thus blocking the main military and logistical route between Spanish Italy and the Spanish Netherlands. The climactic victory was won by Montmorency at **Avigliana** (1630).

1631–1648. French Participation in the Thirty Years' War. (See p. 540.)

1632. Noble Revolt. This was led by the King's brother, and enemy of Richelieu, Duke **Gaston of Orléans.** Montmorency led the rebel army, which was defeated by Marshal **Henry Schomburg** at **Castelnaudary** (September 1). Montmorency was captured and executed.

1642, December 4. Death of Richelieu.

1643, May 14. Death of Louis XIII.

The Early Reign of Louis XIV, 1643–1661

1643–1661. Mazarin's Ministry. Louis was 5 years old. His mother, **Anne of Austria,** became regent, relying completely on Cardinal **Giulio Mazarin.** (Unlike Richelieu, Italian-born Mazarin was a political cardinal, not a priest.)

THE FRONDE, 1648–1653

Resentment of nobles and people against taxation and the accumulation of royal power under Richelieu, and even greater resentment of Mazarin, his replacement and continuer of the policies, led to full-scale revolt as soon as the Thirty Years' War was over, even though the war with Spain continued.

1648, July 12. Beginnings of the First Fronde. Demands of the Parlement of Paris, addressed to Louis and his mother, were rejected by Anne and Mazarin.

1648, July–December. Unrest and Rioting in Paris.

1649, January 8. Rebellion of Parlement. Mazarin was outlawed by Parlement, which also ordered seizure of royal lands. The royal family and Mazarin had fled to St.-Germain. Civil war broke out with many nobles, including **Prince Armand of Bourbon and Conti,** on the rebel side.

1649, January–February. Condé Supports the Queen. Partly because of a feud against his younger Bourbon brother, Armand of Conti, the Great Condé led his army against Paris, captured the fortress of Charenton, and laid siege to the city. When Conti and other rebel nobles appealed to Spain for help, Parlement sought peace.

1649, March 11. Peace of Rueil. Parlement dismissed its troops and made peace with the court. Mazarin was reinstated. The queen declared a general amnesty.

1649, August–December. Friction between Condé and Mazarin. The general, thinking his services warranted a greater voice in affairs, quarreled with Mazarin, then began negotiating with the formerly rebellious nobles.

1650, January 18. Imprisonment of Condé. Mazarin also imprisoned his brother, Conti, and brother-in-law, Duke **Henry of Longueville.**

1650, February–April. The Second Fronde Begins. While nobles raised insurrections in Normandy, Burgundy, and Bordeaux, Turenne took over military leadership of the Fronde, and agreed to join a joint Spanish-Frondist army to invade France from the Spanish Netherlands.

1650, June–October. Inconclusive Maneuvering in Northeastern France. The invasion failed to take advantage of an opportunity to march on Paris largely through mutual suspicions of Turenne and the Spanish leaders.

1650, October 15. Battle of Champ Blanc. Turenne, vainly attempting to relieve besieged Frondeurs in Rethel, was defeated by the much larger and better-trained royal army under Marshal **César de Choiscul, Comte du Plessis-Praslin.** Turenne escaped with only a small fragment of his army.

1651, February–September. Amnesty and Lull. In a general amnesty the princes were released from prison (February 15) and Turenne returned to Paris. Mazarin fled to Germany.

1651, September. Renewal of Civil War. Condé, Conti, and other nobles again revolted, then captured Bordeaux and made it their base. Condé signed an alliance with Spain. Turenne remained loyal to the crown, but the revolt spread throughout France. Louis called Mazarin back to Paris (November).

1652, March–July. Operations between the Loire and Seine. A most complicated and fruitless series of maneuvers and engagements took place between Turenne and Condé.

1652, July 5. Battle of St.-Antoine. A new royal army, brought up from the frontier, joined Turenne to trap Condé outside the walls of Paris, now benevolently neutral toward the royal cause. Condé, after a bitter struggle, was on the verge of defeat when fickle Paris opened her gates to let him escape. He then fled to join Spanish forces and imperial troops of the Duke Charles IV of Lorraine invading France's denuded northeastern frontier. Turenne immediately marched north.

1652–1653. Operations North and East of Paris. Turenne outmaneuvered superior forces of the Spanish, Frondeurs, and Lorrainers, protecting the capital while the rebellion collapsed. Louis re-entered Paris (October 21, 1652). Mazarin returned (February 6, 1653). The Fronde was over, though the war with Spain went on.

CONTINUATION OF THE SPANISH WAR

1653–1657. Condé against Turenne. The pattern of the previous campaign governed. Despite superior strength, Condé, now a Spanish generalissimo, was unable to draw Turenne into combat under unfavorable conditions. In a war of maneuver and siege in northern France, Turenne won a victory at **Arras** (1654, August 25), and was defeated at **Valenciennes** (1656, July 16), but slightly outgeneraled his able opponent, who was hampered by Spanish suspicions and lack of cooperation.

1657. Franco-British Alliance. France and England being separately at war with Spain, Cromwell and Mazarin concluded a treaty of alliance whereby their forces were to attack jointly the coast towns of Gravelines, Dunkirk, and Mardyck. Dunkirk was to be ceded to England.

1657, Fall. Capture of Mardyck.

1658, May–June. Siege of Dunkirk. Turenne advanced rapidly from Mardyck on Dunkirk despite opening of the dikes by the Spanish. Investing the city—garrisoned by 3,000 men—he was joined by 3,000 English troops under Sir **William Lockhart.** The arrival of the English fleet boosted his force to 21,000 as siege operations began. Don **Juan of Austria,** viceroy of the Spanish Netherlands, gathered a relief army at Ypres under himself and Condé. This army consisted of 6,000 cavalry and 8,000 infantry plus 2,000 English Jacobites under **James, Duke of York**

(later James II), furnished by pretender Charles II of England.

1658, June 7–13. Advance on Dunkirk. Don John and Condé moved into a camp site on the dunes, between beach and pasture lands northeast of Dunkirk.

BATTLE OF THE DUNES, JUNE 14, 1658

Turenne decided to seize the initiative by a surprise attack. During the afternoon of the 13th, he collected 9,000 cavalry and 6,000 infantry for battle, leaving 6,000 men guarding the siegeworks. There was some skirmishing before dark.

Early in the morning, just before low tide, Turenne's army—deployed in two lines and a reserve—advanced across the dunes; the English infantry was on the left; the cavalry was divided between his flanks; half on the beach and half in the meadows on the land side of the dunes. Turenne's advance was slow, giving the Spanish time to prepare. This slowness was deliberate because his plan was based upon the changing of the tide.

The Spanish infantry held a line across the dunes, right flank resting on the beach. A cavalry contingent covered the left flank; the bulk of the cavalry was in reserve; none was on the beach, for fear it would be destroyed by fire from the English fleet maneuvering offshore. Don John commanded the right, Condé the left. Against Condé's advice, John had advanced so rapidly that he had left his artillery behind.

Initial contact was made on the Spanish right, where the English attacked, supported by guns of their fleet. The reserve Spanish cavalry belatedly tried to support the infantry but was badly beaten by the French left-flank cavalry, led by the Marquis **Jacques de Castelnau.** In the center the French infantry slowly pushed the Spanish back. On the Spanish left, Condé's cavalry attack against the Marquis **François de B. de Créqui** was foiled by arrival of Turenne with cavalry from his left wing. Turenne's stratagem of using the change of the tide on the beach to enable him to carry out a cavalry envelopment around the Spanish land flank was a manifestation of his skilled adaptation of battle formations suited to the peculiarities of the battlefield. The battle, which lasted from 8 A.M. to noon, was a complete victory for Turenne, who only lost about 400 men. Don John's toll was 1,000 killed and 5,000 taken prisoner; the Spanish tercios were virtually annihilated. Turenne pursued vigorously until nightfall. Dunkirk subsequently surrendered and was ceded to Cromwell. It remained in English hands until Charles II sold it to Louis XIV in 1662.

1659, November 7. Peace of the Pyrenees. Spain ceded much of Flanders and other frontier regions. The Spanish Empire was crippled, the French monarchy stabilized. Louis XIV married Maria Theresa, daughter of Philip IV of Spain. The following year Condé asked and received the forgiveness of Louis XIV.

The Personal Reign of Louis XIV, 1661–1700*

Upon the death of Mazarin, who had ruled in his name for almost 18 years, Louis XIV began his personal reign. His theory of government had emerged from the writings of Richelieu, the teaching of Mazarin, and his own experience. He was not inclined to share his authority with anyone—"*L'état, c'est moi.*" The nation in turn empathized with the person of the king. Louis's finance minister Jean-Baptiste Colbert sought to balance the need for a strong army with a stabilized and increased wealth. Emulating the Dutch, he promoted commerce and navigation, thereby initiating an extensive colonial policy. The colonial companies were repre-

---

* The last 15 years of the reign (1700–1715) are covered in the next chapter.

sented to the king as armies participating in an economic war. A virtually new navy was created for the defense of the colonies, and Vauban constructed great fortified naval bases at Brest, Dunkirk, Le Havre, Rochefort, and Toulon. Colbert had 20 warships in 1661; there were 196 vessels in 1671, and 270 in 1677. The army was reorganized through the efforts of Louvois and Vauban (see p. 528).

The reorganization of the army, the creation of the navy, and the increased wealth were instigated by Louis's ambition for fame and his desire for an increase in territory. His secretary for war, Louvois, was an opportunist who played to Louis's weakness for military expeditions. A feud developed between the practical Colbert, who frowned on military expeditions, and Louvois, who pointed out the failures of commercial enterprises. The most important events were:

1664–1666. Operations against the Barbary Pirates. Because of damage to the commerce of Marseilles, Louis dispatched a naval squadron to bombard Djidjelli in Algeria and made subsequent attacks on Algiers until an agreement was reached with the Dey of Algiers.

1666. War with England. By an agreement of 1662 Louis was obligated to aid the United Provinces in their second war with England (see p. 556).

THE WAR OF DEVOLUTION, 1667–1668

Upon the death of his father-in-law, Philip IV of Spain (1665), Louis demanded the inheritance right of devolution, or succession, and claimed the whole of the Spanish Netherlands. Spain refused; **Charles II** became king (see p. 572).

1667, May 24. Invasion of the Netherlands. Turenne quickly subdued a part of Flanders and Hainault.

1668, January. The Triple Alliance. The United Provinces, England, and Sweden concluded a treaty to check French expansion.

1668, February. Invasion of Franche-Comté. Condé, leading French troops, completed the occupation in 14 days.

1668, March–April. Triple Alliance Demands Peace. Louis entered negotiations.

1668, May 2. Treaty of Aix-la-Chapelle. Franche-Comté was returned to Spain, but France was left with a number of fortified towns on the Spanish Netherlands' frontier and some strongholds in Flanders. The unsettled succession question was deferred.

THE DUTCH WAR, 1672–1678

Louis set about isolating Holland from her allies. The Triple Alliance was undermined by the secret **Treaty of Dover** with Charles II of England (May 22, 1670; see p. 557). A similar treaty was concluded with Sweden (1672), as well as treaties with Cologne and Münster.

1672, March. Declaration of War. The French army of 130,000 men, under Louis's personal command, marched down the Meuse, by-passing the Dutch fortress at Maastricht, to establish a base at Düsseldorf, on allied territory. Louis's army was well armed and equipped. The growing French Navy had the support of the English fleet. The Dutch Navy had 130 ships, but the land army in 1671 comprised only around 27,000 men, badly armed and commanded. When danger of war appeared imminent in February (1672), William III of Orange began to raise the effective force to 80,000 men.

1672, May–July. Invasion of Holland. Three columns invaded the United Provinces: Turenne, with over 50,000 men, down the left bank of the Rhine; Condé, with an equal force, down the right bank; Luxembourg, with an army consisting primarily of Louis's German allies (Cologne and Münster), advanced from Westphalia toward Overijssel and Groningen. William and a weak field army attempted to hold the Ijssel-Rhine line, but the French rapidly forced passage at **Tolhuis** (June 12). Nijmegen, Gorinchem, and other towns fell. General Count **Henri L. de'A. Rochefort** led a cavalry raid into central Holland, took Amersfoort and Naarden, was checked at Muyden, then captured Utrecht. The French advance threatened Amsterdam. However, the Dutch people saved Amsterdam by cutting the dikes and flooding the countryside. Meanwhile, Luxembourg had been stopped at Groningen.

1672, August. Revolution in Holland. William of Orange was placed at the head of the government (see p. 570).

1672, August–September. Support for Holland. Fearful of Louis's ambitions, several princes formed a coalition against France: Elector Frederick William of Brandenburg, the Emperor, and Charles II of Spain.

1672, August–September. Dispersion of the French Army. Against the professional advice of Turenne and Condé, Louis now parceled his army into small packets, trying to deal with all of his enemies at once. Turenne had urged that the Germans be smashed first by the concentrated French army. Instead, he was sent to Westphalia, Condé to Alsace, other units to the Spanish Netherlands frontier, and the remainder of the army waited in Holland for the flood waters to freeze.

1672, September–December. Dutch Raid on Charleroi. William hoped to exploit the French dispersion, but was repulsed.

1672, September–1673, January. Turenne on the Middle Rhine. With forces never exceeding 20,000 men, Turenne outmaneuvered the much larger combined imperial and Brandenberg armies under Count **Raimondo Montecuccoli** and Frederick William. The latter was so discouraged that he sought peace (**Treaty of Vassem,** June 6, 1673).

1672–1673. Winter Operations in Holland. Luxembourg, threatening Leyden and The Hague, was forced to withdraw to Utrecht by a sudden thaw. Condé had similar trouble attempting to take Amsterdam.

1673, June 29. Capture of Maastricht. Louis personally commanded an army of 40,000; Vauban's professional skill overcame the Dutch fortress after a brief siege. Louis then invaded Lorraine and conquered the electorate of Trier (Treves).

1673, July–November. Turenne and Montecuccoli. On advice of Louvois, Louis ordered Turenne, with 23,000 men, to prevent Montecuccoli (who had 25,000) from joining the Dutch. At the same time Turenne was to protect Alsace and do nothing to anger neutral states. In vain Turenne protested that these instructions were inconsistent. He did his best, but able Montecuccoli avoided battle and joined William at Bonn. The allies besieged and captured Bonn (November 12). This isolated Louis's allies (Cologne and Münster), who made peace.

1674, January. Growth of the Coalition. Denmark joined the coalition, many German princes joined the Emperor, the Great Elector (Frederick William of Brandenburg) re-entered the war, and England made peace with the allies by the **Treaty of Westminster** (February 19; see p. 558). Louis withdrew from Holland so as to concentrate against the Spanish Netherlands and Franche-Comté, and to protect Alsace from the Germans.

1674. Other Operations. A French expedition to Sicily surprised the Spanish and gained success. In Roussillon a small French force under Marshal Schomburg repulsed Spanish attacks.

1674, May–June. Campaign in Franche-Comté. Louis, with Vauban providing the professional skill, recovered Franche-Comté in 6 weeks. Besançon fell after a siege of only 9 days.

1674, May–August. Campaign in the Spanish Netherlands. Condé held the line of the Meuse with about 45,000 men. William advanced against him with about 65,000, proposing to invade France.

1674, August 11. Battle of Senef. Seeing an opportunity to strike the allied army on the march, Condé attacked boldly with only half of his army and without artillery. The more-numerous allies rallied after an initial setback and recovered some lost ground. Both armies withdrew during the night. Condé, being joined by the remainder of his army, decided to renew the battle next day. But the allies had withdrawn completely; he could justly claim tactical as well as